WAR THROUGH THE AGES

Historical Books by Lynn Montross

WAR THROUGH THE AGES

THE RELUCTANT REBELS
The Story of the Continental Congress,
1774-1789

RAG, TAG AND BOBTAIL
The Story of the Continental Army,
1775-1783

CAVALRY OF THE SKY

WASHINGTON AND THE REVOLUTION
(teen-age)

U. S. MARINE OPERATIONS IN KOREA
First, second and third volumes with Captain Nicholas A. Canzona, U.S.M.C.;
fourth and fifth volumes in preparation.

THE UNITED STATES MARINES
A Pictorial History

WAR
THROUGH
THE AGES

REVISED AND ENLARGED THIRD EDITION

By LYNN MONTROSS

DECORATIONS BY L. K. HARTZELL

HARPER & ROW, PUBLISHERS
NEW YORK, EVANSTON, AND LONDON

F-O

For

my son,

Alan F. Montross,

in the hope that his world may learn

from books instead of bombs.

CONTENTS

PLANS AND ILLUSTRATIONS

PREFACE

THE first edition of this book was published during World War II, when the issue was in doubt, and a second edition appeared shortly after the end of that conflict. Subsequent events, such as the cold war of the Western nations against Communism and the shooting war in Korea, have provided new material for this revised and enlarged third edition. World War II chapters have meanwhile been rewritten to make use of sources not available when they were prepared, particularly German and Japanese documents and memoirs.

Atomic weapons, guided missiles and jet propulsion, to name only three World War II tactical innovations, may have a more sweeping effect on civilization than the first explosives of the Middle Ages. Still, it would be hasty to assume that all past precepts of national defense are about to be tossed into the wastebasket of history. If the experience of the centuries teaches any enduring lesson about war, it is that the heart of man has never been changed by any weapon his mind has conceived. There is, in short, no reason to believe that the hydrogen bomb has affected Napoleon's famous dictum, "The moral is to the material in war as three to one."

That is the justification for offering a survey of war at a time when the need for world peace has never been greater. The two are not opposite poles, nor are they as different as black and white! Even if we allow that war is a disease of the body politic, as it has sometimes been defined, men of good will cannot hope to escape the ravages by ignoring the symptoms.

A backward glance at the combats of pike and arquebus may seem impractical in a day of intercontinental ballistic missiles. Yet the first war of the new Atomic Age was fought in Korea with weapons and tactics often reminiscent of the Western Front in 1915. Battles were won in that conflict by a reliance on principles which have not changed since the time of Alexander the Great. For in 1950, as in 331 B.C., the decisiveness of weapons depended largely on the use made of such timeless elements as preparedness, secrecy, deception and surprise.

Although Americans like to think of themselves as a peace-loving people, the United States has been involved in three major wars during the first half of the twentieth century without once having been the aggressor. Thus it would have been possible for a young man to have enlisted at the age of eighteen in the first World War and served in World War II and Korea before reaching his fifty-third birthday.

During this 35-year period it would not only have been possible but usually unavoidable for a young man to study four years at an American university without being offered a single historical or analytical course in a subject that might soon claim all his energies, perhaps even his life. Books about war were divided between the heroic and the ethical appeal, giving the reader his choice between a saga and a sermon.

Fortunately, a more scientific approach has been gaining ground since Pearl Harbor, which taught that a war may be forced upon a reluctant nation in the time it takes a bomb to drop. Some first-rate analytical books about World War II and Korea have been published, and colleges and universities are paying more attention to military history.

The purpose of this book is to supplement such studies, scholastic or otherwise, with a general survey of tactics, strategy and battle during the past thirty centuries. For without some knowledge of the military past, citizens of a democracy can hardly hope to deal intelligently with problems of war and peace in the military future.

L. M.

Washington, D.C.
February 3, 1960

PART ONE
THE CLASSICAL AGE

✫

I

THE GYMNASTIC WARFARE OF GREECE

Ah! the generals! they are numerous but not good for much!

—ARISTOPHANES

THE ancient Greeks were one of those fortunate peoples whose situation offered some choice between peace and war. They were not, like the plains dwellers of Mesopotamia, forced by vulnerable frontiers into a struggle allowing only the option of conquering or being conquered. Nor were they, like the Egyptians, so isolated by natural barriers as to run the risk of softness and degeneracy.

Their peninsula was well defended by mountains and sea, giving the invader no easy approach. The sunny climate helped to develop a race of athletes whose physical beauty and perfection have perhaps never been equaled. The valleys were fertile, demanding a wholesome degree of labor without imposing hardships such as would drive a people into warfare for survival. The mountains bred a spirit of independence, yet the sea saved the Greeks from the poverty which is the usual lot of hill dwellers.

As the population increased beyond the ability of the soil to sustain it, the Greeks took to ship. Second only to the Phoenicians, they became the merchants and traders of the Mediterranean. Colonization rather than conquest served the needs of expansion, and at an early date a small Hellenic empire had been established on the Asiatic and African coasts as well as the islands of the Aegean. By the seventh century B.C. these colonies were prosperous enough to succor the homeland with shiploads of grain in years of threatened famine.

Here, apparently, was a people which might have taken a historical middle course between the struggle that burned out the Mesopotamian empires and the softness that led to the bondage of Egypt. But inherent in the peninsula's natural advantages were the germs of civil strife. The mountains and straits defended against invasion but also divided the Greeks into petty states meeting in a spirit of truculent clannishness. The result—the wars of fratricide leading to self-destruction—has been summed up by William James in his famous essay "The Moral Equivalent of War":

> Greek history is a panorama of jingoism and imperialism—war for war's sake, all the citizens being warriors. It is horrible reading because of the irrationality of it all—and the history is that of the utter ruin of a civilization in intellectual respects perhaps the highest the world has ever seen.

To this it might be added that even the extent of Greece's downfall is no more striking than its acceleration. Only 152 years separated the sturdy triumph of Marathon from the defeat of Chaeroneia—a tragically brief period of military health as compared to the endurance of Roman and Byzantine arms.

During this century and a half the Greek warrior declined from his high estate as citizen-soldier to that of a mercenary hiring out to Asiatic despots. Bribery and treachery became commonplace events, as is shown by contemporary writings, and after a few generations of civil war the constant calls for recruits drained the vitality of the leading city-states.

TACTICS OF THE ANCIENT WORLD

If the ancient Greeks failed at keeping the peace, it could not often be said that they set a brilliant standard of war as compared to Hellenic progress in other directions. Their military history is chiefly a record of groping for tactical expression, and it remained for a conqueror to assemble the pieces of a puzzle the intelligent Greeks were never able to solve.

Taken singly, their contributions to the art and science of war were sometimes of a distinguished order. But there is a total lack of that finished symmetry for which Greek sculpture, literature and architecture are famed. It was as if a splendidly muscled athlete had developed the use of only one arm.

That arm found its military counterpart in the hoplite, the foot soldier who made the heavy infantry the dependence of all the states. He was a freeman and hence an aristocrat in the world of his day—a citizen bound by laws of his own making to almost lifelong military service. Slaves carried his bulky armor to and from the battlefield, other slaves bore his baggage and supplies. His self-appointed duty was to fight, though as a citizen he might perhaps have the privilege of helping to banish his general afterwards.

It is one of the few times in history when an aura of caste and elegance has surrounded the infantry. But in nearly every other respect Greek warfare had broken away from the Asiatic past. Greek democracy offered a contrast to the despotic character of Assyrian, Persian and Egyptian armies. Greek mountains and coasts naturally imposed tactics differing from those suited to the Asiatic plains.

For centuries the battles of those plains had been fought to a conventional pattern. Two huge armies laboriously fumbled for each other's throats without a pretense of secrecy or surprise In composition they were as alike as the weapons carried by each. The cavalry took its position on both wings, with massed squares of foot in the centre and chariots drawn up in front of all. Behind the centre, as an indispensable feature of Eastern battle, the king stationed himself with his retinue. He was guarded like a vital organ of war, since his flight or capture usually became the prelude to disaster.

Units of tens, hundreds and thousands were the rule in Asiatic warfare, being frequently mentioned in the Old Testament. Marching in column of fours, though not found in European armies until a relatively modern date, is depicted on Egyptian tombs of thirty centuries ago. Yet for all of their progress in organization, Eastern armies of these centuries give the effect of flabby bulk in most of their operations.

Drawing up a line of battle often became a tedious process which took all day. In that event both forces waited in formation until the next morning. Then the slingers, archers and dart throwers began the contest, swarming out from between the infantry squares to discharge their missiles, and retiring through the intervals. The chariots charged and the cavalry tried to sweep around the enemy's flanks. Finally the masses of foot met in ponderous collision with sword, spear and shield.

Victory customarily went to the side which succeeded in overlapping the opposing line. Panic and rout followed the first sign of adversity, for the irregulars of Asiatic armies were mere human jackals, often serving for the privilege of stripping the slain. As a result the casualties of the victors were few, while the vanquished fell by the thousand in a pitiless pursuit lasting until darkness.

Although envelopment proved the decisive factor, commanders seldom made any effort to rest a flank on some natural obstacle such as a hill or river. Nor did they attempt to provide a reserve which would only have reduced the extended front desired for overlapping the enemy's wings.

It was dull warfare depending in the long run on numbers. But the warfare of slaves has always been dull, and an Oriental host consisted largely of serfs flogged into action by nobles, satraps and mercenaries.

In Greece, on the contrary, the skill and valor of the individual citizen were so exalted as to indicate that the strife of heroes may also have its limitations. Down to the Homeric Age, and in later centuries, the battles of the peninsula resolved themselves into a single great shock followed by hand-to-hand duels between stout-limbed champions of both sides.

It made for great poetry but not for great war. Even the conceptions of wise old Nestor in the *Iliad*—probably the first recorded tactics of the Western world—aimed at no more subtle an end than the restraint of the arrant individualism of the Greek warrior:

> The horse and chariot to the front assign'd,
> The foot (the strength of war) he ranged behind;
> The middle space suspected troops supply,
> Inclosed by both, nor left the power to fly;
> He gives command to curb the fiery steed,
> Nor cause confusion, nor the ranks exceed;
> Before the rest let none too rashly ride;
> No strength nor skill, but just in time, be tried;
> The charge once made, no warrior turn the rein,
> But fight, or fall, a firm embodied train.

By discouraging excesses of zeal, while guarding against the panic of doubtful troops, Nestor hoped to strike a compromise between the extremes of indiscipline. But it will be noted that he aimed simply to build up a more cohesive human wall than the enemy's array, so that his forces might prevail at the first clash. Although Greek commanders were fertile in ruse and stratagem, as symbolized by the legendary horse of Troy, they usually contented themselves in their tactics with a simple collision all along the line.

THE ELEMENTS OF TACTICS

Far back in the racial past, as the tribal army emerged from the armed tribe, men discovered that there were only three basic military formations. Whether a force was composed of four men or four thousand, it could be grouped for tactical purposes only into a line, a column or a square. The variations and derivatives, of course, have been made the subject material of military treatises down to the present day. But the line, the column and the square remain the foundation of tactics.

The first two differ merely by 90 degrees of the compass. Thus a line of men four ranks deep, facing east, has only to execute a left turn to become a column of four files, facing north.

None of these formations is satisfactory for all purposes. The line lacks depth and mobility, while the weakness of the column lies in its narrow front and vulnerable flanks. The even worse defect of the square —men facing outward in all four directions—is found in the fact that it gains strength by sacrificing the ability to march or manoeuvre. For this reason the square (or its counterpart, the 360° perimeter) has always been the resort of a hard-pressed defensive.

Almost without exception the warriors of primitive races group themselves into a phalanx—a heavy and compact line of battle which becomes a column on the march. The virtue of this formation is its solidarity, both moral and physical. The ranks are deep enough so that the individual can see comrades before and behind him. The files are close enough so that he can feel the reassuring touch of the shield on his right and the spear on his left. Again we are indebted to Homer for a glimpse of an early phalanx forming from column into line of battle:

> Thus o'er the field the moving host appears,
> With nodding plumes and groves of waving spears . . .
> Each leader now his scattered force conjoins
> In close array, and forms the deepening lines.

Throughout history the depth of the phalanx has been an accurate measure of the fighting spirit of any people. The Egyptians, whose unmilitary qualities kept them in bondage for many centuries, found it necessary to form masses of a hundred ranks and a hundred files. The hardy and athletic Greeks often relied on a depth of only eight ranks, though more were sometimes added for special purposes.

Sheer lack of population made it needful for them to develop superior skill and courage as compared to the bulky onslaughts of the East. Athens, largest of the city-states, was never able to muster more than 50,000 fighting men at the height of her power. Sparta was so poor in human resources that a ferocious state discipline became the substitute for numbers.

And that the intellectual Hellenes should have evolved a warfare of brawn is not altogether a paradox. The individual was king in democratic Athens, a hero even in regimented Sparta. The individual could and did attain to great art, but his ingrown distrust of authority seldom allowed him to tolerate for long the central command necessary to great war.

Greek Hoplites

Instead, he preferred to deal lusty blows, to fight in the ranks as a hoplite, to endure all his life the gymnastic exercises which fitted him for hand-to-hand combat.

A ten-foot spear and a short cut-and-thrust sword were the hoplite's weapons. On his left arm he carried a round shield large enough to protect his entire body in a kneeling position. Greaves of metal plates sewed on leather, and a bronze helmet and cuirass completed his armor, while the scarlet cloak found such favor as to become virtually the Greek uniform.

All told, the armor and weapons weighed about 70 pounds. The slave who carried this burden on the march also had the duty of foraging for his master.

In early centuries a line of chariots commonly preceded the Greek phalanx. Missile weapons also played a prominent part in every campaign—the javelin, or short casting spear, the dart, the bow and arrow.

Then as Hellenic warfare gradually departed from Eastern influences, infantry shock attack with spear and sword came to be the main reliance. Horse had never been an arm adapted to a mountainous terrain, and for some unexplained reason the Homeric art of the bow and arrow fell into almost complete decline.

By the fifth century B.C. the Greek line of battle consisted of a hedge of spears bearing down upon the enemy. Sometimes the first impact decided the day by shattering the opposing ranks. More often the two forces fought it out with the sword in parallel order until one or the other had been punished beyond endurance. Combats between individual champions, with both armies pausing to watch, were of frequent occurrence. But it was seldom that either general resorted to surprise, manoeuvre, flank attack or any other variation from the plain frontal assault.

As a result, the victory customarily went to the strong and agile, just as victory in the East was decided by right of bulk.

The Battle of Marathon

The two opposing schools of war had their first great test on the field of Marathon in 490 B.C. At the outset of the campaign the chronic handicap of Greek generalship becomes apparent in the lack of unified command which would contribute to many a future defeat. Even in the emergency, with independence at stake, ten *strategoi* divided the leadership of the Athenian army. Only after long persuasion could Miltiades gain approval of his sensible plan for meeting the Persian invaders on the seacoast instead of awaiting their thrust at Athens.

It is not surprising that the city had few allies, for never in history were the Greeks able to combine effectively. On the march, however, the little army was reinforced by a few Plataeans, bringing its strength up to 11,000. Aid had also been promised by Sparta, but due to the observance of a religious festival it arrived too late.

Miltiades took a position on a height sloping gently down to the Persian army, nearly a mile distant. His wings were protected by a hill and a stream, and he had thinned his centre in order that the Greek line might have more width against a numerically superior enemy.

Here another persistent weakness of Greek arms is evident in the lack of cavalry, light infantry or missile weapons, all of which the enemy had in force. Doubtless due to these handicaps, Miltiades decided to seize

the initiative. Down the slope at a run came the athletic Greeks, striking
the Persian line before its cavalry and missiles could become effective.

At the first shock the wings crushed the more lightly armed Asiatics
in their path, but meanwhile the thinned Greek centre had been pushed
back almost to its starting point. Whether or not Miltiades foresaw this
development, he soon turned it to advantage. After his wings had routed
the enemy's right and left, he ordered them to wheel inward and fall
upon the centre.

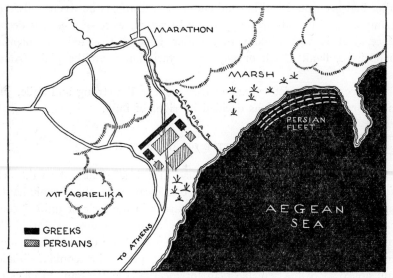

The Battle of Marathon

Thus hemmed in on both flanks, the warriors of the East were crushed
with losses of 6,400 as compared to 192 fallen Greeks. Persian arms,
based on the battle of envelopment, had become the prey of an envelopment by forces outnumbered at least two to one. It was a famous triumph
for the gymnastic warfare of Greece.

But Marathon was more than a battle—it was a saga and a legend.
Even at this early historic period it serves as an example of the patriotic
suppression or exaggeration of facts which must be taken into wary
account throughout military chronicles. For the Greeks gilded their
glory by a tenfold multiplication of enemy numbers which probably did
not exceed 25,000 on the battlefield, thus setting a precedent which has
seldom been neglected down to the present day.

THE BATTLE OF SALAMIS

The Hellenic peoples, like the Phoenicians, had been almost literally thrust into the sea by geographical conditions. In line with the experience of all young maritime nations, they soon found it necessary to build warships in order to protect their merchant vessels from piracy. Land warfare also depended largely on water transport in a peninsula of straits and bays, as is indicated by these lines from the *Iliad*:

> Their troops in thirty sable vessels sweep,
> With equal oars, the hoarse-resounding deep.

The Mediterranean being subject to prolonged calms, oars were needed to supplement sail on all types of vessels. Naturally, a limit was soon reached in the length of vessels with a single bank of oars, and two-banked warships appeared in Phoenicia as early as 700 B.C. A century later, according to Herodotus, the Egyptians added a third bank; and for generations "trireme" served as the name for any naval unit, whatever its equipment.

The extant ruins of Athenian shipyards reveal that four banks were introduced by 330 B.C., while in later centuries the tiers of oars rose to fantastic heights. But for several hundred years the authentic trireme remained the dreadnought of the ancient world, figuring in all the operations of the Graeco-Persian wars.

The Athenian trireme, as shown by the ruins of the docks at Zea, measured 140 feet long with a 20-foot beam. A curiously modern note is added by the discovery that these ships were built to a standard model with interchangeable parts. The maximum crew of 225 consisted of 174 rowers, 20 sailors and a small force of hoplites serving as marines.

"In the ancient world the rower was not usually a slave," we learn from Torr's *Ancient Ships*, "and it is a strange fact that Athenian citizens in the age of Pericles, who were in no wise unconscious of their own transcendant gifts, willingly labored at the oars to generate a mechanical force that was directed by the intelligence of others."

The ram, or rostrum, of the earlier warships protruded above the water line, but a later age found it more effective when wholly submerged. A three-toothed spur of hardwood armored with iron or bronze, it projected about ten feet. The middle tooth was longest and sharpest, being intended to pierce an enemy ship before the other two dealt her a blow which released the weight of the sinking vessel. Naturally the keel and ribs had to be built stoutly, not only to sustain the shock of ramming but also the strain of being constantly drawn up on shore. Not a very seaworthy vessel, due to her narrow beam, the trireme had to be beached at the end of day while the crew slept on shore. Lofty monuments of rocks dotted the coast as lookout stations, and sentries were posted,

> High on the mound; from whence in prospect lay
> The fields, the tents, the navy and the bay.

Thus the naval warfare of Greece was intimately associated with land tactics. Generals became admirals overnight, just as hoplites became marines, and the fleet and army were seldom separated for long.

Although warships cruised under sail, oars were considered the only reliable power for battle manoeuvre. Second to the ram in offensive menace, the stout, projecting catheads could be brought up alongside to shear off an enemy's oars and render her helpless. Boarding tactics, with their resulting disorder, found favor only in emergencies.

During the decade after Marathon, while another and greater Persian invasion threatened, the Greeks decided on a united fleet as the logical first line of defense for a peninsula. A force of 366 triremes was hastily assembled, of which 200 were built and manned by Athens.

The Persians likewise based their attack on co-operation between land and sea forces. Xerxes brought an enormous army supported by double the Greek strength in warships. As an earnest of his determination the despot began operations by bridging the Hellespont and cutting a canal across the peninsula of Mount Athos—two mighty engineering feats for that day.

Still, the usual Greek want of foresight gave the invaders their foothold. Leonidas and his small band of Spartans died to a man at Thermopylae, leaving the Western world one of its most heroic legends. From a strictly military point of view, however, the defense proved only that adequate numbers might have held the famous pass. Indeed, the pages of Thucydides hint that contemporaries regarded Thermopylae less as a saga than a reproach:

". . . the Mede had time to come from the ends of the earth to Peloponnese before any force of yours worthy of the name went out to meet him."

This disaster threw the burden of defense on the fleet, which withdrew to the strait of Salamis on the Attic coast. At least 40,000 men, or nearly every able-bodied citizen, must have been recruited for the triremes of

Athens alone. Hence the impending sea battle promised to be even more decisive than Marathon in shaping the future of Greek civilization.

Hastily trained crews handicapped the warships more than lack of numbers. In view of this weakness the *strategoi* wisely decided not to try conclusions in open waters with the expert seamen of the Phoenician mercenary triremes. By means of a typically Grecian stratagem—the simulation of treason—the great Persian fleet was lured into the narrow strait.

The enemy's numbers thus lost most of their advantage when attacking on a cramped front. Even so, the hard-pressed Greeks found it necessary to resort to the boarding of vessels for hand-to-hand combat. Salamis provided a good opportunity when a thousand ships tried vainly to manoeuvre in the limited space. A wild mêlée of tangled ships resulted, and as an individual fighter the hoplite proved more than a match for the Phoenician hireling.

After their line had been broken, the invading triremes were soon beaten down to a defensive ending in flight. They lost 200 ships, the Greeks 40.

In historical results Salamis ranks as the world's first decisive naval engagement. The Persian fleet was driven from European waters, causing Xerxes' army to postpone operations until the following year. By virtue of this breathing spell the Greek cities were able to unite enough land forces at the battle of Plataea to end forever the peril of Persian domination.

GREECE'S MILITARY DECLINE

Hellenic unity never endured for long, and the next century saw a continual struggle of Greek against Greek. The forces were so evenly matched that tactical supremacy became increasingly sought as the key to victory. Athens led the way until the one potent arm of Greek warfare had the support of a trained and effective light infantry.

In the peltast, with his short spear, small shield and light armor, tactics at last found some basis for mobility. Scouting and skirmishing began to play a larger part as commanders strove to vary the old parallel clash. The Persians, moreover, had taught their victors two important lessons, leading to the increase of cavalry and missile weapons. Lacking native material, the Greeks resorted to mercenaries—bowmen of Crete, horse from the plains of Thessaly—as every army soon included respectable contingents of archers and mounted men.

Lack of population continued meanwhile to make war a grievous burden on a land which knew little peace. While the Greek cities were being drained of resources to pay alien soldiers, their own stout freemen hired out by the thousand in the ranks of Asiatic despots. As a consequence the peninsula presented the spectacle of fighting men wandering from city to city in search of employment which seldom lacked for long. Within a few generations arms had become the Hellenic trade.

This condition has been interpreted as evidence of a perverse love of strife. A closer examination, however, will reveal that Greece's incessant wars were the symptoms of a profound civil decay. Such was the dearth of public spirit that Demosthenes could not overcome the factionalism of his countrymen even when Macedonian invasion threatened. The great statesman's warnings went unheeded, and in the end he had the melancholy duty of delivering the funeral oration over those who had fallen in the fatal defeat of Chaeroneia.

In the military sphere the tragedy of Greece may be charged to a dull sword which prolonged the stalemate of civil warfare. Generalship continued to lag behind tactical improvement, since audacity along intellectual lines was not encouraged by a system which punished honest failure. Success, on the other horn of the dilemma, was only too likely to be taken as proof of dangerous personal ambitions. There remained every incentive for a commander to plod a prudent middle course.

Nor can the waning morale of the citizen-soldier be overlooked as a factor in the decline. Only sixty years after Marathon and Salamis the derisive comedies of Aristophanes echo the groans of the Athenian under the endless burden of war. The chorus of *Peace* pictures conscription in the fifth century B.C. as a character "stops in front of the statue of Pandion, reads his name and starts away at a run, weeping bitter tears." In contrast, the pleasures of peace are sung by the dramatist with evangelical zeal:

> Oh! joy! joy! no more helmet, no more cheese nor onions! No, I have no passion for battles; what I love, is to drink with good comrades in the corner by the fire when good dry wood, cut in the height of summer, is crackling; it is to cook pease on the coals and beechnuts among the embers; 'tis to kiss our pretty Thracian while my wife is in the bath.

Aristophanes has a good claim to recognition as the father of pacifists. Nevertheless, his most ribald scenes are tinged with black despair. His laughter always seems near to angry tears, as if he felt it already too late to check the momentum of Hellenic self-destruction.

"And why have the gods moved away?" asks Trygaeus in *Peace*.

"Because of their wrath against the Greeks," replies Hermes. "They have located War in the house they occupied themselves and have given him full power to do with you as he pleases; then they went up as high as ever they could, so as to see no more of your fights and hear no more of your prayers."

II

MACEDONIA'S HUMAN FORTRESS

The art of war is, in the last result, the art of keeping one's freedom of action.

—XENOPHON

As if in corroboration of Aristophanes, it was too late for purposes of Hellenic unity when Greece finally developed a first-rate general.

Athens, with her superior sea power and commerce, had failed to hold the ascendancy. Sparta in turn tried vainly to dominate the quarrelsome peninsula. Then at the battle of Leuctra, 371 B.C., Thebes won a brief, futile hegemony by a victory which might have been forgotten except for the tactics of Epaminondas.

In the study of war, nevertheless, Leuctra is a landmark of more importance than Marathon. Epaminondas, a man of position and education, appears to have had a moral courage rare among Greek commanders. Facing a larger and better Spartan army, and with Theban independence at stake, he did not hesitate to risk tactics which were a departure from the Hellenic past.

The Spartans formed their army of 10,000 in expectation of the traditional parallel clash, for even at this late date the element of surprise was lacking in Greek campaigns.

Epaminondas brought a force of 6,000, nearly half of which were unreliable allies. His two best units were a small but well-trained cavalry and an infantry *corps d'élite* known as the Sacred Band.

The Theban commander had another and more potent resource in the moral impact of surprise. It had long been remarked in Greek warfare that the usual parallel advance tended always to bring the right wing first in contact with the enemy. The explanation, according to Thucydides, lay in the simple fact that each warrior unconsciously sought the protection of the shield borne by the man on his right.

Epaminondas now proposed to create victory at the expense of the mental habits of his opponents. Toward this end he adopted a strange oblique order of battle in which his left wing, reinforced to a depth of forty-eight ranks, was thrown well in advance. In order to guard the flank of this heavy column he posted the Sacred Band on the extreme Theban left. On his right he placed the cavalry well in front of the "refused" wing made up chiefly of doubtful allies.

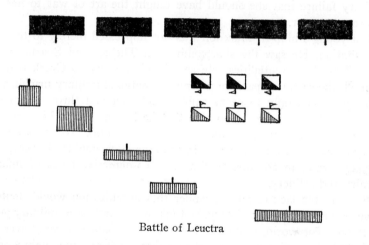

Battle of Leuctra

The battle opened with a brief cavalry clash won by the better trained Theban horse. Then the left wing bore down on the Spartan right, rolling it up on its own centre by virtue of superior numbers.

The muscular tactics of Sparta were helpless against this concentration of force at one point. Yet the victory owed to moral rather than physical pressure as the demoralization of the shattered right wing soon spread to the Spartan centre and left, which had hardly struck a blow. In the end the panic-stricken army fled with losses of 2,000, including the king, before the Theban centre and right became seriously engaged.

It is typical of the trials of Greek generalship that Epaminondas faced charges of laxity shortly afterward, and Diodorus records his dismissal from command. After serving as a common soldier, however, he was reinstated in time to gain a second triumph of the oblique order associated with his name.

The tactics of Mantineia were modeled after those of Leuctra. Again the Spartans became victims of a moral surprise, but Epaminondas received a mortal wound and the battle ended in an incomplete Theban victory.

THE MACEDONIAN TACTICAL SYSTEM

Neither Epaminondas nor his fellow citizens had probably attached any importance to the three years recently spent in Thebes by a young Macedonian hostage. This youth, a prince from the petty and semi-barbaric northern kingdom, had nevertheless been much impressed by the victory of Leuctra. It was thus the last weary irony of Greece's military failure that she should have taught the art of war to her own future conqueror.

But young Philip of Macedon was not impressed merely to the point of imitation. He saw the shortcomings of Theban and Spartan tactics as well as the potentialities. He saw in Greece, as no Greek had ever seen, all the scattered parts of a complete national military machine.

They needed only to be assembled, polished and thrown into gear. At this task Philip proved so able that he bequeathed to his son Alexander an instrument fit for the conquest of a world. It was an army in every modern sense of the word, including a staff, engineering corps and baggage train, in addition to the three co-operative arms of infantry, cavalry and artillery.

Even in the lack of an Alexander this organization would doubtless have claimed its page in history. But led by the first great military genius of the ancient world, it marched 10,000 miles and overcame every foe without losing a single combat or campaign. In sieges, mountain warfare, desert skirmishing, the crossing of rivers—each of these the department of military specialists—the Macedonian machine functioned as effectively as in great pitched battles.

It was, in short, as perfect an instrument as has ever been devised for the warfare of its own day; so perfect, indeed, that military critics have questioned whether Alexander could have been defeated by any of the earlier armies of the age of gunpowder.

Philip's goal, the domination of Greece, was a vast enough ambition in view of his resources. After seizing the throne he found himself master of uncertain frontiers defended only by a rude, skin-clad militia trained for border combats with tribesmen. His single military asset was cavalry, for the young nobles of Macedonia preferred to fight on horseback.

arm of the ancient world he must be credited with genuine tactical creation.

Effective engines of war, it is true, had been known for some centuries. As early as the reign of Uzziah (808-756 B.C.) the Old Testament mentions "engines, invented by cunning men, to be on the towers and upon the bulwarks, to shoot arrows and great stones withal."

Their use, it would appear, had been confined to siegecraft until the Macedonian king saw larger possibilities. The logical Greeks, who might have been expected to excel in mechanical warfare, had seldom resorted to engines even in the assault of cities.

Philip did not stop with the conception of an artillery arm. He also originated the idea of carrying only the essential parts on the march, depending on trees to supply the timbers which made up most of the bulk. A single pack horse was thus enabled to transport gear that could be assembled into one of the cannon of ancient warfare.

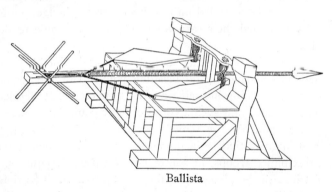

Ballista

War engines of the period fall into two groups according to cause and effect of propulsion. The ballista, or ancient fieldpiece, operated on the principle of tension; the catapult, or howitzer, by means of torsion.

The former was simply a magnified crossbow stretched by a windlass. Upon release of the cord it discharged a projectile, usually a spear, with considerable force. It could be aimed with some accuracy and was generally used for low trajectory effects.

The catapult, in contrast, hurled a missile high in the air for purposes of clearing a wall or hill. Its long upright arm terminated in a spoon-shaped end to contain the missile, the opposite end being entwined in heavy cords secured to posts. These cords were twisted by winches until the arm was parallel to the earth, thus acquiring the torsion-generated force for expulsion.

MACEDONIA'S HUMAN FORTRESS

The cavalry having been the weakness of Greek arms,
it the strength of his new national army. He organized his
a bodyguard called the Companions which became the hamme
donian battle tactics. In support he formed troops of light ho
for scouting and skirmishing.

The former hostage had noted another and equally fatal she
of Greek warfare in the phalanx, an excellent defensive f
serving indifferently for purposes of attack. Philip improved it by
ing a longer spear and extending the depth from eight to sixteer
The Macedonian sarissa, according to Polybius, was 21 feet
compared to a Greek pike never more than two-thirds that length.

The shield of the Macedonian phalangite hung over his left sh
in order that both hands might be free for the heavy weapon. He gr
it about six feet from a butt weighted for balance, so that the
extended some fifteen feet in front. In battle formation the spear
the first five ranks thus protruded into an impenetrable hedge, while
remaining ranks grounded their sarissae at a 45-degree angle to def
missiles overhead.

On level ground this mobile human fortress was invincible when
bore down with locked shields and bristling points. But the formatic
had weaknesses which Philip himself was first to perceive. Its flanks an
rear were open to attack, and such a compact body could be manoeuvred
readily only on a plain. As the remedy for both defects he built up a
supporting light infantry that set a new standard for the ancient world.
Reliable and disciplined troops, in contrast to the usual irregulars, they
protected the wings of the phalanx, lending mobility as well as defense.
Consisting chiefly of peltasts, they also included archers, darters, slingers
and javelin men.

The javelin, or short casting spear, was an ancient fighting tool that
had fallen into decline until Philip began a revival which would be
reflected in Roman tactics. The seven-foot shaft could be hurled with
deadly accuracy at twenty to thirty yards, being also useful for thrusting
at close quarters. No other classical weapon served so well both for
shock and missile attack.

THE ARTILLERY OF ANCIENT WARFARE

Up to this point Philip's innovations had been principally by way of
selection or improvement. But in his development of the first artillery

With changes in name, both the catapult and ballista survived until the late Middle Ages before the introduction of any new principle into the artillery antedating gunpowder. Modern replicas, while unable to recapture the ancient secret of preserving the elasticity of the cords, have established the possibility of ranges up to 500 yards or more with projectiles weighing several hundred pounds.

In addition to artillery, an efficient engineering corps, baggage train and medical service must have been incorporated into the new Macedonian army. There is little mention of these branches in the pages of classical historians, but the results are evidence of their existence. Neither Alexander's marches nor his sieges could have been accomplished without the aid of such trained, responsible specialists.

As early as the Trojan wars the military surgeon had been held in esteem. The *Iliad* mentions Machäon and Podaleirius as leeches whose skill was in constant demand, the former for surgical operations and the

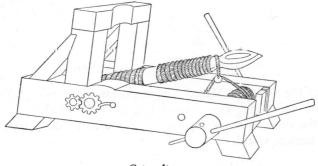

Catapult

latter for his diagnosis of symptoms that today would be in the province of the psychiatrist. Podaleirius it was who noted the wild glare and irrational actions which preceded the suicide of Ajax.

Ancient armor served its purpose so well that wounds occurred in far higher proportion to battle fatalities than is the experience of modern warfare. Heavy death lists were usually the consequence of flight and massacre rather than hard fighting. Moreover, it is evident that the surgery of the ancients managed speedily to restore light casualties to active service. Infection seems to have been no grave problem, nor did epidemics ever check the far-flung operations of the army of Persian invasion. Alexander himself recovered from numerous wounds, and a surprisingly large percentage of his veterans survived years of the most strenuous campaigning.

Likewise judging by results, we may assume that the Macedonian baggage train proved equal to its problems. The sarissa, shield and body armor of each phalangite weighed about 80 pounds, while the cavalry-man rode a barded horse and was equipped with complete scale armor in addition to shield, sword and short spear. These burdens were borne by slaves on the march, and sumpter animals transported supplies for an army operating thousands of miles from its homeland.

Macedonian Heavy Armed Cavalryman

As to the ability of Macedonian engineers and artificers, there is less need for conjecture. The siege of Tyre alone is sufficient to establish in detail the supervision of experts familiar with all the principles known to the ancient world.

THE MACEDONIAN ARMY

Greek training had consisted largely of gymnastic exercises, but Philip placed his faith in drillmasters. Despite the lack of stirrups (which do not appear in military chronicles until the fifth century A.D.) he trained his cavalrymen to develop a firm enough seat for hard-riding shock tactics with sword and spear. And though no other phalanx was ever able to use such a long and heavy weapon, he trained his foot soldiers until they could wield the sarissa with speed and precision.

The organization of the Macedonian army showed as much gain over the past as its arms and training. There had been national armies of conscripted freemen, such as those of the Greek states. There had been standing armies depending chiefly on mercenaries, as in Assyria and Persia. But Philip formed the world's first national standing army, its strength being made up of citizens owing military service, of volunteers from the nobility, of auxiliary troops from tributary states, and of mercenaries employed for some special skill.

For purposes of administration the army was divided into units resembling those of a modern military system. Sixteen files of 16 men each were equivalent to an infantry company of 256. Four of these companies made up the Macedonian counterpart of a battalion, eight a regiment and 16 a brigade, or half phalanx, of about 4,000 men.

As a tactical unit the phalanx became the mobile central fortress of the battle line, the pivot either of attack or defense. The wings were composed of cavalry, the heavy for striking power and the light for mobility. Inserted between the phalanx and the cavalry wings as hinges were the light infantry forces which supplied the flexibility for manoeuvre. Around both flanks hovered the archers and javelin men, ready to harass the enemy from a distance.

These were the limbs and sinews. Directing them was a brain: a staff of wise, experienced old officers who had the privilege and duty of offering advice, though the king retained the supreme command.

THE CONQUEST OF GREECE

Exactly twenty-two years from the time he left Thebes as a hostage, Philip appeared before the city to challenge all Greece. His force of 40,000 included veterans who had already won victories extending his realm from the Euxine to the Aegean.

On the field of Chaeroneia he attacked a numerically superior army of Thebans and Athenians who put up a desperate but losing fight. It is to their credit, in view of the tactical odds against them, that the issue remained in doubt for hours. Finally a counterstroke of the Macedonian left-wing cavalry, led by the eighteen-year-old Alexander, enabled the invaders to envelop and crush the allied centre. In the end the Theban Sacred Band, once Philip's tutors and now the rear guard of Greek freedom, died to the last man.

This was the Macedonian army, with few if any important changes in organization, which crossed the Hellespont four years later to challenge the world.

Its young commander had been uniquely prepared by birth and education for his self-assigned task. Philip's son in reasoned decision, he had a violent and ungoverned side inherited from a sinister mother of barbarian blood. Tutored by Aristotle in Greek logic and culture, he found all the joy of a Homeric hero in the hot actuality of hand-to-hand combat. A dual and inconsistent nature, yet it fitted young Alexander well for his career as conqueror.

If his ambitions were reckless in scope, it may be noted that he spared no pains in preparation. After seizing the throne made vacant by Philip's assassination, the new monarch first put down unruly elements in his own kingdom. Then in a whirlwind campaign which took him across the Danube, he chastised the barbarians and stamped out the last sparks of revolt in Greece.

It also seems certain that a man of his learning would not have neglected historical precepts; for the empire he was about to assault had been founded by a soldier worthy even of the emulation of an Alexander. Before Cyrus the Great there had been no high art of conquest. The Assyrians knew how to win victories, but their brutal and senseless warfare raised up an inverted pyramid, a structure sure to topple from the weight of oppression. Cyrus, in contrast, erected a temple of military statecraft in which the vanquished were free to retain such customs, prejudices and beliefs as did not interfere with the payment of tribute. Cyrus even paid the vanquished the tribute of adopting their various forms of religious worship, as if wishing to offend neither his new subjects nor their gods.

In proof of his policies, the Persian Empire had managed to survive two centuries of generally weak successors to the throne. Nevertheless, Alexander had before him a second historical precept which must have seemed an explicit summons.

Only two generations before, a band of Greek mercenaries had fought in the cause of a pretender to the Persian throne. Although sharing in his defeat at the battle of Cunaxa, the Greek phalanx stood its ground against overwhelming numbers. Then the death of their employer leaving them stranded in a hostile empire, the Ten Thousand had no choice but to begin the homeward march that is the subject of Xenophon's *Anabasis*.

A literary classic, the *Anabasis* is likewise the first of those great military treatises which have had a part in shaping the warfare of every age. For Xenophon was leader as well as historian of the Ten Thousand: he wrote about tactics he had evolved and tested in the heat of action.

These tactics proved so potent that after a terrible 4,000-mile retreat the Greeks cut their way out of Persia, though only half of them lived to cry, "The Sea! The Sea!" Xenophon's cool skill at handling reserves and rear guard operations, as detailed in his writings, may well have left lessons for Alexander. And it is even more probable that Alexander took as a message this line from the *Anabasis*:

"Persia belongs to the man who has the courage to attack it."

THE INVASION OF PERSIA

On the banks of the Granicus, only two marches from the Hellespont, the Macedonian invaders won their first clash with the enemy. The satraps of Asia Minor had hastily assembled a force to oppose the crossing of the shallow river. Their numbers were not in excess of Alexander's 35,000, and they had clumsily posted cavalry in the first line of defense while their Greek mercenary infantry waited uselessly in the rear.

Alexander promptly forded the stream and routed the Persian horse after a hard fight; then it became an easy matter to annihilate the outnumbered Greek phalangites.

As he proceeded unopposed along the littoral, commanding the sea with his fleet, the Macedonian leader demonstrated that he was more than a military adventurer. Every step of his progress offers evidence of careful planning. Method and system, rather than dash, distinguished his operations; he subdued hill tribes which the Persians themselves had never mastered, and behind him he left a line of strategically placed garrisons.

Although the word "strategy" is of Greek derivation, it does not appear in military terminology until relatively modern times. It is therefore appropriate to quote a nineteenth-century writer, Clausewitz, who defines tactics as "the formation and conduct of single combats in themselves" and strategy as "the combination of combats with each other. . . . In other words, strategy forms the plan of the war, maps out the proposed course of the various campaigns which compose the war and regulates the battles to be fought in each."

An even more modern definition is offered by Captain B. H. Liddell Hart, who compares strategy and tactics to the front and back axles respectively of a motorcar. "On the front axle depends the question which way the car goes. On the back axle depends the question whether it goes—whether the car moves at all."

Cyrus the Great doubtless ranks as the first accomplished strategist of ancient warfare. But the historical sources of his campaigns are so scanty and legendary that the student can only begin with Alexander. His operations, in contrast to the incoherent civil strife of Greece, are each a carefully forged link in a chain binding the gigantic limbs of the Persian Empire.

The first real battlefield test, at Issus, becomes merely another and more vital link in the strategic chain. The great king, Darius III, had at last been sufficiently alarmed to take the field in person instead of entrusting the defense to his satraps. But the Persians had learned only one lesson from their defeats at Marathon and Plataea: the employment in larger numbers of Greek mercenaries. Bulk was still the dependence of Eastern tactics, cavalry and missile weapons the merit.

To the Syrian coast Darius brought an army vastly outnumbering the invaders. With a rare flash of strategic insight, he placed his great force directly across Alexander's rear, forcing him to fight to regain his line of communications. Then in his eagerness the Persian monarch marched straight into a geographical bottleneck—a mile-wide coastal plain between the foothills and the sea.

Again, as at the Granicus, the Persians formed their line of battle behind a fordable stream. Again they were so poorly disposed, due to the cramped space, that the rear half of the army could only serve as witnesses to the struggles of comrades in the front ranks.

Even so, the threat of numbers led Alexander to secure both flanks as if foreseeing at least the possibility of disaster. After resting his troops, he opened the battle by plunging through the stream at top speed in order to lesson the effect of the enemy's missiles. The Macedonian right wing was thrown out well in advance, with the spearhead of attack pointed at the Persian left-centre, where Darius had stationed himself.

Alexander obviously aimed at moral results, knowing how quickly an Eastern army could disintegrate after the capture or flight of the king. But at this moment the unexpected changed the entire course of battle. The Macedonian phalanx lost its solidarity while crossing the stream, and the Greek phalangites of the enemy centre pressed forward to take advantage.

This movement opened a fatal breach between the Persian centre and left, and Alexander was not slow of perception. At once he wheeled his cavalry right wing inward, charging in flank the Persian centre and widening the gap between it and the left. Darius and his nobles took to their heels at the approach of personal peril, setting an example soon followed by the rank and file. Only the Greek mercenaries stood their ground, dying silently as their ranks were assailed from all sides.

The Persian rout was so complete that more than 100,000 were slain, as compared to 450 Macedonian losses, if Arrian and Diodorus may be credited. At any rate the possibility of such extremes is established throughout the history of ancient warfare. An orderly retreat was rare except among the most disciplined troops; and the pursuit of broken foemen almost invariably turned into a massacre lasting for miles and for hours.

III

ALEXANDER AGAINST THE WORLD

How doth the city sit solitary, that was full of people!
How is she become as a widow! she that was great among
the nations, and princess among the provinces, how is she
become tributary!

—THE OLD TESTAMENT

WHILE the beaten Persian king began the recruiting of another army, Alexander turned to strategic considerations of a new sort. In order to open up the way into Egypt it had become necessary to reduce two walled cities which threatened otherwise to breed revolt in the rear.

Today a petty port of a few hundred inhabitants, ancient Tyre was described by the Bible as "the crowning city, whose merchants are princes, whose traffickers are the honorable of the earth." The old site on the mainland had been found vulnerable long before Alexander's coming, and the Tyrians built a new stronghold on an island half a mile from shore. Encircled by walls of masonry rising abruptly from the water's edge, and easily provisioned by the ships in its two harbors, this island city had already withstood an Assyrian siege of thirteen years.

There were few precedents in Western warfare to guide Alexander and his engineers in such a formidable undertaking. Hellenic siegecraft had advanced but little since Troy, while in Asia the fortification and attack of cities was more expertly developed than any other branch of warfare. Great strongholds were essential not only for the security of plains dwellers but also as a base for offensive operations. And even allowing for Oriental hyperbole, it may be believed that walls more than a hundred feet high, wide enough on top for the passage of chariots, were not at all uncommon.

The economic attack was the most simple and obvious form of siege-craft. Cities were sometimes surrounded for years by encamped foemen who reared walls of their own to cut off trade and supplies. Assyria, whose appetite for war exceeded her ability, had a peculiar addiction to blockades which endured until a new generation grew up to manhood. But the defenders were at no great disadvantage in a contest of this sort, and often they could better supply themselves than an invading army subsisting on ravaged territory.

Hence the threat of starvation usually had to be supplemented by a physical attack on the walls and a moral assault on the will, nerves and courage of the beleaguered.

The earliest of all besieging weapons were probably the ram and the bore. Hewn from the trunk of a tree and wielded by men grasping thongs, the former was metal-knobbed for battering and the latter metal-pointed for seeking out weak joints in the masonry. The purpose of both was to open up a breach for the entrance of storming parties.

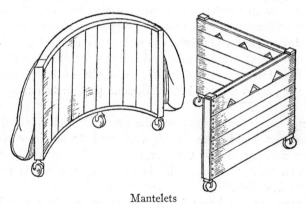

Mantelets

The next logical step was to hang the ram or bore within a stout penthouse to defend the attackers from missiles. Mantelets, or huge shields of wicker covered with wood or hide, were built on wheels as protection for groups of artificers.

If the walls stood firm against frontal efforts the assailants tried to surmount them. Picked troops swarmed up ladders to attempt escalades. Enormous wooden towers were erected by the labor of thousands and wheeled up to the moat by more thousands of men working levers. Great mounds of earth and stone, also the product of infinite toil, enabled the besiegers to rain down missiles and drop bridges for storming parties.

There remained a third dimension to siegecraft, and the attackers neglected no opportunity to burrow under the walls. Tunnels were begun from hidden points and continued beneath the inner works to admit troops for a *coup de main*. Mines were located by digging under the wall, shoring up the cavern with timbers, and filling it with combustibles. After a slow fire had burned out the supports the masonry collapsed and opened a breach.

Meanwhile, of course, the defenders had their tactics. When the wall was seriously menaced, they toiled night and day to throw up a half-moon of masonry behind it. They fired the enemy's towers or nullified the effect of his mound by building their own works still higher. They met the threat of a mine or tunnel with a counter-tunnel, and many a desperate encounter took place beneath the earth's surface. Finally, the artillery of the besieged, operating from a superior height and foundation, could deliver a more deadly fire.

Both sides relied on all manner of missile weapons, and sorties resulted in frequent combats outside the walls. Engines of war were used not only to hurl stones and spears but also fire pots, blazing arrows, caldrons of boiling oil and even infected corpses to spread disease. Flame-throwing devices, known in Greece as well as Asia from the earliest times, usually consisted of a metal tube and bellows for effect at close ranges. Naphtha, found in surface oil deposits, was doubtless the agent of combustion, since it played a small but continuous part in tactics down to the age of Greek fire.

If the masonry proved stout and the granaries well filled, the defense held the upper hand both in physical and economic respects. But throughout military history the moral element has generally been more decisive than either, for especially in siegecraft a chain is no stronger than its weakest link.

In all ages, so persistent is this tradition, resolute attackers have spared no effort to send their spies and secret agents within the walls. Until modern centuries the fate of a fallen city was horrible, yet despite the most urgent incentives to unity more garrisons have been betrayed than were ever starved or stormed into submission. The Old Testament, one of the greatest source books of ancient tactics, presents a famous example of such an outcome:

> And Joshua saved Rahab the harlot alive, and her father's house-
> hold, and all that she had; and she dwelleth in Israel even unto this

day: because she hid the messengers which Joshua sent to spy out Jericho.

Tyre was deemed by Alexander to be proof against either a moral or economic attack. He began operations, therefore, by building a mole

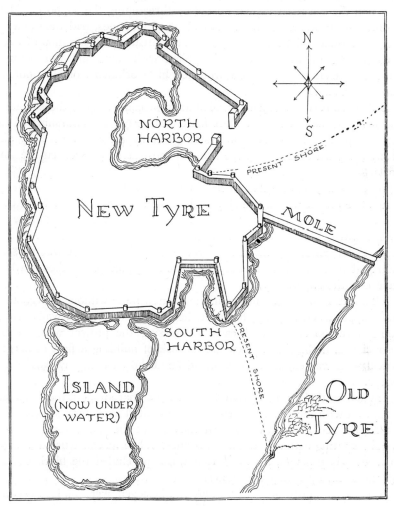

Alexander's Siege of Tyre

200 feet wide from the mainland across the half-mile strait (now a peninsula) to the walls.

The immensity of this labor may be estimated by the fact that the ruins have survived to this day. A city and a forest were swallowed up by the construction as old Tyre was destroyed and a wooded country-side stripped of timber. The population of the entire district served as forced labor along with the Macedonian army.

When the sea itself turned hostile by threatening the supports, Alexander, who professed to be a descendant of Hercules, had thousands of trees uprooted and thrown in whole for a breakwater. He mounted two great towers on the mole, each supplied with rams and war engines, while mantelets of green hide protected his workmen from fire pots or blazing arrows.

But Tyre had the enormous advantage of commanding the sea, since the invaders had sent their fleet back to Greece. The warships of the city constantly drove the artificers to cover by their sorties. They also brought skilled divers to grope beneath the water and weaken the supports.

When such tactics failed to halt the construction, the triremes made a surprise attack with a fire ship and set both towers ablaze. Next they fell upon the mole itself, opening gaps which soon led to its destruction by the waves. Alexander at once gave orders for a stronger and wider mole. After conceding that sea power was essential to success, he soon managed to collect a mercenary fleet from Cypress and Rhodes which gave him the superiority.

This factor enabled him to continue his new mole without interruption. As it approached the city, however, he concluded that the walls at this point were too strong to breach. Dismissing the project with godlike insouciance, he began the tremendous task of building a fleet of barges, armed with war engines, which could be anchored near any part of the works.

He had bottled up the Tyrian fleet in the two harbors, but the defenders fought on with the desperation so often exhibited in Semitic sieges. They sank great rocks in the water near the base of the walls, keeping Alexander's floating batteries at a safe distance. When he constructed dredges to meet this problem, a few Tyrian warships eluded the blockade and cut the ropes operating the cranes.

Alexander substituted chains and the besieged were at last reduced to awaiting the inevitable breach. They put up a frantic resistance, but the Macedonians brought the seven-month siege to an end with the storming of the stronghold.

Alexander proceeded down the coast and encamped before Gaza, the last barrier on the route to Egypt. This plains city depended on walls too mighty to be readily assailed by ram or bore. But again the conqueror conscripted the man power of a province, heaping up a mound estimated at 250 feet in height and 1,200 feet in diameter at the base. This eminence gave his war engines such an advantage that in two months Gaza was taken and destroyed.

THE BATTLE OF ARBELA

During the two years since his defeat at Issus the Persian monarch had assembled an army sometimes reckoned at half a million men. Whatever its numbers, this host possessed a fighting spirit unusual in Eastern warfare. Even the rank and file realized that complete dominion was the goal of invaders who had founded new cities after seizing Syria and Egypt.

Alexander's troops were upheld by motives of another but equally potent sort. Although the great adventure had only begun, recent Macedonian shepherds had already shared in a booty beyond their wildest imaginings—gold amounting to $3,600,000 recovered on the field of Issus alone, and an even larger sum at Damascus. Yet even this loot was insignificant as compared to the treasure that awaited in Susa, Babylon and Persepolis.

The two armies collided on the plain of Arbela, near ancient Nineveh, whose ruins remained as a monument to the fallen Assyrian Empire. Alexander had 7,000 cavalry and 40,000 foot, while the Persian host must have been four or five times as large.

Darius' plan of battle was probably as sound as could have been based on Eastern traditions of bulk. He placed his cavalry on the wings and the great masses of foot in the centre according to standard practice. As a departure he drew up an advance line of chariots with stout scythes protruding from both sides. These vehicles were to charge as the archers released their clouds of arrows. When the enemy had been thoroughly demoralized, Darius counted on his numbers for a vast envelopment.

In preparation he had chosen his own battlefield and leveled off the plain to the smoothness of a parade ground. Then, despite his numerical advantage, he left the initiative to his foemen.

That Alexander should have accepted the encounter on such terms is a measure of his confidence and audacity. His scouts had kept him fully informed as to the enemy's strength and dispositions. His staff officers confessed their trepidation by urging a desperate night attack as the only hope of success. Still, the twenty-five-year-old leader over-ruled them and drew up his army for a pitched battle.

As usual, he placed the phalanx in the centre and the cavalry on the wings, with hinges of light infantry between the two arms. But at Arbela for the first time he formed a reserve at the cost of reducing a perilously narrow front. Behind each wing he posted a flying column consisting of both horse and light infantry, to guard against the enemy's

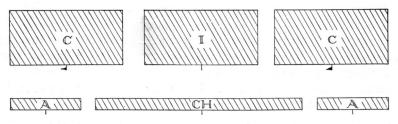

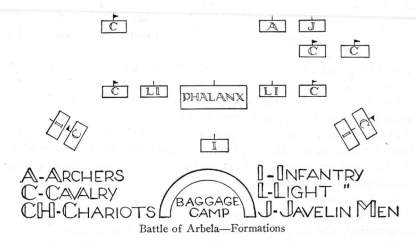

A-ARCHERS   I-INFANTRY
C-CAVALRY   L-LIGHT "
CH-CHARIOTS BAGGAGE CAMP   J-JAVELIN MEN

Battle of Arbela—Formations

expected envelopment. If this did not take place, the columns were in position to wheel inward and reinforce any weak point in the line. In the rear of all a force of infantry guarded the camp and constituted a second reserve in case of disaster.

These dispositions were chiefly of a precautionary nature. But Alexander planned for victory, not mere survival, when he distributed the strength of his wings. The right, led by him in person, he designed to be the instrument of attack. The left, aided by the phalanx, he committed to a stand against the enemy's attack. Thus he intended the army to fight two battles, one defensive and the other offensive, leading up to the climax.

Characteristically, he seized the initiative. His right, followed in echelon by the rest of the army, made a rapid and disconcerting thrust at the Persian left. In view of the much narrower Macedonian front, this movement brought most of the units opposite one enemy wing.

Darius, fearing that he might be cheated of his chariot tactics, felt obliged to make a corresponding shift, though the new ground proved less favorable. The ponderous Persian line, moreover, was at a disadvantage in sparring for position. The ranks became confused and Alexander struck with his cavalry.

Now, too late, Darius ordered his chariot charge. But the Macedonian force was ranged diagonally across the field, its right far in advance of the defensive left wing. This oblique front was less vulnerable to shock effect, while Alexander's archers and javelin men were in a position to harass the flanks of the chariots.

Before long the onslaught of scythes had been reduced to a wild tangle of locked wheels and frantic horses in the middle of the field. The chariots reaching their objective were awaited by foot soldiers who isolated and destroyed each in turn.

The battle entered its second phase when Alexander put all the strength of his right into a supreme effort. Every minute counted desperately, since his left and centre were struggling meanwhile against overwhelming odds. They had sent messages for reinforcements, but the offensive wing was now committed to such an extent that only its victory could save the remainder of the army from destruction.

The crisis came when the Macedonians drove so deeply into the enemy's left-centre that Darius and his nobles took to flight. The bulk of the host kept on fighting stoutly, and the issue remained in doubt until Alexander's right finally cut its way through. Then while portions of his cavalry pursued the beaten Persian horse, he wheeled inward and struck the flank and rear of the infantry masses in the centre.

This threat served at once to relieve the pressure on his own half-defeated left and centre. A panic soon spread through the Persian ranks, ending in the disintegration of a host still retaining a great numerical advantage.

The pursuit lasted until midnight, covering 25 miles and resulting in a fearful slaughter. And though Darius managed to escape with his life, the battle of Arbela in 331 B.C. dated the downfall of the empire conquered by Cyrus.

The Moral Basis of Tactics

So much for the physical side of a contest which remains one of the world's decisive battles. Unfortunately, the most faithful description can scarcely avoid leaving the impression that the victory was forged by hard blows in the heat of combat. Yet it is a demonstrable fact that neither Arbela nor any other great battle has ever been won by material means alone. The action, the impact of flesh and bone, the clash of steel upon steel—all these are but the leverage used by generalship to release far more powerful moral forces.

Even in ancient times, when it may be supposed that instincts were more primitive, few warriors fought for the love of fighting. The large majority fought to win, and their will to struggle waned at the moment when victory was apparently snatched out of grasp.

The test may be found in statistics indicating that most armies lose aggressive spirit before their casualties have reached 30 per cent. They are not physically crushed, since seven men out of ten are still able to bear arms. They are not necessarily overwhelmed, since the survivors may still be more numerous than the enemy's whole force. They are simply convinced! The threat of ultimate defeat has convinced them, and it is the business of the tactician to supply the threat.

If this can be accomplished by means of a military illusion, so much the better. Armies of superior numbers have been put to flight before one man out of ten has fallen. They were not beaten by blows which became more than flesh could bear. They were beaten in spirit according to laws as old as the human heart, and the victor is the one who can best apply those laws.

The methods of creating a conviction of defeat have been studied from the earliest times. Just as all tactics stem from three primitive formations, nearly all the battles of history, however complex their manoeuvres, may be broken down into three basic principles of offense.

There is the flank attack, giving the effect of a great human club striking at the enemy's exposed side. There is the battle of envelopment, comparable to pincers exerting pressure from both sides on the vitals of an adversary. And there is the battle of penetration, in which an army drives a wedge deep into the opposing line.

Plain frontal assaults, though sometimes necessary or even desirable because of tactical limitations, are as a rule the resource of dull generalship. The direct rear attack, on the contrary, is so rare in military chronicles that it may generally be associated with ambush or pursuit.

Finally, even the three most effective plans of battle are capable of being reduced to a single principle. For upon closer examination it becomes evident that the tactical pincers and wedge, no less than the club, are simply forms of the flank attack. Envelopment achieves its effect by blows at both flanks, while penetration seeks to exploit two new flanks after rupturing the enemy's front.

In any event the threat is largely moral. Armies, like the individuals found in their ranks, are made uneasy by the approach of danger from the side or rear. A single approach is not a complete flank attack, however, because the defenders can often face about to meet the menace on equal terms. The moral threat is produced by a compound assault— from the side while the front is simultaneously engaged. An army so attacked is in the position of an individual beset by two foemen, one of them dealing direct blows and the other stealing behind to stab him in the back.

This situation has no end of military counterparts. Epaminondas, it will be recalled, surprised his opponents at Leuctra when they expected a simple frontal battle in the Greek tradition. After fixing their attention by a general advance, he suddenly struck from one side with a local superiority of weight. The material effect was to crumple the enemy's right wing on its own centre, throwing the entire army into confusion. But this result was not as important as the moral threat to the Spartan rear, convincing those hardy warriors that they were hopelessly beaten. They fled, of course, from a foreboding of disaster which had been made to appear much worse than any realities already suffered. At the moment of rout they still retained a numerical advantage, while neither their left nor centre had been seriously engaged.

Marathon in turn is an example of the battle of envelopment. The Greeks had attacked all along the line, only to have their weak centre hurled back. Miltiades, the Athenian commander, created victory out of this reverse by ordering his wings to converge like pincers upon both flanks of the advancing Persians. At once the invaders sensed a trap and hastened to retire before their last avenue of escape was cut off at the rear. The Greek moral threat had overcome at least a two-to-one superiority in material respects.

At Arbela the vastly outnumbered Macedonians had small prospect of succeeding with either a flank attack or envelopment. Penetration, opening up new flanks by shock and disruption, remained the most hopeful means of dislocating the wider Persian front.

Allowing that no diagram can adequately represent masses of

struggling men, the accompanying plan suggests the positions of the two forces at the climax. The Persian archers and chariots, as shown in the preceding plan, have been put out of action. Then Alexander's army has assumed the dual functions of hammer and anvil, the one wing enduring blows so that the other might have the opportunity of delivering them. At the crucial moment the enemy is placed between hammer and anvil and threatened with destruction.

The mere threat sufficed to beat foes who had victory almost within grasp after severely punishing the Macedonian left and centre. Yet it is

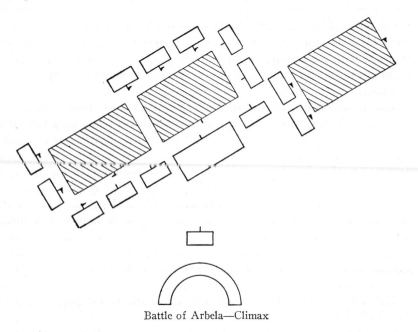

Battle of Arbela—Climax

not likely that Alexander needed more than a few thousand cavalry in the enemy's rear as the moral leverage which led to panic. Nor is it probable, even at the instant of panic, that the enemy's numbers had been much reduced from their original superiority.

Arbela, Marathon and Leuctra, though differing in method, have in common several broad principles which will be found to govern many a future operation of war. All three examples make it plain that the flank attack, however conceived, succeeds in proportion to its menace to an opponent's rear. It is evident, moreover, that the effectiveness of the assaulting troops depends largely upon the endurance of comrades who are meanwhile fixing some other part of the enemy's line. But the most significant lesson may be derived from the fact that in each of these instances the losers held the material advantage up to the climax of panic. Their casualties—and the rule has few exceptions in military chronicles—occurred less as a cause than an effect of defeat.

Napoleon, the most coherent if not the most able of generals, contrived in a later age to put the deduction into exactly a dozen words. "The moral is to the material in war," he said, "as three to one."

THE CROSSING OF THE JAXARTES

After plundering the lush Persian cities the Macedonian army soon resumed its march. Alexander's avowed purpose was the pursuit of Darius and the remnants of organized resistance; but this chase came secondary to his great plan of creating a Graeco-Persian empire.

Toward this end the campaigns of the next six years frequently presented tests more rigorous than pitched battle. Nearly every operation of conquest has to deal with the ancient trinity of time, weather and geography, any one of which may prove more formidable than an armed host. All three usually combine against the aggressor in mountain and desert fighting; and Alexander had now committed himself to endless small war in which the risks were constant and the triumphs petty.

Unfortunately, the classical authorities do not always leave good detailed accounts. But we know that the invaders made artillery their reliance in mountain operations, just as cavalry had been their main arm of battle. It is evident, moreover, that Alexander had reduced his war engines to parts which could be carried on the backs of his men. On at least two occasions, attacking strongholds too inaccessible to be reached by pack animals, he was still able to employ his catapults with decisive results.

The two most urgent problems of mountain warfare—supply and scouting—seem to have been equally well solved. The army continued to live on the conquered country without suffering for food or forage. And though his cavalry was often useless, Alexander proved so apt at securing information that his soldiers fell into none of the ambuscades that are the resort of hill warriors.

By the third year after Arbela his campaigns had taken him to the great range of the Hindu Kush, in modern Afghanistan, within sight of peaks 24,000 feet high. In the early spring his soldiers toiled over a pass rising to the altitude of an Alpine summit. After cruel hardships the frostbitten veterans descended to desert steppes where they met the opposite ordeal of thirst and heat.

At last they reached the limits of civilization at the river Jaxartes (Sir Darya) where Cyrus the Great was defeated and slain by the Scythians. And here Alexander directed an artillery operation, strikingly modern in its results, which compares with any of his battlefield victories.

The stream had been swollen by rains and the Scythians held the other bank in force. They had destroyed all boats but the young Macedonian leader fell back upon an expedient which he had used in crossing the Danube. By his orders the tents of the entire army were filled with straw and stitched watertight to serve as floats for improvised rafts.

Next he faced the problem of crossing a broad river under fire—an ordeal which remains to this day a major test of strategy. The Scythians waited at the water's edge to loose a deadly flight of arrows when the rafts were helpless in midstream. Alexander's war engines were also lined up, waiting for the signal, and at the moment of embarkation they began an intense bombardment. The barbarians, dismayed by the incredible shower of heavy missiles from such a distance, took to their heels and left the passage unopposed.

Never again until the last ages of the Roman Empire do we find such an advanced conception of artillery tactics.

After crossing the Jaxartes the invaders defeated the Scythians with heavy losses. This was no light achievement, for the descendants of those nomad horsemen, using the same maddening tactics, were to destroy a succession of civilized armies. Shunning action at close quarters, and coming to grips only to cut off small detachments, they gave an opponent no rest from their sorties. Yet when attacked in force, they vanished like a mirage after releasing a final flight of arrows over their shoulders.

The difficulty lay in pinning these elusive warriors down to battle. Alexander solved it by cavalry manoeuvres as swift and unpredictable as their own. After numerous feints he finally caught the enemy's main body between his light cavalry and a flanking column of mounted archers and javelin men. The more lightly armed barbarians were cut to pieces and offered no further resistance.

THE ELEPHANT IN TACTICS

The conqueror's last pitched battle, though of minor historical importance, has been called his strategic masterpiece. At Issus and Arbela he had been the grim assassin of empire; but with his task accomplished, Alexander appears in the role of studied military artist.

After the death of Darius the invader crushed the last Persian opposition before retracing his steps and marching down into northwest India. There he soon found a pretext for violating the domain of Porus, the most powerful of the potentates in this region.

Throughout its long march the Graeco-Macedonian army had been strengthened by native levies or reinforcements from the homeland until it probably equaled the Indian king's 50,000 foot and 3,000 cavalry. The invaders camped near modern Jalapur as Porus held the opposite bank of the river Hydaspes, half a mile wide.

Alexander divided his army and made the customary feints at forcing a crossing. Then after thoroughly baffling his adversary, he stole a night march of 18 miles and crossed with 5,000 horse and 9,000 phalangites, all picked troops. This operation is notable for the first recorded use of pontoons—crude boats built in sections which had been secreted for the attempt.

The bewilderment of Porus increased when he learned of the passage, yet saw the main Macedonian force still encamped on the other shore. For Alexander based his hopes of victory on a moral surprise intended to confuse the enemy by its very audacity After defeating a detachment sent to bar his progress, he marched straight to the Indian camp and offered battle to nearly four times his own numbers.

The Macedonian line was drawn up with the phalanx in the centre and the cavalry on the wings. Again, as in his former battles, Alexander proposed to attack the enemy's left-centre as a preliminary to penetration. But at the Hydaspes he varied his tactics by sending a small force of cavalry to ride entirely around the Indian army under cover of the hills, striking first at the right rear and then joining the concerted assault on the left flank and rear.

Porus had placed his infantry in the centre, his cavalry on the wings and 130 elephants across the front. The Macedonian attack succeeded in demoralizing the masses of Eastern foot, but Alexander had not reckoned sufficiently with the elephants. His horses were so terrified by the strange beasts that the cavalry charges lost most of their shocking power. Surprise having thus failed of victory, the battle turned into a bloody eight-hour struggle decided by sheer hard fighting.

The Hydaspes remains one of the few contests in which elephants took a leading part, for Arrian relates that the Indian cavalry fell back on them "as to a friendly wall for refuge." Like a boxer striking with his left and right, Alexander alternated blows with his cavalry and phalanx.

Still, he made no headway until the elephants "began to retire slowly, facing the foe like ships backing water, merely uttering a shrill piping sound."

Following up their advantage, the phalangites locked shields and broke through the dislocated Indian centre while the cavalry attacked in the rear. The main body of the Macedonian army crossed the river just in time to take up a pursuit in which Porus was captured and the remnants of his army scattered. That Alexander had won a costly victory is indicated by his 980 slain, a figure which hints at total casualties of 50 per cent.

IV

THE ROMAN LEGION

The Romans are sure of victory, knowing well that they have to do with men who are not their equals. And they cannot, as we must allow, deceive themselves; for their exercises are battles without bloodshed, and their battles bloody exercises.

—JOSEPHUS

DURING the campaigns of the past ten years Alexander had shared all the hardships of the march and suffered a score of wounds in his dual character as commander and cavalry warrior. Yet his gusto for war remained as prodigious as ever. After the victory of the Hydaspes he was ready to press on to new conquests, but his weary veterans had reached the limit of their endurance. In desperation they mutinied, forcing their young leader to turn back in acknowledgment of his first defeat.

The conqueror devoted his remaining few years to the consolidation of his gains. Nevertheless, his death at the age of thirty-two was followed by revolt and civil strife which led to the shattering of the great empire almost as rapidly as it had been conquered.

The wars of the Diadochi, or Successors, were waged by generals schooled in Alexandrian tactics and endowed with the loot of all Egypt and Persia. Their campaigns as a result were based upon a lavish outpouring of gold. Elephants soon came to play almost as prominent a part as cavalry; the hiring of mercenaries was on an unprecedented scale, and war engines arrived at a high standard of tactical development.

During the next two decades hired armies marched and countermarched over Greece, Persia and Asia Minor as Alexander's former officers made futile war upon one another. It was a cynical strife, with gold serving both as means and end, and treachery becoming as important as strategy.

With the rapid Orientalization of all the forces, cunning grew to be the substitute for strength. The hard-riding Macedonian cavalry, striving for penetration, gave way to horse-archers who were loath to close with the enemy until elephants had broken their ranks. Missile weapons, replacing shock attack, made the wars of the Diadochi memorable for the progress of siegecraft and artillery tactics.

At the famous siege of Rhodes, which began fourteen years after Alexander's death, 30,000 artificers and workmen served the attacking army. The largest of the towers, mounted on wheels, required 3,400 men to move it up to the walls. Another thousand were needed to wield a battering ram 180 feet long. Yet the defense was so ably conducted that Rhodes held out for six years, being finally relieved by allies who gained control of the sea.

Plutarch mentions galleys of 15 and 16 banks of oars in the accompanying naval engagements. Instead of the usual ramming tactics, the warships mounted engines to clear the decks of opposing vessels by "broadsides" of stones and spears. In the land warfare of the period, battles sometimes began with an artillery "preparation" by means of catapults and ballistae to demoralize the ranks of the infantry.

Despite the advance in the use of missile weapons, Alexander's forthright warfare had died with him, never to be revived by any of his successors. Thus for all of their occasional flashes of brilliance, the campaigns of the Diodochi lapsed more and more into routine professionalism. Finally, only a few generations later, the successors of the conqueror had completed the cycle back to its starting point, the simple phalanx.

ROME'S FIRST LESSONS IN WAR

It is always some conception of the human wall that is the beginning and end of tactics. Decadent peoples fall back upon it as a weary refuge; emerging nations, still unsure of their own powers, make it a foundation. Hence as the military heirs of Alexander were returning to phalangial solidarity, the ancestors of Scipio and Caesar had just begun to grope their way outward toward more daring combinations.

Early Roman warfare inevitably suggests a comparison with the Greece of several centuries before. Both peninsulas were defended against invasion by mountains and sea; both were divided by natural barriers into small states warring against one another; and both were peopled by hardy freemen whose distrust of political power was equaled only by their willingness to serve in the ranks as citizen-soldiers.

But here the likeness ends, for the Romans were armed from the beginning with a unity and purpose never developed by any Greek city.

Originally a mere den of robbers and outcasts, Rome soon progressed from plunder raids to campaigns of conquest against her neighbors. And in contrast to Greek citizens who could seldom agree among themselves, the Romans resembled warrior ants in their heroic conception of the duty owed the cause by the individual.

This communal spirit, rather than any marked superiority in weapons or tactics, gave them an early ascendancy in the Italian peninsula. They were beaten thoroughly and often, but no people ever showed a greater genius for profiting from defeat. Only two years after Alexander's death they suffered at the hands of the Samnites a reverse so complete that it led to the surrender of an army and the acceptance of humiliating terms. The disaster also led to the gradual adoption of a new formation which promised to succeed where the phalanx had failed.

This was the beginning of the Roman legion.

At the Caudine Forks a whole army had been trapped by the Samnites in hill warfare, reiterating the historical lesson that the phalanx is unsuited to manoeuvre in rough country. Philip of Macedon met the difficulty by retaining and even increasing the solidarity of the formation, while lending it mobility by means of cavalry and light infantry. The Romans, lacking a Philip, learned painfully from experience. Over a period of several generations, they developed a formation so marvelously supple that it has been compared to the human hand. For the legion was capable either of closing up solidly like a fist, or of feeling out the enemy's weaknesses with the effect of exploring fingers.

The new organization did not, like Philip's army, begin a career of uninterrupted victories. Nor did it wear out in a historically brief period, despite some jolting defeats endured from time to time. The system went on, steadily keeping abreast of changing conditions, to dominate the ancient world for the next five centuries.

And if the early Romans lacked a Philip or Alexander, they made it plain that they wanted neither. Like the Greeks, they preferred the risk of defeat to the danger of a commander seeking undue political power on the battlefield. For that reason the republican armies were led by elected consuls who held supreme authority on alternate days. Such a plan did not encourage brilliant generalship, but it served its purpose of curbing personal ambition. The legion, moreover, was not a military system designed to become the personal instrument of a conqueror. Evolved by a sturdy race of freemen, it depended for its results on minor tactics rather than the great decisions of strategy.

Whatever its numbers, the phalanx always went into action as a unit. The new Roman formation, on the contrary, consisted of forty infantry combat units. They were drawn up in three lines 250 feet apart, as shown in the accompanying diagram, on a front of 1,200 feet.

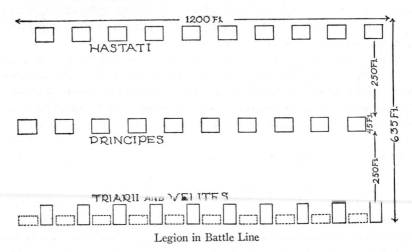

Legion in Battle Line

The first two lines were composed of 20 maniples, each a separate little phalanx of 12 files and 10 ranks. Each unit of 120 men held a front of 60 feet and a depth of 45 feet, giving the soldier ample room for the free use of his weapons. An interval equal to its own front separated every maniple from its neighbor, in order to permit manoeuvre over rough ground.

Nor had solidarity been sacrificed for mobility. The maniples of the second line were arrayed behind the first in chessboard fashion; they could readily move forward into the intervals, presenting a solid phalangial front to the enemy. Likewise, in time of need, the units of the first line could retreat into the intervals of the second. In the third line 10 units of light infantry were alternated with as many of reserves, the former numbering 120 men each and the latter 60.

A further distinction between the three lines depended on the quality of troops and length of service. The *hastati* of the first line were young soldiers of from twenty-five to thirty, and the *principes* of the second line included seasoned troops ranging in age from thirty to forty. The third line consisted half of *triarii,* veteran reserves fighting their last campaigns, and half of *velites,* youths of from seventeen to twenty-five, serving as light infantry.

From front to rear one maniple of each classification formed a cohort, or Roman battalion, of 420 men. Ten such cohorts made up the total infantry strength of a legion; but 20 were usually combined with 900 cavalry and other supporting units into a small, self-sustained army of about 10,000. The numbers and order were constantly varied to meet changing conditions, since the legion proved its adaptability against time and circumstance as well as the enemy.

The consul acting as commander-in-chief was held responsible to the Senate. Under him, and sometimes appointed by him, six tribunes had somewhat the authority of colonels. In active service the most renowned and essential officers of the legion were its 60 centurions, or captains, two of whom commanded each maniple.

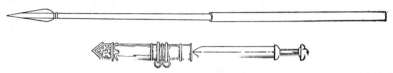

Roman Pilum and Gladius

The two famous weapons of the Roman legionary were the pilum and gladius—the one a seven-foot throwing and thrusting spear, the other a 20-inch cut-and-thrust sword with a broad, heavy blade. In quality and workmanship both were superior to any hand weapons heretofore produced in the ancient world. The pilum was capable of penetrating the stoutest armor when hurled from short distances, and Livy relates that the two-inch blade of the gladius could sever an opponent's arm or leg.

The *velites* were armed with javelins and darts for skirmishing, while the *triarii* bore a pike ranging from 10 to 14 feet in length.

Upon closing with the enemy the legion customarily took the initiative even against numerical odds. The agile *velites* opened the engagement by pouring in a volley of javelins and darts before retiring to the rear to await their duty of caring for the wounded. Then the maniples of *hastati* went into action at a charge, hurling their pila and rushing in with the deadly short sword before the foe had time to recover. They were followed in rapid succession by the *principes,* who added a second shock to the foe's demoralization.

If they found themselves in difficulty, the *hastati* slowly retreated into the intervals of the second line, forming a temporary phalanx. Or in an emergency the veteran *triarii* of the reserve came to the rescue with their pikes.

Although a force of 300 horse supported each 10 cohorts of foot, Roman cavalry remained of small account until a later age when defeat taught the need. Until then the legionary horseman may be considered merely a dragoon, or mounted infantryman.

The Training of a Roman

At seventeen the Roman youth entered upon an obligation of military service which did not end until the age of sixty, although the last fifteen years were usually devoted to garrison duty. The soldier of early centuries went unpaid, and campaigns were conducted during the summer months in the manner of all primitive military organizations. Then as Rome's ambitions and frontiers expanded, and as the citizen-soldier took the field for longer periods, it became necessary to allot a small compensation.

Romans held military service to be a cherished right as well as stern duty of citizenship, both freedmen and slaves being barred from the ranks. Despite the hardships, it was considered such a harsh penalty to be refused that disloyal factions were punished in this manner. Allied peoples of Italy were accepted for service but formed into separate organizations, an allied legion serving with a Roman on nearly equal terms.

Only men of good physique could qualify, but the Romans were unique among warlike races in their approval of short stature. At a later period Vegetius described the military ideal:

> The recruit must have sharp eyes, a head carried erect, broad breast, stout shoulders, big fists, long hands, not a big belly, of well proportioned growth, feet and soles less fleshy than muscular. If he has all this, no stress need be laid on the height, for it is far more important that the soldier be strongly built than tall.

On many a field, indeed, want of stature became an asset when the short and stocky legionary darted under the hedge of opposing spears and came up thrusting with his sword.

"No great dependence," warns Vegetius, "is to be placed in the eagerness of young soldiers for action, for fighting has something agreeable in the idea to those who are strangers to it." In line with this principle, the Romans endeavored to knock any romantic notions out of the recruit's head. Even before reporting for duty he had already undergone a strict preliminary training in running, jumping and climbing exercises. Then upon beginning active service, he served under drillmasters who subjected him to all the exertions of actual war. Sham battles were a favorite test, and Polybius says that the weapons of practice weighed twice as much as those wielded in battle.

Whatever the length of his service, the training of the legionary was never relaxed. Unnecessary public labors or needless marches were ordered simply for purposes of discipline. The burden of the soldier often consisted of cloak, shield, armor, helmet, weapons, ax, spade, scythe, pot for cooking, several weeks' rations, and two stout palisades to be used in making camp. The total could hardly have amounted to less than 75 pounds.

At the end of a long march the weary soldier was put to digging ditches and throwing up earthworks strengthened by the palisades he had carried all day on his back. After the camp had been made and the sentries posted, he enjoyed his one brief luxury—the privilege of eating from a reclining position, since his morning meal was gulped while standing. But even this boon might be taken away as punishment for the slightest offense or mistake.

Wheat, ground daily and made into cakes or porridge, served as the basis of legion rations, being supplemented by fresh meats or vegetables whenever possible. Olive oil was considered a necessity of diet, while vinegar or sour wine was esteemed for supposed medicinal as well as thirst-quenching virtues.

"Bad water is a kind of a poison," wrote Vegetius, "and the cause of epidemic disasters." For though the ancients may not have suspected the existence of germs, they show an almost modern spirit in their military health regulations. All authorities emphasize the need for selecting camp sites with the utmost care.

Roman Legionary

The peculiarly Roman science of castramentation grew out of discipline as well as the practical good sense distinguishing all functions of the legion. A consular army of two legions, or nearly 10,000 men, occupied a site of about fifty acres. In form it was invariably square, with well-guarded gates of entry on each side. And though the camp might be only for a night, walls and ditches were dug to repel an assault in force.

The two main lateral avenues of the military city had always the same name and location. On either side of the Via Retentura were located such special branches of the service as baggage, headquarters, hospital and supply. The Via Principalis, 100 feet wide, was lined with the tents of the tribunes and centurions, each opposite his own command.

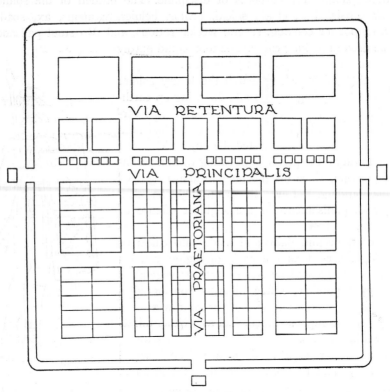

The Legion In Camp

Below this thoroughfare stretched the tents of the soldiery, the same spot being assigned every night to the same troops. Each maniple took up a hundred square feet, and the cavalry had separate grounds for the picketing of horses. The two legions, allied and Roman, were divided by the Via Praetoriana.

Whether the camp was in Gaul or Africa, the soldier always found himself in surroundings so familiar that he could form into ranks on the darkest night. Every man had the number of his cohort painted on his shield, and the units were further identified by different colors. Calls of the tuba and cornu, forerunners of the bugle, rang through the tented streets to summon the troops.

The discipline of the legionary received the same minute supervision as camp sanitation. Floggings with rods were administered for trivial offenses, the death penalty for cowardice or disobedience. Merely being absent beyond hearing of trumpet call could be defined as treason and punished by crucifixion. No other nation of history ever imposed such rules on citizen-soldiers; and a nineteenth century military writer, Colonel Ardant du Picq, has offered a psychological explanation:

> In order to conquer enemies that terrified his men, a Roman general heightened their morale, not by enthusiasm but by anger. He made the life of his soldiers miserable by excessive work and privations. He stretched the force of discipline to the point where, at a critical instant, it must break or expend itself on the enemy.

However this may be, the fact remains that the early legionary, with his cropped head and brown cloak, was almost wholly lacking in the qualities summed up by the phrase "military spirit." He displayed few of those whims of mercy or generosity which varied the routine cruelties of other ancient warriors. Always more the citizen than the soldier, he made it his single-minded aim to crush, if not to exterminate, the enemies of the republic by the most earnest and direct means.

THE VICTORIES OF PYRRHUS

Within a generation the improved Roman tactical system inflicted upon the Samnites a defeat which compensated for the disaster of the Caudine Forks. Once conquered, the subject peoples of Italy were allowed a wise measure of political liberty, and their legions were soon fighting side by side with those of Rome.

As its next test the republic encountered an able invader. Pyrrhus, king of Epirus, had already proved himself to be one of the most talented of the military adventurers who rose to power after the collapse of the Macedonian Empire. In 281 B.C. he brought to southern Italy an excellent army and an Alexandrian dream of conquering a new empire in the West.

Two Roman armies marched out to meet him and were soundly beaten during the campaigns of the first two years. Nevertheless, the invader's gains were so dubious at the battle of Heraclea that the term "Pyrrhic victory" has remained for all time the description of an overcostly success.

The Epirotic king based his strategy upon the supposition that Roman military progress had scarcely advanced beyond the barbarian stage. To his surprise the legions snatched the initiative, diving under the pikes of the Greek and Macedonian mercenary phalangites and inflicting ruinous casualties. The disciplined maniples were not shaken by their first experience against elephants, and only Pyrrhus' superior cavalry enabled him to gain his dearly bought victories.

The resolution of the republic remained stanch even when the invading army threatened Rome. And in the final clash, on the field of Beneventum, the legions won the decisive battle of the five-year war, forcing the disillusioned conqueror to set sail from Italy. Maniple prevailed over phalanx by virtue of hard fighting, and at the crisis the Romans succeeded in driving the elephants back through the broken ranks of the enemy.

In exactly the same spirit, only ten years later, the republic set itself the grim task of mastering a problem more formidable than the one presented by Pyrrhus' elephants. Roman military development had been strictly along the lines of land warfare, yet at the outbreak of the First Punic War in 264 B.C. the nation challenged a power whose warships ruled the western Mediterranean.

That Rome should have created a navy at all was a marvel in view of inexperience and lack of shipbuilding facilities. To have assembled a fleet which won an important sea victory within five years was undoubtedly the greatest achievement of the long war. This triumph remains an outstanding exception to the historical rule that naval strength is in proportion to the growth of a country's merchant marine.

During the two centuries since Salamis warships of four and eventually five banks of oars had replaced the trireme, though the ram remained the chief offensive threat. A Carthaginian quinquereme, driven ashore in a tempest, became a model for Roman shipbuilders, and the first crews were trained in frameworks set up on dry land. A fleet was launched in sixty days from the time the timbers were felled, only to meet with disaster as a consequence of faulty navigation.

But the republic's best asset, as it proved, was ignorance of established naval practice. Romans distrusted the new element too much to place any faith in the complex manoeuvres of ramming: either by land or sea they wished to settle the account with sword in hand. This prejudice led to a revolution in tactics, as is so often the case when novices make war. In the corvus, a huge hook mounted on the prow of a warship, the Romans found a means to grapple on an enemy vessel while dropping a bridge for boarding her. As further preparation for combat at close quarters, the new quinqueremes were equipped with fighting turrets fore and aft to hold picked bands of marines.

These innovations took the Carthaginians by complete surprise at the battle of Mylae, 260 B.C., and their fleet was sunk or routed off the coast of Sicily, giving the Romans command of the sea.

Again, four years later, the republic won a victory at Ecnomus by a departure from standard tactics. Faced by 330 Carthaginian vessels bearing down in a semicircle to envelop the smaller Roman fleet, the defenders formed a wedge by lashing together a group of warships at the apex. As many as 30,000 rowers and fighting men on both sides took part in a hard-fought engagement which ended in another Roman victory with 58 enemy ships sunk or captured.

The new navy continued to find the sea a more redoubtable foe than the Carthaginians. An entire fleet of 117 ships and 20,000 men perished in a single tempest; and during a period of five years no less than 700 quinqueremes were lost to the elements. Such reverses merely caused the Senate to demand added sacrifices, and peace was finally forced upon Carthage as a result of the decisive Roman sea victory of Aegusa.

Meanwhile, to complete the paradox, the seamen of Carthage had improved their land tactics to an extent which enabled them to gain the most impressive victory of the war.

During the early years the legion had overrun Sicily, beating the Carthaginians in nearly every encounter. Goaded by defeat, they at last employed the Spartan general Xanthippus to train an army for the defense of Africa. The Romans landed an expeditionary force under the consul Regulus, and the two armies met near Carthage in the battle of Tunes. The four legions commanded by Regulus amounted to about 17,000 foot, supported by the usual inadequate cavalry arm. Xanthippus brought 12,000 infantry, 4,000 horse and 100 elephants.

The persistent use of elephants in Carthaginian tactics may be traced back to the Orientalized armies of the Diadochi, whose mercenary soldiers became the tutors of Carthage. Yet with the possible exception of the Hydaspes, it is difficult to find a battle in which the huge beasts played a decisive part. They terrified the horses of an untried enemy, but foot soldiers were rarely thrown into grave disorder. On the contrary, the missiles of defenders often tormented the animals into a frenzy of fear and rage, so that they became equally dangerous to friend and foe. In recognition of this factor the mahouts were equipped with a mallet and spike to drive into the brain of an unmanageable elephant.

Regulus at least was sufficiently impressed to have altered the customary checkerwise formation of the maniples by placing them one behind the other. This allowed wide intervals through which he trusted that the elephants could be driven to the rear.

The animals were thus stampeded before doing much harm, but the enemy's cavalry seized its opportunity. After dispersing the inferior legionary horse, the Carthaginians found their way into the lanes between maniples and opened up new flanks. The Romans were cut to pieces and only 2,000 escaped a disaster in which Regulus was made captive.

This reverse had no bearing on the outcome of a naval war, as Carthage was eventually forced to cede Sicily and pay an indemnity amounting to $4,000,000. On the whole the Romans could and did congratulate themselves on progress which had made them masters of Italy and the Mediterranean within a generation. They had every reason to suppose that the nation was entering upon a period of well-earned tranquillity, and for the first time in her violent history Rome relaxed.

V

HANNIBAL CROSSES THE ALPS

*The Romans did not provoke him while he remained
quiet, such power did they consider that single general
possessed, though everything else about him was falling
into ruin.*

—LIVY

IN THE autumn of 218 B.C., when a gaunt Carthaginian army debouched from the Alps into the plains of Italy, the name of its leader meant little to the average Roman citizen. The idea of Carthage ever invading Rome was incomprehensible to a people who commanded the sea and assumed that the inevitable next war would be fought in Africa.

But there was nothing at all miraculous about Hannibal and the force he led. Both were the products of one man's will. That man was Hamilcar Barca, and he had spent his life in the accumulation of the destructive forces which now hung over the republic.

As an epic of hate his career has perhaps never been equaled in history. He had emerged from the last war a ruined Carthaginian aristocrat, after giving an excellent account of himself as commander in Sicily. Then the peace party rose to power in beaten Carthage, and he found no support for his plans to carry a second conflict into the camp of the enemy.

Alone, on his own responsibility and using his own funds, he led an expedition for the conquest of Spain. Carthage had not dared to defy Rome by building a new navy, so he had no choice but to march along the African littoral and cross in small transports at the Pillars of Hercules. Within eight years, by arms and diplomacy, he conquered the tough Iberian tribesmen and created virtually a personal empire out of a third of the peninsula.

Looking back on this achievement a generation later, Cato declared that no king was worthy of being named beside the uncrowned Hamilcar.

Spain provided most of the resources, human, moral and material, for a new Punic war. The revenues from the mines not only financed Hamilcar's operations but also won him the approval of a merchant nation interested in the profits to be derived from a subject people. The Iberian tribesmen made a sturdy infantry nucleus for a new army, and the peninsula became a proving ground for a new tactical system.

After Hamilcar's death in battle, his son Hannibal rose to command at the age of twenty-seven. Already a veteran of the Iberian campaigns, the young general was the final product of the will which had driven one man to plot the destruction of a power able to raise a quarter of a million troops.

Hannibal, like his three brothers of the "lion's brood," had been taught by Greek tutors and trained from infancy in the Barca creed of everlasting war on Rome. Hence as a man of education he must have compared his situation with that of Alexander, who likewise inherited from his father a complete army and tactical system.

In its elements the new Carthaginian army was as motley a force as has ever been assembled: Iberian heavy infantry wearing white tunics and carrying bucklers of bull's hide; tall, half-naked Gauls with their huge swords and spears; Balearic slingers trained from childhood to hurl leaden pellets with amazing force and aim; Libyan foot soldiers with shaved heads and tattooed limbs; Numidian light horse clad in the skins of wild beasts and riding without bridles; African javelin men who fought in the wicker towers borne by the elephants.

A dozen tongues were spoken by the rank and file, yet Hamilcar had managed to weld such strange material into an organization that proved more obedient than the Macedonian army. And just as Philip made himself strong where Greece was weak, Hamilcar built up the cavalry arm neglected by Roman generals.

Both light and heavy horse were found in higher proportion to infantry than in any former army of Western warfare. Gauls, Africans and Iberians composed the heavy arm, having adopted the barbarian tactic of mounting two warriors, one to fight on horseback and the other on foot after the charge.

The light cavalry, made up of wild Numidian irregulars, depended on mobility. These nomads of the African plains, armed with lance, dart and sword, were natural foragers and skirmishers. Like the Scythians, they avoided close combat while menacing an opponent's flank or rear, and in the pursuit of broken troops they showed a pitiless persistence.

Libyans, Gauls and Iberians filled the ranks of the heavy foot. They fought in a close phalangial formation of from twelve to sixteen ranks, though at a later period adopting many of the arms and tactics of the legion. In the infantry as well as the mounted arm the light troops were numerous and effective. The Balearic slingers and the hooded burnoose-wrapped African tribesmen had no equals in a Roman military system which depended upon half-trained youths as skirmishers.

Lightness and mobility, in short, were the most valuable assets of a Carthaginian army which included barely enough heavy horse and foot to serve as a pivot for battle manoeuvre. On the march this army moved with bewildering rapidity, since it carried little baggage and depended on its irregular cavalry for food and forage. The half-savage men in the ranks were better inured to privations than civilized soldiers, and the prospect of loot acted as a sufficient incentive.

THE TREBIA AND LAKE TRASIMENE

Hannibal's troops had need of their hardihood in view of the losses they sustained in the Pyrenees and Alps. Of the large, well-equipped army which left Spain, 46,000 reached the Rhone; and of these only a remnant of 20,000 foot, 6,000 horse and a few elephants survived the October ascent of the Alpine passes.

Polybius, writing a generation later, states that "both in appearance and condition they were brought to a state more resembling that of wild beasts than human beings."

The severity of the ordeal may explain the tardiness of Roman efforts, both before and after the crossing, to oppose Hannibal. The republic did not become fully aroused until the invaders were recuperating on the plains of the Po; then the audacity of a foeman who had undergone such sacrifices did not fail of its full moral effect.

Roman generals had not been idle during the twenty-three years since the last war, but they failed to grasp the strategic purpose of Carthaginian preparations in Spain. As a consequence the invasion seemed to occur with the suddenness of an avalanche, reducing the nation to a hurried defense on its own soil.

Once begun, the measures for resistance were pushed with energy, and the first test came at the battle of the Trebia about two months after the crossing of the Alps.

The Carthaginians had won a preliminary cavalry combat on the river Ticinus against the consul P. Cornelius Scipio. The beaten force immediately united with another consular army under Sempronius, making a total Roman strength of about 40,000. Hannibal, who had been reinforced by Gallic recruits to nearly equal numbers, did nothing to oppose the junction of his enemies. Desiring the moral effect of a victory at the outset, he even permitted the Romans a small cavalry success in the hope of bringing on a general attack.

This bait proved so tempting that Sempronius overcame the protests of his colleague and ordered an impetuous advance. The legionaries waded waist-deep through the icy waters of the Trebia during a snowstorm, yet Hannibal took no advantage of their confusion. His plan aimed at annihilation rather than repulse, and Sempronius was allowed time to form his three lines of maniples with the river at his back.

In ravines near the flat battlefield Hannibal had concealed a force of 2,000 light cavalry under his young brother Mago. While they awaited his command, he began the engagement with his Balearic slingers and African light foot, who quickly drove in the *velites* of the other army. Then the Carthaginian cavalry, lately brought up to a strength of 10,000 by Gallic reinforcements, routed the Roman horse as a preliminary to an infantry attack which bent both legionary wings toward the river.

It is a tribute to Roman discipline that Hannibal's elephants had little effect. But Sempronius' centre was isolated when the wings were pushed back, thus exposing the whole army to envelopment. At this moment Mago suddenly appeared with his detachment and fell upon the rear to complete the work of destruction.

Only about 10,000 men of the Roman centre cut their way through to safety. Of the 30,000 casualties, many were drowned in the river or trampled by the elephants. Hannibal's losses are not given, but they could not have been slight in view of the hard fight put up by the vanquished.

A few months later, before Rome had recovered from the disaster of the Trebia, the nation was horrified by another slaughter which ranks as the greatest ambush of military history. Hannibal had left his winter quarters near modern Bologna and alarmed the republic by marching across the Apennines, through the marshes and down into the peninsula. His wild soldiery devastated the countryside for miles around, causing the consul Flaminius to pursue with more vigor than caution.

The Carthaginian general, having recently lost an eye from an infection, rode in a litter borne by the last of his elephants. In spite of his illness he perceived that the wooded and hilly shores of Lake Trasimene provided a natural trap for an unwary antagonist. Leaving only a rearguard detachment to lure Flaminius into the pass, he accomplished the feat of hiding practically the whole Carthaginian army in the heights overlooking the road.

The Gauls, Iberians and Africans were in their places before dawn, while from the lake rose a heavy morning mist which aided the deception. The signal for attack found the Roman columns strung out helplessly in marching formation. They were speedily cut to pieces by foes who burst out from the woods, and of the army of 30,000 only about 6,000 escaped the general fate of massacre or drowning.

A few days later the republic had an added misfortune when Hannibal inflicted 4,000 casualties on a cavalry force which the consul Servilius had sent to his colleague's rescue.

A less courageous people might have been thrown into a panic by the loss of two armies in so short a time. But at least the legion had not been found wanting, for both at the Trebia and Lake Trasimene a few maniples cut their way through the entire Carthaginian army. Even in defeat the Roman system had proved its merit against incoherent elements made terrible only because of one man's genius for war.

Hannibal himself had already paid his crushed foes the tribute of adopting their arms, armor and formations. With his last success he captured enough Roman equipment to rearm most of his infantry; and in later engagements his three-line battle order bore more resemblance to the legion than the phalanx.

The defects in the republic's military structure were not new. They had simply survived the strain of lesser tests. The inferiority of legion cavalry, apparent enough in the Pyrrhic and first Punic conflicts, now became a fatal handicap against an adversary who made the cavalry his main strength. The Roman division of authority—the custom of two consuls commanding on alternate days—proved an equally grave weakness against a general with absolute supremacy. Intended to discourage rash conclusions, the divided command actually invited reckless decisions (as at the Trebia) when consuls failed to agree.

Finally, a national frame of mind seems largely to blame for the republic's disasters. Tacitus and other ancient writers emphasize the Roman pride in bold and straightforward fighting, the Roman scorn for ruse and stratagem and indirect approach. Subterfuge had always been held a token of weakness—an attitude which made the Roman mentality peculiarly vulnerable to Hannibalic guile.

The reaction, coming after the Trasimene massacre, was terrific. And if the Romans had once erred by fighting too bluntly, they now flew to the opposite extreme of not fighting at all.

This policy, fortunately, was put into effect by a general of wisdom and moral courage when the Senate gave Quintus Fabius Maximum the supreme command and dictatorial powers in the emergency. Keeping to the hills, where Hannibal's cavalry could not follow effectively, he began the campaigns which have made "Fabian" an adjective standing for delaying tactics.

For months he risked only such operations of small war as cutting off stragglers, attacking foraging parties or destroying supplies. He resisted every attempt of Hannibal to lead him into an ambush or general engagement, even though he had to watch the Roman countryside being cruelly ravaged.

The "masterly inactivity" of Fabius won the republic a breathing spell in which to renew its morale. But at last the situation became more than a proud nation could endure, and public sentiment forced the Senate to prepare for a test of strength. The army was built up to an unprecedented total of 85,000, or nearly double the numbers of Hannibal, and ordered to take the initiative.

The Battle of Cannae

Despite this show of force, the cavalry remained woefully weak in proportion to foot. Nor had the system of command been improved, since we still find the partnership of a prudent general, Aemilius Paullus, and a hotheaded colleague, Tarentius Varro.

The latter, on his days of authority, was singled out as the victim and craftily lured into offering battle on the plain of Cannae in the summer of 216 B.C.

Hannibal had in mind an astonishingly bold plan which aimed to profit from the very numerical advantage of the enemy. First throwing out a screen of light troops to conceal his dispositions, he drew up a line of battle which could have been conceived only by a genius or a fool. The unique feature was a convex centre, composed of 25,000 Gallic and Iberian foot and bending outward toward the 70,000 legionaries of the Roman centre. The units at the apex were heaviest, the sides being built up in echelon and linked to the Libyan infantry of the wings.

The tactical idea behind this strange conception might well have been borrowed from an ancient principle of engineering; for the formation was in reality a great human arch, designed to bear the weight of the whole Roman army! The more the enemy pushed this arch inward, the more cohesive it necessarily became, reaching its utmost solidarity when parallel with the wings. Hannibal's plan did not end here, since he had prepared no mere passive resistance. He intended that the convex centre should not only be flattened out, but even forced back into a concave position—to become a terrible trap for the Roman army when the Carthaginian wings wheeled inward.

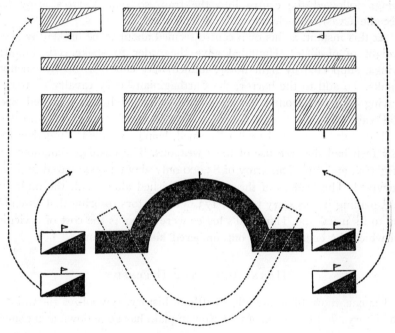

Battle of Cannae

The risks were in full proportion to the expectations of success. Even the most disciplined troops might have offered problems in such a complex array, and Hannibal led alien mercenaries fighting for plunder. If they got out of hand, the collapse of the centre would inevitably be followed by the destruction of the Carthaginian army.

Varro unwittingly aided his adversary by forming his maniples in six files and twenty ranks instead of the usual front of ten men and depth of twelve. Weight was thus gained at the cost of flexibility, and the Roman consul appears also to have reduced the intervals. When the battle opened, the legion had virtually been transformed into a phalanx which bore down massively on the arch of the Carthaginian centre. The Gallic and Iberian infantry gave ground slowly as Hannibal took personal command of a retirement depending on exact order and timing. He showed perfect control over his men, but the danger increased as they withdrew into a concave formation which must grow weaker as the enemy advanced.

The Romans, nevertheless, were in worse peril at the moment they raised the victory shout. Their line had lost all order as the converging wings followed the centre into the trap, so that Varro's army had become a vast, shapeless huddle of humanity.

At this instant, as his own centre seemed about to be broken by sheer weight of numbers, Hannibal gave the order to strike. His infantry wings, supported by light horse, immediately closed in on the enemy's flanks. To add to the horror, the Carthaginian heavy cavalry of 10,000, having returned from the rout of the legionary horse, now fell upon the rear.

The Romans were virtually disarmed, being so crowded together that few men had the free use of their weapons. The ensuing slaughter was frightful, and out of an army of 85,000 only about 15,000 dazed fugitives survived. The leaders of the republic perished along with the rank and file, making it necessary to elect 173 new senators to bring that assembly up to its usual 300. Hannibal's losses were 6,000 as the cost of a victory in which the enemy's slain outnumbered his whole army.

HANNIBAL ON THE DEFENSIVE

Cannae, more than any other battle of history, symbolizes the ultimate in victory; and the name of that Roman plain has gone down as a generic noun to soldiers of all ages.

Polybius interpreted the republic's disaster as "a lesson to posterity that in actual war it is better to have half the number of infantry and a superiority in cavalry, than to engage your enemy with an equality in both."

The tactical resemblance to the Trebia is obvious, and both of Hannibal's great triumphs may have derived from Marathon. Yet nearly all of his operations, even to minor combats, were based upon the same conception. Where Alexander strove for penetration and disruption, the

Carthaginian general seldom departed from the principle of the ambush, the most primitive of tactical ideas.

Savages at a crude stage of development learn to hide behind trees and lie in wait for an unsuspecting enemy. Hannibal, a product of Phoenician and Greek culture, imagined gigantic ambuscades in which deadly forces were hidden behind ideas, though he showed himself perfectly capable of using trees for the purpose. For Cannae was no less an ambush than the Trasimene, the difference being only that one existed in the moral sphere and the other in the physical.

As the fruits of victory he at last gained allies when Capua, second largest city of Italy, led the southern part of the peninsula in revolt against Rome. The Carthaginian Senate sent reinforcements, and former neutrals such as Macedonia began to incline toward his cause.

Rome, in contrast, had become so crushed that slaves were hastily armed to defend the city after the restoration of Fabius to command of the remnants of the army.

Yet only a few months after Cannae the Carthaginian leader must have realized that the victory foreshadowed his own downfall. The very extent and completeness of a Cannae made the greatness of Rome the more convincing, while showing up in pitiless clarity the lack of Carthaginian resources. From the beginning Hannibal had made it plain that he did not hope to conquer Rome on the battlefield. Tactical victories were to be only the strategic means of raising all Italy in arms against harsh conquerors of recent memory. "I come," said the invader, "not to place a yoke on Italy, but to free her from the yoke of Rome."

As a Carthaginian, he reckoned without the moderation and wisdom of a Roman administration. There was no yoke on Italy, and few peoples of the peninsula cared to exchange Roman liberties for a Carthaginian promise.

Such halfhearted allies as Hannibal gained in Apulia and Bruttium proved to be dubious assets, for all of his reinforcements were required to defend them from the vengeance of Rome. Their participation diverted his energies into a war of posts and sieges, the one form of tactics in which he was weak. His supply problems were increased, since he could scarcely forage in allied country with the freedom his army had exhibited at the enemy's expense.

Rome, meanwhile, grew morally stronger and more united. At last the heads of the republic were able to agree on a sound permanent policy in dealing with Hannibal. Though he was not to be given the opportunity for another triumph, Rome did not propose to revert to Fabian tactics.

The new middle-course strategy was to be based upon several small armies hemming him in, keeping him continuously on the defensive but avoiding a general engagement.

It is one of the marvels of military history that the mind which had planned a Cannae could with equal ability adapt itself to a long-drawn defensive against odds. Yet for thirteen more years Hannibal stood off three and four Roman armies simultaneously by means of marches and manoeuvres more brilliant than his battlefield victories. Feinting, dodging, parrying, sometimes narrowly escaping encirclement, he wore out a succession of Roman generals and finally left Italy of his own volition with his remaining force intact.

The fifth year after Cannae he forced the republic to put forty legions into the field, or 200,000 troops, of which 90,000 operated directly against him in four armies, and the rest in subsidiary campaigns made necessary because of his invasion. And even though Roman generals shunned battle for the most part, he managed to trap and destroy two small armies in a single summer.

When Rome laid siege to Capua in 211, as punishment for disloyalty, Hannibal tried unsuccessfully to relieve the city. Then with a flash of his old strategic boldness, he left Capua behind and marched straight upon Rome. The capitol gave way to brief dismay, but Roman generals had learned Hannibal's weakness in siegecraft and war engines. They refused to be drawn from Capua, which was finally taken and its inhabitants slain or sold into slavery.

During these years of ceaseless manoeuvre Hannibal's strength probably never exceeded 40,000, the bulk of his army being composed of unwilling recruits from southern Italy in place of his vanished veterans. Keeping this force together was no small achievement, since he could seldom offer either pay, loot or the certainty of rations.

As time went on, and as his army dwindled, the enemy grew constantly more able and aggressive, until Hannibal himself sought frequently to avoid battle. He had now become a victim of the strategic law which prescribes that a persistent victor must end by teaching the art of war to the vanquished. After years of conducting a school of applied tactics for Roman commanders, he developed in the consul Marcus Claudius Marcellus a pupil who got the better of the master in several small combats. As a final irony the consul Claudius Nero, successor to Marcellus, contrived to lure Hannibal into a typically Hannibalic ambush, and only the nearness of the fortified camp saved the Carthaginian force from disaster.

Improved Roman generalship became a genuinely decisive factor eight years after Cannae when Hannibal at last had a prospect of adequate Carthaginian support. His brother Hasdrubal, with an army larger than his own, had marched from Spain over the Alps and down into northern Italy. Three Roman armies and a distance of 250 miles now separated the two forces. The republic took every measure to prevent a junction, and the consul Livius was charged with the duty of halting Hasdrubal while Nero "contained" Hannibal in southern Italy.

Although Hasdrubal tried to communicate with his brother, the messenger was captured. And with enemy plans in his possession, Nero came to a strategic decision worthy of a Hannibal. He left most of his army facing that unsuspecting foeman, while with the remainder—a detachment of picked troops, 6,000 foot and 1,000 horse—he slipped away to the north to reinforce Livius against Hasdrubal.

Nero's progress turned into a triumphal march. The foot soldiers were carried in wagons by the country people over roads lined with cheering crowds. The 250 miles were thus covered in seven days, and the contingent arrived with added strength as a result of youths and old soldiers volunteering along the route.

Livius benefited perhaps more from moral than material reinforcement when the two Roman consuls combined. Taking the initiative, they out-manoeuvred the invader in the battle of the Metaurus and defeated him by means of Nero's flank attack. Hasdrubal was slain and his entire army reduced to casualties or scattered fugitives.

The Metaurus is the first recorded example in ancient warfare of a campaign on "interior lines"—i.e., an operation in which a general takes advantage of his position between two enemies to attack one before the other can come to the rescue. Nero created the strategic illusion so successfully that he had returned to southern Italy before his absence was surmised. Hannibal received his first news of the catastrophe when the Romans tossed his brother's bloody head over the ramparts of the Carthaginian camp.

Victories of Scipio Africanus

Even this triumph did not free Rome from the menace of her terrible antagonist. Hannibal maintained himself for four more years in southern Italy, withstanding every army the republic could send against him.

During this period he had little aid from his own country, while coping constantly with troops better than his own and led by a high

order of generalship. Yet it is by no means certain that Rome would
have gained the final decision if she had persisted in her warfare of
attrition. Toward the end, fifteen years after the crossing of the Alps,
her own vital resources were being drained more fatally than those of
the invader.

The republic's salvation came as the result of building a backfire of
military genius second only to that which threatened its ruin. Publius
Cornelius Scipio, son of the consul who became Hannibal's first opponent,
represented a new generation which had grown to manhood during the
struggle. And just as Hannibal had been nurtured on hatred of Rome,
young Scipio swore vengeance against the invaders after the Trebia and
Lake Trasimene.

He was first among his countrymen to realize that Hannibal could be
beaten more decisively in Spain and Africa than in Italy. This strategy
might have been borrowed from Hannibal himself, who had struck at the
nerve centres of Rome, knowing that the limbs would wither of themselves after a paralyzing blow.

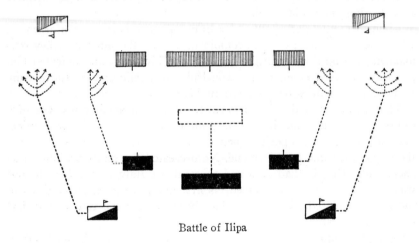

Battle of Ilipa

In Spain the Carthaginian army of the year 206 had been built up
to a strength of 75,000, commanded by Hasdrubal Gisco and Hannibal's
brother Mago. This force had dominated the peninsula since winning
a decisive victory in which Scipio's father lost his life.

As his first feat, the young Roman general captured the great Carthaginian base and arsenal at Cartagena by a bold *coup de main*. The victory
gave him a foothold for recruiting native troops into the ranks of his

small army. After several more minor successes, he gained enough strength to risk a pitched battle at Ilipa with the enemy's main force.

His army numbered 45,000 foot and 3,000 cavalry, while the enemy brought into action 70,000 foot, 32 elephants and 5,000 cavalry. Neither side placed much trust in the unwilling Spanish levies which made up most of their infantry strength. Mago and Hasdrubal met the problem by placing the Iberians on both wings, supported by the cavalry and elephants, and stationing the reliable African troops in the centre. Each morning for several successive days the Carthaginian army marched out from camp in this formation and offered battle. Scipio as regularly refused the engagement, though drawing up his ranks in readiness.

After thoroughly establishing his reluctance to fight, the Roman commander suddenly confronted the enemy in a dawn advance. The Carthaginians were taken by complete surprise and allowed no time for their morning meal. Scipio added to their discomfiture by forcing them to stand in line for several hours, cold and hungry, while he took his leisure about attacking.

He had disposed of his doubtful Iberian elements by placing them in a centre designed to be "refused" while both wings of legionaries were thrown obliquely forward. The success of this plan was as brilliant as its conception. The Iberians of the enemy's wings were immediately crushed when the Romans converged after their double oblique advance. In the meantime the Roman horse had routed the opposing cavalry and driven the elephants in on their own ranks. These successes forced the strong Carthaginian centre to retire without striking a blow. Scipio's withheld centre, never quite coming to grips, had served its purpose of nullifying the enemy's main force.

Ilipa became the most distinguished Roman victory of the war, but Scipio lacked Hannibal's sinister talent for exploiting his tactics to the limits of destruction. In spite of heavy casualties the defeated army retired in order and was beaten in detail only after an extended campaign of pursuit.

Two years later, with the last Carthaginian resistance stamped out in Spain, Scipio overcame the reluctance of the Senate and gained permission to carry the war into Africa. He landed with a small but well-trained army of veterans and for a time was hemmed in by superior numbers on the shore near Utica. But again he showed his mastery of surprise in an audacious attack on the enemy's camp which led to the annihilation of the encircling army.

By dint of diplomacy as well as fighting, Scipio gained Numidian allies and prevailed everywhere in the campaigns of the year 203, forcing the enemy to sue for peace after the loss of another army in the defeat of the Great Plains. The merit of Roman generalship and the improvement of Roman cavalry were the chief factors in bringing Carthage to a situation as desperate as that of the republic at the beginning of the war.

Still, the struggle was not to end without a more fitting climax. Before the peace negotiations could be completed, a reversal of Carthaginian sentiment resulted in the recall of Hannibal from Italy for a last tremendous effort.

The odds were against him from the moment he landed. His numbers were probably about 45,000, as compared to a Roman army of 36,000, but he was much weaker in the cavalry which had always been his arm of victory. The Carthaginian foot, moreover, was of poor quality. Few real veterans could have been left to Hannibal after his years of campaigning, and his Italian remnants had been hastily combined with the military debris remaining from the disasters in Africa.

Hannibal made a tacit confession of his weakness by requesting a parley just before the battle of Zama. When unable to obtain any softening of the Roman terms, he prepared for an encounter which could have but one result.

The engagement opened with a charge of the 80 elephants distributed along the Carthaginian front. These beasts had less effect than usual, since the clamor of the Roman trumpets drove them back upon their own ranks or through to the rear. Scipio then ordered the advance of his cavalry, which had no trouble in routing the mediocre Carthaginian horse. With both wings stripped, Hannibal might now have become an easy victim if his adversary had kept his cavalry well in hand. But the Roman and allied Numidian horse rode off the field, and the battle turned into a piecemeal series of infantry clashes.

The Carthaginian commander had adopted practically a legionary formation by drawing up his foot in three lines with the best troops in reserve. The low quality of his material could not be doubted when the Gallic levies of the first line recoiled from the Roman onslaught and endangered the whole army in their panic. Now came the curious spectacle of the Carthaginian first and second lines contending wildly against each other while the enemy dealt out death to both. When the disintegration of the first line was complete, the second had become so weakened as to be soon overlapped and cut to pieces.

The victory assured, Scipio had so little to fear from his antagonist that he paused with the grim deliberation of an executioner to sound the recall. Almost within bowshot distance he re-formed his veterans into a heavier line before administering the *coup de grâce*.

Hannibal, beaten down to his last reserves, and obviously not strong enough to counterattack even when his opponent's ranks were in confusion, could only await the final blow. Yet his ability to infuse his own spirit into oddly assorted military elements was never displayed more dramatically. Inspired by his leadership, the doomed Carthaginian third line fought with such fury that the issue actually remained in doubt for a time. Only the belated return of Scipio's cavalry, which fell upon the Carthaginian rear, put an end to the battle with the annihilation of the outnumbered survivors. Hannibal barely escaped with his life, and his country came to an abject acceptance of the enemy's terms.

Even the victory of Zama did not enable Rome to settle the account with her tireless foeman. After being placed at the head of the ruined state, Hannibal revealed a talent for peaceful administration that compares with his genius for war. With Carthage practically barred from commerce and seafaring, he built up a new national life on an agricultural foundation. So successful were his efforts that he stood ready within a few years to offer payment of an indemnity calculated to sap the nation's resources.

Rome could not allow such an enemy to remain in power and he was forced into exile in Syria. There he lost no time in fomenting an Asiatic uprising, known as the Syrian War, in which he took part as naval commander. Undoubtedly he hoped to lead Carthage once more against Rome, but his allies were defeated before the conflict could spread to Africa. Hannibal drifted into a hunted career as an outcast in Asia Minor, and at the age of seventy he took his own life to avoid betrayal into the hands of the Romans.

VI

THE COHORTS OF PEACE

The Roman soldiers, bred in war's alarms,
Bending with unjust loads and heavy arms,
Cheerful their toilsome marches undergo,
And pitch their sudden camp before the foe.

—VIRGIL

THE relative merits of the legion and the phalanx offered material for a controversy of absorbing interest to military writers of the ancient world. Polybius, as the tutor of the younger Scipio Africanus, naturally takes the side of the legion. Through conceding the defensive strength of the hedge of spears, he offers strategical arguments for Roman dispersion:

If the enemy decline to come down to it, but traverse the country sacking the towns and territories of the allies, what use will the phalanx be? If it remains on ground suited to itself, it will not only fail to benefit its friends, but will be incapable even of preserving itself; for the transport of supplies will be easily stopped by the enemy, seeing that they are in undisputed possession of the country: while if it quits its proper ground, from the wish to strike a blow, it will be an easy prey to the enemy.

The Pyrrhic and Punic wars had offered several incomplete tests; and it is noteworthy that Hannibal quickly altered his phalanx into a supple three-line infantry formation resembling the legion. As further evidence, two battles were fought in Polybius' own day which had been generally accepted as proof of legion superiority.

Philip V of Macedon had sent aid to Hannibal, an offense that provoked a Roman invasion of his realm. On the field of Cynosceplanae, five years after Zama, the maniples won a sweeping triumph over the phalanx in the Macedonian hills. Due to the rugged nature of the country, Philip's ranks lost their solidarity and his army paid the penalty.

A generation later his son Perseus met another great reverse at the battle of Pydna. This time the legion prevailed on level ground suited to phalangial tactics, and the result has struck many military writers, both ancient and modern, as a conclusive test.

It may still be questioned, however, whether the degenerate phalanx of Pydna, two centuries after Arbela, is worthy of being compared with the legion in its prime. The tactical mechanism of Alexander, gaining mobility from light foot and cavalry, could doubtless have inflicted an equally crushing defeat on the cohorts of the Empire in its last days.

Nor is the issue so limited that it can conveniently be reduced to any particular age. Perhaps it would not be too comprehensive a statement to say that all military history is made up of an endless struggle between the principles of dispersion and cohesion. The swing from one to the other has influenced tactics ever since Troy, and Armageddon will probably consist of a bloody clash between the last phalanx and legion left on earth.

Sometimes the struggle is so entirely in the moral sphere that the ideas of warfare may be traced to legionary or phalangial tendencies in military thought. Sometimes the actual formations are revived, for both the Roman and Macedonian models were faithfully copied by armies of the age of gunpowder. In all events the question is not one for a commander or even a nation to decide. Social, political and economic factors help to shape tactics as well as purely military considerations; and Rome had already begun drifting back toward the phalanx when Polybius wrote his praises of legionary flexibility.

The process was hastened by the granting of citizenship to Italian allies. When voluntary enlistment replaced the old compulsory levy, all free-born Romans gained the right to serve in the army. Even slaves, criminals and aliens were greedily recruited as the republic entered upon a century of revolution and civil war. Physical fitness finally became the only test of soldiers who fought for loot and swore loyalty to the general instead of the country.

Marius, himself an illiterate of low birth, bears most of the responsibility for these changes. In his efforts to retain political power he found it expedient to command troops who would not question a commander's motives. Sulla, Pompey and Caesar followed his example, and soon the patriotic citizen-soldier of Nero and Scipio had become only a memory.

THE NEW ROMAN ORGANIZATION

It now grew as easy for the man of means to avoid serving as for the proletarian to make war his sole occupation. The relaxed standards led inevitably to tactics suited to a lower grade of human material. As the old distinctions between *triarii, principes* and *hastati* were abolished, the legion infantry consisted simply of light or heavy troops.

The former included foreign auxiliaries from Rome's new provinces— Ligurians, Balearic slingers and Numidian irregulars—instead of *velites* fighting their first campaigns. Only the heavy foot remained of solid Italian origin. The practice of combining a Roman with an Italian legion

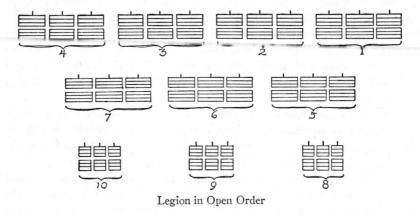

Legion in Open Order

fell into decline, and both classes of citizens mingled in the ranks as soldiers of fortune. Pay, loot, donatives and land grants combined to make the service so attractive that the average legionary had no thought of returning to civil life. He was no less a mercenary, despite his citizenship, than the alien in the light infantry or cavalry.

Gladiators were employed as drillmasters, for the new system did not neglect the training of the recruit. If possible, legionary discipline became even more severe with the lowering of admission standards, so that the extent of Roman public works may often be attributed to the need of occupation for a turbulent soldiery.

Nor had the arms undergone any important changes. The javelin and short, heavy sword were still the principal weapons, though the use of missiles had increased with the reliance on alien light infantry. The scutum, or cylindrical shield, the helmet, scale armor cuirass and greave on the right leg remained as defensive equipment.

It is only in a survey of tactics and formations that the transition becomes really apparent. For the old supple maniples, the fist and fingers of Roman attack, demanded a personal initiative beyond the pleb in the ranks. The cohort was now the basis of a less flexible order, and the legion had halfway reverted to the phalanx from which it evolved.

Ten cohorts composed the legion of Sulla and Caesar. The numbers varied widely but a strength of 360 may be considered a fair average for a cohort in the field. To the 3,600 heavy infantry were usually attached enough contingents of light foot and cavalry to bring the total up to five or six thousand.

Seven Legions in Battle Order

The maniple persisted merely as a convenient unit of a cohort drawn up either in eight or ten ranks. Four cohorts were placed in the first line, three each in the second line and reserve. The intervals had been reduced, in keeping with the deterioration of recruits, giving a front of 1,050 feet for a legion of 3,600 infantry.

A force of 25,000 heavy foot, or seven legions in three lines, occupied about a mile and a half of front. This array was phalangial in contrast to the maniples of Nero and Scipio, yet it averaged only some 11 men to a metre of front as compared to 28 in Alexander's army.

In open order the first two lines were deployed into the intervals between cohorts, allowing each man twice as much room for the use of his weapons. The third line, or reserve, remained in close order, keeping intervals equal to a cohort front.

If the legion had lost much of its mobility, the new formation could readily form a square for a desperate resistance. The first, second and third cohorts continued to face front, the fifth and sixth wheeled into line on the right, the fourth and seventh to the left, and the eighth, ninth and tenth to the rear.

Perhaps because it could be trusted less, the legion of Sulla and Caesar was led with more foresight on the march than the armies ambushed by Hannibal. Preceded by a vanguard of cavalry and heavy foot, the main body of troops and the baggage occupied the centre, followed by a rear guard disposed for immediate action. Light infantry flankers were thrown out like antennae on either side of the column, ready to give the alarm at the approach of a foe.

Even in hilly or wooded country these precautions were observed as faithfully as possible. And as the conquests of the republic increased, the victors built a network of military roads which had no equal in Europe until the nineteenth century.

The usual day's march was 15 to 18 miles in about six hours, with the labor of making camp to follow. Some 500 pack animals were assigned

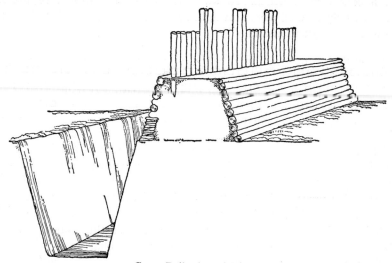

Camp Palisade and Ditch

to each legion for the transport of war engines and the tents made of skins. The burden of the soldier reached the limit of endurance after the adoption of a forked pole—wryly known as "Marius' mule"—for convenience in carrying tools, cooking utensils and several weeks' supply of rations.

When the marching column met with resistance, half of the force beat off the enemy while the remainder dug trenches in the rear. A height or slope was chosen for the site, and by dint of practice the legions could complete their works in an incredibly short time. A low palisade sufficed for men who fought behind shields, though they dug a ditch wide and deep enough to provide a formidable obstacle.

In extended campaigns the fortified camp depended also on redoubts (*castella*) thrown out at strategic points. A cohort occupied an outpost 120 feet square which became a small-scale replica of the main camp.

The combat tactics of the new legionary differed little from those of the vanished citizen-soldier. The short, thickset Roman continued to win battles by diving under opposing spears and stabbing with his sword. The only change lay in the increased use of missile weapons, due to the practice of "preparing" a stubborn foe by a long-drawn discharge of pila. Lingering at javelin-casting distance, the rear ranks advanced through to the front to throw their spears in turn, while the light troops brought up a continuous supply of weapons. The scutum proved so adequate that these missile exchanges resulted in few Roman casualties, though the legionaries often opened gaps in the enemy's line.

The lesson of Cannae had not been forgotten, and the cavalry showed a steady improvement. A *turma* of 32 men in 8 ranks remained theoretically the unit, with 12 *turmae* making up an *ala* (wing), or regiment. But in actual operations the mounted arm consisted largely of allied auxiliaries who kept their own national formations.

At least the generals of the civil wars had learned that unstinted velocity is the secret of cavalry success. The *turmae* were hurled in masses upon the enemy's flanks or upon infantry broken by the three successive shocks of the legionary foot. The intelligent use of the mounted arm in scouting had brought about a corresponding advance in strategy, and the elements of surprise and deception were no longer rare in Roman campaigns.

CAESAR'S CONQUEST OF GAUL

At a glance the improvements in tactics and generalship would appear to have compensated for the deterioration in the ranks. But in spite of stern discipline the civil war soldier was capable of insubordination which did not stop short of mutiny. His commanders might flog or crucify him at will, but they feared the mob spirit in the cohorts and shamelessly courted the favor of their men.

The commanders themselves were politicians taking the Roman road to power. As such, they varied severe punishments with the arts of wheedling and cajoling. Oratory came to the aid of discipline as generals sought to arouse martial ardor by an inspiring address known as the *cohortatio,* and the precedent has not been wasted upon politico-military leaders of later ages.

It follows that a keen and ruthless demagogue would be most likely to succeed in the cynical strife of this period. Julius Caesar was neither the first nor the last of the self-made dictators of the ancient world, but he was probably the most talented. At the age of forty, after dabbling in rhetoric and priestly mysteries, he set out to learn the art of war. Gaul and Britain became his military laboratory, and in ten years of campaigning he brought off conquests which led to the domination of the Roman world.

These victories, gained over vast numbers of barbarians, are of a sort to impress the reader of the *Commentaries,* which was Caesar's purpose in writing the book. Yet they were curtly dismissed by another great soldier-dictator, ending his career as a military critic. "Caesar's glory would be problematical," commented Napoleon, "if it depended solely upon his conquests in Gaul."

This verdict is not as unjust as it may seem. History presents no more traditional spectacle down the centuries than those campaigns in which the barbarian hordes are overcome by the handful of civilized invaders. The result is so monotonous that in all ages the exception has been dramatized out of proportion to its military importance.

In ancient warfare, at least, the outcome could seldom be attributed to novel or terrifying weapons. Barbarian inferiority in arms was usually more than balanced by an advantage in numbers and situation. Yet Caesar, like Alexander and Hamilcar before him, like Cortez and Clive to follow, found geography a more formidable foe than fierce opponents defending their homes and liberties.

In seeking an explanation, the scientist is perhaps a better qualified authority than the practitioner of arms. Anthropologists are fairly well agreed that war is one of the youngest of human institutions, an outgrowth of civilization rather than of savagery. Havelock Ellis, reviewing the evidence, concludes that

> ... war is not a primary aptitude of mankind or a habit of the stock from which man rose. ... The early implements of man are tools; an incalculably long period elapsed before weapons were thought of, and it was during this vast period that the lines of human progress were forever laid down.

Military results confirm the theory that barbarians are handicapped by lack of racial experience of war. Their failures must be charged principally to an underdevelopment of that tenacity of purpose, that relentless will to victory, which distinguishes the warfare of civilization from the strife of primitives. The comparison, not altogether flattering to civilization, goes far toward explaining the historical succession of triumphs won by a few soldiers over a host of skin-clad warriors. Method, organization and discipline are contributing factors; but in the end the physical courage of the defenders is unequal to the moral ferocity of men fighting for power and property.

No better illustration could be found than Caesar's famous bridge across the Rhine. Built in ten days from the time the first timbers were cut, this tremendous labor was intended merely to overawe tribesmen who fancied themselves secure from Roman might. Caesar contented himself with a demonstration of force on the other bank, knowing that the threat would accomplish as much as a victory in the field.

When the Gauls learned the lessons of unity and leadership after seven terrible years of defeat, they still were unable to command that civilized tenacity of purpose which pushes a campaign to its logical conclusion. Under Vercingetorix, a gallant and able chief, they found new strength in the guerrilla tactics that are the best resource of tribesmen pitted against trained soldiers. Their early successes, however, encouraged them to undertake a more ambitious war of posts and sieges—the operations best suited to an organized foe.

The natural defenses of Alesia which seemed impregnable to Vercingetorix and his 80,000 followers were promptly surrounded by a Roman system of walls and trenches. When Gallic allies came to the rescue of the defenders, Caesar in turn shut himself in behind works of circumvallation, until the relieving host dissolved as a consequence of primitive irresolution.

Fifty miles of approaches were spun like a complex web about Alesia before the Gauls were starved into submission. An abject surrender ended one of the most heroic efforts ever made by barbarians; and Vercingetorix was put to death after being chained like a wild beast and exhibited in a Roman triumph.

ROMAN CIVIL WAR CAMPAIGNS

The number of tribesmen slain in the Gallic conquests has been estimated as high as two millions. Even women and children were not spared in massacres which sometimes lacked the scant excuse of expediency. This was a departure from the traditions of ancient warfare, which usually tempered its horrors by granting some degree of mercy to non-combatants.

From such butcheries to the opposite pole of a bloodless campaign may seem an abrupt transition, but the guiding principle remains the same. Theoretically, at least, slaughter is a regrettable adjunct of operations seeking primarily to bend the enemy's will by the threat of force. The flawless victory would therefore be the one in which all objectives were gained without the loss of a man by either side. Only a few such triumphs are recorded in history, and none has ever surpassed Caesar's first civil war campaign.

After crossing the Rubicon with a single legion he mastered all Italy in sixty days by moderate political policies. His enemy Pompey fled to Greece without a show of resistance, though still controlling the fleet and most of the legions. Caesar is said to have summed up the quality of his opposition with the remark: "I am going to Spain to fight an army without a general, and thence to the East to fight a general without an army."

The epigram also illustrates his own contribution to war. For if Alexander was the greatest conqueror of antiquity, and Hannibal the most able tactician, Caesar merits recognition as a superlative leader of men. His competence rested upon that close, reciprocal contact between commander and troops which has always been as important as material assets.

The soldiers who followed him in Gaul did not serve a vague concept of patriotism. They were bound by emotional ties to the personality of the slim, elegant patrician at their head. This union of commander and troops was sometimes affectionate, sometimes stormy, always warm and intimate. Caesar alternately scolded, pampered and beguiled men whom he treated as perverse children. His praises were a boon to incite jealous rivalries, and the Tenth Legion won immortal renown because of his favoritism.

The purity or sordidness of his motives did not concern men who had emigrated from civil life into a military world. So complete was the departure that they had become virtually the forerunners of a new estate —the rejected and the outcast, the poor, the criminal, the oppressed, the unadapted, all the restless men of future ages who were to find their hearth and altar in the regiment. Caesar's vices and foibles were of vastly more interest to the soldiers of the Tenth Legion than questions of his political integrity. They marched through Gaul singing proud and ribald songs about their "old bald-headed adulterer." They fought, suffered and died for the pride of the legion and the personality of its leader.

To such soldiers and such a leader the "army without a general" seemed an affront, and Caesar singled it out for his opening campaign in 49 B.C. At the outset he appears to have had no idea of the conception that was to result in the bloodless capture of 70,000 men. He began conventionally, even dully, by ordering two direct assaults on the enemy's fortified camp at Ilerda (Lerida) which were repulsed with heavy losses.

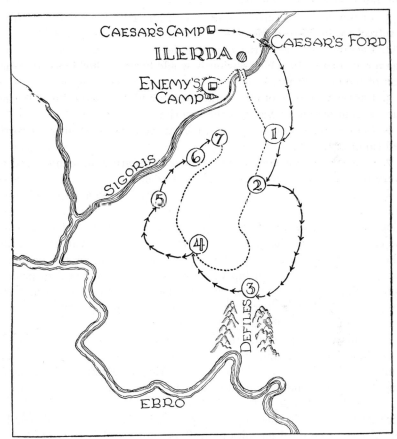

The Ilerda Campaign

His very lack of strength may then have suggested a bolder strategy, since he commanded only 40,000 troops against the legions led by Afranius and Petreius, Pompey's lieutenants in Spain. The first problem was one of dislodging the enemy from the fortified heights, and this Caesar accomplished by diverting the channel of the river Sicoris to create a new ford. With their communications threatened, Pompey's

officers decided to cross the Sicoris and retire toward the rugged defiles
on the river Ebro. Caesar followed closely and the campaign developed
in the following stages:

1. Caesar forces the enemy to take a weak defensive stand, then de-
clines an almost certain victory;

2. Caesar pursues his opponents, harassing their flanks and rear
without ever coming to grips;

3. Caesar makes a rapid countermarch and cuts the enemy off from
a retreat to the Ebro defiles:

4. Caesar again takes the opposing legions at a disadvantage—and
again refuses a battle which obviously would have resulted in the destruction of the other army;

5. Caesar makes another countermarch and heads off his faltering
enemy from obtaining water at the Sicoris;

6. Caesar cuts off his foes from their last resort of regaining the fortified camp at Ilerda;

7. Caesar gains the complete surrender of an army outmanoeuvred at
every turn and twice spared from a bloody defeat.

The entire campaign was designed to undermine the loyalty and resolution of legions which were serving Pompey rather than Rome. Caesar
added to the moral effect by encouraging his troops to fraternize with
the enemy, knowing that the outcome would be in his favor. By sparing
fellow Romans from slaughter he not only won credit for magnanimity
but also for expert generalship which could not fail to appeal to professional soldiers. Finally, he made the dramatic gesture of offering his
70,000 prisoners their liberty and a safe escort to Rome, with the result
that most of them immediately enlisted in his ranks.

After his return to Rome the added strength enabled him to put his
house in order before sailing to Greece to defeat the "general without an
army"—a description which proved flattering to Pompey—in a hard-
fought campaign ending with Caesar's triumph at Pharsalus. He went
on to seek out Pompey's allies and lieutenants in Egypt, Asia Minor,
Africa and Spain. In these operations Caesar was so successful that he
gained deadly political enemies as well as undisputed control of Rome;
and his assassination occurred only six months after the final victory at
Munda.

His tactics are seldom remarkable and his flashes of strategic brilliance
were too often summoned to redeem his own reckless or slipshod dispositions. But in his ascendancy over unruly troops Caesar had a weapon
which he demonstrated with unique effect. When his carelessness in

Africa led to a perilous envelopment by Numidian cavalry, he still could command full faith in his ability to extricate the army. After forming his infantry in a single line, he ordered alternate units to face about. Then as his flanking contingents burst through the enemy's circle right and left, he charged front and rear with the cohorts, winning a victory at Ruspina that remains one of the oddities of military history.

Even when his own men displayed the spirit of the age, Caesar needed only his personal sway to quell the mutiny. He put the malcontents to shame by calling them "citizens," for the designation which was once a Roman's greatest pride had become a term of contempt among professional soldiers. Rome at last had acquired military spirit.

The Battle of Actium

After the dictator's death came another period of revolution lasting until Octavius' great naval victory in 31 B.C. over the combined fleets of Antony and Cleopatra.

Land warfare always led in Roman esteem, but the republic owned vast forests for shipbuilding and waged a constant strife against the swarming pirates of the Mediterranean. It is not surprising, therefore, that piracy should have suggested the new tactics which won the most decisive sea engagement of the ancient world.

The classical vogue for many banks of oars had resulted in warships of incredible dimensions. Plutarch goes so far as to claim that Ptolemy Philopater, ruler of Egypt, built vessels of 40 banks requiring 4,000 rowers. This statement may be politely doubted, though it seems certain that ships of four banks were in use. Owing to the awkwardness of such creations in manoeuvre, missile attack with war engines had come to be as effective as ramming or boarding tactics.

The 200 or more ships of Antony and Cleopatra were typical of the fleets of the last two centuries. Octavius probably brought equal numbers to the Epirotic coast, but he had learned a lesson from the Liburnian pirates. His light, swift vessels, with only two banks of oars, were copies of the agile craft which had been preying upon Rome's commerce. The encounter thus became a naval version of the struggle between the principles of the legion and the phalanx. The Liburnians (for the name was to cling to the new warships) proved as supple in their element as the maniples. They dodged the rams of the enemy's unwieldly vessels and eluded the "broadsides" of heavy missiles. After the famous flight of

Antony and Cleopatra, the engagement ended with most of their fleet in flames.

Mobility and fire ships decided more than the battle of Actium: they began a trend that naval tactics were to follow for ten centuries. The Liburnian, or even the vessel with a single bank of oars, was to become the unit of the Empire and of Byzantine sea operations down into the late Middle Ages. The use of fire ships or of various flame-throwing devices was to become the most effective mode of attack.

Owing to its historical importance, Actium had an almost equally far-reaching influence on land operations of the future. For the victor would soon be better known as Augustus, founder of the Empire, whose reforms gave rise to a new period of military development. Just as the violent and uncouth Marius had created the cohorts in his own political image, Augustus now brought into being a new phase of legionary progress.

Peace, not war, was the state purpose to be served by Rome's remodeled army; defense, not unprovoked aggression, was to shape the course of its operations. Thus during the next two centuries the legion came to resemble a vast constabulary standing guard over the longest period of tranquility the civilized world has ever known.

The *Pax Romana* has always remained the most hopeful achievement of history to peoples of later ages who could see no prospect of an end to strife and tumult in their day. Such war-worn generations could at least remember that the Rome of Augustus had just emerged from a century of revolution and civil war. Even after Actium there was no immediate promise of relief from anarchy and bloodshed. There was nothing to hint that the sly young Octavius would develop into the lordly Augustus of the later busts and engravings. There was, in short, no assurance of anything at all except the misery and despair that had been accumulating for a hundred years.

This was the background of the *Pax Romana*.

In the past the world had occasionally known absence of war, such brief interludes being usually due to sloth, impotence, fatigue or isolation. But peace of a positive nature, peace as a proud and strong state policy, peace even as the basis of a powerful army's strategy—here was a peace such as had never been proclaimed since the beginnings of written history!

The boon, it is true, could be enjoyed only on terms enforced by sword and javelin. As the name implies, the *Pax Romana* was strictly a Roman and not a humanitarian institution, with the dissenter being held criminally liable by the cohorts. Not only were invading foemen met with a vigorous counterattack, but also such ideas and principles as displeased the reigning emperor. Some of Rome's worst tyrants flourished during this period of tranquility; and no peace awaited the early converts to a new faith announced in Judea during the procuratorship of Pontius Pilate.

Even so, the first two centuries of the Christian era, though scarcely measuring up to an ideal of the brotherhood of man, remain the only proof we have that the world is capable of long maintaining calm and order.

THE DEFENDERS OF THE LONG PEACE

The essential part taken by the legion could have been possible only after a transition in military policies. The quality of the army was rapidly restored as troublous civil war elements were weeded out and replaced by enlisted citizens. The new strategy grew out of the plan begun by Augustus, and followed by his successors, of attempting no new conquests on a large scale. The frontiers of the Empire were permanently welded into a vast chain extending from Britain to the Euphrates, from the Rhine to the Sahara. It became the duty of the army to patrol this chain and keep the strategic links in repair. A concentrated force was not required, since the Empire had no other great war power as a potential enemy, and at the height of the *Pax Romana* the legions were apportioned to the following frontier districts:

Britain 3; Lower Rhine 2; Upper Rhine 2; Upper Danube 4; Middle Danube 2; Lower Danube 3; Dacia 1; Asia Minor 2; Syria 4; Judea 1; Arabia 1; Egypt 1; Africa 1; Spain 1.

The field army in 120 A.D. numbered about 180,000 legionaries and 200,000 auxiliaries. Including the "household" troops of Rome and the marines of the fleet, an establishment of fully half a million men enforced the long peace. The frontier garrisons had sufficient strength to beat off the usual plundering raids, but any serious threat resulted in reinforcements being sent by the legions nearest the point of danger. In an emergency the peaceful districts were all but stripped of troops in order to obtain a temporary concentration.

Natural barriers such as the Rhine and Danube were utilized whenever possible by the cordon of defense. The spade continued to be one of the most effective Roman weapons, and the frontier depended on countless redoubts as well as the great wall of Britain or the wooden palisades (*Limes*) of Germany.

The cohort, maintained at a field strength of 500 or 600, remained the unit of tactics which still trusted in the shock of sword and pilum. Each legion of 5,000 to 6,000 heavy infantry was supported, as in the republican past, by at least equal numbers of archers, slingers, light foot and cavalry serving as alien auxiliaries. The only tactical changes of note were to be found in an increased emphasis upon cavalry and war engines, in line with the trend of the last two centuries.

In the early days of the republic the proportion of cavalry to infantry was at most one-tenth, rising to one-seventh during the civil wars. Now the numbers had grown to one-fourth as the legion faced the problem of mounted barbarian raiders able to elude the heavy armed infantry.

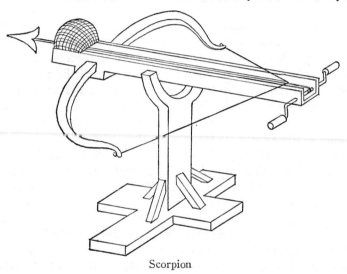

Scorpion

The use of war engines had formerly been confined to siegecraft, but the Empire found them valuable for the defense of border *castella*. By the fourth century, according to Vegetius, 10 catapults and 60 ballistae were assigned to each legion, giving a ratio of a "gun" or "howitzer" to 100 infantrymen. This was a much higher proportion, to use a modern comparison, than the average of three pieces of artillery to 1,000 men in Napoleon's armies.

Tacitus mentions an enormous ballista in a battle of A.D. 69, so the use of war engines could not have been limited to the defense of frontier fortifications. It may also be supposed that the "scorpion," a small ballista which could be worked by two men, was designed to meet the needs of mobility in field operations.

But the disturbers of the long peace were not always barbarians bent on plunder. The vast extent of the Empire included many walled cities which had to be reduced whenever a province rebelled. Siegecraft, of all branches of tactics, was perhaps best adapted to the methodical Roman genius, and the result never varied. The soldiers of the Empire were not remarkable for innovation; they simply proved more thorough and tireless in the employment of all the familiar devices of antiquity—mantelets, penthouses, towers, mounds, terraces, the ram, the bore, the mine.

No pains or labor were ever spared, as is shown by examples from the republican past. Sulla's mound at Massade was 285 feet high, and upon it were erected towers bringing the total construction up to an elevation

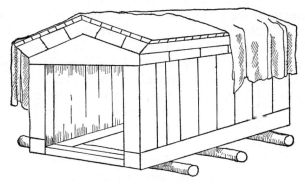

Roman Penthouse

of 441 feet. At the siege and destruction of Carthage the attackers used a ram so enormous that 6,000 men were required to build the emplacement and penthouses. Caesar's soldiers at the storm of Massilia provided themselves with mantelets a foot thick against the missiles hurled from the walls. Roman persistence prevailed even against the genius of Archimedes, who failed to save Syracuse with great burning glasses and war engines which have been described in fabulous terms.

Upholding such traditions, the soldiers of Titus could not be withstood in the famous siege of Jerusalem begun in A.D. 70. After its capture the city endured a cruel sack and devastation, for the Empire punished political rebels with more severity than was meted out to mere border plunderers.

The historian Josephus, who took part in the Jewish uprising, has left convincing accounts of the discipline and morale that enabled his foemen to succeed everywhere:

When they come to a battle the whole army is but one body, so well coupled together are their ranks, so sudden are their turnings about, so sharp their hearing as to what orders are given them, so quick their sight of the ensigns, and so nimble are their hands when they set to work; whereby it comes to pass that what they do is done quickly, and what they suffer they bear with the greatest patience.

Nor did an occasional reverse weaken this legend of invincibility. Sometimes a border cohort died to a man before reinforcements could come to the rescue; and even during the reign of Augustus an entire army was trapped and annihilated by Teutonic tribesmen. But the exceptional disaster only renewed the firmness of Roman efforts, and a victor could seldom boast of any lasting military gains.

The character of the man in the ranks had much to do with the duration of the *Pax Romana*. In every province the "hard shell and soft kernel" of the Empire relied upon soldiers who had a personal share in the maintenance. The legionary of Britain may never have set eyes upon Rome, but he was nevertheless a proud citizen. His father may have been a legionary before him, stationed at the same border camp. The permanence of the military career encouraged him in turn to bring up strong sons who would take his place after he retired to the land granted him in support of his old age.

Soldiers of this type were serving neither a patriotic abstraction nor yet a leader's personality. They were serving power and property in which they had a tangible stake; and it was natural that they should have regarded the Empire's enemies less as military foemen than as a rabble of outlaws and felons.

The Battle of Adrianople

When decline and defeat finally overtook the legion, Rome's military institutions had outlasted the Empire they were preserving. The kernel had rotted before the shell showed signs of cracking.

Nevertheless, the army cannot be wholly absolved from responsibility. It has been the experience of history that large forces of "household troops" are maintained at any nation's peril, and Rome's Praetorian Guard was no exception. Established on a moderate scale by Augustus, these cohorts had grown into an army of 50,000 which made and broke emperors at pleasure, even to the extent of auctioning off the purple to the highest bidder. The pay and privileges of the Praetorians set an example of insolence which spread until it corrupted the fighting men on the frontier.

The years from 235 to 297 were given over to anarchy ruled by sword or dagger. Forty-six emperors or pretenders were slain or assassinated in strife that drew most of the legions away from their posts. With the border left undefended at vital points, the barbarians found an opportunity to add invasion to the horrors of civil war.

Rome's most sacred military traditions crashed as the Goths closed in from the north while the Persians threatened the eastern provinces. Decius became the first Roman emperor to be slain in battle by barbarians when his army was routed at the battle of Forum Trebonii by Goths who overran the middle districts. Only a few years later Valerian was defeated and captured by the Persians, achieving an even more unhappy distinction as the first emperor to die in captivity.

After sixty terrible years Rome's salvation owed to a succession of strong Illyrian rulers who gradually recovered the ravaged provinces. They were followed by Diocletian, the great reorganizer, who restored the realm to some semblance of its former power.

His reforms averted the final downfall for a century, but as an institution the legion all but disappeared. Diocletian had to use any military resources which promised to end the emergency; and the old cohorts were made subordinate to strange units recruited from Gaul, Illyria and Germany—even from among the shaggy barbarians beyond the Danube. The new defenders of the Empire, according to the historian Mommsen, were esteemed "more highly in proportion as they differed the more in nationality, organization and spirit from the old normal Roman legions."

Diocletian's greatest contribution was the abolition of the Praetorian Guard and the formation of a central army of reserves which stood ready to direct a concentration of force on any imperiled point of the frontier. These measures prolonged the Empire's decline, and Rome even knew a few more triumphs. But two generations of chaos had taken a fatal toll of military strength, for the fourth century brought a more formidable peril than the plunder raids of the past.

Migration, a phenomenon often confused with war, now threatened a civilization too decadent to defend itself. The human waves which beat against the frontier were almost impersonal in their impact, like some mighty and restless force of nature. Behind them, lending a tidal impulse to the movement, came more waves of land-hungry barbarians seeking a racial home.

The marvel is only that the weakened resources of the Empire held out until the year 378. Yet it is evident on the eve of Adrianople that the Goths had no intimation of a victory that was to send the Empire tottering to its ruin. They had been literally pushed across the Danube by the pressure of the migrating hordes behind them, only to be hemmed in by the Romans who had imprudently offered them a refuge. Preservation must have seemed their only hope.

Emperor Valens had but to await reinforcements to make his triumph certain. But personal glory appears to have been a compelling motive, and he decided to attack before the enemy's main body of cavalry returned from a foraging expedition. He drew up his army in the accustomed formation, with the infantry in the centre and the cavalry on the wings, while the Gothic foot took refuge behind the wagons of the camp.

Never did time and chance play a more dramatic part in the outcome of a battle. Valens had carried the fight to the enemy's wagon barricade before the main body of barbarian horsemen unexpectedly appeared and struck his left flank, routing the squadrons in their path. The cavalry of his right wing then took to flight, leaving the centre a prey to envelopment as the tribal foot poured out from behind their wagons.

An accidental Cannae resulted after the wretched Roman infantry was surrounded and forced into a mass too dense to permit the use of weapons. Only the thinning of the ranks by slaughter permitted the survivors to make their escape. The emperor and two-thirds of his army perished in a massacre that heaped up 40,000 corpses on the field.

Theodosius, the successor of Valens, did not flinch from a disaster which had stripped the eastern frontier of defenders. After patching up a peace, he attempted a restoration based on the dangerous expedient of employing mercenary horsemen from the hosts of the Empire's assailants. But it had become too late for another Diocletian. The sinking sun of Adrianople was followed inevitably by the twilight of the military power that had ruled the world with sword and javelin for the last six centuries. The tactical supremacy of the infantry had reached an end, to be replaced by a cavalry age enduring for the next thousand years. Already the vanguard was forming, and in another generation Alaric and his Gothic riders would be sweeping at will across Italy to the sack of Rome.

PART TWO

THE CAVALRY
CYCLE

✫

I

THE DARK AGES OF WAR

---

*The emperor came on: a dawn of spears darker than
night rose over the leaguered city.*

—THE MONK OF ST. GALL

THE Franks seemed the logical heirs of Roman infantry tactics during
the years when the Empire lay at the mercy of invaders. The warriors from the fens and forests of the North had developed indigenous
combat methods very like those of the early Romans. They seized the
initiative whenever possible, pausing in their onslaught only to cast the
terrible *francisca*, a battle-ax that could shear through shield or helmet.
Then they flung themselves upon their foemen in one great shock all
along the line, thrusting with the javelin or with a short sword resembling
the gladius.

The blade of the ax was weighted so that it could either be used in
hand-to-hand fighting or hurled with deadly aim and accuracy. Another
curious tactic arose from the fact that the iron head of the javelin extended well down a shaft that could not be cut off when transfixed in a
buckler. The Frankish warrior then stepped on the butt to force down
his opponent's shield and render him a defenseless victim of the sword.

Here, apparently, were the beginnings of a combined shock and missile
attack which might have evolved into an effective infantry system. As
human material of war, the Franks had always been reckoned among the
most formidable of Rome's barbarian adversaries. Noted for gigantic

stature, militant spirit and hardihood, they were enemies respected by
the cohorts for courage which relied more upon hard fighting than defensive armor.

In spite of these natural assets, the Franks were not yet sufficiently
civilized to have developed the essentials of organization and discipline.
Though they had been in contact with Rome for several centuries, their
arms showed little improvement over those of the Jutes, Saxons and
other remote tribesmen. When their one tremendous shock failed against
the ranks of trained soldiers, they had no further resources; and even at
the moment of victory they were likely to be betrayed by the disorder
accounting for their defeats.

As a consequence, the Teutonic infantry fighters had to content themselves with the lesser spoils of empire—Gaul, Britain and Lower Germany.
Their mounted kinsmen from the plains of the Danube and Vistula bore
off the main prizes, not only because of their adherence to cavalry tactics
but also because they had learned political and military lessons from the
vanquished. After the reorganization by Theodosius, indeed, barbarian
horsemen became practically the sole support of an empire too far gone
in decline to defend itself. The barbarians supplied generalship as well
as troops, for some of Rome's last victories were won by Stilicho, the
son of a Vandal officer, over Germanic invaders.

The significance of Adrianople as a military landmark became even
more unmistakable at the battle of Chalons in 451 when Europe united
its forces against the dark threat of Attila. Either the Frankish foot took
no part in the engagement or the ancient chroniclers considered the efforts
of the infantry too unimportant for mention. At any rate the horse of
both sides dominated the field. The light-armed Huns, already in retreat,
were at last overcome by the heavy Gothic cavalry; but Attila retired in
fair order, and the following spring he still had sufficient strength to
ravage Italy. His death two years after Chalons probably compares with
the battle in historical importance, for without his leadership the Huns
ceased to be a menace and soon vanished from the European scene.

Aetius, the victorious general, had come up from the ranks of barbarians, and barbarian troopers played the principal part in the Empire's
last great triumph. Yet Aetius, like Stilicho before him, met death at the
orders of an ungrateful emperor, and within a generation Rome was
being ruled as well as defended by barbarians. Theoretically, the emperors
of Constantinople still held sway over a realm extending from Britain to
Syria, but the actual masters of the West were Gothic and Vandal kings.

THE PHALANX OF THE FRANKS

It had taken Rome centuries to sink into sloth and apathy—the Goths and Vandals became decadent within a few generations. Like so many rude conquerors before and since, the barbarians paid the historic penalty of acquiring the vices as well as the loot of a fallen empire.

Only a hundred years after Chalons the last great Ostrogothic king, Baduila, found it necessary to remind his people of the sturdy and war-like virtues of their ancestors. His efforts were in vain and the Ostrogoths perished by the thousand before the invading horse-archers from Constantinople. The northern Italian plain became so depopulated as a result that the Lombards moved in without a struggle.

The Vandals, who had created a rich kingdom around the site of old Carthage, met an even more shameful fate. So feeble was their resistance that the vastly outnumbered Byzantine invaders prevailed in two battles of scarcely more importance than vanguard skirmishes.

The Visigoths managed to rule in Spain until the eighth century, but only for lack of a real test. They were usually beaten in their border encounters with the Franks, and the Saracen conquest found them an easy prey.

All three peoples disappeared from history, and with them vanished the last cherished traces of Roman military skill in the West. Only the ruins of broad highways and frontier *castella* testified to the legionary past as the Dark Ages settled down over Europe.

Another cycle had been completed, and the methods of warfare reverted to their crudest beginnings. The human wall, in its most primitive form, again became the unit of tactics as the Franks, the Angles and the Saxons extended their holdings in Britain and Central Europe. Their survival owed less to a preference for infantry tactics than to isolation and a smaller share of the booty of empire. They retained a proportionately larger share of warlike spirit while the more successful Teutonic horse-men grew soft and self-indulgent, like athletes lingering too long at the feast.

In the sixth century, which was to see the downfall of the conquerors of Italy and Africa, the Frankish war bands were just merging into a rude kingdom. At the death of Clovis, after thirty years of campaigning, he had made himself undisputed ruler while conquering most of France. His sons developed into such able warriors that the royal domain was extended to include half of Germany and nearly the whole of France, in addition to territory which is now Switzerland and the Low Countries.

Although this realm was treated by the Christianized descendants of Clovis as a vast estate rather than a united nation, it had become the foremost power of Europe at the beginning of the seventh century. The Saxons remained pagan tribesmen, while the Angles and Jutes had won scarcely more than a foothold in Britain.

It thus fell to the Franks to defend Europe against the Moors who had overrun Spain and penetrated into France by the year 732.

The invaders were horsemen depending upon surprise and swift envelopment to demoralize an unmounted enemy. Charles Martel, the champion of Christendom, showed a foresight rare in that day of blunt fighting by refusing to allow his host to be lured out of a strong defensive position near Poitiers. Forming his warriors into a solid square, he took a stand which forced the Moors to decide between attack and retreat.

"The men from the North," in the words of the Spanish chronicler Isadore, "stood immovable as a wall, or as if frozen into ice, but hewing down the Arabs with their swords." The battle thus culminated in a repulse rather than a crushing defeat for squadrons which dashed themselves futilely against the mass of Franks fighting shoulder to shoulder. Nevertheless, the Moors withdrew from the field and never again became a menace to Europe. Charles prudently did not invite disaster by pursuing with his undisciplined host.

The outcome may be considered fortunate in view of the low state of European warfare. Against Saracen skill in siegecraft, flank attacks and the use of war engines, the Franks could oppose only incoherent masses of untrained and largely unarmored men. The Roman science of fortification had survived only in ill-patched ruins, and such was the poverty of the Frankish realm that many freemen had no weapons except clubs.

Until the accession of Charles the Great it is doubtful if Europe could have withstood a really resolute invasion. Charlemagne's conquests welded the Teutonic peoples of the continent into a single empire reaching from the Ebro to the Danube. His intelligent military reforms put an end to the chaos of three centuries and built up the first adequate system of defense the West had known since the fall of Rome.

Before Charlemagne the Frankish host had depended chiefly on bulk. Every able-bodied male of the kingdom owed war service, though as a rule only one man from each free household had to serve. Neither pay nor rations were provided on the march, with the inevitable result that friend and foe suffered alike from pillaging.

Charlemagne retained the principle of universal service but formed his subjects into small groups, each being required to send one well-armed man instead of several wretchedly equipped peasants. As his next step he made the ownership of land, then virtually the only property, the basis of military duty. Proprietors of estates were deemed wealthy enough to send a warrior clad in a byrnie, or mail shirt. Owners of smaller tracts must at least combine to arm a man with spear and shield. Counts, abbots and bishops, as the great landowners, had the duty of supplying their just proportion of retainers protected by a helm as well as byrnie.

In these distinctions we have the germ of the feudal system which was to become the foundation of European arms.

Nearly every imperial military edict derives from Charlemagne's life-long aim of creating a disciplined army of mailed cavalry out of the sprawling host of unarmored foot. The Moors, the Avars and the Lombards, as potential foemen, were all horsemen. Cavalry shock tactics, moreover, had been given an impetus by the invention of the stirrup, which doubtless ranks as the foremost contribution of the Dark Ages to the science of war.

There are no records to show the increase of the Frankish mounted arm, but in his later campaigns the emperor considered it his main strength. Meanwhile, he gave every encouragement to the importation of armor, while forbidding merchants to sell byrnies outside the kingdom on penalty of forfeiting all their property.

Equally drastic decrees were issued against the disorder and insubordination so characteristic of the Frankish warrior. Drunkenness, disobedience or coming late to muster, the most common offenses, might be punished by heavy fines. That some measure of improvement resulted is evident from an imperial summons of the year 806, as quoted in Oman's *History of the Art of War in the Middle Ages*:

> You shall come . . . with your men prepared to go on warlike service to any part of our realm that we may point out; that is, you shall come with your arms and gear and all warlike equipment of clothing and victuals. Every horseman shall have shield, lance, sword, dagger, a bow and quiver. On your carts you shall have ready spades, axes, picks and iron-pointed stakes, and all other things needed for the host. The rations shall be for three months, the clothing must be able to hold out for six. On your way you shall do no damage to our subjects, and touch nothing but water, wood and grass. Your men shall march along with the carts and the horses, and not leave them until you reach the muster-place, so that they

may not scatter to do mischief. See that there be no neglect, as you prize our good grace.

It is further evident that great room for improvement existed down to the end of Charlemagne's long reign, despite his efforts to overcome the poverty and inertia of the age. Not until the emperor's final edict, dated in 812, was he able to decree that no man must appear at the muster armed only with a club. And though he commanded that the poorest warrior must have at least a bow and quiver, Charlemagne's attempt to introduce archery ended in flat failure.

THE INVASION OF ITALY

The emperor's first campaigns were directed against the declining Lombard kingdom that had dominated the Italian peninsula since the annihilation of the Ostrogoths. Like the Goths and Vandals, these mailed horsemen made the sword and lance their principal weapons; but unlike their Teutonic kinsmen, the Lombards had a well-knit national organization from the beginning.

In 773 the main Frankish army, led by Charles himself, marched over the Alps at Mount Cenis. The Lombards under King Desiderius were drawn up at Susa to give battle, but meanwhile a second Frankish force crossed the St. Bernard and suddenly appeared in the defenders' rear.

As compared with the usual strategy of the Dark Ages, this campaign ranks as a rare masterpiece. As a result the Lombard army was forced to divide and retire hurriedly to Verona and Pavia to withstand sieges. The emperor took Verona within a few months, and after a long blockade Pavia surrendered the following summer.

Even in these early operations Charlemagne seems to have organized at least a nucleus of well-armed cavalry. As evidence, Oman's *Art of War in the Middle Ages* quotes a poetic description of the invading army which the Monk of St. Gall derived from some lost contemporary account. In this fragment Charlemagne and the Frankish vanguard are depicted as seen by Desiderius and the defenders of Pavia:

> Then appeared the iron king, crowned with his iron helm, with sleeves of iron mail on his arms, his broad breast protected by an iron byrnie, an iron lance in his left hand, his right free to grasp his unconquered sword. His thighs were guarded with iron mail ... and his legs, like those of all his host, were protected by iron greaves. His shield was plain iron, without device or color. And round him and before and behind him rode all his men, armed as

nearly like him as they could fashion themselves; so iron filled the fields and the ways, and the sun's rays were in every quarter reflected from iron. "Iron, iron everywhere," cried in their dismay the terrified citizens of Pavia.

The conquered Lombard kingdom, as a cavalry recruiting ground, proved a military asset to the victor in his campaigns against the Saxons. From 774 to 799 few summers passed in which he did not send an expedition against the warlike pagans of the Elbe and Weser districts. Their territory was well suited to defense, and the Saxon war bands were capable of uniting under stress into a redoubtable foot soldiery fighting with sword and spear. Under the able leadership of Wittekind they learned to feign submission when attacked in force, only to rebel again when the main Frankish army retired.

Charlemagne's persistence was remarkable. Year after year he launched his campaigns until the Saxon leaders, their strength reduced by battle and massacre, finally submitted to baptism. Few details of these operations are left by contemporary accounts, but at least we know that the emperor made use of converging columns of attack, while his revival of field fortification proved a valuable military lesson.

Taught by bitter experience, Charlemagne learned not to allow a conquered region the opportunity for a new uprising. After receiving hostages and tribute, he selected a strong natural position and built a "burg" with palisade and ditch to serve as headquarters for a permanent garrison. The various posts were linked together with roads, and such well-chosen sites as Bremen and Magdeburg have had a continuous political existence down to modern times.

The emperor's campaigns against the Moors, oddly enough, do not appear to have been a holy war. He allied himself with the Saracen whenever he found it expedient, and the celebrated disaster of Roncesvaux has been traced to an attack by Christianized Basque tribesmen in a pass of the Pyrenees. At any rate (so few and diverse are the military sources of the age) it may be concluded from the *Chanson de Roland* that the once formless Frankish host had grown accustomed to marching with a vanguard and rear guard.

Charlemagne's last expeditions brought about the annihilation of the Avars who had terrorized eastern Europe for two centuries. An Asiatic people, probably of Turkish origin, they had settled along the Danube in "rings," or great enclosures defended by earthworks, the largest of which has been described as 38 miles in circumference. Nevertheless, the Avars

were a spent power at this time, having suffered severe defeats from the
armies of Constantinople. The Franks merely completed the work of
destruction, and after the capture of their chief ring the mounted raiders
disappeared so dramatically that "to vanish like the Avars" is still a
Slavic proverb.

THE RAIDS OF THE NORSEMEN

Upon the death of Charles the Great his empire was divided among
his sons and soon lost its cohesion. Thus the year 814 becomes the last
time in history when Europe acknowledged a single political and military
system, though the ideal has inspired such latter-day conquerors as
Napoleon and Hitler.

The emperor's tactics were primitive as compared to the departed
glories of classical warfare. He fought no great battles and his campaigns
were won either over barbarians or powers long past their military prime.
Even so, the precepts left by "King Charles, that man of iron" pointed
the way to Europe's deliverance from the perils of the next age.

The first recorded Viking raid occurred in 799, but the forays did not
become serious until the middle of the ninth century. At the beginning
of their plundering career the Scandinavian adventurers, like the Angles
and Saxons who invaded Britain, fought in small war bands under a
chief. In contrast to their Teutonic kinsmen, they had adopted the bow
and arrow, though the ax remained the most effective Norse weapon.
Not to be confused with the missile ax of the early Franks, it consisted
of a heavy blade fixed to a handle five feet long. Wielded with both
hands, the heavy blade could cleave horse and rider at a blow. The javelin
and sword were also used on occasion, and in the lack of armor a kite-
shaped shield, painted in bright colors, served for protection.

Stout land fighters, the Norsemen were feared even more for their
development of the earliest sea power of Atlantic waters. As a departure
from the general military inferiority of the Dark Ages, their ships were
better designed than Greek or Roman vessels, overcoming water resistance to a degree not equaled until modern times. The carved prows and
sterns of these single-deckers rose high out of the water, and the bulwarks were hung with gaudy shields. Speed and seaworthiness were built
into them at the sacrifice of size, for the largest of the raiding vessels held
fewer than 200 men. Yet such small craft proved fit either to cross the
Atlantic or to penetrate far up the rivers into the interior of Europe

Contrary to legend, the Vikings were seldom interested in fighting for the sake of fighting. They felt it no disgrace to take to flight with their plunder; but once hemmed in by an aroused countryside, they never refused a battle against any odds. Man for man, they proved more than a match for the soldiery of Europe, and even in defeat their axes took a terrible toll.

Surprise and velocity served them well as moral weapons. Leaving their warships under guard after reaching the limit of a river's navigability, they spread out in fleet bands to sack every village and abbey in the district. Before the peasantry could arm against them, the plunderers were on their way to sea.

The early raids were more cautious, being confined to the seacoast. But the Norsemen esteemed helms and byrnies second only to gold, and before long they became as well equipped as their victims. Hence the expeditions grew progressively more bold, until by 850 the raiders were strong enough to sack London and push far up the Meuse and Loire. Permanent bases were established at the river mouths as the manhood of Scandinavia took up the profitable new career; and though they remained infantry fighters, the Vikings learned to seize horses to speed their forays and retreats.

Europe had no adequate defenses for several decades. The old Frankish general levy was too slow and ponderous to cope with these elusive foemen, the peasantry too poorly trained and armed. The only sound military remedies were to be found in the principles left by Charlemagne —fortification, mailed cavalry, fewer and better soldiers.

The feudal system thus received another impetus as every district found its protector in the local count or duke. Only stone walls and alert forces of mailed riders proved effective against the Norsemen, with the result that the Frankish realm soon disintegrated into small and self-sufficient states, each with its own little army. In time these states became hereditary fiefs, governed by some arrogant lord whose allegiance to the crown was merely theoretical.

So in every age protection becomes the means and end of power when the existing government can no longer guarantee property. The new feudal system almost immediately demonstrated its worth by giving the heathen invaders their first stout opposition. And since the Vikings were businesslike in their operations, they quickly learned to avoid districts offering battle rather than booty.

The growing science of fortification played its part, especially after the invaders were repulsed from the walls of Paris in 886. The English went a step further by adopting Norse sea tactics with such success as to establish the island's first naval tradition. Finally, the Vikings themselves, in line with universal experience, tended to become less bold as they acquired more property. Those who had been bribed to settle in France rapidly took on the status of vassals instead of enemies, soon being numbered among the most faithful defenders of the Cross.

The Norse menace had scarcely abated when another series of raids descended upon Europe from the eastern frontier. The new foemen were the Magyars, an Asiatic people of somewhat mysterious origin, who had occupied the plains of Hungary. These mounted bowmen followed the usual tactics of the East, swirling about an enemy from all sides, pressing every advantage but turning at the first sign of serious resistance.

Once committed to battle, the Magyars were too lightly armed to meet European cavalry on equal terms. But even the Viking incursions seemed slow in comparison to the ravages of foemen who swept across a province, loading their loot on packhorses and leaving a trail of burning villages before the ban could be assembled. In 924 the raiders raced through Bavaria, Alsace, Lorraine and Champagne to the Ardennes before returning by way of Franconia. Another of their expeditions took them in a vast circle through Germany, France and Italy, then back over the Alps to their homeland.

The spreading feudal system met this new test so vigorously that the Magyar depredations lasted but a short time as compared to Viking raids. Henry I, the German king whose domain had suffered most heavily, was forced to pay tribute for nine years, but during this respite he built up a chain of strong outposts manned by cavalry. So thorough were his efforts that he granted land to condemned men on condition that they defend frontier burgs; and it may perhaps be assumed that these felons became the ancestors of a proud future nobility.

At least they gave the Magyars a stern reception on their next visits. Meeting surprise with surprise, the German horsemen surrounded and cut to pieces small bands of plunderers; and the Magyars, like the Norsemen before them, were soon discouraged by unprofitable forays. In the end Henry's son, Otto the Great, managed to force a battle on them and administer a crushing defeat at the Lechfeld.

THE BATTLE OF HASTINGS

During the next century the continued growth of the cavalry arm left England the last stronghold of the national levy of foot. Isolation had permitted the islanders to cling to their old military customs, though the Saxon sword and spear had been supplemented by the adoption of the kite-shaped shield and two-handed ax introduced by the Vikings.

The Normans, in contrast, had departed so far from the tactics of their ancestors as to be considered the best horsemen of France. Hence their

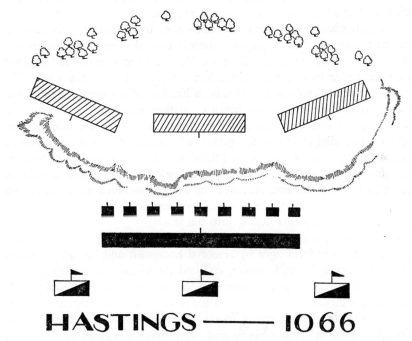

HASTINGS —— 1066

invasion of England in 1066, aside from its general historical interest, becomes the first important clash between the infantry and cavalry of the age.

The Norman force at the battle of Hastings, estimated by contemporaries at 60,000 or more, may have amounted to a fourth of that number. In the first two lines were drawn up the armored infantry, consisting largely of archers, but the invaders placed their dependence in the three or four thousand mailed horsemen of the third line.

King Harold's host, composed almost entirely of foot, was several times as large. He had taken a strong defensive position on the crest of a hill, with a wood behind him and a glacis-like slope in front. Massed deeply in the centre were his picked troops, armed with the ax, while both wings consisted of unarmored shire levies fighting with sword and spear. The bow had not yet become a national weapon, and few if any archers seem to have been included in the English ranks.

Duke William opened the engagement with a flight of arrows and charge of his foot soldiers. The defenders held firm behind locked shields, easily proving their superiority over the feudal infantry of France. English axes lopped off heads and limbs at a blow, driving the attackers back with the shire levies following in rash pursuit.

The Norman cavalry took advantage of the pursuers' disorder to launch a counterattack with such success that William immediately ordered another advance. This time the Normans were instructed to feign flight in order to draw the shire levies out again into the open. The stratagem proved so effective that both English wings were cut to pieces, leaving the centre to bear the brunt of further attacks.

All the rest of the day, from noon until dusk, the massed axmen were subjected to flights of arrows varied with thundering cavalry charges. The invading bowmen discharged their missiles at an angle, like projectiles from a catapult, so that English shields offered small protection against the harassing fire. At last King Harold received a mortal wound and his followers broke ranks, some choosing death at the hands of the enemy and the remnant fleeing into the woods.

As a military landmark Hastings became the forerunner of a series of battles won in later ages by armored horsemen and infantry archers. Contemporary opinion, however, credited the victory to the cavalry and overlooked the decisive combination of the two arms in shock and missile attack. The tactical lesson had been too advanced for its day, and within a generation the heavy armed foot soldier practically disappeared from Europe except in remote Slavic and Scandinavian regions.

It has been said that the presence of two thousand horsemen in Harold's host might have changed the course of history. Likewise, on many a future field, the absence of infantry would prove equally momentous. For the mailed rider was now everywhere supreme, representing an aristocracy which dominated his small world politically as well as militarily.

In the classical age the phalanx, the maniple and the cohort had in turn served as units of battle. Now for the only time in history we find a single human being, the mounted man-at-arms, functioning virtually as a combat unit. Summed up in his iron-clad person were the destinies of a feudal tract of land, tilled by sullen serfs and depending for its defense upon his unimaginative tactics.

The very word "infantry" persists as a heritage from this era when mere lads attended the seigneur on horseback. As a token of the military esteem in which they were held, the battle losses of these unmounted retainers were not deemed worth the mention. The importance of the man-at-arms, on the contrary, was exalted by the economics of a day that held life more cheap than property. His charger and hand-wrought armor represented a sum of money which could scarcely have been comprehended by the serfs whose brutal toil must redeem him from captivity. Encased as he was in iron, looking down upon life from the vantage point of horseback, he naturally tended to develop an arrogance out of all proportion to his military worth.

At a later date the despised peasants and burghers were to demonstrate that this self-esteem was largely misplaced. Meanwhile the mailed rider continued to dominate by virtue of moral rather than material superiority. The tactics of his age grew more and more conservative, until finally he came to be manoeuvred with all the ponderous caution of modern naval operations—a human dreadnought whose shadow fell darkly across the warfare of the Middle Ages.

II

THE BYZANTINE HORSE-ARCHER

The first blessing is peace, as is agreed upon by all men who have even a small share of reason. . . . The best general, therefore, is that one who is able to bring about peace from war.

—BELISARIUS

GLANCING back at the long period between the battles of Chalons and Hastings, the observer is most struck by the military helplessness of Europe. Throughout these six centuries it would seem that the West was seldom in sufficient strength to withstand a determined conqueror. The raids of the Vikings and Magyars, which terrorized a continent, were sometimes conducted by bands of only a few hundred men. Even the battle of Poitiers, the one field that might be considered a test, represents scarcely more than the repulse of a large-scale plundering expedition.

Yet despite the vulnerability, no resolute challenger appeared during those six centuries. This boon was by no means due to chance, for never were foemen more to be dreaded than the Asiatic hordes of the Dark Ages. The threat was not lacking, but during the entire period Europe's future found able defenders in the East-Roman Empire.

Constantinople, with its strategic location, served as the bulwark between East and West, the link between the ancient and modern worlds.

Alone and unaided, Constantinople beat off the onslaughts of Slav, Avar, Bulgarian, Persian, Saracen, Russian and Turk, thus permitting Europe to develop its civilization along Western lines.

As a great warpower, staking its survival on cool skill and intellect, the East-Roman or Byzantine realm has left a record unsurpassed in military history. From the accession of Justinian in 527 until the Turkish invasion of 1071, its generals never suffered a fatal defeat or enjoyed a long respite from strife. And even after disaster finally overtook its forces, the Empire managed to endure with many vicissitudes until 1453, when the Turks battered down the walls of Constantinople with cannon.

A comparison with ancient Rome naturally suggests itself, since there is little to choose between the two empires in duration and effectiveness of armed might. If the operations of Constantinople were on a smaller scale, so also was the strength of a nation which could seldom raise more than a fourth of Rome's numbers. Nevertheless, it may be doubted if the legions faced a more formidable succession of enemies than those hurled back from the gates of Constantinople.

Some historians, indeed, have treated the Eastern Empire as merely a political extension of ancient Rome, despite the differences in language, customs and religion. But at least in a military sense the break had been complete. The one was a conquering power depending upon infantry tactics, the other a defensive realm trusting to its cavalry for salvation. Rome's stern discipline and drill became legend, while Constantinople's victories were due to studied strategy and generalship.

Byzantine warfare, in short, was essentially Greek rather than Latin in character—as if the gymnastic armies of Athens had known a reincarnation based less upon muscular than cerebral audacity! Not even the intellectual vices of the sly Hellenes were missing, for the generals of Constantinople showed a fondness for ruse and stratagem that often went to extremes. If bribery or trickery promised to serve their ends better than fighting, they felt it no shame to resort to the most dubious dodges.

In their defense it may be urged that no military power in history ever stood off such overwhelming numbers over a period of so many centuries. The soldiers of Byzantium, moreover, must be credited with humanitarian impulses going far beyond any mercies granted by Greece or Rome. But these mitigations were forgotten and the trickery remembered by a school of historians whose verdict has been summed up by Gibbon: "The vices of Byzantine armies were inherent, their victories accidental."

Fortunately, the research of later years has brought to light newer authorities studied with less prejudice. Gibbon and Hallam have sometimes been discredited as a result, and the opinion of most present-day military historians is expressed in Sir Charles Oman's comment:

> So far is this sweeping assertion from the truth that it would be more correct to call their defeats accidental, their successes well deserved. . . . For centuries war was studied as an art in the East, while in the West it remained a matter of hard fighting. . . . The men of the West, though they regarded war as the most important occupation of life, invariably found themselves at a loss when opposed by an enemy with whose tactics they were not acquainted. The generals of the East, on the other hand, made it their boast that they knew how to face and conquer Slav or Turk, Frank or Saracen, by employing in each case the tactical means best adapted to meet their opponents' method of warfare.

It is chiefly due to Oman's research that we are acquainted with the military textbooks which constituted virtually a Byzantine weapon of war during the Dark Ages. Written by generals and emperors for the conduct of actual field operations, these treatises overlooked no detail, moral or material, that might contribute to victory. The national characteristics of potential foemen were analyzed with shrewd detachment, their arms and tactics scrutinized for every weakness. Even the weather, in its influence upon an adversary's resolution, was not deemed too trivial a topic for the speculations of a strategist.

The textbooks take it for granted that the enemy will always possess the numerical advantage, but there is no lack of confidence in the eventual triumph of the East-Roman organization. If opponents are regarded with caution, they are also held in disdain as military inferiors. And presumptuous as this attitude may seem, the Byzantine military system met the tests of five hundred years with but few and unimportant changes.

The Campaigns of Belisarius

This system is further unique in that it was not founded upon any such sturdy yeomanry as had upheld Roman and Macedonian beginnings. Sixth-century Constantinople had added the vices of the East to those inherited from decadent Rome. The urban populace was idle and vicious, subsisting on the grain dole and exhibiting its fighting qualities only in street riots. The government was often corrupt or oppressive, representing a top-heavy nobility and priesthood supported by a burden of taxation that crushed the peasantry.

The Eastern Empire had escaped the fate of Rome by bribing the most formidable of the barbarians and persuading them to move on to the occupation of Italy. During this period of stress the emperor Zeno also laid the cornerstone of the future military organization by recruiting a native element into an army otherwise composed of *Foederati,* or mercenary Teutonic horsemen.

At the accession of Justinian the many weaknesses of Constantinople were balanced by such assets as a fleet, a nucleus of native soldiery and a strategic position astride the land and water crossroads of the world. Two generations of comparative peace and quiet had enabled the realm to recuperate from barbarian ravages; and in 530 Justinian's forces won the first of a series of successes leading to the reconquest of Italy, Africa and southern Spain.

The victor was a twenty-five-year-old general of Thracian peasant birth who had risen from the ranks of the emperor's bodyguard. It would thus appear that merit gained unusual recognition in the new Byzantine army, for Belisarius developed into the greatest tactician of the century, a knightly figure whose career became legend.

His first decisive success was won over 40,000 Persians threatening the eastern frontier fortress of Daras. Belisarius marched an army of 25,000 to the relief of this important outpost, and the two forces clashed on a plain outside the city.

In his dispositions the young East-Roman commander, like Scipio at Ilipa, placed his most doubtful troops in a "refused" centre while both wings were thrown well forward. Belisarius apparently distrusted his infantry, for he protected their entire front by a deep ditch, leaving passages for the cavalry of the wings. The Persians came on in two lines, the cavalry wings advancing while the infantry centre was held up by the ditch. As a result two breaches were opened in the opposing line, and Belisarius led his reserve cavalry to the rout of the Persian left wing before taking the exposed centre in flank and rear. The losses of the enemy were so severe that during the remainder of the campaign the Byzantine general never found another opportunity for battle.

At Daras the infantry had scarcely struck a blow, and in his African campaigns Belisarius relied entirely upon horse. After landing on the coast with only 15,000 troops, he advanced with the cavalry third of his army to challenge the rich and populous kingdom which occupied the site of old Carthage.

The first encounter at Ad Decimen was hardly more than a series of skirmishes in which Belisarius gained the upper hand with his mercenary

Huns. The result justified his daring invasion, making it plain that only a century after their sack of Rome the Vandals were too far gone in ease and sloth to defend themselves.

At the decisive battle of Tricameron they halted their entire cavalry host behind a shallow stream. Belisarius, whose infantry lagged a march behind, did not hesitate to seize the initiative against an enemy passively awaiting his attack. Plunging into the stream with his 5,000 horse, he led a general assault which soon had the more numerous Vandals in flight. In sixty minutes they paid with their kingdom for violation of the axiom providing that velocity is the secret of cavalry success.

Procopius, the historian of these campaigns, who served as secretary to Belisarius, has left excellent accounts of Byzantine arms and tactics. Apparently as early as the sixth century there were fogies who worshipped the military past, for Procopius speaks with scorn of "those who call the soldiers of the present day 'bowmen,' while to those of the most ancient times they wish to attribute such lofty terms as 'hand-to-hand fighters' and 'shield-men' and other names of the sort." He continues:

> But the bowmen of the present time go into battle wearing corselets and fitted out with greaves which extend up to the knee. From the right side hang their arrows, from the other the sword. And there are some who have a spear also attached to them and, at the shoulders, a sort of small shield without a grip, such as to cover the region of the face and neck. They are expert horsemen, and are able without difficulty to direct their bows to either side while riding at full speed, and to shoot an opponent whether in pursuit or in flight. They draw the bowstring along by the forehead about opposite the right ear, thereby charging the arrow with such impetus as to kill whoever stands in the way, shield and corselet alike having no power to check its force. Still, there are those who take into consideration none of these things, who reverence and worship the ancient times, and give no credit to modern improvements.

An added testimony to the merit of Belisarius' horse-archers is to be found in the numerical odds he overcame during his invasion of Italy. To the conquest of a Gothic kingdom able to raise 100,000 fighting men, the East-Roman general brought an army of less than 10,000. Yet so swift and sure were his moves that he swept the enemy before him and took Rome without a battle.

Even granting that the Ostrogoths had lost most of their barbarian hardihood, it is astonishing that Belisarius should have been able to withstand a year's siege, beating his foes constantly in cavalry combats outside the walls. In his own words, as quoted by Procopius, he attributes his superiority to the horse-archers of the small Byzantine army:

In the first skirmishes with the Goths, I was always on the look out to discover what were the strong and weak points in their tactics, in order to accommodate my own to them, so as to make up for my numerical inferiority. I found that the chief difference between them and us was that our own Roman horse and our Hunnish *Foederati* are all expert horse-bowmen, while the enemy has scarcely any knowledge whatever of archery. For the Gothic knights use sword and lance alone, while their bowmen on foot are always drawn up to the rear under cover of the heavy squadrons. So their horsemen are no good till the battle comes to close quarters, and can easily be shot down while standing in battle array before the moment of contact arrives. Their foot-archers, on the other hand, will never dare to advance against cavalry, and so keep too far back.

As a consequence of this lack of co-operation between cavalry and infantry, the Gothic host failed consistently against Belisarius and was forced to raise the siege. No pitched battles took place and the numerous skirmishes were decided by the effectiveness of the Byzantine mounted bowmen.

The invaders pressed on to Ravenna, the capital, which surrendered without a blow. The submission of the rest of the realm followed, and the Gothic king soon joined the deposed Vandal ruler as a captive in Constantinople.

That the gallant Belisarius should have been recalled after such triumphs seems a flagrant instance of royal ingratitude. The decision also points to a grave weakness of Justinian's armies. Their numbers were made up chiefly of *Foederati* attached to the service of the general, thus constituting a threat to the throne as well as a drain on the treasury. At a later date the danger of such mercenary bodyguards became an incentive to a truly national army serving the Empire. Meanwhile, though his suspicions of Belisarius proved unjustified, Justinian sought to prevent intrigue by sudden changes of command.

It is a comment on Byzantine court life that the emperor saw no inconsistency in appointing Narses, a septuagenarian eunuch without previous experience of generalship. His judgment was vindicated when the former grand chamberlain won two victories distinguished for their tactics.

After ten years of submission to Constantinople, the Goths revolted under the heroic Baduila and set up a new kingdom. At Taginae in 552 their army was drawn up on a plain, facing an East-Roman force which held a comfortable numerical superiority. In the face of odds King Baduila attempted a surprise assault all along the line, but Narses had prepared a unique formation.

In his centre he placed masses of dismounted cavalry armed with lances, and attached to them were wings of infantry archers extended in a crescent toward the enemy. The Gothic horsemen charged impetuously into this semicircle and were met by a converging missile attack. The infantry of the second line, dismayed by the shower of arrows, lagged behind until they were ridden down during the pursuit by the East-Roman cavalry. Baduila was slain and his kingdom perished with him.

Narses went on to gain a second triumph a year later, using almost identically the same troops and tactics. At the battle of Casilinum his opponents were Frankish unmounted warriors who had invaded Italy in the hope of plunder. Again the assailants were caught between showers of arrows from both curving wings, and again Narses ordered a cavalry charge after the enemy had been thoroughly demoralized by the infantry attack. The destruction of the Franks was so complete that only five warriors are said to have survived.

The merit of the Byzantine formation lay in its balanced combination of infantry and cavalry tactics, of shock and missile effect. The dismounted centre, deeply massed with lances, served as a defensive phalanx during the early stages, insuring against disaster and giving the wings their opportunity for a prolonged missile assault. Then at the turning point the lancers took to horse again, resuming their true cavalry function of pursing a broken enemy.

MAURICE'S MILITARY REFORMS

At the crest of Byzantine victories it appeared that the grandeur of the ancient Roman Empire might be restored. Yet within another decade most of the conquests were lost as Constantinople fought off invaders who had ravaged up to the walls of the city. The last victory of Belisarius, in fact, was won against Bulgarian hordes encamped outside the gates. Recalled from disgrace in the emergency, the prematurely aged hero had only 300 veteran troops at his disposal. These he placed in hiding on the enemy's flanks while commanding peasants and citizens to build campfires, raise shouts or otherwise simulate martial ardor. The Hannibalic ruse succeeded so well that the Bulgarians fled in a panic after losing a few hundred horsemen in ambuscade attacks.

Several years later Belisarius and his master died with the knowledge that the fruits of their triumphs had been lost. For the Lombards had moved into Italy without a struggle, and neither Africa nor southern Spain long remained possessions.

The abrupt descent to such an anticlimax must be charged to the lack of human and economic reserves which usually kept the Eastern Empire on the defensive. Justinian, who achieved unique immortality in war, law, theology and architecture, so bankrupted his realm that the consequences were inherited by his successors.

Their plight brought into gradual being the great military system that was to endure almost unchanged until the eve of the twelfth century. After Justinian the Empire slowly turned its back on the West, becoming every year more Greek in character as well as language. Its arms and tactics departed correspondingly from the traditions of ancient Rome, gaining intellectual values in compensation of material weakness.

In the next generation appeared Maurice's *Strategicon*, the first of the great Byzantine military treatises. Written about 578 by a general who later became emperor, this work describes the reforms which were the foundation of the new system.

First of all, there was to be an end to the alien mercenaries whose hire had drained Justinian's treasury and threatened the security of his reign. No longer were troops to pledge obedience to their officers instead of the realm. In turn the officers were to be appointed by and held responsible to the central government. And though Maurice's dream of universal military service failed of realization, the new policies gave rise to a dependable native soldiery raised within the borders.

Strict codes and penalties restored a discipline which had been lax among aliens loyal to their own military leaders and codes. According to Bury, Maurice was "obliged to introduce the custom of entrenching a camp; the laziness and negligence of soldiers and officers had, it seems, come to such a pass that they dispensed with the fosse as a useless expenditure of labor."

Such lapses were so severely punished that the Byzantine army soon rivaled the legion in field fortification. In time a chain of 52 fortresses defended the Danube line, with 27 farther south in Moesia as a second line of resistance. Frontier posts were organized into a permanent cordon of defense, new forts being added and old ones repaired. Castles and walled towns were armed to repel barbarians whose siege tactics had improved through contact with civilization. Permanent garrisons held strategic points, including a force of 2,000 at the famed pass of Thermopylae.

Constantinople itself, as Europe's greatest city, depended on a mighty triple system of walls. The moat, 60 feet wide and 20 feet deep, could be filled with water piped from distant hills, though it was generally used as a dry ditch. Behind the scarp a battlemented wall 6 feet high furnished cover for archers. Sixty feet back of this obstacle rose another wall, 27 feet high and studded with 96 towers projecting to permit flanking fire. The towers were 180 feet apart and varied from 30 to 35 feet in height above the wall.

The third great wall, connected to the second by a covered way allowing safe passage of troops, was 30 feet high and nearly as thick, with a rear drop of 40 feet to the level of the city. From this barrier protruded another system of 96 towers, twice the height of those of the second wall and placed checkerwise.

But Byzantine generals did not rely too much on masonry. The heavy armed horse-archer remained the real defense of the Empire. His mail shirt hung from neck to thighs, with gauntlets and steel shoes completing the armor. All active branches of the service wore the conical Byzantine helmet, tufted in various colors to distinguish units. The horses of front-rank men were furnished with frontlets and poitrels, and the well-built saddle had steel stirrups.

Broadsword, dagger, lance, bow and quiver were the trooper's weapons. He was issued a light linen surcoat to wear over his armor in fair weather, in addition to a woolen cloak strapped behind his saddle for protection against cold. The lance-pennon and surcoat, like the tuft of the steel helmet, were of various distinguishing colors.

The infantry ranked as a secondary arm, since the Empire's enemies were chiefly mounted men, but neither its arms nor training show neglect. The heavy armed foot soldier, known as a *scutatus* from his round shield, wore a mail shirt and occasionally greaves and gauntlets. As weapons he carried a lance and sword in addition to an ax with a spike opposite the cutting edge. The light armed infantry consisted almost entirely of archers.

The cities supplied few recruits as compared to such provinces as Thrace, Isauria, Cappadocia and Armenia. Small landowners filled the ranks, receiving pay as well as exemptions from the burden of Byzantine taxation. The officers represented an aristocracy which handed down a professional tradition from father to son. They brought servants into the field, and even the troopers often hired an attendant for every four or five men.

East-Roman generals, like Napoleon in modern times, avoided organizations of identical numbers on the theory that they became a source of information to the enemy. Under Justinian the largest tactical unit had been the numerus of 300 to 400 troops, resembling a modern battalion. After the reforms of Maurice, six to eight *numeri* were grouped into the equivalent of a brigade, while three such brigades formed a small "division" of 6,000 to 8,000.

The next step was based less upon arbitrary units than the actual strategic needs of the territory to be defended. Under this system, which became to Constantinople what the legion had been to Rome, the Empire was divided for purposes both of recruiting and defense into military provinces known as themes.

The troops assigned to each of these geographical divisions may be compared to a modern army corps—a complete and self-sustaining force capable either of repelling a local raid or supplying its contingent of soldiers for large-scale operations elsewhere in the realm. The *strategos* commanded within the borders of his own theme, and under him were the *turmarchs*, each in charge of a *turma* or "brigade" of perhaps 2,000 men.

The themes varied in numerical strength, as did the *turmae*, both being adapted to strategic demands rather than the uses of military bookkeeping. A frontier district, it appears, usually had an establishment of from 8,000 to 12,000 troops, while half of those numbers might serve an inland district. It was constantly emphasized, moreover, that only the fittest men and horses should ever be ordered into action. In line with Byzantine preference for quality over bulk, untrained or poorly equipped soldiers stayed behind as garrison troops.

As the themes were subdivided into *turmae*, so in turn were the latter broken down into still smaller defense stations called *clissurae*. Each consisted of some important outpost, such as a ford or mountain pass, guarded by a few hundred troops under a *clissurarch*, a young officer of about a captain's rank. If changing conditions suggested the need, ɑ *clissura* might be enlarged into a *turma*, or a *turma* into a new theme.

Named for the troops quartered in them, the themes rose to 30 in number by the ninth century, gradually taking over many of the functions of the civil administration. The divisions of Asia Minor were most important, both as a recruiting ground and a bulwark of defense. Though the *strategos* dared not strip his province of troops even in a national emergency, he was expected to reinforce the main army at a moment's notice. As an example of the workings of this plan, ten themes concentrated their strength in 863 to encircle and annihilate an invading host of Saracens.

One of the themes, a coastwise area named Cibyrrhaioton, seems to have operated entirely as a naval base and recruiting ground for sailors and marines. As the world's greatest sea power from the fall of Rome to the rise of the Italian maritime cities, the Empire followed the tactical principles laid down at Actium. Speed and ability to manoeuvre were esteemed over size in the design of vessels; and the word *droman*, which came to designate all Byzantine warships, simply meant "racer."

Usually a two-banked galley, with two lateen-rigged masts and 30 to 40 oars on a side, the *droman* carried a crew of about 300. The fire ship and various flame-throwing devices were methods of offense, but the larger warships also had revolving turrets to contain war engines or bands of heavy armed marines for boarding tactics. A lighter class of *droman* served the purpose of the cruiser, and still smaller craft operated as scouting or dispatch boats.

The effectiveness of the East-Roman navy may be measured by the fact that it became virtually a fleet without a history. Over a period of six centuries its supremacy was seriously challenged on only two occasions. No better test could be found, for the worth of a fleet is best established by its results as a preventive rather than a curative instrument of strategy.

THE MORAL WEAPONS OF BYZANTIUM

In a like spirit, East-Roman generals studied the hearts as well as the weapons and tactics of their foemen on land. Unceasingly they analyzed every trait of an enemy's national character, every prejudice that might lead to weakness on the battlefield.

As early as the sixth century, when Maurice's *Strategicon* appeared, the potential antagonists of Constantinople were being shrewdly classified. Hunnish and Scythian horsemen, it was urged, should be attacked in February or March, as their neglected mounts were then gaunt and half-dead for lack of forage. Frozen rivers were to be utilized in campaigns against those Slavonic marsh dwellers whose ambuscades depended on hiding under water while breathing through hollow reeds. Winter operations were also advised against mountain tribesmen, since the snow revealed their tracks and the leafless trees offered poor concealment.

Asiatic raiders from hot desert regions, on the other hand, could best be assailed during chill or rainy weather; for their volatile natures became subject to depression on gloomy days.

Impetuosity, indiscipline or any other shortcoming merited the keen appraisal of Byzantine strategists, who proceeded to list such methods as promised the utmost advantage. Fraud, ruse or simulated routs were suggested without apparent shame, and it was thought no disgrace to buy off an adversary if tribute appeared to be less costly than war. Such principles are not always in harmony with Western ideals, but drastic economy of means had to be practiced if Constantinople hoped to survive in the midst of overwhelming enemies. And if the ethics of survival are not always heroic, much remains to be admired in the East-Roman military character as described by Oman:

> Of the spirit of chivalry there was not a spark in the Byzantine, though there was a great deal of professional pride, and a not inconsiderable infusion of religious enthusiasm. . . . Courage was considered at Constantinople as one of the requisites for obtaining success, not as the sole and paramount virtue of the warrior. The generals of the East considered a campaign brought to a successful issue without a battle as the cheapest and most satisfactory consummation in war. They considered it absurd to expend stores, money and the valuable lives of veteran soldiers in achieving by force an end that could be equally well obtained by skill.

III

CONSTANTINOPLE AS A BULWARK

The commander who has five or six thousand of our heavy cavalry and the help of God will need nothing more.

—NICEPHORUS II

THE repulse of plunder raids, launched on a much larger scale than those which terrified Europe, became routine Byzantine warfare at all times. These border clashes, with their unsung heroes and nameless combats, were the price paid for security by the richest city of the Dark Ages.

Then late in the sixth century began a series of struggles testing East-Roman skill and organization to the utmost. For a hundred years, with scarcely a breathing spell, the Empire fought for its life. Plunder, trade rivalry, migration, conquest, religious fanaticism—every compelling motive of war lent moral force to invaders pressing in from all sides.

The prelude to disaster came with the incursions of Slavs and Avars from the North while the realm warred against Persia on the eastern frontier. These conflicts, waged side by side for some twenty years, show how profoundly the character of strife may be shaped by its causes. The Slavs were primitives driven by the relentless and mysterious urge of migration. The Persians, on the contrary, battled in the interests of their merchants for the control of the trade routes to India and China. Ironically, silk had become the cause of dispute between the two great civilized empires; for this importation had come to be regarded as a necessity in luxury-loving Constantinople.

Hence we have in these two simultaneous conflicts the opposite poles of strife; the stark and brutal hungers of instinct as distinguished from the cultivated appetites of aggrandizement.

The methods and results show corresponding contrasts. The Persians, whose expectations were limited, kept within like limits in their expenditure of force. If they once penetrated as far as Antioch, the East-Roman forces revenged themselves by driving deep into Media, their farthest eastward advance in two centuries. On both sides a spirit of cool, professional warfare prevailed, with honors about even.

On the northern frontier no such moderation existed. The Slavs. though the most backward people of their day, were nevertheless a greater menace than the plundering Avar horsemen. The tactics of these unmounted spearmen and bowmen were clumsy, but they came on with a surge reminiscent of the Germanic migrations of the fourth century.

Slaughter grew to be an end rather than a means. Priscus, the general commanding the forces of Maurice, won three successive victories in which the Slav losses were 4,000, 9,000 and 15,000. In a following campaign he gained three added triumphs, leaving 30,000 barbarian dead on a single field. Then as a last resort he crossed the Danube and struck at the source of invasion, burning and butchering in a grim strife of extermination.

Still, the barbarians were merely checked after enduring two decades of such chastisement. In turn their ravages had all but depopulated Thrace and Illyria, the only Latin-speaking provinces in the realm outside of Italy. Not only were the chief remaining cultural influences of the West lost to Constantinople, but also two of the army's most dependable recruiting grounds.

The Persian war ended in a stalemate at about the same time. It had been fought for merchandising profits and neither side felt justified in using a large outlay of force. A few years of uneasy truce, however, released deeper antagonisms resulting in a new war to the hilt. Religious causes had been added during the interlude, leading to a death grapple between two profoundly antagonistic peoples, the Christians and the worshipers of the Sun.

The opportunity was provided by an East-Roman revolt occurring in reaction to the sacrifices of the last conflict. The emperor Maurice lost his life during the uprising and his throne went to a usurper, the "brutal and imbecile" Phocas. With troops being drawn from the frontier to put down the insurrection, the enemies of Constantinople found their opening. The Persians rushed in for the kill, followed by the Slavs and

Avars, and within a few years the hostile campfires were reflected in the waters of the Bosphorus.

The Victories of Heraclius

Never a great conquering power after Cyrus, Persia shared with China the historical distinction of outlasting her conquerors. Greece and Rome had run their course, but in 602 A.D. Persia began its eighth continuous century of power under the Parthian and Sassanid dynasties alone.

This longevity owed in large part to the realm's arms and strategic situation. A score of aspiring conquerors had been defeated by the deserts defending Persia on the west; an equal number had survived the deserts only to be harassed and cut to pieces by Parthian horsemen. The legion, even in its day of glory, fared little better than other invaders. In 53 B.C. Crassus and his cohorts were annihilated at Carrhae; in 36 A.D. Antony was beaten; in 232 Alexander Severus went down to defeat; and in 258 Valerian and his whole army were made captives.

Julian the Apostate, who gained Rome's last great infantry victories, demonstrated by his failure that Persia possessed a final resource of defense. Julian crossed the deserts safely and won several battles, only to be starved into submission when the defenders devastated their own most fertile provinces. The able young emperor fell mortally wounded, and his encircled legions were forced to beg for terms.

The Persian army of the year 602 was made up chiefly of cavalry, the heavy armed lancers serving as the striking arm of a host of Parthian horse-archers. Naturally, the generals of King Chosroes met little resistance in a realm torn apart by civil strife. Their first two campaigns took them across Syria to the sea, and the next advance swept across provinces of Asia Minor that had not known an invader for generations. By 608 the Persians were burning the Asiatic suburbs of Constantinople itself, while only a few miles away to the north the Slavs and Avars had ravaged up to the walls.

The Empire made a first move toward military solvency by putting its civil house in order. Africa, the sole province to escape revolt or invasion, led a revolution which ended in the overthrow and execution of the usurper. Phocas was succeeded by the hero-emperor Heraclius, who began his task with an empty treasury and the defeated remnants of an army.

Paradoxically, two great new disasters enabled Heraclius to build up the first truly national army of Byzantine history. Egypt fell to the enemy, then Jerusalem was sacked and the relics of the "True Cross" borne away by the followers of Zoroaster.

The military benefits were immediate. With a holy war in prospect, the Byzantine church melted down its treasures as a loan, while emptying its monasteries of thousands of shirkers. And with the grain dole cut off by the loss of Egypt, the urban populace had to choose between hunger and service in the army.

Even after these gains, the situation remained so desperate that Heraclius fought twelve years on the defensive before acquiring the means for carrying the war to the enemy. When at last he struck, his campaigns of the next six years were distinguished for perhaps the most brilliant strategy of the Dark Ages.

Instead of launching a direct attack in Asia Minor, he made use of the fleet to land at Cilicia in the Persian rear, threatening the invaders' communications. The enemy's main army was thus forced to retire from its strong situation opposite Constantinople, but Heraclius did not accept battle on Persian terms. Only after weeks of swift manoeuvre did he find his opening, with the result that the invaders were defeated and cleared out of Asia Minor.

Continuing the same strategy, the emperor made no attempt to liberate Syria and Egypt by assailing the despoilers of those provinces. In order to accomplish this purpose he turned invader himself, pushing far into Persian territory and compelling Chosroes to withdraw his forces from Syria and Egypt for home defense.

In his next campaign, the boldest of all, Heraclius feinted to fix the enemy's attention elsewhere, then made a swift and secret march across the Armenian highlands. Descending by surprise into Media, he destroyed the fire temples of Thebarmes, the birthplace of Zoroaster. Chosroes desperately recalled his armies from Syria, where they were still awaiting Heraclius, but the Persians went down to defeat in two great battles.

The Eastern monarch gathered his forces for a last tremendous effort in 626 by bribing the Slavs and Avars to besiege Constantinople, while from the Asiatic shore a large Persian army attempted to cross on rafts. But the land and naval forces of the city beat off all attacks, and Heraclius refused to be drawn away from the enemy's territory. He continued steadily to ravage the fairest Persian provinces, forcing Chosroes again to return to the defense of his own soil. His battered Slav and Avar allies gave up their siege meanwhile and retreated across the Danube.

The last levy of Persia had been put into the field when the two armies met near the ruins of ancient Nineveh, not far from the spot where another Persian empire had been destroyed by Alexander's army. Heraclius led the decisive charge and with his own hand slew the opposing general in single combat. The Persians were routed, their defenseless cities yielding a plunder which has been estimated as equal to the booty gained by the Graeco-Macedonian conquerors.

Heraclius granted peace only upon the payment of a huge indemnity and the evacuation of all East-Roman territory. The holy relics of Christendom were brought back to Constantinople, which celebrated a triumph in honor of an emperor who had led his troops farther eastward than any soldier of ancient Rome.

THE CONQUESTS OF ISLAM

Although both empires were exhausted after a war lasting twenty-six years, no surcease awaited either. While they had been putting every resource into efforts to destroy each other, Mohammed reached the height of his career in Arabia. He died in 632, only six years after the peace, and his fierce converts immediately spread out in all directions for the conquest of the unbelievers.

Persia succumbed first. Weakened by previous defeats, the realm hastily raised new armies only to have them cut down by the Saracens in two battles. In the final and decisive engagement, Isdigard, last of a line which had ruled for three centuries, fled into exile after the annihilation of his remaining forces. Persia as a result was overrun to the frontier of India.

The armies of Constantinople fared little better at first. Heraclius sent 60,000 veteran troops to contest the Saracen advance near the river Jordan. A terrific all-day battle occurred, with the Byzantine horsemen gradually pushing the invaders back to their camp. The victory seemed almost within grasp when a last fanatical charge of the Arabs broke the East-Roman ranks.

All Syria east of the Jordan was lost in this one battle. Damascus fell next, then Jerusalem after a desperate resistance of a year.

By this time it had become evident that Heraclius, sixty years old, ill with dropsy and worn out by his campaigns, was not destined to save his country a second time. A fatalistic lethargy seems to have overtaken both the emperor and his subjects, and within a few years Syria and Egypt were lost permanently to the Empire.

These developments came with a terrible sense of despair to Constantinople. East-Roman generals had long been familiar with Arab tactics and had not regarded them as formidable. Like all Eastern horsemen, the desert raiders attacked in agile swarms of lancers and archers, stinging rather than battering an enemy into confusion. Such fighters, though effective in their hour of victory, were contemptible opponents when the fortunes of battle went against them.

Neither their methods nor weapons showed much change, yet a mighty transformation had taken place during the years of the East-Roman war against Persia. Mohammed had touched off one of those explosions of human energy which transcend ordinary considerations of arms and tactics. Outbursts of this sort, mysterious and dreadful in the new forces they are capable of generating, have never failed to shatter existing military values.

Their true origins, like those of electricity or atomic energy, must remain largely in the nature of a cosmic enigma. Their causes and effects are more open to analysis, and it is noteworthy that such explosions have inevitably led to aggression. Defenders, however brave and patriotic they may be, are never charged with quite the same mystic fury.

Man, it has been said, is the only animal on earth willing to fight and die for an idea. The distinction offers a further clue to those hurricanes of conquest which have occasionally swept through history, leaving the wreckage of empires behind them. For the most potent weapon of a Mohammed, a Jenghiz Khan or a Hitler is an idea generated into human energy.

The first impulse is invariably the outgrowth of a previous state of shame or ignominy. The seed of violence is there, lying dormant and awaiting only the cultivation by some gifted tiller of mass misery. The deeper the degradation, the more immoderate are the powers of fertilization—a point that victors would do well to remember when imposing terms.

There is no dependable military remedy, or at least none has been revealed by historical experience. Conquerors of this type, it seems, are not restricted at first by the usual laws of tactics and strategy. They continue to conquer just as long as they are able to keep alive the idea. When that impulse withers, they become merely veteran soldiers with a victorious tradition; and then it is not long until they will have an opportunity of renewing their acquaintance with defeat.

Time and tenacity, therefore, are the best approach to a strategic defense. Even an idea, given enough time, finally fades and dies, leaving a seed to be nursed into life by some future evangelist of destruction. Fortunately for the peoples in their path, such conquerors are not many in the pages of history, and most attempts in the way of artificial dissemination have met with failure.

Centuries before Mohammed, his people had known an era of greatness which remained only a far, faint legend to ignorant tribesmen living like wild beasts of the desert. This legend, according to James Westfall Thompson, had a solid foundation of fact:

> Evidences of a former great prosperity in southern Arabia are not lacking. All the classical writers, Herodotus, Pliny and Strabo, frequently allude to it under the name Saba or Sheba as the richest country on the globe. . . . An innumerable population in this favorable territory, in hundreds of cities and villages, carried agriculture to its highest perfection. Merchants of great wealth sent their fleets to China and their caravans across the Syrian and African deserts.

Such a heritage of past glories, in contrast to a debased present, provided incendiary material for a messiah. Mohammed attacked the prevailing vices of sloth and drunkenness, while appealing to the mingled mysticism and materialism of the Arab character. Trade and war were the chief outlets for the energies of a desert people, so the Prophet proclaimed them highly pleasing in the sight of God.

The warrior had a divine mission in spreading the new gospel, but worldly inducements were also held forth to him. All spoils, after a fifth had been deducted for pious purposes, were to be divided among those who had won the victory or guarded the camp. The widow of a fallen warrior received his just share, and the Prophet was not constrained in describing the rewards awaiting the soul of the slain:

> The sword is the key of heaven and of hell: a drop of blood shed in the cause of God, a night spent in arms, is of more avail than two months of fasting and prayer: whosoever falls in battle, his sins are forgiven: at the day of judgment his wounds shall be resplendent as vermilion and odoriferous as musk; and the loss of his limbs shall be supplied by the wings of angels and cherubim.

That Mohammed was not unmindful of tactical problems is evident from his assignment of a full share of plunder to horse as well as rider, thus encouraging the development of cavalry. The quality of weapons likewise improved under his leadership, and at a later date Saracen armorers were to be reputed the most skillful in the world.

In general, however, the Prophet confined himself to the moral side of war and left few changes in age-old Arab fighting habits. In their first encounters with the Byzantine armies the invaders came on in irregular waves, sweeping around flanks or pouring into any gap in the line. Of discipline they had little, and still less of routine or organization. Their effectiveness lay almost entirely in numbers, mobility and a wild fervor carried far past any charted limits of morale.

In modern times there have been recrudescences of Moslem fury which won the respect of soldiers armed with repeating rifles and machine guns. It is understandable, therefore, that Byzantine bow, sword and lance were hard pressed by the first fierce missionaries of Islam. Nearly every engagement of the first ten years went against the Empire, exhausted as it was from the long Persian war.

After the death of Heraclius his son and grandson, both worthy descendants of the hero-emperor, waged a ceaseless struggle. Historians have remarked the almost entire lack of chronicles during this period, for both Byzantine and Saracen were too busy creating history to write it. Africa, Syria and Asia Minor were the battlegrounds, and the East-Roman armies appear to have contested every foot of soil bitterly.

Patriotic and religious enthusiasm had inspired the soldiers of Constantinople in their war against Persia. Now with a more frantic holy war being fought against them, Byzantine troops fell back on their old professional skill and organization. Finally, after twenty-two years of constant campaigning, they gained a respite when the Saracens themselves sued for a truce, even offering a small annual tribute for the boon.

No greater victory was ever won by East-Roman arms.

But if the first keen edge of fanaticism had worn off the Moslem sword, it was by no means dulled. With the resumption of strife, the Saracens showed a new polish to compensate for any decline in zeal. Learning from the Empire, they had already developed a heavy armed cavalry of their own. Even more astonishing, these former desert dwellers had armed and manned a strong fleet based upon their newly won province of Egypt.

Nor had the East-Roman forces been idle during the truce. The theme system reached maturity at this time, and the Empire also discovered a weapon that was to become the marvel of the age, its secret being kept not only from the enemy but also from posterity.

The test came in 673 when a great combined land and water expedition was launched against Constantinople. The Saracen armada managed to force the passage of the Dardanelles, but a terrible surprise awaited in the first naval engagements. From the prows of the East-Roman galleys protruded brazen tubes which emitted jets of liquid fire. The Arab marines rolled on their decks in agony, helpless against flames which water incited rather than extinguished.

Because of this affinity, Greek fire was sometimes known as "sea fire" or "wet fire." The invention of a Syrian architect named Callinicus, its formula remained a Byzantine state secret for centuries, and even present-day authorities seem none too clear as to its exact components. Colonel Hime, in his *Gunpowder and Ammunition,* has concluded that quicklime was the ingredient distinguishing the Byzantine weapon from flame-throwing devices of the ancient Greeks and Chinese. A compound of such materials as naphtha and sulphur apparently took fire from the quicklime after sea water had been pumped into the tubes to serve both for kindling and propulsion.

These brazen tubes, sometimes carved into dragons' heads or other fantastic shapes, protruded from the city walls as well as the prows of ships. After disastrous experience the Saracens learned that sand, urine or vinegar were the only extinguishing agents.

The important part played by the new weapon has left a legend that Greek fire was the sole means of saving Constantinople. But since the investment of the city lasted four years, it may be concluded that Byzantine tactics and generalship deserved their usual credit. In the end the defenders won a decisive battle fought simultaneously on land and water, and after leaving 30,000 slain, the remnants of the caliph's forces returned to Egypt. In the peace which followed, the Saracens agreed to restore all conquests of the expedition and pay an annual tribute of 3,000 pounds of gold for thirty years.

The final effort of Islam in 717 brought to Constantinople the most formidable armada of the Dark Ages. Eighty-three years after the first clash between Byzantine and Arab, the Moslems appeared in the Dardanelles with a fleet of 1,800 vessels supporting an army of 80,000. Wary by this time of East-Roman tactics, they were resolved to avoid fighting while starving the city into submission.

Constantinople was fully prepared, its granaries having been filled with provisions to last two years. Hence the besiegers themselves were first to feel the pinch of hunger, and an unusually cold winter caused thousands of deaths among the lightly clad Arabs.

During the following spring the invaders were reinforced by a reserve fleet and another army. Nevertheless, the East-Roman forces seized the initiative as their fire ships destroyed an enemy squadron while it lay at anchor. This success paved the way for another victory gained by troops which landed on the Bithynian coast and surprised the Saracen army watching on the other side of the strait.

After a year of reverses the enemy withdrew, having suffered losses of 70,000. On the homeward voyage the shattered fleet ran into a tempest in the Aegean, and out of the great armada only five vessels ever returned to Syria.

The exhausted Empire had at last won a period of recuperation after more than a century of battling Slav and Avar, Persian and Saracen. These terrific struggles, so little known to readers of European history, deserve to be ranked among the most decisive events of Western civilization. For if the Byzantine army had not constituted a first line of defense, it seems almost certain that the Continent must have fallen to Eastern conquerors.

This conclusion, of course, rests upon hypothesis. But at least we know that a full hundred years after the Prophet's death the Franks found it a major undertaking to repel a single Moorish incursion. And with Poitiers as an example, it is impossible to believe that seventh century Europe, still generally unarmored and fighting with clubs, could have resisted Mohammed's zealots at the height of their momentum.

The Tactics of Byzantine Survival

Though its African, Syrian and Egyptian provinces were lost, the shrunken realm had won comparative security which lasted for two centuries, when Constantinople herself turned to conquest. Plunder raids were of almost annual occurrence, some of them involving thousands of mounted invaders, but the efficiency of the theme system reduced these clashes to routine small war.

During this golden age of Byzantine arts and letters several new military treatises appeared, the most important being the *Tactica* of Leo the Wise, written about 900. In this work the emperor gives a detailed account of the cavalry tactics which consistently overcame the Moslem.

Supposing that the *strategos* of an Asiatic border theme has to deal with a formidable force of Saracen horsemen, Leo emphasizes that only the very fittest men must be chosen for field duty. Leaving behind all doubtful elements for garrison service, it is assumed by the *Tactica* that 4,600 picked troops might be mustered out of a total theme strength of 7,000. This force is to be arrayed in a three-line battle order, as shown in the accompanying plan based upon Oman's description:

(1-1). First line, 6 bands of 250 each   1,500
(2-2). Second line, 4 bands of 250 each   1,000
(3-3). Third line reserves, 2 bands of 250 each   500
(4-4). Flanking troops, 2 bands of 200 each   400
(5-5). Ambushing troops, 4 bands of 200 each   800
(6-6-6). Troops to fill intervals   400
                                                        ―――――――
                                                              4,600

Byzantine Cavalry Battle Plan

Three successive shocks, it will be recalled, were at the basis of the infantry tactics of the early Roman Republic. This same principle, but allowing for the possibility of five separate cavalry shocks, is carried out in the battle plan outlined by Leo:

(1-1). The first line, drawn up with small intervals so as to present an almost solid front, is charged with seizing the initiative. Each of the six bands is to send out a third of its archers as skirmishers, the rest being held in readiness for an advance.

(2-2). The second line, its wide intervals allowing for the passage of troops to and from the rear, is to add a second impact before the enemy has recovered from the shock delivered by the first line. The small bodies of troops masking the intervals (6-6-6) are intended with Byzantine guile to give an adversary the illusion of weight and numbers.

(3-3). The third line is to add its shock to a victorious advance or serve as a reserve in case of difficulty.

(4-4). Of the two flanking forces, one is to fall upon the enemy's left flank while the other guards against a similar attempt on the part of the enemy. (Flank attacks were customarily directed against the left in order to take the defenders at a disadvantage in the use of their weapons.)

(5-5). The four ambushing units are to post themselves in hiding far out on the right and left. Their duty is to seize the chances of battle for a surprise attack on the enemy's flank or rear.

The effectiveness of such tactics is scarcely to be doubted against Saracen horsemen whose suicidal courage was matched by an almost total lack of order and generalship. Although the Byzantine infantry often proved useless against mounted raiders, its tactics were not allowed to fall into decline. Whenever possible, the *strategos* sent units of foot to occupy a ford or mountain pass necessary to the Saracen retreat. With this force serving as tactical anvil, the East-Roman cavalry was able to pound the invaders unmercifully. As one of many instances, just such a combined attack annihilated an entire Moslem army in the year 963.

That the Byzantine infantry was also capable of taking the decisive rôle is shown by a great victory won over the Russians. In 941 these northern invaders, led by Vikings and using the same weapons and tactics, had suffered a terrible naval defeat on the Black Sea, their light boats being destroyed by the imperial fleet. Exactly thirty years later, Swiatoslaf, the Russian king, sought revenge by leading an army of 60,000 into the plains of Thrace. All foot soldiers, arrayed in great squares and fighting with ax and spear, they were met at the battle of Silistria by a mixed force of 30,000 cavalry and infantry.

The outcome foreshadowed Hastings both in historical and tactical respects. For the Byzantine foot-archers dominated the day, thinning the dense Russian ranks with their arrows until the cavalry could deal fatal blows. After a fearful slaughter King Swiatoslaf was forced to surrender, and the peace treaty brought his rude followers under Byzantine influences. As a result, Muscovite art, theology and architecture may often be traced back through the centuries to this decisive field.

Leo's *Tactica* makes it evident that in addition to light and heavy foot, the East-Roman army had an efficient engineering corps and supply train. Both contributed to a system of field fortification comparing favorably with that of the legion. The engineers accompanied the vanguard to lay out the night's fosse, while inside the palisade the wagons of the supply train were placed laager-fashion to serve as a second line of defense.

Not even an ambulance corps was lacking in a military organization which had no modern counterpart until the seventeenth century. A surgeon served each band of 250 men, in addition to six or eight stretcher bearers who were rewarded for saving severely wounded men. It is a further comment on Byzantine humanity that the enemy was conceded rights which had seldom before been recognized even in principle. The *Tactica* states that no truce should be broken, no hostage or ambassador unjustly harmed, no noncombatant slain and no female captive mistreated.

In all periods of Byzantine warfare the fine art of analyzing a foeman's national characteristics is made an important department of strategy. Where Maurice's *Strategicon* is concerned with the Slav, Avar and Persian, the *Tactica* deals with such later adversaries as the Frank, Lombard, Saracen and Turk. For example, Leo's shrewd, almost cynical estimate of our ninth century European ancestors is quoted from *The History of the Art of War in the Middle Ages*:

> The Franks and Lombards are bold and daring to excess. . . . So formidable is the charge of the Frankish chivalry with their broadsword, lance and shield, that it is best to decline a pitched battle with them until you have put all the chances on your own side. You should take advantage of their indiscipline and disorder; whether fighting on foot or on horseback, they charge in dense, unwieldy masses, which cannot manoeuvre because they have neither organization nor drill. . . . Hence they fall readily into confusion if suddenly attacked in front and rear—a thing easy to accomplish, since they are utterly careless and neglect the use of pickets and vedettes and the proper surveying of the countryside. They encamp, too, confusedly and without fortifying themselves, so that they can be easily cut off by a night attack. Nothing succeeds better against them than a feigned flight, which draws them into an ambush; for they follow hastily, and invariably fall into a snare. But perhaps the best tactics of all are to protract the campaign and lead them into the hills and desolate tracts, for they take no care about their commissariat, and when their stores run low their vigor melts away. They are impatient of hunger and thirst, and after a few days of privation desert their standards and steal away home as best they can. . . . On the whole, therefore, it is easier and less costly to wear out a Frankish army by skirmishes, protracted operations in desolate districts, and the cutting off of its supplies, than to attempt to destroy it at a single blow.

If this diagnosis appears too contemptuous, it must be remembered that Byzantine strategists amply proved their case. For four centuries, with surprisingly little trouble on the whole, they managed to hold their distant Italian provinces against the bone-crushing tactics of the Frank and Lombard.

THE BATTLE OF MANZIKERT

It is this continuity of the East-Roman military system, as revealed by the various textbooks, which most impresses the student of war. Leo's *Tactica* of 900, written in consideration of new foemen, shows few departures from the methods and organization described by Maurice in 578. Eighty years after Leo, the military handbook of Nicephorus (Phocas) II mentions still fewer innovations, though the Russian, Serb and Bulgarian have replaced the Saracen as enemies.

In short, it was the adversaries of Constantinople who were broken, not the marvelously flexible system which overcame each in turn for five hundred years.

As compared to Macedonian or Roman warfare, it is notable that Byzantine operations seldom aimed at conquest. The textbooks usually take it for granted that East-Roman territory is to be maintained rather than extended; and even the victories of Heraclius, won on enemy soil, were based upon an intelligent defensive.

The wisdom of this policy was demonstrated when Constantinople finally developed several swashbuckling rulers in the eleventh century. Their successes, far more than any defeats suffered by the realm, proved the lack of resources essential to a great conquering power. The loss of the Egyptian, Syrian and African provinces, in fact, had been due less to military reverses than a harsh civil administration which made alien subjects glad to exchange masters. The frequency of palace revolutions is another recurring symptom of weakness; and Byzantine taxation, according to Bury, "aimed at making the treasury full instead of making the empire rich."

Still, there were no defects in the military system which imposed limitations, as was shown by the victories of Basil II. This warrior prince, who wore a monk's garb under his armor, vowed to devote his life to arms and religion, and during the next forty years he was seldom out of the saddle. Known as the Bulgarian Slayer from his monstrous cruelties, he waged a war of conquest for three decades against the strong realm uniting the peoples of the Balkan Peninsula.

The Bulgarian monarch, King Samuel, proved to be a stubborn foeman after adopting the tactics of Constantinople. His hill forts and castles put up such a stout resistance that Basil fought twenty campaigns before conquering up to the Danube. For twelve more years the Bulgarians held out in their central provinces, being beaten by a frightfulness in contrast to past Byzantine mercies. So pitiless was Basil that after his final victory he blinded 15,000 captives, leaving only a one-eyed man in each hundred to guide the host to Samuel with news of the battle. The aged Bulgarian ruler died on the spot from rage and grief.

At the death of the sanguinary Basil in 1025 the borders of the realm proper had reached their greatest expansion of history. His sword had won more new territory than had been gained since the triumphs of Belisarius; yet these very conquests were to prove a liability, both civil and military, leading to disaster.

Not only had the Empire been drained of resources, but the new territory added enormously to the burden of defense. The conquest of Armenia merely created an unruly province out of a free buffer state resisting Turkish inroads. The Syrian conquests substituted an uncertain eastern frontier for the strong natural advantages of the Taurus Range.

These strategic weaknesses were incurred just as the Seljuk Turks, once despised as mere raiders, became a menace to the security of the Empire. Using the familiar sword, lance and bow tactics of Asiatic horsemen, they had grown rapidly in numbers and unity until by 1065 they made themselves masters of Persia and Armenia.

At the battle of Manzikert, therefore, the Empire was contending with a rising Eastern war power whose sultan, Alp Arslan, had been proclaimed Commander of the Faithful at Bagdad. He appeared with at least 100,000 Turkish horsemen on the eastern frontier, where the emperor Romanus Diogenes had gathered a force of 60,000.

Better Byzantine troops had never been led into action, and the numerical odds were no greater than Constantinople's armies often faced. But at Manzikert the realm had the misfortune to be ruled by a young hotspur who aspired to military glory. Like Valens on the equally fatal field of Adrianople, he rejected the peace proposals of the enemy and prepared for headlong attack.

The two decisive battles were likewise similar in that the losers at first swept everything before them. After rashly pursuing the Turks until dusk over plains suited to their tactics, Romanus ordered a retirement to camp. The fierce Asiatic horsemen immediately rallied, closing in from all sides. Although the young emperor led gallant counterattacks, his left was separated from his centre and routed. The remaining squadrons were reduced to a desperate stand in the darkness which culminated in total disaster. Romanus became a captive and all Asia Minor lay open to the ravages of the enemy.

Sword and dagger ruled the Empire during an ensuing decade of anarchy in which the enemy was seldom molested. The walls and fleet saved Constantinople, but after Manzikert in 1071 the great Byzantine military system practically disappears from history.

The realm, it is true, retained a shadow of its former power, and the final downfall was to be postponed for 382 more years. Nor had East-Roman generalship lost its skill and cunning, for many a future triumph remained to be won with mercenary troops. But the old Byzantine system, based upon a native soldiery organized into themes, had been destroyed at the roots when the empire lost its great recruiting ground in Asia Minor.

For centuries that peninsula had supported a large population with its industry and agriculture. In the past such mighty empires as Lydia and Cappadocia had sprung from those fertile plains. Now after ten years of war and anarchy all prosperity vanished, never again to be fully revived down to the present day.

Usually the patient toil of peasants may be trusted to heal the wounds of the earth. This time, however, sword and torch seem to have done their work too thoroughly for redemption. Only a generation after Manzikert, when the Crusaders marched through Asia Minor, they found a bitter, man-made desert in which brambles were growing out of the ruins of once thriving cities.

IV

THE CRUSADES

God fed the Christians with the bread of tears, and gave
them to drink without stint of the cup of repentance, till
the dawn of tribulation came again.

—BOHA-ED-DIN

PROPAGANDA, the science of forging the idea into a weapon of war,
is popularly supposed to be a modern development. Yet a glance at
eleventh century Europe on the eve of the Crusades will disclose most of
our present-day methods for creating the martial mood. Allowing for
improved methods of communication, few basic principles were overlooked in the moral campaign that shaped the opinion of a continent.

At the very outset an embarrassing problem confronted the churchmen
who supplied the leadership. They faced the undeniable fact that the
Moslem custodians of the Holy Places had been comparatively tolerant
and hospitable in their reception of Christians. As early as the eighth
century six pilgrimages had safely made the journey to Jerusalem,
followed by 12 in the ninth century, 16 in the tenth and 117 in the
eleventh, including a single expedition of 11,000 worshipers. In short,
Christians had only to pay a reasonable tax in order to visit their shrines
at will. In return for this payment they received protection from banditry
such as was seldom enjoyed in contemporary Europe.

It was essential, nevertheless, that the Moslem be re-created into the
archenemy of Christendom. Into the new creation went a pinch of fact
and a wealth of imaginative detail. Racial, religious and economic preju-

dices, all were invoked by means of every known medium of emotional appeal.

This is not to say that the fathers of the Church were altogether designing and artful. They doubtless entertained a sincere aversion to the infidel; and a great many other motives, economic, social and political, entered into the movement. Not the least of these was the militant pacifism of the age. For a century clergymen had been using their most potent theological weapons in an attempt to check the ceaseless strife of medieval Europe. To a modern observer, accustomed to unrestricted slaughter, there is of course an element of absurdity in the notion of a week-end peace or an abstinence from arms during Lent. Yet the eleventh century Truce of God represents social leadership of the highest order, achieving results which at least mitigated the lot of feudal humanity.

The conception of a great war to end small wars may likewise seem dubious, but here again the Church stood on sound psychological footing. Europe's accumulated resentments, the mass of running sores on the body politic, were too far advanced to respond to theological remedies. The only cure was to be sought in the fiery idealism of a common cause.

With this end in view, the most fantastic inventions were circulated Matthew Paris and other writers lent their pens, accusing the Saracens of such atrocities as poisoning the pepper exported by the Orient. All Christendom was deluged with papal bulls, circular letters, bulletins, legends, poems, narratives and supposed epistles from pilgrims. Paintings were sent from town to town—forerunners of the modern poster— depicting a hideous Moslem in the act of trampling upon the True Cross. For the common folk, there were itinerant evangelists, usually monks or hermits, who could be trusted to arouse mass emotions.

The response of the people seems devout and genuine. The lords and gentry, somewhat less simple in their reactions, were at any rate inspired by a wholehearted desire for plunder, conquest, adventure and the remission of sins.

Militarily, the times could hardly have been more propitious. In Europe the mailed rider was everywhere supreme, and the baptism of the Slavs and Magyars had opened up a land route to Jerusalem. Sea power also favored the Crusaders, with the ships of Genoa and Venice at their disposal. A potential ally awaited in the East Roman Empire, and Constantinople provided a base both for land and water operations.

To these advantages may be added the development of an effective new weapon in the arbalest, or crossbow. Simply a ballista on a small scale, with the cord drawn back by a winch and released by a trigger, the crossbow shot bolts which pierced the best Eastern armor. More power-ful than the ordinary bow of the day, it differed also in that it could be fired from a reclining position, and the bolts were cheaper and less bulky than arrows. The crossbow was slower, however, since the winch must be wound while placing one foot on the steel arm supplying the force of propulsion.

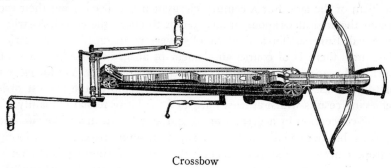

Crossbow

The weapon is mentioned at the battle of Hastings, but it remained a novelty until the Crusades. And even at this early date we have an example of the timeless horror of new fighting tools, resulting eventually in the prohibition of the crossbow by several popes. There would seem to be little choice between being transfixed by a steel bolt and an ordinary arrow; but every age, including the present, has its prejudices. Despite this abhorrence of military change, no restriction has ever yet succeeded in abolishing a weapon which once proved its worth on the battlefield.

The Crusaders in the Field

In contrast to the advantages of Christendom, the Mohammedan world was never more weak. The victory of Manzikert, far from creating a great Moslem empire, led to discord between Turk, Arab, Syrian and Egyptian, and even these racial groups split into factions.

At a glance, therefore, it is hard to understand why the Crusades should have resulted in one of the most gigantic military failures of all time. Only after a survey of the tactical unit, the mailed horseman, do the limitations of Western warfare become apparent.

As a physical specimen, the man-at-arms must have been incredibly tough, wiry, resistant to disease. The medieval lord in his castle tolerated filth and hardship which left weaklings small chance for survival; and the metabolism of the age is indicated by the fact that Europe imported spices in order to stomach dangerously tainted foods. That the knight was not usually a large man, we know from suits of armor in modern museums. It may also be concluded that he had muscles of steel, since he wielded a lance and broadsword that would exhaust a heavier man of today. He was, in short, a sheer fighting animal bred by a relentless process of selection.

Of the courage and endurance of the man-at-arms there can be no doubt, and he may also be credited with practiced skill in the use of his weapons. But throughout the Crusades these military virtues were to be offset by arrogance, stupidity and a total scorn for the intellectual side of war. Five great armies perished almost to a man because they ignored the most elementary principles of strategy. Merely losing a well-traveled route accounted for the bleached bones of thousands, and the most decisive battle of the movement was decided by thirst rather than force of arms.

The weaknesses of Europe were first made evident in the Crusades of the people which preceded the armies of the princes. The zeal of these low-born converts, which might have been utilized in a light infantry system, was permitted to go to waste. Early in 1096 many thousands of pilgrims—poor Crusaders of both sexes, led by monks and hermits—failed even to reach Constantinople, the majority being massacred by Slavs and Magyars in just retribution for their excesses.

The men-at-arms drifted overland in small bands until by the spring of 1097 a host of perhaps 150,000 had gathered near Constantinople. Godfrey of Bouillon and his brother Baldwin led the men of Lorraine; the Provençals were under Raymond of Toulouse; and Bohemund and his nephew Tancred commanded the Norman contingent.

Momentarily the warriors of the West became united in their hostility to the Eastern Empire. Byzantine and Crusader, each displaying his worst side, behaved more like enemies than allies with a common cause. Far from learning military lessons from Constantinople, the Franks (a name that was to be applied to all Crusaders) could scarcely be restrained from sacking the city. The East-Roman generals, while shunning the hard fighting, relied upon trickery to claim a jackal's share of the spoils.

Under the circumstances it is remarkable that all factions forgot their differences long enough to besiege Nicaea, on the Asiatic shore opposite Constantinople. With the capture of this western outpost of Islam, the Empire was relieved of a threat that had existed since Manzikert, and the Crusaders had a free passage into Asia Minor.

While awaiting reinforcements, the Turks slowly fell back, ravaging an already horribly ravaged countryside. The Crusading army met the forage problem by marching in two parallel columns, and this division of strength offered the Moslems their first opportunity at the battle of Dorylaeum.

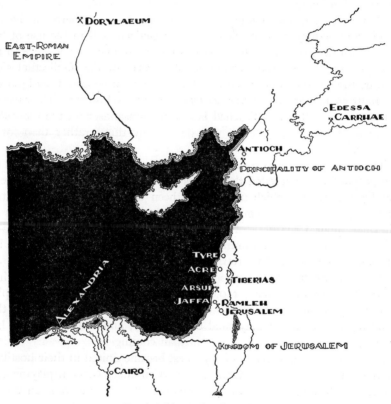

Battlefields of the Crusades

Bohemund, leading about half of the invaders, was suddenly beset on an upland plain by a much larger army of Seljuk Turks. Using the swarming attack which had won at Manzikert, the Eastern horse-archers soon had the Franks surrounded. It was the Crusaders' first experience with such tactics, and Bohemund prudently ordered them to keep their formations. The men-at-arms thus escaped a complete disaster, but their losses were heavy while the opposing bowmen suffered scarcely at all.

Messengers had been sent to the column led by Godfrey and Raymond, but Western efficiency may be measured by the fact that it took the rescuers five hours to ride seven miles. Meanwhile, Bohemund and his men were giving ground. Their assailants had broken into the camp, slaying women and priests, when reinforcements finally arrived to turn defeat into victory. The very delay proved an advantage, since the enemy was taken in flank and rear while in complete disorder. Caught between the two divisions of the Crusading army, the Turks were cut to pieces by repeated charges.

The success proved as valuable as it was undeserved, for the Crusaders met no further opposition until they reached Antioch.

Here two combats were fought which would indicate that the Franks had learned a lesson from Dorylaeum. The emirs of Syria had raised an army to relieve the blockaded city, but Bohemund did not wait for the Moslems to choose a field suited to their horse-archers. After a march in the darkness he surprised the enemy at dawn in a defile between a lake and the river Orontes. The results were added proof that the light-armed Moslems could not stand against Western shock tactics. Crowded into a narrow space, they lost 2,000 slain or drowned before the routed survivors could make their escape. A few days later, in a second combat, they were again pinned against the river and defeated with severe losses.

Antioch, which could neither be stormed nor starved into submission, fell by treachery. Once inside the walls, the Crusaders in turn were blockaded; and soon they lost so many horses from want of forage that their chiefs decided upon a sally.

In previous engagements the European foot had consisted only of a rabble of pilgrims left to guard the camp. But with a majority of the knights dismounted, the Franks were forced to improve their tactics. Advancing upon the Moslem camp several miles from the city, their 25,000 warriors were drawn up in three lines of infantry—archers and crossbowmen—mingled with dismounted knights trusting to sword and lance. The cavalry, numbering only a tenth of the force, was posted on the wings to open the engagement, while in the rear Bohemund stationed a small mounted reserve to guard against flank attack. As an added precaution, both wings rested on natural obstacles.

Necessity had thus brought about a balanced combination of shock and missile tactics which swept everything before it. The left and centre of the much larger Turkish army were immediately driven back, leaving the camp and baggage undefended. On the right the Moslem horsemen broke through to the rear, but Bohemund's reserves held firm until reinforcements came to the rescue. In the end the defeat of the Turks was so complete that the remnants of their army scattered to the hills. As a result of this great victory, the Crusaders were able to push on to Jerusalem without serious opposition, and the city fell in July, 1099.

The ensuing slaughter became one of the bloodiest in military chronicles. The men of the West literally waded in gore, their march to the Church of the Holy Sepulchre being gruesomely likened to "treading out the wine-press." Such massacres, it may be noted, cannot be charged entirely to the inhumanity of a past age, for the nineteenth and twentieth centuries are not without examples. The psychologist is perhaps best able to explain, but the historian can at least assert that these excesses usually come as the climax to the capture of a fortified post or city. For long the assailants have endured more punishment than they were able to inflict; then once the walls are breached, pent-up emotions find an outlet in murder, rape and plunder which discipline is powerless to prevent.

The Loss of Jerusalem

In the lack of horses the knights of the First Crusade developed a victorious combination of infantry and cavalry tactics. When the necessity no longer existed, they promptly relapsed into old heresies and suffered two sharp defeats.

All of Baldwin's men-at-arms were well mounted on captured horses at the battle of Ramleh in 1101. Their opponents were troops sent by the Fatimite ruler of Egypt—Bedouin and Moorish light horse, black Soudanese infantry fighting with bow and mace, mailed heavy cavalry from the caliph's guard. The overconfident Franks staked everything on headlong cavalry charges, only to be severely handled by the enemy's better balanced combination of horse and foot. Baldwin withdrew from the field after leaving behind most of his force as casualties.

In 1104 Baldwin and Bohemund lost another battle on the field of Carrhae, where Crassus and his legions had been annihilated by Parthian horsemen nearly eleven centuries before. The defeat of the Crusaders became one of history's most faithful repetitions. Lured by horse-archers out into the desert, the Christians were surrounded and cut to pieces. Baldwin was taken prisoner and only a handful of his men fought their way through to safety.

Neither of these disasters proved decisive, and the next three generations saw more trading than fighting with the enemy as the men of the West acquired a taste for Oriental luxuries. Indeed, the burly barons of Provence and Normandy found silk robes so much less irksome than armor that only two battles of importance are recorded between 1104 and 1187.

During this armed interlude the assets and liabilities of both sides grew more apparent. The Crusaders continued to hold the upper hand in missile weapons and defensive armor. So pronounced was this advantage that the Moslem chronicler Boha-ed-din leaves descriptions of unconcerned Franks marching with arrows stuck in the thick felt cassocks they wore over their mail shirts.

The Christians likewise left no doubt of their ability to ride down Oriental cavalry when given the opportunity for their favorite shock tactics. Yet while the invaders won inconclusive victories in the only two tests of these eighty-three years, Moslem harassing tactics gained far more deadly results. No less than five Christian armies, estimated at a total of 200,000 men, were destroyed on the march. Although able to repel enemy attacks in force, the undisciplined Franks melted away as a result of stragglers being cut off and foraging parties surrounded.

With the resumption of active warfare, the Kingdom of Jerusalem had cause to regret these potential reinforcements lost during the Second Crusade. Islam at last had found unity under the leadership of the gifted and chivalrous Saladin. The great *jehad*, or counter-crusade, was being preached; and from the Nile to the Tigris the followers of the prophet acknowledged one rule.

By race a Kurd of Armenia, Saladin had been educated in Damascus according to the best traditions of Mohammedan culture. Most of his career was devoted to fighting his fellow Moslems, and only after two decades of civil war could he present a solid front to the invaders.

In 1187 he swept through the Kingdom of Jerusalem with 60,000 warriors from Egypt, Syria and Mesopotamia. One by one the fortresses fell to him, and when he blockaded Tiberias, the capitol of Galilee, King Guy came to the rescue with the *levy en masse* of the realm—1,200 knights, 18,000 foot and some thousands of mercenary horse-archers.

After concentrating near Nazareth, the outnumbered Christians marched behind the True Cross through arid regions laid waste by the enemy. Saladin let the terrain and July heat fight for him as he slowly fell back, luring the Crusaders into the stark hills near the Sea of Galilee.

Both the men and horses of King Guy's army were tormented by thirst, but on the eve of battle he chose to encamp rather than risk a march through the dusk to water. The Moslems fired the dry grass for miles around, and all that night the clouds of stifling smoke added to the misery of the encircled army. Sleep was further made impossible by

Saracen archers who hovered outside the campfires, their bowstrings twanging in the darkness as ceaseless flights of arrows fell.

By dawn the Crusaders were morally defeated before striking a blow. Through black and swollen lips the foot soldiers told Guy that they had no strength left for battle. Even a majority of the knights gave up the struggle and huddled like lost sheep about the True Cross. The only survivors were a small band of men-at-arms who sought an escape, sword in hand. Apparently the Saracens let them pass in order to make sure of the remainder, who were speedily reduced to corpses or captives along with their king.

The strange battle of Tiberias (or Hattin) proved the most decisive of the Crusades, leading to the capitulation of the Holy City after only a fortnight's siege. Saladin's mercy came in contrast to the great massacre of 1099, for the Christian inhabitants were generally extended clemency. By the close of 1187 nearly the whole of the Kingdom of Jerusalem had fallen to Islam, with Tyre remaining the single stronghold of importance held by the Christians.

Saladin and Richard

Saladin's victories were largely due to the intelligent use he made of the terrain and the natural fighting qualities of his men. More often than any other Moslem leader, he gave the Crusaders every opportunity to accomplish their own defeat. In this expectation he seldom met disappointment.

As an example of the inability of the Franks to learn from disaster, a whole century passed before they profited from their sea power. During this time enough reinforcements perished on the overland march to have insured an ultimate triumph, yet not until the Third Crusade of 1189 did most of the Crusaders take to ship. Then, too late for victory, the men of the West also discovered under Richard the Lionhearted the tactics which might once have led to tremendous results.

This lusty hero of troubadours and romancers has seldom been given credit for his generalship. When he arrived before Acre in 1191, the city was being ineffectually blockaded by 30,000 Franks who had landed since the defeat of Tiberias. They had been badly mauled by a relieving army under Saladin, and the English prince found them scarcely more than a leaderless mob.

Due entirely to his energy and discipline, Acre capitulated within a few weeks. For his next campaign Richard set himself the task of recovering Jerusalem. Jaffa seemed the logical base for such an operation, and

toward this seaport the army set out along the great Roman road beside
the Mediterranean. Within sight of the marching columns a fleet brought
supplies.

According to precept Saladin had every right to anticipate another
victory over indiscipline. He brought a numerically superior force which
moved parallel to the Franks, following an inland route and watching
for the first sign of disorder.

But this campaign was to reveal one of the greatest miracles of the
Crusades—a disciplined European army, capably led. Realizing that
fatigue had resulted in many a former defeat, Richard marched only in
the cool of the day and gave his men frequent rests. He placed his porters
and pack animals nearest the sea; the next column consisted of cavalry,
while the infantry marched still farther inland as a first line of defense.
All three columns, extending for miles, were kept well in hand to guard
against straggling.

After waiting three weeks in vain for disorder, Saladin determined to
create it. He planned to swarm out from the forest of Arsuf, located
about a mile from the sea, and harass the Franks until their confusion
offered an opportunity for assault in force. With wild yells the Moslems
burst out of the woods—Bedouins, Turkish horse-archers, black Soudanese bowmen, mailed Mamelukes. The Franks had been prepared for
such a surprise and the long columns continued their march in perfect
array. The crossbowmen paused only to aim, then made ready another
bolt and fell into ranks again. The knights plodded along watchfully,
keeping their intervals in spite of casualties from Moslem arrows.

After more punishment, the men-at-arms began sending messengers to
Richard, begging for the word of command. He withheld his counterattack until finally the Moslem host fell into the disorder Saladin had
hoped to create in the enemy's ranks. Then the battle cry of St. George
was raised and the knights spurred into the masses of light horsemen
filling the narrow plain. A fearful slaughter followed as the crossbowmen
poured in their bolts while the mailed riders delivered charge after
charge. Yet even in the moment of victory Richard kept his men in hand,
and the columns were re-formed before the Crusaders became the victims
of their usual rash pursuit.

Arsuf was Saladin's first great defeat, and he attempted nothing more
ambitious than skirmishing operations during the remainder of his opponent's march.

Having demonstrated the proper defense against Moslem harassing
methods, Richard proceeded to win a combat based upon a combination

of shock and missile tactics which might well have changed the history
of the Crusades. Surprised by a dawn attack at Jaffa, he could muster
only 55 knights and 2,000 infantry against several times their numbers
of Turks. He ordered his infantry spears to kneel in the first line, and
behind them he placed expert crossbowmen to fire weapons loaded and
handed up by the soldiers of the third line. His small body of horse was
held in reserve for a counterattack.

The hedge of spears kept the enemy at a distance, while the crossbows
delivered a concentrated hail of missiles. The Turks were thrown into
complete disorder, their ruin being completed by the charge of the 55
knights. Within a few minutes the losers had left 700 men and 1,500
horses on the field at a cost to Richard of only two men slain.

The Sack of Constantinople

Arsuf and Jaffa had little influence on future tactics, including those
of Richard himself. In general the English prince preferred boldness to
brilliance, so that the rest of his career presents a record of hard but
uninspired fighting.

After he gave up his Jerusalem campaign and returned to Europe, few
operations of interest took place in the Holy Land. The time for compromise had come, since both Moslem and Frank were weary of war.
And though new expeditions were to be launched in the next century,
the last crusade of military importance accomplished the ruin of a Christian ally.

The French, Flemish and Italian warriors of the Fourth Crusade
assembled in good faith, being detained in Venice because of inability to
pay their passage to the Holy Land. The Venetian doge, Henry Dandolo,
furnished supplies as a prelude to holding the men virtually captives on
an unhealthy island in the lagoon while their stores dwindled.

History has seldom revealed a more ruthless character than this almost
sightless octogenarian, for Dandolo plotted to bend the Crusaders to his
will. When they were in no position to demur, he proposed that they pay
their debt to Venice by taking part in a great expedition against Constantinople. With guilty consciences, but with their imaginations inflamed
by the enormous prospects of loot, the Christian warriors allowed themselves to be persuaded.

The moment could not have been better chosen by Venice for the
destruction of a commercial rival. The Crusades had contributed almost
as much as Manzikert to the decline of the Eastern Empire, and in 1203

it no longer ranked as a first-rate military power. The fleet was too weak to oppose the invading armada's passage of the Dardanelles, while the army consisted of but a few thousand mercenary troops.

Only the great walls and towers remained intact from Constantinople's former glory. Against them the Crusaders' first combined land and water attack failed. Led by the warship of the blind old doge, they captured a few towers by throwing bridges from their ships across to the ramparts. When the garrison still held firm, the 30,000 invaders withdrew after setting fires which resulted in a terrible conflagration.

Both sides prepared two months for the final test of strength. The garrison beat off wave after wave of assailants, but again the Crusaders made the torch their principal weapon. Advancing behind the flames, they had barely secured a foothold when the Varangian Guards, the best troops of the city, chose this moment to demand arrears in pay. With mutiny added to fire, the morale of the defenders collapsed and Constantinople fell.

The sack that followed was costly to future generations. For the Crusaders were destructive as well as rapacious, with consequences which have been summarized by James Westfall Thompson:

> The pillage is one of the blackest chapters in European history. Constantinople was the one city in Christendom which represented an unbroken continuity of higher culture and material civilization from the time of the ancient Greeks. Nearly the whole wondrous heritage was destroyed. . . . Libraries, baths, palaces were reduced to heaps of ruins.

Historians feel certain that most of Greek art and literature survived until that winter day in 1204. But after their first frenzy of wreckage the Crusaders proved miserly plunderers. When the gold and silver had all been divided, they stripped tombs and altars of priceless art objects to be melted down into copper coins.

Posterity, cheated of such treasures, is left only a gloomy satisfaction in the weak and miserable existence of the Latin empire set up by the conquerors. This creation, which included a mere scrap of territory outside the city walls, endured but fifty-seven years before falling ignominiously to 800 Byzantine soldiers. The restored Eastern Empire held together two more centuries; but events were to prove that the sack of 1204 had fatally undermined the ancient bulwark of Christendom against the Moslem. It was, ironically, the most impressive military result of the Crusades.

V

THE FAR EAST

The greatest happiness is to vanquish your enemies, to chase them before you, to rob them of their wealth, to see those dear to them bathed in tears, to clasp to your bosom their wives and daughters.

—JENGHIZ KHAN

DURING the years when Frank, Byzantine and Moslem were rending each other, a greater war power was emerging on the other side of Asia. In 1240 Matthew Paris recorded Europe's impressions of the horsemen who had swept from the Pacific to the Mediterranean in two decades:

> Swarming like locusts over the face of the earth, they have brought terrible devastation to the eastern parts, laying it waste with fire and carnage. . . . For they are inhuman and beastly, rather monsters than men, thirsting for and drinking blood, tearing and devouring the flesh of dogs and men, dressed in ox-hides, armed with plates of iron, short and stout, thickset, strong, invincible, indefatigable.

Allowing for exaggerations in this description, it may still be doubted if the human race has ever produced more repulsive specimens than those nomads whose grandsons ruled urbanely in China. Predatory, drunken, incredibly filthy in their habits, the Mongols also possessed warlike virtues which were to make them the greatest conquerors of the Far East. A brief outline of the career of their leader might be mistaken for some dark fantasy out of the Arabian Nights tales. Fighting his first petty combats at the age of thirteen, the sub-chief Temudjin warred forty years before establishing his rule over his own people. In the decline of his life, as Jenghiz Khan, it took him only another decade to conquer the world, or at least such parts of the world as he deemed worth conquering.

A more stark personality the earth has never known. In China alone his victims have been estimated at 18,000,000 souls, for the war creed of the Mongols was not evasive: "The vanquished can never be the friends of the victors; the death of the former is necessary therefore for the safety of the latter."

The campaigns of Jenghiz Khan and his successors were too far-flung to be measured in terms of miles or leagues. Mongol armies moved according to degrees of latitude and longitude. Their conquests were on a correspondingly large scale—peoples and areas of the earth's surface, rather than kingdoms or empires.

Yet the beginnings both of the leader and his people were unpromising. The events of the early years reveal a man of terrific resolution, but we see few glimpses of creative military talent. The rising young Temudjin was apparently satisfied for the most part with the tactics of his ancestors. These differed in few essentials from the fighting habits of all warriors of the steppes.

In that bitter plateau region men took to horse as naturally as coast dwellers become sailors. The distances were vast beyond the comprehension of a European, the plains so bleak that constant movement was required in order to find pasturage. Such conditions, combined with a climate of fierce extremes, evolved tough breeds both of horses and men —the Scythians, the Huns, the Parthians, the Tatars, the Turks and the Mongols.

It is a truism of military history that herdsmen have always been more warlike than tillers of the soil. Existence itself is a struggle for such peoples, partaking of the character of war. The Mongols, like their kinsmen of the steppes, enjoyed few more civilized comforts than the half-wild beasts which represented their only wealth. Boys took early to the bow and saddle, since riding and archery were necessary to survival. Hunting, herding and theft were the only occupations, and all three called for the elements of surprise, ambush, stratagem and missile attack.

The strength of the steppes warrior thus derived from the fact that he was not a trained soldier, snatched from a softer life and drilled in the use of unfamiliar arms. For that reason his tactics have always been effective against trained soldiers. From Alexander down to Napoleon, those same harassing advances, swirling envelopments and elusive retreats have never failed to confuse a formal opponent.

The weaknesses of the Asiatic horseman may likewise be traced to environmental causes. His life made him an individualist, acknowledging little discipline beyond the observance of a few tribal codes and taboos. Brave when bravery was expedient, he had small love for adversity and no shame at turning skulker, deserting such comrades as had not already preceded him in flight. Finally, his poverty made plunder more desirable than victory, and a nomad success often led to fatal disorder.

The Mongols, through contact with the Chinese, were more advanced militarily than the remote warriors of the steppes. But in general the early battles of Temudjin followed a pattern that is monotonous to anyone familiar with Hunnish, Parthian or Turkish arms. The Mongols were no better disciplined than their nomadic cousins, and they appear to have had the same tender regard for a whole skin.

Then came the amazing transition. After struggling forty years to establish his tribal supremacy, the Great Khan turned conqueror. The Mongols had been paying tribute to the Kin Empire of China: Jenghiz insultingly demanded that the process be reversed.

In the spring of the year 1211 he took advantage of treachery to cross the Great Wall; but the invaders were no more successful at first than other plains warriors who occasionally raided China. Their ignorance of siege tactics and the use of war engines was demonstrated by failure before fortified cities, and that autumn Jenghiz withdrew after few and minor successes.

The turning point of his career came in a following campaign when he discovered that Chinese ancestor worship could be made to serve a conqueror. The Great Khan, who was not inhibited by the usual mercies, conceived the plan of forcing captives—women, children, aged fathers, favorite sons—to march ahead of his army as the first potential victims of resistance. The effects of such pragmatic tactics led to the overwhelming of northern China in two years.

The usefulness of the vanquished to the victors did not end here. Jenghiz Khan went a step further by incorporating into his army not only Chinese officers but also Chinese mechanics, Chinese artificers, Chinese engineers and Chinese scholars of the art of war.

In short, it remained for a barbarian conqueror to perceive that the ideas of the conquered were a greater plunder than their cities. Militarily speaking, the result was the grafting of a wise and subtle Chinese head

Apathy has its uses, nevertheless, and more than one successful invader had reason to conclude that a conquest of China was like plunging a sword into the sea. There was little seeming resistance, yet the steel soon rusted and was absorbed. So complete was this process that after a few generations only a philosopher could have told who was the conqueror and who the conquered.

Taken singly, neither the Mongol nor the Chinese had proved a formidable warrior, but the fusion resulted in military forces of earth-shaking potentialities. The Mongol had always been cruel, but his ravages were merely brutish until he came under Chinese intellectual influences. The Chinese had always been war-like, but his tactics were anemic until they partook of Mongol vigor. The combined effect was one of cold and malignant power, the product of civilized craft mated with barbarian sinew.

As a result, the horsemen who invaded China in 1211 were a horde of skin-clad primitives as compared to the military machine which set out in 1220 for the conquest of Asia. In every detail the operations of this organization reveal a profound knowledge of war. For the army was not the only instrument of aggression. Before the warriors went into action the ground had been prepared by another and more furtive host— the spies and secret agents who undermined the enemy's will to resist.

Nor were the lance and bow the only weapons. Even more deadly was the terrorism which the Great Khan's men distilled, drop by drop, to poison the resolution of the defenders. In the past the Mongols had been noted for casual massacre, the Chinese for rare refinements of mental torture. Now these extremes were to be combined in a studied policy of frightfulness which resulted in the supreme military effort of the Far East.

The Fall of Bokhara and Samarkand

The machine had been nine years in the building, and in five months it overcame the great Khwarismian Empire of Persia, which included as recent conquests the territory of modern Iran, Afghanistan, Turkestan and parts of northern India.

The work was half done before a single warrior crossed the border, as is evident from the number of walled cities delivered by treachery. The invaders, moreover, had secured through their spies full information of an enemy left in military darkness.

Mohammed, the shah of Khwarizm, had a superiority in numbers after mobilizing his vassal states. But he weakened his strategy by placing a thin cordon along the frontier of the river Jaxartes, thus committing himself to a passive defense.

The invading forces, numbering perhaps 150,000, were divided into four columns. The first, under Chépé, struck the shah's southern or right flank. The other three, taking the northern route, debouched on the left of the Khwarismian line. Juji and Jagatai, sons of the emperor, worked south with their armies, reducing fortresses and gradually wheeling in to meet Chépé's converging spearhead. Close on their heels followed a fourth Mongol force, led by Jenghiz Khan in person, which suddenly vanished into the vast desert of Kizil-Kum, only to reappear even more dramatically in Mohammed's left rear.

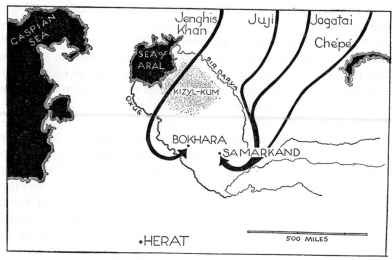

The Mongol Campaign of Invasion

The movements executed by these four columns have never been bettered by any modern army of invasion. Both the shah's flanks were turned, his communications severed and his two principal cities caught between swiftly closing pincers.

Mohammed, perceiving himself about to be crushed between Jenghiz and Juji, desperately offered battle to the latter, only to be routed with fearful losses. He was compelled to leave Bokhara to its fate, and that fabulously rich and populous city fell to Jenghiz after a brief siege. The Great Khan himself mounted the steps of the central mosque and issued a succinct invitation to plunder: "The hay is cut: give your horses fodder."

After sacking Bokhara, his army moved east toward Samarkand, which was threatened from that direction by the junction of the other three Mongol forces. Treachery led to the surrender of the second mighty stronghold of Khwarizm, and it remained only to stamp out isolated sparks of resistance.

The entire campaign is remarkable for economy of means. Yet manoeuvre appears no more important to the final outcome than the moral weapon of frightfulness. The sack of Bokhara served as a first object lesson. The few who survived that horror bore tales of infamies which made death seem a reward. As a climax of terrorism the great city was burned to the ground, with the loss of a priceless heritage of Islamic art and manuscripts. Even the outlying gardens of apricots, cherries, melons, roses and poppies were laid waste, leaving the site a wilderness.

The result bears no resemblance to the senseless ravages of barbarians. Nor can it be compared to a hot-blooded outburst such as the massacre perpetrated by the Crusaders in Jerusalem. Mongol excesses were cool and systematic, aiming at definite moral objectives. Hence an abject surrender did not save Samarkand from pillage and slaughter, though that city fared somewhat better than Bokhara.

Herat, on the other hand, became an example of the punishment dealt out to really obstinate defenders. After first capitulating, the city revolted and stood off an army of 80,000 for six months. When the besiegers at last gained an entrance by storm, they condemned the inhabitants to seven days and nights of bloody atonement.

That such massacres resulted from policy is further shown by the tempting terms offered cities seeking mitigation. Persuasive Mongol agents rode in advance of the columns, promising mercy to the fearful or treacherous. But once the invaders entered the gates the program never varied. The inhabitants were classified according to their useful ness; and the customary slaughter took place after the sparing of a few hundred virgins and mechanics to join the woeful trains of captives.

It might appear that such horrors would defeat their purpose by driving defenders to a suicidal desperation. But the Mongols did not err in supposing that the result would more often be capitulation, saving the trouble of a storm or siege. As a monotonous instance, the historian Howorth records that " . . . one Mongol, entering a street in which there were a hundred individuals, proceeded to kill them all without any resistance."

The physical effects left permanent scars. Today only an arid region and a few dull provincial towns survive from a Moslem civilization which once supported several cities claiming a million people each. But the moral aspects are equally dreary, for the ruin of an empire had been largely accomplished with the consent of its own fear-drugged inhabitants.

THE MONGOL TACTICAL SYSTEM

The victims of Mongol aggressions sincerely believed that they had been overwhelmed by countless hordes. But this illusion owed to tactics and mobility, since the Mongols themselves usually contended against numerical odds. Howorth estimates their largest total establishment at no more than 230,000 troops, including alien auxiliaries.

The *touman* of 10,000 may be considered a Mongol division, with the decimal system prevailing all the way down to the unit of ten horsemen. The bow, scimitar and lance were the principal weapons, though front-line troops carried lances equipped with a hook for dragging an adversary out of his saddle. Two sorts of bows were used: a light one for rapid-fire use on horseback, and a more powerful siege weapon reinforced with horn or steel. Likewise, the three different "calibres" of arrows served various tactical purposes.

Each trooper had his own tools, rations and camp kettle, his extra clothing being packed in a watertight bag of sewn skins which could be inflated for crossing rivers. The armor consisted of tanned hide covered with overlapping plates. Both men and horses in the first two ranks were completely armored for shock attack, while the three rear ranks wore lighter equipment for missile and skirmishing tactics.

The Mongol tactical system, rigid in conception, had been designed to foresee any problem which might arise in the field. The officer had only to give the indicated command at the proper moment, his thinking having been done in advance for him by military scientists.

The entire system was built up around the natural fighting qualities of the individual warrior of the steppes. His virtues, it will be recalled, were mobility and hardihood; his vices, indiscipline and skulking. The faults were first guarded against by the sternest penalties ever imposed on Eastern soldiers. These were described by John of Carpini, who had been sent by Innocent IV in 1246 to bring back a first-hand account of Mongol tactics:

For if one or two or three out of the ten fly on the day of battle, all the rest are tried and executed. Unless there is a general retreat ordered, the first to fly are always so punished. And if two or three out of the band make a gallant assault, and the rest do not follow them, the laggards are likewise put to death. And if one or more are taken prisoners, and the rest fail to rescue them, then also are they executed.

But after establishing the principle, it would appear that commanders earnestly desired to spare the warrior's courage from too severe a test. For in contrast to Byzantine cavalry tactics, founded on successive shocks, the Mongol horse-archer came in contact only with a demoralized foe.

The first wave of attack was of a nonmilitary nature—the spies and secret agents seeking to divide and conquer. Next came the strategic assault—those flying columns of invasion capable of advancing fifty miles a day. Far from attempting to close with the enemy at the outset, they resorted to such stratagems as feigned flights leading to ambuscades.

But if the foe is very powerful, they will turn aside from him two or three days' march, and burst into another part of his lands and slay and burn there. And if they find that they cannot accomplish even this, they will retreat ten or twelve days' march, and lurk for some time in a safe spot, till they think that the hostile army will have dispersed, and then come out by stealth and ravage again.

Only after an enemy had been two-thirds beaten by strategy—his communications cut, his frontiers devastated, his line turned and his people terrified—were Mongol tactics brought into play. And even at this stage, John of Carpini makes it evident that the exchange of blows was avoided whenever possible:

But if the enemy fights well, they will open their circle and let him break through, but will set upon him the moment that he scatters, and they will slay him more by this sort of flight than in close combat. For you must know that they are not particularly fond of a mêlée, but prefer to shoot and kill from a distance.

This preference was made the foundation of the whole tactical mechanism. From the three rear ranks were thrown out clouds of skirmishers who harassed an advancing foe with arrows and javelins. When they had fully accomplished their duty of breaking the opposing line, the warriors of the first two ranks went into action with lance and scimitar. If by any chance the enemy still showed fight, the skirmishers again advanced through the intervals to pour out a deadly harassing fire.

A more effective combination of shock and missile tactics, each supporting the other, was never produced during the Middle Ages. The entire lack of infantry may seem a shortcoming, but Mongol strategists shunned operations demanding too much from their single arm. In general they contrived to make the cavalry serve every purpose, since the swiftness and endurance of the steppes rider were almost beyond belief. Extra animals were often led as remounts, hundreds of them being spurred to death in a single campaign.

In siegecraft, as on the battlefield, the system operated with cold efficiency. First came the secret agents to take advantage of cowardice or treachery. If they failed, the next step was a blockade and bombardment by the war engines whose essential parts were carried on pack horses. Finally, if a city could neither be betrayed, battered nor starved into submission, the terrible "endless storm" took place.

This continuous day-and-night attack was carried on by troops serving in relays. Here again the Mongol esteem for a whole skin is apparent, for there appears to have been little idea of forcing an entrance by hard fighting. The object was rather to exhaust the defenders by fatigue and sleeplessness; and captives were sometimes pushed ahead of the troops to serve as flesh-and-blood mantelets.

THE MONGOL INVASION OF EUROPE

No individual created such a mechanism, and no individual was necessary to its continued operation—not even Jenghiz Khan. When the leader died in 1227, seven years after the invasion of Khwarizm, the Mongol machine rolled on to more impressive conquests than ever before.

The army seems to have been imbued with a professional spirit rather than the fervor which had been the driving force of Moslem victories. Racial or ethical cohesion could not have been possible, since Mongol and Chinese elements were a minority in a rank and file made up largely of Turks, Kirghiz, Manchus, Bashkirs and other tribesmen of the steppes. Military effectiveness remained the only common bond, with the problem of so many tongues being met by a wordless code of command. The officer communicated an order by means of signaling flags, so that a ghostly silence has been described as one of the most distinguishing features of Mongol operations.

Christianized Russia became the next victim of aggression. Nor is it a coincidence that the Russian duchies were at this time split apart by dynastic quarrels, just as Khwarizm had been disunited in the hour of peril. Mongol spies in both instances brought back information which decided the schedule of invasion. Mongol generals, as a result, probably knew more about the internal dissensions of Islam and Christendom than did the princes most nearly concerned. So thorough was this intelligence system that agents took advantage of Venetian and Genoese trade rivalry to secure information of Europe's defenses.

Contemporary Russian arms were about on a level with those of the early Franks. Axmen and spearmen made up the bulk of a general levy fighting in dense phalangial formation. Stone being scarce both in Russia and Poland, forts consisted for the most part of log palisades vulnerable to the torch.

The Mongol horsemen had never before met an infantry host, but the Russians gave them little trouble. Shattered by disunion and often by treachery, the duchies fell one by one before superior numbers at the point of contact. Their wooden stockades were burned, their infantry masses shot down by mounted bowmen with impunity. Kiev, the metropolis, surrendered in 1240 after being deserted by a cowardly prince. The usual sack and massacre took place, ushering in an enslavement which held most of Russia in bondage to the Golden Horde for a century and a half.

As the victors spurred westward, Europe was next to be gripped by dread and doubt. Even Roger Bacon shared the general belief that the invading horsemen were the soldiers of Antichrist, appearing to fulfill certain dismal Biblical prophecies.

Sabutai and Batu, the Mongol generals, had as their main objective the plains of Poland. They seem to have had remarkably accurate intelligence, and their concentration in the Lemberg-Przemyzl area was a model of swiftness and precision. The campaign depended upon four flying columns like those employed in Khwarizm. Again a single army had the task of destroying resistance on one flank, while the other three were delivering the decisive blows at the opposite end of the line.

The single army under Kaidu crossed the Vistula and encountered its first resistance at the battle of Szydlow, near Cracow, in March, 1241. The defenders were Polish feudal horsemen who went down to utter defeat after their king fled from the field. Cracow and Breslau were taken, then Kaidu swept on like a hurricane until he collided with a second Christian army near Liegnitz.

The ensuing battle had no effect of checking the Mongol momentum. The motley force of Germans, Templars, Hospitalers and Polish remnants outweighed the invaders, but lack of cohesion led to another disaster. Within a month Kaidu had cleared the Polish and Silesian right flank, freeing his column to cross the central Carpathians for a junction with the other three Mongol armies.

These forces had meanwhile crossed the eastern Carpathian passes and debouched into Hungary. Advancing in a triangular pattern, with the main body as the apex preceded by flying columns on either side, the three armies converged upon reaching the Danube.

On the other bank King Bela waited with the levy of Hungary, a mounted host of mailed lancers and archers. It was the most formidable defense the Mongols had yet encountered, and Batu made no attempt to force a crossing and fight with his back to the river. Instead, he began a strategic retirement combined with devastation.

Bela was lured into a rash pursuit ending at the river Sajo. Here the Hungarians took a strictly defensive stand, hoping to hold the line of a fordable stream. They possessed a numerical advantage offset by low morale and poor leadership.

The invaders, for their part, were never more confident. Batu is said to have given his young officers a tactical lesson on the eve of battle, pointing out the errors of foemen crowded together like sheep. Under cover of darkness he sent detachments to seek fords on both flanks, then at dawn he engaged the Hungarian front with a missile attack. Bela had thus been "contained" when the flanking detachments struck his rear, throwing the army into confusion as the main Mongol body crossed the river to the attack. By noon the great host was scattered and the kingdom lay open.

Small bands of the invaders plundered as far as the Adriatic, meeting little resistance. Then as swiftly and silently as they had emerged, the Mongols evacuated Hungary and vanished forever into Asia. Europeans attributed this boon to a timely miracle, but history records that a question of the succession caused the Mongol princes to hasten back to the Far East.

Nevertheless, it would be a mistake to suppose that Europe could have been conquered at will. Three crushing defeats gave proof indeed that Western feudal horsemen were not the equals of the invaders in pitched battle. But the Mongols themselves had no illusions as to their own invincibility, and it is likely that they renounced further European conquests for sound military reasons.

As evidence we have several reverses which seem hardly worth mentioning in contrast to Mongol victories. Yet the fact persists that Batu's columns were sharply harassed in the Carpathians, while Kaidu's army met with flat failure before the fortified Moravian cities of Olmutz and Brunn.

Indecisive as these checks proved, their lesson at least was not ignored by the Mongols. On the plains of Russia, Poland and Hungary they had easily outmanoeuvred the immobile feudal levies of their opponents. The wooden castles and log palisades of those regions offered few difficulties. But the remainder of Europe was principally a terrain of forests and mountains, of miserable roads and massive stone fortifications. The invaders, it appears, prudently took note of these obstacles and decided not to venture outside their own tactical element.

In a word, the legend of unbroken victory which has grown up around the followers of Jenghiz Khan cannot bear too close scrutiny. They turned their backs on the problems awaiting in western Europe, while in the Near East they were repulsed by the Eyubite Sultanate of Syria and Egypt, the only first-rate Moslem power of the day. In Japan a generation later they met a defeat with heavy losses inflicted by the Sumarai warriors whose domain they attempted to violate.

That the Eastern horsemen were not invincible is scarcely a matter for wonder. But in their recognition of this fact they stand almost unique in the annals of conquest. Most other victorious hosts have sooner or later been lured beyond their tactical depth because pride could not suffer an occasional reverse. The Mongols alone refused to be betrayed by those considerations known in the West as "prestige" and in the East as "face." The Mongols were interested in the harvest of loot and victory, not in the glory to be gained by the reaping.

In Persia and China they were soon overthrown or absorbed, and they lasted longer in Russia only because the environment suited a return to barbarism. Unlike the armed zealots of the Prophet, who gave more than they took, and who came in time to be praised by the vanquished, the men of Jenghiz Khan appear little better than bandits and slave drivers. The world of the thirteenth century might have benefited by the spread of Chinese culture, but the Mongols themselves had derived only lessons in the craft and guile of conquest. Except for a sword they came empty-handed, and within a few generations they followed the Goths and Vandals into that limbo awaiting the conqueror who has nothing to offer save force.

VI

LONGBOW AND HALBERD

---

*Lo, behold the great evil adventure that fell that Satur-
day! For they slew as many good prisoners as would well
have been worth, one with another, 400,000 francs.*

—FROISSART

THE influence of tactics on thought and progress has never been
better illustrated than by the extremes of the thirteenth century. The
Mongols offered an example of an attack so destructive as to resemble
some diabolical force of nature. In Europe, on the contrary, the offensive
had become too weak to maintain order or enforce the collection of taxes.
The consequence was private war waged by barons from strongholds
able to defy the state. Ideas, dammed by military stone and steel, grew
stagnant. Culture dried up at the source for lack of an outlet, and from
an entire continent rose the stench of intellectual decay.

Colonel E. M. Lloyd in his *History of Infantry* has remarked that the
state of the unmounted arm is an index to conditions in any age. "When
men are slumbering, careless or brutalized, it [the infantry] is abject
and despised; and it only shows what it is capable of when privilege and
inequality have been replaced by a social system which pays more attention to the dignity of man."

In all the world of the thirteenth century there was no infantry worthy
of the name. True, there were men who fought on foot—serfs and barbarians, for the most part—but they played an humble part in the
outcome of battle. Their presence on some fields was ignored by con-

temporary chroniclers, and seldom did anyone trouble to estimate their numbers. Except for a few mercenaries, hired for a special skill, they remained the drudges of war.

Bouvines (1214) was a typical battle of the age. The only unusual feature lay in the fact that the engagement was preceded by a glimmer of strategic sense. King John of England tried to draw Philip Augustus, the French monarch, south against himself in order to give his Flemish allies the opportunity to take Paris. When this plan failed, the allies reunited and accepted battle on a plain between Lille and Tournay.

Like most clashes of the Middle Ages in Europe, Bouvines actually consisted of three separate battles waged by the mounted wings and the infantry centres of the opposing armies. These unrelated contests were in turn made up of hundreds of single combats in which individual strength or skill counted for more than tactics. The French knights, the best mailed horsemen of the day, proved their superiority by routing both allied wings, leaving the wretched foot a prey to slaughter. As usual, the thousands of fallen infantry were not deemed worth counting, while the death of 170 English and Flemish knights amounted to an exceptionally high casualty list.

Of more interest, from the viewpoint of the age, was the fact that three counts, 25 barons and 100 knights were captured. All accounts make it plain that ransom played a leading part in medieval warfare, influencing both causes and tactics. As a result, men of quality were all but immune from the usual hazards to life and limb; and it could truthfully be said that friend and foe alike mourned their death.

Not only did the unmounted retainers suffer most of the bloodshed, but their miserable toil earned the gold for the great lord's release. The price came high, in view of the poverty of the age, being usually fixed at the limit of a fief's supposed resources. Sometimes, indeed, the captors were too greedy in their expectations, as when Richard the Lionhearted languished for two years in Austrian prisons. His subjects never managed to raise the full 150,000 marks, though they groaned under taxes before a compromise was reached.

A dismounted knight might be at the mercy of a serf fighting on foot, but it would not have occurred to humble folk to profit by the advantage. The retainer who brought in an enemy noble contented himself with a small reward, leaving the bulk of the ransom money to be divided among his betters.

War thus became the principal business of the day, with marriage portions and agriculture ranking as secondary sources of income. Naturally, the medieval merchant of violence did not care to invest his capital without reasonable hope of gain. Even small forces were costly to equip and maintain, and pitched battles did not as a rule offer returns commensurate to the risk.

For sound business reasons, therefore, general engagements were so shunned that the exception looms as a landmark. Such rare encounters depended virtually on mutual consent at a time when defense dominated and surprise seldom seemed either desirable or possible. The roads of the continent enforced a snail's pace, hours being required to deploy an unruly host into line of battle. Once committed, both wings promptly disintegrated, as at Bouvines, while the foot remained huddled in the centre as a tactical afterthought. Neither generalship nor central command were in evidence, and it was not uncommon for one wing to raise the victory shout while comrades were being routed at the other end of the line.

The great lesson of the Crusades—the effective combination of foot and horse—was not observed even by Richard, its leading exponent, in the dynastic brawls of Europe. Competition and not cohesion remained the spirit of a medieval army, and tactics reverted to elements more primitive than the phalanx.

The profit of arms lay not only in ransom but also bribery and the sack of cities. These ends were sought in an endless warfare of posts and sieges, varied by occasional sorties or stratagems. Opponents being regarded less as enemies than trade rivals, it appeared at least a negative victory to ravage the lands of a military competitor from whom no gain could be extorted. Famine thus came to be a common military result, and warring districts were known by their charred villages and sear fields.

MEDIEVAL SIEGECRAFT AND FORTIFICATION

Although the infantry was held in a contempt proportionate to the stigma attached to human toil, medieval siegecraft relied chiefly on the wretched foot soldier. For that reason the bulk of every army consisted of an unmounted rabble. An impediment to marching or manoeuvre, these retainers became literally the sinews of war in the assault of forts or cities.

Siegecraft, which is remarkable for greater continuity than any other form of tactics, had departed but little in the thirteenth century from the methods of Alexander. It was not until the early Middle Ages, indeed, that Europe fully restored a science which had been in decline since the fall of Rome. Then all the old familiar devices of antiquity were gradually revived—the tower, the mound, the mine, the penthouse, scaling ladders, fascines, mantelets, the ram and the bore, the catapult and the ballista. Mechanical improvements were sometimes introduced, but barring changes in nomenclature the essentials had not varied in two thousand years.

Not until the twelfth century was a basically new weapon developed in the trebuchet, a war engine operating on the principle of counterpoise instead of torsion or tension. It consisted of a horizontal beam pivoting on two great uprights. One end was fitted with a sling or spoon-shaped cavity to contain the missile; and from the other end hung weights of iron or stone to supply the power of propulsion when suddenly released. The projectile, usually a large stone, described a parabolic curve in its flight. A winch pulled the sling back to earth for reloading, and a trigger served to drop the weights. The size and velocity of the missile, of course, depended on the amount of counterpoise, though the trebuchet appears to have been a better "mortar" than the catapult.

The ram and the bore had been the great offensive weapons of the early Middle Ages, but their effectiveness waned with the improvement of fortification. Besiegers then began to rely largely upon mines similar to those employed by the ancients. Of the three divisions of attack, however, the moral continued to prevail more often than the physical or economic. As in all other ages, assailants found it easier to betray than to starve or storm a city into surrender.

Richard, whose career dramatizes the military trends of his day, returned from the Crusades to apply the principles of Byzantine engineering which had baffled the Franks in the Holy Land. His Château Gaillard, dominating Rouen, became one of Europe's earliest examples of rounded keeps and concentric fortification. A curved surface proved less vulnerable than corners to the ram or bore, while also permitting the defenders more fire power with crossbows. The advantages of concentric over single walls are obvious, for the victory no longer seemed so probable when an assailant breached the outer barrier.

Richard's stronghold, built in 1197, also introduced outer wards and foreworks beyond the main walls. Occupying a well chosen strategic position on a steep height defending Rouen from every direction, the castle consisted of three distinct *enceintes* or wards in addition to the keep. The outer defenses included a bridgehead covering the Seine.

Within the next half century concentric fortification spread until it overshadowed the warfare of the period. Added to an already overwhelm-

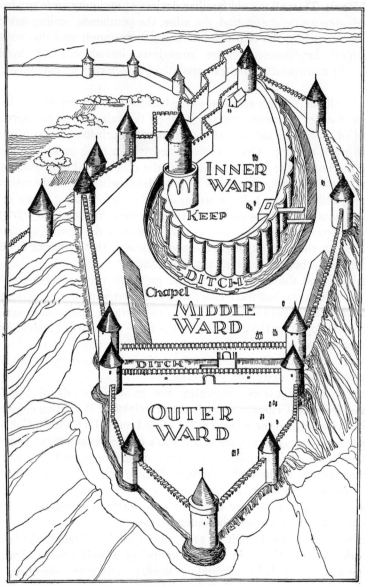

Plan of Chateau Gaillard

ing defensive, it meant that Europe was left little hope of armed protest against tyranny and injustice. In 1204 the forces of Philip Augustus successfully mined the Château Gaillard, but the triumph must be considered a rule-proving exception. Most of the barons were able to defy either king or commoner from their tiny despotic states crouching behind moats and walls.

The body armor of the man-at-arms reveals a similar emphasis on the defensive at the expense of other military values. By the tenth century the simple mail shirt had been improved by the addition of a coif or hood of chain mail for the protection of the neck, throat and sides of the face. Next the shirt and coif were joined into a single garment, and the crestless conical helmet acquired the nasal—a piece of iron to guard the nose from sword cuts deflected by the headpiece.

The kite-shaped shield, permitting better vision and more freedom of movement than the round shield, found universal favor with men of quality at this time. The lance, which at Hastings had been so short that the Norman knights used it for casting, gradually took on length until it became solely a shock weapon, being couched in a rest when the horseman charged. The sword also gained length and acquired a rounded point, so that it became useless for thrusting. The crossbow remained the single effective missile weapon, and Genoese mercenaries hired out as specialists to all the monarchs of Europe.

In the twelfth century the mail shirt was extended nearly to the knees and divided front and back for riding. The conical headpiece gave way to a "pot-helm," or casque, so heavy that the knights donned it only for actual combat. This innovation offered almost complete defense against sword cuts, but the wearer grew the more dependent on lowborn attendants, since he could be momentarily blinded when his eye-slits were knocked awry.

As the art of the armorer advanced, mittens and later gloves of finely wrought chain mail were added to the panoply. The shield became smaller, in proportion to the improvement of body armor, until it could no longer be used as a stretcher for a wounded comrade.

Returning Crusaders introduced the gambeson, a short cassock made up of layers of quilted rags sewed to leather and covered with linen. This garment was worn under the armor as added protection, though it constituted the sole defense of attendants and foot soldiers. Woolen or linen surcoats, representing a Byzantine influence, covered the armor in inclement weather.

The thirteenth century ushered in the earliest plate armor. At the outset the intention was merely to supply added protection for such exposed parts as shins, elbows and kneecaps. Then the cuirass or curved breastplate found favor, and soon plate had begun to supersede chain altogether, though its full development was left until the fourteenth century.

Even in the age of chain mail the weight and discomfort of armor molded tactics as wellborn men became reluctant to fight on foot under any circumstances. The relatively high cost of a barded horse and panoply added to the social cleavage of the day, and the words "varlet" and "villain" have survived as terms of lordly contempt. Hence the ultimate product of the armorer's craft was the creation of a mobile human fortress; a man of iron dwelling in a house of stone—a man defended not only from foemen but also from the invasion of ideas.

It is the more to his credit, therefore, that at least he paid lip service to the mercies extended by the code of knighthood and chivalry. Granting that these humanities were perhaps honored more often in principle than practice, it remains a magnificent fact that they were offered *voluntarily* by military men in a position to extort rather than make concessions.

War is not a compassionate trade and the disgusting butcheries of a Jenghiz Khan leave no doubt as to the decisiveness of frightfulness. For that reason, every concession made by men of violence is worthy of being remembered as an outpost in human progress. The Byzantines, surrounded by numerous and savage foes, could still announce a war creed of immunity for women and other noncombatants. The followers of Mohammed, furious zealots though they were, could establish a moderate tribute as the alternative to the Koran and the sword. Viewed in the same light, the lapses or absurdities of chivalry seem trivial in comparison to a code which assumed some pity for the weak and some responsibility for the helpless.

The Battles of Courtrai and Bannockburn

In theory the feudal levy was adequate as a system of raising troops for a national effort. Each serf owed military service to his master for the land he tilled, and each proprietor in turn agreed to send the monarch a specified number of armed men according to the size of his fief.

In practice no central government of the period had enough power to command the full allegiance of its nobles unless the campaign promised to serve their selfish ends. Such military duty, moreover, proved too limited for large-scale operations. In England the feudal warrior could be compelled to serve only forty days a year, and on the Continent an army seldom remained in the field long enough to complete a siege.

The penalties were felt in that department of war which is sometimes known as "logistics"—the science of transport, commissariat and supply. In all times these factors have had as much influence on operations as strictly military decisions, and never were armies more wretchedly nourished than in the Middle Ages.

The consequence was strategic chaos. When a province had been eaten bare, the hungry horde straggled on to a less ravaged district, though its task might be only half finished. Neither enemy nor fellow countryman were spared by these locust tactics, and the very beasts of the field learned to hasten toward the walls at the first melancholy sound of the alarm bell. Such conditions speeded the development of fortification, thus completing the vicious circle by shutting off remaining sources of supply.

The prolonged supremacy of the mailed horseman, despite all military shortcomings, must be attributed in large part to his monopoly of the privilege of bearing arms—a prerogative guarded as jealously as the priestly mysteries, since other classes were allowed to fight only in a menial capacity. But it must have occurred to many a serf or merchant that the knight was not invincible, and early in the fourteenth century the chivalry of France and England bowed to crushing defeats.

As the prelude to the battle of Courtrai in 1302, Count Robert of Artois led a French army into Flanders to put down a revolt. His opponents were members of the despised merchant class which was just then gaining a foothold in Europe. They had managed to hire a few mercenary crossbowmen, while placing their chief reliance in the pike and a curious weapon called the godendag. Probably only a burgher could have thought of such a practical fighting tool, for the club-like staff served well to knock a knight out of the saddle, and the stout spike at the end proved horribly useful for dispatching a prone man in armor.

The Flemish infantry made a stand behind a morass in the centre and streams on either side. In their arrogance the French knights did not wait for their crossbowmen to demoralize the enemy's inferior force. As a consequence the defenders promptly counterattacked when the impetuous charge bogged down in disorder upon reaching marshy ground. Within a few minutes the field had become a shambles as the invaders were unhorsed and pitilessly slain. So heavy were the losses of the routed French nobles that the burghers hung up 700 pairs of golden spurs as a victory offering in the near-by abbey church.

The lesson of Courtrai was reiterated only twelve years later in a strikingly similar battle. This time the defenders were Scottish clansmen under Robert Bruce, their king, and the invaders the chivalry of England led by Edward II. The two forces met at Bannockburn, near Stirling, in a clash which influenced the tactics of the age.

The English feudal levy of about 25,000 outnumbered the Scots more than two to one. This force consisted largely of veterans who had acquired an extensive experience of irregular warfare in the Welsh campaigns of Edward I. After subduing the Welsh archers, Edward enlisted them in his own ranks and inflicted a great defeat on Sir William Wallace's Scots at the battle of Falkirk in 1298. Here the defenders, arrayed in a phalangial formation of "schiltrons," or deep masses of spearmen, were enveloped and cut to pieces with arrows at point-blank range. Their pikes proved useless against the bowmen, and after a fearful slaughter the remnants of Wallace's army were ridden down by the English knights.

The victory-flushed invaders, again reinforced with Welsh and Irish archers, expected to repeat this performance at Bannockburn. But in Robert Bruce they were dealing with a foeman who was a tactician as well as legendary hero. In keeping with his dual character, he first slew an English knight in single combat before both armies, then with keen insight he prepared for the larger test.

After placing his four schiltrons behind a marshy brook in the centre, he rested one flank on a wood and the other on a bend of the stream. Pikemen in solid array held the Scottish front, as at Falkirk, but Bruce did not intend that they should fall helpless victims to enemy archery. To guard against this danger he kept 500 mounted men-at-arms in reserve and disposed bowmen of his own.

Surprise proved to be his best resource against opponents who expected him to fight a purely defensive battle. All night the English pioneers labored to bridge wet spots so as to permit a cavalry charge across the marsh against the Scottish flank. At dawn, however, Bruce seized the initiative by attacking with three schiltrons in oblique order. The invaders, caught in confusion while forming for advance, were hurled back by the oncoming hedge of spears. Their archers tried to save the situation but Bruce rode them down with his reserve horse as Scottish bowmen added to their demoralization.

Although the English infantry fought stubbornly, King Robert had a final surprise in store. His fourth schiltron suddenly emerged on Edward's right flank, plunging the entire army into a helpless mass of struggling men and horses. At this moment the "gillies," or Scottish camp followers, poured out of the wood for the kill, and soon the battle had become another Cannae. Nearly 1,100 earls, barons, knights and esquires perished or were captured, in addition to 10,000 slain among the English rank and file. Edward escaped but thousands of the survivors were cut down by peasants while fleeing to the border. The losses of the Scots amounted to 4,000, which would indicate that their liberties had been preserved by hard fighting as well as Robert Bruce's tactics.

Courtrai and Bannockburn offered no new lesson. Ever since Troy historical experience had taught that velocity is the strength of cavalry; that mailed horsemen brought to a standstill by unbroken infantry are at a disadvantage equaled only by the plight of broken infantry pursued by horse.

The only historical novelty lay in the fact that a lesson actually was learned from Bannockburn, since it is usually left for another generation to profit from a disaster. The first proof came in 1332. Even the fact that the rival forces were composed of Scottish adventurers is significant, for plunderers and pirates have often led in the revision of tactics. Unhampered by tradition, such opportunists of war are less concerned with form than results; and in time their ideas are legitimatized by the military family.

On this Scottish field the victory went to dismounted knights who fought as mailed spearmen defending the archers on both wings. When the enemy had been demoralized by arrows the knights took to horse again in their proper cavalry function of charging a shattered infantry.

A year later, at Halidon Hill, Edward III gained a triumph based on a faithful copy of these tactics. The Scottish war had been resumed after Bruce's death and his overconfident countrymen came off losers in a minor Bannockburn. The dismounted English knights, as defenders, stood firm against advancing schiltrons as the archers poured in a deadly fire. After the Scots were thrown into disorder, Edward's men-at-arms leaped into the saddle and turned the demoralization into a rout.

CRÉCY AND POITIERS

These were essentially the tactics which overcame the chivalry of France during the next decade, placing that kingdom in bondage to invaders possessing only half the national resources. But the tools of war are always more impressive than the methods of using them, and the English victories have been attributed by popular verdict to the longbow.

Certainly this national weapon played a large part. It satisfied a long-standing need for more effective missile attack than could be supplied either by the crossbow or the comparatively weak bow of past ages. For the six-foot longbow with its cloth-yard shaft not only increased accuracy but also distance and penetration. Sometimes its legend exceeds the credible, but at least we know that fully armored French knights were pinned to their horses under combat conditions.

English Longbowman

Strange as it may seem, the English had neglected archery until a late date, as their defeat at Hastings indicates. During the campaigns in Wales they adopted from the enemy the weapon which had thinned their ranks in hill ambuscades. The Welsh used an elm bow so short and heavy that it could be wielded as a club at close quarters. The English preferred yew and made a rule that the length should equal the archer's reach with both arms outstretched.

The vogue of the longbow spread through the land as yeomen vied with each other at a standard practice range of 220 yards. Misses were not

many at this distance, though an arrow could be sent twice as far with
less accuracy. In comparison, the crossbow had a much slower rate of
fire, as well as a handicap in force and accuracy. Its single advantage lay
in the fact that bolts were cheaper than cloth-yard shafts and more of
them could be carried by the archer. On occasion, too, the compactness
of the crossbow was better suited to siegecraft and the defense of castles.

Still, for all of the superiority of their new weapon, the English owed
far more to tactics, organization and national spirit. While the lowborn
man of Europe remained a serf, the Englishman was emerging into a
yeoman with the right to sell his own toil and produce. The Magna
Charta had been one result of this smashing of fetters; and now for the
first time in the Middle Ages the man in the ranks began to serve as a
paid soldier rather than a mere bearer of military burdens.

Thus it was a truly national army that Edward III led to France.
From baron and bishop down to archer, every man received a fixed and
regular daily wage in addition to his prospects of sharing plunder. In the
case of bowmen and other foot soldiers the pay approximated the earn-
ings of a laborer in civil life, with the result that soldiers were found
without difficulty for long-term foreign service.

Edward I had been first to perceive the inadequacy of the feudal levy
in his Welsh and Scottish campaigns. Of the 2,400 men-at-arms he
brought to the battle of Falkirk more than half received pay. In England
military service soon came to be considered a freeman's duty rather than
a prerogative of aristocracy, and a commander could now begin an operation with some certainty that his force would remain with him to the
finish.

After landing in Normandy in 1346, Edward III made it evident that
his invasion was a large-scale plundering expedition. Despite his absurd
claim to the French crown, he showed more concern over loot than the
garrisoning of captured towns and fortresses. To meet the threat, Philip
of France called out the feudal ban of the realm—a total of at least 12,000
mailed horsemen, 6,000 Genoese crossbowmen and 20,000 foot. King
John of Bohemia joined the host, and the Holy Roman Empire also sent
contingents.

The English army consisted of 3,900 men-at-arms, 11,000 archers and
5,000 foot. Edward took a defensive position at Crécy, near Abbeville,
with both wings resting on villages. As at Halidon Hill, he dismounted
his horsemen and arrayed them solidly in the centre. The wings, which
projected on either side like horns, were made up of bowmen ranged
behind ditches and pointed stakes.

The day was nearly spent but the French knights chose to advance by the last rays of a setting sun which added its symbolism to the occasion. The battle opened with a tactical duel between crossbow and longbow which clearly proved the superiority of the latter. The English archers, sending six arrows for every one they received, pinned helmets to heads and pierced enemy breastplates. The Genoese were put to flight with heavy losses, only to be ridden down by oncoming French knights who scorned them as a cowardly rabble.

English Dismounted Man-at-Arms

The men of gentle blood fared no better themselves against the long-bow. Ignoring the archers of the wings and advancing on the withheld centre, they were stopped midway by a deadly cross fire of arrows that heaped up slain horses and riders. Charges followed in desperate succession until sixteen separate attacks developed, yet at no time was the English line ever shaken. When darkness put an end to the agony, 1,542 French knights and nobles lay dead on the field, among them John of

Bohemia. The losses of the foot soldiers were not reckoned but they must have amounted to thousands.

Fifty Englishmen perished as the price of a victory which established their homeland overnight as a great war power. Nevertheless, the French missed the tactical lesson of Crécy entirely. Supposing their disaster to have been due to some mysterious merit of knights fighting on foot, they determined in the future to dismount their own horsemen before charging. The error of this deduction was to be revealed ten years later in another tragic defeat.

In the early autumn of 1356 Edward the Black Prince conducted a plunder raid into central France. At Poitiers, near the field where Charles Martel hurled back the Saracens, he encountered a French army of about 16,000 led by King John and his son Philip. The Black Prince's numbers were only 6,500 but he chose to fight rather than abandon an enormous booty. Taking a strong defensive position behind hedges and hollows, he dismounted his horsemen as usual and awaited the attack.

Comparatively few longbows were included in his force, but the French made no effort to exploit a great superiority in missile weapons. Though the crossbowmen might have dispersed the English archers, King John's men-at-arms attacked before many bolts could be fired. A narrow front robbed them of most of their numerical advantage, and the terrain added to the disorder of heavy armored knights laboriously advancing on foot.

A handful of English archers, shooting from behind hedges on both wings, poured in a flanking fire which brought the attempt to a standstill. A second wave of assault, led by the dauphin, fell back after some sharp fighting. Then King John came on with all his remaining strength, forcing the defenders to throw their reserves into a desperate hand-to-hand struggle. At the climax, with victory still in doubt, the Black Prince sent 60 horsemen and 100 archers under cover of the hedges to deliver an audacious counterattack on the enemy's flank. This decision, a brilliant move for its day, achieved moral rather than physical results followed by the collapse of the French army. After an English cavalry pursuit lasting until nightfall, 2,000 nobles and knights were slain, while the 1,961 wellborn captives included the king and the dauphin.

Poitiers offered proof that the invaders' triumphs were not entirely due to the longbow. The engagement also demonstrated that armored men are at a worse handicap on foot than horseback when attacking a foe using balanced infantry and cavalry tactics. But the losers in their despair could only conclude that they faced an invincible enemy. From stupid arrogance they flew to extremes of caution, and during the next four years they suffered all France to be ravaged without offering another battle.

Swiss Halberdier

THE SWISS TACTICAL SYSTEM

In the half century since Courtrai a succession of reverses left no doubt that the thousand years of cavalry supremacy were drawing to a close. No more could a headlong charge of mailed horsemen serve as the final verdict of progress; for with the rise of infantry a new race of freemen demanded the right to be heard in a force-ruled world.

The English had gained their successes with tactics in which the two arms strengthened and supported each other. In Central Europe at this time another sturdy people began winning battles with the infantry alone.

The Swiss were first known for heavy masses of spearmen like those of most primitive military organizations. Then, contrary to historical experience, they added tactical weight as they acquired skill and confidence. The outcome was a compact medieval phalanx which has been compared to the Macedonian instrument of conquest.

As a national weapon, the halberd suited mountain dwellers whose foes were encroaching horsemen. The eight-foot shaft had a heavy steel head with the blade of an ax, the point of a spear and a hook for pulling a rider out of the saddle. Wielded by brawny arms, this murderous tool of war could cleave the best plate armor.

In their first test the Swiss burghers and peasants defeated the Austrian knights at Morgarten in 1315. Even at this early date the House of Hapsburg exhibited its famous appetite for all territory to be acquired by war or marriage. Duke Leopold of Austria led a force of horsemen to chastise the cantons and met disaster in a defile between the mountains and the lake of Egeri. The defenders had thrown a stone barrier across the road and hidden themselves along the slope. Suddenly they rolled down boulders and burst out upon the flank of the half-mile column. The men-at-arms were helpless, being able neither to charge nor retreat, and those who survived the halberd were drowned. Only the duke and a few of his retainers escaped.

Such ambuscades are conceived by hill warriors in all ages, but the Swiss soon improved their tactics by adopting the pike for front-rank soldiers and the crossbow for light infantry units. As to the proportions, an old Zurich muster roll shows that a force of 2,770 men consisted of three-fifths halberds, one-fifth pikes and one-fifth missile weapons.

The depth of the files depended on the numbers, since it became the custom to form an approximate square. The army usually formed for combat into three of these heavy columns advancing in echelon and preceded by crossbow skirmishers. The vanguard and rear guard, serving as detached wings to the central mass, were thus in a position to guard against flank attack.

The 18-foot pike was held shoulder-high with a downward slant so that the weapons of the first four ranks projected in a thicket of 12-inch points. In the interior of the phalanx the pikes were held upright by warriors who stepped forward to take the place of fallen comrades. The halberdiers waited in the rear ranks to turn the battle into a hand-to-hand slaughter after the enemy's front had been broken.

The comparison with Macedonian formations is obvious, but in more important respects the Swiss were the successors of the early Romans. Like those firm republicans of ancient times, they derived their strength less from strategy than a beelike cohesion combined with the most devout patriotism. Both peoples considered a relentless attack the best defense, and both sought victory in minor tactics rather than brilliant generalship. Even their military vices were similar, for the Swiss also left a tradition of cruelty, truculence and pettiness of outlook.

Their leaders, like the Roman consuls, were elected officers. Each warrior served under the pennon of his own town or valley, and in time of peril the entire levy of the cantons could be mustered without delay or confusion. This gave the Confederacy a tremendous advantage over the slow, uncertain ban of neighboring feudal states. Before their barons and knights could respond to the summons, a Swiss army might be marching toward the border at the rate of thirty miles a day.

To this strategy of celerity was added tactical surprise. In a century when men wore increasingly heavy mail, the Swiss came near to discarding armor altogether. Only a helmet and breastplate protected a warrior who deemed rapidity of movement a better defense than iron. As a result the hedge of bristling points often bore down upon a medieval host before it could form into line of battle. Thus if the Swiss lacked a mounted arm, their warfare did not suffer either in respect to mobility or shock effect.

Swiss skirmishing tactics, moreover, showed a real appreciation of light infantry values. The swarm of crossbowmen in advance of the main body served both to screen the assault and clear the way. Then came the moral impact of the three forests of spears surmounted by countless flags and pennons, including on occasion the great red banner with the white cross. If the enemy was not already demoralized, he had in a very short time to deal with onrushing steel points guided by men who gave no quarter.

This was essentially the sort of army that met the Austrians and their Burgundian allies at Laupen, near Berne, in 1339. The engagement took place on a level plain which severely tested the tactics of phalangites outnumbered three to one by armored riders. Half of the small Swiss force attacked the Burgundian foot, while the remaining 900 pikes and halberds stood for hours against every assault the Austrian chivalry could deliver. When the ranks of the armed peasants thinned, other warriors pressed forward to replace the slain. Finally the survivors were rescued when their comrades returned at the quickstep from defeating the Burgundians. Reunited, the men of the cantons attacked so savagely that the Austrians were routed with a loss of 80 barons and hundreds of knights.

Laupen offers an example of the Swiss tactic of "forming the hedgehog" by facing outward in four directions with their pikes when reduced to a desperate defensive. For though the mountain warriors spared no captives, they proved on many a future field their ability to die with equal grimness.

That Austria should have stirred up such a military hornet's nest a third time was due to Hapsburg obstinacy. Duke Leopold the Valiant summoned his full feudal levy in 1386 and hired many mercenaries. With this force he marched against Lucerne, the strategical centre of the Confederacy, at a time when the bulk of the Swiss army had departed for a distant campaign.

Only the men of four forest cantons were left to meet the invaders on the hillside of Sempach, but without hesitation they attacked in a single deep column. Leopold, who had been impressed by the tactics of Crécy and Poitiers, accepted the defensive and dismounted his knights as spearmen. The vast numerical superiority of their pikes hurled back the Swiss, who returned again and again to the attack despite losses. At length the two fronts became locked in a weary stalemate; and at this moment, according to patriotic legend, Arnold von Winkelried gathered the enemy's spear points to his breast.

Whatever the facts may have been, the historic truth remains that the Swiss prevailed in the end by dint of courage and endurance. After breaking the opposing line, they swung their halberds to such effect that Leopold and half his army were slain. The victors had won not only the few trampled acres of Sempach but also their country's independence for centuries to come.

VII

THE DAWN OF GUNPOWDER

And it was great pity, so it was,
This villainous saltpetre should be digg'd
Out of the bowels of the harmless earth,
Which many a good tall fellow had destroy'd
So cowardly.

—SHAKESPEARE

IN THE year 1249 the English friar Roger Bacon made a cryptic announcement which has been accepted as the first indisputable mention of gunpowder. Within a generation the explosive had become well known, and after some sixty years its powers were being utilized for the propulsion of missiles.

The claims of the German monk Berthold Schwarz to the discovery have been dismissed as too vague by Colonel Hime in his *Gunpowder and Ammunition*. Likewise, the skepticism of military historians as to any possibility of Eastern origins has been voiced by Sir Charles Oman:

> All attempts to prove that the credit of discovering gunpowder should be assigned to the Chinese, the Arabs or even the Hindus come from misconceptions as to the meaning of certain words describing military devices. . . . There would seem to be no doubt that the Chinese possessed incendiary compounds, as did the Byzantines, long before the tenth century of our era. But that they had explosive compounds is nowhere proven.

The appearance of the first firearms is equally a subject of mystery and controversy, but they may be dated with assurance to the first quarter of the fourteenth century. Colonel Hime offers historical evidence to show that "guns with powder" were imported into England from Ghent in 1314. At any rate, the new weapon soon spread throughout western Europe, since bombards are mentioned in the account of a siege of Metz in 1324 and in a Florentine document of 1326.

The earliest pictorial proof, according to Oman, is found in the Mille-mete Manuscript of 1327, portraying an armored knight touching the linstock to a crude, vase-shaped piece loaded with a stout, feathered bolt. In all ages men have created their inventions in the image of familiar and outworn devices, so it is not surprising that the fire pot and the arrow should have left their imprint on early cannon. Even the nomen-clature suggests such influences, for the first French weapons of gun-powder were called *pots de fer* and the Italians applied the word *vasi*.

Literally "pots" they were, those squat, wide-mouthed pieces which could have been effective only for battering at doors or walls from very close ranges. After 1325 the new tool of tactics made its way rapidly, and by the middle of the century it had grown so common as to be mentioned chiefly in inventories.

Astonishing, from a modern point of view, is the calm with which the medieval mind accepted an innovation that was to revolutionize warfare. This lack of excitement goes far toward explaining the obscurity sur-rounding the origin of firearms—apparently many chroniclers did not deem them worth reporting in any great length or detail. The grumbling of contemporary soldiers is more understandable, since military men have never been hospitable to inventions which clash with their tradi-tions. Yet the scholars of the Middle Ages appear likewise to have had small prescience of the part gunpowder would play in the future of civilization.

Perhaps most curious of all, the medieval imagination leaped at a single bound from the first *pots de fer* to the idea of repeating firearms. In 1339 occurs the report of a weapon called the *ribaudequin*, consisting of tubes so clamped together that all could be touched off at a single sweep of the linstock. Three huge pieces of the sort were constructed in 1387 at Verona. Each was made up of 144 tubes permitting twelve separate discharges of twelve balls, and four horses were required to draw the mechanism.

The notion of multiple fire soon went into the discard along with a few breechloaders cast during this period. In general, the first proved weapons of gunpowder may be divided into two types, as represented by the bombard and the handgun. And though both were known by various names in several languages, it is less confusing to view them simply as primitive forerunners of the cannon and musket.

EARLY TYPES OF ARTILLERY

Bombards were of fairly large diameter from the beginning, and the practice of casting them from brass or copper rather than iron was widespread. Wheels had been attached to many of the early pieces, but for some unexplained reason the principle of mobility did not find permanent adoption until the next century. Ponderous wooden sledges were substituted, the gun being secured to them by metal hoops or bands.

This framework must have been speedily jolted to pieces in a day when the force of recoil could not be controlled. Moreover, the bombard could have been aimed only approximately by such makeshifts as digging out earth or employing wedges to depress the muzzle or gain elevation. Despite these obvious disadvantages, the carriage continued to lag behind the gun in mechanical improvements for two hundred years.

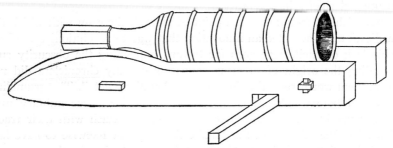

Bombard, Late Fourteenth Century

Wrought-iron bombards appeared in the late 1300's, gradually replacing copper or brass castings. As a safeguard, the barrel was reinforced with iron hoops until advances in the science of metallurgy made such precautions needless. That misfires and disasters were all too common is hinted by the fifteenth-century *Livre du Secret de l'Art de l'Artillerie et Cannonrye* (as quoted in Fortescue's *History of the British Army*), which solemnly emphasizes the perils of the gunner's occupation:

> In the first place, he ought to honor, fear and love God, and to have Him always before his eyes, and go in fear of offending him, more than other soldiers, for every time that he fires a bombard,

cannon or other piece of artillery, or is engaged in making gunpowder, the piece may be burst by its great force, or if it is not burst
he is still in danger of being burned by the powder, and the very
breath is a deadly poison for men.

Armies did not receive artillery into full standing until a much later
era, and meanwhile the gunners considered themselves members of a
guild or craft rather than an arm of the military service. A distinct spirit
of freemasonry prevailed among these specialists who imparted their
knowledge to apprentices under oath of secrecy. In view of the atmosphere of necromancy, it would appear that the new profession involved
more than the usual conspiracy against the layman. Only an alchemist

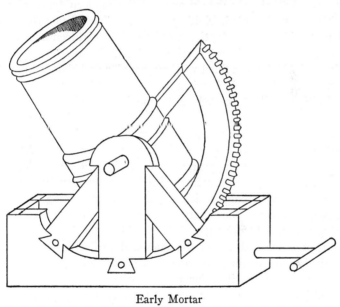

Early Mortar

or soothsayer could have been regarded with more awe, and it may be
noted that master gunners were able to demand high pay as well as
servants to perform the menial tasks.

Although Roger Bacon had made it plain that the compound of saltpetre, charcoal and sulphur should be wetted, gunners ignored this
advice for two centuries. As a penalty the dry ingredients often shook
down into separate layers, rendering the explosive useless. Thus it became the habit to mix the gunpowder on the battlefield, which not only
increased the risks but also made it difficult to secure a uniform product.

Such shortcomings, added to the lack of aiming devices, could only have resulted in dubious force and accuracy.

As an outgrowth of the *pot de fer* came the mortar, the tactical ancestor of the modern howitzer. These blunt, wide-mouthed pieces were useful in siegecraft when high trajectory fire was desirable for dropping a ball over ramparts.

In the early fifteenth century the introduction of the culverin provided the first fieldpiece of the Middle Ages. Standard bores were still far in the future, but a diameter of one to three inches appears to have been the rule. The first examples were mounted on sledges, with wheels to be revived before the middle of the fifteenth century.

At a remarkably early date nearly all the modern types of artillery ammunition were invented. Neither the word "shell" nor the projectile itself found widespread adoption until the late eighteenth century, yet gunners of the Middle Ages experimented with hollow iron spheres, the two halves of which were filled with gunpowder and clamped or screwed together. Called "grenades" when round and "bombs" when oblong, these primitive shells depended on a time fuse which had to be lighted separately.

Loose fragments of iron and flint, known as "langridge," were rammed into the bore and secured by a wad of moss before firing. As the next step, case shot made its appearance about the middle of the fifteenth century. A bag or metal container fitted to a wooden base was filled with stone or leaden balls which scattered after leaving the cannon's mouth. Not even crude incendiary shells and red-hot shot were lacking, both being reported before 1470.

Solid shot continued to be the standard projectile, however, until comparatively modern times. Throughout the Middle Ages stone cannon balls were preferred to iron for reasons of economy, and every town maintained its own ammunition quarry. Culverins were few as compared to mortars and bombards of large caliber, for the best results of medieval artillery were secured in siegecraft. The "Mons Meg," an early fifteenth-century wrought-iron bombard now preserved in Edinburgh Castle, had a bore of 20 inches and fired a stone ball of 300 pounds. Even larger bores were known, but these monsters had a range of only a few hundred yards.

Infantry firearms show a much slower development. The first handgun consisted simply of an iron tube clamped to a long staff and fired by a match applied to the touchhole. The butt of the staff rested upon the ground, to absorb the recoil, and only aim at a high trajectory could have been possible. The French and Italians led in the development of the *bombarde portative*; and in the early fifteenth century the true handgun appeared with a shortened stock which permitted firing from the shoulder or breast.

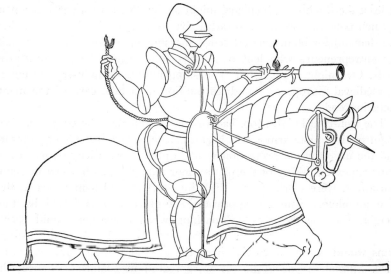

Hand-Gun, Late Fourteenth Century

In 1364 the city of Perugia ordered the construction of 500 "little bombards of only a palm's length." But these early pistols, like medieval breechloaders and repeating firearms, represented an experiment too advanced for its day.

FIRST TACTICAL EFFECTS OF GUNPOWDER

The implements of the military past had been relatively cheap and available. Although armor proved too expensive for the commoner, bows, arrows, darts and spears could be turned out by hand in quantity, and even war engines did not present serious difficulties to a lord commanding the toil of serfs. With the dawn of gunpowder, the economic factor began to make itself felt in tactics. Bombards and handguns were not only costly but few—too few indeed for any but the larger towns and wealthier barons to own. Hence the first victim of the new weapon was destined to be the petty feudal noble who had survived less because of his own strength than the weakness of his attackers.

Every province had its castles and minor strongholds which existed by preying upon commerce. These dens, like the spider webs covering a windowpane, had shut off all but the dimmest light from a continent; but the development of siege artillery meant that their days were numbered. Their walls were often crammed with loot as an incentive, and at least the threat of a bombard might suffice to extort a peace payment.

Such potential profits were attractive in an age of private war. Soon the demand for bombards exceeded the supply, creating an opportunity for entrepreneurs who lent both guns and gunners on a gain-sharing basis. Overnight a small but flourishing munitions industry sprang up in medieval Europe as foundries multiplied to take care of the manufacturing end.

The iron-clad knight, too, had reason to tremble. The transition from chain mail to plate armor had begun before Roger Bacon's cryptogram, and the urge toward protection went to preposterous lengths when firearms appeared. Many of the plate-armor panoplies, as modern museums can attest, were works of art. Full in the chest and slim of waist, they give an almost feminine appearance of grace that is belied by their weight. For the day was approaching when a charger would bear a burden of from three to four hundred pounds, and a prostrate man-at-arms would be unable to rise from the ground without lowborn assistance. Special breeds of horses were reared in Flanders to meet this crisis, their descendants having come down to us as Belgian and Percheron draft animals.

The pomp of chivalry had increased in proportion to its weakness, and at Agincourt in 1415 the French host of 40,000 was literally an army with banners. But even though a pennon or standard fluttered over every contingent, the display only served to commemorate one of the last great efforts of a dying feudal age.

France still groaned under English and Burgundian domination as the Hundred Years' War entered upon its seventh decade of ravages tempered by uneasy truces. Since Crécy the realm had won its only successes under Constable Bertrand du Guesclin, whose nibbling strategy won back most of the territory the invaders had taken by gulps. Avoiding battle with the longbowmen, while constantly pinching off offposts and inciting revolt, this medieval Fabius managed to make the war unpopular among the conquerors.

French pride could not long endure such a strategy, with the result that the kingdom suffered another terrible defeat at Agincourt. Plate armor now offered such protection that the shield served merely for heraldic show, while the custom of dismounting horsemen had revived

Plate Armor Panoply

such weapons as the leaden mace and two-handed ax. Knightly cerebral
processes had not improved, however, and once again the French advanced in several unco-operative waves on a front too cramped for their
numbers. The outweighed English, making their usual defensive stand,
were given the opportunity for deadly execution with the longbow when
the attackers piled up in deep mud. Their confusion invited a counterattack which ended in the death or capture of 6,000 Frenchmen of gentle
birth at a cost to the victors of 13 men-at-arms.

Some authorities mention a few handguns at Crécy in 1346, though
they had not the slightest influence on the outcome. Likewise at Agincourt the result owed nothing to the firearms brought into action chiefly
by the losers. Not until the siege of Orleans 13 years later do we find
an operation in which weapons of gunpowder took a leading part.

The ancient city on the Loire had withstood many assaults since
Roman days, including an attempt by Attila's Huns in 451. Walls six
feet thick rose from 13 to 33 feet above the moat, while five gates and 34
towers completed a system of outer defenses topped by stone battlements
and parapets. Besides war engines of all sorts, the city had provided
itself with 70 mortars, bombards and culverins. This was doubtless as
impressive a concentration of artillery as had yet been seen in the Middle
Ages, since many of the pieces were borrowed from other towns.

The works were manned by a strong garrison when an English army
of about 4,000 appeared in October, 1428 with a siege train of mortars
and bombards drawn by oxen. Immediately the assailants conscripted
the labor of the district to build two huge stone and wood bulwarks from
which they hoped later to storm the walls.

Anatole France's *Joan of Arc* presents from contemporary writings
a vivid picture of life during the siege. Into a town normally housing
15,000 people had been jammed 40,000, most of them men-at-arms or
refugees from outlying regions. Tempers were worn thin by overcrowd-
ing, and constant friction occurred between the townsmen and soldiers.
Yet despite a shocking lack of sanitary precautions, Orleans escaped the
usual epidemic; and the English blockade could not prevent merchants
from entering the gates with grain, cattle and gunpowder. The besiegers
were in worse straits for food and supplies.

The women and children had as their task the manufacture of the
thousands of darts, arrows and crossbow bolts shot from the battlements.
The populace also became an enthusiastic audience for the artillery duel
which continued all winter. Twelve master gunners, with many apprentices and menials to do their bidding, served the pieces of the city. Chief

among them was a Lorrainer by name of Jean de Montesclère, whose pay of 12 livres a month represented more money than a laborer might expect in a year. Several times an English stone ball weighing 150 pounds crashed through a roof and killed three or four people huddled in a room. It is also recorded that with but two discharges of leaden balls from his culverin Maitre Jean brought down five armored foemen.

Despite such exceptions it is plain that the artillery of 1428, while potent against smaller strongholds, had not yet become a threat to walled cities of any strength. Attrition was the only result of the seven-month gunnery duel at Orleans, as compared to a decision brought off within ten days by moral factors.

THE LIBERATION OF FRANCE

From the beginning the material advantage had been on the side of defenders who were superior in numbers, guns and supplies. Yet so thoroughly had France bowed to a tradition of defeat that Orleans might have fallen to the hated *Godons* if Joan of Arc had not appeared. Her very innocence of military affairs proved an incentive to burghers who distrusted their own men-at-arms. They rallied behind her and stormed by sheer weight of numbers the two English bulwarks commanding the walls. After severe losses the invaders lifted the siege in May, 1429, and retreated in the conviction that they had been overcome by sorcery.

Clad in white armor, the Maid rode with the leaders of an army which took the field to win several small successes. Then at the battle of Patay this force surprised and annihilated an English column of 5,000 archers and horsemen at a loss to themselves of one man-at-arms. The towns of central France made haste to welcome the victors, and Charles VII was crowned at Reims barely two months after the relief of Orleans.

These results have been accepted by several modern writers as paradoxical evidence of a peasant girl's merit over the soldiers of her day. Yet witless as the French men-at-arms often were, they averted a disaster several times by declining the attack she urged regardless of tactical circumstances. There is nothing to show that Joan had military ability, but in the end her moral ascendancy served France better than the most gifted generalship.

After her martyrdom fifteen dreary years of anarchy and civil strife intervened before Charles could bring his nobles into line. Then in a series of swift campaigns his forces cleared the land of invaders, leaving the enemy only Calais as the prize of a century's conquests.

This triumph represents a miracle in material respects comparable to the spiritual transformation wrought by Joan of Arc. Another woman, Agnes Sorel, had a leading part in bringing it about. First of the royal mistresses who have molded French history, she helped to urge upon Charles the necessity for a military establishment capable of keeping his own house in order. As a result the first standing army of the Middle Ages came into being—9,000 permanent troops, paid and equipped by the king, which could be used to crush the king's foes either within or without the realm.

The raising of this small force, which set a precedent for other monarchs, is one of the landmarks of military history. The feudal age might perhaps have struck a compromise with gunpowder, but the impact of the standing army dealt a death blow.

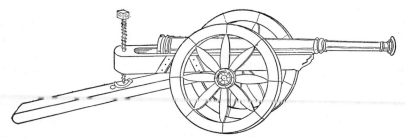

Culverin, Mid-Fifteenth Century

France's new regular soldiers were not slow to perceive the possibilities of artillery fire power, and the gun founders of the country soon led in creative experiment. By the middle of the century they had improved the culverin until it became an effective fieldpiece. Wheels replaced the awkward sledges, and a screw permitted quick adjustments for elevation or depression of the muzzle. The recoil no longer presented such a problem as gunners learned to check it by allowing the piece to roll up an inclined plane.

English decline also favored the French. Tactically speaking, the longbowman's St. George had contracted the diseases of the dragon he slew, and after a century the conquerors had grown as arrogant as the French knights of Crécy. Their fighting methods had resisted change ever since that triumph, though a national army of yeomen had degenerated into a plundering host. At the battle of Formigny in 1450, therefore, the situation was reversed when 7,000 invaders met a French force of 4,000 near Caen.

The English chose their familiar defensive position behind natural obstacles with dismounted horsemen in the centre and archers in the extended wings. But this time the French did not oblige with a thundering charge. Instead, they brought up a culverin on either wing and coolly raked the enemy line with enfilade fire. When this punishment grew beyond endurance the longbowmen tried to capture the guns without support from the rest of the army. They were taken in flank by horsemen and cut to pieces, leaving the English centre an easy prey for the enemy's culverins and cavalry. Four-fifths of the invading army fell in contrast to twelve French men-at-arms. Hence the encounter, despite its small numbers, ranks as one of the tactically decisive battles of history.

Once again the artillery played a decisive part in the field before the English were expelled from France. In 1452 the veteran John Talbot, Earl of Shrewsbury and sole surviving general of Agincourt, landed at Bordeaux with an army soon reinforced by Gascons up to 6,000. Hastening to the relief of Castillon, besieged by the French, he departed from the usual methods. But the moment was ill chosen for assuming the tactical offensive, since the besiegers were entrenched behind 100 pieces of artillery. Within a few hours Agincourt had become an anachronistic memory as the English and Gascons, massed in a single column, were riddled by cannon fire. Talbot was killed and scarcely a man escaped the destruction of the last invading army of the Hundred Years' War.

THE TACTICS OF JÁN ŽIŽKA

For centuries eastern Europe had lagged far behind the western nations in military affairs. On the field of Tannenburg in 1410 the contending hosts of German and Polish horsemen showed few tactical advances over the dull feudal levies swept aside by the Mongols in 1241. The Poles prevailed by sheer hard fighting, and the prestige of the Teutonic Knights never recovered from the disaster sustained in that muscular battle.

Yet only a decade after Tannenburg a peasant army of eastern Europe discarded its flails and led the entire continent in the creation of a tactical system based upon weapons of gunpowder. This system not only overcame every foe without a single check; it proved fully two hundred years ahead of its own day, teaching lessons that were never understood by soldiers again until the seventeenth century. A greater miracle has not been recorded in the annals of war.

But genius itself is a miracle that has never failed to shatter existing military values and reassemble them in terms of the future. Alexander needed no precept to show him how to use ancient war engines according to modern artillery principles. Likewise, the accomplishments of blind Ján Žižka and his Bohemian wagon-forts have been summed up by Sir John Fortescue:

> Throwing all military pedantry to the winds he fought as his own genius dictated, and in the rapidity of his movements and the unrelenting swiftness with which he followed up a victory he bears comparison with Napoleon. He was the first to make artillery a manoeuvrable arm, the first to execute complicated evolutions in the face of an enemy, and the first to handle cavalry, infantry and artillery in efficient tactical combination.

Little is known of Žižka's early years. A petty noble, poor and uneducated, he spent most of his life as a mercenary soldier in Poland and probably took part at Tannenburg. When he returned to his own country, then on the verge of anarchy, the bearded, one-eyed veteran of sixty-five had still to begin his prodigious career.

After John Huss died at the stake in 1415 the first premature challenge of the Reformation was sounded in Bohemia. The martyr's followers, modeling themselves after primitive Christians, held their simple rites in the fields with married priests officiating in the language of the people. Their renunciation of such established beliefs as canonization, purgatory, indulgences and paid prayers soon caused them to be hunted down as heretics by the Church. Far from shrinking, the Hussites issued a counter-proclamation, "In this hour of vengeance it behooves us neither to show pity nor imitate the mercy of Jesus. For these are the days of fury, of fervor and of violence."

During the ensuing civil strife Ján Žižka first appears in 1419 as the leader of a few hundred peasants armed with scythes and flails. Religious zeal seems to have inspired him less than a pan-Slavic dream of uniting the Czechs and Poles against Germanic oppression. Perceiving that novices stood no chance against armored horsemen, he retired with his followers to the inaccessible hill town of Tabor, about five days' march from Prague. There he created a stronghold which developed into the famous arsenal and tactical laboratory of Hussite warfare.

An old campaigner, Žižka had no doubt observed that indiscipline remained the chief weakness of feudal armies. At any rate he began by imposing the sternest order known since Roman times. Battle drill went on constantly at Tabor, each man being assigned his own permanent place in the ranks. Straggling and disobedience were punished as severely as brawling, wining or wenching. Officers gained promotion solely on merit, with Žižka setting an example of selfless service by declining title, honors or rewards.

Hordes of camp followers encumbered other armies of the day, but idleness could not be tolerated in a military community which recognized the former serf as the equal of the apostate noble. Women and old men were trained to throw up field fortifications, and even the children had their drill as ammunition bearers.

In an age of sorcery Žižka's approach was that of the military scientist basing his formula on precise analysis and experiment. Instead of pushing untried troops into battle, he tested them by planning operations within their tactical means—forays from the base at Tabor against the walled and armed monasteries which dotted Bohemia. Such successes not only built up a morale of victory but also armed Žižka's peasants with the enemy's crossbows, handguns and bombards. The large loot of gold and jewels went into a war chest to finance more ambitious campaigns.

The distinguishing feature of the Hussite system was the adoption of the wagon-fort as the unit of tactics. For centuries migrating tribesmen had fought behind their wagons, and the laager of the Goths even became a factor in Roman downfall at Adrianople. Hence Ján Žižka did not originate this primitive method of defense, though he was first to see in it the key to a new offensive based upon fire power and manoeuvre.

The Hussite wagon-fort bore little resemblance to its crude military ancestor. It might more accurately be described as an armored car pierced with loopholes for crossbows and handguns. Twenty warriors were attached to each unit, half of them being pikemen who manned the gaps between vehicles to guard against cavalry assault. In line of battle a ditch protected the front of wagon-forts linked by chains, though both drivers and horses were also trained for offensive manoeuvre. Contemporaries have left a fantastic legend of complex movements executed at a gallop, but the results at least allow us to believe that all possible mobility was realized with the heavy iron-clad cars. Moreover, Žižka shared the preference of most great generals for the strategical offensive combined with the tactical defensive, and his skill at manoeuvre usually forced opponents to choose between attack and retreat.

Armor had now become so stout that at ordinary battlefield ranges it resisted both arrows and crossbow bolts. Only the handgun remained effective, and Žižka eventually armed a third of his infantry with this weapon. Here the mobility of the wagon-forts had its tactical effect, since those rolling fortresses permitted cool and deliberate aim by sheltered men firing from a rest.

But Zižka's appreciation of fire power did not stop with the handgun. He was also first to manoeuvre with artillery in the field—not mere culverins on sledges, such as the French later used, but bombards of medium caliber. All of his cannon were mounted on four-wheeled carts which could be brought up into the gaps between wagon-forts for a concentration of fire upon any part of the enemy's line. Stone balls weighing upwards of 100 pounds were thus sent with deadly effect into massed squadrons of feudal cavalry.

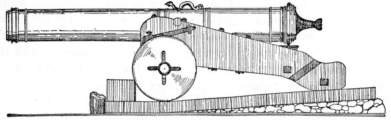

Medium Bombard, Showing Inclined Plane to Depress Muzzle and Check Recoil

As a third arm the Hussites relied upon a small but well-organized cavalry of their own, including light horse for scouting as well as armored riders for shock effect with lance and sword.

A typical campaign began with the strategic assault in which Zižka seized the initiative and overran his opponent's territory with bewildering swiftness. The Bohemians, like the Swiss, considered mobility a better protection than body armor, and they were often across the border before their foemen had assembled. Siegecraft developed into one of the strongest departments of Hussite warfare, and the large artillery train served to reduce vital towns or fortresses while the cavalry devastated fields and cut communications. The object was to force the enemy to attack at a disadvantage, and Zižka's strategy seldom failed of this result.

His battle line consisted of wagon-forts across the front, pikemen or artillery in the gaps, and cavalry on the wings. But the Hussite commander planned to stand on the defensive only long enough to shatter the enemy with superior fire power. His tactics also contemplated a counterattack to be delivered at the moment of demoralization, and Zižka's cavalry pursuits inflicted savage losses in religious warfare which neither granted nor sought quarter.

The fervor and morale of his troops cannot be overlooked; for the hymn-singing Hussites, like the Moslems of the seventh century, were

fighting for convictions which meant more to them than life. Nor can
the importance of Tabor be too much stressed, since that war city evolved
in two years the principles which placed the Bohemians two centuries
ahead of their foes. Yet the greatest factor of all was the genius of a
man who towers like a mountain over the military thought of his own
age.

The Wars of the Hussites

In 1420 Pope Martin V proclaimed a crusade of all Christendom
against the heretics and entrusted the command to Sigismund, Roman
emperor and king of Bohemia and Hungary. At least half a million
potential foemen in eastern Europe were thus arrayed against a war
establishment which never exceeded 25,000 troops.

Sigismund's reputation as a crusader against the Turks enabled him
to raise an enormous feudal host which moved on Prague. Zizka hastened to the defense with 9,000 warriors and entrenched outside the city
walls. It is evident that at this early date Hussite methods had not yet
been perfected, for the capital owed its salvation to courage and hard
fighting rather than tactical skill. Even the women took part as the small
army repulsed all assaults on a palisaded height known to this day as
Zizka's Hill. In the end the besiegers retired because of dissensions
within their own ranks.

A second and greater crusade followed a year later, all volunteers
being offered indulgences and absolutions. The German princes took
command of a polyglot host which has been estimated with the usual
exaggeration at 200,000. No doubt this force possessed an actual five-to-
one numerical superiority, but the Hussite tactical mechanism was now
prepared to demonstrate that fire power counted for more than feudal
lances backed by a few handguns. Zizka advanced with his wagon-forts
and met the invaders near the Bohemian border before they could concentrate. Operating on interior lines, he struck first at one force and
then at another. In four days the Hussites won two great pitched battles,
took two fortified towns and slew uncounted thousands of the crusaders
before they scattered in full flight. In view of these results it is understandable that the world of the Middle Ages should have believed Zizka
and his followers to be in league with the devil.

Only the barest accounts have been left by contemporaries who had no
comprehension of the new tactics. But it is plain that both Luditz and
Kuttenburg were large-scale battles. On each field the Hussites chose

the defensive with their bombards and wagon-forts, then launched a counterattack to exploit the confusion created by fire power.

Perhaps most astonishing of all is the fact that this vigorous campaign was directed by a blind man. Zizka had recently lost his other eye from an arrow wound, and during the rest of his career he based his decisions on the reports of subordinates.

His victories over the crusaders did not end operations. Meanwhile, Sigismund led another army into Moravia to chastise the heretics of that land. He had already perceived the error of fighting the Hussites with mere bulk, and the force of 23,000 consisted largely of skilled mercenaries directed by a famed *condottieri* captain, Pipa of Ozora. Zizka marched immediately into Moravia with a force of about 10,000 and defeated the emperor. Again most of the details are lacking, but the decisiveness of the victory may be judged by the fact that Sigismund left 12,000 slain on the field and narrowly escaped capture.

Three lesser crusades were launched against Bohemia during the next few years, but each time the feudal host dissolved without striking a blow. The mere sound of approaching wagon-forts and Hussite battle hymns sufficed to turn the German knights into a mob of fugitives racing back to the frontier.

After 1422 the heretics themselves were usually the aggressors and invaders. Zizka's first great offensive was an expedition into Hungary to punish the men-at-arms of that kingdom for their part in the crusades. On the march his wagon-forts advanced in two parallel columns which enclosed the rest of the army and presented a square whenever an attack threatened. Owing to this formation the Hussites were able to ravage the lands of cavalry warriors without once receiving a serious check.

The campaign became the prelude to twelve years of ceaseless offensive warfare—invasions of Germany varied by cruel interludes of civil strife in Bohemia. Although the Hussites could unite against a common foe, they were hopelessly divided among themselves according to religious and political beliefs, and their bloodiest battles occurred on the home front.

Considerably less trouble was experienced with the once insolent German masters of Bohemia. Even the Teutonic Knights, who had taken the lion's part in eastern Europe for a century, were reduced by Zizka to the rôle of hares. Favoring odds of ten-to-one were not enough to prevent the customary flight; and Austria, Silesia, Saxony, Bavaria, Thuringia and Franconia in turn were plundered by small bands of Hussites who met with almost no resistance. Only once during this decade did the terrified Germans make a real stand, and at the battle of Usti their army of 70,000 was routed with grievous losses by 25,000 Hussites.

Late in 1424 Ján Zizka died of illness at the age of seventy, and medieval legend has it that he left orders for his skin to be made into a drum to frighten his German foes. Such a measure seems hardly necessary, for that result was achieved with monotonous regularity by the tactical system he created. Once a blind man had led the Hussites to victory, and now for all military purposes a dead man rode at the head of the wagon-forts! Even Zizka's affliction proved an asset in that the sightless leader had thoroughly taught his methods to the subordinates upon whom he leaned. The mechanism as a result continued to function without a break.

The new Hussite commander was a married priest, known as Procop the Great, whose talents were political rather than military. With an invincible army behind him, he managed to wring concessions even from the pope and emperor, but Bohemia paid the price of success in the drain on her man power. More and more Polish or Hungarian mercenaries found their way into the ranks, lured by the loot being taken from the helpless German states. Greed became a more prominent motive than faith or patriotism, and some of Zizka's former officers were active in organizing opposition to Procop.

A violent end was the inevitable climax to an era of such violence, and the battle of Lipany in 1434 amounted virtually to Bohemian national suicide. The nobles and conservatives raised an army commanded by Borek of Miletinek, a trusted general under Zizka. Procop led his combined forces to a fratricidal clash in which both sides used wagon-forts and wheeled cannon. After a terrific struggle the priest's overconfident men were trapped by means of a feigned flight, and he perished as one of the 18,000 victims. The Bohemians themselves had accomplished what their foemen were unable to do, so that within a generation the exhausted land came again under German and Catholic domination.

The Fall of Constantinople

In fourteen years Zizka's tactics had won at least 50 combats while accounting for the sack of 500 walled towns or monasteries—all without suffering a single noteworthy defeat. Yet this system was destined to flame like a rocket across the medieval sky, creating panic and terror rather than light. After the final explosion only a legend remained, and it became of no more worth than a charred stick to the soldiers of the future.

Other men, to be sure, used wagon-forts after 1434. Other men brought cannon to the battlefield. But neither Žižka's foes nor his countrymen learned how to co-ordinate the tactics of those weapons, and it may accurately be said that the Hussite system itself perished at Lipany.

Historically, too, the sacrifices and perils of the fourteen years led to empty victories. As a final irony, the one result of great permanent importance was unsought; for Constantinople fell to the infidel largely because Eastern Europe had spent its efforts in campaigns against Christian dissenters.

In the last century a foothold had been won in the Balkan peninsula by the Ottoman Turks, whose swift rise to power will be discussed in following pages. Christendom made several attempts to dislodge the invaders, including an expedition which Sigismund led to defeat in 1396. But six years later the Turks themselves were overwhelmed by the Tatars, and throughout the next few decades their European possessions lay open to reconquest.

The opportunity was neglected by a pope and emperor who chose to crusade in Bohemia. The Turks as a result gained time for full recuperation, and even in 1453 they were opposed only by the shrunken Byzantine Empire.

Reckoning from the reign of Justinian, that realm had now survived its foes for a thousand years—the longest period of military endurance ever recorded by history. But the sack of Constantinople in 1204 had been a crippling blow, and two centuries later a mere scrap of territory remained outside the city gates. The navy had long since fallen into decay, while the army consisted only of garrison troops to man the ramparts against 80,000 invaders.

The siege thus resolved itself into a contest between the new weapons of gunpowder and Europe's mightiest system of fortifications. Even in their decline the walls were more formidable than any masonry yet conquered by cannon, though the Turks brought a siege train of 70 pieces which also merited superlatives. One enormous bombard, named Basilica, was drawn by 60 oxen and fired a stone ball weighing 800 pounds. This monster cracked after a few days, but eleven other bombards continued to send projectiles crashing into the outer works.

At first it appeared that the defenses might resist this battering, then with experience the besiegers learned better how to direct their fire.

After forty days four towers were leveled, and so many breaches opened that a general land and sea assault succeeded in a few hours.

Militarily, the result was impressive. The French and Hussites had already demonstrated the power of artillery in the field, and now the fall of Constantinople gave proof that the mightiest walls no longer offered a refuge against gunpowder. Yet that May morning in 1453 is remembered as more than a tactical landmark. For a last spiritual link with the ancient world had been broken, and henceforward men would turn their eyes toward the future rather than the past.

PART THREE
THE MILITARY RENAISSANCE

*

I

PIKE AND ARQUEBUS

War being an occupation by which a man cannot support himself with honor at all times, it ought not to be followed as a business by any but princes or governors of commonwealths; and if they are wise men they will not suffer any of their subjects or citizens to make that their only profession.

—MACHIAVELLI

WHILE the Hussite campaigns were anticipating a new age of tactics, the pomp of chivalry had already reached its anticlimax in Renaissance Italy. At the battle of Zagonara, 1423, two large forces of *condottieri* horsemen struggled all day with results which have been reported by Niccolò Machiavelli, "In this great defeat famous throughout all Italy no deaths occurred, except those of Ludovici degli Obizi, and two of his people, who having fallen from their horses were smothered in the morass."

On the field of Castracaro in 1467 a record was set which must remain forever unique in military annals. After hours of mock-furious cavalry charges, the day was decided without a drop of blood being shed on either side. "Some horses were wounded and prisoners taken," writes Machiavelli, "but no deaths occurred."

The most obvious explanation for such curiosities is to be found in the increased weight of armor. With the spread of firearms it had become necessary either to seek added body protection or discard all except the most vital defenses. The Swiss and the Hussites took the latter course, while the Italian horseman strove to make himself into a human citadel.

Another and greater cause may be traced to the highly professionalized warfare of Italy. The close of the Hundred Years' War flooded Europe with thousands of "outcasts and broken men" who knew no other trade than fighting. These scarred campaigners drifted to Italy, where the quarrels of the city-states insured a brisk demand for their services. The natural leaders raised and equipped bands which were available to any despot, and subsequent events proved the *condottieri* to be shrewd dealers in a merchandise of military flesh and blood.

In this as in other respects Renaissance Italy has seldom failed to remind historians of ancient Greece. Both scenes were painted in gorgeous colors of artistic and intellectual progress against a background of the blackest greed, treachery and violence. Men lived and created prodigiously, as compared to other ages, and their crimes were on as bold a scale. Only their warfare was petty, and its futility led in both cases to downfall.

From beginning to end the likeness is striking. Just as Greece gained everlasting glory by hurling back the Persians, so Italy under the Lombard League defeated the German invaders of the Hohenstaufen emperors. But Italy, like Greece before her, was able to unite only long enough to repel an outside foe. After winning the long struggle against odds, the peninsula promptly repeated the Hellenic tragedy by shattering into a score of disputing city-states.

The analogy continues faithful as Venice and Milan and Florence—like Athens and Sparta and Thebes of old—were bled white by their wars and forced to hire mercenaries. Once again dissension and tyranny created the opportunity for a conqueror, and the last act of both dramas was the same. Philip of Macedon mastered Greece, while Charles V found Italy an equally ready prize for his great Hapsburg empire.

Viewed in this light, the intrigues of the Visconti, Medici and Sforza despots seem tinged with a desperate fatalism. Only the *condottieri* derived any real profit, and they displayed their zeal by cherishing a goose which laid so many golden eggs for adventurers. Operations were often conducted so as to prolong rather than decide a campaign, since tactical results appeared less desirable than impressing a present or prospective employer. Toward this end, apt captains learned to stage a most convincing battle without putting their military capital to grave hazards. Armored cavalry best suited such theatrical purposes, and the foot companies of the earlier bands were almost entirely replaced by horse.

The more unscrupulous leaders did not stop short of extortion. Walter of Montreal, a Provençal free lance, raised an army of 7,000 men-at-arms and 2,000 crossbowmen called the Grand Company. Marching from city to city, this rogue was able to demand tribute even from the rulers of Pisa and Florence. His establishment included not only well-paid and disciplined troops but also secretaries, accountants, a council, a provost marshal and a hangman. Walter's amazing career ended on the gallows, but his Grand Company exemplified the peril of mercenaries uniting against their masters. The lords of Italy needed no second warning, and the poison vial or assassin's dagger came to be prescribed when a captain was suspected of dangerous personal ambitions.

In turn the *condottieri* leaders exhibited skill as well as insolence in preserving a delicate balance of power among their employers. There was of course no incentive to tactical improvement in a warfare of cleverness which aimed never to crush tomorrow's patron. Not all encounters were as innocuous as Zagonara, but the usual battle appears scarcely more than a large-scale tournament of tilting lances and prancing chargers. Native Italian soldiers, who might have restored some reality to these operations, preferred the pay and safety of a *condottieri* career.

MACHIAVELLI'S WRITINGS

When the Greek city-states approached their doom, Demosthenes gave the world his most famous orations in an attempt to bring unity out of chaos. Likewise, in a similar emergency, Renaissance Italy produced another great intellect who devoted his genius to warning his countrymen. Though Machiavelli's very name has come down through the ages as a synonym for guile, he also deserves recognition as a patriot who read with prophetic clarity the signs of his times. The Florentine writer reasoned correctly that national armies and improved tactics had already made medieval thought obsolete. He aimed, therefore, to create with his pen a politically united peninsula defended by a militia of citizen-soldiers modeled after the Roman legion.

In his *Principe* Machiavelli concluded that the warfare of Europe would take on the character of armed diplomacy as the various monarchs gained the centralized power to defy not only their own feudal barons but also the Church and Empire. He foresaw the rise of a new age of nationalism, replacing the medieval ideal of a Christian community; and the *Principe* expounded a sword-sharp political philosophy for rulers contending in the struggle for power.

The *Arte della Guerra* ranks as the first of a long line of military treatises urging a compromise between weapons of gunpowder and ancient formations. Throughout the next two centuries, following Machiavelli's lead, adaptations of the legion or phalanx were to be recommended by theorists who often proved more familiar with the pages of Arrian, Polybius and Vegetius than the tactical trends of their own day. Not until the French Revolution did the soldiers of Europe entirely awaken from their dream of restoring the glories of a classical past.

The *Principe*, with its cold-blooded morality of expediency, might have served to instruct twentieth century dictators, but Machiavelli's military ideas enjoyed no such longevity. As a remedy for the weaknesses of *condottieri* warfare, he advocated a conscripted national army—a new legion whose units were to consist of 2,000 pikes, 1,000 "shot" and 3,000 men armed with sword and buckler in Roman fashion. A very minor part was allotted to weapons of gunpowder, for the Florentine critic deemed artillery useful merely for opening a battle and small arms effective chiefly in skirmishing. The cavalry was likewise to be reduced to secondary importance as a scouting or raiding arm.

Only in his vision of conscription did Machiavelli anticipate the military future, but he proved a discerning observer of the follies of *condottieri* warfare. Hence he considered Italy's plight already desperate, and like Demosthenes before him he saw his worst forebodings come true during his own lifetime.

The Swiss and the Landsknechts

One of the most decisive factors in the forthcoming conquest of Italy was the presence in Europe of a large and formidable army which remained at the call of any royal bidder. For the Swiss, finding profit a more compelling motive than patriotism, were now a mercenary force to be reckoned with in power politics.

The soldiers of the cantons had not welcomed changes in their national tactics, but some concessions to gunpowder had been made. A muster roll of the year 1444 shows that 61 handguns were included with the crossbows of a light infantry force numbering about 500. Gradually a few culverins were brought into the field, and by this date the 18-foot pike had largely replaced the halberd.

Paradoxically, a total defeat became the best Swiss advertisement. In the minor battle of St. Jacob, 1444, a mercenary corps was hemmed in by French foes possessing a 15-to-1 numerical advantage. Nevertheless, the pikemen "formed the hedgehog" and fought until their phalanx had been reduced to a mound of corpses surrounded by twice as many enemy slain. This combat, as a contrast to *condottieri* methods, convinced employers that Swiss soldiers were worth their hire.

Charles the Bold, Duke of Burgundy, remained one of the few masters of Europe who were not awed by the Confederates, and his error in judgment cost him his life after three crushing defeats. His duchy, which had been for a century one of the great war powers of the Continent, including Flanders, Brabant and the Somme towns among its holdings, was reduced as a consequence to the level of a province.

With large resources at his disposal, Charles formed the grandiose conception of a standing army in which mercenaries were to be hired for their national specialties. English archers, French artillerymen, Flemish pikemen, Italian cavalry and German handgun men were thus combined with a nucleus of Burgundian men-at-arms. To this military potpourri was to be added the duke's own generalship, and in his first clash with the Swiss he imitated the most imitated victory of history.

But the battle of Granson in 1476 did not become another Cannae. Lacking either cohesion or zeal, the mercenaries of the wings took alarm at the retirement of a "refused" centre, and the affair ended in an almost bloodless Burgundian rout.

Charles's second invasion of Swiss territory had a more disastrous climax at Morat, where his army of 20,000 was surprised by 25,000 foemen and beaten in detail with heavy losses. Even though the Burgundian cannon tore holes in the opposing ranks, the duke's mercenaries were unable to withstand an assault which did not pause to count the cost.

The final encounter near Nancy became one of the few engagements in which the Swiss varied their customary methods with manoeuvre. Possessing a comfortable advantage in numbers, they divided their forces and executed a turning movement under cover of the woods. The unfortunate duke's army was taken in front and flank by relentless pikemen who won a complete victory. Among the dead lay the snow-shrouded body of Charles the Bold, his head cleft to the chin by a single blow from a halberd.

The three battles are distinguished less for tactics than historical results. Most states, however badly the fortunes of war may turn against them, manage at least to retain their national existence. But after a third smashing defeat in a year the bankrupt and demoralized Duchy of Burgundy sank to a provincial status in the French realm.

Nor did victory prove altogether an asset to the Swiss. Their fighting methods resisted progress, since success did not encourage change; and the sturdy virtues of this mountain people were gradually corrupted as arms became the national trade. Nearly every boy was now trained from childhood for the state profession, learning a military pride which combined the stoutest courage with avarice, truculence and revolting butcheries of prisoners.

After their triumph over Burgundy the Swiss could have challenged any army on the Continent. Yet barring a few minor annexations they showed a curious indifference to political or territorial aggrandizement. For the next two centuries they were content to remain wage earners of war; and *Point d'argent, point de Suisse* became an adage commemorating the hard bargains driven with employers by the Confederates.

Their prosperity, at least from a limited point of view, inspired the German states to raise competing mercenary forces known as "landsknechts"—a term of vague origin which came to denote hired pikemen and handgun men fighting in heavy columns after the Swiss manner. At first the Germans were clumsy imitators, being beaten in most of their early encounters with the Confederates. But in time they earned a comparable reputation as firm infantrymen, while responding more alertly to changes in tactics and new weapons of gunpowder.

In their military customs and organization, the German bands were to become the tactical ancestors of the modern regiment. The colonels (*Oberst*) were commissioned by the state to recruit troops, and each unit of several thousand men was divided into companies commanded by captains (*Hauptmann*) and lieutenants (*Fahnrich*). As a substitute for national loyalty, the colors (*Fahnlein*) of these hirelings symbolized military spirit and pride in the regiment.

Mercenary traditions also influenced the coming age in less fortunate respects. The availability of so many competent swashbucklers, willing to serve any state or cause, was scarcely a factor to encourage neighborly relations between countries. Even in time of peace a monarch often found it prudent to employ such troops as a precautionary measure, or simply to deprive another state of their services. The financial burden was heavy, yet the penalty might be mutiny or disorder if the hired bands were not promptly paid.

Both the Swiss and landsknechts were capable of revenging themselves on a niggardly master by deserting to the enemy on the eve of battle.

Mercenary ethics could also be stretched to include double-dealing or the plundering of the civilian populace. Nevertheless, it was seldom that either corps lacked for a patron. The ambitions of Europe's princes were on a larger scale than their resources in native troops, and by the dawn of the sixteenth century every army depended on alien hirelings. Inevitably, these men set an example of greed, brutality and indiscipline which other soldiers were not slow to follow, so that loyalty to king or country became generally subordinated to the lure of loot.

THE ITALIAN WARS, 1494-1525

Another factor in the new era was the growing complexity of diplomatic motives. In contrast, the wars of the fifteenth century had been comparatively isolated affairs. While Spain was expelling the Moors, the French and English were able to settle their differences without interference on the other side of the Pyrenees. And while Germany and Hungary launched their crusades against the Hussites, the Turk found an opportunity to steal into Europe's unlocked back door and take Constantinople.

But the ink had scarcely dried on Machiavelli's pages before the theories of the *Principe* hardened into acts. France invaded Italy in 1494 and became embroiled not only with the city-states but also Spain, the Papacy and the Empire. Within a few years the strife had spread to the opposite ends of Europe as England and the Ottoman Empire contracted alliances with the main belligerents. Every ruler of the Continent had grown sensitive in regard to strategic flanks, and only cold self-interest determined the very slight difference between an enemy and an ally.

Improved weapons of gunpowder were meanwhile working a similar revolution in tactics. During the War of the Roses the Lancastrian party regarded it as an atrocity that the Yorkists were ". . . traitorously ranged in bataille . . . their cartes with gonnes set before their batailles." Yet within a generation wheeled cannon were being used by all the armies of Europe, even though aiming devices showed little progress and the recoil was still a disturbing element.

At this same period the crude handgun was being widely superseded by the arquebus, or hackbut, the first of the matchlocks which dominated infantry tactics for two centuries. The curved and shortened stock of the new weapon permitted better aim from the shoulder, and the touchhole gave way to a steel cock which held the "match." The latter was simply a smoldering cord, made from strands of twisted tow and prepared by boiling in vinegar or the lees of wine. Each soldier carried a "link" of several yards attached to his belt. After the tedious process of loading, he fitted the lighted end into the cock just before taking aim. A pull of the trigger brought the match down in contact with the "flash powder" contained in the firing pan, thus setting off the charge in the barrel.

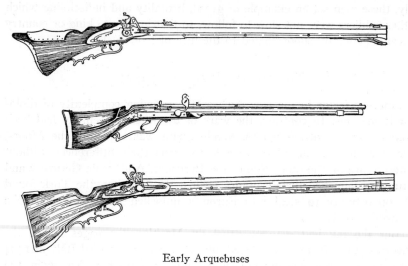

Early Arquebuses

The early arquebuses differed in size according to the whim of the maker, but weapons of standard bore soon were introduced. Called "calivers," or *arquebuses de calibre*, they weighed from nine to twelve pounds in various countries and fired a ball of about an ounce. The lighter and shorter *demihaque* was a primitive carbine designed for mounted men, while at the other extreme the *arquebus à croc* weighed fifty pounds and took four-ounce bullets. These ponderous pieces were equipped with a steel hook so that they could be fired from a wall or rampart to withstand the recoil.

Accurate aim was out of the question, but the ordinary arquebus proved fairly effective against formations at ranges up to 100 yards. Then for several minutes the soldier had no defense against shock attack, since muzzle-loading with a wooden ramrod involved many motions. This delay offered a tactical problem solved by the long, heavy spear of the Swiss and landsknechts; and pike and "shot" were to become inseparable on the battlefield until the invention of the bayonet. Various methods were employed of grouping the two arms, but the underlying idea was always to protect the arquebusier while charging his piece.

More than three centuries had now passed since the invention of gunpowder, yet during this period generalship advanced little beyond a bow-and-arrow past. Ján Zizka towers like a giant over the late Middle Ages because he alone understood the possibilities of handguns and wheeled cannon. But just as the Renaissance released a torrent of impetuous ideas in art and literature and politics, so the soldiers of that day experimented with daring new tactics of fire power. Within a few years intellectual valor became a requisite of victory as each battle made the preceding engagement obsolete.

Pedro Navarro, foremost engineer of the day, aided the Spanish invaders of Italy by contriving new techniques of siegecraft and fortification. Gonsalvo of Cordova, known as the Great Captain, adapted Roman sword-and-buckler tactics to weapons of gunpowder. Fernando Devalos, Marquis of Pescara, became famed for infantry reforms and innovations which molded the warfare of the entire century. The French, not to be outdone in the clash of military minds, won victories as a result of the improvements in artillery mobility conceived by the Duke of Ferrara.

Nor was the prevailing interest in arms confined to professional soldiers. Leonardo da Vinci, though he considered war a "bestial frenzy," designed a mortar and a flying machine. The stormy Cyrano de Bergerac took part in several Italian campaigns, and the Chevalier de Bayard figured in equally prodigious exploits. Only the Renaissance could have produced such oddly assorted hosts in which mercenaries were combined with patriots, lances with cannon, crossbows with arquebuses, and military scientists with the last fond exponents of chivalry.

The expedition which Charles VIII of France led to Naples in 1494 became the marvel of the age. Swiss masters had long been employed to drill the infantry of the standing army, and such famous old regiments as Picardie were already in existence. Scottish archers and Swiss pikemen served as mercenaries, supporting French men-at-arms organized into a heavy cavalry force. But the wonder of all was an artillery train such as the world had never seen before. The largest pieces weighed 6,000 pounds and required twelve horses to draw the four-wheeled carts on which they were mounted. The smallest were two-wheeled guns firing a ball not much larger than an arquebus bullet. Ranging between these extremes the French had cannon for every imaginable purpose of the siege or battlefield.

Stone projectiles had now become obsolete along with those early wrought-iron bombards secured by metal hoops against the danger of bursting. Breechloaders, depending on a movable charge-case in the lower end of the barrel, had not proved practical because of the escape of gas. By the end of the fifteenth century, therefore, cast-iron shot and muzzle-loading guns of cast iron or bronze had become fairly well standardized. As compared to the ponderous bombards of the past, these pieces were slender and graceful in design, being frequently ornamented with the most artistic Renaissance workmanship.

Already the French had conceived the principle of the limber; and two wheels of the heavy carts were removable, while the light artillery could be manoeuvred in the field. Another innovation of vague date and origin was the trunnion—the cylindrical protection on either side of the piece which fitted into a socket in the carriage. Prior to this time the gun had been immovably secured to the stock, but the trunnion supplied an axis connecting it with the carriage and wheels. The muzzle could readily be elevated or depressed for more accurate aim, and less disturbance resulted from the recoil.

The stilted tactics of the Venetian and Milanese *condottieri* had no chance against such an array of force as the French king brought. At the battle of Fornova in 1495 the Italians were routed in ten minutes, and the real contest did not begin until Gonsalvo of Cordova gained a foothold in Calabria with 600 cavalry and 1,500 foot. Some pikemen were included in the Spanish ranks, but the Great Captain won his first victories with a curious revival of legionary tactics.

Vegetius, writing his *De Re Militari* in the fourth century, after the disaster of Adrianople, could scarcely have imagined that his glorification of the legion would bear fruit a thousand years later. Ignored by the decadent Romans for whom it was intended, this nostalgic and confused work was preserved in manuscript form throughout the Dark Ages, to be translated into English and French before the invention of type. By 1489 printed editions had appeared in Utrecht, Cologne, Paris and Rome as Renaissance soldiers groped back to classical warfare for inspiration.

The cohorts were but a memory when Vegetius wrote, yet in 1502 a combat took place near Barletta which became a historical echo of the clash between Roman gladius and Macedonian sarissa at Pydna in 168 B.C. In this later contest Spanish sword was pitted against Swiss pike with the same tactical result, as recorded by Machiavelli: "By the help of their bucklers and the agility of their bodies, having got under the pikes and so near that they could come at them with their swords, the Spanish had the day with the slaughter of most of the Swisses."

For several years most of the Spanish foot was armed with a buckler and short thrusting sword, and even the body armor bore a striking resemblance to Roman equipment. But the Great Captain, unlike many of his contemporaries, proved no slave to the classics. A veteran of the War of Granada in which the Moors were driven out of Spain, he was enough of a practical fighting man to perceive the advantages of arquebus tactics combined with Roman field fortification.

When the two forces met again at Cerignola, a year after Barletta, the Spaniards were entrenched in a vineyard behind palisades. The French infantry and Swiss mercenary pikemen charged only to be mown down in bloody windrows by a hail of arquebus bullets. At the moment of demoralization a Spanish counterattack ended the affair with the capture of the enemy's magnificent artillery train, which had never got into action.

Louis XII sent reinforcements to the remnant saved from Cerignola, but the following January the French were outmanoeuvred and forced to capitulate. Again the Great Captain's field fortifications and arquebuses brought off the victory. Spinning a web of trenches about the French, despite the abhorrence of Renaissance generals to winter campaigns, he placed the enemy in a position allowing only the alternatives of surrender or destruction.

In the next great encounter, the battle of Ravenna in 1512, it is understandable that the Spaniards under Pedro Navarro and the Marquis of Pescara should again have relied on entrenched arquebusiers. But during the nine years since their surrender the French had raised another large invading army and worked out new tactics of artillery mobility.

The Spanish and Italian forces gave battle in order to relieve the beleaguered city. In front of their trenches they opened fire with cannon and 200 *arquebuses à croc* mounted on wheels after the German mode. For three hours the French infantry endured without breaking the deadliest pounding yet known on a battlefield. The landsknecht mercenaries stood firm and closed the gaps in their ranks even though 38 out of 40 captains were slain.

Meanwhile, the Duke of Ferrara moved 24 French cannon to a position on the enemy's extreme right. He caught the Spaniards by surprise with an enfilade fire which all but blasted their foot soldiers out of the trenches. Ferrara's landsknechts then rushed in to make short work of the Spanish sword-and-buckler men, while the French cavalry struck in the rear to complete the disaster. Pescara's army was nearly exterminated, since only a few companies managed to withdraw behind steady volleys. The victors were so battered, however, that Ravenna won a gloomy renown as one of the bloodiest battles of the century.

Ferrara's artillery mobility proved itself again in 1515 against the best shock troops of Europe. Usually the Swiss were employed by the French, but in this campaign a large force had taken the pay of the pope and emperor. These mercenaries were about to accept a French bribe and return to the cantons when reinforcements arrived from the homeland and influenced a decision to fight.

The engagement began at Marignano, near Milan, as the three columns of pikemen advanced in echelon with their customary headlong valor. The French cannon tore great holes in their ranks, yet a cavalry counterattack was necessary before the Confederates could be hurled back. All afternoon the Swiss renewed their attempts and were repulsed by blasts of artillery followed by charges of the men-at-arms. The battle went on until midnight and continued at dawn along the same obstinate lines. Francis I, the young French king, took part in 30 cavalry attacks before the wreck of the Swiss army retired after 28 hours of fighting. The pikemen were said to have saved only 3,000 out of an army of 25,000, and the exhausted victors admitted losses of 8,000.

Marignano put an end to the Swiss legend of invincibility. After one or two more experiences of frontal attacks against cannon or entrenched arquebusiers, the ancient prestige of the Confederates was lost forever, though they were still to be esteemed as firm mercenaries.

The French in turn were allowed only a few years in which to profit from their victories. When the decisive battle of the Italian wars occurred at Pavia in 1525, the Marquis of Pescara prepared to meet artillery mobility with new arquebus tactics. The engagement as usual resulted from an attempt to relieve a blockaded city. Francis had entrenched before Pavia with an army of 20,000 when a Spanish force of equal numbers penetrated his outer works in a dawn surprise. Still, the French scored first with a concentration of artillery such as had prevailed at Ravenna. The advancing Spanish columns were thrown into disorder, but the king lost this advantage by ordering a premature cavalry counterattack which interfered with the fire of his own guns.

Pescara chose this moment to deploy 1,500 arquebusiers organized into a special corps. In the words of the chronicler Brantôme, these picked troops had been trained "without word of command . . . to wheel round, to face about from this side to that, now here, now there, with the utmost rapidity." Taking cover behind walls and hedges, the arquebusiers riddled the ranks of landsknechts whose pikes were useless. The battle turned into a mêlée dominated everywhere by Spanish firepower, and only remnants of the enemy escaped the general disaster. Francis himself was taken prisoner, leaving to posterity the melancholy saying, "All is lost save honor."

THE SPANISH PHALANX

The great victory resulted not only in the winning of Italy by Charles V but also in a reaction toward military conservatism. After 1525 Renaissance generals made it evident that they had had their fill of smashing campaigns, of ruinous defeats and costly triumphs. Within twenty-three years the Spanish armies alone had bridged the tactics of as many centuries. Beginning with their revival of Roman sword-and-buckler methods at Barletta, they finally evolved at Pavia the most effective infantry fire power yet known in the age of gunpowder. But the cost of the Italian wars had been great both in money and bloodshed, and the next generation welcomed a return to phalangial thought.

In 1500, when Charles V was born, the minor kingdom of Spain had only lately achieved unity after ridding itself of the Moors. Nineteen years later the ugly Hapsburg youth was elected emperor over his French rival. And in 1525, with Francis a captive after Pavia, Charles had become ruler not only of Spain but also Italy, Germany, Hungary, Bohemia, the Netherlands and vast new discoveries in the Americas. Half of Christendom acknowledged the imperial rights of this plodding young man whose territory exceeded by far the lands dominated by Charlemagne. Never since Charlemagne had Europe seemed so near to the age-old dream of a single mighty empire.

This result had largely been brought about by the Spanish army, which now emerged as the only force capable of holding together such an enormous domain.

All the energies of the kingdom had been turned into military channels after the expulsion of the Moors and the explorations in the New World. Trade and agriculture came to be despised at a time when shiploads of gold were arriving from America. The youth of the land aspired only to warlike adventure, and men of quality considered it an honor to serve as simple soldiers. The infantry was preferred over other arms, and at a later date the author of *Don Quixote* carried a pike in the ranks. Even the emperor once shouldered an arquebus until ordered by his superior officer not to take undue risks.

Men of this mettle fired the first shots ever heard in the forests of the New World. The triumphs of Caesar's legions in Gaul were surpassed as small bands of Spaniards left their ships behind them and marched into the unknown against populous empires. Yet in Peru, as in Gaul, the foreordained result was a victory in the moral sphere of civilized will and tenacity over barbarian indecision. The terrifying effect of Spanish firearms and horses proved a minor factor as compared to an "absolute" concept of war which neither the Incas nor the Aztecs could comprehend until the time had passed for unified resistance.

Spanish campaigns in Germany and Africa, though not as spectacular, offer more of real military interest. All the recruits for these operations were instructed by drillmasters in home garrisons. After they were passed as fit for active service, an equal number of novices took their places in the training barracks. This was the beginning of the depot system that eventually found adoption in all European armies.

The tercio, or Spanish tactical unit of about 3,000 foot, set many other traditions for the modern regiment. Composed of twelve companies of some 250 men each, the fighting strength in the year 1534 was divided equally between pikemen and arquebusiers. Company officers consisted of a captain and ensign, and a sergeant and ten corporals filled the non-commissioned ranks.

The *maestro de campo* (colonel) commanded the tercio, assisted by a *serjeanto mayor* (major), a *furriel mayor* (adjutant) and several lesser staff officers. Music was supplied by 24 drummers and fifers under a drum-major, while eight halberdiers served the colonel as a bodyguard. Spanish solicitude for the warrior's soul is shown by the fact that 13 chaplains were attached to each tercio, though the medical staff was limited to a surgeon, physician and apothecary.

In 1536 the entire military establishment amounted to 67,000 troops. Of this total 53,000 were made up of non-Spanish elements—German, Italian and Walloon mercenaries, for the most part—but the scantily populated Iberian peninsula furnished the quality and command of the army.

All ranks were supposed to be regularly paid and supplied. In practice, however, frequent lapses caused mutinies in the tradition of the landsknechts, whose organization had been the model for the tercio. The stream of gold pouring in from the Americas had already brought the poverty of inflation to Spain while enriching the merchants and carriers of the Netherlands. Militarily, the consequences were indiscipline and curtailed operations. Rome was brutally sacked only two years after Pavia by an unpaid imperial army, and a sequence of such excesses gave Spanish troops a reputation for cruelty.

Although Pavia had been won by mobility as well as fire power, the reaction which set in after that victory led toward cohesion. In other words, the tactics of conquest had been replaced by the tactics of consolidation. So marked was this tendency that by 1536 the native Spanish horse had dwindled to 580 men-at-arms. Including mercenaries, the entire cavalry force numbered only 5,300, or one-twelfth of the infantry strength. A corresponding decline took place in the artillery, despite the lesson of Ravenna.

Not only had the responsibility of maintaining the vast empire been entrusted to one arm, but this arm gained solidarity at the expense of mobility. The agile combat groups of Pavia were soon replaced by tercios massed into great squares known as "battles"—the first phalanx of the age of gunpowder. In further keeping with the conservative bent, foot soldiers wore heavier armor consisting of morion (open helmet), corselet and thigh-pieces.

Fire at will gave way to volleys at the word of command. Afterwards each rank filed back to the rear to reload, gradually moving forward with successive volleys until its turn came again. Due to the slowness of the reloading process, a formation many ranks deep was required to allow even the best drilled troops enough time to charge their pieces. Various ideas of mingling the "shot" with the pikes were put into practice, but all plans recognized that the spearmen must protect the arquebusiers from shock attack.

Although this function was defensive, the pikes served also to deliver the counterstroke. The eighteen-foot shaft, weighing ten pounds, appeared a fearsome thing to foemen awaiting the oncoming thicket of steel points. The arquebus, in contrast, seemed no more than a harassing weapon. After its work had been done, then came the turn of the iron-clad pikemen to advance shoulder to shoulder with a majestic tread described by Sir John Smith, writing in the late sixteenth century:

> Moving forward together pace with pace and step with step, carrying their pikes firmly with both their hands breast-high, their points full in the enemy's face, they do altogether give a puissant thrust.

But the merit of the inflexible Spanish system lay neither in its tactics nor its generalship. Better tactics failed against the tercios, and no outstanding generals appeared until after decline had created the necessity. The real explanation of a century's military domination by so small a kingdom is to be found in morale—a morale which refused to concede even the possibility of defeat.

This is simply another way of saying that the Spanish forces were imbued with a keen professional spirit. People's armies, to be sure, have written some of the most thrilling pages of history. But in every age when supremacy has been long demonstrated, it is upheld by men who consider themselves regulars as distinguished from mercenaries or citizen-soldiers. Such were the phalangites of Arbela, the legionaries of Ilerda, the longbowmen of Poitiers. And such were the tercios which defended the enormous Hapsburg empire after Pavia.

They were beaten on occasion, though they declined to admit it. Nor were their successes of a dramatic sort, since the emperor's German and African campaigns amounted to hardly more than punitive expeditions. Yet throughout these years—a most critical period for Christendom—their superiority was so well established that no other army felt capable of offering battle on equal terms. Thus the Spanish military system, like a "fleet in being," served by its very presence to secure Europe against the last great threat of Moslem conquest.

II

THE MARCH OF ISLAM

He who rules on the sea will very shortly rule on the land also.

—KHEYR-ED-DIN

BY THE first half of the sixteenth century the Mohammedan world had reached its greatest expansion of a millennium. Arabia, Egypt, Syria, Asia Minor, Turkestan, Persia, Moorish Africa and parts of India acknowledged the spiritual leadership of a Turkish sultan as the successor to the caliphs. Constantinople thus became the religious and political capital of an Islam extending from the Atlantic coast of Africa to the Asiatic islands of the Pacific.

Turkish conquests in Europe included most of the Balkan territory up to the Danube. A foothold was even gained for a short time in the very citadel of Christendom when a sea-borne expedition raided Italy and seized Otranto.

This outgrowth may be traced to a small political seed deposited by the winds of conquest. Othman, who gave his name to the Ottoman Turks, was the son of a petty chief driven from central Asia by the ravages of the Mongols. The enforced migration led to Asia Minor, where the progenitor of future sultans began his career in 1289 with a strength of 400 horsemen. His life was devoted to wresting small scraps of territory from the decrepit East-Roman Empire; and he died in 1326 as the master of nearly all Bithynia, the only remaining Byzantine province in Asia.

His son Orkhan represented the second of seven unbroken generations of talented rulers. It was due to his political acumen that the army increased from 400 to 40,000 within fifty years of the original settlement, while the new state gained a foothold in Europe.

Orkhan has been credited with originating the plan of military colonization which attracted adventurers from all parts of the Moslem world. In addition to the usual lure of plunder, he held forth the inducement of conquered lands to be divided among the conquerors. In return, the recipient of each timar, or fief, owed the state the service of a completely equipped cavalry warrior.

So far the scheme seems to be merely a copy of Europe's creaking feudal system of this period. But the shrewd Orkhan introduced two amendments which changed the results entirely. First, he avoided the dangers of limited military duty by demanding that his vassals agree to serve for any length of time deemed necessary. Secondly, and more important, he made his fiefs nonhereditary, so that future generations of nobles would never gain enough power to challenge the central authority.

All holdings reverted to the state upon the death of a beneficiary, and his sons were expected to help conquer new territory if they hoped for a like reward. In order to guard against a local hegemony, a son never received his father's identical fief.

Due to Turkish polygamy, the timariot class multiplied with incredible rapidity. Naturally each new generation clamored for wars of conquest as the only means of acquiring lands; and the Ottoman state was soon encroaching on its Moslem neighbors while plotting aggrandizement across the Dardanelles.

Orkhan's crafty diplomacy opened the way for the invasion of Europe. By pretending friendship and lending military aid to tottering Byzantium, he put that empire in his debt and learned the roads as well as weaknesses of the Balkan provinces. When he seized Gallipoli and the peninsula below it in 1353, Constantinople had little choice but to acquiesce. Then only eight years later the real assault was launched. So well had the spade work been done that in a single smashing campaign Orkhan's son Murad reduced all of Macedonia, Thessaly and western Thrace up to the walls of the imperial city.

Louis the Great of Hungary chose this moment to make war on Serbia and Bulgaria, with the result of weakening rather than crushing those kingdoms. Murad saw his opportunity and promptly added Bulgaria to the list of Turkish conquests. Serbia fell next when the invaders won a victory at the battle of Kossova which gave them the mastery of the

Balkans, Both Murad and his opponent lost their lives, and that June day in 1389 began a Serbian bondage which endured in some degree until 1909.

Within three generations a few hundred fugitives had founded a Turkish empire ranking as one of the world's great war powers. The permanency of the European conquests was to be proved only seven years after Kossova when Emperor Sigismund led a crusade of some 50,000 Hungarian, Polish, German and Italian warriors in an attempt to recover the lost kingdoms. These lands had as usual been parceled out among deserving vassals, and the Christians were met at Adrianople by Turks defending their homes. The outcome was a tremendous defeat for Sigismund.

Fortunately for Europe, the sultan did not follow up his victory. Bajazet was more interested in Asiatic expansion, and this policy led to a collision with another and greater conquering host.

THE TATAR CAMPAIGNS

By the year 1400 the Tatars had already overrun Russia, Persia and India. Under the leadership of Timur the Lame, also known as Tamerlane, they swept aside every people in their path, winning a series of triumphs which rivaled the Mongol victories.

Timur, like Jenghiz Khan before him, found it harder to master his own people than to reduce the rest of Asia. Most of his life was devoted to the petty combats of provincial wars, and not until his declining years did he emerge as a conqueror on a vast scale. Then he proved irresistible in campaigns taking his horsemen from the Ganges to the Hellespont. When he died undefeated at the age of sixty-nine he was preparing a Chinese invasion which doubtless would have been as successful as his other attempts.

The phrase "world's greatest conqueror" has been applied to Timur as well as Jenghiz Khan. Yet the similarity of Tatar and Mongol conquests leaves room for skepticism. The student of these monotonously successful operations can only wonder if the oppressed and fatalistic masses of the East were not more susceptible to invasion than Western peoples. Again we read the same dreary accounts of whole villages submitting like sheep to being slaughtered by a few foemen. Again we learn of "defenders" riding forth to join rather than oppose the plundering host. In the end it would appear that an Asiatic conqueror of these centuries had only to gather some momentum to be assured of half-beaten opponents.

Timur imitated and even improved upon Mongol tactics of frightfulness. Legend has it that he reared great pyramids of human skulls as an object lesson, and certainly this ferocious cripple buried thousands of captives alive as punishment for a brave resistance. The sack of Bagdad alone accounted for possibly 100,000 victims who succumbed to all manner of hideous tortures.

The Tatar host, like the Mongol army, included a motley assortment of horsemen from the steppes of Asia. There was little difference in the arms carried by each, though Timur never developed a tactical mechanism which equalled the Mongol system. He depended on the age-old mobility and hardihood of Eastern tribesmen, adding as his own contribution a genius for war greater than the ability displayed by any Mongol leader. In every operation his approach proved unerring, and throughout his career he contrived to force all adversaries to take the tactical offensive at a disadvantage.

After subjecting his own people and mounting the throne of the old Khwarismian realm at Samarkand, Timur enlarged his domain at the expense of Jenghiz Khan's descendants. Most of the Mongol conquests had endured only a few generations, but the Golden Horde of Russia still retained its power and vigor. In a remarkable campaign the Tatar leader marched 1,500 miles in a few weeks to offer battle to this formidable foe. Each of his horsemen led a spare mount, and the entire force depended on hunting for provisions.

The ensuing three-day engagement on a great plain near Kandurcha followed the general pattern of Tatar tactics. In his youth Timur had been a lusty warrior, but after being badly lamed by a wound he devoted himself to generalship in the manner of a modern commander. At Kandurcha his army was arrayed in the familiar Oriental crescent formation, with the lancers and mounted archers of both wings extended toward the enemy. As a unique feature of Tatar operations the centre was defended by entrenchments, while in the rear Timur massed a substantial force of reserves which he used to strengthen either wing. He appears to have shown great skill in directing the action, and by the third day the superior numbers of the Mongols were exhausted and put to rout.

After the Golden Horde had been subdued, Timur's easy conquest of India may be attributed to his generalship in respect to manoeuvre and siegecraft. Bagdad, Damascus and Aleppo were next to fall, being sacked with terrible slaughter during a three-year campaign in which the Tatars drove steadily westward toward the Mediterranean. At no time did they meet first-rate opposition, and the invading army was constantly swelled by plunder-lured deserters from the ranks of the defenders.

It was thus an enormous and polyglot host of Asiatic horsemen that Timur brought to the battle of Angora in 1402 against equal or perhaps superior numbers of Turks under Sultan Bajazet. Probably no greater cavalry battle has ever been recorded in history, for it does not appear that weapons of gunpowder had anything to do with the outcome.

Timur virtually won the day by manoeuvre before striking a blow. After devastating the Turkish lands near Angora, he placed Bajazet in such a position that the sultan had to attack in order to secure water at the river Halys. His troops were half defeated by thirst as they went into action, both men and horses being tortured by the dust rising from the plain. Treachery played a part when a number of squadrons went over to the enemy, and the struggle ended in a disaster for Bajazet, who died in captivity.

So complete was the rout that the Ottoman state seemed on the way to a collapse as dramatic as its beginnings. Civil war followed invasion as Bajazet's sons disputed for the succession, and rebellions of conquered subjects broke out in Syria and the Balkans.

The empire escaped ruin only because of boons such as fate has seldom extended to a prostrate power. Timur's death three years after his great victory was followed immediately by the disintegration of his conquests. At this same period Christendom entered upon the Hussite crusades that were to drain the energies of eastern Europe for a generation. The combination of these timely circumstances gave the next two Ottoman sultans a respite which they used to advantage in building up a new tactical system. Fifty years after Angora the Turks were stronger than ever before, and Constantinople fell an easy prize to their great siege train.

THE SPAHIS AND JANISSARIES

The Ottoman army of 1453 became the first Eastern force to balance age-old steppes tactics with a well-developed shock attack. Heavy armed cavalry were included in respectable numbers along with the usual mounted bowmen, and the new Turkish infantry arm compared with the best regiments of Europe. Ottoman generals did not lag behind their Western foemen in appreciation of artillery values, and within a few generations Ottoman admirals commanded fleets strong enough to contend for the mastery of the Mediterranean.

The resulting victories were never as spectacular as the conquests of a Timur or Jenghiz Khan; but Turkish forces held their own against far abler opponents, maintaining an empire that endured for centuries after Mongol and Tatar conquests had become a memory.

The feudal levy of landowners continued to make up the bulk of the army. Before 1453 most of them were mounted bowmen, using the familiar swarming tactics of Eastern warfare. Then shock weapons gained in favor, and by the end of the century at least half of the timariot warriors relied upon the lance, sword or mace.

Orkhan, the great organizer, is said to have created the first companies of the mailed horsemen known as Spahis. Formed at the outset as the sultan's bodyguard, they gradually expanded into the heavy cavalry of the Turkish army—a dependable reserve of paid troops armed with the lance and scimitar for hand-to-hand combat. This volunteer force included loyal vassals or veteran adventurers.

By far the most unusual branch of the army was the famous corps of Janissaries, or tribute-children. Beginning in the fifteenth century, the empire adopted a fixed policy of seizing Christian boys between the ages of seven and ten. For ten years the young captives were given strict military discipline while being instructed in the Mohammedan faith. After this term of apprenticeship they entered the ranks of infantry companies which had no equal in contemporary Europe.

Boys from the mountains of Albania, Bosnia and Bulgaria were preferred; and in view of the opportunities for advancement, Christian parents eagerly offered their sons to the sultan's recruiting agents. For it is a paradox of this strange corps that former slaves should eventually have acquired a power over their masters which may be compared only to the prerogatives claimed by the Praetorians of ancient Rome. As their influence grew, the Janissaries made and unmade sultans with supreme insolence, while over a period of three centuries fully half of the Ottoman grand viziers came up from their ranks.

Originally trained as foot-archers, they adopted the arquebus early in the sixteenth century. Yet the brains of these military monks proved more valuable than their brawn, since they were virtually recognized as the staff college of the Ottoman army. Few campaigns were planned without their advice, and it was largely due to their progressive spirit that the Turks appeared before Constantinople with the heaviest artillery train of the age.

A century after Angora the Turks won a battle which illustrates the tactical advances made since that disaster. Sultan Selim II, who doubled the territory of the empire by Eastern conquests, invaded Persia in 1514 with a force of about 50,000, including Janissaries, Spahis, timariot horsemen and an artillery train. His opponent, Shah Ismael, founder of the Sefavi dynasty, had won a series of victories in Mesopotamia which marked him as an emerging Timur. The Persian force, a typical Eastern cavalry host, far outnumbered the invaders; but Selim achieved a strategic surprise by crossing the Armenian mountains to threaten Tabriz.

Ismael advanced to defend his capital and the two armies met on the plain of Tchaldiran. The Turkish force was arrayed in a manner new to the East: light infantry and irregular cavalry formed a thin first line, while in the second the timariot horsemen of the wings were strengthened by Janissary arquebusiers and Spahi cavalry in the centre. Artillery, massed in batteries, covered the front of this line, and both flanks were protected by baggage carts chained together, wheel to wheel.

The shah's horn-shaped attack, aiming at envelopment, showed no departure from traditional Eastern tactics. He broke through the thin Turkish first line with ease, then superior skill told over superior weight as arquebuses emptied Persian saddles and the Turkish batteries tore gaps in the oncoming columns. Ismael received a bullet wound, and the rout of his horsemen was completed by a counterattack of Spahis. After this devastating defeat Tabriz fell without resistance to the invaders.

The merit of the new Ottoman tactics was further demonstrated as Selim the Terrible campaigned for seven years in Armenia, Mesopotamia, Syria and Egypt, beating the best cavalry of the East without suffering a serious reverse. When the sultan died in 1520 he left to his son a mighty empire spread out over three continents.

The Fall of Belgrade and Rhodes

It is one of history's most noteworthy coincidences that Islam should have reached this height at a time when Christendom was defended by the most powerful empire since the time of Charlemagne. In military resources the rival powers were fairly well matched. The Ottoman establishment included about 12,000 Spahis and 20,000 Janissaries (not counting recruits in training), while at least 50,000 timariot horsemen and as many irregular foot could be raised for a distant campaign. The Hapsburg empire had built up a standing army of about 55,000, and the feudal levies of Austria, Bohemia and Hungary equaled the timariots both in quality and numbers.

Only a few months after the crowning of Charles V, Soliman the

Magnificent became the new head of the Ottoman state. Immediately the two youthful rulers—each the most able of his line—began a duel for supremacy which continued for forty years.

Border warfare had gone on intermittently since the fall of Constantinople, with the Christians holding firm under such resolute champions as John Huniades, the Hungarian regent, and Scanderbeg, the Albanian patriot. Ottoman expansion had generally been toward the East, ignoring Europe altogether, and in 1520 the Turks still held only the lower Danube near its mouth. Hungary had been considered a sufficiently strong buffer state to halt further inroads, so that Christendom was lulled into a false sense of security when the real contest began.

Past attempts proved that Europe's flanks were well guarded against Turkish invasion by the mountains of Croatia on the west and Transylvania on the east. The centre remained the only avenue of approach, and this region relied on the supposedly impregnable fortresses of Belgrade and Shabetz.

In 1521 the young sultan appeared with a large army before Shabetz and carried the walls by storm. Marching 40 miles east, where Belgrade commanded the junction of the rivers Danube and Save, he bridged the latter and cut the great fortress off from supplies or reinforcements. Belgrade, like Shabetz, was woefully undermanned, and the Turkish sappers created breaches by means of gunpowder mines. The inevitable surrender, after a resistance of a few weeks, found only 400 able-bodied defenders left in the citadel.

At last Christendom was thoroughly aroused, but after opening the way in a single summer's campaign Soliman did not threaten Europe again for five years. This delay brought little comfort, since the sultan devoted his time to the establishment of Islam's first formidable sea power.

For a thousand years, following Saracen defeats at the hands of the Byzantines, the Mediterranean had remained a barrier to Moslem ambitions. But the Moors soon turned to piracy after their expulsion from Spain, and by the end of the fifteenth century corsairs from African ports were raiding the coast of Italy and France. Their vessels were rowed by Christian captives; and just as the Janissaries became Ottoman strategists, many a former galley slave rose to leadership among the Barbary pirates.

Soliman saw larger possibilities than plunder in Moslem sea raids, and after capturing Belgrade he took the first steps toward gaining naval supremacy in the eastern Mediterranean. The shipyards of the Golden

Horn had already been rebuilt under his orders, making it possible to construct a respectable fleet of galleys and transports. Without hesitation, despite his inexperience, the sultan immediately launched a sea-borne expedition against Rhodes, the last great outpost of Christendom in the Aegean and reputedly the world's strongest fortress.

Since the fall of Constantinople the science of fortification had gradually acquired a new set of values. Medieval walls and towers, however stout, grew increasingly vulnerable as improvements were made in the casting of cannon and manufacture of gunpowder. The resulting gains in accuracy enabled besiegers to duplicate the effect of the battering ram by concentrating their fire on one spot. As a consequence, military architects were forced to exchange the trowel for the spade, digging in for protection instead of building upward to create targets. For purposes of active defense, detached stone bulwarks, semicircular in form, were thrown out both as a shield for the gates and an advanced position for the guns of the garrison.

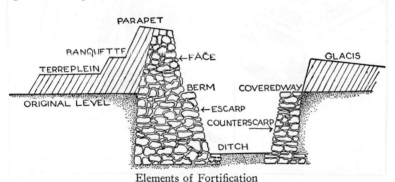

Elements of Fortification

Although the ditch had not been reckoned an essential feature of medieval fortifications, it became of the utmost importance to a new system based upon low, screened works which crouched half hidden in the terrain. Part of the earth dug from the ditch was piled up behind an escarp of masonry to form the rampart, which not only added strength but also provided a place for the artillery of the defense. The rest of the earth was thrown up beyond the counterscarp as a glacis—a gentle downward slope exposed to a plunging fire from the rampart. Behind the glacis, and sheltered from the guns of the rampart, a covered way protected garrison troops either for defensive combat or counterattack.

Such a system offered a formidable series of traps and obstacles. But mere passive resistance did not suffice, and neither the bulwark nor the curtain (a straight section of the rampart) solved all the problems of garrison fire power. The former proved too detached for full security, while the latter gave no opportunity for flanking shots.

Sixteenth century engineers found a solution for both weaknesses in the bastion, described by an English authority, Colonel Kelly, as "an element of fortification which dominated the science for 300 years." In effect, the new work was simply a projection of the curtain into two flanks and two faces forming a salient angle at the front. A defensive advantage was gained by doing away with the bulwark's isolation, while for purposes of flanking fire the guns of the rampart could now rake any section of the ditch.

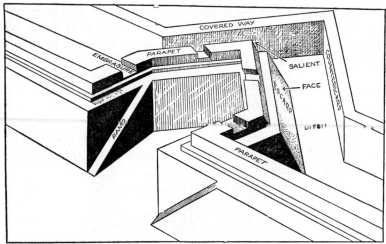

Plan of Bastion

The Knights Hospitalers, as masters of Rhodes, had incorporated all of these improvements into the fortress at an enormous expenditure of time and money. On the other hand, Soliman crossed from the Asiatic shore with a great artillery train and an army of 150,000 which included a host of sappers from the mines of the Balkans. The siege continued throughout the summer and autumn, clearly proving the superiority of the new fortifications over the most powerful offensive. Although the invaders brought huge mortars firing stone balls, the bastions stood firm and returned a cannonade which caused frightful losses among the assailants. The Turks excavated 54 gunpowder mines without gaining a permanent lodgment, being frustrated in most instances by countermines. In desperation, Soliman at last made several attempts to carry

Rhodes by storm, but few of his troops were able to penetrate beyond the shot-swept glacis and ditch.

The fortress might have held out indefinitely except for a dire shortage of gunpowder, which caused the Knights to accept the remarkably easy terms of victors whose losses were estimated as high as 60,000 slain. Ottoman sea power rather than siegecraft deserved the credit, since neither Venice nor any other Christian state chose to risk a naval encounter with the blockading galleys. This lesson did not escape Soliman, who continued to strengthen his fleet while resuming the land attack on Europe.

THE SIEGE OF VIENNA

In 1526 the sultan marched from Constantinople to the Danube with an army estimated at 150,000 and actually amounting to perhaps two-thirds of that figure. Charles was as usual occupied with an Italian war, so the burden of the defense fell upon Hungary, aided by Bohemia and Moravia.

King Louis of Hungary had only forty days in which to raise an army, and the inevitable bickerings between allies weakened his plan of campaign. Thus while the Christian leaders disputed, Soliman gained time to bridge the river Drave near its junction with the Danube. With Hungary open to invasion, the allied commanders had little choice but to accept battle on a plain near Mohács. Fearing an envelopment by the sultan's superior numbers, they decided to seize the initiative after drawing up their force in two long, thin lines. The 80 Christian guns opened the engagement, then the Bohemian and Hungarian cavalry led a general attack which broke through the Turkish first line.

Soliman had adopted a formation of three heavy lines after throwing out a flanking detachment far to the left. The allied advance met with serious trouble, therefore, when it came up against the 15,000 Janissary foot and massed batteries of the second and third lines. Point-blank salvos worked a maximum of destruction, followed by a counterattack of the Janissaries just as the flanking detachment struck the right rear of the Christian army. The outcome was a wild rout from which only half of the king's force survived as fugitives. Louis himself perished and most of the nobles of Hungary were slain in a disaster which left Buda a prey to occupation without further resistance.

Soliman promptly annexed the fallen kingdom as a tributary state governed by a puppet ruler in the person of a malcontent Hungarian noble. Again it is puzzling to note that three years passed before the

Ottoman Empire followed up its great victory, but the sultan had his hands full on other fronts. Throughout these years Soliman waged an almost continuous strife with Persia, and his most vigorous efforts were devoted to putting down revolts of newly conquered subjects in Asiatic provinces. Charles meanwhile was equally engaged in his wars against France and the German Protestants. Only at intervals did the two antagonists find an opportunity to resume the great contest between Islam and Christendom.

After Mohács the sultan subdued an uprising which had spread from Asia Minor to the Euphrates, but in 1529 he invaded Europe again with a host computed at 120,000 troops and 20,000 baggage camels. Ferdinand, archduke-king of Austria and brother of the emperor, accepted the responsibility of the defense with stout resolution. Realizing that the medieval walls of Vienna were not impregnable, he determined to rely upon men rather than masonry. Charles had sent Spanish foot from his army in Italy, and veteran German infantry regiments made up the remainder of a garrison of about 20,000.

The Turks spread out on both sides of the Danube, but before they could move their 300 guns into position a sortie of 2,500 defenders inflicted a sharp defeat on advance posts. This blow was followed only three days later by a surprise attack of Spanish units which added to the discomfiture of the besieging forces. Henceforward the defenders snatched the initiative away from their assailants at every opportunity. Ferdinand's engineers proved so successful at counter-mining that many of the enemy's mine-heads were detected and blown up before doing any harm. Whenever a breach was opened, the garrison threw up new works while beating off storming parties. Finally a great Christian sortie of 8,000 foot fell upon the invaders at dawn one morning with enormous destruction of Turkish troops and material.

Seldom has there been a more convincing demonstration of the adage holding that the best defense is a vigorous attack. When as a last resort Soliman ordered a general storm, his men were too dispirited by past reverses to make way against Spanish and German arquebuses. The assault failed with heavy losses, and that night the Ottoman host began a retreat which became one of the catastrophes of military history. Snow fell in October, weeks earlier than was to have been expected in the Danube country. Horses and camels floundered to their death in roads resembling morasses, while Austrian horsemen hung on the flanks of the beaten army to cut off stragglers. The sultan's entire transport had to be burned, and most of his artillery was destroyed or captured before the shrunken remnant of the expedition reached Constantinople in December.

The valorous defenses of Vienna in 1529 may be considered the first turning point in the struggle between Moslem and Christian. Once again, three years later, Soliman launched a major land assault, but this time the invasion met a united front. Past differences were forgotten as Martin Luther exhorted the German Protestants to give sincere aid, and Charles himself hurried to the Danube with his best Spanish and Italian veterans.

Soliman was too discreet to risk an encounter against such opposition. At a tremendous loss of prestige he kept his distance from Vienna, contenting himself with devastating the countryside and capturing a few border towns. This choice marked the beginning of a new phase of limited operations—large-scale raids varied with a warfare of posts and sieges—which prevailed until the sultan's death thirty-two years later during a campaign in Hungary. The real strategic victory had been won without a fight by the Spanish tactical system, which interposed a bulwark too formidable for even the greatest of Ottoman conquerors. Thereafter, contrary to the historical rule, land warfare took the passive role while the decisive engagement occurred on the sea.

The Battle of Lepanto

Already the New World was becoming a factor in the power politics of Europe. Spain had seemed well on the way to acquiring an African empire when discoveries in America claimed the naval energies of the realm. As a consequence, the ports of Tunis and Algiers soon swarmed with Moorish and renegade Christian pirates whose raids grew increasingly bold.

The year after his unsuccessful attempt on Vienna the sultan recognized the fighting qualities of these corsairs by heaping honors on their natural leader—Kheyr-ed-din, better known as Barbarossa—and appointing him to the supreme command of the Turkish fleet. As added evidence of political breadth, Soliman formed a naval alliance with the "Most Christian King" of France, who had been awaiting an opportunity to stab the emperor in the back ever since his defeat at Pavia.

These two moves foreshadowed a maritime threat to Europe which Charles correctly diagnosed as far more serious than Turkish land invasion. Barbarossa proceeded within a few months to justify his new honors by ravaging the Italian coast almost to Naples with a fleet of 84 galleys manned by Janissaries. Reggio was sacked in this great raid, and a total of 11,000 Christian captives carried away to the slave markets of Constantinople.

Legend has it that the red-bearded pirate, then over seventy years old, descended from a French Christian family. At any rate he has gone down in history as the most able of Ottoman admirals, for his depredations of the first two years proved so alarming that Charles felt it necessary to invade Africa. In 1535 the emperor set sail with 600 ships commanded by Andrea Doria of Genoa. Tunis fell after the defeat of Barbarossa by the invading army, yet even as the victory was being celebrated the old corsair delivered a successful attack on Minorca in Spanish waters.

In 1537 the sultan deemed his naval strength sufficient for an invasion of Italy, but after ravaging the countryside around Otranto and Brindisi the Ottoman force withdrew because of threatened communications. Charles countered with a second African expedition in which his gains were nullified by the loss of 130 transports and 3,000 men in a tempest. Meanwhile the cynical diplomacy of the French king played a part as Francis alternately betrayed both the emperor and sultan in his efforts to profit from their strife. Only once did the Ottoman and Christian main fleets meet during this preliminary period; and in the inconclusive battle of Prevesa the Turks under Barbarossa sank seven galleys without losses of their own before Doria retired from the action.

On the whole the Ottoman fleet had a little the better of the intermittent clashes of the following three decades, but it was left to another generation to decide the issue. Both Charles and Soliman were dead, and their admirals as well, when the battle of Lepanto brought the struggle to a climax in the greatest sea engagement of fifteen centuries.

After failing to take Malta in 1565, the Turks invaded Cyprus five years later with 116 galleys and 50,000 troops. The Republic of Venice appealed to the whole Christian world for aid to its island possession, and during the summer of 1571 a force of 200 warships assembled under the command of Don John of Austria.

The last stronghold of Cyprus had been taken and the island overrun with frightful slaughter before the Christian fleet set sail, but the twenty-six-year-old admiral sought out the enemy in the Gulf of Lepanto. The Turkish vessels, commanded by Ali Mouezinzade, numbered about 290, though averaging smaller than the European ships and containing many inexperienced crews. More important to the outcome, Don John brought

20,000 of the empire's best land-service troops, while the Ottoman force included 16,000 soldiers, chiefly Janissaries.

Not a single galleon, or broadside-firing vessel depending on sail, took part in the affair. In the comparatively calm waters of the Mediterranean the galley had survived as the tactical unit long after being superseded in the Atlantic. The usual warship of this type averaged about 150 feet long, with two or three masts carrying a lateen-rigged sail for cruising purposes. For battle manoeuvre the galley relied entirely on its 54 oars, 27 on a side, manned by slaves chained to the benches. Each ponderous oar was served by as many as six men, who were flogged into wild activity during an engagement by boatswains pacing up and down the gangway. A full crew of officers, sailors and slaves numbered

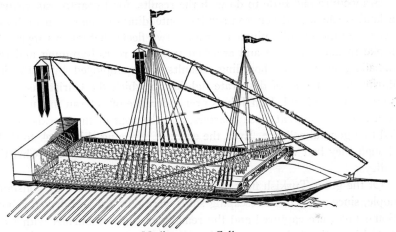

Mediterranean Galley

400, in addition to the fighting men stationed in the prow with the guns. Ramming and boarding were still reckoned an effective attack, though arquebus fire power had come to play a decisive part.

As their unique tactical contribution, the Turks introduced the "galleot" of 18 to 24 oars and a crew of 200 men. Essentially a half-size galley, this raiding vessel was speedy and easily managed. At the other extreme, the Venetians developed in the "galeass" a double-size galley whose unwieldy qualities were balanced by a larger complement of rowers and marines.

Six of these large warships held the front of the Christian line at Lepanto. Behind them the remainder of the Venetian, Spanish and papal fleet took a crescent formation, with 70 galleys in the centre, separated by three ships' breadth from the wings of some 50 galleys each. About half a mile to the rear Don John stationed a reserve of 30 ships.

The enemy array, also crescent-shaped, consisted of 100 galleys in the centre, 55 in the right wing and 95 in a left wing obviously intended as the striking force. The Turks had a reserve of 40 vessels.

The westerly wind was favorable as Don John's line advanced, churning the sea with thousands of oars. The shock of the six galleasses proved disappointing, but at least each of them outfought several Ottoman ships during the course of the day. When the two main lines clashed, however, the Turks won the first advantage as their heavy left wing turned the Christian right. Then the two centres came together in a furious mêlée dominated by arquebus fire and boarding tactics.

Manoeuvre had little to do with the results, for Lepanto was virtually a land battle waged between armies contending on their own or hostile decks. So thoroughly mingled were the two fleets that galleys repeatedly broke through the line and attacked from the rear. Ramming and cannonading as well as boarding assaults were employed by both sides during three hours of desperate fighting in which the Christians slowly won the upper hand. Don John's preponderance of veteran infantry gave him the advantage at close quarters, and the rout of the Turkish centre led to a general collapse. Even the enemy's left-wing ships took to flight, though they had won a local superiority and captured several Christian galleys.

Of the great Turkish fleet only 40 vessels ever returned to Constantinople, since many of the escaping ships were pursued and driven ashore. Some 110 were captured and the remainder sunk or burned with troop casualties estimated at 25,000 slain and 5,000 prisoners. Fifteen thousand Christian galley slaves were freed by the victors, whose losses amounted to 17 ships and 7,500 dead.

Thus ended the most decisive naval engagement since the battle of Actium in 31 B.C. A year after Lepanto the Turks managed by a prodigious effort to launch 160 new galleys, but they refused a second meeting with Don John. Following that defeat Moslem sea power declined as rapidly as it had risen, so that within a few decades Europe had to deal only with intermittent pirate raids.

Time also proved that Ottoman land warfare had reached its zenith under Soliman the Magnificent, whose three successors were a drunkard, a lecher and a madman. True, the Hungarian frontier was to be repeatedly crossed during their reigns, and Vienna withstood another siege as late as 1683. But never again was Christendom in real peril, for the deterioration of the Turkish tactical system became more and more apparent. And though the individual soldier continued to be regarded as a tough foemen in border campaigns, it grew plain to future generations that Islam's last fervent dream of conquest had ended at Lepanto.

III

THE HUGUENOT UPRISINGS

Indiscipline spread to the noblesse, some of whom, after a first taste of the dish of plunder, refused to sup on any other meat.

—LA NOUE

IN 1562 the massacre of a congregation of Calvinists plunged all France into civil war, and only six years later the Protestants of the Netherlands revolted against Spanish rule. This was the beginning of an era in which the ideas of the Reformation were threshed out with military flails.

The long-drawn French and Dutch conflicts had scarcely ended before the entire continent became involved in the Thirty Years' War, closely followed by the Great Rebellion in England. All four outbreaks are generally treated as separate struggles, but viewed from a historical distance the period emerges as a great European revolution lasting a century. The impact of Luther, Calvin and Machiavelli upon an age just discarding medievalism had been tremendous. Religion and state politics thus were prominent causes, but men also fought for a confusing variety of the most exalted and sordid motives—for freedom, for tolerance, for commerce, for pay, for plunder and even for bare subsistence.

In France such paradoxes were present to a bewildering extent. Catherine de Medici, whose name is stained with the Massacre of St. Bartholomew, hated and feared Catholic zealots nearly as much as the extremists among the Protestants. On the other hand, the later Huguenot leaders sometimes commanded armies made up in large part of Catholic volunteers. French religious reform had originally gained converts among sober and humble folk, yet the ranks of revolt were filled with Puritans fighting side by side with looters, mercenaries, swashbucklers and the proudest nobles of the land.

Out of this maze of inconsistencies one man emerges as guide and mentor—François de la Noue, called *Bras-de-Fer* because of the iron hook which replaced an amputated arm. As a soldier this versatile Huguenot campaigned for thirty years, fighting in the Netherlands as well as France. As a hero he became famed for one of the boldest exploits of the wars by capturing Orleans with only 15 horsemen. As a general and tactician he contributed in no small measure to the Protestant victories, and finally as a military writer La Noue ranks as the greatest figure of the age.

His *Discours Politiques et Militaires*, written while he was a prisoner of war, went into many editions and eventually influenced Cromwell, Montrose and Gustavus Adolphus. The work is equally valuable for its comments upon the social and economic aspects of the age. One of the chief causes of Europe's unrest, thought La Noue, was the presence of so many idle soldiers who had fought in the wars between the Valois kings and Hapsburg emperors. These men, particularly the non-noble officers, felt it a social degradation to return to the plodding life of a farmer or tradesman. Such a widespread prejudice, combined with the incendiary ideas of the times, helped to start the conflagration which swept over the Continent.

At the outset, according to the *Discours*, the Huguenot forces observed prayers and a discipline so strict as to interdict swearing. The Catholics likewise made a sincere effort to prohibit pillage and violence to noncombatants. But after a few campaigns both sides fell into disorders which foreshadowed the wolf tactics of the Thirty Years' War. "It sometimes caused me to laugh bitterly," concludes La Noue, "to think how 'soldier' meant the same thing as 'brigand' in our Days of the Troubles."

Nor was the lust for loot confined to men in the ranks. Maximilian de Bethune, Duke of Sully, who later became prime minister of Henry IV, notes with businesslike candor the sums which represented his share of the plunder of a fat town. Nevertheless, he relates an anecdote in his *Memoirs* pointing out the futility of such practices:

The inhabitants of Ville-Franche having formed the design of seizing upon Montpazier, another little neighboring town, by surprise, they chose for their execution of it the very same night which the citizens of Montpazier, knowing nothing of this, had pitched upon to make themselves masters of Ville-Franche. Chance, moreover, so ordered it that, the parties taking different ways, did not meet; all was executed with so much the less difficulty, that the walls both of one place and the other were wholly without defense. They pillaged, they glutted themselves with booty; it was a happy world till day appeared and discovered their mistake. The composition was, that each should return to his own home, and that all should be put in its first state. This is an image of war as it was carried on at this time: it consisted of seizing by subtlety or assault the towns and castles of the enemy.

The savage soldiery hired by all armies contributed further to the turbulence of the times. Rivalries between these mercenaries led to butcheries of captives in nearly every battle. Both the Swiss and the landsknechts had deteriorated in military virtues, yet their greed remained boundless. Serving any cause without scruple, they showed their resentment of arrears in wages by mutinies comparable to a modern strike. Operations frequently came to a standstill for this reason, and many a lost campaign may be traced to a meager pay-chest. As a last resort, unruly hirelings did not stop short of attacking the civilian population in order to revenge themselves. Europe had already been given an example of such an outrage when 30,000 unpaid Spaniards and landsknechts sacked Rome in 1527 with a hideous loss of life and property.

Early Huguenot Reverses

The Protestant cause faced heavy odds in France. From the beginning nearly all the material advantages were on the side of the Holy League, representing the uneasy alliance of the monarchy, the Guises and other Catholic factions. The old established regiments of the standing army were at their command, giving them a superiority in infantry numbers which the rebels never overcame. Even more important, the Leaguers retained the tax-collecting machinery of the realm, which meant that they were better able to hire mercenaries. Paris and most of the other large cities remained loyal, and Philip II of Spain proved an active and helpful ally.

In view of these Catholic assets, it is not surprising that the Huguenots were beaten in the campaigns of the first ten years. Their strength lay in a cavalry force composed of nobles and gentry who combined the most reckless courage with an aristocratic contempt for reconnaissance or any other routine task. Family and sectional quarrels had the Protestant camp in constant turmoil, and local interests usually took precedence over the main issue.

Louis of Condé, the Huguenot commander, personified the weaknesses of his army. A prince of the blood, he lent political distinction to "the Religion," but as a tactician Condé rose scarcely above the level of a dashing cavalry colonel. Taken prisoner in his first defeat, he was exchanged in time to lead his horsemen into another bootless battle against five times their own numbers. Finally, even a broken leg, resulting from a horse's kick, could not keep this fiery prince out of action; and he was slain as a crippled captive after riding at the head of his men in a third Huguenot reverse.

The devout and prudent Admiral Coligny, who succeeded Condé, had no better fortune. Although he managed to raise an army of 18,000, including many German mercenaries, the Huguenots were outnumbered in the battle of Moncontour, 1569, and suffered a fourth disaster. La Noue became a prisoner and half of the rebel infantry perished in a cold-blooded slaughter.

This blow was followed in 1572 by the Massacre of St. Bartholomew, in which Coligny and most of the other Protestant leaders were numbered among the victims. At the moment the cause must have seemed utterly lost to the hunted survivors, yet already the Huguenots had developed two sources of strength.

First, the insincere truces which followed each of the "Troubles" provided for such lenient terms that the rebels were said to have "lost every battle and won every peace." This was largely because the various Catholic factions preferred to favor the enemy rather than concede one another any political advantage. Eventually their discord grew until thousands elected to fight in the Protestant ranks.

Secondly, a decade of defeat taught the losers new and better tactics. Out of their very military poverty they evolved methods, based on recent mechanical improvements in arms, which led to a series of unbroken successes.

MUSKET AND PISTOL

Siegecraft and fortification, though secondary to the outcome, favored the more adaptable Protestants. La Rochelle, Havre and Marseilles had rebuilt their defenses according to the latest ideas, but most of the inland towns still depended on medieval walls. Such antiquated places the rebels often maintained against artillery by means of improvised earthworks known as *fortification à l'Huguenotte*. Instead of defending obsolete masonry, they surrounded the *enceinte* with outlying palisades, entrenchments and gun emplacements. Not only were the Huguenots generally the winners in this duel of spade against cannon, but they also learned lessons which made them more resourceful in attacking enemy towns. As a result their battle losses were balanced by the possession of strongholds enabling them to bargain for moderate peace terms.

At the outbreak of the war the regiment was the French infantry unit, composed of about 1,000 pikes and "shot" in fairly equal numbers. In combat the foot soldiers formed into squares, according to the Spanish system, and after discharging their pieces the arquebusiers retired to the rear to reload. These standardized tactics favored the Catholics, who retained the old royal regiments and could better afford to hire mercenaries.

The native Huguenot infantry took readily to firearms, but commanders seldom had the funds to hire a proper complement of pikemen. Again necessity led to tactical invention as a solution was found in the scheme of posting groups of arquebusiers between cavalry squadrons and on both wings. These units, called *enfants perdus* because of the danger of their position, were trained to take advantage of all available cover and pour a fierce fire into advancing horsemen. Undefended by pikemen, they became a helpless prey if the enemy's charge succeeded; but experience proved that infantry fire could be a decisive factor in breaking up a cavalry attack.

Both sides eventually made use of such groups, though the Huguenot proportion of "shot" to pikes rose as high as nine-tenths in several combats. The rebels also showed a more progressive spirit in adopting the musket: an invention of about 1550 which did not come into general use until the end of the century. For all practical purposes the new weapon was simply an enlarged arquebus, since the matchlock principle remained unchanged. But with the introduction of a portable iron fork, serving as a rest while the soldier took aim, it was possible to bring into the field a piece five and a half feet long, weighing 15 pounds. A two-ounce ball could be fired with effect at distances up to 200 yards, thus doubling the former range and load.

The problems of reloading also were doubled, so that two soldiers had to be assigned to the clumsy weapon with its fork, ramrod and "link" of smoldering match. The bullets were carried in a leather bag with drawstrings, while separate cases held the priming powder and the coarser powder which went into the charge. Upwards of a hundred motions were required before the ball was finally tamped down, and the best musketeers of the day needed three minutes to complete the operation.

The effect depended a great deal on the care used in reloading, for haste resulted in many bullets dropping harmlessly to earth without ever reaching the foe. Misfires added to the uncertainty. Perhaps four times out of five, under combat conditions, the soldier could expect a discharge vigorous enough to make recoil bruises a common complaint. But rain or mist were likely to render the match useless, and a puff of breeze at the last moment might blow the priming powder out of the pan. Sometimes, too, a wind-borne spark found its way into the company powder barrel.

Enormous quantities of match had to be provided for every campaign. Especially during a siege an alert garrison might burn hundreds of pounds daily. In night operations the glowing links were a handicap to surprise, though lighted strands left in bushes served as a stratagem to cover withdrawal.

Such drawbacks of the matchlock principle were of course less apparent in the sixteenth century than today. From the viewpoint of the Huguenots, fighting a cavalry war, the merit of the heavier weapon lay in its ability to stop enemy horsemen. The two-ounce balls had a frightful shocking power, penetrating the stoutest cuirasses at close range and smashing bone and sinew as they plowed through a man's body. Thus in spite of its faults the musket gained increasing favor as an infantry firearm, while the more convenient arquebus continued to be used by skirmishers.

Rebels, defying the accepted order, are traditionally more hospitable to tactical change, so it is not surprising that the Huguenots also profited from a small artillery revival. Each of their three main victories owed in some measure to a few fieldpieces which were placed, timed and aimed to advantage.

At about this period gunpowder had been much improved. Men at last remembered Roger Bacon's injunction to wet the three ingredients before mixing, thus washing away many of the impurities which had formerly fouled the bore and touchhole. After it had dried and caked, the compound was broken into tiny pellets known as "corned" powder. The new product provided not only a more certain but also a more violent explosion; and at a later date the grains were compressed and hardened for uniformity in reaction.

Although corned powder would rule the battlefields of the next three centuries, the innovation had no immediate or startling effect on tactics. Since the first bombards the artillery had been the most confused and neglected of all arms, if indeed it could properly be called an arm of the military service. Its development remained in the hands of hired specialists who sometimes owned as well as operated a cannon hired for the duration of a campaign. These gunners preferred siege to field operations because the rewards were greater; but the hard-pressed Huguenots managed to show a superiority over their opponents on every field.

Wheel lock Pistol

Another sixteenth century invention aided the cavalry, which had been a secondary arm in Europe ever since a series of disasters proved the futility of pitting lances against improved firearms. Even the adoption of the horse-arquebus, or early carbine, still left the mounted soldier at a disadvantage: for that weapon demanded the use of both hands, and the burning match added to the difficulties. About 1550, however, the appearance of the wheel-lock pistol began to work a revolution in the cavalry tactics which dominated France's wars of religion.

The new firing principle was based upon the sudden release of a steel-toothed wheel wound up by a key to tighten a spring. A pull of the trigger brought the revolving teeth in contact with a lump of pyrites, thus showering sparks on the priming powder in the pan. The horseman could fire with one hand while holding the reins, and two pistols were carried in holsters as well as a third in the right boot.

The name of the new weapon, derived from a Bohemian word, points to its origin in eastern Germany. Soldiers soon recognized the worth of the invention, and within a few years German horsemen "armed with little arquebuses only a foot long" were being employed by all the armies of Europe. These "reiters," wearing helm and cuirass and high leather boots, became the mercenary rivals of the Swiss and landsknechts by the end of the century.

Although a great deal of ornamentation went into the early pistols, they could scarcely have been convenient for firing. The butt, surmounted by a metal knob, was almost on a line with the barrel, so that accurate aim must have been impossible. There were repeated efforts to utilize the wheel-lock principle for muskets or arquebuses, but the mechanism revealed defects which discouraged wider adoption. The spring weakened after being wound up too long; the lump of pyrites might be shaken out in the excitement of action; and the wheel itself could easily be put out of order by rough handling. Hence the matchlock, despite its shortcomings, was to remain the prevailing infantry weapon for another century.

The German reiters not only introduced the pistol but also a new cavalry attack known as the "caracole" and designed to shatter squares of pikemen. Riding up in successive lines, the mercenary horsemen fired their pistols point-blank at the enemy, then swerved off to the rear to reload and re-form their ranks. The effect depended on exact timing and co-ordination, for the practitioners of the caracole laid themselves open to counterattack if they failed to maintain steady waves.

France was an ideal testing ground for new cavalry tactics, since the pistol found favor among the rebels, while the Catholic *gendarmerie* clung to the old charge of lancers in two thin lines. La Noue declared against the caracole, citing ancient examples to prove that impact has been in all ages the secret of cavalry success. His advice may have had some weight, but it is more probable that the caracole could not be reconciled with Huguenot dash and indiscipline. At any rate the Protestant horsemen took to hurling themselves upon the enemy in columns, following up vigorously with the sword after discharging their pistols. Even in defeat these shock tactics were so effective that at Moncontour the victors suffered more cavalry losses than the vanquished.

This same Huguenot disaster led within a few months to a campaign in which Admiral Coligny left a lesson for the coming century. After the battle he retreated south with the wreck of his army, pursued by the enemy's reiters. The Catholics supposed him to be still helpless when he burst upon them the next spring in a raid which terrified the entire country. Around a nucleus of 3,000 horse he had recruited a like number of arquebusiers, mounted on country nags. The word "dragoon" did not come into use for a hundred years, but Coligny's mounted infantrymen served the same tactical purpose. Their great sweep began at Nimes, continued through Languedoc, Burgundy and Champagne, and ended by threatening Paris itself after the repulse of the only Catholic army barring the way. The Huguenot force was too small to attempt a storm or siege, but the moral effect of the raid went far toward wiping out past reverses.

HENRY OF NAVARRE

After seven weary and indecisive "Troubles" the turning point of the French civil war came with the generalship of Henry of Navarre. This prince, like Richard the Lionhearted, has been made such a hero of romance that he is seldom given his due as a tactician. Yet it was largely due to his eye for ground, his quick perception of any battlefield advantage, that Huguenot resourcefulness won out against material odds.

Since the Massacre of St. Bartholomew the rebels had been beaten down to a defensive aiming less at victory than survival. Then in 1586 Henry III allowed dissenters only fifteen days in which to profess the Catholic faith, and the Protestants took up arms for the eighth time. In this crisis there was little to recommend their new commander. The shabby King of Navarre was even accused of cowardice, having saved his own skin during four years of captivity by a feigned abjuration. Nevertheless, any doubts either as to Henry's courage or ability were dispelled on the field of Coutras in 1587.

His opponent, the Duke of Joyeuse, was marching toward Bordeaux with 8,000 foot and 2,000 horse. The Huguenot leader, with a total force of only 6,300, did not hesitate to contest the advance. Taking a strictly defensive position on a 700-yard front between wooded heights, he formed 800 of his best mounted men into three squadrons with a depth of six ranks. Between them he placed small detachments of musketeers and arquebusiers—the front ranks kneeling—with orders not to fire until the enemy came within 20 yards. The left flank was defended by combat groups of *enfants perdus*, and the main infantry force held the wooded slope on the right.

While the Catholics were laboriously deploying, Henry drew first blood in a brief artillery duel. His small battery, much better placed and served than the enemy's guns, accounted for at least a hundred enemy casualties. This punishment caused Joyeuse to hasten a general advance, led by his cavalry in two thin lines and followed by the infantry squares.

The oncoming horsemen were terribly staggered by the point-blank fire of the musketeers and arquebusiers which Henry had posted between his squadrons. Then the Protestant horse spurred forward to the counterattack. Six-deep columns, armed with pistol and sword, found little difficulty with disordered lancers in two-deep array. After breaking through, the rebels whirled to strike again and again from the flanks and rear.

In ten minutes Joyeuse's army had ceased to exist as a fighting force. The duke and 3,500 of his men were slain, the rest put to flight or captured at a cost to the victors of 200 killed and wounded. The blows exchanged by the infantry of the wings had little to do with a triumph gained by a combination of musketry with cavalry shock. Some of his tactics Henry had inherited from former Huguenot leaders, but the scheme of posting arquebusiers between cavalry squadrons appears to have been original, as was his idea of instructing front-rank men to fire from a kneeling position. Both of these conceptions will bear watching in their influence on the military future.

Two years of desultory small war passed before the king's ability met a second test against three-to-one odds. Henry III had been assassinated meanwhile, and Henry of Navarre, as heir presumptive, was fighting for a throne. In a political sense rebels and royalists had traded places, and the struggle was further complicated as many Catholics enlisted with their former enemies.

The king had invaded Normandy, hoping to win Rouen, when the Duke of Mayenne, new head of the League, threatened him with an army of 20,000 foot and 4,000 horse. Henry, whose strength did not exceed 9,000 troops, retreated nearly to Dieppe; then making a stand in the defile of Arques, he won a dramatic though indecisive victory. Mayenne was lured into attacking on a 400-yard front, where his numbers were at a disadvantage, and beaten by a succession of cavalry counterattacks. At the critical moment the fire of a small Huguenot battery, concealed in a castle overlooking the field, helped to turn the tide of battle.

The results were chiefly moral, and Arques caused prudent men such as Sully to deplore the valor which carried "the white plume of Navarre" into every mêlée. But if ever a commander was justified in taking the risks of a cavalry captain, the king had good reasons for making his name a legend among scarred fighting men. Huguenot indiscipline had become too deep-seated to be reformed (even if Henry himself had been a disciplined character!) and the Catholic half of the army served a man rather than a cause. Such an establishment could be held together only by personal ascendancy.

In 1589 Henry and Mayenne met again near Paris in the most decisive battle of the wars. An army of 25,000 Leaguers, including 4,000 horse, opposed a royalist force of about 9,000 foot and 3,000 cavalry. Despite the odds against him, the king was confident enough to accept a formal engagement on a plain affording neither protection for his flanks nor cover for his arquebusiers.

From a tactical standpoint the encounter became one of the most instructive of the century. Not a single lance was carried by royalist horsemen depending on pistol and sword; and in the infantry the proportion of pikes to "shot" rose scarcely above a fourth. Mayenne's foot consisted of the usual heavy columns of pikemen and arquebusiers in about equal strength. The best squadrons of his horse were still armed with the lance, though he placed some dependence in reiters practicing the caracole.

Each army was drawn up, with little regard for a reserve, in a single line of cavalry squadrons alternated with infantry units—chiefly pikemen on the League side, chiefly arquebusiers in Henry's ranks. Mayenne, counting on numbers, extended his front with a view to envelopment of his opponent's flanks. The royalist commander obviously planned to await attack, relying on his musketeers to create an opportunity for his cavalry.

Again Henry's skillful placing of a few guns won him an initial advantage. Mayenne was galled into ordering a general advance, but the reiters of his left wing were quickly thrown into confusion by the flanking fire of arquebusiers. Their caracole tactics had failed, and in falling back the German mercenaries blocked the path of the League lancers of the centre, so that Mayenne's cavalry lost momentum all along the line.

Henry lost no time in exploiting the enemy's disorder. His right-wing squadrons rode in knee to knee, making short work of reiters with empty pistols and lancers too crowded together to use their weapons. With the king's white plume always in the fore, his horsemen cut their way through and returned to attack again from the rear. Mayenne's squadrons were soon in full flight, and a majority of his foot soldiers threw down their arms without having struck a blow. The League army was virtually annihilated, since the battle and pursuit took an additional toll of 4,000 slain in contrast to only 500 royalist casualties. Both the caracole and charge of lancers had failed against cavalry using the pistol as a prelude to shock attack; and again the volleys of a few arquebusiers contributed more to the outcome than the pikes of both sides.

As usual, the king demonstrated that he knew better how to gain than use a victory. After his smashing triumph at Coutras he let his army break up while he bore the captured standards to his mistress. After his inconclusive success at Arques he had been encouraged to attempt a dangerous and futile blockade of Paris. And now, after destroying the last field force of the enemy at Ivry, he turned his back on the undefended capital and marched away to besiege a petty stronghold in Champagne.

At last such lapses in strategy were about to be punished. Philip II of Spain, horrified at the prospect of a Protestant monarch in France, ordered his main force in the Netherlands to come to the aid of the League. Thus when Henry belatedly invested Paris he had to deal with a relieving army of 15,000 Spanish veterans commanded by Alexander of Parma, the master strategist of the day.

Although the city was in distress, the royalists were forced to lift the siege; for Parma had been strengthened by a new army of 12,000 Leaguers under Mayenne. The king tried to compel his adversaries to fight, regardless of their superior numbers, but at every turn he was frustrated by a stealthy and feline sort of warfare. If Henry advanced, Parma coolly awaited him behind field fortifications which his veterans had thrown up overnight. If Henry stood firm, Parma appeared as if by a miracle on his flank. If Henry tried to manoeuvre, Parma seemed to anticipate and parry his most secret thoughts.

During this contest between the bear and the leopard Paris was fully reinforced and revictualled. The king had no choice but to confess his defeat: he had met a general who knew how to gain direct ends by indirect means.

Henry laughed, swallowed his pride and proceeded to learn strategy from a strategist. The next campaign developed when he had Rouen at the point of yielding—again Parma came to the rescue, and again the Spaniard avoided battle while striving for all his objects by manoeuvre. This time, however, Henry took a lesson from Coligny and threw out a detachment of mounted arquebusiers to cut the enemy's line of communications.

Parma was not to be trapped, but after relieving Rouen he found himself in one of the tightest places of his career. For the king proved so apt a pupil that his master escaped encirclement only by the remarkable engineering feat of bridging the broad Seine. The royalist army, with victory apparently within reach, faced empty entrenchments after 16,000 Spanish troops had been taken across the river in a night with perfect secrecy.

The sickly Spanish general had won the strategic duel, but the campaign killed him. He retired a broken man after the strain of those Norman operations, and his death occurred a few months later from the effects of exhaustion aggravated by a wound. The Spanish monarch had lost his greatest general, yet the capitulation of Paris and Rouen was merely postponed until 1594, when Henry united all factions by his famous compromise with the Church.

In the sphere of grand strategy—the great international chessboard where the moves are made by nations—the price paid by Spain for Parma's two campaigns was ruinous. Not only had France become a strong and united kingdom, but the rebels of the Netherlands had been granted a breathing spell. During this interlude they built up a precise new military system under Maurice of Nassau, and within the next several years they won their independence by force of arms.

IV

REVOLT IN THE NETHERLANDS

I have tamed men of iron in my day—shall I not crush men of butter?

—THE DUKE OF ALVA

FOR a generation the French and Dutch wars raged simultaneously and even merged at times. Reinforcements were sent on several occasions by the Huguenots to their Protestant brethren of the Low Countries, and stout old *Bras-de-Fer* La Noue won one of the few land victories gained by the rebels over Spanish troops. On the other hand, William the Silent created a diversion in 1568 by leading an army into Picardy and Champagne, while a Dutch fleet came to the aid of Henry of Navarre during his siege of Rouen.

At intervals the strife took on an international aspect which foreshadowed the Thirty Years' War. Queen Elizabeth supported both rebellions in somewhat parsimonious measure with English soldiers, money and maritime help. On the Catholic side, the fanatical Philip II devoted all the resources of Spain to the extirpation of heretics—a policy which brought him into conflict with England and France as well as the Netherlands.

All over Europe theological differences had taken on a new and vehement meaning in response to the spiritual reaction which followed the materialism of the Renaissance. Religion had become a reality for which men were willing to lay down their lives. Yet it would be a mistake to view the clashes of the Counter-Reformation altogether in the light of a holy war, despite the prominent part taken by Calvinist and Lutheran against Jesuit and Capucin. The Huguenots of France were feared as much for their mounting trade prosperity as their doctrinal opinions. In a like spirit, grandees of Spain resented the fact that most of the treasure wrung from the New World eventually found its way into the pockets of Dutch merchants and carriers.

Actually the very foundations of European society were being shaken by a threefold revolution—political and economic as well as religious. Ever since the fall of Rome authority had been based upon the land which for centuries represented the only form of wealth. Meanwhile, a more potent and fluid source of power emerged in the money accumulated by the landless merchant classes. The long pendulum of history had completed another ponderous swing, and a new industrial order was uttering its first strident cries as a challenge to an old agricultural economy.

During this transition period a pall of frustration hung over the Continent. The hereditary landowning aristocrats lacked the wealth to impose their full will. The merchant classes possessed the means but lacked both the tradition and machinery of authority. In such a struggle for power it was natural that Protestantism, itself the product of controversy, should in general take the side of change. Quite as inevitably, the established Church chose to uphold economic and political institutions with which it had been closely associated for a thousand years.

Philip II of Spain, who inherited the sixteen provinces of the Netherlands when Charles V divided his vast empire, regarded them as dynastic if not actually personal property. He depended on them for an annual sum in taxes which sometimes exceeded the gold and silver brought from the Americas. In return, as a loyal son of the Church and the Inquisition, he felt an earnest responsibility for the spiritual as well as temporal welfare of his Dutch subjects. When they rebelled both against his rule and the Church's authority, he could only view the uprising as combined anarchy and heresy meriting the most severe chastisement.

His opponent, William the Silent, came up to manhood with a belief in exactly these same codes. As a youth he was a gourmet, military dilettante and favorite of the emperor Charles. Not until the age of thirty-five did he commit himself wholly to the cause of revolt, and then only after having labored long to reach a compromise. Hence in the metamorphosis of William from a luxury-loving courtier into one of the most somber of all national heroes, the history of Protestantism is written in terms of a personal choice which faced millions of bewildered Europeans.

Owing to his birth and wealth, William's choice was more dramatic though perhaps no more painful than the one confronting a peasant or burgher. A hereditary landed aristocrat as well as representative of the merchant classes, he had seen Flemish and Dutch cities grow from fishing ports into rich centres of world commerce. He had seen his own holdings grow simultaneously into one of Europe's first large family fortunes. He might, by throwing in his lot with Spain and Catholicism, have added to his wealth and political stature. He decided instead for Protestantism and independence at the cost both of his fortune and his life.

LAND DEFEATS OF THE REBELS

Battles were neither many nor decisive in the Low Countries. This factor was foreordained by military geography, since normal troop movements were next to impossible in territory so cut up by canals, dikes, marshes, estuaries and broad tidal rivers. Sea power and the twin sciences of fortification and siegecraft were destined to be more important means of controlling a water-girt area dotted with large, prosperous towns. The first of these assets the Seven Provinces possessed from the beginning, and in the end they gained their independence by bringing the defense and attack of cities to the highest development of the century.

The deadlock grew so dreary meanwhile that the moral element became of vital concern to both sides. Four Spanish governors tried every imaginable method of breaking the rebellion, and all four were themselves broken by the passive resistance of a land overrun by foemen. The Duke of Alva, who condemned an entire population of 3,000,000 as heretics and outlaws, was recalled after his mass executions failed of their purpose. Next came Don Luis of Requesens and Don John of Austria, the hero of Lepanto, both of whom fared little better with milder policies based upon bribery, intrigue and persuasion. Finally, even the high military talents of Alexander Farnese, Duke of Parma, could not gain a decision; and he followed his two predecessors to an early grave which was largely the consequence of strain and bafflement.

The Dutch genius for war found expression in seafaring, and attempts to take the field with hastily raised native forces ended in catastrophe. At the combat of Tisnacq an army of students, rustics and burghers was annihilated by a small Spanish detachment which had only one man wounded while inflicting losses of 2,000 slain. No better fortune attended early Dutch efforts to raise mercenary armies composed principally of German landsknechts and reiters, with a sprinkling of English, Scottish, Huguenot and native volunteers. Louis of Nassau, son of the Dutch leader, chose a strong defensive position at Jemmingen in 1568 but allowed his retreat to be cut off by the river Ems. Alva, with a smaller Spanish force, skillfully dislodged the opposing mercenaries from their trenches with a flank attack, then turned the ensuing panic into a slaughter which filled the stream with corpses. Seven Spaniards and 7,000 of the vanquished fell in this affair, according to a dispatch sent by the duke.

Spanish Pikeman

Ten years later an equally incoherent and badly led rebel army was defeated by Don John. The Dutch troops were retreating when a surprise flank attack scattered their covering force, exposing the main column to attack before it could form into line of battle. Again the same astonishing disparity of losses occurred, for the Spaniards acknowledged two men killed at Gemblours in contrast to 8,000 enemy slain or captured.

William the Silent took the field himself in 1572, after using personal resources to build up Dutch numerical superiority with an army of 20,000 landsknechts and 9,000 reiters. The prince's military ability fell far short of his political leadership, and he was outmanoeuvred by Alva, who hung on his flanks all summer while studiously avoiding battle. In the autumn, having lost thousands of men by desertion, William disbanded an army which had not struck a blow.

During these reverses the rebels could at least console themselves that they were not lacking in dogged courage. Unfortunately for their cause, the enemy combined courage with discipline, confidence and audacity, as was demonstrated by one of the most remarkable exploits in all military history. In 1575 Requesens determined to reduce Zierikzee, the capital of the islands off the coast of Zeeland. The Dutch controlled the sea, but a traitor informed the grand commander of a submerged dike which permitted wading at a depth of four or five feet. The attempt was made at night by 3,000 troops who held their powder and muskets over their heads. Any unforeseen delay might have resulted in the loss of the entire force when the tide came in, and even a misstep on the narrow bank meant almost certain drowning. Yet the steady Spanish veterans made the crossing of two leagues before daylight, though suffering all the way from the attacks of Dutch boatmen armed with harpoons and arquebuses.

Zierikzee fell after a siege of nine months, but the indirect results of the campaign led to a new unity in the Netherlands. From the beginning the nine southern provinces, largely royalist and Catholic in sentiment, had been only half converted to the rebellion. Trading with the oppressors was of such common occurrence that William pleaded, "Our enemies spare neither their money nor their labor: will ye then be colder and duller than your foes?"

This situation existed until the hardships of the Zierikzee campaign, aggravated by arrears in pay, caused a mutiny which spread through the Spanish army. Even the most loyal regiments were infected by the mercenary spirit; and after electing their own officers the mutineers decided to reimburse themselves by looting Antwerp, the largest city of the Netherlands. The ensuing sack, known as the Spanish Fury, became the most memorable outrage of a war distinguished for cruelty. After two days and nights of violence which respected neither Catholic nor Protestant, the streets were heaped with more dead than fell in Paris during the Massacre of St. Bartholomew. The property damage, both by fire and plundering, amounted to incalculable millions.

These atrocities ended for the time being all differences of opinion between Netherlanders. Only four days later the signing of the Pacification of Ghent united the sixteen provinces in a common front which marks the political zenith of the revolt.

The Development of Siegecraft and Fortification

A similar horror, though on a smaller scale, was to make the defense and attack of cities more important than battle in the conduct of the war. In 1572 the burghers of Naarden first defied the enemy before concluding that supplies were lacking for a prolonged resistance. Seeking to escape the recent fate of Zutphen, which had been brutally sacked in punishment for its defense, they opened the gates after receiving promises of clemency. The Spaniards partook of a feast prepared in their honor, then tolled the great bell to summon Naarden's citizens. This was the signal for a deliberate massacre lasting until practically all had perished, regardless of age or sex.

The example of frightfulness, far from paralyzing resistance, served to incite a frantic defense which enabled Haarlem to hold out for seven months against 30,000 besiegers. Although the fortifications were antiquated and the garrison weak, the burghers of this important city hanged the messenger who demanded capitulation. All the inhabitants flew to arms, including even 300 women formed into an arquebus corps; and the Catholic churches were defiantly stripped of images for use in the repair of outworks.

Just as Vienna had relied on counterattacks rather than walls to repel the Turks, the people of Haarlem made frequent and effective sallies. The city had scarcely been invested when the surrounding forces were surprised by a band of Dutch arquebusiers on skates, who left several hundred Spanish dead on the ice. Throughout the remainder of a cold winter both skates and sleds were utilized to supply a city located on a narrow isthmus.

Even in the matter of cruelties the aroused burghers proved a match for the enemy. Gibbets were erected above the ramparts and all prisoners hanged in full view of their comrades. Hoops, daubed with pitch and set on fire, were thrown to encircle Spanish necks; and showers of live coals helped to defeat a general assault which Alva ordered after three days of cannonading.

Due to their heavy losses, the besiegers gave up storming attempts and resorted to gunpowder mines. Here again the civilian populace held its own against trained soldiers. Counter-mines were sunk in the frozen soil, resulting in strange subterranean combats, or explosions which blew up whole parties of assailants. On every occasion when the Spaniards succeeded in opening a breach, they met new works manned in force. Sorties were of almost daily occurrence, and in one great counter-attack the defenders captured seven cannon and many wagonloads of supplies after killing 800 of the enemy. "Never," wrote Alva to his king, "was a place defended with such skill and bravery as Haarlem, either by rebels or men fighting for their lawful Prince!"

The city faced slow starvation when the ice melted, since a local Spanish control of the sea barred any hope of relief. Still, the burghers continued their mad and hopeless resistance until the last rat had been devoured. The enemy not only offered comparatively lenient terms but kept their word by pardoning most of the 35,000 citizens after the execution of leaders and garrison troops. An estimated 12,000 of the victors succumbed to wounds, disease or the gallows during the course of a siege in which 10,000 cannon balls failed to reduce the old-fashioned works.

This costly triumph became the prelude to a succession of sieges distinguished for such stubborn and heroic resistance as to nullify Spanish gains. Antwerp managed to defy Parma's main army for fourteen months, and Ostend set a record for the age with a defense lasting three full years. Nor were the rebels always the losers in these contests of endurance. During a siege of seven weeks the burghers of Alkmaar repulsed all assaults and so threatened enemy communications that a retreat was ordered. Leyden held out for eleven months, suffering all manner of privations before cutting the dikes and flooding the Spaniards out of their positions.

Valor alone does not explain these obstinate defenses. Even more important is the fact that the Dutch, building new works under combat conditions, soon became the masters of Europe in practical fortification.

The glacis, ditch and rampart had remained the elements of the science since proving their merit at the siege of Rhodes. Then as engineering skill advanced, soldiers began to think in terms of integrated systems rather than component parts. It is at this time that we first read of the "trace," or general plan on the ground, in respect to the mutual relation of flank and face.

The ideal of military architects was to obtain the utmost protection combined with defensive fire power. Toward this end the simple star trace led up to the tenaille trace, in which the flanks were placed back to back between the faces. The objection to both was that a certain amount of "dead ground" in the ditch could not be reached by fire from the ramparts. Casemates at the ditch level were deemed unsatisfactory, and engineers eventually found a solution in the bastioned trace, with its flanks directly opposite each other and linked by curtains. This

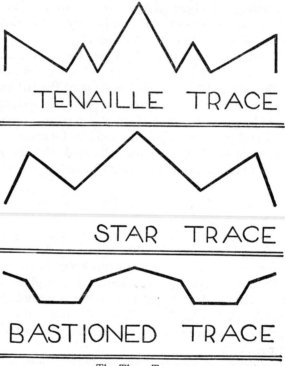

TENAILLE TRACE

STAR TRACE

BASTIONED TRACE

The Three Traces

design permitted the guns of the faces to cover the glacis, while the flanks were in position to rake any section of the ditch.

The bastioned trace remained supreme for a century, with Paciotti's citadel at Antwerp, built in 1568 at a cost of 1,400,000 florins, becoming Europe's first famous example. As time went on, theorists vied with one another in proposing new "systems," all of them based on the mathematical relation of flank, face and curtain. Fortification in detail became increasingly stressed, giving rise to a maze of gates, sally ports, ravelins, demilunes, hornworks and bastions.

As viewed by a modern age, the plans of these fortresses suggest monstrous geometrical flowers thrusting out petals in the form of bristling salients. In its functions each ravelin, bastion, hornwork or demilune might more properly be compared to the watertight compartment of a ship divided by bulkheads. For each was a self-sustaining little fortification with its own garrison, though all were mutually supporting units of the same system.

The Dutch, fighting for their lives, were necessarily more intent upon practice than theory. At the outbreak of the war few cities had completely rebuilt their old works, so that in nearly every siege the rebels simply made the best of existing facilities. The mighty citadel of Antwerp never

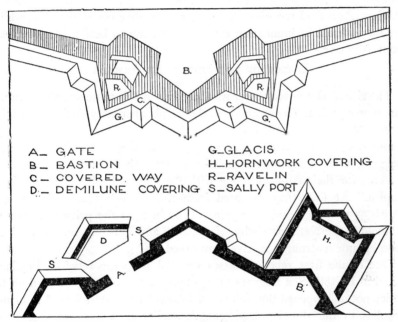

Details of Fortification

had a test, since it served only to shelter the mutineers of the Spanish Fury and was afterwards destroyed by the citizens themselves. At a later date the long resistance of the city was due to a combination of two causes—the utilization of water defenses to limit the attack to a narrow front, and the resourcefulness of the defenders in building new works as old ones were breached. After fourteen months Parma prevailed only by throwing a fortified bridge across the broad Scheldt to cut off all supplies.

Water has always been the greatest ally of the Netherlands in time of war, and nearly every fortress depended on wet ditches that were drained before they froze. At Maestricht, where a garrison of 1,000 held out for four months against an army of 30,000, the river Meuse filled deep moats which limited the approach. Parma's veterans suffered losses of 4,000 in an unsuccessful general assault, carrying a single gate only to be confronted with a new triple-walled ravelin derisively named after the Spanish commander. The besieging army had to surround Maestricht with a chain of eleven forts before starving the city into surrender.

The sea itself protected Ostend, cramping the assailants' front to such an extent that for three years the burghers were able to contrive added barriers. As a final resource, the cutting of the dikes saved Leyden, while the mere threat of inundation caused the enemy to beat a hasty retreat from Alkmaar.

WRECK OF THE INVINCIBLE ARMADA

The rise of Dutch sea power was based upon this same practical genius for improvisation. The enemy held the naval superiority during the early months of the war, and thousands of Zeeland's sailors were driven by commercial ruin into a career of piracy. Calling themselves the Sea Beggars, after a Spanish term of contempt, these outlaws adopted a crescent for their emblem, along with the motto "Rather Turkish than Popish." At first they operated from the English coast, preying on Dutch as well as Spanish shipping. Then in 1572 the privateers won a foothold in the Netherlands by seizing Brill and Flushing, and patriotism soon became a stronger motive than greed.

One of the first rebel successes resulted from the relief of Leyden. Admiral Boisot's Sea Beggars manned an armada of flat-bottomed boats which not only opened the sluices but followed the waters inland to bring supplies to the starving burghers. A similar fleet was raised by the Spaniards, and for days both forces were stranded until an easterly wind combined with the springtide to flood the countryside. The following "naval" combat, fought far from the ocean by flotillas manoeuvring among half-submerged trees and farmhouses, ranks with the skating arquebusiers as a military curiosity. At midnight, during a storm which lit up the turbid waters with lightning flashes, the Sea Beggars, using harpoons as weapons, annihiliated the enemy in pitiless hand-to-hand fighting. Food reached Leyden the next morning, and the city founded its renowned university to commemorate the deliverance.

Boisot won a more decisive victory this same year which marks the beginning of a Dutch naval supremacy lasting throughout the war. Middelburg being besieged by the rebels, Requesens collected a fleet of 75 small vessels to supply the famished garrison. Opposite Romerswael in the mouth of the Scheldt a slightly smaller squadron was drawn up by Boisot in waiting. With the grand commander watching from the shore, the two forces exchanged broadsides at close range before resorting to boarding tactics. In the mêlée the rebels mastered their foemen both in seamanship and savage hand-to-hand combat. Fifteen enemy ships were captured and 1,200 Spaniards slain before the rest of the battered fleet took to flight, abandoning Middelburg to a surrender.

Boisot gained a third triumph in 1574 when his Sea Beggars defeated a Spanish squadron of 22 vessels in the Scheldt, sinking or burning 14 of them. Such successes led to a Dutch control of the inland waters and surrounding sea which seriously affected enemy operations on land.

Queen Elizabeth had meanwhile adopted a policy of making privateering raids serve the purpose of an undeclared war on Philip II. In the New World the king's commerce and treasure fleets were at the mercy of such adventurers as Drake and Hawkins, secretly backed by the queen. And in the Netherlands the mutinies of the king's armies may be traced to English and Dutch interception of ships bringing money lent by Italian bankers. It is not surprising that after a decade of these depredations Philip resolved to destroy Protestant sea power with his Invincible Armada.

England's naval history is often dated from this period, yet the last three centuries of maritime progress cannot be entirely overlooked. As far back as 1214 a fleet of vessels commanded by Hubert de Burgh won a great victory over 80 French ships under a monk named Eustace, noted as a medieval naval tactician. This engagement of sailing ships, as chronicled by Matthew Paris, is said to have been the first recorded instance of manoeuvres to seize the "weather gage"—i. e., the offensive advantages of a wind allowing ships to steer straight for an opponent. The English succeeded in their purpose, bearing down on the enemy with discharges both of arrows and unslaked lime, the latter being borne by the wind to blind opposing seamen. The Frenchmen were speedily boarded, their rigging and halyards cut, and their crews beaten in hand-to-hand combat with losses of 65 ships.

English preference for sail power and vigorous tactics was demonstrated again in 1340, when 200 ships under Edward III annihilated a combined French and Genoese force in the battle of Sluys. In this encounter, the naval prelude to Crécy and Poitiers, the allies lost 25,000 men and nearly their whole fleet.

During the reign of Henry V (1413-1422) not a single galley flew the English flag, though Mediterranean battles were to be decided by oars for two more centuries. The *Jesus*, of 1,000 tons, led a royal fleet which ranged in general from 400 to 520 tons. In preparation for the invasion of France that resulted in the victory of Agincourt, every vessel of 20 tons or more in the kingdom was impressed, composing an armada of 1,400 sail.

Despite their progress in other directions, English seamen were not the first to use cannon. As a consequence, they lost the earliest engagement in which guns played a decisive part—a battle off New Rochelle in 1372, won by French and Spanish ships over a smaller English squadron. A few of the Spanish galleons mounted cannon which gained the credit for the victory; and only five years later the galleys of Genoa and Venice are known to have adopted the new naval weapon.

Organized navies were not to appear for several more centuries, but in late medieval times the larger nations followed England's lead and began to build warships instead of depending on armed merchant vessels in an emergency. Cannon were at first placed in the bows and upper decks to fire over the bulwarks, but the necessity for cover soon suggested portholes. In the Tudor period English warships of four or five masts mounted several tiers of broadside-firing cannon, in addition to enormous forecastles and deckhouses for the fighting crews. A captured Portuguese carrack of this age, carrying 32 brass guns and 700 men, measured 165 feet in length and 47 in beam.

When open hostilities broke out between England and Spain in 1587, Queen Elizabeth could count on some 200 ships of from 100 to 1,000 tons. The *Ark Royal*, flagship of the fleet, was of 800 tons and carried 55 guns. Philip had hoped to build up a larger force with the united resources of Spain and Portugal, but his preparations were interrupted by Sir Francis Drake's audacious raid. Sailing into the harbor of Cadiz, the English explorer destroyed upwards of 10,000 tons of shipping, so that the departure of the Armada had to be postponed until 1588. The total strength then numbered 130 ships, including eight galleys or galleasses, manned by 7,000 sailors and 17,000 soldiers.

In material assets the opponents were well matched, since the Spanish superiority in tonnage was offset by an English advantage in numbers of ships and weight and distribution of armament. But the Armada was simply an army afloat, directed by military minds and depending on seamen only for transport. The English ships were manned by blue-water sailors and commanded by men such as Drake, Howard, Hawkins and Frobisher, whose very names stood for daring on the high seas.

The first skirmishes occurred off the English coast, but the loss of a few ships did not prevent the Armada from proceeding toward Dunkirk, where a Dutch squadron blockaded Parma's main army. The Spaniards planned to convoy these troops across the Channel, while the defenders were equally determined to strike before a junction could take place. In

Spanish Galleon

this purpose the English were successful, and Drake came up with the Armada as it straggled up the Flemish coast near Gravelines.

The following encounter, like so many other great naval clashes, has an historical importance out of proportion to the losses inflicted. Spanish tactics were based upon the recent victory of Lepanto, which had actually been a land battle fought on decks. But while the invaders attempted to close and board, Drake anticipated naval warfare of the future by depending entirely on gunnery. For several hours the English ships kept their distance, firing alternate long-range broadsides which damaged enemy hulls and rigging. Spanish gunnery and seamanship were helpless against such an attack, and only a sudden squall saved 16 ships from being captured.

Indecisive as these results may appear, English strategy won a complete victory when the battered Armada, beset by storms, drove on past Dunkirk and left Parma blockaded with his expeditionary force. The homeward voyage around Scotland resulted in the wreck of many vessels, and only a woeful remnant of the great fleet ever returned safely to Spain.

MAURICE OF NASSAU

The failure was clearly the turning point of the Dutch revolt, since the Invincible Armada had been as much of a threat to the Low Countries as to England. After the disaster Philip ordered Parma's army into France, where it managed only to postpone the collapse of the League for a few years. This interval, following the assassination of William the Silent, gave the United Provinces a breathing spell in which they found new military leadership under his son, Maurice of Nassau.

The transition led straight to independence, for Maurice proved to be not only the greatest general of the war but also the creator of a new school of tactics. Appointed to command at the age of twenty-one, he never arrived at a decision that might be charged to impulse or immaturity. Only once, and then with the utmost reluctance, did he accept a pitched battle, and a successful outcome left him unimpressed. Yet his prudence was combined with a talent for bold and original strokes which became equally important to the final victory.

Maurice began by organizing the first dependable standing army of the rebellion. Using the same human material which had failed his father —German mercenaries plus English, Scottish and Huguenot volunteers —he fared better because of his insistence upon long-term enlistments and the strictest obedience. In order to uphold a rigid discipline, he paid and supplied his troops punctiliously, thus guarding against the usual causes of mutiny or desertion.

Dutch infantry reforms aimed at two definite results: better manoeuvre in the field, and improved siegecraft. Toward these ends the young prince adopted small and supple units as compared to the massive tercios of the enemy. His companies were first cut down from 150 to 115 men, then to only 80 musketeers and pikemen in equal proportions. The width of the front was increased meanwhile by reducing the depth of the "shot" to ten ranks and drilling pikemen to take three-foot intervals instead of standing shoulder to shoulder.

Spanish generals of this period relied on infantry squares in which the musketeers found protection by retiring inside the formation behind an envelope of pikes. Maurice reversed this process by training his musketeers to take refuge outside of the pikemen on both flanks, stationing themselves parallel with the fourth or fifth rank. In this position, guarded on either side by protecting steel points, they continued to fire even during close combat. Their drill developed speed and precision in reloading, while preserving perfect order as the ranks filed back to the rear. Added fire power was realized by arming most of the foot with muskets, though the arquebus still found favor among skirmishers.

Soldiers had written praises of legionary formations for a century, yet it is notable that the new Dutch standing army came nearest to a practical combination of Roman tactics with weapons of gunpowder. Not only were Maurice's regiments comparable in size to the cohort, but he also used a similar checkerwise array in line of battle. The resulting mobility and availability of reserves enabled him to win the foremost Dutch land victory of the war at Nieuport in 1600. In strength the two armies were fairly equal, each being composed of about 10,000 foot and 1,500 cavalry. But the fighting took place among seaside dunes, and the four great blocks of Spanish infantry were at a handicap on broken ground as compared to regiments of only 800 to 1,000 men deployed in "crossbattles." Wide intervals had been left between Dutch units which offered less of a target to the enemy, while Maurice's highly trained musketeers delivered more and steadier volleys. At length the tercios fell into disorder under the punishment and gave away after enduring heavy casualties.

Even this triumph did not swerve the Dutch commander from his conviction that manoeuvre and siegecraft were more important to the cause than winning pitched battles. Before he took command, the fortunes of the rebels had sunk to their lowest ebb. Parma's sieges had been long and costly, but one by one the key towns of the Netherlands fell into his hands—even such vital strongholds as Nymegen, Zutphen, Deventer and Steenwijk. The reduction of these enemy-held cities came first in Maurice's strategy, since he intended his army to be primarily an instrument of siegecraft. This conception represented a break with past traditions, for the Spaniards regarded their sappers and engineers as auxiliaries rather than members in good standing of the military family. Nevertheless, the new Dutch system found vindication as its organizer began taking cities in a few days which had held out for months against the foe.

Breda fell first, being seized by a stratagem in 1590 when Maurice concealed troops in turf barges which passed the unsuspecting sentries.

Within a few more months Dutch effectiveness was better demonstrated by the capture of Zutphen in seven days, closely followed by the successful eleven-day siege of Deventer.

In both cases the prince pushed forward his approaches at astonishing speed, then brought a tremendous concentration of artillery to bear upon one section of the defenses. His opponents, expecting the customary snail's pace of siegecraft, were thrown off balance by a high order of engineering science combined with surprise and velocity. Maurice even made humanity a moral weapon by hanging marauders among his own troops, while protecting the town folk and granting full honors of war to a capitulating garrison. Such treatment, in contrast to enemy abuses, did not fail to influence future operations.

Spanish appeals for help forced the Duke of Parma to leave his Paris campaign and make a feint at the province of Utrecht. The Dutch general was not to be outwitted even by a master at this game. The moment that Parma turned his back, Maurice loaded the entire Dutch army and siege train in barges. Taking advantage of inland waterways, he crossed the country and suddenly appeared before Hulst, near Antwerp, at the opposite end of the Spanish line. This town surrendered in five days before Parma could hasten to its relief; then the prince was off again in his barges, reappearing far to the north in the province of Gelderland. Here he surprised Nymegen, the most important city held by the enemy in this district, and captured it after six days of terrific bombardment.

During the next few years Maurice roamed the Netherlands at will with a compact force seldom exceeding 10,000 men. He kept the initiative throughout these campaigns, regaining provinces as he captured city after city with scarcely a failure. Following Parma's death, other Spanish generals tried to crush the prince in the field, but he did not choose to put a proved strategy to the risk of pitched battle. At every challenge he threw up field fortifications too strong to be stormed, though orthodox soldiers might sneer at "those digging moles whom with undeserved fame the spade hath raised."

Yet the enemy soon had reason to learn that a cautious adversary would not decline a fight on his own terms. The brisk action of Turnhout occurred when the Dutch commander suddenly caught up with unwary foemen after making a forced march of 24 miles in nine hours. A large Spanish detachment was taken completely by surprise and cut to pieces with losses of 3,000 at a trivial cost to the victors.

Maurice did not allow this brilliant little victory to interfere with the methodical reduction of enemy garrisons. In 1592 he captured Steenwijk, which put up a stout defense of thirty-four days. Next he laid siege to Koevorden, a marsh stronghold so difficult of access that the inevitable surrender was deferred for forty-six days. Geertruidenberg and Groningen fell during the following year, and with the capitulation of these fortresses the Spaniards were practically cleared out of the northern provinces.

As the rebels regained control of their cities and communications, the conflict lost all character of an insurrection and began to resemble a war between established nations. In 1596 the seven United Provinces were recognized for the first time as a sovereign state when they concluded the Triple Alliance with England and France. On the other hand, Spanish arms and diplomacy could claim at least a partial victory, having won back the nine southern provinces to their original Catholic and royalist sympathies.

Maurice's successes continued, until by 1597 he had added to his list of captured towns Breedevoort, Oldenzaal, Meurs, Enschede, Ootmarsum and Grol. Three years later he struck deep into enemy territory to win the greatest pitched battle of the war at Nieuport. But the Dutch could no more hope to gain ground in the southern Netherlands than Philip could hope to reconquer his lost provinces. The struggle had already turned into a deadlock which lasted until the truce of 1609, when at last the Spanish monarch virtually conceded the independence of the new republic.

V

GUSTAVUS ADOLPHUS

Here strive God and the devil. If you hold with God, come over to me. If you prefer the devil, you will have to fight me first.

—GUSTAVUS ADOLPHUS

EUROPE remained at peace only nine years, then the whole continent was plunged into the most confused and horrible of all modern wars. The strife flared up from an apparently local dispute. Ferdinand II, Roman emperor, claimed the vacant throne of Bohemia, while the Protestant magnates of that land offered the crown to Ferdinand, the elector palatine. Both candidates resorted to arms in 1618, and within three years the Protestants were badly beaten.

This would seem to have settled the question, but in reality the Thirty Years' War had only begun. For Bohemian rule was merely a side issue in a long-deferred struggle for political, religious and economic power which concerned all Europe.

The Jesuit-influenced Ferdinand, "pattern prince of the Counter-Reformation," had a vast twofold purpose: the suppression of German Protestantism, and the realization of the old Hapsburg dream of actual instead of nominal rule over Central Europe. Thus in the larger sphere were represented the principles of monarchy and militant Catholicism which had lost ground in the last two wars. Spain and Bavaria found it to their interests to support the emperor, who appeared to them to be the champion of unity, of conservatism, and of peace.

On the other side, the strangest of political bedfellows combined to uphold what they believed to be the cause of progress, of balanced power —and of peace. Catholic France and Protestant Sweden joined forces to give the Empire its most persistent opposition, with Bohemia, Denmark, England and the United Provinces taking a lesser part. Even Pope Urban VIII, who was also an Italian prince, extended his tacit blessing to the heretics resisting further Hapsburg expansion.

The Germany of 1618 consisted of 21,000,000 people divided into no less than 2,000 interdependent states, many of which included but a few villages and fields. Only in a single respect were these hundreds of fiefs united in sentiment: they all found the emperor's twin aims contradictory. Catholic princes who might have welcomed the downfall of Protestantism were disturbed by a vigorous concept of Hapsburg authority. Protestant princes who might have supported the Empire were alarmed at the threat to their religious liberties. Hence Germany was fated to be the prize and battleground of the war, her people torn apart by dissension, her lands overrun by the most brutal armies of modern history.

Count Tilly, the "monk in armor" commanding the forces of the Catholic League, proved to be a stern and devout old campaigner who sincerely trusted that he was fighting God's battles. Christian of Anhalt, his opponent of the Protestant Union, could also lay claim to a blameless private life and devotion to his faith. Unfortunately, both sides strained their resources to put large numbers of hired soldiers into the field, and plundering soon became an accepted means of obtaining supplies. In time the very strategy of the war was dictated not by state policy, or even military expediency, but by the amount of food left in a district. Mercenary leaders grew in political stature to be the rivals of princes, and armies were recruited according to a current adage, "Whose house doth burn, must soldier turn!"

Such conditions were foreshadowed in 1620 when the Spanish general Spinola invaded Germany as Tilly defeated Anhalt in Bohemia. Although the Protestants seemed crushed between these two forces, thousands of homeless men were driven by privation to join the beaten army. Nor was its new commander, Count Ernst von Mansfeld, prevented by lack of finances from continuing in the field. A landless adventurer, he led his famished troops into enemy territory, followed by a horde of doxies, thieves and other camp followers. When the German Protestants could no longer put up with him, he ignored his dismissal and raised regiments serving no cause except their own appetites. This outlaw army swept like a swarm of locusts through Alsace and Lorraine, at last finding employment in the United Provinces.

Emperor Ferdinand, whose treasury could not support his ambitions, turned up the very prince of plunderers in Albrecht von Wallenstein, the central figure of Schiller's trilogy. Pale, neurotic, mysterious, the Czech noble won distinction less for generalship than a genius for recruiting and subsisting troops at small expense to his patron. In the fashion of the times, Ferdinand signed a stipulation as to regular pay and supplies; but Wallenstein's methods are suggested by the lines which Schiller put into the mouth of his sinister hero:

> This Emperor
> Did perpetuate by my arm in the Empire
> Such deeds as rightly ne'er should have been done,
> And even the princely mantle that I wear
> I owe to services that are misdeeds.

The depredations of a Mansfeld or Wallenstein were not lacking in a certain vicious effectiveness; for hunger made recruits even in hostile regions, while looting cowed the inhabitants and left nothing to nourish the enemy. But campaigns which might otherwise have been gainful were robbed of their results by this stomach strategy. Opposing armies tended to diverge rather than clash, and operations became increasingly impotent as more and more provinces were stripped of supplies. Europe was at last reaping the whirlwind after a century's dependence on ruffianly mercenaries.

Following the Protestant reverses in Germany and Bohemia, the war entered a diplomatic phase guided by Machiavelli's dictum that "men must either be caressed or be destroyed." Cardinal Richelieu of France, whose policy it was to undermine Hapsburg power, made tentative overtures to England and the United Provinces. Those two countries also drew closer to Denmark, though as rival maritime nations they were too intent on self-interest to build up a strong alliance. Little came of such halfhearted moves, and in the field of action the Protestant states paid the penalty of divided councils. In 1526 Christian IV of Denmark invaded Germany with 25,000 men; and the incredible Mansfeld, who had found Dutch discipline odious, chose this moment to lead a bootless expedition against Vienna. The two ventures were ill-timed and uncooperative, foredoomed to failure for lack of helpful allies. Mansfeld was defeated by Wallenstein in the battle of Dessau Bridge, while only a few months later Tilly routed the troops of the Danish king.

Never did the Hapsburg dream of European and Catholic empire appear closer to reality. As the Danish remnants fell back upon Jutland, the German Protestants were being stripped of lands by the Edict of Restitution. Outside of the Netherlands, where both Maurice of Nassau and Spinola had died of illness after fighting each other to a stalemate, not a single Protestant army of any size remained in action. Tilly and Wallenstein joined forces after their triumphs, and in 1628 nearly 100,000 imperial troops stood on the shores of the Baltic Sea.

A Protestant catastrophe was averted only by the enemy's lack of naval power. Wallenstein had adopted the imposing title "Admiral of the Baltic," but he had no ships with which to attack the Danes in their island refuges and force the capitulation of German coastal cities. Stralsund, though a second-rate fortress, had been so well supplied by Danish and Swedish fleets that the imperial army abandoned a siege lasting seven months. The Danes secured remarkably lenient peace terms from a land-bound foe, and the great turning point of the war came when Sweden intervened.

Gustavus Adolphus and the Swedish Army

Historians are still not agreed as to the motives which impelled this northern realm of only 1,500,000 population to enter the struggle without prospect of worth-while allies. But there seems to be no reason to doubt the causes given by the king to his estates:

Sweden is in danger from the power of the Hapsburg; that is all, but it is enough. That power must be met, swiftly and strongly. The times are bad; the danger is great. It is no moment to ask whether the cost will not be far beyond what we can bear. The fight will be for . . . house and home, for Fatherland and Faith.

Gustavus Adolphus, then thirty-five years old, was no novice at the art of war. Since the age of seventeen he had been successfully campaigning in Norway, Poland, Russia and East Prussia to uphold an aggressive Baltic policy. Still, the twice-wounded royal commander had not won any triumphs to indicate that he would smash the Hapsburg power within thirty months. Nor did his homespun-clad army, in contrast to the plumed and bedizened imperial forces, bear much resemblance to a conquering host. Gustavus cheerfully admitted, "My troops are poor Swedish and Finnish peasant fellows, it's true, rude and ill-dressed; but they smite hard and they shall soon have better clothes."

Perhaps the most hopeful sign was to be found in the fact that a disciplined and regularly paid army had challenged forces whose victories had brought chaos rather than peace. As a poor agricultural country Sweden had an annual revenue of only 12,000,000 rix-dollars (a monetary unit equaling three and a half English shillings), of which five-sevenths had been set aside for the army. This sum supported a total establishment of about 40,000 troops. The human resources of the kingdom were correspondingly limited, and all males between the ages of fifteen and sixty with no settled dwelling owed military duty. Of the remainder, one out of ten was chosen by drawing lots, allowing for exemptions favoring certain trades. Tax reductions were granted to nobles who became officers, and Lutheran clergymen served virtually as recruiting agents.

Gustavus has sometimes been credited with the introduction of uniforms, but Oman records in his *Art of War in the Sixteenth Century* that white coats were worn by some English companies during the reign of Henry VIII. Red and blue coats were later assigned to shire levies to distinguish the troops of various districts; and an order of 1584 anticipated the modern science of camouflage by prescribing a "sad green color" for contingents about to take part in forest fighting.

The Swedish regiments were known by silk ensigns of white, blood-red, yellow, green, old blue and black in solid colors with embroidered emblems and mottoes. With the exception of a uniformed royal bodyguard, foot soldiers wore a sleeveless peasant's smock, loose knee breeches and woolen stockings, all of homespun drab. This dress caused them to be described as "ill-appearing clods," but its warmth permitted sustained winter operations.

The king found armor irksome to an old wound, and his example was followed by musketeers who relied only on a pot-helmet. The growing efficiency of firearms, combined with the gruesome surgery of the day, led foot soldiers of all countries to question whether the weight of the breastplate could be justified by the protection it afforded. Thus the Thirty Years' War dates the modern decline of armor, though pikemen and heavy cavalrymen continued for many more years to wear the cuirass.

Taking the lead in this movement, the Swedes held an advantage in mobility over their opponents. Further gains resulted from a discipline which prohibited not only looting but also the usual rabble of camp followers. One imperial army of 30,000 fighting men is said to have been encumbered by 140,000 noncombatants—women, children and cripples who had been reduced to vice or beggary by past devastations. The Swedish army permitted a man's wife and family to follow the regiment, but thieves and harlots were drummed out of camp. The children attended regimental schools, and a special soldiers' prayer book was printed in Stockholm to be issued to all ranks. The king himself, as the author of hymns sung in Sweden to this day, often knelt on the ground to lead regular morning and evening worship.

Theft, looting, cowardice and violence to women were punished by hanging, while minor culprits might be shackled or made to "ride the wooden horse" with a musket tied to each foot. Accused men had the right of trial by court-martial and final appeal to the monarch. The troops were provisioned from magazines established at points along the route and kept filled both by imports from Sweden and enforced contributions from the countryside. A staff of commissaries distributed supplies, and sutlers were licensed to set up booths for the sale of small luxuries. Huts or tents sheltered the troops in fortified camps, though as a rule the army was quartered on the populace of towns. According to regulations, a soldier could demand bed, salt and vinegar, in addition to the right of cooking at his host's fire. All other exactions were regarded as looting.

This system, which originated for the most part with Gustavus, enabled him to cut down his baggage train to an unprecedented extent. Yet despite his strict orders against plundering, the king pursued a systematic and successful policy of "making war nourish war." Subsidies from allies as well as payments from conquered districts footed a large part of the cost, so that within two years Sweden cut down her military budget from five-sevenths to one-sixth of the national income.

Considering that a military instrument represents the spirit as well as sinew of a nation, it is not surprising to find that the northern kingdom had made astonishing progress in all directions. As late as 1535 Gustavus I ruled a rude and semibarbarous people who waylaid merchants venturing within the borders. The founder of the Vasa line did his own clerical work for lack of able assistants; and the low standard of learning among the nobility forced him to hire foreign adventurers as ambassadors. He introduced Protestantism during his long reign, made trade treaties with surrounding nations and built up a Baltic commerce.

From these beginnings the realm developed so rapidly that his grandson Gustavus Adolphus, born thirty-four years after his death, was educated in one of the most cultured courts of Europe. Instructed in seven languages, as well as the royal trades of war and diplomacy, the youth became ruler at the age of seventeen of a small Baltic empire. Nevertheless, Sweden remained essentially a middle-class country with a high degree of parliamentary government for that day. Four estates, *bourgeoisie* as well as nobles, clergy and peasants, had some voice in national decisions; and the power of the Vasa kings did not ignore individual rights. Thus after deciding on war against the emperor, Gustavus Adolphus submitted the question to the council, "I did not call you together because I had any doubt in my mind, but in order that you might enjoy the freedom of opposing me if you wished."

This sturdy and reciprocal spirit built up the first truly national army of modern times—the world's first modern fighting machine as compared to the tradition-ridden hosts of mercenaries supported by every other nation of Europe. All four estates were represented in its ranks very much as in the national life. A council of officers acting as a general staff planned every campaign, though the final decision lay with the king as commander in chief. Merit gained promotion more often than seniority or birth; and a twenty-six-year-old former page, Lennart Torstensson, became chief of artillery, while the command of the cavalry fell to a rough old professional soldier, Johan Banér.

"The Swedes do not defend their men with walls," ran a contemporary saying; "the Swedes defend their walls with men." As the foremost representative of the nation's manhood, Gustavus Adolphus occupied a unique and paradoxical position. He championed a revolution against the divine right of kings, yet no Hapsburg lord of Europe could have boasted a tenth of the worship accorded him by a liberty-loving people. He became the first great exponent of scientific warfare in the modern age, yet no more Homeric figure has ever emerged from the pages of military history. Everywhere, on the march, about the camp, in the thick of the cavalry mêlée, the green feather and worn leather buff coat of the king were always visible to his men. The blond and burly king was to them a symbol not only of the cause and the faith but also of a stirring national adventure. For the king, like any other Swede of his day, loved nothing more than a good fight.

Gustavus' Military Reforms

Preparations began in the homeland. The nation's young industries, both government armories and private firms, were pushed to the limit to supply equipment. As an example of military demands in a day of hand labor, it has been calculated that an infantry regiment of 576 muskets used 3,000 pounds of gunpowder a month, 2,400 of lead and 3,400 of match.

Late in May, 1630 Gustavus handed over the government to an unusually capable prime minister, Axel Oxenstiern, and sailed with an expeditionary force of 13,000 troops—92 companies of foot and 116 of horse. The audacity of the attempt was made possible by Swedish control of the sea lanes. Throughout the coming campaigns the Royal Navy of 54 vessels, with the *Mercury* of 32 guns as flagship, maintained unbroken communications.

Legend has it that after setting foot on German soil the king set the example by kneeling in thanksgiving before seizing a spade. At any rate the Swedes proved from the beginning to be a digging as well as praying army. Gustavus had been taught his first lessons of war by veterans of the Netherlands campaigns, and the Dutch prince became his leading model. Not only were Swedish organization, discipline and pay influenced by Maurice's reforms, but the Dutch engineering system was copied almost in detail. Hence a large corps of sappers accompanied the expeditionary force, while troops of all arms, including even the cavalry, had been drilled in pontoon-bridging and throwing up field fortifications.

Despite his admiration for Maurice, the Swedish monarch proved to be no dull imitator. He saw with ready perception that the prince's cavalry—German mercenaries practicing the caracole—had been the weakest link in the Dutch army. Gustavus preferred the hard-riding shock tactics introduced by the Huguenots, and his horsemen were likewise trained to charge home with the sword after firing their pistols. Nor did he overlook the Huguenot precept of mounting foot soldiers to take part in long raids, for in the Swedish army we find the first example of a trained dragoon corps. A tactical hybrid, this force consisted of men who fought as light horse on the attack and dismounted infantrymen on the defensive. They wore little or no armor and carried a carbine and saber.

The availability of such units, useful for raids, skirmishing or foraging, allowed Gustavus to organize his regular cavalry entirely for shock tactics. With the pistol and sword as weapons, and the helmet and cuirass as protection, the Swedish troopers advanced at a trot in a three-rank formation of two lines. A total of 115 men composed a company, and the average field strength of a regiment totaled 800 to 1,000.

During his Polish wars Gustavus had already made important changes in infantry tactics. In 1526 his armorers invented a lighter musket with mechanical improvements permitting faster loading by a single soldier.

The heavy iron fork was replaced by a thin spike, known as a "Swedish feather," which served both as a rest and a double-pointed palisade stake to ward off enemy cavalry. These reductions in weight were achieved without much sacrifice of fire power, so that both the arquebus and old unwieldy musket were superseded by a matchlock taking a one-ounce ball.

Gustavus does not appear to have been the inventor of paper cartridges, but he was probably first to use them as standard equipment. Fifteen such prepared charges, together with spare powder and ball, were carried by the Swedish soldier in a cloth bandolier slung across his chest. When reloading, he had only to bite off the end of a cartridge and push it home with the ramrod, thus saving many motions and making sure of more effective fire.

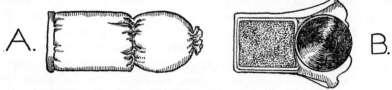

The First Cartridge: (A) Paper Wrapper; (B) Cross Section

With his duties simplified and his burden lessened, the musketeer could now carry a saber. This weapon, in addition to the double-pointed "Swedish feather," provided the regimental "shot" for the first time with some means of defense against shock attack. The eighteen-foot pike was no longer so necessary as a supporting arm, and Gustavus reduced the length of the shaft to eleven feet, while also decreasing the number of pikemen in an infantry unit.

In the imperial armies a proportion of about four pikemen to three musketeers had been the rule. The king reversed this ratio by arming 75 men with muskets and 59 with pikes in a company of 150 foot, the rest being petty or commissioned officers. Further gains in fire power were realized by the introduction of an entirely new tactical conception known as the brigade order.

For a century the depth of the infantry unit had depended on the time it took the musketeer or arquebusier to file back to the rear, while protected by pikemen, and recharge his piece. Due to intensive drill, Maurice of Nassau managed to cut down his array to ten ranks. Gustavus, profiting by mechanical improvements, trained the Swedish "shot" to advance in an open order of six ranks which closed up into three on the firing line. When delivering a volley the front rank knelt and the other two stood. thus adding to musketry effect while lessening confusion.

The brigade, as the basis of the new method, was a tactical rather than administrative unit. It might be composed of one full-sized or two weak regiments, with numbers ranging from 1,000 to 1,500 or more. Weight had little importance as compared to the mobility gained by combining small battle groups of musketeers and pikemen in a wedge-shaped formation. Lord Reay, a contemporary English observer, has left diagrams showing a brigade of 1,512 foot drawn up in three lines. The three groups of pikemen, totaling 648, form a protective triangle. Behind them, in the intervals, and on the flanks, are 864 musketeers in five groups occupying positions from which they can sally forth, deploy, fire, and retire once more within the formation to reload.

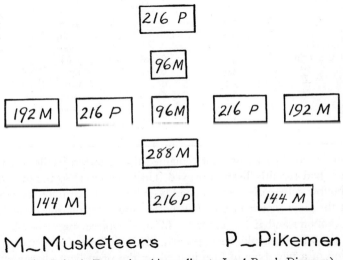

M_Musketeers   P_Pikemen

Swedish Brigade Formation (According to Lord Reay's Diagram)

This was one plan for drawing up the mobile human bastion. But there appears to have been no sacred rule, and the positions as well as proportions were varied to meet different tactical problems. The advantages of such flexibility are obvious, enabling the brigade to pour in more and deadlier volleys than a like number of imperialists massed in a square.

So far, with few exceptions, Swedish military reforms owed in some measure to the experiments of La Noue, Coligny, Henry of Navarre and Maurice of Nassau. As a talented organizer, Gustavus began where his predecessors left off, taking the best of their ideas and combining them with his own. In his development of field artillery, however, the king had few precedents to guide him. Since the introduction of that arm by Ján

Žižka, very little tactical progress had been made in 200 years as compared to improvements in ordnance and ammunition. Hence a wider variety of guns existed than the soldiers of Europe knew how to use effectively, as is evident from a seventeenth century English list:

Name of Piece	Caliber inches	Length of Piece ft. in.		Weight of Metal pounds	Weight of Shot pounds
Cannon Royal	8.5	8	6	8000	66
Cannon	8	"	"	6000	60
Cannon Serpentine	7	"	"	5500	53.5
Bastard Cannon	7	"	"	4500	41
Demi-Cannon	6.6	11	0	4000	33
Cannon Petro	6	"	"	4000	25
Culverin	5.2	10	11	4500	18
Basilisk	5	"	"	4000	15
Demi-Culverin	4	"	"	3400	10
Bastard Culverin	4	8	6	3000	11
Saker	3.6	6	11	1400	6
Minion	3.4	6	6	1050	4
Falcon	2.5	6	0	680	2
Falconet	2	3	9	500	1.5
Serpentine	1.5	"	"	400	.8
Robinet	1	"	"	300	.5

Although solid cast-iron shot remained the usual projectile, the primitive shell had recently been improved. Up to about 1580 the gunpowder in the hollow sphere of sheet iron had been ignited separately. The gunner lighted the slow match in the shell before touching off the main charge in the cannon; and if the latter misfired, the piece might be blown up before the missile could be extracted. This objection was met by the invention of a new type of fuse ignited by the propellent charge, and by the end of the century such projectiles were being commonly used in sieges.

The earliest hand grenades also made their appearance, being provided with an ordinary slow match. The soldier lighted the fuse and whirled the two-pound missile about his head to speed ignition before throwing. Accidents were frequent, and even such tactical pioneers as Gustavus seem to have regarded the grenade as an experiment.

Late improvements in case shot found a more cordial reception, for the effectiveness had been increased in 1573 by the invention of a bursting charge which filled half the container. Both the modern time fuse and percussion fuse were proposed at this period, but the ideas proved too advanced for the chemistry of their day.

All of these innovations came in time to help the Dutch win their independence. With water transportation at his disposal, Maurice was able to bring into action an unusually heavy artillery train which raised siegecraft from a venture into a science. No such gains were made on the battlefield for the simple reason that a practical field gun had not yet appeared. The Duke of Ferrara overcame this difficulty by manoeuvre, and Henry of Navarre showed uncommon skill in placing his small batteries. But these examples were wasted on professional gunners who continued to use an assortment of pieces too heavy for field purposes. They usually placed the artillery in front of the army to fire a few preliminary salvos; then as the action developed, the guns remained silent and stationary, a prey to capture or recapture according to the changing fortunes of battle.

Gustavus approached the problem during his Polish wars by inventing a light gun consisting of a copper tube reinforced by iron bands, rope set in cement and a final binding of sole leather. The tube was made to screw in and out, since it became heated by a few discharges and had to be removed for cooling. Without the carriage the "leather cannon" weighed only 90 pounds, but it soon had to be discarded as too fragile for field use.

The king continued his experiments, discovering that advances in metallurgy had made possible a shorter cast-iron piece without any sacrifice of effect or safety. In 1624 he recalled most of his old ordnance to be recast into four-pounders of 2.6 inches caliber, 3 feet, 10 inches in length and 400 pounds in weight. Four men or a single horse could handle the new gun in action, though the four-pounders used by other armies weighed upwards of half a ton.

This was the first regimental piece of military history, and Gustavus developed the first artillery cartridge as its ammunition—a thin-turned wooden case holding a prepared charge wired to the ball. Due to convenience in loading, the Swedish four-pounder could be discharged eight times while the best musketeer fired six volleys. Each infantry regiment of 1,000 men brought its own gun into action, while at a later date the proportion rose to a gun for every 500 troops.

Thus in 1630, nearly four centuries after Roger Bacon's announcement, the artillery at last showed signs of becoming a recognized arm of the military service. Even Gustavus could not rid himself entirely of the hired gunners and carriers who had so long stultified field tactics, but at least he placed soldiers in command and introduced a high degree of co-ordination with other arms.

THE INVASION OF GERMANY

Upon learning that the Swedish king had crossed the Baltic with only 13,000 men, Emperor Ferdinand is said to have exclaimed, "So we have another little enemy!" The invaders could not have been taken very seriously, for they were not opposed during the first six months by the main armies of either Tilly or Wallenstein. During this period Gustavus devoted himself to a methodical warfare of position, taking some 80 strong places in Pomerania and Mecklenburg. In several instances a storm was necessary, but a majority of the towns surrendered after appearances had been saved by a show of force.

The apathy of the German Protestants disappointed the king during these months. In Leipzig 62 princes of the reformed faith met to discuss policies, but they did not once mention the name of Gustavus during eight weeks of debates.

His first help came from Catholic France. It is a tribute to Richelieu's perception that he recognized the Swedish monarch's ability before proofs had been given on the battlefield. A French observer had accompanied the army since its landing, and in 1631 Louis XIII agreed to pay the invaders a lump sum of 120,000 rix-dollars, in addition to annual subsidies of 400,000 for the next six years. In return, Gustavus contracted to keep at least 30,000 foot and 6,000 horse in the field, while promising to respect the Catholic faith in districts where it was already established.

Emperor Ferdinand also aided indirectly by dismissing Wallenstein, whose ambitions alarmed Germany's Catholic princes. Some 40,000 of his troops were turned over to Tilly, bringing that general's total up to 70,000, while enough imperialists enlisted in the Swedish ranks to form several new regiments. Despite their recent habits, these volunteers served Gustavus well, for the German soldier by this time had become more concerned with subsistence than causes.

Lack of numbers remained the king's greatest handicap as Tilly advanced in the spring of 1631. Gustavus, hoping to avoid battle and draw the League commander into a campaign of manoeuvre, moved against the outstanding fortresses of Mecklenburg. New Brandenburg, Prenzlau, Treptau and Klempenau fell in rapid succession. Frankfort-on-Oder was stormed and 3,000 of the garrison put to the sword in reprisal for an imperialist massacre. Landsberg capitulated next after a ten days' blockade, and good Catholics prayed to be delivered "from the devil and the Swedes, the Finns and the Lapps." Even the German Protestants had reason to feel uneasy when Gustavus marched on Berlin, then a wooden town of 10,000 people, and forced the Lutheran elector to give possession of Spandau, his strongest fortress.

Nevertheless, the campaign failed of its main purpose. Tilly refused to be distracted from his siege of Magdeburg, largest and most prosperous city in northern Germany, which Gustavus had sworn to protect. The king thus had to choose between abandoning his Protestant allies or risking the entire cause in a battle against perilous odds.

Instead of coming at once to the relief, he negotiated with timorous Protestant princes for passage through Saxony. The delay proved fatal, for Magdeburg was stormed, sacked and burned as the imperial troops got out of control, only 5,000 out of 30,000 inhabitants being spared in a massacre which filled the Elbe with hacked corpses. Most of the survivors found themselves impressed into virtual slavery, and Vienna heard the *Te Deum* without joy as the full extent of the horror became known.

The Protestant world clamored for vengeance, but Gustavus, his army further weakened by an epidemic, could only retire sorrowfully to Werben and take a defensive stand in an entrenched camp on the banks of the Elbe. Tilly followed and Swedish field fortifications were put to the test when his infantry twice attacked the maze of earthworks. For the first time the new regimental gun gave bloody proof of its merit as Tilly's veterans twice swarmed up to the redoubts, only to be cut down in swaths by case shot at murderous range. After being twice repulsed, the imperialists fell back in confusion, leaving 6,000 dead and wounded out of an assaulting force of 22,000.

Mecklenburg was too wasted by the summer's campaigns to support an army, so with reluctance Tilly led his hungry troops into unravaged Saxony. As he had feared, their excesses drove the elector into an alliance with Gustavus, who derived enough reinforcements to offer battle at last. The Swedish army of 26,000, plus 16,000 Saxons, immediately marched on Leipzig, which had been taken with an enormous plunder by the imperialists. Tilly would have preferred to retreat, but realizing that his men might mutiny rather than abandon their booty, he chose an advantageous position on a plain six miles from the city.

The Battle of Breitenfeld

The seventy-two-year-old Walloon general, who had learned his trade under Parma, drew up his 35,000 troops on a two-mile front in two lines of infantry squares averaging about 1,500 each. Also in accordance with Spanish custom, he posted his cavalry on both wings and the artillery along the front. A gentle downward slope favored the imperialists, and both the sun and the wind from the dusty plain were in the faces of the enemy.

The September morning was already bright and hot when the allies appeared. Gustavus' homespun-clad men, who had slept in plowed fields, presented a rustic appearance as compared to the brilliant cloaks and plumes of the Saxon regiments. Nevertheless, Swedish fighting qualities

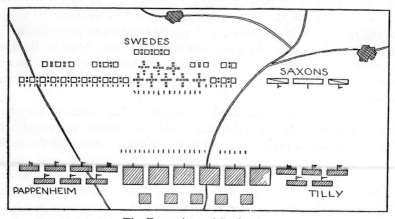

The Formations of Breitenfeld

were exhibited when Tilly sent out 2,000 cavalrymen as skirmishers. At once the king's new-formed dragoon corps went into action, supported by Scots mercenaries, and drove the imperialists back.

In full view of the foe Gustavus drew up his men in two lines and a reserve, the Swedes to the right of the Saxons. Tilly's veterans gaped at the strange chessboard formation which took shape as the brigades fell into position. Never before had soldiers of this age seen cavalry, artillery, pikemen and musketeers supporting each other in self-sustained little combat groups, but more surprises were in store as an artillery duel began at noon. Not only did the 100 Swedish cannon outnumber those of Tilly, but the mobility and quick-firing qualities of the regimental gun resulted in three shots to his one. Soon the battered imperialists could stand no more of this unequal punishment, and the cavalry of both wings spurred forward.

On the allied left Tilly's advance won an immediate and inspiring success. The untried Saxon troops first wavered as the Croat horsemen came on in an avalanche of crimson cloaks and gleaming blades. Then despite the efforts of the young nobles to rally them, the whole 16,000 broke into a blind rout when the enemy turned their own cannon against them. Gustavus and his Swedes were left alone to contend against a numerical superiority.

On the other side of the field the imperialists met a sterner reception. The fiery Count Pappenheim, whose 5,000 Black Cuirassiers were reckoned the best cavalry in Europe, swung far out to the left and thundered down upon the Swedish flank. Gustavus' alternate combat groups of musketeers and horsemen had been drilled to meet such an emergency; they wheeled about coolly so that the second line stood at right angles with the first, forming a V-shaped salient of defense. Pappenheim, the scarred veteran of a hundred charges, endured the worst half hour of his life as his men dashed themselves to pieces against this flexible human redoubt. The Swedish regimental guns poured a hail of death into his massed squadrons; the musketeers darted out, deploying, kneeling, firing, retiring to reload; the horsemen counterattacked, then fell back upon the protection of their own cannon and musketeers—all three arms fought together with bewildering speed and precision.

Six more times Pappenheim re-formed the dwindling remnants of the Black Cuirassiers and returned to the attack. When the seventh attempt shattered against still unbroken formations, the surviving imperialists took to flight, seeking only to escape the pursuing Swedish cavalry.

In the centre meanwhile Tilly led an oblique advance of infantry squares, swinging rightward to profit from the Saxon rout which had laid bare Gustavus' left flank. It was a timely movement, but again the flexibility of the Swedish order allowed musketeers and horsemen to change front and await the onslaught. The king himself, helmetless and wearing only his buff coat, rode up and down the lines, shouting hoarse encouragement as he galloped with reddened saber into every mêlée. The infantry brigades, clashing with the enemy's massive squares, kept up an unfailing rattle of musketry with deadly effect. Torstensson's guns tore great holes in the imperial front, and soon he had recaptured the Saxon cannon, using them to enfilade the opposing line. Caught between these two fires, the imperialists were beginning to break when Gustavus dealt them a last crushing blow with his reserve cavalry after a sweep around the left. Tilly's infantry and horse were cut off from each other, and as dusk fell over the field the Swedes rode into the milling fugitives to inflict "Magdeburg quarter."

Of the 35,000 imperial troops, 7,000 were captured and 12,000 killed or severely wounded. But even these figures do not tell the full story of the disaster; for Tilly, who suffered three wounds, could rally only 600 survivors, and Pappenheim 1,400. All of their baggage and artillery fell into the hands of victors whose losses amounted to about 2,100.

Both in tactical and historical respects Breitenfeld ranks as one of history's most decisive battles. In the fashion of the times Tilly had launched more or less separate attacks not only of his wings and centre but also of his cavalry, infantry and artillery. Each of these assaults, though pushed by veteran troops with desperate tenacity, failed against a fighting machine in which each tactical part had been geared to the operation of the whole. A new era of warfare had dawned, and henceforward Gustavus Adolphus was to be the preceptor of every thoughtful soldier.

VI

THE THIRTY YEARS' WAR

Ay, our life
Was an unresting march; like blustering winds,
Homeless, we stormed across the war-shaken earth.
—SCHILLER'S *Wallenstein*

VIENNA was "struck dumb with fright" by the news of Breitenfeld, while the Protestant world rejoiced with a fervor that knew no bounds. To add to the exultation, the tidings came that the Dutch had sunk an entire Spanish fleet preparing to land an army in Zeeland. This victory proved to be the turning point of the war in the Netherlands, where Maurice of Nassau had shown little of his old vigor in the campaigns just before his death. His brother Frederick Henry succeeded him, and the republic entered upon a series of sea triumphs under Admiral Martin Tromp.

Like Hannibal after Cannae, Gustavus had placed himself in a position to choose between an assault on the head or the limbs of a reeling enemy. And like the Carthaginian, he took the less dramatic of the alternatives by turning his back on the capital to strike at the richest provinces. His decision was guided partly by distrust of his Saxon allies, partly by a desire to succor co-religionists while wintering his troops at imperial expense. This course did not please Richelieu, who considered southwest Germany his own sphere of influence. Nevertheless, Gustavus marched westward from Breitenfeld, receiving the capitulation of Erfurt, then southward into the "Priests' Alley" of Franconia.

Königshofen, the key city, surrendered after a few well-aimed shots from Torstensson's siege guns. The capitulation of Würzburg followed shortly; then a general panic set in as the Catholic lords and bishops sent their valuables to the supposedly impregnable fortress of Marienburg. Here the Swedes and Scots mercenaries carried the works in a bloody two-day storm, taking a tremendous booty after putting the garrison to the sword.

This was the one serious lapse from discipline, and a majority of the hostile towns welcomed victors who were able to guarantee religious toleration and immunity from violence. Still, it could not be said that Gustavus proved an easy taskmaster. With grim humor he demanded from each city at least the contribution it had hitherto been paying the Catholic League, which was never a trifling sum. Thus Mainz was assessed 80,000 talers, in addition to another 80,000 collected equally from the Jesuits and Catholic clergy, while at a later date Munich had to raise no less than a quarter of a million. Already Germans were beginning to wonder, as historians have wondered ever since, as to the ultimate designs of a conqueror who addressed small Protestant states:

Up for the Gospel, those of you who believe in it, or it will be the worse for you! I shall treat neutrality as equivalent to a declaration of war against me.

Before going into winter quarters at Mainz, the king had made himself master of nearly all Germany. Within eighteen months his little expeditionary force had swelled into an army of 108,000, of which 18,000 troops stood on the Rhine, 20,000 on the Main, 8,000 in Hesse, 13,000 on the Elbe, 17,000 in Mecklenburg, 20,000 in Bohemia and 12,000 in various garrisons. Less than a quarter of the total were Swedes, for so successfully had war nourished war that within another year the king expected to double his numbers at small expense to the realm.

Tilly and Pappenheim had of course been able to recruit new forces soon after their defeat. Homeless men flocked to their standards as readily as the 7.000 imperialists captured at Breitenfeld took up arms for Gustavus. Meanwhile, Emperor Ferdinand had found it necessary to swallow his pride and beg Wallenstein to raise a second army.

Since his dismissal that uncrowned king had shut himself up at Prague, surrounded by courtiers and astrologers. As lord of Friedland, a duchy composed of lands given him in reward for past services, he became perhaps the first man in Europe to grasp the idea of the modern totalitarian state, organized for war. Alternating fantastic prizes and penalties, Wallenstein put the entire population to work at weaving clothing, preserving food, manufacturing arms. Roads, mills, foundries, granaries and warehouses multiplied until, within two years, the little state had stored up enough military supplies for a kingdom.

It was as a rival prince rather than loyal noble that Wallenstein received his emperor's overtures. The terms of their agreement have never been fully revealed, but the adventurer apparently gained absolute control of the army, the power to conclude treaties, and the promise of such Hapsburg lands as Bohemia and Brandenburg with the title of elector. Seldom in history has a soldier of fortune carried insolence so far.

Gustavus, faced with two hostile armies, broke up winter quarters in March, 1632. Singling out Tilly for his first campaign, he crossed the Danube unopposed and marched to the Lech, where the League general and Maximilian of Bavaria had fortified the steep heights overlooking the river. It had not occurred to them that the king would dare to storm such a position, but overnight he built a bridge of boats and sent across 300 Finns under cover of a smoke screen created by burning damp straw. Working under heavy fire, these picked troops succeeded in throwing up earthworks, then following a six-hour artillery duel in which Gustavus himself helped to aim the regimental guns. Tilly fell mortally wounded as the enemy won a foothold, and after enduring 3,000 casualties the Bavarian king saved the army at the expense of its baggage and guns. The Swedes came on in relentless pursuit, being cheated of an annihilation only by a windstorm which left the road blocked with uprooted trees.

The imperial remnants were too shattered to put up further resistance in the field. Augsburg, Landshut, Mosburg, Freising and finally Munich surrendered to the invaders, who acquired vast military stores as well as enforced contributions of gold. In this campaign the Swedish monarch began to be troubled with serious indiscipline among the German mercenaries who now made up two-thirds of his numbers. "They are no Swedes who commit these crimes, but you Germans yourselves," he declared. "Had I known that you were a people so wanting in natural affections for your own country, I would never have saddled a horse for your sakes, much less imperiled my life and my crown and my brave Swedes and Finns."

Wallenstein perhaps understood the Germans better. As the first modern leader to exploit their credulity, obedience and hunger for leadership, he soon built up a personal following of 40,000 veteran troops. After ravaging Saxony with fire and sword, this formidable force marched southward toward Nuremberg to meet Gustavus and his army of 20,000.

Despite the difference in numbers the Swedish king would not have shirked a fight to save his Protestant allies in the city. Wallenstein, however, had planned a more passive and sinister campaign. First laying waste the countryside for miles around, he entrenched on a steep ridge called the Alte Veste, allowing his opponent a choice between starving or abandoning Nuremberg. All summer the two armies faced each other

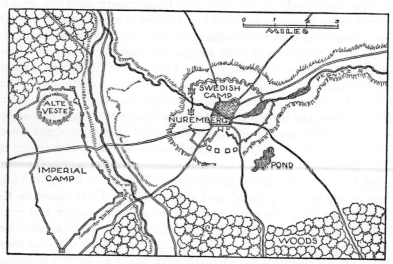

The Nuremberg Campaign

with no other activities than those of the burial parties who disposed of scores of corpses every day. Wallenstein had the advantage in this duel of privation because of his reserve supplies in Friedland. By September the king had been reduced to such straits that he summoned reinforcements and ordered an assault.

For ten hours his best storm troops, the Swedes and Scots and Finns, charged up the ridge time after time under a murderous fire. Thrice they gained enough temporary positions to bring up a few cannon, but at dusk Gustavus had to concede a repulse after leaving 4,000 dead on the Alte Veste. Assigning a strong garrison to the defense of the city, he led his gaunt army away for recuperation. That same week Wallenstein also broke up camp, having been able to starve just three days longer.

THE FOG OF LÜTZEN

Although the imperial forces resumed their ravages in Saxony, Gustavus had not given up hope of bringing them to a decisive battle. In probably the greatest forced march of a slow-motion war he made the 250 miles from Bavaria to Erfurt in 18 days, causing Wallenstein to exclaim, "The Swedes came as if they had flown."

The imperial commander, accustomed to more deliberate movements, concluded that his adversary would pause for rest and reinforcements. Accordingly he allowed Pappenheim to detach himself with 8,000 troops, principally cavalry, for a plundering expedition against Halle. Gustavus saw his opportunity and pressed forward to surprise Wallenstein at Lützen, fifteen miles west of Leipzig. Given only two more hours of daylight, the Swedes might have attacked before the enemy was prepared; but the early autumn dusk intervened, and all that night the two armies waited in line of battle.

Accounts of the affair are contradictory, though it would appear that the Swedes were drawn up in essentially the formations of Breitenfeld. Gustavus took charge of the right wing, placing the left under Bernard of Saxe-Weimar, a German Protestant nobleman who won a reputation for bravery at the Alte Veste.

Wallenstein, whose couriers were hastening after Pappenheim with orders for his return, formed the remaining 20,000 imperialists behind earthworks and a shallow drainage ditch. The cavalry was divided between the two wings, one of which rested on a stream and the other on the town. The centre consisted of four great infantry squares in "lozenge formation," while a fifth supported the cavalry of the right wing. Parties of skirmishers took cover in the ditch, while as usual the artillery was ranged along the front.

Seldom has the outcome of a battle been more affected by visibility. A paltry sun rose out of the mist, shedding its watery light over the Saxon flatlands; then the November fog combined with the smoke from the burning town to shroud the field. All day the two armies groped for each other in a murky hell lit by stabs of flame from the guns, and the recollection of the participants seems to have been correspondingly clouded.

The morning was far along before the gunners could see well enough to begin their preliminary cannonade. The Swedish brigades advanced in the centre, driving back the skirmishers and capturing most of the imperial cannon. They swept on to attack the infantry squares at close quarters, losing contact for the moment with cavalrymen who had dismounted to lead their horses across the ditch. Wallenstein's squadrons took advantage of the confusion to pour into the gap, and this threat brought Gustavus himself galloping from the right wing with mounted reinforcements. His countercharge made such headway that the Swedish heavy guns were brought up at close range. The enemy had begun to waver all along the line when the word spread through both armies that the king's riderless horse had been seen.

At once the Swedish advance lost momentum. The imperialists had recovered their lost guns as Bernard took command and ordered a new advance. A second time the battle rolled back over the same ground, and Wallenstein's artillery changed hands again before Pappenheim arrived on the field with the first units of his 8,000 fresh troops. This became the most desperate moment of all for the exhausted brigades. Fighting doggedly, they were forced back across the ditch to their original starting point. There was little thought of tactics on either side, for the battle now consisted of combats between small groups contending in the fog and smoke. Darkness had almost blotted out the scene when Bernard, though painfully wounded, rallied his men for a final effort that drove the imperialists from the field.

No accurate estimate exists of losses which were frightful on both sides. Pappenheim fell mortally wounded and some of the imperial captains found their companies reduced to two or three survivors. With all their artillery and baggage lost, the tatters of the army could doubtless have been annihilated by victors strong enough to pursue. But several of the Swedish brigades had lost five-sixths of their strength, and late that night the weary survivors discovered the riddled body of the king under a heap of enemy slain.

Whatever may have been the real motives of Gustavus Adolphus, his death left Germany in chaos. Whether he was the Protestant liberator or merely a conqueror aspiring to the Hapsburg powers, the king had supplied a leadership which no rival could approach. After his thirty months had ended, the fog of Lützen seemed to have settled permanently over Europe, plunging the whole continent into a twilight in which men struggled without much hope or aim for fifteen more years.

Wallenstein ventured, failed and paid with his life. Broken in nerve and health after Lützen, he began negotiations with the Swedish generals to betray the emperor. But at last his stars had deserted him, and Ferdinand rewarded the assassins who provided a violent death not included in the adventurer's horoscope.

Europe's confusion increased as Bernard of Saxe-Weimar developed into a lesser Wallenstein. After Lützen, which he claimed as a personal triumph, the German duke demanded to be recognized as generalissimo of the Swedish forces. This title was denied him, but his influence prevailed when the main army of 25,000 men attacked 30,000 entrenched Spaniards and imperialists at Nördlingen in 1634. According to Bernard's plan, the troops were divided for a combined frontal and flank assault on the strong enemy positions. Both attempts failed as a consequence of bad timing and direction, though the Swedes charged fifteen times against a hill which dominated the opposing line. After the final repulse they lost the initiative to a counterattacking enemy who profited by their division to turn the affair into an utter rout.

At Nördlingen perished almost the last remnants of the disciplined national army which Gustavus had brought from the homeland. Thereafter the forces of the kingdom were Swedish in name only, being composed of the usual mixture of German, Scottish, English, Irish, Croatian, French and Polish mercenaries. By this time soldiers fought for a general rather than a cause or country, and it had become the universal practice for prisoners to take the pay of their captors.

Nördlingen appeared at first to have canceled even Breitenfeld, so complete was the Swedish disaster. In the next battle of any consequence, however, the tables were turned by old Johan Banér, former cavalry commander under Gustavus. Again the imperialists had entrenched behind batteries on a hill. Again the Swedish forces were divided, as if for a storm; but after luring the enemy regiments out on the plain, Banér fell upon them from three directions to inflict a terrible defeat. All the imperial stores and cannon fell into his hands as the beaten army broke up in a general flight.

Yet Wittstock proved no more decisive than Nördlingen toward ending the war. After eighteen years of strife Germany had become a pit of despair in which a losing commander could always recruit another army. Wild beasts lurked in the blackened ruins of towns whose inhabitants had taken to the woods like wild beasts. Plague and famine carried off thousands of victims every month, in addition to those maimed and butchered by a wanton soldiery. Cannibalism grew so rife that bodies were torn from the gallows by hunger-maddened folk, and throughout the Rhineland the very graveyards were guarded because of the traffic in human flesh.

The Swedes alone were charged by their foes with the destruction of 1,500 towns and 18,000 villages. Bohemia claimed the loss of three-fourths of her people during the war, Nassau of four-fifths, Württemberg of five-sixths. Bavaria estimated that 80,000 families had been wiped out, and only one-fiftieth of the inhabitants are said to have survived in the worst devastated regions of the Palatinate. No doubt these figures were exaggerated, yet a modern historian of the war, C. V. Wedgwood, has placed Germany's total deaths at 7,500,000, or more than a third of the entire population.

Although the moral ravages cannot be calculated, a whole generation came up from birth to maturity in an appalling atmosphere of filth, disease, starvation and violence. The lords and commanders themselves set a vicious example. Following in the footsteps of Mansfeld and Wallenstein, Bernard insisted on Alsace as his reward, and Banér considered the enemy's bribe of an imperial title. Such precepts of greed and treachery were reflected in the ranks by mutinies or wholesale desertions to the foe. Often the prevailing reign of force crumbled into anarchy as unattached bands of armed men wandered about the country with no other aim than filling their pouches.

Among the other inevitable penalties were the ruin of trade and agriculture, the enforced changes of religious and political belief, the breaking up of family ties and the thousands of illegitimate births. Whether these results have had any effect on Germany's development since 1648 has always been a matter of conjecture. At any rate it is certain that no other European people of modern centuries has ever had such a concentrated experience of war's brutality.

THE BATTLE OF ROCROI

Millions of common folk had been praying all their lives for peace, yet it remained to the interests of statesmen to prolong the strife. In 1635 matters took a more decisive turn when France passed from covert to open hostilities. The struggle now developed into a candid contest for power between the House of Bourbon and the Spanish and Austrian Hapsburgs. Meanwhile, the spiritual issues of the Counter-Reformation were being thrust to the background by an emerging age of science and philosophy—the age of Grotius, Hobbes and Descartes, of Harvey, Kepler and Galileo.

It was, in fact, virtually a new war which had flamed up from the ashes of the old. One by one, nearly all the old leaders had followed Mansfeld, Gustavus and Wallenstein to the grave—Banér, Bernard of Saxe-Weimar, Cardinal Richelieu, Emperor Ferdinand. The fighting had spread from Germany to Italy, France, Spain, Switzerland, Denmark and the Netherlands. And now Louis XIII lay on his deathbed as the reorganized French army faced its first great test under the command of a young man born in 1621, when the dreary struggle was already three years old.

The brief career of the twenty-two-year-old Duke of Enghien did not recommend him for such a responsibility. A great-grandson of the reckless Huguenot leader, and soon himself to be known as Prince of Condé upon inheriting the title, he had been suspected of madness as a boy. Moody and impulsive by turn, young Enghien overruled generals old enough to be his father when he decided on battle at Rocroi against the best infantry left in Europe.

The Spanish general Melo, with 9,000 horse and 18,000 foot, had been besieging this important frontier fortress on the line of the Meuse. Enghien came to the relief with 7,000 horse and 16,000 foot. First he had a problem of approach, since the Flemish village was surrounded by woods and marshes except for a single narrow defile. The risks of a trap were obvious, but against the advice of his lieutenants the young French commander led his army through safely and formed for battle.

Melo, who expected 6,000 reinforcements in addition to already superior numbers, may have been too confident of crushing his opponent to offer any premature resistance. The Spanish infantry, carrying on the traditions set by Parma and Spinola, had yet to suffer a serious reverse during the war. Past operations had taught the tercios only scorn for the hastily raised mercenaries of other armies, and Melo placed his main trust in the 10,000 Spanish veterans of his centre. Behind them, as a reserve, he drew up 8,000 allied foot in two lines, while dividing his cavalry about equally between the two wings.

Enghien adopted practically the same formations—infantry in the centre, cavalry on the wings—with only the difference that his foot units averaged much smaller than the Spanish squares. But the French troops were not as contemptible as the enemy supposed, for Richelieu's last gift to his country had been the organization of a disciplined national army modeled frankly after the Swedish system. First weeding out alien hirelings as rapidly as possible, the cardinal offered inducements to Frenchmen to take up a military career—young peasants and artisans in the ranks, impoverished young nobles as officers. Camp followers met with severe discouragement, and prisoners were either exchanged or sent to the galleys instead of being taken into service according to the general custom. After a decade of this rebuilding process the army had developed a new pride and cohesion which faced a first major trial on the plain of Rocroi.

The action opened with cavalry clashes on both wings. Enghien, leading eight squadrons on the French right, scattered the Spanish left, only to discover that his own horsemen of the left had been hurled back upon their reserves. It was necessary for the young commander to hasten to the aid of these routed troops, but instead of circling behind his own centre he spurred on recklessly to cut a path through the Spanish lines. Striking the tercios in flank, he drove a wedge between them and the German, Italian and Walloon foot of the reserve. The allied infantry broke before this surprise assault, and without drawing rein Enghien continued entirely around the field to charge the victorious enemy horsemen from the rear.

This stroke of genius decided the battle. The Spanish squadrons, caught between two fires, followed their comrades of the other wing in flight, leaving the infantry of the centre hemmed in from three sides. The veterans of the tercios were still able to repulse the French foot, but repeated cavalry charges on both flanks made their situation hopeless. Dusk had dimmed the field when the Spanish commanders asked for quarter. Enghien came forward to grant terms just as several Spanish companies mistook their orders and opened fire again. At once the French rank and file suspected treachery and fell upon the tercios with a fury which their officers could not check. When darkness put an end to the massacre, the flower of the Spanish army had been cut down with losses of 7,000 slain and 6,000 prisoners, nearly all of whom were wounded.

Within a week, as hoofs pounded to every corner of Europe with the news, diplomats sensed that Rocroi had been one of those rare battles which date a new era in international affairs. Not only had the century-old Spanish tradition received a deathblow, but too few veterans were left to train new tercios according to the old standards. This disaster, following the sinking of a fleet of 77 vessels by Admiral Tromp in 1639, made it evident that the long period of Spanish greatness was drawing to an end. On the other hand, the victors paid with 4,000 casualties for a triumph establishing a French military superiority which endured with few breaks for the next two hundred years. Their young leader won a reputation which was to make him celebrated as the Great Condé, and the masterly handling of his squadrons ushered in a new emphasis on cavalry tactics.

The Daimonism of Lennart Torstensson

Although Gustavus had been in his grave for a decade, the spirit of his reforms influenced the last years of the war. The French had profited from lessons in organization; and meanwhile a Swedish revival, based upon mobility and discipline, led to victories as effective even if not as dazzling as Rocroi.

Lennart Torstensson, former artillery general, became commander-in-chief after Banér's death. Taking leave of a war-weary and nearly bankrupt kingdom in 1641, he arrived in Germany with 7,000 raw Swedish recruits only to be confronted with a mutiny of the main field force. Torstensson himself, one of the few survivors among the great names, had grown prematurely old and sick and disillusioned. As if the evil of the war had entered into his own flesh, he was so racked by gout that he could neither walk nor sign his name. Despite these handicaps, he managed to put down the mutiny. Then after a period of reorganization, he invaded Saxony, Moravia, Denmark and Bohemia, winning four victories which took him nearly to the gates of Vienna.

Second only to the conquests of Gustavus, no greater military achievement was recorded during the thirty years. But Torstensson would have none of his old master's moderation, and his operations were based upon a destructiveness which has gained him but a grudging renown. From the outset he made no pretense of paying troops, thus legalizing a long existing situation by inviting his men to plunder. This principle brought into his ranks the worst ruffians of every nationality, and Torstensson relied on the lash, the rack and the gallows to enforce a discipline of terror. Pitiless to the "licensed robbers" who served and hated him, he showed himself equally pitiless to the enemy and noncombatants. Tilly could plead that his men got out of hand at Magdeburg, but by his own cool admission Torstensson's sack of Kremsier was comparable in ferocity.

Behind him, as he marched through Saxony in 1642, he left a trail of blazing villages. His men plundered even the dead, ripping open tombs and stripping the rings from ancient skeletons. The crippled commander drove them relentlessly as he rode in a cumbrous litter and planned the rapid and unpredictable movements which confused every opponent. At Schweidnitz the Saxon army made a stand and was routed by a few swift blows, leaving its artillery on the field. Torstensson lunged into Moravia, burning, torturing and pillaging as he went. Olmütz fell and the Swedish mercenaries advanced within twenty-five miles of Vienna before Archduke Leopold could assemble a force of superior numbers. Tempering audacity with prudence, Torstensson fell back into Saxony. He had already invested Leipzig when the archduke caught up with him, and on the field of Breitenfeld a second Swedish triumph was won by smashing cavalry charges. The invalid himself led the victorious squadrons, clinging to the reins with pain-knotted hands as his horsemen shattered the enemy's left wing and separated the right from the centre. Leopold barely escaped with his life after losing half his army either as slain or prisoners who reinforced their captors.

Torstensson invaded Moravia again before being ordered against Denmark, which, like Saxony, had become a Hapsburg ally during the last years of the war. Sweeping across Germany at his usual disconcerting speed, he paralyzed the Danish land defenses within a few months by manoeuvre alone. The emperor had sent an army to attack him from the rear; but after leaving a force to hold Denmark, the Swedish general eluded his foes and struck at the undefended Hapsburg lands in Germany. When at last the imperialists overtook him they met a decisive defeat at Juterbog, and Torstensson broke into Bohemia with his ravages.

Here another army of imperialists and Bavarians awaited his advance at Jankau, only a few miles from Ján Zižka's old citadel of Tabor. Both in quality and numbers this was the strongest force Torstensson had encountered, yet his fourth victory became the most complete of his career. First confusing and separating his adversaries by manoeuvres under cover of the woods, he fell upon their detachments one by one until the day became an imperial catastrophe. The outcome has been compared with Rocroi, for at Jankau in 1645 perished nearly the whole of the veteran Bavarian cavalry, which had been considered as valuable to the Hapsburg cause as the Spanish foot.

Although the way to Vienna lay open, Torstensson had pushed himself and his army so mercilessly that both collapsed within sight of the imperial city. One end of the Danube bridge had been seized when the bleak heart and wasted body of the leader broke down just as his ruffianly troops reached the limits of exhaustion. The attempt was abandoned, and after resigning his command the sick man returned to Sweden as indifferent to his new honors as to the curses heaped upon him by half of Europe.

TURENNE'S STRATEGY

On all fronts—Germany, Bohemia, Denmark, Italy, Flanders, Spain— the Hapsburgs and their allies were beaten but not yet crushed. Peace negotiations had begun as early as 1636, but France and Sweden made no secret of their desire to prolong the conflict in order to demand better terms. This policy, foreshadowing the "armed diplomacy" of the coming century, was carried out in the operations of the Vicomte de Turenne, whose studious generalship dominated the final campaigns.

The tact, patience and serenity of the thirty-two-year-old French commander came as a relief after Torstensson's cold ferocity. A younger son of the Huguenot family of Bouillon, which ruled the little principality of Sedan, Turenne had been apprenticed at the age of fourteen to learn the trade of war from his uncle, Maurice of Nassau. Beginning as a private in the Netherlands in 1626, he rose by sober merit within five years to a colonel's commission under Richelieu. Thus by 1643, upon taking over the French forces on the Rhine, he had gained a reputation as a trustworthy plodder rather than a brash genius of the Enghien type.

The young duke had scaled the heights of military glory in a few hours, while Turenne took such a beating at Marienburg, his first battle as an independent commander, that he thought of resigning. The contrast between the colleagues was further exhibited in 1644 when Enghien brought the flower of the French army to reinforce Turenne's motley assortment of mercenaries. As a Catholic and prince of the blood he had the final decision; and after overruling the older soldier he ordered an attack of the combined forces on the Bavarian field fortifications near Frieburg. The assault developed into a three-day battle in which the French finally captured the enemy positions at the cost of half their troops. This Pyrrhic victory was followed a year later by an even more disastrous triumph on the field of Nördlingen, the scene of Bernard's defeat in 1634. Again Turenne would have preferred a campaign of manoeuvre, but Enghien dreamed of another Rocroi as he sent the French infantry up the slope against the Bavarian batteries. As it proved, the affair came perilously near to being another Nördlingen; for only the death of Franz von Mercy, the able enemy commander, saved the French from a repulse. The defenders were able to fall back in good order to prepared positions, leaving Enghien a hill occupied with losses of 5,500 out of 7,000 veteran foot.

Ill health caused his retirement soon afterwards, and Turenne became free to develop his own ideas. As human material he inherited mercenaries of a dozen nationalities, the débris of every field since Lützen. Mutiny was one of the first problems to be met, since tax-burdened France could not pay her troops regularly. A year of reorganization proved necessary, then during the summer of 1646 his manoeuvres reduced Bavaria without a battle, causing the king to sue for an armistice.

There was nothing spectacular about such methods as compared to the bloody onslaughts of the past decade. Where other generals strove to duplicate the victories, Turenne had studied in detail the troop movements of Maurice and Gustavus. Avoiding encounters unless he possessed an overwhelming advantage, he relied upon caution, surprise and logistic precision to manoeuvre the enemy into wasted territory while retaining his own sources of supply. The confusion of the imperialists opened the way to Munich and gave Turenne an opportunity to unite with the Swedish general Wrangel. Meeting little opposition, the two armies subjected Bavaria to a devastation which forced Maximilian to ask terms.

The rulers of Europe observed with interest this new type of generalship. Turenne cut a modest figure as compared to a Bernard or a Wallenstein—but he did not dictate policies or set himself up as a rival of princes. He seemed a soldier of limited talents as compared to an Enghien or a Torstensson—but he knew how to win campaigns while shunning the pitched battles which had often proved as punishing to the victors as the vanquished. He was, in short, a painstaking master of small war; and in 1648 his strategy brought the struggle to a close with an almost bloodless triumph of manoeuvre.

Maximilian having broken his armistice, Turenne united with Wrangel to drive the 30,000 enemy troops back to the Danube. At the village of Zusmarshausen the imperial field marshal Melander, commanding the last Hapsburg army left in Germany, was surprised in wooded country and threatened with annihilation. He fell mortally wounded while trying to extricate himself, and the Italian general Monticuculli saved the hopelessly demoralized remnants only by sacrificing their guns and supplies.

After Zusmarshausen the end was inevitable. Enghien, now Prince of Condé, won another victory over the Spaniards at Lens; and the Swedes were besieging Prague when the emperor at last agreed to sign the peace. But after three decades of chaos Europe could not hope to regain tranquillity so easily. The Continent swarmed with unemployed mercenaries, so that nearly six years passed before the last alien garrison could safely be withdrawn from Germany. England and Scotland were in the midst of a rebellion, and even in victorious France the *Te Deums* had scarcely been heard before the streets were barricaded for the civil war of the Fronde.

VII

ENGLAND'S NEW MODEL

I have not the particular shining bauble or feather in my
cap for crowds to gaze at or kneel to, but I have power
and resolution for foes to tremble at.

—OLIVER CROMWELL

ON THE Continent, generally speaking, the rebels had been the underdogs throughout the religious wars. Against them were arrayed all the moral and material resources accumulated for generations by Church and State.

In England this situation was reversed. There the century-old triumph of Protestantism had become so complete that the religious struggle derived from various shades of dissenting opinion. On the political side, the divine right of kings had been challenged with such success that Parliament wielded more actual power than the crown. From the beginning the rebels controlled the navy, the finances, the large cities and most of the militia bands. Moreover, they had as powerful allies the Covenanters, those zealous disciples of John Knox who ruled Scotland after repudiating the king.

Law, sentiment and tradition were the mainstays of a monarchy fighting for its life, but the weight of these moral factors was not to be despised. "If," said the Earl of Manchester, "we beat the king ninety and nine times, yet he is king still, and so will his posterity be after him; but if the king beats us then we shall all be hanged, and our posterity made slaves."

The advantages of Parliament may be further discounted by the fact that England possessed no standing army to compare with the establishments of Europe. Both Charles I and Parliament had to depend on armed rustics and tradesmen; and the first clashes between these inept bands were of course decided more by chance than skill.

In contrast to Continental nations, England had long been a land barren of military tradition. This lack may be charged in part to a feeling of insular security, since the navy was never suffered to fall into the same decline. An even greater cause may be traced to that deep-seated distrust of standing armies which has colored the history of the English-speaking peoples.

This prejudice had its inception at an early date. The first brilliant victories of the Hundred Years' War were followed by a long-drawn stalemate ending in defeat and disillusionment. Such glories as were afforded by the Wars of the Roses had likewise been forgotten by generations which remembered the slaughter and privations. The end of both struggles found the island kingdom overrun with unemployed fighting men who had little choice but to resort to crime or beggary. These broken-down warriors became an added affront to the honest yeoman when he considered the possibilities of a tyrant using them for purposes of civil oppression.

Shakespeare, drawing his characters from the life about him, doubtless reflected popular sentiment when he portrayed the soldiery of his day with such incomparable satire and contempt. Almost without exception the warriors of his pages—Nym and Falstaff, Pistole and Bardolph—are transparent rogues, frauds or swaggerers. His opinion of the profession as a whole is perhaps best summed up by the famous lines:

> Then the soldier
> Full of strange oaths and bearded like the pard;
> Jealous in honor, sudden and quick in quarrel,
> Seeking the bubble reputation
> Even in the cannon's mouth.

But Shakespeare does not confine himself to satire. He is also worthy of consideration as a military historian, for we have no better account of contemporary recruiting methods than Falstaff's confession in *King Henry IV*:

I have misused the king's press damnably. I have got . . . such a commodity of warm slaves, as had as lieve hear the devil as a drum; such as fear the report of a caliver worse than a struck fowl or a hurt wild duck. I pressed me none but such toasts-and-butter, with hearts in their bellies no bigger than pins' heads, and they have bought out their services; and now my whole charge consists of ancients, corporals, lieutenants, gentlemen of companies, slaves as ragged as Lazarus in the painted cloth, where the glutton's dogs licked his sores; and such indeed as were never soldiers, but discarded unjust serving men, younger sons to younger brothers, revolted tapsters and ostlers trade-fallen, the cankers of a calm world and a long peace. . . .

These were the pressed men who fought England's foreign wars. For home defense the kingdom relied on even more dubious troops—the local militia bands whose entire training amounted to one day's drill each month. Such military amateurs inspired the ridicule of a later poet, John Dryden, who came up to manhood during the Great Rebellion:

> The country rings around with loud alarms,
> And raw in fields the rude militia swarms;
> Mouths without hands; maintained at vast expense,
> In peace a charge, in war a weak defense;
> Stout once a month they march, a blust'ring band,
> And ever, but in times of need, at hand.

The want of trained soldiers in 1642 did not prevent the opposing forces from rushing blindly at each other to seek a decision. Every war waged by recent civilians has an inevitable first encounter of this sort—an overconfident collision whose only decisive result is to teach sober men of both sides the need for discipline.

The Royalists numbered 13,000, the Parliamentarians 20,000. Neither army had any military objective in view; and the quality of the intelligence may be judged by the fact that the rival forces lost contact for ten days, though seldom more than twenty miles apart in open country. At last the desired clash took place at Edgehill, near Oxford. After forfeiting the advantages of a dawn surprise, the Royalist cavalry prevailed on both wings, only to lose all discipline and cohesion during the pursuit. This left the infantry of the two centres to carry on a confused struggle which ended in a stalemate at dusk. The king's losses had been the heavier, but he claimed a victory by virtue of his possession of the field.

That evening Charles knighted as one of his heroes a squire who had not heard of the war until the day before, when the Royal Army interrupted his fox-hunting. The incident is typical of the state of the nation at Edgehill, since it has been estimated that only one-fortieth of the population took an active part even in the later stages. The conflict was waged by determined minorities on both sides, and after the first outburst of volunteering both were to resort to the press gang to fill their ranks.

THE RISE OF OLIVER CROMWELL

The tremendous influence of Gustavus Adolphus on his age is evident from the beginning in the tactics of the Great Rebellion. Every seventeenth century gentleman considered the science of arms a part of his education; and the publication of the *Swedish Intelligencer*—to this day one of the best sources—had given Englishmen a good idea of the reforms which revolutionized warfare on the Continent.

As early as Edgehill the infantry of both sides had adopted the Swedish six-rank formation, deploying into three on the firing line and delivering their volley while standing, stooping and kneeling. The proportion of musketeers to pikemen was never less than two to one; and lightly armed dragoons, protected by a padded buff coat, served as scouts and skirmishers.

From start to finish the infantry remained the most neglected arm of the war. Only the lowest elements of the population were pressed into service; they were poorly paid and trained as compared to the cavalry, and their vulnerability to cavalry flank attacks shaped the entire course of the struggle.

At Breitenfeld, it will be recalled, Gustavus' brigades of foot were able to change front and shatter Pappenheim's horse. At Rocroi the famous Spanish tercios held out for hours against encircling foemen. But every battle of the Great Rebellion reveals the impotence of the infantry in any situation demanding manoeuvre. Once assailed from the flank, the foot of either side was soon reduced to helplessness.

Nor had Swedish ordnance reforms made headway in England. Both armies were encumbered with pieces too heavy for manoeuvre, and only in sieges did the artillery play a decisive part.

By a process of elimination the cavalry became the all-important arm. Its methods were borrowed directly from Gustavus Adolphus—the same three-rank line, the same dependence on close formations and the discharge of pistols followed by the shock of steel. A troop of 60 sabers, under a captain, cornet and quartermaster, was the unit; and seven troops, or about 420 sabers, made up a regiment under a colonel.

Unfortunately, wages were often in arrears, especially in the Royalist army, with the usual consequences of plunder and indiscipline. Despite this factor, English operations were distinguished for the most part by a moderation unknown in the Thirty Years' War. The rights of civilians and prisoners were generally respected, and commanders at least made a sincere effort to prohibit looting and devastation.

The lack of generalship became painfully apparent in the early clashes. Charles himself possessed no military ability to match his personal courage, but at Edgehill he discovered a dashing cavalry leader in his nephew, Prince Rupert. Only twenty-three, this young noble was the son of the first woman of the age—Elizabeth of Bohemia, whose intellect won the praises of Descartes in his dedication of *Principles of Philosophy*. Artist and scientist as well as swashbuckler, Rupert has been credited with introducing the mezzotint process of engraving, and his "Head of St. John the Baptist" remains one of the best early examples.

More important to the Rebellion, he proved to be a born cavalry commander, as fiery as Pappenheim and a great deal more intelligent. His shock tactics, driven home with naked steel at Edgehill, not only made chaff of the roundhead horsemen but also taught a lesson to the beaten enemy. For on that field an unknown Parliamentary captain, Oliver Cromwell, perceived that Rupert's tactics could be improved and used against him.

It would be hard to imagine a more unpromising candidate for military glory than this solid English squire at the age of forty-three. Rather above the average of Parliamentary gentry in family, wealth and education, he affected a rustic plainness of dress and manners which deceived his contemporaries. His sole distinction had been election to the House of Commons; and afterwards few of his fellow legislators could recall the "swollen and reddish countenance" of the member from Huntington.

A lifelong farmer with no experience of war, Cromwell at least had a conviction that sound breeding principles could be applied to an army as well as a flock or herd. This meant starting with the very best human stock: ". . . not old decayed serving men, and such kind of fellows" but "men of a spirit . . . that is likely to go as far as gentlemen will go, or else you will be beaten still."

After Edgehill he dropped out of sight for some months. In the eastern counties, where he was personally known, Cromwell devoted the winter to recruiting and training cavalrymen up to his own rigid standards. This interlude became a turning point in the war, since by spring his 400 horsemen were the most disciplined body in the Parliamentary ranks. As a colonel Cromwell repulsed twice his own numbers in the minor cavalry action of Grantham, and a few weeks later his troopers won an even more important clash at Winceby. But these were only the preliminary tests, for in the battle of Marston Moor (July, 1644) the Cambridgeshire squire gained a national renown.

Even after two years of strife the amateurish qualities of both armies were evident on this field. There had been no real strategic plan on either side, so that the struggle actually consisted of a dozen separate little wars waged in as many districts. Men deserted wholesale when asked to serve outside their own shires, and thousands of troops were immobilized to garrison petty strongholds in every corner of the realm.

An equal lack of tactical direction was shown when the two forces faced each other all afternoon at Marston Moor without either daring to seize the initiative. Finally, more by accident than design, the battle began in the summer dusk; and the first advantage went to the Royalists, despite the fact that Prince Rupert's 18,000 troops faced 25,000 foemen. The cavalry of both Parliamentary wings recoiled, and on the right the reverse turned into a complete rout. Afterwards the king's horse wheeled in and struck the flank of the shaken infantry, creating such havoc that the battle appeared to have been decided.

The three main Parliamentary generals fled, and only Oliver Cromwell, commanding 4,000 horsemen on the left wing, refused to abandon hope. He had also been driven back in the general Royalist advance, suffering a slight wound in a mêlée which threw his squadrons into confusion. But at the moment of disaster his superior discipline enabled him to re-form for a counterattack. Rupert's troopers had become badly disorganized by their supposed triumph, and the unexpected onslaught sent them streaming back in full flight. Cromwell then fell savagely upon the flank and rear of the Royalist infantry, and before dark the forces of Parliament snatched a complete victory from the jaws of defeat.

The glory was deservedly shared by David Leslie, whose allied Scottish horse contributed in large measure. But any doubts as to Cromwell's ability were removed a year later, when at Naseby he won another victory which virtually ended the First Civil War.

The engagement became almost a replica of Marston Moor. Again the Royalists were outnumbered, having only 9,500 troops to Parliament's 13,000. Again they won a seeming triumph when their infantry broke the opposing centre as Rupert's right-wing cavalry swept aside all opposition. Meanwhile, the only Parliamentary stroke had been delivered by Lieutenant-General Cromwell, whose squadrons routed the horse on the other side of the field.

At this crisis the discipline of the two cavalry leaders decided the day.

Rupert as usual overshot the mark, being unable to re-form his men after their impetuous charge. Cromwell, who had drilled his troops to overcome this very weakness, sent a few squadrons in pursuit and returned with his main body to strike the rear of the enemy centre. Before the prince could come to the rescue, the Royalist foot had been annihilated and the battle lost. Half of the beaten army was captured, and after Naseby Charles lacked the resources to put another force into the field.

MONTROSE'S CAMPAIGNS IN SCOTLAND

Not until the eve of disaster had the unhappy Stuart monarch discovered a general who might perhaps have saved his cause. And then, characteristically, Charles neglected the opportunity.

Only a prophet, to be sure, could have foretold that the Marquis of Montrose would destroy six armies in a year and master all Scotland. At the age of thirty-two he remained a dilettante in politics, poetry and war. A graduate of St. Andrews, he had traveled on the Continent and gained a broader outlook than most of his Scottish peers, but his military talents were as hidden as Cromwell's.

Marston Moor had been lost before he received a general's commission and powers to deal with the northern rebels. These powers, unfortunately, did not include material aid of any sort. When he recrossed the border, disguised as a groom, he had only two followers and four lean nags with which to combat an enemy holding every town north of the Tweed. In such a venture he had need of the philosophy expressed in his own spirited lines:

> He either fears his fate too much,
> Or his deserts are small,
> That dares not put it to the touch,
> To win or lose it all.

The political situation in Scotland was not lacking in possibilities. Although the Covenanters ruled the land, supporting Cromwell against the king, Montrose knew that thousands of malcontents awaited a leader. He himself had been a Covenanter until concluding that those religious zealots were tyrants; and allegiances changed so rapidly that Cromwell was soon to destroy the Scots who were now his allies.

Unlike England, the poor and sparsely settled northern kingdom owed its existence to a vigorous military tradition. Three centuries had passed since Bannockburn, yet every Scot still committed to memory the testament in which the victor left his descendants a national system of warfare:

> On fut suld be all Scottis weire,
> By hyll and mosse themselff to reare.
> Lat woods for wallis be bow and speire,
> That innymeis do them na deire.
> In strait placis gar keip all store,
> And byrnen ye planeland thaim before.
> Thane sall thai pass away in haist
> When that thai find na thing but waist.
> With wyles and waykings of the nyght
> And mekill noyis maid on hyght,
> Thaim sall ye turnen with gret affrai,
> As thai ware chassit with swerd away.
> This is the consall and intent
> Of gud King Robert's testiment.

In other words, Bruce urged his countrymen to take cover in hills, woods and swamps rather than trusting to walls; to lay waste the fertile and level plains which might nourish an invader; and to place their dependence in ambushes, stratagems and night surprises instead of formal operations. Better military advice could not have been given to a vastly outnumbered people threatened by powerful neighbors across a border which provided no natural defenses.

With few and grievous exceptions, King Robert's Testament had been faithfully observed. As a result Scotland preserved her national existence long after Ireland, protected by the sea, had fallen to the English conqueror.

During the past century, indeed, arms had become a trade in the northern kingdom. When not engaged in plundering raids on other clans, the kilted warriors hired out by the thousands, like the Swiss of old, to fight the battles of other countries. Enough Scots to form a brigade served under Gustavus Adolphus, and the French standing army always included large contingents of those rugged mercenaries.

As king's commander, Montrose soon found himself in the paradoxical position of being hunted down as a rebel by the rebels against royal authority. It appeared certain that no quarter would be given his recruits, since the Covenanters had already excommunicated him from the Kirk and put a price on his head.

His new status as outlaw acted like a magnet on the anarchy of Scotland. At once he was joined by a thousand Macdonald warriors—half-savage Catholic tribesmen from Ulster and the Western Isles—who needed a leader as much as Montrose needed troops. Loot-lured Highlanders brought his numbers up to 2,700; and six weeks after Marston Moor he turned without hesitation to attack the nearest of three Covenant armies advancing on him.

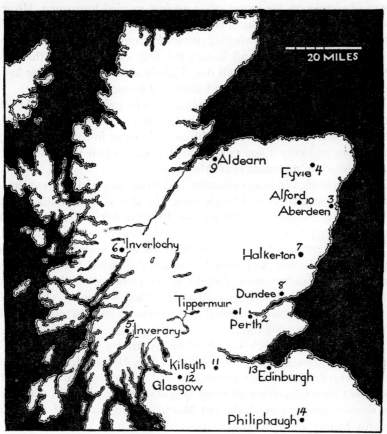

Montrose's Year of Miracles

The ensuing battle, fought at Tippermuir on September 1, 1644, doubtless ranks as the last victory of history won by a European army with battle-axes and arrows. Montrose's "cavalry" consisted of the four nags with which he had entered Scotland; and only a single round of ammunition was available for the few matchlocks in his ranks.

The Covenanters under Lord Elcho numbered 7,000 well-armed foot, 700 horse and nine pieces of light artillery. The rebels were not first-rate troops, however, most of them having been lately raised in the Lowland towns.

As Elcho advanced, his men were brought to a standstill by a volley of stone and arrows, mingled with scattered musket shots. Then Montrose ordered an immediate assault on the enemy's centre, staking his hopes of victory on the moral effect against untried townsmen. He was not disappointed, for the lean, red-shanked men of the hills raced to the attack with wild yells, swinging their claymores and Lochaber axes. They crumpled the Lowland line at the first shock, turning the affair into a bloody pursuit lasting all day. Elcho's army scattered after losses of 2,000 slain, while Montrose had scarcely a dozen casualties.

He took the town of Perth that night with its military spoils. At once the Highlanders left for the hills to deposit their loot, according to a custom as much to be reckoned with as their valor in battle. The king's commander had only 1,500 troops left, but within two weeks he won a second victory in a combat near Aberdeen.

Lord Burleigh, his next opponent, had 2,000 foot and 500 cavalry of much better quality than Elcho's men. He also showed more tactical wisdom by attempting a feint on the Royalist left while sending his horsemen along a sunken road for a surprise attack on the other wing.

Montrose now had 70 horse, and his men were armed with firearms captured from the foe. As Burleigh's cavalry debouched from the sunken road, the Highlanders opened ranks to let them gallop through, then wheeled to empty their saddles with a point-blank volley from both sides. Meanwhile, the clansmen routed the Covenant foot to complete the annihilation of the rebel force.

After a three-day sack of Aberdeen by troops who could not be checked, Montrose's strength dwindled to 800. His third adversary, the Earl of Argyll, headed the Covenant as well as Scotland's most powerful clan, the Campbells. With an army of 4,000 he succeeded in surprising the Royalist remnant at Fyvie, but Montrose again came off victorious. Against five-to-one odds, usually reserved for Gaelic ballad rather than reality, he took a defensive position on a hill between bogs, concealing his reserve force under cover of the scrub. Argyll advanced into the tactical trap, and a premature volley of the Highlanders spoiled Montrose's plans for destroying another Covenant army. The enemy managed to retire intact, and the losses of neither side were heavy.

Instead of seeking a new test, Montrose launched a strategic campaign which was never surpassed in the Great Rebellion. Leaving the rebel leader waiting with his superior army, he vanished into the mountains to strike at the very citadel of the Covenant, the Campbell lands on the other side of Scotland.

The clan capital, Inveraray, had no thought of danger until the Royalist leader descended upon it out of a gray December sky. Next, the waters of Loch Awe reflected the flames of castles and fortresses abandoned by defenders too stunned for resistance. Within a few days the territory was laid waste and the power of the Campbells broken for all time.

When Argyll came belatedly to the rescue Montrose took to the hills in January. Again his strategy was based on audacity, for he chose an "impossible" route over the highest and wildest mountains of the British Isles. Skirting Ben Nevis along single-file trails through snow and ice, his men had no food except raw oatmeal eaten from the point of a dirk.

This time he had 3,000 Highlanders to fight, chiefly Campbells burning for vengeance. But the surprise proved so complete that tactics were needless when he fell upon Argyll like an avalanche out of the February dawn. The combat of Inverlochy turned into a slaughter of Campbells who stood to the last man, leaving more dead on the seashore than Montrose's whole force.

The alarm of the Covenanters caused the raising of two new armies, composed largely of veterans from Cromwell's campaigns and led by competent professional soldiers, Hurry and Baillie. After recrossing the mountains in the early spring Montrose flung himself between them and seized the initiative.

In a brisk fight at Halkerton Castle he repeated his favorite tactics of hiding part of his force behind the brow of a hill, thus enticing Hurry into a cavalry attack repulsed with heavy losses. Once more his men were destitute of supplies, so he turned to his only source, the enemy. Leaving the weaker half of his force with the baggage, he set out at midnight with 750 foot. Before noon he had stormed Dundee, 24 miles away, and withdrawn his loot-laden clansmen.

The pursuit continued all day and night. One Covenant army nipped at his heels, while the other took a parallel route to cut him off from the hills. Montrose succeeded in eluding both. First beating off Hurry, he halted in the darkness until Baillie drew ahead, then doubled in his tracks and slipped away between them. In 36 hours he had marched 70 miles, captured a walled town, fought several rear-guard actions and made good his escape.

In May, 1645, he gained his most brilliant tactical triumph by defeating Hurry at Auldearn. With only 2,000 foot and 250 horse against double those numbers led by a veteran officer of the Thirty Years' War,

Montrose boldly dispensed with a centre. Instead he posted a few of his weakest troops in the village with orders to fire repeatedly. On the right, behind bogs, he stationed 500 Macdonalds to fight a desperate holding battle. Montrose himself took the left with his entire cavalry and the bulk of his foot skillfully concealed behind the slope.

As he had hoped, the Covenanters launched their main attack on the right wing. The Macdonalds were hard pressed, but Montrose waited until the intuitive moment before coming to their relief with his hidden force. The surprise was devastating, and Hurry's army became a mob of routed fugitives, suffering more than 2,000 slain at the cost of few Royalist casualties.

Within a few weeks the king's commander forced a decision on the reluctant Baillie. The combat at Alford is notable as the only engagement to which Montrose brought equal numbers—about 2,000 to a side—though the Covenanters had their customary advantage in cavalry. A fourth time he contrived to hide a reserve force, while dividing his cavalry between the wings. The first clash had developed into a fierce struggle when the flank attack of the concealed Royalists turned the tide. Baillie's veterans were cut to pieces almost to a man.

That same month Cromwell won his great victory at Naseby. Upon receiving the news, Montrose began recruiting desperately for an invasion of England. Although Charles had appointed him viceroy in honor of his victories, he received none of the promised aid which still lay within that beaten monarch's resources. Nevertheless, he managed to build up the strongest army of his career—5,400 infantry and 500 horse, nearly all of them troops seasoned in his own campaigns.

The Covenanters, too, had prepared for a supreme effort with an array of 7,000 veteran troops under Argyll. It is an amusing note that the war council consisted of the five generals whom Montrose had defeated in recent months. Despite the object lessons they had accumulated, the rebel leaders showed an excess of confidence which brought defeat in the decisive battle of Kilsyth. Their eagerness led them to risk a flank march across the Royalist front without even the covering fire of their artillery. It was a fatal move against so keen an adversary, for the royal commander ordered a charge which cut Argyll's army squarely in two.

His greatest triumph thus became his easiest, since only a few hundred Covenanters ever survived the relentless all-day pursuit. Glasgow and Edinburgh capitulated without a blow, and Montrose had become master of Scotland almost on the anniversary of his entrance with two followers.

During the "year of miracles" his troops had been held together only

by the will of the slim, handsome nobleman at their head. Protestant and
Catholic, Scot and Irishman, mountaineer and townsman, they combined
the most antagonistic elements of the land—unruly men fighting only for
plunder or to pay off ancient clan grudges. Had the king not neglected
him, Montrose might conceivably have been able to raise paid, disciplined
forces and challenge Cromwell. As it proved, his downfall was to be even
more startling than his rise.

The moderation of his policies as conqueror soon alienated even his
small nucleus of dependable soldiers. When he hanged looters after letting off captured cities with a fine, the clansmen deserted by the hundreds. Only a month after his decisive victory Montrose found himself
reduced to 600 ill-equipped troops. Scotland remained in his grasp, but
David Leslie was marching northward with 4,000 Covenanters who had
served under Cromwell.

Lacking the horsemen for reconnaissance, the Royalist leader was overwhelmed in a dawn surprise at Philiphaugh, near the southern border,
in September, 1645. He managed to cut his way through and escape to
the Continent, where Mazarin offered him the captaincy of the king's
guard with the rank of marshal of France. Montrose declined, and after
the beheading of Charles I he landed in Scotland with a few retainers.
Another year of miracles was not to be, and the marquis met his end on
an Edinburgh gallows, following his betrayal to the Covenanters for a
price of 25,000 pounds Scots.

Fortescue, in his *History of the British Army,* ranks him as: ". . . perhaps the most brilliant natural genius of the Civil War." Gardiner, the
historian of the Rebellion, declares that he ". . . had all of Cromwell's
promptness of seizing the chances of the strife, together with a versatility
in varying his tactics according to the varying resources of the enemy,
to which Cromwell could lay no claim, while his skill as a strategist was
certainly superior to that of his English contemporary."

Certain it is, at any rate, that no soldier of history ever displayed a
brighter talent for handling the small army and fighting the small battle.
During the next two centuries the future of the Western Hemisphere was
to be decided by forces seldom exceeding 5,000 in numbers. Yet so persistent is the tradition of weight, few commanders of such bands have
made the most of their opportunities. Montrose, almost alone in the
chronicles of his century, realized that numerical handicaps were compensated by an added ability to march, manoeuvre and take cover.
Against opponents who knew only how to trade blows, he carried his
preference for rapid movements to such lengths as to bury all captured

cannon. Against opponents who copied the tactics of larger brigades, he found his inspiration in Scotland's clan-fighting methods, the ancient precepts of ambush and stratagem and surprise. And in a military age which considered a battle a year a progressive pace, Montrose won eight combats during that period to demonstrate the advantages of velocity over bulk.

THE "CROWNING MERCY" OF WORCESTER

It was left to Oliver Cromwell to destroy the dour tyranny of the Covenant with a professional soldiery such as England had never seen before. Prior to Naseby the victor had helped to legalize the Parliamentary national army known as the New Model. A limited conscription served to raise the full strength of 21,000—6,000 horse, 1,000 dragoons and 14,000 foot, who were to be regularly paid with an appropriation of 45,000 pounds monthly. The supplies and discipline were also fixed by law, and for the first time the scarlet coat came to be worn as the uniform.

The organization was too recent to have any effect on the outcome of Naseby, though its existence doubtless influenced the decision to execute Charles I. Not until the Second Civil War, when Cromwell faced his former Scots allies, did the New Model give an account of itself in the field. Then at the battle of Preston in 1648 an English force of 8,500 administered a crushing defeat to 20,000 invaders.

The difference in numbers hardly gives a fair picture of the relative merits of the two armies. Despite its advantage in this respect, the Scottish force consisted of raw levies which David Leslie had refused to lead. Poorly armed and worse provided, these recruits had scattered for subsistence when Cromwell struck them after a forced march through the Midlands. Hence it was actually three separate armies which the English overwhelmed and beat in detail. The retreat of the losers became a rout through a hostile countryside until the remnant laid down their arms.

Up to this point the Rebellion had been distinguished for mercies to captives and neutrals. But after Preston a number of enemy leaders were executed; and at a later date Cromwell put down the Irish revolt with a harshness which culminated in the massacres at Drogheda and Wexford. The beheading of the king became a final incentive, and in 1650 all Scottish factions united behind the exiled Charles II. The threat served to bind Englishmen together as never before, so that the strife developed into a fierce national war between the two kingdoms.

Religious causes also played a more prominent part, since Charles had gained Covenant support by swearing to impose Presbyterianism on England. Five days after the pact, Cromwell hastened to the border to put his army in motion. With 5,000 horse and 10,000 foot he marched upon Edinburgh, following a coastal route and receiving supplies from his fleet.

His capable opponent, David Leslie, with whom he had shared the credit at Marston Moor, emerges as perhaps the most luckless general of the war. Although he commanded much larger numbers than Cromwell, most of them were the unwilling and untrained products of a harsh conscription. To add to his woe, he had barely felt out the enemy's strength when the all-powerful Kirk called a halt for three days to examine the spiritual state of the army. During the ensuing "purge," held within musket range of the foe, Leslie lost the services of 80 officers and 3,000 men who were found wanting in theological respects. Thereafter he remained under the thumb of the ministers, who ruined his best opportunity by forbidding him to fight on the Sabbath.

It must not be supposed, however, that the English commander-in-chief had a sinecure. Leslie proved to be a resourceful adversary, and the Scots still held a great numerical superiority. They had forced the invaders into a tight corner, hemming them in by the sea, when Cromwell achieved a surprise in a dawn attack. By precise timing and dispositions he rendered the Scottish right and part of the centre ineffective while shattering the other half of the army. Then turning on the remainder, he completed a victory at Dunbar which ended with 3,000 Royalists slain and 10,000 captured.

Leslie devoted the winter to training a new army as scattered forces of Scots followed a Fabian strategy of harassing the invader. Their main stronghold was at Stirling, but in the spring of 1651 Cromwell manoeuvred them out of this position by throwing a force to the north and cutting off their supplies. This move left Leslie and Charles only the choice between an immediate battle in Scotland, with few prospects of success, or a desperate invasion of England in the hope of acquiring Royalist allies.

The king chose the latter horn of the dilemma and bolted southward late in July. A week later Cromwell broke camp and set out in pursuit.

The result was one of the most dramatic races in the chronicles of war. The Scots followed the western coast, marching at the rate of 15 miles a day. On the other side of the island, along the eastern littoral, Cromwell's veterans covered their 320 miles in only three weeks.

Charles soon discovered that he could hope for no support in England.

With only 16,000 half-trained men against Cromwell's 31,000, he decided
to take refuge in Worcester for a last stand. There was, of course, little
doubt as to the outcome; and the lord general's fame rests upon the
completeness of his victory. Dividing his army, he moved up both banks
of the river Severn while sending out a third detachment to cut off retreat
to Scotland. The timing and co-ordination of the converging forces,
always a difficult military problem, was solved by means of bridges of
boats thrown across the stream. On September 3, 1651, the anniversary
of Dunbar, Cromwell ordered his general assault, and all Royalist
resistance ended within a few hours. Charles escaped with a few hundred
fugitives, but the last army of his cause had ceased to exist. The victors
admitted only 200 losses in the campaign which put an end to the Great
Rebellion.

GOVERNMENT BY THE SWORD

Seven years to the day passed from the "Crowning Mercy" of Worcester to Cromwell's death on September 3, 1658. During this period he
ruled as a military dictator, first in effect and later officially, over a
people whose remote ancestors had won the Magna Charta.

The instrument of the lord protector's government was a professional
standing army, always ready, always equipped and disciplined, which
has had few equals in history. Cromwell himself, after ordering his
soldiers to dismiss Parliament, foresaw the possibility of nine men out
of ten turning against him. "But what," he said, "if I put a sword in this
hand of the tenth man?"

At a later date, in one of his rare passages of self-justification, he
declared, "If nothing should ever be done but what is according to law,
the throat of a nation might be cut while we send for someone to make
a law."

As compensation for the loss of their ancient liberties Englishmen
could console themselves with an aggressive foreign policy which won
military, naval and diplomatic triumphs out of proportion to the size of
the country. Scotland, bled white by her battle losses, had at last been
reduced to the status of a province. Irish rebels dared raise their heads
no longer. Holland, the great maritime rival, was crippled by Blake and
Monk in a series of glorious actions on the sea. France and Spain, both
of them larger kingdoms, sank their pride to bid against each other for
an alliance with England.

As added solace, Cromwell's "subjects" might take pride in a soldier
whose deeds were on the grand scale even in an age of military greatness.

The extent of his genius has been very fairly estimated by a modern biographer, John Buchan:

> In the Worcester campaign . . . he opened the door to the invader, and by a precise concentration at the right point made victory certain. He could be very bold, and also very cautious; he was a master of the strategy of indirect approach, and also of manoeuvre in bulk—both novelties in his day. So obvious indeed did his methods seem that we are impressed by their simplicity, and are apt to attribute his successes largely to the stupidity of his opponents. But that is the highest tribute that can be paid to a great captain.

Nevertheless, the contemporaries of Cromwell made it plain that they considered the dictatorship a bad bargain. Only a few years after his death the lord protector's remains were barbarously exhumed and exhibited to public fury. At the same period the remains of Montrose, hanged as a champion of law and tradition, were treated almost as saintly relics.

The reason is evident after a glance at England's internal affairs during Cromwell's seven years of power. In time of peace no less than 57,000 soldiers—a huge force for that day—were quartered on the nation for the obvious purpose of stamping out the first spark of revolt. The upkeep of this army added a million pounds annually to an already intolerable tax burden.

Trade was bad and unemployment a national scandal. The prisons were so overcrowded with debtors that Cromwell had to condemn his thousands of political suspects to virtual slavery in the West Indies. Thus with the wry humor which is a people's only defense against a dictator, the verb "to barbadoes" crept into the language as a synonym for unjust banishment.

Still, the country gentry might have forgiven the fines and confiscations. The masses might have endured a poverty resulting in widespread beggary and vagrancy. What most infuriated the English freeman was the invasion of his personal life, the watch over his private affairs by a host of invisible agents.

At the height of the tyranny the nation was divided into eleven districts, each under a major general whose decisions were backed up by cavalry sabers. Betrayal and petty espionage became the order of the day, and even the most innocent public amusements could not escape the interference of the state. The old Merry England had vanished, and in its stead emerged a melancholy and sullen land which only awaited the day when it would welcome back the loser of Worcester.

The reaction is historically significant in view of the times. For the seventeenth century was an age when men were discarding the last traces of medieval thought and forming the first ideas of nationalism. Already the characteristics had begun to appear, some of them racial and hereditary, some shaped by such environmental factors as trade and climate and geography, which would soon set the nations apart more sharply than boundary lines on a map.

In the study of war these characteristics will be found as important to the outcome as weapons and tactics. Condé's thrilling victory at Rocroi began a French tradition of *élan* that was to result in some famous disasters as well as triumphs. Wallenstein's exploitation of German submissiveness left an example that would not be neglected in the military future of that land. Hence it is not surprising that Cromwell gave his countrymen an added distrust of martial glory, at least until such a time as a general could be safely canonized.

Twelve generations have lived and died since Worcester, yet the shadow of the lord protector, sword in hand, still falls heavily upon the warfare of Britain and the United States. Never since that time has a British or American government been prepared at the outbreak of hostilities for the tests to come. For the English-speaking peoples have made it plain that they would rather risk defeat than dictatorship; and the dread of a second Cromwell has influenced the campaigns of Marlborough and Wellington, of Washington and Grant and Lee.

PART FOUR
ARMED
DIPLOMACY

☆

I

WAR FOR PROFIT

---

*When a general makes no mistakes in war, it is because
he has not been at it long.*

—TURENNE

FOR a century and a half men had been fighting with more zeal than
discretion, as is generally the case in conflicts waged to uphold principles.
Blood had been spilled without stint by pitiless armies which recognized
few rights of the captive or civilian. Massacre had become the rule rather
than the exception, and whole provinces were depopulated as a consequence of plague, famine and pillage.

From this extreme it seems to the modern observer only an overnight
transition to the most temperate military era since the Renaissance.
Beginning about the year 1660, men appeared by tacit consent to have
agreed upon a warfare of moderation which lasted until the outbreak of
the French Revolution in 1789. Armies were composed entirely of long-
term troops held in such discipline that hanging for the theft of a barn-
yard fowl was not unknown. Looting and devastation reached a minimum
among forces which received their pay, food and clothing from the state.
And where of late the battle of annihilation had been the ideal—a Naseby
or Kilsyth or Dunbar—generals now strove to avoid bloodshed while
gaining their ends by manoeuvre and siegecraft.

Unless an exception is made of the *Pax Romana*, when the legions
stood guard over a world welded into a single empire by conquest, history
records no peace worth mentioning since the dawn of civilization. Yet

there is no lack of evidence to show that strife can be kept within reasonable bounds. Clausewitz, the nineteenth century military analyst, made a careful distinction between the "limited" and the "total" or "absolute" conflict in which both adversaries put forth the last ounce of effort, regardless of cost, to obtain a complete victory. As a Prussian he naturally concluded that such matters should be foreseen by the state, which would then prescribe for its soldiers the exact amount of force to be applied in winning specified results. It has been the experience of time, however, that restraints are more often imposed by economic or ethical conditions than political decisions.

The ancient world offers a wealth of examples. In view of the cheapness of human life in an era of universal slavery, we are likely to forget that restraint prevailed during most of the long classical age. Greek and Roman armies were small in proportion to the population; and the cost of such weapons as bows, spears and catapults did not become a grievous economic burden. Not until decay had set in, with its symptoms of civil anarchy, did either empire pass from limited to total war.

The most notable exception is to be found in the three Punic conflicts, which show the transition in process. The first was a limited war, waged for aggrandizement and logically concluded with the payment of tribute and cession of territory. Then after a brief truce deeper antagonisms were aroused which resulted in two absolute wars ending in Carthaginian extermination.

Throughout the centuries of Byzantine supremacy, moderation proved a military asset to a small empire beating off hordes of barbarians. As their textbooks reveal, the soldiers of Constantinople took pride in a restraint based on skill and intellectual valor. But even Byzantium was forced into total war when beset by the fanatical Moslems and Persian Sun worshipers. And at a later date the empire met its downfall after being weakened by the victories of a conquering son who scorned limitations.

During the early medieval period, when Europe found some cohesion in a common faith, we have an excellent example of a moderation imposed on humane and ethical grounds. In its results the Truce of God fell considerably short of peace; but it did reduce suffering by confining war to certain periods of the calendar. As further alleviation the churchmen managed, by dint of vigorous propaganda, to divert the family quarrels of Christendom into crusades against the infidel.

Nor can the voluntary mercies of chivalry, during later medieval centuries, be overlooked in a survey of ethical limitations. Even allowing for frequent violations, these codes served to mitigate the violence of an age when petty warfare was ceaseless.

It is only when we turn to the clash of ideas that total war appears to be the universal rule. Revolutions, civil struggles and religious conflicts are always more deadly than the strife of aggrandizement, which at least indicates that humanity places a higher value on belief than property. During the century and a half ending at Worcester the Continent had actually been shaken to its foundations by a prolonged revolution. The fighting had been savage, the suffering intense; and doubtless the survivors could see few benefits to compensate for all the misery. Yet from this historical distance it is apparent that religious toleration and the security of parliamentary institutions owe largely to those cruel times.

In contrast, if the warfare of the new era was moderate, so also were the results. For the next 130 years highly trained troops disputed without heat for the prizes of armed diplomacy. After a succession of summer campaigns waged with leisured art, a few fortresses or provinces changed hands at the peace table, and the belligerents began at once to prepare for a resumption. At its best this strife was urbane and economical, meriting the complacency of the historian Gibbon, who wrote in 1782:

> In war the European forces are exercised by temperate and undecisive contests. The Balance of Power will continue to fluctuate, and the prosperity of our own or the neighboring kingdoms may be alternately exalted or depressed; but these partial events cannot essentially injure our general state of happiness, the system of arts and laws and manners, which so advantageously distinguish, above the rest of Mankind, the Europeans and their colonists.

But this is an idealistic view, and Gibbon takes no account either of the cynical causes or the sterile results. Nor does he refer to those military excesses which sometimes occurred in spite of all efforts at constraint.

THE WARS OF THE FRONDE

The man whose name is most often associated with the age had passed his fifth birthday when the couriers brought the news of France's triumph at Rocroi. Nearly seventy years later, as a weary and disillusioned patriarch, he heard the tidings of his last victory. Between those dates his country had been continually in arms, a condition for which he was chiefly responsible.

In any event his abilities would not have been hidden, but as a monarch for seventy-two years—the longest recorded reign in Continental history—Louis XIV was to become a symbol and byword as well as ruler of France. For half a century his court dictated Europe's modes in art, taste, dress, manners and thought; and above all the Sun King set the pace for the warfare of his day.

As a youth his most formative years were spent amid the alarms of the Fronde, that incoherent civil struggle which dated the last outbreak of feudalism in France. So called from a word denoting a boy's sling, this uprising was described by Michelet as "a burlesque war . . . a war of children, with a child's nickname . . . comic in its origin, its events, its principles." Nevertheless, the decade proved tragic enough to the young king who on two occasions had to abandon Paris, sharing with his court the hardships and humiliations of a flight into the provinces.

The memory of those occasions was to lead in later life to a centralization of power which would end the danger of the nobles asserting themselves again. Meanwhile, the boy monarch arrived at his first conclusions about war by appraising the operations of the rival Fronde commanders.

Colleagues on fields of the Thirty Years' War, the foremost soldiers of France had become enemies in the civil strife. Condé, a prince of the blood, took the side of the rebels against Cardinal Mazarin's policies. Turenne, as a Protestant and minor noble of a frontier duchy, supported the royal cause.

Two more opposite approaches to victory could not have been found in the realm. The hero of Rocroi made the battle his medium, taking audacious risks for the opportunity of dealing a final blow. His adversary preferred the campaign, hovering always on the enemy's supply lines and avoiding all but the most promising actions. And though Condé had unquestionably the larger share of native genius, Turenne remained all his life a student who learned in the school of trial and error.

As a spectator in this contest between the artist and the scientist, the adolescent king scarcely realized that he was choosing for the future between two schools of military thought. The operations of the Fronde were petty, confused and often farcical; but in the end Turenne clearly had the better of the duel. The secret of his success has been described by a modern biographer, General Maxime Weygand, as "a tenacity which wore down an adversary by a process of slow usury."

In a first encounter, fought near Bleneau, Condé became a victim of his own luster. Having just beaten another Royalist army, he pressed on with 14,000 troops to overwhelm Turenne's force of 4,000 and capture the king. But in his haste he allowed himself to be trapped in a defile by infantry posted behind bogs. At the critical moment Turenne unmasked a battery of artillery which completed a bloody repulse of the Frondeurs.

The opponents met again at the Faubourg St. Martin after Turenne manoeuvred Condé into a desperate position with his back to the closed gates of Paris. The rebels were badly mauled when the Duchesse de Montpensier, better known as *La Grande Mademoiselle*, ordered the gates to be opened and the cannon of the Bastille turned on the victors. This bit of melodrama saved Condé from destruction, but his defeat ended the civil strife.

Thereafter the uprising took on the character of a national conflict as the rebels appealed for aid to Spain, which had been conducting a lackadaisical war against France for a generation. Treacherous as this alliance may appear today, it must be remembered that in 1653 patriotism was still subordinated to family and dynastic loyalties. Turenne himself had been a Frondeur at the outset, and his rival now led alien forces without considering himself an outcast.

For three years the opponents waged a tedious warfare of posts and sieges in which the honors were about even. If Turenne succeeded in a well-planned dawn attack on Condé's lines of circumvallation at Arras, the prince revenged himself the next summer by storming the French lines at Valenciennes. Neither won a lasting advantage, and the decisive battle of the Dunes did not occur until 1657, when Mazarin ceded Dunkirk to England in return for Cromwell's aid.

Turenne was besieging the port when Condé and Don John of Austria came to its relief with a Spanish army. The prince had a great superiority in cavalry, his favorite arm, while Turenne was the stronger in foot and artillery. Both forces had large contingents of English soldiers, since 6,000 redcoats under Turenne faced several corps of Loyalists led by the Duke of York, afterwards James II.

Condé drew up his lines among the dunes, his right resting on the sea and his left on a canal. The French advanced and were hurled back on the left wing by a counterattack of the prince's squadrons. But this was his last gain of the day, for Turenne's pressure on the left and centre already had the Spaniards in retreat. The position of Condé's horsemen soon became hopeless, and he joined the general rout. After ten years of strife and anarchy France at last had won a weary tranquillity reflected in Turenne's battlefield message to his wife:

> The enemy came to us and, God be praised, they have been defeated. I was pretty busy all day, which has fatigued me. I wish you goodnight: I am going to bed.

The nineteen-year-old king, a spectator at the Dunes, had no further doubts as to the sort of generalship he favored. Although he generously pardoned Condé, restoring him to past honors, Louis made it plain in his future military decisions that he considered the tortoise swifter than the hare.

THE REFORMS OF LOUVOIS

On the death of Cardinal Mazarin in 1661 the young monarch began to rule with an absolutism which France welcomed after the disorders of the Fronde. One of his first acts was to name Turenne marshal general of the camps and armies, and that soldier's ideas influenced the coming decade of reorganization.

In all his operations Turenne had singled out the enemy's stomach as his weakest point. The aim of his ceaseless manoeuvres was to cut opposing forces off from supplies, thus undermining their vigilance and creating the opportunity for a favorable action. At Zusmarshausen, the campaign which ended the Thirty Years' War, this strategy worked so perfectly that the French general won a well-nigh bloodless victory by manoeuvring a Bavarian army into disintegration.

Naturally, a commander who attacks an enemy's supplies will give thought to conserving his own; and the new marshal general discovered the first great war minister of modern centuries in François Michel Le Tellier, Marquis of Louvois. Within a few years the young civil servant had outdistanced Turenne's instructions and become the master of his age in the science of training and providing armies.

Law and custom in contemporary Europe held the king responsible for the national defense, his funds for that purpose being limited to the Royal Treasury's regular sources of income. In order to fill his ranks the monarch depended on colonels who not only raised but also bought and sold regiments. In effect these men were contractors of military labor; they often had no tactical knowledge, and the field command usually rested with the lieutenant colonel. Civilian contractors furnished arms, food and clothing, while officers' commissions were purchased much like shares in the stock market today.

In view of the limitations on taxes a monarch found it hard enough to make both ends meet, and his difficulties were increased by peculations. Not only did the merchants cheat scandalously in the matter of supplies; the colonels and captains pocketed the pay of dead or even imaginary soldiers.

Louvois could not abolish this proprietary system, but he put a stop to the recognized swindles. The new war minister did not content himself merely with working a revolution in honesty; he also introduced an efficiency which the army had never known before. After creating a quartermaster general's department, he went on to train a commissariat staff to supervise the price, quality and transport of supplies. This reform led to the improvement of the roads over which those supplies were to be moved, and the establishment of magazines at strategic points for the storage of large reserves of food, arms and ammunition.

The new magazine system alone was sufficient to change the warfare of Europe, for it meant that a general no longer had to remain in the district which promised enough provisions. With reserve stores at his disposal, he could manoeuvre from fixed points and concentrate on military instead of forage problems. Added benefits to the health, morale and discipline of troops were certain to result. As a final advantage, though the French minister had few altruistic motives, noncombatants would be spared the ravages of the military hordes which had devoured fair provinces.

For several centuries soldiers had been citing precepts from ancient warfare, but it remained for Louvois to restore the methods by which classical armies were supplied. He foresaw the monotony of a diet of biscuits and salt pork, and his quartermasters were instructed to buy vegetables and fresh meats, paying current prices even to the inhabitants of enemy districts. Such expenses were to be met by contributions of money levied on the conquered, but in the interests of discipline soldiers were forbidden to pillage. Louvois' reforms found ready imitators among other armies, so that the Swiss jurist Emeric de Vattel was able to boast a century later in his *Law of Nations*:

> At the present day war is carried on by regular armies; the people, the peasantry, the townsfolk take no part in it, and as a rule have nothing to fear from the sword of the enemy. Provided the inhabitants submit to him who is master of the country, and pay the contributions demanded, and refrain from acts of hostility, they live in safety as if they were on friendly terms with the enemy; their property rights are even held sacred; the peasants go freely into the enemy camp to sell their provisions, and they are protected as far as possible from the calamities of war.

During the past century, it will be recalled, whole armies had disintegrated almost overnight as a consequence of looting and indiscipline. Hence the practical values of the new moderation were not exaggerated in Vattel's comment:

Such treatment is highly commendable and . . . is even of advantage to the enemy. For a general who protects unarmed inhabitants, who keeps his soldiers under strict discipline, and who protects the country, is enabled to support his army without trouble and is spared many evils and dangers.

Benefits of this sort appealed far more to Louvois than any notions of mercy to the vanquished. Within a few years he had removed the usual causes of insubordination by building up the best fed and best housed army in Europe, and now he set out with equal vigor to make it the best trained.

Nobody saw more clearly that two recent improvements in weapons had increased the necessity for drill. The first was a native French invention. For many years the hunters of the Pyrenees had thrust a knife into a musket barrel to fight off wounded bears. Gradually the plug bayonet (named after the city of Bayonne) won army recognition; and at a later date Vauban is said to have perfected the socket which allowed the blade to be fixed while the piece was discharged.

The musket itself had been bettered meanwhile by the invention of a new lock to replace the cumbersome and uncertain match of the past two centuries. A sharp piece of flint was firmly clamped between the jaws of the cock, which upon a pull of the trigger struck sparks to ignite the priming powder. Even more important, the fall of the cock simultaneously uncovered a firing pan which up to this instant had been kept closed, thus protecting the powder against wind and rain.

The effect of the two innovations on infantry tactics was to render obsolete the pike which had remained in use ever since Roger Bacon's day. At last the foot soldier could contribute to his unit's fire power while still possessing in the bayonet a ready defense against shock attack. The flintlock eliminated most of the misfires which had previously occurred; and night operations would no longer be robbed of surprise by the glow of burning matches.

An invention of vague date and origin, the new lock had been approved by every other army before Louvois' prejudices were overcome. In regard to the bayonet he showed a more progressive spirit, and the French forces took the lead not only in discarding the pike but in adapting their tactics accordingly.

Foot soldiers of the past had fought in column because of the necessity of combining pikemen with musketeers. Gustavus varied the order somewhat with his brigades, but for the most part the unruly infantry of the religious wars could be manoeuvred only in masses. With the adoption of the new weapons, both Turenne and Louvois perceived that the day of line formations had arrived. Henceforward the infantry of France would be trained to advance in three ranks, firing volleys at the word of command.

The difficulties, of course, were formidable. Soldiers who failed to keep a meticulous line might aim badly or even fire at one another in the excitement of combat. The effect depended upon a mathematical rigidity of approach, so that the volley crashed out as one shot, and the bayonets leaped forward as a single hedge of gleaming points. Such precision was possible only to men who had been drilled until they became automata—an ideal which Louvois demanded of the French army.

The days dragged into months, the months into years, and still the bark of commands rang out on every parade ground of the realm. In response the long lines marched forward in stately unison, every musket at its identical angle, every foot keeping a stately cadence of 80 steps a minute. For Louvois had discovered the very Lucifer of drill masters in Jean Martinet, whose name has come down as an odious byword to generations of grumbling recruits.

Once again, though that result may have annoyed him, the ferocious minister had helped to make war more humane. During the religious struggles the lives of troops had been held in scant esteem because replacements could be so easily obtained. But at least five years were needed to perfect a soldier for linear tactics, and Louvois was not the man to despise such an investment. Not only did he exhibit an increasing solicitude for the well-being of his rank and file; he also became one of the first military leaders to make a practical study of morale.

In theory the soldiers of the day were recruited by voluntary enlistment, though most observers agree as to the hypocrisy of the system. Apparently only a minority joined of their own free will, the others being secured by fraud, trickery or various forms of official blackmail. Vagrants, tosspots and petty offenders were considered fair game by the king's agents; and after serving a long first enlistment term, few men had either the will or means to resume civil life.

Officers could not complain of the same compulsion, yet as a class they represented the younger sons of the nobility who had no other career open to them. In a more exalted sense they were social outcasts as well as their men, even though war ranked as the most aristocratic of all trades. The pay was necessarily small, the future hazardous; and Louvois well knew that a bid for morale must appeal to vanity rather than sober reason.

He found his solution—and no better exists to this day—in those bits of bronze and ribbon awarded for distinguished service. Louvois was not the originator of French military medals, but he reorganized and popularized the orders to such an extent that they are associated with his name. As a next step toward inspiring *esprit de corps,* he made the French army the first on the Continent to be completely uniformed. Various colors were worn at first, depending on the unit, but immaculate white coats came to be the pride of the old regiments. Epaulets, lace, plumes and embroidery adorned the officers with a splendor which military dress has seldom known since that era.

As a final effort to make army service more attractive, the minister founded the famous Hôtel des Invalides. Hence at a time when other nations condemned their outworn warriors to an old age of beggary, the crippled or ailing French veteran could look forward to a haven among his comrades.

Since Gustavus Adolphus, whose ideas he borrowed and developed in many instances, no man has had a better right than Louvois to be called the "father of modern war." Almost singlehanded, thanks to a Herculean capacity for toil, he created an entirely new French army and supply system in a few years. In its drill, its arms and its morale, this army had advanced half a century beyond any rival force in Europe. And yet during these last years of peace, Louvois produced still another innovation which has been copied down to the present day. Each autumn he held a gigantic series of war games and manoeuvres on the plains of Châlons to complete the training of his troops under simulated combat conditions. With the king and great lords in attendance, and with the troubled diplomats of other nations looking on, the new French army displayed a precision which brought a gleam even to the fierce eye of Inspector General Martinet.

There remained only one further step, since it is an adage of history that no perfect military instrument has ever been suffered to rust from disuse. And in line with ancient precedent, Louvois soon began to suggest to his sovereign the advantages to be gained from aggression.

COLBERT, MAN OF PEACE

It was irony enough that the ruthless minister of war should have done so much to soften the strife of his day. But the paradox is completed in the career of France's Man of Peace, Jean Baptiste Colbert, whose efforts served only to push his country into long and terrible years of war.

As the son and grandson of merchants, the minister of finance and the marine would have been barred from an officer's commission in the navy he created for France. No self-made man in a democracy ever rose more swiftly by his own merits; and it is to the glory of Louis XIV that he backed the upstart against the most snobbish court of Europe.

After holding confidential posts under Mazarin, Colbert found his opportunity at the age of forty-six. He had long known, as had everyone else in the realm, that the Royal Treasury was being systematically robbed by tax-gatherers who fancied themselves immune from justice. Colbert presented evidence of their peculations to Louis, who appointed him controller general with powers to prosecute the offenders. These inquisitions added enormously to the young king's popularity, while filling his treasury to overflowing. Soon he was able to buy back Dunkirk from Charles II, thus winning even more fervent applause from subjects who had always resented that bit of England on French soil.

In recognition of his minister's bleak incorruptibility, the king virtually turned over the country to him to be run as a business. Within a short time Colbert had France nearly out of debt, her internal affairs on a sound basis, and her revenues increased.

Next he set himself the larger task of augmenting the national wealth from which all revenues flowed. His conceptions of state prosperity were harsh and narrow; and far from believing in a community of nations, he preferred that France prosper at the expense of her neighbors. In the same spirit, he remained all his life a frigid pacifist—not because war resulted in suffering, but because it seemed to him a less effective means of aggrandizement than his own policies.

It was inevitable, therefore, that the Man of Peace should have turned to those industrial subsidies and protective tariffs which have fomented so many wars ever since. In rapid succession the edicts fell from his pen. He revived the moribund weaving trade with transfusions of state money; he made a national industry of the Gobelin tapestry works; he endowed all manner of model new factories to turn out goods which France had been importing; and from the king he won a grudging decree that nobles might engage in commerce without disgracing their birth.

During this same period he surrounded the nation with high tariff walls which resulted in the customary reprisals from other countries. In further aggravation, he poured immense sums into the trading companies of the Indies, while building a network of roads to encourage industrial self-sufficiency in France.

As an observer of the maritime duel between England and Holland, the minister concluded that his sea-borne commerce must be protected by a navy. France had a few warships, but neither any naval traditions nor merchant fleet to compare with her rivals. With only a few years at his disposal, Colbert set out to remedy conditions which had been centuries in the making. He somehow found the shipwrights, whom he subsidized by allowing a premium for vessels built at home, while imposing duties on those purchased abroad. Seamen risked a death penalty for serving in the ships of other nations, and laborers were forbidden to emigrate.

The best naval architects of the realm worked out problems of design and ordnance for the new warships. Training academies sprang up at Rochefort, Dieppe and Saint-Malo; the ports of Calais, Dunkirk, Brest and Havre were fortified, and the arsenals at Toulon and Rochefort completely rebuilt. To attract recruits, Colbert devised a scheme by which seamen were pensioned and held in reserve after finishing their terms of service. In the higher ranks young nobles were offered inducements to study for commissions in the royal schools.

The minister spared neither himself nor others in this tremendous undertaking. As an example of his pitiless energy, he instructed his Canadian agents to entrap Iroquois barbarians for a living death in the galleys of the Mediterranean, where oars still supplemented sail. But if the means are overlooked, the acomplishment is without an equal in modern maritime history—the singlehanded creation within a decade of a navy and merchant marine able to challenge the fleets of old seafaring nations.

In his own sphere the Man of Peace held practically the powers of a dictator, since the king and Louvois had other interests. And like all dictators before and since, he built up an imposing façade of prosperity with spectacular public works intended both to dazzle and create employment. His Languedoc Canal—a ditch 150 miles long, connecting two seas—has been called a greater achievement, in view of comparative engineering facilities, than the Suez or Panama projects. He filled Paris with new bridges and boulevards, began the building of the Louvre, and later applied his tremendous zeal to the construction of the palace at Versailles.

In his efforts to add to the census Colbert may even have left a lesson for twentieth century dictators. Already France's 19,000,000 souls made her by far the largest united nation in Europe, but the minister was not satisfied. He announced the family of ten as a patriotic goal to be attained by every loyal subject, who would then be exempted from personal taxes. Less fruitful progenitors were to be rewarded in proportion, and the state encouraged early marriages by offering prizes.

The fault did not lie with Colbert's approach, but the campaign ended in disappointment. Still, this was a minor rebuff for a man accustomed to moving mountains, and the tragedy of the great minister's career may be traced to his successes. They were all too convincing at the time, while the penalties of official swaddling did not become apparent until later. Meanwhile the Man of Peace managed to create more enemies for France with his policies than Louvois ever made by whetting the sword.

THE ROYAL STATESMAN

The third figure of the triumvirate was the monarch himself. For in spite of the latitude that Louis granted to his ministers, he had every right to utter the words which legend has put into his mouth, *"L'état, c'est moi!"*

Never as an adult could he forget those hunted years of the Fronde when the boy king fled from hoarse Parisian mobs and rebellious armies led by nobles who had sworn allegiance. The memories still haunted Louis when he came to power with two fixed ideas—he wished all his days to shun his capital city, and he desired equally to humble the provincial lords.

The answer has been written in stone and mortar for following generations to read. For it would be a mistake to assume, as so many thousands of tourists have assumed, that Versailles was built entirely as a monument to the Sun King's vainglory. No doubt he hoped to make a crushing impression, knowing that men are image worshipers in respect to power as well as faith. But the king also found in the new palace a statesman's answer to his two resolves. By removing the court to a country village, he secured himself against another outbreak of Parisian turbulence; and the splendor of the edifice could not help but emphasize the authority of the crown over the nobility.

Versailles thus became the tomb of feudalism in France, and Louis must have considered it cheap as compared to the cost of another Fronde.

For that matter, the huge structure would have been well worth the expense as a means of overawing other rulers. The sincerity of their admiration was expressed by imitation as a hundred shoddy little copies sprang up in Central Europe. The formal etiquette of the French court set the mode for such small fry, and the French language supplanted their native tongues.

The practical advantages of such a result were not lost upon Louis, who made statecraft and diplomacy his provinces. Although he had an able man in the foreign minister Lionne, trained by Mazarin, the king granted him no such freedom of action as Colbert and Louvois enjoyed. Hence it was the monarch himself who decided when at last the question of war arose.

Louvois professed to be alarmed at the state of the northern border. In that region the Spanish Netherlands maintained such fortresses as Lille, Charleroi and Armentières, while France possessed no sites for comparable bases. As a military remedy, the war minister proposed the outright seizure of a strip of Spanish territory, thus creating a new strategic front which would make Paris less vulnerable.

Louis saw the need with quick perception, but Colbert had yet to be persuaded. And here an agreeable surprise awaited, for the Man of Peace lent a sympathetic ear. Like so many advocates of a high tariff, he had become annoyed at the retaliations of competing nations, particularly the Dutch and Flemish merchants. He also dropped a hint that France needed another port on the North Sea—a port like Ostend in Spanish territory, or perhaps even such a splendid prize as the Dutch city of Rotterdam.

Louvois promised the utmost economy both of time and money. The king and Lionne set the diplomatic machinery in motion, citing justifications and seeking promises of neutrality. And in the summer of 1667 the armies of France swept across the frontier, making short work of an inadequate Spanish defense.

All objectives of the War of Devolution were taken by Turenne within six weeks, but the monarch had still another trump up his sleeve. Early the next spring, after a comfortable winter in quarters, he sent advance agents to corrupt the officials of Franche-Comté, an isolated Spanish province adjoining Switzerland. These missionaries were promptly followed by Condé with an army of 20,000 which overran the territory and claimed it for France.

Louis had no designs on Franche-Comté at this time, but the seizure served its purpose at the peace table. With a great air of generosity he offered to return the province to Spain in fair exchange for her fortresses of the Netherlands. Naturally the diplomats were not deceived by any such legerdemain, though the king gained not only his original ends but even some credit for magnanimity in less sophisticated circles.

The disappointed minister of finance was advised to be patient in regard to his seaport. For France's first aggression had alarmed half of Europe. Already the other nations were increasing their armaments, and as a good strategist Louvois reminded his sovereign of the advantages to be gained by striking first.

II

THE GRAND MONARCH

Thus our attacks reach their end by the shortest, the most reasonable, and the least bloody methods that can be used.

—VAUBAN

SHORTLY after the War of Devolution it grew apparent that Louis had singled out Holland for his next blow. Not only was there a sharp commercial rivalry between the two countries, but the king felt a personal antipathy to the democratic ideals and stiff-necked Protestantism of that small maritime nation.

On land the Dutch faced hopeless odds. Their army was a corporal's guard as compared to the 180,000 fully equipped men whom Louvois could now put into the field. By this time, moreover, Colbert had built up his navy to a formidable strength. In addition to these assets, the French monarch sought an alliance with England, which meant that the defenders would be outweighed nearly ten to one on a basis of population.

But perhaps the greatest contrast lay in the two forms of government. As a commercial oligarchy, then dominated by a peace party, Holland could arrive at military decisions only after the long and grave deliberations of assemblies. France, of course, could move swiftly and secretly as soon as the king and his ministers gave the word. In short, the coming clash was to test the relative wartime merits of democracy and absolutism, with all the advantages as usual appearing to favor the latter.

Before forming too hasty an opinion, however, it might be well to glance back through the past few centuries. In any such survey the observer will be struck by the disproportionate share of victories won by four small peoples, the Swiss, the Scots, the Dutch and the Swedes. This result cannot always be attributed to geography, since three of these countries had frontiers not entirely defended by mountains or sea. Only a single common denominator can readily be found for all four, and that is an early preference for representative forms of government. All four were fierce opponents of political or religious tyranny; all four were pioneers in the establishment of republics or limited monarchies. Yet despite such supposed handicaps, they gained some of the most thrilling triumphs of military annals, not only against numerical odds but also against the forces of despotism.

The plain lesson of history is that peoples perish because they grow soft and dull, not because they follow the instincts of freemen. No better illustration could be had than that of Holland, the most vulnerable of the four doughty little nations. Eighty years of war were required to win Dutch independence, and the effort broke the heart of Europe's mightiest despotism. Thus the long age of Spanish military supremacy actually came to an end in the Netherlands, even though a few stout tercios remained for Condé to destroy at Rocroi.

While Spain toppled into decline, her former colonies emerged from the conflict into the "golden century" of Dutch progress. During this period Holland produced such names as Hooft, Vondel and Huygens in literature; Hals, Steen, Vermeer and Rembrandt in painting. As a great humanist, Hugo Grotius laid the foundations of international law in his *De Jure Belli et Pacis*, which influenced the thought of Europe. Five chapters of this work urged military mercies as a policy of enlightened self-interest, and Grotius must be given large credit for the new era of moderation.

By 1660 the commercial genius of the "modern Phoenicia" had built up a trading fleet of 10,000 vessels, manned by 168,000 seamen and transporting goods valued at a billion francs annually. The nation's herring fisheries, supporting 260,000 inhabitants, brought in another billion francs each year. The Dutch East India Company alone was a world power surpassing most of the German principalities, for in 1669 these traders maintained 150 merchantmen, 40 warships and an army of 10,000 troops.

At the height of this period Admiral Martin Tromp, scourge of the Spaniards, is reputed by legend to have fixed a broom to his masthead to signify that he had swept the sea clean of enemies. But while history reveals no inherent military weakness in a democracy, there is a danger in the prosperity which had been created more often under representative than absolute forms of government. When large groups of citizens prosper from trade, they are only too likely to wax complacent, neglecting the national defense in favor of profits. Such symptoms were already apparent in Holland, the land of 40 per cent dividends, when in 1652 that nation faced the threat of Cromwell's military dictatorship.

England's motives were stated with forceful lucidity by Admiral George Monk, a former general under the Protector. "What matters this or that reason?" he inquired. "What we want is more of the trade which the Dutch now have."

There followed a 22-month sea struggle in which six battles were fought by fleets numbering from 70 to 120 warships on a side. Since Lepanto the world had not seen the like of these clashes for fury and endurance. Tromp, the "father of naval tactics," displayed all of his old fiery ability before he fell in action. Michel de Ruyter, his successor, gave proof of the talents which have caused analysts to acclaim him the greatest admiral of the century. But genius alone could not atone for the inferiority of Dutch ships, or the penny-wise policies of the merchants ruling the republic. Although Blake and Monk were beaten twice and severely handled even in their four victories, England was able to impose humiliating terms of peace.

The temporary ruin of her commerce and fisheries taught Holland a lesson which led to reforms before the struggle was resumed twelve years later. Nevertheless, De Ruyter labored under handicaps which he overcame by sheer skill and audacity. In a first engagement, fought near Lowestoft in 1665, he was forced by the defection of several captains to retreat from the Duke of York. The following year, however, he gained a smashing victory in the Four Days' Battle, a running encounter in mid-Channel between about 80 sail on a side. Taking full advantage of the dispersion of Monk's fleet, the Dutch admiral struck with a local superiority and sank 20 ships before driving the enemy to refuge in the Thames.

A few months later the victor in turn suffered a reverse in the battle of North Foreland, though the final honors of the war rested with him after one of the most daring exploits of naval history. The English, already exhausted by commercial losses, had laid up their fleet for the winter of 1667 when De Ruyter suddenly appeared in the Thames. Forcing an entrance past supposedly impregnable forts, booms and shore batteries, he pushed up the river nearly to London. For two weeks the glow of the burning shipping, including some of the navy's first-raters, lit up the night skies over a city recently devastated by the great plague and fire. Samuel Pepys' diary has left an account of the ensuing panic, for it was largely as a result of this raid that public opinion forced Charles to sue for peace. Naturally the Dutch were able to dictate terms, and it seemed to them a triumph of diplomacy—as it doubtless was in the year 1668—to cede the area of New York and New Jersey in exchange for Surinam and other large holdings in the East Indies.

WILLIAM OF ORANGE

The ink had scarcely dried on the treaty before the United Provinces faced the prospect of a new struggle against both England and France. In a despairing effort to escape this calamity the Dutch peace party made every concession, however revolting to the national pride. The aggressors were not to be cheated of their prey, and for lack of a pretext the English attacked a Dutch convoy in March, 1672. A few weeks later both Charles and Louis declared war as Turenne's 100,000 troops crossed the Rhine on copper pontoons invented by Inspector General Martinet.

According to their secret agreement the two monarchs were to divide the best Dutch ports between them, while Charles stood also to receive large subsidies as the price of his naval aid. Louis had not forgotten his own designs on the Spanish Netherlands, whose territory he took good care not to violate until he had first disposed of Holland. Hence he bargained with the elector of Cologne for a passage through neutral lands which enabled him to turn the Dutch flank and open the way to Amsterdam.

The defenders added bad strategy to weakness by scattering their 20,000 soldiers among obsolete fortresses which fell like overripe fruit. Soon the advance turned into a triumphant procession in which Louis played the conqueror's role with the pomp of an Assyrian despot. This time Colbert had proved reluctant, despite the lure of a seaport or two, but the campaign offered no reverses to justify his misgivings. On the contrary, the Dutch peace party went down on its knees, offering to cede Maestricht and other strongholds which would have given Louis the keys both to Holland and the Spanish Netherlands.

This was the turning point, for the refusal of the French king led to revolution in the United Provinces. The humble folk of the republic— the seamen and fishermen and toilers who supplied the sinews of prosperity—rose on all sides to repudiate the cringing offers of the merchants in power. Several of the leading pacifists were literally torn to pieces as the nation found new leadership by appointing William of Orange its stadholder in supreme command of the army and navy.

Never has there been a more breathless climax in Europe's affairs, since at this moment the French monarch still held the destiny of Holland in his hands. For several weeks the main sluices of Muyden lay within easy reach, and one French detachment even occupied the town for a short time. But Louis turned aside to capture a few second-rate fortresses, and the opportunity passed. The first act of William of Orange was to cut the Muyden sluices, so that once again the desperate little nation made an ally of its ancient enemy the sea.

Ship-of-the-Line, Seventeenth Century

All the flaming courage of the Spanish wars had been recaptured as Dutchmen rallied behind the twenty-one-year-old stadholder and a battered admiral who would soon observe his sixty-sixth birthday. Already the great-grandson of Holland's famous liberator showed signs of a cold and precocious ability which caused him to be respected by all men and loved by none. Having secured Amsterdam by flooding hundreds of square miles, young William set about grimly to raise troops and form defensive alliances. Meanwhile De Ruyter drew first blood by shattering the combined English and French fleets in the battle of Solebay.

Strange as it may seem, the age of sail had only lately revised naval warfare. Up to the time of Tromp admirals still thought in terms of the head-on attack adapted to vessels aiming to ram or board. The Dutch commander introduced the first line formations suited to broadside-firing ships, though he was never reluctant to turn a battle into a general mêlée at close quarters. Tromp also became a pioneer in the direction of unified fleet tactics by means of codes and signaling flags.

The English, who never scorned to learn from a worthy adversary, borrowed these ideas and added some of their own. Thus the experience of the first two Dutch wars went into the *Fighting Instructions* written by the Duke of York who was soon to be crowned James II. This manual prescribed an advance in line abreast, then a sharp swing into a single column proceeding on a course parallel with the foe. The effect depended on precise seamanship, since obviously the broadsides would be more concentrated when fired from ships sailing as close to one another as skillful navigation permitted.

At Solebay, with the fate of his country in the balance, the old Dutch sea dog never lost the calm for which he was renowned. The morning of the action he swept his own cabin as usual and fed the chickens he always kept on board the flagship. Near the east coast of England his lookouts sighted the 101 allied ships of the line which he had deceived by a feigned retreat. De Ruyter commanded 91 sail of a generally lighter or inferior class, but without hesitation he gave the order to attack. Using his advantages of surprise and a favoring wind, he drove a wedge between the English and French squadrons at the beginning of the action. Then detailing a division to "contain" the latter, he fell upon the Duke of York with such fury that the English escaped a complete disaster only by the arrival of reinforcements.

The losses on both sides were heavy, but De Ruyter had won a timely victory in strategic as well as tactical respects. By putting the allies to flight he prevented an intended descent on his own coast; and after administering the defeat he was able to convoy a Dutch merchant fleet bringing direly needed supplies.

Throughout the next twelve months De Ruyter managed to keep the sea lanes clear for his hard-pressed countrymen. The allies attempted no more large-scale operations until June, 1673, when a fleet attempted to open the way for the landing of English troops in Holland. The nation was then in such straits that William lacked ammunition for both land and sea forces; but he made his choice by ordering the old admiral to block the invasion at all costs.

In any contest between allied and Dutch fleets the importance of the locale must not be overlooked. English and French vessels were built for deep coastal waters, while the shoals off Holland made it necessary to design flat-bottomed warships of lighter and less seaworthy construction. In the Channel this factor worked out to De Ruyter's disadvantage, but now he stood on the defensive in his own shallow bays with craft better suited to such waters. Also in his favor was the historical lesson that allies never pull together as well as the forces of a single nation.

The odds against him were thus somewhat reduced, though his genius must be given chief credit for one of the most brilliant campaigns in naval chronicles. In the first two actions, fought in the Schoonveldt Channel, the allies with 81 ships of the line sought to draw his 55 vessels out of their protective shoals. De Ruyter as usual chose his own time and place, surprising the enemy squadrons on June 7 before their line had formed. They suffered a sharp repulse; and again a week later the Dutch admiral attacked with such success that the allied fleet had to return to England for repairs, while his own losses were light.

In both engagements De Ruyter used fire ships to good effect. This ancient mode of attack, revived by Tromp against Blake and Monk, was of course reserved for the side holding the weather-gage, or windward position. The results depended on exact timing, but the blazing hulks were capable not only of creating disorder in an opposing line but also of working a great deal of destruction.

The decisive battle of the Texel took place near the mouth of the Meuse on August 20. De Ruyter, with not more than 60 ships of the line, faced upwards of 90 commanded by the French vice-admiral, D'Estrées, and Prince Rupert, former cavalry leader in the English civil wars. The object of the allies was to land troops from a convoy of transports, while the Dutch admiral stood on the defensive in coastal waters too shallow for their heavier craft.

The action began at dawn when he seized the weather-gage and bore down on the three enemy divisions—30 French ships in the van, Rupert with about the same number in the centre, and Sir Edmund Spragge commanding the rear. De Ruyter attacked in three squadrons, sending 12 ships under Bankert against the French while he launched the main assault against the two English forces. As at Solebay, he planned to "contain" the French, who in turn attempted to divide their strength and place Bankert between two fires. This proved to be a fatal move against so resolute an opponent, for the Dutch vice-admiral put up his helm and ran through the larger detachment of 20 sail, creating such havoc that the French van took no further part in the action. With this result gained, Bankert wore around to the aid of his chief, who meanwhile had cut Rupert off from the English rear.

Thanks to such enterprise, the Dutch now had equal numbers for the attack on the English squadrons. The affair turned into a furious gunnery duel lasting until late afternoon, with the English taking the major part of the punishment. At last Rupert contrived to reunite his scattered forces, and after a few hours of more cautious fighting De Ruyter had to withdraw at sundown for want of ammunition—a handicap which during the day had saved the enemy from more serious damage. Reports of the sinkings are too conflicting for mention, though the allies unquestionably had the heavier losses in a battle which the naval critic Mahan has likened to Nelson's masterpiece:

> He [De Ruyter] went to this final strife of the two great seapeoples in the fulness of his own genius, with an admirably tempered instruments in his hands, and with the glorious disadvantage of numbers, to save his country. The mission was fulfilled not by courage alone, but by courage, forethought and skill. The attack at the Texel was, in its general lines, the same as that at Trafalgar . . . but as the odds against De Ruyter were greater than those against Nelson, so was his success less.

Even if he had sent the whole allied fleet to the bottom, the victor could scarcely have added to his far-reaching results. Nine days after the battle William of Orange was enabled to form an active alliance of the United Provinces with Lorraine, Spain and the Empire. At once Louis hastened to offer terms which would have been a wild dream a year before, but the stadholder sternly refused. Six months after the Texel, following a period of inactivity and bickering between allies, the English signed a separate peace, remaining neutral for the rest of the war. As a final benefit, the French monarch, now on the defensive himself, withdrew the last of his armies from Dutch soil just twenty-two months after launching the invasion.

VAUBAN'S THREE PARALLELS

During the breathing spell won for him by his admiral, William raised a large army of Dutch, Danish, Spanish and German troops. In 1674, with Holland out of danger, he marched to the aid of his new allies in the Spanish Netherlands, then occupied by Condé. Both commanders were spoiling for an action, and the clash became William's first and Condé's last battle.

It was also the first important test of the new training and tactics introduced by Louvois, which by this time had been copied throughout Europe. The Dutch general held a large advantage in numbers, though his men were inferior in every other respect to the superb regiments drilled by Martinet. Despite this fact, coupled with his own youth and inexperience, William attempted a surprise and was himself brought to bay near Seneffe. After hours of bloody fighting Condé claimed a triumph by virtue of capturing the enemy's baggage; but he took no joy in losses which amounted to 17 per cent in slain alone for both armies. Nor could it be denied that William had drawn off his remnants in good order.

The glory did not interest Europe's soldiers as much as the professional lessons taught by Seneffe. At the outset it was evident that the staggering casualty list had been no accident. Battle losses were bound to be severe when soldiers advanced shoulder to shoulder, halting at the word of command to trade volleys at distances suited to dueling pistols. Only an iron discipline could nerve men to keep on reloading and firing while they stood firm amid the heaped-up bodies of writhing or motionless comrades. Only years of drill could school them to close up their tattered ranks and march forward with the bayonet at that slow and solemn pace of eighty steps a minute.

As compensation it became apparent that battles would not be joined as often as before. Obviously the line of infantry was even more vulnerable than the column to cavalry attack. The thinner formation had to be protected at all times by horsemen against the bloody and hopeless confusion wrought by the charge of enemy squadrons. Even when secured from this peril, the line could gain its best results only on level, unbroken ground. Both the volley and bayonet charge depended on a precision which might be thrown into fatal disorder by an insignificant ditch or mound. Hence the encounter battle had become largely a relic of the past; and future actions would depend virtually on mutual consent when either general could refuse by retiring to wooded or rolling country.

The king pondered these tactical problems and reached his own conclusions. He felicitated the victor of Seneffe, but he also placed him on the list of retired generals.

Louis himself, as nominal commander of a French army, had recently been given credit for a triumph which seemed to offer the utmost in military profit at a minimum hazard. Just thirteen days after investing Maestricht, one of the strongest fortresses in Europe, his forces had surrounded the works with a maze of open trenches which rendered the defenders helpless. The capitulation had been obtained, moreover, at a total cost in lives which was less than many a battalion had paid at Seneffe.

At least the king did not deceive himself as to the identity of the victor at Maestricht. He realized that the success had been made possible by an engineering officer, Sébastien le Prestre de Vauban, who knew more about the related sciences of siegecraft and fortification than any other man on the Continent.

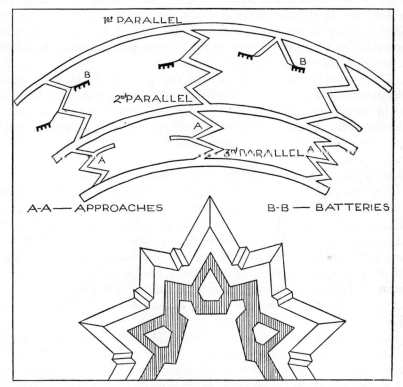

Vauban's Parallels and Approaches

Under a more narrow sovereign Vauban might have missed his opportunity for want of blue blood. The son of poor landowners, he had been left an orphan in childhood and brought up among peasants whose outlook he retained all the rest of his days. At the age of seventeen he enlisted as a simple soldier and gradually climbed to a lieutenant's commission. Soon his talents were brought to the attention of Louvois, and Vauban's rise thereafter became a proof of the recognition given merit in the new French army.

Before 1673 he had both built and taken smaller strongholds, but his real fame began at the age of forty with the siege of Maestricht. There Vauban introduced the system which was to govern siegecraft for the next 150 years. After cutting off a fortress from outside aid, he planned to begin operations with a first trench, or parallel, dug just beyond the range of the defenders' artillery. From this protection the approaches were pushed forward to a second parallel, linked in the same manner to a third within striking distance of the outer works. As shown in the accompanying sketch, the approaches were opened in a zigzag fashion, especially as they drew nearer to the fortress guns, in order to afford a maximum of cover against cannon balls.

This system of trenches gave the attackers a sheltered line of communications all the way up to the fortifications. Then batteries were brought up to the second parallel in an effort to breach the ramparts and silence the fire of the defenders. While the artillery duel went on, underground galleries were dug from the third parallel to the vicinity of the glacis and counterscarp. Picked troops were brought up from the rear, and gunpowder mines located under the sectors chosen for the assault.

Now the climax of the siege had arrived. With his preparations complete, the attacking commander summoned the garrison to surrender. The answer depended on the progress the defenders had made with their artillery fire and the sorties sent out against the opposing batteries and parallels. If the terms were refused, the besiegers exploded their mines and special groups of volunteers known as "Forlorn Hopes" charged through the débris to storm the remaining works. At this crisis the fate of the stronghold was decided in several hours of hand-to-hand fighting.

Seldom in the new age of moderation did events reach such a stage. Vauban, one of the most sympathetic soldiers of all time, believed in conserving lives from motives of humanity as well as mere cold economy. A former private in the ranks, he never lost the viewpoint of the humble pawn of war; and during the course of years his four published treatises made him the mentor of Europe in all questions regarding siegecraft.

Owing chiefly to his influence, military men accepted a detailed etiquette ruling the conduct both of the besiegers and the besieged. Surrender, far from being held a disgrace, was considered praiseworthy when further resistance could end only in needless slaughter. The defenders were usually accorded all the honors of war, marching out with drums beating and flags flying. Officers were at once paroled, and soldiers stood a good chance of exchange after a brief period of not too burdensome captivity. Meanwhile it became the duty of the victors to protect unarmed inhabitants from pillage or acts of violence.

The rare exceptions may be traced to occasions when the governor of a stronghold displayed a stubbornness which his age held neither heroic nor practical. Then the storming troops were likely to get out of hand after their sanguinary ordeal and pay back a captured city with the torch and sword.

In every age military geography has shaped the trend of tactics, and circumstances destined the late seventeenth century to be an era of siegecraft. With all armies provided by their own magazines, fortresses served as depots for food and ammunition rather than refuges for troops. The roads of the Continent were still in a miserable state as compared to Roman highways, so that canals and rivers remained the principal avenues of military supply. On the other hand, these waterways made it possible to transport on barges the heavy cannon which otherwise could never have been brought up for a siege. Hence the warfare of the day developed into a contest for the possession of fortified river and canal towns which held the same strategic importance as the railway junctions of the present time.

Maurice and Gustavus had broken the ice of tradition, but Vauban organized the first engineering corps of uniformed soldiers whose operations were combined with those of other arms. There was nothing infallible about his system of parallels and approaches; and a long series of triumphs can be attributed in nearly every instance to superior skill, foresight and timing. His capture of Maestricht, a fortress dominating vital inland waterways, served France better at the time than if he had won a victory in the field. A few months later he took Trier after another brief siege, thus gaining control of the river Moselle for the supply of Turenne's forces in Germany. The following year Vauban directed the one defense in which he ever took part, the successful resistance of Oudenarde.

In many of his operations fewer soldiers were killed and wounded than perished of illness during the building of the palace at Versailles. Campaigns of this sort appealed to the king's love of moderation, and beginning with Maestricht it grew to be the custom for Louis and his court to appear soon after the investment of a famous fortress. In turn the nobles and their ladies brought a throng of valets, seamstresses, hairdressers and purveyors whose livelihood depended on luxurious tastes. Before long the rude accommodations of the troops were flanked by another and more elegant tent city peopled with courtiers wearing velvets, brocades, silk stockings and powdered wigs.

Racing has been called the sport of kings, but in this age the term might more accurately have been applied to war. The bitter scent of death could scarcely be recognized amid all the lotions, perfumes and pomades. Every day the nobles and their ladies gathered on some hilltop to enjoy the panorama of Marshal Vauban spinning his web of parallels and approaches around the entrapped city. Every day the nobles and their ladies awaited the arrival of a courier galloping into camp with news of Marshal Turenne's latest manoeuvre on the Rhine. Wagers were laid on the outcome with a feverishness ordinarily reserved for duels, flirtations and palace intrigues. And when at last the doomed stronghold laid down its arms, the nobles and their ladies were still in attendance to watch the captives march past with dull drums and trailing banners.

Strangest of all, the man who provided these royal pageants remained simple and unspoiled. In contrast to the servile courtiers surrounding the king, he spoke his mind with blunt honesty, as many surviving letters reveal. Louis not only accepted this frankness without rebuke; he repaid it with a measure of confidence which the scowling Louvois or chill Colbert had never enjoyed. Thus for the next thirty years we have the spectacle of Europe's most despotic ruler showing his admiration for the peasant who found a marshal's baton in his knapsack.

Turenne's Last Campaigns

After leading the French invasion at the outset of war, Turenne marched to the Rhine and defeated the Great Elector of Brandenburg, then the only ally of Holland, in an easy campaign. But William's diplomacy soon raised a coalition of enemies, and the victor fell back on the defensive with inferior resources.

His opponent in the autumn of 1673 was Count Raimondo de Montecucculi, the general who had saved the Bavarians from annihilation after Turenne's triumph at Zusmarshausen in 1648. This prince of the empire had begun his career as an unknown Italian adventurer, becoming a simple soldier in the Austrian army at the age of sixteen. Ten years later, rising to the command of a regiment under Tilly, he distinguished himself in the operations against Gustavus. After being taken prisoner, Montecucculi devoted a long captivity to military studies; and his own *Memoria della Guerra* won a lasting reputation as a treatise on the art of war.

Now after the lapse of a generation the two veteran commanders met again on Bavarian soil, each with nearly a half century of experience behind him. Both were too wary to be enticed into battle at a disadvantage, and the campaign became wholly a duel of manoeuvre between the foremost masters of the Continent.

Montecucculi scored first. With greatly superior numbers he drew Turenne to the river Main, then outguessed his opponent by making a surprise crossing to the right bank. Next the imperial commander stole a rapid march to Frankfort, turning Turenne's position and forcing the French to beat a painful retreat to the Rhine for supplies. Montecucculi came on as if in hot pursuit, but suddenly left his adversary waiting and advanced on another French force at Trier. Turenne, who could do little now except conform to his enemy's bewildering moves, followed with the intention of defending the city. Again he was outwitted, for Montecucculi vanished from the Trier vicinity to join forces with William of Orange, far to the north. The combined armies then besieged Bonn, taking that stronghold after reducing Turenne to the rôle of helpless onlooker.

Without a single action being fought, the imperial general had gained all the objectives sought by the school of manoeuvre. He had repeatedly cut his opponent off from supplies; he had worn him down by deceptive marches and countermarches; and he had thrice managed to leave Turenne in the dark as to imperial intentions. The results of the campaign were worth several battlefield victories, for the allies had established an unbroken line from the North Sea to Bavaria. Cologne and Munster had been knocked out of the war as Louis' allies, while Denmark and most of the German princes were encouraged to join the coalition against France.

Throughout the strategic duel Turenne and Montecucculi exchanged almost daily courtesies by messenger, often congratulating each other on some happy move. Such amenities, so hard to understand in a day of mass hatreds, were common at a time when the bulk of the population scarcely knew that a war was in progress. National lines were not closely drawn, and every famous general had among his officers a number of foreign volunteers serving as apprentices. Thus Turenne made a favorite of a young colonel whom he called his "handsome Englishman," and who was to be better known to history as the Duke of Marlborough.

Early in the spring of 1674 the French commander crossed the Rhine with some 10,000 troops and fell upon an equal number of allies under the

Duke of Lorraine. After storming the entrenched camp at Sinsheim, Turenne forced the enemy to accept battle on a steep hillside covered with vineyards. Line formations being impossible on such ground, he placed his cavalry between two wings composed of infantry platoons mingled with squadrons of horse. This unusual array carried the heights to win a complete victory, killing or capturing nearly 3,000 of the enemy.

Shortly afterwards, in obedience to Louvois' instructions, Turenne laid waste the Palatinate to prevent that region from supplying an imperial army. This was the first of the occasional exceptions to a rule of moderation, though the war minister had been harsh enough in the requisitions he wrung from Holland. The king expressed his regret, but royal disapproval did not save the region from the torch. Many of the homeless inhabitants took ship for America, setting a precedent of emigration which would be followed by thousands of war-weary Europeans.

Turenne fell back across the Rhine as two imperial armies converged on him, each larger than his own. Until October he fenced skilfully with both to prevent a junction. Then as the situation grew more urgent, he singled out the nearest force for a battle at Enzheim in which his 20,000 troops won an indecisive victory over 36,000 allies. Neither side improved its prospects, and Turenne had only the satisfaction of inflicting 6,000 casualties at a cost of 3,500 to himself.

He continued his retirement into Alsace, being unable to keep the enemy forces from combining, and in late November both sides prepared as usual to go into winter quarters. At any rate the sixty-four-year-old French commander went through the motions, for he was planning a campaign which caused Napoleon to proclaim him "the only general who ever grew bolder with age."

He masked his intentions by repairing the forts of middle Alsace, as if determined to stand on the defensive. Then stealing away into Lorraine, he swung behind the Vosges and divided his troops into small detachments for purposes both of speed and deception. The three-week march over the mountains proved an ordeal for men struggling through snowstorms, but Turenne reunited his army at Belfort and debouched into Alsace from the south.

The imperialists meanwhile had split up among the villages for a comfortable winter. The festivities of the Christmas season had reached their height when the incredible news came that the French were ten miles from headquarters. In wild alarm the allied generals gathered their scattered forces for battle; but on January 5, 1675 Turenne won a splendid and decisive victory at Turkheim, gaining all Alsace at a blow.

Thirty squadrons of his cavalry pursued the beaten remnants to the Rhine, and the victor moved into the quarters which the enemy had so hastily vacated.

In the spring Turenne and Montecucculi met again. The latter had the numerical advantage over a French army of 20,000, but neither strategist attached much importance to mere weight. As supreme imperial commander, Montecucculi had the more valuable assets of a friendly countryside and a better chain of magazines. His object being to retake Alsace, he moved down the left bank of the Rhine to menace Philippsburg with its French stores. Turenne in turn threatened the Strasbourg region, where the enemy's supplies were concentrated.

Such feints did not deceive either veteran, and the turning point came when the French general suddenly threw his forces astride of the Rhine, controlling both banks by means of a pontoon bridge. After this surprise he had his dazed adversary following French moves, always a trifle too late. The duel continued for two more months, nearly every advantage going to Turenne. At last Montecucculi betrayed his frustration by essaying a desperate night attack, which the French repulsed with ease. A few days later Turenne manoeuvred his opponent into a position near Sasbach which left the enemy few hopes either of victory or escape. Usually cautious in his predictions, he exulted to his officers on the eve of battle, "It is done! I have them now!"

These were his last recorded words, for he was killed by a cannon shot while drawing up his forces. Thus perished an old campaigner whose operations Napoleon advised every military student to "read and reread." Esteemed as a great artist in his own war-loving era, Turenne was mourned by a court which included such lights as Corneille, Racine, Molière, Boileau and La Fontaine. His appeal to following ages has been that of a "soldier's soldier" rather than popular hero, a preceptor in the sciences of manoeuvre and logistic precision.

Owing to his personal ascendancy over troops calling him "our father," Turenne's officers lost the opportunity he had created at Sasbach. The imperial general suffered double the casualties, but he won the battle and sent the French streaming back into Alsace. In order to save that region Louis found it necessary to summon Condé out of retirement and raise reinforcements. But Montecucculi soon gave up his command because of age and illness, and in the end Turenne's gains were preserved.

The war dragged on for three more years, its pace growing slower as the various state treasuries diminished. In 1676 Louis' brother, the Duke of Orleans, revealed an unsuspected talent by defeating William at

Cassel and overrunning Flanders. The king remained adamant in his prejudice against costly battles, and the victor was promptly recalled.

The only other action of importance took place on the sea when William sent De Ruyter to dispute the French command of the Mediterranean. The Dutch fleet proved woefully inadequate for the mission, but no protest was heard from a stout old fighter who in his day had ordered several captains shot for flinching. His Spanish allies became an encumbrance, and De Ruyter received a mortal wound at the age of sixty-nine while directing the decisive battle off Sicily. The able French admiral, Duquesne, followed up his victory a few months later by destroying the allied fleet at anchor.

By 1678 all belligerents were weary of the struggle. The French held a comfortable advantage on every front, and Louis decided that the time had come for negotiations. In order not to risk any territorial gains, he appealed to the Dutch merchants by sacrificing Colbert's protective tariffs. They rose to this bait, and in 1679 a pact was signed which gave the aggressor nearly every prize he had sought in the war. Nor, on the other hand, did the United Provinces lose a single village, though the nation had been fighting for its life at the beginning.

William of Orange, the most bitter opponent of the treaty, swallowed his rage for three days after the conclusion of peace. Then he swiftly assembled his battalions and attacked an unsuspecting French army near Mons. The outcome of this strange affair merely demonstrated that talented new generals were ready to succeed Turenne and Condé. Although caught off balance, the French commander Luxembourg made a notable recovery; and after a bloody day's work he administered a sound beating to his assailant at the cost of several thousand lives on each side.

THE STRIFE OF DIPLOMACY

In his fashion the French monarch kept the peace no better than William. For it was during the uneasy interlude between wars that his armed diplomacy got in its best efforts.

Louis depended on the ancient technique of the *fait accompli*, which has never been bettered by aggressors down to the present day. As a result Europe had to endure an anxious decade in which his diplomatic tactics of the last war were repeated and varied at the expense of Spain, the Empire and smaller states.

In 1668 he had seized Franche-Comté with the intention of bartering Spanish territory at the peace table for other Spanish territory which he more earnestly desired. At the same time he staked a specious claim to the province through possession, and now in 1678 he gained a permanent title at the Peace of Nymegen.

Louis took care that many clauses of the treaty were left vague enough to permit future triumphs of this sort. He had not been awarded full possession of Lorraine, but pretexts were readily found which "justified" interference. French soldiers poured over the border, reducing the unhappy duke to exile as a mercenary general in the imperial army.

Nor had Louis been granted all of Alsace, though he lost no time in discovering dynastic "rights" which led to the devouring of that province in hasty gulps. Fragment after fragment of imperial and Spanish territory vanished from its owners in the same manner. First came the preliminary "interpretation" of the peace clauses. Next the French claims were solemnly "legalized," and Europe was confronted by still another *fait accompli* as the king's troops moved in overnight.

Moderate in diplomacy as well as arms, Louis limited his provocations to many and small seizures. Though his appetite for territory proved insatiable, he confined himself to a mouthful at a time, so that the victims would scarcely feel that their loss warranted the redress of arms. Only when a prospective dupe had his back turned did the monarch abandon his customary caution.

Such an opening came in 1683 as Vienna faced the last great Ottoman invasion. The emperor called on Europe for a latter-day crusade; but the Most Christian King of France sent his troops to lay hold of Strasbourg, an imperial stronghold from time immemorial. He firmly established himself on the Rhine while John Sobieski, king of Poland, marched to the Danube with a force of 40,000. This army, combined with the imperialists led by the deposed Duke of Lorraine, finally defeated the Turks under the very walls of Vienna.

Never had Louis seemed more the insolent Grand Monarch, invincible either in peace or war. So far his armies had not lost a single major engagement, nor had his diplomacy met with a real reverse. But the king was not infallible, and even at this height of his power he made blunders which brought grave consequences.

One of the most serious was his revocation of the Edict of Nantes, that great compromise which guaranteed civil and religious rights to both Catholic and Protestant. By proclaiming it a crime to profess the reformed faith, Louis lost at a stroke of the pen more loyal subjects than he had gained in all his conquests. Civil warfare flared up in France; and despite the laws forbidding emigration, a total of nearly half a million Protestants fled the realm. These pilgrims included a high percentage of skilled workmen and trained soldiers or sailors, many of whom took up arms against France as a result of persecutions which had been deplored by Pope Innocent XI.

The king's second great error lay in his underestimate of the Dutch stadholder. Perhaps Louis is not to be blamed, since only a seer could have foretold the part which would be played by this ugly duckling of history. For a parallel it would be necessary to go back to ancient times, when in another mercantile nation the hatred of the Barca family for Rome had forged a Hannibal. In the United Provinces the House of Orange had already produced a William the Silent and Maurice of Nassau as foes of oppression. And now their young descendant bore the French despot an enmity so relentless that he would never rest until all Europe took up arms once more against the aggressor.

Personally a gloomy and repellent character, William seemed to have been created as an avenging fury. Asthmatic, tubercular and partly crippled, he endured physical ills which would have broken most men. Yet it was this wasted body which bore the main burden of Europe's struggle against French designs. It was this implacable will which did most to unite the nations against Louis, so that war broke out again in 1689, with France beset by England, Holland, Spain, Sweden, Savoy, the Empire and certain Italian and German states.

III

MARLBOROUGH AND EUGENE

I am now at an age when I find no heat in my blood that gives me temptation to expose myself out of vanity; but as I would deserve and keep the kindness of this army, I must let them see that when I expose them, I would not exempt myself.

—THE DUKE OF MARLBOROUGH

THE odds against Louis XIV seemed crushing, as they always do when an aroused continent turns on an aggressor. Without allies of her own, France faced enemies on six fronts, while on the sea her fleets had to contend against the two foremost maritime powers of the world.

Yet a closer analysis will disclose that the most worth-while assets remained on the side of the French. Louvois had at last brought to a climax his lifelong task of reorganizing an army now numbering 375,000 trained soldiers—a larger total than the nations of the Grand Alliance could hope to put into the field. Colbert's navy had likewise reached its peak with 60,000 sailors manning ships of much better design than those flying the Dutch and English flags.

Two other factors aided the French, as they have every encircled war power since that day. First, the armies of the Grand Monarch were under a single head, which gave them an incalculable advantage over allies split by the usual suspicions and disagreements. Even more important, these armies had the benefit of interior lines against divided enemies. In other words, France held the hub of the strategic wheel, sending out her forces

347

along routes comparable to the spokes, while the opposing nations had to operate around the rim.

Such sources of strength must be given consideration when one is inclined to pity an outweighed belligerent, hemmed in from all sides. Time and distance also enter into the equation, and the actual numerical advantage goes to the side which can respond with the most men at the moment when they are most needed.

France, in short, had superior force in 1689 to pit against superior bulk. The strategic difference between the two became evident as the armies of the Sun King rolled forward on all fronts, taking their limited objectives with ease. Louvois, as usual intent on depriving the enemy of supplies, ordered a second devastation of the Palatinate, and the country around Mannheim, Spires and Worms was cruelly laid waste. Only a generation ago this would have been considered a routine operation, while now a universal outcry arose. Old military vices died hard, but at least such devastations were no longer endured as legitimate warfare.

The great event of the first year proved to be the bloodless coup which ended in the crowning of the Dutch stadholder as William III of England. During the last war he had won a diplomatic victory by wedding Mary, the Protestant daughter of the prince who became James II. Opposition to that Catholic monarch grew steadily in England, and in 1688 James had to flee the country after the conspirators crossed the Channel. A few months later William and Mary began their reign.

Louis had been well aware of the plot to overthrow his royal brother. He offered to reinforce James with French warships, but an excess of confidence led the English king to refuse. Both monarchs believed that the revolution would be easily put down, bringing England into the war on the side of France.

On the contrary, James had become a refugee whose only prospect of regaining the throne lay in an Irish counterrevolution. He landed in that troubled island in March, 1689, with the aid of a French fleet bringing 6,000 soldiers. Admiral Herbert tried to resist the invasion with English ships but met defeat in the battle of Bantry Bay. James then made Dublin his capital and began recruiting Irish troops to supplement his French battalions.

The Jacobite rebellion spread with such rapidity that William himself had to desert the main theaters of war and sail for Ireland. As a general he had Marshal Schomberg, a Huguenot who joined the enemies of Louis XIV after his expulsion from the French service. One of the most able soldiers of the day, he brought James to a stand on the river Boyne in the summer of 1690. The Jacobites numbered about 25,000 against the 35,000 English, northern Irish, Dutch, French Huguenot and Danish contingents of the enemy. The battle was decided by skill rather than numbers, however, as Schomberg and William launched a left-wing cavalry attack across the river, striking the rebels in their right and rear. The Huguenot general lost his life in the fighting, but his victory compelled James to seek refuge in France after abandoning the routed remnants.

The importance of the Boyne lies in its historical results, for the losses of neither side were heavy. As a diversion the campaign had been a blow to the allies, yet Louis did little to take advantage of their distress, even though his troops won a great victory in Flanders on the very day of the battle in Ireland.

During the last war the Duke of Luxembourg had shown an ability matched only by his unpopularity, and history has likewise neglected one of the strangest of all military geniuses. Not only had he won the battle of Mons after repelling William's treacherous attack; he exhibited an even brighter talent during the famous retreat to Maestricht in which his 20,000 men evaded every attempt of 70,000 allies to cut off or surround them.

The marshal's belated recognition may be traced to a character which Louvois found repulsive and the king barely tolerated. A hunchback from birth, undersized and distorted in mien, Luxembourg first acquired an evil reputation as a suspect in poisoning plots. Only his high birth and close association with Condé got him out of prison, but he continued to make enemies at court. In time his ill fame spread to the people, and verses were hawked about Paris which compared him to the legendary Faust, intimating that the duke had sold his soul to the devil for military glory.

At any rate he remains one of the few generals who never lost a single action of importance. He also merits historical distinction as the first general to command the larger armies of the new age. In 1690, at the age of sixty-two, he retained a fierce vitality which enabled him to sit his horse for long hours. Harsh to his own men and unfeeling in his attitude toward the conquered, he still exacted a grudging admiration for an intellect which cut through military problems like a sword.

In the Fleurus campaign he originated a marching order, copied by all armies down to the time of Napoleon, which gave rise to the famous maxim, "March always in the order in which you encamp, or purpose to encamp, or fight." The French army advanced for four days in close order, covered on all sides by a cavalry screen in addition to front, flank and rear guards. Its numbers amounted to 45,000, though Luxembourg commanded as many more men in combined operations. At Fleurus he caught up with the 40,000 allies under the Prince of Waldeck, who had taken a stand behind a double barrier of marshy brooks, his flanks resting on villages.

The position was a strong one, but the French marshal conceived a plan of battle which for boldness and scope has few equals during the century. First launching a frontal assault, he sent his left-wing cavalry through the woods to envelop Waldeck's right. Meanwhile he himself led the cavalry of the French right, supported by infantry and artillery, in a wide sweep around the enemy's left. The execution was so perfect that the three shocks struck Waldeck's lines in rapid succession, and all his efforts to repair the damage led to worse. At the end he had been reduced to a quarter of his cavalry and only 14 battalions of foot, which formed a square and retired to broken ground. Luxembourg's losses were 2,500 in a victory which cost the allies 48 guns, 150 colors, 5,000 slain and 8,000 captured. But instead of following up the success, he was ordered by Louvois to keep in line with the other French armies.

The following month a very ordinary general, Marshal Catinat, won the battle of Staffarda over the allies in Piedmont. He contributed little to an outcome which mainly proved how superior the French troops were to any men the Grand Alliance could put into the field. In morale as well as training and equipment, Louvois had created an almost invincible host; and many of the nation's military traditions and marching songs date from this period.

The first French artillery regiment had been formed in 1684, at last putting an end to the guilds of semi-civilian cannoneers which had served armies since the invention of gunpowder. Yet for all of Louvois' improvements in organization, it cannot be said that he bettered field tactics. Cannon continued to be used chiefly in preliminary bombardments, for no soldier since Gustavus had ever recaptured the mobility and effectiveness of his guns.

Under Louvois the regiment was administrative, while the battalion of 17 companies numbering 60 men each, or a total of 1,020, became the infantry tactical unit. In the cavalry the squadron of 180 horsemen, divided into three companies, served the same purpose. As late as 1690 a few pikemen remained in the ranks, though the bayonet had generally replaced that ancient weapon in all armies.

Some of the greatest changes of the new era occurred in the sphere of command. As was observed by the military writer Guibert, small armies carrying out large operations had suddenly been replaced by large armies performing small tasks. Nevertheless, the responsibilities of the general had been much increased. In a past age he had commanded forces of from 15,000 to 30,000 in massed formations which presented an infantry centre between two cavalry wings. With such an array, covering a very small front, one man could supervise every detail of the shifting scene.

Then came the army of from 40,000 to 100,000 in line, occupying several miles of front. Results depended far more on precision, yet every move still had to be directed by a single commander-in-chief stationed in the rear where he had a full view of the field. There were as yet no staffs in the modern sense of the word, though he was assisted by several generals and perhaps a score of younger officers. This tense little group of mounted men watched the fighting, reporting any unusual turn to the commander. He formed his decisions instantly on the basis of their information rather than advice, transmitting his orders by means of runners who sought out the battalion officers in the smoke veiling the action.

It is the privilege of every age to scorn the military past, yet one cannot help wondering how well a great many latter-day generals might have fared in 1690. Command under such circumstances must have been a moral and physical trial, but the crippled French marshal continued to prove his fitness for directing the larger armies. The summer after Fleurus he won another victory over Waldeck in the battle of Leuze; and in 1692 Luxembourg defeated William III in the bloodiest clash of the war.

The English king brought off a surprise at Steenkirke after misleading his opponent with false information. As a result Luxembourg was caught with his forces separated when the allies attacked at dawn. William did not strike with his entire weight, and the battle developed into a race as each commander speeded fresh troops to the scene. No more exacting test of generalship could have been had, while terrible sacrifices were demanded of infantry battalions exchanging volleys at close range. Luxembourg at last brought up enough reinforcements to repulse the allies and capture most of their guns. Only a part of each army got into action, but 8,000 troops were killed or wounded out of the 15,000 leading William's attack. The French losses, though less severe, caused Louis to impose further restrictions on the victor.

THE BATTLES AT SEA

Colbert died of overwork in 1683, having already seen many of his policies nullified by the king and Louvois. But the greatest achievement of the Man of Marble remained intact—a navy which during his lifetime had grown to surpass the combined English and Dutch fleets. England's naval architects frankly copied French designs, and the French naval academies anticipated by two centuries anything of the sort in England.

The first encounter at Bantry Bay in 1689 had been a weak affair. Not a ship was sunk by broadsides fired at long distances, and the English fleet retired from the action after granting the enemy all objectives. Yet in honor of this "victory" Admiral Herbert became an earl.

The following year he suffered a defeat off Beachy Head that could not be glorified by English pride. With 56 ships of the line he met Admiral Tourville's fleet comprising 70 sail of equal or better quality. Herbert bore down in line abreast, bringing his van into action with little support from the centre and rear. Tourville made the best of this dispersion and only a calm saved the allies from disaster. As it proved, Herbert reached port with most of his fleet after burning 16 ships to prevent their capture. The French did not lose a vessel.

The two battles ushered in a new naval era which would have astonished such fighters as Blake, Tromp and De Ruyter. Where ships had once been expendable, their value being judged by the hurt they inflicted on the foe, the primary object now grew to be the conserving of one's own forces. Toward this end admirals became preoccupied with the niceties of approach, so that the ends of battle were subordinated to the means.

De Ruyter had shown that decisive actions could be fought with line tactics, but his successors preferred to burn gunpowder at ranges too long for much damage. After Beachy Heady the island kingdom was seized by an exaggerated fear of French invasion, and the command of the naval forces passed to Admiral Russell. He withdrew the beaten squadrons to the Thames, adopting a passive defense and conceding Tourville the freedom of the sea lanes. Thus was announced the celebrated doctrine of the "fleet in being" which has inspired so much controversy ever since. Instead of risking his remnants in combat, Russell held that their mere presence in port constituted a threat which would deter the French from landing troops. The outcome supported his belief, and the "fleet in being" theory still has its place in naval strategy.

At the time the result may be charged to the fact that the French navy took its orders from Versailles. Louis proved no more eager than Russell to hazard his ships, and for two years the victorious fleet did little to exploit its success. Tourville, though lionhearted in action, dared not assert his prerogatives, and by 1692 the opportunity had passed. For the English had meanwhile built up a superiority which gave them a two-to-one advantage at the next meeting.

From an excess of prudence Louis flew to the opposite extreme, sending Tourville an unconditional order to seek an engagement. With 44 ships of the line the French admiral sighted an English fleet of 99, which he attacked without hesitation. Despite his handicap in numbers, he displayed such tactics and seamanship that the fighting ended at dusk without a single French ship having been sunk or captured. The enemy had sustained at least equal damage when Tourville retired; but during the retreat 15 of his vessels were cut off by an adverse tide in the Race of Alderney, making it necessary for their crews to burn or scuttle them.

The battle of La Hogue could scarcely have been called a glittering allied triumph, and Tourville's subsequent losses were not fatal. Yet from that date French sea power declined as swiftly as if it had been blasted away by the guns of the enemy.

The real reasons go back to a centralized control which had already nurtured French commerce so lovingly that it could not survive in competition with the weedlike growth of Dutch and English trade. In the same spirit the French navy had been tended by Colbert like a hothouse flower. Entirely a military organization, it had no reserves of merchant seamen to draw upon, as did the more rugged English and Dutch fleets. Hence it lost vitality as the war progressed, especially since the persecutions of the Huguenots had robbed it of more trained men than fell in all the battles combined. Naval construction, moreover, is the most expensive form of national aggrandizement; and after having been pampered until it became delicate, the French fleet was now being starved for lack of funds.

La Hogue had little to do with that result, but never again would the gallant Tourville challenge foes who grew stronger year by year. Money could not be found either to build new French ships or repair old ones. The sea-borne commerce of the nation dwindled for lack of protection, thus completing the vicious circle; and during the remainder of the Grand Monarch's reign his warships took part only in privateering operations.

Growth of Military Engineering

Although it was not so apparent at the time, the armies of Louis XIV had also passed their zenith. These last great victories wear an autumnal brilliance, as if their very splendor were a symptom of decay. Vauban continued to take his cities and strongholds. Luxembourg continued to win every engagement. And yet the roots of the French military system were already withering for want of nourishment.

The causes were much the same as those which had brought about the naval decline. But they do not entirely explain a curious reluctance on the part of French strategists to take any advantage of the most smashing land victories. Allowing for all possible obstacles, France lost several opportunities to bring the War of the Grand Alliance to a successful conclusion. Luxembourg at various times had both the troops and ability to break Holland, the centre of resistance, whereupon the weaker allies might have sought terms. But Luxembourg merely won battles while his royal opponent, defeated on every field, won the war.

This failure must be ascribed to a certain meanness of outlook on the part of Louvois and the king. From the outset the two men directed nearly every operation from Versailles, insisting that each campaign be synchronized to the creeping advance of six armies on as many widely separated fronts. Such a master plan, however logical in theory, could not help but penalize enterprise and exalt an unthinking obedience.

As economies grew more and more desirable, the king and Louvois met the issue by curtailing operations rather than striving for a decision. Hence they both favored a limited strategy aiming at the methodical reduction of bases and strongholds. Louis loved the pageantry of a siege, while the capture of magazines appealed to a minister specializing in the logistic side of war.

Vauban profited from their attitude, becoming the only French general whose campaigns were not stifled by too much supervision. Long before hostilities began, he had been kept busy at fortifying the new frontier won by the king's acquisitive diplomacy. Military engineering thus was given an impetus such as it had never known before.

Vauban's mastery may be traced to his long experience both as a destroyer and builder. During his career he directed 40 sieges as chief engineer without a single failure being recorded against him. On the defensive, he constructed or repaired more than 160 strongholds, incorporating into them all the ideas he had formed while overcoming enemy fortifications.

As a penalty of fame he had a school of imitators whose admiration of his methods often exceeded their understanding. These disciples promptly reduced his principles of fortification to "Vauban's three systems," and engineers were labeled according to their preference for the First, Second or Third. But Vauban wrote nearly as well as he built, and his treatises prove him to be less limited than his followers.

"One does not fortify by systems," he insisted, "but by common sense." As evidence, a study of twenty-eight fronts constructed by him revealed that no two were identical, while all had been varied to take advantage of local conditions.

The single "system" found in all his fortifications consisted of an emphasis on active rather than passive defense. Beginning where his predecessors left off, he shared their preference for the tenaille trace, though adding unique touches of his own. Ditches 18 feet deep and parapets 18 feet thick were typical dimensions, and Vauban went beyond previous builders in providing for enfilade fire. Each of his fronts stressed not only the possibilities of artillery defense but also of infantry counterattack. Every provision was made for the concentration of garrison troops at threatened points, for sorties outside the works, and for hand to hand fighting at the crisis.

In his defensive theories Vauban ranks as a talented developer rather than originator, for his greatest creative powers were devoted to the attack. After perfecting his parallels and approaches, he turned to experiments in mining, publishing the findings in his *Traite des Mines*. Due to his influence, companies of trained miners were incorporated into all French engineering regiments.

"Place besieged, place captured" became a French adage to celebrate the parade of Vauban's captures. His only worthy rival was the Dutch soldier Menno Coehoorn, inventor of a small siege mortar bearing his name. To this engineer were also attributed three systems of fortification featuring complex works suited to the Low Countries. In his attacks he depended on great masses of artillery to prepare the way for costly advances across the open.

The theories of the two engineers were tested in 1692 at Namur, built by Coehoorn and defended by him against Vauban. The latter took the fortress in 36 days at a cost of 2,600 killed and wounded, while the garrison had double the casualties. Three years later Coehoorn attacked his own stronghold, though Vauban was not present. The Dutch general required 60 days to gain a surrender, suffering some 18,000 casualties in comparison to 8,000 French losses.

The first siege is famous for the introduction of ricochet fire, which became Vauban's most effective method of assault. Before 1692 he had relied on a concentration of cannon to breach the escarp with a succession of shots making a knifelike cut through the revetment. The new attack consisted of reduced charges which dropped a ball just over the parapet to ricochet along the terreplein, destroying the men and guns in its path. When accurately aimed, such fire could cause terrible execution, and some years passed before adequate defenses were found.

Vauban also has a good claim to recognition as the father of grenadiers. His capture of Namur owed in large part to the training of picked infantrymen in the tactics of the comparatively new weapon. The French used no less than 20,000 grenades in this operation alone, giving such a convincing demonstration that Louvois soon formed special battalions of men who today would be described as storm troopers. Only the strongest and bravest could qualify for this dangerous duty, so that the tall grenadier guards came in time to be known as the élite of every European army.

While Vauban went on taking fortresses, Luxembourg won a victory over William which represents probably his greatest tactical achievement. The allied leader, though he loved war with an unholy fervor, had never become more than a plodding general. Still, by all the standards of the day he had every right to feel secure in his fortified and entrenched camp at Neerwinden. A hundred cannon stood along the convex front; the right wing lay behind the small river Geete, and the left had the protection of a marshy stream.

After reconnaissance Luxembourg judged the position to be too crowded to be impregnable. He opened the battle with an attack on the village in William's centre, enduring two repulses with heavy bloodshed before gaining a precarious foothold. Meanwhile, as he had hoped, his opponent drew troops freely from both wings to support his centre. This provided the opening for the main French assault against the extreme left, where the defenders fell into confusion as they changed front. Soon the flight of the allied left-wing cavalry led to a rout in which the bulk of William's foot was driven into the Geete with losses of 18,000 slain, wounded and prisoners in addition to 104 guns. The French casualties also were grievous, but after Neerwinden the victor became known as "the upholsterer of Notre Dame" because of the captured colors he had sent to that cathedral during the war.

As usual no advantage was taken of the success. Nor did Louis encourage Catinat to follow up the second beating he administered to the allies in Italy at the battle of Marsaglia.

The war settled into routine campaigns which dragged on for several more years with few military events worth noting. In 1697 the French general, Vendôme, captured Barcelona. That same summer Vauban brought his career to a climax by taking the strong fortress of Ath in 23 days at a cost of only 50 men. On other fronts the French armies managed in general to hold their gains, for the king clung to a defensive strategy during the latter stages of the conflict. That autumn he himself offered sacrifices in territory which led to the Peace of Ryswick.

Europe considered this treaty a triumph for William III, whose victories in diplomacy offset his defeats in the field. His native United Provinces had again given France her stiffest resistance, aided by the sea power of his adopted country. But even though French finances were badly depleted, the nation had suffered no reverses to warrant the renunciation of previous conquests in Alsace and Lorraine. Time was to prove that the Grand Monarch had other motives for seeking peace, so that Europe would soon be faced with a new *fait accompli* which dwarfed all past aggressions.

THE WAR OF THE SPANISH SUCCESSION

Toward the end of the War of the Grand Alliance it had become plain to Louis that Charles II of Spain could live but a short time. This imbecilic monarch was the last of his line, and in the lack of an heir the French royal family had a strong hereditary claim to the Spanish throne. Bavaria and the empire also had their candidates, while all the other nations were profoundly interested. With indecent haste the ministers of Europe flocked to Madrid, each trying desperately to advance his own interests.

The Peace of Ryswick led to several years of diplomatic warfare in which threats, bribes and promises took the place of bullets. In this contest Louis XIV emerged as victor. Despite the fact that France had been continually at war with Spain for three quarters of a century, the dying Charles II made a will naming as his successor Louis' seventeen-year-old grandson, the Duke of Anjou.

Europe was now confronted with the gravest menace of the century. Spain alone would not have been a formidable French ally, but her empire still included Milan, Naples, Sicily, Sardinia, the southern Netherlands and vast holdings in the Americas. As the head of this powerful combination Louis would have control of the Mediterranean as well as American trade. Never had the Grand Monarch's diplomacy won a greater triumph, and he added to it by forming secret alliances with Bavaria, Savoy and Cologne.

World domination now lay within his grasp, yet for some months the other powers seemed too paralyzed to unite against him. Although war had become inevitable as the new century dawned, Louis might have postponed its outbreak if success had not led to insolence. Again Europe awakened to the spectacle of French troops crossing the frontier in sudden little rushes. One by one the fortresses of the Spanish Nether-lands were seized in defiance of the terms of Ryswick, their Dutch garrisons ousted and their works strengthened.

The Empire struck the first blow in 1701 when an Austrian army marched into Italy without a declaration of war. By the next spring England, Holland, Denmark, Portugal and most of the German states had also taken up arms against France and her allies.

The Sun King and his subjects faced their fourth war in a somber mood. All the famous French military leaders of the past had died— Turenne, Condé, Colbert, Louvois, and within recent months Luxem-bourg and Tourville. Only Vauban and the monarch himself were left, and the two old men quarreled. The great engineer, moved by the misery of the realm, dared to suggest that the Protestants be restored to their former liberties. Next he sounded the first note of the Revolution by writing a book advocating a more equitable system of taxation. Louis could not tolerate such ideas even from a favorite, and Vauban remained in retirement until his death in 1707.

Including reserves, France could raise some 400,000 troops for the new campaigns, but the quality had degenerated. In order to find funds the king revived the pernicious system of selling offices, both civil and military. As a consequence mere children held nominal commands, while both the training and equipment of the army were neglected by Louvois' successors.

The very first battle on the Rhine produced a wild panic and flight of French infantry battalions—something which would have been unthink-able in past wars. Only the timely charge of General Villars' cavalry turned the rout at Friedlingen into a victory over mishandled German forces. At least this commander showed promising talents, but Louis could not be sure of the new generation of military leaders. In Italy one of his favorites, Marshal Villeroi, was defeated at Chiari by Prince Eugene with losses of 3,000 as compared to 150 fallen imperialists. As a worse humiliation, Villeroi was afterwards surprised at Cremona and taken prisoner in his nightshirt.

THE BLENHEIM CAMPAIGN

The enemies of France held an undeniable superiority at sea, and no longer were they so outweighed in the field. Thanks to the lessons taught by disaster, these powers now had armies of veteran troops whose training and equipment Louvois would not have scorned.

Their weaknesses were moral rather than material. Like all allies of history, they suffered from a lack of cohesion and leadership, and inevitably a tradition of defeat had grown up during the last two conflicts. This spirit is understandable when we reduce the era to terms of individual experience. Thus a Dutchman who had reached the age of eighteen at the time of Louis' first aggression would now have become a man of fifty-three. His whole adult life, including the troubled interludes which passed for peace, would have been spent in dread of the Grand Monarch's next move. Yet never during this period, however devoutly he may have wished it, would the armies of France have taken a single decisive beating.

The turning point came with the naming of fifty-two-year-old John Churchill, Earl of Marlborough, to the command of the Dutch and English armies. As yet, though he had risen to the rank of captain general, this handsome courtier was distinguished chiefly for such unmilitary traits as tact, charm and serenity. In 1688 he won promotion by betraying James, but a few years later was imprisoned in the Tower by William III on an unproved charge of treason. Not until the death of the latter and the accession of Queen Anne in 1702 did Marlborough find his opportunity. Then as commander-in-chief he took several important fortresses without a failure, being raised to the title of duke as a reward.

Already Marlborough had disclosed a knack for smoothing out the differences of allies which has never been surpassed by any soldier. It proved a thankless task, since his supposed inferiors were often upheld by the Dutch deputies who supplied most of the troops of the army. The rulers of Holland, having copied the vices of French strategy along with the virtues, insisted on a methodical warfare of posts and sieges throughout the first two years. France had recovered meanwhile from her early reverses, and in 1703 Marshal Villars won a second great victory over the imperialists at Höchstett, losing only 1,000 men to the enemy's 11,000.

By the following spring the armies of France held the initiative on eight fronts. They seemed on the way to repeating their triumphs of the last three wars when Marlborough asserted himself. His Dutch masters, who paid him 10,000 pounds a year to insure their authority, would have preferred another campaign of siegecraft. Instead, the English general decided to challenge the French and Bavarian forces on the Danube who were preparing to seize Vienna.

The conception of a thrust from Flanders into Bavaria was so bold that the Dutch would not allow their troops to take part. With only English or English-paid soldiers, Marlborough crossed the Meuse on May 12, 1704, and reached the Rhine on the twenty-third. On June 22 his army joined forces with the Germans under Margrave Louis of Baden, finishing the long march in surprisingly good condition.

Here for the first time Marlborough conferred with Eugene of Savoy to begin a famous collaboration. This imperial prince, born a French subject, had taken service in the Austrian army as a youth. Now at the age of forty-one he had reached the prime of a career which lasted half a century and included thirty campaigns as commander.

The two generals agreed to separate operations until the moment came to unite for a decisive battle. While the prince manoeuvred along the Rhine, Marlborough and the margrave decided to capture Donauwörth as their base on the Danube. The town was defended by the entrenched hill of the Schellenberg, held by 12,000 Bavarians; but the allies stormed the position, regardless of losses which amounted to 6,000. Only a fourth of the Bavarian survivors cut their way through to the main army.

In this bloody assault battalions of English grenadiers took a prominent part. Already the new weapon had made its way from siegecraft into regular infantry tactics, proving especially useful in the assault of entrenched positions. Special pay and privileges were accorded the grenadiers of European armies, and the tall men chosen for this service soon set the style in military dress with their lofty shakos and swaggering uniforms.

After establishing his magazines around Donauwörth, the English general marched through Bavaria, burning and destroying with a harshness reminiscent of Louvois' devastations. His object was to bring the elector to terms, and neither bribes nor entreaties obtained any mercy for the blackened countryside.

In August the enemy looked forward only to a few more leisured manoeuvres before going into winter quarters. The two mediocre French commanders, Villeroi and Tallard, were examples of the king's growing tendency to choose his generals on a basis of birth or personality rather than ability. With three armies at their disposal, these marshals permitted Marlborough and Eugene a junction in Bavaria for the purpose of forcing a battle on Tallard alone near Blenheim.

Even so, the 52,000 allies were slightly outnumbered by a Franco-Bavarian army holding a position of unusual natural strength. One of Tallard's flanks rested on the Danube, the other in the hills; but he made the mistake of drawing up his French and Bavarian contingents as

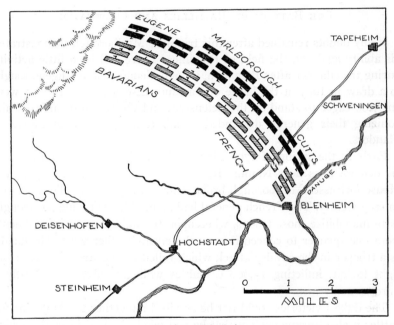

Battle of Blenheim

separate forces. Marlborough selected the weak joint in the centre for his main attack, ordering Eugene first to fix the enemy's attention on the right wing, while Lord Cutts performed the same duty on the left.

The French fought magnificently behind their uninspired leader, and Cutts fell back after two costly repulses. Eugene also became heavily involved on the Bavarian side of the field. But Marlborough's purpose had been accomplished, for Tallard had stretched his line to repel the assaults on both wings. The duke himself now delivered the decisive stroke in the centre, where his fresh squadrons opened a fatal breach between the French and Bavarian lines. Into this gap the victorious horsemen poured, wheeling left to drive thousands of fugitives into the river.

Marlborough's losses were 12,000 in a victory which destroyed Tallard's force and virtually knocked Bavaria out of the war, depriving France of her only stout ally. At least 15,000 of the losers were killed, wounded or drowned, in addition to the 11,000 who laid down their arms. The French marshal himself became a captive as the rags of his army fell back in disorganized retreat.

THE BATTLES OF RAMILLIES AND OUDENARDE

If any doubts remained after this triumph, Marlborough demonstrated his ability again on the field of Ramillies. There had been little activity during the summer after Blenheim, though Vendôme and Eugene fought to a draw in Italy at the battle of Cassano. Elsewhere the French were only too eager to stand on the defensive; and the Dutch deputies, while lionizing their general, demanded a dull campaign of manoeuvres in Flanders.

Early in the spring of 1706 Marshal Villeroi at last ventured out of his defense lines near Namur. Before he could reach the safety of the Meuse fortresses Marlborough brought him to bay at Ramillies and won an easy victory. The French general had secured his left wing so strongly as to immobilize those troops, whereupon the duke drew reinforcements from that quarter to concentrate on the enemy's other wing. He fought as a trooper in the cavalry attack which rolled up the French army from right to left, inflicting 15,000 casualties while the allies lost hardly a third as many men.

The duke's victories could not be ascribed altogether to his genius for battle; it also became evident that he had taken the lead in tactics which the French had held so long. In all Europe there was no infantry to match his Dutch battalions, and the English cavalry had established a like supremacy.

These results were due to training as well as a personal ascendancy over motley allies who loved the man for his tact, justice and courage. Where the French infantry depended on the bayonet, Marlborough placed his faith in disciplined musketry. Where the French fired rank by rank, his men fired platoon by platoon. And where the French volleys were hasty, he drilled his men to let the other side shoot first, even at the cost of painful losses. Then while the enemy reloaded, Marlborough's soldiers brought up their pieces with the air of executioners whose aim could not fail.

The merits of platoon fire may be traced to the superior discipline made possible by the smaller unit. In his cavalry tactics the duke reversed the order, depending on cold steel and shock effect where the French had grown to rely less on the saber than the pistol. In this choice Marlborough was upheld by the experience of history, and the victories of his squadrons led to the greatest cavalry revival since the time of Cromwell.

After their beating at Ramillies the French had been briefly encouraged by a success which Vendôme won in Italy. This unpredictable marshal, who has been aptly called "a sluggard in camp and a giant in combat," took advantage of Eugene's absence to shatter the imperialists at Calcinato. The remnants were driven into the mountains, where Eugene rallied them with difficulty. But Vendôme was soon rewarded with a command in Flanders, and the prince fell upon his weak successors to win the decisive battle of Turin, which put an end to French hopes in Italy.

In 1708 the centre of gravity shifted to Flanders, where Vendôme boldly laid siege to Oudenarde. Marlborough and Eugene, as usual in perfect harmony, moved at once on his strong defensive position. The French essayed a right-wing advance to throw the allies off balance before they could form in line. The attempt resulted only in the other wing remaining inactive while the right and centre took the brunt of the allied assault. Next the Dutch marshal Overkirk was sent by Marlborough entirely around the enemy's right, and at the crisis these squadrons charged from the rear to complete Vendôme's defeat. The allies took 8,000 prisoners and inflicted 6,000 casualties while losing but 3,000 men.

The naval situation meanwhile served more effectively than lost battles to increase France's misery. At the beginning of the war a French and Spanish fleet had dared an indecisive action with the English off Malaga, but heavy losses discouraged a second venture. Thereafter the ships of the island kingdom ruled the seas. They transported troops across the Channel with impunity. They sailed audaciously into Vigo Bay, capturing a whole Spanish treasure fleet on which Louis had counted for funds. They even won a foothold on the shores of the Mediterranean by their seizure of Gibraltar in addition to Minorca with its harbor of Port Mahan.

The French were helpless except for the harm their privateersmen could do to enemy commerce. Often this damage was impressive after raids carried out by several ships of the line, and the English merchants complained bitterly. But as Mahan and other critics have pointed out, such destruction is in itself a confession of naval impotence. At least the injured nation is able to maintain a commerce worth raiding, while at this period the ports of France were filled with merchantmen rotting at their piers.

The economic consequences, added to the terrible burden of expense, brought the nation to the brink of ruin in 1708. The war had already been lost on land and sea, and Louis swallowed his dynastic pride to save his subjects further suffering. The terms he offered were more than reasonable, they were abject. He consented to give up territory right and left, to cease all aid to his grandson on the Spanish throne, even to subsidize the allies in their efforts to unseat that monarch.

But the victors had waited too long for this moment. They were in no temperate mood, and Louis learned that peace would be granted only on condition that he take up arms with his former foes against his grandson. To this the king would not agree. "If I must fight," he said, "I will fight my enemies and not my children."

Armed with a conviction of right, he appealed directly to his own subjects—a rare resort for a ruler of that day. All classes responded with remarkable loyalty, and the allies now faced a conflict which fore-shadowed the people's wars of the future.

The nation lacked only a leader, and this gap was promptly filled by Claude Louis Hector, Duke of Villars, whose advancement had lagged far behind his self-admiration. At the age of fifty-five his record included distinguished service under Condé, Turenne and Luxembourg, but pro-motions had been tardy because of Louvois' dislike. Even in the present conflict, despite his high birth, Villars reached the rank of marshal only after winning two great battles. Hence he remained a junior to such dullards as Villeroi and Tallard, who led the main armies while rele-gating him to secondary fronts.

In the emergency France rallied to his magnificent courage. The oppor-tunity was created for him by the winter of 1709, which added the last bitter drop to the nation's cup of woe. The cold gripped the entire con-tinent in December, continuing with an intensity never known before. The canals in Venice were frozen solid, even the mouth of the Tagus in Portugal. Cattle and sheep perished in the fields, and after the fourth month of glacial temperatures the seed corn died in the soil of France. This frightful winter was followed by a cold, rainy spring in which the new crop rotted before it could sprout. The death rate mounted in French cities as the peasants subsisted on roots and herbs. For the enemy had ships in which to import food, while the blockaded realm faced a slow starvation.

Still, France had one son who could strut and boast. Marshal Villars, a Gascon by birth, shared the miserable rations of his soldiers and bragged so loudly that the whole kingdom heard. His quips and vaunts were repeated everywhere by haggard countrymen who alternately laughed, wept and believed. Never, in truth, since Joan of Arc had Frenchmen given their trust so devoutly as to this greathearted Falstaff. Genuine volunteers joined the ranks, and it was not altogether a gesture when the Grand Monarch himself offered to serve if the need arose.

Louis stripped the palace of jewels and gold to raise funds. He taxed the nobles and debased the currency. Meanwhile he kept up a modern propaganda campaign with circulars explaining his rejected peace offers; and angry countryfolk armed themselves with forks and flails as the allied tide swept on toward Paris.

Lille had fallen that winter, despite the heroic resistance of the aged Marshal Boufflers. During his whole career Marlborough did not incur a failure in siegecraft, and Tournay capitulated in the spring after a costly attack. The victors moved on Mons in August, but this time Villars was willing even if not prepared to fight. With an army of 90,000 including a large proportion of raw and ill-equipped recruits, he stood squarely in the path of the 100,000 allies led by Marlborough and Eugene. There were two taut days of hesitation, then the final test came in the greatest struggle ever waged so far by armies of the modern world.

THE BATTLE OF MALPLAQUET

As a preliminary error the allied councils misjudged the temper of France and her new leader. The idea of mass patriotism was incredible in 1709, and Villars appeared a blusterer trying to stiffen dubious and untried troops. Marlborough and Eugene decided therefore to attack the French army in woods and marshes defended by palisades, trenches, abattis, cannon and every manner of obstacle that military skill could contrive. The allied commanders agreed on a plan of battle which contemplated a false attack by Eugene on the French right. After the enemy had been committed in this quarter, Marlborough planned to aim the real blow at the left by concentrating heavy forces in combination with a turning movement through the woods.

On this decisive day Villars' generalship proved worthy of his own high estimate. Far from being beguiled by the containing attack on his right, he managed without weakening the other wing to involve Eugene's troops in grave difficulties. The French fought like demons, recruits as well as veterans, hurling back the Dutch infantry time after time with fearful slaughter.

Marlborough launched his main attack against resistance such as he had never met before. In the crisis Villars took personal command of men who sold every trench and palisade at a terrible cost. When the valiant braggart suffered a bad wound, he continued to command from a chair until falling over insensible. Next, Eugene was wounded in the head, and Marlborough nearly collapsed in the saddle from exhaustion. By this time the bloody affair had turned into a "soldiers' battle" in which the opposing lines surged back and forth with more fury than direction. After seven hours of fighting the allied centre, until then but little engaged, advanced across the open with serious losses to push back the weary defenders. Old Marshal Boufflers, who had succeeded to the French command, wisely decided to withdraw in good order.

The allies laid claim to a victory on the usual grounds of possessing the field, but all the other benefits of Malplaquet went to the French. Their losses were 10,000, while no less than 24,000 Dutch, Austrians, English and Prussians lay dead or wounded after a battle that was not matched in bloodshed until the year 1812.

At first the slaughter seemed barren of results. It did not even save Mons, which the duke took before going into winter quarters. But as time went on, the far-reaching effects justified Villars' boast to the king, "If it please God to give your majesty's enemies another such victory, they are ruined!"

The Dutch army—the best that maritime power ever raised—had been too riddled to recover fully. The Prussians were also sore and disgruntled losers. Disputes between the allies multiplied, for all spirit as well as justice appeared to have fled from the cause. But the worst consequence came months afterward when Marlborough was recalled in disgrace. Malplaquet had furnished his political foes in England with just the sort of ammunition they needed to topple the duke from his pinnacle.

Shattered in health, he commanded a last brilliant campaign in 1711. Villars had established a fortified line from the Scheldt to the sea which he derisively named *Ne Plus Ultra* after his opponent's taste in dress. The chain was too strong for frontal assault, and Marlborough resorted to such strange ruses as to acquire a reputation for madness. Dashing hither and yon, he pursued a game of military hide-and-seek which had Villars bewildered. Finally the English general doubled in his tracks, penetrating the *Ne Plus Ultra* after a march so strenuous that hundreds of men fainted on the road. But the success resulted only in the capture of Bouchain; and a few weeks later the duke was dismissed from the service, remaining in exile until the end of the war.

Although Malplaquet had been the decisive battle, the struggle dragged on for several more years. On the southeastern front, where invasion threatened, France was saved by the talents of the Duke of Berwick. The natural son of James II and Malborough's sister, this English soldier led a French army to victory over an English army commanded by the French soldier Ruvigny at the battle of Almanza. But as a rule Berwick shunned combat while depending on complex manoeuvres to deceive or wear down the enemy.

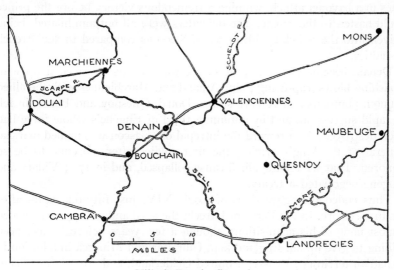

Villar's Denain Campaign

At this type of warfare, which has always been appreciated more by professionals than laymen, the duke ranks as one of the great masters. He earned the praise of his illustrious uncle with whom he corresponded affectionately. Napoleon also became a later admirer who approved Berwick's habit of shooting profiteers. The only first-rate soldier of the House of Stuart, which stood so much in need of military genius, the royal bastard literally marched the enemy out of Spain in three campaigns, bringing his task to an end with the storming of Barcelona.

On the northern front Eugene took charge of the allies after Marl-borough's fall. Their forces still amounted to 120,000, and the French had to maintain a passive defensive in 1712 while the prince took Le Quesnoy. Next he moved on Landrecies and Villars decided to fight. Still suffering from the effects of his wound, the marshal had a grave numerical handicap to overcome. This he accomplished by a succession of rapid feints which resembled and equaled Marlborough's manoeuvres on the *Ne Plus Ultra* lines.

Threatening here and there, Villars finally lured the prince into divid-ing his forces. Eugene expected an attack at Landrecies, where he moved the bulk of his troops, and even the French were deceived as to their commander's intentions. But Villars left a mere detachment behind and slipped away in the darkness with his main force. After an all-night march he reached Denain late in the morning and took the entrenched allies by complete surprise. Without rest his columns stormed the enemy lines in a bayonet attack, winning a tremendous victory before the prince could hasten to the rescue. The defenders were all but annihilated, being driven into the Scheldt with losses of 8,000 as compared to 500 French casualties.

Denain became the last battle of the war. Villars followed it up with smashing blows, capturing Saint-Amand and Marchiennes with the allied cannon, pontoons and reserve stores. Douai, Quesnoy and Bouchain fell in rapid succession, and by autumn a third of Eugene's whole force had been destroyed. As a reward the intrepid old Gascon was named marshal general of the king's armies, the first soldier after Turenne to be so honored. That winter the allied cause collapsed, and in 1714 Villars and Eugene negotiated a treaty.

Thus ended the aggressions of Louis XIV, just fifty-one years after his first seizure. In the Peace of Utrecht the aged and weary ruler yielded almost none of his acquisitions, though a few years before he had been willing to give up all. England kept Gibraltar and Minorca in addition to Canadian territory; Prussia acquired Gelderland, and Austria the Span-ish Netherlands and Naples.

Spain had been badly shorn, while little Holland emerged from the struggle too exhausted to remain in the first rank of European powers. Nor could it be said that France's new cities and provinces compensated her for the misery of those darkest years. At any rate, we have the testimony of the Grand Monarch himself, who confessed to posterity on his deathbed, "I have been too fond of war. . . ."

IV

THE KING AT ARMS

Few men are gifted with sound reasoning powers, thus it is the human heart that we must search. Without having studied this most profound and sublime side of war, one can scarcely hope for the favors of fortune.

—SAXE

THE term "world war" became a later conceit, yet it may be noted that every nation of Europe resorted to arms during the first years of the eighteenth century. Asia, Africa and the Western Hemisphere had some part in operations; and though the campaigns are recorded in terms of one cipher less than those of today—armies of a hundred thousand instead of a million—the impact was proportionately as heavy on the small world of that age.

Side by side with the War of the Spanish Succession, the Great Northern War involved the principal kingdoms of the Baltic. From 1700 to 1718 Sweden fought Denmark, Poland, Saxony and Russia, at last losing a struggle which cost her most of her empire.

The northern nation's prestige had suffered in 1675, when as an ally of France she was invaded by Denmark and defeated by Brandenburg at the battle of Fehrbellin. Her fleet was destroyed, her commerce ruined, her southern provinces laid waste, and some of her territory in Germany lost.

During the reconstruction period of the next two decades, Charles XI assumed almost despotic powers while putting the army, navy and finances back on a sound footing. On the death of this able monarch in 1697, the *Riksdag* ended a brief regency by crowning the fifteen-year-old Charles XII after declaring him of age. Two years later Denmark, Poland and Russia formed a coalition to take advantage of the supposed weakness of Sweden and the inexperience of her ruler.

The moment was not as propitious as the heads of those nations imagined. Not only had Sweden's armed strength been fully restored, but the heir to the throne showed an uncommon precocity. Trained under his father's direction from the age of four, he began his reign with a fierce scorn for peace, diplomacy and Parliamentary institutions. And though the sword had been forced upon him, young Charles was first to strike. Singling out Denmark for his blow, he compelled a protesting admiral to risk the fleet in a channel of the sound which had never been navigated before. In August, 1700, the army landed only a few miles from Copenhagen, accomplishing as much by the surprise as if a victory had been won in the field. Within two weeks Denmark signed a humiliating peace which provided for an indemnity of 200,000 rix-dollars.

This treaty became the king's last compromise. Without returning to the homeland, he set out on the fantastic military adventures which were to keep him away for fourteen years.

From Denmark he hastened to Livonia with only 8,000 troops to combat Poland and Russia. The forces of Peter the Great were besieging Riga and Narva, and in November Charles marched to the relief of the latter through a wasteland of bogs. His passage was disputed at one point by 6,000 Russian cavalry, but the king put them to rout with 400 horsemen. And at Narva he won his first battle by storming the Russian fortified camp in a snowstorm, overcoming numerical odds and inflicting several times his own losses.

His advisers urged him to follow up this victory, for the wretched quality of the Russian troops had been revealed at Narva. At this time the violence of Peter's reforms had demoralized his realm, and a Swedish invasion might have incited widespread revolt. But the very weakness of Russia decided Charles in favor of attacking Poland, which seemed the more dangerous of his two foes.

The King of Saxony and Poland typified the worst German despotism of the age. Called Augustus the Strong because of his gross appetites, he left 354 illegitimate children as his chief claim to historical fame. The moral tone of the court at Dresden is suggested by the fact that one of his natural daughters became his mistress after marrying her half-brother.

The royal glutton and lecher had no love for war, however, and took the field reluctantly after his Polish crown was declared forfeited.

Charles had been able meanwhile to overrun Livonia, Lithuania and Courland. In the spring of 1702 he occupied Warsaw and summoned the Polish diet to depose Augustus. The elector at last appeared to defend his crown, and at the battle of Klissow the combined Saxon and Polish forces were easily routed.

Up to this point the stern, ascetic young king presents an appealing picture, his face set resolutely against the storms of Europe's power politics. But now it grew evident that war had become a passion as he rejected every peace offer made by Augustus.

Madness as well as genius ran in the Swedish royal family, and diplomats began to suspect the former when Charles kept the field after both honor and profit had been satisfied. During the years from 1703 to 1706 he campaigned constantly, defeating the Saxons and Poles in two more battles, and pursuing a beaten Russian force through the forests of Lithuania. So easily were these victories obtained that some historians have not found them convincing. Indeed, a startling explanation has been advanced by Winston Churchill, the biographer of his great ancestor Marlborough:

> In their fear of Prussian dominion both the Czar and King of Saxony had adopted the most desperate expedient open to statecraft. They had deliberately courted defeat at the hands of Charles XII so as to bring Sweden and Prussia face to face.

This prospect so alarmed the enemies of Louis XIV, who were themselves courting Prussian aid, that Marlborough was sent to woo Frederick I away from a Saxon alliance. With threats, bribes and promises he accomplished this mission; and Prussia prepared to fight France while Charles marched unopposed to Dresden, forcing Augustus to renounce his Polish crown.

The conqueror could doubtless have made political capital of his position, but at no time did he seem interested in such gains. Europe's diplomats felt easier when he left Saxony in 1707 to invade the dominions of the czar. After receiving reinforcements from his anxious kingdom, Charles assembled his largest army, 20,000 foot and 24,000 horse. On the first day of 1708 he crossed the Vistula over treacherous ice as the enemy fell back before him. Not until July did he encounter resistance near Holowczyn, where the king won the last pitched battle of his spectacular career.

The way to the Dnieper lay open, but the Swedes were already suffering as the enemy retired, laying waste the country and cutting off detachments of foragers. By December the march had become a nightmare of hardships, and Charles abandoned the direct route to Moscow. Turning southward, he planned to unite with the Cossock hetman Mazeppa, then in revolt against the czar. Peter anticipated this move by putting down the uprising, so that Mazeppa was reduced to a few hundred men. As an added disaster the Russians cut off and destroyed a Swedish army bringing supplies.

Europe's terrible winter of 1709 now trapped the invaders. Throughout this ordeal the slim, blond king slept on the frozen ground with his men and shared their meager rations. The army had only half its original numbers left by spring, but in June the king laid siege to the fortress of Poltava, hoping to gain a base while awaiting fresh troops from the homeland. Peter marched to the relief with much larger numbers, and the decisive battle occurred when Charles attacked the Russian fortified camp.

Since his defeat at Narva the czar had worked miracles of modernization. His "window to Europe" had been opened at St. Petersburg; he had built a new navy, and reorganized the army beyond all recognition. It was thus a force of well-drilled troops, armed with 120 guns, which Charles faced at Poltava. Peter's generals, moreover, had introduced a tactical novelty with their redoubts—isolated field fortifications in which picked troops were posted at intervals along the front.

Although he had been wounded in a recent skirmish, the Swedish monarch insisted on being borne into action on a litter. His hardy veterans charged with their usual courage, but the enemy redoubts poured a murderous fire into the flanks of the advancing columns. The left wing became separated while trying to carry these enclosures, and during the confusion Peter's main force gradually enveloped the attackers in a vast semicircle.

Russian artillery supremacy was such that the Swedes could now hope only for survival. Most of the infantry fell on the field, and a few days later 14,000 exhausted horsemen were forced to surrender. Charles himself cut a way through with 1,500 followers, at last finding a refuge in Turkish territory.

Few battles have had such far-reaching results, for on that June day in 1709 a new European war power came into being as an old one declined. Never again would Sweden play more than a secondary part, and never would the Continent take up arms without looking anxiously in the direction of Russia. In short, the cost of armies and navies had mounted so rapidly within the last few decades that the valiant small nation must depend hereafter on alliances with the more populous countries.

At Poltava for a moment Charles XII had struck an authentic note of tragedy. As an exile in Turkey during the next four years he came very near to farce. Thrice he managed to persuade the Turks to declare war on Russia, but Peter the Great adopted the Oriental tactic of bribing an opponent in preference to fighting. During this period the Swedish king acquired the nickname of "Ironhead" because of his obstinacy. Finally the Ottoman authorities found him an embarrassing guest, and Charles was imprisoned when broad hints did not serve to speed his departure.

His country meanwhile had reached the point of distress. Such prolonged operations could not be supported by a nation of only 1,500,000 people, particularly when its autocratic ruler spurned every chance for a profitable peace. After Poltava enemies rose on every side to share the spoils. Prussia declared war; Augustus marched into Poland; the Danes crossed the sound for an invasion; and the Russian fleet won a naval victory on the Baltic.

These were the consequences which awaited Ironhead when he returned to the homeland attended by a single squire. After prodigious sacrifices the kingdom raised another army of 20,000 for him, and Charles fell back on a dogged defensive. The usual disputes between allies won him some respite, but Sweden was still in a sore plight when her once precocious monarch fell dead in the trenches from a bullet which may have been aimed by an assassin.

The nation had little choice in the end but to accept terms which cost her nearly all the Baltic empire conquered by Gustavus Adolphus. Livonia, Estonia and Ingria were divided among victors who also seized most of the Finnish and German territory. Sweden's sole gain from the long war was a fierce reaction toward peace and democratic institutions which has lasted down to the present day.

THE RISE OF PRUSSIA

Charles was not a great strategist. He was not a creative or original tactician. His victories owed chiefly to a fabulous audacity in an age of formal and calculated warfare. But the results were not such as to encourage imitators, and the heavy losses of Poltava served as an object lesson for the future.

Europe's next conflict, the brief War of the Polish Succession (1733-1735), became an example of the operations which Clausewitz later described as "a stronger form of diplomatic note." On the death of Augustus the Strong, two candidates appeared for the Polish throne, with France, Spain and Sardinia taking sides against Russia and the empire. Marshal Villars at the age of eighty led an army into Italy, but died of illness in the field. Eugene also put in a last appearance, and the Duke of Berwick met his death during a siege. Otherwise there was little of interest in trivial operations concerning only the various diplomats and professional armies.

The Europe of 1740 had begun to assume modern outlines. Spain, for all of her great American empire, had withered into a feeble Continental power. Sweden could now be considered a minor Baltic state along with Denmark, and the weary United Provinces would never again be able to recover their former influence. England had established herself as the leading maritime nation; and the acquisition of Alsace, Lorraine and Franche-Comté added to France's stature as a military power.

The Holy Roman Empire had also been a gainer from the wars of Louis XIV. This sprawling federation of Central Europe—"neither holy nor Roman nor yet an Empire"—consisted of member states which elected an emperor for life. Since the ruler was almost invariably a Hapsburg, the Empire included roughly the territory of modern Germany, Belgium and Austria, all under the leadership of the latter. In addition, the Hapsburgs claimed Bohemia, Hungary, Silesia and some Italian lands.

As the bulwark against Ottoman invasion, this vague political structure came to be identified with the pope's spiritual aims. At the same time the dynastic rivalry between the Hapsburgs and Bourbons weighed heavily in Europe's balance of power.

The various states of Italy teetered between these two royal houses, making and breaking alliances in an effort to profit from the antagonism. Politically as well as geographically, therefore, the peninsula was destined to be a battleground.

The large but weak kingdom of Poland, stretching from the Baltic to the Ukraine, had likewise come to be regarded as legitimate prey for diplomatic intrigues. Ruled by an elected monarch, often an alien, the government of this feudal realm has been described as "despotism tempered by anarchy."

With the dawn of the eighteenth century, two new powers had arisen with startling suddenness. To the east the enormous Muscovite empire, knouted into modernity by Peter the Great, became a force in power politics. In northern Europe the kingdom of Prussia had been created out of the mark of Brandenburg in 1701 as a reward for military aid to the Empire. More territory was acquired in the Peace of Utrecht, and a few years later the realm won a foothold on the Baltic at the expense of Sweden. Thus within two Hohenzollern generations a German war power emerged with a population of more than two millions.

Catholic Austria naturally viewed the rise of this aggressive Protestant state as a threat to the Empire. The southern German lands, so loosely united under Hapsburg rule, were placed in much the same position as ancient Greece when confronted by the threat of Macedonia. Surly, avaricious old Frederick William, who built up the Prussian army, was a recognizable counterpart of Philip of Macedon; and in 1740, when the young crown prince became Frederick II, the analogy lacked only a second Alexander.

The unhappy boyhood of this ruler is an old story, but the tyrannical father has seldom been given his due. If he brutally caned his son in public, Frederick William nearly lost his reason at the spectacle of an heir to the throne who despised the German language and people. As an organizer the old king made even religious toleration a cold-blooded policy for attracting potential soldiers. Crimps lay everywhere in wait for the unwary, not only in Prussia but even small neighboring states. When their efforts did not suffice, a limited form of conscription was introduced, so that every Prussian shouldered a musket unless the authorities deemed him more useful to the country in trade or agriculture.

In such a grim realm it was to be expected that the army would deal in hard-knuckled realities. Once the recruit put on a blue uniform, he entered a military bondage without a parallel in Europe. Flogging, caning and running the gauntlet were common punishments, and sergeants prolonged the stiff Prussian drill to the extent of torture. The total result was an organization of nearly 100,000 well-equipped troops backed up by a surplus of a million and a quarter pounds sterling in the Royal Treasury.

Upon coming into this inheritance at the age of twenty-eight, Frederick disbanded the famous regiment of giants, his father's only extravagance, while recruiting the rest of the army up to war strength. Nervous diplomats, who speculated as to his intentions, had not long to wait. In May, 1740 he began his reign; in October the Emperor Charles VI died unexpectedly; and two months later the young monarch seized the Austrian province of Silesia.

Frederick justified himself by citing old treaties, but in his *Histoire de Mon Temps* he candidly mentions the desirability of Silesia, the weakness of Austria and the prospect of French aid. "Add to these reasons an army quite ready for action, the money all found, and perhaps the desire to make a name."

The Austrian emperor died without a male heir, and the succession of his daughter Maria Theresa had not been accepted without dispute. Conflicting dynastic claims led to another general European war, and during the confusion Frederick overran Silesia without meeting serious resistance for four months. At the battle of Mollwitz the Austrian cavalry held an advantage both in numbers and quality, though the army as a whole amounted to only 15,500 against the enemy's 22,000. At the first shock these squadrons swept both wings of Prussian horse off the field; but the infantry stood firm, firing steady volleys which finally turned a defeat into a costly victory.

Henceforward the brief struggle might well have been called the War of the Iron Ramrod. Never has such a slight improvement played a more important part, for it gave the Prussian foot a fire superiority which proved decisive everywhere.

Iron ramrods were by no means a novelty, having been Prussian equipment for forty-two years; but the Austrians still clung to an obsolete wooden tool which broke under strain or warped in a single campaign. Their opponents, being able to load and fire twice as fast, presented a problem in arithmetic which Maria Theresa's generals could not solve. Soon they suffered another defeat at Chotusitz as the queen's dominions were invaded by France and Bavaria. Her affairs reached such a critical state that she opened negotiations with Frederick in 1742, ceding him most of Silesia.

The Prussian triumph seemed inexpensive, but all Europe realized that this was merely the first round. Even so, it could hardly have been supposed that Silesia would continue to be a cause until blood had been spilled from the Ganges to the Ohio.

THE CAMPAIGNS OF MARSHAL SAXE

The War of the Austrian Succession began in 1741, dragging on for eight weary years with most of the nations of the Continent involved. The causes consisted of the old dynastic jealousies and trade rivalries which awaited only some such occasion as the emperor's death. For this was the age of "benevolent despotism," and every monarch aspired to follow in the footsteps of Louis XIV.

Among the larger countries France, Prussia, Spain and Bavaria were arrayed against Austria, England, Saxony and the United Provinces, while smaller states entered or dropped out of the lists in a bewildering fashion. Actually only five powers were much concerned : France fighting Austria, England and Holland; and Prussia again defending her seizures from Austria in the Second Silesian War.

Under the "priest and petticoat regime" of Louis XV and his minister Fleury the armies of France had deteriorated. The commanders were ancient or ailing noblemen distinguished only for birth, the troops so poorly trained and equipped that the days of Louvois seemed a distant memory.

The first French drives, profiting from Austria's misfortunes, were robbed of their results by the over-prudent Fleury. He recalled an invading army which came within six leagues of undefended Vienna, diverting it to the capture of Prague. But the garrison was left unsupported, and Marshal Belle-Isle barely managed to cut a way through encircling foes. Only a fourth of his force survived one of the most terrible winter retreats in history.

During the Rhine campaigns of 1743 the aged Marshal Noailles had a miraculous opportunity to redeem two years of French futility. It was, in fact, a general's dream come true. George II of England, leading in person some 37,000 British, Dutch and Hanoverian troops, stumbled blindly into a trap which would have been avoided by a more competent general. For a tremulous moment old Noailles held the drawstrings as the allies marched into a defile between an unfordable river and steep, wooded hills. At the far end of the narrow valley he had posted the Duc de Grammont with instructions to await the advance with his detachment of 28,000, while he himself disposed the remaining 20,000 French troops to fall upon the allied rear and cut off escape.

The plan was Hannibalic in conception and its fulfillment would doubtless have resulted in another Lake Trasimene at the expense of the English king. But Noailles' good fortune suddenly deserted him as Grammont disobeyed orders and launched a premature attack to win personal glory. Before the marshal could hasten to the rescue, his subordinate had been crushed by superior numbers and driven into the river Main. The routed detachment suffered losses of 5,000, the victors about half that number.

The only French gain from the battle came about indirectly when the disgusted loser urged the advancement of a proved professional soldier, Maurice de Saxe. A natural son of Augustus the Strong and a Swedish countess, this forty-seven-year-old adventurer had begun under Eugene at the age of twelve, taking part at Malplaquet. After campaigning from Sweden to Turkey in later wars, he raised enough money to buy a French regiment. Paris was delighted with the amiable giant who could twist horseshoes into bracelets with his hands, or nails into the corkscrews for which he had such companionable use. Adrienne Lecouvreur, greatest tragic actress of Paris, became Saxe's mistress; and he could probably have married either of the women who were the next two empresses of Russia.

During the War of the Polish Succession he rose to a lieutenant general's rank after dislodging Eugene's relieving army at the siege of Philippsburg. Further recognition came in 1742 for leading the escalade of Prague, and Noailles recommended Saxe to command a proposed invasion of England.

This recurring dream of French strategists was revived at a time of frustration on every front. Dettingen led to a complete retirement from Germany, and Louis abandoned an invasion of the Austrian Netherlands after setting out with an army of 90,000. Hence the attempt at a Channel crossing aroused high hopes. While Saxe waited with his troops at Dunkirk, a fleet of 20 warships actually put to sea before the English were ready. But winter gales threw the invaders off their course, giving Admiral Norris enough time to assemble 25 sail and drive the enemy back to port.

Again French sea power had not been equal to the test, and during the rest of 1744 Saxe campaigned in Flanders without risking an engagement. The following May he laid siege to Tournay as an allied army marched to the relief under the Duke of Cumberland, a younger son of George II. The ensuing battle of Fontenoy, one of the classics of the age of linear tactics, established the French general as the foremost soldier of the war.

Varying figures are given, but it appears that each side had about 50,000 effectives. Saxe chose a strong defensive position, his right resting on a river and his left on a wood. Across the front he located four great redoubts, showing that he had read correctly a lesson of Poltava which escaped other commanders. The guns of these outposts subjected the advancing British, Dutch and Hanoverians to a terrible enfilade fire. For two hours the allies endured this pounding, their confusion increasing as they met repulses in attempts to storm the redoubts.

At last Cumberland resolved to push on between them, regardless of losses, in a suicidal attack on the French main force. He drew up 14,000 infantry in a compact oblong measuring only 500 by 600 yards. The cavalry followed with a few guns dragged by hand. From this moment the battle became an epic of the bright, hard insouciance affected by professional soldiers of the time. With colors flying and drums beating, the crimson column came on in a stately parade step. Meanwhile the

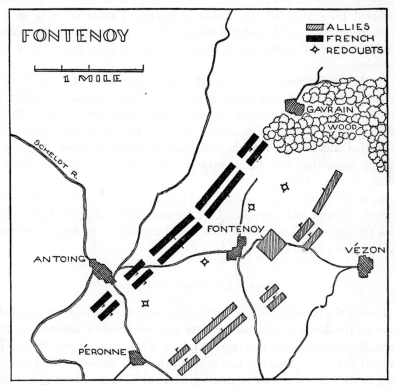

Battle of Fontenoy

redoubts kept up a withering cross fire which caused a shrinkage in the human rectangle as the survivors shouldered inward and dressed their ranks.

When they drew within sixty paces of the French line, Lord Charles Hay stepped out of the allied formation, swept off his hat and drank a toast from his pocket flask. He called for a cheer, which his men gave lustily. The French officers, not to be outdone in international courtesies, returned his salute and ordered a cheer from their ranks. There followed a taut moment when the opponents stared into the muzzles of muskets at the ready; then just before the volley an English voice was heard in mock prayer, "For what we are about to receive, may the Lord make us truly thankful!"

These amenities were not as feckless as they may seem, for one of the objects sought in linear tactics was to induce an enemy to fire first. He could then only reload while awaiting a return volley at even closer range, perhaps followed by a bayonet attack. At Fontenoy the French withheld their fire, but the British aim proved more effective in the musketry exchange. The column continued well into the French position, discharging more volleys as it gained immunity from the guns of the redoubts.

In this crisis Saxe took personal charge. Seriously ill from dropsy, he had been carried into battle in a wicker chaise, chewing a bullet to relieve his thirst. By his orders counterattacks were directed at the flanks of the column as cannon blasted at its face. Within a few minutes the formation was broken, and the remnants withdrew in stubborn groups, leaving more than half the 14,000 in dead and wounded. The French losses also were heavy.

So ended an encounter which grew into a barrack-room legend among both the victors and vanquished. Paris went wild with joy at the news of a triumph after so many reverses, and a poem of celebration written by Voltaire sold 21,000 copies in a day.

SAXE'S MILITARY THEORIES

During the remaining three years of the war the "prodigious marshal" overran the Netherlands, taking forts and cities with a leisured air and defeating the allies on the two occasions when they offered battle. In reward Louis XV honored him with a princely château on the Loire as well as the rank of marshal general which only Turenne and Villars had held.

All of these victories were won with an indolent ease which deceived contemporaries. After besieging and capturing Brussels with 15,000 prisoners, Saxe set up a theater at headquarters in which the latest Parisian farces were played by imported troupes. On the eve of the battle of Roucoux in 1746, it amused him to give his officers their first hint of the impending action by means of an actress's announcement from the stage, "There will be no performance tomorrow—but next day, in celebration of the victory which you are sure to gain, we shall have the honor of presenting a new play to as many of you as remain alive."

The officers and their mistresses applauded, and after an evening's absence the survivors were back in their seats. Meanwhile they had overwhelmed the allies under Charles of Lorraine with losses of 5,000, following up the triumph with a hot cavalry pursuit.

Only once after Fontenoy did Saxe extend himself. His opponent of that battle returned to the Netherlands in 1747, having gained the nickname of "Butcher" Cumberland while putting down a Jacobite rebellion in Scotland. Led by the Stuart Pretender known as Bonnie Prince Charlie, the Highlanders won two combats and marched within 125 miles of London. But they had neither the numbers nor the leadership for a prolonged effort, and Cumberland defeated them at Culloden. Afterwards the disgusting cruelty of his repressions caused him to be loathed even in England.

Upon resuming operations in the Netherlands the corpulent duke joined forces with the Austrian general Daun to isolate a French detachment of 30,000. An allied victory seemed certain until Saxe came to the rescue after a remarkable concentration of troops. Some of his battalions marched 50 miles in two days, and at the hard-fought battle of Laufeld the French won a victory in which they inflicted 6,000 casualties.

In his final campaign of 1748 Saxe invaded Dutch territory, taking several key fortresses. Unfortunately for his adopted country, he died only two years after the peace at the age of fifty-four, leaving as his greatest soldierly accomplishment a book. This treatise, *Mes Rêveries*, published posthumously in 1756, has been esteemed by military scholars ever since as the classic of its century.

Described by Carlyle as "a strange military farrago, dictated, I should think, under opium," the work actually presents ideas so far in advance of their own time that they were not put into effect until the Napoleonic campaigns. While his own generation strained to follow a Prussian example of rigidity, Saxe foresaw the flexibility of futuie warfare. "Few persons will understand me," he proclaims in his preface, "but I write for the connoisseurs, trusting that they will not be offended by the confidence of my opinions."

Although the great generals of the age of Louis XIV expressed their ideas in deeds, the next generation brought forth two military treatises discussed by every soldier in Europe. In his *Mémoires de la Guerre*, based on his service under Luxembourg, the Marquis de Feuquieres endeavored to teach war by historical lessons. Next the Chevalier de

Folard wrote a book urging an infantry column formation amounting to a modern phalanx. Both authors cited no end of classical precepts, and Saxe likewise begins with long quotations from Polybius. But where his predecessors confined themselves to technical aspects, he blames the military deficiencies of the pre-Revolutionary era on social conditions:

What a spectacle do the nations present today! We see a handful of rich, idle and voluptuous men enjoying themselves at the expense of a multitude which flatters their passions and can only live by pandering to their appetites. This assembly of oppressors and oppressed constitutes what is called Society, from which the vilest and most miserable elements are selected to make soldiers.

The warfare of his own day was held by Saxe to be "a science so obscure and imperfect" that "custom and prejudice, confirmed by ignorance, are its sole foundation and support." After deploring the general practice of recruiting "volunteers" by means of fraud or force, he advised a system of universal service. "Would it not be better to oblige every man, of whatever condition, to serve his king and country for five years?"

The citizen-soldiers enlisted under this plan were to be trained in tactically self-sufficient units, each made up of infantry and cavalry, both heavy and light, with a complement of artillery. Ten of these modern legions, amounting to a total of 34,000 foot and 12,000 horse, seemed to Saxe a sufficiently large force for any purpose. "A general of parts and experience, commanding such an army, will always be able to make head against one of a hundred thousand, for multitudes serve only to perplex and embarrass."

Nor did Saxe hold with Feuquieres' theory (and Frederick's practice) that battle was the ultimate test to be sought by a commander. "I am not in favor of giving battle, especially at the beginning of a war. I am even convinced that a general can wage war all his life without being compelled to do so."

This statement he qualified by adding that no good opportunity for a victory ought to be neglected; but in general Saxe believed that manoeuvre based upon rapid movements could be made to serve most of the ends sought by large actions.

His proposed system of universal service included three successive stages: skeleton organizations of officers and veterans to drill citizen-soldiers in time of peace; then a more complete establishment upon the threat of war; and finally the recall of previously trained men to bring each legion up to full strength when hostilities began. The economies realized by doing away with a great standing army were to go toward improving pay and equipment.

For purposes of morale as well as protection, he recommended the adoption of modern armor consisting of leather helmets and buff coats covered with thin steel plates. His skirmishers were to be armed with rifles, which had then been used as fowling pieces for a century without finding favor in military circles. Individual target practice at ranges up to 300 yards was to become standard training, and Saxe preferred fire at will to a commanded volley which "detains the soldier in a constrained position and prevents his aiming with any exactness."

Up to this time there had been no organized light infantry in the armies of Europe, though irregulars sometimes served in a guerrilla capacity. Saxe created this arm in imagination, giving it a prominent part in his tactics. Instead of the usual advance, conceived by Luxembourg, of a compact army prepared either to encamp or fight, he visioned widely separated legions able either to manoeuvre or concentrate. When contact had been made with the enemy, the waves of light infantry were to cover the entire front in small and supple combat groups, taking advantage of natural protection to pour in a deadly rifle fire. After preparing the attack, these trained skirmishers were to fall back through the intervals as the heavy infantry advanced in a dispersed line of modern maniples, accompanied by hand-drawn fieldpieces and squadrons of cavalry. Thus the two processes, the preparation and the actual attack, were to be synchronized so closely that the enemy would have no time to recover from his initial confusion.

This was essentially the new warfare which swept linear tactics into the discard after Saxe had been in his grave for half a century. During his own career he had to be content with theory rather than practice. Most of his vast energies were consumed by dissipation, for as an alien and a Protestant he lacked the influence at court to bring about tremendous reforms in tactics.

At least he managed to train a few light troops for his Netherlands campaigns; and his successes were largely due to experiments with a unit which became the forerunner of the modern division. Two brigades of infantry and one of cavalry were combined with artillery into a formation intended to be self-supporting in local operations, yet capable of swift concentrations for battle. In his later campaigns a chain of these divisions held the strategic line, keeping the enemy constantly off balance and often exposed to serious danger. The victory at Laufeld owed to the concentration of Saxe's divisions from distances as far as 50 miles, and his light troops had a part in disorganizing the enemy both at Laufeld and Roucoux.

But as the French marshal had arrogantly predicted, few were able to understand his ideas. Meanwhile the Prussian king had also won victories which would soon make him known as Frederick the Great. His methods had more appeal for imitators, since they consisted simply of the old linear tactics carried out with the precision of infinite pains. Thus within a few years every army in Europe began to copy Prussian drill, Prussian formations, and (not to miss any detail of the formula) Prussian modes of infantry hairdressing.

PRUSSIA'S MILITARY CODES

In his military testament, intended solely for his own officers, Frederick communicated the secret of Prussian training:

All that can be done with the soldier is to give him *esprit de corps* —*i. e.*, a higher opinion of his own regiment than all the other troops in the country. Since the officers have sometimes to lead him into the greatest dangers (and he cannot be influenced by a sense of honor) he must be made more afraid of his own officers than of the dangers to which he is exposed.

This fear was induced by a discipline which seldom failed to crush out the last spark of individuality. Soldiers were enlisted practically for life, being held under a surveillance which amounted to captivity.

At a glance such a military rule is reminiscent of Roman sternness. The difference lies in the fact that the Romans were citizen-soldiers, so proud of their arms that they deemed it a disgrace to be barred from serving. The Prussian soldier, in contrast, was held in contempt by superiors who regarded him as hardly more than a military beast of burden. Frederick himself referred to his subjects as *canaille*, setting an example for officers drawn from a poor, prolific and ignorant nobility.

This attitude came as an abrupt departure from the traditions of the past. One of Turenne's best assets had been a warm paternalism repaid by the worship of his men. Marlborough, Vauban, Eugene and Villars had all shown a sympathy and respect which earned the love of the common soldier. Saxe, on being told by a harsh general that a proposed raid would cost only fifty grenadiers, replied, "I might consent if it were to cost only fifty generals."

The Prussian spirit may be traced to a sense of rudeness and inferiority which tormented a raw military aristocracy. Such commanders of royal blood as Condé, Berwick and Charles XII might mix with the rank and file without demeaning themselves, but the petty noble of the new northern kingdom felt it necessary to abase his men in order to exalt his own uneasy self-esteem.

"If my soldiers began to think," said Frederick, "not one would remain in the ranks." This danger was averted by the poorest food and pay of any army in Europe, combined with the most brutal drills and punishments. In another country such a policy might have led to mutiny, but the Prussian king did not err in judging the temper of his people. Desertions reached a high percentage, but in general the German soldier's devotion to his masters rose in direct proportion to their contempt for him.

Prussian training aimed to produce an automaton which could not make a mistake. The steps of loading a musket were practiced in endless drills until Frederick's men could fire five rounds a minute as compared to two or three in other armies. But such haste led to poor aim and many misfires, so that the Austrian foot actually inflicted the heavier casualties in the earlier clashes.

Material improvements were no more important in the Prussian scheme than a moral determination which did not shrink from violations of the established codes. In his secret instructions to officers, revised at this period, Frederick sometimes verges upon sentimentality in upholding certain mercies. "Think also of the poor wounded of the two armies," he counsels. "Especially have a paternal care for your own, and do not be inhuman to those of the enemy." Yet in questions involving a military advantage, the king was capable of writing this advice:

In the countries where the people are opposed to you . . . it is very difficult to keep informed of what is happening. If greed for silver does not work, it is necessary to employ fear. Seize some burgomaster of a city where you have a garrison, or some mayor of a village where you camp, and force him to take a disguised man, who speaks the language of the country, and under some pretext to conduct him as his servant in the enemy camp. Threaten him that if he does not bring your man back, you will cut the throat of his wife and children whom you hold under guard while waiting, and that you will have his house burned. I was obliged to employ this sad expedient in Bohemia and it succeeded for me.

The Second Silesian War

After the onset of so many foes had forced Maria Theresa to ask terms from Prussia, the two powers remained at peace until 1744. Then as Austria gathered strength, Frederick began to fear for his Silesian prize. Choosing a moment when the imperial armies were occupied elsewhere, he suddenly crossed the border without provocation, beginning the Second Silesian War. This move accorded with the instruction to his officers in which the king advised that Prussia should always gain the advantages of a surprise assault planned with care and secrecy:

> The whole strength of our troops lies in attack, and we act foolishly if we renounce it without good cause. . . . The one aim of their drill is to enable them to manoeuvre and form up more quickly than the enemy, to attack him with energy while he is unprepared, and to settle the affair more speedily than has hitherto been the custom.

The invasion was so unexpected that the three Prussian columns met almost no opposition. Prague surrendered with its Austrian garrison, and Maria Theresa had reason to tremble for Vienna. But the weakness of the French in 1744 allowed an Austrian army to be diverted against the new foe, and Frederick had to retire into Silesia after abandoning his gains. The following June, with an army of 65,000, he fought 80,000 Austrians and Saxons at Hohenfriedberg, the greatest battle of the war in respect to numbers.

The Prussian king leaped into international fame by winning a crushing victory over Prince Charles of Lorraine. The Saxons proved weak allies, and even the best Austrian regiments, still using the wooden ramrod, were inferior to the enemy in equipment and discipline. The Prussian foot no longer relied so much on rapid fire; but each soldier carried 30 rounds of ammunition (as compared to 24 by the British at Fontenoy) in addition to a like amount brought up by transport and issued just before the action. Frederick's men loaded and fired with fixed bayonets, following up their advantage in musketry with charges which cleared the field.

No troops in Europe showed such machinelike precision when it came to wheeling from column into line or reversing that process. This superiority alone caused the forces of Maria Theresa to be outmanoeuvred on every field. At the battle of Soor, when Prince Charles at last placed Frederick in a perilous position, the Prussians turned defeat into victory by a rapid change of front in the face of the enemy. Nor was the generalship of the king essential to success. In the final engagement, fought at Kesselsdorf, a subordinate commander completely routed a larger allied army. This result decided Maria Theresa to offer a peace which again recognized Frederick's possession of Silesia.

The arms of France had meanwhile prevailed on all sides with a glitter which belied their actual decline. The victories in the Netherlands had been due to Saxe's personal mastery, while in Italy the able Marshal Maillebois outmanoeuvred the Austrians and Sardinians, defeating them at the battle of Bassignano. Even in India, despite British naval superiority, the French captured Madras and repulsed the enemy's land and sea attack on Pondicherry.

The Austrian commanders, Marshal Daun and Charles of Lorraine, had been beaten in every battle of importance. Nor had England fared much better in the War of the Austrian Succession. Her only notable victory, in fact, had been won by the American colonists with their capture of Louisburg, the great French fortress on Cape Breton Island. Even on the sea, where the island kingdom held the superiority, the war was confined largely to privateering operations in which the British suffered heavier losses than their French and Spanish enemies.

THE ROYAL PROPAGANDIST

Historical legend has it that a trinity of scorned women, two empresses and a king's concubine, became the furies who paid off Frederick with a new European war because of their feminine pique at his insults. This story, however fascinating, ignores the efforts of a great Austrian envoy during the years following the peace of Aix-la-Chapelle. For the deft diplomacy of Prince Kaunitz did most to bring about the coalition of Austria, Russia, France, Sweden and Saxony against Prussia.

He began with Maria Theresa, convincing her that the ancient feud between the Hapsburgs and Bourbons had become secondary to the enmity between Austria and Prussia. Next he persuaded Louis XV and his mistress Madame Pompadour that the interests of France ran parallel to those of Austria. As a final triumph, Kaunitz helped to gain the co-operation of Elizabeth, the Russian empress.

The feminine fury was supplied chiefly by Frederick, whose father had found him a "womanish fellow." For a decade his cries of outrage could be heard all over Europe in the form of letters and poems. Behind this torrent of words were motives as purposeful as those of Kaunitz, for the Prussian king merits recognition as the first great propagandist of modern warfare.

There was, of course, no possibility of appealing directly to European masses which were then illiterate. Frederick aimed his message at the few thousand leaders in every country whose opinions counted in world affairs. The output of his pen during these years reached an astonishing bulk, most of it consisting of correspondence and historical writings. Naturally the king's contemporaries regarded Prussia as an aggressor nation defending seizures which had no justification except force. Despite such embarrassing facts, Frederick made it his task to create a more sympathetic picture of a righteous small kingdom encircled by cruel, vindictive and infinitely more powerful foes:

> Destiny, or a demon, has resolved upon the downfall of Prussia; alliances contrary to nature, hatreds for which no cause has been given, secondary influences and real bad luck.

Boastfulness, rage and despair are the king's prevailing moods, for no diarist ever became more personal and introspective. Thus in his anger he refers to the Russian empress as "the infamous whore of the North." When his enemies make a mistake, he writes to Voltaire in an arrogant vein, "I have to do with such stupid people that it naturally follows that I shall get the best of them in the end." And at the moment of adversity Frederick is capable of a boundless self-pity:

> I have no further resources, and we must expect from day to day an increase of our misfortunes. Heaven is witness that it is not my fault, but I have been badly served. There has been in addition much ill luck, and I have had the whole of Europe against me.

The modern reader is likely to agree with Voltaire, who replied to Frederick's threats of suicide with the blunt reminder:

> Nobody will regard you as the martyr of liberty. The truth should be faced: you know in how many courts it is obstinately maintained that your entry into Saxony was an infraction of the law of nations.

Nevertheless, the Prussian king had hit upon a technique of war propaganda which has never been bettered since his day. As a pioneer in the use of words for weapons, he discovered that repetition is more persuasive than reason. An occasional Voltaire might remain a skeptic, but Frederick held that the bulk of mankind, resenting new ideas, will accept the most preposterous statement after the novelty has been worn off by endless reiteration.

As a result the monarch's talents as a propagandist served his country better perhaps than his generalship. Among his own countrymen, who have always been uniquely credulous, Frederick succeeded to such an extent that the seizure of a neighbor's territory was transformed into a holy war. Among the subjects of other realms, including enemy nations, he created doubts and dissensions when he did not actually convince. Even among posterity he made such friends as the hero-worshiper Thomas Carlyle, who accepted Frederick's message in a spirit of admiration rather than inquiry.

Yet for all the odds in population against Prussia, the contest appears fairly even. The Austrian treaty with France made it inevitable that England, as ever anxious about the balance of power, would take sides against her old enemy across the Channel. Frederick could thus count on large subsidies, on control of the sea lanes, and on troops from George II's dynastic possession of Hanover in western Germany.

These benefits offset any help that Austria might reasonably expect from her allies. The coming struggle, therefore, promised to be essentially a duel between the new war power and the old empire of diplomacy, with most of the worth-while military assets on the side of the former. Where Austria devoted a third of her funds to war purposes, Prussia spent four-fifths. Where Austria could raise 132,000 fully trained and equipped soldiers, Prussia now had an army of 154,000. And where Austria's revenues were limited, Prussia had a long-standing surplus in the treasury as well as the assurance of English gold.

There remained an even more decisive difference between the two belligerents. Austria, of all the nations, had become the leading exponent of the new moderation in arms. Not only had the Empire suffered most from the excesses of the Thirty Years' War, but the Hapsburgs preferred the gains of negotiation or marriage to those extorted by force.

Prussia, in contrast to this sprawling and loosely knit power, was a compact state created by and for war. The lives and fortunes of all subjects were at the disposal of an absolute ruler who combined the powers of diplomat, financier and generalissimo. Like most propagandists, moreover, the little man with the pursed lips and bright, nervous eyes had come to believe his own exaggerations. Already he had begun to cite the plea of military necessity against odds; and as a next logical step Frederick would feel justified in seizing any advantage which might be gained by violating the humane codes of the age.

For eight years after the peace of Aix-la-Chapelle the armies faced one another tensely across the frontiers. Then the first shot was fired in the wilderness of America by an obscure provincial officer named George Washington. Within a few more months Europe had gone to war again, and the tramp of marching men could be heard from the plains of Bengal to the forests of Pennsylvania.

V

FREDERICK'S BIG GUNS

The maxims of our Government have degenerated, not our natives. I want to see that breed restored, which under our old principles carried our glory so high.

—PITT

THE Prussian forces took their places according to long preconceived plans: 26,000 watching the Russian frontier; 11,000 on guard against the Swedes in Pomerania; 37,000 in Silesia commanded by Marshal Schwerin; and Frederick's main army of 70,000 pressing on in three columns to the invasion of Saxony. Against these numbers the surprised and widely distributed allies could muster but two detachments amounting to some 54,000 Austrians and Saxons.

The larger of these met the Prussian advance column in the first battle of the Seven Years' War, fought at Lobositz in October, 1756. The rival armies counted about 30,000 each, but the Austrians now had iron ramrods and the Prussians a much more effective cavalry arm as compared to the last war. A thick fog made manoeuvre all but impossible, so that the engagement became a dogfight whenever groping battalions clashed. As at Mollwitz, the king concluded that the day had been lost; but the tenacity of his infantry left him in possession of the field after losses of 3,000 on both sides.

Before winter the Prussians occupied Dresden, took over the national archives and subjected the entire country to a pitiless and systematic looting. All the kingdom's resources were seized, and after the last Saxon

army of 14,000 surrendered, Frederick impressed even these foemen into
his own ranks. Thus within a few weeks he had set the clock back a
century, undoing traditions of mercy which had been gaining acceptance
since the Thirty Years' War. Lack of numbers could not serve as a
justification, for he enjoyed a comfortable superiority at the time.
Originally it had been the grandiose plan of the allies to put half a million
men into the field, but nearly a year passed before either the French or
Russians appeared in any strength. Meanwhile Frederick plundered
Saxony, letting the winter go by without profiting from the unprepared-

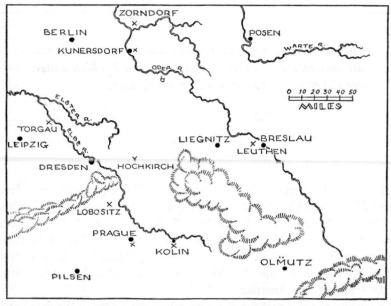

Battlefields of the Seven Years' War

ness of his foes. Not until April did he lay siege to Prague and by that
late date the Austrians were able to send a relieving army of 65,000 under
Prince Charles of Lorraine.

Frederick had at least equal numbers, but his hasty reconnaissance got
him into trouble. After a brief survey from a church steeple, he ordered
a general advance on the Austrian right. Soon the attacking troops were
floundering in moss-grown bogs which had been mistaken for grassy
meadows. Marshal Schwerin and thousands of his men were cut down by
the hail of grape and canister from the Austrian guns; and the survivors
fell back in disorder, leaving their guns behind them.

It speaks well for Prussian discipline that Frederick managed to reform his shaken army and advance again over firmer ground. This time Marshal Zieten's cavalry swept the Austrian horse off the field and turned the flank of the infantry. The Prussian foot came on to complete the confusion of enemies who retired into Prague after losses of 9,000 in addition to 4,000 captured. The victors' casualties were 14,000, including 2,000 prisoners.

The king resumed his siege of the city and the 48,000 enemy troops now behind its walls. After Prussian bombardments failed to make a breach, Marshal Daun came to the rescue with another relieving army, and within six weeks of the battle of Prague a second bloody engagement took place at Kolin.

Here it may be noted that Austrian commanders were not always to blame for the slow and over-prudent movements which distinguished their campaigns. Too often they had to await the decisions of the Aulic Council, an executive and judicial body of twenty members sitting in judgment on imperial questions of grave import. Composed of elders whose combined age represented many centuries of experience, this august assembly did not hesitate to direct field operations from Vienna Sometimes the situation had changed before a courier could reach the scene, but the edicts of the Aulic Council never erred on the side of daring or impetuosity. It was an exception bordering on the miraculous, therefore, when Daun received orders to risk a defeat in an attempt to save the large Austrian force threatened with capture at Prague.

The Hapsburg empire had no monopoly on lapses in military judgment, and Frederick's strategy has been held up to later ages as an object lesson. Although he stood between two enemy forces with numbers superior to either, he took no advantage of the brilliant possibilities of a campaign along interior lines. Instead he divided his army, leaving nearly half to continue the siege of Prague while he marched to Kolin with a force of 35,000 to meet Daun's 53,000.

On reaching the field, his tactics proved no better than his strategy. The battle became a repetition of the flank attack at Prague, with even less concealment and more hasty reconnaissance. Afterwards the king confessed that he had ordered the advance after satisfying himself with a glance at the enemy lines from an inn window. The blue-clad columns swept forward in full view, their intentions so obvious that the attack was broken up before the troops could wheel into line.

Frederick had not reckoned on the "pandours," those Croatian irregulars who had won a reputation as light troops in the last war. Wild and undisciplined, feared even by their own officers, they had little aptitude for formal manoeuvres. But in dislocating a formal manoeuvre the pandours were as able as the Parthians against an unwary phalanx. At Kolin they fell in swarms upon the solid columns of the enemy, harassing the Prussians beyond endurance. During the confusion the advancing troops took three divergent directions, each separate attack being shattered by superior numbers. After five hours of fighting the king was badly beaten, losing 40 per cent of his army in slain, wounded and prisoners.

The siege of Prague had to be lifted as a consequence, releasing Austrian reinforcements which brought Daun's strength up to 100,000. Frederick was forced to abandon Bohemia, for his enemies now threatened on all sides. After months of delays, the French and Russians at last were on the move; and it became plain that the next battles would be fought in defense of Prussian soil.

The king had been a severe critic of the tedious warfare of his era, particularly of the lost opportunities resulting from delays. Yet in this emergency he had only himself to blame. For six months he had remained idle while holding the numerical advantage. Afterwards his foes were still unready, but Frederick made no use of 70,000 Prussian troops which he dispersed on fronts not even remotely threatened. When finally he invaded Bohemia, his carelessness and contempt for the enemy were punished by a costly victory leading up to a ruinous defeat.

The wholesale looting of Saxony and brutal treatment of prisoners also brought consequences which might have been foreseen. Aside from ethical considerations, Frederick stood to lose more than the enemy by violating the humanities of the age. He might hold up his hands in horror, but reprisals were not slow in developing at the expense of invaded Prussia. The Russian armies burned and plundered horribly, and even the gentle Maria Theresa did not object to the ravages of her pandours.

After Kolin the Prussian disasters multiplied. In Saxony the Russians defeated a retiring force under Prince August William. East Prussia lay helpless before a Russian column which hurled back 30,000 defenders at the battle of Gross-Jägerndorf. Berlin was occupied for a few days by Austrian cavalry raiders who overpowered the garrison and enforced a requisition of 200,000 thalers. But the worst news of all came from western Germany, where the French invaders overran Hanover after the capitulation of an entire British army.

The Battles of Rossbach and Leuthen

Although Frederick must have found it difficult to choose between so many enemies, he never acted with more courage and resolution. The greatest peril seemed to him the possibility of the triumphant French uniting with a motley host of 60,000 representing the Holy Roman Empire. The route to Berlin lay open before them, and Frederick planned to combine with Ferdinand of Brunswick in western Germany to prevent the junction of these foes.

In 12 days the king's small army marched 170 miles, but instead of joining Ferdinand he accomplished his object by defeating a detachment of allies at Rossbach.

The Battles of Rossbach and Leuthen

The 11,000 imperialists proved to be troops of wretched quality, while the 30,000 French were described by one of their officers as "assassins fit only to be broken on the wheel, who will show their heels at the first musket shot, and are in a chronic state of incipient mutiny." Still, these deficiencies cannot detract from the merit of tactics with which Frederick might have beaten worthier adversaries. The hardships of the forced march left him only 21,000 effectives, yet his victory was won so brilliantly that half of the Prussian infantry did not fire a shot.

With the confidence of numbers, the French general, Soubise, attempted a blow at the Prussian left flank. Frederick watched from a housetop in Rossbach as the allied columns swung toward him like a ponderous scythe. Soubise, fearing the escape of his prey, hastened the movement at the cost of some confusion. Actually his own troops were in more urgent need of escape, for Frederick had left only a detachment to mask the withdrawal of the bulk of his army in a rearward detour. Thus as Soubise's columns aimed at the Prussian left flank, their own right flank was exposed to assailants stealing around under cover of the hills.

The concealment and timing were perfect as the 38 Prussian squadrons burst out upon foes too surprised for effective deployment. Behind them came the infantry, marching over the hills in an echelon of battalions while the 18 heavy guns tore gaps in the allied files. In only a few minutes the enemy broke and fled in wild disorder, though most of the Prussian foot never came in contact. Soubise's casualties were 7,700, chiefly prisoners, in comparison to only 550 losses for the victors.

As an example of a tactician being hoist with his own petard, the French general's defeat has few equals. But at the moment of victory Frederick learned that his subordinate Bevern, commanding an army of 40,000 in defense of Silesia, had been beaten and captured by the Austrians at the battle of Breslau. During the Prussian retreat the fortresses of Schweidnitz and Breslau capitulated with 5,000 garrison troops.

These disasters made it necessary for the king to retrace his footsteps, and again he marched the 170 miles in 12 days. At Liegnitz he joined forces with Bevern's defeated and leaderless remnant, which gave him a total of 43,000 troops more fit for barracks than battle duty. Nevertheless, the royal commander resolved to attack the Austrian army of 72,000 under Daun and Prince Charles.

Audacious as this decision seems, it may again be noted without prejudice to Frederick that his enemies in this campaign were famed more for bulk than quality. Soubise's army had been a traveling bazaar of hairdressers, sutlers, dancers and singers, in which the women camp followers nearly equaled the troops. And now a raid on the Austrian baggage train brought to the king's attention such strange booty, according to the military critic Jomini, as monkeys, parakeets, lavender water, parasols and muffs. Promotions were based chiefly on birth in the imperial forces, and the most insignificant of Daun's generals demanded luxuries which were not enjoyed by the Prussian monarch in his faded, snuff-stained uniform.

On December 5, 1757—a month to the day after Rossbach—the Prussian forces were on the march at dawn. Daun and Charles had taken a defensive position on a 5-mile line running from north to south across the Breslau road. Their 167 guns, chiefly light artillery, thus averaged 33 to the mile on a front of wooded hills linked up by fortified villages.

Frederick had more heavy artillery as well as a slight advantage in cavalry. His army approached from the west in two parallel columns hidden by pine-clad knolls, the entire 43,000 in formations so compact as only to cover a few miles of snowy country roads. When the columns came opposite the enemy's centre, they made a sharp turn to the south. As yet their intentions had not been guessed by Austrian scouts who warmed themselves at the campfires while their right wing prepared to receive the assault.

Frederick reached a point opposite the extreme Austrian left before closing in for the attack. Knowing his opponents so well, he had not troubled to make the conventional feint on the other flank, where the tense Austrian gunners now crouched behind pieces pointed at the empty woods. Instead he was preparing an innovation in tactics—the bringing forward of an entire battery of ten fortress guns to support his spearhead infantry battalions. Each of these battalions in turn dragged up a six-pounder to supplement the heaviest concentration of artillery ever seen on a battlefield until that December day.

The action began with a clash between Zieten's dragoons and the enemy horse. At last the surprised Austrian left flank realized that it was about to receive the blow for which the right had been reinforced. Even so, the abatis of felled trees seemed sufficient to hold up the attack —until the giant guns roared into action. Then the Austrian works were blasted into splinters as the Prussian infantry executed a left wheel into their three-deep fighting line.

The bluecoats came on in a strange stairwise formation, the battalions fifty paces apart and staggered in alignment so that the left was "refused." History was being introduced to "Frederick's Oblique Order," destined to become the military talk of Europe for a generation, and praised the more because it had first been used by Epaminondas in 369 B.C. For that matter, it had been attempted by Frederick both at Kolin and Rossbach, but without enough success to make the manoeuvre conspicuous. On the snow-muffled day of Leuthen the heavily weighted right wing bore down on defenders outnumbered four-to-one at the point of contact. More and more battalions, each with its own blazing six-pounder, added to an impact which began irresistibly to roll up the Austrian line from left to right.

Daun's forces made a desperate stand in the village of Leuthen while trying to form new lines facing south instead of west. Now occurred the only critical moment of the battle as the Prussian infantry stormed the fortified houses and churchyard, led by the king himself through a hail of bullets. Here again the fortress pieces, each drawn by twelve horses, decided the issue by demolishing the works of the defenders.

With the village lost, the ruin of the whitecoats became complete when a charge of the Prussian horse swept away their last squadrons. The remaining infantry battalions were outnumbered and beaten in detail, being reduced to a horde of fugitives before the winter dusk ended the fighting. Each side had about 6,000 killed and wounded; but the Austrians also lost 116 guns in addition to the amazing total of 20,280 prisoners.

It is not surprising that Leuthen became an epoch in military circles, beginning a controversy which lasted until the French Revolution. Frederick's tactics seemed to provide something which neither Turenne, Marlborough nor Saxe had ever been able to offer—a parade-ground formula for victory. For the diagonal advance of battalions moving up in rapid succession could only be brought off by troops drilled to Prussian perfection. Such a solution appealed to the routine general, since it promised a minimum of thinking on his part combined with a maximum of effort on the part of the troops.

There were dissenters who insisted that the ancient efficacy of surprise and fire power had won a success attributed to the oblique order. According to these heretics, a similar attempt at Kolin met with a well-deserved defeat for lack of concealment. Napoleon afterward ranged himself on the side of the skeptics, declaring that Frederick was laughing up his sleeve at admirers who copied every sacred detail of Prussian tactics.

The best answer is probably to be found in the subsequent practice of Frederick himself. And it is a significant fact that the modern exponent of the oblique order never used it again on a large scale after his famous victory. All the rest of his life he was content to let others discuss the manoeuvre while he preserved a mysterious silence. This reticence cannot be charged altogether to military secrecy, for in his confidential messages to Prince Ferdinand the king emphasized another lesson of Leuthen:

> Do not forget your dogs of big guns, which are the most-to-be-respected arguments of the rights of kings! . . . We must tempt fortune once more under favorable auspices and with big guns. . . . In this cursed war, it is impossible to succeed without having a great train of heavy artillery and of projectiles. . . . The only thing I have to repeat to your army, and about which I advise you to think seriously, is the big gun. . . . I cannot refrain from repeating once more what I have already so often recommended for your advantage; that

is, to augment your artillery, without which you will have no success in your enterprises.

This would appear to be the last word in the controversy, which makes it the more astonishing that none of Frederick's imitators seems to have appreciated the part played at Leuthen by the fortress pieces. Not until the nineteenth century would the world ever again see such an effective use of heavy artillery on the battlefield.

PRUSSIA'S DISASTERS

The six-week campaign raised Frederick's prestige to the heavens. His iron guns and wooden soldiers had struck such a blow at Austrian morale that Daun remained inactive until late the following summer. The extent of France's military deterioration had been fully revealed, and never again would the king have to face a French army. Saxony had been knocked completely out of the war, while already it grew evident that Sweden's part would be only nominal.

Thousands of real volunteers—adventurers, allied deserters or starving refugees—flocked to the victorious army much as soldiers changed sides during the religious wars. Frederick became a popular hero in England; and his subsidy was increased to an annual 670,000 pounds, in addition to the 8,000,000 thalers he had wrung from unhappy Saxony. These sums went three times as far after the coinage had been debased, so that Prussia remained the only belligerent to avoid borrowing. The importance of this factor cannot be overlooked in a war which the king shrewdly predicted would be won by the longest purse.

In view of such gains, it seems incredible that the victor should have relapsed into the tactical vices which had proved so costly at Kolin. Yet during the next two campaigns he fought a bloody drawn battle and incurred two terrible defeats which dragged his country to the brink of absolute ruin.

Russia's efforts so far had been spasmodic, depending on the whims of the weather or the empress. With Poland as a base, the spring months heralded the annual advance, the autumn a retirement which allowed only a few months for campaigning. The army was weak in cavalry, weaker still in transport; and the command sank to a level of incompetence which would have been tolerated by no other nation. Russia's chief strength, in fact, consisted of the moujik in uniform. Mild-eyed and submissive, he had helped to build the wall of flesh which stopped Charles XII; and now at the battle of Zorndorf, fought eight months after Leuthen, he stood squarely in the path of the Prussian conqueror.

Frederick showed his contempt for the new enemy by exposing his army of 36,000 in an arrogant march around the Russian flank. In response General Fermor's 42,000 troops ponderously formed a new front of three great irregular squares so separated by marshes as to be incapable of mutual support.

After a fierce preliminary cannonade, the Prussians advanced with orders to give no quarter to the "barbarians." Seydlitz's cavalry led the infantry assault on the nearest square, meeting a sharp repulse and bayonet counterattack. Tactics were soon forgotten as charge followed charge until the battle degenerated into savage local combats. When darkness put an end to the agony, the defenders were still showing a firm resistance among the mounds of corpses.

Frederick endured losses of 38 per cent, the enemy of 50 per cent, with the slain amounting to a shockingly high proportion. Both armies were in position next morning, each claiming a victory as a truce was declared for the appalling task of the burial parties.

The news of this slaughter spread like a slow, dark stain as men wondered if Europe were returning to the military anarchy of 1648. Voltaire seized his pen in protest, writing his most famous satire during the summer of Zorndorf. His trustful hero, it will be recalled, was seized by crimps and subjected to such a taste of "Bulgarian" army discipline that he begged death as a favor. It is not hard to identify the slyly malicious portrait of the "monarch possessed of a vast genius," and no other battle but Zorndorf could have inspired the description:

> The cannon first of all laid flat about six thousand men on each side; then the musketry removed from the best of worlds some nine or ten thousand blackguards who infested its surface. The bayonet also was the sufficient reason for the death of some thousands of men. The whole might amount to thirty thousand souls. Candide, who trembled like a philosopher, hid himself as best he could during this heroic butchery. At last, while the two kings each commanded a *Te Deum* in his camp, Candide decided to go elsewhere to reason about causes and effects.

Unfortunately for his cause, Frederick learned nothing from the battle. Only two months later, almost as rapidly as Leuthen followed Rossbach, he was attacked by Daun and ignominiously beaten at the battle of Hochkirch.

That Austrian nobleman, as Frederick knew only too well, held his command by virtue of prudence and persistence rather than any great inspiration. The king's scorn for his opponent led him to neglect the most basic precautions as he planned to take the offensive with 37,000 troops against 90,000. While preparing to surprise the whitecoats, he was himself surprised by enemies who left their campfires burning as they formed in the woods for a dawn attack. Prussian discipline saved the army from annihilation, but Frederick lost nearly 10,000 killed or wounded as well as 101 of his cherished guns.

The new year began gloomily. Prussia could still put a total of 150,000 troops in the field, but their quality had declined as the crimps seized boys, old men, prisoners and neutrals. The summer brought a new defeat with losses of 6,000 as General Wedell attempted a too faithful copy of royal audacity and hurled 26,000 Prussians against a much larger Russian army. Frederick hurried to the scene, arriving too late to prevent the junction of Austrian and Russian forces numbering 68,000. His own strength amounted to only 45,000 after calling in all detachments, but he determined to take the initiative against an entrenched enemy.

Beginning with a prolonged bombardment by guns of every caliber, including fortress pieces, the prospects of victory were bright as the Prussians swung around to envelop and surprise the enemy on both flanks. Then after some preliminary successes, the concentric columns lost their way in the woods, falling into a confusion which resulted in disjointed and piecemeal attacks. Seydlitz's squadrons could not save the day, and the king had two horses killed under him while leading the last futile infantry charges.

The Prussian defeat at Kunersdorf became the most crushing of the war as enemy reserves swept the field. Frederick joined the headlong flight of survivors who left 20,720 dead, wounded and prisoners (48 per cent) and 178 guns behind them. The allied losses were 15,700 (23 per cent) in a triumph which became the more humiliating because it was accomplished almost entirely by equal numbers of Russians. The small part taken by the Austrians led to Frederick's salvation, however, when the allies quarreled. Although reinforced up to 90,000 troops, the disputing victors still neglected to enter defenseless Berlin or pursue an adversary who by his own admission had been reduced to 3,000 effectives.

In his hopelessness the king even resigned the command. "To recover from this misfortune is not possible," he explained as he turned the shattered little army over to General Finck. And yet the very extent of the disaster eventually gave him new courage. As week after week passed without an allied blow to end the war, Frederick realized that foes who could not profit from a Kunersdorf would never be able to defeat a resolute opponent.

Nevertheless, the defeat brought about an abrupt change in military policy after he resumed the leadership. In the past three years he had fought seven costly battles—more than Marlborough or Saxe accepted in a lifetime—during a period when 150,000 Prussian lives were being sacrificed in all operations. The next four years were to see him offer only one more engagement. Frederick had learned from despair that craft is the substitute for numbers, and endurance the strength of the weak.

At the age of forty-eight the monarch had become old and bent in appearance, peering out from under his campaign hat with tired, disillusioned eyes. He also had become a greater soldier than on the glorious day of Leuthen. For the coming years of stalemate were to bring his two most solid contributions to the science of arms—contributions which would be praised long after the oblique order had been dismissed as a military curiosity.

Frederick had rightly blamed a want of artillery mobility for his calamity at Kunersdorf. Remembering the horse-drawn fortress guns, he now applied the same principle to field artillery, which in the past had been pulled into action by soldiers tugging at ropes. Henceforward, four horses in file were hitched to each piece, the two leaders being ridden by gunners. About 100 rounds of shot and 30 of grape or canister completed the load, yet the light guns could be manoeuvred with almost the speed of cavalry.

Operating in broken country against entrenched foes, the king had further noted that ordinary guns were often powerless. To fill this gap, he experimented with the howitzer—a piece capable of being fired at such an angle of elevation as to drop a shell over a hill or into a redoubt. The mortar principle had been known since the earliest bombards, but howitzers had formerly been weapons of siegecraft. Thus in adapting them to the battlefield—and by 1762 he had a single battery of 45— Frederick again merits recognition as a military pioneer.

Unfortunately, he required an added object lesson before moderating his faith in the concentric columns which had failed him at Kunersdorf. In 1760 at Liegnitz the Austrians attempted another Hochkirch in a night attack on his marching army; but arriving too late to be surrounded, the king repulsed his assailants with heavy losses. This success encouraged him two months later to resort again to his sovereign remedy of battle as the cure for all strategic ills. Hence at Torgau he took the risk of dividing his army for a front and rear attack on a great Austrian fortified camp.

While Zieten engaged the foe's attention in one quarter, Frederick stole around with the bulk of the army to deliver the main assault from the opposite side. But like so many schemes of the sort, the operation suffered from want of perfect co-ordination. Zieten allowed his forces to be drawn off and delayed by the Austrian light troops, and meanwhile the king launched 6,000 grenadiers at a thoroughly prepared enemy. Within a few minutes the force was almost exterminated, losing nine-tenths of its strength as the 400 Austrian guns swept all approaches with canister and grape.

Frederick renewed the attack at sunset, bringing up his heavy guns. He had hurled in his infantry reserves when Zieten arrived in the early darkness to take part in an incoherent slaughter. His fresh troops saved Frederick from destruction, and the Austrians were finally driven within their works at the fearful cost of 13,120 casualties, or nearly a third of the Prussian army. The enemy lost only about 4,000 killed and wounded, but during the confusion some 7,000 whitecoats were cut off and captured.

This Pyrrhic victory taught Frederick the value of light troops and field fortifications. Both had combined to thwart him at Torgau, and he needed no further reprimand from fate.

By the summer of 1761 desertions were reducing his forces more seriously than casualties, so that his numbers dwindled to 60,000. Only English aid pulled him through this campaign, and the inevitable downfall was averted by an unexpected stroke of fortune. That winter the Russian empress died, and her successor, Peter III, not only made peace with Frederick but even signed an alliance which provided for Russian armed assistance.

This pact left the king only an exhausted Austria to deal with, and he never forgot the lessons of Torgau as the struggle dragged on to a weary stalemate. Throughout the remaining two years he clung to a grimly defensive strategy, manoeuvring with caution and conserving his forces behind redoubts bristling with big guns.

England's World Strategy

Perhaps the most bitter pill for Frederick to swallow at this time was the blazing triumph of his English allies. While he fought for bare survival, they won dramatic victories everywhere. While his operations crawled through towns and provinces, their strategy soared over oceans and continents. And while he could hope at best only to hold his own, they gained a vast empire which included the treasure house of the world. Worst of all, Frederick could not help realizing that he himself had been a pawn in the English scheme—a subordinate paid to conduct local operations.

When William Pitt came into power in 1757, England had reached the lowest ebb, patriotically and militarily, of a century. One army had been destroyed, another had surrendered, while mercenaries were actually employed for the defense of English soil.

To say that the fifty-year-old minister changed such conditions would hardly be adequate. He destroyed them as something defiling and unclean; and after conquering England, he went on to conquer England's foes. Within two years his armies were winning victories on three continents, while his ships carried troops to Canada, Africa, India, Cuba and the Philippine Islands. These operations were on such a scale as to reduce Europe to a secondary theater, with Frederick the Great and Prince Ferdinand serving Pitt's frankly avowed policy of "winning America in Germany."

England's disasters began with the defeat of General Braddock in the Pennsylvania woods, not far from the spot where George Washington fired the first shot of the war. The British commander, refusing to take advice from the despised colonists, lost his life and most of his army in an ambuscade prepared by French and Indians. Only the desperate fighting of young Washington and his Virginia militiamen saved the regulars from annihilation.

The first sea operation of the war ended in a national disgrace when Byng abandoned Minorca to a capitulation after breaking off a listless action with a French fleet. The unfortunate admiral was sacrificed to popular rage and condemned to death, as Voltaire explained, *"pour encourager les autres."*

A more worthy candidate for the firing squad appeared in 1757 when "Butcher" Cumberland surrendered an entire army after his defeat at Hastenbeck by the French under D'Estrées. England's only gain from this humiliating affair was the retirement of the king's son from command and the rise of Pitt to power.

The political career of the new war leader owed largely to a bequest of 10,000 pounds left him by the Duchess of Marlborough "upon account of his merit . . . and to prevent the ruin of his country." A scathing critic of administration policies during the last conflict, he was one of those rare souls who seem to have been created for a crisis. "I know that

I can save this country," he declared, "and that no one else can." Ever theatrical, he shouted his defiance of defeatists in government circles, "If feeble or narrow-minded measures take hold of our councils we are undone, and I will break the heart of him who is so!"

One of his first official acts—a landmark in the history of the British army—was the recruiting of soldiers from the Highlands, considered a nest of outlaws since the rebellion of 1745. Pitt allowed these clan fighters to wear their kilts, appointed Gaelic-speaking sergeants to train them, and put the regiments under their own native leaders. This policy accomplished more than all the repressions of a century. Within a few years, indeed, the part taken by Scotland in British affairs inspired Benjamin Franklin's quip, "Jonah has swallowed the whale."

In the American colonies Pitt saw another neglected resource, and his appeal for 20,000 troops met an enthusiastic response from the provincial assemblies. Two regiments of colonial redcoats were formed on a basis of equality with units from the mother country.

An aroused patriotism in England helped to bring the army up to a strength of 100,000 within a year, while the navy numbered 60,000 seamen. The press gang had a part in this increase, but never in history had volunteering been so spontaneous. A warlike but not a military people, the English had never forgotten Cromwell's armed dictatorship; and only the flamboyant Pitt could have created a people's war out of two years of defeats.

His strategy had the force of simplicity: he aimed to crush France on land and sea, at home and in the colonies, with every means in his power. Toward this end he increased Frederick's subsidies, though the national debt leaped toward the figure of 150,000,000 pounds it would reach before the war ended. But Pitt was endowing victory, not striking a bargain with defeat; and in the same unstinting fashion he supplied Ferdinand, Duke of Brunswick, with the troops and money to beat the French in western Germany.

The war minister's selection of this prince can only be explained by an uncanny ability to recognize undeveloped talent. A subordinate and protégé of the Prussian king, Ferdinand had never held a large independent command until Pitt raised him to the leadership of the British and British-paid forces in Europe. Taking charge of troops demoralized by the recent surrender, he seized the initiative to begin a military career which has been compared favorably with Frederick's.

After Rossbach the French gave Frederick no further trouble, being sufficiently occupied with Ferdinand. The following year he beat them at the battle of Crefeld and gained the rank of field marshal. In 1759 he again assumed the offensive, meeting a defeat at Bergen. His opponent, Marshal Broglie, won by virtue of putting into effect Saxe's theories of concentration by divisions. Ferdinand was thoroughly outmanouevred and forced out of every position he defended during a stubborn retreat.

That summer he had his revenge by defeating Marshal Contades at the battle of Minden. The French, holding a numerical advantage of 60,000 to 45,000, allowed Ferdinand to attack. Contrary to all orthodox practice, the British infantry charged the opposing cavalry as the result of a mistake in orders. Even more surprising, neither shock attack nor artillery fire could stop redcoats who plodded steadily onward, pausing only for platoon volleys which demoralized the opposing horsemen. Finally the advancing battalions broke the French line, and Ferdinand ordered up the British cavalry under Lord George Sackville. For some unexplained reason this officer disobeyed, being afterwards cashiered from the service. The victory was thus robbed of its fruits, though the French never again became a dangerous threat after Minden. Ferdinand won lesser successes over them in following campaigns, so that the Prussian king's survival may be traced in large part to his ally's efforts.

CLIVE'S CONQUEST OF INDIA

Behind all of Pitt's operations against France was a force which has been described by Mahan as "that noiseless pressure on the vitals . . . that compulsion, whose silence, once noted, becomes to the observer the most striking and awful mark of the working of Sea Power."

The only naval action of any importance ended in a British victory—"the Trafalgar of the Seven Years' War"—when Admiral Hawke destroyed an enemy squadron at Quiberon Bay three months after Minden. Once again the French had revived their plans for invading England, and Admiral Conflans tried to slip past the blockading fleet. Hawke pursued him to his own coast, where Conflans sought refuge in the shallows and reefs of waters known only to his navigators. An English seaman of the last two generations might have given up the chase, but Pitt's admiral had been imbued with the spirit of Monk and Blake. At the cost of two wrecked ships, he made straight for the enemy, sinking two vessels while scattering or driving aground the rest of the French squadron.

English fleets took Guadeloupe in the West Indies and Senegal in Africa. During the last months of the war, when Spain became a maritime foe, redcoats were landed for the capture of both Havana and Manila. But these successes were not decisive as compared to the "noise-less pressure" on the French coast. This sea strategy was not originated by the Great Commoner, of course, but he threw a net around the enemy such as had never been known before.

The fortitude required of crews engaged in patrol duty is more remarkable, even if less remarked, than the courage of battle. Under the horribly crowded conditions of eighteenth century sailing vessels, buffeted by storms, living for months on a flinty ration of biscuit and preserved meats, Pitt's watchdogs of the sea won by sheer endurance over an enemy snug in port. In the pride of this fortitude the British sailors grew to regard their foes not as equals but as prey to be confined or hunted down.

The price paid by the nation came so high as to make the war minister unpopular within a few years, and his resignation was accepted before the strife ended. For the French seamen could only turn to privateering for a livelihood, with the result that a tenth of the entire British merchant fleet is estimated to have been sunk or captured. Yet even these losses proved to be a trifling cost for the acquisition of India and France's empire in America.

The fantastic exploits of Robert Clive were made possible only by his country's sea power. The great French administrator Dupleix had been first to dream of seizing India's wealth, and in the last war France gained the victories. But after the fall of Madras a twenty-one-year-old Shropshire clerk escaped the capitulation of his countrymen with a wild vision of conquest. Young Clive had no resources except a recent ensign's commission, yet in a little over a decade he realized his ambition.

Although Dupleix was the greater organizer, he lacked his young rival's unique genius for commanding native troops. The contest between them continued after the peace in Europe, with both men finding allies among the Indian princes. Clive won a reputation in England with his gallant defense of Arcot; and in 1754 the turning point came when Dupleix was recalled in disgrace, his lifework undone because France feared to violate the peace.

English efforts, on the contrary, were redoubled. Pitt called Clive a "heaven-born general" and backed him with troops and ships. Thus at the critical engagement of Plassey in 1757, the conqueror was in a better position than might be indicated by the odds he faced. With only 1,100 Europeans, 2,100 sepoys and nine fieldpieces against 68,000 native troops armed with 53 guns, he could scarcely be blamed for a momentary loss of his audacity. Yet after resolving to fight he won an easy victory.

Except for the 40 Frenchmen who manned the guns, his foes did little except scatter before the English cannonade. Clive did not lose a single white soldier; and only some 70 of his native troops fell in a battle, if such it may be called, which decided the future of India.

THE WINNING OF AMERICA

Such triumphs over masses have a tremendous romantic appeal, but the victor of Plassey, like Cortez and Pizarro before him, continued to prevail by virtue of European will and method. The two million English-speaking colonists of the New World had a more difficult military problem, though they vastly outnumbered the French in Canada. The enemy not only had a compact organization but also the aid of redskins who were much better fighters than the natives of India.

The American Indian, armed by traders with the latest firearms, had an instinctive knowledge of such tactical values as stratagem, concealment and surprise. As a consequence the colonists paid a terrible price during the mother country's wars in Europe. Even during the intervals of peace the long frontier never gained immunity from the ravages of the tomahawk and scalping knife.

In this age Boston was famed as the Sparta rather than the Athens of the New World. The small city's pugnacity so impressed the foe that all colonial fighting men were known as "Bastonnais." Hence it is not surprising that the most ambitious American expedition, aiming at the capture of Louisburg, should have been composed of 4,000 volunteers recruited by the Massachusetts port. Under the command of a lawyer and merchant, they set sail in 90 fishing vessels, being supported later by three small British warships.

Lacking ordnance of their own, the Americans took ammunition to fit the French artillery. Optimistic as this may seem, they promptly carried by storm a battery of 30 large pieces. In teams of several hundred, the invaders dragged their prizes through marshes to positions commanding the strongest man-made fortress on the continent. Instructors from the British ships taught the novices how to load the cannon, and farmer and fisher lads scrambled for the privilege of serving them. The bombardment went on by day and night, though several crews were blown sky-high after learning the art of double-shotting. Brawls between the New Englanders and British seamen also enlivened a bucolic Troy which has found its Homer in the historian Parkman:

While the cannon bellowed in front, frolic and confusion reigned in the camp, where the men raced, wrestled, pitched quoits, fired at marks—though there was no ammunition to spare—and ran after the French cannon balls, to be returned to those who sent them.

After enduring a cannonade which hit every house in the town save one, Louisburg capitulated in the summer of 1745, only to be returned to France in the treaty of peace.

The colonials gave a much better account of themselves than did the regulars in Braddock's disaster; and on September 8, 1756, they won the first pitched battle fought by Americans on the soil of the present United States. While George Washington held a 400-mile frontier with a few hundred militiamen, his comrades of the northern districts raised a force of 2,500, including 300 Indians. Under the command of William Johnson, they set out to take Crown Point, a lake fort defended by Baron Dieskau, formerly a staff officer under Saxe, with 3,500 French regulars, Canadian militia and Indian allies.

The American volunteers were the usual untrained farmers and artisans, armed with their own fowling pieces and carrying hatchets as a substitute for bayonets. As they advanced, Dieskau moved out to await them with an ambuscade near the head of Lake George. Scouts kept Johnson informed of the enemy's intentions, and the action began with a vanguard skirmish in the forest, both sides using Indian tactics. Johnson was wounded and Colonel Ephraim Williams fell in action. In his will, Colonel Williams left a bequest to found the college named after him.

This clash became the prelude to the battle proper as General Phineas Lyman, a Yale instructor, formed his line of rustics who had never faced fire before. The French whitecoats, marching steadily and delivering volleys by platoons, led the enemy advance out of the woods. Dieskau tried to turn both American flanks, but the line miraculously held, beating off his attacks with hatchet and musket. The two sides were so well matched that the fighting lasted all day until the French commander was wounded and captured. Then at sunset the colonials swept forward in a desperate charge which cleared the field. They had lost 262 men and the enemy about 500, chiefly French regulars. Afterward Dieskau said of his opponents, "In the morning they fought like good boys, about noon like men, and in the afternoon like devils."

The battle of Lake George also convinced Pitt that the Americans were good military material. When he came into power it represented Britain's sole success, yet a captain of regulars still outranked a colonial major general. One of the minister's first aims, therefore, was to strike a more just balance between provincial and English officers. He appealed to the colonials as equals, and in response they voted him a far larger proportions of troops and money than the mother country supplied.

After recalling officers of the Braddock type, he appointed to American command four men so apparently ill-suited that only success could have redeemed his choices. First there was an elegant young aristocrat, Lord Richard Howe, selected to lead backwoodsmen in forest campaigns. Next came a petulant invalid, James Wolfe, whose entire sanity had been questioned. Then another invalid, Brigadier John Forbes, nominated to conduct a wilderness campaign over ground where Braddock had failed. And finally a commander-in-chief, Jeffrey Amherst, who had been snatched from obscurity and promoted over the heads of generals.

In an age of patronage not one of Pitt's choices had been a friend or close personal acquaintance. Yet even his perception of their talents is not as remarkable as the inspiration he gave them in interviews before they sailed for America. Three were to die for him, and all four to lift themselves far above the British army level of the day. In contrast, Frederick named as his subordinates a list of generals who managed to lose five out of the six main Prussian battles fought apart from his guidance.

Geography had been the great ally of the French in America, compensating for lack of numbers. Pitt's opening campaign of 1758 thus called for a three-headed offensive on such a scale that 1,200 miles separated the wings. At Cape Breton a fleet and army struck at Louisburg; in the Pennsylvania wilderness another army moved against the frontier outposts; and in the centre a combined land-and-water expedition aimed to reduce the French forts on Lake Champlain.

Louisburg could not hope to hold out against Amherst's 11,000 regulars supported by Admiral Boscawen's warships. The British parallels were pushed forward with such energy that a French garrison of 5.600 surrendered unconditionally within a few weeks.

The campaign of the 1,900 regulars and 5,000 provincials in the Pennsylvania woods also had an easy triumph. Fort Duquesne was taken without a blow and renamed Pittsburgh to celebrate the freeing of the frontier from the Indian menace. Nor was success the only difference between this expedition and Braddock's campaign. For Pitt's officers were too busy for professional snobbery, and the colonials dropped their truculent provincialism to acquire some much-needed discipline. Englishman and American became comrades in arms as Colonel Bouquet of the regulars turned the march into a traveling laboratory of light infantry tactics. Forbes, dying of a "cursed flux," clung grimly to a last spark of life until all the objects of his mission had been accomplished.

The middle campaign, perhaps the most deserving of victory, became the only one to fail. As a political concession, Pitt retained the dull General James Abercrombie in nominal command while delegating the real authority to Howe. This young peer was undoubtedly the most brilliant of the minister's four men, meriting his appraisal as "a character of ancient times; a complete model of military virtue."

Within a short time he brought about a revolution in training such as the British army had not known since Cromwell's day. Officers as well as men were ordered to wear leggings, leave off wigs, brown the barrels of muskets, crop their hair and cut their coats off at the waist. They were each to carry 30 pounds of meal, to be cooked by themselves in order to make the army independent of supplies. From private to general, all luxuries and needless encumbrances were forbidden, with Howe setting the example by washing his linen in the brook.

No other British commander ever won from Americans a fraction of the worship accorded this fervent brigadier. The colonials took to drill until they compared in discipline with the regulars, who had meanwhile been practicing American tactics of mobility.

The force which embarked at the head of Lake George in July, 1758, was Britain's finest and most colorful army of the war. The surrounding woods echoed fife and drum, bugle and bagpipe, as the 15,000 got under way with a large train of artillery. Indians in war paint and feathers, scarlet-clad regulars, Americans in green uniforms or linen hunting shirts, Highlanders in kilt and plaid—the armada filled 1,200 bateaux and a swarm of canoes reaching from shore to shore in a procession 6 miles long.

At the foot of Lake George a portage of a few miles led to Lake Champlain, where the Marquis de Montcalm labored desperately to defend Fort Ticonderoga with only 3,600 troops. Already Pitt's strategy had isolated him by involving most of France's battalions in Germany while the blockade cut off reinforcements to Canada. A British victory seemed foreordained until the first exchange of skirmishers' shots brought down Lord Howe, who had gone ahead with Colonel Robert Rogers and the American rangers. His death, according to Rogers, created "an almost general consternation."

Abercrombie, the forgotten politician, now became commander in reality as well as name. Leaving his own artillery behind, where he remained in a state of panic throughout the débâcle, he could think of nothing better than to order six successive frontal assaults against abatis defended by cannon. More than 2,000 redcoats or colonials were left among the felled trees and pointed stakes before the shattered army retired. Montcalm, a heroic marquis in shirt sleeves that summer day, had fought with his men and saved Canada for another year at the cost of only 300 casualties.

As Parkman has put it, "the death of one man was the ruin of fifteen thousand." For the spirit of victory gave way to one of mutiny and desertion as Abercrombie beat a retreat and hastily fortified against non-existent pursuers. The only gain from the expedition came later in the year when Fort Frontenac, with 9 French ships and the command of Lake Ontario, fell to 2,500 colonials.

THE BATTLE OF QUEBEC

Throughout the next summer Wolfe and Montcalm faced each other at Quebec in a duel more of nerves than of arms. From the beginning of the siege it grew apparent that the great rock's natural strength was a match for the British army of 8,500, supported by Admiral Saunders' warships. Accordingly the French commander refused to be drawn out, while the ardent Englishman could only bombard him from the opposite side of the river.

The most bigoted of Pitt's generals, Wolfe was saved from pedantry by a burning devotion to his profession. To him all informal tactics were distasteful, and he missed entirely the significance of the experiments conducted by Howe, Bouquet and Amherst. Thus during the months of inaction he drilled his troops until they became letter-perfect in all the manoeuvres of linear tactics.

Despite a deep scorn for irregulars and provincials, Wolfe owed his opportunity to American rangers who discovered the famous path up the cliff to the Plains of Abraham. Picked troops crossed the river under cover of darkness, and in the morning Montcalm was confronted by an army of 4,500 drawn up outside the walls.

The French commander might still have declined the challenge, since his foes had been able to bring up only two days' supplies and almost no artillery. Montcalm alone had an advantage in numbers, while a large body of French reinforcements under Bougainville, the future explorer, approached toward the British rear. In short, Wolfe had placed himself between two enemies trusting to a single-file path as his line of communications

What possessed the cool, collected victor of Ticonderoga to throw away his advantages can only be conjectured. It is a reasonable guess, however, that Montcalm had been driven to despair by a British strategy which rendered his cause hopeless. At any rate, the gallant Frenchman accepted an action on the terms of an adversary who had taken risks beyond the limits of mere audacity.

Once the two armies formed on the Plains of Abraham, the advantage passed to Wolfe. Even so, Montcalm fought exactly the sort of battle his opponent desired. Making little use of his Canadian irregulars, he tried to match the British infantry in the linear tactics for which they had been trained. The redcoats stood firm, enduring Montcalm's ragged fire until the enemy came within forty paces. Then in two terrible volleys they cut the French line to pieces with the most deadly musketry ever known in a battlefield up to that time. Both commanders fell mortally wounded, and as they lay dying the British charged to drive the tatters of the beaten army into a city which fell four days later.

It is customary to write finis after this climax, assuming that the struggle virtually ended with the fall of Quebec. On the contrary, Wolfe's successor General Murray was in turn besieged by 10,000 irregulars under the Chevalier de Lévis and defeated in battle the following spring. Illness and bad fare had reduced the garrison to pitiful straits before a British frigate came to the rescue with food and ammunition.

The real conquest of Canada was being pushed meanwhile by the most competent soldier of the war in America. His colonial admirers did well to name one of their new colleges after him, for Jeffrey Amherst had the patient and inquiring mind of a scientist. Fortescue, the historian of the British army, has called him England's greatest military administrator between the time of Marlborough and Wellington.

Amherst alone seems to have realized that the glitter of eighteenth century arms hid filth and disease which would never have been tolerated in a Roman camp. Soldiers subsisted on monotonous as well as unhealthy food, while the sick or wounded might feel grateful for the unusual privilege of lying on clean straw. The consequences, which were accepted in a spirit of fatalism, made themselves felt in every campaign. During the two sieges of Quebec in 1759, for instance, both sides suffered more losses from epidemics than the bullets of the enemy.

Hence the British commander waged his first campaign against dirt. He made his officers responsible for the cleanliness and sanitation of encampments. In an age when even the gentry often relied on perfume rather than soap, he compelled his men to take a daily dip in the nearest brook or lake. At a time when troops were fed wormy biscuit or foully preserved meats, he insisted on fresh vegetables as well as a regular diet of game supplied the army by American scouts. Even cold weather did not excuse his soldiers from bathing, and when vegetables were lacking he depended on the tonic qualities of a brew made from spruce tips.

As a strategist Amherst proved to be equally methodical. He fought no dramatic actions for the simple reason that he usually placed the enemy at too much of a disadvantage to resist. One by one, beginning with Ticonderoga, the French forts were evacuated before his concentric advances. He shared Howe's esteem for American woodcraft, and Colonel Rogers' rangers became the antennae of the main army of regulars and provincials. The exploits of these frontiersmen border on the fabulous; they traveled by means of skates, snowshoes and canoes, neither asking nor giving much quarter in their forest campaigns. At the climax of Rogers' operations, his scouts swam out in the Richelieu River with tomahawks to capture five armed ships.

But this feat was not typical of an offensive distinguished more for precision than thrills. Cerebral daring is seldom heroic as compared to the physical risks taken by a Wolfe, so that Amherst's victories have been outshone by the clash on the Plains of Abraham. Yet it is not often that a soldier saves more lives than he destroys to gain his ends; and the war was not won until a year after the surrender of Quebec, when Amherst's well-scrubbed warriors took Montreal without a fight. Like the Romans of old, he had conquered by virtue of planning and administration, which makes it appropriate that this middle-aged British general should have laid the cornerstone of the world's greatest empire since the fall of Rome.

PART FIVE

THE
REVOLUTION
IN TACTICS

I

THE AMERICAN RIFLE

An army all of captains, used to pray
And stiff to fight, but serious drill's despair,
Skilled to debate their orders, not obey.
—JAMES RUSSELL LOWELL

C AN we gain Independency?" the New Hampshire *Gazette* inquired rhetorically in January, 1776. The answers, if not always accurate in detail, give a fair summary of the odds faced by the American colonies as they took up arms against the mother country:

A Continent of 1000 miles Sea Coast defending themselves without one Ship of War against 300 Battle Ships compleatly manned and fitted—A Country that can pay but 30 Thousand men, at War with a Nation that has paid, and can pay 150 Thousand—A Country of Three Millions of Inhabitants, fighting with a Nation of 15 Millions—A Country that can raise but 1 Mil. of Money at War with a Nation who can raise 20 Mil. in specie. A Country without Arms, without Ammunition, without Trade, contending with a Nation that enjoys the whole in the fullest Latitude.

But the difficulties were not all on the side of the rebels. Lord Jeffrey Amherst, who was perhaps best acquainted with the strategic problems, declined the chief command for practical as well as sentimental reasons, though George III pleaded with him personally.

"Our army will be destroyed by damned driblets," croaked Adjutant

General Harvey, the highest military official of the kingdom. "America is an ugly job—a damned affair, indeed."

The liberals of the land, representing the Whig minority, were outspoken in their sympathy with the grievances of the colonists. Edmund Burke, the orator and statesman, won everlasting renown with his speeches urging conciliation. Pitt, now known as Lord Chatham, declared in 1764:

> I rejoice that America has resisted. Three millions of people so dead to the feelings of liberty as voluntarily to submit to be slaves, would have been fit instruments to make slaves of the rest.

Lord Germain, director of the war, was none other than the Lord George Sackville who had been cashiered for disobedience at Minden and adjudged "unfit to serve his Majesty in any capacity whatever." Assuming the new name under the terms of a will, he rose only sixteen years after his disgrace to a post giving him control of the expeditionary forces. The tactical reforms worked out by Howe, Bouquet and Amherst had meanwhile been buried in the pigeonholes of bureaucracy. Wolfe had become the popular hero of the war, his linear tactics being accepted by British generals of 1775 as ultimate proof of the volley by word of command.

But after fully allowing for British difficulties, the colonists still faced grave military odds. John Adams estimated that only a third of the population could be classified as active rebels. Another third remained indifferent, waiting to hail the victor, while the remainder actually supplied more soldiers to the mother country than the revolutionists were ever able to raise on a permanent basis.

Thus the advocates of independence must fight not only a foreign war against a major European power, but also a savage civil war against larger and better equipped forces of their own countrymen. Only in frontier districts did the terrain offer serious obstacles to an invader, for the bulk of the population, dwelling along the seaboard or navigable rivers, had no defense against the incursions of British sea power.

"A mixed multitude of people, under very little discipline, order or government," George Washington described his recruits. Like Cromwell before him, the American commander-in-chief had the problem of creating an army out of such dubious material, but he never forgot the object lessons left by the lord protector. Never once did Washington falter in choosing between military inefficiency and military tyranny, so that any estimate of his generalship must take into account his sacrifices to political liberties.

During the war, according to Upton, no less than 395,859 American enlistments were recorded, but most of them represented the three-month terms of militia service upheld both by the people and the Continental Congress. So wasteful was this method that Washington could seldom put 15,000 troops into the field, and at times he faced numerical odds of four to one. The penalties paid in the training of troops were summed up by his statement:

> It takes you two or three months to bring new men in any tolerable degree acquainted with their duty. . . . Before this is accomplished, the time approaches for their dismissal, and you are beginning to make interest with them for their continuance on another limited period; in the doing of which you are obliged to relax in your discipline, in order as it were to curry favor with them, by which means the latter part of your time is employed in undoing what the first was accomplishing.

As an added handicap, the commander-in-chief had to accept as his subordinates a long list of officers who owed their rank either to legislative action or popular mandate. The former process resulted in generals who might be considered politicians in uniform rather than soldiers. So many colonels were created by the obliging lawmakers that De Kalb afterward declared it safe to address any strange American officer by that title.

The people's choices led to even more serious consequences. In their impatience to end the war with a fortunate stroke, armed civilians showed an early preference for the hero over the soldier, for the man of impulse over the planner or technician. Thus the border captain Ethan Allen leaped into fame with his bold seizure of Fort Ticonderoga. Israel Putnam, known affectionately as Old Put, won a brighter renown than officers of twice his ability. Benedict Arnold, though his name has become a synonym for treason, probably did the cause more actual harm by his insubordination and bickering. Following the example he set, other leaders sulked, postured and quarreled about questions of rank or privilege until Washington was moved to the outburst:

> Such dearth of public spirit, and such want of virtue, such stock-jobbing, and fertility in all the low arts to take advantage of one kind or another . . . I never saw before and I pray God's mercy that I may never be witness to again!

LEXINGTON AND BUNKER HILL

Only a few early successes were needed to multiply Washington's troubles, and these were not lacking. In April, 1775, the militiamen of Lexington were routed by a volley, and the British regulars accomplished their mission of destroying rebel stores. Then began the unhappy retreat in which the invaders had their first taste of colonial guerrilla warfare. The "embattled farmers" aimed their muskets from behind trees or stone walls, killing or wounding several hundred redcoats and making it an achievement to have saved the rest from annihilation.

Although a British light infantry regiment took part in this expedition, only the name and a few differences in equipment distinguished such units. The actual tactical lessons taught during the last war by Austrian pandours and American rangers had been forgotten by European armies drilled after the Prussian model. This fact had another costly demonstration a few months later when the British charged the American entrenchments on Bunker Hill.

The militiamen astonished the enemy by their boldness and enterprise in throwing up earthworks on the peninsula north of Boston. Yet a mere ensign of regulars might have pointed out that the surrounding waters were navigable for vessels of light draught, so that troops could readily have been landed in the rebel rear.

Nevertheless, the British generals ordered a plain frontal assault to uphold a military prestige which became the principal casualty of that June day. Twice the scarlet-clad ranks advanced with beautiful precision up the slope. Twice the militiamen waited until the last instant before pouring in a fire so sustained and accurate that the attackers fell back in disorder. The third attempt succeeded only because the Americans ran out of powder and ball, but 1,054 out of 2,500 redcoats had fallen. The defenders withdrew in fair order after losing 450 men, including prisoners.

Saxe's theory of the superiority of fire at will over the commanded volley had been proved by farmers and villagers. The British regiments taking part in all three charges lost more than half their numbers; and 89 commissioned officers were cut down in obedience to the rebel command, "Aim for the handsome waistcoats!"

The moral effect was tremendous on both sides. The British, though learning few tactical lessons, gained a new respect for the "rabble in arms" which led to an excess of prudence in their defense of Boston. And where the Americans had once held the regulars in almost super-

stitious awe, they now rebounded to extremes of indiscipline confirmed
by brash overconfidence.

It is one of the mysteries of war chronicles that revolutionists should
so often resolve upon invasion before they are able to maintain their
own territory. In line with this persistent tradition, Congress now
decided to attempt the conquest of Canada. Even Washington seems to
have shared the fond belief of the legislators that the French inhabitants
would rise to welcome forces which came to redeem them from "slavery."

The campaigns were approved on the basis of information volunteered
by those two inveterate opportunists, Ethan Allen and Benedict Arnold.
Both men pretended to intimate personal knowledge of Canadian conditions, giving such roseate reports that three expeditions set forth in the
late summer of 1775.

Allen's premature effort came to an end when he was forced to surrender his inadequate force. Montgomery with 2,000 militiamen managed
to take Montreal, though he found the Canadians indifferent to the war.
Meanwhile Arnold's detachment pushed through the Maine wilderness,
reaching Quebec after severe hardships. The two American armies united
before the city, but both had been reduced to a handful. In desperation
they attempted a combined assault during a snowstorm, meeting with a
complete defeat on the last night of 1775 after Montgomery had fallen at
the head of his men.

Although the campaigns were based on intelligence which had proved
false, the rebels continued to send troops and supplies. Not until spring
did they abandon their futile blockade of Quebec, and that summer the
remnants were driven back across the border.

This failure was obscured by Washington's success at Boston. Throughout the winter, with his own forces constantly on the verge of disintegration, he drew a cordon about the small city which starved, bombarded and finally manoeuvred the British into an ignominious evacuation.

Despite their overwhelming sea power, the beleaguered forces soon
felt the pressure. Coastal raids met with poor results, since the forewarned inhabitants retired to the interior with their cattle. The seafaring
New Englanders meanwhile fitted out several schooners as privateers to
prey upon enemy ships bringing supplies to the city. Thirty prizes were
taken almost under the guns of the warships, one of which gave the rebels
3,000 round shot and 32 tons of bullets.

The crisis of the blockade came when a long train of ox-drawn sleds
reached Cambridge with the cannon captured at Ticonderoga. Gunnery

appears to have been the one formal lesson learned by Americans in the last war, for enemy accounts testify as to the superiority of the rebel fire. Nevertheless, the deadlock continued until Washington sprang a decisive surprise by seizing Dorchester Heights and throwing up fortifications overnight. The new gun emplacements dominated the city and harbor, allowing the British only a choice between carrying the position or abandoning Boston. After some hesitation they chose evacuation rather than the risk of another Bunker Hill; and the great fleet sailed away to Canada, leaving 125 serviceable cannon as prizes for the victors.

The New York Campaign

The losing general had been Sir William Howe, a brother of the fallen leader of 1757 whom the Americans honored with a memorial tablet in Westminster Abbey. On the British commander's advice, the next campaign was directed at New York "with an olive branch in the right hand and a sword in the left." On July 4, 1776, a few hours after the declaration of American independence, the 130 warships and transports appeared off Staten Island with 30,000 troops, Britain's largest foreign expeditionary force up to this date.

Washington, having anticipated the move, stood on the defensive with some 17,000 raw militiamen. His decision to resist seems to have been dictated wholly by political considerations, for the city obviously could not be held against such a powerful army and fleet. In order to protect his left flank the American general threw most of his regiments across the East River to occupy the site of the present borough of Brooklyn. Howe singled out this point for attack when his conciliatory efforts met with rebuffs. After landing 20,000 troops, he struck the American front with two columns while sending a third in a secret all-night march around the left rear. Caught between these detachments, the rebels were routed by skill rather than weight. Both sides lost about 400 killed and wounded at the battle of Long Island, and the Americans also left 1,000 prisoners in the enemy's hands.

Howe has been criticized for not following up his victory, but he decided with apparent logic that the works on Brooklyn Heights were strong enough to warrant a siege. Before he could begin his approaches, the defenders made good their escape in another night surprise as bewildering as the seizure of Dorchester Heights. Stedman, a historian who served as an officer under Howe, has recorded the enemy's admiration of the achievement:

The retreat was effected in 13 hours, though 9,000 men had to pass over the river, besides field artillery, ammunition, provisions, cattle, horses and carts. The circumstances of this retreat were particularly glorious to the Americans. They had been driven to a corner of the island, where they were hemmed in within the narrow space of two miles. In their front was an encampment of 20,000 men; in their rear an arm of the sea, a mile wide. . . . Notwithstanding these difficulties, they secured a retreat without the loss of a man.

Washington concealed his intentions even from his own officers by ordering the beaten army to stand in readiness for a night attack. The success of the evacuation was also made possible by Colonel Glover's Amphibious Regiment. Composed of Massachusetts fishermen wearing blue pea jackets and "trowsers," this corps of specialists seized every small boat in the harbor and ferried the entire army to the Manhattan shore.

Both the Greeks and Romans had troops trained especially for combined land and water operations. As early as 1664 the British Admiralty formed the first marine unit of modern warfare—1,200 "land souldgers prepared for sea service"—and by 1702 six regiments were in existence. Two battalions of American marines were authorized by Congress in 1775, but Glover's amphibians may also be considered the tactical ancestors of the modern corps. Like the versatile American marine of today, the Marblehead fisherman became a military jack-of-all-trades, fighting as a gunner or infantryman when the army did not require his special skill in inland water operations.

Washington had eluded almost certain capture, but even the most brilliant evacuations do not win campaigns. By crossing to the narrow island, moreover, he placed his forces in a strategic bottle, with the British fleet holding the cork.

On September 15 the warships beat up the East River, landing troops which occupied the city and nearly cut off all retreat. After a wild flight most of the demoralized militiamen escaped. They held at Harlem Heights and the next day Washington's tired troops rallied magnificently by defeating the redcoats in a small battle fought over the buckwheat fields of what is now uptown New York.

Howe gave the Americans a breathing spell of nearly a month at Harlem Heights. When at last he embarked four brigades comprising about 4,000 picked troops, it soon became evident that he intended to land at Throg's Neck and turn the American position from the rear. The British and Hessians were frustrated in their first attempt by

American riflemen defending a narrow causeway. Taking to their ships again, they landed on October 18 at Pell's Point. There they were held up the entire day with heavy losses by the 750 troops of four skeleton Massachusetts regiments, supported by three fieldpieces, which Colonel Glover had posted on opposite sides of the road behind stone walls. This delay gave Washington the opportunity to escape with his army.

Howe followed as far as White Plains, winning a skirmish before he gave up the chase. On returning to Manhattan Island in November, he brought the campaign to a close by taking Fort Washington with 3,000 prisoners.

Desertions and expired enlistments had reduced Washington's army to about that number as he retreated across New Jersey. Behind him General Cornwallis' detachment pressed so close that the last rebels had not left Newark before the enemy entered. The American cause never sank to a lower ebb; and most of its disasters could be charged justly, if indirectly, to a Canadian invasion which wasted the military resources of the first year.

THE EPIC OF TRENTON

Washington ordered all boats to be seized for 70 miles up and down the Delaware, and in December he crossed just ahead of the British vanguard. Yet the Pennsylvania shore could offer only a temporary haven; for Cornwallis held the left bank with his German mercenaries, and soon the ice might permit the passage of troops.

Howe went into winter quarters in New York, and the various British detachments in New Jersey had no thought of danger as Washington planned to take the offensive. "Christmas day at night, one hour before day, is the time fixed for our attempt upon Trenton," he wrote to Colonel Reed. "For Heaven's sake keep this to yourself, as the discovery of it may prove fatal to us; our numbers, I am sorry to say, being less than I had any conception of; yet nothing but necessity, dire necessity, will, nay must, justify an attack."

The three Hessian regiments at Trenton felt particularly safe behind a river filled with racing cakes of ice. The mercenaries made merry until the winter dawn, and not until broad daylight did Washington's scarecrow army appear. After crossing the river in boats manned by Glover's amphibians, the miserably shod and clothed militiamen were delayed by a night march through a blinding snowstorm. Nevertheless, the surprise proved so devastating that the rebel columns compelled the surrender of practically the entire detachment at a cost of only two deaths from exposure.

Washington fell back into Pennsylvania with his prisoners as Cornwallis hastened to take command of the shaken British forces in New Jersey. Only three days after his victory the American leader again crossed a river so packed with floes that 48 hours were required for the passage of troops, horses and cannon. The audacity of this attempt is as remarkable as his Christmas venture, for he had but 3,800 footsore and frostbitten recruits with which to resume the offensive against a thoroughly aroused foe.

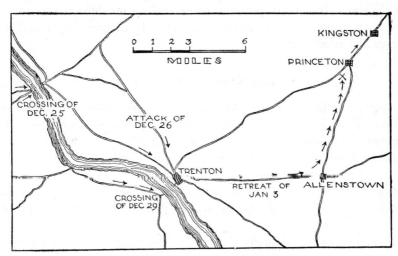

The Epic of Trenton

Cornwallis swiftly concentrated nearly 8,000 regulars against the new American camp at Trenton. All the night of January 2 the two armies supposedly faced each other in the darkness as the British prepared for a morning attack. The rebels left a few men to keep the campfires burning, and Cornwallis did not suspect their escape until daybreak, when sounds of cannonading came from ten miles in his rear. Washington had slipped away over frozen roads to strike enemy reinforcements at Princeton, where he defeated three regiments and took 300 prisoners in a savage little battle of encounter.

Next Cornwallis learned with alarm that his adversary had pushed past Princeton in an advance on the ill-defended British base at Brunswick with its stores and baggage. At Kingston, however, Washington held a council of officers on horseback; and he accepted their decision that the attempt could not be made with ragged and barefoot militiamen in the final stages of exhaustion. Accordingly the army turned off toward

Morristown, where the highlands provided a refuge on the flank of the British advance in New Jersey.

The eight-day campaign lacks the grandeur conferred by large numbers, but no more stirring episode exists in military history. The moral effects of the two victories were incalculable, since thousands of doubting Americans recovered their faith in the cause. But even an epic has its tactics, and second only to Washington's bold generalship the efforts of Glover's amphibians deserve the major credit for Trenton and Princeton. Without those hardy fishermen, the swollen, ice-choked river could never have been crossed three times in a week by an army depending on barges and small boats.

The National Weapon

Another regiment of specialists saved the new nation the following autumn. Early in 1777 Washington placed 500 picked riflemen under the command of Colonel Daniel Morgan, recently released from captivity at Quebec. A cousin of Daniel Boone, this burly, self-educated Virginia pioneer had served as a wagoner in the last war. Now at the age of forty-one he became a natural leader of Virginia and Pennsylvania frontiersmen whom he disciplined with a patriarchal firmness enforced by his own hard fists.

The formation of this unit—the first of its kind in history—came just in time to meet the greatest British threat of the war, a concerted effort to occupy the Hudson-Lake Champlain line. According to the original plan, Howe's forces were to march northward from New York to meet the army of General John Burgoyne, invading from Canada. Such a result would have split the colonies hopelessly, laying them open to conquest in detail.

The rifle was not a new weapon. Even in classical times it had been remarked that the velocity and accuracy of a projectile were increased by the imparting of a spinning motion. Ancient armorers tried to apply the principle to the spears shot from war engines, and sixteenth century gunsmiths made the first experiments with spiral grooving in the bore of wheel-locks. They found that any gains were offset by a slow rate of fire; for in order to prevent the escape of propelling gases, the ball had to be driven into the grooves with a ramrod and wooden mallet. Due to this defect the European rifle was rejected by soldiers and used chiefly for target or sporting purposes.

During the last war the advantages of the American rifle had been noted by Howe and Bouquet, though it played a minor part in the outcome. The real development of the national weapon did not begin until afterward, when the victory opened the frontier to the first great wave of westward migration.

It was a backwoods invention—a slight improvement of epochal significance—which established the superiority of the American arm over its short-barreled counterpart of the Old World. Some unknown genius of the border discovered that a "greased patch" could be placed over the

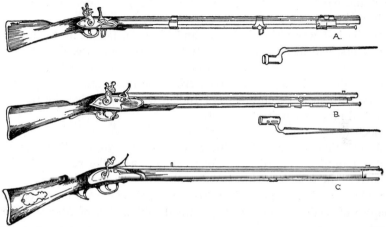

Flintlocks of the American Revolution: (A) French Regulation Musket; (B) British "Brown Bess" Musket; (C) American Frontier Rifle

muzzle as a temporary wrapping for a ball driven home by a few light strokes of the ramrod. This bit of lubricated linen or leather not only made the bullet fit the grooves but also cleaned out the fouling from the previous discharge and acted as a "gas check" to utilize the full force of the explosion. The patch had thus created history's first firearm of precision.

Not until the perfection of the breechloader, three generations later, was the "long rifle" ever excelled. The speed of charging still lagged behind that of the smoothbore, but the gains in range, accuracy and penetration were impressive. At 100 yards, the battle range of the musket, tacticians expected only 40 per cent of hits, and even this average suffered from misfires. The rifle accounted for 50 per cent at 300 yards, while at two-thirds of that distance the border marksman aimed with deadly certainty for a foeman's head or heart.

American "patch-loading" also resulted in economy of ammunition. Because of the increased gas pressure, it was found that the caliber could be reduced to .54, taking a half-ounce ball, whereas most smoothbores of the day fired a one-ounce bullet of about .70 caliber. The smaller projectile, with less air resistance to overcome, developed much more velocity and striking power.

Such gains may be traced in part to expert Pennsylvania gunmakers whose masterpieces are still cherished by collectors. Even so, the effectiveness of the rifle in Revolutionary campaigns owed to a generation of Americans who rank among the natural warriors of history. Like the Parthians or Mongols of old, they were shaped by a daily existence of peril and hardship for the tactics which soldiers of later ages have had to learn by rote.

In the last war Colonel Rogers and his men, taught by their savage opponents, had made a scientific study of ruse, surprise, deception and taking cover—the "modern" methods which were to be taught to the Commandos and Rangers of 1943. After the peace the long border still flamed with sporadic outbreaks of Indian warfare, so that the frontiersman had no opportunity to forget.

Such warfare, of course, was alien to the farmers and villagers of the seaboard. Smoothbores were the weapon of Lexington and Bunker Hill, and not until afterwards did Congress authorize the recruiting of ten companies of riflemen from frontier districts. These units took part in the Quebec, Boston and New York campaigns, but an entirely new chapter of tactics begins in 1777 with the formation of Morgan's regiment.

Up to this time the riflemen had been considered an auxiliary to formal operations—a scout or sharpshooter whose usefulness lay chiefly in skirmishing. It was left to Morgan and his command to prove that the new weapon could also become a decisive factor on the battlefield.

The Surrender at Saratoga

The tactical value of the corps soon had a first test. Burgoyne's army had invested Ticonderoga as Howe moved out against Washington's smaller force in a New Jersey campaign of manoeuvre. The American general made it his object to delay his skillful adversary as long as possible while sending orders for 1,000 woodsmen to place obstacles in Burgoyne's path.

"If I can keep General Howe below the highlands," he wrote, "I think their schemes will be baffled." Toward that end he refused an engagement while sending out Morgan's troops as a cloud of skirmishers to hang on the flanks of the advancing regulars. The success of his strategy, according to the historian Fisher, cost Howe as many losses as if he had fought a battle.

Owing to this result, as well as the blunders of Lord Germain, the British general evacuated New Jersey. Early in July, to Washington's relief, the enemy transports departed in a southerly direction. Instead of trying to meet Burgoyne, Howe had decided to sail up Chesapeake Bay for an attempt on Philadelphia.

The division of the British forces lessened the peril, though it meant that the rebels also had to keep two widely separated armies in the field as Washington crossed New Jersey to defend the colonial metropolis. With a force of green militiamen he could hardly hope to repulse Howe, yet the commander-in-chief sent Morgan's riflemen to the aid of General Horatio Gates' northern army.

Washington did not err in assuming that Burgoyne's invasion remained the greater danger. This veteran general had profited from past British errors to create his country's finest instrument of the war. Composed of 7,200 troops, including 3,000 German mercenaries, the force was supported by an artillery train such as the New World had never seen before —138 pieces manned by 600 gunners. As an even more formidable threat, Burgoyne had organized 650 Indians and Canadians into a scouting arm so effective that the rebels were temporarily beaten at their own game.

In this campaign, perhaps the most decisive ever fought on American soil, the invaders also brought a few Jägers, or Continental riflemen, among the Hessian contingents. These marksmen appear to have given little trouble with their shorter weapon and slower rate of fire. Nor were the German light infantrymen, armed with carbines and swords, ever able to challenge the American supremacy in the reconnaissance and skirmishing tactics of wooded country.

The British lake flotilla appeared before Ticonderoga in June. The artillery train compelled the evacuation of the fort without a fight, and the army pressed overland toward Saratoga.

On the march the column advanced only a mile a day over trails blocked by trees felled at Washington's orders. Burgoyne soon learned, moreover, that detachments were not safe in a hostile countryside. On August 16 a co-operating force under Colonel St. Leger had to retreat from the Mohawk Valley after being defeated by General Herkimer's militiamen at Oriskany. That same week a foraging expedition of Hessians was surrounded by New England volunteers at Bennington and destroyed.

Despite these reverses the invaders retained a superiority in every respect when at last they approached the American lines. Most astonishing, we learn from Gates' messages to Washington that the rebel forces were tactically blinded by the enemy scouts. The savages in particular proved a disturbing element to militiamen who knew little about frontier fighting methods.

Morgan's riflemen arrived early in September to reinforce an outnumbered, demoralized and badly led army of recruits. The first effect of the regiment's participation was dramatic in its suddenness—the British scouts deserted wholesale rather than face grim border men who took a peculiar delight in stalking Indians. Within a few days the tables were turned, so that during the rest of the campaign the invaders groped in tactical blindness.

Lack of intelligence caused Burgoyne to send out three columns on September 19 for a reconnaissance in force. In wooded country he made contact with Morgan's corps, as usual deployed along the skirmish line, and an incoherent combat developed.

On the American side the most striking feature of the clash, known as the battle of Freeman's Farm, is the lack of central command. Throughout the six-week campaign the two generals, Gates and Arnold, neglected their duty for petty bickerings, and neither deserves much credit for the final outcome. In this critical fight the regiments straggled up, one by one, and only the cohesion supplied by Morgan and his corps saved them from disaster. For that reason the day emerges as a landmark in tactical history, becoming the first occasion when riflemen bore the brunt of battle.

Morgan's outweighed men fell back before the main enemy column, but quickly rallied as he formed a line in the woods. To the amazement of the regulars, their opponents exchanged strange gibbering sounds—the wild turkey calls used by the frontiersmen for signaling. The British infantry advanced in close order across the clearing, each scarlet uniform presenting a fine target as the thin, vicious crackling of the rifles sounded. The Americans, taking cover in the autumnal foliage, were almost invisible in their brown linen hunting shirts and buckskin breeches.

There is a curious air of modernity about this scene, foreshadowing a still distant era when the heavy infantry of all armies would be replaced by thin lines of deployed light troops. Allowing for improved weapons, the riflemen of 1777 might have given a good account of themselves in an action of the twentieth century. Burgoyne's 62nd Regiment, which fought opposite Morgan's corps, could muster only the strength of a single company at the end of the day; and of the 48 gunners in one battery of British light artillery, but 12 were left alive and unhurt.

All afternoon the battle swayed back and forth in the forest. Morgan's men held until fresh regiments came to their support—first two, which formed on the left, then others until nine were engaged, giving the rebels a numerical advantage. In the lack of central command the newcomers took their cue from the riflemen and adopted similar tactics. Had they been properly supported by artillery a victory might have resulted; but rifle and musket could not prevail against enemy guns pouring in a hail of canister. Even so, the encounter ended at dusk in a tactical draw, the British losing nearly 600 men and their opponents about 350.

Strategically, the Americans gained nearly as much as if they had swept the enemy off the field. For it must be remembered that the "battle" of Saratoga consisted of two combats separated by 18 days. During this interval the recruits rallied behind Morgan's riflemen, now recognized as the *corps d'élite* of the army. The former spirit of demoralization was replaced by an aggressive confidence as volunteers flocked from all sides. The new American superiority in numbers swelled until 15,000 were hemming in a British army which could not advance and dared not retreat. Throughout these 18 days the riflemen harassed the enemy to the point of desperation, sniping at pickets and depriving Burgoyne of either intelligence or forage.

His situation had become grave when on October 7 he made a final effort to break through the cordon. Gates accepted Morgan's plan for a double flank attack; and the rebel forces were set in motion with his message, "Order on Morgan to begin the game."

Again the weird gobbling of the turkey calls rang through the forest as the leader of the riflemen made a wide turning movement to envelop the British right. Simultaneously General Poor's brigade struck the enemy's left as General Learned advanced on the centre. All three attacks made rapid headway, driving the redcoats back with losses of 400. The battle of Bemis Heights was already won and the foe in full retreat when Benedict Arnold put in a melodramatic appearance to lead a charge on the British fortified camp. For lack of planning or artillery preparation, the first attempt met with a bloody repulse of Americans mown down by grapeshot at close range. Returning to the assault, Arnold fell wounded while dislodging 200 Germans from a redoubt; but his intervention added little except needless casualties to the results previously gained.

Burgoyne hung on for ten more days as the forces of his enemies grew to 22,000. Then on October 17, 1777—a date as important to American independence as July 4, 1776—the remaining 5,700 British troops, many of them sick or wounded, laid down their arms. This outcome, as every schoolboy learns, led directly to an alliance with France which supplied the sinews of ultimate victory.

WASHINGTON AT VALLEY FORGE

During the course of these operations the commander-in-chief fought and lost two engagements. In September he attempted a stand against Howe's forces advancing on Philadelphia, and the battle of the Brandywine became a repetition of Long Island after the British general launched a deft flank attack. Howe occupied the city without further fighting, but early in October Washington made a surprise attack on the British headquarters in the near-by village of Germantown. The American plan called for the converging night march of four columns over as many roads, to be followed by a combined assault at dawn. Such an operation would have tried the best regulars, for it will be recalled that Frederick's veterans failed at Torgau to co-ordinate the attack of two columns. Nevertheless, the militiamen might have succeeded except for a fog which threw them into confusion. They retreated in fair order after both sides had suffered losses almost identical with those of the Brandywine—about 500 British slain and wounded, and 1,000 American casualties, of which half were prisoners.

The two encounters merely reiterated the lesson that short-term volunteers could not meet the regulars in formal combat. Many of the militia units, still lacking bayonets, became easy victims for redcoats who charged with cold steel before the Americans had time to reload. The colonial officers were as uncertain as their men, and mistakes in command contributed to both defeats.

It has been suggested, too, that Washington erred in fighting the British on their own terms. Such successes as Lexington and Bennington support the plausible theory that the rebels might better have trusted to irregular warfare. Yet the commander read the precepts of history correctly when he refused to be swerved from his purpose of creating an army of American regulars. Guerrilla victories, however beguiling, run the risk of degenerating into military anarchy. The strategic ideal is a combination of both in judicious measure, so as to place the enemy between the upper and nether millstones of tactics. Thus at Saratoga, when the central command failed, a single unit of riflemen set an example of firmness which welded irregulars into an effective striking as well as harassing force.

The very name of Valley Forge symbolizes the hardships endured by Washington's troops in their winter quarters twenty miles northwest of Philadelphia. Although supplies were not lacking, the hastily organized systems of transport and commissariat could not cope with the problems of distribution. The sufferings of the army also bear witness to the success of the British economic warfare. Not only had American trade been ruined by the blockade, but American money sank rapidly in value as enemy printing presses flooded the country with spurious notes. Counterfeiting was not a new weapon, but the invaders employed it with an effectiveness which has perpetuated the phrase "not worth a Continental." Meanwhile they added to the pressure by paying for their own supplies in gold.

In spite of its somber legend, Valley Forge is more deserving of renown as the birthplace of the United States Army. The colonies found their Martinet in the person of "Baron von" Steuben, a lovable impostor who invented his title, though he had seen real service under Frederick. With the aid of an interpreter to translate his good-natured oaths, the new inspector general managed within a few months to make soldiers out of ragged, half-starved recruits. The secret of his success was an adaptability amounting to genius. Where other armies, including the British, copied Prussian methods in a spirit of blind emulation, this Prussian volunteer selected and revised with a view to American conditions.

"His drill regulations show his good sense and humanity," declares William Addleman Ganoe's *History of the United States Army*. "On them are based all subsequent ones in our service."

In place of the former crude marching formations, he introduced a column of platoons with a step and cadence conforming to rough country. He reduced the motions of loading a musket, prescribed uniformity of equipment, and reorganized the infantry regiment into two battalions and eight companies of two platoons each. As a disciplinarian, Steuben did more than adapt—he abolished the old rule of fear and created in its stead a new bond of mutual sympathy and respect between officer and citizen-soldier.

The colonies were equally fortunate in having as an artillery and engineering instructor one of the foremost military scholars of the age— Thaddeus Kosciusko, who had studied tactics in Prussia, France and Italy for six years at the expense of the Polish state. After offering his services to America in 1776, he planned the works at West Point which developed into the strategic centre of the rebellion. Before him the sciences of siegecraft and fortification had been little known, but the gallant Pole trained officers who became the founders of American military engineering. Of all the European volunteers he was probably the most accomplished; and his *Manoeuvres of Horse Artillery*, published in New York after the war, served as a text for the next generation of American soldiers.

The belated development of an American cavalry arm also dates from Valley Forge. Up to this time the militiamen had been at the mercy of enemy dragoons, but during the winter of privations the "market shoppers" of Allan McLane helped to relieve the situation by daring raids on British provision trains. And though heavy cavalry took no part in the war, the legions of light horse raised by Henry Lee and William Washington gave the rebels an equality in later campaigns.

For all of the progress made at Valley Forge, the army discovered that a general cannot be trained in a few months. In the past the rank and file had often failed the command, and now on the field of Monmouth the reverse proved true.

The opportunity came when Sir Henry Clinton replaced Howe as the British decided on a limited strategy calling for the evacuation of Philadelphia. In June, 1778, the 10,000 redcoats began a perilous retreat to New York with a baggage train ten miles long. Washington broke up camp with a force of at least equal numbers and took a parallel route through New Jersey on the exposed enemy flank.

Never during the war did victory beckon more alluringly, yet at the council of officers only Anthony Wayne and young Lafayette favored the commander's proposed battle. A like spirit of indecision became manifest during the action. The rebel attacks were delivered piecemeal, with such disjointed tactics as to leave Morgan's riflemen stranded without orders on the opposite British flank. The day ended in an empty American success, for though Clinton suffered nearly double the 300 casualties of the aggressors, he had saved his army from disaster.

The disappointed Americans found their consolation in the firm behavior of Steuben's pupils. In fair fight with musket and bayonet, Wayne's men shattered a Guards regiment which lost more than half its numbers. After Monmouth the Continental, or American regular, never failed to give a good account of himself against the best trained troops of Europe.

Fortune could hardly have been expected to smile a second time, yet an even greater opportunity awaited after the British army reached New

York. Washington at last had the prospect of sea power as Admiral d'Estaing's fleet crossed the Atlantic. Pushing his army by rapid marches, he hemmed in the city from the land side while the French admiral prepared to force an entrance into a harbor defended by a much weaker British squadron.

If the combined attack had succeeded, Clinton might soon have been starved into another Saratoga. The British ships made ready for a desperate defense, but French seamanship proved unequal to the test. Although Mahan presents convincing evidence to show that the harbor shoals need not have balked a more able admiral, d'Estaing gave up the attempt and sailed away to Rhode Island. There he essayed another land-and-sea operation which ended with both the French and British fleets being scattered by a storm.

From this moment the American cause fell into a decline lasting nearly three years. Washington's finest army of the war slowly disintegrated from expired enlistments until such famous units as Morgan's riflemen and Glover's amphibians are heard from no more. Throughout this dreary period the personality of the commander gave the only assurance that Americans might some day win their independence. Fortunately for their cause, the British efforts were limited to small war on the northern front; and in the interests of morale Washington managed to plan several brilliant little surprises such as Wayne's storming of Stony Point.

In the southern colonies, meanwhile, the reverses multiplied. Charleston and its large garrison surrendered in 1779, and at Camden the following summer the British won their most smashing victory of the war when Cornwallis routed a larger force under Gates. The news of this disaster, coming on the heels of Benedict Arnold's attempted betrayal of West Point, seemed to nullify all the American gains made since Saratoga.

THE WAR IN THE SOUTH

British sea power had accomplished the reduction of the three southern colonies. Beginning with the capture of Savannah, the invaders landed troops and supplies for a methodical advance northward which now threatened Virginia. In this purpose they were supported by a large loyalist population, so that the strife took on the character of a civil war attended by cruel reprisals with torch and noose.

The defeat of Gates left only a few rebel guerrilla bands in the entire region. But out of the few thousand troops at his disposal, Washington sent some of his best Continentals under his most trusted subordinate,

General Nathanael Greene. A student of Turenne's campaigns, this Rhode Islander of Quaker birth brought to his task the cool spirit of a professional. Holding no councils and enforcing the strictest discipline, he at once began a campaign of manoeuvre with Cornwallis in the Carolinas.

The first American victory came from a wholly unexpected source—the wild district west of the Alleghenies. Colonel Patrick Ferguson, a British raider, had hanged several kinsmen of the pioneers in that region, and under their own leaders they pursued him to King's Mountain to settle accounts.

Of all the British officers in the war, Ferguson showed the most intelligent grasp of the new tactics. The inventor of an early breechloading rifle, he had recruited 1,100 loyalists into a legion modeled after Morgan's regiment. The affair at King's Mountain thus became exclusively a civil war battle, with the rifle the chief reliance of both sides. Ferguson had trained his troops well, but they proved no match for "over-mountain men" who had been waging a continual Indian warfare. Taking advantage of all cover and shooting with deadly accuracy, the frontiersmen swarmed up the slope to annihilate the loyalist force. After Ferguson's death his remnants surrendered, only to have 100 prisoners shot down or hanged in revenge.

Three months later, in January, 1781, Daniel Morgan brought off the tactical masterpiece of the Revolution by destroying another little British army at the battle of the Cowpens. Commanding a detachment of Greene's force, the American general was pursued by Colonel Banastre Tarleton, whose name is still a legend of dash and cruelty in the Carolina back country. The British strength included 700 regular infantry, 300 loyalist dragoons and two fieldpieces. Morgan led nearly equal numbers, though two-thirds of his army consisted of raw militiamen who were certain to run at the first enemy volley.

His solution of this tactical dilemma ranks with any of Montrose's small battle triumphs. First he violated every rule by defending a rolling plain suited to his opponent's dragoons. Both rebel flanks were left "in the air," while a few miles to the rear the Broad River cut off all retreat. Next Morgan placed the unreliable militiamen in front, with the Continentals and 80 dragoons in support. Far from forbidding his raw troops to retire, he gave permission after they had fired two rounds.

Tarleton advanced with his usual impetuosity, never suspecting a psychological trap. The regulars endured many casualties from the two militia volleys, but were heartened by the flight of the whole American first line. This left but 300 Continentals, who made a desperate stand with musket and bayonet against overwhelming odds. Meanwhile Morgan was busy reorganizing his militiamen behind a low hill in the rear. In ten minutes he inspired them with new confidence, and under cover of the ridge the 600 followed him entirely around the field to envelop the British left rear just as the American dragoons struck the right. Thus at the moment of victory the redcoats were surprised and hemmed in from three sides, losing nearly 300 killed and wounded in addition to 600 prisoners. Only Tarleton and a few scattered riders escaped a disaster which cost the victors 60 casualties.

Despite the small numbers involved, Cowpens had an unusual importance because of Greene's adoption of the plan in his two principal battles. After a skillful retreat to the North Carolina border, the American commander awaited Cornwallis at Guilford Courthouse. Morgan had resigned on account of illness, but the Americans were drawn up according to his advice. Greene made the mistake of placing his militiamen too far in front, however, and some units did not recover from their panic. The fight then turned into a savage struggle between Continentals and British regulars, with honors about even. Greene might perhaps have won a decision, but he chose not to throw in his reserves. The enemy suffered losses of 30 per cent to gain a victory which Tarleton called "the pledge of ultimate defeat."

Cornwallis abandoned the campaign and marched to Virginia to recruit his broken army back to strength. And with this adversary removed, Greene began the operations which cleared the foe from the three southern colonies before autumn.

Tactically, he incurred new reverses at every turn. In April he was surprised and defeated by Lord Rawdon at Hobkirk's Hill, both sides taking equal losses. In May he attempted to storm the strong British post at "Ninety-Six" and met another repulse. In September, during the last and bloodiest battle of the war at Eutaw Springs, Greene used the Cowpens formations with such success as to drive the enemy off the field. Then his half-starved men took to plundering the enemy camp, and were themselves dislodged in the counterattack. Greene's casualties were 600, or 23 per cent, while the 1,000 British slain, wounded and captured amounted to no less than 45 per cent.

"We fight, get beaten, and fight again." Thus Greene summed up his efforts, yet each tactical defeat led to a strategic victory. Rawdon withdrew to the coast from Hobkirk's Hill; the stronghold at "Ninety-Six" was evacuated soon after the American attack; and Eutaw Springs resulted in the remaining British forces being penned up in Charleston under the guns of their ships.

Such gains, achieved with a strength seldom exceeding 3,000 men, are not paradoxical. Greene had simply provided the axis for a genuine people's war which drove the invaders out of the South. While he marched and countermarched against the main armies, the partisan bands led by Lee, Pickens, Sumter and Marion harassed the flanks, cut off supplies, fell upon isolated posts and put down all loyalist aid. This combination of regular and irregular warfare, so unfailingly potent through history, speedily reduced the British occupation to a hollow shell.

The credit must go not only to Greene's generalship but also the 1,600 Continentals who were his mainstay. Better soldiers never fought in the Revolution. Unpaid, famished as wolves, almost literally naked except for breechclouts and pads of moss under their cartridge belts, these men had plodded hundreds of miles over frontier trails. During the campaign they fought four desperate actions and many lesser combats, yet on every field they proved themselves the equals of the British regulars.

The Climax at Yorktown

A corresponding improvement in the American command is evident as Cornwallis overran Virginia with his reinforced army. To meet this threat Washington placed Lafayette at the head of a force equipped largely at his own expense. For several months the enthusiastic young French volunteer, later assisted by Wayne and Morgan, held his own against the invaders in a campaign which has thus been evaluated by Sidney George Fisher:

> With 3000 men he had, by caution, quickness and skilful manoeuvring, tired out a British general with 4500 and compelled him to seek some place of protection.

Cornwallis could hardly have chosen a less safe place than Yorktown, and his colleague Clinton afterwards condemned the Virginia operations in bitter terms. Still, nothing must have seemed more improbable at the moment than a descent of the impoverished rebel army from New York into Virginia. That bold conception was Washington's idea. Ever since his disappointment in 1778 he had dreamed of trapping another British army, and immediately he formed the plan of a vast campaign along interior lines with Cornwallis as the victim.

After gaining assurances of French co-operation on land and sea, Washington went to elaborate deceptions to convince Clinton that the blow was meant for New York. Then on August 19, with only 4,000 men left behind to guard the Hudson forts, he pressed southward in forced marches, closely followed by Rochambeau's army. At the head of the Chesapeake the allied troops embarked in French ships to Williamsburg and reached Yorktown on September 28.

This remarkable concentration owed to a French sea victory. Too late, the British suspected Washington's design, and on August 31 Admiral Thomas Graves put out from New York with 19 ships of the line. Five days later he encountered Admiral de Grasse with 24 ships of the line, and the action known as the battle of the Capes took place. Not a single vessel was sunk, and the cannonading did only moderate damage to hulls and rigging, yet the affair remains one of the world's most decisive naval engagements. As a result Graves had to return to New York to refit, leaving Cornwallis at the mercy of his combined foes.

The beleaguered general had strongly fortified Yorktown, but from the beginning his plight was hopeless. While the 11,000 Americans and 5,000 Frenchmen began their approaches on the land side, De Grasse's warships commanded the sea lanes to cut off British aid. Within a week the storming of the defenders' main redoubts exposed them to a fearful bombardment; and on October 17, 1781—the fourth anniversary of Saratoga—Cornwallis wisely consented to a surrender. Two days later the fighting of the Revolution came virtually to an end as the 7,000 British troops laid down their arms to the music of *The World Upside Down*.

II

FRENCH HORDE TACTICS

Just as lightning has already struck when the flash is seen, so when the enemy discovers the head of the army, the whole should be there, and leave him no time to counteract its dispositions.

—GUIBERT

IF NUMBERS be taken as a criterion, the American Revolution emerges as a small conflict indeed. During the eight years scarcely as many men fell in action as were left on the field of Kunersdorf alone in the preceding war. Yet not a single hamlet changed hands as an outcome of Frederick's operations, while Saratoga and Yorktown brought into being a new nation.

It is not surprising, therefore, that political and military events across the Atlantic should have overshadowed Europe's greatest modern naval war, which went on concurrently. Shortly after Burgoyne's surrender France passed from secret to open strife against England. Spain and Holland soon followed her example, though neither country formed an American alliance. Until 1783 the four maritime powers carried on a contest in European, Caribbean and Asiatic waters which led to remarkably mild results in view of such extensive operations.

Opposing the 150 British ships of the line were 80 French and 60 Spanish vessels. It thus fell to the French navy to bear the brunt of allied efforts, since the Spanish ships were of poor quality and the Dutch took only a minor part. Yet considering the vast empire which British seamen had to protect, the rival forces were fairly well balanced.

After the last war had revealed French impotence on the sea, a popular movement led to the building of a new fleet under Louis XVI. This monarch showed a progressive spirit in approving the reforms of his minister Choiseul, and the glories of Colbert and the Sun King seemed about to be restored.

Unfortunately, too many of the higher officers were still appointed because of noble birth rather than ability. Count d'Estaing, for example, had been a general until his sudden elevation to command of the fleet which aided the Americans in 1778. Brave as a lion in combat, he displayed a timid seamanship which accounted for the barren results of the New York and Rhode Island campaigns.

De Grasse undoubtedly struck the hardest French blow of the naval struggle by making possible the concentration of the allied armies in Virginia. As early as May, 1781, he promised the co-operation of his West Indies fleet, though at the time Washington expected to aim a joint attack at Clinton's army in New York. Then upon learning that Cornwallis had fortified Yorktown, the American commander obtained De Grasse's consent to the amended plans which led up to the British surrender in October.

After showing such a bold and far-reaching grasp of naval strategy, the French admiral met defeat the following April as a consequence of hesitant tactics. Commanding 33 ships of the line off Dominica, he was attacked by Admiral Rodney with 35 sail of similar class. The two fleets fought a running, eleven-hour battle which ended with five French vessels being taken and one sunk. The gallant De Grasse became a prisoner after surrendering his great flagship, the *Ville de Paris*, with only himself and two others left alive on the upper deck.

For a century all navies had more or less followed the rules laid down in the *Fighting Instructions* written by the Duke of York who became James II. This manual prescribed vigorous action on occasion, but the interpretation often resulted in long-distance gunnery duels between single columns of ships taking a parallel course. Hence the great days of De Ruyter had become a memory when a Scottish civilian, John Clerk, wrote a pamphlet urging a return to the tactics of breaking an opponent's line. Naturally, this piece of presumption was greeted by a scornful silence on the part of naval men, yet Rodney owed his victory in the battle of the Saints to just such a manoeuvre.

This is no evidence to show that the British admiral was influenced by Clerk's criticisms, and it has even been intimated that a mistake in orders led to his anticipation of future tactics. At any rate Rodney broke the French line, after a morning of futile cannonading, by sailing several of his ships directly through the centre. This surprise completed the demoralization of a fleet which had fought an overcautious defensive battle.

Meanwhile, at the memorable siege of Gibraltar, the principal Spanish effort of the war, an old artillery tactic of the fifteenth century was revived to hold the fortress. After the resistance had endured for three full years, the Spaniards built ten ships armored six feet thick with green timbers reinforced by iron, cork and raw hides. Mounting heavy siege artillery on these gunboats, they anchored near the British works in July, 1782, and began a pounding which must soon have demolished them. Ordinary round shot buried themselves harmlessly in the wooden armor, but the garrison had been experimenting with cannon balls heated in furnaces. The shore guns changed to red-hot shot, and after 8,300 rounds the grand assault failed with every Spanish ship blown up or burnt down to the water line. The siege lasted seven more months, but never again was "the Rock" in serious danger.

Such dramatic moments were few in the naval contest, since both sides clung to a cautious defensive. It remained for a tough old French sea dog, Admiral Suffren, to provide what Mahan has termed "by far the most noteworthy and meritorious naval performance of the war," adding that it "failed through no fault of his own to affect the general issue."

Early in 1782 Suffren reached India with 11 ships of the line, having surprised and beaten a British squadron under Commodore Johnstone in the Cape Verde Islands. This vigorous attack broke up an enemy expedition planning to raid the Dutch at the Cape of Good Hope.

In the harbor of Madras a British fleet under Admiral Hughes had the advantage of bases and supplies, but the French veteran took the offensive in four furious battles during the next seven months. Described as "prodigiously obese," Suffren displayed none of the easy good nature attributed to fat men. He drove his own captains as relentlessly as his opponents, cashiering three of them for want of zeal. Lacking a harbor, he achieved the "impossible" by refitting on the beach with supplies captured from the foe. Lacking seamen after losses thinned his crews, he impressed natives and even toiled himself under the tropical sun.

None of his onslaughts brought about a decision, though both sides suffered heavy casualties as well as damage to hulls and rigging. Six British captains were killed, and Hughes had been reduced to an uneasy defensive when the signing of peace ended the combats. Outnumbered by 18 ships to 15 in the fifth encounter, Suffren forced his battered opponent to withdraw to Madras with India in danger from a revolt incited by the French.

The campaign made it evident that past French failures had often been due to a conservative naval policy which placed the saving of ships above winning battles. Suffren had the advantage of being far removed from the interference of Paris; and when at last ordered back to Mauritius, he disobeyed on the grounds that he could better judge the situation. As a final tribute to his resolution, he received a spontaneous ovation from late enemies who solemnly visited his flagship to shake hands.

In the same redoubtable spirit John Paul Jones took the new American colors into action within sight of English shores. After distinguishing himself by destroying enemy shipping in American waters, the young captain had been assigned the fast *Ranger* which sailed to France with the news of Burgoyne's surrender. Then with orders for "distressing the foes of the United States," he boldly struck at Whitehaven. Surprising the forts commanding the harbor, he raided the town, spiked the British guns and set fire to shipping. Four days later the *Ranger* met the sloop of war *Drake* off Belfast and sank her in spite of heavier British metal.

Due to Benjamin Franklin's aid, Jones next obtained an old French merchantman which he armed and renamed *Bon Homme Richard* in honor of his patron. Several smaller vessels completed the squadron with which he made an attempt on Leith in the summer of 1779, failing because of contrary winds. On the return voyage he encountered a British convoy and promptly attacked the much superior *Serapis*. There followed the moonlight duel, lasting nearly four hours, in which Jones shouted his famous defiance from the sinking *Richard*, "I have not yet begun to fight!" Finally the British captain asked for quarter, and the victor transferred the remnants of his crew to the captured ship.

Such exploits, to be sure, had little effect on the war as a whole except in their moral value. Privateering raids accounted for most of the damage inflicted by the Americans on the sea. As early as Valley Forge, testimony before the House of Lords revealed that during the first two years the rebels had captured or destroyed 733 ships, of which 174 were ransomed or retaken. During the entire war the records of Lloyd's showed a loss of 3,087 British merchantmen, about a fourth of them being restored.

Impressive as these figures may appear, they go far toward explaining why a captain of Jones' ability had to sail in such a leaky old tub as the *Bon Homme Richard*. The new nation could not hope to build fleets able to challenge British sea power, but practically all the American energies went into privateering at the expense of the infant navy. The leading men of the colonies, including Washington and Greene, found it hard to resist a speculation which might turn an enormous profit in a single voyage.

Measured by results, the most decisive American "naval" action took place on Lake Champlain. Benedict Arnold and his little squadron were defeated after a heroic fight against odds, but he delayed Sir Guy Carleton long enough to frustrate a British invasion in the fall of 1776.

The New Age of Invention

Resourcefulness in mechanical directions has always been a feature of revolutionary warfare, and the first submarine attack of history occurred off New York in 1776. David Bushnell, the inventor, constructed an enclosed, one-man boat propelled from within by pedals turning a paddle wheel. Named the *Turtle* because of its shape, this curious craft submerged to screw a bomb with time fuse to the bottom of the British warship *Eagle*. The attempt failed because the copper sheathing could not be penetrated, and the charge exploded harmlessly after the *Turtle* rowed away. But the idea persisted in the American imagination, giving Robert Fulton the inspiration for his *Nautilus* a generation later.

A few years after the war an experiment of far more influence on modern warfare took place in a small Connecticut arms factory. Eli Whitney, inventor of the cotton gin, had signed a contract to turn out flintlock muskets for the army of the new republic. Instead of delivering the complete weapons, each made entirely by one craftsman in the fashion of past ages, he showed the inspectors a jumble of springs, locks and barrels. These he speedily assembled into several muskets whose interchangeable parts had been made by workmen specializing in a single operation.

Thus without fanfare the age of mass production was born. The first assembly line had come into being, to revolutionize peaceful as well as warlike pursuits of the new century.

It is understandable that contemporaries should have overlooked the significance of this quiet experiment. Even historians have sometimes failed to pay full tribute to a change in production methods which created a new era. For in its influence on strategy, the theory of interchangeable parts could not help but work an upheaval. The small armies and conservative outlook of the past had been largely due to two causes: the expense of training a soldier for linear tactics; and the limited output of arms manufactured by a few master mechanics. Thus Eli Whitney had made it possible to arm millions instead of thousands! With the exception of conscription—mass production of war's human material—no other factor has done so much to shape the fighting methods of the present day.

France on the eve of the Revolution also shows the past crumbling away rapidly. In 1783, as the physicist Charles ascended in a balloon filled with hydrogen gas, the octogenarian Maréchale de Villeroi stood watching at a window of the Tuileries. Passing at once from skepticism to boundless faith, she cried out, "Yes, it is decided! They will discover the secret of never dying—but it will be when I am dead."

And though the zealots of the French Revolution did stop short of immortality, only a decade after Charles' flight the first military observation balloons were aiding armies which fought off the rest of Europe.

Another invention of strategic importance was the signal telegraph perfected by Chappe. On an upright post a transverse bar held at each end an arm moving on pivots. The position of these arms represented words or letters, with lanterns being attached to permit communication at night. In 1793 the earliest line ran from Paris to Lille, being extended to Brussels later. The first message, with typical Revolutionary fervor, reported to the Committee on Public Safety the surrender of Quesnoy: "Austrian garrison of 3000 slaves has laid down its arms."

New lines soon linked Paris to Brest, Lyons and Strasbourg, the last being carried well into Germany by 1805. For though Napoleon rejected the military balloon and Fulton's submarine, he depended on Chappe's device for his rapid movements. Until the electric telegraph, no other means served so well to annihilate time and distance. The stations were placed about six miles apart, and it is recorded that in 1800 an eighteen-word report of an action in Belgium reached Paris in three hours.

Less spectacular, but equally important to the new Revolutionary tactics, were Gribeauval's artillery reforms. By this date canister, ball, shell and grape had become standardized types of ammunition, but there remained a wasteful variation in the models of guns. Hence the French professional soldier anticipated Whitney in perceiving the advantages of interchangeable parts, though he made no other changes in manufacturing methods.

Upon his appointment in 1776 as inspector general, Gribeauval retained only pieces of smaller caliber than 12-pounders in the field artillery, his guns being drawn by four horses in pairs instead of file. Carriages were improved and built to a uniform model, with the "trail" lengthened and the hardwood axle replaced by iron. To improve aiming, he introduced the tangent sight—a brass rule with graduations to indicate angles and tangents, and equipped with a metal slide to allow the gunner to "lay" the piece for direction or elevation.

These improvements brought the French artillery well in advance of other armies as the Revolution began. In the field of military engineering the Marquis de Montalembert revised principles of fortification which had been held sacred since Vauban. Where his great predecessor strove by means of an intricate trace to minimize the attack, Montalembert

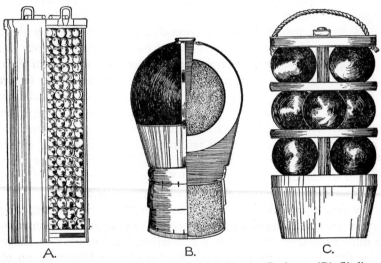

Types of Artillery Ammunition: (A) Case-Shot, or Canister; (B) Shell; (C) Grapeshot

depended on simple tenaille or polygonal lines to construct an "immense battery" designed to pour a superior fire into the works of a besieger. His *Fortification Perpendiculaire*, which is said to have launched more new ideas than any other treatise on the subject, found a brilliant follower in Lazare Carnot. This engineering officer went even further with his "Carnot wall" in providing for an active defense based on strong tenaille lines. As an outgrowth of French thought the polygonal school of fortification prevailed throughout Europe during the early decades of the nineteenth century.

THE WRITINGS OF GUIBERT

French scientists had likewise discovered new principles in chemistry, physics and higher mathematics which had a tremendous though indirect effect on Revolutionary warfare. And in line with this progress, military theory acquired its most creative writer since Saxe in the youthful Comte de Guibert.

In 1770, at the age of twenty-seven, he published his famous *Essai general de tactique,* and within a few years the treatise had been translated even into the Persian. Europe's salon intellectuals and professional soldiers alike discussed a work which exploded a bomb under current ideas of warfare. Nor did the author limit himself to military theory, for in his preface he sounds one of the first notes of the Revolution:

> In the midst of the general feebleness the various governments, themselves feeble but prolific in petty methods, extend the dull weight of their oppression. They seem to be engaged in a secret war against their subjects, corrupting one faction only to tyrannize over another.

The armies of Europe, declared Guibert, were composed of "the most vile and miserable class of citizens . . . onerous to those nations in time of peace, insufficient to reassure them in time of war." As for the conflicts of the age, he dismisses them in several contemptuous sentences:

> Conqueror or conquered, it makes little difference. The mass of national debt accumulates. Credit declines. Funds are lacking. The fleets cannot recruit more sailors, nor the army more soldiers. The ministers, between themselves, sense that it is high time to negotiate. Peace is made. Several colonies or provinces change hands. Often the cause of the quarrel is not mentioned, and each side remains seated on the debris, occupied by paying its debts and whetting its dull sword.

In his very next paragraph, however, Guibert foresees a possibility which became historical fact a generation later:

> But suppose there were to arise in Europe one vigorous nation, of method and genius and sound government: a people who combined simple virtues and a national militia with a fixed plan of aggrandizement; who never lost sight of system; who knew how to make war at small expense and subsist on their victories; who were not reduced to sheathing their sword by calculations of finance. We would see this people subjugating their neighbors . . . as the north wind blows down the frail reed!

Nobody accomplished more than this young man to inspire the victories he predicted. Disclaiming any great originality, he acknowledged his debt to past writers and declared it his purpose to assemble and

revise. Yet despite his modesty, Guibert had had an extensive military
education. At the age of sixteen he accompanied his father, serving as
Marshal Broglie's chief of staff, on the campaigns against Ferdinand
which put into effect Saxe's principles of divisional concentration. As a
result France's only victories were won by Broglie, and Guibert advocated the divisional system as the basis for a new warfare of mobility.

Where Saxe recommended light infantry units, his disciple went a step
beyond by urging that all infantry be trained for such tactics. Like Saxe,
he favored fire at will over commanded volleys, though the bayonet
appeared to Guibert to be a relic of "the custom of the pike. . . . Bodies
of infantry seldom make use of naked steel, for on the charge they
seldom meet near enough to cross bayonets."

In his larger tactical ideas Guibert had obviously been influenced not
only by Saxe but also Pierre de Bourcet, who has been called the first
of the great chiefs of staff. This professional soldier, not well enough born
to gain rapid promotion, had learned war in Italian mountain campaigns.
Planning operations during the War of the Austrian Succession, he
evolved new methods of concentration which are summed up in his own
words:

> The plan is to threaten the enemy at all other points of his posi-
> tion. . . . This will make him divide his forces, and we can then
> take advantage of the geographical conditions to reunite our own at
> the critical point before he can unite his.

Here in two sentences, as various modern critics have pointed out,
is the essence of the warfare which was later to be described as "Napoleonic." After serving with distinction in the Seven Years' War, Bourcet
became director of a school for staff officers established as one of the
reforms of Choiseul. While holding this position, he incorporated his
principles of mobility and concentration into a treatise called *Principes
de la guerre de montagnes*. The book never found its way into print,
though secret manuscript copies were kept for French staff officers.

Guibert had obviously derived from Bourcet, but again he developed
and enlarged. After outlining an imaginary campaign in which self-
sustained divisional columns seize the initiative, he continues:

> Coming within reach of the enemy, the general either draws off
> or strengthens certain columns according to his judgment, advancing
> one, leaving another in the rear, directing this toward one point, that
> toward another. . . . The troops . . . form for battle in an instant,

beginning their attack before the enemy has had time to determine the point where the blow is being aimed, or, even if he has discovered the point, before he has time to change his dispositions to ward off the blow.

This sort of lightning warfare, combining the advantages of dispersion and concentration with those of mobility, Guibert defined as "grand tactics"—a term later adopted by Napoleon along with the method itself. The phrase was apt, for such an attack fell neither within the limits of tactics nor strategy, according to past standards. Actually it proved to be a hybrid: the product of tactical velocity mated with strategic deception.

In concluding his argument, Guibert anticipated another favorite Napoleonic manoeuvre by proposing the advantages of a sudden sweep to the enemy's rear, throwing the army astride the hostile line of communications:

> What will the enemy be able to do if surprised by this new kind of war? . . . Will he change his position? If so, he will lose the advantages of the ground on which he has relied, and be obliged to accept a battle wherever he can.

Unlike so many military theorists, the author did not ignore the logistics behind his suggested moves. Attacking the existing magazine system, he held it an anomaly to "have separated the science of subsistence from the science of war." Guibert contended that the army should live at the enemy's expense in the enemy's country, with its baggage reduced to a minimum and its line officers thoroughly trained in matters of supply.

As he had borrowed from Bourcet, so Guibert in turn contributed to a treatise afterward published by the Chevalier du Teil. The later writer made it his task to suggest artillery tactics suited to the new warfare of mobility. Most of his material could interest only a gunner, but among the technical details one paragraph left its mark on history:

> We must unite the greatest number of troops and the greatest masses of artillery on the points where we wish to force the enemy's position, while creating an illusion of attack on the others. . . . The moment when our troops should assault is determined by the ravages that the artillery has made on the troops and defenses of the foe.

Here was a formula for blasting away resistance which would eventually be put into effect on such fields as Friedland and Wagram.

France's Levy en Masse

Guibert died in 1790 before seeing any of his proposals translated into victories. For a time he had been the lion of the salons, with even Voltaire writing verses in his praise. But the professional soldiers of France were not so receptive to new ideas, and toward the end the "modern Bayard" had become embittered by a lifetime of controversy.

As if by common consent of historians, Valmy has been accepted as the decisive battle of the Revolutionary wars. Most readers of history, however, have found a disappointing lack of drama or significance in that cannonade. Late in the summer of 1792 the Prussian column of 35,000 crawled sluggishly across the border, dragging behind it an enormous wagon train with tents for all ranks. Magazines and bakeries were set up along the route, further adding to the delays of a march which exhibited the worst defects of eighteenth century warfare.

The fortresses of Longwy and Verdun surrendered as a French army of equal strength fell back through the Argonne. Up to this time nearly every Revolutionary force had retired in wild panic from the Austrian or Prussian regulars. On the Belgian border one mob of armed civilians even slaughtered three of its generals who tried to halt the general flight.

Hence it seemed a stirring event when the retreating French made a stand at Valmy on September 20. At a range of 1,400 yards the two forces bombarded each other for several hours, each side enduring a few hundred casualties. The Prussian infantry advanced, only to halt well out of reach of enemy musket balls. And nothing more happened to enhance the news which sent the whole French nation into a delirium of joy. The invaders remained in the locality ten more days as dysentery added to a seriously mounting sick list. Then negotiations were begun for a peaceful withdrawal, and the Duke of Brunswick and his Prussians crawled back across the border.

But Valmy, like Washington's little success at Trenton, had a moral importance out of all proportion to the military results. Within a few more weeks Frenchmen had carried the fight to foreign soil. In the south advances were made into Nice and Savoy. In Germany a daring expedition led by Custine captured Mainz. And in Belgium the first real battlefield victory of the war was gained by Dumouriez, the hero of Valmy, when his army of 40,000 surprised 14,000 Austrians at Jemappes and drove them out of their trenches.

That winter Louis XVI went to the guillotine, and the new republic faced a coalition of determined enemies—England, Holland, Spain and

Sardinia in addition to Prussia and Austria. Here again it is puzzling to note that France seemed indifferent to the odds against her, even declaring war first in several instances. Such a spirit is partially explained by the belief of a few extremists that union within would be strengthened by peril from without. But it must also be remembered that this was the winter of Poland's agony, that unhappy kingdom being reduced to a third of her original territory by the Second Partition.

The First Partition of 1772, instigated by Frederick, had found the pious Maria Theresa willing to subordinate her personal ethics to the interests of Austria. Two decades later another enlightened empress, Catherine of Russia, sent soldiers to crush the Polish patriots who had voted a new constitution. Against heavy odds Thaddeus Kosciusko and Prince Joseph Poniatowski put up a heroic fight, winning three pitched ·battles in as many months before retiring to Warsaw in good order. But the cause was betrayed by their own king, and early in 1793 Prussia and Russia divided most of Poland's remaining territory.

With these seizures reminding them of the treatment which a helpless nation might expect in the age of benevolent despotism, Frenchmen can scarcely be blamed for their fear and hatred of the allied monarchies. Such emotions, unfortunately, did not serve to repel the armies closing in like hands about the republic's throat. The fact grew increasingly plain that France lacked the trained infantry. The famous old royal regiments had vanished, though some battalions of whitecoats remained to stiffen the ranks at Valmy. The officers, representing the younger nobles, had either emigrated or become victims of revolutionary suspicion. And despite the impressive "paper strength" of the National Guard, voluntary enlistments had not filled the gap.

It is not surprising, therefore, that the early campaigns of 1793 wiped out the gains made the previous autumn. In Belgium the Austrians drove the French before them with ease, aided by inhabitants who had become disgusted with revolutionary looting. Dumouriez attempted a stand east of Brussels, lost the action and followed Lafayette's example of choosing exile to further support of the immoderate policies being voted at Paris. Such generals as did not take this prudent course were promptly hustled to the guillotine after a defeat.

Some of the flights of recent civilians appear both ludicrous and pathetic. During the British advance the Guards encountered frightened boys whom they "cuffed and jostled . . . without condescending to kill them." As a consequence of such panics the republic had to abandon the volunteer system in favor of a limited form of conscription. The first

law called for 300,000 men, with provisions being made for the purchase
of substitutes. This measure, by penalizing poverty, brought in a large
percentage of outcasts and malcontents who deserted at the first opportunity. The edict, moreover, aroused such opposition among royalists of
the western provinces as to bring on the full-fledged civil war of the
Vendée.

By April the situation had grown so serious that France went under
the dictatorship of the Committee on Public Safety. Still, the nation's
salvation owed less in this crisis to her own efforts than the jealousy
and distrust which divided her enemies. There can be no doubt that
already many of the allied leaders were visioning another and greater
partition at the expense of the sorely beset republic. Far from co-operating in their advances, they gave every indication of placing themselves
in a favorable position to scramble for the spoils.

Despair had become the prevailing mood of France when on August
23, 1793—one of the most memorable dates in the chronicles of war—
the Committee on Public Safety issued a decree announcing universal
conscription for the first time in modern history. Even when read today,
the words of the proclamation convey some idea of the urgency of the
situation:

> The young men shall fight; the married men shall forge weapons
> and transport supplies; the women will make tents and serve in the
> hospitals; the children will make up old linen into lint; the old men
> will have themselves carried into the public squares to rouse the
> courage of the fighting men, and to preach hatred of kings and the
> unity of the Republic. The public buildings shall be turned into bar-
> racks, the public squares into munitions factories; the earthen floors
> of cellars shall be treated with lye to extract saltpetre. All suitable
> firearms shall be turned over to the troops; the interior shall be
> policed with fowling pieces and with cold steel. All saddle horses
> shall be seized for the cavalry; all draft horses not employed in culti-
> vation will draw the artillery and supply wagons.

Thus with a few strokes of the pen the entire military past was
abolished. All the faults and virtues of eighteenth century warfare, the
moderation along with the cynicism, the humanity as well as the greed,
were swept into the discard of history. The modern nation-in-arms, half
god and half monster, had been evoked to dominate the battlefields of
Europe.

THE FORERUNNER OF NAPOLEON

Even this drastic decree could not supply the military leadership which France needed as much as trained troops. But on August 14 a quiet captain of engineers became the new member of the Committee on Public Safety, and his appointment marks the turning point of the Revolutionary campaigns.

It is not altogether a coincidence that Lazare Carnot began his duties just nine days before the announcement of universal conscription. Although no individual bears the full responsibility for that decision, most authorities agree that he had the principal part. Within a short time the "organizer of victory" had become minister of war and virtually commander-in-chief of the new armies which hurled back their opponents on every front.

A Burgundian of good family, noted for his treatise on fortification, he had risen no higher than a captain's rank at the age of forty because of radical political beliefs. During the next few years he worked in the shadow of the guillotine because Robespierre and Saint-Just found him too conservative. A comparison with Washington is inevitable, not only in stern republican virtues but even such personal traits as a reserve which chilled contemporaries. Of all France's heroes, in fact, Carnot most nearly resembles the Anglo-Saxon ideal.

His first move, before conscription had been in effect a week, was to take an active part in the Hondschoote campaign. Late in August the allies captured enough border forts to open a lane to Paris. At this point each national contingent began to consider its own interests, and the Anglo-Hanoverian force turned off toward the coast to besiege Dunkirk.

Carnot hastened to the scene to encourage the garrison and aid the concentration of relieving French armies under Houchard and Jourdan. In spite of the general indiscipline some 40,000 troops were assembled. Advancing in eager but disorderly columns, they attacked at Hondschoote on September 6 and dislodged the allies. The victory was mainly psychological, since the French were unable to pursue an enemy who retreated in order after moderate losses. But Dunkirk had been saved, and the year's nightmare of flights, defeats and surrenders seemed at an end.

On October 15, only a few weeks later, Carnot's novices won an even more convincing triumph at Wattignies. An allied army of 66,000 had invested Maubeuge, the single remaining fortress of any strength which barred the way to Paris. Again the new minister of war fought in the field, and it was due to his tactics as well as resolution that the besiegers were beaten.

In their contempt for military amateurs, they assigned 26,000 troops to "contain" a garrison of nearly equal numbers, the remaining 40,000 being dispersed about the region as a covering force. Carnot and Jourdan at once began to concentrate every available French unit from distances as far as 130 miles away. For the moment they were denounced as traitors at Paris, since the near-by towns had been stripped of their garrisons and left defenseless. But thanks to the Revolutionary quick-step, some battalions covered as many as 70 miles in a little over three days.

The French thus contrived to attack the 26,000 allies with a local superiority of nearly two to one. Despite this advantage, they were repulsed the first day by the steady regulars holding the plateau of Wat-tignies. That night Carnot conceived the plan of transferring 8,000 men from his beaten left to the other wing in order to overlap the Austrian left near the village. Under cover of darkness the weary young troops completed the march; and at daylight Carnot himself, wearing civilian dress and shouldering a musket, led the columns which stormed Wattignies and rolled up the allied army from left to right. Not once but three times the French returned to the attack, displaying a wild courage which blotted out the memory of past disgraces. And though too tired and battered to pursue, they had freed Paris from danger as the allied army went into winter quarters.

These two last battles of 1793 established Carnot as the essential link between the theory of Guibert and the practice of Napoleon. Carnot it was who first perceived in the awkward evolutions of a Hondschoote and Wattignies the promise of a future Austerlitz.

The minister of war had of course read all the treatises of his age. He knew all the arguments as to the relative merits of line and column formations. But in the field one could not choose during the summer of 1793. It required long months of drill to train a soldier for linear tactics, and every attempt to pit novices against regulars in formal battle had led to wild routs. In the end the recruits took matters into their own hands, fighting as best they could; and Carnot saw the germ of an ultimate decision in the "horde tactics" scorned by a disciplined foe.

Self-preservation is not a bad foundation for victory, and at Hond-schoote most of the French forces showed a marked distaste for coming within range of enemy muskets. Only the more adventurous souls swarmed out in a ragged wave of skirmishers to take cover in ditches and behind hedges. From such positions they peppered the long lines with a fire which left the enemy helpless. Return volleys were a waste of ammunition, and the regulars advanced only to find that their opponents had scrambled back to new cover. Less valiant Frenchmen soon saw the advantages of a new military game which promised to be safe as well as interesting. They joined their comrades of the ditches and hedges until the allied casualties grew serious. When enough troops had plucked up courage, their officers ordered an advance; and the recruits surged forward in masses which by courtesy were called columns.

On this field the allies were almost literally mobbed by numbers, but in only six weeks Carnot's raw forces showed a notable improvement. At Wattignies they not only outmarched and outmanoeuvred but also outfought the enemy. And here for the first time may be seen the crude beginnings of those swift and deadly concentrations which would later be known as "Napoleonic."

The influence of the American Revolution is evident in the skirmishing tactics. In addition to Lafayette, Jourdan and Berthier, scores of lesser officers had seen service in Rochambeau's expeditionary force. They returned with enthusiasm for American methods; and as the organizer of early National Guard units, Lafayette included a rifle company in each battalion. The weapon itself does not appear to have been widely adopted in the new French armies, but Hondschoote and later fields indicate that lessons had been learned in marksmanship and taking cover.

Most of the Revolutionary tactics, however, sprang from necessity rather than precept or theory. Lacking magazines, Carnot's troops became less dependent on bases and lines of communication. Lacking tents, they learned to bivouac in the field where all units could be readily concentrated. Lacking supply wagons, they marched at twice the speed of better provided opponents. Thus were Guibert's doctrines of mobility put into effect—not through army reforms, as he had hoped, but by dint of military poverty!

By the following summer universal conscription had increased French numbers to nearly three quarters of a million—the greatest horde ever seen in Europe since the barbarian migrations. Of the 531,000 in the main fighting forces, 323,000 were infantry (100 three-battalion demi-brigades), 97,000 light infantry, 29,000 artillery, 20,000 engineers and 59,000 cavalry. The last traces of the old régime had vanished along with such famous regiments as Picardie; and all units now wore the blue uniform of the National Guard, being designated by numerals instead of names.

As technical branches which had never attracted nobles, the artillery and engineers preserved many of their royal army traditions throughout the Revolution. The cavalry, on the other hand, had been so aristocratic an arm as to lose most of its officers by emigration, so that the Revolutionary squadrons remained inferior for several more years. This delay threw an added burden on infantry recruits, yet the first great battle of 1794 reveals a further improvement in the command as well as rank and file.

In April a French army advanced to capture Menin and Courtrai, thus creating a salient in the main lines. The allied generals, now fully awake to the dangerous potentialities of "horde tactics," made plans to surround and cut off these troops with a concentration of their own. Preceded by picked skirmishers, with field artillery at the head of each striking force, three columns closed in from the allied left. On the right the fourth and fifth columns, the latter led by the Archduke Charles of Austria, were to complete the encirclement.

The great "annihilation plan" might have succeeded if the French had waited for the blow to fall. But mobility and elasticity were inherent in their tactics, and Souham struck back as soon as he divined the enemy's intentions. With 12,000 men against 21,000, his subordinate Vandamme came to grips with the column on the allied left, fighting and retreating so stubbornly as to ruin the co-ordination of the entire operation. On the other wing the two enemy columns met delays, leaving the two in the centre to bear the brunt of the main French counterattack launched by the superior numbers of Souham and Moreau. Two-thirds of the allied forces were thus immobilized at the battle of Tourcoing, and the remainder given a beating in which they suffered 5,500 casualties. Not only had the young French generals covered themselves with glory, but Vandamme's desperate stand was to become the forerunner of many a Napoleonic defense planned to permit an offensive movement elsewhere in the field.

The Triumph of the Revolution

Tourcoing had by no means crippled the losing army, and in May the French met a reverse near Charleroi. The allies could still muster 140,000 regulars in Belgium against 200,000 poorly equipped recruits; but in view of the new multitudes being raised by conscription, the Austrian commander-in-chief Coburg sought a quick decision in battle.

On June 26, after Jourdan's army of 73,000 had taken Charleroi, Coburg attacked at Fleurus with forces totaling 52,000. Again he trusted to the advance of five columns according to plans worked out so minutely that few changes could be made after the forces were committed. The French stood on the defensive in entrenched positions, and the battle resolved itself into separate actions as each column came in contact. After six hours of slugging the young recruits on the French right gave ground, allowing the Austrian general Beaulieu to combine his column with that of the Archduke Charles. The defenders rushed up reinforcements in this quarter as the enemy made three costly attacks across ground bare of cover. When a fourth effort failed, Lefebre led a counterattack just as Coburg gave the order for a general retreat.

The allies withdrew in excellent order, having endured only half the casualties of the victors; but Fleurus became the decisive French victory of the Revolutionary wars. Coburg retired unpursued over the Meuse as the Austrian government made arrangements to evacuate its Netherlands provinces, which were formally annexed by France. The English contingent went home in disgust that summer, and the Dutch capitulated to the French who pressed forward to overrun their homeland. Prussia ceased all hostile activity after her English subsidies were stopped, signing a treaty of peace the following spring. As the climax to this series of triumphs, a few French hussars captured the Dutch fleet that winter by riding over the ice to gain the surrender of well-manned warships frozen in the Texel.

Carnot can hardly be given too much credit for directing operations, not only at the front but also in France, where every man, woman and child made his contribution. Working night and day, sprawled at full length on the floor over his maps, the minister of war had advised and encouraged his generals without tying them too closely to instructions from Paris. The results of his first seventeen months were summed up, with no more than customary exaggeration, by the Committee on Public Safety:

> Twenty-seven victories, of which 8 were pitched battles; 120 combats of minor importance; 80,000 enemies killed; 91,000 prisoners; 116 fortresses or strong towns taken, 36 of which had to be besieged or blockaded; 230 forts or redoubts captured; 3800 guns of various sizes; 70,000 muskets; 1900 tons of gunpowder; 90 flags.

Due to Carnot's energy, new sources of saltpetre were discovered, and copper supplied by melting down church bells. He established the first signal telegraph and gave orders for General Marlot's ascent in the first military observation balloon at Fleurus. Even these efforts were secondary, however, as compared to the war minister's development of new military talent.

In June, 1791, no less than ten future marshals of France were fighting in the ranks, while six were as yet civilians. Carnot instituted the system of rapid promotions under which Jourdan, the former peddler, and Moreau, the recent law student, shot over the heads of older and duller officers. In his abhorrence of fanaticism, Carnot abolished the rule of terror which made every officer fear for his life, while gradually ridding the army of the political representatives who acted as informers. Vandamme, Lefebre, Macdonald, Masséna and Desaix all owed their rise in some measure to Carnot; and by 1795 he had marked for advancement the two youthful officers who proved to be the most able of the early Revolutionary era, Hoche and Bonaparte.

Finally, the great war minister knew when to stop—a rare virtue in a leader who has once experienced victories of his own creation. He had been first to grasp the possibility of tactics growing out of necessity, and with equal foresight he soon began warning his countrymen of the dangers of carrying aggression too far. A moderate in war as in politics, he approved an offensive policy aiming at the establishment of stronger natural frontiers. But this was no age of moderation, and France's new ambitions were to launch a world struggle which would last with few and brief intermissions until the final act of Waterloo.

III

GENERAL BONAPARTE IN ITALY

*Many good generals exist in Europe, but they see too
many things at once: I see but one thing, and that is the
masses; I seek to destroy them, sure that the minor matters will fall of themselves.*

—BONAPARTE

ALTHOUGH it has been said that soldiers of all ages are influenced
by the war before the last, the continued emulation of Prussian methods
in 1796 is a little difficult to understand. On a basis of cold results, Frederick and his generals had won exactly half of their sixteen battles, and
even the Prussian numerical inferiority may sometimes be traced to error
or defeat. Yet a generation later not only the drill but the two favorite
resources of European armies went back to the Seven Years' War.

Concentric columns of attack were still widely used in tactical operations, though Frederick had found reason to regret them on several
occasions. As a defensive strategy, the "cordon system" of dispersed
but mutually supporting units appealed to military minds which did not
believe in trusting too many eggs to one basket.

In theory this plan had the merit of the utmost flexibility combined
with the least risk. Minor assaults could be met in equal strength, while
an adversary who concentrated against any part of the cordon exposed
his flanks to the counterattack of reinforcements drawn from near-by
supporting units. Such expectations, of course, were based on the assumption that the enemy would also march at a rate of 70 paces a minute,
considering every move in relation to his magazines of supply.

French strategists reasoned that the Revolutionary quickstep and practice of living "on the country" gave them a great advantage. Nevertheless, the offensives of 1795 made little progress in spite of their emphasis on mass, concentration and repeated blows. On some fronts, indeed, the invaders maintained a cordon of their own; and when both sides fall back on the defensive, the results are not likely to be impressive.

The explanation for this lull is to be found in a loss of moral momentum. The French citizen-soldier had fought valiantly to defend his homeland, sharing in sacrifices such as no modern European nation had ever made before. Not only had he driven the last foeman over the border, he had also made it possible for France to annex more new territory than had been gained since the wars of Louis XIV. Only England, Austria and Sardinia remained of the determined enemies which once threatened, and these countries showed signs of weariness.

From the viewpoint of the conscripted peasant or artisan in the ranks, the great adventure of the Revolution had passed its climax. France had been received back into the family of nations at the Concert of Europe in 1795, and that summer Hoche put down the civil war in the Vendée. It seemed the logical time to call quits; but the Directory, which had replaced the Committee on Public Safety, sought new victories to compensate for the weakness and corruption of the government. Carnot's powers and influence had been much curtailed, and within two years he would be driven into exile. Meanwhile, as a stout republican, he uttered a warning which became prophecy:

> If we carry out these great projects of invasion, it will be necessary ... to maintain an enormous armed host exposed to new alternatives of defeat or success which allow us no hopes of an end to political crises. Such a plan is contrary to the principle under which France has renounced the spirit of conquest. This principle, in fact, forbids us all aggrandizement which is not governed by a duty of insuring the safety of our own possessions.

Too great an extension of the frontiers, said Carnot, would lead to a dangerous spreading out of the forces required to defend them as the enemy learned the new warfare. Eventually, he predicted, Frenchmen would be compelled "to abandon precipitately all conquests and retire to their own borders after enormous losses."

If his gloomy forecast did not come true until 1813, the reason may be traced principally to the minister's own recognition of young Bonaparte's ability. After distinguishing himself at Toulon in 1794, this artillery officer had presented several memoranda for campaigns in Italy which Carnot read with approval. Next the favor of the Directory had been gained by the "whiff of grapeshot" which dispersed a Parisian mob, and at the age of twenty-seven young Bonaparte rose to the command of the army in Italy.

The prospects of an ambitious soldier were hazardous in February, 1796. Only four days before Bonaparte's appointment, the Directory proclaimed a condition of national bankruptcy. The Revolutionary fervor of the early years had been replaced by a spirit of materialism on the part of rulers and discontent among the masses. Uprisings were becoming frequent in Paris, while the "White Terror" in the south of France did not stop short of appealing for English and Austrian aid.

The armies of invasion were in no better state after the disappointing offensives of the previous year. Treason had been added to defeat in Germany as General Pichegru, the commander, revealed French plans to the enemy. In Italy the troops were ragged and half starved, on the verge of mutiny.

Bonaparte's first and not his most insignificant victory thus became the conquest of his own sullen army. He did not make the mistake of appealing to patriotism or dead Revolutionary principles. In his first famous proclamation, issued in March, the new general promised food, fame and spoils to men who had tired of liberty, equality and fraternity:

> Soldiers! You are naked, ill-fed; the government owes you much, it can give you nothing. Your patience, the courage you exhibit in the midst of these rocks, are admirable, but they bring you no glory; no lustre is reflected on you. I will lead you into the most fertile plains of the world. Rich provinces, great cities will be in your power; there you will find honor, fame and riches. Soldiers of Italy, shall courage or constancy fail you?

In a somewhat less masterful tone, Bonaparte penned a second communication which likewise reflects the new spirit of the age. This time he addressed the Directory in Paris with the air of a respectful yet confident and alert young servant of the state:

> I have found in Oneille some marbles which are valued at quite an amount. I have ordered them to be estimated and put up at auction. . . . That might give you a sum of thirty to forty thousand francs.

The next day, showing his grasp of administrative detail, he cracked the whip over Commissary Lambert:

> The general-in-chief orders you to make an official report of the bundles of hay which remain. . . . You will have Citizen Michel arrested until you can find out who bundled the hay and the storekeeper who received the lettuce. It is important, Citizen Commissary, that not a single rogue escape.

Behind the torrent of words flung out by that tireless pen was a devastating personality. At an historical distance it is hard to estimate the effect of a man's voice or gaze, but we have the testimony of those two hard-bitten campaigners, Masséna and Augereau. As older and more experienced officers, the ex-smuggler and former soldier of fortune felt some condescension about taking orders from an unknown *arriviste*. Yet after a first personal interview they confessed to each other, as adventurers of proved courage, that the impact of those cold gray eyes had been frightening.

Within a few days nobody in the army of Italy disputed the ascendancy of the small, slender commander with the lanky hair and restless hands. All ranks had become so infused with his nervous energy that on April 11, scarcely a month after his arrival, Bonaparte began his first offensive.

THE WEEK OF DEGO AND MONTENOTTE

The French army was strung out along the Riviera for 50 miles, holding the coastal highway and the Ligurian spur of the Apennines. From the summits could be seen Bonaparte's promised land—the historical amphitheater of the Lombard Plain, bounded on three sides by mountains. The Kingdom of Piedmont and the hereditary Austrian possession ot Milan occupied the western half of this region, with their combined armies facing the French along the northern slope of the Ligurian hills.

The allies were drawn up in cordon fashion for the defense of the two capital cities, Turin and Milan. On the left the Piedmontese force of 25,000 under Colli lay between Mondovi and Ceva, while to the right Beaulieu's 30,000 Austrians held from Acqui nearly to Genoa. The long chain consisted of widely extended forts or cantonments at strategic points in the foothills and narrow valleys.

Against the 55,000 allies and their 150 guns Bonaparte could muster only 40,000 troops and 60 guns after summoning all reinforcements and stripping his line of communications to France. He was particularly weak in cavalry, being able to mount less than 3,000 men on animals which had nearly starved during the winter. But ragged and barefoot armies are always dangerous, and the young commander's first move gave him the equivalent of an extra division.

Since manoeuvre must take the place of numbers, he began by seizing Carcare, where he commanded a good transverse road linking up the four

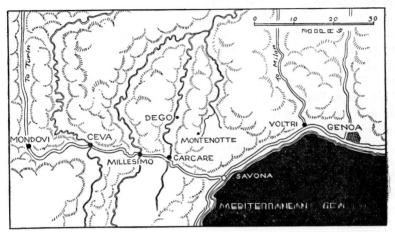

The Dego-Montenotte Campaign

river valleys held by the enemy. Hence his position had been likened to the base of a fan, while to the north the allied cantonments were located along the divergent sticks. From Carcare and the upper waters Bonaparte could send a column into any one of the narrow valleys and recall it for an operation in another. The allies had to depend on mule trails over the foothills to unite their dispersed forces, with the difficulties increasing as the arc of the strategic fan widened.

Beaulieu interpreted the French concentration as a threat to Genoa and sent a large detachment to the coast. This error further weakened his forces in the hills, and the first action occurred on April 12 at Montenotte as a French column surprised a much smaller Austrian force and routed it with losses of 2,500.

Colli had written to his colleague that the enemy "would never dare to place himself between our two armies"—an amusing prediction in view of Bonaparte's passion for operations along interior lines. For the next blow fell the following day on Colli's Italians near Millesimo, compelling a detachment of 1,500 to seek refuge in the near-by fort of Cosseria. Again Bonaparte struck with superior numbers, taking advantage of his position to use many of the troops which had fought at Montenotte the day before.

Having aimed lightning blows at the allied left and right, his third move—on the third day—was directed at the centre. Here a French column, marching without sleep, took the fortified town of Dego with 3,500 Austrians and 30 guns, and a few hours later the Piedmontese at Cosseria surrendered to another column.

So far everything had gone according to plan. The French, shuttling from one valley to another with bewildering rapidity, had inflicted losses of 7,500 at a cost of 400. But on the fourth day the young general met the test of an unexpected reverse when an Austrian force of 6,000 recaptured Dego. The news found him on the way to Millesimo with the bulk of his troops. Bonaparte doubled in his tracks, pressing his men furiously, and drove the enemy out of Dego with losses of 1,000 men and 18 more guns on the very afternoon of their success.

Without checking his momentum, despite the exhaustion in the ranks, the French commander retraced his steps toward Millesimo. On April 16, just 96 hours after the opening clash at Montenotte, he hurled nearly his whole weight at Colli's army, compelling that dazed opponent to pull back to Ceva.

The allied contingents were now separated beyond hope of rendering each other effective aid. Only by marching around the hills in the rear could the Austrians reinforce the outnumbered and badly demoralized Italian columns which Bonaparte pursued relentlessly. Within a few days he had driven the foe into the plains, and Colli asked for a truce as the French advanced on Turin. The beaten general requested several hours in which to arrange terms, but Bonaparte made his famous reply: "I may lose battles: I do not lose minutes."

The Bridge at Lodi

With Piedmont knocked out of the war, the victor turned again to the Austrian army. In view of his inferior numbers Beaulieu had abandoned the hills and taken a defensive stand on the north bank of the broad Po. Along this line the seventy-one-year-old general drew up the usual cordon and awaited his youthful opponent.

Bonaparte's promises were already partly fulfilled, for his men were now well fed, shod and clothed as a result of spoils or new stores. On reaching the Po, he had little choice but to make the conventional feint. But while feinting on his left, the real crossing was completed far to the right by six picked battalions which marched 44 miles in 36 hours. The Austrians, never dreaming of such celerity, found their cordon turned at a stroke.

Only the French lack of pontoons enabled Beaulieu to withdraw after a loss of 3,500 captured. Next he took a stand behind the river Adda, leaving a strong rear guard with 14 guns to hold the bridge at Lodi until the last Austrian had crossed.

As yet Bonaparte's casualties had been astonishingly small, for he manoeuvred where another general might have put up a blunt fight. Now he chose again to violate the established rules by making a direct frontal assault on a position which might readily have been turned. Some of the French units actually had crossed the Adda elsewhere as he sent his men in a cramped column across a bridge a hundred yards long. Hundreds of cheering grenadiers were shot down by grape or canister, but others climbed over their bodies or slid down the piles to wade the shallow stream. At last the human torrent swept across the blood-splashed planks to bayonet 2,000 Austrians at their guns, though the French had sustained at least equal losses.

At a glance this affair seems a cruel and needless butchery, yet no action was ever less regretted by Bonaparte. Lodi, in fact, was a coolly planned triumph of military psychology, intended to create a tradition of superhuman French valor both among his own forces and those of the enemy. In this purpose it succeeded so well that Bonaparte won the proud nickname of "Little Corporal" from troops whose flesh he had pitted against the Austrian cannon.

As a profound reader both of history and the human heart, he knew one military rule that allows of no exceptions—men love the general who leads them into danger and hardship, not the general who places their welfare above victory. Thus Lodi marks a new era in the Revolutionary wars. From that moment Frenchmen began to serve a man, not a nation or a political creed.

Bonaparte himself must have partaken of the general elation, for even at St. Helena he treasured the memory. "Only after Lodi did the idea come to me that henceforth I should be a decisive player on the political boards; then rose the first sparks of high ambition."

THE FIVE DAYS OF CASTIGLIONE

From the Adda the Austrians fell back to the Mincio, drawing up their third cordon. Beaulieu's retreat had shortened his lines, and on this river he had the further advantage of the great fortress of Mantua. Nothing daunted, Bonaparte made the crossing on May 30, forcing his opponent to abandon the Mincio. Fearing for his communications with Austria, Beaulieu strengthened the garrison at Mantua and fell back to Trent on the road to the Brenner Pass. During these moves neither side hesitated at violating the neutrality of Venice, just as neither would hesitate the following year at destroying that ancient oligarchy.

The campaign ended when Bonaparte again entered Milan, to be hailed as a liberator by crowds which had not as yet fully experienced French looting and indiscipline. The city had been taken just after Lodi, and now the victor laid siege to the citadel to capture the heavy artillery needed for an investment of Mantua. Thus in each operation he made "war nourish war," while never neglecting to send the impoverished Directory his regular offerings of jewels and Italian art treasures to be turned into cash.

At no time during the past six weeks had Bonaparte produced any method not already discovered by his French predecessors. Two modern books, Captain Jean Colin's *L'Education militaire de Napoléon* and B. H. Liddell Hart's *The Ghost of Napoleon*, have traced in detail the conqueror's debt to Bourcet, Guibert and du Teil. The victories of Carnot's armies left further precepts which were accepted almost without change, and yet Bonaparte had injected something new and vital into the warfare of his day. The answer has been supplied in his own words:

> The essence of strategy is, with a weaker army, always to have more force at the crucial point than the enemy. But this art is taught neither by books nor by practice: it is a matter of tact.

This rare quality of tact, or intuition, was the young general's most distinguished contribution. Approach to battle became more important than battle itself in his combinations, for he seemed almost to read an opponent's mind. Up to this time the French had not fought a single action in the old manner, unless one counts the storm of the bridge at Lodi, yet most of northern Italy had fallen into their hands.

Bonaparte's selection of subordinates had much to do with these results. Already, during the past six weeks, he had promoted in his own mind many of that hierarchy whose names would reverberate like thunder from one battlefield to another—Lannes, Victor, Berthier, Joubert, Masséna, Augereau, Marmont, Bessières, Suchet, Junot, Murat. Most of them were young and dashing, those Frenchmen of generally humble birth who would never have risen beyond a noncommissioned rank in the old Royal Army. Or if not young in years, like the forty-three-year-old Berthier who served as chief-of-staff, they retained a youthful vigor and endurance. A few, like Masséna, Suchet and Joubert, developed a high order of generalship. Others, like Lannes, Junot and Augereau, had more heart than brains. But at least one thing Bonaparte demanded of all alike: they must not shrink from exposing their own bodies to the perils met by the lowest private. Ney became known as "bravest of the brave," and Oudinot survived no less than thirty-four wounds.

The rank and file could not help sharing in the zest. In contrast to the ragtag who drifted into the old long-term armies, the French soldier was likely to be a clean, healthy young workman or peasant, possessed of native intelligence if not some schooling. Already he had begun to speculate as to the strategic purposes of the long, sleepless marches he made as a pawn of war. Bonaparte commented with pride and amusement on the shrewdness of one private who did not hesitate to advise the commander-in-chief.

"A chasseur approached my horse. 'General,' he said, 'you ought to do this.' 'Wretch,' said I, 'hold your tongue!' . . . For what he had told me was just what I had ordered to be done."

If more was expected of the French soldier and officer than their counterparts in other armies, so also were the rewards greater. Already the army of Italy had won a booty such as had been gained by no European conqueror in generations. Personal violence to noncombatants was rare, but all ranks thieved like gypsies, with Bonaparte and the Directory setting the example in spite of punishing an occasional culprit. Milan, Turin, Pavia and Bologna were stripped of gold, jewels and objects of art in addition to the usual requisitions of provisions. Even the pope, on making his peace, had to deliver 12,500,000 francs, 500 ancient manuscripts and 100 precious statues, paintings and vases.

On the debit side, such exactions led to reprisals which seriously hampered operations. Italians who had been eager for political reform soon longed for the return of the Austrians. Three infantry battalions were needed to cope with an uprising in Milan, while at Pavia 8,000 armed peasants broke into the city and overcame the French garrison. At a critical period of the campaign Bonaparte lost nearly a week of his cherished minutes in putting down the revolts of cities which had lately cheered him.

After a stubborn resistance the citadel of Milan fell late in June, providing 140 large guns for the investment of Mantua. With 42,000 well rested troops, including a few reinforcements from France, Bonaparte moved on the great fortress in the marshes of the Mincio. The works were defended by 316 guns and a garrison of 8,000, so that the French toiled during July on their parallels. The test was nearly at hand when

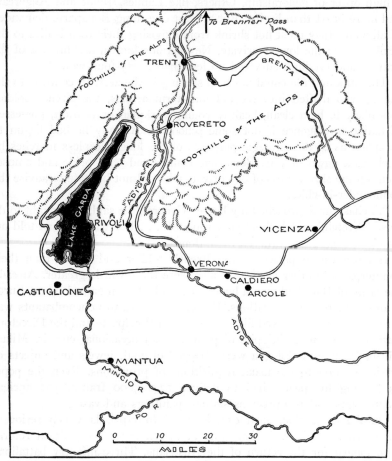

The Struggle for Mantua

Bonaparte learned that an Austrian army of 50,000 had debouched from the Alpine passes.

It is not a coincidence that Beaulieu's successor Wurmser had also passed his seventieth birthday. Austria's generals were advanced on a basis of seniority, though the real elders of the empire met in the Aulic Council to devise the strategy. This time their object was to relieve

Mantua, and Bonaparte's late victories along interior lines were ignored by orders directing Wurmser to divide his forces. Hence the old cavalry general took the main road down the Adige Valley, while his lieutenant Quosdanovich marched down the western side of Lake Garda to join him at Verona.

For the first time in his blazing career Bonaparte doubted. He even asked counsel of his subordinates, and all the rest of his life he recalled gratefully that tough, growling Augereau voted to fight when more able officers advised retirement.

The gunner and the general fought for mastery in Bonaparte's soul, but he spiked his hard-won siege pieces and marched against the new enemy. Once the decision had been made, he recovered his mastery and gained a series of victories so breathless that only incomplete records remain of the achievement. For in five days of running combats and manoeuvres, the whole being known as the battle of Castiglione, he separated his enemies and inflicted on them total losses which he estimated, with some hyperbole, at 70 guns and from 18,000 to 20,000 slain, wounded and prisoners.

The Aulic Council had not been wholly blind to such a peril, and either Austrian general was directed to move on the French rear if Bonaparte turned to attack the other. Still, the elders of Vienna had no conception of the bursts of speed which their foeman demanded and got from his men. Hurling his masses of manoeuvre from the foot of the lake, he caught Quosdanovich by surprise on August 1. The broken country suited Pijon's skirmishers, including a few companies of riflemen, as they harassed the Austrians until the French columns could close with the bayonet. In an explosion of isolated small combats Quosdanovich was forced back for three days until he decided to rejoin his chief by retiring around the head of the lake.

He did not know it, but for forty-eight hours Bonaparte's forces were actually fighting both in front and rear. While the main mass drove at Quosdanovich, stouthearted Augereau battled against odds to delay and "neutralize" Wurmser, approaching from the east side of the lake. The success of this operation made it possible to concentrate most of the French strength against that opponent alone on August 5, when the final engagement took place near Castiglione.

This encounter more nearly resembled an old-fashioned pitched battle than any action Bonaparte had yet fought. In a few hours he might count on superior numbers—the local superiority he maintained throughout the five days—if he could hold Wurmser until the reinforcements arrived. This he accomplished by a series of attacks designed to engage the whole Austrian front and compel his opponent to use his reserves. Meanwhile the French reserves, after an all-night march, struck the enemy's rear and Bonaparte ordered the decisive blow on the left centre.

Defeated but not broken, Wurmser retired eastward over the Mincio. His only gain during the brief campaign had been the reinforcing of Mantua with seven battalions which slipped in at the beginning of the running fight.

French minor tactics of the five days had not differed greatly from Hondschoote's swarms of skirmishers followed by impetuous masses of attack. The improvement over that early Revolutionary battle may be found less in method than velocity—an unheard-of velocity which multiplied the striking power of the French on ground too rough to give the superb Austrian cavalry many openings. Bonaparte himself rode five horses to exhaustion, and Augereau's division completed a march of 50 miles in about 36 hours.

The postscript to Castiglione was dashed off with the same fearful celerity after Bonaparte paused to rest troops too weary to pursue. Leaving a detachment to blockade Mantua without siege artillery, he pounded northward in three columns to Trent, where Wurmser and his new subordinate Davidovich were believed to have reunited the beaten Austrian forces. But the Austrian general had again divided his strength, ordering Davidovich to hold Trent with 13,000 men while he marched with his remaining 22,000 in a second attempt to relieve Mantua.

These moves gave Bonaparte another opportunity to get between two enemy armies. He drove Davidovich from Trent on September 5, assigning a detachment to hold him, and turned southward into the Brenta Valley with the bulk of his forces in pursuit of Wurmser. During the next six days Masséna marched 100 miles and Augereau 114, both of them fighting three actions. Wurmser attempted a stand at Bassano on the eighth, being beaten with severe losses. The chase continued until the twelfth, when the old general and his remaining 12,000 troops found a refuge in the beleaguered fortress he had hoped to relieve.

The Battles of Arcola and Rivoli

At almost the same time a campaign took place in Germany which proved that Bonaparte had no monopoly on operations along interior lines. There the twenty-five-year-old Archduke Charles separated the armies of Moreau and Jourdan and drove both back across the Rhine after winning two brilliant victories.

All summer the Directory had considered Italy a secondary theater. On several occasions orders were even given Bonaparte to co-operate with his colleagues in Germany, though he managed to retain his independence of action.

Carnot's plans for the invasion of Austria show less ability than his defenses of French soil. Nor did Jourdan and Moreau exhibit the same fire as their armies of 45,000 and 50,000 slowly forced the archduke over the Danube. Charles commanded a total of 68,000 troops, half of which he manoeuvred as a separate force under Wartensleben. On August 11 the archduke alone risked a delaying action near Neresheim, and the following day he began concentrating at Ingolstadt to hurl most of his strength at Jourdan. Leaving 30,000 men to fend off Moreau, he recrossed the Danube with the remainder and advanced cautiously before finding his opening. Then on the twenty-fourth he engaged Jourdan's front while the Austrian left curled like a whiplash around the extended French flank.

The battle of Amberg turned into encounters between columns, with two French battalions being destroyed to a man. Still, it could not be said that Charles had won a great victory—his chief gain had been the driving of a wedge between the French armies. Following up his retreating enemy, he won a more convincing triumph on September 3 at Würzburg, where he sent Jourdan reeling back across the Rhine with losses of 2,000 men and 7 guns.

Moreau, on receiving the news of these reverses, had good reason to fear for his communications with France. Already the archduke's army was pushing up the Rhine Valley to head him off, but in the nick of time he beat a hasty retreat to Strasbourg, abandoning the gains made by France during the summer's operations.

Bonaparte himself might have been proud of the results won by the Austrian prince. If they fall far short of a Castiglione in destructiveness, it must be remembered that Charles had not inherited the tactics, marches and concentrations of Carnot's armies. As an opponent of those armies in 1794, however, he had become the first of France's foemen to learn lessons in the new warfare.

Early in November the Italian front again flared into activity as the Austrians made a third effort to relieve Mantua and the 28,000 troops now blockaded in that stronghold. Losses and lack of reinforcements had gravely reduced Bonaparte's strength, and he could oppose only about

30,000 field troops to enemy forces totaling 47,000. Davidovich marched southward from Trent with 18,000 of these, while the new commander Alvinzi crossed the Piave with the main army after debouching from the eastern Alpine passes.

The French at last were beginning to show the strain. Panic accounted for the flight of a detachment sent to stop Davidovich, and Bonaparte ordered that it be written on their colors, "These men are no longer of the Army of Italy."

A week later he lost the first combat of his career in an attempt to stop Alvinzi at Caldiero. The two forces clashed at dusk in a sleet storm, and the French retired with sharp casualties after failing to carry the enemy position. Bonaparte listed Victor, Murat, Pijon, Lannes and Joubert among his wounded.

Neither Austrian general took any advantage of this reverse, and the French fell back into Verona before their converging forces. Here Bonaparte conceived the plan of a wide swing across the Adige to fall upon Alvinzi's rear from the south, cutting his communications. The French march led through a swampy country of few roads in which a detachment might at places stop an army. This was exactly what happened at Arcola, where for three days a force of Alvinzi's Croats held the bridge and causeway over the small river Alpone and its surrounding marshes.

After the repulse of the first day's assaults, Bonaparte grasped a standard and led the charge on the following morning. Still the enemy guns piled up heaps of corpses, and the commander narrowly escaped capture in a counterattack. Not until the third day of bloody fighting did the French win the bridge and approach to the high road, though the victory derived from an almost ridiculous ruse. With both sides exhausted, Bonaparte sent a few trumpeters to sound the charge in the Austrian rear, and panic routed defenders who had beaten off an army.

The delay ruined the French plan of reaching dry ground in time to surprise Alvinzi, who easily met the threat to his communications. As consolation Bonaparte had placed himself in a position to retrieve a disaster arising from the failure of his subordinate Vaubois to contain Davidovich. The defeat of this French detachment at Rivoli left the road open to the northern Austrian army, but Bonaparte reunited his forces to hurl Davidovich all the way back to Trent. Returning to Verona from the pursuit, he found Alvinzi retiring eastward across the Brenta, and Wurmser withdrawing into Mantua after several hopeful sorties.

Thus the Arcola campaign ended with both sides fought out and neither deriving any great satisfaction from the results.

The fourth attempt to relieve the fortress did not come until January, 1797, though it may be noted that the Austrians no longer remained in winter quarters. During the breathing spell Bonaparte's ceaseless pleas obtained him a few reinforcements, despite the obvious failure of universal conscription under the Directory. So many leaks had developed, in fact, that a French commander might now feel fortunate to bring equal numbers into the field.

The new Austrian forces amounted to 43,000 divided into three detachments—Alvinzi's main army of 28,000 advancing from the north on Trent and Rivoli; Bayalic's 6,000 moving from the east against Verona; and a third group of 9,000 under Provera approaching from the south toward Mantua.

With about the same numbers at his disposal, Bonaparte had to disperse his forces dangerously until he could foresee the direction of the main enemy attempt. Leaving 8,000 men to blockade Mantua, he flung out detachments in three directions. Then on concluding that Alvinzi would strike the principal blow, he demanded more than the usual speed of French columns hastening toward a concentration at Rivoli. Only one thing had been lacking in previous campaigns made up of a series of small combats; and now at last the issue was to be staked on a single decisive battle.

The clash promised also to be a final test of the tactical merits of concentric columns as opposed to French grand tactics. The very terrain of Rivoli—a lakeside plateau approached by good roads from three directions—made it inevitable that the Austrians would rely on their favorite converging attack. Quite as inevitably, Bonaparte planned to make use of his interior lines in the hope of bringing up a local superiority of numbers at each threatened point.

The fields of Tourcoing and Fleurus had already seen a trial of these rival theories, with the verdict favoring Carnot's awkward but zealous recruits. At Rivoli, however, Bonaparte's greater skill was balanced by an enemy numerical advantage of more than two to one at the beginning of the battle. Shortly after daybreak the Austrian columns emerged out of the mist—one on the left, three in the centre, and a fifth moving on the right flank of French forces drawn up in a semicircle. The three central columns struck first, but Bonaparte rushed up troops from his wings to hurl the enemy down the steep slopes after hours of terrific fighting. Meanwhile the French concentration began to take effect as new brigades reached the field. Masséna arrived at nine o'clock, just in time to save Joubert and the French right rear from envelopment. The two forces caught the Austrian column between them and pounded it to pieces with a terrible converging fire. On the other side of the field this drama was repeated as later units helped to crush the last enemy column with the irresistible masses the French had everywhere brought into action.

Providing a final fillip to the victory, a regiment under Murat fell upon the Austrian rear after crossing the lake in boats. Alvinzi's forces became so demoralized in the end that 12,000 surrendered, though no more than 2,000 had been killed or wounded.

As a tactical test Rivoli left no further doubts. The rigid Austrian columns, like horns seeking blindly to gore the foe, aimed scattered blows that were met by a united defense. The French efforts, even at the risk of mixing metaphors, can only be compared to flame—vivid, searing flame which darts through crevices and leaps over barriers, which flows around and behind every obstacle in its path. At moments Bonaparte's forces seemed more scattered than those of the enemy; but this illusion is also given by tongues of flame racing together to merge into a destructive blaze. Hence the military lesson of Rivoli was summed up by the victor in advice to his brother Jerome:

> I see that you think that two columns which shall seize the enemy between them are at an advantage; but this does not occur in war, because the two columns never act in unison, and your opponent can beat one after another. Of course you must turn the enemy, but concentrate first.

The French forces proved that they knew how to use as well as gain a victory. Provera and his 9,000 Austrians, not yet having learned the outcome, were on their way to Mantua to co-operate with the garrison. Since this union would produce an army nearly equal to his own, Bonaparte determined to reach the fortress first. Some of his units had fought near Verona on the thirteenth, marching 14 miles that night to fight again at Rivoli next morning. Yet these troops pelted back over the same road, covering 31 miles after another sleepless night, to arrive at Mantua on the fifteenth before Provera had news of his superior's defeat.

The Austrian general promptly surrendered when he realized that Bonaparte's main army had him surrounded. All hope thus vanished for the blockaded citadel, yet Wurmser resisted until the last artillery horse had been eaten. Then on February 2 the garrison laid down its arms;

and in honor of the stout defense, Bonaparte freed the old warrior to return to his homeland with an escort.

THE MARCH ON VIENNA

Even at this early date the blaze of Rivoli gave signs of spreading into a conflagration which would eventually sweep over the Continent. On that field Bonaparte had demonstrated his mastery of grand tactics. Within a few more weeks he would seize the prerogatives of grand strategy— the science of combining political and military means to gain the ends of warfare.

An avid reader of history, Bonaparte must have remarked that the world's greatest conquerors, such towering figures as Alexander and Jenghiz Khan, possessed full powers in statecraft as well as strategy. As an unknown young general, he had gained his will with the Directory by methods strongly suggesting bribery. Now as an acknowledged god of battles, he proposed to show his contempt for France's rulers by dictating terms of peace.

Two weeks after the fall of Mantua he literally crossed the Rubicon to punish the pope a second time, imposing an indemnity of 30,000,000 francs and bearing away more art treasures, including a bust of Caesar. He also established justifications which could later be used against the Venetians—a "wretched and cowardly population, unfitted for freedom."

The expedition to Vienna began in March. Recent reinforcements brought his numbers up to 90,000, of which nearly half were left behind to guard Italy and the long line of communications. Even so, the invader enjoyed a comfortable advantage in bulk over the forces of the Archduke Charles. In the quality of troops he held a greater superiority, for the ranks of the new Austrian army were filled largely with militiamen and recent recruits.

The thin, frail prince, who wrote essays on the Gospel as well as military treatises, would have liked nothing better than a contest. But his green soldiers behaved badly, deserting in droves before the veterans of Rivoli. Charles had to content himself with futile rear-guard operations or threats at the French rear as his strength dwindled to a third of his opponent's. Bonaparte, meanwhile, sent him a strange message:

> Our valiant soldiers are waging war and want peace. Has not this war lasted six years? Have we not killed enough people; have we not brought enough suffering upon mankind? . . . You, who stand so near to the throne, uplifted above the petty passions of statesmen

and governments, are you not disposed to win for yourself the title of benefactor of mankind, savior of Germany? I regard it as quite possible for you to save your country by force of arms. But, even then, Germany will be laid waste. If these lines could save the life of but one man, I should pride myself more upon my civic crown than upon the melancholy renown of the battlefield.

These sentiments from the victor of Lodi were referred to Vienna by Charles, who very properly replied that as a soldier he had no authority to discuss terms. Whatever may have been the personal reactions of Austria's diplomats, they recognized that Bonaparte had scored a victory in the field of propaganda. His letter, if published over Europe, would inevitably stamp the empire as a feudal and militaristic power which spurned humanist ideals.

At the time Austria had further reasons for desiring peace. On the Rhine another young French general was making disconcerting progress. Only a year older than Bonaparte, Lazare Hoche had displayed a comparable ability under much less glorious circumstances. As a loyal officer, he accepted the Vendée assignment which Bonaparte evaded; and after winning that civil war, he led an invasion of Ireland which collapsed for lack of French sea power. Now at last he had made his entrance on the great European stage, driving his opponent Warneck from the Rhine to the Lahn with the "incessant blows" urged by Carnot. The Austrian fell back to the Nidda, only to find Hoche's right wing wrapped around him. Almost certain destruction or surrender faced the beaten general when an armistice saved him. Thus ended the brief moment of the only French soldier who might have become a rival to Bonaparte, for Lazare Hoche died of illness a few months later.

The truce had been unexpected. After a four-week march over the high road from Trieste, Bonaparte found the Austrian envoys awaiting him at Loeben, 80 miles from Vienna. Without consulting the Directory, he agreed to terms which later went into the peace of Campo Formio. Like Louis XIV, who preferred to barter territory he did not own, the Republican general coolly offered to trade Venice for a formal Austrian cession of Belgium. The bargain was accepted, and the recent enemies became partners in several lesser deals which promised a mutual profit.

Barely a year had gone by since Montenotte, but young Bonaparte showed no diffidence before the plenipotentiaries of the ancient Hapsburg empire. "Strike out that passage," he ordered when they included a gracious preamble recognizing the new French form of government.

"The Republic is like the sun, which shines of its own light—only the blind fail to see it!"

THE SEQUEL IN ITALY

Other soldiers might err through ignorance of the past, but it has been truly said that Bonaparte was the slave of history. At no time in his career did this subjection reveal itself on a more grandiose scale than in his expedition to Egypt. Sound military reasons existed for a blow at the communications of the British Empire, but the adventurer's own words hint at personal motives:

Only in the East have there been great empires and mighty changes; in the East, where six hundred million people dwell. Europe is a molehill!

The corrupt Directory, veering from Left to Right, showed itself willing to be rid of an embarrassing hero and 40,000 veteran troops who might overthrow the government. This alacrity in itself proved that Bonaparte had chosen his moment badly from the viewpoint of ambition. Already such farsighted plotters as Sieyès, Fouché and Talleyrand knew that France would soon need her traditional strong man, yet the leading candidate sailed away with his soldiers and savants on a dubious Oriental venture.

As a rule the spotlight of history promptly follows him to Egypt, though far more stirring events, both political and military, took place meanwhile in Europe. After Austria's separate treaty the English ambassador agreed even to recognize the conquest of Belgium, and honest Carnot declared it the best peace France had been offered in two centuries. But the last champion of moderate republicanism was denounced as a "minister of Albion," and before long he had to flee for his life. France, devoured by disorder and unrest, had committed herself to a policy of endless foreign aggression.

As usual the directors needed gold, and the largest available sum reposed in the treasury at Berne. Before Bonaparte's leave-taking the first moves were made to provoke resistance, but the patient Swiss complied with every demand. Finally it became necessary to invade without a good pretext, and the Continent's oldest republic went down fighting, to be replaced by another of the puppet states which France created out of her conquests.

The other powers could not tolerate this bastion in the heart of Europe, and in the autumn of 1798 a new general war broke out, with Austria,

England, Russia, Portugal, Turkey, Naples and the papacy forming the Second Coalition.

The last year of the century began gloomily for France. The Directory found no enthusiasm for its conflict, and only 160,000 troops could be raised in four armies. The principle of universal conscription had been established in 1793, but most of the 770,000 men under arms had long since become civilians. Desertions were even welcomed by generals unable to provide for their troops, and the government failed to compel new enlistments.

As a remedy General Jourdan introduced a law in September, 1798, which has set a pattern for conscription legislation in all countries. Young men of from twenty to twenty-five were obliged to register, with conscripts to be drawn annually from the youngest class. This was the measure which provided no less than 2,613,000 French troops over a period of 14 years for the Napoleonic campaigns.

Ironically, the author took a beating for lack of numbers because the directors could not enforce his law. In March, 1799, Jourdan's army of 40,000 fell back before the superior strength of the Archduke Charles. Although burdened with orders from the Aulic Council which prescribed cordon methods, the prince managed to concentrate 60,000 men at Stockach, near Lake Constance. In a widespread "strategic" battle of clashes between columns, the French accepted defeat after losses of 5,000.

Bonaparte could doubtless have done better than Jourdan, but it is hard to see how he might have improved on Masséna's generalship in Switzerland. With but 20,000 men at his disposal, France's "mountain goat" seized the initiative against double his numbers of Austrians aided by bands of Swiss irregulars. By all the laws of war he should have been destroyed in detail, but his rapid thrusts all but annihilated several of the detachments which the enemy had to use in rugged country. In the combat of Nauders he sent his troops over the crests to cut off an unwary foe, and at Tauffers 4,500 Frenchmen emerged from a ravine in the Austrian rear to capture 6,000 men and 16 guns.

After Jourdan's defeat Masséna succeeded to the general command with total forces amounting to 45,000. In May he was brought to bay at Zurich by the archduke's 88,000, though the necessity for detachments reduced both main armies to half of those numbers. The Austrians attacked the French entrenched position on a five-mile front and were repulsed with grievous casualties. Illness soon made it necessary for the archduke to accept a minor rôle in the war, and Masséna remained in full control of Switzerland.

By this time it had become apparent that Italy would be the principal theater of operations. The puppet republics set up by France demanded 35,000 men for their defense, leaving 80,000 in northern Italy. The Austrians under Kray numbered 84,000, with Russian reinforcements being expected when Suvárov arrived to take over the allied command.

Neither side had won any lasting advantage before the celebrated old Russian general brought his contingent of 17,000, affording the strange spectacle of Cossacks on the plains of Italy. At the age of seventy, after half a century in arms, he was remembered for campaigns against the Turks in which he outdid their cruelties. While storming Ismail in Bessarabia, he permitted a massacre which ranks with the Spanish Fury and sack of Magdeburg; and his chastisements of Kosciusko's beaten Poles in 1794 were not much milder.

"Advance! Strike!" The two words summed up the creed of a soldier who saw war as an act of mystical violence. Yet in spite of the sinister fame gained by the "modern Attila" in the combats of eastern Europe, he proved no more barbarous than his contemporaries in Italy. The mere threat of a sack by Suvárov brought about the surrender of several French posts, and it can only be concluded that the old Russian made shrewd use of his reputation.

It is a fixed belief of all ages, ignoring the victories of Dandolo, Barbarossa and Zižka, that only young generals can adapt themselves to tactical change. Suvárov added another exception to the list by driving the French out of Italy after winning three great battles before autumn. As a first step, recognizing that the slow marches of the whitecoats had accounted for many of Bonaparte's successes, he issued one of his characteristic orders:

Fair weather is for my lady's chamber, for dandies, for sluggards. He who dares to cavil against his high duty is, as an egoist, to resign his command at once. Whoever is in bad health can stay behind. These so-called reasoners do no army any good.

All Russians were thought to be a little mad in 1799, since the complete insanity of Czar Paul could not be doubted. It came as a shock to the aristocratic officers of Austria, nevertheless, to be scolded by a gnome-like commander, barely five feet tall, who retained the habits of a private in the ranks. Suvárov did not win their complete respect until he stormed from Lake Garda to the river Adda in April, driving the French before him everywhere.

At Cassano, not far from Lodi, the rôles of that fight were reversed when Moreau tried to defend a strongly entrenched position. The moral supremacy had passed to whitecoats who endured 6,000 casualties to win the passage of the river. Moreau lost half of his outnumbered army, including 7,000 prisoners, and Suvárov and his Cossacks entered Milan in triumph.

The difficulties of the retreating losers became aggravated by a general revolt of the mock republics set up by Bonaparte. On all sides the peasants turned against Moreau's remnants, who were saved only by the Aulic Council's demand that Suvárov pause to besiege several forts in his rear, including Mantua. Not until the middle of June could the disgruntled Russian resume his campaign, and by that time a second French army had marched up from central Italy under the command of Macdonald, the French-born son of a Scottish immigrant.

Suvárov, with 25,000 men, found himself between Macdonald's 35,000 and Moreau's 15,000. The old campaigner showed that he could also play the game of interior lines as he singled out Macdonald's army before the French forces could join. On the river Trebia, near the scene of Hannibal's first victory over Rome, a terrific two-day battle was launched by the Russian general's order, "The opposing army will now be taken prisoners."

Until long after midnight a wild and bootless combat went on in the darkness as Frenchmen, Cossacks and Austrians struggled in the shallow stream and its sandy islands. Friend and foe alike were mown down by the artillery of both sides before the commanders could extricate their forces. All the next day the grapple continued as each army failed after repeated attempts to gain a foothold on the opposite bank. That night Macdonald withdrew in token of defeat after losing nearly half his army —4,000 slain and 12,000 wounded, missing and prisoners.

Suvárov, who had suffered 6,000 casualties, sent his battered army in pursuit, but could not prevent the junction of the French generals. Again the Aulic Council felt it wise to correct the "Russian madman," and to his disgust there followed another interlude of the prudent warfare approved by the elders of Vienna.

Not until mid-August could Suvárov force a decisive battle on the French, and the delay enabled them to assemble a last army of 35,000 under Joubert, regarded by Bonaparte as one of the most dynamic of his young officers. Nearly all Italy had been lost, including Mantua, when he awaited the allies in the Ligurian hills where Bonaparte's first victories had been won. After 16 hours of desperate fighting, Suvárov's superior numbers finally carried the fortified heights of Novi at a cost of 8,000 men. Joubert and four of his division generals were killed in a disaster which took a toll of 11,000 casualties and 37 guns.

St. Cyr and Moreau led the tatters of the army to safety in the mountain passes, leaving the French frontier open for a time. Only a few weeks later Bonaparte returned from Egypt, and on arriving in Paris he took good care to be overheard as he cried, "What have you done with this France I left so brilliant? . . . I left you victories; I find defeats! I left you the millions of Italy; I find spoliation and misery!"

IV

SWORD OF THE EMPIRE

---

*Had we taken ten sail and allowed the eleventh to escape,
being able to get at her, I could never have called it well
done.*

—NELSON

BONAPARTE'S own failure in Egypt had been as complete as the
French defeats in Italy, even if less conspicuous at the time. From the
outset he realized that an army of 40,000 could make no headway unless
the hordes of the East were won over to his side. Hence he began by
dating his proclamations according to the Mohammedan calendar, while
organizing an Institute of Egypt for the exchange of cultural ideas.

This phase lasted but a short time when it grew evident that the masses
were too fatalistic to be stirred by promises of a liberty they neither
understood nor trusted. The despised Orientals, in short, proved more
clear-sighted than their contemporaries of Europe when it came to
estimating Bonaparte's ambitions.

They gave him their answer by a general uprising which began with
the massacre of a convoy of French wounded. Bonaparte put down the
revolts without hesitating to shell the mosques which he had only lately
caused to be respected. In further confession of political failure, he abandoned persuasion for age-old Eastern methods of terrorism. There is
even a frantic note in his order for the heads of executed rebels to be
rolled into the public squares of Cairo as an object lesson.

The army upheld the tradition of invincibility which civilized forces have always maintained against the hordes of barbarism. This process Bonaparte explained with his usual keenness of analysis. One Mameluke, he said, was more than a match for a Frenchman in single combat. Ten Mamelukes could perhaps hold their own against ten Frenchmen. But two hundred trained soldiers, forming a small tactical unit, would beat several times their numbers of opponents who had not been schooled to act in unison. Drill and discipline, in other words, were the levers which enabled a Cortez or Pizarro to uproot vast populations of rude foemen.

No better illustration could be found than Bonaparte's own victory in the battle of the Pyramids. On that field, beset by a crushing weight of Mameluke riders and fanatical Arabs, he formed five division squares in echelon. From the inner ranks men loaded muskets and passed them up to the soldiers in front, who poured a deadly fire from four sides into horsemen dashing themselves to pieces against the human bastions.

The Turks proved to be no better tacticians, though they had small excuse for ignorance of European methods. The army landed by the grand vizier at Alexandria included 10,000 infantry drilled and armed up to the best contemporary standards. Yet in the test the Turkish commanders adopted a passive defense which allowed Bonaparte to stretch both their wings as a preliminary to ripping through the centre. In a few minutes the invaders had been reduced from an army to a stricken mob, and only a handful escaped drowning or massacre.

The War on the Sea

From the beginning the fate of the Egyptian expedition was decided less by land warfare than the naval developments of the past five years. At the outbreak of the Revolution the French were not at a hopeless disadvantage in material respects with their 76 ships of the line and 6,000 guns as compared to 115 British sail with 8,700 guns. It has been the experience of history, however, that revolutionists do not fare as well on the sea as on land. This may be explained by the fact that fleets are more intricate fighting mechanisms than armies, depending to a greater extent on long traditions of discipline and skill. A beaten army may often be recruited up to new strength and infused with new fighting spirit, as Carnot proved in 1793. A beaten fleet can lose the naval war in a few hours, exposing the coasts and commerce of the nation to enemy ravages for several years to come.

In 1793 the French navy suffered less from a lack of ships than the shock of political upheavals on a delicately adjusted organization. Three-fourths of the former royal officers had been replaced by seamen promoted from the ranks or transferred from the merchant marine, most of them selected for their Revolutionary fervor. In every squadron several political representatives from Paris had the duty of reporting any deviations from faith or zeal. As a last ludicrous touch, the marines and auxiliary gunners were removed wholesale by fanatics who saw a violation of equality in "the exclusive privilege of fighting at sea." The places of these highly trained specialists went to sans-culottes from the National Guard who had never been aboard a ship.

Under such circumstances it is not remarkable that the new crews were beaten tactically in their first fight. The marvel is that they fought with such resolution as to justify their claim of a strategic victory in the battle of the First of June.

A poor harvest having brought France to the brink of famine, 120 grain ships sailed to the Chesapeake in 1794, being met on the return voyage by the entire Brest fleet of 26 warships. The action developed when Lord Howe's fleet of exactly the same strength caught up with the convoy about 400 miles off Ushant.

The British admiral ordered his captains to "lock yardarms" with their opponents for a brief, decisive combat at close quarters. These instructions, following Rodney's breaking of the French line in 1782, show that naval men were gradually departing from the conservative tactics of the past century. Howe's first onslaught threw the enemy into confusion, and six of the British ships sailed through the formation. In the mêlée ten damaged French craft were cut off, but by prodigious efforts Admiral Villaret de Joyeuse escorted three of the cripples to port as well as his grain ships. Having fought with the threat of the guillotine hanging over him, he lived to boast with melancholy pride, "I saved my convoy and my head."

The French vessels, bearing such new names as *Tyrannicide* and *Vengeur du Peuple*, owed their losses of six prizes and a sunk ship to unskilled gunnery and seamanship. But even the enemy paid a tribute to Revolutionary valor, reporting that the *Vengeur* went down with all hands shouting *"Vive la République!"*

The British navy was also undergoing a transition at this time. For a century other nations had wondered at the devotion of seamen recruited by brutal press-gang methods and ruled by a discipline of savage severity. Only victory redeemed the hardships, low pay and monotonous food of crews made up of the criminal and depraved as well as unfortunate elements of the population. Such a system gave an impression of gold-braided aristocracy at the top, yet the officers came largely from the middle classes and honors were based on achievement more often than birth.

Young Horatio Nelson may be taken as a fair example. The son of a Norfolk clergyman, he became a midshipman at thirteen, serving a valuable apprenticeship as a Thames river pilot. Invalided home after several years of foreign duty, the delicate, sensitive youth recalled in later life "a long and gloomy reverie in which I almost wished myself overboard." This mood gave way to "a sudden glow of patriotism" as Nelson passed his lieutenant's examination and reached the rank of post captain in 1779 at the age of twenty.

Neither officers nor crews were spared by the system, and in May, 1797, the accumulated grievances of the seamen broke out into the most widespread mutiny of the British navy. Even so, the affair resembled a well-planned general strike rather than an armed uprising, since surprisingly few cases of violence occurred. The sailors quietly took charge of the ships, even showing their respect for many officers by voluntarily restoring them to authority. That the officers in turn must have felt some sympathy for the men is evident from their acquiescence.

In the end Parliament and the Admiralty had to grant reforms which were long overdue. Only a few disaffected leaders were executed, and the crews proved their complete loyalty a few months later by defeating a Dutch fleet in the battle of Camperdown.

Although they resented the French domination of their country, the sailors of Holland had old scores against England. Hence they fought their 15 ships with fierce resolution in the encounter off the Texel with 16 British sail of a much superior class. Again the transition in tactical ideas is shown as Admiral Duncan gave the order to break through the enemy line for "close action." The outcome was inevitable, but the outweighed Dutch vessels gave such a good account of themselves that all 11 prizes taken by the victors were too damaged to be towed to port. Several of the British ships also suffered serious injury in their head-on attack.

Spain had meanwhile concluded an active alliance with the French Republic which endangered the communications of the Mediterranean fleet commanded by Sir John Jervis. In February, 1797, the British admiral, with 15 ships of the line, caught up with 27 enemy sail off Cape St. Vincent. In the chase seven Spanish vessels became separated from the rest, and Jervis sent his single column between the two enemy groups. Toward the end of the file was the *Culloden* under Horatio Nelson, now advanced to the rank of commodore. In violation of orders he broke out of the column, displaying an initiative which resulted in the surrender of two of the four prizes taken by the victors.

While their allies fought two battles in eight months, the French resorted to a fleet-in-being strategy varied with raids on British commerce. Their only active effort of 1797 took place in December as Hoche revived the perennial dream of landing troops on British soil. A fleet of 17 ships of the line convoyed transports containing 15,000 soldiers, but the ships became scattered by rough weather and only a few reached the Bay of Bantry. Not a single man landed in Ireland, though the flotilla managed to return without losses to home ports.

The first real contest between the ancient foes was postponed until 1798, when the British learned of a great armament being assembled at Toulon for an unknown purpose. Jervis recommended Nelson for command of the Mediterranean fleet, but the new admiral could learn nothing of the enemy's well-concealed plans.

At the age of forty he had arrived at his rank by seniority, though his enterprise at the battle of Cape St. Vincent gained him popular recognition. Shortly afterwards he lost an arm in the blockade of Cadiz, and the sight of one eye had gradually failed as a consequence of a former wound. Nelson's forthright tactical principles were already known in the service, but the paternal interest of Jervis played no small part in the molding of his career.

This great organizer stands in much the same relation to future naval events as Carnot to the subsequent victories of Bonaparte. A martinet by reputation, Jervis tempered his firm discipline by a unique breadth of character and mastery of his profession. More than any other commander, he restored morale and fighting spirit after the great mutiny; and he first recognized in his young protégé the talents which would become common knowledge after Trafalgar.

If Jervis may be compared to France's Organizer of Victory, the parallel is completed by the likeness between the doctrines of Nelson and Bonaparte. Neither felt that a victory was complete unless the opposing force had been destroyed for all purposes of the war. Both introduced a close and reciprocal relationship with subordinates as a departure from the stiff exclusiveness of past commanders. Bonaparte left many warnings as to the danger of delay, while Nelson declared, "Time is everything! Five minutes may spell the difference between victory and defeat."

The similarity is added proof that no man had created this new age of war. All had been created by it, just as young and vigorous shoots find their way to the light after a fire has cleared away the dead growth of the past. The pious Austrian prince, the ex-smuggler Masséna, the seventy-year-old Russian general, the ardent English admiral—all were as legitimately the offspring of a revolutionary era as Bonaparte himself.

The very impetuosity of Nelson's pursuit led to disappointment after his discovery of the French departure from Toulon. Guessing at Alexandria as the destination, he reached that port two days ahead of the 400 enemy transports escorted by 13 ships of the line. Then retracing his course too hastily, the British admiral missed his prey by a few miles in the darkness.

Not until weeks later did he finally sight the French fleet at anchor in Aboukir Bay on August 1, 1798. Although the sun had set, Nelson sent his fleet into action without pausing to change the order in which the vessels arrived on the scene.

The British strength consisted of 14 ships, of which 13 were 74's and one a 50. The French admiral, de Brueys, thus had a superiority in metal with his four frigates in addition to nine 74's, three 80's and the huge flagship L'Orient mounting 120 guns. Despite this advantage, he trusted to the shoals for a passive defense. The bay at the Rosetta mouth of the Nile had filled up with silt, and the French ships took a position which seemed to limit the enemy to an attack from seawards. De Brueys felt so safe on the land side that he did not even clear for action in that quarter. As added assurance, he depended on the French shore batteries for a deadly enfilade fire.

Nelson had neither reliable charts nor pilots, but at dusk he sailed into the bay with a favoring breeze. His orders were for part of his captains to attack from the land side while the rest came in from the sea. All were to begin at the head of the French line, moving toward the centre and subjecting each enemy ship in turn to a double assault.

The battle of the Nile developed exactly according to these plans, even though one ship grounded. The Goliath, leading the advance, sailed between the Guerrier and the shore, raking that French ship while passing on to the next. Closely following, the Zealous fired a second crippling broadside into the Guerrier as three British newcomers broke through the line to take positions between the enemy and the shoals. Almost simultaneously Nelson's flagship Vanguard led an attack from seawards which poured more broadsides into already helpless French hulls.

In the darkness the shore batteries had no such effect as de Brueys had hoped. His L'Orient was engaged by three British captains, and at ten o'clock the huge flagship blew up with a flaming explosion which revealed the French fleet being destroyed in detail. Two ships were burned and nine captured, and even the four which escaped were sunk or taken by the victors in subsequent operations.

Not a single British vessel went down in a triumph which surpassed any naval success of the past century both in method and results. When the news reached Europe, the English diplomats were able immediately to form the Second Coalition against France. Bonaparte thus had his communications cut at a blow, with the Turks added to the enemies he must face in the East.

The French general had a second unhappy experience with enemy sea power the following spring when he crossed the desert to meet the new foe in Turkish Syria. His troops won several combats, but at Acre they found the Turks aided by two British ships of the line under Sir Sidney Smith. For two months Bonaparte fretted while this second-rate fortress held out, though he crushed a Turkish relieving army at the battle of Mount Tabor. The delay made it necessary to lift the siege, and after returning to Egypt he received news which caused him to board a frigate in the dead of night and set sail for France. Taking only a few favorite officers, he left his demoralized army in a hopeless situation which ended two years later with the surrender of the remnants to a British expeditionary force.

THE MARENGO CAMPAIGN

Even the news which decided Bonaparte owed to England's sea power, for Sir Sidney Smith chivalrously sent a bundle of the latest European publications. From them the French general pieced together the events which made him realize that his hour had struck.

After the summer's defeats the prestige of the Directory had sunk to such an ebb that Sieyès sought a military figurehead. The middle-aged Masséna had won France's only successes, but he combined republican principles with an entire lack of political ambition. In the lack of a hero Sieyès determined to create one out of Joubert. This personable young soldier fell in with the scheme, promising to win a victory over Suvárov. But instead of gaining fame, Joubert met defeat and death on the field of Novi, leaving France in worse peril than before.

As a last resort the colorless Moreau had been approached when dispatches brought the unexpected word of Bonaparte's landing. At least this general had a few tactical triumphs to clothe the bare bones of strategic failure, and Sieyès realized that France had found her strong man. The preliminary steps toward dictatorship were taken with almost indecent haste, and a month after his arrival Bonaparte emerged from the *coup d'état* of the Eighteenth Brumaire with the new title of consul.

Sieyès and his group had naturally counted on retaining most of the actual power, but in this expectation Bonaparte disappointed them. Within a short time he made himself virtually the head of the state in civil as well as military respects. Nevertheless, he knew that his position could only be secured by a victory which would win peace and stability. Even in this emergency France had grown so weary of war that out of a population of thirty millions less than five hundred men answered the latest call for volunteers.

The only improvements in the military situation since the disaster of Novi had resulted less from French exertions than disputes between allies. After that battle Czar Paul ordered his victorious general to return home by way of Switzerland and Germany. Obeying against his better judgment, Suvárov decided to cross the mountains at the St. Gothard and fight his way through French detachments. While toiling toward the summits, he relied on an allied covering force of 30,000 under Korsákov to contain Masséna near Zurich. But that adversary, ever dangerous, left a division to defend the St. Gothard and concentrated to rout Korsákov at the second battle of Zurich with losses of 8,000 killed and wounded, 100 guns and many prisoners.

The whole allied line fell back after this defeat, leaving Suvárov unsupported at the foot of the St. Gothard. There followed a nightmare of hardships and reverses as the French harassed the Russian column on mountain roads. The fighting was continual, and Suvárov lost half of his 28,000 troops before resigning himself to the only enforced retreat of his life. After a winter in quarters, his destitute army marched home by a safer route; but Russia's greatest soldier soon died in disgrace, broken by the czar's condemnation.

During the first days of the new century Bonaparte began the tremendous task of creating the victory so essential to his power. Not only was the treasury empty and credit exhausted, but France's 229,000 troops were in a low state of morale and equipment. Desertion had become such a problem under the new conscription law that but 310 men reported out of one draft of 10,250.

In six weeks the First Consul, aided only by the faithful Berthier, finished a colossal labor which today would be divided among a host of well-trained staff and administrative officers. In addition to reorganizing his troops and enforcing the conscription law, he drew up a detailed plan of campaign embracing the operations of all armies. Such permanent reforms were introduced as the grouping of divisions and army corps, the replacing of civilian artillery drivers by soldiers, and the abolition of the practice of hiring artillery horses from contractors. During this period Bonaparte administered civil affairs so ably both at home and abroad as to win public confidence in the stability of his dictatorship.

Moreau's army of the Rhine, holding the upper river, constituted the strategic left wing of France's force. In the centre Switzerland was occupied by detachments, and on the right Masséna's depleted army of Italy defended a line from the Alps to the Mediterranean. Bonaparte's plan contemplated the formation of an army of Reserve to take advantage of the Swiss passes. While Moreau contained the enemy in Germany, and

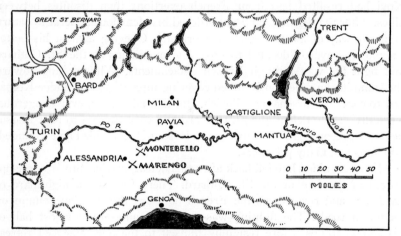

The Marengo Campaign

Masséna held in western Italy, the consul proposed to lead the new army over the Alps and fall upon the rear of the Austrians attacking Masséna.

The fact that the execution fell short of the conception may be blamed on one of those accidents of war which even genius cannot foresee. The pass of the Great St. Bernard had been nearly traversed by Bonaparte's army when the advance units were held up by the tiny fort of Bard, defended by those tough Croat soldiers who had played havoc with French plans at Arcola. With the Italian plains nearly in sight, this mountain outpost put up such a stout resistance as to delay the French artillery for two weeks—long enough to ruin the element of surprise on which Bonaparte had counted.

The old Austrian commander Melas, a veteran of the Seven Years'

War like most of the empire's generals, thus gained time to cope with
the threat to his right flank and rear. In his front he had Masséna
besieged at Genoa, while the able young French general Suchet defended
Nice and the Var with small forces.

Melas' first mistake—a natural one according to his lights—lay in
assuming that the army of Reserve would hasten directly to the relief of
the hard-pressed Masséna at Genoa. Instead, Bonaparte cut one of the
two main Austrian lines of retreat by seizing Milan and Pavia, with
their large military stores. As a second error Melas underestimated the
tenacity of Masséna and the brilliance of Suchet—two factors which
robbed him of the successes he expected in western Italy. Bonaparte was
able meanwhile to threaten his other line of retreat, and early in June the
Austrian had to abandon his western campaign in a belated effort to
break the perilous embrace of the army of Reserve in his rear.

Thus had Bonaparte relieved Genoa by striking in another quarter.
The two generals now engaged in a race of concentration. This contest
the consul won easily by gathering his forces from the Milan district
and marching westward while Melas was still assembling about Alessandria. A French victory now seemed assured, but at the last moment the
leader's future hung in the balance as a result of errors which nearly
cost him the battle.

At Montebello on June 9 the French advance units and Austrian rear
guard fought a combat which ended with 2,100 of the latter slain or
wounded and a like number captured out of the 12,000 on the field. This
small victory, won at a cost of 500 casualties, gave Bonaparte an overconfidence which increased as Masséna and Suchet advanced to threaten
Melas from the opposite direction. As a result the French commander-in-
chief, placing too small a value on his opponents' numbers and resolution,
detached two of his six divisions to prevent an Austrian escape to the
right or left.

Melas soon proved that he had no intention of escaping. Advancing
from Alessandria on June 14 with his main force of 30,000, he struck
Bonaparte's remaining 23,000 troops on the plain of Marengo. The
Austrian superiority in guns and cavalry soon had the French on the
retreat in spite of a desperate defense. All but five of Bonaparte's guns
were taken as the whitecoats came on with irresistible momentum. After
three hours of the advance Melas believed his victory so assured that
he retired with a slight wound, leaving a subordinate to manage the
pursuit of the battered foe.

At this moment, perhaps the most bitter of his life, Bonaparte could only curse the mistakes which had wiped out all the gains of a masterly campaign. Without much hope, he sent a courier galloping to Desaix's division—the only one of the two detachments which could return in time—with the frantic plea, "In the name of God, come if you can!"

During the next two hours Bonaparte took personal charge of the retirement, using his few reserves with the utmost skill. Still the French gave ground, and still the Austrians pressed forward with invincible battalions. Bonaparte's men had reached the breaking point when Desaix joined in the fight after a forced march of heroic endurance. His 6,000 weary troops and 8 guns were not enough to balance the enemy's weight, but the miracle of his arrival became the turning point. As their reinforcements stormed into action the beaten French found new courage, and suddenly the battle began to swing in the other direction. Desaix fell with a bullet through the brain, but the more numerous Austrians were seized by an unaccountable panic. So compelling was the moral factor on both sides that only 400 horsemen and 2 guns led the final assault that sent the whitecoats streaming back to Alessandria in rout.

The old Austrian general, as broken and bewildered as his men, signed an armistice next day in which he abandoned all of Italy west of the Mincio. Bonaparte, in view of his narrow escape, showed himself willing for once to allow an enemy force to withdraw intact.

Marengo cast a curious spell over both belligerent nations which cannot be explained by its numbers or results. From that day onward the French were the moral victors of the war, the Austrians the all but acknowledged losers. In view of this spirit, the victory won by Moreau at Hohenlinden the following December seems a mere sequel in spite of its grand scale. This French general, torpid in strategy but forthright as a tactician, had one of his decisive moods in the gloomy defiles of the Black Forest. Aided by appalling storms of snow and rain which only French mobility could overcome, he crushed the straggling Austrian columns one by one to inflict total losses of 20,000 men and 90 guns.

On Christmas Day, three weeks later, hostilities came to an end with the armistice of Steyer. Bonaparte had Hohenlinden to thank for his peace, but never could he forget that at Marengo he had won an emperor's crown.

The Battle of Trafalgar

Austria signed the Peace of Luneville the following February, but the war on the sea lasted another year. During this period Bonaparte attempted to cripple English commerce with his Armed Neutrality in which Russia, Denmark, Sweden and Prussia pledged themselves to resist belligerent rights in the Baltic.

The island kingdom, threatened with the loss of vital markets and supplies, delivered an ultimatum to Denmark with 20 ships of the line, which Nelson called the "best negotiators in Europe." The hero of the Nile ranked as second in command, a position which could be blamed on his own insubordination. For Nelson resembled Bonaparte not only in tactical doctrines but also such characteristics as vanity and egoism. After his celebrated victory he gave naval assistance to schemes in the Mediterranean which promised more private glory than national advantage; and as a result of disobeying a direct order of the Admiralty, he returned to England with a tarnished reputation.

Another man might have redeemed himself by more respectful conduct, but as a naval genius Nelson took a short cut with a new act of insubordination. When Copenhagen defied England's ultimatum with shore batteries mounting 696 guns, Sir Hyde Parker had no choice but to use force. Nelson had drawn up the plan of attack, but at a critical stage of the bombardment his superior flew the order, "Leave off action." Then occurred the famous incident of Nelson's placing the telescope to his blind eye with the remark, "I really do not see the signal!" From that moment he took virtual command of the fleet, silencing most of the enemy batteries with his better gunnery. Proving no less able as a diplomat, he induced Denmark to sign an armistice the next day. Nelson soon succeeded Parker, and after sailing into the Baltic he managed the armed negotiations which ended in a satisfactory agreement.

In March, 1802, the Treaty of Amiens gave a warring generation the longest truce it would ever enjoy. Although the formal peace lasted only fourteen months, three years passed without the tramp of marching hosts being heard in Europe. During this interlude Bonaparte rebuilt France with the same fierce energy he had once devoted to battle. Roads and canals, great public works, a revised code of laws and solid industrial prosperity all combined to make Paris the "new Rome of a new Caesar." Order and discipline were often restored at the cost of political liberties, but Frenchmen preferred authority to the chaos left by the Revolution. As a result Bonaparte found no difficulty in crowning himself Napoleon I, and in 1804 the dictator became the anointed of the Lord in a ceremony sanctified by the blessing of the pope.

Unquestionably he hoped to extend his power by methods which fell short of war, but England could not long tolerate peaceful aggressions in the manner of Louis XIV. France had retained most of her conquests.

and Napoleon soon strengthened his position by annexing Piedmont, invading San Domingo and compelling Spain to agree to the Louisiana Purchase. When he showed intentions of taking over Egypt next, England made her attitude clear by recalling William Pitt to the ministry.

The son of the Great Commoner, this implacable enemy of Napoleon soon brought into being the Third Coalition of England, Austria and Russia. Following his father's policy of making sea-borne commerce pay for the subsidizing of continental allies, Pitt faced as his first problem a threatened invasion of England. At Boulogne and near-by ports Napoleon concentrated 130,000 troops to be taken across the Channel in 2,000 specially built flat-bottomed boats. In defense, England armed 700 small craft along her shores, while five fleets comprising 65 ships of the line watched the ports of Brest, Boulogne, Corunna, Cadiz and Toulon.

"Let us be masters of the Strait for six hours," said Napoleon, "and we shall be masters of the world." But as months went by without an attempt, it grew plain that he did not underrate the practical difficulties. Finally the news came as no great surprise when he turned his back on Boulogne in the summer of 1805 to march against the armies of Austria and Russia.

In his writings the emperor afterwards contrived to give the impression that his admirals were to blame for the failure. A more candid analysis, however, must trace most of the responsibility to his own door. Although he had been in control of France's destinies for five years, the fleet had not gained from his vast administrative talents. Training and discipline had improved since 1794, but the navy of 1805 shows little progress over the fleet of Louis XVI. Napoleon simply renewed the policies of overcentralized control and timid strategy which had hampered past admirals.

Villeneuve, the French commander at Trafalgar, displayed the same pathetic eagerness to please a royal master as his predecessors of the old régime. Taking his instructions from the emperor, then far away in Germany, he emerged from the security of Cadiz to risk the brief voyage into Mediterranean waters. Napoleon, like the Sun King on several occasions, had suddenly varied a prudent policy with orders which placed an admiral on his honor to fight:

> His Majesty wishes to destroy that circumspection which is the reproach of the navy; that defensive system which paralyzes our fleet and doubles the enemy's. He counts the loss of vessels nothing if lost with honor; he does not wish his fleet blockaded by an enemy

inferior in strength; and if that is the situation at Cadiz, he advises you and orders you to attack.

Still doubtful, Villeneuve drew up a plan of battle which stressed the desirability of keeping open a line of retreat. Nelson, on the contrary, ignored the possibility of defeat while devoting his genius to the problem of preventing the enemy from escaping. "No captain can do very wrong," he told his subordinates, "if he places his ship alongside that of the enemy."

The 18 French and 15 Spanish vessels slipped out of Cadiz, and on the morning of October 21, 1805, Nelson's fleet sighted them making southward off Cape Trafalgar. Villeneuve awaited the attack with a slightly concave line of 21 ships supported in the rear by a reserve of 12 which he intended to reinforce any part of the fleet. The British admiral also fought in two divisions. Collingwood, with 15 ships, had freedom of action to strike at the allied rear as he saw fit, while Nelson with the remaining 12 proposed to keep the van and centre from going to the assistance of the rear.

At noon the two British columns bore down on the allied line. Collingwood broke through first and engaged 16 ships. Nelson succeeded meanwhile in deceiving the enemy as to his intentions, and both the centre and van expected his attack. Ten of the leading ships became separated as a result, so that the allied fleet had been split into three sections incapable of mutual support. At this moment Nelson found a gap opposite the French flagship *Bucentaure*, twelfth in line, and led the advance with his *Victory*.

The battle now turned into a confused mingling of ships pouring broadsides into one another at close range. The superiority of British gunnery in these exchanges is shown by the 400 casualties inflicted on the *Bucentaure* at a cost of 50 on the *Victory*. Before the ten ships of the allied van could be of any aid, the centre and rear had been beaten in detail. Firing continued until 4.30, according to the *Victory's* log, when Nelson died of a bullet wound after learning of his complete triumph. Eleven crippled allied vessels escaped to Cadiz, 18 surrendered and the remaining 4 were captured afterward by a British squadron off Corunna.

Trafalgar established the supremacy of British sea power so convincingly that it became the last great naval action of the Napoleonic wars. During the next ten years the emperor had to content himself with counter-blockades and the ravages of privateers. Such raids accounted for an average loss of 500 ships a year, yet as in past wars the trade of

Britain thrived at the expense of French merchant ships which dared not venture out of port.

THE SUN OF AUSTERLITZ

England's joy over Trafalgar was tempered by the news that only a day later Napoleon had cut off and captured an Austrian army.

Before leaving Boulogne the emperor paced the floor all one night, dictating a detailed plan of campaign. Out of that restless brain came every decision guiding the marches, halts and manoeuvres of the columns which soon began pouring through Germany at the rate of a steady fifteen miles a day.

Only a man at the peak of his mental and physical powers could have performed such a feat, and only troops keyed up to the highest pitch could have come up to his expectations. Napoleon declared the Grande Armée of 1805 the finest instrument the world had ever known, and surely it has few equals in history. All of his forces had fighting discipline, but this one had also a foundation of training acquired during the months of waiting at Boulogne. From the thirty-six-year-old leader down to the last drummer boy, the ranks were filled with a spirit of youthful zest and swagger. Among the corps commanders, only Bernadotte and Augereau had passed their fortieth birthdays; Ney, Lannes and Soult were exactly the emperor's age, while Davout was thirty-five and Marmont thirty-two. Half of the divisional commanders were in their early thirties, and some of them still younger.

In its tactics this army remained an infantry host, for the day of great cavalry and artillery masses had not yet arrived. Those arms were still secondary to the battalion columns of foot whose advances have been described by a contemporary, General Foy:

The action was opened by a cloud of skirmishers, on foot and mounted. . . . They harried the enemy, escaped from his masses by their speed, and from the effect of his guns by their scattered order. They were reinforced so that their fire should not die out, and they were relieved to give them more efficacy. The mounted artillery rode up at a gallop, firing grape and canister at point-blank range. The line of battle moved in the direction of the impulse given; the infantry in column, for it did not depend on fire, and the cavalry units mingled so as to be disposable everywhere and for everything. When the rain of enemy bullets began to thicken, the columns took to the double-quick with the bayonet, the drums beating the charge and the air reverberating with cries, a thousand times repeated, "Forward! Forward!"

In other words, French tactics had not changed essentially since 1794. The Grande Armée of 1805 still relied on columns of bayonets to collect the victory after its skirmishers had brought suit with methods borrowed from the American Revolution. The only difference lay in an infinitely improved co-ordination of the three arms.

Nor had the Austrian armies stood still since the last war. After adopting the French organization of corps, they cut down their baggage trains by deciding that all troops should subsist in the manner of the enemy. As a final concession, the Aulic Council copied French equality by promoting Marshal Mack von Leiberich to command after his rise from the ranks of Europe's most caste-ridden army.

Even this republican gesture could not change Austrian marching habits, which remained lamentably slow. As a consequence Mack's army of 60,000 was cut off by Napoleon's swift movements, and after the combat of Elchingen a detachment of 10,000 surrendered. With the balance, minus thousands of fugitives, Mack took refuge in his fortified camp at Ulm, where the French surrounded him. The Austrian commander, exposed to artillery fire, agreed to an armistice of 21 days, but by means of trickery Napoleon introduced armed parties which opened the gates. Mack then had no choice but to surrender his remaining 25,000 troops, giving the enemy a victory which compares with Caesar's bloodless triumph of Ilerda.

"The strength of an army, like that of a moving body in mechanics, is expressed by the mass multiplied by the velocity." These were Napoleon's words, but his grenadiers had a more simple explanation for their successes, "The emperor has discovered a new way to make war: he uses our legs and not our bayonets."

The latter definition came nearer to the mark as the victorious columns bore down on the Austrian capital so rapidly that its defense had to be abandoned. The retreating whitecoats planned, of course, to blow up the great bridge over the Danube, but French audacity cheated them even of this effort. Two gaudily uniformed marshals, Murat and Lannes, coolly walked across as an officer stood ready to light the fuse. While they confused him with glib talk, a rush of French soldiers overpowered his men and saved the structure.

Napoleon rested his footsore troops in Vienna, then pressed on to meet the combined Austrian and Russian forces near Brunn. By the end of November the allies had concentrated about 83,000 men, including 16,000 cavalry, with the French total amounting to 68,000.

Since his hairbreadth escape from disaster at Marengo the emperor had given much thought to the art of battle, particularly in its psychological aspects. On that field only the hard fighting of his soldiers saved him until Desaix could come to the rescue. But the chief lesson lay in the fact that a mere 400 horsemen and two guns had led the counterstroke which turned defeat into victory. The minds and not the bodies of the enemy had been overcome, for the narrow margin between success and failure could be traced to the imagination. Napoleon speculated as to the possibility of another Marengo, created by art instead of circumstance, and the name of that masterpiece was Austerlitz.

West of the Moravian village the allied armies, accompanied by the two emperors, held a plateau known as the Pratzen Heights which overlooked frozen bogs and ponds. On December 1 Napoleon saw that his opponents intended to turn his right flank, cutting him off from Vienna. All that day, therefore, he simulated the doubts and hesitations which had been real enough at Marengo. By evening the allies were fully committed to the movement, and the French emperor issued a proclamation to his troops, pointing out the enemy's mistakes and explaining his plans for beating them.

Each private thus became a partner in operations, and that night the soldiers in their shelters were visited by the leader, wearing a campaign hat and gray-green riding coat. In wild enthusiasm the men made torches of their bivouac straw, but the deluded enemy interpreted the flares as a ruse to mask retreat.

The morning of the second was misty, but at eight o'clock the sun suddenly lighted the snow-clad hills as the French formed up for battle. The superstitious Corsican read a symbolism into this phenomenon, particularly since the allied columns were already moving on his right. Every grenadier knew that this wing had been purposely stripped of troops for a mock defensive. The duty of containing the enemy was assigned to Davout and his magnificent III Corps, which had arrived late the night before after marching the 90 miles from Vienna in 68 hours. The French left had been fortified as a part of Napoleon's "calculated timidity," while behind the centre were massed Soult's divisions for the counterstroke which should split the allied army squarely in two.

"While they march on my right," the emperor had told his men, "they present me their flank." And the dullest French soldier knew that the great blow would be delivered against the allied centre on the Pratzen Heights after both enemy wings had been stretched.

Once the plan of Austerlitz has been told, there is little to add except the statistics of a battle which came up to its conception. On the French right Davout and his 12,500 men battled desperately to hold off 40,000 Austrians and Russians. With ponds and marshes to aid his defense, he gave only about a mile of ground, never losing touch with the centre. The battle was actually won in this quarter, for the allied centre had been fatally weakened when Napoleon ordered the assault on the Pratzen. After the capture of that plateau the separated wings of the enemy were beaten in detail by a tremendous local superiority at every point. The winter dusk finally sheltered the flight of losers who had left behind 12,200 killed and wounded, 133 guns and 15,000 prisoners at a cost to the French of about 6,800 casualties, chiefly in Davout's corps.

Austerlitz killed William Pitt, who died a few days later after asserting prophetically that the map of Europe "would not be wanted these next ten years." For with the news of the battle he learned that his Third Coalition had been broken when Austria sued for terms at a considerable sacrifice in territory.

JENA AND AUERSTEDT

Napoleon had departed far from the traditions of the Revolutionary past. Where Carnot's armies were inspired by a fierce patriotism and hatred of the foe, the Grande Armée gives the impression of a fine professional instrument serving an adored leader. Pillaging and disorder had been largely suppressed by imperial decree, though the requisitions of supplies still bore heavily on an occupied province. The greatest change, however, may be seen in a new attitude toward the enemy which is reminiscent of eighteenth century amenities. During the Austerlitz campaign Napoleon kept up a friendly correspondence with both opposing emperors, writing them such messages as the following to Czar Alexander:

> Sire, I send my aide-de-camp, General Savary, to compliment you on your arrival in the army. I charge him to express my esteem for you, and my desire to find occasions which will prove to you how much ambition I have to gain your friendship. I pray you to receive him with the kindness which distinguishes you, and to hold me as one of the men most desirous of being agreeable to you.

It is hardly necessary to add that these sentiments were composed for a diplomatic purpose, since Napoleon supervised the political situation

as closely as the military. During the Ulm and Austerlitz operations he
had been sensitive to the danger of Prussia on his left flank, though the
neutrality of that kingdom had been bought by a bribe of territory. After
the peace with Austria, while the Russian forces remained inactive, he
left the entire Grande Armée encamped in readiness along the Bavarian
border. Prussia had already begun calling her 200,000 troops to the
colors, and in the summer of 1806 Napoleon learned that a secret treaty
of alliance with the Russian enemy had been signed.

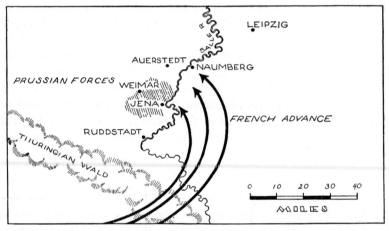

The Jena-Auerstedt Campaign

Little doubt existed in the northern kingdom that armies upholding
the traditions of Frederick would make short work of foemen who only
a few years ago had been regicides fighting in rags. Napoleonic equality
of opportunity was so despised in an army led by petty nobles that
Marshal Blücher boasted that he "would dig the graves of the French
on the Rhine." Crowds in Berlin cheered during those last weeks of peace
as a procession of well-born young men whetted their swords on the
steps of the French Embassy.

As the last exponents of pure linear tactics, the Prussian soldiers were
still beaten into obedience with "the stick" and drilled by officers who
used surveying instruments to correct the dressing of the ranks. Volleys
by command remained the dependence of an infantry which could load
and fire faster than any rival force, its battalions being trained to manoeuvre in the field with machinelike precision. On the other hand,
equipment had been allowed to deteriorate, the officers lacked field

experience, and Prussian marches lagged behind even Austrian standards.

Napoleon had won his last war by a single battle. With equal confidence he now proposed to crush the new enemy in a single breathless campaign which should sweep from one end of the kingdom to the other, paralyzing all resistance within a few weeks. Toward this end, he conceived a new strategic formation which he called the "battalion square"—a great onslaught of marching columns advancing behind covering forces which were to attack the enemy wherever he appeared, gripping and immobilizing him until Napoleon could concentrate his masses of manoeuvre for a decisive blow. It became the duty of other French covering forces to prevent the enemy detachments from concentrating meanwhile.

In September the Prussians and their Saxon allies, amounting to about 130,000, began marching southward in accordance with the national policy of seizing the initiative before the declaration of hostilities. On October 7 their ultimatum was delivered, and the next day Napoleon's 150,000 troops crossed the wooded Thuringian hills in three great columns.

The Prussians were drawn up in cordon for a first mighty battle southwest of Weimar. Instead, Napoleon swung toward the east after emerging into the plain, then around toward the rear of defenders threatened with being cut off from Berlin. The French columns, marching at the rate of twenty-five miles a day, had already closed in toward Jena and Naumburg before the war was a week old.

While awkwardly facing about to meet the new danger, the Prussians were handicapped by the magazine system on which they relied solely for supplies. Ironically, even their famed discipline proved a liability when the troops went cold and hungry rather than disobey regulations which forbade the taking of wood or provisions. The invaders, not being tied to any such restrictions, showed a much better morale when the two forces made contact.

On October 13 Napoleon concluded that he had most of the enemy before him and prepared for battle the next morning. He proposed to strike with his main force and drive the Prussians back toward Naumburg. Davout and his III Corps were already approaching that town, and Napoleon ordered his marshal to circle around to the west and cut off all retreat after the action at Jena.

The emperor concentrated in the darkness, and at daybreak on the fourteenth some 60,000 French troops were densely packed on a narrow plateau, being hidden from the enemy gunners by a fog. The remainder of his forces formed in the ravines on either flank. As the Prussians came forward in rigid lines, their commanded volleys had little effect on swarms of skirmishers firing from shelter. Four times in succession their advances were thrown into disorder before counterattacks of French columns drove them off the field. Early in the afternoon Napoleon delivered a final charge of vastly superior weight which swept away the last traces of enemy resistance.

Although puzzled by the ease of his victory, the emperor did not learn until evening that at Jena his main army defeated a large detachment which he outnumbered two to one. The main Prussian army had been defeated that same day west of Naumburg by Davout's detachment in a magnificent fight against similar odds.

Napoleon's error lay in the assumption that the enemy would not make the mistake of dividing his forces. Only two days before, the Prussians had been 100,000 strong between Weimar and Jena; then the threat of envelopment sent the Duke of Brunswick's main army retreating to the north, leaving behind the containing force which Napoleon defeated. Thus the 30,000 men of Davout's corps received the shock of 58,000 Prussians at Auerstedt, 18 miles from Jena. For six hours the little, bald-headed marshal, his face blackened with powder smoke, handled his men with such skill and resolution as to hurl back every advance. After Brunswick fell mortally wounded, Blücher and the Prussian king led cavalry charges which failed to shake the defense. At each threatened point Davout took advantage of French mobility to bring up reinforcements from elsewhere in the line, and after severe casualties the enemy retreated without interference from exhausted victors.

Of the twin disasters which befell Prussia that day, Auerstedt became the more demoralizing. It was no disgrace to be beaten by Napoleon, but the second calamity proved beyond dispute that the might of France did not consist wholly of the emperor's genius. Count von Gneisenau, who had experienced another revolution as a mercenary in America, drew the moral of Auerstedt in a few words:

> What infinite aptitudes slumber undeveloped in the bosom of a nation! In the breasts of thousands resides real genius. . . . The Revolution has set the whole strength of France in motion; and by the equalization of all the different classes and the equal taxation of property, it has converted the living strength in man and the dead strength of resources into a productive capital, thereby upsetting the old relations of States.

As he joined in the rout following the two reverses, Gneisenau saw the opposite effects of Prussian oppression. The servility of the masses, once the pride of the petty nobility, now led to the most abject humiliation a modern nation has ever known. Not only did the inhabitants refuse food to their retreating countrymen, they turned even the wounded out of doors to make room for advancing conquerors who responded with disgust and contempt.

In theory Prussia had a people's army, since every subject owed military duty under a recent law. Yet in the emergency all classes turned against the nation's defenders. The burghers of Berlin, headed by the mayor, met the invaders with an effusive welcome. French soldiers were cheered in the streets as the newspapers "lavished adulation on the victors and abuse on the beaten army."

Such exhibitions, far from moving Napoleon to pity, resulted in the harshest treatment he had ever meted out to a vanquished country. Officers and men looted at will, being permitted to plunder Lübeck as if it had been taken by storm. Large indemnities were levied on Prussia and her allies, and the emperor did not hesitate even at appropriating Frederick's sword and trophies.

The strategic pursuit began the day after Jena and Auerstedt. Davout marched the 166 miles to Berlin in 12 days, fighting two actions on the way, and arrived a few hours after the first courier brought news of the defeats. With like rapidity, other French detachments made a great sweep toward the Baltic, occupying cities and compelling the surrender of troops. On November 7, just one month after Prussia's ultimatum, the last force of the kingdom laid down its arms when Blücher's 10,000 men were hemmed in with their backs to the sea.

EYLAU AND FRIEDLAND

Without giving his soldiers time to rest, Napoleon struck at Russian enemies who had got no farther than Poland in their efforts to aid Prussia. On November 2 the reliable Davout led the march on Warsaw, followed by the other corps after the surrender of the last Prussian contingents. Recent conscripts were left to occupy the prostrate kingdom, and by December the whole Grande Armée was based in Warsaw.

While the emperor proclaimed himself the champion of Polish liberties, his able opponent Bennigsen moved into East Prussia to harry the French communications. With an army of 100,000, including 10,000 Prussians who had escaped across the border with their king, the Russian general forced Napoleon to form a defensive line south of the Baltic between Danzig and Königsberg.

The whole French scheme of making war had to be transformed overnight. Where the troops had been accustomed to marching on metaled roads and living on fertile provinces, they now found themselves on a bleak northern plain crossed only by dirt trails. All supplies had to be brought by transport from distant bases, and the invaders suffered unwonted hardships because of their lack of experience with the magazine system.

Napoleon, in short, was compelled to adopt the enemy's way of making war under circumstances most favorable to the enemy. Naturally the Russians felt at home in an environment reminding them of their own steppes. Warmly clad and inured to sub-zero weather, they took in their stride the privations which placed thousands of the French on the sick list. Bennigsen led virtually a professional army of long-term volunteers, for even in time of peace his troops had been kept in condition by long

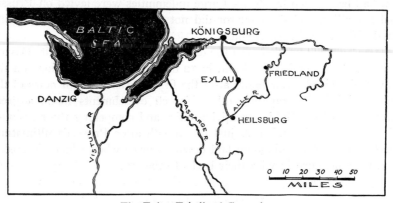

The Eylau-Friedland Campaign

marches through the empire. The Cossacks soon proved their superiority as scouts and skirmishers over the French light horse; and the Russian commander held a further advantage with his great artillery train of 18- and 24-pounders.

In view of such conditions, it is not surprising that both the Grande Armée and its leader appear to have suddenly declined. Early in February, however, he saw an opportunity which promised a great victory. With amazing rapidity, considering the miserable roads, Napoleon threw the bulk of his forces across Bennigsen's communications to Russia. He had never conceived a better plan, but his opponent escaped disaster because the French masses of manoeuvre were delayed. Thus on the snow-covered field of Eylau the emperor had only 50,000 troops against 67,000. With this strength he hoped to fix the enemy until the detachments of Ney and Davout, totaling an additional 28,000, could arrive for attacks on the rights and left.

The battle began during an early morning snowstorm in a dismal country of frozen lakes and swamps. In the centre Augereau's VII Corps advanced through the swirling flakes but lost its direction. Taking an oblique course across the Russian front, the column was horribly punished by the fire of 200 guns. During the confusion the enemy cavalry charged downhill with the wind, and only 3,000 of Augereau's 14,000 men were left unhurt. The Russian horsemen penetrated nearly to Napoleon's headquarters, sending his staff into a panic, but he coolly ordered a counterstroke by the Guard which cut the Cossacks to pieces. All day the fighting surged back and forth with the same fury. Ney could not arrive in time, but Davout's smash at the enemy's left led rapidly to the rolling up of the entire line. A French victory seemed assured when 7,000 Russian reinforcements appeared just as both sides had reached utter exhaustion after pushing through deep snowdrifts in the extreme cold. At dusk Bennigsen withdrew with losses of 18,000, and the 15,000 French casualties forbade any pretense of pursuit.

Neither army derived the slightest profit from this slaughter. Napoleon spent the winter recuperating his troops and bringing up reinforcements which gave him a large numerical advantage. In May he took Danzig after a long siege, and by the first of June his columns were in motion again.

On the fifth the emperor began a sweep to the right with the intention of cutting Bennigsen off from Königsberg and the Baltic. The 147,000 French troops swung around like a great scythe, causing the Russian to take refuge in a hastily entrenched camp at Heilsburg. Napoleon made the mistake of supposing his adversary more vulnerable, and on June 11 Murat's cavalry led the advance with Soult's corps close behind. In the absence of artillery preparation the attackers met a repulse from the enemy guns and trenches. Fresh troops could not redeem the failure, and dusk put an end to the attempt after 12,000 had been killed and wounded.

Napoleon continued an envelopment which forced Bennigsen to retreat toward his Königsberg base of supplies. The French pursued so hotly that several columns overshot the mark as the enemy made a stand on the river Alle with Friedland as a centre.

The ensuing battle is one of the finest examples of Napoleon's ability to turn a chance encounter into a decisive engagement by means of lightning concentrations. Stopping his columns in their tracks on the night of the thirteenth, he issued to each the orders for its appearance on the field next day in a co-ordinated effort.

In the morning, sure of an eventual superiority, he advanced with 33,000 troops to contain Bennigsen's 50,000. The concentration began to take effect at noon as the first columns reached the field; but Napoleon did not strike until five o'clock, when he had massed 68,000 men against an opponent with his back to the river. The enemy left being cramped into a bend of the stream, the emperor selected this spot for his main blow. The Russians resisted with more than their usual valor, and several assaults by Ney had been thrown back when a new tactical development turned the tide.

On his own initiative the French artillery general Sénarmont collected 36 guns in two batteries at a distance of 250 yards. These pieces, just out of musket range, were soon opening gaps in the helpless ranks of the enemy infantry with canister and grape. After a few minutes of this carnage, the French battalions had little difficulty in routing a shattered foe. The Russians attempted a cavalry counterattack, but Sénarmont changed front with his guns to take the horsemen in flank with a murderous discharge.

This was the beginning of the terrible artillery preparations which would soon result in masses of cannon, wheel to wheel, firing salvos of case shot from point-blank ranges. Napoleon perceived the advantages of the innovation as his infantry forced the Russian centre across the river while the other wing broke into flight. Bennigsen's losses amounted to nearly 30 per cent of the army, but the obstinacy of his defense is shown by French casualties of 12,000 in the final battle of the war.

V

THE WAR ON THE PENINSULA

The habit of Napoleon had been to astonish and deceive mankind, and he came at last to deceive himself.

—WELLINGTON

A FEW days after Friedland the victor and Russia's ruler met on a raft in the river Niemen. Far from taking a narrow advantage of his triumph, Napoleon offered an alliance as a climax to the policy of persuasion he had been following since Austerlitz. This time the young and idealistic czar responded to the conqueror's wooing. Where he had lately visioned himself as fulfilling a divine mission to defend "the sacred rights of mankind," he now agreed that France and Russia were geographical allies.

The other nations could only look on helplessly while the emperors of the East and West gave every appearance of dividing the world between them at the Peace of Tilsit. Prussia was dismembered, being stripped of all territory west of the Elbe and most of her Polish acquisitions. A new Polish state, with a liberal constitution dictated by France, was created in the Grand Duchy of Warsaw. In return for these concessions, Russia was to have the Danube principalities and her own will with Finland. Yet even these stupendous changes were dismissed by Napoleon as trivial. Soon, he declared, the two emperors would join forces for the conquest of India.

In less than seven years a French soldier had won all this power in fair fight. As Pitt predicted on his deathbed, the map of the Continent had become obsolete. It now consisted of France and Russia, with Austria lying between them as an unhappy buffer nation. Only Sweden and Portugal, protected by remoteness, dared assert any friendship for England, the single nation remaining at war with France. The rest of western Europe had become a hodgepodge of duchies and principalities which Napoleon either ruled or held in a bondage of fear. In many instances the authority over these puppet states had been given as a reward to marshals or members of the Bonaparte clan.

Civilians might profess to see signs of military weakening in the costly draw of Eylau and the repulse of Heilsburg, but soldiers knew better. They knew that Napoleon's campaign in East Prussia had been one of his greatest triumphs over colossal difficulties. Never had he shown more tactical adaptability.

Since 1800, under his administration, the conscription law had brought in a minimum of 60,000 recruits annually, rising to a total of 210,000 in 1805. Many of these veterans, lured by loot and victory, became professional soldiers for life, forming a permanent cadre of the finest military material in Europe. Toward this result, no modern leader has ever equaled Napoleon in his ability to fire men's imaginations while not neglecting to fill their pockets. Heroes such as the redheaded, tobacco-chewing Ney might thrive on a religion of glory, but most of the marshals preferred riches and titles. Subordinates and the rank and file shared in proportion, while in his Legion of Honor the emperor revived the system of decorations which Louvois had found an incentive to morale.

Even the uniforms bespoke the transition in French military ideals since Carnot's exile. Plain republican blue had been replaced by a rainbow gamut of costumes in the triumphant mood of grand opera. Vanquished capitals now were treated to a pageant of sabretache and dolman, of lofty shako and nodding plume, of brass helmets and gleaming cuirasses and the enormous bearskin busbies of the Guards. The climax was not far distant when Murat would impress the childlike Cossacks with his aigrette of ostrich and heron feathers, gold collar and belt, pink riding breeches, canary-yellow boots, gilded stirrups, sky-blue saddle cloth and final trimmings of leopard fur hung with crimson tassels.

Hidden by such overwhelming trappings, a few early symptoms of decline had indeed begun to appear, but they could be traced back to Austerlitz rather than Eylau. Up to his greatest triumph of sheer skill, Napoleon depended on manoeuvre to produce the "heaviest battalions" in which he trusted so implicitly. After that success he shocked Metternich with his cool comment, "I can use up 25,000 men a month."

Conscription promised an endless supply of French cannon fodder, and the next two campaigns reveal a growing emphasis on weight. The "hurricanes of cavalry" were not yet in evidence, but Napoleon had begun to increase his squadrons of heavy-armed cuirassiers. At Jena 60,000 foot soldiers were huddled together within range of enemy guns, and Friedland began a new artillery era in which brutal masses of cannon would gradually replace skirmishers depending on speed and marksmanship.

But these signs were faint as yet, and in 1807 few observers could have foretold from Napoleon's tactics that there would never be another Austerlitz. His mistakes in grand strategy were more apparent. Intuitive as he was on the battlefield, the emperor often showed himself insensitive to the political aspirations of his own day. Judged by his later writings, he seems seldom to have realized that his conquests were due not only to military might but also a message of hope brought to Europe's millions on the points of French bayonets.

"We come to give you liberty and equality," growled old Marshal Lefebre in a Franconian town. "But don't lose your heads about it—the first person who stirs without my permission will be shot!"

This naive proclamation, of course, illustrates the growing tyranny of Napoleonism. But it also offers a clue as to why so many thousands of Poles, Germans and Italians fought for the conqueror of their own free will. They could not forget that Lefebre himself, beginning as a private in the Royal Army, had taken fifteen years to reach the rank of sergeant. After the Revolution he needed only half that time to win a marshal's baton and a title. His wife, though retaining her hearty mannerisms, had stepped up meanwhile from battalion washerwoman to Duchess of Danzig.

Frenchmen, in other words, were freemen as compared to European masses whose serfdom had been tempered only by the whims of benevolent despotism. Already an uneasy stirring could be felt throughout the Old World, as if these masses vaguely sensed the approach of some springtime of the human race. The political and industrial growths of the last thousand years were putting out new roots; and if the conqueror had but known it, Europeans stood ready to welcome the prophet of the new age of steam.

Up to this time Napoleon appeared a promising candidate. He had revised not only the warfare but also the laws and finances of his day. Beginning with his money difficulties of the Italian operations, he had learned how to make francs serve him like soldiers. so that his cam-

paigns became wholly self-supporting without imposing an intolerable
burden on the vanquished.

Naturally the new source of mechanical power, now past the experimental stage, was regarded with dread as well as hope. The dullest
peasant or artisan could see that the thermodynamic engine threatened
to overthrow systems of industry and transportation which had served
with few changes since the Dark Ages. Europe cried for a new Moses
to lead its troubled masses into the Promised Land, and Napoleon
listened without comprehension!

The proof of his deafness came abruptly in 1808. For only a few
months after reaching the pinnacle of his influence, the conqueror took
his first step toward Waterloo by invading Spain.

Then, for all of his audacity, he revealed the limitations which account
for his downfall. Far from becoming the prophet of the age of steam, he
showed himself to be merely another benevolent despot. Where Europe
asked for a vision of the future, he groped back into the past for a
Carolingian legend that had been embalmed since the Dark Ages. And
since history punishes stupidity even more swiftly than evil, the world
soon had the unprecedented news of a French army laying down its
arms. The reaction had begun, and all the revolutionary promises which
Napoleon had sown like dragons' teeth were about to sprout into armed
hosts for the destruction of Napoleonism.

THE SURRENDER AT BAYLEN

The occupation of Spain lacked even the excuse of military expediency,
since that country had been France's most consistent ally. But being
helpless on the sea, Napoleon resolved to starve England's trade with
his continental system. Portugal represented a weak link in this counterblockade, and in a secret treaty France and Spain agreed to divide the
kingdom between them. Not only were French soldiers to be given free
passage through Spain, but the weak and corrupt government agreed to
furnish troops and supplies.

Even these concessions did not satisfy the emperor, and early in 1808
he treacherously occupied Spanish fortresses. By April 100,000 French
troops were in the country, and Napoleon interfered to place his brother
Joseph on the throne after an uprising caused the abdication of Charles IV.

Although the Spanish people detested their former rulers, the entire
country rose in revolt at the prospect of an alien monarch. Within a few

weeks 100,000 rebels were in the field—brave but untrained and ill-equipped volunteers under inexperienced leaders.

In this crisis Napoleon might well have recalled that he had ridden to power on the crest of a people's war. France fought with all her might, both human and material, against nations which held war to be no affair of the ordinary subject. These monarchies left the fighting to groups of specialists which served the ruler; and once such forces were beaten, the ministers had little choice but to ask terms. Sometimes a few hours of combat might decide a war, as when the Hapsburg empire made peace after Austerlitz. But when a French army met defeat, another soon marched out to replace it, as Carnot demonstrated in 1793.

It seems incredible that Napoleon should so imprudently have taken the risk of his own best weapon being turned against him, yet he reacted like a Charlemagne chastising the pagans. After giving orders for the Madrid insurrection to be put down with ruthless severity, he set his other forces in motion to cope with the disturbances in the provinces.

Unfortunately for the emperor, the instruments of his wrath consisted largely of recent conscripts, sent to Spain to complete their training. These forces made little headway against patriots defending their homes. Gerona and Valencia beat off French attacks; Saragossa resisted with memorable tenacity; and the misfortunes of the invaders were capped by an event which stunned all Europe—the surrender of a Napoleonic army which had hardly struck a blow.

After crossing the Morena chain into Andalusia, a detachment of 20,000 under Dupont sacked Baylen and Cordova with the ferocity shown in all these operations. Then retracing his steps in the blasting heat of July, the French general sent part of his strength ahead to hold the mountain passes while he followed with an enormous train of booty. Two Spanish forces, made up in part of regulars, took advantage of this dispersion to close in from front and rear. Dupont's untried conscripts failed him in the emergency, and after a weak effort to break through, he consented to the parleys at Baylen which resulted in the surrender of his remaining 18,000 men.

The revolts in Spain and Portugal gave England the opportunity to land small expeditionary forces, and the following month another French army capitulated near Lisbon. As a preliminary General Junot's detachment of 13,000 took a sound beating from the 17,000 troops of Sir Arthur Wellesley. The victor had good prospects of capturing the French remnants, but at the Convention of Cintra his superiors sent Junot's men home by sea on condition that they evacuate Portugal.

This general had driven a good bargain in view of his hopeless situation, but the disgrace at Baylen ranks with a decisive battle in its moral significance. On receiving the news, the emperor gave way to rage and grief. "When honor has been lost by a shameful capitulation in the open field," he declared, "nothing can restore it."

Although the next day had been set for Joseph Bonaparte's entry into Madrid, the surrender had an electric effect on the Spanish uprising. Enthusiasm and weight of numbers soon drove the French back across the Ebro, and within a week the new monarch had to flee from his capital.

"A conqueror, like a cannonball, must go on. If he rebounds his career is over." This remark, made by Wellington years later, applies to Napoleon's predicament in the late summer of 1808. He solved it by taking personal command of new armies totaling a quarter of a million, while England placed an expeditionary force of 40,000 under Sir John Moore.

The rebound at Baylen had brought on total war.

Napoleon's Campaign in Spain

The emperor himself must be held responsible for the French policy of terrorism. "You will never get to the end in Spain except by vigor and energy," he instructed his brother. "This attitude of clemency and kindness leads to nothing."

The French generals needed little encouragement, since their opponents had not shrunk from any excesses. Within a few months both sides had exhausted every resource of reprisal. The invaders sacked nunneries and butchered civilians, while the Spanish guerrillas went to such fantastic lengths as poisoning wells, plunging prisoners into boiling water and sawing a captured officer in two. The horrors of the period were depicted with great art as well as propaganda by the Spanish painter Goya, whose weird and appalling etchings have left a permanent record.

When Napoleon crossed the Pyrenees in late October the rebels were drawn up in four armies along the line of the river Ebro. The success at Baylen had led to the delusion that raw levies could face the emperor's veterans in the field. This belief was brutally shattered by a succession of rapid French blows which routed all four forces within a few weeks. Napoleon scarcely troubled to use his skill against opponents who took to flight after the first shock, just as eager but undisciplined recruits have always fled from disciplined soldiers.

The way to Madrid lay open and French advance guards occupied the city on December 2. Then at the climax of his easy triumph the emperor had the astounding news that Moore's army was advancing on his rear. At once the French dispositions had to be changed to deal with the new opponent.

Early in November the English general had marched out of Portugal with vague orders to aid the Spanish armies. Leading 22,000 troops, he counted on a junction at Salamanca with 18,000 reinforcements under Sir David Baird which had landed at Corunna. The news of the Spanish defeats and the fall of Madrid left Moore without an objective, and he formed the bold plan of moving on Napoleon's communications at Burgos.

On December 17 he joined forces with his subordinate as an intercepted dispatch from Berthier gave him knowledge of the French dispositions. Learning that Soult's corps of 20,000 held an isolated position, Moore resolved to fall upon this opponent. He had no illusions as to the risks, since more than 100,000 enemy troops lay within striking distance, but the English commander planned to "run for it" if threatened with encirclement.

All preparations had been made for attacking Soult when news came that Napoleon was advancing with every division within reach. Moore realized that audacity had reached its limits, and on Christmas Day he began one of the most famous retreats in history.

The emperor, with his disdain for British land forces, could not at first credit his adversary with such daring. Then he took personal command of 42,000 troops and assigned an equal number to Soult and Junot for an enveloping movement.

During the ensuing chase Moore not only outwitted but also outmarched his pursuers. Evading first one and then another while fighting rear-guard actions at every step, he crossed the mountains of Galicia in rain and snow. Within a week Napoleon found the pace too strenuous and left Soult with orders to continue. On January 11, after fearful hardships, Moore reached Corunna with his thinned and exhausted ranks, only to find the fleet of embarkation delayed by storms. Soult attacked with superior numbers and met a complete repulse in the battle of Corunna, though the British victory was saddened by the commander's death from a wound.

Wolfe's well-known poem about the midnight burial created a romantic legend, so that Moore has been remembered as a hero rather than a general. Nevertheless, the scientific spirit of the fallen leader lived on long afterward, making possible the methods which balked Napoleon on the Peninsula. No greater military scholar and trainer of men ever wore the British uniform, for Wellington's successes may be traced directly to his reforms.

It has been noted that French skirmishing methods owed to lessons taught by the American Revolution. Seldom in history has a war had such a potent influence, for Moore's doctrines were also derived from his participation in that struggle. Returning to England as a twenty-two-year-old captain, he saw the losing army discredited and starved for funds during the next fifteen years. Colonels became the proprietors of regiments bought and sold like cattle; and "army brokers" fattened on a traffic in enlistments which filled the ranks with boys, old men, weaklings, criminals and even lunatics.

Almost singlehanded, Moore attacked these abuses with the zeal of a crusader as he slowly rose to a brigadier's rank. His opportunity finally came in 1803, when public indifference to military affairs was dispelled by the threat of a Napoleonic invasion. Then as commander of the famous camp at Shorncliffe, he created the tactical laboratory of the Peninsular operations.

At this time linear tactics were on the decline in European armies which now copied Napoleon's methods as frantically as they had once imitated Frederick's. Moore had been second in command of the expeditionary force which cleared the French out of Egypt, but he did not share in the prevailing awe of enemy formations. On the contrary, he saw in the line and its fire power the most effective defense against bayonet attacks in column.

Cornwallis had already applied an American lesson by introducing two ranks instead of the three prescribed by Prussian infantry regulations. Moore went a step further at Shorncliffe by training three regiments of riflemen for his Light Division, soon to become the most celebrated British unit of the Napoleonic campaigns.

The two-rank formation—the "thin red line" of the Peninsula—gave a much wider front for musketry with the same number of troops. But Moore foresaw the need of missile effect at longer ranges to break up French shock attacks before they could be pushed home. The American operations had shown that the rifle doubled the distance and accuracy of infantry fire power, and the Light Division became the largest body of troops in Europe to be armed exclusively with the new weapon.

British standards of marksmanship would doubtless have been held in contempt by Morgan's frontiersmen, nor could the short-barreled British rifle compare with the American firearm. Later results on the

Peninsula were to prove, however, that the soldiers of the Light Division had received sound training in skirmishing, mobility, scouting and woodland fighting.

Moore's conceptions were also aided by an English artillery invention which became the single effective new weapon of the Napoleonic wars. In 1784 Major Henry Shrapnel perfected a spherical case-shot shell, named after him, which enabled a burst of leaden balls to be fired into enemy infantry at an extreme range of 1,200 yards, or about three times the maximum of ordinary case shot. The time fuse exploded an opening charge which scattered the bullets and the fragments of the hollow iron container to cause deadly execution under favorable conditions. Military conservatism delayed the adoption of the shrapnel shell until 1803, but both Moore and Wellington were quick to recognize its value.

The Congreve rocket of this period proved to be less successful, though its "red glare" has been immortalized in the American national anthem. Invented by the artillerist for whom it was named, the weapon was discharged much like an ordinary signal rocket to explode a small shell by means of a time fuse. But neither its force nor accuracy were satisfactory, and Congreve's innovation came to be esteemed chiefly for moral effect.

At the Shorncliffe camp Moore not only reorganized the tactics of the army but also took a leading part in building up a national militia as a secondary line of defense against the expected invasion. Within a few months 342,000 civilians were armed and given rudimentary training under their own officers. The chief benefit of this undertaking, as it proved, was to unite the English people in their determination to fight to the end against Napoleon.

In a like manner Moore managed within a year to inspire a neglected army with new professional pride and fighting spirit. Opposing the lash as the main resource of discipline, he insisted on the moral as well as physical development of the rank and file. For a generation it remained a distinction to have been an officer promoted by Moore, and the influence of Shorncliffe may be traced directly down the years to the final victory at Waterloo.

WELLESLEY'S CAMPAIGN OF 1809

After the English debarkation from Corunna the French overran the Peninsula. The Spanish armies had been beaten in four battles during the winter as Sir Arthur Wellesley landed 26,000 troops at the mouth of the

Tagus in April, 1809. That month Austria went to war again, and the British expeditionary force had as its object the detaining of Grande Armée units which might otherwise have been sent to reinforce Napoleon on the Danube.

England's new commander-in-chief, exactly the emperor's age, had gained a reputation for safe rather than dashing generalship in India. He held an uncertain position with his small army on the Tagus, for Soult had invaded Portugal as far south as Oporto, while Marshal Victor lay at Merida, forty miles from the eastern frontier, with another French detachment of superior numbers. Between these two enemy forces on the British right and left were only a few bands of discouraged Portuguese rebels.

The prospects of an immediate British victory seemed dubious, but Wellesley had already remarked two grave enemy handicaps. First, no co-operation existed between the armies of Soult and Victor, although both were under the nominal command of King Joseph. As a second and more fatal weakness, the French forces had been compelled to spread out dangerously in order to wrest supplies from a hostile and impoverished countryside.

Moore had recognized that line fire power offered the antidote to column shock attack, and Wellesley now saw that an army regularly supplied from the sea had a tremendous advantage over forces providing for themselves in the French manner. In rich provinces Napoleon gained mobility as a result of living on the country; but the hills and arid plains of the Peninsula could only limit the movements of soldiers who had no other source of food or forage. Troops could not be massed for long campaigns, while small detachments invited the vengeance of native guerrillas.

A master of the logistic side of war, Wellesley organized mule pack trains to bring provisions over Portuguese trails too poor for wheeled vehicles. Thus only a few weeks after his landing, despite the seeming odds against him, he won a smashing victory over Soult in which food played a larger part than gunpowder.

This marshal, vexed by the usual French supply problems, had no choice but to scatter his forces to the north and south of Oporto. Wellesley brought his strength up to 40,000 by uniting with raw Portuguese levies, and on May 7 he advanced northward with complete secrecy. Crossing the river Douro above the town, he took Soult by surprise and soon had the entire French army in flight. Only the timidity of a British subordinate, General Murray, saved the routed troops from destruction, but Soult lost 6,000 men and all of his artillery before finding a refuge at Lugo.

Wellesley halted his pursuit because of news that Victor was advancing in his rear. He naturally assumed that this move aimed at co-operation with Soult, but events proved it to be merely an independent reconnaissance. Soult and Ney had quarreled meanwhile as they drifted southward toward the Tagus. Thus by coincidence rather than strategic design,

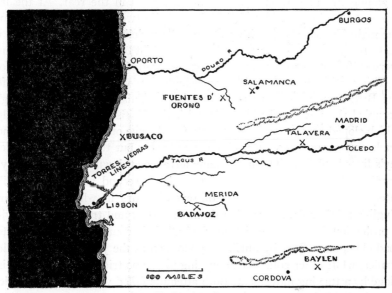

The Peninsular Operations

the French soon had 100,000 men within striking distance of Wellesley.

The British commander, made overconfident by the wrangling of his opponents, now proposed an audacious march on Madrid in combination with General Cuesta. On July 17 the 56,000 allies, about 36,000 being Spanish troops, drove Victor up the Tagus Valley. During the march Wellesley experienced the handicaps of the enemy as he and his aged colleague disagreed. Victor retreated until reinforced by King Joseph up to a strength of 46,000, then the allies in turn were pushed back to a defensive position. The monarch pleaded with his supposed subordinate to wait until Soult's arrival would insure an overwhelming French superiority, but Victor declined to share the expected glory with another marshal. Hence on July 28 the first test of line and column took place at Talavera.

Wellesley is unique among generals in that he managed to select the same sort of ground for most of his major engagements. From this first Peninsular battle down to Waterloo, he habitually posted his troops behind a low ridge which protected them from ricocheting cannon balls while compelling the French columns to advance uphill. A screen of British riflemen was thrown out along the forward slope to meet the enemy skirmishers on their own terms. If possible these light troops lingered to harass advancing columns which were also being subjected to a galling fire of shrapnel shells from the guns in the rear. At the last moment the sharpshooters fell back, and the two ranks of infantry met the main French shock with platoon volleys delivered from distances of 50 to 100 yards. A bayonet counterattack might be ordered if the columns were sufficiently shaken, and the cavalry awaited to pursue a broken foe.

This tactical formula, with surprisingly few variations, accounted for the British successes on the Peninsula. At Talavera the Spanish right occupied the town and vineyards, with the British left holding a ridge which sloped gently down to a brook. On the eve of the battle the French made some progress with preliminary attacks, but the next day Wellesley's lines held firm. The first enemy advance at dawn was repulsed by a deadly volley and infantry counterattack. A second assault met a like fate. Then came a curious lull of several hours in which French and English soldiers drank together from the brook and traded tobacco with a professional courtesy which marked all their contacts. At noon Victor made his great effort by hurling 14,000 men at the junction of the allied armies, while other columns amounting to 16,000 tried to take the British ridge by a turning movement. Both attempts failed with heavy casualties, though the British were severely handled as a consequence of pushing their counterstroke too far.

The French losses were given as 7,268, and the 5,363 British killed and wounded represented a fourth of Wellesley's strength. The small extent of the Spanish participation is shown by casualties of less than 1,000. Next day both armies remained in position, and that evening Victor and Joseph retreated to cover Madrid.

Cuesta refused to advance farther, though his colleague had been rejoined by the Light Division after a march of 43 miles in 22 hours, equaling the best Napoleonic records. Wellesley's disgust soon turned to chagrin when news came that Soult and Ney were endangering his communications. Hundreds of wounded were left behind in the haste of a withdrawal accompanied by disputes which ended all co-operation between the allies. The British general reached Portugal after a perilous retreat, and in honor of his victory he was created Viscount Wellington of Talavera.

THE BATTLES OF ASPERN AND WAGRAM

Many accounts of Frederick's and Napoleon's campaigns leave the impression that Austrian armies existed chiefly for the purpose of providing their opponents with victories. Nevertheless, it must not be supposed that the whitecoats were soft adversaries; for the empire which lost battles had a habit of winning wars. Thus in the end neither Frederick nor Napoleon took much joy of their triumphs, while Austria emerged from both struggles without serious losses in prestige or territory.

Austerlitz marks a break with tradition, but after that defeat Vienna made determined preparations to fight Napoleon again at the first good opportunity. During the brief war Archduke Charles had won his country's sole victory by beating Masséna in the hard-fought battle of Caldiero in Italy. As a reward, despite his comparative youth, he was made generalissimo of the armed forces and president of the Aulic Council which had so often hampered his moves.

Charles set himself the immense task of creating a nation-in-arms out of an empire in which the average peasant or burgher had no concern with war. Due to his influence, political reforms were granted to give Austrians some measure of the Revolutionary liberties which Napoleon now found so annoying. A mild form of conscription supplemented the volunteer system, with promotions being based more often on merit. The French plan of corps was adopted, even to the units of varying strength which Napoleon favored as a means of deceiving the enemy. French formations of skirmishers and columns were likewise prescribed for troops made independent of their former magazines and unwieldy baggage trains.

Although handicapped by ill health, the thirty-eight-year-old prince built up an establishment of 300,000 within two years by using cadres of professional troops to train his new citizen-soldiers. Both the cavalry and artillery were much increased to cope with recent Napoleonic mass tactics, and Charles placed particular emphasis on improved staff work.

His army was not yet ready in 1809, but the surrender at Baylen convinced the archduke that his opportunity had come. Thus the French emperor's intervention in Spain had the immediate effect of raising Austrian as well as English land forces against him.

Napoleon began preparing with his usual resourcefulness to meet the new danger. As early as January, on arriving in Paris from his Spanish campaign, he issued orders for calling up the 1810 class of conscripts a year in advance. Forces totaling 63,000 had been left across the Rhine since the Peace of Tilsit, and these corps were strengthened as new ones were formed.

By March both nations were rushing headlong toward a collision without much pretense of secrecy. During these final preparations Napoleon had a unique advantage in the signal telegraph (now extended into Germany) which enabled Paris to receive news in hours while Vienna waited days. As reports of the Austrian moves reached him, the emperor issued complex orders for a French concentration about Ingolstadt to counter a threat from any direction.

It is a truism of history that nearly all generals are bolder in theory than action. Exactly the reverse proved true of the Austrian prince, who now prepared to snatch the initiative away from his redoubtable adversary, though his military treatises were noted for prudent doctrines. In March Charles moved most of his forces into western Bohemia with the plan of crossing the mountains and advancing in a single great mass of

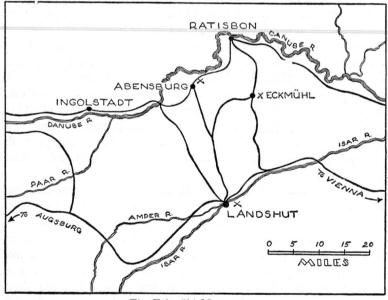

The Eckmühl Manoeuvres

manoeuvre while the French were still dispersed. Battles were to be forced on the enemy wherever encountered between the river Main and Black Forest, the object being to detach from their reluctant French alliance the 100,000 troops of Saxony and the Confederation of the Rhine.

It was a conception worthy of Napoleon himself, and subsequent events proved that it had an excellent chance of succeeding. At the last moment, however, the emperor and Aulic Council interfered after finding the design too daring. Over his protests the archduke's forces were ordered from Bohemia to the south bank of the Danube for an advance toward the Isar. A month's time was lost in making the change, and it is a justifiable conjecture that Austria also lost the war as a result.

In spite of Napoleon's instructions to Berthier, named commander-in-chief in his absence, the French units were badly dispersed as the enemy crossed the river Inn. Davout's left wing near Ratisbon was separated by seventy miles from Masséna's right at Augsburg, while only light covering forces remained in the centre to prevent the Austrians from splitting the army asunder.

The signal telegraph having brought him reports, Napoleon left Paris at 5 A.M. on April 13. Night and day the carriage sped toward the Danube with frequent changes of horses as the emperor dictated orders. At 4 A.M. on the seventeenth he reached Donauwörth to complete a trip which takes 18 hours by a modern express train. By the nineteenth, after 48 hours of running fights between covering detachments, he had reunited his right wing and centre near Ingolstadt and taken the initiative away from the archduke.

Not only had Charles missed his opportunity, but the lengthening of his lines placed him in the peril which the French had just escaped. Napoleon did not fail to perceive such openings, and on April 20 he concentrated after all-night marches to strike the enemy's centre near Abensburg and drive a wedge between the right and left wings. About 7,000 Austrians fell in this straggling fight which left the archduke's forces near Ratisbon completely separated from General Hiller's troops about Landshut.

Now came a curious historical repetition of the Jena-Auerstedt situation as the emperor fell upon Hiller's detachment with most of his strength, not realizing that Davout's corps was beset by the archduke's main army near Ratisbon. On the twenty-first Napoleon's much superior forces inflicted losses of 5,000 on Hiller's retreating Austrians at Landshut; and that same day Davout sent word to the emperor, "All the enemy's army is in front of us. I am occupying the height of Eckmühl, which is on my right. The battle is very lively."

At this point one cannot help wondering what Napoleon's career might have been without Davout, who has received small credit either from his patron or historians. The aristocrat of the marshals in birth and education, the stern, smooth-pated little man had no interests in life except war and the waltz. In both he achieved a cold and meticulous distinction, though his aloofness caused him to be respected rather than liked by associates. Entirely lacking in political ambition, he displayed a generalship which ranks him among the most talented soldiers of the age, for at Eckmühl his dispatches guided Napoleon to the foremost French victory of the war.

After Davout had pointed out the opportunity, the emperor moved from Landshut by forced marches to unite with his hard-pressed marshal and overwhelm the archduke on the twenty-second. By dusk the Austrians had been routed with losses of 5,000 prisoners and 6,000 slain and wounded. A French pursuit might have brought on a disaster, but Napoleon contented himself with limited results.

Within a week he had split the enemy forces squarely in two while defeating them in three combats. Years later, at St. Helena, the emperor was still to tingle at the memory: "The greatest manoeuvres which I ever made, and for which I gauge myself the highest, took place at Eckmühl, and were infinitely superior to those of Marengo or other actions which preceded or followed."

The whitecoats had fought well in every engagement, but the new army and its untried generals could not manoeuvre against Napoleon and his veteran officers. As consolation the Austrian rear guard repulsed the French at Ebelsburg, giving the archduke time to reunite the two parts of his army on the north bank of the Danube.

The way to Vienna lay open, and Napoleon pushed down the south bank, receiving the only slight wound of his career in the storm of Ratisbon. On the march his edicts against straggling and disorder hint at the deterioration in the ranks since Austerlitz. Hardships could not be blamed for such lapses, since an imperial order of May 14 fixed the daily ration of the soldier at 24 ounces of munition bread, 4 of soft bread, 16 of fresh meat, 4 of rice or dried vegetables, an ounce of brandy and a bottle of wine or beer.

A better explanation may be found in the fact that Frenchmen were weary of endless warfare, as their growing opposition to conscription showed. Austrian morale, on the other hand, had improved perceptibly since 1805. Instead of capitulating as before, Vienna put up a stout resistance in which civilians took part; and the garrison surrendered only to save the city from fires started by three days of French bombardment.

Napoleon had counted on the enemy's asking for terms after the occupation of the capital, but Charles stood across the river with a reinforced army. Captured freight boats were used by the French engineers to build a great pontoon bridge 2,000 yards long between the right bank and the large wooded island of Löbau. From this position only a minor channel remained to be bridged to permit the passage of troops to the Marchfeld, a broad plain dotted with villages of stone construction.

The emperor's successes around Eckmühl seem to have given him an almost fatuous confidence, for on May 21 he sent 30,000 troops across from Löbau as if the enemy did not exist. The archduke's lack of interference was interpreted as sloth, but he had actually been waiting to trap as many of his foemen as possible. At noon he struck with the full force of 85,000 men, and the out-numbered French battled desperately to hold Aspern and Essling.

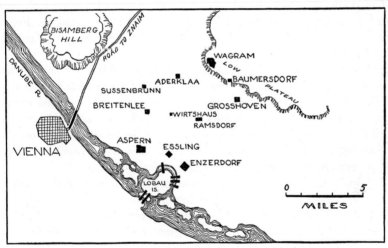

The Aspern-Essling Campaign

The villages lay too close to the river to be turned, so that the Austrian columns were compelled to deliver costly frontal attacks. Aspern changed hands several times before dusk, and every stone house in Essling served as a stronghold of bloody street fighting. As a final effort Napoleon hurled masses of cuirassiers in the centre against Austrian cannon defended by infantry squares, but the horsemen eventually had to retire after fearful losses.

During the night, as the opposing forces bivouacked within musket shot of one another, the emperor put across reinforcements which brought his strength up to 77,000. At 7 A.M. he launched an assault of sheer weight at the enemy centre as Lannes pushed forward with a ponderous column of infantry. The Austrian line had been broken when the slim, blond archduke, hatless and holding aloft a standard, led his last reserves in a counterstroke which repulsed the mortally wounded Lannes. Next the whitecoats recaptured Aspern, and worse news came when Napoleon learned that his great bridge to the south bank had been cut by enemy barges.

The French retirement to Löbau began in the afternoon as the archduke inflicted grievous casualties on both flanks. By nightfall more than 100,000 men were huddled together on the island, sharing the stunned realization that the emperor had met his first major defeat. The Austrian losses were given as 22,000, and Napoleon's can scarcely have been fewer, though he did his best to minimize the extent of the reverse.

That night the darkness of Löbau fell over one of the most glooomy scenes in military chronicles. The beaten army, cut off from the French forces on the south bank, had neither provisions nor hospital facilities. It had lost even the moral support of leadership, for the shock plunged Napoleon into a stupor of depression. The hero of this black hour proved to be an agent of healing as Surgeon General Larrey took virtual command. Without pausing to ask the emperor's leave, he ordered cavalry horses to be killed for soup boiled in the cuirasses of dead troopers. Until dawn Larrey and his aides labored with the thousands of wounded, performing amputations by lantern light; and it is to Napoleon's credit that he rewarded the surgeon by making him a baron.

Although communications were resumed next day over the repaired bridge, the emperor was so shaken that for the second time in his life he asked advice of his generals. Without an exception they urged retreat, but he at last decided that another and greater attempt must be made.

If the Eckmühl manoeuvres had revealed the inexperience of the new Austrian army in staff work and command, Aspern demonstrated that Charles and his citizen-soldiers were the equals of the French on the battlefield. In tacit admission, Napoleon made it plain that he would rely on his superior bulk in the forthcoming clash. By stripping his long line of communications he concentrated nearly a quarter of a million men, of which 182,000 were to take part in the battle. Against this array the archduke could raise only 128,000, with the bare possibility of 40,000 weary reinforcements if his brother, Archduke John, reached the field by forced marches from Hungary. Charles had 410 guns to his opponent's 470, but his 4,600 cavalry must meet 29,000 French horsemen.

Following Aspern the island of Löbau had been transformed into a fortress bristling with cannon. On July 5 Napoleon cleverly feinted in the direction of Essling, but during the night he had put up seven new bridges over which his troops poured to occupy a line to the east, stretching from Enzerdorf to Grosshoven. The archduke, deceived into awaiting the attack between Aspern and Essling, showed remarkable adaptability in changing front. During the first day, however, he confined himself chiefly to defensive fighting in which his outweighed left wing repulsed a massed assault.

That night Napoleon gave orders for a great effort in the centre at dawn on July 6, but his adversary forestalled him by taking the offensive before daybreak with an attack aiming to cut the French left off from the bridges. By 11 A.M. the whitecoats were making such progress, led by the wounded archduke in person, as to place Napoleon's whole army in danger. Again he faced the stark possibility of defeat as the outnumbered Austrians swung in to separate his left from his centre. Only on the right, where Davout made headway toward Wagram, could the emperor find encouragement.

In his anxiety the French leader ordered a counterstroke based on human tonnage rather than any pretense of skill or surprise. Summoning every infantry battalion within reach he gave Macdonald the command of 30,000 men advancing shoulder to shoulder in a gigantic hollow square against the Austrian centre. At the head of this tactical monster 104 guns breathed grape and canister, while dense squadrons of cuirassiers brought up the rear.

With cool resourcefulness Charles hurried forward batteries on both flanks which ploughed red furrows through the helpless ranks. No soldier witnessing this sickening spectacle could escape the realization that Napoleon was buying victory with blood after art had failed him. Like a great wounded beast dragging its entrails behind it, the column lurched past Wirtshaus with ponderous halts and starts, leaving a ghastly trail of wounded and dying at every step. Finally the Austrian foot fought the mass to a standstill, and Macdonald appealed for still more guns and men.

"Tell him that the battle is won!" said the emperor. And so it was, thanks to Davout's generalship on the right wing, where his advance had already taken him past Wagram. At 2 P.M., facing the peril of his whole line being rolled up from left to right, Charles retired in perfect order toward the Bisamberg Heights, unmolested by any pursuit. Every French officer knew meanwhile that Napoleon had been more clearly outfought and outgeneraled than at Aspern, for the victory of Wagram owed principally to the failure of the archduke's reinforcements to arrive. When their advanced patrols at last put in an appearance at 5 P.M., the strain on French morale was revealed by a widespread panic such as the Grande Armée had never known before.

Napoleon's casualties were 30,000, including 7,000 prisoners, while the Austrians lost 19,000 killed and wounded in addition to 5,000 captives. Five days passed before the emperor risked another encounter. He found Charles still full of fight after withdrawing to a strong position in the hills near Znaim. Several tentative French attacks had been repulsed on July 11 when Emperor Francis sent an envoy to propose an armistice which Napoleon eagerly accepted. In the end a financial crisis rather than military reverses had driven the Hapsburg ruler to ask for terms.

THE TORRES VEDRAS LINES

Austria's greatest soldier never took the field again, for his health soon forced him into retirement. Even so, he had toppled Europe's god of battles from his pedestal of invincibility, with moral effects which would become increasingly fatal. Never after Aspern and Wagram would Napoleon's opponents believe him invulnerable. Never would the Grande Armée itself, from marshals to grenadiers, recover a faith that had once been a shining sword.

Only two such dramatic struggles could have accomplished this result, but on the Peninsula the strength of France continued to be drained by the slow poison of attrition. It has been conservatively estimated that an average of 100 conscripts a day left their bones on those tawny plains in proof of a contemporary saying, "Spain is the death of the soldier, the ruin of the officer, and the fortune of the general."

Certainly the cupidity of the marshals had much to do with arousing hatred, for towns were sacked without any military excuse. Napoleon's subordinates, those fearless young blades of the early years, had modeled themselves only too faithfully in the image of the imperial master. By 1810 most of them were on the way to becoming middle-aged opportunists, more interested in loot and luxury than their profession. The custom of bringing mistresses into the field grew so common that a captured French officer remarked to Wellington, "You, sir, have an army—we are a traveling brothel!"

Napoleon's supervision from Paris only proved that autocracy as well as democracy has its limitations in making war. At a glance it would seem that every advantage must go to the dictator with absolute powers, since the fumblings and hesitations of a parliament are painfully obvious. Yet it remains a fact that marshals in Spain received orders based on reports about Wellington which the emperor derived from English newspapers. Such intelligence, of course, was likely to be somewhat stale after completing a circuit of several months by way of Lisbon, London and Paris.

Napoleon displayed a similar lack of realism in dealing with every Peninsular problem; and his scoldings of beaten marshals (long after the event) bear a curious resemblance to the "armchair criticism" which soldiers despise when it is of civilian origin. Hence it is significant that the best results in Spain were gained by the commander most neglected by the emperor.

In 1809 a ragged and unpaid French army of 10,000 was assigned to General Suchet, who had distinguished himself in the Marengo campaign. Two days later this demoralized force ran from Spanish guerrillas, yet the new leader soon made it into an instrument of victory. Operating in Aragon and Catalonia, he reconquered both provinces without a single serious reverse. His opponents were British generals—Blake, O'Donnell, Murray and Mackenzie—who tried to duplicate Wellington's successes. Although they had the same advantages of supply, sea power and native allies, Suchet beat them in two pitched battles, five sieges and a score of combats. In four years his small army captured 82,000 prisoners and 1,415 guns to win him the belated reward of a marshal's baton.

Napoleon himself might have learned a lesson from this commander's administration. Suchet not only put an end to French looting, including that of King Joseph, but actually refunded money extorted by his predecessors. Treating the conquered with scrupulous fairness, he created employment by transforming the sad ruins of Saragossa into new parks, hospitals, orphanages and schools. By admitting Spaniards into a share in the government, he won their respect to such an extent that soldiers of the army of Aragon were able to go unarmed among the peasantry.

The brutal contrast in other parts of occupied Spain accounts to a large extent for Napoleon's most costly military failure. Soult, who aspired to become King of Portugal, could not send a message without an escort of several hundred cavalry. Masséna, Ney, Victor and Marmont all suffered more from the reprisals of irregulars than the efforts of Wellington. These partisan bands, numbering from a few hundred up to several thousand, often showed real skill and discipline under their own natural leaders. Fighting in mountain districts which every man knew intimately, they could disperse when hard pressed, only to reunite the moment the invaders' backs were turned. As to the value of such operations, no less an authority than Sir John Fortescue has declared that the guerrillas were the real heroes of the final victory on the Peninsula.

Wellington's appraisal of this asset, combined with his advantage in supply, left him confident in 1810 when his force of 60,000 faced two armies under Soult and Masséna of about 65,000 each. During the winter he had thrown up the famous lines of Torres Vedras about 25 miles north of Lisbon. Two low ranges of hills were studded with 87 connected redoubts mounting 290 guns. This system defended the Lisbon peninsula from the Tagus to the sea; and with the consent of the Portuguese government, Wellington devastated the outlying provinces after evacuating the unfortunate inhabitants.

Masséna thus marched into a man-made desert of empty towns and barren fields with an army depending on the country for food. Before retiring within his lines, Wellington ventured and won a defensive battle at Busaco on September 27. The British general took his favorite position behind a ridge, and Masséna could not dislodge him with a superiority in numbers. The riflemen of the Light Division had the better of the preliminary contacts; then Ney's assaulting troops climbed the slope under a storm of shrapnel before being repulsed by the steady volleys of the redcoats. The French forces accepted a reverse with 4,600 casualties, while the losses of the victors amounted to only 1,200.

The consequences of absentee generalship were shown during the following winter, when Masséna "blockaded" the Torres Vedras lines in stubborn obedience of the emperor's orders. How the French army subsisted is a mystery which has puzzled historians, but the besieged were meanwhile enjoying regular sea-borne supplies from their homeland. In April even the resolute marshal had to withdraw with his army in rags and near to literal starvation. He had lost 25,000 men slain, captured and dead from disease or malnutrition in operations which Napoleon dismissed with the criticism, "This campaign was not reasoned out, therefore it was not methodical."

Wellington cautiously pursued, and on May 5 Masséna retraced his steps from Salamanca to deliver a general attack at Fuentes de Orono. The British commander made mistakes in his dispositions which he freely confessed afterwards; but the steadiness of his infantry enabled him to repulse his adversary with losses of 2,200 as compared to 1,500 casualties of his own.

The British remained on the defensive throughout 1811. During the Torres Vedras campaign the Spanish fortress of Badajoz had secured the southern gateway to Portugal, but the loss of this stronghold now forced Wellington to divide his army. After twice failing in attempts at recapture, he found it a sufficient task to defend both main lines of entry with his limited numbers. Sometimes, indeed, he escaped defeat only because of his foreknowledge of the enemy's next move. For the French, subsisting on a meager country, must plan their strategy according to the harvest, and Wellington had only to estimate the food at their disposal.

Not until 1812, with war between France and Russia imminent, could he attempt a prolonged offensive. In February he besieged Badajoz for the third time, at last capturing it by escalade on April 5 with losses of 5,000. For 48 hours his troops were out of hand, and Wellington saw drunken excesses which a sensitive nature could never pardon. He condemned his men in public terms of loathing, and their respect for him was seldom warmed by affection. Even so, all ranks had a faith in his ability which found justification on the field of Salamanca.

Wellington's greatest Peninsular battle took place in July after a race for position in which Marmont's army of 47,000 marched parallel to him for several days, often in plain sight. The British general, with about equal numbers, finally saw an opportunity to isolate his adversary's left wing. Sending Pakenham's division around in a long flanking march, he drove through the gap between the French left and centre, and a final cavalry charge completed the enemy's ruin. Marmont's losses were 15,000 at a cost to the allies of some 6,000 casualties.

The victor might perhaps have destroyed the routed army with a vigorous pursuit, but he wisely chose the political benefits. The route to Madrid lay open, and on August 12 his forces made an entry which marks the turning point of the war. From that moment the initiative remained with the allies, and in less than a year the last invader had been driven from the soil of Spain.

VI

THE ROAD TO WATERLOO

Had I died at Moscow I should have left behind me a reputation as a conqueror without a parallel in history. A ball ought to have put an end to me there.

—NAPOLEON

STATISTICS, so seldom to be trusted throughout military history, are particularly open to doubt in Napoleon's campaigns. The French conqueror, like Frederick before him, added or subtracted for purposes of shaping opinion, leaving historians the task of arriving at an estimate. But even allowing for this factor, it would appear that at least 450,000 troops were assembled in June, 1812, for the invasion of Russia. Frenchmen composed no more than a third of this host, for their growing opposition to war forced the emperor to make his allies provide most of the men and funds.

Of the 363,000 who crossed the Niemen on the twenty-fourth, only the Polish contingents, still believing in Napoleon as their liberator, showed any zeal for the work ahead. The Germans, Austrians and Italians marched as a result of compulsion, and thousands deserted at the first opportunity. Even the French rank and file revealed a declining morale, for the emperor's Russian adventure had been deplored by most of the marshals and generals.

The causes of the war may be traced to the continental system which had been indirectly responsible for the invasion of Spain. Napoleon had already annexed Holland in his efforts to enforce the blockade, thus destroying his last hope of peace with war-weary England. Next his divorce from Empress Josephine and marriage to Marie Louise led to a lukewarm Austrian alliance which alarmed Russia, so that hostilities became inevitable after Czar Alexander's renunciation of the continental system.

As a master of propaganda, Napoleon proclaimed a modern crusade in which he represented his "army of twenty nations" as upholding the liberation of nationalities against Asiatic despotism. Unfortunately for his ends, the invasion of Spain and annexation of Holland were still fresh in memory, while Alexander had shown himself to be a sincere if somewhat bewildered European liberal. Hence a majority of the emperor's alien troops proved to be a military encumbrance, for even his Austrian allies had no intention of taking more than a nominal part.

Napoleon's growing preference for bulk over quality is evident in the Grande Armée of 1812. Berthier is authority for the statement that many conscripts of the past few years went into action without ever having fired more than a few shots intended to teach reloading. Even in its great days the French infantry had never depended on musketry, but a similar laxity may be noted in the training of skirmishers. In 1809 the new Austrian army held its own with the French in irregular tactics, while on the Peninsula the English demonstrated a marked superiority. In a combat of 1811, for instance, 3,000 riflemen of the Light Division attacked 11,000 infantry of Regnier's corps at Sabugal and administered what Wellington described as a "handsome dressing."

French losses had not yet been so severe that the decline could be blamed on a poorer quality of conscripts. The explanation is rather to be found in the deterioration of the emperor's powers as a commander. While brooding over his first defeat in the gloomy hour of Löbau, he evolved new tactical theories which were later summed up with his usual coherence:

The invention of powder has changed the nature of war. Missile weapons have become the principal ones; it is by fire and not by shock that battles are won today. . . . In the open field, as in siege warfare, the gun plays the chief part; it has effected a complete revolution. It is with artillery that war is made.

No fault could be found with this doctrine, for every great captain since Ján Žižka has eventually come to believe in the supremacy of fire power. Frederick's early victories were won by musketry combined with the shock of bayonet and saber, but ruinous losses taught him to trust to his big guns for salvation. A similar transition is evident in Napoleon's military creed after Aspern, though he put his ideas into effect with much less consistency.

The gap between his theory and practice has convinced many critics that the French conqueror was not a great tactician as compared to his genius in strategy and the hybrid art known as grand tactics. For if he increased his guns to a proportion of three to each thousand troops, he also added enormously to the strength of the heavy cavalry, an arm which had no usefulness except in shock attack. Meanwhile the emperor neglected the missile effect of the musket and rifle in spite of his assertion, "The power of infantry lies in its fire."

Even in his emphasis on artillery the former gunner displayed remarkably little adaptability. He missed entirely the lesson of the howitzer left by Frederick, though Wellington did not fail to benefit from it. Nor did

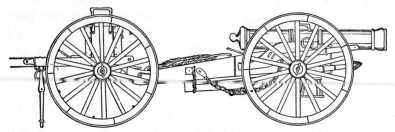

French 12-Pounder

Napoleon profit from the shrapnel shell, an enemy invention tested at his expense in Peninsular battles. His new appreciation of fire power, in short, led simply to a multiplication of the 12-pounders—the emperor's "pretty girls"—which at Friedland had blasted gaps in the ranks of the opposing foot.

Whether or not there is any psychological connection, his skill seems to have declined in direct proportion to his reliance on mass. At Wagram the victory, if such it may be called, had been won by Davout's flank attack without much aid from the emperor's monstrous column of bayonets preceded by cannon. There was a singular lack of co-ordination between the two efforts, yet the column came to a halt under terrible punishment while Davout made headway with the old Revolutionary tactics of mobility.

Three years after this costly triumph Napoleon repeated all of its worst mistakes on the field of Borodino. It is a curious circumstance that on the eve of action Davout urged the desirability of a flank attack which would have made the engagement almost a copy of Wagram. The imperial master refused because of his fear that the enemy might escape him, since by this time he had come to regard battle as the sole key to decision.

The Romans had taken centuries to complete the historical transition from formations of mobility to phalangial density. Napoleon needed less than a decade, for at Borodino he created virtually a single great column out of his army by massing 130,000 men on a front of about two miles, giving an average of more than 20 men to the yard. With this solid array he delivered an attack on the centre in simple parallel order—an attack so devoid of all tactical art that it can only be explained by the French aphorism, "Nothing fails like success."

The Retreat from Moscow

The events leading up to Borodino show a corresponding deterioration. That the time for the advance had been unwisely chosen was revealed when a third of the horses died from eating green forage. In the heat of the steppes hundreds of men perished from sunstroke, and from the outset straggling became a serious problem. The two Russian columns retreated meanwhile into the emptiness of the plains after devastating the countryside—Barclay over the road taken by Napoleon, and Prince Bagration on a parallel southern route.

It had long been remarked in the Grande Armée that Pauline Bonaparte's lovers advanced from her couch to positions on the imperial staff. Nepotism had less amusing consequences when Napoleon gave his brother Jerome the command of a detachment sent to destroy Bagration's column before the two Russian forces could unite. Jerome showed his incompetence by four days of complete inertia, and the opportunity passed before he was replaced by Davout.

In the first five weeks Napoleon lost a third of his troops while covering 200 miles. During this time his strategy miscarried so badly that he missed three chances to beat in detail the foemen who as yet had taken no losses worth mentioning. Even the French occupation of Smolensk, the first goal of the advance, became a hollow triumph when the burning town was evacuated without a fight by the united forces under Marshal Kutuzov.

The Russian generals at last decided to make a stand before Moscow, and early in September their army of 121,000 awaited the French at Borodino, 70 miles from the city. After some preliminary fighting on the fifth, Napoleon launched a direct frontal attack the following morning, depending on his 400 guns to open the way for cavalry shock. Closely as he had massed his troops, the Russians huddled even more densely on their centre, where the principal French efforts were aimed at the "great redoubt." The guns of both sides thus had a perfect target for discharges of ball and canister, and after a fearful slaughter Murat's cuirassiers swept the field in a thundering charge which broke the enemy line. The infantry followed to swarm up the face of the redoubt, which fell only when the defenders were annihilated.

These gains were the only results the French had to show for their 32,000 casualties. The Russians, despite losses of 42,000 in the bloodiest battle of the age, fell back to a new line and continued to return the French fire until dusk. Napoleon has been criticized for not making his victory decisive by a final attack of the Guard, which had seen no action all day, but he concluded that a further outpouring of blood would not be justified. At least he had opened the way to Moscow, for Kutuzov retreated under cover of darkness without pursuit by the exhausted French cavalry.

In several of his early battles Napoleon had shown that a frontal attack need not be artless if planned by a general who knows how to use up his opponent's reserves while conserving his own. Hence the fault of Borodino lies not so much in the method as a lack of central direction which left the marshals on their own resources. Napoleon's stupor during the critical hours was so pronounced that it has been attributed to preliminary symptoms of the ailment which ended his life.

However this may be, the emperor still gave the appearance of a sleepwalker upon entering Moscow a week later. In spite of his experiences in Spain, the fires set by the Russians failed to convince him that he faced another people's war which could not be concluded by a fortunate stroke. For nearly six weeks he lingered amid the charred ruins, hoping for peace overtures from a czar who declared, "My campaign is only beginning."

The legend of the climate defeating Napoleon is so firmly established that historians have never quite been able to overcome it, though all agree that Russia had seldom known such extended mild weather. Indiscipline and the breakdown of command were actually responsible, since the army had been reduced to 90,000 effectives before ever reaching Moscow. Supplies for six months remained in the city, but the golden autumn days passed by while the emperor could not decide whether to retreat or go into winter quarters. Once the order for retirement had been given, he could not bring himself to abandon the loot and guns which soon accounted for the death of his overworked horses.

The memoirs of survivors leave no doubt that the domes of Moscow were scarcely out of sight before the army began to disintegrate into a disorderly mob. Neither the weather nor the pursuing Cossacks inflicted a fraction of the losses which resulted daily from insubordination. Again, as in Egypt, Napoleon found that troops marching in a hollow square could easily repel irregular horsemen; but thousands chose to throw away their muskets and risk death or capture for the sake of their stomachs.

Ney's prodigies of valor in rear-guard operations enabled some 50,000 gaunt troops to reach Smolensk, the sick and wounded having long ago been sacrificed in a heartless *sauve-qui-peut*. Light snows and cold nights were encountered, yet the climate remained miraculously clement all the way to the Russian border, where the unfrozen Berezina could be forded by horsemen. Firm and intelligent direction might still have saved the wreck of the army, but the crossing of the river on November 26 revealed the final failure of the command. While Surgeon General Larrey operated on the wounded in the open air, many line officers had become too concerned with their own salvation to enforce order. The result was a terrible panic on the bridge as thousands of men died by drowning or being trampled underfoot.

On December 8 Napoleon set out for Paris after placing Murat at the head of the starving troops. The cold had now grown severe as the retreat turned into a headlong rout; and though Russian pursuit ended at the Niemen, the Grande Armée had already accomplished its own destruction so thoroughly that only a few hundreds ever lived to see France again.

THE DOWNFALL OF THE EMPIRE

During the winter, as the storm gathered about France, Napoleon worked at top speed to create a new army. In spite of the losses in Spain and Russia, the astonishing fact remains that he had not yet drawn as heavily upon national resources in man power as did French generals of a century later. His lack was in trained soldiers rather than the raw material of conscription; and he solved it in part by appealing to the patriotism of National Guards who had volunteered for home defense only. Using these units as his cadres, he called up fresh drafts not only from France but also Italy and the German states. Thus by the end of March he confounded his enemies by marching toward the Elbe with

200,000 troops, few of which had received more than the rudiments of instruction.

Napoleon was equally surprised when he realized that Prussia had secretly armed against him. Shame having been added to defeat by the exhibition of cringing after Jena, the emperor felt it safe to limit the Royal Army to the size of a national police force. While appearing to obey the imperial edict, General Scharnhorst contrived to train thousands of men from the underground societies of defense which honeycombed the realm. By 1813 his system had produced a hidden national army, and the Russian débâcle provided the opportunity for a general uprising.

French ideas had worked a more lasting conquest than French bayonets, for Stein and other German patriots blamed past oppressions for the disgrace of 1806. Hence we have the strange spectacle of Revolutionary boons being extended to Prussians in a spirit of benevolent despotism, with the paradox completed by the fact that neither Stein nor Scharnhorst were natives of the kingdom. As crusaders for Germanic liberties, both men supported the Edict of Emancipation, which freed Prussian serfs in 1810. The abrogation of class distinctions soon followed, and degrading punishments were abolished in the army.

Although the petty nobles groaned at such reforms, they were ready to take any steps to expel the invaders. Early in 1813 the surrounding of several garrisons led to a general French withdrawal, and in April Napoleon faced Prussian forces among the 200,000 allies opposing him in Germany. Bernadotte, now crown prince of Sweden, also joined the list of France's enemies as Austria and the German principalities awaited only a good opportunity.

"I shall conduct this war as General Bonaparte," said the emperor in tacit admission of past lapses. Certainly his first swift moves recall the slim young commander of 1796, able to do without sleep and take an active part in the next day's fighting. Again he seemed to have recovered his old energy as the French drove ahead in the familiar order of an advance guard of all arms followed by masses of manoeuvre poised to strike.

On May 1 the first units entered Lützen. Wittgenstein, who had replaced Kutuzov, planned to contain the advance guard and send the bulk of his Russians and Prussians around to surprise Napoleon's right rear. The following morning, on the battlefield where Gustavus fell, the emperor became aware of the enemy's design. At once he massed for a counterstroke in his right rear while ordering the advance guard to fight a defensive battle in front. Within a few hours the allies had been out-generaled as Napoleon first beat off their flank attack, then marched in his reserves behind 100 guns firing canister at musket range. The assault tore a great gap in Wittgenstein's line, and only the French lack of cavalry permitted the defeated army to make an orderly retreat after severe losses.

The emperor outdid his marshals in this engagement by appearing everywhere in the field to encourage young conscripts who behaved well in their first test. Legend even has it that he helped to serve the guns, applying the toe of his boot in several instances to scared recruits who needed persuasion.

While still possessing a superiority in numbers, he followed the beaten allies to Dresden, where they gained four days in their retirement by blowing up the stone bridge over the Elbe. On the twentieth Napoleon at last caught up with them at Bautzen, and in spite of their strong position he planned a battle of destruction.

The 100,000 Russians and Prussians occupied trenches and redoubts behind the river Spree, with marshes offering additional obstacles to an advance on their left and centre. Nevertheless, Napoleon began his attack in that quarter with the 100,000 troops of the main army, and by dusk he had crossed the stream to force the defenders back to secondary positions. His object in this first day's fighting had been to fix the enemy while Ney's detachment of 60,000 completed a wide sweep around the allied right rear to cut off all retreat.

At daybreak on the twenty-first the emperor made a pretense of resuming the fighting as he awaited Ney's decisive stroke. In the confidence of success he took a morning nap, but at that very moment his favorite marshal committed one of history's most memorable blunders. Having received penciled orders to arrive in Blücher's rear by 11 A.M., he duti-fully halted because he had reached his destination an hour early in a crushing surprise. Even the protests of Baron Jomini, his chief of staff, could not budge the redheaded marshal from this fatal decision.

Never were lost minutes more costly to Napoleon, for his subordinate's delay gave the enemy barely enough time to avert destruction. Thus when the emperor launched his main blow with 80,000 troops and massed guns, he achieved only empty gains in the centre. Ney had no better success, upon resuming his advance, against forewarned opponents who had been preparing ever since his appearance to make good their retreat.

Bautzen might have been the victor's greatest triumph since Austerlitz, but he failed to capture a single trophy as the allies retired in good order. The casualty list proved a further disappointment, since the French had 20,000 killed and wounded as compared to 13,500 enemy losses.

Shaken by the narrow margin of their escape, the allied generals continued to fall back during the last days of May. Then to their astonishment Napoleon presented them with the equivalent of a victory by opening negotiations for an armistice of six weeks. This decision, which many critics have termed the most serious military error of his whole career, was motivated by the emperor's "want of adequate cavalry," according to the excuse he gave afterward. In more vital respects, however, the suspension of arms could scarcely help but favor the enemy. The retreating army had already been pushed back into a weak position, and another French victory would probably have kept Austria out of the war.

That want of energy rather than cavalry had been the reason was to be hinted by the emperor's subsequent actions. The promise of his opening burst of activity had not been fulfilled, for two incomplete successes restored the lethargy which led to ruin in Russia. The summer of 1813, indeed, can only be compared to the delay in Moscow when Napoleon could not decide whether to remain or withdraw. Now he faced an even more momentous decision as the allies agreed on terms of peace which were surprisingly moderate from their point of view.

As Austrian mediator between the belligerents, Metternich asked for the independence of Spain and Holland, the restitution of Illyria, the reconstruction of Prussia with an Elbe frontier, and the renunciation of the French protectorate over the Duchy of Warsaw and the Rhine Confederation. The acceptance of these conditions would still have left Napoleon with power and territory beyond the wildest dreams of Frenchmen when he became consul in 1800. Even a year of recuperation at this time might have renewed his armed strength, but again the conqueror could not make up his mind. Again the days passed in indecision, and only when it was too late did he send a note of virtual acceptance. The message reached Prague just a day after the Peace Congress had broken up, and the procrastinator had his answer as Austria's 200,000 troops were added to his foes.

At least his failure as a negotiator had been compensated by military gains during the past six weeks. When hostilities were resumed on August 16, he had a much larger force of cuirassiers under Marshal Murat, whose photographic eye for terrain made him the greatest cavalry leader of the age in shock attack. The French artillery had been increased to 1,200 guns, and reinforcements brought the total strength up to about 350,000 of all arms against nearly half a million allies.

As a final strategic asset, Dresden had been fortified with a view to a vast campaign along interior lines. Around this central bastion on the Elbe the French forces were grouped in readiness to spring at any of the three armies approaching in concentric columns from the north, east and south.

It was by no means a hopeless military situation that the emperor faced in his first purely defensive campaign. Again, as at Lützen, he began operations with a seeming recovery of his old audacity as 100,000 French troops advanced on Berlin. The moral effect of such a capture would have been tremendous, but after years of defeat the generals of Europe were becoming familiar with the "Napoleonic touch." Far from being disconcerted, the allies had anticipated this very move and set a trap. Thus while Blücher simulated a desperate retreat toward his capital, the 200,000 Austrians and Russians under Schwartzenberg planned to cross the Bohemian mountains and move down the Elbe to surprise Dresden.

Napoleon was not so easily to be taken in, and on comprehending the situation he decided to cross the mountains and fall upon Schwartzenberg's rear. This bold conception had to be amended when he learned how near the allies were to his fortress, but the emperor showed all his old skill and daring in the counterstroke. Leaving Macdonald to contain Blücher and sending Vandamme's corps to cut off Schwartzenberg's retreat, he hastened back to Dresden with the bulk of his forces to offer a decisive battle. No more remarkable march is recorded in his career, for the young French troops covered 90 miles in 72 hours, moving in mass across the country. On August 26, just as the allied attack commenced, the army reached Dresden in time to win the last great victory of the empire.

At 5 P.M. Schwartzenberg sent six columns against the southern suburbs, and 300 guns covered the assault of allies who had adopted Napoleon's artillery tactics. The first impact struck St. Cyr's vastly outnumbered garrison troops, but reinforcements poured in as Napoleon's advance units entered the city to join in the fighting without a moment's rest. The emperor himself set an inspiring example by riding up and down the lines, and French soldiers never fought more fiercely. The redoubts in the centre were taken and retaken, but at dusk a counterattack led by Ney drove the enemy out of all captured positions.

Heavy rains that night gave the more mobile French forces an advantage, and reinforcements continued to arrive in the darkness. Even so, Napoleon could oppose no more than 97,000 men to double those numbers when he seized the initiative at daybreak.

The allies had meanwhile fallen back to the heights overlooking the town. For the first time in his life the emperor planned an attack on both flanks combined with a holding battle in the centre. This conception, imposed largely by the nature of the ground, was carried out with brilliant success. While the guns of the French centre kept up an incessant cannonade, Ney opened the engagement with an infantry assault which made rapid gains on the allied left. On the other flank Victor's infantry and Murat's cavalry advanced through the mud to break up and capture whole battalions. In both operations the superior mobility of French field guns played the decisive part.

Late in the afternoon, after a worried council of war, the beaten generals ordered a retirement. In 24 hours of fighting they had lost 38,000 men, including 20,000 prisoners, at a cost to the French of less than 10,000 casualties.

At this moment Napoleon undoubtedly had a chance to end the war by delivering one of the vigorous pursuits of his early years. His troops were exhausted, to be sure, and the wretched state of the roads did not invite further efforts. On the other hand, the distress of the equally exhausted losers became so acute that 1,000 wagons and 200 guns or caissons were left along the route.

In the allied rear Vandamme waited with 40,000 troops, providing the strategic anvil against which a Napoleonic pursuit might have pounded the retreating army to destruction. Instead, Vandamme himself was destroyed when the emperor delayed so long as to leave him without support in the midst of overwhelming numbers.

This same week news reached Napoleon that the detachments of Oudinot and Macdonald had both been beaten with heavy losses by Prussian forces. The gains of Dresden had thus been wiped out by three defeats taking a toll of 60,000 casualties.

For these reverses the emperor had only his own system of warfare to blame. From the beginning he had emphasized physical over intellectual valor to an extent which stifled all initiative on the part of subordinates. Only four of his marshals ever showed ability at independent command, and their talents were developed without encouragement from the imperial master.

At this time the prematurely aged Masséna had retired from active service, and Suchet had his hands full in Spain. Both St. Cyr and Davout remained with the emperor in Germany, and it is a significant fact that he assigned these able field commanders to fortress duty, the one at Dresden and the other at Hamburg. Ney was still the Napoleonic ideal of a marshal, and only ten days after the battle of Dresden that brave blunderer led a fourth detachment to defeat at Dennewitz with new losses of 15,000.

The emperor's last triumph had surpassed either Friedland or Wagram, but no longer did his enemies seek peace after a smashing reverse. For in 1813 he faced a people's war in which most of Europe found a common cause; and the moral effect of Dresden was outweighed by the four allied victories over subordinates. The emperors of Austria and Russia had taken the field with Schwartzenberg's army, making plain their determination to press forward, regardless of losses, until Napoleon had been thoroughly beaten.

As an ominous portent of the future he learned now that Wellington's army had invaded France after defeating King Joseph at the battle of Vittoria. Only a miracle of generalship could have saved the emperor at this late date, but he seemed utterly unable to grasp the imminence of disaster.

Various reasons have been advanced by historians for the periods of inactivity which multiplied after Dresden. At the age of forty-four the corpulent emperor had doubtless lost some of his physical vigor, yet the seventy-one-year-old Blücher proved to be the most energetic commander in the field. It is more likely that the explanation lies in the field of psychology; that the French conqueror, like so many lesser men facing failure in middle age, took refuge in a happier dreamworld. Once he had made an ally of mud and snow while pressing the enemy harder, but three weeks after his victory a September rain brought the revealing admission:

> Yesterday and this night are so frightful that it is impossible to move. . . . Write to Murat, to Mortier, Macdonald and Poniatowski, that the frightful weather which continues today makes every movement impossible, and that if tomorrow the weather betters, preparations are to be made for the day after.

The enemy did not let such conditions halt the armies gradually closing in from three sides to threaten Napoleon's communications. Meanwhile, though the French troops were starving in a district picked bare of supplies, their leader let a month pass in vacillation. It had become apparent that he must abandon Dresden and fall back toward Leipzig, yet not until October 7 could he make the decision. Even then he left St. Cyr and 30,000 garrison troops behind to be captured at Dresden, while an equal number were immobilized at Hamburg under Davout. In his hour of need the emperor had formed the habit of scattering his forces, though his early victories were won from generals who gained nothing by trying to hold everything.

The climax came swiftly. Bernadotte closed in from the north, Blücher from the east, and Schwartzenberg from the south—a total of about 325,000 troops led by their crowned heads as well as commanders. Napoleon, having missed several openings to strike back in detail, could only withdraw his 214,000 men in a semicircle about the bridgehead on the Elster.

On October 16, the first day of the battle, the French outfought and outgeneraled their encircling foes. Napoleon seemed aroused to his full powers as he shifted units from one point to another to gain a local superiority. His artillery kept up a continuous thunder such as Europe had never heard before, and at the close of the day a tremendous counter-stroke had the allied left in distress. The Russians and Austrians finally had to call on their last reserves to save themselves from disaster.

A French victory might still have been possible, but on the seventeenth the emperor became a prey to one of his fits of lassitude. Far from exploiting the confusion he had wrought among his foes, he allowed them a full day of rest and reorganization. The next morning Bernadotte's forces added their weight to an assault which slowly forced the defenders back into a constantly narrowing semicircle in front of Leipzig. In the left centre the struggle became so furious that Russians and Austrians advanced over the bodies of comrades who had been repulsed in previous attempts. The last French hopes vanished that afternoon when 35,000 Saxon allies went over to the enemy; and after sitting in a stupor for several hours the emperor gave the belated order to retreat.

Unfortunately, no new bridges had been built to supplement the single span over the Elster. Throughout the night the beaten forces streamed across the river, but on the nineteenth thousands remained to add to the confusion in the narrow streets as the allies stormed the town. Still, nearly all might have escaped but for the mistake of an excited subaltern who blew up the bridge too soon, condemning 20,000 rear-guard troops to capture or drowning. These losses, added to the killed and wounded, made a total of 50,000 French casualties. Varying figures are given for allied losses which could hardly have been less than 30,000.

Although Leipzig stands out as the most prodigious battle of the age, the issue was decided by minor tactics. Only numbers redeemed the weakness of allied generalship, for Napoleon's broken army was suffered to retire without interference from victors who might readily have won peace for Europe.

After a few days the allies followed in a leisurely manner, trusting to the fact that Wrede and his 50,000 Bavarians stood in the path of Napoleon's retreat. This army, which had lately deserted its French alliance, held a strong position with 100 guns as the emperor's vanguard of 30,000 approached Hanau, with the Rhine only two marches away.

Never in any past triumph did a Napoleonic host appear more magnificent than this tattered remnant which almost literally rode over the forces barring the way. In a swift artillery manoeuvre General Drouot galloped up with 50 guns to enfilade the whole Bavarian line. The infantry fell to its work with an air of silent fury, preparing the way for a final cavalry charge organized by Napoleon himself. Within a few hours Wrede's army had been cut to pieces in atonement for Leipzig as French soldiers fell back to defend their own soil for the first time in twenty years.

THE CAMPAIGN IN FRANCE

Even now Napoleon could have had terms of conciliation from the war-weary allies. The Russian and Austrian emperors had been fighting primarily for peace, and memories of 1793 made both hesitate at the prospect of invoking another people's war in France. The emperor thus had a final opportunity to spare his country the ravages of invasion, but again he demanded too much until the time for negotiation had passed. In the end Prussia's hunger for spoils and revenge dominated the allied councils, and Blücher crossed the Rhine on the first day of January.

For all of his pretensions to modern thought, Napoleon revealed a concern for his territory and dynasty which might have been expected from a Hapsburg ruler of the sixteenth century. With most of Europe in arms against him, he still had thousands of veteran soldiers immobilized in such distant outposts of the empire as Danzig, Hamburg, Catalonia and the Italian fortresses. In the event of defeat these garrisons must share the fate of St. Cyr's men at Dresden, and meanwhile they could only subtract from the numbers needed so sorely to win an ultimate victory.

In his desperation the emperor decreed a *levy en masse* which filled his ranks with "mere children," for the campaign of 1813 had finally drained France's resources in man power. After the neglected fortresses of the border had been manned, he could count on scarcely 70,000 field troops to meet more than three times their numbers of veteran foemen.

Not a moment could be spared for training the new forces. The brigades were stiffened with the old soldiers who remained, and in his need for officers the emperor accepted volunteers from the Invalides whose wounds had not fully healed. Where once he had commanded his hundreds of thousands, he now instructed his brother Joseph as to the defense of Paris, "Place 50 men at each gate armed with muskets, 100 with fowling pieces and 100 with pikes. Thus each gate will be defended by 250 men."

In his German campaign Napoleon's failure had been one of execution, for his plan was sound and his strength sufficient. Now during these winter months of 1814 the reverse held true. With a fantastic lack of resources and a plan almost hopeless of accomplishment, he achieved a brilliance of execution which can only be compared to the victories of

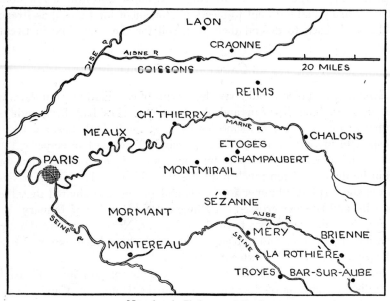

Napoleon's Defense of Paris

1796. Never once did he falter or lose faith against crushing odds. Never did he spare himself or become a victim of the indecision which had nullified his efforts of the last few years. In short, General Bonaparte had at last come back to redeem the errors of Emperor Napoleon; and only a dead soul could fail to be stirred by the military drama of the next few weeks.

In keeping with the atmosphere of Greek tragedy, he fought his first action on the grounds of the military school at Brienne which he attended as a homesick boy. Late in January the armies of Blücher and Schwartzenberg united on the Aube after a converging march from the Rhine. Their vast superiority in weight made them careless until Napoleon surprised the Prussian headquarters on the twenty-eighth. Blücher and his chief-of-staff Gneisenau narrowly escaped capture in the reverse, and next morning they fell back to La Rothière to accept a battle which could not be avoided because of the traffic blocking roads to the rear. The emperor attacked again on February 2, but snowdrifts prevented him from bringing up enough artillery to win a decision.

The new French troops were surprisingly steady in both encounters. In a few days, so remarkable was Napoleon's genius for leadership, he had imbued this mixed force of peasant lads and old troopers with a spirit of victory. Over country roads which had become bogs after a recent thaw, they followed him tirelessly as the leader launched a bold new offensive against the Prussians.

The Cossacks had never been gentle invaders, but the worst atrocities in France were committed by the Prussians and other Germans whose submission to Napoleon had been the most abject in Europe. Blücher's route from the Rhine was marked by burning villages, and violence to noncombatants led to reprisals which could not be checked by wholesale executions. These excesses were in contrast to the moderation of Austrian troops and the humane treatment of inhabitants as Wellington pursued Soult's beaten Peninsular army toward Toulouse.

The expediency of the Prussian methods might have been doubted as operations were transferred to the valley of the Marne. In general Frenchmen had proved too exhausted after twenty years of strife to wage a people's war, but local uprisings of the peasantry handicapped Blücher everywhere.

The question of spoils having become of paramount interest, the Prussian monarch wished his army to reach Paris first. While carrying out these orders his general met delays both from the weather and the harassing of francs-tireurs. Hence he had separated his columns widely for subsistence and protection when Napoleon struck like a hurricane to inflict four defeats in five days.

Starting from Troyes, the emperor's 20,000 foot, 10,000 horse and 120 guns overcame terrible hardships in a march of complete secrecy. On February 10 he surrounded Olsuviev's corps so swiftly that scarcely a man escaped being killed or captured. This blow cut the Prussian army in two, and Napoleon defeated Sacken's corps on the eleventh in a battle at Montmirail. Without checking his momentum, despite the hunger and fatigue in the ranks, he struck Yorck on the twelfth at Champaubert to win a third victory. The thirteenth was devoted to pursuit, but the following day the French took Blücher both in front and flank near Étoges, punishing that general so severely that he barely saved his force from destruction.

Although the Prussians had double the total numbers, they were beaten with a local superiority in each of the four clashes. The sum of Blücher's losses amounted to 20,000 as he abandoned his Marne campaign and withdrew toward Châlons in a retreat which fell little short of a rout.

The disaster led to an allied council of war on the fifteenth in which a general retirement was advocated. Before this plan could be put into effect, Napoleon took advantage of his position between the two armies to strike Schwartzenberg's flank and win three new victories at the expense of the Austrians and Russians.

On the fifteenth he began a march in which some units covered 60 miles in 36 hours over miserable roads. The cavalry kept moving all day and most of the night, while the infantry rode in wagons when not marching. From Meaux the advance turned southward, and on the seventeenth the French scattered the Russian van at Mormant. The following day Napoleon beat an Austrian detachment in the battle of Montereau, and a third success at Méry drove his opponents all the way back to Bar-sur-Aube.

In eleven February days the emperor's little army had marched 170 miles, won seven combats and relieved Paris from the threat of two great invading armies. Summing up these feats in his critical writings, Clausewitz delivered the solemn judgment, "We do not believe that there is anything like this in history."

Early in March the Prussian general finally rallied his battered forces to move against the detachments of Mortier and Marmont. Napoleon could bring up only 30,000 men against 100,000, but he determined to unite with his marshals in an attempt to knock Blücher out of the war. After a rapid march from Sézanne he drove the Prussians back on the French garrison at Soissons, which was to have been the anvil for his battle of destruction. The weak capitulation of an aged subordinate at Soissons having ruined this plan, the emperor followed the enemy to Craonne, where he won his final victory of the campaign over the Prussian rear guard.

Blücher took a strong defensive position at Laon, and on March 8 Napoleon prepared an assault in combination with a flank attack by Marmont. Unfortunately, his orders were intercepted by Cossacks, so that a night surprise routed Marmont's detachment. The following day, after meeting a repulse at Laon, the emperor renounced his offensive and withdrew to Reims for rest.

Although the French forces were worn out, the allies had little cause for congratulation. In six weeks they had incurred nine humiliating reverses, with only three minor tactical successes to their credit. At this point Czar Alexander realized that the political situation offered a short cut to victory. All reports made it clear that France had lost faith in a leader whose obstinate rejection of terms had brought the nation to ruin. The Russian ruler therefore proposed a moral campaign in which the united forces of the invaders were to march to Paris in the role of peacemakers.

Napoleon played his last card by dashing at the communications of an enemy who ignored this futile threat. The political move, curiously enough, had developed into the most effective military thrust the allies had yet attempted. More by accident than design, they drove between the emperor and his marshals, and the detachments of Macdonald, Mortier and Marmont were severely handled. Napoleon, still gambling with destiny, advanced with 20,000 men against 80,000, only to lose a fourth of his numbers. All hope of resistance now vanished from the minds of reasonable Frenchmen, and on March 31 Paris surrendered when the remnants led by Mortier and Marmont gave way on the heights of Montmartre.

Napoleon alone refused to accept the inevitable. Not until his marshals demanded his abdication did he finally sign the agreement which reduced him to the rule of Elba's few miles. Thus in the end, for all of his amazing victories, the conqueror's own definition perhaps explains his failure in the crisis of 1814: "The art of war is simple and executive. There is nothing ideological about it."

WATERLOO: THE END OF THE ROAD

Whether the usurper might have regained power in 1815 by winning a great opening battle has always been a moot question. Certainly Europe showed no hesitation about accepting the challenge on his return from Elba, and a victory in Belgium would only have led to new tests against the Austrians and Russians. Nor is it sure that military successes alone could have restored unity in France. where the change of rulers had been accepted doubtfully.

But if Napoleon's political position was insecure, both at home and abroad, he possessed more real military strength than at any time since Leipzig. The moderate peace of 1814 had granted amnesty to thousands of French veterans immured in fortresses or held as prisoners, and a year of Bourbon rule had been dull enough to make ardent Bonapartists out of the majority. There could be no doubt that Napoleon's "old moustaches" were with him heart and soul as he staked his future on the campaign in Belgium.

England, Prussia, Austria and Russia had each pledged 150,000 troops for another invasion of France, but the contingents of the last two nations could not arrive before July. Hence the allies realized that Napoleon's first blow must be aimed at the Prussian and Anglo-Dutch armies disposed in cantonments to a depth of 30 and a width of 90 miles in southern Belgium. Early in June these forces included 93,000 men under the Duke of Wellington and about 116,000 in Blücher's ranks.

Of the 124,000 men Napoleon concentrated near Charleroi for the invasion, nearly all were old soldiers. The principal weakness of the army lay in the fact that few of the officers and men had ever worked together. In this respect the Prussian army was the strongest of the three, since Blücher and Gneisenau led most of the units of their last two successful campaigns. Wellington, in contrast, commanded a mixed array of 31,000 English troops, 29,000 Dutch and Belgians, and smaller contingents from Hanover, Nassau and Brunswick.

Napoleon's methods were so well known that the enemy fully anticipated a secret concentration followed by a rapid advance designed to separate the allied armies and beat them in detail. Yet in spite of their precautions, the emperor caught them unprepared. He made the expected moves, but made them with such unexpected surprise and swiftness, such masterly co-ordination of all forces, that his enemies were confounded. On the night of June 14 the French columns reached Soire and Philippeville, and the next morning they crossed the Sambre after storming the Charleroi bridge. Thus before a shot had been fired, Napoleon's strategy nullified the 8-to-5 numerical superiority of widely dispersed foes.

But this was not all. To crown his masterpiece of manoeuvre, the conqueror prepared a subtle trap by leaving open the main highway from Namur to Nivelles. After his passage of the Sambre he could easily have cut this road, but such a result would doubtless have caused the retreat of fatally separated allies. Instead, he wished to leave just enough hope to lure them into the dangerous expedient of a forward concentration on the battlefield itself. In preparation to meet such an attempt, his right and left wings were thrown slightly forward, and behind them he grouped the masses of manoeuvre for the knockout blow.

On the night of the fifteenth the French army occupied a square whose sides measured about twelve miles. The left wing under Ney extended to Frasnes, while Grouchy's right straddled the Sambre at

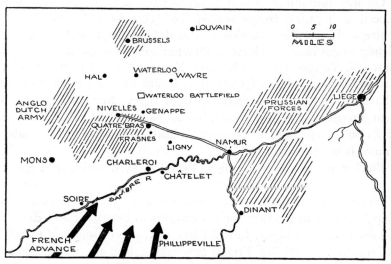

Napoleon's Strategy at Waterloo

Châtelet. The centre and reserve, including the Guard, were concentrated about Charleroi. This dominant strategic position still encouraged the allies to risk a forward concentration, yet Napoleon could hurl most of his strength at either.

Of the millions of words which have been written about Waterloo, the most prominent is "*if*—." Critics and readers alike have speculated as to why the emperor lost the campaign after opening moves which were never surpassed at Austerlitz. Many answers have been given, but it is too seldom emphasized that he left behind three marshals whose talents might have insured a victory.

The first was Murat. This general's defeat in a premature Italian combat so angered Napoleon that he made no use of the best cavalry leader in Europe. The other two were Davout and Suchet, neither of whom had ever been beaten in an independent action of any importance. The one remained in Paris as minister of war, the other on the inactive frontier of the Alps.

The blunders and losses of subordinates had accelerated the emperor's downfall in 1813, yet at Waterloo he placed his trust in Soult, Ney and Grouchy. Such a choice seems hardly a coincidence, and it can only be assumed that the emperor deemed it an intrusion when his marshals showed any capacity for the intellectual side of war. Much less explicable is the fact that he also left behind at least 30,000 veteran troops who could have been employed at Waterloo without endangering other fronts.

On the sixteenth Napoleon began to pay the price. At noon he advanced with 71,000 troops against the 83,000 of Blücher's right and centre at Ligny. His intention was to destroy the Prussian army in a victory so complete as to leave Wellington unaided when the next French blow fell. Toward this end he gave Ney explicit orders to master the British advance units at Quatre Bras before swinging eastward behind Blücher's right for the decisive stroke at Ligny. Ney commanded sufficient strength for both purposes, having been assigned the 30,000 men of Erlon's corps, and the emperor added the warning, "The fate of France is in your hands."

Blücher put up a stouter fight than had been anticipated, and the inexcusable delay of Ney's operation gave Wellington time to bring up reinforcements at Quatre Bras. On learning of these circumstances, Napoleon sent new orders for his marshal to detach Erlon's corps for the flank attack at Ligny. In that battle the emperor soon had to call on his reserves, though the French gradually gained the upper hand. At 6.30 P.M. he anxiously awaited Erlon, who had been sighted only to disappear toward the west. Finally, realizing that no co-operation could be expected from his left wing, Napoleon went on unaided to smash the enemy centre with a charge of the Guard. By dusk Blücher was badly beaten with 12,000 casualties, but the emperor had failed to destroy the Prussian army even at a cost of 8,000 killed and wounded.

That night he had dismal news from Quatre Bras which must have reminded him of the lost opportunity at Bautzen. Ney had wasted the hours in which he might have won an easy victory, and by 6 P.M. Wellington's reinforcements gave the enemy the numerical superiority. As a result the hard-pressed marshal recalled Erlon after he had almost reached Ligny, and the corps of 30,000 men oscillated between the two battles without deciding either. At nightfall Ney had been repulsed with 4,300 casualties, and Napoleon's success fell far short of his conception.

After the day's losses the French army still held an advantage over Wellington alone if the blow could be delivered before Blücher had time

to rally his shaken forces. The brief June nights permitted early movements, yet Napoleon missed his chance to attack at Quatre Bras on the
morning of the seventeenth. At the late hour of 10 A.M. the British
commander realized the peril of his isolation and began a withdrawal to
the north. That evening, while pursuing, the emperor was served dinner
by the very waiter who had attended his adversary at breakfast.

A terrific thunderstorm prevented any decisive action in the late afternoon, though a French reconnaissance in force unmasked Wellington's
new position a few miles south of the village of Waterloo. There on a line
from Hougoumont to La Haye the main Anglo-Dutch strength of 67,000
troops and 156 guns awaited battle in the morning. Both armies bivou-

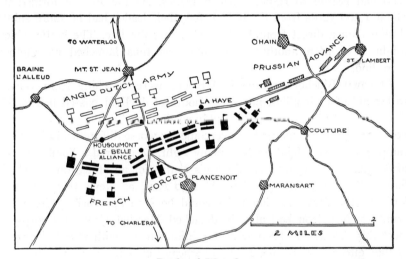

Battle of Waterloo

acked in the wet fields of rye, the French striking force of 74,000 men
and 246 guns being drawn up between Rossome and Genappe.

Wellington's most admiring biographers have seldom found him a
sympathetic character. At the outset of the campaign he referred to his
command as an "infamous army," and his public reprimands were
resented both by officers and men. In his defense it might be added that
the harsh reactionary of 1815 had entered the army as a shy, sensitive
younger son, aspiring to a musical career. Self-discipline made him
intolerant, but it could never be said that he spared himself. His mastery
of minor tactics is revealed by the dispositions of June 18; and if the
rank and file did not love "Old Nosey," at least they trusted him.

Again the redcoats were drawn up in a "typically Wellingtonian position," with most of the infantry concealed from the enemy by a low ridge. All along the line the weaker and less experienced allies had the support of veteran Peninsular units. Yet for all of his tactical skill, the British commander misunderstood the enemy's strategic plan, as is shown by his detachment of 17,000 badly needed troops to Hal in anticipation of a French turning movement on his right. On the other hand, most critics contend that Napoleon erred even more seriously in failing to strike Wellington's left, thus completing his purpose of separating the Anglo-Dutch and Prussian armies.

Nor did the emperor trouble to ask advice of his Peninsular generals who had reason to respect British tactics. As the French formed up about 1,300 yards from the hidden foe, their leader had no more subtle design than a direct frontal attack all along the line. The battle which might have been another Austerlitz was thus launched as another Borodino.

At dawn Blücher's reorganized troops were marching from Wavre to the aid of their allies, but seven hours of daylight passed before the French attacked at 11.30 A.M. Muddy roads served as the excuse for this delay, though the emperor had overcome far worse difficulties in his 1814 campaign. After a feint on the enemy right, he ordered a bombardment of 80 guns to "prepare" Wellington's centre for an attack on La Haye Sainte, the key to the position. At 1.30 P.M., as Ney's troops moved forward, the first Prussian units could be seen approaching from St. Lambert. Napoleon had already detached Marshal Grouchy's corps to meet this threat, and he now sent reinforcements with renewed orders to that effect. Meanwhile, Ney's overheavy columns were repulsed by Wellington's infantry, supported by a cavalry counterattack.

A second attempt by Ney failed, and at 4 P.M. Napoleon hurled 43 squadrons of horse against La Haye Sainte. They rode through a tempest of shrapnel and case shot, only to shatter themselves against British infantry formed into squares. When a counterattack of allied cavalry swept the field, the emperor made an even greater effort with 80 squadrons. This assault might perhaps have succeeded with infantry support, but again the horsemen could not break squares which fired deadly and continual volleys.

It would be hard to improve on Wellington's description of this phase "Never did I see such a pounding match," he wrote afterward. "Both were what the boxers call gluttons. Napoleon did not manoeuvre at all.

He just moved forward in the old style, and was driven off in the old style."

Even the most devout hero-worshipers have found little to praise in the emperor's tactics. As at Borodino, the French attacks were delivered piecemeal, with a glaring lack of co-operation between the arms. Massed guns failed of their usual effect, since the enemy lines were sheltered by the ridge; and the subsequent advances of unsupported foot or horse met a unified resistance which Wellington directed with cool precision. In short, the Iron Duke was at his best on the field of Waterloo, Napoleon at his worst.

The crisis came at 6 P.M. when the emperor ordered Ney to take La Haye Sainte at any cost. By this time he realized that Grouchy had failed either to contain the Prussian main body or return to the aid of the French at Waterloo. Hence the two allied armies had already made contact, gaining a numerical superiority which would increase as fresh Prussian brigades arrived.

French fighting qualities were displayed at their best in the storming of La Haye Sainte by Ney's men. With the key to his position lost, Wellington admitted next day that " . . . it had been a damned nice thing—the nearest run thing you ever saw in your life." Napoleon had meanwhile driven the Prussians from Plancenoit with a bayonet attack, and the shaken Anglo-Dutch forces had to bear the brunt of a French advance all along the line. Their repulse of this attack must be attributed to Wellington's success in re-forming his lines and strengthening his centre. As the French fell back at 8 P.M. the initiative passed to the allies, who swept forward to claim their victory.

Two grenadier battalions of the Guard fought on to the death, and other units held Plancenoit long enough to keep open a route of retreat along the Charleroi road. But the emperor's last chance had vanished as he joined the flight of his routed army. The comparatively fresh Prussian troops took up a pursuit which lasted all night, driving the beaten forces out of seven successive bivouacs and compelling them to seek a refuge across the Sambre.

The French losses were at least 40,000, including prisoners. Wellington reported 15,000 casualties and the Prussians 7,000. Some 45,000 dead and wounded lay in an area of three square miles about La Haye Sainte, so intense had the fighting been in the centre.

Even Napoleon had no serious thought of another attempt as his carriage sped toward Paris. In his writings he blamed Ney, Erlon and Grouchy for the failure of the campaign, but a more candid appraisal does not absolve him from blame. As a battle Waterloo offers the final proof of the decline in the emperor's ability which had been increasingly evident for seven years. The struggle is more memorable as a human drama, for history offers no clearer reassurance of the lesson that power cannot long be maintained by force over peoples determined to resist.

PART SIX
WAR'S MACHINE AGE

☆

I

SOUTH AMERICAN REVOLUTION

I called the New World into existence to redress the balance of the Old.

—CANNING

THE problems of maintaining neutrality during a world war were illustrated by the plight of the United States throughout the Napoleonic period. Even before the age of the steamship and cable the young republic found the Atlantic an inadequate barrier for preserving a policy of isolation.

Two proclamations made the American attitude clear during President Washington's first term, yet ship seizures and border disputes nearly brought on another conflict with England as early as 1794. Four years later the new nation fought a brief and undeclared war with France for similar causes, and within a few months 80 armed ships flying the tri-color were sunk or captured. The crisis grew so serious that Washington resumed the chief command after authorizing the recruiting of soldiers and building of frigates. Only the value of American trade to France led Talleyrand to avert open hostilities by repudiating his policies.

These foreign emergencies added enormously to the trials of a country which had not yet put its home affairs in order. Then in 1803 the fortunes of war conferred a boon so great that it might have ruined a people less accustomed to self-government. President Jefferson sent negotiators to Paris to buy New Orleans, but in a most irregular transaction Bonaparte ceded the vast domain known as the Louisiana Purchase—potentially the richest area of the earth's surface—for a price of only a few cents an acre.

This decision amounted to a confession on the part of the First Consul that he lacked the warships to defend the colonial empire so dubiously acquired from Spain. At the moment neither he nor his American beneficiaries could have realized that the principal historical effect was to be the creation of a major world power across the Atlantic.

Owing to a caprice of destiny a neutral nation thus gained the largest material profit of the Napoleonic wars. But the republic's difficulties were soon multiplied by the blockade and counter-blockades announced by England and France. After Austerlitz and Trafalgar the seizures of ships presented such a problem that the United States adopted perhaps the most drastic measure that has ever been conceived in the name of neutrality. The Embargo Act of 1807, by abruptly suspending commerce with both "the tiger and the shark," had the immediate effect of plunging a prospering maritime nation into an economic vacuum.

Although thousands of merchants, shipowners and seamen faced ruin, Jefferson trusted that this step would convince the belligerents of the necessity of American trade. English statesmen, on the contrary, held that American self-denial would not prove equal to such a heroic test. Whether the embargo might have succeeded if fully enforced is a matter for conjecture, since the result was to turn the United States into a nation of smugglers. Internal dissension grew so rife that the seafaring New England states actually discussed secession, and after a year the act had to be repealed without ever having known a real test.

England's seizures of American ships and seamen continued in spite of President Madison's policies of "peaceful coercion," and the breach between the two nations widened. Wiser statesmanship might have made a valuable ally out of the United States, for public sentiment in America overlooked the fact that Napoleon was the greater offender. During the five years preceding 1812 he had taken 558 American vessels and the British 389, but the island kingdom too often added insult to injury. The final and unforgivable provocation came when British agents in Canada supplied arms to the Indians on the frontier. The western Congressmen, representing districts in peril of massacre, were unanimous in demanding a conflict which historians have generally condemned as a blunder.

THE WAR OF 1812

The ensuing struggle has its chief interest as a study in unpreparedness. Although the nation had a population of seven and a quarter millions in 1810, only 23 warships, of which three carried more than 40 guns, could be opposed to the 800 British sail.

As recently as 1804 the small American fleet had distinguished itself in a successful war against the Barbary pirates at a time when European nations were paying tribute. The woeful lack of development since that war may be charged to President Jefferson's ideas. An incorrigible amateur in invention and architecture, he authorized the building of 165 gunboats to replace standard warships. A more unfortunate experiment has seldom been recorded, for these small craft proved too unseaworthy to carry the weight of their single gun.

The few remaining warships outsailed and outfought the enemy to such an extent that after the war British naval architects copied American frigates—the "terrible nondescripts"—almost in exact detail. Of the 16 duels on the high seas, the Americans were victors in 12; and the tiny navy captured no less than 254 merchantmen. The 517 privateers accounted for an additional 1,300 prizes, while a total of 30,000 prisoners were taken as compared to 6,000 in land warfare. So disturbing were these results to English pride that the London *Times* declared editorially in 1813:

> The fact seems to be but too clearly established that the Americans have some superior mode of firing, and that we cannot be too anxiously employed in discerning to what that superiority is owing.

Such victories, however glorious, could not prevent American commerce from being ruined. Nor did they seriously affect the ocean strategy of a war in which enemy frigates patrolled the American coast without often being challenged. Thus the only two decisive naval engagements were fought on the lakes which lie between the American and Canadian border.

In 1813 Commodore Perry's triumph on Lake Erie recovered the Northwest after that region had been lost in land reverses. The ten small American vessels, mounting 57 guns, were opposed by the 63 guns of the squadron commanded by Captain Barclay, who had served under Nelson at Trafalgar. After a terrific three-hour fight the heavier weight of the American metal, combined with more accurate gunnery, forced every British ship to strike her colors.

As a direct result the British land forces were compelled to beat a hasty retreat from Detroit. The energetic Perry took General Harrison's small American army aboard his ships, crossed to the Canadian shore and led the decisive charge of the battle of the Thames, in which the redcoats and their savage allies were routed. This victory secured the Northwest for the remainder of the war and freed the frontier from the Indian menace.

The following year the most decisive engagement of all took place on Lake Champlain. By 1814 the abdication of Napoleon had released comparatively large numbers of Wellington's veterans for service in America. An army of 12,000 under General Provost crossed the New York border in September to repeat Burgoyne's strategy of cutting the vital Champlain-Hudson line. The Americans had no troops which could hope to repulse such an invasion, but General Izard's little army threw up redoubts for a desperate stand at Plattsburg. Both sides realized meanwhile that the issue must be decided on the water, since poor roads and communications made control of the lake an essential factor.

In all American history no commander ever had a heavier responsibility than the thirty-year-old Lieutenant Macdonough as his squadron awaited the British lake fleet in Plattsburg Bay. Not only did he have fewer ships, but his 45 long-range guns with a broadside of 759 pounds faced 60 enemy guns throwing a weight of 1,128 pounds. Against these material odds Macdonough won a memorable triumph of skill. After his flagship *Saratoga* had apparently been silenced by the much larger *Confiance,* he swung her about by an ingenious device of springs in her cables and fired unexpected broadsides. The surrender of the *Confiance* and three other vessels led to a British flight, and the next day Provost's army began an enforced retreat to Montreal. The news of this reverse reached Ghent in time to hasten the signing of a peace treaty in which the American envoys gained their chief demands.

The operations on land presented a series of disgraceful object lessons reiterating the futility of the American militia system. During the three years an impressive total of 527,654 men enlisted, according to Upton, but 400,000 of the one- to three-month volunteers saw little or no active service. Of the remainder so few reached the firing line that in the two principal battles the Americans were outnumbered two to one by foemen who had crossed the Atlantic. Flights and disorders of green recruits reduced some of the early campaigns to the level of comic opera; for the able General Winfield Scott described the militia commanders as "sunk in either sloth, ignorance or habits of intemperate drinking. . . . Swaggerers, dependents, decayed gentlemen . . . utterly unfit for any military purpose whatever."

The twenty-eight-year-old Virginia volunteer, educated for the law at William and Mary College, showed what disciplined American soldiers could do when his brigade routed a larger force of British regulars on the field of Chippewa in July, 1814. A giant in character as well as physique, Scott obtained permission from his commanding officer, General Jacob Brown, to institute a period of training almost within sight of the enemy. Like Steuben at Valley Forge, he began with the officers. Sweating colonels and majors shouldered a musket for ten hours a day at the camp near Buffalo, learning the rudiments of drill. The energetic brigadier taught them the intellectual side of war from his own European military treatises; and his insistence on camp hygiene reduced an appalling sick list so abruptly as to puzzle army surgeons.

The turn of the rank and file came next, after Scott had ended a plague of desertions with several executions. The men had been given two months of training when the little American force crossed the Niagara River into Canada. The attack at Chippewa on General Riall's redcoats was pressed with such steadiness that he exclaimed, "Those are regulars, by God!" Advancing behind a superior fire, both of musketry and artillery, Scott's brigade sent the enemy into flight with a bayonet attack.

Three weeks later the 2,000 Americans met Drummond's army of 3,000 at Lundy's Lane. Both sides claimed a victory in a bloody fight which lasted from afternoon until long after darkness. The troops led by Brown and Scott repeatedly drove the British from their guns, retiring only after both commanders had been wounded.

The two concluding land engagements offer a dramatic study in contrasts. In the affair known derisively as the "Bladensburg races," a force of American militiamen fled from half their numbers of invading regulars, abandoning the nation's capital to be burned by the enemy in August, 1814. Only a few months later the situation was exactly reversed at New Orleans. In that battle an equally untrained American army, fighting double its numbers of the same Peninsular veterans, inflicted the most crushing defeat ever endured by British arms since Bannockburn and Castillon.

The explanation is to be found simply in the ability of Andrew Jackson, a border captain who emerged as the best general on either side. Like Daniel Morgan at Cowpens, he disciplined his troops on the battlefield, inspiring them with a confidence which led to the foremost American triumph of the war.

Just as Washington's recruits were scorned for running on several occasions, so historians have been notably severe on the victims of the Bladensburg rout. Such terms as "poltroon" are usually reserved for this disgrace by critics more accustomed to the shedding of ink than blood. The experience of war, however, teaches that the nation itself is far more culpable than the citizens it sacrifices to unpreparedness. Battle is a business for specialists, and in taking to his heels the untrained man is justified by the traditions of thirty centuries.

Andrew Jackson seems to have had an instinctive understanding of this truth at New Orleans. Except for 700 regulars, his motley force of 5,700 consisted of frontier militiamen, Gulf pirates and even armed merchants,

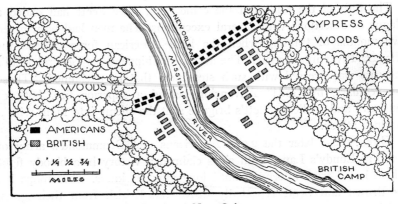

Battle of New Orleans

planters and slaves. Nevertheless, he struck the first blows against a British expeditionary force of 14,250, including 500 riflemen from the Light Division as well as the best line regiments of Wellington's campaigns.

Foolhardy as Jackson's attacks may appear, he risked only night operations at first—the one department of tactics in which the undisciplined man has an equal chance with the trained soldier. On December 23 the American general learned that the redcoats were within a few miles of the city after making a skillful landing. Some 2,200 of his troops had yet to arrive, but in spite of his numerical inferiority he ordered an advance that night.

In the darkness the Americans fell upon the enemy with rifles and hunting knives, their assault being supported by the guns of the schooner *Carolina* in the Mississippi River. There followed a confused two-hour struggle in which, as Jackson had expected, his men more than held their own. Not only were the invaders treated to a dismaying surprise, but their losses amounted to 50 per cent more than the 211 casualties of the assailants.

The moral importance of this prelude cannot be overestimated. During the next two weeks the border captain continued to give his troops a conviction of victory without ever exposing them beyond their tactical depth. Nearly every evening small groups of volunteers penetrated into the enemy lines, making the nights sleepless for foemen whose drill fitted them for more formal operations. By day the keen-sighted frontier riflemen took cover in the woods to harass the British outposts.

Jackson's men gained a daily advantage in these skirmish-line encounters as the remainder of his forces threw up earthworks south of the city on both banks of the Mississippi. On December 28 the British attempted a reconnaissance in force, only to be driven back with sharp casualties. And on January 1, 1815, the American troops stood like veterans during an artillery duel in which the invaders were again compelled to retire.

These preliminaries are often disregarded in accounts of the main battle, yet by the eighth the moral ascendancy had passed to militiamen who believed that they had thrice proved their superiority. With complete assurance they awaited the grand assault ordered by General Pakenham on both sides of the river.

Saratoga had been decided by the rifle, but the tactical interest of New Orleans lies in the fact that it was history's first battle to be fought almost exclusively with that arm. Practically all of the Americans carried the long-barreled, patch-loading frontier weapon; and as the foremost riflemen of Europe, a majority of the enemy light troops were equipped with the Baker model, 2½ feet in length of barrel and using 20 bullets to the pound of lead. Not only did this piece have a much shorter range, but a British sharpshooter could qualify by hitting a target 4 feet in diameter at 200 yards—a standard which would have been scorned by marksmen of the New World.

The fatal error of Pakenham's plan seems to have been due to an underestimate of American range and accuracy. At nearly 300 yards the scarlet ranks were subjected to a small-arms fire such as had never been known on a European field. On the left bank the main force advanced between the river and woods with stolid courage, but within a few minutes the leading units lost 50 per cent of their numbers. Pakenham and most of his officers fell; and when the smoke lifted, more than 2,000 redcoats were stretched out on the field. The remainder broke into flight after 500 surrendered to victors who had lost only 7 men killed and 6 wounded. On the other bank the American detachment had been driven back by superior numbers, but Pakenham's successors ordered a general withdrawal. While neither side knew yet that peace had already been signed, the British accepted their defeat and Jackson wisely did not risk a pursuit.

South America's Wars of Revolution

New Orleans left precepts in rifle tactics and the handling of green troops which might well have been adopted in South America, where the various Spanish colonies were now fighting for independence. Instead, the wars of that continent present as dismal a picture of unpreparedness as may be found in military annals. Courage and resolution were not lacking, but even after years of effort the patriots suffered ghastly losses and hardships because of their persistent lack of organization or training.

Bolivar, the great liberator, emerged as the hero of some 200 bloody encounters; and a modern Colombian authority has estimated that more than 600 combats took place in his country alone. Two crossings of the Andes rank among the most difficult marches of all time, while some of the operations in tropical jungles demanded a superhuman endurance. Pillage, anarchy and massacre added to the trials of the rebels—and yet it is a reasonable conclusion that most of these sacrifices might have been avoided with a modicum of planning.

As a greathearted patriot Simon Bolivar dedicated his life and fortune to the cause. His zeal has not often been matched in history, but it is equally plain that the Liberator created a majority of his own troubles by his failure as a general and military administrator.

During the first four years his country alone changed hands four times, falling on each occasion to guerrilla forces of only a few hundred troops. Undoubtedly a small but disciplined army could have held Venezuela and preserved order, but only at the end of his headlong career did the Caracas aristocrat pause to build up an establishment of trained soldiers. Most of his campaigns show the same impulsive lack of preparation, so that the student of these prodigious efforts can only echo the famous French criticism, "It is magnificent, but is it war?"

South America as the background of revolution offered no unsurmountable difficulties to absolve Bolivar from his neglect. On the contrary, the rebel recruits proved to be excellent military material. That the fault lay with the leader himself is further shown by the career of his great rival, José de San Martín, the liberator of Argentina, Chile and Peru. This soldier-statesman, like Cromwell at the outset of the Great Rebellion, began by creating a force of disciplined troops. As a result he accomplished more in two combats than Bolivar in two hundred.

The long struggle started in 1809 when the mother country's war of liberation against Napoleon offered the opportunity for a general revolt of her South American colonies. During these early years the military situation rather favored the rebels, for even in normal times Spain had never maintained large bodies of troops in her overseas possessions. Religious and commercial oppression, rather than military tyranny, caused the most valid grievances of colonials who found it fairly easy to overthrow the various provincial governments. In Caracas, as a typical instance, an almost bloodless uprising of armed civilians forced the Spanish captain general to abdicate in 1810.

In every province the leaders of revolt were the Creoles, or subjects of pure Spanish lineage. Denied a share in the government, they had become the social, economic and intellectual aristocrats of the capitals. The mestizos, or natives of mixed Indian and Spanish blood, made up the bulk of the population, and beneath them were the Indians and descendants of Negro slaves.

The new republic of Venezuela had scarcely been proclaimed when it fell in a brief counterrevolution which demonstrated that the mestizos offered both sides the key to military success. In 1812 an unknown royalist adventurer named Monteverde, beginning with 230 followers, reconquered the entire country in a few months. After his first successes enough plunder-lured recruits flocked to his ranks to give him a formidable guerrilla force, and the surrender of the main republican army opened the way to Caracas.

Bolivar, who had taken but a small part in these events, fled into exile. The following year he gathered 800 men in New Granada (modern Colombia), crossed into Venezuela and increased his strength until he drove the royalists out of the capital in a 90-day campaign. Unfortunately, the mestizos who had supported him were equally ready to rally behind his enemy, the former pirate Boves, and the country was mastered for a fourth time in 1814.

Operations on both sides were conducted with revolting cruelty. Boves earned his nickname of "the Butcher" by barbarous massacres, and in 1813 Bolivar issued a proclamation of war to the death which resulted in a slaughter of 866 prisoners, including civilians. In reality a state of armed anarchy prevailed in Venezuela, with the combats between guerrilla bands being decided less by skill than numbers and the fortunes of war.

Under comparable conditions Washington and Greene had shown what could be accomplished by untrained troops. The difference lay in the fact that each of these revolutionary commanders realized the necessity of keeping at least a small force of regulars in the field. Such a nucleus may be compared to the hub of a wheel, and the various guerrilla bands to the spokes. For the lessons of history make it plain that irregular warfare leads to anarchy unless it is supported by a central establishment of dependable soldiers. A few of the strategic spokes may be broken and replaced, but without the hub the entire wheel collapses.

The warfare in South America entered a second phase after Waterloo when both sides gained reinforcements from Europe. Up to this point the cause of the mother country had been upheld chiefly by native royalists, but the arrival of expeditionary troops found the rebels also strengthened by veterans of the Napoleonic wars. In the year 1817 a total of 5,088 such volunteers reached Venezuela alone, and the other rebelling provinces were helped to a lesser extent. These adventurers consisted largely of British soldiers recruited in London during the depressed economic conditions of the early peace years. Most of them proved to be troops of the highest quality, so that the rebels had somewhat the better of Spain in the new turn of events.

Funds having also been contributed to the cause, Bolivar returned from his second exile to command at least a military equality. Enormous stores of unwanted war supplies could be had from Europe at low prices, and the rebel armies were soon better equipped. Despite these advances, two more years of chaotic small engagements passed without a decision. In the only important battle of this period Bolivar's forces were routed at La Puerta in 1818, losing most of Venezuela as a penalty.

The following spring he set out on his most celebrated exploit, the crossing of the Andes into New Granada. The route led across the flooded plains of the Orinoco basin during the rainy season, then over icy mountain passes at an altitude of 11,000 feet. Only a third of the original army of 3,200 survived the ill-planned march of 700 miles, but the Liberator recruited local forces before meeting a more numerous enemy on the field of Boyacá in August, 1819. In this hard-fought engagement the steady valor of the British rifle battalion had most to do with a rebel victory which ended forever the Spanish domination of New Granada.

Bogotá, the capital of the new republic, supplied men and money for the relief of Venezuela, and in June, 1821, Bolivar won independence for his homeland at the battle of Carabobo. The royalist general La Torre took a defensive position among ravines with 5,500 troops, chiefly native Venezuelans. Bolivar's army of 6,500 included 900 British riflemen and 1,500 *llaneros*—half-savage horsemen from the tropical plains who had no superiors in the world as irregular cavalry. These two contingents won the battle virtually unaided after Spanish volleys routed the main rebel force. The British battalion formed into a square and stood off the whole royalist army for an hour, losing a third of its numbers. The last cartridges had been fired when the *llaneros* came to the rescue, and a combined charge dislodged the enemy. In the plain the shattered royalist infantry surrendered by the battalion, giving Bolivar a victory so complete that he entered Caracas in triumph.

SAN MARTÍN'S CAMPAIGNS

Neither of the two decisive battles in the North shows much evidence of generalship. The rebel efforts were so badly scattered on both fields that the superior discipline of the British volunteers conveys the illusion of superior bravery. Only after turning to San Martín's campaigns do we see the possibilities of trained and well-led South American soldiers functioning together as an army.

This patriot had been born in Paraguay of a poor Creole family and sent to Spain as a boy for a military education. At the age of sixteen he became an officer in the regular Spanish army, gaining a lieutenant-colonel's rank for bravery in the Baylen operations. On the outbreak of the revolution in Buenos Aires (modern Argentina) San Martín returned to South America and took part in the uprising which resulted in an easy victory for the rebels.

Some of the more enthusiastic accounts of the revolts give a picture of unmitigated Spanish tyranny backed up by large expeditionary forces of "Peninsular veterans." On the contrary, the mother country appears to have been honeycombed with secret revolutionary societies at this time, and only in Chile and Peru did the royalists have any great military advantage. San Martín was one of many Spanish officers who were converted to the cause of South American independence; and he offered his sword to a homeland which he had not seen since the age of eight.

In 1814, having already won distinction as the first soldier of Buenos

Aires, he led a revolutionary force into upper Peru. There he became convinced that scattered guerrilla efforts could only end in anarchy; and after resigning his command, he set out singlehanded to organize South America's first disciplined army.

Two years passed in which he seemed to have dropped out of sight. During this interlude he created at Mendoza—a remote frontier town in the Argentinian foothills of the Andes—a military laboratory in the tradition of Tabor and Valley Forge. In his character, indeed, San Martín deserves comparison with Washington or Carnot, not only in honor and integrity but also an unfortunate austerity. Argentinian and Chilean refugees found their way into his unpaid ranks, and sixty-two volunteer officers from Europe and the United States helped to drill the flotsam of South American revolution.

By the end of 1816, on his own initiative and with little aid from Buenos Aires, he had trained a compact little army of 3,000 foot, 1,000 Gaucho cavalry and a small artillery force. Where Bolivar had wasted his resources in colorful but futile local combats, his fellow liberator realized that no province could hope for permanent independence while Spain held Chile and Peru as her central bastions. Most of the loyalist power, both political and military, was concentrated in these two departments as San Martín began his ascent of the Andes in January, 1817.

If his three-week crossing seems tame in contrast to Bolivar's feat, the explanation lies in months of careful planning. San Martín even took remedies against mountain sickness at an altitude of 12,700 feet, and a train of 9,000 mules brought provisions and ammunition for every soldier. The losses were astonishingly small as the army reached the Chilean side to find a larger royalist force drawn up in the Pass of Chacabuco. In the ensuing battle the discipline of Mendoza told as the rebels won a complete victory in a single concerted attack.

Method and precision brought about the permanent conquest of Chile in a year at a minimum of bloodshed. San Martín based his strategy on a small navy acquired by construction and the capture of enemy ships. Commanded by a brilliant English adventurer, Lord Cochrane, the fleet swept the Spaniards from the sea and transported troops up the long coast line. Only in one engagement did the rebels ever waver, and on this field the flight of surprised recruits was redeemed by San Martín's trained battalions. The decisive victory of Maipo, fought near Santiago in April, 1818, likewise owed to the commander's better discipline and more skillful use of reserves against a numerically superior foe.

Before advancing northward, the victor paused a year to secure his gains and reorganize his army. This seeming delay actually saved time as well as lives, for the combined land-and-sea attack on Peru was made in such overwhelming strength that the royalist forces fled to the hills without much show of resistance. In 1821 Callao and Lima were evacuated before the rebel army and fleet, and San Martín proclaimed the independence of Spain's oldest and most loyal province.

As an idealist he wished this conquest to be accomplished without bloodshed. Thus instead of pursuing his foes into the mountains, he offered them a compromise of conciliation. The enemy leaders were invited to participate in a plan for a Peruvian limited monarchy, a form of government which San Martín favored over a republic for a people denied political experience by three centuries of Spanish oppression.

During the following negotiations his failure in diplomacy is as noteworthy as Bolivar's lapses in strategy. The Argentinian soldier's reserve gave the effect of hauteur, for he possessed none of the rhetorical arts which enabled the northern liberator to win men. As a consequence his policies of conciliation came to nothing. Months of idleness corroded the morale of the army, and some of his most trusted officers plotted his assassination.

This was the situation in July, 1822, when at last the two revolutionary leaders met at Guayaquil. San Martín, whose worst enemies had never accused him of aspiring to personal power, offered to serve under Bolivar as a general, and their combined talents would doubtless have hastened the ultimate victory. But the fiery Venezuelan's ambition could tolerate no rival, even in a subordinate capacity. The events of the conference have never been fully revealed, though it is evident that San Martín became the victim of some rather shabby political trickery. Within thirty-six hours he took ship for Peru, leaving the glory to Bolivar as he resigned all authority to end his life in impoverished European exile.

Thirty months of bloody fighting were necessary in Peru before the last royalist army went down to defeat at Ayacucho in December, 1824. Antonio José Sucre, as Bolivar's lieutenant, displayed a much higher order of generalship than his master in the past. Even so, the departed Argentinian soldier cannot be denied his share of the credit. Not only had Bolivar fallen heir to many of his rival's veterans, but for the first time he made an effort to keep a trained and equipped army in the field. San Martín's precepts thus lived after him, and some authorities have gone so far as to proclaim him the true hero of South American independence.

The Monroe Doctrine

Viewed from today's historical distance, the republics created by the South American revolts have succeeded in overcoming unique difficulties. Before 1810 there were only a few printing presses allowed on the entire continent, and Spain took particular pains to deny her New World subjects any such training in self-government as had become the foundation of the United States. Naturally these handicaps led at first to chaos, so that even Bolivar declared before his death, "Independence is the only thing we have acquired, and that at the cost of everything else."

While the new nations were convulsed by frequent outbreaks of civil war or even anarchy, their weakness invited European intervention for selfish ends. This danger was foreseen by the United States in 1822, when the northern republic became the first power to recognize the South American governments. That same year the Quadruple Alliance of Europe considered the plan of sending expeditionary forces across the Atlantic to restore Spain's former colonies to her. Rumor had it that Russia expected Californian territory as compensation for her part in the enterprise, with other parts of Mexico to be allotted to France. Already the czar had issued a decree claiming the Pacific coast as far south as the fiftieth parallel, and forbidding ships of other nations to approach within one hundred miles of shore.

These European moves were made in the name of pacifism. Since the *Pax Romana* no dream of universal peace has been revived more persistently than the hope of an alliance to outlaw war. Each generation fondly believes that it has discovered a plan which had been urged prior to 1800 by Henry IV of France, William Penn, the Abbé de St. Pierre, Jeremy Bentham and Immanuel Kant. With the exception of Bentham, who favored moral persuasion, all of these leaders believed that nations, like the individuals composing them, could be made to obey laws forbidding armed aggression. All agreed that the enforcement could be left to an international constabulary—the counterpart of the policeman who compels the citizen to respect the rights of his neighbor.

It is a popular conviction that the plan has never been given a fair trial in modern times, yet the Holy Alliance of 1816 was formed with such ideals in view. The leading rulers of Europe, with the exception of the pope, the sultan and England's prince regent, signed a pact declaring that "the precepts of Justice, Charity and Peace . . . must have an immediate influence on the councils of Princes and guide all their steps."

Henceforward the various governments were to consider themselves "members of one and the same Christian nation."

The sincerity of the inception has never been questioned, though Europe's diplomats did not share in the exaltation. Metternich described the document as a "loud-sounding nothing," and Castlereagh called it "sublime mysticism and nonsense."

The Holy Alliance merely announced the principle, but the enforcement did not depend on moral persuasion alone. Within a few more months the Quadruple Alliance of Russia, Austria, Prussia and England (with France being later admitted) undertook the task of maintaining world peace by means of armed might. Thus during the years following the Napoleonic wars Europe was policed by an all-powerful league of nations which could—and did—send its soldiers to put down every threatened disturbance.

At last an age-old dream had come true, and yet both alliances have been condemned ever since as conspiracies against progress and political liberties. Their failure may be charged to the fact that each generation has its own idea of what constitutes international justice, order and liberty. Even such apparently opposite poles as peace and war are capable of widely varying interpretations, so that today's "intervention" may go down in history as "aggression."

As Europe's foremost crowned liberal, Czar Alexander reaffirmed his belief in "free institutions." But in the next breath he added the amendment, "Liberty should be confined within just limits. And the limits of liberty are the principles of order."

This attitude is understandable when one remembers that the world had just emerged from twenty-three years of continual bloodshed. It is also understandable that revolution and republican principles should have been in bad odor at this time. Monarchial institutions must have seemed the only proven safeguard; and the Quadruple Alliance doubtless represented a majority of war-weary Europeans when it chose to regard political revolt as an offense against order. Thus in 1821 soldiers were sent to crush uprisings in Naples and Piedmont which now appear to have sprung from genuine grievances. Europe had gained peace and stability at the cost of man's right to protest against tyranny.

England withdrew from the conferences when the question of restoring "order" in Spain and South America came up for discussion. The island kingdom had built up a prosperous trade in the Western Hemisphere, which gave it a common interest with the United States in resisting encroachments across the Atlantic. The outgrowth was the Monroe

Doctrine, a political instrument which has long outlasted the Quadruple Alliance.

The British foreign minister, George Canning, claimed the credit in his famous boast to Parliament, but Washington, Adams and Jefferson had already stated the principle. "Our first and fundamental maxim," said Jefferson, "should be never to entangle ourselves in the broils of Europe. Our second never to suffer Europe to meddle in cis-Atlantic affairs."

These are the familiar tenets. Less well known, but equally important, is the fact that the document has so often operated virtually as an unwritten naval and military alliance of the two English-speaking peoples. This effect, which neither Canning nor Monroe foresaw, has been due to the "implications" and "interpretations" read into the act by following generations. As a result Captain Mahan would be justified in declaring nearly a century later that the Monroe Doctrine "adapts itself with the flexibility of a growing plant to the successive conditions it encounters." The influence on the development of the Western Hemisphere and Pacific areas can hardly be overestimated. Assured of British co-operation, the United States was able to warn the powers of the Quadruple Alliance that "we should consider any attempt on their part to extend their system to any portion of this hemisphere as dangerous to our peace and safety." The young republic took an equally firm stand with Russia, and in 1824 that nation retreated by signing a treaty which limited its Pacific coast claims to the southward by the parallel 54° 40′ north latitude.

Republican institutions were thus given a chance to develop, while in Europe the Quadruple Alliance turned the clock back by restoring the benevolent despotism of a past age. Yet in at least one respect the Old and New Worlds agreed. Both made it evident that they wanted no more of the intemperate warfare of the Napoleonic era. The conqueror's forthright methods seemed to have died with him, and the nation-in-arms to have vanished like a violent dream. Invention followed invention with bewildering rapidity, but even the improvements in weapons had little effect on tactics after Waterloo. The reaction had set in, and for two generations the conflicts on both sides of the Atlantic were waged by small professional armies with a moderation reminiscent of the eighteenth century.

II

THE TACTICS OF REACTION

Into the valley of death
  Rode the six hundred;
For up came an order which
  Some one had blundered. . . .

—TENNYSON's "Charge of the Light Brigade"

IN 1807, after years of experimenting, Alexander Forsyth perfected a new method of ignition which superseded the flintlock. The Scottish clergyman's invention, which has been called the most important advance in firearms since Roger Bacon's announcement, consisted of a detonating powder which sent a flash through the touchhole after being struck a smart blow. Within a few more years copper caps containing mercury fulminate came into use, so that small arms were no longer subject to misfires due to wind and damp.

Not the least advantage of the new system was the fact that a village gunsmith could readily transform a flintlock into a percussion-firing weapon. Owing to military conservatism the improvement had no effect on the Napoleonic wars, but after exhaustive tests the British army gave its approval in 1836.

The percussion cap made possible the first repeating firearm of precision when Samuel Colt produced his revolving pistol in 1835. Ever since the fourteenth century men had been experimenting with multiple fire, and the American inventor is said to have been inspired by an ancient weapon in the Tower of London. The old priming system with exposed powder had doomed former attempts to failure, while the Colt pistol utilized the Forsyth principle with immediate success. Cocking the hammer caused the muzzle-loading cylinder to revolve so that each successive chamber formed a continuous bore with the barrel. A few years later English inventors perfected the "double-action" system in which a pull of the trigger not only detonated the cap but also revolved the cylinder, bringing a fresh charge into line.

The United States army immediately adopted a few revolvers which proved their reliability in the Seminole War of 1836. Despite an original price of $130, the .44 caliber Colt soon became the weapon of the frontier. The demand made it necessary to introduce mass production by means of machinery; and in 1847 the manufacturer contracted to supply the army with a much improved pistol at a cost of only $28.

From the beginning the Americans had led in the development of the rifle, and about 1830 they produced the first successful long bullet. It had always been recognized that the round missile of past ages lost velocity and accuracy through air resistance, but no other shape could be made to fit the grooves of the rifling. In the new "sugar-loaf bullet" only the base came in contact with the bore, and the usual greased patch acted as a gas-stopper. A special ramrod with a cup-shaped head forced the projectile into position with ease and exactness. Without any loss in accuracy, this discovery increased the range of the American weapon to nearly five hundred yards at a time when riflemen of other nations were still driving the ball into the bore with a ramrod and wooden mallet.

Scott's Invasion of Mexico

The new weapons had their first real test in the war between the United States and Mexico in 1846. The great westward migration had led to frequent border clashes, and the Americans who poured into Texas won their independence from Mexico at the battle of San Jacinto in 1836. When the new republic petitioned to be admitted into the Union, Congress passed the Annexation Act in 1845. The step precipitated not only hostilities with Mexico but also the chain of events which brought on the Civil War.

Of all American conflicts the one with Mexico has been most often condemned as dishonorable. This tradition may be traced back to the rabid politics of the day, for the Whigs and Abolitionists came dangerously near to treason in their opposition. Such leaders as Clay and Webster denounced the struggle as a conspiracy to bring more slave-holding states into the Union; and a Whig newspaper declared that it would be "a joy to hear that the hordes under Scott and Taylor were every man of them swept into the next world."

That such strictures are not to be taken too seriously is shown by the fact that both victorious generals became Whig candidates for the presidency. Nor is there any more reason for accepting at face value the denunciations of American motives by Whig orators. The fact is that slavery had been the "burning issue" of the republic ever since its foundation, and the actual causes of Mexican strife were obscured by the causes which would soon lead to Secession.

An understanding of this background is necessary to dispel a commonly held belief that the United States crushed a weak and unprepared neighbor by overwhelming bulk. On the contrary, the actual odds in the field weighed heavily against the Americans. The northern army faced four times its own numbers in the principal battle; and as a triumph of skill over obstacles, Scott's campaign had no equal in the world during the half century after Waterloo.

The impression of might was given by an absence of the traditional blunders, combined with discipline in the ranks and efficiency in the command. For this war remains unique in American history in that it was fought chiefly by regulars instead of the usual militia hordes. Had the same skill been shown in 1812, the country would have been spared many humiliations, for the operations of 1847 presented more difficult military problems.

Nor could it be said that the Mexicans were unworthy opponents. A generation of civil war had trained a hardy native soldiery which defended a formidable terrain with ability as well as courage. In the critical campaign the Americans found the enemy particularly strong in engineering and artillery—two arms which are not the resources of a military rabble.

The Mexicans struck first by crossing the Rio Grande in April, 1846, and capturing 60 prisoners. The American forces in Texas consisted of about 2,000 regulars supported by frontiersmen. Under the command of General Zachary Taylor, a border captain whose bravery and resolution compensated for lack of technical knowledge, they drove the invaders across the river after winning two combats.

In the summer and autumn California and New Mexico were occupied by small American forces which met no resistance. Taylor's reinforced army continued into northern Mexico, taking Monterey after three days of street fighting. During these preliminaries President Polk's efforts to negotiate a peace were balked by Santa Anna, the exiled Mexican dictator. As the Napoleon of the West, this adventurer made no secret of his desire for a war which would restore him to power. He took command in the field, and after the failure of Polk's overtures the first battle occurred at Buena Vista in February, 1847.

Upon learning that Taylor had been reduced to less than 5,000 troops by detachments and withdrawals, Santa Anna made a swift and secret march northward with an army of 20,000. Although the Americans were surprised near Saltillo, they retired in good order to a mountain pass. In the absence of Taylor they found a more expert leader in Colonel Wool of the regulars, but the fury of the first day's assault forced them out of the pass. The next morning Santa Anna put to flight a militia regiment in the centre and threatened the rear. On his return Taylor wisely left the conduct of the battle to trained officers, and better cavalry and artillery tactics at last gave the small army the victory at a cost of nearly 40 per cent in killed and wounded.

The Mexicans were well armed with imported weapons, so that the two-day engagement emerges as the first in history to be fought with percussion firearms. American riflemen used the long bullet, but the superiority of Taylor's infantry fire may be attributed to marksmanship rather than any material advantage. The merit of the Colt revolver had a more dramatic success, since it played a decisive part in the counter-attacks of the American dragoons.

Buena Vista interrupted Polk's plan to abandon the northern campaign and strike at the heart of Mexico with an expeditionary force under Winfield Scott. General-in-chief for the last seven years, the huge Virginian had been the intellectual leader of the army since 1815. After Waterloo, while still suffering from a wound, he visited Europe at his own expense to study tactics. His insistence on punctilio and military scholarship earned him the nickname of Old Fuss and Feathers, but the veteran's high opinion of his own ability found proof in 1847.

Vera Cruz surrendered in April after a brief siege, while about two marches inland Santa Anna defended the highway to the capital with an army estimated at from 15,000 to 18,000. The Mexican commander, who had just been elected president, held the mountain pass of Cerro Gordo in a wild country of jungle-clad defiles and steep cliffs. His engineers had fortified the position well, and three batteries guarded against frontal attack.

Scott halted his army of 8,500 until he could make thorough reconnaissances. A brilliant young engineer, Captain Robert E. Lee, finally

discovered a route which offered a possibility of a wide turning movement. While the bulk of the army threatened in front, a brigade swung
far around to the west in an attempt to carry the cliffs. Although surprised, the Mexicans resisted with such resolution that the first day's
assault failed. Scott sent reinforcements and the following morning the
Americans scaled the heights in the Mexican rear to rout a retiring
enemy.

Sixty cannon, 5,000 prisoners and thousands of muskets were taken
by victors who suffered fewer than 500 casualties.

Now came an interlude of nearly three months while the American
president again tried to negotiate a peace. Scott aided by enforcing a
discipline which respected not only the personal and property rights but
even the pride of the high-spirited Mexicans. Desertion, rape and murder were punished by some fifty executions during the campaign, and
pillage or violence by confinement at hard labor. All supplies were
purchased at fair rates by invaders who interfered as little as possible
with local laws and customs.

The resulting order did not fail of appealing to a people who had
known little but civil war and anarchy under Santa Anna. The Mexican
church co-operated openly with the Americans against the dictator, but
he retained a firm enough hold on the country to reject peace offers
while organizing a last army of defense.

Early in August the American commander cut loose from his base at
Puebla to advance on the capital. He had drilled his troops constantly
during the three months, so that he now had a force of regulars supported by dependable militiamen. In his esteem for merit over bulk
Scott even went so far as to send home unreliable volunteer units whose
enlistment terms would soon expire, though at one time his field
strength dwindled to 6,000. This process of elimination gave him one
of the finest instruments of American history; and as its leaders he
trained such promising young officers as Lee, Grant, Jackson, Meade,
Beauregard, McClellan, Longstreet and Joseph E. Johnston.

THE CAPTURE OF MEXICO CITY

The army had been reinforced to a strength of about 11,000 before
crossing the mountains, but the attempt remains one of the most
audacious undertakings of the century. The Duke of Wellington, after
estimating the perils ahead, is said to have commented, "Scott is lost!
He cannot capture the city and he cannot fall back upon his base."

Certainly it would be hard to find a terrain offering more difficulties than the approaches to the Mexican capital. Despite its high altitude and the lofty mountains in the background, the plateau about the city consisted largely of marshy land crossed only by stone highways built upon raised embankments. Three lakes further aided the defense by limiting the invader to as many roads. Turning movements were next to impossible, and cavalry or artillery mobility were denied an attacker making frontal advances in cramped columns.

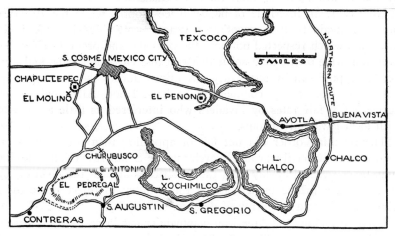

Scott's Mexico City Campaign

Although Bonaparte had failed against comparable difficulties in his Arcola campaign, the American army and its sixty-one-year-old leader staked their very survival on the success of the campaign. Lacking the troops to garrison his line of communications, Scott brought only enough supplies to last him over the mountains. The invaders met no resistance in passes rising to an altitude of 10,000 feet; but upon reaching the crossroads of Buena Vista (not to be confused with Taylor's battlefield) they discovered that Santa Anna stood on the defensive with from 25,000 to 30,000 troops drawn up behind a shield of field fortifications.

Scott's chances of victory depended on the reconnaissances of his riflemen and dragoons. Again Captain Lee distinguished himself by bold surveys which revealed that the main route was strongly defended by the fortified hill of El Penon, bristling with guns and surrounded by marshes. The long northern highway around Lake Texcoco presented a series of redoubts held by artillery and good troops. There remained only the little-used road south of Lake Chalco, which Santa Anna had neglected because much of it lay under water at this season.

Scott concealed his intentions by sending a division toward El Penon; and on August 15 he accomplished the "impossible" by turning the main Mexican defenses. Wading for long stretches, and dragging the artillery through mudholes, the entire army reached San Augustin after only a few skirmishes with guerrillas.

Upon recovering from the surprise, Santa Anna took advantage of his interior lines to rush troops to San Antonio and the Contreras region. Between the two points a wilderness of lava beds, known as El Pedregal, had long been deemed impenetrable. Only a mule trail led from San Augustin to the Contreras highway, making it necessary to build a road for the artillery.

Scott divided his army, sending a detachment to open the way to the Contreras route while he feinted against the strong position at San Antonio. In 48 hours the Americans not only built their road but also established communications between the two forces across the wastes of El Pedregal. On the nineteenth the first battle took place north of Contreras. About 5,000 Mexicans and 22 guns were entrenched near the highway, and two American divisions met a costly repulse in a preliminary effort. That night Scott sent reinforcements across El Pedregal, and at daybreak on the twentieth a flank attack routed the enemy with losses of 1,500 men and all 22 guns. The victory not only opened a main highway to the city but also forced Santa Anna to withdraw in haste from his untenable position at San Antonio.

It may be noted that Contreras was the third two-day battle of the war, showing the intensity of the fighting on both sides. That same afternoon, before the enemy could recover, Scott stormed Santa Anna's new position at Churubusco without taking time for reconnaissance. Nearly 1,000 Americans fell before the guns of a bastioned fieldwork, but after a hard struggle the Mexicans were dislodged and pursued to the city gates. Since dawn Santa Anna had lost more than a third of his total strength, for his casualties at Churubusco alone have been estimated as high as 10,000, chiefly prisoners.

Scott, who suffered a slight wound, made use of his success by trying again to negotiate a peace. Two weeks passed in which the victors deferred to the vanquished, but the armistice served only to confirm the obstinacy of Mexico's dictator. For Santa Anna still had about double the numbers of his adversary, and the fortifications about Chapultepec were thought invulnerable.

On September 8 the Americans attacked El Molino del Rey, an old gun foundry which had been converted into the principal outwork of Chapultepec. The defenses proved more formidable than had been anticipated, and Scott's men endured several bloody repulses before carrying the position at a cost of 900 casualties. About 2,000 of the enemy were killed and wounded in addition to the 700 captured.

The American bombardment of Chapultepec commenced on the twelfth in preparation for an escalade the following morning. The rocky mass of the fortress rose 200 feet above the plateau, its level top being surmounted by the national military academy which had turned out so many excellent artillerymen and engineers. As new evidence of their skill, they planted land mines among the almost vertical approaches, though the Americans managed to cut most of the fuses.

The assault was delivered from two sides against a garrison which kept up a heroic resistance to the last. Once the ditch had been crossed, the Americans swarmed up the ladders with such spirit that Chapultepec fell after an hour of hand-to-hand fighting. The losses of both sides were heavy, particularly among the officers.

Even after this success two more sharp combats were necessary at the city gates before the capital surrendered. Santa Anna commanded in person at the San Cosme fortifications, where a cannon dragged to a church tower by Lieutenant Ulysses S. Grant ended a struggle of several hours. On the next road to the south another American detachment had to battle its way from house to house. Scott had made ready for a resumption the next morning when a white flag appeared as Santa Anna withdrew his remnants.

The casualties of six hard-fought actions could have left the American commander no more than 7,000 effectives to hold a city of 180,000 inhabitants. In this emergency his good order and moderation repaid him, for a majority of the people preferred American occupation to the dictator's ferocious exactions. At a later date, indeed, a group of leading citizens proposed to Scott that he become their president as a prelude to annexation of the entire country by the United States. The general declined this unusual offer, but his administration created a memorable chapter of good will in the relations between victors and vanquished. As a climax Scott arranged for the final terms to be signed in an outlying town, so that the peace treaty would not be named after a capital which had put up such a gallant resistance.

THE WRITINGS OF JOMINI AND CLAUSEWITZ

In 1854, on the eve of the Crimean War, Napoleon would have found startling changes in the continent he had aspired to rule. His signaling semaphores had been superseded by wires which transmitted messages in minutes instead of hours. The logistics of his famous marches were relegated into the past by railways which linked the principal cities. On the sea the smudge of steamships could be seen as often as the white sails of a vanishing maritime age.

Perhaps most astonishing of all, no war of any consequence had taken place in Europe since Waterloo. All of the marshals were dead, and the few surviving veterans of Rivoli had come to be regarded with that mixture of wonder and tenderness which is the due of relics. Only in the political field would the emperor's ghost have trod upon familiar ground, for the ideas of 1789 were still potent enough to have frightened half the monarchs of Europe at the barricades of 1848. History had repeated itself with strained fidelity, moreover, as another Bonaparte made himself emperor of France by declaring, "The name of Napoleon is in itself a programme."

Still, it may be questioned whether the conqueror would have deemed his nephew a worthy successor. The ideas of the French Revolution would have been as distasteful to him as any other ruler of the day; and in spite of their new weapons, the generals of 1854 were obviously dullards and reactionaries.

In all Europe but a single military institution remained to comfort anyone who had seen the sun rise over Austerlitz. For Baron Antoine Jomini still occupied his pedestal as the foremost living analyst of Napoleonic warfare. He had begun his first treatise the year after Marengo, and the last word would not have been written until a few months before the outbreak of the Franco-Prussian War. During these sixty-eight years the critic's industry equaled his longevity, but his *Précis de l'art de la guerre* (1836) has generally been accepted as the masterpiece of a large shelf of books.

As a young Parisian bank clerk in 1798 the Swiss writer returned to his homeland to resist French aggression, rising to the command of a battalion at the age of twenty-one. In 1801 he began his *Traité des grandes opérations militaires,* the publication of which brought him such recognition that he served as Ney's aide-de-camp at Austerlitz. During the Jena campaign he was attached to Napoleon's headquarters. The emperor created him a baron and general at the age of twenty-eight, and after the Peace of Tilsit the czar also retained him as a military coun-selor. He acted as Ney's chief-of-staff in Spain and during the German operations of 1813, though his advice did not save that marshal from some costly blunders. Berthier's jealousy finally made Jomini's position so difficult that he took advantage of his neutral standing to join Alexander in the campaign leading up to the battle of Leipzig.

Although he refused to take part in the violation of Swiss territory and subsequent invasion of France, Jomini had been a participant in nearly the entire Napoleonic era. His approach is consistently that of the military scientist seeking to condense his observations into a work-able formula for other soldiers. Hence his books are filled with a pro-fusion of diagrams, axioms and geometrical allusions which often obscure the human side.

As if aware of a weakness in psychological respects, he warned that "war is an impassioned drama and by no means a mathematical equa-tion." In spite of such qualifications most of Jomini's followers have erred in the direction of a rigid precision. The master himself cannot escape this reproach, for he concluded that "the skirmishers made the noise, but the columns carried the position." And though pointing out the error of "making war trigonometrically," he emphasized his arcs, angles and diameters at the expense of such values as surprise and mobility.

His tremendous appeal in his own age was based on the understand-able desire of contemporary soldiers to recapture the skill of Napoleonic warfare without the excesses. The miseries of those years were too well remembered in the middle of the nineteenth century for any government to risk a recurrence. If a further object lesson were needed, Europe's revolutions of 1848 had proved that masses trained by universal con-scription might rise in arms against their divinely appointed rulers.

Jomini's revised but authentically Napoleonic formula seemed to offer the advantages of a rose stripped of its thorns. Despite a long and flattering association, he saw the conqueror's faults plainly enough to comment, "One might say that he was sent into the world to teach generals and statesmen what they ought to avoid." That these short-comings could be avoided was the lesson of the analyst's shelf of books. It could not fail of impressing a generation which wished to believe in the possibility of another Austerlitz without the subsequent embarrass-ment of another Waterloo.

Jomini's great rival and contemporary, Karl von Clausewitz, did not live to see the publication of his masterpiece *Vom Kriege* in 1832. Nor did he ever enjoy a tithe of the immediate fame, though the Prussian writer's theories have endured to shape the warfare of a day which has forgotten the *Précis*. This outcome, which would have amazed the soldiers of 1854, may be explained by the fact that Jomini produced a system of war, Clausewitz a philosophy. The one has been outdated by new weapons, the other still influences the strategy behind those weapons.

Born in 1780 of a Polish family which had emigrated to Magdeburg, Clausewitz entered the army at the age of twelve. As aide-de-camp to Prince August he served in the Jena campaign, being captured and held prisoner in France for two years. After assisting Scharnhorst in the reorganization of the Prussian army, he became a staff officer in the campaigns of his country's War of Liberation. During the years after Waterloo the solitary, red-faced general was reputed to be a secret drinker because of the midnight hours he devoted to his writing. He died of cholera in 1831 with the task uncompleted, and the following year his widow published the two volumes which have been translated into English as *On War*.

Although Clausewitz hoped "to write a book which would not be forgotten in two or three years," that very fate seemed at first to have overtaken his masterpiece. Even in Prussia the work gained no great renown for a decade, and not until the end of the century did it interest French and English soldiers. This interim of oblivion cannot be attributed to dull contents, for Clausewitz sounded a defiant challenge to critics of the Jomini school who contended that art might gain the ends of slaughter:

> Let us not hear of generals who conquer without bloodshed. If bloody slaughter is a horrible sight, then that is a ground for paying more respect to war, but not for making the sword we wear blunter and blunter by degrees from feelings of humanity, until some one steps in with one that is sharp and lops off the arm from our body.

Breaking with the precepts of Saxe and Guibert as well as Jomini, the Prussian writer ridiculed as "philanthropists" all theorists who believed in "a skilful method of disarming and overcoming an enemy without great bloodshed." Clausewitz held that

> . . . in such dangerous things as war, the errors which proceed from a spirit of benevolence are the worst. . . . He who uses force unsparingly, without reference to the bloodshed involved, must obtain a superiority if his adversary uses less vigor in its applica-

tion. The former then dictates the law to the latter, and both proceed to extremities, to which the only limitations are imposed by the amount of counteracting force on each side.

Describing war as "a trinity of violence, chance and reason," he further showed his contempt for Jomini's axioms of precision by stressing the element of unpredictability. "There is no human affair which stands so constantly and so generally in close connection with chance as war."

Clausewitz developed his doctrine of the "annihilation principle" by urging that "the military power must be destroyed, the country con-quered so that it cannot produce a new military power, and even the *will* of the enemy destroyed. . . . The decision by arms is for all transactions in war, great and small, what cash payment is for bill transactions."

As a departure from Saxe, who believed and demonstrated that manoeuvre could take the place of combat, Clausewitz insisted, "We have only one means in war—the battle. . . . The bloody solution of the crisis, the effort for the destruction of the enemy's forces, is the first-born son of war."

The Prussian writer also differed in italics from predecessors who emphasized the possibilities of skill prevailing over mass. "An unbiased examination of military history leads to the conviction that the *superiority in numbers becomes every day more decisive.*" Lest the lesson be underestimated, he drives it home by repetition. "The principle of assembling the greatest possible numbers may therefore be regarded as more important than ever."

It would be unfair not to add that Clausewitz, as well as Jomini, tempered his conclusions with many and significant qualifications. Thus if the Prussian writer seemed to advocate a savage and unlimited onslaught of bulk, he also maintained that an "absolute and real" war could be justified only by a great national emergency. "If we require from the enemy a small sacrifice, then we content ourselves with aiming at a small equivalent by the war, and we expect to attain that by moderate efforts." He made it plain, furthermore, that the statesman and not the soldier should prescribe the application of a nation's armed might:

> To leave a great military enterprise or the plan for one to a *purely military judgment and decision* is a distinction which cannot be allowed, and is even prejudicial; indeed, it is an irrational pro-

ceeding to consult professional soldiers on the plan of a war, that they may give a *purely military opinion* upon what the cabinet ought to do. . . .

Clausewitz could be subtle and logical as well as forceful, and no critic has ever shown a deeper understanding of the moral side of war— the fears and fatigues of the soldier, the doubts and hesitations of the general. In his tactical deductions, based on sound judgment and long experience, he often reveals as keen an appreciation of dexterity as Saxe or Guibert. Nor is he an unyielding dogmatist even in respect to his own principles. "Pity the warrior who is contented to crawl about in the beggardom of rules!   . What genius does must be the best of rules, and theory cannot do better than show how and why it is so."

Yet in the long run a military theorist must be judged not only by his writings but also by the interpretation of them on future battlefields. If Jomini's axioms and diagrams produced geometrical soldiers, it is because his exceptions proved less convincing than his main system. And if Clausewitz fathered the most bloody and wasteful era of warfare in modern times, it is because lesser minds accepted his philosophy rather than his tactics, his flashing phrases rather than his sober modifications.

Prussia was uniquely open to persuasion in the early nineteenth century. As the laboratory of the Clausewitzian doctrines, that kingdom had already entered upon a new and ruthless era of nationalism following the Napoleonic wars. Only a spark would have been needed to touch off such explosive material, and the nation's military theorist had provided a conflagration.

THE CRIMEAN WAR

The causes of the war which France, Turkey and Great Britain declared on Russia in 1854 were nearly as confused as the results. It is clear at any rate that the czar's threatened occupation of Constantinople would have endangered the British overland route to India. The French emperor, for his part, needed few pretexts to enter a conflict which promised without undue risks to carry on the Napoleonic tradition.

The recently launched *Himalaya*, largest iron screw steamer in the world, helped to transport the redcoats to Black Sea regions. With dimensions of 340 by 46 feet and a speed of nearly 14 knots, this pioneer vessel proved so well constructed that she remained in service as a naval collier at the late date of 1918.

As a further example of mechanical progress, most of the British and

French infantry were now equipped with the rifle. This improvement had been made possible by the perfection in 1849 of a cylindriconoidal lead bullet which required no special skill in loading. Named after its French inventor, the "Minié ball" was an elongated projectile with a deep hollow at the base to receive an iron plug. Although small enough to slide down the bore without being driven in by the ramrod, the bullet was expanded by an explosion which pushed the plug into the indenture and spread the base into the grooves of the rifling.

For a century the greased patch had utilized the principle of expansion, but only the American frontiersman had mastered the art of loading by this method. The cylindriconoidal bullet, by making the rifle a universal weapon, thus ranks with the percussion cap as an advance in the development of firearms. Within a few more years American experiments proved that the iron plug had been unnecessary, for the pressure of the gases served as well to spread a hollow base. By 1851 the "rifle musket" had been adopted for the entire British infantry, and the French equipped twenty battalions which were trained to manoeuvre as the *pas gymnastique* of five miles an hour.

Events in the Crimea soon demonstrated that generalship had not kept pace with mechanical improvements. Memories of Waterloo so obsessed the British commander, Lord Raglan, that he had a regrettable habit of referring to his allies as "our enemies, the French." They in turn were under the spell of recent operations in Algeria, and the war seemed to them another colonial adventure. The Turkish general, Omar Pasha, occasionally injected a note of realism, but his opinions were calmly ignored.

At the outset a curious stalemate developed as both sides maintained a stubborn defensive on opposite shores of the Black Sea. When at last the allies broke this deadlock, their expeditionary force landed in the Crimea without maps or other information about the region. Never since the Crusades have armies lost their way with more persistence, for the Russians refused to be outdone in the memorable blunders of the campaign.

The action centered about the eleven months' siege of Sevastopol, attacked both from the land and sea. Attempts at relief by field armies led to such actions as Alma, Balaklava and Inkerman, with the French and British riflemen holding a tremendous advantage over Russians depending on the smoothbore. Even so, the allied troops were so miserably led that England's poet laureate made a recitation piece for schoolboys out of the tactical error which sent the Light Brigade to its destruction.

The telegraph, appearing for the first time in modern warfare, only added to the confusion by bringing Paris and London within a few hours of the battlefield. Napoleon III kept the wires warm with advice, and a crisis threatened when he proposed to take command in person. General Simpson, successor to Raglan, grumbled that the new means of communication had "upset everything," and the French commander Niel complained bitterly about being placed "at the paralyzing end of an electric cable."

If the misadventures of the generals sometimes came near to farce, at least the sufferings of the rank and file supplied a note of authentic tragedy. Thousands of allied troops died of disease as a consequence of improper food, clothing and sanitation. At one time more than half the British army was unfit for service, and two out of every three Russian recruits were prostrated by illness or starvation on the way to the front. All told, more than 100,000 men were lost in the defense of Sevastopol, the majority of them succumbing to epidemics.

It would hardly be an exaggeration to say that the only generalship of the war was shown by Florence Nightingale in her efforts to overcome the apathy of the British War Office. The English nurse had an able ally in William Howard Russell, who ranks as the first great war correspondent of modern times. Since Waterloo the advances in popular education had created a great new reading public, so that future generals and statesmen would have to reckon with the power of the press. During the winter Russell reported the horrors of the Crimea in such fearless detail as to cause the downfall of the Aberdeen ministry. Although the commanders at the front accused him of actual treason, his revelations of mismanagement paved the way for the reforms brought about by "the angel of the lamp."

The story of Florence Nightingale's superhuman labors has been told too often to need repetition. Up to this time, shocking as it may seem, the care of the sick and wounded in European wars had not caught up to the high standard of responsibility maintained by Byzantine armies of the so-called Dark Ages. Within five months in 1855 the English nurse reduced the hospital death rate in the Crimea from 42 to a mere 2 per cent. Even this victory is insignificant as compared to her greater triumph in establishing the right of the ill and maimed to decent hospitalization. It is the single redeeming result of a war which otherwise would be remembered only for object lessons.

THE ITALIAN WAR OF LIBERATION

After the fall of Sevastopol the conflict drifted into an inconsequential peace, and four years later the French emperor began a new military adventure in Italy. Sardinia had led an uprising against Austria in which the Italian patriots were defeated as a result of Radetzky's able generalship. A decade later Cavour found Napoleon III willing to intervene in the hope of territorial gain. The French and Sardinian forces concentrated on the Po in May, 1859, as the emperor took the field in person. They defeated the Austrians in the battle of Magenta on June 4, and on the twenty-fourth the war came to an abrupt end with an allied triumph on the field of Solferino.

At this zenith of the Second Empire the "false Napoleon" seemed to have fully restored his uncle's glories as he dictated terms to young Emperor Franz-Joseph. It would be left to history to reveal how ill-prepared the victorious army had been. The great Jomini, then past eighty, supplied a plan of campaign so rigidly Napoleonic that it met the unorthodox issue of railways by ignoring them altogether. In their sweep across Lombardy the French often invited flank attack, but the enemy obligingly took no advantage. As Philip Guedalla has remarked, "the French enjoyed in 1859 the pleasing experience of defeating with the methods of 1809 an adversary whose military thought was that of 1759."

The sudden peace, far from being the triumph it appeared, owed less to Austria's predicament than the victor's fear of Prussian intervention. Hence he compromised by accepting the cession of Lombardy, though he had promised Cavour to conquer to the Adriatic. France received Nice and Savoy in full payment for work which had been only half done.

Even in their diagnosis of the brief campaign the emperor and his generals revealed a lack of military judgment which would meet a sterner reception in 1870. As the legitimate heirs of First Empire precepts, they attributed their victories to columns of bayonets, though the introduction of the first rifled cannon deserved more credit. The advantages of rifling and elongated projectiles had long been recognized by gunners, but all previous attempts failed to overcome the handicaps imposed by muzzle-loading. The sponsors of the improvements found a patron in Napoleon III, who had written two treatises on artillery while still a pretender. Concluding that the short range of the smoothbores had prolonged the siege of Sevastopol, he ordered secret experiments to be made in Algeria. These tests resulted in the adoption of a rifled, breech-loading fieldpiece which proved its practicability at Magenta and Solferino.

In both battles the new French guns had double the range as well as an advantage in accuracy. Firing from well-protected positions in the rear, they broke up Austrian cavalry and infantry concentrations with grape and canister. The enemy's demoralization was completed by the tactics of French skirmishers who had learned irregular warfare in the Algerian campaigns. Thus the victory had been three-fourths won before the columns of bayonets advanced.

On the day of Solferino, however, the emperor showed more concern with humanitarian than technical aspects. Sitting his horse in the brilliant sunshine, he smoked countless cigarettes and muttered, "Poor fellows! Poor fellows!" Napoleon's sympathy went no further, but a Swiss spectator named Henri Dunant wrote a booklet recording his distress at the lack of medical attention for the wounded. The publication of *Un Souvenir de Solférino* aroused the conscience of Europe to such an extent that the foundation of the international Red Cross may be dated from that bloody field.

Dunant urged that "the leaders of the military art of different nationalities agree upon some sacred international principle, sanctioned by convention, which, once signed and ratified, would serve as the basis for the creation of societies for the aid of the wounded in the different European countries." During the next few years he traveled from one capital to another, appealing to governmental officials. The French emperor lent his influence, then at its height as a result of Solferino, and delegates from twenty-six nations met at Geneva in August, 1864.

As an outcome of the conference, the Geneva Convention announced the adoption of such principles as care for the wounded of both sides, respect for the rights of prisoners, immunity of military hospitals from bombardment, and protection for the materials of medical services. Thus another flag had come into being, and the white banner with the red cross would soon be known throughout the world as a symbol of international mercies.

III

THE NEW WARFARE OF THE WEST

I consider the central idea pervading this struggle is the necessity that is upon us of proving that popular government is not an absurdity. . . . If we fail it will go far to prove the inability of the people to govern themselves.

—LINCOLN

I T HAS truthfully been said that Napoleon might never have lived, for all the influence his actual methods had on the soldiers who deified him two generations later. The Europe of the mid-nineteenth century seemed to have recaptured the caution, the detachment, the moderate efforts and results—everything except the skill of the wars conducted by Louis XIV.

Although universal conscription had been retained in principle, the armed hordes of 1813 were but a memory. In 1860 so many exemptions were allowed, combined with inducements to re-enlist, that most of the continental armies had become fairly small professional forces supported by a reserve of trained citizens. Indeed, a contemporary observer might have supposed that war had been reduced to a secondary rôle in a changing world. Inventions multiplied as the factories of Europe opened up new markets for the products of the machine. Already the nations were beginning to reach out for newly explored African territory; and so briskly did trade follow the flag that Commodore Perry's warships visited Japan with a request for more friendly commercial relations.

Battle seemed as archaic as a gladiatorial contest in comparison, for Europe's masses were no more involved than if watching a bloody spectacle in the arena. As the telegraph brought daily reports from the Crimea, the newspapers were read with a fascination once reserved for sporting events. England's booming textile industry responded to the popular interest by naming a new style of greatcoat for the absent-minded Lord Raglan. In Paris, then fascinated by the new chemical dyes, the modistes found a similar inspiration in the Italian War, so that *magenta* became the latest shade for the *garibaldis* worn by fashionable ladies on the boulevards.

There was, in short, no hint of the tremendous struggle impending at this moment in the New World. Nobody could have supposed in 1860 that four million men would soon be under arms, fighting a people's war with extraordinary violence.

As measured by anything in Europe's past, the American Civil War was fought on a tremendous scale. The theater of operations embraced an area so vast that a single flanking movement covered a distance of 800 miles. More than 2,000 combats took place, of which 149 were engagements of enough importance to be called battles. Half a million soldiers gave their lives, either on the battlefield or as a direct consequence of the campaigns. The cost in money to the North alone amounted to nearly five billion dollars; and the South did not admit defeat until every resource, both moral and material, had been exhausted.

In its tactics as well as weapons this struggle is the first in history which can readily be identified with the warfare of the present day. The railway and telegraph at last came into their own, after having confused and annoyed the professional soldiers of Europe. Hundreds of steamships, plying the great rivers and the 3,500-mile coast line, supplied and transported the armies of both sides. Eli Whitney, the father of mass production in arms, had inadvertently helped to bring on the strife by his invention of the cotton gin, which provided the Confederates with the sinews of war. Cyrus McCormick's reaper, by opening up the prairies of the West, added enormously to the strength of the Federal cause.

The first duel between ironclad warships was followed by the first railway gun, the first electrically exploded torpedo and the first recorded instance of a vessel being sunk by a submarine. The first metallic cartridges were invented for the first breech-loading repeating rifles to meet the test of war. The machine gun had its first demonstration on the battlefield, and wire entanglements made their first appearance.

To this list might be added such recent arms as the revolver and rifled cannon, neither of which had as yet proved its worth in large-scale operations. Nearly as much originality was shown in the adaptation of weapons which had been thought obsolete. Among these revivals were the military observation balloon, lamp and flag signaling, the land mine and the hand grenade.

Generalship reached such a high degree of skill as to threaten a stalemate. At least three commanders on each side displayed an ability seldom matched in the Napoleonic wars, though the spirit of professionalism was entirely lacking. For it is a remarkable fact that nearly all the American military leaders remained civilians at heart, sincerely deploring the bloodshed and destruction they wrought. Even the rank and file—the "thinking bayonets" of the North and South—sensed that they were fighting for causes which concerned the whole world. Not only was the age-old institution of slavery making its last stand, but also a patriarchal and agrarian civilization menaced by the machine. Thus on the battlefields of Virginia and Tennessee the eighteenth century contended against the nineteenth, the future against the past. On both sides the conflict was waged with fury, with faith in ultimate victory, and with a conviction of righteousness which Julia Ward Howe immortalized in her "Battle Hymn of the Republic":

He is coming like the glory of the morning on the wave;
He is wisdom to the mighty, he is succor to the brave;
So the world shall be his footstool and the soul of time His slave;
    Our God is marching on.

The Awakening at Shiloh

In nearly all material respects the North held an obvious advantage. Twenty-two states were arrayed against eleven which had only a third of the total population. The enlisted men of the small army and navy remained with the North, as did a majority of the officers. Most of the industries of the nation were located in this region, as well as the financial and shipping centres.

The strength of the seceding states lay in the fact that they must be invaded and conquered in detail before the Union could be restored. The reduction of such a vast area, thinly populated, poorly served with roads and railways, presented more difficult military problems than those which had awaited Napoleon's army of half a million in Russia. To solve them the North could count on but 17,000 men in the regular army (most of them guarding frontier outposts) and a navy of 40 steam vessels manned by 7,600 sailors.

Despite the general unpreparedness, both sides were further weakened by an excess of confidence. The Confederacy sacrificed its initial political advantage by firing the first shot at Fort Sumter, and Northern pacifists could no longer plead that "the wayward sisters be allowed to depart in peace." In turn the Union politicians accused Winfield Scott of senility when he predicted that a large army of regulars would be needed for three years to put down the rebellion.

The general-in-chief was now rounding out a half century of leadership which gives him a unique position in the history of the United States Army. At the age of seventy-five, his huge frame tortured by dropsy, the pompous veteran could no longer take the field, though he had trained nearly every officer who rose to fame during the next four years. Events were to prove that Scott's advice might have led to a much less costly effort, but the Union statesmen believed that 75,000 three-month volunteers would suffice. With like fatuity the Confederacy also placed its faith in untrained recruits.

The Edgehill of the American war took place in July, 1861, when two mobs of armed civilians blundered into contact at Bull Run, thirty miles south of Washington. The ensuing grapple gave no hint of the tremendous military events which would develop in later months. Forces amounting to about 20,000 on each side fought on a ragged three-mile front, with the honors fairly even. After several hours of awkward advances and flights, the Confederates won by virtue of the fact that "the mob which fled first was the loser."

The result gave neither any cause for congratulation. The victors were so demoralized that a single regiment of Federal regulars succeeded in keeping open a line of retreat. In the North humiliation was heaped upon defeat when the routed militiamen were joined by a horde of spectators who had made a picnic out of an occasion promising an easy triumph.

Bull Run had such a sobering effect on the generals that an eight-month lull now began in the eastern theater as both sides turned grimly to the recruiting and drilling of large volunteer armies. This interlude suited the purposes of President Jefferson Davis of the Confederacy, who favored a defensive strategy in expectation of aid from France and Great Britain. The two European powers, depending on Southern cotton for their prosperity, had already made it evident that they favored the cause of rebellion.

From the beginning the political duel between Davis and Abraham Lincoln had an unusual influence on the outcome. Both leaders owed their power to universal suffrage, and both made every move in a flood-light of publicity directed by the newspapers. As a graduate of West Point and hero of the Mexican War, the Confederate appeared to hold an advantage over his unknown opponent, yet Lincoln scored first by detaching the border states from a possible Southern allegiance. His unfailing tact, in contrast to ill-timed enemy encroachments, secured Maryland, West Virginia, Kentucky and Missouri for the Union, though the four states supplied thousands of soldiers to the armies of Secession.

This political victory gave the Federal forces an early ascendancy in the western theater. By the end of 1861 bases had been established in Kentucky and Missouri, and General Ulysses S. Grant won the first great military success of the war when 12,000 Confederates surrendered at Fort Donelson in February, 1862.

It might accurately be said that this triumph was gained by the West over the South. The volunteers from the prairie states were fighting for economic as well as moral causes, and control of the Mississippi seemed to them a more vital issue than slavery or states' rights. Here again Jefferson Davis suffered a political defeat, for the gaunt, homely man in the White House knew how to appeal to his own section of the country.

The victor of Donelson also represented the democratic West, which preferred that its heroes be of common clay. After gaining distinction in the campaigns of 1847, Grant had resigned from the army, his good name tarnished by reports of intemperate drinking. In civil life he failed even more dismally, for the outbreak of war found him scarcely able to support his family as a clerk at the age of nearly 40. Life had given this dusty, thickset little man few reasons for self-confidence, yet it was exactly this quality which distinguished his first important action as a commander.

His superior, General Halleck, dubbed Old Brains because of his military pedantry, had singled out for attack the rebel forts on the navigable Tennessee and Cumberland rivers, only ten miles apart at this point. Fort Henry fell easily to Commodore Foote's gunboats, the garrison taking refuge in the bastioned earthwork dominating the Cumberland. On February 12 Grant violated all strategic rules by investing Donelson with a force which at first did not equal the numbers of the defenders. Foote's gunboats met a costly repulse from the plunging fire of the fort, and the beleaguered army nearly succeeded in cutting its way through. At this crisis the Federal brigadier's comment reveals the bold assurance which became his most valuable resource as a general:

> Some of our men are pretty badly demoralized, but the enemy must be more so, for he has attempted to force his way out, but has fallen back: the one who attacks first now will be victorious and the enemy will have to hurry if he gets ahead of me.

Never has character played a more decisive part in strategy, for the opposing commanders of the four years were intimately acquainted with one another as a result of youthful associations at West Point or in the Mexican campaigns. Thus Grant based his next moves on an appraisal of his adversaries' probable reactions:

> I had known General Pillow in Mexico, and judged that with any force, no matter how small, I could march up to within gunshot of any entrenchments he was given to hold. . . . I knew that Floyd was in command, but he was no soldier, and I judged that he would yield to Pillow's pretensions.

Grant's assault on the fifteenth came as the final touch of a campaign won by psychology rather than heavy blows. Riding up and down the blue ranks, he impressed his shaken recruits with the foe's weakness rather than the difficulties ahead, "Fill your cartridge boxes quick and get into line—the enemy is trying to escape, and he must not be permitted to do so!"

The raw Federal volunteers crashed through the abattis like veterans, taking the key point of the fort. That night, faithful to Grant's analysis of their character, Floyd turned over the command to Pillow, and that general resigned in favor of Buckner, who accepted the victor's terms of unconditional surrender.

Two months later Grant had reason to learn that confidence can be carried too far. After Donelson the ambitious Halleck prepared to cut the South's principal lateral railway at Corinth, Mississippi. Union forces amounting to 33,000 were sent up the Tennessee River to Pittsburgh Landing under Grant and his second in command, William Tecumseh Sherman. There they awaited reinforcements of 20,000 and 7,000 led by Buell and Lew Wallace.

Only recently the nervous, irascible Sherman had been accused of insanity because he continually imagined himself imperiled by vast enemy armies. Now under the spell of Grant's assurance he swung so far to the other extreme that the dispersed Federal forces were not entrenched in a position of strong defensive possibilities. Neither of the two commanders dreamed that the Union concentration might be interrupted as 40,000 rebels burst out of the woods on the morning of April 6 to achieve one of the most incredible surprises in the annals of war.

The Confederate generals, A. S. Johnston and Beauregard, had advanced over miserable roads from Corinth. Having given up all hope of a surprise, they would have abandoned the attempt except for the difficulty of extricating green troops. Hence they were nearly as confused as the enemy commanders when the Southern advance caught the Federal outposts eating breakfast.

It has been estimated that 80 per cent of the troops on both sides had never seen action before. Discipline may be judged by the fact that company officers were often elected by their men. Sanitation was wretched, and the messes served by inexperienced cooks made dysentery a common complaint. In short, two mobs of military innocents met at Shiloh, and it is small wonder that they were soon out of control. The miracle is only that both stood up to two days of terrific fighting, enduring casualties which would have appalled regulars.

Flights and surrenders quickly reduced the Union forces to scarcely more than half the numbers of their assailants. The reinforcements of Buell and Wallace were still miles away, and only the wild disorder of the advancing rebels enabled a few firm Federal officers to form some semblance of a line. Sherman atoned for his carelessness by holding desperately to frustrate Johnston's plan of rolling up the Union army from right to left. Grant coolly assembled guns for a final stand with his back to the river after his troops had pushed back a mile. Meanwhile the battle resolved itself into savage and disconnected scuffles.

The crisis came after nine hours. Johnston fell mortally wounded and Beauregard saw that his exhausted recruits could make no further headway. That night, as a chill rain drenched both armies, Grant again showed his grasp of the moral factor, "Whichever side takes the initiative in the morning will make the other retire, and Beauregard will have to be mighty smart if he attacks before I do."

In proof of this prediction the reinforced Federals recovered their lost ground the next day. The Confederates fought valiantly for eight hours, but the pressure of fresh enemy troops forced Beauregard to retire early in the afternoon.

It would be hard to find another instance of war's amateurs battling with such tenacity. At dusk on April 7 not far from 20,000 dead and wounded lay exposed to the sleet. The Confederate casualties amounted to 22 per cent, and the Union brigades which fought on both days lost about a third of their numbers.

THE GENERALSHIP OF LEE AND JACKSON

Politically and geographically, the eastern theater seemed to have been created as a battleground of civil war. The two capitals faced each other at a distance which invited attack, yet the material advantages of the Union were balanced by the Confederacy's natural resources of defense. For the Blue Ridge range crossed Virginia like a partition dividing the state into strategic compartments. On the western side the Shenandoah Valley slanted toward Washington and away from Richmond. Thus the Federal invader taking the shorter route risked an enemy sweep which might cut his communications or threaten his capital. If he provided against this peril, his army had still to overcome a desolation of second-growth thickets, known as the Wilderness, which proved to be worth an army to the South.

Nevertheless, the burden of the offensive rested upon the Union, and prospects of victory were bright in the spring of 1862. While Shiloh could not be called a convincing triumph, Beauregard's retreat had been a moral blow to the South. Corinth and Memphis fell during following weeks, and in the trans-Mississippi region the Confederates suffered a crushing defeat on the field of Pea Ridge. Still farther west, the rebel invaders of New Mexico were driven back into Texas and the entire Southwest secured permanently for the Union.

As an even more irreparable disaster, the metropolis of the Confederacy surrendered in April to Admiral David Farragut. In 1813 the "American Nelson" had won his first renown at the age of twelve by commanding a British prize. Before reaching his majority he was recognized as a leader, having mastered French, Italian and Arabic in addition to his tactical studies. Sixty years old at the outbreak of the Civil War, Farragut demonstrated at New Orleans that he had lost none of his daring. In defiance of the War Department, which held that the forts of the lower Mississippi should be slowly reduced by bombardment, he ran past them at night with a fleet of wooden ships to gain the capitulation both of the strongholds and the city.

This success enabled the Northern blockade to reduce to a trickle the munitions the South had been receiving by way of Mexico. Meanwhile the new Union general-in-chief, George B. McClellan, launched a long-prepared offensive against Richmond with an army which he had drilled all winter. An accomplished organizer and trainer, the dapper young commander also showed good strategic sense. Alert to the

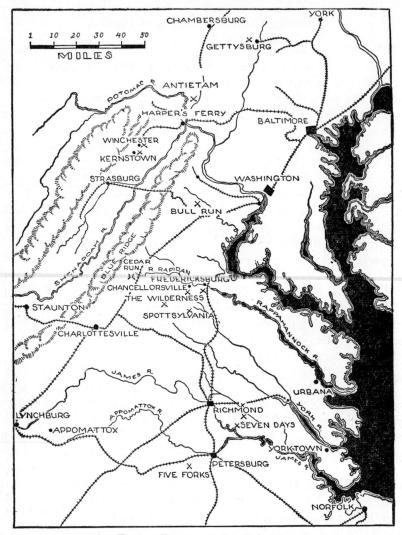

Eastern Theater of the Civil War

perils of the direct overland route, he relied on Federal sea power to transport his main force to a point on the coast opposite the enemy capital.

With this peril added to its late reverses, the prospects of the South were gloomy. Any hope of European intervention had become faint when the North was thrown into a brief panic by the appearance of the Confederate ironclad *Merrimac* in Hampton Roads. In an afternoon the new naval monster created tactical history by destroying two helpless wooden sailing ships, and Secretary of War Stanton predicted a bombardment of Washington.

Contrary to a popular impression, the *Merrimac* was not the first armored vessel. Wooden and leather armor had been used in ancient times, and in 1859 the French covered the steam warship *Gloire* with iron plates. A few months later the British navy launched the *Warrior*, whose 4.5-inch sheathing gave 42 per cent of the visible target full protection against any naval guns then in use.

Late in 1861 the North and South began a similar race in construction which the *Merrimac* won over the *Monitor* by a few hours. Protected by four inches of iron over 22 of wood, the Confederate ship mounted six smoothbores and four rifles. Of even more interest to naval men was her 1,500-pound cast-iron beak, reviving ramming tactics after a lapse of centuries.

The workmen were driving in the last rivets as the *Merrimac* steamed out of Norfolk to sink the sloop-of-war *Cumberland* with her ram. Next she drove the *Congress* aground and riddled her with round shot. The Federal frigate was burning at midnight when the *Monitor* arrived for the first duel between ironclads the following morning. From her low, flat hull projected a revolving turret armored with 8-inch plates and mounting two 11-inch smoothbores. Yet even these heavy guns merely damaged a few of the *Merrimac's* plates in 20 direct hits. The 22 hits scored by the Southern ship did no more harm, and at noon the contest ended in a draw.

Not a man on either side had been killed, and both ironclads soon vanished from history, the *Monitor* sinking in a storm and the *Merrimac* being blown up by her crew during the evacuation of Norfolk. The importance of the duel lies in the fact that wooden sailing vessels had become obsolete in four hours. Under Farragut's leadership the Federal shipyards immediately began to turn out armored, steam-propelled gunboats and larger turret ironclads known as monitors, setting an example which European navies were not slow to follow.

With the North again in full command of the sea, McClellan's expeditionary force landed on the Yorktown peninsula early in April. Lesser Federal forces converged on Richmond from the north and west, so that the Confederate lines, facing double their own strength, were stretched from the Alleghenies to the Atlantic.

Behind this impressive show of might was a fatal lack of harmony. Lincoln and Stanton had already lost faith in a commander whose unruly egotism gave the excuse for their interference. Hence the Federal chiefs were at cross purposes when the South found leadership in the appointment of Robert E. Lee as military adviser to President Davis.

Although Winfield Scott had considered him the foremost American soldier, the fifty-five-year-old engineer officer failed in his first Civil War campaign. Commanding raw troops in mountain warfare, he lost West Virginia to McClellan, who leaped into national prominence as Lee retired to supervise coast fortifications.

In the spring of 1862 the commander of the main rebel army, Joseph E. Johnston, could think of no better defense than awaiting the foe near Richmond. Lee persuaded Jefferson Davis that a passive resistance could lead only to disaster. With cool audacity he urged a diversion in the Shenandoah Valley which would cause the enemy to be more concerned about the safety of Washington than the capture of Richmond. In combination with this thrust he advised that Johnston march boldly out to meet McClellan in the peninsula. The Southern defense was thus conceived as a far-flung campaign on interior lines, relying on manoeuvre to take the place of numbers. And while Lee could not have known of the dissension among Northern leaders, he correctly read the doubts and evasions behind McClellan's Napoleonic airs.

The Shenandoah operations were assigned to General Thomas J. Jackson, who had gained the imperishable nickname of Stonewall at Bull Run. A latter-day Covenanter in his stern piety, he took the fierce joy of an Old Testament warrior in the craft and guile of combat. Immediately grasping Lee's purposes, he pushed up the Valley to Kernstown and flung his 3,500 troops against double their numbers. The Confederates were beaten with sharp losses, but the defeat amounted to a strategic victory before McClellan landed. For Lincoln and Stanton became so alarmed about Washington as to exaggerate the enemy's strength and intentions.

This illusion Jackson fostered by the swift and deceptive dashes of his "foot cavalry" during the next two months. With forces never larger than 17,500 he outwitted three Federal generals commanding a total of 65,000, the bulk of which were intended to reinforce McClellan's right wing. Even more astonishing, the Southern general contrived to bring a large numerical superiority to each of the four combats in which he defeated his opponents.

Early in May he drove one Union force into the mountains of western Virginia before turning on Banks with 17,000 men against 9,000. While pursuing this adversary northward, Jackson suddenly wheeled to overwhelm another small enemy detachment. Then pressing on to Winchester, he struck Banks and hurled the Federal remnants across the Potomac.

McClellan was now within sight of Richmond's steeples, but Jackson had created a panic in official Washington. Far from strengthening the army in the peninsula, Lincoln and Stanton appealed for reinforcements to defend the capital. All available troops were set in motion against Jackson, who not only made good his escape but defeated the Northern advance units in two final rear-guard clashes.

Although Washington had never been in actual peril, the celebrated "Valley campaign" neutralized the great Federal advantage in weight. McClellan advanced slowly and timorously, sharing in the alarm of the Union capital while thousands of his troops sickened from fever in the swamps. So cautious were his decisions that the retreating Johnston struck the first blow on May 31 at Seven Pines. The two-day battle ended indecisively, its most noteworthy result being the appointment of Lee to field command after Johnston fell severely wounded.

As his first move the new leader pretended to reinforce Jackson while secretly ordering him to hasten by road and rail to Richmond with his best troops. By this time the Shenandoah campaign had succeeded in depriving McClellan of the reinforcements he expected on his right wing as he advanced up both sides of the Chickahominy. Lee could thus count on 87,000 men against his adversary's 109,000. By brilliant utilization of the works south of the river he stationed 28,000 of his total to hold 75,000 of the enemy. With the remaining 59,000 he struck the 34,000 Federals on the north bank to launch the savage encounters known as the Seven Days' battle.

From June 26 until July 2 the sleepy little swamp villages were overrun with the most terrific contest ever known in the New World up to this time. On the opening day President Davis watched 2,000 of his men fall in frontal attacks, yet Lee continued to rain blows on the enemy's right flank. On the twenty-eighth the Union forces withdrew across the Chickahominy after losing 5,000 prisoners in a desperate action at Gaines' Mill. By his own admission McClellan now fought to "save the army" as he abandoned any designs on Richmond and retreated toward the James. In spite of costly checks, Lee followed him with relentless attacks which culminated on the seventh day with a repulse at Malvern Hill as 6,000 rebels were mown down within a few hours by entrenched riflemen.

Although the grand tactics of the Seven Days appear awkward in comparison to Lee's later triumphs, he fully accomplished his object of delivering Richmond. The losses of each side were at least 15,000, and in addition McClellan had a fifth of his total forces incapacitated by fever. As the measure of his frustration he sent hysterical messages of reproach to Lincoln and Stanton which had much to do with his subsequent removal from command. Undoubtedly he had been much handicapped by civilian interference, but Lee's strategy must be given the major credit for the result.

LEE'S INVASION OF THE NORTH

As its great tactical precept the Seven Days' battle demonstrated that Napoleonic warfare was dead. The merit of Robert E. Lee as a soldier is largely due to the fact that he needed no second lesson, whereas the generals of Europe continued to kneel before the historically embalmed corpse until 1918.

The flaming victories of the First Empire, it will be recalled, were based on the successive blows of massed guns, columns of bayonets and squadrons of heavy cavalry. All three were made possible by the short range of smoothbore muskets and cannon, permitting the attacker to concentrate within a few hundred yards of the foe. Lee became the first soldier to realize that the rifled musket and cannon had restored the balance between the offensive and defensive by multiplying the range of missile effect.

The fruits of his perception were a Fredericksburg and a Chancellorsville—the logical successors to a Saratoga. For the new warfare was as American as names like Shenandoah and Chickahominy; as American as the ears of green corn roasted over the campfire by bearded youths in slouch hats and homespun butternut brown. In 1862 the national weapon had simply arrived at a tactical maturity promised as early as 1777.

This growth may be attributed in part to mechanical improvements. The accuracy and reliability of the breech-loading Sharps rifle of 1848 had given "sharpshooter" to the language to denote an expert marksman. Next the Spencer repeating carbine of 1860 increased the soldier's rate of fire to 16 shots a minute. And with the American invention of the metallic cartridge, the bolt-action principle would soon come to be universally accepted.

Still, the defensive power of the infantry in Civil War operations cannot always be attributed to such innovations. Repeating firearms found no favor with Confederate generals, who feared the wastage of their limited supply of ammunition. Nor did the men in blue need anything more potent than single-shot rifles at Malvern Hill to work a fearful slaughter among their opponents.

It is in the entrenchments as much as the weapon itself that we find the clue to Lee's greatest victories. Just as the backwoods invention of the greased patch had given the American rifleman of 1777 an advantage, so in 1862 the equally practical "head-log" revolutionized tactics. This improvement consisted merely of two logs so placed on the parapet as to allow the entrenched soldier to fire from a slit between them. Thus protected from the hasty and scattered shots of advancing foemen, he could aim from a rest with a sense of security. Ax and spade soon became almost as important as the rifle itself, since nearly all the Civil War campaigns took place in wooded country. With constant practice the troops of both sides learned to throw up log-faced earthworks in an incredibly short time, and even the Northern revival of hand grenades did not solve the problems of the offensive.

Ever since Saratoga, when Morgan's men took cover in the autumn woods, concealment has been an essential of sound rifle tactics. More by necessity than design, the Confederates became the first great army of modern history to benefit from protective coloring in their uniforms. The butternut brown homespun worn by most of the troops actually owed to lack of manufactures, but in the field it helped to reduce casualties and permitted many a surprise.

Lee's generalship rested largely on his ability to make use of such factors. For the Southern leader did not depend on the rifle pit solely for defense; he also made it the pivot of attack. Relying on the proved fact that a marksman in a trench could take care of several foemen, he planned to neutralize a large portion of the enemy's bulk and create the opportunity for a decisive counterstroke. On several fields he carried his daring to such lengths as to divide his army in the face of a more numerous foe, knowing that a regiment in the trenches was worth a division in the open.

Of course two could play at this game, but in 1862 the leading Federal tacticians were still worshiping at the shrine of Austerlitz. Both

McClellan and Halleck had written treatises based on Jomini's interpretations of Napoleonic warfare, and even the kepis of the Northern soldiers showed the French influence. It is not surprising, therefore, that Federal columns of bayonets were sometimes sent forward in the best traditions of the Empire, only to be torn to tatters by unseen opponents. On the other hand, the riflemen themselves developed such confidence that the war presented several instances of troops firing in turn from parapet and parados to repel an encircling enemy.

The two other pillars of Napoleonic warfare, massed guns and charges of heavy cavalry, fared no better than the bayonet column in the Civil War. Great artillery concentrations at close range could readily be broken up by rifled cannon; and onslaughts of horsemen were suicidal against infantry weapons which killed at nearly 500 yards. The Confederate armies, holding an early cavalry superiority, needed only a few costly lessons before limiting their operations to raids aiming at securing information or destroying supplies. Thus during the Seven Days the 3,000 sabers of General J. E. B. Stuart rode entirely around the Union army in a spectacular sweep.

But if Lee rejected outworn tactics of the past, no soldier over showed a better grasp of timeless strategic principles. The Shenandoah and Richmond operations are often treated separately, yet both derived from the same conception. Now planning a new campaign on interior lines, the Southern leader decided soon after the Seven Days to strike the Northern army on the Rappahannock before it could be reinforced by troops returning from the peninsula.

The self-seeking Halleck, accepting the credit for Grant's victories, had been named general-in-chief after McClellan's debacle. Another Western soldier, John Pope, took command of the Army of Virginia with a boastful and tactless general order hinting that Northern defeats were due to fainthearted efforts. At a stroke of the pen he lost the respect of his troops, and a few weeks later Lee and Jackson demolished the remnants of his military reputation at the second battle of Bull Run.

Just as Carnot's armies had profited from poverty, so the Confederates, living on the country, outmarched enemies tied to their wagon trains. On August 25 Lee detached Jackson, and that general made a wide detour to the Federal rear, destroying the stores of the advanced base at Manassas Junction. Pope immediately advanced to trap his daring opponent. Although Jackson could have escaped, he invited attack in order to lure Pope toward Lee, who followed with the bulk of the Confederate army.

The Union commander had just been strengthened with troops disembarked at Aquia Creek, bringing his strength up to 70,000 against Lee's 55,000. On the twenty-ninth he fell upon Jackson alone with overwhelming numbers, but never did the defensive power of entrenched riflemen prove itself more effectively. Holding behind a railway embankment, the detachment stood firm until the next day, when Lee's fresh divisions delivered the counterstroke. Only the magnificent fighting qualities of Federal troops prevented the victory from being complete, but Pope retreated with losses of 14,000 men and 30 guns at a cost to Lee of about 9,000 casualties.

A few days later, having been reinforced from Richmond, Lee carried the war to the North. Without hoping for a military decision, he aimed at such political objects as influencing the coming elections and detaching Maryland from the Union.

The time could not have been more propitious, for Northern morale reached a low ebb after Second Bull Run. Already the distracted man in the White House had found Halleck a pompous pedant as military adviser. In the field it became necessary to reinstate McClellan, who at least had shown ability as an organizer.

Meanwhile Lee again divided his army, sending Jackson in an attempt to capture Harper's Ferry with its strong garrison. By a prodigious stroke of luck, the order for the separation fell into McClellan's hands, giving him the cue to redeem himself with a battle of annihilation. Yet even this amazing opportunity went begging as the Northern general advanced with his wonted caution. So slow were his movements that Jackson took Harper's Ferry and reunited with Lee on September 16 to accept battle the next day.

Due to the Confederate vice of straggling, Lee's army had melted away until he could bring but 41,500 troops into line on a strong defensive position at Antietam Creek. McClellan's numbers were 81,176, but the story of the day is told by the fact that not more than two of his six corps were ever engaged simultaneously. Two remained in reserve, seeing almost no action in a battle fought in detail by the other four. Often the advancing Federals were outweighed at the point of contact by riflemen taking every advantage of excellent natural cover. Lee handled his army faultlessly and the following morning his troops awaited a resumption which McClellan declined. On the nineteenth the invaders fell back across the Potomac without molestation, having suffered about 10,000 casualties as compared to 12,000 for the North.

Among the other distinctions of the war, Antietam became the first battle of history to be photographed. Matthew Brady's camera, focused on the windrows of dead behind Maryland rail fences, has left a pictorial record never equaled by any written description. By this time the newspapers had scores of war correspondents in the field, so that problems of censorship became urgent for both sides. Thus every effort was made to present Antietam as a great Union victory, though even Lee's retreat could not save the North from a profound disappointment at the result.

FREDERICKSBURG AND CHANCELLORSVILLE

With infinite patience Lincoln left McClellan in charge until November in spite of his dilatory strategy. Then having failed with conceited generals, the president placed the Army of the Potomac under Ambrose Burnside, who had twice declined a command for which he felt himself unfitted.

The only Union victory of the autumn months had been political, when the Emancipation Proclamation gained world sympathy for the cause. The military situation had grown more gloomy as a Confederate offensive swept over Kentucky to install a provisional governor. Grant and Sherman were making little progress in their attempt on Vicksburg, and Missouri faced the threat of invasion. The Northern faults in the conduct of the war were exhibited at their worst when Lincoln pushed the reluctant Burnside into an ill-planned advance against Lee on the Rappahannock. Delays ruined any element of surprise, and the Union commander's modest estimate of his talents found a tragic justification at Fredericksburg.

Behind the river the 79,000 Confederates held a ridge on a six-mile front. On December 12 the advance units of the 122,000 Federals were severely harassed while crossing, and after issuing conflicting orders Burnside decided on an assault the next morning. On the rebel left, held by General James Longstreet, the Union divisions swept forward time after time against riflemen firing from behind a stone wall. The attempts had no adequate artillery support, and not an attacker reached the objective in this critical quarter. That night Burnside withdrew his wrecked army, having lost 12,650 dead and wounded, and the enemy about a third as many.

A few weeks after "the horror of Fredericksburg" came the news of an even greater slaughter in Tennessee. General William Rosecrans, advancing with an army of 43,000, encountered the 37,000 Confederates who had retreated from Kentucky under Braxton Bragg. On the last day of 1862 a desperate struggle took place at Murfreesboro, with losses of 13,250 to the Federals and 9,865 to the foe. Both armies remained in position after this bloody and indecisive affair, and several days later Bragg retreated from an adversary too exhausted to pursue.

In the eastern theater the winter passed quietly as the two armies faced each other across the Rappahannock. The new Northern commander, "Fighting Joe" Hooker, took every measure to restore the morale of his troops for a supreme test in the spring. Lee and Jackson had meanwhile been planning an invasion of Pennsylvania, but the enemy moved first in an attempt to turn their right flank and open up a route to Richmond.

Hooker's strength consisted of 120,000 infantry, 400 guns and a newly organized cavalry force of 12,000. Lee had recently sent Longstreet's divisions on a distant foraging expedition, so that he could count on total numbers of only 55,000.

Over the Union lines swayed an observation balloon, and in imitation of rebel raids Hooker detached most of his horsemen to destroy railways in the enemy rear and cut off retreat. On his left he assigned Sedgwick's 40,000 troops the task of crossing the Rappahannock to act as the tactical anvil. Simultaneously the commander proposed to lead an advance of 70,000 men from the right, with the design of crushing Lee between two overwhelming forces.

The three-day battle began on May 1. Lee gave Early's division the difficult duty of "containing" Sedgwick. With the balance of his army he moved boldly out to meet Hooker.

That afternoon the action took a new course when the Federal general encountered enemy skirmishers in the tangled thickets of the Wilderness. Believing himself to be threatened by Lee's whole force, he fell back to Chancellorsville in an excess of prudence. There he awaited an assault as his troops occupied previously entrenched positions of great strength. Sedgwick had meanwhile been checked by Early, so that the original Federal plan had already failed as a consequence of tactical blindness.

The engagement entered its second phase early the next morning. With audacity which has seldom been approached, Lee sent Jackson and 26,000 troops on a 15-mile detour around the enemy right from the west and north. Closing in with his remaining 17,000 men, he demonstrated in front of Hooker's 70,000 as if preparing an assault from the east and south. During this critical interval Stuart neutralized the detached Union cavalry, while Early managed to hold Sedgwick at a distance.

At sunset the Confederate surprise revealed itself with the effect of an explosion. The enveloper became the enveloped as Jackson smashed into the Union right rear while Lee fixed the front. By dusk the enemy flight had become a panic, but in the failing light Stonewall Jackson was mortally wounded by accidental shots from his own lines. The attack faltered as subordinates took up the pursuit, and before nightfall Lee had lost his chance for a victory of annihilation.

On the morning of May 3 he resumed the attack as Hooker fell back to a line of inner works protecting his retreat. At once Sedgwick abandoned his efforts against the hard-pressed Early and prepared to withdraw across the Rappahannock. And though Lee continued in motion until the fifth, his rapid marches and counter-marches added little to the results already gained. The Federal losses have been estimated at 16,000, those of the Confederates at 12,000.

Chancellorsville clearly ranks as the masterpiece of Lee's career. In all history few battles compare with it for the daring utilization of every moral weapon against crushing material odds. Immediately afterwards the victor planned his second invasion of the North. Again his objects were chiefly political, but it also appears that he had some hope of a military decision which might win independence for the Confederacy in a peace of compromise.

IV

THE DECISION IN AMERICA

We have good corporals and sergeants and some good lieutenants and captains, and those are far more important than good generals.

—SHERMAN

THE Confederates who marched through the rolling farmlands of Southern Pennsylvania in June, 1863, had already established their claim to immortality as one of the great armies of all time. A tattered and dusty host, ill-shod and worse provided, they had still to meet a major reverse in two years of terrific fighting. Yet even at this pinnacle, the Southern soldier had limitations which have been very fairly analyzed by one of his battle leaders, General D. H. Hill:

Self-reliant always, obedient when he chose to be, impatient of drill or discipline, he was unsurpassed as a scout or in the skirmish line. Of the shoulder-to-shoulder courage, bred of drill and discipline, he knew nothing and cared less. Hence, on the battlefield, he was more of a free lance than a machine. Who ever saw a Confederate line advancing that was not crooked as a ram's horn? Each ragged rebel yelling on his own hook and aligning on himself! But there is as much need of the machine-made soldier as of the self-reliant soldier, and the concentrated blow is always the most effective blow. The erratic effort of the Confederate, heroic though it was, yet failed to achieve the maximum results just because it was erratic. Moreover, two serious evils attended that excessive egotism and individuality which came to the Confederate through his training, association and habits. He knew when a movement was false and a position untenable, and he was too little of a machine to give in such cases the whole-hearted service which might have redeemed the blunder. The other evil was an ever-growing one. His disregard of discipline and independence of character made him often a straggler, and by straggling the fruit of many a victory was lost.

Robert E. Lee commented even more gravely on such shortcomings. "The greatest difficulty I find is in causing orders and regulations to be obeyed. This arises not from a spirit of disobedience, but from ignorance."

Sometimes these lapses may be charged to Lee's own tolerance. As the direct heir of the Washington tradition, he went even further than the Revolutionary hero in his aversion to anything smacking of military tyranny. Only a few occasions are recorded when he reproved a subordinate, and several of his most trusted officers took liberties which few commanders would have allowed. Stonewall Jackson seemed to have an intuitive access to his superior's very thoughts; but men like the able and opinionated Longstreet were capable of causing friction in their very zeal for victory.

It was Lee's misfortune in Pennsylvania that a series of such incidents changed the entire course of his campaign. First, the boisterous Jeb Stuart chose this moment for one of his celebrated rides around the Federal army. This misunderstanding cost Lee dear, for he entered enemy territory in ignorance of Union troop movements.

Next, one of his corps commanders, A. P. Hill, decided on his own initiative to drive an opposing cavalry force out of the comfortable red brick town of Gettysburg. The invaders, some of whom were skylarking in plug hats taken from village shops, hoped to renew their supply of shoes. Instead, they met an unexpectedly stiff opposition from the Federal horsemen.

Early in the war the Northern squadrons had given such a poor account of themselves as to inspire Hooker's jibe, "Whoever saw a dead cavalryman?" The South, on the contrary, took a particular pride in an arm based upon aristocratic traditions. The saber was still more esteemed than the ugly and utilitarian revolver, and dashing raids were held to be a leader's greatest glory. Two years of success had given the Confederates a dangerous degree of self-esteem, for out of painful experience the enemy developed dragoon tactics which were to prove more effective. Discarding the saber altogether, they dismounted to pour in a deadly fire from Spencer repeating carbines, with the revolver being reserved for combat at close quarters.

These methods had delayed Lee's main cavalry force under Stuart, who was severely handled in several brushes before rejoining the main body. And on July 1 the enemy horsemen put up such a stout resistance at Gettysburg that Hill had to bring up reinforcements. Soon the Federals were strengthened by infantry arrivals; and in the afternoon fresh Confederate troops joined an impromptu fight which swelled to the proportions of a battle. By evening the defenders had been driven out of the town to a position on Cemetery Ridge, but the plans of both Lee and the Federal commander were upset. The soldiers had taken matters into their own hands, and a chance encounter committed both sides to the most memorable contest of the Civil War.

THE BATTLE OF GETTYSBURG

In its fashion the long-suffering Army of the Potomac also has a claim to immortality—a more remarkable claim, perhaps, than that of Lee's men. In two years the Northern veterans had fought six battles, incurring five defeats and a draw that could only be called a bitter failure. During this time they had served under as many commanders, each of whom had demonstrated his inferiority to enemy generals.

The Northern political leaders had failed as dismally in their use of a great numerical advantage. During the first year of the war some 500,000 three-year volunteers came forward, but the government suddenly adopted a policy of enlisting nine-month recruits. The South had meanwhile discovered the faults of the militia system, and early in 1862 an effective plan of universal conscription was adopted. Not until March, 1863, did the Union pass a similar law, but the provision allowing for the purchase of a substitute had the usual result of penalizing poverty. In reaction came the New York draft riots which resulted in 1,000 persons being killed or wounded.

Even these mistakes did not end the fatuity of the Federal policies. On several occasions whole armies of veteran troops were split up for such distasteful duties as hunting down guerrillas or serving as replacements. Add to these stupidities the fact that the Union had neither a strategic plan nor a unified command until the final year, and it is small wonder that military disasters occurred.

In spite of all, the men in blue had no air of being a defeated army. Eastern city dwellers, New England farm lads, midwestern villagers, they had somehow found a pride and cohesion which upheld the Southern forces from the beginning. This miracle had been wrought by the corps and divisional leaders—men like Sedgwick, Sickles, Hancock and Slocum. On the first day of Gettysburg such subordinates chose and occupied a position which Napoleon might have praised. For the Northern line has been likened to a fishhook, with Culp's Hill as the barb, Cemetery Ridge the shank and Round Top the eye. From the interior of this rough semicircle troops could readily be shifted to reinforce some other quarter, while the enemy must operate around the circumference.

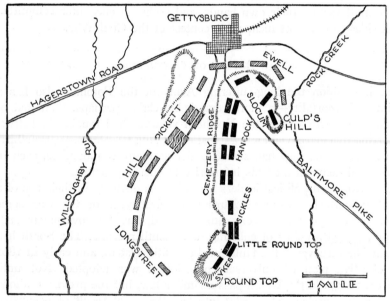

Battle of Gettysburg

The Army of the Potomac had need of every advantage. Its latest commander, George G. Meade, had been appointed on June 28 when Lincoln realized that the enemy had outmanoeuvred Hooker. A studious but uninspired soldier, he could not count on the numerical superiority enjoyed by his predecessors. Lee brought some 75,000 troops, and during most of the battle his army equaled Union forces which finally amounted to 82,000. Meade had not had time to cope with his new responsibilities, yet a decisive struggle had been thrust upon him without warning.

Under these circumstances it is not remarkable that his subordinates should have taken the initiative on the first day. That night both armies brought up all available troops, and the real contest began the next afternoon, after the Confederates had lost precious time by delays. Longstreet's corps advanced on the Union left, where contrary to Meade's orders his men occupied the famous salient of the "Peach Orchard" and "Devil's Den." Here a desperate grapple took place, with the defenders being pressed back after contesting every inch of ground.

During the action a Union brigadier influenced the course of the battle by seizing the Round Top heights, a key position which had been curiously neglected by his superiors. For a few minutes Longstreet's men won a foothold in the main line, being soon driven out by a determined charge. Then on the Federal left the firing died down as the troops of both sides became too exhausted for further efforts.

At the other end of the line the attack was also late, since it had been planned to await Longstreet's advance. Ewell took Culp's Hill without great difficulty, many of the defenders having been withdrawn to reinforce the other wing. But the Federal riflemen of Cemetery Ridge repulsed all attempts to storm the positions of the right-centre, and the second day ended with only the single Confederate gain.

This consolation was snatched away at dawn on July 3 when a relentless counterattack, well supported by artillery, recaptured Culp's Hill after four hours of fighting. The moral ascendancy now passed to the Union side, for it became clear even to the rank and file that Lee was not at his best. So far the Confederate attacks had been launched in detail, without benefit either of good timing or co-ordination. Longstreet's obstinate delays have been blamed, but at no time does Lee seem to have believed in the battle which had been forced upon him against his better judgment.

In support of this hypothesis, there is a false and alien note about his plans for the third day. Having failed on both enemy flanks, he now decided to aim the decisive blow in an attempt to break the centre. This has been called a "pseudo-Napoleonic" conception, since neither Federal wing had as yet been badly shaken in spite of heavy losses. The risks of defeat were multiplied by new delays, moreover, as Pickett's 15,000 attacking troops formed up in the morning, only to wait four hours for the order to advance.

At 1 P. M. the 140 Confederate guns began an intense preliminary bombardment. The 77 Union pieces in this quarter replied for half an hour, then held their fire for the enemy infantry. As the rebel lines swept forward, 1,200 to 1,400 yards separated them from their objective. The Federal guns raked this expanse with shot, shell and grape, and from the rifle pits came a hail of Minié balls when the attackers drew within range.

The story of the famous charge is best told by the bare statistics. In any age of war, including the present, losses of more than 30 per cent will usually suffice to stop assaulting troops. Yet out of the 4,500 men in General George Pickett's own division, 3,393 were left on the field—a casualty list of 75 per cent. All 18 of the brigade and regimental commanders were killed or wounded, and one regiment lost nine-tenths of its total numbers.

Even more amazing is the fact that these Virginians were not shattered in spirit. The survivors actually penetrated the Federal first line, falling back when Hancock's prompt counterattack deprived them of assistance from their supporting brigades.

The three-day battle virtually ended with this epic. Lee remained in line but his opponent did not assume the offensive. By the fifth the Confederates were in full retreat, with Meade still declining to attack even when they were held up for several days by the flood waters of the Potomac. The Federal casualties exceeded 23,000, and the invaders had about 30,000 killed, wounded and missing during their brief campaign.

THE SURRENDER OF VICKSBURG

Gettysburg has always been remembered more devoutly than any other military event in American history. A "soldiers' battle," noted neither for generalship nor decisive results, the struggle has its deep moral significance in the sacrifices made by armed citizens of both sides. Lincoln's noblest words were spoken as their epitaph; and the field itself, preserved as a national shrine, is still visited by many thousands of Americans annually.

The rejoicing in the North was intensified by the news of a second victory which ranks as the turning point of the war in material respects. On July 4 Vicksburg and its garrison surrendered to Grant, which meant that the Confederacy had been severed as a consequence of losing the Mississippi. From that moment the European powers based their diplomacy on the almost certain prospect of the Union prevailing in the end.

Vicksburg, from its situation on the bluffs, commanded a waterway which Sherman called "the spinal column of America." In his first attempt, late in 1862, Grant took the obvious approach from the high ground to the northeast. Two Federal columns set out from Memphis and Grand Junction with a long, single-line railway as their communications. The enemy soon cut this tenuous line of supply; and Sherman's force of 30,000 met a costly repulse at Chickasaw Bayou, on the bluffs of the Yazoo River.

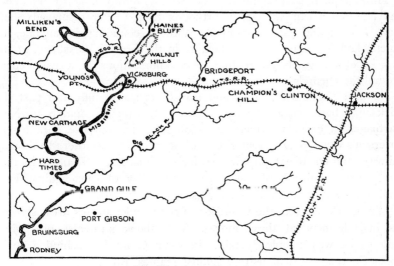

The Vicksburg Campaign

Due to Halleck's intrigues, military politics had a sordid influence on Federal strategy in the West at this time. Grant's simple and trustful nature placed him at a disadvantage in such dealings, and only Lincoln's faith saved him from sinking back into obscurity. Even so, his future was uncertain as he took command of a second expedition against Vicksburg in February, 1863.

With three corps at his disposal, the Federal general located his main base at Milliken's Bend. Here he could depend on the river for supplies, though surrounded by an appalling terrain of swamps, creeks and bayous.

As his first effort to reach the uplands east of Vicksburg, Grant began work on a canal across a bend of the river opposite the rebel left flank. In the light of later events it is apparent that he planned this colossal project chiefly to keep his army busy and in good spirits.

Next, and for similar reasons, he ordered the digging of a channel from the Mississippi to the upper Yazoo. The attempt so alarmed the enemy that the Confederates hastily constructed a new fort to protect their right flank. Following these two seeming failures, Grant crossed again from Milliken's Bend in an advance through the lowlands against Haines' Bluff. This third feint the enemy easily broke up by harassing operations in a dismal country of woods and bayous.

Throughout these preliminaries the stubby, untidy Union commander had in mind a campaign so unorthodox that it later dismayed Sherman, his leading hero-worshiper. Without confiding in anyone, he quietly laid his plans for a manoeuvre in the rear of Vicksburg, at the risk of exposing his entire line of communications in a wide curve around the enemy's flank.

Admiral Porter's gunboats and transports successfully ran past the Vicksburg batteries as the army began its overland march to New Carthage. In order to divert attention from his purpose, Grant sent Grierson's cavalry in a great circuit of 600 miles with orders to destroy railways and cut telegraph wires as far south as Baton Rouge. Another Union force under Banks advanced from New Orleans against Port Hudson, second only to Vicksburg as a river stronghold.

John C. Pemberton, the Confederate commander in this area, showed his bewilderment at these moves. A textbook strategist of limited outlook, he was completely taken in when Grant left behind a corps under Sherman to demonstrate against Haines' Bluff.

The Federal advance units had meanwhile crossed the river below Grand Gulf after routing rebel brigades appearing from Port Gibson to contest the advance. With Sherman's arrival early in May the army was reunited. Up to this time its supplies had come down the Mississippi on barges, but with only five days' rations, Grant cut loose altogether from his base.

The significance of this step cannot be overestimated. All European armies of the day had long ago returned to the magazine system in reaction to the excesses of the Napoleonic wars. The Federal forces of the first two years, influenced by continental models, likewise depended on bases and wagon trains. Early in the war Northern political leaders still hoped to gain converts in border regions, and generals were warned against offending the inhabitants. The Confederates, subsisting for the most part in friendly territory, were first to supply themselves at the expense of the enemy. This policy gave them an advantage in mobility which General Ewell summed up in his comment, "The path to glory cannot be followed with much baggage."

In proof of the epigram many a Northern general had been made to appear slow and soft by an adversary like Stonewall Jackson. Now for the first time on a large scale a Union army advanced without encumbrance while foraging for a living. Grant even went so far as to discard most of his remaining wagons after concluding that light vehicles could be collected to fill any temporary need.

The effect on Federal mobility was immediate and startling. Confederate officers, having grown accustomed to a snail's pace on the part of their opponents, were disconcerted by this advance. Their confusion increased when Grant turned toward Jackson instead of making the expected moves against Vicksburg.

Using the Big Black River as a strategic shield on his left flank, he planned to isolate his adversary and cut Vicksburg off from aid. Too late, Pemberton realized the danger and telegraphed for reinforcements. His own detachments were scattered in anticipation of another feint, and he could think of no better counterstroke than to threaten a line of communications which had ceased to exist. On May 14 the Union army reached Jackson, held by an inadequate force under Joseph E. Johnston. Grant stormed the town and gained control of Vicksburg's main railway.

Without checking his momentum, he drove between Pemberton and Johnston to prevent a junction. This stroke left the 45,000 Confederates separated into three groups. With a concentrated force of equal numbers, the Federal commander at last turned west to complete his great strategic circle by closing in on Vicksburg.

Johnston had now been manoeuvred completely out of the fight. As Pemberton's superior he ordered that fumbling general to unite his forces for resistance in the field, and on the sixteenth the outweighed Confederates were beaten by Grant with losses of 4,000 in the battle of Champion's Hill. The loser might still have saved his army by taking Johnston's advice and evacuating Vicksburg. Lacking the moral courage for this painful decision, he retired to await a siege which would have but one outcome.

By deception and manoeuvre Grant had already won his main objectives when he reached high ground at Walnut Hills and occupied Haines' Bluff as his new base of supplies. A few days later, counting too much on enemy demoralization, he made the single mistake of the campaign by ordering a general assault all along the line. From three miles of trenches the rebel riflemen replied with a murderous fire. Grant stubbornly tried again, and on the twenty-second he had to accept a second repulse with heavy losses.

Pick and spade served him better as weapons. Throughout June his parallels and approaches drew ever closer to the Confederate entrenched camp. In the Federal rear Johnston was assembling an army of relief, but after a heroic resistance Vicksburg came to a choice between surrender and starvation.

Grant showed his mastery of the moral side of war by offering terms which tempted Pemberton to capitulate on the national holiday. By paroling the 37,000 prisoners, moreover, the victor "hoped to demoralize the whole interior country still in rebellion, by spreading this dispirited mass of men among the yet unconquered remainder."

GRANT AS COMMANDER-IN-CHIEF

When Banks took Port Hudson five days later, most of the West had been lost to the Confederacy by shortsighted policies. From the beginning Richmond had treated this area as a secondary theater, too often assigning green troops and mediocre generals to its defense. Even when the region developed a first-rate soldier of its own in Nathan Bedford Forrest, the leaders of the South chose to regard him as a raider unfitted for higher command. It was left to Sherman and the enemy to estimate him at his true worth.

The neglect may be blamed to a great extent on the patrician codes which sometimes stultified rebel cavalry tactics. As a former horse trader and slave dealer, Old Bedford betrayed his lack of formal education by remarks which gave rise to many amusing legends. In compensation for errors in grammar, he destroyed a succession of Union detachments and preyed constantly on the main supply lines. These victories were usually gained by small armies which he recruited himself and armed with captured weapons. Receiving little aid from Richmond, he planned his own strategy and trained his men according to his own ideas. Only in this respect may Forrest be considered a guerrilla, for his mobile forces often included well-led infantry and artillery as well as mounted troops.

By the summer of 1863 he had at last made enough of an impression on his superiors to be used as a subordinate in major operations. Serving as a cavalry general under Bragg, he did much to bring about the first great rebel victory since Chancellorsville.

For several months Bragg and Rosecrans had contented themselves with a mild campaign of manoeuvre in middle Tennessee. Then the news from Vicksburg aroused the Federal general to an advance in which he took Chattanooga and drove his opponent into northern Georgia. In September both were watching for an opening when Bragg received five brigades of reinforcements under Longstreet. Attacking before Rosecrans had fully concentrated, he won a smashing victory in the bloody two-day battle of Chickamauga.

The movements of both armies being hidden by pine woods, Forrest's hard-riding cavalry gave Bragg the advantage in securing information. On the second day of furious fighting he learned of a wide gap in the enemy line, and Longstreet drove through to rout the centre and right. This disaster isolated General George Thomas on the left with only five divisions and a few brigades to withstand most of the Confederate army. In the next few hours the "Rock of Chickamauga" won his nickname by saving Rosecrans from destruction. Though at times his entrenched riflemen were beset from three sides, he defended the Federal retreat and even managed to extricate the bulk of his own forces. The desperation of the struggle is shown by losses of 16,000 for Rosecrans and nearly 21,000 for Bragg out of fairly equal numbers which did not exceed 65,000 on either side.

Thomas, like Farragut, was one of the many native Southerners who remained loyal to the Union. In reward for his stout defense, he soon succeeded Rosecrans to the command of the army he saved.

The battle also resulted in Grant's being appointed to supreme command in the West after the beaten army was besieged at Chattanooga and threatened with starvation. In October, when he arrived, Rosecrans' plight had grown urgent as the enemy hemmed him in from heights overlooking the valley. Grant established a new and effective line of supplies as his first move. Next he reorganized the strengthened army into three masses of manoeuvre under Hooker, Thomas and Sherman. By the middle of November he completed his plans to break the grip of an outnumbered but strongly entrenched adversary.

Opposite the Union right the Confederates held Lookout Mountain, 2,400 feet in height. The rifle pits of the centre covered the steep slope of Missionary Ridge, while the other rebel wing occupied earthworks extending from Tunnel Hill nearly to the Tennessee River. Two months of toil plus every resource of engineering skill had gone into these defenses, and Grant's plans reveal a confidence in keeping with his nature. In the centre he posted Thomas to fight a holding battle as Hooker and Sherman dealt alternating blows leading up to a double envelopment. All advances were to be closely co-ordinated with a view to avoiding the losses of Vicksburg.

Humor is seldom a feature of great military operations, but the "Battle Above the Clouds" had moments bordering on absurdity. The action began on November 25 with a limited gain by Sherman on the Union left. Meanwhile Hooker swept up to the summit of Lookout

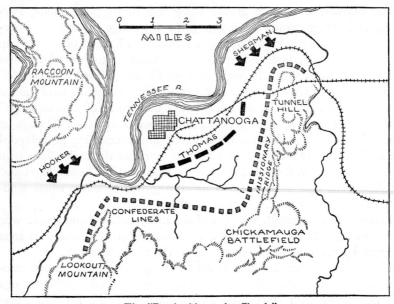

The "Battle Above the Clouds"

with unexpected ease. Sherman now moved forward for the decisive stroke at Tunnel Hill, and Grant sought to relieve the pressure on him by directing Thomas to advance on Missionary Ridge.

According to verbal orders the troops in the centre were to halt and consolidate their position after carrying the first line of rifle pits. Instead, the attackers ignored their officers and followed the evicted rebels up the slope. In a moment a scene of the wildest confusion ensued as pursuers and pursued alike drove the panic-stricken Confederates out of all their remaining works up to the summit. The result had been gained by sheer disorder, for in the excitement few shots from either side did any harm.

The Federal generals could only look on in stupefied wonder as their men broke the enemy centre, making the whole position untenable. The officers of the beaten army were equally helpless, and most of their 8,654 casualties consisted of prisoners taken in flight.

Grant's relentless pressure on both rebel wings had actually caused the collapse of the centre, and the victory gained him the chief command. Unquestionably Lincoln had erred in the past by interfering in military matters, though he declared that all he "wanted, or ever had wanted, was some one who would take the responsibility." In Grant he had found his man, and late that winter the recent tanner's clerk became the first soldier of modern history to command the army of a million troops.

THE STRUGGLE IN THE WILDERNESS

The new leader insisted from the beginning on regarding the far-flung Federal forces as one army with a single objective. For the past three years they had been acting as a score of independent and unharmonious groups which co-operated, in his own words, "like a balky team, no two ever pulling together."

With only a few weeks at his disposal, he planned a series of co-ordinated moves which aimed at no less a result than the military destruction of the Confederacy. Lee's superb army in Virginia remained the chief obstacle to such an outcome, but the Federal chief did not propose to supervise operations from Washington. Leaving Meade in nominal command of the Army of the Potomac, he allotted to himself a task in the field which six of his predecessors had conspicuously failed to master.

Grant hoped of course to be able to defeat Lee in battle. But this purpose was secondary as compared to the all-important object of "containing" that adversary while a second Federal army under Sherman completed a great flanking march through the heart of the Confederacy. Meanwhile the movements of two subsidiary armies were to be geared to the progress of the main campaigns.

Naturally, all the details of this vast plan were not perfected at once, and subsequent events proved it to be elastic in conception. To Sherman, then making final preparations in Tennessee, Grant merely wrote, "I do not propose to lay down for you a plan of campaign; but simply to lay down the work it is desirable to have done and leave you free to execute it in your own way."

Early in May Sherman advanced into northern Georgia as the Army of the Potomac crossed the Rapidan. Grant had considered the possibility of a sea expedition, but dismissed it in favor of the shortest overland route to Richmond. The enemy's army rather than the capital was his true objective, and he concluded correctly that Lee would fight every step of the way in its defense. Both Confederate flanks were also to be threatened by secondary Union armies—Sigel's corps pushing southward in the Shenandoah Valley, and a force under Butler demonstrating on the south bank of the James River.

Grant led about 115,000 men of all arms, including a cavalry corps of 13,000 under Sheridan. He hoped to avoid battle in the Wilderness, but his opponent was not one to sacrifice the advantages of those dense thickets, eroded gullies and abandoned surface mines. For while the Federal commander strove for attrition, Lee, with half the numbers, could only trust to endurance. After Gettysburg the Southern leaders realized that their main hope for independence lay in a strictly defensive strategy. Both sides had grown weary of the war, but the rebels were fighting for their homes, while upon the North fell the burden of invasion. Moral exhaustion might well decide the issue, and the South still had faith in an ultimate victory as Lee and Grant came to grips.

The world had grown accustomed to the battle of two or even three days, but the battle of a month foreshadowed the warfare of the next century. The casualty lists of the past had often been recorded in five figures, but the total losses in this colossal grapple were then believed to have reached 100,000. Hence it is not surprising that the chroniclers of 1864 tried to comprehend the deadlock by reducing it to four engagements between May 5 and June 3—the Wilderness, Spottsylvania, North Anna and Cold Harbor.

Actually these were but the high points of a fight which raged without intermission from the Rapidan to the Chickahominy. During the opening days in the Wilderness hundreds of wounded perished when the underbrush caught fire. Smoke filled the gloomy thickets as the two blind armies battered ceaselessly at each other. Without rest for his men, Grant swung swiftly over to the southeast, but Lee was not to be outflanked. At Spottsylvania his log-palisaded trenches faced the enemy in a "hog's snout" salient, so that troops from one wing could readily reinforce the other. Here the action went on for thirteen consecutive days, and at its height the struggle for the "Bloody Angle" lasted forty hours without a pause to bury the dead. Again Grant resorted to a well-executed flank march, and again his adversary awaited him at North Anna Creek behind a new semicircle of earthworks which repulsed all attacks with heavy losses.

All this time the Federal commander had manoeuvred with skill and daring, only to be checked by concentrations on interior lines which were never surpassed in Lee's greatest triumphs. Then on June 3 Grant made his single blunder by ordering a blunt frontal assault at Cold Harbor. A few hours later 6,000 slain and wounded were stretched out before the rebel rifle pits at a trifling cost to the defenders. And with this final slaughter the month's battle ended as the exhausted armies faced each other in trenches less than a hundred yards apart.

The Federal dead, wounded and missing have been estimated at 50,000, the Confederate losses at 32,000. Lee had retreated nearly to Richmond, yet both in tactical and political respects he must be credited with the victory. Grievous as his casualties were, amounting to 46 per cent of his original strength, he had won even the temporary advantage in the duel of attrition. For after Cold Harbor the Northern general was execrated as a "butcher" by newspapers which had recently lauded him to the skies. Throughout the Union the heart-rending casualty lists were blamed on the Administration; and in view of the approaching presidential election, the hopes of the Confederacy grew brighter than at any time since Chancellorsville.

Few soldiers of history have been the victims of an injustice such as has permanently clouded Grant's military reputation. Although he admitted his error at Cold Harbor, the blunder had been no more costly than Lee's frontal attacks at Malvern Hill and Cemetery Ridge. Throughout the entire war, moreover, Grant's total losses amounted to a smaller proportion than those of his great opponent. Yet in 1864 he had to endure a storm of abuse from his countrymen which has even been echoed by critics and historians.

In his defense he might have cited the fact that two Federal subsidiary armies had failed through no fault of his own. Franz Sigel and B. F. Butler were both political generals, the one because of his German-American following in the Middle West, the other in recognition of his influence with New England voters. Lincoln has been criticized for such promotions, yet in his sphere the president was making every effort to win the war.

Grant's plan of invasion had counted on pressure to be exerted on Lee's flanks by these two subordinates. Instead, Sigel's advance in the valley met an early defeat at New Market by a hastily improvised rebel force. On the James the 40,000 Federals under the Massachusetts lawyer gave Lee no concern in his rear. After a hesitant attempt Butler allowed himself to be bottled up in the Bermuda Hundred peninsula by Beauregard's little army.

Nor did Grant's troubles end here, for the reverse in the Shenandoah invited an enemy counterthrust a month later. The forthright Jubal Early swept Hunter out of the way and administered another beating to Sigel at Martinsburg before crossing the Potomac. By this time Washington had grown accustomed to rebel feints, but the alarm of 1864 became the most serious of the war. For a few hours, had he but realized it, Early probably held it in his power to capture the Federal seat of government! Only militiamen and civilians defended the outer works in the suburbs, but the invader hesitated until six Federal brigades put in an opportune appearance.

This humiliating episode was also blamed on Grant and Lincoln, thus adding to the complexities of a war in which moral and political decisions were as vital as strategy. The Democratic party, with the disgruntled McClellan as presidential candidate, had already announced a platform condemning the Union effort as a failure and urging a negotiated peace which would have meant a Confederate victory. In such an appeal to voters, the narrow escape of Washington served as well as Cold Harbor to arouse prejudice.

Grant met the crisis with magnificent moral courage. Only nine days after his repulse he won the most brilliant strategic success of his career—a triumph of skill which did more to ruin the South than a victory on the battlefield.

As a preliminary he ordered Sheridan's cavalry to threaten Charlottesville as Hunter created a diversion in the valley. These efforts were planned to draw Lee's attention northward while Grant further entrenched his Chickahominy position as a base for manoeuvre. With the utmost swiftness and secrecy he began on June 12 to transfer troops from lines within earshot of the foe. By the fifteenth the movement was well under way, yet Lee did not learn until the eighteenth that the whole Union army had crossed the James and swung around to his strategic rear in an advance on Petersburg. The importance of this withdrawal to the future of the war has been soberly estimated by a Southern critic, General E. P. Alexander:

> Thus the last, and perhaps the best, chances of Confederate success were not lost in the repulse of Gettysburg, nor in any combat of arms. They were lost during three days of lying in camp, believing that Grant was hemmed in by the broad part of the James below

City Point, and had nowhere to go but to come and attack us. The entire credit for the strategy belongs, I believe, to Grant.

The dangers and difficulties of the Federal general's plan were in proportion to the rewards. If detected by the enemy he ran the risk of being attacked in flank and beaten in detail with disastrous results. Yet in order to accomplish his purpose he had to move 115,000 men

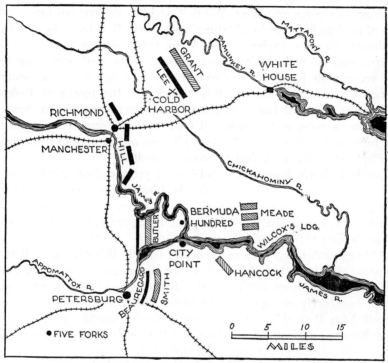

Grant's Crossing of the James

across the Chickahominy swamps, bridge a tidal river 2,100 feet wide, and shift his base of supplies 150 miles.

On the thirteenth Lee had word of enemy activity. Interpreting it as a threat to Richmond, he detached Hill's corps to defend the works east and south of the city. Beauregard first warned of the peril to Petersburg, though on the seventeenth his superior telegraphed in reply, "Have no information of Grant's crossing James River, but upon your report have ordered troops to Chaffin's Bluff."

Grant gave the command of his advance guard to General W. F.

Smith, who had distinguished himself at Chattanooga. These troops marched to Wilcox's Landing and were transported by water to City Point, whence they advanced on Petersburg works from which most of the defenders had been stripped. At this crisis the salvation of the Confederacy owed to Beauregard's audacity. With but 2,400 men against ten times their numbers, he counterattacked so boldly that Smith became paralyzed with indecision.

Hancock's corps was next. When it arrived, Beauregard made bold use of his interior lines to withdraw troops from the Bermuda Hundred positions opposite Butler. Hancock in turn allowed himself to be bluffed, and the main Union attack did not begin until Meade reached the scene with forces which brought the total up to 80,000 against 14,000 Confederates. Despite this superiority, the piecemeal Federal efforts met the usual fate of columns attempting to carry entrenchments by frontal asaults, and Beauregard held until Lee sent reinforcements. By June 19 Grant's aides had not only lost an opportunity to shorten the war but also incurred a total of 10,000 casualties.

Lee had clearly been outgeneraled, and yet the final result owed a great deal to recent battles in which he broke the nerve of the Union corps leaders. At no time could Grant count on such subordinates as Beauregard, Hill or Early; but without indulging in recriminations he drew up lines of investment.

Although much has been made of his bulk in this campaign, it may be noted that he lacked the numbers for a true siege. For three years the enemy had been fortifying the Richmond-Petersburg area, and Grant had barely enough strength to fix rather than surround an entrenched foe. Both sides could manoeuvre at will, and his opening moves were directed against the railways which brought supplies from Danville, Lynchburg and the port of Wilmington.

This decision was typical of the Union commander's strategy. Where his predecessors had aimed at Richmond, the moral objective, he took the surer method of attacking the enemy's economic resources. During the remainder of June his forces succeeded in destroying several junctions as well as sixty miles of track on the three principal routes. Lee countered with daring sorties which cost the Federals a total of 5,000 casualties; but his confidential message of July 21 to President Davis is testimony that Grant's crossing of the James had been decisive:

I hope your Exc. will put no reliance on what I can do individually, for I feel that will be very little. The enemy has a strong

position & is able to deal us more injury than from any othe: point
he has ever taken. Still, we must try & defeat them. I fear he will
not attack us but advance by regular approaches. He is so situ-
ated that I cannot attack him.

Lee, the master of surprise, daring and deception, had been immobilized by those very strategic weapons. For the opposing forces of the
Petersburg lines, sometimes only 50 yards apart, carried on a system of
warfare which their grandsons would inherit almost intact in 1918.
Even the wire entanglements, trenches, dugouts, listening posts and
bombproof shelters of 1864 differed in few respects from those which
would be seen fifty years later on the Western Front. Then in July the
Union army set another precedent by exploding an enormous mine, but
before the assaulting troops could climb out of the crater they were
counterattacked with losses of 4,300. This debacle brought Grant's
total casualties up to 75,000 in three months; and with Lincoln despairing of re-election, the Army of the Potomac settled down to an autumn
and winter of siege operations.

SHERMAN'S MARCH TO THE SEA

Public opinion in the North had already condemned Grant as another
Hooker or Burnside. The popular mind could more readily comprehend
a Cold Harbor than the crossing of the James, and the deadlock at
Petersburg seemed to have no connection with Sherman's gains in
Georgia. Yet even in the sphere of strategy a flank attack depends upon
the fixing of the enemy's main body, which had been Grant's primary
purpose when he crossed the Rapidan. Lee was now held powerless
to interfere as Sherman advanced to capture Atlanta in September.

Before setting out from Chattanooga the invader had planned so
thoroughly as to reconstruct in advance the parts of the railroad bridges
which he anticipated that the enemy would destroy. With Western
exaggeration Sherman's troops boasted that he had even equipped
himself with spare tunnels. Instead of fighting, as the enemy had expected, he used his superior strength to manoeuvre his way through
northern Georgia. While his centre threatened the main army, one
Federal wing or the other wrapped itself around the rebel flank.

With only half the numbers, Johnston continued to fall back to entrenched positions after parrying every thrust with remarkable skill.
Unless he could accept a battle on his own terms, the Confederate gen-

eral was prepared to retreat all the way to Atlanta, which he considered "too strong to be taken by assault and too extensive to be invested."

A sounder defensive strategy could not have been devised; and after seven weeks Sherman grew impatient at his progress over miserable hill roads while depending on the rebuilt railway for supplies. On Kenesaw Mountain, near Marietta, he attempted a plain, unvarnished frontal attack, only to meet the bloody repulse which is the familiar result of such efforts in the Civil War. Once again the two armies resumed their duel of manoeuvre, though in May and June the constant skirmishing cost Sherman 17,000 casualties and the enemy not far from as many.

By July 17 the invader had been delayed for ten weeks, with the main test still to come; but the Southern Fabius now rivaled Grant as an unpopular figure among his own countrymen. On that date President Davis yielded to public clamor and replaced him with a "fighting general," John B. Hood, who led the army to three defeats within the next ten days.

The new leader struck as Sherman crossed Peachtree Creek, the last water barrier, with his flanks ten miles apart. On the twentieth Hood fell upon the strategic right wing, only to learn to his cost the defensive power of entrenched riflemen. He withdrew his beaten forces, made a march of 15 miles on the night of the twenty-first, and surprised the Union left the next day. The Confederates had a local superiority in numbers; but again, as at Chickamauga, the sharpshooters of the rifle pits demonstrated their ability to repel combined attacks from the front and rear. After this repulse, known as the battle of Atlanta, Hood ordered a third futile attempt on the twenty-ninth which caused Davis to impose a policy of caution.

Sherman now abandoned his base and suddenly moved against the railways south of Atlanta. This strategy so bewildered his opponent that during August the Federal forces succeeded in cutting off most of the city's supplies. On September 2 Hood had to evacuate a manufacturing and railway centre which meant more to the Confederacy in material respects than Richmond.

This Northern victory came only a few weeks after the news of Farragut's greatest exploit, the opening up of Mobile Bay. Considering her inferiority in ports and shipyards, the South had put up an effective resistance on the sea. Not only did blockade-runners maintain a flow of supplies from Europe, but the first submarine success of history occurred in February, 1864. As the victim the *Housatonic* was sunk off Charleston by a spar torpedo fitted to the bow of a partly submerged Confederate craft propelled by nine men turning cranks along the screw shaft. A few minutes later the victor swamped through an open hatch, and during the war four other crews of volunteers were lost in experiments.

Allowing for such rare counterattacks, Southern naval efforts were devoted to keeping open a few fortified ports for blockade-running. Mobile was the most important harbor on the Gulf, and Grant originally intended that an army should co-operate with Farragut. This plan had to be dropped when the interference of Napoleon III in Mexico kept large Union forces on the alert in the Southwest. Thus on August 4 the Union admiral led a purely naval expedition made up of both monitors and wooden ships. Two of the former were moving on the heavy rebel ironclad *Tennessee*, guarding the approach to the forts, when a mine blew up the leader. The whole Federal column had hesitated when Farragut made his decision with the famous words, "Damn the torpedoes!" Heading straight for the mine field, he reaped the reward of audacity when all of the attackers crossed without further losses. Ramming tactics soon forced the *Tennessee* to surrender, then one by one the forts were isolated and captured by combined land-and-water assaults. This triumph left Wilmington the sole port of any consequence now supplying the Confederacy.

In the land warfare Sherman's capture of Atlanta had scarcely been announced when Sheridan proceeded to win three battles over Early in the valley. The consternation caused by the July raid on Washington had caused Grant to create the new Army of the Shenandoah to end the rebel threats from this quarter. As its commander Sheridan naturally emphasized the Northern dragoon tactics, based on the revolver and repeating carbine, which he had helped to develop. Hence the most instructive cavalry operations of the war occurred when the two small armies manoeuvred for a favorable opening.

Sheridan found his chance near Winchester on September 19 and inflicted a first defeat on his able opponent. The confidence of the Union horsemen was shown when one division literally rode down a hostile battery to take 1,200 prisoners. In the pursuit the victors caught up with Early three days later and routed him again at Fisher's Hill. A month followed in which Sheridan cruelly devastated the rich farming region; and on October 18 the Federal forces rallied to win the decisive battle of Cedar Creek after Early had at first swept everything before him.

The political effects of the timely succession of Union victories were immediate. Atlanta's fall had especially stimulated Northern morale, and President Lincoln could now look forward to the November elections without the slightest anxiety.

After his occupation of the Georgia city Sherman pursued Hood westward for more than 100 miles. Then on his return he prepared to cut loose from his base with the main army and march to the sea, leaving Thomas a barely adequate force to cope with Hood in the rear. Both Sherman and Grant have received the credit for this strategy, which seems to have been the natural outgrowth of a flexible campaign. The relationship of Lee and Jackson is more renowned, but the Western soldiers had an equally close understanding. Their correspondence reveals the gradual maturing of the idea, so that the march through Georgia may properly be called a mutual conception.

On November 15 Sherman began his 300-mile sweep with an army of 60,000. No opposition worthy of the name was encountered, and the troops spread out to lay waste a strip 60 miles wide through the granary of the Confederacy.

Sherman has justly been censured for the needless suffering he inflicted, though Sheridan's devastation of the Shenandoah was even more harsh. For all military purposes the thorough destruction of railways would have sufficed to deprive the Confederate armies of food, while the burning and looting of local supplies could only leave a tradition of bitterness for following generations. Enemy chroniclers admitted that cases of personal violence were few, but it could not be denied that thousands of civilians had been reduced to the hardships of malnutrition.

For a month the North remained in suspense, since Sherman had no means of sending a message. Then in December he suddenly emerged at Savannah. The storming of Fort McAllister caused the evacuation of the city after a brief siege, and Sherman established communications with the fleet.

Almost simultaneously the plodding Thomas won a victory over Hood at Nashville which came near to being a battle of annihilation. Following his defeats at Atlanta, the Confederate planned a bold advance into Union territory as the best means of frustrating Sherman's purposes. He hoped to destroy Thomas' insufficient army before threatening Ohio and marching into Virginia to join Lee. A three-week delay to collect supplies in Alabama proved fatal to this conception, giving his opponent the time to organize reinforcements for a stand in Tennessee. Meanwhile Grant lost his wonted composure while urging Thomas to attack, for neither friend nor foe could budge this soldier until he consented. When at last he struck near Nashville, the two-day battle resulted in an overwhelming Federal triumph. The collapse of the outflanked rebels became so complete that Forrest's cavalry barely managed to keep open a line of retreat for the survivors.

The news of this decisive victory left Sherman free for his next logical move. And on February 1, after hurried preparations, he crossed into South Carolina for a northward advance on Lee's rear—the consummation of the 800-mile flank attack which had been launched at Chattanooga nine months before.

The Surrender at Appomattox

After the fall of Wilmington, last great port of supply, neutral observers realized that the end was near. Not only had the material resources of the South been shattered, but even the causes of rebellion. For the theory of states' rights became a mockery when governors might browbeat Jefferson Davis by threatening to secede from the Confederacy. Nor could the doctrine of slavery be upheld when several Southern leaders advocated the freeing of Negroes to fill the thinned ranks of the armies.

Grant's strategy had accomplished no more toward the final result than Lincoln's political genius. Throughout the war the Northern statesman had appealed to the small farmer of the South who had no stake in slavery. Men of this type found a natural military leader in Nathan Bedford Forrest, while Jefferson Davis seemed to them to be the mouthpiece of a cotton aristocracy. Desertions multiplied in the early months of 1865, and all over the Confederacy could be heard the bitter refrain, "A rich man's war but a poor man's fight!"

Although Lee's background had been far more aristocratic than the president's, he supplied a moral leadership which the austere Davis could never offer. Men who had lost faith in the Confederacy could still find a cause in the greathearted humanity of Robert E. Lee. He repaid their devotion with an unfaltering courage. As one of his last thrusts, he aimed a moral blow at the Union by a sortie which had as its primary object the capture of Grant himself. And despite his few remaining resources, Lee contributed a notable innovation by ordering the first railway guns of history for use in the Petersburg lines.

His position became more precarious daily as the forces of the enemy closed in from all sides. He could give Johnston only a token force to resist Sherman's advance into North Carolina, and Sheridan had now brought his cavalry from the valley to add to the foes hemming in Petersburg. The defenders continued their sorties, but Sheridan's victory over a detachment at Five Forks severed a vital railway to Richmond. On April 2 Grant broke through the Petersburg lines, hurling the Confederate forces all the way back to the outskirts of the capital. That night Lee had no choice but to evacuate the city in order to save his army from capture or destruction.

Only 28,356 men now remained of the 55,000 who had composed the Army of Northern Virginia on February 20. As a last desperate chance Lee hoped that by retreating westward he might still join forces with Johnston for a stand in the mountains. Such an operation involved a march of 100 miles across the enemy's front, yet he beat off his pursuers for four days in running fights. On April 7 Sheridan's cavalry finally cut off all escape, leaving only the alternatives of battle or surrender. Lee held out without food for forty-eight more hours, then on April 9 the war came virtually to an end as his remnants laid down their arms at Appomattox. Of all the many tributes written to the valor of these ragged, half-starved survivors, none is more convincing than the statistics showing that they had inflicted 10,000 casualties on the Federal forces in the last ten days. Down to the very end the man in the rifle pits had proved himself the equal of at least two attackers.

Johnston asked for an armistice the following week, and Forrest soon came to terms in Alabama. Yet neither of these events could compare with a ceremony in South Carolina as a symbol of the restored Union. For on April 14 Major-General Robert Anderson, summoned from retirement, raised the flag again over Fort Sumter—the identical flag he had hauled down four years before on that date.

V

GERMAN BLOOD AND IRON

To introduce into the philosophy of war a principle of moderation would be an absurdity. War is an act of violence pushed to its utmost bounds.

—CLAUSEWITZ

ALTHOUGH most of the European powers had sent observers to the battlefields of the Civil War, its lessons of defensive fire power were not accepted. Professional soldiers have always preferred to believe in the offensive, and two wars waged in Europe at this time left more convincing precepts.

In the New World it had taken the Federal forces four weary years to overcome an adversary with much inferior material assets. By way of contrast, the armies of Prussia needed scarcely as many months for the campaigns which humbled empires with resources seemingly greater than her own. Between these two examples there was but a single choice; and the victorious generalissimo summed up current military opinion when he dismissed the Civil War as a conflict of "armed mobs chasing each other around the country, from which nothing could be learned."

Helmuth von Moltke himself was seriously compared to Napoleon, not only by his own countrymen but even the critics of neutral nations. Otto von Bismarck, as chancellor of a united Germany, became the most feared and admired figure in world diplomatic circles. German culture, German ethics and German ambitions set the pace for a new era

633

of nationalism; and German military thought created a new age of warfare.

The unexpectedness of the irruption had much to do with these results. On the eve of 1866 the prospect of a unified Germany under Berlin's domination seemed so remote that Europe's statesmen were taken unawares. Prussia seemed a second-rate military power when measured beside France, so that Europe's soldiers were equally stunned by the victories of 1870. In their bewilderment they could only ascribe the outcome to material might; and Moltke's methods were soon being copied as earnestly as Frederick's had been two centuries before.

Berlin's triumph might have been less of a surprise to anyone who had studied the German temperament. Arms and tactics may change in every generation, but the test of war brings out national characteristics which run remarkably true to form. The Englishman's bulldog grip has redeemed his military unpreparedness often enough to support the adage that his country "always loses the first battle and always wins the last." The mercurial nature of the French soldier makes him an extremist, scaling the heights of martial glory or plunging into equally drastic defeats, according to the merit of his generalship. The American's lack of discipline in formal operations finds its compensation in his precision as a marksman and resourcefulness as an individual fighter. By the same token the German is most formidable as the automaton of a military machine, carrying out long-preconceived plans of invasion.

Such conclusions will not please internationalists who hold that boundary lines are but the artificial barriers which divide the human family like the partitions of a home. Yet those who would challenge these generalities must often quarrel with the history of the last two hundred years. Beginning with Frederick's seizure of Silesia, the German soldier has on thirteen occasions been the tool of aggressions planned in Berlin. Only twice during this period has he fought a purely defensive war that was free from motives of aggrandizement.

This record has sometimes made him seem more of an alien to his neighbors than the Slav or Turk. As an individual in his own community he has an enviable reputation for thrift, order, cleanliness and an amiability bordering on sentimentality. As a political unit in international relations he gives the impression of conflicting traits—arrogance combined with self-pity, discipline with hysteria, boastfulness with a sense of inferiority, and a failure at self-government which finds its solace in the urge to govern others. No doubt such opinions are frequently colored by prejudice, yet other peoples cannot be blamed for finding it difficult to reconcile the German of the Christmas tree legend with the German who justifies his harsh treatment of "inferior races."

Germans themselves are aware of such inconsistencies, often exhibiting a melancholy and introspective pride in them. It has been suggested that the national dualism owes to the fact that the northern regions did not come under Latin and Christian influences until after the conquests of Charlemagne. This theory might satisfy a philosopher, but most present-day observers will conclude that the following eleven centuries should have sufficed to convert the most stubborn pagans from beyond the Elbe.

A more convincing explanation may be found in a strange gap which appears throughout the chronicles of the Germans. Of all the leading Western peoples, they are the only one which has never struck a memorable blow for political liberties. The United States is regarded as a young nation, yet in 1776 England's recent colonies had already experienced a century and a half of local self-government. In rebelling against the mother country they were denouncing the most liberal rule of the day, and Englishmen tacitly agreed with them afterwards by adopting many of the reforms sought in the struggle. At this same period the German remained a serf under dull princelings whose tyrannies were accepted with docility. A determined uprising might have swept these weak and petty despots into the wastebasket of history; but the Germans of 1776 allowed themselves to be sold like cattle to fight as mercenaries against the freemen of the New World.

Prussian serfdom was abolished in 1810, and the outward forms of parliamentary rule and the ballot were granted in 1850. But these belated boons were not wrung from the rulers by the protests of the people—they were extended by the rulers in the gracious mood of benevolent despotism. And since nations, like individuals, do not value benefits for which they have not struggled, such gains soon proved to be empty. The army continued to hold the actual power, and the peasant remained nearly as much of a serf as he had been a century before.

The penalty has been a dangerous degree of political immaturity as compared to the progress of other Western peoples. Lacking the healthy skepticism taught by self-government, Germans have blindly followed a succession of leaders, from Wallenstein to Hitler, who used them as the dupes of conquest. By the end of the nineteenth century this process had gone so far that Nietzsche could say of his countrymen:

> The Germans are always so badly deceived because they *try* to find a deceiver. If only they have a heady wine for the senses, they

will put up with bad bread. Intoxication means more to them than nourishment; that is the hook they will always bite on. A popular leader must hold up before them the prospect of conquests and splendor; then he will be believed. They always *obey*, and will do more than obey provided they can get intoxicated in the process.

GERMANY'S FÜHRER OF 1817

Wallenstein and Frederick had left examples of the advantages held by the totalitarian state, completely organized for war, over nations trying to maintain a partial peace economy. Both of these leaders had demonstrated the sacrifices which Germans were willing to make for a conqueror. But it remained for a later and more obscure figure to lay the moral foundations for Bismarck's three wars leading up to a united empire ruled by Berlin.

Unfortunately for three generations of Europeans, Frederick Ludwig Jahn has never been widely known outside of his own country. Had his lifework been understood in 1860, in 1910, or even as late as 1930, nobody could have been surprised by the "sudden" onslaughts of German invasion which occurred in those decades. For it is one of history's saddest paradoxes that the threats and preparations of the aggressors should thrice have been so obvious that the imperiled nations failed to take warning.

The son of a Lutheran preacher, Jahn studied at the universities of Halle, Jena and Griefswald for six years. His career as an early Führer did not begin until the age of thirty, when he declared that grief over the Jena-Auerstadt disaster turned his beard gray overnight. Like most German patriots, he had been shocked less by the military defeat than the servility with which all classes greeted the victors. From that moment he dedicated his life to the task of building up a conquering German spirit by means of political propaganda as well as physical culture.

A later age applied the epithet "Huns" to German invaders as a supreme insult, but Jahn exhorted his followers to emulate the rude virtues of their barbarian ancestors. Setting the example, he lived in a cave for a time and wore a gown of coarse cloth which he tried vainly to introduce as a national costume. In spite of such boorish affectations, the champion of primitive Teutonism soon proved that he could not be dismissed as a mere eccentric. Within a few years after founding his first *Turnverein*, he indoctrinated all Germany through his gymnastic societies which had as their actual purpose the "moral regeneration" of the fatherland. Volunteers from these clubs formed Free Corps battalions, aiding in Scharnhorst's secret reorganization of the Prussian army which helped to overthrow Napoleon after the retreat from Moscow.

Up to this point "Father" Jahn had been lauded as a hero by the conservative ruling classes of Prussia. They did not regard him with disfavor until after Waterloo, when he not only continued his efforts with the gymnastic societies but also organized university student leagues as centres of nationalistic propaganda.

The history of the next four years bears a dismally familiar aspect for the present-day reader. Youth movements sprang up all over the land, displaying a hysteria which aliens have too seldom associated with the national character. In 1817 occurred Germany's first book burning as delegates from student leagues met to make a bonfire of publications despised as pacifist or reactionary. The various youth congresses subscribed to Jahn's belief that the new Germany needed a dictator who would be worshiped by his people as a savior. Equally popular were the leader's twin doctrines of Teutonic racial superiority and violent anti-Semitism, both of which have been revived in every following generation. Music, literature, history and sculpture were not overlooked, for it was urged that all art and scholarship should be nationalistic in tone.

Only one thing seems to be missing in this picture of 1817, but the nineteenth-century Führer did not lack for bands of strong-armed disciples—Germany's first Brown Shirts—who were capable of using gymnasium-trained muscles to convince dissenters. By the next year the virtual mobilization of the nation's youth had gone so far as to alarm Metternich, the guiding spirit of the Quadruple Alliance and its conservative tenets. In 1819 his influence had much to do with the sentencing of the agitator to two years in prison. Although the term was never served, the Prussian authorities detained Jahn in a fortress until 1824, afterward forbidding him to live within ten miles of Berlin.

The time had not been ripe for the full-fledged dictator of the leader's vision; but Peter Viereck's *Metapolitics, From the Romantics to Hitler* makes it evident that Jahn's ideas lay dormant in the German soul after his death in 1852 at the age of seventy-four. Nobody did more to prepare the people for the creation of a permanent nation-in-arms, functioning in time of peace as well as war.

German scholars, who might have restored some sanity to the new era, had meanwhile found their Clausewitz in the philosopher Hegel. Thus by the middle of the century the humanist ideals of Immanuel

Kant had gone into a decline shared by the works of Schiller and Goethe. The former members of Jahn's student leagues were now the nation's intellectual leaders, and Hegel's complex theories gave them a Jesuitical formula for a creed of state worship.

Such thought processes, which are traditionally described as "mystical" by Germans themselves, had a most practical effect on the state educational system. Writers of textbooks supplied the elementary schools with doctrines of chauvinism and race superiority which had no counterpart in any other country of Europe. In the universities the high standard of research which had inspired such American disciples as Mott and Parkman sank to a scholarship which could praise the partition of Poland as a boon to the Poles. Soon even Bismarck would sneer at the servility of intellectuals who promptly found pan-German justifications for his proposed seizures of French territory. "What we want are the fortresses," he declared bluntly. "The idea about Alsace having been primitively German is an invention of the professors."

The so-called Revolution of 1848, so widely misunderstood in other countries, had small effect of halting such developments. Paradoxical as it may seem, this muddled protest was inspired as much by motives of nationalism as liberalism; and the monarch himself gave proof of more enlightened political ideas than those held by some of the leading "revolutionists."

Emigration rather than revolt became the hope of the subject who cherished his liberties. Where once Germans had fled to the New World to escape the ravages of invading hosts, they now sought relief from the oppressions of their own army in time of peace. During these years the United States offered a sanctuary to thousands of families from Prussia and the north German states influenced by that aggressive kingdom. Despised as pacifists and reactionaries by their more docile countrymen, these pilgrims formed whole regiments of German-speaking volunteers in 1862 to fight for the moral causes of the Civil War. Men like Carl Schurz emerged as their leaders, and the United States has profited ever since by the wave of emigration.

The effect on Germany's future was equivalent to that of a major political amputation. Within a few decades enough progressive citizens to form a small nation had departed, and their loss could only confirm a submissiveness which has been at the root of most subsequent aggressions. Not all men of spirit chose the sad road of voluntary exile, but there remained a liberal minority which could seldom hope to overcome the serf mentality of the masses.

The inevitable result of this sum in human subtraction was the con-
firming of the army rule which held the actual power, regardless of
the outward form of government. Thus the first factories of the Machine
Age were supervised by the army as potential means of military supply.
The first railways, which in other countries had spread in a haphazard
fashion, were controlled by the army with a view to the mobilizations of
a Clausewitzian offensive.

In 1793 the French Revolution had drawn upon the man-power of
the nation as a last desperate defense against encircling foes. Two generations later the United States decided questions of such grave import
that both sides resorted to universal service. But the new Germany
was not threatened by enemies in 1860, and no great moral issues were
at stake. The new Germany restored the nation-in-arms as an instrument
for putting into effect Clausewitz's theories of the superiority of mass.
And since other countries could not long tolerate a weaker military
status, man himself now came to be regarded as matériel of war—a living
projectile to be employed without stint because of its very cheapness.

THE BATTLE OF SADOWA

For centuries it had been the belief of humanists that popular education would strike a blow at the basic causes of war. Exactly the contrary
proved true in the new Germany, where even the textbooks were regimented. Within a decade Bismarck found it possible to convince his
countrymen that Danes, Austrians and Frenchmen in turn were their
mortal enemies. So wholehearted was the public response that Moltke
foresaw perils as well as advantages:

> Today the question, "Is a nation strong enough to make war?"
> is of less importance than that, "Is its government powerful enough
> to prevent war?"

This military scholar was equipped to survey the contemporary scene
with a detachment shared by few Germans. Born of a Prussian family
living in Holstein, he had been brought up as a Danish subject and
educated at the cadet school in Copenhagen. At the age of twenty-one
he entered the Prussian service, and again in 1835 he changed his
allegiance by beginning a long term as a Turkish officer. Returning to
Berlin with an international viewpoint, he rose to leadership because
of the fact that in his youth he had been a favorite pupil of Clausewitz.
But even though he had sat at the feet of the master, Moltke made it

his task to put the brake on the blind zeal of Prussian disciples. Due to his recognition of the increasing effect of infantry fire power, the Clausewitzian theories of mass were amended to envision an offensive strategy of envelopment. Thus the army was schooled to advance in a chain of distributed corps for the purpose of gripping the enemy and sweeping around his flanks.

Moltke's influence also had much to do with Prussia's adoption of the first practical breech-loading rifle of European warfare, the famous "needle gun" of 1841. So called because of the thin steel needle in the bolt which a pull of the trigger drove through the powder to strike the percussion cap at the bullet's base, the mechanism had a serious defect as compared to early American breech-loaders. For the needle often broke after becoming corroded by explosions, making it necessary to change the entire bolt. Despite this fault, the new weapon gave the Prussian army an obvious advantage over rival establishments which would continue to depend on muzzle-loaders for two more decades.

In 1850 it appeared for a time that the needle gun might have its first test. The revolution of 1848 had been waged largely for the nationalistic cause of compelling German princes to accept a union under Prussian domination. Frederick Wilhelm IV refused the imperial crown, but the movement brought the kingdom to the verge of war with Austria to decide the question of German leadership. The Prussian forces were partially mobilized when soldiers and statesmen agreed that shortcomings in the military machine made it unwise to take the risk. As a result Prussia's humiliating submission led to sweeping army reforms planned by an unusually able organizer, Count Albrecht von Roon.

Up to this time conscription had been limited for reasons of national economy. Against bitter Parliamentary opposition the new war minister succeeded in training double the number of men for three years with the colors and four in reserve. Methods of instruction were improved until Prussia actually had a large standing army of professional caliber, supported by a Landwehr for home defense. This expansion hastened the promotion of officers, so that the organization profited from a new aggressive spirit. In the command Moltke laid the foundations of the precise staff work for which his forces were soon to be famed. Thus where rival armies contented themselves with hypothetical plans of defense against vague future enemies, Prussian generals studied the actual roads and towns of neighboring countries with a view to directing the advance of invading corps.

During these years the war-state derived an even greater advantage from Bismarck's rise to political leadership. Born in the year of Waterloo, the burly Prussian squire had begun his career with a fierce opposition to all Parliamentary institutions. Later he modified his attitude to a belief that such processes had their value as a sop to the public, though holding that all questions of gravity should be decided by the monarch, the generals and the ministers. This conviction he put into practice when the legislators imposed conditions on the granting of funds for the army reorganization. William I met the crisis by appointing Bismarck minister-president, and within a few years the crown and the army had been made independent of Parliamentary meddling in all issues of importance.

In his foreign policies Bismarck soon revealed Europe's greatest political intellect of the age. Other statesmen could not be sure about the next war, but the Prussian thought in terms of the war after next. So well laid were his plans that he was already weighing the prospect of crushing Austria while inviting that empire to share in the guilt and spoils of an attack on Denmark.

The perennial Schleswig-Holstein question gave the opportunity. For centuries the two "Elbe duchies" had been associated with the Danish crown, and in 1848 a premature Prussian invasion failed because of the intervention of other powers. The matter was clearly one for arbitration, since Holstein had a large German population while Schleswig was peopled almost entirely by Danes. The issue concerned all Europe, but only Bismarck knew exactly what he wanted. "From the very beginning," he declared at a later date, "I kept annexation steadily before my eyes."

Austria's jealousy of Prussia impelled her to take a hand, and in 1864 the allied powers made short work of a gallant but hopeless Danish resistance. Then as Bismarck had anticipated, the question of the despoiled provinces, held jointly by the recent partners, soon led to his desired war for the domination of Germany.

The Prussian minister had a delicate task. He wished to hasten hostilities while his country held the material advantage, yet to make the Hapsburg empire appear the aggressor. In both of these purposes he succeeded adroitly, though even Prussian credulity found it hard to accept a lately lauded ally as a sudden enemy. Most of the south German states threw in their lot with Austria, but Bismarck's alliance with Italy diverted enough opposing troops to create a balance of about half a million trained men on each side.

The generals had no precedent to guide them in the mobilization of these hosts by railway. As an example of the problems involved, it has been calculated that if the French army of Waterloo had invaded Belgium by one highway instead of three, the 124,000 troops and 350 guns would have extended in a column 55 miles long. Much more ammunition was used by the weapons of 1866, and the Prussian staff found that an army corps of 42,510 men, 13,802 horses, 90 guns and 1,385 vehicles occupied no less than 27 miles of railway. The superior organization of the war-state gave it a tremendous advantage, yet the troop movements which began on May 16 were not completed until June 5.

Bismarck had foreseen that Austria would be slower, and he allowed the enemy a full week's start in order to support the claim that Prussia was being attacked. Both he and Moltke knew that the risk was justified by their weapon superiority. In the two Silesian wars of the past century the merit of iron over wooden ramrods had been a decisive factor. Now in 1866 history repeated itself as the Austrian infantry brought into action a slow-firing muzzle-loader. In order to reload the soldier must expose himself, though his adversary could both charge and fire the needle gun from a reclining position while utilizing natural cover.

In the first skirmishes the difference proved to be exactly the difference between victory and defeat. The Austrian organization had already shown its inefficiency in the Magenta-Solferino operations, and six years later a low morale was added to material inferiority. Benedek, the commander-in-chief, having risen from the ranks of a caste-ridden army as a Protestant doctor's son, found himself handicapped by the passive obstruction of subordinates from the nobility. The early clashes in Bohemia convinced him that his efforts were doomed to failure, and in a telegram to the emperor he urged that Austria make peace before incurring a disaster. Franz-Joseph refused on the grounds that the national honor demanded a decisive action; and at the battle of Sadowa (or Königgrätz) on July 3, Benedek's forebodings were justified by an Austrian defeat which virtually put an end to the Seven Weeks' War.

Armies which expect to be beaten are seldom disillusioned, and the fumblings of the victors were a more surprising outcome. Their sixty-six-year-old commander, who resembled an elderly professor rather than a soldier, set an example for future generals by remaining far back in the rear areas. This was a drastic change from the methods of Grant and Lee, who carried their preference for personal reconnaissance so far as to be recognized on occasion by enemy sentries. In all other respects the conflict of 1866 shows that no lessons had been learned from the Civil War. Both the Prussians and Austrians held their cavalry in reserve for Napoleonic shock action, with the almost incredible result that for forty-eight hours the two great hosts were only a few miles apart in open country without either being aware of the other's presence. Finally the advance units stumbled into touch to bring on an engagement which neither commander had sought.

Only its huge scale rescues Sadowa from mediocrity, for the armies of nearly a quarter of a million each were the largest ever known on a European battlefield up to that time. Moltke's mistakes seem to have come from a lack of adaptability as well as reconnaissance. Once his preconceived plans had been upset by circumstance, he missed several brilliant opportunities to take advantage of his opponent's vacillation. When contact had been made, such lapses were amply redeemed by the fact that one Prussian with a needle gun was the tactical equal of three Austrians with muzzle-loaders. Afterward the victors themselves called the brief struggle "the captains' war" because so many vital decisions were made on the firing line by company officers. On the rainy day of Sadowa the Prussian units were guided into action by the sound of the guns rather than any central plan, and contrary to their training the infantry had the good sense to scatter into thin skirmish lines. By the middle of the afternoon their fire power had the Austrians in full retreat after casualties of 45,000, including 20,000 prisoners, at a cost to the Prussians of less than 10,000. The superiority of Benedek's cavalry and artillery saved the vanquished from a pursuit, and no further action of consequence took place before the signing of the armistice three weeks later.

THE FULFILLMENT AT SEDAN

The 1,550 guns of Sadowa had scarcely ceased roaring when Bismarck began preparations for the third of his trinity of wars—the victory over France which he intended to be the seal of German unity. As a preliminary step, even before the armistice with Austria, he made every effort to salve the pride of losers who might be lured into an alliance with the prospective next enemy. The victorious army did not press its advance on Vienna, and strict orders were issued against the triumphal entry which otherwise would have been to the Prussian taste.

Already Bismarck, Moltke and Roon were well aware of France's military and political weaknesses. They knew that the gilt of the Crimean and Italian victories hid structural defects which probably could not stand the strain of a serious test. These faults became even more apparent in the Mexican campaign as the French met a bloody preliminary repulse at Puebla. With several times the resources, Marshal Bazaine could not accomplish a fraction of Scott's results; and the invaders prudently withdrew when the end of the Civil War freed American veterans to uphold the Monroe Doctrine.

By the summer of 1866 Napoleon III had grown too ill and prematurely old to put into immediate effect the reforms urged by his military advisers. Unquestionably he would have preferred to end his reign in peace, but during the next four years Bismarck cleverly played upon his very doubts and fears. Meanwhile Moltke and Roon made it evident that they were aware of Prussian failures at Sadowa which might have been exploited by a more capable adversary. The numbers of their cavalry were increased afterward, and the new training methods paid more attention to reconnaissance. In the artillery all smoothbores were replaced by rifled steel breechloaders, superior both in range and accuracy to the bronze muzzle-loaders of France.

Prussia's population had been increased to 24,000,000 as a result of the Seven Weeks' War, including the 6,000,000 in the allied states of the North German Federation. After the military system had been extended over this area, Moltke could depend on a million trained troops under thirty-three years of age for his next effort.

Although the French emperor was kept well informed of German preparations, he had to deal with a rising tide of discontent at home during these critical years. In 1868, when he finally managed to pass a new conscription law, opposition in the Chamber reduced it to a flabby compromise. Events were to prove, moreover, that it had come too late to improve the military situation, though adding enormously to the ruler's unpopularity.

The imperiled nation found its most practical measure of defense in the adoption of the chassepot, a breech-loading rifle with a longer range and faster rate of fire than the needle gun. By placing the percussion cap at the base of the paper cartridge, and by introducing a rubber ring in the breech as a gas-stopper, French inventors were able to reduce the caliber from .66 to .43, thus enabling the soldier to carry 90 rounds of ammunition into action as compared to 75 for the German weapon.

In the diplomatic field Napoleon counted on an active alliance with Austria and Italy, but his confidential agent reached Vienna to find that Bismarck had succeeded in isolating France. A month later the candidature of a Hohenzollern prince for the Spanish throne gave the Prussian chancellor his opportunity for a war in which France would be placed in the rôle of aggressor. For four years his diplomacy had made Napoleon the dupe of clumsy efforts to restore French prestige, but there is little evidence to support the claim that Bismarck "falsified" or even unfairly deleted the famous Ems telegram. Such an accusation is a reflection on his skill as an international angler, for the fish had already risen to the bait.

Only recently the French historian Thiers had declared of his country's foreign policy, "There are no blunders left for us to make!" On July 19, 1870, he had reason to retract this statement when a woefully unprepared nation, both morally and materially, went to war with a state which had been preparing since Sadowa. In the first three weeks France's machinery of mobilization broke down so badly that only 220,000 troops reached the frontier, including a regiment which detrained by mistake in a town just occupied by the foe. During the next three weeks the two main French armies were separated, confused, outgeneraled and beaten in detail by three German armies totaling more than half a million troops. And on September 1 the fiasco came to an end with one French army surrendered and the other rendered helpless as the prelude to a similar fate.

These are the stark outlines of the Second Empire's downfall. They do not hint at the surprising fact that this military failure contained many elements of a successful resistance. Man for man, the French soldier outfought the German in nearly every encounter; and if the nation's resources had been used intelligently, the invaders might have been taught some severe lessons.

Before a blow had been struck, the alarms of France's leaders were communicated to the public. Outside of the Paris boulevards the war had not been accepted with enthusiasm, but Frenchmen have always been valiant in the defense of their own soil. Nevertheless, the emperor betrayed more concern over the possibility of revolution than the problems of repelling the foe. Rejecting all the advantages of a people's war, he made no use of the civilian rifle clubs which had recently become a popular movement. Most of France's millions were reduced to a spectator's rôle, for the two main armies consisted chiefly of long-term troops imbued with a professional rather than a patriotic spirit. The national unpreparedness imposed a defensive strategy, and Napoleon added to the chaos by hastening to the front in the manner of his illustrious uncle.

The emperor's natural hesitancy was aggravated by a bladder ailment which made it agony for him to sit his horse. Past wars had demonstrated his lack of military ability, and the empress' frantic telegrams from Paris had more weight with him than the advice of his two marshals. Thus in urging a brief invasion of German soil he seems to have been thinking entirely of the moral effect upon the boulevards. On August 1 a French corps dispersed a mere battalion at Saarbrücken, and Napoleon reported the skirmish with all the fanfare appropriate to a great opening triumph.

At least the minor success had a melancholy distinction, for it was the last to be gained by his armies. The victors fell back across the frontier, and on August 6 they were outnumbered and beaten in the battle of Spicheren. A disorderly affair, fought with little art on either side, the clash demonstrated the ability of the invaders to bring more men up to the firing line. Out of 42,900 Germans in the vicinity, 27,000 got into action. The French corps leaders, each thinking of his individual problems, were able to engage only 24,000 troops out of 64,000 within striking distance.

On the other wing the Germans isolated a French detachment at Weissenberg on August 4, hurling 25,000 men against 4,000. In spite of these odds the French put up a heroic resistance for six hours, launching repeated counterattacks and retiring in good order on Marshal MacMahon's main army. The victor of Magenta, a French descendant of an exiled Irish family, halted his forces for a determined stand, and on the sixth the first great battle of the war took place at Wörth. Moltke had not planned for the encounter, but as at Spicheren his corps commanders responded alertly to the sound of the guns when the outposts made contact at dawn. Again the story of the engagement is told by the figures, for the French were able to concentrate only 37,000 men out of 50,000, while the enemy brought up 77,500 out of 82,000 within reach of the battlefield. The German advantage in artillery was even greater, with 234 rifled breechloaders being massed against 101 outdated French guns.

The marvel of Wörth is only that the defenders managed to hold their own for eight hours, so that the issue remained in doubt until 3 P. M. The chassepot proved to have double the effective range of the needle gun, and the French counterattacks were delivered with such fury that several regiments lost up to 90 per cent of their numbers. Time after time MacMahon's men had the best of local fights in a wooded terrain, only to be enveloped by sheer bulk after their losses had reached the appalling total of 20,100.

As a further blow to the vanquished, Wörth and Spicheren dashed the high hopes placed in a secret weapon. For two generations the popular imagination had been fired by the wonders of the Machine Age, and even professional soldiers dreamed of a war being decided by some invention utilized as a surprise. The vision seemed to have materialized on the eve of 1870, when the French mitrailleuse became the first machine gun of European warfare.

In 1862 Dr. Richard Gatling of Chicago had invented a gun consisting of ten rifled barrels revolving about a fixed and central axis. At the rear of the piece a turn of the crank brought each barrel in successive alignment with the breech mechanism, while the others completed the process of ejecting empty cartridges, receiving fresh ones and inserting them into the chamber. A maximum of two hundred shots a minute could be fired, and the revolutions gave every barrel time to cool before its turn came again. At his own expense the inventor demonstrated the gun on several Civil War battlefields, but not until after the peace did the United States Army place an order.

The mitrailleuse operated on much the same principle, though as many as thirty barrels were used. Napoleon himself approved the invention, but he forgot the historical lesson that new weapons are no better than the tactics guiding them. Because the weight of the piece made a horse-drawn carriage necessary, France's generals regarded it as an artillery rather than an infantry arm. There is a danger in keeping a military secret too well, moreover, and the troops soon showed that they had not been thoroughly trained in firing. Often they opened up at ranges too long for effect, and the enemy learned to bring up fieldpieces to knock out every mitrailleuse before the infantry advanced. As a consequence the French secret weapon proved to be a positive detriment on some fields, since it weakened the batteries by replacing direly needed fieldpieces.

By far the most decisive factor in the war was the enormous German superiority both in the quantity and quality of artillery. Added to these advantages were much better tactics, for the invaders employed their guns in overwhelming masses which usually silenced the French batteries. Thus the counterattacks of the defenders seldom had adequate support from their own guns, while the German envelopments were made possible by terrific preliminary bombardments.

Cavalry reconnaissance had improved since 1866, yet both sides were too frequently in the dark as to the other's movements. This deficiency may generally be attributed to caution, since a few disastrous experiences had taught mounted men to be wary of fire power. Charges of cuirassiers merely invited a futile casualty list, and neither army had placed enough emphasis on scouting.

Such a lack does not wholly explain the disorders seen on every battlefield. German apologists found their excuse in the long-range and rapid-firing qualities of the rifled breechloader, declaring that the "new fire power" made precise manoeuvre an impossibility. This analysis ignores the recent American precepts, for the taunt of "armed mobs" might more justly have been applied to Moltke's forces than those of Grant and Lee. As compared to Civil War battles, both Wörth and Spicheren present a spectacle of forces out of the control of their commanders. Afterward, far from following up his twin victories, Moltke wasted forty-eight hours in which he had no knowledge of the enemy's movements. During this critical interval, with a wide gap left open in the German centre, 130,000 French troops within striking distance were prevented only by the incompetence of their own generals from taking advantage of the greatest lost opportunity of 1870.

Not until August 12, after a week of confusion and altered plans, did the advancing Germans locate Marshal Bazaine's forces falling back on Metz. This French commander, though the accusations of treason were never proved against him, had taken up arms with a conviction of defeat equal to Benedek's doubts in 1866. In retreating toward the Moselle he had no more optimistic an aim than to stand on the defensive and inflict all possible damage on an enemy whom he tacitly admitted to be his superior.

The events of the next few days did not support this belief. On the fourteenth, in the battle of Columbey-Borny, Bazaine's men fought with such determination that the attackers were fortunate to hold their ground. Two days later, at Vionville-Mars-la-Tour, the French for once held a numerical superiority when the usual lack of intelligence betrayed the German advance units into an attack against twice their own strength. With victory beckoning all day, Bazaine allowed the enemy to bring up reinforcements while fully half of his own troops remained idle until the opportunity had passed.

Even in the final test of August 18 at Gravelotte-Saint Privat, the French cause was not lost except in the minds of leaders who had reached a state of moral bankruptcy. Moltke, Bismarck and the king passed hours of "terrible suspense" as their best brigades met bloody repulses. On the left wing the charge of the Prussian Guards at Saint Privat came to a standstill after losses of 30 per cent from the fire of French riflemen. The assaulting troops were helpless until they had the support of Saxon reinforcements and twenty-four batteries of artillery. The Germans of the right wing met a more stern reception at Gravelotte, where concealed mitrailleuses added to the hail of bullets from the chassepots. The advancing forces wavered, then broke and fled in one of the worst panics of the war—infantry, cavalry and artillery mingled in wild disorder as the French pursued on the initiative of company officers. Had their commander taken advantage of such moments, the story of Gravelotte-Saint Privat might have ended differently, but at nightfall Bazaine ordered a retreat with his own main positions intact and the enemy too exhausted to renew the struggle in the morning.

The French general had reached his fateful decision, and his withdrawal into the Metz fortress provided the strategic tomb for 130,000 men who would never strike another blow for their country. In view of the Civil War lessons, it may be wondered why the offensive had prevailed with such seeming ease over defenders armed with machine guns as well as breech-loading rifles. The answer is that intelligent defensive tactics were seldom employed in 1870. In spite of the costly repulses so common on American fields, European strategists believed that field entrenchments would sap the fighting spirit of an army.

This attitude is understandable on the part of German soldiers who made a shibboleth of the attack. But French military literature of the period is also filled with offensive doctrines based less upon realism than a romantic appraisal of the national soul. According to these treatises, the heirs of Grande Armée traditions were at their best only when permitted to hurl themselves at the foe with the bayonet. References to the *arme blanche* and "irresistible French *élan*" were allowed to become a substitute for reasoning, especially since the victories of 1859 had been mistakenly attributed to the use of cold steel.

As the penalty a decade later, the invaders were often conceded the advantages of a strategic offensive combined with the tactical defensive. Wörth, Spicheren and Columbey-Borny present a spectacle of French counterattacks pressed with the utmost gallantry, only to be shattered by Germans armed with an inferior rifle. Not until the battle of Gravelotte-Saint Privat, when France's leaders had become too demoralized to be concerned with *élan*, do we find a single example of effective defensive tactics. For on that field the retreating forces at last made an extensive use of entrenchments and natural cover. During those final forty-eight hours the French infantry fired nearly two million cartridges —more than the total expenditure of the Prussians in 1866—with the result of inflicting costly repulses on both enemy wings. The battle was actually unfinished when Bazaine gave the order to retreat, and there is good reason to believe that a more resolute general might still have wrung a victory from a battered and exhausted foe.

Hence the experience of the American conflict was confirmed rather than disproved, so that France's greatest modern military historian, Jean Colin, later gave as the lesson of 1870, "Well-chosen and well-arranged defensive positions, even when very weakly held, could not be carried."

After recovering from their surprise and gratitude at the outcome of Gravelotte-Saint Privat, the victors wasted no time. Assigning about equal numbers the task of investing Metz, they immediately formed the new Army of the Meuse for an advance on Chalons, where MacMahon had paused to reorganize his beaten forces. Meanwhile a third German army marched on Paris.

The logical course would have been for MacMahon to fall back in defense of the capital, or at least to have made every effort to save France's last held army. But again the uneasy political conscience of the nation's rulers played its part. From Paris the empress telegraphed that retreat might be punished by revolution; and Napoleon became persuaded that the situation called for a desperate attempt to relieve Bazaine at Metz. The unexpectedness of this move threw the whole German machine out of gear, as so often happened when the French did not respond according to the plans and alternatives of the invaders. For a few days the opportunity actually existed for Bazaine to break the enemy ring and unite with his rescuers. Once it had been lost by indecision, both French armies were doomed as Moltke recalled his forces advancing on Paris and turned on MacMahon with all available troops.

On August 29 the Army of the Meuse, cutting the French off from Metz, drove them northward into the path of the German army which had turned back from the capital. Caught between these two superior forces, MacMahon sought a refuge and found a trap in the small border fortress of Sedan, noted as the birthplace of Turenne. Mobility offered the only French chance of escape, since four depleted corps were menaced by seven enemy corps imbued with a conviction of victory. But even with a line of retreat to the northwest still open on the morning of September 1, the commander allowed his forces to be crowded in confusion around the inadequate works. The beleaguered army fought back with futile bravery, but any doubts as to the outcome were removed at noon when the Germans completed their encirclement. At 4:30 P. M., after vainly seeking death in action, the sick emperor applied rouge to hide the pallor of his face. Then with rare moral courage he flew a white flag to save 82,000 helpless troops from a German artillery pounding which amounted to massacre.

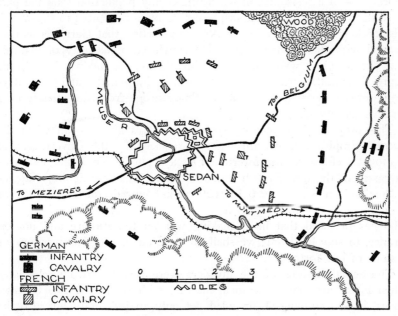

The Envelopment of Sedan

Considering the inept decisions of the military chiefs, the end of the Second Empire came with the inevitability of a Greek tragedy. The only surprising feature is the combative spirit still shown by the beaten army in its hour of humiliation. French officers ran the risk of personal violence from men who believed that they had been betrayed, and the prisoners went into military captivity with the conviction that they could have fought their way out of the encirclement.

FRANCE'S ARMIES OF CIVILIANS

In less than six weeks Prussia had won the war, or so it seemed on the day of Sedan. Bazaine had not yet been starved into submission, but the fall of encircled Metz could not be long averted. As the two northern armies of invasion began their leisured march on Paris, Moltke's assurance led him to announce that by the end of October he would be "shooting hares" in his homeland.

The victory had clearly been gained by the nation-in-arms over badly led professional armies. The forces of a united Germany, including the Saxons and Bavarians who fought against Prussia in 1866, had made short work of a resistance in which the enemy population took the part of stunned onlookers. Hence in presenting his masterpiece to the world, Bismarck won widespread sympathy by asserting that Germans had no quarrel with the French people. He convinced a majority of neutrals that the invaders were only defending themselves against Napoleonic aggression; and as a final virtuous touch he intimated that his country-men were conferring a boon by freeing Europe from the menace of a tyrant's ambitions.

This propaganda edifice collapsed three days after Sedan when the Second Empire was overthrown and replaced by the Government of National Defense as the forerunner of a republic. To Bismarck's em-barrassment the new French leaders outdid him in arraigning Napole-onism; and on September 6 Jules Favre announced policies which were a direct challenge to German motives, "It is for the King of Prussia, who has declared that he is making war on the Empire and not on France, to stay his hand; we shall not cede an inch of our territory or a stone of our fortresses."

The actual designs of the invaders were revealed two weeks later when Favre arranged a personal meeting with Bismarck. The German terms, it was announced, included not only an indemnity but also the cession of Alsace and most of Lorraine. There followed a moment of dismay, then the war entered upon a second phase as the French people flew to arms under the leadership of Léon Gambetta.

On October 7 the fiery orator escaped from encircled Paris in a balloon and called on every citizen to fight. The response was so fervent that within a few weeks the nation had raised and equipped twelve corps, numbering 600,000 men and 1,400 guns, to fill the strategic vacuum created by the surrender or neutralization of all the organized forces. As a greater military miracle, these awkward but fanatically brave volunteers won France's first notable victory of the war on November 9. Advancing from Tours, an army of recent civilians routed an outweighed Bavarian corps with heavy losses at the battle of Coul-miers, fought near Orléans.

In its political effects the ragged engagement became a second Valmy.

The French nation, which no longer seemed a first-class power after Sedan, won world-wide respect and sympathy. The invaders, by their own admission, were placed in the position of aggressors warring for money and territory.

Even in military respects Moltke's armies lost much of the prestige gained during early weeks. Confronted by an unexpected resistance of the people, they betrayed their alarm by the "gravest errors" of judgment. Such was the confusion that the phrase "fog of war" came into use to describe the invaders' ignorance of enemy movements; and had the victors of Coulmiers been well-organized troops, they might have been able to relieve Paris.

Up to this time the war had been conducted with moderation by both sides. If the Germans lived on the country and exacted large sums from captured towns, they also enforced a strict discipline. After the national uprising, however, their frustration led to drastic measures. Just as Alva had once condemned an entire nation as outlaws, the victors of Sedan now virtually denied the right of Frenchmen to defend themselves in any manner not approved by the foe. Justifying this policy by a thin legalization, they shot thousands of prisoners whose offense consisted of not being fully uniformed or led by regular army officers. German company commanders, as judges, prescribed the death penalty even for a refusal to betray comrades. Communities as large as Châteaudun were sacked or burned merely as punishment for a gallant resistance, and a thorough system existed for the transportation of loot to Germany.

While the individual reprisals of the francs-tireurs often matched these excesses, a comparison of the national casualty lists places most of the guilt on the enemy forces. Their own total losses of 28,000 dead and 101,000 wounded show a fairly normal proportion. In contrast, the French losses of 156,000 dead and 143,000 wounded can only be explained by an official German ferocity without a parallel in the nineteenth century.

These violations of accepted codes had their usual historical result of inciting a more desperate defense. The francs-tireurs, or irregular riflemen, most of them members of the civilian clubs neglected by Napoleon III, were brought under military discipline as Paris prepared for a long siege. Open quarrels between Moltke and Bismarck were symptoms of enemy anxiety as Gambetta announced a *levy en masse* and sought European alliances.

At first it appeared that the *Défense nationale* might overcome the terrific odds against an occupied country whose regular armies had collapsed. Then the German advantages of organization and training gradually prevailed as Gambetta found it necessary to use improvised forces utterly lacking in those qualities. Not only did the time element work against him, but also a winter of unusual severity which imposed terrible hardships on the miserably equipped *mobiles*. As the heroism of their effort won a moral victory for France, the capitulation of Bazaine on October 14 added another German army to the material might of invaders whose numbers rose to nearly a million men. By the end of the year the eventual outcome could no longer be doubted, for after Coulmiers the new French corps met reverses at every turn. Poor staff work, civilian interference and the misgivings of professional soldiers all contributed to the failure, though Gambetta insisted that the admission of defeat had been premature.

At least the armed citizens had put the regular forces to shame with their valiant defense of five months. On January 28, 1871, the sufferings of besieged and bombarded Paris led to an armistice, and the advocates of compromise were upheld in the elections a few days later. The national honor had been saved, but a helpless France could only await the terms of victors who were no more disposed to be moderate in peace than in war.

VI

THE PRUSSIA OF THE ORIENT

---

*The true speed of war is not headlong precipitancy, but
the unremitting energy which wastes no time.*

—MAHAN

ON JANUARY 18, 1871, Prussia became the success story of the age
of nationalism when William I was proclaimed emperor over 41,000,000
united Germans. Bismark's lifework reached its climax at this historic
moment. Using essentially the methods of Louis XIV and Napoleon I, he
had wrought a tour de force which ranks with the achievements of
those conquerors. And if they had not known when to stop, the Prussian
statesman now planned a secure and peaceful future for the empire
created by blood and iron.

But mass emotions are more easily aroused than quenched, as the
aftermath of the Civil War had already proved. The brotherly peace
envisioned in Grant's and Sherman's terms of surrender had been
repudiated by the shortsighted policies of Reconstruction within five
years. Only Lincoln could have prevented such abuses of power, and
the assassin's bullet which ended his life also made an end of justice and
honor in the treatment of vanquished Americans. Aside from ethical considerations, the ultimate cost of that vengeance could not help but fall
upon the whole United States as a bill to be paid by following generations.

With this ugly example before him, the great chancellor revealed his
limitations by subscribing to a peace designed to shame as well as crush

a proud nation. For it was obvious to the world that the unprecedented indemnity of five milliards had been imposed with a view to grinding France under the conqueror's heel for years to come. German troops, stationed in the country at its own expense, were to be withdrawn only when the last franc had been paid. Nor were Alsace and Lorraine seized entirely for their economic value to the new empire. Bismarck's writings make it evident that he attached more importance to the possession of border fortresses which promised a permanent mastery over a prostrate foe. As a final degradation, the beaten nation had to agree to a clause providing for a triumphal parade of the victors through the streets of Paris.

Whether Bismarck could have modified these terms is not even a question. The fact is that he made no effort worthy of the wisdom he had shown after the defeat of Austria. Thus despite his complaints that the German generals excluded him from their councils, he alone must bear the chief responsibility for a ruthless peace which became the cornerstone of the next great European conflict.

The Bitter Fruit of Sedan

Contrary to a general impression, wars of revenge are not of common occurrence. Popular memories being short and statesmen being guided by pragmatic motives, a vanquished nation is more likely to seek an alliance with the victor. History's greatest modern exception may be found in the undeviating course followed by France for two generations after the Treaty of Frankfort.

In May, 1871, the brief and brutal civil war of the Commune seemed to have completed the German purpose of ruining the nation. For all of his political genius, Bismarck could hardly have imagined that only a month later a national loan for paying part of the indemnity would be oversubscribed two and a half times. So determined were Frenchmen to deliver their soil from the hated invaders that in 1872 a second loan of three milliards was fourteen times oversubscribed by a people noted for financial caution.

That same year a new conscription law was passed in a grim spirit of popular approval. Frenchmen who had heard the tread of alien troops in the shuttered streets of Paris did not flinch from the prospect of five years with the colors. Few exemptions were allowed, so that the vanquished of 1870 could look forward to a truly national army of two million trained men, in addition to as many more territorial reserves.

Throughout the two decades after the Peace of Frankfort this specter of vengeance haunted the German peace which Bismarck had sought to secure. While the aged William I reigned, only the chancellor's vigilance prevented France from making alliances. Even so, he lived long enough to see his lifework threatened with disaster. For in 1888, when William II came to the throne, it grew apparent that Bismarck's methods were too conservative to please the new ruler and the new generation of Germans. Where he had clung to a defensive military policy, they alarmed the world with the most extravagant threats of aggression. And where he had planned for a continental empire, they had visions of naval expansion at the risk of antagonizing Great Britain.

As a final irony, his lifelong policy of strengthening the imperial power at the, expense of popular rule brought about his downfall. The headstrong young ruler did not hesitate to display his ingratitude by a virtual dismissal, and Bismarck's fellow ministers refused to support him. At a loss of dignity the old man made every effort to regain his position; but German public opinion upheld the new Caesar whose blustering speeches promised a more glorious Sedan on some future field.

From that moment French diplomacy took the commanding position in Europe which the chancellor had held for three decades. His most sacred tenet had been the securing of Russia's neutrality, so that Germany would not be menaced by an enemy in her rear. Yet before he had been in retirement three years, the signing of a Franco-Russian pact confirmed his distrust of the new régime. And before his death in 1898, Bismarck must have realized that William II's naval policies would soon drive the world's greatest sea power into the camp of the enemy. The next war awaited but one of the "incidents" which the imperial braggart provided so often, and France held the trump military cards.

The statesman who knew how to temper ruthlessness with discretion could only have closed his eyes with a profound sense of failure. In 1866 and 1871 his country had held an overwhelming advantage, but at the turn of the century every rival power likewise trusted to well-armed masses. Peasant lads and factory workers who had scarcely heard of Sedan were spending several years of their lives in barracks because the surrender of an emperor and an army had changed the course of military thought. Soldiers and statesmen were themselves uneasy as they contemplated the army of five million, for it had already occurred to them that today's conscript might become the revolutionist of tomorrow. Fear dulled the glitter of Europe's bayonets, fear tainted the councils of the diplomats; and where once generals had built upon a foundation of disciplined skill and bravery, they now based their tactics on fear:

> In modern battle, which is delivered with combatants so far apart, man has come to have a horror of man. He comes to hand-to-hand fighting only to defend his body, or if forced to it by some fortuitous encounter. . . . It may be said that he seeks to catch the fugitive only for fear that he will turn and fight.

Such comments, written from observation by Colonel Ardant du Picq, were published in a book called *Battle Studies* after his death in the Franco-German campaigns. As his troubled vision of the military future, the French officer saw war in terms of a struggle between the conscript's moral endurance and the terror induced by destructive new weapons:

> Today the soldier is often unknown to his comrades. He is lost in the smoke, the dispersion, the confusion of battle. He seems to fight alone. Unity is no longer insured by mutual surveillance. A man falls, and disappears. Who knows whether it was a bullet or the fear of advancing farther that struck him down?

Writing at a time when French strategists regarded the bayonet as the national weapon, this heretic scoffed at their creed of *élan*: "Each nation in Europe says, 'No one stands his ground before a bayonet attack made by us.' All are right . . . Whether the bayonet be fixed or in the scabbard makes no difference." Nor did the author of this unique treatise believe that the hordes of Europe could be inspired by an outworn legend of martial glory:

> It would be a service to humanity and to one's people to dispel this illusion and show what battles are. They are buffooneries, and none the less buffooneries because they are made terrible by the spilling of blood. The actors, heroes in the eyes of the crowd, are only poor folk torn between fear, discipline and pride. They play some hours at a game of advance and retreat, without ever meeting, closing with, even seeing closely, the other poor folk, the enemy, who are as fearful as they but who are caught in the same web of circumstance.

If such thoughts had appeared in print before 1870, France's professional soldiers would doubtless have resented them. But in a chastened spirit the generals of the new national army paid respectful heed to

Ardant du Picq's conclusion, "Tactics is an art based on the knowledge of how to make men fight with their maximum energy against fear, a maximum which organization alone can give."

The reconstructed French army did not lack organization and system. No troops in Europe were better armed, and yet the statesmen of the Third Republic could only view the future apprehensively. With Germany setting the pace, every great power had now become the victim of the strategic Frankensteins which glared at one another across the frontiers of 1898. However petty the causes of the coming conflict might be, the generalissimo who remembered Sedan could not afford an hour's delay in rushing his forces to the front. The very mobilization of these vast hosts involved such complicated problems of transport and supply that it was tantamount to a declaration of war. Once well launched, the process could not readily be halted because an opportunity for an honorable peace had arisen in the meantime.

Nor could preparedness for total war be attained without paying a price in social consequences. The necessity for secrecy, conceded by the most liberal citizens, threatened in every country to establish a military hierarchy which acknowledged only the half-gods of victory. The danger attracted world-wide attention when revealed in the proceedings of France's famous Dreyfus case. For the imprisonment of a Jewish officer on manifestly unproved charges of treason brought up the greater issue of how far an army might go in flaunting national ideals and institutions. It is to the glory of Frenchmen that they risked national security in meeting the challenge, and the accused man went free after a struggle which reached the proportions of a bloodless civil war.

No such trial could have been possible in Germany at this time. The ideals sown by Jahn had been harvested by Bismarck, and all classes accepted an army rule which would have driven a less submissive people to revolt. The liberal minority wrested an occasional reform of compromise, it is true, but emigration continued to be the hope of the subject who valued his rights as an individual. Civilians were openly treated with contempt by officers, and the emperor himself announced that the German woman's sphere was bounded by the church, the kitchen and the cradle.

With few exceptions, the nation's leaders made no secret of their belief in a creed of aggression. Moltke, one of the mildest of German militarists, expressed this faith in a rebuke written to a Swiss liberal, "Perpetual peace is a dream, and not even a beautiful dream. . . . In war man's noblest qualities are developed." Among the youth of the land the peculiarly German institution of the student duel indicated the trend of national thought. Barred to Jews and other social inferiors, these solemn contests were judged on a basis of the participant's stoicism rather than skill; and anthropologists might have found a marked resemblance to the torture ordeals endured by young barbarian tribesmen to prove their manhood.

Germans, in short, were thoroughly convinced that the total war of aggression promised a national profit both in moral and material respects. Humanists might dispute this doctrine, but they could not deny that the indemnity of 1870 had amounted to double the actual expenses of the victors, not to mention the acquisition of two provinces at a very moderate cost in blood.

In an age when nationalism had the appeal once exerted by religion, such statistics were infinitely more persuasive than ethical arguments. The spectacle of a strong and united Germany could not fail to impress those submerged European peoples who yearned for a government, a capital and an army of their own. If any further precepts were needed, it could not be forgotten that two aggressive new powers had been inspired by the example set at Sedan. Only a few weeks later the storming of Rome led to the unity of Italy; and it might as truthfully be said that the Japanese Empire also came into being on that September day which looms as the most portentous date in the history of modern warfare.

THE BOXER REBELLION OF 1900

The founders of Italy soon made it evident that they looked to Germany for security as well as guidance. Despite the financial difficulties of the recently created kingdom, the army bill adopted in 1882 provided for the formation of two new corps, while increasing the annual military estimate to the crushing sum of 200,000,000 lire. That same year saw the signing of the Triple Alliance with Germany and Austria, and the beginnings of an Italian policy of imperialism. After the murder of several explorers had supplied the conventional pretext, an expeditionary force occupied Massawa and Beilul. The extension of the Italian zone alarmed the Negus of Abyssinia, whose tribesmen annihilated a detachment of 524 troops, only a single man escaping.

Within eight years such border clashes had grown into a full-fledged war culminating in the Italian disaster at Adowa. Overwhelming forces of Abyssinians, armed with rifles and artillery, surrounded three columns comprising 20,000 soldiers. More than half of the invaders were slain or captured by savage foemen who made a practice of mutilating prisoners. A few months later Italy sued for peace, paying an indemnity of 10,000,000 lire.

Japan's early attempts to play the game of the great powers also ended in humiliation. Following the two visits of Commodore Perry's warships, the island empire abandoned its long isolation to the extent of sending envoys to Washington and the European capitals. Then in 1864 the murder of a British subject brought a drastic reprisal when 16 British, French and Dutch warships bombarded Shimonoseki to enforce a demand for an indemnity of $3,000,000. The money being used to apply pressure for added concessions, Japan learned European lessons which were promptly applied in Korea.

As traditional enemies, the two Oriental peoples had often clashed before. In 1592 an army of 200,000 Japanese invaders was equipped with the island's first arquebuses, manufactured in imitation of models brought by Portuguese traders. This force overran the peninsula, winning a victory which resulted in the ears of 38,000 dead foemen being cut off and buried in a memorial mound at Kyota. On the sea the Koreans won a great naval engagement with copper-armored warships mounting bronze rocket guns, and after a struggle of six years the expeditionary forces were withdrawn.

Japanese culture had been borrowed from Korea as well as China, but in 1875 the islanders sent a gunboat in the manner of a civilized nation dealing with a backward Asiatic people. The Koreans not only fired on the vessel but replied with contemptuous messages which nearly led to hostilities. In the end the Japanese cabinet had to swallow these insults, since internal conditions were too unsettled to permit a, foreign war at this time.

Within the past decade the empire's progress in modernization had clashed with the narrow codes of the Samurai, or hereditary warrior caste. Torture had been abolished, Christianity permitted, the first railway built with the help of English engineers, and newspapers, postal service and the telegraph introduced. This rapid and indiscriminate adoption of Western institutions threatened the very existence of the Samurai, who took up arms against the government in the Satsuma Rebellion of 1877. Despite their feudal traditions, the malcontents formed an army of 40,000 men trained in gunnery and modern tactics. A desperate strife of eight months ensued, and the complete victory of the 65,000 government troops meant that the Samurai no longer held exclusive privileges in military affairs.

The Japanese peasant or artisan having shown himself worthy of bearing arms, a new conscription law struck at the roots of the feudal system by making every male subject liable to army service, though the ideals and leadership of the Samurai were largely retained. This policy so strengthened the military system that the empire soon wiped out the Korean humiliation. In line with Western methods a formidable squadron was sent to demand a trade treaty, and by 1880 three ports had been opened to foreign commerce.

European observers, warming to the flattery of imitation, viewed such beginnings with condescending approval. Scholars might insist that the empire's official name was Nippon, but "Japan" remained in general usage. At a later date the Gilbert and Sullivan light opera popularized the title of "mikado" for a ruler called the tenno. Such bland misconceptions were less serious than the belief that Japanese modernization had bridged a gap of centuries in a decade. Actually the islanders were no more than fifty years behind the rest of the world in most mechanical respects when they emerged from their two centuries of self-imposed withdrawal. Throughout this period their leaders had never been wholly out of touch with European methods. Japanese cities compared with those of the West both in size and organization, and Japanese armies of 300,000 troops were known at a time when half as many would have been considered a large force in the West.

Japanese isolation—a phenomenon without a parallel in modern world history—must be charged to moral rather than material misgivings. The Jesuit missionaries of the sixteenth century, far from meeting popular hostility, had made thousands of eager converts. But Christian doctrines threatened the power of the shoguns, who ruled as military dictators; and the creed could not easily be reconciled with the legend of a divine emperor descended from the Sun Goddess. Hence the war lords closed their ports in 1630 and forbade their subjects to travel abroad. Christians were ferociously persecuted, while every encouragement was given to the Shinto priests who taught abject submission to superiors.

After the long interlude a similar problem confronted the dictators of 1880. Railways, steamships and telegraph lines were deemed harmless influences as compared to the democratic ideas upheld in Great Britain, France and the United States. The Japanese leaders met the issue by deriving most of their new civil and military codes from Bismarck's Germany, where the forms of Parliamentary consent were seldom allowed to interfere with army rule. In the same spirit the Japanese people were finally granted a legislature of two houses, peers and commons. German officers were imported as preceptors for the army, and German advisers helped to reorganize the imperial household and court ceremonial according to the Berlin model. For if the German "kaiser" did not claim divinity, he at least came closer than any other Western ruler to assuming the lofty prerogatives of the mikado.

The awakening of the European nations dates from 1894, when Japanese squadrons and armies easily humbled China in a war of only a few months. The astonishment of the West may be attributed chiefly to blindness, for even during her years of seclusion Nippon had remained a first-class power of some 25,000,000 inhabitants. Cannon had been manufactured in quantity during the eighteenth century, and the island's first naval academy was founded in the year of Perry's visit. A people of such proved adaptability did not find shipbuilding beyond its powers. At the outset British financiers lent the money for vessels constructed on the Clyde, but the Japanese insisted on sending observers to watch every step of the process. Within a few years they were turning out ironclads in their own yards, despite the amusing tales of errors being copied with earnest fidelity.

In view of her potential resources, Japan might have become the defender of Oriental interests. Instead, she chose to range herself with the European powers scrambling to exploit China's weakness. The victorious war of 1894 brought a large indemnity as well as territorial gains, but Russia and Germany regarded the triumph as inimical to their own ambitions. Their protests forced Japan to disgorge her most cherished spoils, and the empire had no other recourse but submission.

A proud people, united by a fanatical patriotism, the islanders were also patient. Six years later their turn came again when the great powers united to put down the Boxer Rebellion of 1900. This first military event set an ominous tone for the new century with a display of force and greed which some of the participating nations have had good reason to deplore in later years. For the adaptable Japanese, as impressionable to ideals as to methods, had another lesson in civilization when the German emperor addressed his marines about to embark for China:

> Give no quarter! Take no prisoners! . . . Even as, a thousand years ago, the Huns under their King Attila made such a name for themselves as still resounds in terror through legend and fable, so may the name of German resound through Chinese history a thousand years from now. . . .

Spokesmen for other countries were not so hysterical and indiscreet, but this was the age of "the white man's burden" in Britain and "manifest destiny" in the United States. Profitable "spheres of interest" remained to be claimed in Africa and Asia; and as newcomers to the feast of the nations, both Japan and Italy sent forces to share in the rending of prostrate China.

THE NEW AGE OF NAVAL WARFARE

At least the late arrivals were at no great disadvantage in sea fighting. Within the age of living men a new age of tactics had revolutionized naval construction, and the multiplicity of inventions favored the chances of such recent maritime nations as Germany, Italy, Japan and Russia.

In the ancient world, when oars supplied the power of propulsion, fire ships, ramming and boarding had been the resorts of fleets able to manoeuvre at will. Then came the age of sail, when the most aggressive captain must wait on the whims of the wind. Either the mêlée or the bombardment at long range depended for its results on expert seamanship, and a sudden calm or storm might become as decisive as a superior weight in metal.

In 1862 the duel between the *Merrimac* and the *Monitor* seemed at first to demonstrate the triumph of armor. The fact that neither ironclad had been seriously hurt, though two Federal wooden warships were destroyed, led naval men to place too much emphasis on the mere factor of protection. Yet even at the time the most astute observers realized that the Federal frigates were handicapped less by their wooden construction than the inability of sailing ships to manoeuvre against a steam-driven vessel such as the *Merrimac*. The real lesson of the famous fight was the triumph of mechanical means of propulsion; for during the remainder of the Civil War, wooden steamships gave a good account of themselves in competition with monitors.

Ramming tactics were of brief duration, and any remaining illusions as to the supremacy of armor vanished during the decade following the war. For the effectiveness of rifled steel guns showed corresponding gains; and tests proved that no warship could hope to achieve full protection against the havoc wrought by shells.

The development of the self-propelled torpedo, named after its Scottish inventor, Robert Whitehead, gave a further advantage to the naval offensive. The spar and stationary torpedoes of the Civil War had already proved how devastating an underwater explosion could be as compared to a hit above the water line. The resistance of the element being much greater than that of the armor, the entire force of the detonation is directed against a few square feet of the ship's surface. Whitehead's first torpedo, containing 18 pounds of dynamite, traveled underwater at 6 miles an hour, the engine being driven by compressed air. By means of a hydrostatic valve and pendulum balance mechanism, the 300-pound weapon could be set to run at any desired depth.

From this beginning has grown the complicated modern torpedo, equipped with a gyroscope-controlled rudder for direction. By the end of the century a speed of 25 miles an hour could be attained for 5,000 yards with projectiles containing several hundred pounds of the newer and more deadly types of explosive.

The underwater, self-propelled weapon suggested the warship utilizing the same principles. In 1875 John P. Holland built his earliest type as another American, Simon Lake, began a lifetime of research. European inventors were also at work, and the first submarine to receive official naval adoption was the French *Gymnote*, launched in 1888. Of 30 tons' displacement, this pioneer craft had a screw propeller driven by an electric motor which used current from secondary cells.

Before a single ship had been sunk in combat, the menace of the torpedo boat and submarine caused an upheaval in naval construction. Thus within a few decades the 100-gun three-decker, the "superdreadnought" of the age of sail, had become as obsolete as the trireme. Until 1875 naval architects retained sail for auxiliary power and still hoped to find eventual safety in armor. Then as the weight of protection reached its inevitable limit, only the vital parts were armored with plates up to 24 inches in thickness, and steam became the sole power of propulsion.

By the last decade of the century the outline of the modern battleship had taken shape, with the *Majestic* class of Great Britain serving as a model for rival powers. Armor of an improved type known as the Harvey process covered the most vulnerable sections in a belt which had a minimum thickness of 9 inches and a maximum depth of 15 feet. Four 12-inch guns of the new quick-firing type and twelve 6-inch guns were carried in heavily armored casemates. The nine vessels of the *Majestic* class were of high freeboard, 14,900 tons, 390 feet long, reaching a speed of 17 knots.

All the mechanical advances of the age had gone into the building of these floating steel fortresses powered by steam and electricity. Their "rifles" were capable of hurling tons of screaming steel at moving targets from a distance of 4,000 yards. Not only did the modern battleship represent the most concentrated unit of armed force ever conceived by man, but also the most impressive symbol of a nation's pride and prestige.

For all of their terrific striking power, the new monsters had no adequate defense against the swift little torpedo boat. Naval tacticians found an answer in the creation of an auxiliary craft, the destroyer. Despite its aggressive name, this vessel was originally intended to be the unit of a protective screen covering the advance of the main battle line. Speed and deception were the destroyer's resources, and her light, quick-firing guns proved so effective that the torpedo boat soon disappeared from tactical history. Its offensive functions were taken over by the destroyer itself, which could either deliver or parry an attack after torpedo tubes were added to its armament. Submarines did not become a serious threat until after the turn of the century, when the speed, manoeuvrability and light draught of the destroyer fitted it to hunt down underwater craft with depth charges.

The battleship had a further tactical limitation, since its armor limited the speed desirable for purposes of raiding or scouting. The lack brought another permanent addition to the fleet in the cruiser. An intermediate type, veering between the destroyer's swiftness and the battleship's power, this lightly armored vessel was designed at first to prey upon armed merchantmen. Then in the 1890's the competition between nations led to the development of a heavy type. Displacing as much as 12,000 tons, carrying 10-inch guns and armor belts 8 inches thick, these newcomers were in reality small battleships and took their place as such in the line. Eventually the light and heavy cruiser were recognized as distinct types, though no other warship has been subject to so many upward or downward revisions according to the times. Different national requirements have also led to varying standards, but in any event the tactical purpose of the cruiser is comparable to that of the cavalry in land warfare.

THE WRITINGS OF CAPTAIN MAHAN

Perhaps the most striking feature of the new naval age may be found in the fact that these first modern fleets had to depend largely on theory or peacetime tests for guidance. The Civil War had left but few and elementary lessons, and no further sea engagements of any consequence were recorded until 1898. Between those dates the term "war games" took on an unusual significance as admirals sought to anticipate the conditions of some future test which might decide a nation's destiny in a blazing hour of combat.

The possibilities of such manoeuvres as "crossing the T" were thus recognized before they ever developed in action. Given the hypothetical situation of a faster squadron crossing the bows of an enemy column, it is obvious that the leading warships of the latter must endure a terrible converging fire. No effective reply can be made, since so many guns of the column are obstructed by the ships ahead. The most plausible solution is to wheel sharply into a parallel order, but during the movement the first few ships will still be subjected to heavy punishment

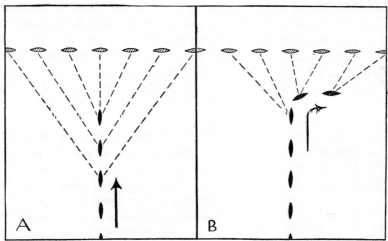

The Naval Manoeuvre of "Crossing the T"

before their own fire can be fully effective. In the long run a superior or at least equal speed is doubtless the most reliable defense.

This was one of the tactical problems discussed at the War College founded by the United States Navy in 1885, with Captain Alfred Thayer Mahan as its first president. A more fortunate appointment could not have been made, for even at this early date the dignified, scholarly officer had qualities which would later rank him alongside Clausewitz as a theorist of modern warfare. His father, a West Point instructor in engineering, had written two treatises on field fortification and entrenchment which influenced the tactics of the Civil War. From this atmosphere young Mahan went to the new naval academy at Annapolis, graduating just in time to take an active part in Federal sea operations. His own early career having thus bridged the gap between the ages of sail and steam, he could write from personal experience of the transition.

It is a comment on the times that when the forty-five-year-old Mahan began lecturing on history and strategy at the War College, there was almost no modern naval warfare to study. So few and confused were its precepts in 1885 that he persuaded his superiors to "borrow" a young army lieutenant, Tasker H. Bliss, as an instructor in land tactics. Mahan himself acknowledged a debt to the writings of Jomini and Napoleon, so that he approached the blank page of modern naval theory with a broad sense of the relationship between operations on land and sea.

His own lifelong ambition to write found a first outlet in *The Influence of Sea Power upon History, 1660-1783*, compiled from lectures he had given at the War College. Two years passed before he found a publisher willing to take the financial risk of bringing out the book. Nevertheless, its appearance in 1890 gained him a world-wide acclaim which can only be compared to the reception given Guibert's treatise. Two years later the publication of *The Influence of Sea Power upon the French Revolution and Empire, 1783-1812* established the American author as the acknowledged authority in his field. Even more remarkable, his reputation has not diminished with the years, despite the sweeping tactical changes of the next half century.

It has been said that Mahan wrote twenty books to expand from historical examples a theme presented in the first ninety-five pages of his first book. Where former naval writers had more or less ignored the economic background, he began by asserting that a navy can only justify its existence by the protection of merchant shipping. Describing the sea as a network of trade routes, he cited precepts from the ancient world to prove that true national greatness has been in all ages based upon water-borne commerce. The most powerful navies, he maintained, have grown out of thriving merchant fleets, while the purely military navy is foredoomed to failure.

In the development of this theory, Mahan's first and best known book is devoted chiefly to the long duel between the British navy and the artificially created fleets of Colbert and his successors. With few exceptions, the results of these wars offer convincing evidence in support of his main theme. For in the last chapters the reader sees France stripped both of her commerce and colonial possessions, while her rival has become mistress of a vast empire.

The second book, as its title implies, takes up in even greater detail the struggle between a French army dominating the Continent and a British navy in control of the sea lanes, with Napoleon and Nelson as the protagonists. Deriving his material from French as well as English sources, Mahan shows the effects of "the noiseless, steady, exhausting pressure with which sea power acts, cutting off the resources of the enemy while maintaining its own, supporting war in scenes where it does not appear itself, or appears only in the background, and striking open blows only at rare intervals." So well established are these conclusions that few critics have ever dared to challenge them; and Mahan's most frequently quoted words reiterate that "those far distant storm-beaten ships, upon which the Grand Army never looked, stood between it and the dominion of the world."

This familiar passage may be considered an exception, for if Clausewitz ranks as the most quotable of war theorists, Mahan is surely the least. In general the American writer avoided the aphorisms, paradoxes and smashing phrases which distinguish *Vom Kriege,* and their absence has been to the benefit of his writings. Never is the reader beguiled into attaching too much importance to a half-truth presented as a rhetorical thrust. He may be crushed by the weight of twenty books, he may feel that the theme is as relentless as sea power itself, but he is not likely to carry away any such misinterpretations as have often stultified Clausewitz's message.

It is seldom indeed that Mahan asserts himself as a lawgiver, though his own convictions are not hidden. For the most part he is content to let his main premises be revealed by historical events—the decisiveness of the economic attack as exemplified by the blockade, the limitations of the "fleet in being" school of strategy, the delusive victories gained by privateering and similar raids on the commerce of a stronger maritime enemy.

Although he has left some surpassing tactical descriptions of sea battles, Mahan is at his best in dealing with questions of national policy and grand strategy. Hence his first two books found a warm and immediate welcome in England, where the issue of naval expansion was then being debated. Honorary degrees were conferred on him by Oxford and Cambridge; and it would be no exaggeration to say that modern British naval policy has been profoundly influenced by books read with the respect usually paid to classics.

Nor did the many object lessons drawn by Mahan from France's sea warfare bar him from favorable comment in that country. On the contrary, French naval men accepted them in the spirit of disciples, while praising the impartiality of his research. An even more flattering tribute came from Germany when the kaiser quoted Mahan to justify a policy of naval expansion. And in 1892 *The Influence of Sea Power upon History* was officially adopted as a textbook in the new German navy.

Deeply patriotic as well as religious, Mahan had served as an officer in 1880 when his own country's fleet could not measure up to the standard set by second-rate powers. He had seen its merchant marine sink into mediocrity after the Civil War as England's iron steamships crowded out the wooden sailing vessels which had been the pride of America in the days of the clippers. These conditions the theorist set out to remedy. Regarding the United States as an insular rather than a truly continental power in naval strategy, he tried to impress his countrymen with a sense of their responsibilities as well as opportunities on the sea. All of his books were written at least indirectly for this purpose, and in 1897 he published a direct appeal in *The Interest of America in Sea Power, Present* and *Future.*

Mahan's success was all that he could have asked. If Americans lagged a few years behind Europeans in their applause, they eventually subscribed to most of his tactical principles. His influence was equally potent in questions of policy, so that the events leading up to the annexation of Hawaii, Puerto Rico and the Philippines were colored by his imperialistic views.

The transition from theory to practice took on a new vigor in 1896 when Theodore Roosevelt became Assistant Secretary of the Navy. As Mahan's most ardent follower, this forceful young crusader reorganized the system of navy rank and promotion, ordered great reserves of coal and ammunition, began new projects at the arsenals and navy yards, and spent $800,000 for target practice. Due largely to his efforts, the fleet had reached an advanced stage of preparation when the United States declared war on Spain in April, 1898.

The most sharply criticized of recent American foreign ventures, the conflict could undoubtedly have been avoided by a willingness to arbitrate. But American public opinion had been inflamed by newspaper accounts of Spanish colonial oppressions, while the "strong" policy of the Administration was to some extent based on Mahan's advice as a member of the War Board. The mysterious explosion of the United States battleship *Maine* in Havana Harbor supplied the "incident," and within three months of the declaration of war both Spanish squadrons had been completely destroyed at a cost of only one man killed.

As the first important fleet actions since the Civil War, these operations were too one-sided to be tactically instructive. Admiral George Dewey showed great enterprise in penetrating the defenses of Manila Bay on May 1, but the obsolescent Spanish ships were no match for his four protected cruisers. The superior American gunnery sank or burned every enemy vessel, then quickly silenced the shore batteries. In the Caribbean the issue remained in doubt for a few weeks until a much more powerful American force bottled up Admiral Cervera's four armored cruisers in Santiago harbor. On July 3 the badly handled

The Battleship of 1898—U.S.S. *Iowa*

Spanish squadron attempted an escape, only to be annihilated by the fire of the battleships *Iowa, Indiana, Oregon* and *Texas*. More than five hundred Spaniards were killed and wounded, the rest being taken prisoner along with their commander.

THE RUSSO-JAPANESE WAR

Six years passed before modern naval strategists at last had an opportunity to study great actions between fleets of fairly equal strength. Even this brief period brought enough changes to inspire the complaint of a German admiral that "ships became obsolete before they were launched."

Japan had awaited an opportunity for further expansion on the Asiatic continent ever since being robbed of the main rewards of her victory over China in 1894. During the following decade, though her own shipyards were now in operation, the empire floated loans with which to buy warships from the United States and European nations. In 1902 her growing prestige was recognized by a British alliance, and the next two years saw Japanese relations with Russia strained to the breaking point.

Port Arthur and the eventual domination of Korea loomed as the prizes on the misty morning of February 6, 1904, when six battleships and four cruisers with their destroyers and torpedo boats silently put out to sea under Admiral Togo. The fifty-seven-year-old Japanese commander, the product of an English naval education, had been the hero of an attack which his cruiser launched on Chinese transports in 1894 without the formality of a declaration. And now as the Russians still deluded themselves with hopes of peace—hopes not discouraged by Japanese diplomats—Togo's flotilla reached Port Arthur on the night of February 8 without having been detected. At once his torpedo boats raced into action against the seven battleships and six cruisers at anchor outside the harbor with all lights ablaze. Thus began the first great war of the twentieth century—two days before the Japanese declaration.

Under the circumstances it is remarkable that not a single Russian ship went down. The protection of the new torpedo nets proved so adequate that only two battleships and a cruiser suffered hits, though in the lack of dry-dock facilities even this damage amounted to a paralyzing blow.

At daybreak, when Togo's main force steamed forward, the Russian shore batteries had belatedly been made ready, and their fire repulsed the assault. The Japanese admiral has been criticized for failing to annihilate an unsuspecting foe, but the strategic problem called for prudence. His total "paper strength" exceeded that of the enemy's Pacific fleet, which had been divided between Port Arthur and Vladivostok, a thousand miles apart. The Japanese ships had the advantage in speed, modernity and fire power as well as leadership, but there remained an x in the equation as represented by the czar's Baltic fleet. Togo's squadron, moreover, had the added duty of keeping the sea lanes open to Korea for an amphibious operation involving the transport of large armies. In view of these responsibilities, he adopted a strategy of the utmost caution by blockading Port Arthur while a second Japanese force kept watch over the four Russian cruisers at Vladivostok.

The incompetence of the Russian command at Port Arthur had not prepared the invaders for the abrupt change when Admiral Makárov replaced Starck. The new leader steamed outside the harbor nearly every day, but in April his boldness incurred a fresh disaster. Both sides had sown many submerged, electro-mechanical mines; and during a sortie the Russian flagship *Petropavlovsk* went down with six hundred

men, including the energetic "Cossack admiral," while another battleship was badly damaged. These results confirmed the passivity of the
port's defenders, who did not know that on May 15 two of Togo's largest
and newest battleships had also been sunk by mines.

The Japanese admiral, combining the stature of a dwarf with a
giant's imperturbability, managed to keep his losses secret, since the
land operations had now become of primary interest. World-wide sympathy favored the cause of the invaders, yet for all practical purposes
the Russians were actually in the position of "underdog." General
Kuropatkin could count on but 100,000 widely separated troops at the
outset, while the Japanese had a first-line army of 270,000 highly
trained men in addition to 200,000 reserves. The difference between
these strengths dictated a Russian strategy of delay until a corrupt and
bureaucratic government could send reinforcements over the long Trans-
Siberian railway.

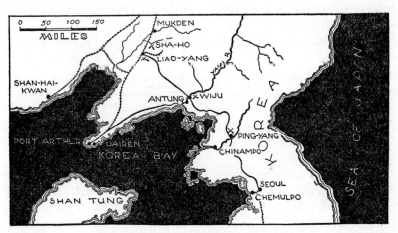

Battlefields of the Russo-Japanese War

Neither by land nor sea could any effectual resistance be offered to
the landing of General Kuroki's army at Chemulpo. As the expeditionary
force pushed up the Korean peninsula over miserable roads, Kuropatkin
sought to gain a respite by concentrating far back in the rear at Liao-
Yang. He sent only a covering detachment to contest the crossing of the
Yalu, and the first land battle occurred on the banks of the river which
constituted the Manchurian frontier. Since 7,000 Russians were opposed
to some 40,000 Japanese, the outcome could hardly be in doubt; but in
its far-reaching moral effects the battle of the Yalu ranks as an Oriental

Valmy. For the first time in modern history European troops had been beaten by Asiatics using their own methods.

On May 26 the empire celebrated a second victory as 30,000 troops landed under the guns of Togo's warships and stormed Nanhan Hill, held by 3,000 entrenched Russians. Although gained at a cost of 4,500 casualties, the success gave the invaders a foothold for siege operations against the outdated works of Port Arthur.

Instead of retiring within his neglected defenses, General Stössel wisely moved outside to hold a system of improvised trenches and redoubts in the rugged hills encircling the town. This decision gained him two months in which to strengthen his permanent lines before the suicidal Japanese assaults forced a retirement. But the attackers had won one advantage to compensate for grievous losses, since their guns could now drop shells among the Russian ships in the harbor. Admiral Vitheft put to sea with Togo in pursuit, and the first real naval battle of the war resulted from an attempt of the Port Arthur and Vladivostok squadrons to unite.

Up to this time the mine and torpedo had appeared the most effective naval weapons. It was not so well known that the Japanese were making use of an invention which had proved too modern for most European fleets. Then in the experimental stage, Marconi's wireless had been installed in the fishing boats so often utilized by Japanese strategists. With trained naval men as operators, these craft relayed the messages of a spy system which included Japanese officers posing as servants in high Russian circles.

Added to his information of enemy plans, Togo's superior speed enabled him to overtake Vitheft's squadron only 20 miles south of Port Arthur. The battle of the Yellow Sea on August 10 developed into a cautious duel of gunnery at extreme ranges of nearly three miles. The new Japanese armor-piercing shells did not come up to expectations, and only a single Russian ship was crippled. Togo refused an excellent prospect of a victory of annihilation, for he still felt that he could not risk the loss of a vessel while the threat of the Baltic fleet impended. That night his decision found justification as most of the beaten ships limped back to the dubious security of Port Arthur, the rest being soon forced into neutral harbors for internment. Four days later the Vladivostok squadron also returned to port after losing a cruiser to a secondary Japanese squadron, so that the enemy's Pacific fleet had virtually ceased to exist as a fighting force.

The Battles of Mukden and Tsushima

Marshal Oyama, generalissimo of the Japanese armies, had by this date mastered his formidable supply problems and begun an advance toward the railway with Liao-Yang as a first objective. His staff having absorbed the German spirit as well as method, Sedan became the model for a vast enveloping movement launched by a chain of seven deployed divisions.

Although Moltke's victories continued to inspire twentieth-century soldiers, Petersburg might still have taught more instructive lessons. Only seven years after Sedan, moreover, the Russo-Turkish War had offered new evidence as to the defensive power of modern arms. During the siege of Plevna 40,000 Turks had been able to hold an open town for six months against 100,000 Russians with 440 guns. Depending only on trenches and redoubts, the defenders inflicted 38,000 casualties, most of them as the result of rifle fire, before being finally starved into surrender.

A decade later the general adoption of smokeless powder might have been interpreted as a further warning to generals dreaming of a swift and crushing offensive. Described as being "neither smokeless nor a powder," the new explosive consisted of perforated pellets manufactured from a mixture of nitroglycerin and diluted guncotton. Although the smoke had not been wholly eliminated, so few traces were left that the soldier's position would not be revealed by day. Far greater advantages resulted from the slow-burning qualities, since the great defect of black powder had been a rapid explosion which forced the missile out at the first impact, thus wasting much of the force of the propellent gases. Smokeless powder, in contrast, started the bullet gradually on its way, set it firmly in the grooves of the rifling, and accentuated the spinning motion by maintaining a pressure which reached a maximum at the muzzle.

The benefits were many. Due to a lesser strain on the gun itself, a flatter trajectory, longer range and higher velocity could be obtained with a smaller projectile. In 1886 France took the lead by adopting the Lebel magazine rifle of only .310 caliber. A few years later the Germans issued a .30 caliber bolt-action repeater, and the Japanese went even further by approving a .25 caliber arm which enabled the soldier to carry nearly double the usual amount of ammunition. The new small-bore rifles had a range of 3,000 yards, which meant that concealed infantry could keep fieldpieces at a more respectful distance. On the other hand, the gains were shared by ordnance in equal measure, so that both larger and smaller artillery than the usual 15-pounder could be brought into the field.

These tactical changes came just in time to be a decisive factor in South Africa as 90,000 Boers compelled the British to put nearly half a million regular troops and auxiliaries in the field. Dismissed by European generals as mere large-scale guerrilla operations, these campaigns left no doubt as to the effects of smokeless powder and the repeating rifle. Surprise, mobility and concealment were the resources of marksmen who made skillful use of a difficult terrain, and the British expenditure of small arms ammunition came to 66,000,000 rounds, or double the amount used by the Germans in 1870-1871. Khaki uniforms were adopted for protective coloring as early reverses taught the regular troops to advance in thin skirmish lines, taking advantage of all cover. Both sides brought heavy, long-range guns into the field as well as the rapid-firing one-pounders known as pompoms. The British eventually found the key to victory in punitive expeditions based on chains of blockhouses, but the fire power of modern arms enabled the Boers to resist for two and a half years.

Although the new types of recoil-operated and gas operated machine guns had been invented before the Spanish-American War, neither found wide favor until the Russo-Japanese operations. Hiram Maxim, an American who later became a British subject, brought out the first single-barrel gun in which the functions of loading, firing and ejecting the cartridge were performed automatically by utilizing the force of the recoil. Another American, John M. Browning, discovered a way to employ part of the propellent gases for the same purpose; and his invention established the air-cooling principle as distinguished from the water jacket which cooled the Maxim model. Both types were at first mounted on wheels and later on tripods.

The new open order of fighting, combined with the introduction of so many new weapons, meant that the old systems of lamp, flag and semaphore signaling must give way to more modern methods. As early as 1867 the British had conducted successful experiments with the field telegraph in colonial campaigns. The South African War saw dispatch riders carrying messages on motorcycles, and field telegraph cables were laid across country "at a speed limited only by that of the six-horse teams which drew the wagons."

The Japanese, in spite of their reputation as mere imitators, took the next forward step by adopting the field telephone for land operations, while depending on the wireless for communication at sea. The armies of Manchurian invasion, comprising picked troops of professional caliber, were equipped not only with the most modern artillery but also the Hotchkiss machine gun, an air-cooled, gas-operated weapon of Austrian manufacture. The staff work, training and organization of Marshal Oyama's forces measured up to German standards, while every soldier was imbued with a morale of self-sacrificing zeal. The world of 1904, in short, could not produce a more modern fighting machine than the seven divisions which gave battle at Liao-Yang on August 28. The open country favored the annihilation plans of the attackers, and Oyama called for another Sedan to reach its climax on the anniversary of that military landmark.

Kuropatkin at least had an equality in numbers, since reinforcements had been arriving over the Trans-Siberian railway at the rate of 30,000 a month. But his best asset proved to be the repeating rifles and Maxim machine guns of an army which was otherwise outclassed both in equipment and organization. Always stubborn defensive fighters, the Russians gave ground grudgingly and inflicted heavy losses at every backward step. Japanese attempts at envelopment were met by an extension of the Russian lines as the battle turned into a chaos of local encounters. On September 1, after two days of bloody repulses, the Japanese Sedan was so far from realization that the enemy began a terrific counterstroke. During the next forty-eight hours Oyama had to use up his reserves in defensive fighting, and on September 3 the first great engagement of the war ended in a stalemate of exhaustion. Although the Japanese claimed a victory as Kuropatkin fell back toward Mukden, their 23,000 casualties exceeded by 20 per cent the losses of a foe able to retire in good order.

A month later the conflict entered upon a new phase as Kuropatkin took the offensive along the Sha-ho River. He had no better success with his envelopment schemes, and both armies learned from costly experience that the spade offered the only defense against the rifle and machine gun. As the autumn rains set in, the opposing forces faced each other on a far-flung front of parallel trenches behind formidable mazes of barbed-wire entanglements.

Meanwhile the Japanese had been using up an average of 12,000 men a month in their efforts to carry the trenches and redoubts of Port Arthur's hills. Enormous mines were exploded by the attackers, and 11-inch howitzers kept up a ceaseless battering with shells weighing 485 pounds. Still, the defenders of 203-Metre Hill managed to make that prosaic name famous by the obstinacy of their resistance. At last the position fell on December 5, exposing the trapped battleships in the basin to an accurate artillery fire directed by field telephone. Within a few more days all four had been sent to the bottom, and the fall of Port Arthur came in January after a seven-month siege which cost the victors losses of nearly 100,000.

Throughout a severe winter the main armies contented themselves with the combats of trench warfare while preparing for the supreme test. On February 21 the 350,000 troops of Oyama's reinforced divisions surged forward in a general advance against equal numbers of Russians holding a 47-mile front. Despite the telephones and observation balloons of the attackers, the Japanese lost cohesion within a week, making serious mistakes in the disposal of their reserves. By March 1 the great battle had become a slugging match between entrenched forces, with attrition proving everywhere more decisive than manoeuvre. Oyama sent in his last reserves against a still unshaken foe as he made his final bid for victory with a prodigious pincers movement on March 6. After long and exhausting marches his right and left met north of Mukden on the tenth, only to discover that their completed circle enclosed no enemies. Kuropatkin had withdrawn his forces after heavy casualties in rear-guard actions, conceding his opponents the town but not their expected triumph. Even so, Oyama could claim a victory of attrition in the three-week battle, having inflicted about 90,000 casualties at a cost of 50,000.

As the battered but unbowed Russian army took up a strong new position north of Mukden, it became probable that the decisive battle would occur on the sea. In October, after long vacillation, Nicholas II had sent his Baltic fleet on the long voyage around Africa to the Far East. Admiral Rozhestvenski reached Madagascar just in time to learn of Port Arthur's surrender, and several months of waiting in tropical ports did the armada no good either in moral or material respects. But the czar lacked the courage necessary for retreat; and after the arrival of reinforcing units via Suez, the united fleet steamed for the Straits of Malacca.

Togo had been refitting and conducting target practice ever since the battle of the Yellow Sea. In that engagement his primary concern had been the saving of Japanese ships, whereas he now considered himself free to concentrate on the destruction of the enemy. In terms of mass Rozhestvenski had an impressive force which included seven battleships, six cruisers and a flotilla of destroyers among the forty-five vessels.

The Japanese could show no more bulk even in their home waters, but Togo's superiority lay in speed, fire power and training. Nor can the difference in morale be discounted, for Rozhestvenski and his officers were oppressed by a sense of futility as the fleet coaled for the last time in Cochin China.

Considering that all world history presents only a score of great sea battles, it is hardly a wonder that a vast literature has been devoted to each. Edwin A. Falk's *Togo and the Rise of Japanese Sea Power* gives an excellent detailed account of the moves leading up to the crossing of the Russian T. On the morning of May 27, 1905, the first enemy ships were sighted in the waters between Japan and Korea, and the Japanese fleet went into action at a rate of 16 knots as compared to 10 for the enemy. Early in the afternoon contact was made east of Tsushima Island. Togo's superior speed as well as judgment gave him the opening for steaming diagonally across the bows of the battleships in the first Russian division. Although the T was not crossed with typographical accuracy, several of Rozhestvenski's ships were placed at a grave disadvantage in firing. During that fatal half hour he lost the greatest sea battle since Trafalgar as one battleship sank and another dropped out of formation. The demoralization of the remainder led to near-collisions as the opposing columns swung into concentric circles, their vision obscured by smoke and overcast skies.

By nightfall three more crippled battleships had been sent to the bottom, and the balance of the fleet sought only an escape to Vladivostok. Togo now put into effect the next step of his plan by withdrawing his larger ships and sending in his torpedo boats and destroyers. All night these swift killers harassed a stricken foe, accounting for the destruction of three armored units. The following day the entire Japanese fleet hunted down surviving enemy vessels which were practically all sunk, captured or driven into internment. In the end the beaten admiral, wounded and unconscious, became the prisoner of victors who had lost but three torpedo boats in gaining a triumph which would long be hailed as the most complete of the age of steam.

Where the battle of Mukden had failed of a decision, Tsushima ended the war. The United States had a direct interest in preserving a Pacific balance of power, and President Theodore Roosevelt acted as mediator between the warring nations. Russia appeared to be in a much inferior position, yet she had not exerted a tenth of her strength in land warfare, while her adversary put forth a supreme effort to gain limited results. Hence the island empire also had good reasons for accepting a peace of negotiation; and the Treaty of Portsmouth awarded her half of Saghalien, the surrender of the Russian lease of Port Arthur, and the recognition of a Japanese sphere of influence in Korea.

In past conflicts the prowess of the victor had been reckoned in terms of losses inflicted or territory occupied. But the twentieth century, which brought so many innovations, provided a new standard. Pacifists of the day fondly believed that wars were fomented by selfish little groups of international financiers, yet thousands of middle-class investors had a stake in the outcome of the Russo-Japanese War. Both nations borrowed about half a billion dollars, and three weeks before the outbreak Russian four per cent bonds stood at 98½ as compared to 78½ for the Japanese. The surprise attack on Port Arthur caused a Russian drop of six points and a Japanese loss of ten. The fall of the fortress led to quotations of 90½ and 77¾ respectively, but the climax arrived with the news of Tsushima. For after that event the bonds of the two powers reached an equality at 87¾. Togo's thudding guns had won for his country the ultimate respect of the Western World.

PART SEVEN
WORLD WAR I

☆

I

1914: THE LIGHTS GO OUT

Modern war is too serious a business to be entrusted to soldiers.

—CLEMENCEAU

IT IS a sad commentary on the events leading up to 1914 that questions of "war guilt" were being disputed before ever a shot had been fired. The inevitability of the struggle was generally recognized, and thoughtful observers could only regard the assassination of the Austrian archduke as an incitement to be compared with the pebble which starts a long-impending avalanche.

Every warring power managed to cite the most plausible justifications. But even allowing that Germany had taken the lead in aggression for fifty years, all of the other nations were more or less tarred with the same brush. If any one basic cause could be assigned to Europe's first great conflict since Waterloo, it might have been found in the consent of the various peoples. For half a century they had given their rulers full powers in the secret dealings of diplomacy and strategy, and during the summer of 1914 the blank check was presented for payment.

This indictment applies as much to the masses of Russia as to the more privileged citizens of France and Great Britain. No country of Europe, however autocratic its form of government, could afford to risk a general war without the support of public approval. Statesmen and military leaders were acutely sensitive to fluctuations of morale, and in every capital the order for mobilization was applauded with an excitement bordering on frenzy. Shopkeepers who bore names suggesting an enemy nationality were made the victims of mob violence; and stranded citizens of hostile nations had to endure official as well as popular persecution, regardless of their age, sex or conduct.

Such outbursts might be more charitably dismissed if the peoples of Europe had not long ago demonstrated their willingness to assume the sacrifices as well as enthusiasms of power politics. From Germany the creed of state worship had spread until the peasants and workingmen of all nations proudly identified themselves with their own armies, navies and diplomatic corps Where once the luxury of making war had been restricted to kings, the twentieth century seemed to bring even this privilege within the reach of the masses. If the price came high, no murmur was pitched loud enough to alarm the various capitals. Nor could it truthfully be said that the people had been deceived or betrayed by their rulers. More often the statesmen and generals had to brace themselves against a popular clamor for war, as in France during the period of Boulanger's ascendancy. The fact is that Europeans had shouldered the burdens of high taxes and universal conscription for half a century without complaint; and in August, 1914, they went to war with full confidence in the efficacy of force as a remedy for fear.

The juggernauts thus set in motion were too huge to be comprehended even by the state servants who pressed the buttons of mobilization. In France the trains followed one another day and night at intervals of eight minutes—7,000 trains transporting 3,781,000 men in sixteen days. In Germany, where four new double-track lines had significantly been laid during late years, 550 trains a day rumbled across the Rhine bridges. Cologne alone received a new train of conscripts every ten minutes for two weeks. Altogether, nearly four million German soldiers were carried to the front, and the quantities of food, arms and ammunition reached astronomical figures.

So tremendous was the machinery of mobilization that its operators were unable to put on the brakes. When France perversely upset the calculations of Berlin by a last-minute display of reluctance, it was too late to halt the forward movement of troops. The first patrols had already crossed the border as Germany sent an ultimatum so insulting that it could only be answered by force. The General Staff had planned a war on two fronts, and even a prospect of French neutrality could not be allowed to interfere.

Singularly few expressions of regret were heard as the bright morning of the twentieth century slowly blurred into a red mist. The most convincing of these were voiced not by the people but by the men later accused of leading the people into war. Germany's emperor, who had played the fool more often than the knave, wrote in bitter self-pity:

> Wantonness and weakness are to engulf the world in the most terrible of wars, the ultimate aim of which is the ruin of Germany. For now I can no longer doubt that England, France and Russia have conspired to fight together for our annihilation . . . and so the notorious encirclement of Germany is at last an accomplished fact.

The kaiser, characteristically, thought of the consequences to himself and his country. Sir Edward Grey, the British foreign minister, spoke for his entire generation as he sat in his London office, staring out into the summer dusk. "The lights are going out all over Europe," he said. "We shall never see them again in our lifetime."

THE OPPOSING FORCES AND PLANS

The leading optimists of the Continent were the generals. Almost without exception they shared the belief of the people that their armies would surge on to victory within a few weeks. Germany, as usual, had a plan. The dread of "encirclement," coupled with a genuine peril of imports being cut off, made it more than ever desirable to strike a knockout blow before the enemy could gather his full strength. Hence the General Staff counted heavily on its strategic blueprint for another and greater Sedan at France's expense. Not even another Moltke was lacking, for a nephew of the dead hero had risen to the chief command.

The author of the conception, Count Alfred von Schlieffen, had faced the bleak prospect of a war on two fronts during his long term as chief-of-staff. Noting the growing emphasis on offensive doctrines in France, he evolved a strong and simple plan for utilizing even the efforts of the enemy to insure the success of a German invasion. On the customary plea of necessity, Schlieffen felt no shame in urging a violation of Dutch as well as Belgian territory at the outset. He proposed the sweep of an overwhelmingly strong right wing through those countries, thus gaining time by avoiding the Ardennes and the formidable chain of French forts stretching from Luxembourg to Switzerland. Counting on an enemy offensive meanwhile, he insisted that the numbers of the German left wing be reduced to the lowest margin of safety. As they slowly fell back toward the Rhine, hard-pressed by the French, the main German mass of invasion was to complete its great wheel through Belgium to the south of Paris. Then, too late, the foe would discover that his own advancing armies were in deadly peril from the rear as the German right wing swung east to cut their communications and pin them against the frontier.

The French, in short, were to be given every opportunity to accomplish their own destruction after being lured forward by a few illusory gains. Schlieffen was enough of a realist to allow for Belgian resistance and a British expeditionary force of 100,000 men. Even so, he believed that a six-week campaign should suffice to crush France, whereupon the victors would hurl their full strength at Russia before that country had fully mobilized. If by any chance the plan should fail, its author advised that the fatherland accept a compromise peace and begin secret preparations for another attempt.

Had the war broken out in 1900, France would unquestionably have been in less danger. The deterioration during the next fourteen years may be charged to an almost incredible excess of confidence on the part of the General Staff. Since the Russian and British alliances promised an advantage both in numbers and sea power, the harsh lessons of 1870 were easily forgotten. The new school of French strategists, replacing a generation which had held the foe in sober respect, went to extremes in advocating an offensive policy based on faith rather than works. Grandmaison and Foch took the lead by professing a mystical belief in the moral supremacy of the attack. The recent "discovery" of Clausewitz had been an exciting event to these staff officers; and the writings of Ardant du Picq now seemed to them to demonstrate the triumph of spirit over matter in the military sphere. Even the philosophy of Bergson, then being widely discussed, added its contribution by praising intuition and instinct as opposed to cold reason.

"When on the offensive," declared Grandmaison, "recklessness is the best safety." Foch in his turn invited a rebuke from history by asserting that the deadly effect of modern weapons favored the chances of the attack. "Formerly many guns were needed to produce an effect. Today, a few suffice."

The scope and direction of the German invasion had been divined with surprising accuracy as early as 1911, but the optimistic new school of French thought underestimated by nearly half the numbers that would be employed. As an equally fatal miscalculation, it was supposed that the Germans would be obliging enough to take the laborious route through the Ardennes. Reassured by these premises, the General Staff of 1912 adopted its famous Plan XVII, which contemplated a great counterstroke in the centre to paralyze the enemy's communications in Lorraine and roll back both of his wings.

But if France's soldiers staked the national future on a military philosophy rather than a strategy, they must be given credit for a most persuasive influence over their allies of the Entente. English civilians of 1912 would doubtless have been dismayed to learn how far their generals had gone in abandoning a traditional policy of isolation. Where once their country had subsidized allies or planned moderate amphibious strokes as its part in continental wars, Sir Henry Wilson, the director of military operations, pledged a maximum strength of 150,000 trained soldiers to fight under French supervision on the Allied left wing. As an ardent Francophile he established close relations with Ferdinand Foch, then commandant of the French Staff College, whose *Principes de la Guerre* was adopted as a text for British officers. So amiable did this Briton prove, as compared to his countrymen in the past, that French confidential documents paid him the compliment of referring to the proposed expeditionary force as the *Corps d'Armée* Wilson.

Russia showed an equally astonishing complaisance. For the czar's generals promised within eighteen days of mobilization to relieve the pressure on France by advancing against East Prussia with a minimum of 800,000 troops.

Bismarck could scarcely have rested in his grave as these commitments were gained by the nation he had tried to isolate and render helpless. Even the realistic Schlieffen had not counted on any such developments, and the failure of his renowned plan must be attributed in large measure to the aid which France secured from her Allies. Germany, on the other hand, had already faced the fact that Italy would not take an active part in the Triple Alliance at the beginning. Nor did the strategists of Berlin have any illusions as to the support which might be expected from their other partner. The wars of 1859 and 1866 had long ago revealed the extent of Austria's military decline, and in the twentieth century the Hapsburg empire gave the appearance of a feudal relic. Once a common religion had supplied some cohesion, while now the nationalistic clamor of Czech and Slav and Magyar threatened to shake the ancient structure to pieces on the eve of its final military effort.

In view of the commanding positions taken by France and Germany, the coming struggle promised to be a duel to the death between those powers in the western theater, with all other operations ranking as subsidiary. If France held the potential superiority in numbers, sea power and allies, it must be remembered that these factors could not make their weight felt at once. The German advantages in organization, training, weapons, tactics, strategy and central location were of far more immediate value.

The Collision on the Marne

"Make the right wing strong!" Schlieffen had admonished just before his death in 1913. The younger Moltke, however, introduced the first of many amendments to his preceptor's plan by deciding against a violation of Dutch neutrality. On the grounds that Germany might need "a last air-hole through which we can breathe," he struck first at Liége after crossing the Belgian frontier.

The small country's decision to resist had heartened the Allies, who hoped to gain time by a prolonged resistance of the fortress defending the crossings of the Meuse. Ever since the great days of Vauban, Montalembert and Carnot, the sciences of fortification and siegecraft had been in decline. The Napoleonic era had restored a warfare of movement, while in 1870 the fate of Sedan, Metz and Paris did not encourage soldiers to place much trust in permanent works. The masonry of the past was obviously vulnerable to modern artillery, and a new age of fortification did not begin until builders learned how to use steel armor and reinforced concrete.

A Belgian engineer, General Henri Brialmont, became the most celebrated exponent of the methods prevailing at the end of the century. Even before 1870 the detached fort had taken on more importance than the *enceinte* as cities multiplied their population during the new industrial age. Brialmont led in the development of the "ring fortress," or girdle of strongholds thrown out at distances of several miles from the citadel. Far from attempting to build works of unlimited resistance, he regarded the fort, like the battleship, as an expendable unit which justified its existence by the damage it could inflict upon the enemy. Hence the new defenses consisted of underground galleries protected by a crown of concrete. Casemates for flanking batteries were provided with fixed portholes, the surrounding terrain being measured in advance so that gunners could find any target with deadly accuracy. Revolving steel cupolas with domed tops could be raised or lowered by machinery for fire in every direction.

As Belgian inspector-general, Brialmont made Antwerp, Liége and Namur his masterpieces, and the London *Times* predicted that these strongholds might delay the enemy as much as six months. The German host of invasion included 1,500,000 troops divided into seven armies. The three southern groups were to carry out Schlieffen's ideas by making a short advance followed by an elastic defense on a wide front. The remaining four had the task of pivoting on Metz for a wheel through Belgium and France, with the main burden falling upon the powerful right wing—Kluck's army of 320,000 men and Bülow's army of 260,000.

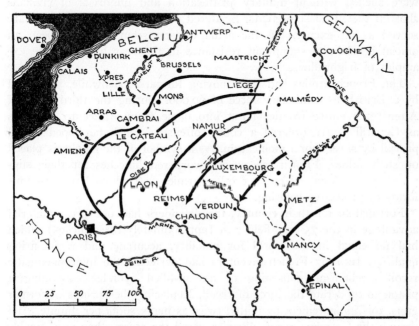

The German Invasion of France—August, 1914

These forces were held up for four days by the twelve armored forts of Liége, despite the seizure of the city and bridges in a daring *coup de main* which won General von Ludendorff his first notice. Then the enemy sprang the first tactical surprise of the war by employing 17-inch howitzers. Within eight more days these monsters were able to smash the cupolas and turrets so completely as to compel the surrender of the dazed garrisons.

After a success costing 40,000 casualties, the Germans followed up the retreating Belgian army and occupied Brussels on August 20. That same day they appeared before Namur, which fell after only two days of pounding by the huge howitzers. This second disaster led to a premature loss of faith in armored concrete forts, and the French stripped some of their strongholds of guns to be used in the field.

The invaders were well ahead of Schlieffen's timetable as they reached French soil. So far their only error had been political. In the confidence of ultimate victory they treated the conquered Belgians with a brutality which aroused the horror and condemnation of neutrals. Even on the evidence of facts admitted by the Germans themselves, towns were shelled without military justification and hundreds of civilians shot on the flimsiest pretexts. Scattered outbreaks of guerrilla warfare served as an excuse, but the actual reason seems to have been an official decision to stamp out resistance in the rear by deliberate examples of frightfulness.

The French armies had been moving forward meanwhile, supported by a British expeditionary force of 90,000. During the third week of August the entire frontier burst into flame from Alsace to Flanders as General Joffre ordered a counteroffensive which he hoped would prevail by sheer moral momentum. As a symbol of the emphasis placed on such values, French troops still wore red breeches for their supposed inspirational effect after other armies had adopted modern uniforms of protective coloring.

Fortunately for their country, the defenders had one great material advantage in the 75-mm. field gun (approximately three inches) which had no equal in the world for mobility, accuracy and rapid firing qualities. In 1897 French inventors had perfected the hydropneumatic recoil mechanism, consisting of an oil-filled cylinder containing a piston to moderate the force of recoil. Replacing the springs of former guns, this improvement permitted twice as many shots per minute. And though the Germans eventually discovered the secret, they were unable or unwilling to duplicate the manufacturing process for the improvement of their own field artillery.

In nearly all other respects Moltke's forces owed their material superiority to the inventions of enemies or neutrals. But if they fell short in creative powers, the invaders showed themselves to be more adaptable. Both in numbers and tactics they held an enormous advantage over the Allies in heavy artillery and machine guns. As an even more modern asset, their 1,000 planes and 30 lighter-than-air machines gave them practically an equality with France and England, combined, in military aviation.

Although man's attempts to fly may be traced back to ancient times, it is sufficient to begin with the year 1903, when the Wright brothers made their famous flight of 120 feet at Kitty Hawk. In 1908 Wilbur Wright remained in the air for two hours and twenty minutes, and the following year Blériot won world-wide acclaim by flying across the English Channel. Even at this date the military potentialities were not overlooked; for in 1909 an Italian theorist, Giulio Douhet, addressed a prophetic message to his countrymen:

> To us who have only armies and navies, it must seem strange that the sky, too, is about to become another battlefield no less important than the battlefields on land and sea. But from now on we had better get accustomed to this idea and prepare ourselves for the new conflicts to come. If there are any nations which can exist untouched by the sea, there are certainly none which can exist without the breath of air. In the future, then, we shall have three instead of two separate and well-defined fields of battle.

As early as 1913, when the Balkan nations won their independence from Turkey, a Russian aviator in the Bulgarian service dropped propaganda leaflets warning Adrianople to surrender or be bombed. On February 6 a biplane actually did release six small bombs, causing a panic but little damage. The pilot returned safely to his own lines with two bullet holes in his wings. That same week occurred the first recorded attempt to attack a warship from the air as two Greek aviators dropped several bombs without success.

The Warplane of 1914: British Bristol Scout

These developments proved premature, for all the belligerents of 1914 depended on two-seated biplanes designed solely for reconnaissance, plus a few single-seaters acting as aerial scouts. Not a plane in Europe was equipped with a machine gun, and the combats between exposed pilots and observers were waged with such weapons as pistols, carbines, hand grenades and even shotguns.

Of the 2,300 German, French and British aircraft supporting the armies of 1914, only a few could have survived a flight across the Channel. The pilots, including many recent adventurers and showmen, bore much the same relationship to the military system as the guilds of cannoneers in the Middle Ages. Hence these specialists were seldom able to overcome the prejudices of the various general staffs during the critical battles of the Frontier, better known by the names of Mons, Charleroi, Guise and Le Cateau. Although a dense "fog of war" blinded the opposing forces, both sides placed their trust in cavalry patrols rather than air reconnaissance, with many opportunities being lost as a consequence.

On the extreme right wing the French penetrated to the Rhine before being hurled back, while in the centre Joffre staked his hopes of victory on a pincers movement. As the British converged from the west, he expected to swing to the northwest and surround large German forces. But since the enemy had meanwhile begun a wider pincers movement with double the numbers, this ambitious scheme nearly led to a national disaster. Only the intuitive anxiety of General Lanrezac, commanding the French left wing, made possible an Allied withdrawal just as the Germans were springing the trap. For this service to the country he was promptly dismissed by Joffre, who could not bear to be put in the wrong by a subordinate.

If the French generalissimo's strategy had been bad, his tactics were even more deplorable. Massed troops went into action without adequate artillery preparation, their red breeches presenting a splendid target for enemy machine guns. Some regiments lost up to 80 per cent in futile bayonet attacks which proved the limitations of valor, and the total French casualties of the opening month have been placed at 300,000.

Plan XVII having failed, Joffre had little choice but to order a general retreat. During the last week of August his battered forces and their weary British allies fell back, halting only to defend themselves against the foe's relentless pressure. In a few more days Paris had been evacuated by the government and half a million civilians as the Germans approached within twenty-five miles. The British also prepared for the worst by changing their base from Le Havre to Saint-Nazaire.

At this stage Moltke made further amendments to the Schlieffen plan. After detaching seven divisions to invest Maubeuge and Antwerp, he sent another four to East Prussia, where an unexpected Russian advance threatened. Then in the belief that the Allied left wing had been shattered beyond repair, he allowed his right-wing generals, Kluck and Bülow, to wheel eastward for an envelopment *north* of Paris which promised to bag thousands of prisoners. Moltke also altered the conception of a defensive left wing by strengthening those armies and permitting them to close in on Verdun and Nancy.

The invaders, in short, may now be considered victims of the optimism which had all but ruined Joffre. Moltke cannot wholly be blamed, since the reports of his subordinates indicated that it remained only to gather the fruits of a victory already won. The kaiser himself appeared in the field to bless the anticipated break-through at Nancy, and on the enveloping wing Kluck and Bülow began a race as each sought the lion's share of the glory.

On September 3, as France seemed doomed to endure a new Sedan, the strategy of her defense suddenly advanced a full fifty years. So far, despite the improvements in weapons, the war of 1914 had been waged with the ideas of 1870 by commanders who were nearly all veterans of the last conflict. Then came the "miracle of the Marne" when supposedly beaten armies turned on their pursuers. And after failing with the bayonet, the imperiled nation found salvation in the airplane, the telephone and the motor vehicle.

It would not have been surprising if the gulf of half a century had been bridged by some brisk young modernist. Instead, the hero of the hour proved to be a warrior past the retirement age who had been relegated to a defensive rôle. General Joseph Galliéni, military governor of Paris, first deduced from the reports of French aviators—the reports which had been ignored or distrusted by other officers—that the impetuous wheel of the German enveloping wing had left the enemy's right flank exposed. Making use of the telephone to save vital minutes, he persuaded Joffre on September 4 to begin a daring counteroffensive two days later. As his final and most dramatic contribution, Galliéni became the war's pioneer of motorized transport by rushing a French division to the front in six hundred taxicabs commandeered in the streets of Paris.

The strategic elements of the battle were simple enough. On September 6 the growing pressure on his right flank caused Kluck to take hasty defensive measures. The abrupt halt of his advance soon created a gap between him and Bülow, with only a thin cavalry screen interposing. Into this gap poured the French, followed by their British allies, so that Bülow in turn was seriously menaced. By September 10 the whole machine of invasion had been thrown into confusion, and Moltke sanctioned a general retreat after losses which included 38,000 prisoners.

Unfortunately, the usual account does not make it plain that the battle of the Marne was also fought on the Meuse and Moselle. For the crown prince's attempts to envelop Verdun ended in bloody failure, and Prince Rupprecht's forces met an even more costly repulse in their assaults on the Grand Couronné forts before Nancy. The French defenders at these points not only outfought the foe but managed to send troops to the armies engaged north of Paris.

It was perhaps inevitable that the war's most decisive field should have become fertile ground for legends. Galliéni deserves the credit for the conception, while Joffre's massive calm is no more to be dismissed than his readiness to assume the fearful responsibility. But laurels can be cultivated in a day of facile publicity, and Foch's staff officers nourished a myth which assigned him the main part in the victory. Soon it grew to be a general belief that he had "won the battle by driving the enemy into the marshes of St. Gond," though his part had been chiefly defensive and no less worthy for that reason. The fact is that the Marne, like so many other great contests of history, was essentially a "soldiers' battle," and the glory of the confused fight belongs to French conscripts staggering in the last stages of exhaustion.

The blame for the defeat likewise became a moot question, and it has too often been assumed that Moltke would have won by adhering strictly to the Schlieffen plan. No doubt his departures led to blunders as well as improvements, though he would have been lauded for moral courage in the event of victory. Perhaps a greater shortcoming may be charged to a rigid Prussian mentality and its dependence on such plans. The elder Moltke, sensing a danger in this tendency, had insisted on unusual freedom of decision for subordinates in the field. Even this reform contributed to the ruin of his nephew half a century later, for Kluck, Bülow and the two princes asserted themselves almost to the extent of insolence. Thus in 1914 were expiated the military sins of 1870, and the Marne became a strategic as well as national revenge for Sedan.

THE BATTLE OF TANNENBERG

As consolation for a defeat which precipitated the mightiest siege of all time, the Germans could point to a "second Cannae" won on the Eastern Front. During the preliminary stages they went through an agony of anxiety. Moltke never made a more serious mistake than that

of the deified Schlieffen in his estimate of the time needed by the
Russians for preparation. The czar's generals were not as dilatory as he
had supposed, and in August the minimum German forces left in East
Prussia had to meet a great two-headed invasion. Refugees choked the
roads leading westward, so that Moltke could hardly refuse reinforcements from his armies in France.

At the outbreak of war the Russian plans had not contemplated an
offensive against both Germany and Austria. The extraordinary influence
of France over her ally led to the decision to invade East Prussia as

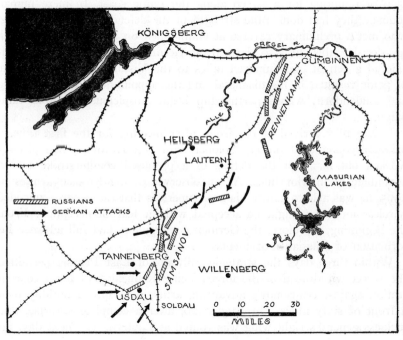

Battle of Tannenberg

well as Galicia. The latter campaign alone would have strained Russian
resources, but the strategists of St. Petersburg agreed that an effort
must also be made to help France.

If Schlieffen had erred in his calculations, events were soon to prove
that he had not been far off the mark. The czar's armies were provided
with less than half the German strength in artillery. Reserves of ammunition were incredibly low, and even the supplies of rifles and

bayonets could not keep up with demands. Corruption and pro-German sentiment had crept into the highest military circles, while at a later date several officers were to be convicted of treason. In short, the Russian organization labored under all the handicaps which had frustrated its efforts in 1905.

Rennenkampf, who commanded the northern army of invasion, was himself a German sympathizer, if not actually disloyal. While his hastily improvised forces crawled toward Königsberg, another miserably equipped army under Samsonov advanced south of the Masurian Lakes. After passing this strategic barrier the two generals had a vague plan of reuniting for a sweep along the Baltic coast. In mere human tonnage they had double the strength of the defenders under Prittwitz, who met a preliminary reverse at Gumbinnen on August 20. Although not decisive, this check so alarmed the German commander that he considered a retreat of a hundred miles to the Vistula. His obvious state of panic resulted in his dismissal and the appointment of Hindenburg and Ludendorff, whose partnership began auspiciously in this campaign.

Before they arrived at the front, after meeting for the first time, a brilliant young staff officer, Colonel Otto von Hoffman, had already worked out many of the details of a proposed counterstroke taking advantage of interior lines. As an observer of the Russian armies in 1905, he was able to assure his new superiors that the enemy's uncoded wireless messages might be accepted without fear of deception. From the beginning, therefore, the German commanders had full advance information of Russian movements.

Within three days the strategic railways of East Prussia permitted the secret withdrawal of the forces facing Rennenkampf for a concentration against Samsonov's advancing army, now spread untidily over a front of sixty miles. On August 26, after a complete surprise, that luckless general's right wing was routed at Lautern. The next day, far to the south, his left suffered an even worse disaster near Usdau, being entirely cut off from the main body. The centre resisted doggedly, but the quality of its generalship may be judged by the fact that Samsonov, ignorant of the forces arrayed against him, still supposed that he was attacking! By August 30 his famished and exhausted columns had been nearly surrounded, and it remained only for the victors to round up their bag of 92,000 prisoners. During the flight of the Russian remnants the beaten general stepped aside into the woods, and his aides heard a single shot fired in atonement for his blunders.

After the battle Colonel Hoffman had another happy idea. Recalling the humiliating German defeat by the Slavs in the fifteenth century, he suggested that the victory be named after that ancient field, which lay close at hand. For similar reasons of morale, he helped to cultivate the legend which represented Hindenburg, during his years of retirement, as having studied the Masurian lake region with a view to saving the fatherland on some vague future occasion from the Russian hordes. It made a pleasing and inspirational story which the German people accepted without reservations; and before long the old *Junker's* national leadership served the cause more effectively than his military ability.

So did art come to the aid of fact as all countries strove to "humanize" the remote and godlike figures of the supreme command. Only the methods of modern publicity could accomplish this purpose in a war of such vast dimensions that many a conscripted citizen never set eyes on his general during the course of a campaign.

With Samsonov's army destroyed, Ludendorff hastened to complete his battle on interior lines by turning on Rennenkampf, who had not made a move to aid his colleague. As early as August 29 German troops were detached to the north, and the reinforcements sent by Moltke arrived just in time to take part. On September 5 the first German attacks north of the lakes gained the advantages of surprise against enemy lines sprawled over a sixty-mile front, and four days later Rennenkampf ordered a general retreat. Ludendorff missed his opportunity for another battle of annihilation, but by September 14 the Russian casualties amounted to 125,000, chiefly prisoners, as Rennenkampf fell back across the frontier. Throughout the ragged fight his supply system functioned so poorly that the retreating troops were sometimes near to literal starvation.

The news of the German success might have been more satisfactory if the Russians had not won an even more smashing victory in Galicia. The triumph had been gained, moreover, by using the envelopment methods so dear to the heart of the Prussian strategist.

The plans of the Central Powers envisioned a resolute Austrian defense against Russia while Germany crushed France. But Conrad von Hotzendorff, chief-of-staff of Franz-Joseph's armies, shared the belief of his allies in the efficacy of the attack. His able adversary, the Grand Duke Nicholas, trusted in similar theories, so that the opposing forces moved toward a terrific collision.

The four Austrian armies made good preliminary progress. For the enemy's superiority in numbers and generalship did not become evident until September 1, when the first decisive battle ended at Lemberg. After five days of sanguinary fighting Conrad's forces were beaten at their own game of encirclement by the energetic Russian field commanders. General Brusilov drove in the Austrian right and Ruzsky crushed the left to gain a victory resulting in the capture of the empire's fourth city as well as 120,000 prisoners.

The rear of his left wing being threatened, Conrad tried again to outflank the advancing phalanx, and again his armies were severely handled. On September 11 he extricated himself by ordering a general retirement; and the Austrians fell back nearly to Cracow, leaving behind a garrison of 150,000 men to be surrendered in the great fortress of Przemysl as the invaders overran Galicia.

THE BEGINNINGS OF TRENCH WARFARE

By the end of September all five of the principal warring powers had been frustrated in their original plans. All faced the grim realization that the struggle probably could not be decided before winter. The remaining operations of 1914, therefore, may be summed up as hastily improvised efforts to salvage every possible advantage in preparation for the next year's campaigns.

In the east Germany's strategy was shaped largely by her ally's plight. Early in the war an Austrian "punitive expedition" had invaded Serbia, only to be repulsed with losses of 42,000 by defenders outweighed in all material respects. This disaster brought the empire's total casualties up to 400,000 in the first six weeks. Morale sank to a low ebb, particularly among the troops recruited from Slavic regions; and early in October Hindenburg and Ludendorff tried to redeem the situation with new offensives in Galicia.

For two months the opposing forces surged back and forth to a depth of two hundred miles on a thousand-mile front stretching from the Baltic to the river Dniester. Like contending mastodons, huge armies attacked and counterattacked at a cost of casualty lists which once would have been considered a respectable total for a nation's entire armed strength. Austria suffered a second humiliation in Serbia meanwhile as invading forces of 200,000 were shattered in a three-day battle and sent streaming back across the frontier in rout.

In view of his material handicaps the grand duke's generalship in Poland deserves high praise. Twice he nearly turned the tables on opponents who attempted great double envelopments; and if his losses in men and territory were greater, he forced the Germans to draw upon reserves which might have won the decision in France.

The end of the year found all the armies digging into the frozen soil to establish winter lines as Nicholas fell back to positions defending Warsaw. In the west a similar stalemate had been in the making during this same period. After their victory on the Marne the Allies were too spent to pluck the fruits; and Moltke retired in good order to the heights of the Aisne, the natural bastion of northern France. Yet even though the invaders' plans had miscarried, about one-tenth of the country remained in their hands, including 80 per cent of the coal resources and nearly all the iron. Several of the most essential French railways were at their disposal for lateral troop movements, in addition to the best grain-producing districts.

All historians have found it curious that throughout this critical period both sides neglected to seize the Channel ports. Winston Churchill, First Lord of the Admiralty, could not convince British leaders of the urgency; and not until the end of September did the Germans strive for strategic prizes which once could have been occupied without a fight.

Had a part of the British expeditionary force been originally landed at these ports to fall upon the invaders' right flank, the battle of the Marne might have had a much more conclusive ending. But during the ensuing "race to the sea," as each side strove to outflank the other, it was said that the Allies were always "an army corps too few and twenty-four hours too late." On September 28 the Germans began a bombardment of Antwerp with their mighty howitzers. The valiant little Belgian army resisted for twelve days, but the belated arrival of a few thousand British reinforcements could not prevent the evacuation of the fortified camp by survivors who escaped down the Flemish coast. At least their defense had gained time for the Allies to rush troops to the left of the line, and this narrow margin probably saved them at the first battle of Ypres.

From October 19 until November 22 the enemy battered ceaselessly at the gateway to Dunkirk, Calais and Boulogne. General von Falkenhayn, who had replaced Moltke after the Marne, brought up 16 divisions and 250 heavy guns to attack six and a half Allied divisions supported by 50 heavy guns of obsolescent types. In spite of this superiority the highly trained British troops of the old regular army held most of their ground. A limited German break-through on October 31 was patched up by counterattacks, and the final effort of November 11 resulted in bloody repulses of the Prussian Guards. Even the British cooks and grooms took part at this climax, for two-thirds of the expeditionary force had fallen in the defense of Ypres.

The little regular army had not been sacrificed in vain. Its dying efforts gave the French a much-needed interval in which to stabilize the front and send reinforcements. November brought an early onset of snow and rain, and both sides were compelled to accept a deadlock of trench warfare from the sea to the Alps.

THE FIRST GAS ATTACK

Before the war civilians had wondered shudderingly if flesh and blood could withstand the new weapons. The answer was recorded in the zigzag lines which scarred the surface of Europe. Soldiers had simply taken refuge in the bosom of the earth, since in all ages the size of the casualty list is determined by moral rather than material factors. Destructiveness may thus lead to stalemate rather than victory, and some of the most deadly modern arms have slain no more men in proportion than the pike and arquebus.

The Allied generals faced the new year with undiminished optimism. Sir Douglas Haig, a cavalry officer, still had so much faith in the saber that the prewar standard of two machine guns to a battalion struck him as "more than sufficient." It was left to British civilians in the Ministry of Munitions to multiply his estimate by sixteen while providing other modern siege weapons such as trench mortars, signaling flares and improved hand grenades, all of which the enemy had in much larger quantities.

Only Lord Kitchener's intuition (as opposed to his colleagues' dreams of an early victory) had led to the creation of a new British national army of volunteers. Early in 1915 a million men were in training, some of them with wooden guns, as thirteen infantry divisions and five cavalry divisions of regulars and territorials held a small front in Flanders.

Joffre and Foch, while still trusting in the bayonet, believed that the artillery offered the key to the deadlock. It seemed to them a mathematical certainty that if enough shells were hurled at the enemy's trenches a path could be blasted for the infantry. The benign visage of the French commander-in-chief reassured countrymen who called him "Papa" Joffre. So imperturbable that he refused to be called from his meals or sleep for any emergency, he never shrank from responsibility.

Such virtues might have been questioned, however, when the new artil-- lery doctrines failed in two bloody offensives. In eastern Champagne the attack began on February 16 with a prolonged "drumfire." But the enemy found shelter in his trenches and dugouts, emerging only when the bombardment lifted to permit the advance of the French infantry. Then the German machine guns had their turn at the expense of heavily laden men plodding through shellholes and barbed-wire en- tanglements. Only a few trenches and villages were taken in 44 days of fighting at a cost reckoned as high as 100,000 casualties.

This slaughter did not discourage commanders who held that the Allies had a potential two-to-one advantage in numbers, counting the ill-equipped Russian hordes. Japan had declared war on Germany, and as a French writer put it somewhat prematurely, Italy "came to the rescue of the victors" in the spring of 1915. France's generals made this potential superiority in man power the justification for a strategy of *grignotage*—a ceaseless gnawing at the enemy lines until attrition led to a decision. With dauntless optimism, but without secrecy or surprise, Joffre directed his next attack at the St. Mihiel salient which hung like a hornet's nest between Nancy and Verdun. Again the defenders had little trouble in beating off repeated frontal advances with heavy losses.

The enemy was first to comprehend that modern armed force is measured in terms of mechanical horsepower and ammunition produc- tion rather than the muscles and bayonets of a past age. On this basis there was no comparison between the German soldier, the unit of a highly industrialized nation, and the Russian soldier who might feel fortunate to be supplied with a rifle. The German output of arms and ammunition exceeded that of all the Allies combined; and the inferiority of the Central Powers in mere man power was balanced by strategic railways which permitted troops to be shifted rapidly from one front to another on interior lines.

General von Falkenhayn, upon whose shoulders had fallen the burden of Schlieffen's and Moltke's errors, trusted to attrition in the moral rather than material sphere. Unlike colleagues and foemen who had not awakened from a Clausewitzian dream, the handsome, urbane German commander foresaw in 1915 that the war had already become a contest in endurance. For the Western Front he prescribed defensive operations to take advantage of the enemy's willingness to beat out his brains against a wall of trenches. In the east he overruled Hindenburg and Ludendorff, who wished to gamble all for a final victory, by approving a limited offensive designed to maim rather than annihilate.

Falkenhayn, in short, wished to shun the scaffold while allowing the foe enough rope to hang himself. As Germany's reward he visioned a favorable peace of compromise after the Allies had become sufficiently exhausted and disillusioned. In order to hasten this outcome he encouraged tactics which would prey upon civilian morale; and on Christmas Eve, 1914, an airplane dropped the first bombs of the war on English soil without causing casualties. Three weeks later several Zeppelins—lighter-than-air machines driven by motors—killed four civilians in a raid on Yarmouth and Cromer.

By April the Allies had learned to expect Zeppelin attacks, and that same month they became the victims of the war's first effective use of poison gas. It is not widely known that the Germans had already experimented with the new weapon in Poland, where the intense cold so nullified the results that the Russians did not know they had been gassed. Nor is it generally realized that the French and British had ample warning in April, 1915. Several prisoners told of the preparations, and a German respirator was captured as even more convincing evidence. General Ferry, much alarmed, reported the danger to his Allies and French superiors, only to be removed by Joffre after events had proved him right.

The Germans were aware of the plans for a new Allied drive near Arras. In order to dislocate this attempt they decided somewhat dubiously to try chlorine gas in the Ypres sector. Only the enemy's skepticism saved the Allies on April 22, for no reserves awaited to exploit the four-mile gap created by the greenish-yellow clouds released from cylinders and borne by a favoring breeze. Two French divisions, including Algerian troops, were the principal sufferers. The wretched survivors, gasping and choking, threw away their arms and stumbled toward the rear; but the Germans themselves were nervous as to the effects and did not pursue vigorously.

The war produced no greater heroes than those French and Canadian troops who prolonged their flanks that night until the rear areas were held by a frail chain of outposts. These men had no protection other than wetted towels and handkerchiefs, yet they staved off disaster for six days until a new line could be established. By this time the Germans had awakened as to the possibilities, and the second battle of Ypres developed from their belated efforts to break the Allied cordon. During the next three weeks their gas, artillery and infantry assaults inflicted 70,000 casualties at a cost of half as many, though the French and British yielded no ground of strategic importance.

It has been plausibly argued that the Germans lost an opportunity to end the war by their local and premature use of gas. But such a weapon could be tested only in the field, and the results surpassed all reasonable hopes. Even so, the practical gains were small as compared to the moral odium always incurred by the nation sponsoring a military innovation. The Germans of 1915 were also believed to have originated the flame-thrower, one of the most ancient of weapons; and the horrified peoples of neutral countries began to credit the wildest tales of "Hun atrocities."

Respirators were soon issued to all front-line troops. And after the novelty had worn off, neither cloud gas nor liquid fire inspired as much terror as high explosive shells. Both new weapons played only a minor part in the long-awaited Allied offensive which opened near Arras on May 9. The 1,200 French guns hurled 700,000 projectiles, for it was assumed that an average of 18 shells to every yard of front would paralyze all resistance. General Pétain's corps did advance three miles in two hours, but other French and British divisions were not so fortunate. After the first day the battle disintegrated into the usual local struggles for trenches and ruined hamlets, with the losses of the attackers amounting to 102,500 when the fighting came to a standstill late in June.

Before winter the French casualty list alone reached a total of a million after the failure of two more offensives in the same pattern. On September 28, following 72 hours of drumfire with 850 heavy guns and 1,600 fieldpieces, Joffre's stirring proclamation was read to the 500,000 troops about to assault the enemy's strong Champagne positions:

> Your *élan* will prove irresistible! It will take you at the first effort beyond the foe's fortified lines and to his batteries. You will then allow him neither truce nor repose until the victory has been achieved.

In combination with this attempt the Franco-British forces had already begun an offensive in the Lens-Loos area north of Arras. Widely separated as the two drives were, Joffre had no doubt that his concentric prongs would "compel the Germans to retreat beyond the Meuse and possibly end the war."

Both drives won a few immediate successes. Particularly in the Champagne district the German front-line trenches were penetrated in places and the secondary positions threatened. Then as usual the enemy rushed up reserves, and the battle turned into a series of "nibbling actions." At Loos the final British thrusts merely added to losses of 60,000, many of whom had been gassed on the opening day when the wind failed to carry the chlorine from their own 5,000 cylinders. Nor had the French achieved any results of strategic importance in either sector beyond the inflicting of 120,000 casualties at a total cost of 192,000.

German Offensives on the Eastern Front

So few were their precedents that Allied staff officers might have been pardoned by history for failing to solve the material problems presented by an age of transition. It is harder to condone their indifference to such ancient military principles as deception and surprise. Even less forgivable is their lack of economy in spending the final currency of national wealth—the human lives entrusted to every commander by universal conscription.

In the east Ludendorff and Hindenburg took the most elaborate precautions to insure secrecy as they transferred large forces from France. General von Mackensen and his able chief-of-staff, Colonel Seeckt, were allotted 700 guns and countless trench mortars for the opening drive in Galicia on May 2. The intense four-hour bombardment found the Russians utterly unprepared, and the Austro-German forces began an advance which covered ninety-five miles in the first two weeks. By the end of the month Mackensen's army had taken 153,000 prisoners and 128 guns.

The peoples of the Allied nations had looked forward confidently to "the Russian steam-roller" reaching the plains of Hungary before summer. Instead, the disorderly retreat of the grand duke's armies continued throughout June as Przemysl and Lemberg fell, making it necessary to evacuate nearly all of Galicia.

The explanation was simple enough. For even the German commanders, informed by a tireless intelligence system, had no conception of the inefficiency and corruption which betrayed the Russian soldier. The campaigns of the autumn and winter had used up most of the ammunition reserves, so that batteries were limited to a few shells daily per gun. Only two-thirds of the six million troops could be issued rifles, and cartridges were usually lacking for the obsolete Mexican and Japanese arms carried by thousands of men. Less fortunate troops were reduced to fighting with clubs until a rifle could be had from a fallen comrade. Yet while such victims were heartlessly sacrificed, the officials of a tottering régime allowed mountains of supplies to rot or rust.

All summer the dreadful and fantastic *danse macabre* continued on the Eastern Front. Even the victors were sometimes moved to pity by the dumb, fatalistic courage of half-starved moujiks fighting a twentieth-century war with weapons of the Stone Age. In July a new Austro-German offensive overran Poland, and Warsaw fell the following month. The grand duke's generalship had not declined, but he could only choose retreat as a lesser evil than encirclement.

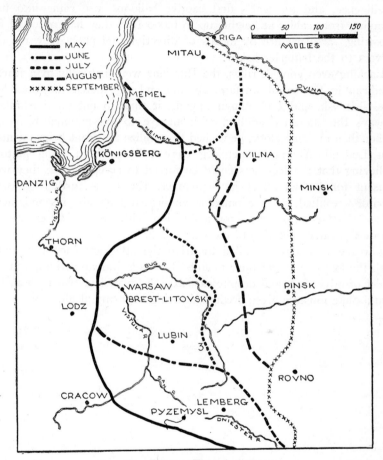

The Eastern Front in 1915

Added to their other advantages, the Germans had recently gained command of the air on all fronts. Early in 1915 the machine gun was introduced as an aerial weapon, the first types being fired backwards over the pilot's head, so that the plane had to fly away from its target. Next came a swivel mounting, and that summer the Germans brought out the Fokker monoplane, equipped with a synchronizing gear which allowed the gun to be fired through the propeller blades.

The mastery of this machine lasted until early in 1916, when the Allies improved their models. Meanwhile, both sides made great strides in perfecting aerial photography to supplement older methods of securing intelligence, and the war's first captive balloons also came into use. Swaying from cables at heights up to 6,000 feet, they had no equal for "spotting" artillery fire by means of directions telephoned by the observers to the batteries below.

Lacking even enough rifles, the Russians were naturally at a fearful handicap in the aerial warfare. By the end of August they had lost Brest-Litovsk, and Falkenhayn thought it time to put on the brakes. Always the statesman-soldier, with an eye to the national resources rather than military glory, he wished to stabilize the front before winter. But Ludendorff and Hindenburg were still far from being glutted. Believing that the Russians could be forced to accept terms, they won consent for a final effort in September. Enormous further gains in territory resulted, yet the outcome vindicated Falkenhayn's judgment. When the Germans strove for a decision with 30,000 horsemen—the greatest cavalry operation of the war in Europe—the dragoon tactics of the weary Cossacks prevailed to drive the attackers back fifty miles with the loss of most of their mounts. It was a dramatic triumph in the midst of adversity; and despite casualties estimated at two million, the grand duke must be given credit for saving his army at all.

II

DEADLOCK ON THE WESTERN FRONT

We are the Dead. Short days ago
We lived, felt dawn, saw sunset glow,
Loved and were loved, and now we lie
In Flanders fields.

—JOHN MCCREA

By 1916 it could hardly be doubted that the war would eventually be decided in France and Belgium. Vast as the operations were on the Eastern Front, the three main belligerents regarded it as a secondary theater. France and Great Britain neglected their Russian allies, while Germany had never used more than one-fourth of her strength in the Polish and Galician campaigns. Hence the chief result of those tremendous casualty lists had been the weakening of both Russia and Austria.

Japan made it evident that she was interested only in seizing German possessions in the Far East. Italy, having entered the war in the hope of gaining Austrian territory, limited her operations to an assault on that empire. Handicapped by an awkward strategic position on the northern frontier, she soon found herself reduced to trench warfare in difficult mountainous terrain after losses of 240,000 in badly planned offensives of 1915. Serbia's efforts came to an even more unfortunate ending in October of that year. After having twice repulsed the Austrians, the small Balkan kingdom was crushed by Mackensen's invasion in October, and only a retreat to the Adriatic coast saved the remnants of the army.

Just as Italy had been bribed by the Entente in a secret treaty of dubious ethics, so the Central Powers won Bulgaria over by inducing her to share in the spoliation of Serbia. Among the secondary participants, however, Turkey proved the most formidable because of the help she had given the Central Powers since her entrance in October, 1914. Due to her strategic position, the Ottoman power had been able from

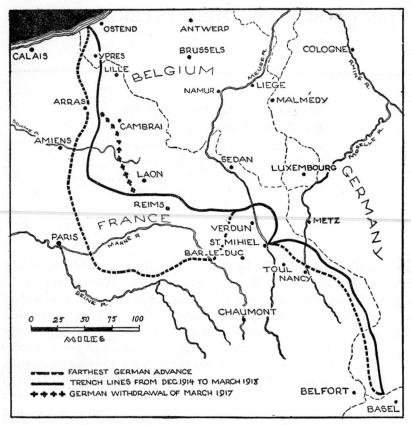

The Western Front, December, 1914, to March, 1918

the beginning to menace Russia in the Caucasus and Great Britain both in Egypt and Mesopotamia. Large forces had to be diverted by both Entente nations to meet these threats, and the early encounters showed the Turks to be stout fighters.

At various times during the war the minor theaters offered opportunities for major results, yet the Western Front remained the area of decision. Reaching from the North Sea to Switzerland, this diagonal gash of trenches did not shift as much as ten miles from December, 1914, to March, 1918—with the single exception of a voluntary German retirement from a salient. During those twenty-nine months the very term "Western Front" came to symbolize a new way of living and thinking for several million Europeans who had departed far from a former existence as civilians. By day the opposing lines were marked by the "sausage balloons" rising from shattered woods, and at night No Man's Land was lighted nervously by colored flares and the uncanny white brilliance of star shells. The chattering of machine guns announced every impulse of anxiety, and nightly raids or patrols accounted for hundreds of casualties during the intervals of comparative calm. Even the diseases of the Western Front had a significance of their own, so that "trench foot" and "trench fever" were known as the plagues of the human moles who inhabited muddy ditches and damp dugouts.

Each province of this military world had a character of its own. Soldiers spoke with grim respect of the Lens or Champagne sectors and referred to the Vosges areas as "rest camps." For both sides concentrated the most and best of their troops from Ypres to Verdun, while tacitly agreeing that the eastern positions were to be lightly held. And since the continuous line of entrenchments offered no flanks, the warfare of the Western Front gradually evolved into a series of direct assaults striving for penetration. Generals hoped that by butting hard enough they might open up new flanks, and each successive failure led to an increase in the volume of artillery fire which blasted the way for the infantry.

It first occurred to a few British leaders in 1915 that the Allies faced a long siege war in which their potential material advantages were discounted by Germany's central position and long preparations. With the Western Front offering only a possibility of costly local attacks, it seemed logical to utilize the Allied preponderance in sea power for creating new flanks in distant theaters, thus gaining the strategic leverage with which to break the deadlock.

But the French, who prided themselves on logic, took a more parochial view. While granting that British amphibious operations had won some economical triumphs in past conflicts, French generals were swayed emotionally by the fact that the foe occupied a tenth of their soil. On the eve of 1914 Joffre did not value the British navy as worth a single bayonet except for moral purposes, according to Sir Henry Wilson, and that ardent Francophile raised the estimate only to 500 bayonets.

Wilson, as chief liaison officer, must bear much of the responsibility for altering British traditions of making war, though Kitchener often concurred against his better judgment. The brilliant, forty-year-old Churchill became the leader of Britons who advocated more reliance on amphibious operations. The events of 1914 soon proved that he had been right in urging a land-and-water flank attack on the invading enemy. Next, Churchill sponsored the venture which has since been recognized as perhaps the most promising of all Allied campaigns, the Dardanelles expedition.

THE FAILURE AT GALLIPOLI

Considering the vast potentialities, it hardly seems possible that opinion could have been so divided. The French General Staff might have been expected to oppose any withdrawal from the Western Front, but Churchill and other British advocates met almost as much opposition in London. Even those leaders who approved the venture in theory were of widely differing convictions as to methods of procedure. Thus the attempt had been weakened by many evasions and compromises before an Allied squadron struck the first great blow on March 18, 1915.

All witnesses agree as to the majestic spectacle of the eighteen British and French battleships bombarding the Narrows, with seaplanes "spotting" for their blazing guns. Behind this spectacle of might, unfortunately, was a fatal lack of planning and harmony. The Allied intentions as well as bickerings had been trumpeted abroad, and since November several local attacks by British warships had ruined any possibility of surprise. Worst of all, no co-operation existed as yet between the land and sea forces, though troops had already been disembarked at the Lemnos base.

As late as February, according to enemy testimony, the Allies might have had the Gallipoli Peninsula almost without a fight. But even the lethargic Turks had at last been prodded into preparations for a defense supervised by German officers. Still weak both in troops and ammunition, they had given up hope on March 18 when a succession of mysterious explosions decided not only the day but the entire campaign. A small Turkish steamer, undetected, had laid mines in the recently swept channel, and four Allied battleships blew up, only one of them being beached and saved afterwards.

At the moment of victory the British admiral abandoned the attempt, and the soldiers were informed that their turn had come. Five more weeks of grace were granted the Turks before the five divisions of English, French, Australian and New Zealand troops landed on April 25. Meanwhile the enemy had been able to bring his strength up to six divisions, which inflicted heavy casualties on the invaders before they gained two precarious footholds. The deadlock of trench warfare soon set in, with the Turks holding the commanding heights of the interior.

Several times during the next few weeks the Allies came heartbreakingly close to gaining a decisive advantage. But lack of numbers, coupled with inexperienced troops, accounted for a series of minor reverses. And when the British and French were reinforced up to twelve divisions in July, the increase was so delayed that the enemy now had fifteen divisions taking part in the Gallipoli operations.

The difference between these figures explains the failure of the great Allied attempt in August to push across the peninsula north of the Narrows and cut off thousands of Turks. A complete surprise was realized in the opening attack, and the enemy barely managed to hang on to several vital points. Then the Allied strength proved unequal to an effort further weakened by the usual lamentable want of co-ordination. From that moment the generals and admirals had no further hope of victory, and it became merely a question of when the evacuation would be ordered. Ironically enough, this operation was the first to benefit from secrecy, skill and perfect co-operation between land and sea forces, so that nearly 100,000 troops were withdrawn in December with astonishingly few losses.

Even during a war in which Allied opportunities so often went begging, Gallipoli remains perhaps the most dismal failure. Half of the ultimate land and naval force, led by men respecting the basic principles of strategy, could unquestionably have forced the Dardanelles in February and taken Constantinople. Turkey, cut off from German aid, would soon have been reduced to a minor part. Greece, Bulgaria and Rumania, then waiting to hail the victor, would have joined forces with the Entente. Russia could have been helped directly, once the Allies were linked geographically, and a demoralized Austria would have been open to attack from the rear.

Unfortunately for the Entente, the enemy did not neglect such openings. After a summer of driving back the wretchedly supplied Russian forces, the Germans found it easy to overrun Serbia with the assistance of a bribed Bulgaria. And where the Allies had failed in spite of overwhelming sea strength, the Central Powers were now linked geographically from the North Sea to the Persian Gulf.

The Battle of Jutland

The lessons taught by Tsushima gave rise to the most feverish decade of naval construction history. Immediately afterwards the British *Dreadnought* lent its name to the new era of the all-big-gun battleship designed for speed as well as terrific striking power. Of 17,900 tons displacement and 490 feet in length, the vessels of this class were driven by turbine machinery of 23,000 horsepower developing a speed of 21 knots. The armament consisted of ten 12-inch guns in five turrets, supplemented by twenty-four 12-pounders distributed over the ship for defense against torpedo boats.

Even these formidable specifications did not satisfy, and the *Iron Duke* class of super-dreadnoughts introduced ten 13.5-inch rifles with twelve 6-inch guns as secondary armament. The length was increased to 580 feet and the displacement to 25,000 tons. As a more radical departure came the *Queen Elizabeth* class, begun in 1912 and completed after the outbreak of war. These five battleships used fuel oil to develop a speed of 25 knots from 75,000 horsepower. The armor belt had a maximum thickness of 13 inches, and 15-inch guns appeared for the first time in the main armament.

A range of 4,000 yards had been considered long at Tsushima, but these giants could hurl their tons of armor-piercing projectiles five times that distance. Meanwhile the stealthy and prowling enemies of the battleship had likewise grown more deadly. By 1914 the torpedo boat had been largely superseded by the destroyer making 40 knots and carrying six torpedoes capable of sinking a ship five miles away. Submarines had been developed with a greater cruising radius, so that they could lie in wait on cargo routes or sow miles of a vastly increased explosive force in enemy waters.

Nor had the cruiser lagged in the world-wide armament race. The British Committee on Designs which planned the *Dreadnought* also recommended a new type known as the "battle cruiser" which had more speed and striking power than the battleships of a few months before. Although the number of guns and thickness of armor were reduced in the interests of mobility, the *Princess Royal* class of 1910 carried eight 13.5-inch rifles in addition to an anti-torpedo-boat armament of 4-inch guns. In 1912 the *Tiger* class burned fuel oil as well as coal, and the experience of 1914 led to the *Renown* and *Repulse*, making 32 knots and carrying 15-inch guns.

After a decade of such technological advances, Tsushima seemed almost as outdated as Trafalgar. For no admiral in the world could pretend to know all the tactical possibilities of the new naval monsters. Great Britain had 20 dreadnoughts in 1914 as compared to Germany's 13, as well as a slight superiority in battle cruisers. But these advantages were offset by a greater vulnerability, since the British Isles risked starvation within a few weeks if the sea lanes were not kept open for food imports.

Well might Winston Churchill remark that the commander of the Grand Fleet was the only man "who could lose the war in an afternoon." In view of this appalling responsibility, the post was given to an admiral of cautious doctrines, Sir John Jellicoe. Under him, as commander of the battle cruisers, Sir David Beatty displayed a lust for combat which carried on the Nelsonian tradition.

As the natural weapon of the weaker sea power, the submarine caused alarm in England when three old armored cruisers were sunk off the Dutch coast by the *U-9* on September 22, 1914. But never again did the enemy have such a good day's hunting, so that the British were able to charge off these losses to their own boldness. No such explanation could be advanced for the mine explosions which began with the destruction of the super-dreadnought *Audacious* on October 27. Only an eternal vigilance could cope with this hidden menace, and the contest between mine-layer and mine-sweeper continued throughout the four years.

Three cruiser actions of the early months might have given the British more reason for concern. Although they were victors in two of the engagements, their armor-piercing shells had a tendency to explode on contact, thus failing to penetrate to the vitals of an enemy ship. The Admiralty did not take steps to remedy this deficiency, which more than any other factor accounts for the disappointing British results in the war's one great fleet action.

In January, 1916, the appointment of an aggressive new German commander, Admiral von Scheer, made such a meeting inevitable. The prudent Jellicoe could hardly have asked a better opportunity, for his 37 capital ships encountered 23 German battleships and battle cruisers off the Norwegian coast on May 31. The 272 British guns of 12-inch or larger caliber were opposed by 176. Jellicoe could count on 8 armored and 26 light cruisers against 11, and 80 destroyers against 63. Finally, he had a comfortable advantage in speed, since Scheer's force included 6 pre-dreadnought battleships.

Beatty's advance squadron first sighted Hipper's inferior force, and in a savage action of battle cruisers two British ships went down. As compensation for these unrequited losses, Beatty managed to draw the entire High Seas Fleet toward Jellicoe's battleships. Scheer did not suspect his peril until the enemy shells fell about his van. In order to save himself, he executed a long-practiced manoeuvre as each ship turned about simultaneously. Ten minutes later the German fleet disappeared into the mist, and Jellicoe did not risk a pursuit, having lost a third battle cruiser.

Had the battle been broken off late in the afternoon, as it appeared to be, the Germans could have claimed a one-sided tactical triumph. But the crisis came at sunset as Scheer blundered back into the trap he had just escaped. This time his T was crossed by enemy battleships disposed in echelons at a range of from 8,000 to 12,000 yards. Again the German admiral "turned a tactical somersault" as his van took a terrific pounding. In order to cover the manoeuvre he ordered his destroyers to attack while emitting a smoke screen. As a last desperate measure, his battle cruisers were sent on a "death ride" straight for the enemy. During the next few minutes the German capital ships suffered heavy damage without one of them sinking, but Jellicoe allowed 11 destroyers to cheat his 27 battleships of their prey as he made a 45-degree turn.

Night settled over the battlefield after the two fleets again lost touch. During the hours of darkness there were several confused minor clashes, and just before dawn a British torpedo sank an enemy capital ship. But the new day broke over an empty ocean, for Scheer had succeeded in slipping through his cordon of foes. His losses were a battleship, a battle cruiser, four light cruisers and five destroyers. The British list included three battle cruisers, three armored cruisers and eight destroyers. Jellicoe's losses were even more humiliating in terms of tonnage and personnel—115,025 tons against a German total of 61,180, and 6,945 casualties against 3,058. As a final blow to British pride, not a single opposing vessel had been sunk by gunfire alone, though Beatty's battle cruisers had proved especially vulnerable.

The explanation of these results may be found largely in three German material advantages—better range-finding instruments; a more scientific distribution of the armor belt; and shells with delayed-action fuses which inflicted greater damage than the British ammunition. But while the battle of Jutland might be called a German victory in tactical respects, the strategic situation was not changed. Britannia continued to rule every sea except the Baltic, and Scheer himself reported to the kaiser that the enemy could never be brought to terms by means of naval battles. He urged a resumption of the underseas raids on commerce, promising "a victorious end to the war at not too distant a date."

It had once been hoped in Berlin that the submarine might reduce the British naval superiority. But its victims consisted largely of old or isolated warships, and German strategists recognized that the U-boats could inflict more serious damage on shipping. With only twenty-four of them available for the 1915 effort, the means were lacking for enforcing a decision. The British took prompt measures such as arming merchant vessels and closing the Straits of Dover with a barrier of mine and net. Hence the premature campaign had already failed when President Wilson protested after the sinkings of the *Lusitania* and *Arabic* with Americans on board. German leaders were not yet prepared to risk the intervention of the United States, and they promised that no more unarmed ships would be sunk without warning and without saving lives.

The most far-reaching strategic result of Jutland, therefore, was a renewal of German faith in unrestricted submarine warfare. For if the campaign of 1915 had failed, only 19 U-boats had been lost while 54 new ones were being built. At this rate of increase, tremendous results might be expected from a resumption.

The "Sausage Grinder" of Verdun

Falkenhayn had gained his main ends in 1915 at an expenditure of less than half the casualties suffered by the Allies. Two million prisoners helped to ease the labor shortage in Germany; and as the new year dawned, the far-seeing generalissimo decided that the time had come to cripple France. His conception has never received a tithe of the renown accorded the Schlieffen plan, yet no more subtle and psychological design was ever proposed during the war. Falkenhayn hoped, in brief, to take a terrible advantage of French generals who held that morale would decline if each inch of ground were not defended to the last drop of blood. Limited German resources were to be used on a limited front for the purpose of "bleeding France to death." Knowing that her generals would make a national issue of the defense, pouring reserves into every breach, Falkenhayn regarded the prospect of a break-through as secondary to the damage which could be inflicted on the enemy's dwindling man power.

The Verdun area was selected for the attempt because of the miserable French communications. Before dawn on February 21 the German guns opened a bombardment on an eight-mile front east of the Meuse, and tons of shells had been fired when the infantry began advancing in the early winter dusk. As a departure from the costly mass assaults of the enemy, Falkenhayn's troops went forward in specially trained little combat groups of from fifteen to fifty picked men. Flares were used for signaling, and officers meeting a determined resistance could demand further artillery preparation.

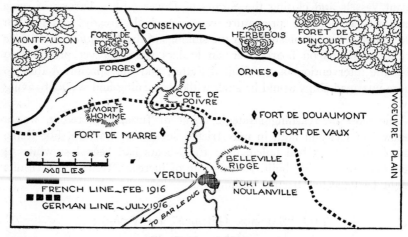

The Battle of Verdun

The German commander did not err in supposing that his opponent would rush up reinforcements, regardless of losses. Although Joffre had scoffed at warnings of the attack, he now threatened his officers with a court-martial if they retreated. But flesh and blood had their limits, and the defenders were compelled to give ground until their main line east of the Meuse had been broken on February 24. That night the situation became so serious that Joffre's subordinates dared to rouse him from his sleep, and General Henri Pétain was sent to Verdun to take charge of a rapidly crumbling defense.

The new leader had been an unknown infantry colonel at the outbreak of war. No believer in the mystical doctrines of the offensive upheld by his superiors, he won distinction for a businesslike economy of life which his men repaid by an unusual devotion. Pétain had need of their trust, for Fort Douaumont fell a few hours before his arrival at the front. Stripped of men and guns by Joffre, this dominating height was occupied by a German patrol which overpowered the handful of exhausted defenders without firing a shot.

After the loss the French General Staff showed a belated appreciation of fortification. Even in 1914 it might have been assumed that the disillusionment caused by the fall of Liége and Namur had been premature. Only a few weeks later the Grand Couronné forts of Nancy put up a resistance which played a vital part in the battle of the Marne. More modern than the Belgian works, built of heavier concrete and armor plate, they were little damaged by the German fire. Nevertheless, Joffre chose to regard similar forts at Verdun as deathtraps; and not until after Pétain's coming were they properly garrisoned as links in the defense system.

During his first anxious week the new French commander also regrouped his heavy guns west of the Meuse to pour a deadly enfilade fire into the Germans advancing on the other side of the river. Within a month scores of the enemy's heavy guns had been put out of action, including all of his famous 17-inch howitzers. A far more dramatic success was scored by a single shot from a railway gun, which blew up no less than 450,000 fused shells of the main German ammunition dump in the Forêt de Spincourt.

Certainly Verdun could never have been held except for Pétain's immediate reorganization of the supply system. All French railways being closed by enemy fire except one second-rate route, motor transport came into its own through dire necessity. The road from Verdun to Bar-le-Duc, later known as the "Sacred Way," was kept in constant repair by a small army of toilers using stone from near-by quarries. Trucks bringing both troops and ammunition followed one another every fourteen seconds night and day at the height of traffic, with regular stations being set up for the unloading of men and materials. Any vehicle unable to keep up the pace found itself ruthlessly shoved into the ditch, for the pulsating flow of military lifeblood could not be interrupted for a minute.

Although the Germans had an excellent network of railways in their rear areas, French motor transport proved superior in many respects. This fact had its demonstration when Pétain relieved his men more frequently, launching counterattacks of fresh troops against weary Germans who began to refer to Verdun as the "sausage-grinder."

The battle entered its second phase on March 6 after the Germans dragged their heavy guns across the crater field left by previous bombardments. And though the evidence is contradictory, the attackers now appear to have become victims of their own psychological offensive. The crown prince, as field general, wished to win glory for the name of Hohenzollern, while there is good reason to believe that Falkenhayn himself had gradually come to trust in a break-through rather than attrition. The world-wide publicity given every move made it difficult to withdraw without a national loss of prestige; and like the man holding the tiger's tail, Falkenhayn also feared a large-scale counterattack by the quarter of a million troops which Joffre had thrown into the fray.

At any rate the German commander repaired a grave omission of his first attack by a new advance on both sides of the Meuse. The next three months saw the most desperate fighting of the war up to this date. The trained German combat groups had nearly all been wiped out, and the crown prince sent forward dense waves of infantry on narrow fronts as cannon fodder for the voracious 75's. The name of Mort Homme became a sinister legend on five continents as the French held the long ridge in spite of enemy bombardments which created fearful plumes of gas and smoke to a height of half a mile. Across the river the Côte de Poivre also won a grisly fame by repelling incessant attacks. The German losses of April and May were at least as severe as those of the defenders, while the psychological battle continued to go against its author.

Not until June 7 did Falkenhayn make a single gain of strategic importance to compensate for the butchery of his men. On that date Fort Vaux fell after a fabulous resistance, and the German tide swept perilously near to the last heights defending Verdun on the east bank. Both sides now regarded the forts with a new respect as they withstood prolonged poundings. Douaumont endured a total of 120,000 shells during the eleven months—including one bombardment of 1,000 tons a day over an area of 150 acres—without serious damage to its subterranean works.

In May the pressure on the French had been somewhat relieved by a successful Russian drive in Galicia, and Falkenhayn knew that he must soon make ready to meet a British offensive on the Somme. Every hour counted as the Germans used a tremendous weight of men and shells in a final effort to smash the remaining defenses of Verdun. The battle reached its crisis on June 23. After being informed that further enemy advances would mean the loss of the city along with six hundred guns and vast materials, Joffre took the responsibility with his wonted composure. The weary Frenchmen in the lines justified his confidence. Fighting without sleep for days, they shattered the German assaults;

and on June 24 Falkenhayn admitted failure by abruptly stopping the flow of reinforcements to Verdun. Local attacks and counterattacks continued all summer, but subsequent events were to prove that the French had already won the greatest defensive battle in their history.

For the first time since 1914 an Allied army had profited from better tactics and generalship. Despite the great masses of guns brought forward by the enemy, the French artillery held a decisive advantage in precision. French scientists aided by developing the first deadly gas shells to be used on the Western Front. By 1916 both sides realized the limitations of cloud gas, and the Germans experimented with lachrymatory shells. It remained for their foemen to carry the idea to its conclusion by providing a bursting charge just sufficient to release a small cloud of phosgene—a much more toxic gas than the chlorine formerly in use. The new ammunition surprised the Germans during the early weeks of Verdun, inflicting thousands of casualties and subjecting the advancing troops to the handicap of wearing masks. So impressive were the results that wind-borne gas became obsolete overnight as the warring nations strove to produce more lethal types of gas shells.

The French also took the lead in the new military science of camouflage. Dummy guns and similar devices had been employed for centuries, but aerial photography created the need for specialists making a study of deception. Artists in the French artillery first saw the possibilities of concealing gun positions, and in 1915 their efforts won official recognition. Wire screens served as a foundation for foliage, with great care being taken to avoid suspicious shadows which would show up in photographs. Roads and machine gun nests under direct observation were likewise blended into the landscape with a skill once reserved for theatrical property making. Merchantmen and warships, which had formerly worn a dull gray, were thought to be more effectively protected by "dazzle-painting"—the application of violently contrasting colors in irregular patterns. Although the vessel became more conspicuous, the broken lines made it difficult for enemy submarines to estimate the exact course. When the Germans introduced color screens in their periscopes to reduce a dazzle-painted ship to a silhouette, the Allied experts fell back on blue, black and white designs which defied such attempts at neutralization.

Camouflage helped the French to win the prolonged artillery duel at Verdun, for their losses in heavy guns were only a fraction of those inflicted on the enemy. German infantry casualties led to an ever-increasing reliance on the spade, so that some of the dugouts of the Verdun lines provided a refuge for an entire battalion. All armies now wore uniforms of khaki, blue, gray or green in subdued shades, and the general adoption of steel helmets signaled the first revival of armor since the Thirty Years' War. Experiments with shields and bulletproof vests were less successful, since the soldier had already been burdened too heavily.

While the emphasis on protection had begun long before Verdun, the results of the battle made it more evident that the artillery was the decisive arm of the war. Tacticians admitted that the infantry merely occupied the ground gained by the thundering guns; and it was aptly remarked that the traditional Queen of Battles had become a drudge fit only for "mopping up" after the storm of steel.

The Russian and British Offensives of 1916

The French, never reticent as to their sacrifices, appealed to both of their main Allies for relief. As usual, the request found the Russians acquiescent even if not ready, and the battle of Lake Norotch resulted in March from an ill-timed offensive in the Vilna district. The spring thaw fought on the side of Germans who needed only their local reserves to repulse all attacks with losses of 100,000.

After the disasters of 1915 the czar himself had assumed nominal command while finding a scapegoat in the competent grand duke. This change, of course, only rendered the army more helpless against court intrigues. A single antiaircraft battery stood guard over all Russia, and the lack of planes placed the ground troops at a terrible disadvantage. More machine guns had been made available by the Allies, and in 1916 it could at least be said that every Russian soldier carried a rifle. But ammunition reserves were still unbelievably low, so that General Brusilov had to hoard shells from his daily allowance while preparing for a new attack south of the Pripet marshes.

The operation was intended merely as a large-scale diversion while the bulk of the Russian forces planned another advance in the Vilna sector. Without much encouragement or aid from his superiors, Brusilov began a general advance on a three-hundred-mile front with a view to seeking weak spots for a possible break-through.

The brief bombardment and absence of any concentration gave no warning on June 4, and 200,000 prisoners were taken in the first three days. Within a week both Austrian flanks collapsed, so that Ludendorff had to throw in all possible reserves to prevent a débâcle. The Russian high command was almost equally embarrassed by the unexpected success. Brusilov had attacked with no advantage in numbers, and reinforcements must go southward if the victory were to be fully exploited. The miserable Russian communications proved unequal to this task, and Ludendorff's strategic railways enabled him to plug all gaps before the end of the month. The Russians continued their efforts in Galicia until the end of September, taking a total of 450,000 prisoners and regaining much of the southern territory lost in 1915. But their own losses mounted toward a million, for the assaults continued long after the opportunity had passed. Hence at the moment when the Allies were rejoicing over the return of "the Russian steam roller," the czar's forces had actually shot their last bolt. Not victory but revolution was to be the next vision of the long-suffering moujik in uniform.

On July 1 the Franco-British drive on the Somme began without a pretense of surprise after a seven-day bombardment. The original conception had included forty French divisions, but the drain of the Verdun operations reduced this figure to five on the opening day. The main burden thus fell on the new British army of volunteers as its first major effort.

It is still a puzzle as to why the Somme area was chosen, for the Allies had to advance uphill against positions which the enemy had strengthened during two years of comparative calm. Although the British were reluctant at first, the French generals had their way; and eventually Haig became so optimistic as to plan for a pursuit by his favorite arm, the cavalry. Incredible as it may seem, the mounted brigades were ordered on July 1 "to gallop right through to Cambrai, encircle it, and cut the railway lines to the east." The staff officer who penned these innocent lines probably did not dream that two more years of anguish would be required before Cambrai finally fell to clanking iron monsters whose lifeblood was gasoline.

Lack of realism on the part of the British commanders accounted to a large extent for the frightful casualties of the first assault. The chalky soil of the Picardy uplands lent itself admirably to the creation of immensely deep and roomy dugouts which sheltered the Germans throughout the week's bombardment. Hence their machine guns were quickly manned when the attackers swarmed out of the trenches in broad daylight, each soldier bent under sixty-six pounds of ammunition, grenades, picks, shovels and sandbags. As an added handicap to the burdened troops plodding through barbed-wire entanglements, Haig's rigid plan

called for an advance in equal strength all along the front. The courage
and morale of the British citizen-soldier were high, but inexperience
plus faulty training led to an attack in dense waves which the enemy
bullets shattered. By evening the main attempt had been repulsed, and
the casualty list of nearly 60,000 amounted to 40 per cent of the British
troops engaged. The more flexible French tactics had some success
south of the Somme, where a surprise was achieved, though the Allied
results could only be described as a costly failure.

The events of the next five months showed all the contending forces
to be under the spell of the Western Front psychology. The British and
French, having abandoned all hopes of quick decision, turned the battle
into a slugging match. The German generals, with like obstinacy,
demanded that their men hold every wood and hamlet, regardless of
cost. Thus the action which had begun in July sunshine finally bogged
down in the mud and snow of November, with casualties of half a million for the Germans and 600,000 (about three-fourths British) for the
Allies. And though a strip 30 miles long had been overrun to a maximum depth of 7 miles, the territorial gains were unimportant as compared to the depressing effect which the "Somme blood bath" had on
enemy morale.

In 1916 the Allies also gained a temporary mastery of the air by
virtue of mechanical and tactical improvements as well as a numerical
advantage. Goaded by the success of enemy Fokker planes, both
the French and British now had fighters in which the machine gun
fired through the propeller, while the two-seated reconnaissance aircraft were provided with a second machine gun aimed toward the rear
by the observer. During the Verdun operations the French organized
the first squadron operations as patrols flew far into hostile territory
to attack aerodromes. The Germans countered with their "circus
system"—roving squadrons of fighters under a picked leader—and champions of both sides won a bright fame for prowess in individual combats.
This outgrowth of aerial tactics has been criticized as the "knight-
errantry phase," and certain it is that more practical possibilities were
being neglected. As evidence a few German bombers dealt the British a
severe blow on July 21 by blowing up 8,000 tons of ammunition in a
central dump at Audricq. Despite this example, all the air forces of 1916
continued to pay more attention to Homeric duels than opportunities for
destroying matériel or personnel.

The first tanks likewise failed for want of tactical vision. In October,
1914, Colonel E. D. Swinton had already perceived that the machine gun
was an unsurmountable barrier to a warfare of movement. Although he

cannot be called the sole originator, the British engineer took the lead in urging the necessity for some sort of armored car to cope with the war's dominant weapon. Military history presented several remote examples, the most notable being the wagonfort of the Hussites. Swinton and his associates, however, found their inspiration in a familiar agricultural implement, the American caterpillar tractor. From the beginning the technical problems were simple as compared to the difficulties of overcoming military prejudice. For the British rather than the German army proved to be the tank's main foe, and only Winston Churchill's support enabled the conception to survive into the experimental stage.

In February, 1916, the Mark I passed all tests. Called the "tank" for purposes of secrecy in dispatches, the "male" type carried two 6-pounders was well as machine guns. Twenty-six feet long and 28 tons in weight, this first steel-armored landship could cross a ditch 6 feet wide and reach a speed of 4 miles an hour on the level. The light or "female" tank, armed only with machine guns, was intended to be paired with the heavy model as a destroyer of personnel. Both were operated by crews of seven men.

Wisdom after the event being cheaply bought, popular opinion is often too severe on soldierly conservatism. For it is a military leader's business to take only calculated risks, and nations would perish if every inventor's dream were welcomed in an uncritical spirit. The growing pains of the tank, on the contrary, were prolonged for lack of intelligent skepticism on the part of Haig and his staff officers. After having blindly opposed the innovation at first, they flew to the opposite extreme of using it prematurely in the hope of winning a local success. Thus on September 15 the rhomboidal machines went into action on the Somme with half-trained crews and tactics which disregarded Swinton's instructions. Of the 49 out of 60 tanks which reached the front, only 18 fired a shot, the others having mired down in the muddy crater field. One captured a village and another mopped up a trench with 300 prisoners, but the attempt was obviously a failure which confirmed the General Staff's earlier prejudices. The verdict of the British "fox-hunting generals" found expression in the removal of Swinton, whose brain-child also seemed doomed to pay the penalty of official displeasure.

As a happy contrast the French of Verdun showed what could be accomplished by a fully exploited tactical surprise. After the June crisis the battle took on a secondary importance for several months as German troops were sent to the Somme and Eastern Front. During this lull the French artillery generals worked out the details of a new conception known as the "creeping barrage"—a rolling curtain of fire timed to protect the troops advancing just behind the exploding shells.

Of course the innovation demanded the most precise co-ordination between the artillery and infantry if the assault troops were not to become victims of their own guns. Hence the weeks of preparation paid rich rewards on October 24 when General Nivelle's forces took Vaux, Douaumont and thousands of prisoners, regaining in a single blow the ground which had cost the Germans months of bloody effort. In a second thrust the attackers advanced their lines two more miles, and an additional 15,000 prisoners and 115 guns fell into their hands. The low casualties of these drives justified the French in claiming a final victory at Verdun. The enemy could not even boast a favorable balance in attrition, for the total losses of each side were about 350,000 during the eleven months.

Germany's Submarine Campaign of 1917

After the trials of 1916 Ludendorff described the German army as "absolutely exhausted." Falkenhayn, the champion of attrition, was removed from command as the casualty list on all fronts exceeded a million. Yet the Allies had small cause for rejoicing, since their weary foe could still muster enough reserve strength to knock Rumania out of the war in a swift autumn campaign.

That small kingdom entered the lists on August 28 after long vacillation, having been promised aid from Russia and the Allied expeditionary force at Salonika. Again Germany induced Bulgaria to take part, and in September the Central Powers struck from the north and south with two armies. Mackensen took Constanza, the chief port on the Black Sea, while Falkenhayn drove deep into Transylvania. Allied aid came too late to save the oil fields and grain-producing regions, though a large part of the beaten Rumanian army made its escape after most of the country had been overrun.

Behind the forced optimism of British and French propaganda an atmosphere of doubt could be sensed as the new year began. The midwinter cabinet crisis in London ended in the granting of almost dictatorial powers to a new War Cabinet headed by Lloyd George, the most outspoken critic of Allied generalship on the Somme. Next, Joffre was compelled to resign in favor of General Nivelle, whose recent successes at Verdun seemed to promise quicker and less costly methods of winning the war.

These revelations of Allied anxiety had scarcely been announced before the Germans began a new submarine campaign. Regarding American intervention as practically certain, they waited until the 1915 total of U-boats had been multiplied by five. With this strength, including new underseas raiders of a more formidable type, the emperor's advisers believed that the Allies could be brought to terms before American aid had any great influence.

The losses inflicted during the first six months appeared to warrant this conviction. From January to June no less than 3,855,000 tons of British, Allied and neutral shipping were sent to the bottom—a rate of destruction which could never have been endured until the end of the year. In April alone, as the United States declared war, 850,000 tons were destroyed; and at a first meeting Jellicoe informed Admiral Sims of the American fleet that the Allies were in imminent peril of losing the war.

Nor could the British and French leaders derive any consolation from the land operations of this critical period. Haig's forces advanced on the Somme in March, only to discover to their chagrin that the enemy had vanished, leaving a horribly devastated salient behind. Hindenburg and Ludendorff, who replaced Falkenhayn, did not subscribe to the Western Front creed that morale would be injured by a profitable retirement. Exactly the contrary proved true as the Germans cut down orchards, poisoned wells and leveled villages, creating a military desert filled with booby traps. Such destruction set a new standard of viciousness, and it is to the credit of Prince Rupprecht that he refused to sign the order. From a cold-blooded viewpoint, however, the success of the evacuation could not be denied.

The new German positions, known to the Allies as the "Hindenburg line," introduced the war's first well-planned system of defenses in depth. The principle might have been traced directly back to Vauban, though Ludendorff learned his lesson from the improvised French strongpoints linking up the forts of Verdun. For weeks he employed thousands of prisoners in the creation of integrated dugouts, tunnels, trenches and machine gun nests—a maze of concrete and earthen traps to a depth of several miles. The bristling new line was much shorter, and the strength of the artificial defenses made it possible to use thirteen fewer divisions.

MUTINY ON THE WESTERN FRONT

While the Allied propagandists tried to present Haig's recovery of the salient as a victory, the British and French made their final preparations for a combined offensive. For weeks it had been boulevard gossip that Nivelle promised a break-through on the Aisne. Indeed, the persuasive general talked so freely at a Paris luncheon that the absence of secrecy might have been farcical except for its tragic consequences. Naturally, the enemy had full advance knowledge, including even a detailed plan of assault listing every French unit and its objective. Yet when Nivelle learned that the Germans possessed this information, he made no effort to change his dispositions. With half a million men and 3,500 guns concentrating on a front of 25 miles, he adopted as his slogan, "Laon in twenty-four hours and then the pursuit!"

The British struck first on April 9 in the Arras sector. A week's preliminary bombardment ruined any prospect of surprise, but the news of the American declaration had left the men in high spirits. The new British gas shells disconcerted the enemy gunners, and a perfectly timed creeping barrage protected the advancing troops. Under the vigorous leadership of General Allenby, they stormed Vimy Ridge and captured 200 guns as well as 13,000 prisoners the first day. Then the battle followed the familiar Western Front pattern as resistance stiffened. And though Allenby's attacks continued in support of his Allies, no further gains of importance were announced to justify total losses of 84,000.

Meanwhile the French attempt ended in a national calamity. For instead of buying victory with his 118,000 casualties in two weeks, Nivelle drove his army to mutiny.

Following a ten-day bombardment, the troops advanced amid belated snow flurries on April 16. Ludendorff was ready with a system of elastic defenses, and the overrunning of his first-line positions proved to be an illusory gain. The difficulties did not multiply until the attackers reached the three inner zones, each complete in itself, forming a belt two miles in depth. Strongpoints and concrete machine gun nests subjected the French to a deadly enfilade fire at every step. The German planes, which had won a local mastery of the air, flew low over the lines to signal the guns or swoop down on the French infantry with a hail of bullets. If the assailants survived these ordeals, they had to meet surprise counterattacks from storm troopers who rode to each threatened area in fast trucks and debouched from cunningly placed tunnels or communication trenches. These combat specialists were armed with a recent weapon in the automatic rifle, which had all the effect of a machine gun when fired in short bursts. Picked men, trained for violent onslaughts, they held a great advantage over ordinary infantry burdened with equipment.

Under the circumstances it is not surprising that Nivelle met a defeat which led to his dismissal. Within a few weeks disaffection had spread through sixteen corps, and one authority states that but two divisions remained trustworthy on the entire front between Reims and Soissons. Political agitators were blamed by French officers who sought a face-saving excuse, but unbiased research makes it plain that the outbreaks amounted to a military strike. The Aisne drive simply added the last drop to an indignation of long standing; and after having exhausted every other means of protest, the man in the ranks asserted himself as an outraged citizen.

III

THE SORROWS OF VICTORY

---

*Neutrality is no longer feasible or desirable where the
peace of the world is involved and the freedom of its
peoples.*

—WOODROW WILSON

THE gravity of France's situation in May, 1917, may be judged by
the fact that no widespread revolt had been known in an army of
western Europe since the Thirty Years' War. Yet far from being disloyal, the mutineers were willing to man the trenches in defense of their
own soil. They balked only at such offensive operations as had inspired
a memorandum addressed in 1916 by Abel Ferry to the Viviani cabinet:

> They claim that to fire human grapeshot at the enemy without
> preparation, gives us a moral ascendancy. But the thousands of
> dead Frenchmen, lying in front of the German trenches, are instead
> those who are giving moral ascendancy to the enemy. If this waste
> of human material keeps on, the day is not far off when the offensive
> capacity of our army, already seriously weakened, will be entirely
> destroyed.

The author of this solemn warning (as quoted in Douhet's *The Command of the Air*) was a French deputy serving as an infantry lieutenant. More coherent than the average poilu, he voiced the principal griev-
ance of soldiers whose courage and devotion could not be doubted. The
real miracle of the Marne, in fact, had been the hardihood of French

728

conscripts so recently snatched from home life. They astonished even their own commanders during those first chaotic weeks by enduring casualties and privations which might have broken regulars. And therein lies the tragedy of the World War, for it did not take the generals long to adopt a spendthrift attitude toward their living matériel. Losses once regarded as appalling were soon thought inevitable, and the years of attrition saw human lives being "traded" like the pawns of a chess game played by inept opponents.

It would be an injustice, nevertheless, to accuse these middle-aged staff officers of mere callousness. Almost without exception they were men of rigid honor who had dedicated their lives to duty. Unfortunately, they were also narrow men, uneducated in economics, history and the social sciences, uneducated even in the broader lessons taught by war. Their schooling, received in such academies as St. Cyr, Sandhurst and West Point, had not prepared them for leadership in the huge armies of conscripted citizen-soldiers, and the moral gulf between command and ranks was never bridged throughout the war. The consequence was a tragic misunderstanding.

From the time of Alexander it had been an axiom that a commander could not hold the respect of his men without sharing to a reasonable extent their perils and hardships. So universal is this rule that no outstanding exception can be found in all military history down to 1870. Marlborough, Frederick and Sherman, among others, put the principle into words which make it evident that they justified their risks on psychological grounds.

Grant, the first general to lead a million citizen-soldiers, wore a private's uniform and based his decisions on personal reconnaissance. A civilian at heart, hating war and despising the traditions of the profession, he accomplished his tremendous results with the aid of a staff which today would hardly be thought fit for a divisional commander. It must be remembered, moreover, that the typewriter and field telephone had not yet appeared to ease the burdens of administrative detail.

Moltke was the first great captain to break with the past. In his emphasis on planning, he located his headquarters far back in the rear, leaving the supervision of the fighting to subordinates. And since there is no more convincing justification than victory, the method gained converts as armies swelled in numbers.

In some respects the benefits were apparent. Modern staff work can hardly be said to have begun until after Moltke showed the way. Military cartography developed into a science, while precision and co-ordination improved in every army which followed the Prussian model. Yet in his genius for specialization Moltke went to such lengths as to create a gap between staff and regimental officers—a tendency which his imitators accepted along with the tactical virtues.

Obviously the generalissimo of several million troops cannot charge at the head of his men in the eighteenth-century manner. But when even the divisional staffs of 1917 sought comparative comfort and safety, combatants felt that they were being thrust and not led into battle. Resentment of such conditions ate like a canker at the fighting spirit of every World War army; and to complete the sad paradox, most of the commanders were too far removed from war's realities to know the truth.

Worst of all, staff work itself lost rather than gained in effectiveness as generals forfeited the respect of their men. According to B. H. Liddell Hart's *The Real War*, a high-ranking British officer paid his first visit to the front at the close of a four months' attack which cost 300,000 casualties. After one look at a Flemish terrain which shellfire had reduced to a ghastly swamp, he burst into tears with the exclamation, "Good God, did we really send men to fight in that?"

Precision in organization and logistics could not compensate for such ignorance of the human difficulties; and it is a safe assertion that thousands of needless casualties on the Western Front could be charged to the "aggressiveness" of sedentary commanders.

In nearly all other respects the armies of western Europe showed a lively concern with problems of morale. Medals were awarded in such profusion as to lose much of their distinction. Never in history had the soldier been so well clothed and fed. The granting of home leaves entered into the calculations of strategy, and an efficient army postal service delivered letters in the trenches. Supplementing the efforts of the Red Cross, a score of sectarian and charitable organizations distributed gifts, games and athletic equipment. Famous actors and actresses volunteered to perform in improvised theaters just behind the reserve lines, and army-supervised canteens sold small luxuries at reduced prices to men drawing the low pay of universal conscription.

International codes regulated the treatment of prisoners, setting minimum standards which included pay from the enemy for voluntary labor. War's victims benefited to an even greater extent from advances in military surgery, though only two generations had passed since Florence Nightingale and Henri Dunant fought to establish the right of casualties to the bare decencies of care. By 1914 preventive medicine and sanitation had conquered such epidemics as smallpox, typhus and typhoid, so that only isolated cases were reported in the armies of western Europe. The importance of this result is shown by the contrasting record on the Serbian front in 1915, when an outbreak of typhus took a heavier toll than the guns. World War surgeons, moreover, no longer tolerated a high mortality rate from infected wounds. Immediate first-aid treatment, followed by scientific care and cleanliness, saved so many of these cases that a vast majority were returned to duty. New techniques of facial surgery worked miracles for the disfigured; and after being provided with artificial limbs, crippled men were trained for suitable occupations in civil life.

Most of these organized mercies, which today are universally accepted in theory, do not date back beyond the airplane. Nevertheless, the armies of 1917 had reached such a low ebb of morale that four of the six principal warring nations were actually on the verge of a collapse. Of the original belligerents, only the British and German forces retained much combative spirit; and some of their units were so war-rotted that surgeons encountered that most morbid of symptoms, the self-inflicted wound.

PÉTAIN'S REORGANIZATION

After replacing Nivelle on May 15 Pétain faced a situation without a precedent since the time of Turenne. Happily for the imperiled nation, the new commander was one leader who had consistently held the respect of the man in the trenches. Far from being the "democratic type," he was stern and reserved to the point of severity. But he was also firm and just, and the French soldier soon made it plain that these were the qualities he demanded. Thus in a miracle of reorganization Pétain managed to restore order within a month while keeping the extent of the revolt a secret from the enemy.

By way of contrast his methods explain the previous failures of generalship on the Western Front. In his first few weeks, visiting ninety divisions in the lines, the commander-in-chief invited frankness from soldiers who had seldom seen a major general at the front. Both officers and men were encouraged to present their grievances to a patriarchal leader who promised reforms. That he could be rigorous is shown by his execution of twenty-three men convicted of treasonable motives. But for the most part Pétain endorsed the complaints of the mutineers by putting into effect sweeping tactical and administrative changes. As a final contribution, he wrote an article reaffirming the causes and objectives of the war for uniformed citizens whose faith had been all but destroyed. By July 1 he had the army in hand, and the following month a successful offensive showed how fully confidence had been restored. Choosing the Verdun area for its symbolic values, Pétain made good use of the tactical suggestions received from regimental officers. The infantry platoon was reorganized into a self-supporting group of specialists—riflemen, automatic riflemen, bombers and rifle grenadiers—which set an example for other Allied armies. Within the division the proportion of light artillery increased until in some instances the gunners actually outnumbered the infantry. After several weeks of intense training, the French swept forward at Mort Homme nearly to the old lines of 1915, their casualties being kept at a minimum by surprise and precision. In October the new commander won one of the most worth-while strategic successes of the war by pinching off an enemy salient northeast of Soissons. Not only did he take 20,000 prisoners, but the Germans were compelled to retire beyond the Ailette, leaving the Chemin des Dames heights to victors who had neatly turned their position.

Legend has credited Joffre with the remark that it cost ten thousand casualties to train a major general on the Western Front. At any rate the French army of 1917 had paid some such price, for more than half the infantry consisted of soldiers past the age of thirty-two. Even Pétain could not restore the fire of youth to these sober heads of families, but at least he had given them back their belief in France and her military ideals.

THE COLLAPSE IN ITALY AND RUSSIA

It was the tragedy of Italy that no leader of Pétain's ability appeared in time to save the country from the most humiliating rout of the war. The major contenders had shown little interest in this area, so that the operations of the Italians and Austrians might be described as a war within a war—a minor front in all respects except numbers. For two years large armies had been achieving small results on the Isonzo, where both sides found the foothills as much of a barrier as the enemy. Italy's strategic aims were vague, but no less than eleven offensives had been launched toward Trieste to carry out a policy of attrition only too faithfully modeled after the Western Front. Nearly a million Italian casualties were incurred without reducing more than half of the disheartening distance to the objective.

Cadorna, the chief of the General Staff, was a Piedmontese aristocrat who prided himself on his reputation as a martinet. His generals drove their men too hard in difficult mountain terrain, issuing orders based on maps and strategic formulas rather than a firsthand knowledge of the human problems. As the ultimate stupidity, striking industrial workers were sent to the front lines for punishment, and their subversive doctrines aggravated a war-weariness which reached its climax in the autumn of 1917.

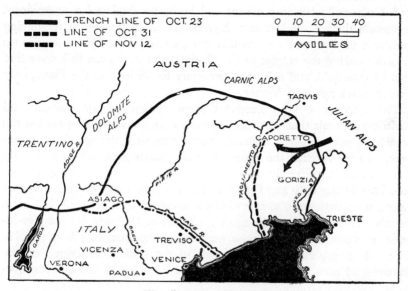

The Caporetto Campaign

So wide was the moral gap between the supreme command and regimental officers that even in his memoirs, written after the war, Cadorna denied that any grave discontent existed. If the enemy had not been equally ignorant of conditions, Italy would doubtless have been brought to terms in a single campaign. But Ludendorff had his own worries over Austrian morale, and his decision to send seven picked German divisions seems to have been based on a fear that his allies might collapse. Certainly he had no anticipation of the Italian demoralization which took place as the attackers poured down from the Julian Alps on October 24. In the Caporetto sector, which gave the débâcle its name, they ripped through the centre of a front which fell into indescribable chaos. Thousands of men crowded every road in a wild mass flight, and within a few days the whole fortified hill system had fallen with 3,000 guns.

From the first hour Caporetto resembled a pursuit rather than a battle. For the statistics leave no question as to the real causes of defeat —50,000 Italians killed and wounded as compared to nearly 300,000 prisoners and more than 400,000 deserters! Where the argumentative poilu had denounced his generals, the Italian peasant simply threw away his rifle and turned his feet homeward.

If Cadorna had been a tyrant and bully, he displayed a magnificent resolution during the last few days before his dismissal. After having hundreds of deserters shot as examples, he somehow kept a semblance of order during the retreat to the Tagliamento. But even this river line could not be held, and it became necessary to fall back to the Piave, only twenty miles north of Venice.

The outcome so far exceeded the expectations of the German and Austrian generals that adequate reserves were not at hand to exploit the breach. A new and less welcome surprise awaited the attackers, moreover, as they reached the Piave. For the Italian remnants, so recently jeered in flight, suddenly stood with stout courage to defend their own soil. Numbering only 423 battalions against 736, and 3,500 guns against 7,000, they outfought victory-flushed invaders in a struggle lasting a month. Much of the credit must go to Diaz, the new commander-in-chief, a rough old soldier who understood the man in the ranks. He appealed so successfully to the pride of the Italian conscript that the menace had been largely overcome before French and British reinforcements got into action.

After Caporetto, with its total of nearly 600,000 Italian losses in two months, the other Entente powers maintained contingents on the Southern Front. But the valorous defense of the Piave had redeemed the flight to the Tagliamento, and during the winter Diaz created a new fighting spirit by introducing reforms similar to those approved by Pétain.

On the Eastern Front it had long been a question as to whether Russia or Austria would collapse first. The ancient Hapsburg empire was saved in the summer of 1916 only by Ludendorff's frantic efforts. A few months later the death of the aged Franz-Joseph broke the last emotional link with the past. His reign had begun during the revolutions of 1848, and as he lay on his deathbed the survival of his dynasty owed solely to the fact that Russia was in a worse plight.

France and Italy had expressed their dissatisfaction with the conduct of the war by mutiny and desertion. The huge Russian army, with much more provocation, simply crumbled away. The causes were of course largely political, but again it is evident that strictly military events played their part. Men who lack even rifles cannot see their comrades mowed down by machine guns without feeling resentment. And it was in the ranks of the army that political exiles found their most fertile field for revolutionary propaganda. So well had their work been done that the overthrow of the czar in April, 1917, owed to disaffection in the armed forces rather than the empire as a whole.

France and Great Britain at first cherished the delusion that their ally would remain a force in the war. The scandals of Romanoff rule having been an embarrassment to Allied propagandists, it seemed logical that Russian efforts would gain from the ousting of incompetent and dishonest court favorites. The appointment of the able Brusilov as commander-in-chief confirmed this hope, and on July 1 the reorganized forces began their last offensive of the war. Within a few days it appeared that mere military tonics could not cure Russia's long political sickness, for a brisk counterattack reduced the Galician armies to a demoralized mob. The Germans, who had full intelligence of revolutionary plots, wisely contented themselves with a limited victory in the field. During the remainder of the summer they adopted a deliberately passive policy on the Eastern Front, fearing to arouse the patriotism of opponents who were now deserting by the thousands.

It was at this stage that Hoffman had perhaps his most brilliant idea of the war. Although his reactionary superiors were shocked at first, they finally consented to the transporting of exiled revolutionists across the frontier in sealed railway carriages. Thus did Lenin and Trotsky return to their homeland—as the wards of *Junker* officers who did not suspect that their own country might some day be infected by deadly political germs.

Before the end of the year the most optimistic Allied observers admitted that no further military aid could be expected from Russia. And with France and Italy still convalescing, the two English-speaking nations realized that they must bear the brunt of the effort against a German army which could soon bring a numerical superiority to the Western Front.

CAMBRAI: THE TRIUMPH OF THE TANK

At dawn on June 7, 1917, the German forces holding Messines Ridge had an awful impression that their whole world had gone up in a searing blast of flame, débris and mangled bodies. Before they could recover from their panic, khaki-clad foemen poured into the breach to round up captives too stunned for resistance. By means of this resounding success the British army announced that it had reached full stature as the most formidable of Germany's opponents.

The survivors among Kitchener's million volunteers were now battle-hardened veterans, and the conscription law of 1916 had since provided an enormous increase in total numbers. In addition to the armies defending some of the most critical sectors in France, large expeditionary forces had been transported to Egypt, Palestine, Greece, East Africa and Mesopotamia. British civilians had meanwhile made the painful transition from a peacetime economy to a united war effort in which the nation's factories were devoted almost entirely to the production of munitions.

Along with the other warring countries, Britain found it necessary to employ thousands of women as industrial workers if the appetite of the guns were to be satisfied. The island kingdom took the next logical step by organizing the first national corps of uniformed women volunteers. Subjected to military discipline and trained for the many skilled tasks required to support combat troops, these auxiliaries proved so useful that after 1916 it could no longer be said that woman's rôle in war was passive.

As added evidence of tactical maturity, Messines became the first important all-British offensive, since former drives had been more or less pointedly suggested by the French as large-scale diversions. The adjective "brilliant" is customarily applied to an operation distinguished rather for method, realism and uncommonly good judgment—qualities less often encountered than brilliance in the shambles of the Western Front. General Plumer and his chief-of-staff Harington neglected no detail of intelligent planning; and after a long bombardment 19 mines containing 600 tons of explosive literally blew the crest of the ridge into the air. The British infantry followed so rapidly that within an hour most of the limited objectives had been taken. Reversing the usual rule, the casualties of the attackers were fewer than two-thirds of the 25,000 inflicted on the foe. To cap the triumph, Plumer resisted all temptation to stretch his gains, thus avoiding the costly anticlimax of operations pushed too far.

From a tactical viewpoint, as many critics have remarked, Messines is the single authetic siege attack of a siege war. Where other strategists thought only in terms of a break-through, the two British generals accomplished more by making certain of modest results on a limited front. But it is noteworthy that they had to withstand pressure from general headquarters; and the following month Haig committed himself to an offensive which today is remembered as the supreme folly of the British war effort.

Despite the accumulated object lessons, many staff officers still trusted implicitly in the artillery formula. Past failures being charged simply to a lack of sufficient fire power, Haig massed 2,300 guns on a 15-mile front in preparation for the third battle of Ypres, better known by the soldiers' name of Passchendaele. Although the Belgians had warned that the attempt would destroy the complex drainage system of reclaimed Flemish lands, no less than 103,000 tons of shells were used during the preliminary bombardment alone. For ten days the guns thundered ceaselessly, then the hapless infantry paid the penalty by advancing through a man-made swamp dotted with stagnant pools.

In all military history it is doubtful if soldiers were ever condemned to a more grisly ordeal. So slow was their progress that London headlines reported gains of a hundred yards by attackers wallowing through mud and slime. A more unsuitable area for an offensive could not have been chosen, for on the level plain the British positions were visible six miles in the rear. By day and night the German planes swept down to bomb batteries and troop movements. In the front line the water-filled craters offered the only refuge from the fire of enemy "pillboxes"—concrete machine gun emplacements which resisted even a direct hit from field artillery. To add to the difficulties, the Germans made their first use of mustard gas, a skin irritant that remained in the soil to inflict painful burns and blisters.

A hundred days the agony of Passchendaele lasted, with 4,300,000 shells being fired before general headquarters admitted that the tactical duel between the machine gun and cannon had ended as usual. At a cost of 300,000 casualties the attacks gained a few worthless kilometers. By way of attrition the enemy had been punished to the point of describing the battle as "the supreme martyrdom of the war." But perhaps the most favorable outcome was one which Haig and his officers would hardly have approved. For Passchendaele destroyed public confidence to such an extent that Lloyd George kept a tighter rein on his generals thereafter. In France the dour Clemenceau showed a similar distrust, so that 1917 dates the rise of a vigorous civilian leadership in Allied war circles. Professional soldiers grumbled bitterly among themselves about the "interference of politicians," but history has recorded that Passchendaele was the last of the futile slaughters.

As the final irony, an offshoot of the main battle won a far brighter fame as the tactical landmark of the year. For at Cambrai a British tank attack, intended as a diversion, achieved a complete rupture of the Hindenburg line. At last the iron cavalry had come into its own, and the most conservative staff officers had to concede that a new era of warfare had dawned.

It was the good fortune of the armored corps to have received more than its share of the soldiers whose opinions were regarded as unorthodox. The General Staff still had little faith in the new weapon, and the transfer of a career to this orphaned branch amounted to a decent burial.

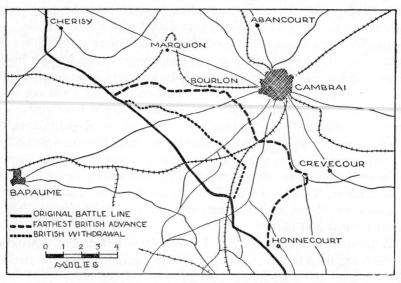

Cambrai: the Triumph of the Tank

Thus the tanks gained from the most searching and original mind in the army, as revealed by later writings, when Major General J. F. C. Fuller became chief-of-staff of the corps in April. During the summer he urged the Cambrai attack so persistently as to add to his reputation as an impractical visionary. The plan might never have been approved, in fact, if the ghastly failure in Flanders had not made it advisable to detract British public attention from Passchendaele.

Fuller held that Swinton's tactical instructions had never been observed. He added ideas of his own, and during the night of November 19 some 600 guns were secretly moved up in support of the 381 tanks hidden in a wood just behind the lines. At dawn the phalanx burst out on a dazed foe along a six-mile front, each wedge-shaped formation of three machines being followed by two platoon columns of infantry. Not until this moment did the gunners begin a hurricane barrage without preliminary registration.

The surprise proved so crushing that the German first-line troops swarmed out with uplifted hands. Nor did the steel monsters hesitate when they reached the wide trenches of the "impregnable" Hindenburg line. Each dropped a huge fascine of brushwood to form bridges, then the tanks ripped through defenses in depth which had been designed to hold up an army for weeks. Before dusk the clanking cavalcade had taken 7,500 prisoners and 120 guns while penetrating to a maximum depth of 7,000 yards—the greatest single bound ever made as yet on the Western Front! The British casualties were light, for whole battalions had only five or six men wounded.

If the battle had ended here it might have been celebrated more jubilantly. But Fuller's original conception of a gigantic raid and withdrawal had been amended by General Byng, who envisioned the prospect of a cavalry exploitation. Almost no reserves were available, while the six infantry divisions consisted of battle-worn troops from the horrors of Passchendaele. Thus a woefully inadequate force was pushed into a narrow salient where it became the prey of counterattacks. Neither the tanks nor the cavalry being adapted to such a defensive, the British soon had to give up most of their territorial gains after total losses matching those of the enemy. Even so, the opening triumph left no doubt that the tank had won its way, and both the British and French armies placed large orders for the future.

Cambrai was more than a vindication of a new weapon. The battle also restored the ancient principles of secrecy and surprise which had been so neglected on the Western Front. As a result the ten-day bombardment became an anachronism, and both sides depended on a tempest of steel followed by a precise creeping barrage.

LUDENDORFF'S OFFENSIVES OF 1918

Behind the German lines the new year began with terms being dictated to two recent enemies. In the Treaty of Brest-Litovsk, signed with the new Bolshevik masters of Russia, the Central Powers made the

Ukraine a puppet state while also severing Finland, Livonia, Esthonia and the Caucasus from the former czar's empire. In addition, Russia agreed to pay an indemnity of 300,000,000 gold rubles.

If these conditions seem harsh and vengeful, they were benevolent as compared to the economic slavery in which a shorn Rumania found herself after the Treaty of Bucharest. Not only were large slices of territory awarded to Bulgaria and Hungary, but Germany secured control of the nation's railways, oil and grain for years to come.

It might have been supposed that after digesting these spoils the Central Powers would be imbued with a victorious morale. On the contrary, they derived no more consolation from the events of 1917 than their enemies. Both Bulgaria and Turkey were exhausted, and only the support of a stern ally postponed the disintegration of Austria. Even in Germany the first mutterings of defeatism could be heard, for a meager harvest and the British blockade caused 1917 to be known as "Turnip Year." Teutonic self-pity exaggerated the privations, but there can be no doubt that the national diet was monotonous even if sufficient.

While the attrition of the Western Front had hurt Allied morale, the Germans were also badly battered. But the worst disappointment came from the comparative failure of the submarine campaign during the last six months. After enduring losses until July which would soon have brought disaster, the Allies found a belated salvation by modernizing an eighteenth-century tactic—the convoy system which had protected sailing ships from privateers. The American navy, ready from the moment that war was declared, aided in the planning of routes and schedules. Soon large fleets of camouflaged freighters were being safely escorted across the Atlantic by destroyers which dropped depth charges to cripple a submerged foe. Armed merchantmen and vast mine fields were also found effective, and the sharp rise in U-boat losses led to demoralization of the crews. Thus by December the German strategists had to admit that they could neither starve England into submission nor prevent great numbers of American troops from crossing the sea.

This threat alone meant that the Central Powers must either win or lose all in 1918. Only the seizure of the Ukrainian grain fields, indeed, promised enough supplies for the planning of a final effort. And while the Allied leadership gradually passed to civilians, Hindenburg and Ludendorff used threats of resignation to make themselves virtually the military dictators of Germany. The old *Junker* remained a symbol of paternalistic authority to the people, but his rude, emphatic colleague wielded the power. Only fifty-three years old in 1918, Ludendorff had surmounted the professional handicap of a middle-class origin to become recognized as the war's leading tactician. Close contact with regimental officers gave him his ideas, and early in 1918 he felt confident enough to promise a complete victory before autumn on the Western Front.

His assurance owed to the perfection of an entirely new plan of offensive tactics. Again the Allies had created while the Germans adapted, for the conception first appeared in a pamphlet written by a French infantry officer, Captain Laffargue. As a remedy for the frustration which pervaded the Western Front, this unhonored theorist suggested a method which he called "infiltration." Trained spearheads of infantry specialists were to precede the main body, their function being to penetrate weak spots in the opposing line and attack machine guns from the flank or rear. Thus the foe would be beset from two directions, and the plan also called for closer infantry co-operation with the trench mortars and artillery.

In his most fanciful moments the French captain could never have supposed that he was proposing a system which would dominate the warfare of the coming age. Even his name "infiltration" found adoption along with the method. Unhappily, the benefits went to France's hereditary enemy when a copy of the pamphlet fell into their hands. After being translated, it atttracted Ludendorff's notice; and according to Captain Wynne's *If Germany Attacks*, the commander incorporated the ideas into his next manual of instructions.

The basic principle could not fail to appeal to a tactician who had already shown his faith in storm troopers. It happened also that German gunners had recently been working out the details of a better co-ordination between field artillery and advancing infantry. So it was that Laffargue's pamphlet came just in time to crystallize the enemy's half-formed thoughts along similar lines. By the early summer of 1917 Ludendorff had proceeded from theory to practice, and in secret areas behind the Eastern Front thousands of picked young men were being trained for infiltration.

The first test came on March 21, 1918. The British had long known that the blow would fall on their front, and even the exact date had been learned. But a surprise can be achieved in method as well as time or place, and no one in General Gough's Fifth Army had any conception of the havoc which would soon be wrought.

On a front from Arras to La Fere the German guns laid down a hurricane bombardment of such unprecedented violence that British communications were paralyzed. Thus rendered mute, the defenders were blinded by a dense morning mist as the storm troopers burst upon them. These mobile groups of specialists, armed with grenades, automatic rifles and light mortars, had orders to pour into any gap they

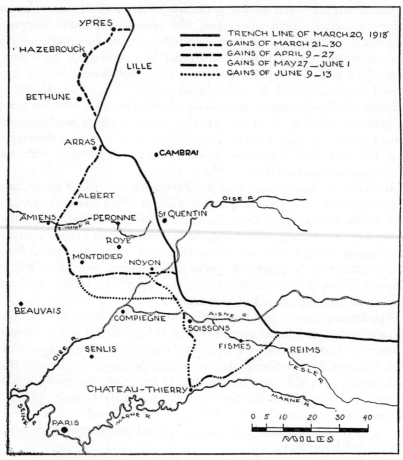

Ludendorff's Four Offensives in the Spring of 1918

could find or create, leaving the task of mopping up strongpoints to successive waves of infantry. The field artillery, carrying out its new tactics, had already begun to move up where it could render vigorous support, while field telephone wires were hurried forward by other highly trained groups.

The total effect has been likened by a British historian, John Buchan, to a racing flood. Just as water follows the course of least resistance, rushing into every crevice, swirling around obstacles, so the German torrent of infiltration swept through long-prepared defenses. Within forty-eight hours the attackers had penetrated to the unheard-of depth of ten miles in places, and Gough's entire front was plunged into a nightmare of confusion.

To add to the alarm in Allied circles, a mysterious German weapon now began to drop shells in Paris, though the nearest enemy lines were sixty-two miles away. Since the farthest previous range of artillery fire had been about twenty-five miles, all manner of speculations were rife. Not until after the war was it confirmed that the Germans actually had constructed a monster long-range gun principally for its moral effect. Concealed in a forest, the piece required an enormously long barrel weighing 200 tons to fire an 8-inch projectile filled with only 22 pounds of explosive. Hence the damage and casualties were comparatively light; and after the novelty wore off, Parisians began to accept "Big Bertha" with derision.

Much more dismaying were the reverses in Picardy. The German tide continued to race onward, inundating rear-area towns sacred to generals and their staffs. Yet even in this dark hour it could not be said that the attackers were invincible, for the British held firm at Arras, giving up only a few kilometers at a frightful cost. The crisis came in the south at the weak joint between the French and British forces. For hours a gap of several miles existed between the two armies, but by this time the Germans had also become victims of the chaos they created. Pétain rushed in French reinforcements before the crack could be widened into a chasm, and after the first terrible week the attack began to lose momentum. During the last days of March it reached a standstill within sight of Amiens Cathedral as the Australian infantry repulsed all assaults.

The German captures included 70,000 prisoners, 1,100 guns and enormous stores. Nevertheless, the amazing tactical success had ended in strategic failure for want of nourishment. As Cruttwell's *History of the Great War* has put it, ". . . the battle-flame burned lower and lower. The problem of adding fresh fuel, to which Ludendorff had given such thought, proved insoluble."

The British losses, though serious, were not fatal; and the enemy now occupied a pocket which would be vulnerable to counterattack if he lost the initiative. As an added comfort, the Allies at last achieved unity of command when Foch was named generalissimo at the historic Doullens Conference. This step had been praised in theory ever since 1914, but not until they felt the hot breath of the foe at their backs could the Allies agree.

Thrice again in the next three months Ludendorff demonstrated that he held the long-sought key to a break-through. Before the fighting died down in Picardy he struck in Flanders on April 9. In three days the attack penetrated to a depth of eleven miles between Ypres and Béthune, threatening Haig's forces with being driven into the sea. Finally the British brought up enough reinforcements to hold the new line as local actions continued throughout April.

Ludendorff's next blow fell by utter surprise on the Chemin des Dames front in May. Ironically, the Allies had thought this area so safe that divisions crippled in the last two battles were sent there for rest. Few reserves were available after these troops broke, and the German centre covered thirteen miles in a single day, though three rivers intervened. Ludendorff was nearly as disconcerted as the Allies, for he had not counted on any such dramatic results. Success beckoned so alluringly that he turned his intended diversion into a full-scale offensive by reinforcing the divisions in the new bulge between Reims and Soissons. They continued their triumphant progress until June 1, when German troops again stood on the Marne, only thirty-seven miles from Paris.

The very extent of the advance made a fourth drive necessary. For the narrow salient was forty miles deep, with but a single railway near the western face to serve the area. Hence on June 9 the Germans made another bound in the direction of Compiègne for the purpose of widening the pocket. This time, as an ominous portent, they not only fell short of the goal but lost two miles of their new gains to a French counterattack.

There is a remarkable similarity between the four German offensives. On each occasion the tactical successes of the first few days promised overwhelming results. Then the advance rapidly lost momentum as strategy failed to overcome what Clausewitz has called the "friction of war." And finally the assaults were stopped cold, after having created still another bulge as a potential trap for its occupants. Ludendorff, in short, had won spoils, territory, prisoners, renown—everything except the decisive victory he must have before time fought on the side of his enemies.

If the methods of infiltration have a vaguely recognizable aspect, it is because the principle goes back to classical warfare. Actually the armies of 1918 were bringing up to date the ancient tactical duel between the legion and phalanx! Just as the Romans had darted under the hedge of spears, so Ludendorff's modern maniples took the line of least resistance against a trench system bristling with mechanical weapons. In both cases mobility found a way to outwit solidarity which could not be outfought by frontal assault; and the machine gun of the twentieth century proved no more invincible than the sarissa of the ancient world.

Infiltration alone cannot be credited with the greatest advances made on the Western Front since 1914. Ludendorff also had introduced a degree of co-ordination between arms which no other organization had attained. And though the cry of "Germany against the world" was already a familiar plaint, it may be noted that 164 battle-frayed French and British divisions were beset in March by 208 German divisions. These figures do not tell the whole story, for much of Ludendorff's strength consisted of well-rested troops from the Eastern Front who had seen little action in two years. German trustfulness had been thoroughly exploited by official propaganda, and all ranks had an intense conviction of victory.

It is understandable that both the troops and their commander should have been confident as they stood almost within view of the Eiffel Tower. In less than three months they had inflicted not far from a million casualties. As trophies they could point to 200,000 prisoners, 2,500 guns and fabulous captures of supplies. Yet even at this moment Ludendorff had lost his race against time. For the Americans were already in action on the Marne, and new arrivals at the rate of 300,000 a month had more than made good the total losses of the Allies.

THE ALLIED MARCH TO VICTORY

Warned by the example of England, which clung to an inadequate volunteer system for nearly two years, the United States passed a universal conscription law soon after declaring war. While the first recruits were in training, four divisions of regulars, marines and National Guard militia volunteers landed in France before the end of 1917. They completed their training in quiet sectors, and the nation's first casualties occurred that autumn in the minor combats of trench warfare.

General John J. Pershing's plans for maturing his expeditionary force were interrupted in March by the Allied reverses in Picardy.

Without hesitation he offered his half-trained troops to the older Allies to be used as they saw fit.

Despite the urgency, Foch wisely kept them in reserve until late in May. Then occurred the first American attack of the war when a division of regulars took the village of Cantigny in the Montdidier sector. A few days later, as the foe threatened Paris, another division of regulars and marines counterattacked so often and so fiercely at Château-Thierry as to throw Ludendorff's latest drive off balance.

In contrast to the active partnership of the American fleet, the land forces had been chiefly a moral support to their Allies up to this time. Now during these first troubled days of June the young army distinguished itself in a difficult assignment. Fighting under French command, supported by French artillery and planes, the Americans gave the enemy no rest on the Marne. It has been justly observed that their inexperience often resulted in too many casualties, but never has their resolution been questioned.

New units arriving from the United States were sent to the front soon after they disembarked. By July seven divisions (each the equivalent in numbers of two European divisions) had seen action between Reims and Soissons, while two more reinforced the British in Picardy.

Although he later denied that his calculations were upset by the Americans, Ludendorff undoubtedly hastened his next effort in the fear of losing the initiative. In May he launched the Chemin des Dames attack as a diversion while preparing the real blow in Flanders, where the British stood so perilously near to the sea. But the unexpected successes on the Aisne and Marne were a snare, since they lured him into using up reserves for the creation of his most vulnerable salient. Hence in July he returned to the original conception by planning a second diversion in the south to mask a final bid for victory in Flanders.

The attempts were presented to the army and people as the *Friedensturm*, or peace offensive: the supreme effort which would compel the enemy to grant favorable terms. This approach proved so convincing that the troops were keyed up to a sacrificial pitch on the eve of July 15. Forty-seven divisions had orders to attack between Château-Thierry and the Argonne, supported by the heaviest concentration of artillery the war had known up to this time. So terrific was the bombardment which began at midnight of France's *Fête Nationale* that somber observers in Paris watched a man-made aurora borealis light up the eastern sky.

Nevertheless, the assault failed dismally in the Champagne sector, where Pétain had long ago prepared an elastic system of defenses made deadly by mustard gas and the war's most extensive use of land mines. The German losses in this quarter were estimated at fully ten times the French casualties. West of Reims the attackers managed to cross the Marne near Château-Thierry and advance three miles toward Épernay, their objective. Then the desperate American counterattacks of the next two days forced a withdrawal.

Ludendorff could not have realized, as he fell back across the river, that he had lost the initiative forever. For the next day brought Foch's dramatic riposte at Soissons, and from that moment the Allies continued to rain blows until they won the war.

So far, in his brief term as generalissimo, Foch had not enjoyed a popular triumph even among his own countrymen. Yet while parrying the foe's thrusts, he never lost his almost religious faith in the offensive. His tact helped to adjust the conflicting problems of the Allies, and an unfailing optimism in the crisis further added to his fitness for the supreme command.

The timeliness of his "revenge" made it seem an inspiration of the hour, but Foch had long before decided to smash in the western face of the enemy's Soissons-Reims salient. Even at this date he took great risks in disposing of his strength, for the British were left with fifteen divisions to face thirty-one on the critical Flanders front, now suspected to be Ludendorff's next objective. Never during the war did the success of an entire cause hang so much on a single day's fighting; and Foch chose the two most experienced American divisions, composed of regulars and marines, to act as the spearhead of assault along with General Mangin's Moroccans. For purposes of secrecy, these troops were rushed up to the front on the night of July 17 in long columns of trucks. Without pausing for food or rest, they deployed at dawn to begin the decisive counterstroke known as the second battle of the Marne. The absence of artillery preparation made the surprise complete as the Franco-American forces, following a creeping barrage, broke through to a depth of four miles.

All historians have exclaimed over the strategic resemblance of this action to the first battle of the Marne. Again at a critical moment the Germans exposed their right flank, and a second time they paid dearly for underestimating the enemy's resources. Even the locale did not differ, for on both occasions the small river Ourcq was the scene of the counterstroke. Only a single contrast is apparent, for in 1914 the victors had been too exhausted to press their advantage. In 1918 they redoubled their efforts as half a million American troops took part in a ten-day convergent advance which inflicted 100,000 casualties, including 35,000 prisoners. As a consequence Ludendorff had to cancel his plans for the Flemish offensive (already scheduled for July 20) and hasten a withdrawal from the Marne to the Vesle.

On August 2 he completed his forced evacuation of the Soissons-Reims salient. Six days later the British struck in Picardy to gain a victory which the German commander called the "black day" of his army. And on August 14, despite his confidence of a month before, he privately admitted to the emperor that the Central Powers could not hope to win the war. Thus did events rush toward a climax with a velocity which would have been thought fantastic during the long months of deadlock.

The Germans between Albert and Moreuil had no intimation of peril on the morning of August 8 when hundreds of enemy tanks emerged from the mist without the ceremony of a preliminary bombardment. Simultaneously the 2,000 British guns laid down a creeping barrage for the advance of 13 divisions, largely Canadian and Australian, on a 15-mile front. Even more disconcerting, armored cars filled with automatic riflemen spread confusion in the rear areas, so that a German army corps staff had its breakfast interrupted by a hail of bullets. The British reserves followed closely behind the shock troops to consolidate the first day's advance of six miles. Only north of the Somme did the attack meet much opposition; and on August 9 an American infantry brigade stormed Chipilly Ridge after a thirty-hour overnight march.

At a glance it is hard to see why this offensive, brilliant as it was, should have plunged the German supreme command into such gloom. Neither the territorial gains nor the bag of 21,000 prisoners at a cost of 20,000 casualties would appear to be a crippling blow. But the German generals were alarmed at the methods, not the results. Twice in three weeks the Allies had demonstrated that they could smash through with great masses of tanks—352 in the attack of July 18, and 456 on August 8. In the new "whippet," moreover, both the French and British now had a light tank capable of making six miles an hour under combat conditions. Both armies followed the Cambrai pattern of tactics, and the antitank weapons of 1918 gave the enemy no prospect of an adequate defense. Nor did German shortages of labor and materials allow any hope of competing with the foe in the manufacture of the new weapon.

Quite as dismaying was the improvement in Allied strategy. Where deception and surprise had been the exception, they were now the rule.

Thus a calm sector might be overrun the next morning by troops brought up in the darkness by endless caravans of motor vehicles. Foch's attack doctrines, so costly during a siege war, at last had found their moment. Changing conditions likewise justified the new audacity revealed by Haig's instructions to his generals, "Risks which only a month ago would have been criminal to incur ought now to be incurred as a duty."

As a final menace, the Allies proved that they could use as well as win a victory. Much as the Franco-American forces had followed up the July 18 triumph, the British added to their August 8 gains by wiping out the salient pointing at Amiens. The results were almost identical, for during the next few weeks the enemy's losses totaled 100,000, including 40,000 prisoners. The French joined in the offensive south of Moreuil, and by the end of the month Roye, Péronne and Bapaume had been taken.

No longer could the hard-pressed foe pursue a strategy of interior lines by shifting reserves from one threatened point to another. On September 1 General Plumer's offensive in Flanders reduced the salient between Ypres and Arras. And on the twelfth, at the opposite end of the line, the American forces fought their first action as an independent army by pinching off the St. Mihiel bulge which had interrupted the Paris-Nancy railway ever since 1914.

The new organization had not come up to maturity without growing pains. General Pershing, in his devotion to professional ideals, sometimes made his preference for regulars so obvious as to offend the great majority of citizen-soldiers. On the other hand, he won the admiration of his countrymen by refusing to allow the army to be dispersed under French and British command. This prejudice came as a shock to French generals, who were accustomed to a rather meek attitude on the part of allies. The clash of opinions led to a stormy interview when Foch tried to limit the St. Mihiel attack after final preparations had been made. The generalissimo objected, not without reason, to a divergent drive toward the northeast. Instead, he proposed a mere local St. Mihiel operation as the prelude to a converging offensive of the British and American armies—a vast pincers movement with two hundred miles separating the wings in Flanders and on the Meuse.

The controversy ended in a characteristic compromise when Pershing adopted all possible features of both plans. So boundless was his faith in the American soldier that he promised to wipe out the St. Mihiel salient on September 12 and be ready for the greater offensive within two weeks—a test in strategic scene-shifting which had never been met by any of the older armies!

Fortunately for the national honor, performance did not fall short of pride. The St. Mihiel attack caught the enemy in the act of withdrawing; and during a two-day attack the American forceps closed on 15,000

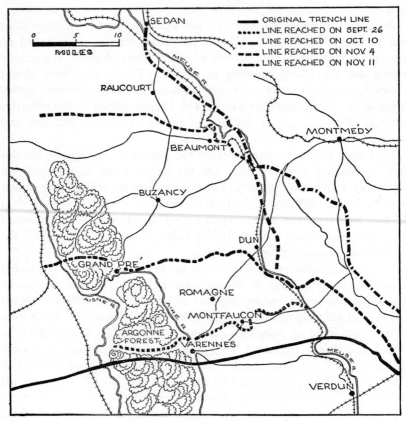

The Meuse-Argonne Campaign

prisoners and 450 guns. At a cost of 7,000 casualties, the success ranks as one of the most thrifty of the war. The next ten nights were devoted to the transfer of half a million men in army trucks a distance of 100 kilometers to the new front. And on the twenty-sixth, though some units arrived on the eve of battle, the Americans opened the Meuse-Argonne drive by breaking through to a maximum depth of five miles in a complete surprise.

It is not likely that a greener army ever began a major offensive, for only three of the nine divisions had seen much action prior to St. Mihiel. But the enemy having been deceived into expecting an attack in the Woëvre area, his lightly held Meuse-Argonne lines gave way at the first shock of greater numbers supported by 2,700 guns and 189 whippet tanks.

As yet no army had solved the strategic problem of maintaining its momentum after the first rush, and the American woes began on September 28, after the Germans were reinforced. During the next six weeks the nation's greatest battle of history proved to be another Wilderness—a dark and bloody struggle against a cunning foe holding a cramped front of ridges, ravines and dense thickets. The German defenses in depth, stretching back for 14 miles, included the great Kriemhilde line and three lesser systems linking up heights. Tanks could seldom be used on this ground, and the artillery lost much of its effectiveness. Hence it remained for the infantry to pit flesh and nerve against machine gun nests.

The Americans slugging away at an invisible enemy could not have supposed that peace was so near. Yet even as their commander planned on his army bearing the brunt of the 1919 spring offensives, Germany had begun to disintegrate. The iron-willed generals were first to break, not the apathetic civilians toiling in munitions factories or the retreating troops. Ludendorff, the very incarnation of daemonic energy, suffered a collapse at his headquarters on September 29. His officers found him writhing on the floor with foam on his lips, and that night he urged that Germany capitulate. Hindenburg, no less shaken, declared that "a peace offer to our enemies must be issued at once." Thus on October 3 the nation's military heads came to an open admission of defeat when a tentative appeal for an armistice went to President Wilson.

The events which influenced the decision had happened with incredible rapidity. In September, after long inactivity, the Allied expeditionary force at Salonika struck northward to compel the surrender of Bulgaria on the twenty-ninth. The next day Turkey sued for terms, having been shattered by Allenby's victory in Palestine. On the Western Front, as the Americans inched their way forward, the British left wing broke the Hindenburg line with astonishing ease. Aided by two American divisions, the attackers gave Ludendorff a lesson in his own infiltration tactics. Tank assaults created the gaps, then the infantry poured through to take the foe from the flank and rear. By October 5 the whole mighty system of concrete defenses had fallen with the further loss of 36,000 prisoners and 350 guns. As a result the French forces which formed the strategic centre were able to occupy hundreds of towns and villages hastily evacuated by an outflanked foe.

Nor were the minor Allies denied a part in the final act. The little Belgian army, after retaining a scrap of its own soil throughout the war, joined General Plumer's advance on Ghent. The Italians, who had repulsed an Austrian offensive on the Piave in June, now launched a great drive of their own which split the opposing forces in two. Soon the retreat turned into a rout, and on October 30 the tottering empire asked for an armistice, having miraculously become the last of the Central Powers to admit defeat.

After four gloomy years the Allied peoples were dazzled by the sudden brightness. Even the old-school generals, the die-hards who insisted that tanks would never supplant their favorite arm, could exult as the dispatches came from Palestine. For General Allenby had brought off the war's greatest victory of annihilation, and to the cavalry belonged the glory. Fighting on ground suited to their tactics, the British mounted forces advanced 300 miles in a month to take 75,000 prisoners. Less apparent but no less potent in the final reckoning were the modern guerrilla methods introduced by that gifted scholar and explorer, T. E. Lawrence, the organizer of the Arab revolt.

Only on the Allied right wing in France did fortune seem to frown. Pershing removed generals right and left, and gradually he replaced the new divisions with battle-hardened troops. Still, more than two-thirds of the distance to the objectives remained to be covered at the end of ten days.

Out of the travail came the most advanced aviation tactics of the war. General William Mitchell, commanding the American squadrons, attributed the painful progress to the immunity of a hidden foe from artillery fire. As a remedy he put into effect his own conception of an air-borne artillery arm. On October 10, to cover American crossings of the Meuse, two formations of 322 and 338 planes dropped a total of 81 tons of bombs on enemy munition dumps and troop concentrations in a single day. No such terrific blow had ever been dealt from the air before, and American forces not only crossed the river but also passed the barrier of the Argonne Forest.

Actually, of course, the pressure on this sensitive area had a tremendous influence on operations elsewhere in France. In the realization that they must defend the Rhine instead of the frontier if the attack prevailed, the Germans employed fully a fourth of their divisional strength on the twenty-mile front. November 1 brought the crisis, following an interlude in which Pershing again overhauled his army. Then in a leap of six miles the Americans advanced through Buzancy to drive a fatal wedge in the opposing centre.

The struggle which had cost the new army a total of 117,000 killed and wounded now took on the character of a pursuit. Meanwhile occurred the mutinies in the imperial navy and the abdication of the kaiser. And as the envoys left Berlin to treat for an armistice, it seemed more than a coincidence that Pershing's men were storming the heights commanding Sedan—the battered town whose name had once been the symbol of a Germanic triumph.

IV

GERMANY WINS THE PEACE

Every up-to-date dictionary should say that "peace" and "war" mean the same thing. . . . It may even reasonably be said that the intensely sharp competitive preparation for war by the nations is the real war, permanent, unceasing; and that the battles are only a sort of public verification of the mastery gained during the "peace" interval.

—WILLIAM JAMES

ON THE morning of November 11, 1918, the unreal hush that fell over the battlefields seemed the first promise of enduring peace. The millions of citizen-soldiers suddenly released from peril supposed of course that life would go on much as it had before. In common with all postwar generations, they did not suspect that peace has its own strife and sacrifices.

It has been remarked by historians that German aggressors of past centuries were twice so fortunate as to be rescued from disaster by their enemies. In 1762 Frederick the Great had admittedly been defeated when the death of Russia's empress made possible an immediate alliance with his most formidable foe. Again in 1807 the beaten kingdom was saved from destruction at the hands of Napoleon by the intercession of the Emperor Alexander.

The Allied nations went even further during the twenty years following the Armistice. After disarming Germany, they looked on sympathetically while that country laid the foundations of a military might which would soon be superior to their combined strength. And after demanding reparations in the peace treaty, they collected but a fraction of the total sum while "lending" Germany a much larger amount to be spent almost openly for rearmament.

Future generations will doubtless find this period one of the most incredible chapters of history. For the years from 1918 to 1938, when viewed in perspective, can only appear as a brief and troubled truce linking two phases of the same war.

Germany's intentions were made sufficiently clear from the beginning. When the beaten troops paraded in Berlin, President Ebert of the republic reviewed them at the Brandenburger Tor, decorated as if for a national triumph. "As you return unconquered from the field of battle, I salute you!" he cried.

These words, uttered months before the signing of the Versailles Treaty, may be accepted as the nation's declaration of the next war. Surprising as it may seem, the military events of 1918 proved no embarrassment to German leaders who explained that the army had been betrayed at home, not vanquished in France. And since most of the people had remained stanch after the generals admitted defeat, the "stab in the back" was publicly charged by Ludendorff to Jews, Jesuits and Freemasons within the country—the minorities which have been denounced by every minor Führer since "Father" Jahn.

Although the Armistice terms required immediate demobilization, the republic showed its teeth within four months by calling for volunteers in a proclamation of January, 1919. The new German units took the name of *Freikorps* after the bands of 1813 which had furtively armed against Napoleon. Their leaders made no secret of similar motives, and the response of the people is shown by the growth of the army to a strength of 450,000 during the winter. Not only did former imperial officers resume their authority, but many of the units went by the names of old regiments. Nor could the full approval of the republic be doubted when President Ebert reviewed well-armed veteran troops the following June—before the much-criticized terms of the Versailles Treaty were announced.

In reality the German warmongers were vexed by the relative mildness of the conditions imposed by the victors. Adolf Hitler has seldom been credited with a sense of humor, but in his autobiography *Mein Kampf* he exhibits a sardonic glee when relating his attacks on the treaty. Then an unknown Munich spy and informer, the future leader had just discovered his powers as an orator. Pacifist sentiment seemed to him the greatest stumbling block to rearmament, for the reasonable citizen had to admit that the Versailles terms were not severe as compared to those visited by a victorious Germany on Russia and Rumania in 1918. Other orators had dodged this delicate subject, but Hitler prided himself on a bold approach when addressing his early meetings. By appealing to the emotions of his hearers with a message of German racial superiority, he managed to convince them that the Treaty of Brest-Litovsk had been just, while the Versailles Treaty was the weapon of "international Jews" conspiring for Germany's ruination.

The national duality never revealed itself in a more tragic light than during the next few critical years. All authorities agree that millions of Germans, perhaps even a majority, were weary of war and willing to take the peaceful road to recovery. Opposed to them at first was a determined clique of army officers who could not reconcile themselves to the loss of their old aristocratic privileges.

Ludendorff himself set the tone in his *Der Totale Krieg*, a post-Armistice treatise presenting doctrines of total war which made Clausewitz' theories seem old-fashioned. Bluntly differing from the former master's deference to state policies, the loser of 1918 summed up the new German military code in a few words, "War is the supreme expression of the national will to live and therefore politics must serve war-making."

The *Putsches* which exploded like bombs during these years were nearly all instigated by former officers with the aim of overthrowing the despised republic. Despite their aristocratic pretensions and scorn of politics, they courted the support of the mob while associating themselves with the lowest rabble rousers of the slums. General von Lüttwitz led a volunteer army to Berlin in 1920 and actually seized the government for a few days after the flight of President Ebert. Ludendorff took a leading part in two other attempts, marching with Hitler and Goering in the unsuccessful Munich "beer-hall" *Putsch* of 1923.

The peoples of democratic countries might view such uprisings as isolated disturbances, but the officers of Germany knew better. They referred to this preliminary phase as the "war in peace," and it is significant that men guilty of open treason were seldom condemned either by law or public opinion. The next world war had actually begun.

The Sinews of World War II

It has been estimated that the interval of "peace" between the two world struggles saw an average of a war a year in various parts of the globe. Some of them, like the Soviet repulse in Poland and Turkey's defeat of Greece, might have been called major conflicts in normal times. But none had as much influence on the future as the victory won by "defenseless" Germany in the fields of finance and propaganda.

There is still a question as to how much manipulation entered into the German inflation crisis of 1923. At any rate the financiers and industrialists as a group emerged unscathed, and many profited enormously. The middle classes paid with their life savings as the value of the paper mark sank until four trillion were worth a dollar. Then at a stroke of the pen came "stabilization," which left millions of ruined and embittered citizens, once the bulwark of conservatism, in a mood to welcome a dictator.

The former Allies could not be called harsh creditors. In 1921 the total bill for reparations had voluntarily been scaled down by more than 40 per cent. Two years later the financial crash, occurring as the French troops occupied the Ruhr to enforce coal deliveries, gave Germany's bankers their opening. Under the masterly leadership of Dr. Hjalmar Schacht, they begin a campaign of "organizing sympathy" which eventually netted their country a handsome profit on the entire reparations transaction.

This outcome is a testimonial to the fact that truth is the best propaganda in time of war. For Schacht's astonishing victory owed in large measure to a change of heart experienced by recent foes. Middle-class Britons and Americans resented the official lies which had once goaded them to such extremes as refusing to listen to German music. In 1914, for instance, it should have sufficed to tell the truth about the German occupation of Belgium. While the invading troops had been well disciplined, enough cases of official frightfulness occurred to make a revolting story. Instead of being presented with these facts, civilians were treated to fantastic tales of women and children being mutilated, supposedly as one of the diversions of a brutish soldiery.

Allied leaders of high ideals, swept away by the passions of the hour, lent their names in good faith to arraignments which at best were based on rumors. The eminent Lord Bryce, author of *The American Commonwealth*, removed the last doubts in the United States when he endorsed many of the accusations as chairman of a committee examining the evidence.

From uncritical error it was but a step to outright distortion. All too soon the limits of credibility and decency were reached with the legend of the "German corpse factory"—a macabre tale which represented that the enemy utilized his slain for purposes of recovering the fats needed by munitions makers.

The difficulty of keeping popular hatred at a white heat throughout a long struggle is apparent from such excesses, and the desirability might have been questioned. The inevitable reaction came after the Armistice, when thousands of Allied soldiers returned to their homes in a mood of skepticism. They had encountered little firsthand evidence of the enemy outrages which drillmasters cited to work up the proper fury for bayonet practice. For that matter, few of them had ever seen a man bayoneted, though their sedentary generals retained a sentimental faith in the ability of "cold steel" to solve a machine-gun war.

Even some of the more convincing atrocity charges, when subjected to analysis, could be ascribed to Allied urgency rather than enemy ferocity. The vulnerability of the submarine made it a suicidal risk to warn intended victims, and lack of space limited the possibilities of saving lives. Yet the U-boats nearly decided the war while inflicting about 17,000 fatalities—a modest total as compared to the German deaths which might have been traced to the Allied naval blockade.

By 1923 the pendulum of public opinion had swung far in the opposite direction. Few people remembered that Belgian hostages actually had been butchered, Russian captives starved and overworked, French industries systematically destroyed, and whole populations of eastern Europe held in virtual slavery. These crimes were not the acts of individuals who could be described as sentimentalists more often than sadists. They were official military policies carried out with the habitual obedience of the German people, as Ludendorff made clear in his subsequent treatise on total war.

The occupation of the Ruhr proved to be mild in contrast, and France had the justification that many of her mines, destroyed without a shadow of military reason, were still unproductive. Nevertheless, the Germans seemed martyrs to a world weary of violence; and the first serious rift between the former Allies occurred when British and American opinion condemned the occupation.

Schacht did not need a second invitation. Presenting a highly colored picture of an avaricious France plundering a helpless Germany, he won a great propaganda victory over those very Britons and Americans who were fiercest in denouncing Allied propaganda of the last war. As the first rewards his country received a loan of $200,000,000 under the Dawes Plan, plus a breathing spell of four years in which reparations payments were to be much reduced.

It might have been supposed that some of this money would benefit the impoverished middle classes. Instead, $10,000,000 went immediately to the Krupp munitions works, and $12,000,000 to Herr Thyssen, who was soon to endow Hitlerism. Chancellor Stresemann had much to do with the next gains at the expense of late enemies. In a diary entry of 1924 (quoted by Borsky in *The Story of German Reparations*) he filed an interesting suggestion offered him by an American banker:

> The thing to do now is to win over the individual American sub-scriber to the idea of an American loan. The granting of a loan would give us an army of 300,000 people in America who would make propaganda for Germany because they would be interested in her welfare.

The persuasive Dr. Schacht proved to be just the man for such a mission. From 1925 to 1930 he became a transatlantic commuter, busily conferring at the White House and addressing the more important luncheon clubs. Chamber of Commerce executives were particularly impressed by his firm stand for democratic ideals, and it was a shock only a few years later when he lent himself to Hitler's strong-armed financial policies with the same decorous zeal.

Germany's financial flank attacks of the late 1920's are recounted succinctly in Lilian T. Mowrer's *Rip Tide of Aggression*. At intervals the artful Dr. Schacht reminded his creditors that a balky pump needs frequent priming. If they showed signs of obduracy, he darkly hinted that another collapse might plunge his country into Bolshevism, dragging all Europe down with her into ruin. This veiled threat usually sufficed to send British and American bankers hurrying to their money-bags. As commercial loans poured into Germany, Schacht taught the lenders to refer to reparations as "political" debts, with the intimation that nothing would be left for private obligations if they were paid.

Now an orgy of spending began in a nation which solemnly reiterated that it could not honor its commitments. Public buildings, parks, high-ways and athletic stadia were constructed without regard to cost. Housing developments in industrial regions were laid out on a scale that made similar projects in war-scarred France appear flimsy. Seven great planetaria were built at a time when the United States could afford but one, and Germany's state railways adopted equipment too expensive for England or France. Throughout this strange era of prosperity, the German citizen paid slightly more than one-fourth of the taxes which burdened an Englishman. And in 1927, before it seemed prudent to withhold such facts from prying creditors, national savings of nearly two billion dollars were reported by the Reichskredit Bank.

By 1930, indeed, Germany had received so many transfusions of British and American capital that inflation again resulted, this time without a suspicion of manipulation. Wild spending and overproduction brought on unemployment; and as a remedy the Young Plan provided a new loan of $300,000,000, while further reducing reparations payments. In view of depression conditions in America and Britain at this time, the Germans did not experience unusual hardships. But few people in Germany, least of all President Hindenburg, had ever shown any faith in government by the people. The republic had long been dead, and the remains were buried with indecent haste when Adolf Hitler became chancellor in 1933.

Even as he began open preparations for war, his potential victims still hugged the delusion that Germany was broken and impoverished. Yet as mistress of half Europe in the last conflict, wringing most of her supplies from occupied regions held in a harsh bondage, the loser emerged with a lighter burden of debt than any of the major victors. The amount was largely wiped out in 1923 at the expense of her own middle classes, so that the state and private loans of the next few years, most of which were never repaid, represented a clear even if dishonorable profit.

After making himself dictator, Hitler found Schacht useful in carrying out even more gainful financial policies based on bribery, coercion and underselling. And in 1939, though the nation's creditors had been bilked by pleas of poverty, the Führer could reveal to his adoring people that he had spent forty billion marks on rearmament.

PACIFISM AS A CAUSE OF WAR

This boast came as a challenge to British and American pacifists who supported their ethical arguments with the contention that "war does not pay." Such a premise could not be expected to convince Hitler's followers. In 1871 Germany had emerged as a great power after wresting two provinces from France in addition to an indemnity which returned a profit above all military expenses. Even in 1939, after losing the last war, Germans could claim that ever since 1914, with the exception of the five years between the Armistice and the Dawes Plan, the country had progressed partly at the expense of other nations.

But if the bankers of the democracies were duped, so were many of the pacifists and liberals. During the interlude between wars it was a prevailing belief that Germany meant only to right the supposed wrongs of the Versailles Treaty. Nonaggression doctrines went to such morbid and unreal extremes that hundreds of American university students pledged themselves not to take up arms even in defense of their own soil. A few years later, some of these same young men died in flaming planes over German and Japanese territory.

The irony of this outcome is not softened by the fact that the United States has produced the greatest pacifist of modern times. In a single essay, published in 1910, William James gave his countrymen a philosophy of peace which has made *The Moral Equivalent of War* a classic. Differing with zealots who held war to be an international crime or disease, he believed that many martial virtues could and should be preserved:

A permanently successful peace-economy cannot be a simple pleasure-economy. In the more or less socialistic future towards which mankind seems to be drifting we must still subject ourselves collectively to those severities which answer to our real position on this only partly hospitable globe. We must make new energies and hardihoods continue the manliness to which the military mind so faithfully clings.

Where his contemporaries urged such cure-alls as universal disarmament or an international police force, James suggested a "moral equivalent of war" in the possibility of drafting young men, rich and poor alike, for national labor projects ". . . to get the childishness knocked out of them and to come back into society with healthier sympathies and soberer ideas."

British and American pacifists of the 1930's seemed to be idealizing the very "sheep's paradise" which the Harvard philosopher deplored At any rate, a survey of their doctrines reveals an almost pathological emphasis on comfort and safety. The causes of war are ascribed, at least by insinuation, to the plots of bankers, diplomats and munitions makers.

Such propaganda helped to create a "pleasure-economy" in the 1920's which remained deaf to the loudest threats of aggression. The fact that

Mussolini's trains ran on time impressed many Americans and Britons more deeply than the castor-oil executions ordered by a brutal Fascist tyranny. Even when the first blow was struck—the Japanese invasion of Manchuria on a cynical pretext in 1931—the warnings of Secretary of State Stimson had no effect. People who had been persuaded that all war was wrong did not protest at the seizure of thirty million Chinese and a fertile area twice as large as California.

All too soon the respectability of the pacifist organizations exposed them to "boring-from-within" tactics by propagandists of a less naïve character. Both Fascists and Communists hid behind the white mantle of universal peace, and new "cultural fronts" were created until many a worthy humanist became an unwitting crusader for revolution. Such possibilities were not overlooked by the forces of aggression, with the result that more than one high-sounding movement proved to be a Trojan horse sheltering agents paid by the Germans or Japanese.

Prophets of the Coming Warfare

Generalship had been in bad enough repute in the democratic nations since 1918, and strictures in the name of pacifism handicapped military preparations. As a consequence, three of the most gifted tactical theorists of their generation had to combat public apathy as well as professional conservatism.

General J. F. C. Fuller of Great Britain, Colonel Charles de Gaulle of France, and General William Mitchell of the United States—all three had distinguished themselves in World War I. Fuller, it may be recalled, had taken a leading part in planning the battle of Cambrai in 1917, usually accepted as the genesis of tank warfare. The following summer, as chief general staff officer of the tank corps, he worked out the details of a gigantic blow on a front of from 80 to 160 kilometers. Hundreds of fast tanks, accompanied by bombing planes, were to rip through the main enemy lines and surprise corps headquarters, railheads and vital communications. While these machines paralyzed the brain and nerve centres, some 2,500 heavy tanks accompanied by infantry in armored cars would follow up by crushing the body and limbs of the opposing army.

General Mitchell had meanwhile submitted an idea for an equally devastating surprise to be carried out by the opposite Allied wing. Commanding 1,500 aircraft at St. Mihiel, including 414 bombers, he evolved the principle of airborne artillery which he applied so effectively in the Argonne. The parachute was still at the experimental stage in 1918, but

Mitchell envisioned airborne infantry taking part in Pershing's proposed advance on Metz the following spring. Sixty squadrons of bombers, each of the 1,200 planes carrying ten men, were to make a dawn flight over the enemy lines, the great armada being protected by fighters. The 12,000 specially trained troops would then descend in parachutes to attack from the rear while the main American force delivered a frontal assault. Mitchell calculated that a total of 2,400 machine guns and their ammunition could be taken, and that the airborne army could be maintained by supplies dropped from planes.

Neither of these two plans can be dismissed as a mere dream. Foch had already approved Fuller's tank assault for the spring of 1919, and Pershing assured Mitchell of full support in organizing and training the parachute troops.

After the war the American brigadier flew several thousand miles a week while his restless mind strove to create the world's most modern air force. As a pilot he established a new world speed record of 224 miles an hour in 1922; and as a leader he experimented before that date with the dive bomber, the two-ton bomb, the aerial cannon, the ski-equipped plane for northern service, and the fighter armed with eight machine guns.

It had been a shock to Mitchell in 1918 that not a single high-ranking general of the American forces showed enough enterprise to inspect the enemy positions from the air. Three years later he learned more about the brass-hat mentality after announcing that his bombers could sink the largest battleship.

Several German warships remained to be destroyed according to treaty terms, and official tests were held off the Virginia coast in July, 1921. It was of course the duty of Navy officers to be skeptical until Mitchell proved his case, but their attitude betrayed an unwarranted hostility as the airmen sank a submarine and cruiser with comparative ease. There remained the sturdy battleship *Ostfriesland,* and in twenty-one minutes Mitchell's planes wrote a new chapter in tactical history by sending it to the bottom with six one-ton bombs. Without a direct hit having been made, the underwater explosions of the "near misses" ripped great holes through the four steel skins of the hull.

As the shuddering wreck went down, the observers felt that they were watching the end of an era. Although battleships and cruisers had carried seaplanes during the last two years of the World War, the machines were forced to land on the nearest shore. The first landing on the deck of a ship occurred in 1917, and just before the Armistice the British launched the converted liner *Argus* as the world's first aircraft carrier. Naval men of 1921 were still dubious as to the new type of warship, however, until they had more evidence as to the effects of bombs. The tests provoked by Mitchell thus had their influence on sea tactics, though he met resentment from officers later described by Admiral Sims as "hidebound, unfitted and uneducated." The retired naval commander, a lifelong champion of tactical progress, declared himself for carriers and a strong air arm; and in 1925 the converted battle cruisers *Saratoga* and *Lexington* were launched with a capacity of from seventy to eighty planes.

No doubt Mitchell's methods of publicizing the issue were flamboyant and often insubordinate, but genius is customarily pardoned by history after its ideas are adopted. In 1925 President Coolidge ordered the flier court-martialed, though editorial comment had it that the Army and Navy were actually on trial. Mitchell listed a hundred recommendations he had made for the betterment of military aviation, all of which had been ignored. He testified as to the strained relations between army and navy officers of Pearl Harbor, warning that the vital Pacific base could be surprised. And as the climax of a trial reported in headlines, the defendant accused his accusers:

There are two kinds of treason. The first is constitutional and means betraying one's own country. The second means action whereby a party "betrays their trust." The Army and Navy are treasonable under that head for not giving proper improvements to the air service. Of course, I refer to the system and not to any individual.

The judges, having little choice but to find Mitchell guilty of indiscipline, sentenced him to a five-year suspension from duty without pay. The aviator promptly resigned, and his remaining ten years were devoted to carrying on the crusade by means of lectures and articles in periodicals. Before his death from illness in 1936 he had seen many of his ideas adopted, and the experience of the second World War has upheld the judgment of General Johnson Hagood, who declared that Mitchell "has done more for aviation in the army than any other man since Wright invented the airplane."

During the same period the British tank officer found his own army undergoing a like decay, and he reacted as vigorously as Mitchell. In *The Reformation of War*, appearing in 1923, General Fuller compared the British organization to the heir of a stately but outdated Jacobean mansion:

It has been in the family for three hundred years, and he is naturally very loath to part with it and inhabit some horrible ferro-concrete house. He cannot afford to modernize it, and, to make both ends meet, he shuts up room after room, and so "economizes" his reduced income and hopes for better times. He cannot tear himself away from its memories and traditions and family ghosts, and so the dry-rot creeps through its foundations and the rain percolates through its roof.

Fuller's *Tanks in the Great War* (1920) is probably the best work on the early progress of the landship. From this tactical treatise he went on to books such as *The Dragon's Teeth* and *War and Western Civilization*, both published in 1932, which deal as much with social, political and economic aspects as the military. In an age of myopic pacifism the professional soldier inquired more thoroughly into causes and effects than many of war's opponents.

Like Mitchell, the British theorist appealed to the public rather than to any esoteric cult of military readers. In the preface to *The Reformation of War* he announced his purpose:

I have not written this book for military monks, but for civilians, who pay for their alchemy and mysteries. In war there is nothing mysterious, for it is the most common-sense of all the sciences. . . . If it possess a mystery, then that mystery is unprogressiveness, for it is a mystery that, in a profession which may, at any moment, demand the risk of danger and death, men are found willing to base their work on the campaigns of Waterloo and Sedan when the only possible war which confronts them is the next one.

Fuller's published writings during the interlude between wars amount to well over a million words, including works on military history and biography as well as tactical treatises. It would be hard to cite a war that is not discussed in the encyclopedic range of his critical comments. Above all, his books are notable for their insight into the nature of the storm which burst upon a dazed world in 1939. He made no pretensions to being a prophet, and some of his speculations, particularly as to the future of chemical warfare, were not borne out by the next conflict. But in an era when the English-speaking peoples drugged themselves with delusions of an impregnable defensive, Fuller insisted that a modern nation could be overwhelmed by a mechanized and aerial attack.

In 1917, when his theories vexed cavalry generals, he was accused of being "visionary." Hence it is instructive to glance at the results achieved by him and his associates of the world's first tank corps. The following statistics, quoted from *The Reformation of War,* are self-explanatory when it is recalled that the tactics of armored warfare had to await their opportunity until 1918:

July to November, 1916—475,000 British casualties as the price of 90 square miles, or an average of 5,277 to the mile;

July to November, 1917—370,000 casualties to gain 45 square miles, an average of 8,222;

July to November, 1918—345,000 casualties and 4,000 square miles, an average of 86.

Four years after the Armistice the British soldier was appointed chief instructor at the Staff College, and in 1926 he became military assistant to the chief of the imperial General Staff. The lectures of his *Field Service Regulations III* (republished in the United States under the title of *Armored Warfare* in 1943) were also adopted for study by the general staffs of the German, Russian and Czechoslovak armies. In his own country, unfortunately, he ceased to be officially regarded as a prophet when soldiers and civilians of the 1930's placed their faith in a defensive gospel. Fuller, the apostle of the mechanized offensive, was retired on half pay with the rank of major general. His subsequent adventures in politics were no more fortunate than those of most soldiers, and the outbreak of the new conflict found him writing critical articles for a London newspaper.

Colonel Charles de Gaulle of France, much younger than Fuller and Mitchell, was graduated with honors from St. Cyr. Assigned in 1914 as a lieutenant to an infantry regiment commanded by Colonel Henri Pétain, the young career officer distinguished himself as a combat leader in World War I.

During the 1920's he deplored the postwar spirit of defeatism which found expression in the Maginot Line—a great underground steel and concrete barrier which too many Frenchmen trusted to stop the hereditary enemy if he struck again. De Gaulle did not share in the prevailing belief that the Germans would choose to wreck themselves against the Maginot Line, which stretched only from the Rhine to Sedan in its greatest width. He warned in *The Army of the Future* that his countrymen courted disaster by depending on the Ardennes to halt invaders striking in the gap between the main French and Belgian fortifications. These wooded hills, he declared, would not stop mechanized columns; and instead of relying upon permanent works, France would be safer behind an entirely armored force of only 100,000 career soldiers—the "army of the future" urged by his book:

As compared to the total number of troops that France sent into action in the month of August, 1914, this army will possess a firing capacity three times larger, nearly ten times its speed and an immeasurably greater degree of protection. When one adds that the whole will normally operate on one-tenth of its front and that the professional soldiers get enormously increased results from their equipment, one can gather some idea of the power which the professional army of tomorrow will be able to wield.

De Gaulle's theories made few converts in a country which placed its faith in frontier fortifications. Great Britain had no Maginot Line, but the nation's most widely read military writers stressed the advantages of the defensive until the public believed that an aggressor would suffer crippling casualties.

THE PROPHET OF TERROR BOMBING

It remained for an Italian theorist to shape the military future to a greater extent than any of his contemporaries. As early as 1909 Giulio Douhet had predicted that aircraft would take a decisive part in tactics. In *The Command of the Air*, translated into nearly all European languages during the 1930's, he wrote:

> Let us leave poetry to the poets. The population can and must be inured to the horrors of war, but there is a limit to all resistance, even human resistance. No population can steel itself to endure aerial offensives forever. A heroic people can endure the most frightful offensives as long as there is hope that they may come to an end; but when the aerial war has been lost, there is no hope of ending the conflict until a decision has been reached on the surface, and that would take too long. A people who are bombed today as they were bombed yesterday, who know that they will be bombed again tomorrow and see no end to their martyrdom, are bound to call for peace at length.

The Italian theorist did not, as popular opinion supposed, justify the ethics of bombing civilians. As the first soldier to recognize the potentialities of air power, he warned his countrymen that the new dimension of tactics would respect neither age nor sex nor distance from the battle line:

> Any distinction between belligerents and non-belligerents is no longer admissible today either in fact or theory. Not in theory

because when nations are at war, everyone takes a part in it: the soldier carrying his gun, the woman loading shells in a factory, the farmer growing wheat, the scientist experimenting in his laboratory. Not in fact because nowadays the offensive may reach anyone; and it begins to look as though the safest place may be in the trenches.

While noncombatants had been bombed throughout the last war, the results were far from being decisive. The 154 tons of bombs dropped on England by Zeppelins during the first two years caused property damage of only a million and a half pounds sterling. After 1916, as the lighter-than-air machines proved too vulnerable, the largest raid of all was carried out by fewer than 40 planes. Total casualties of 1,413 killed and 3,406 injured were inflicted during the entire war; but from a strictly military viewpoint the German raids accomplished little except the neutralizing of 414 British planes and 700 searchlights maintained in the London defense area.

A pamphlet published by the Italian town of Treviso probably offers the best study of bombing conditions in the first World War. From April, 1916, to October, 1918, the community of 40,000 people endured 32 Austrian raids. About 1,500 bombs, or an estimated total of 75 tons, were dropped on an area of a square mile. Yet the casualties amounted to only 30 dead and 50 injured before civilians were evacuated. As Douhet points out, the air forces of that day were not equipped to drop the whole 75 tons in one night; and long intervals between attacks gave Treviso time to control fires, remove wreckage and provide for the safety of its citizens.

Had the war lasted a few more months, this consolation would no longer have existed. For the Allies were preparing to raid Berlin in 1919 with forces of 100 planes or more, each carrying a half-ton bomb or its equivalent in smaller projectiles.

The next fifteen years brought much greater technical improvements, so that the Italian aviators actually did drop 75 tons of bombs in a single day during their Ethiopian operations. Three years later, as the great raid on Barcelona (March 17-18, 1938) inflicted civilian losses of nearly 900 in slain alone, there could be no further doubt that non-combatants would soon be subjected to horrors without a precedent in military chronicles. The evidence of the Barcelona attacks led to vast increases in the numbers of German bombing planes; and the official character of such tests was shown when the Third Reich decorated the participating airmen. Meanwhile the Nazi propaganda machine did not neglect an opportunity to intensify the "war of nerves" directed at the shocked civilian populations of neutral nations.

Douhet's plausible theories, coupled with the results of the Spanish Civil War, gave the democratic nations a dread of strategic bombing which influenced the decisions of statecraft. More than any other factor, this fear was responsible for the concessions of the 1930's which permitted Germany to rearm and threaten world peace.

The Medievalism of Modern Germany

The Fourteenth Edition of the Encyclopaedia Britannica, published in 1929, devotes just sixteen lines to the biographical sketch of a "Bavarian politician" named Adolf Hitler. Yet there was nothing miraculous about the rise of this obscure figure to the dictatorship of all Germany only five years later. Total war could not be waged until someone won the total acquiescence of the people; and the nation's brooding ex-officers considered that Hitler had demonstrated his fitness over all other candidates. Even men who prided themselves on hardness were impressed by such sentiments as the former corporal proclaimed as early as September 19, 1933:

Brutality is respected. Brutality and physical strength! The plain man in the streets respects nothing but brutal strength and restlessness—women, too, for that matter, women and children.

It is scarcely surprising that other countries were unable to take this demagogue seriously at first. Only in Germany, which has historically preferred obedience to liberty, could a leader have won the worship of crowds which he held in a contempt revealed by his words of April 14, 1934:

The people need wholesome fear. They *want* to fear something. They want someone to frighten them and make them shudderingly submissive. . . . Why babble and be indignant about torturing? The masses need something that will give them a thrill of horror.

That such theories were not mere talk had already been demonstrated by Hitler's Brown Shirts—one of the private armies of modern *condottieri* which contended for mastery in the streets and beer halls of Germany during the postwar years. Young thugs and ruffians from the slums filled the ranks; but it is not so well known that the seven commanders in 1930 were all former career officers of the kaiser's army, including three who belonged to the old nobility. Fried's *The Guilt of the German Army* also discloses that President Hindenburg, then accepted by other nations as a figure of austere respectability, wired his "comradely thanks" after the bloody purge of 1934 in which Hitler slaughtered enough rivals to make his power absolute.

Thus the dying republic, betrayed by its own sworn officials, ended by congratulating its assassins. During its fifteen feeble years of existence it had not only failed to keep order but even winked at the factions plotting its downfall. As a final legacy it left to Hitler the cadre of a great national army as well as the financial backlog for rearmament on a gigantic scale.

From Germany's past the half-educated Führer also inherited such moral weapons as anti-Semitism and the legend of a master race. His own contribution, the quality which made this little man terrifying, was his intuition—his strange power to energize the Teutonic opposite poles of subservience and aggressiveness which had served every German war lord since Wallenstein.

The seventeenth-century mystic had found his followers among men weary of the materialism of the post-Renaissance era; and the prophet of a new Thirty Years' War appealed to masses nauseated with the materialism of the Machine Age. In no country had the worship of the "bitch-goddess" taken a more gross form than in the Germany of 1910, where burghers ate five heavy meals a day and prided themselves on girth as a measure of success. Though scorning Jews for their commercialism, this Germany could even commercialize Paul Ehrlich's discovery of a cure for syphilis by making it a profitable state monopoly. Then came the World War, wiping out such values and leaving in their stead only a sickness of the spirit. Hitler, with his pasty face, absurd mustache and glassy, hyperthyroid stare, was the very incarnation of this disease—a human caricature of the mass frustrations which made the Germany of 1933 a menace to civilization.

Again, as in the time of Bismarck and William II, a brave but hopelessly small minority fought against militarization. These "underground" rebels risked torture as well as death, and even their families were made the victims of a hideous Nazi persecution. But as usual the bulk of the people followed their war lords.

The hardships endured by the nation during the postwar years have sometimes been cited in extenuation. Yet the areas later organized into the new states of Poland, Yugoslavia and Czechoslovakia had undergone a worse ordeal, having been under the Teutonic heel as victims of a harsh exploitation. All three of these peoples, despite their inexperience, made a better showing at self-government than Germany, and Czechoslovakia emerged as one of the model democracies of the world.

Defeated individuals often find a refuge from reality in a dream-world of the past. And after failing both at war and self-government, a sick Germany crept back into the womb of history when it gratefully accepted Hitler's creed of a perverted medievalism. For the new political faith restored the violence of the Middle Ages without the innocence, the tortures without the humility, and the mental poverty without the necessity. Henceforward the fury of mass emotions would take the place of reason in Germany, and citizens of the twentieth century would find their solace in grandiose plans for the slaughter or enslavement of conquered peoples.

Had the democratic nations themselves been in good political health at this time, the peril might not have been so great. But two decades of an economy based upon comfort and pleasure had infected them with a malaise of the will. Though angrily rejecting most of the tenets of World War propaganda, middle-class citizens of France, Britain and America still clung to an ostrich-like conviction that the German people, as distinguished from their rulers, were guiltless of warlike intent.

If the screaming Hitler now emerged as the incarnation of an aroused Germany, the democratic nations also had their symbolic man of the hour. Neville Chamberlain, more than any other, represented the stunned incredulity and helplessness of the millions listening at their radios in France, Britain and America. The British prime minister, believing that all things have their price, tried to bargain with the new madness and met humiliation. For his concessions only encouraged bolder forays, until men of good will realized that the umbrella of Munich was not a shield which could defend them from bombs. Thus in 1938 did Germany win the peace, and in another year the losers would be fighting for survival.

General von Seeckt has been given a great deal of the credit for a war effort which seemed cyclonic in its suddenness. After the *Freikorps* units were outlawed by the Versailles terms and the national army limited to 100,000 troops, Mackensen's former chief-of-staff trained the entire force to be the commissioned and noncommissioned officers of a mighty future host. Yet the cadre idea was by no means new, and the street fighting which had been raging in Germany since the Armistice is more worthy of recognition as the foundation of the new warfare. In these sanguinary battles young men learned from storm troopers the advantages held by the audacious few over the bewildered many. They learned the military values of surprise, of deception, and of ferocity. This was the school of warfare which produced the blitzkrieg, and the Spanish Civil War became the rehearsal for World War II when the Germans, Italians and Russians secretly intervened.

V

THE RESUMPTION IN 1939

---

*Those who cannot remember the past are condemned
to repeat it.*

—GEORGE SANTAYANA

EVER since Waterloo it had been disputed as to whether another
conqueror would ever dominate Europe. Curiously, the soldier whose
victories are most comparable to an Austerlitz or Rivoli was neither an
offensive strategist nor an imitator of Napoleon. Robert E. Lee, by
making the defensive power of the entrenched rifleman serve him as a
pivot for counterstrokes, brought off the greatest triumphs against
material odds won in the nineteenth century. Napoleon's imitators
failed because this same tactical supremacy of the rifle, and later of the
machine gun, made it impossible to concentrate the field guns which the
conqueror used to blast a path for his cavalry and infantry.

In 1937, two decades after Mitchell taught the first lesson, German
strategists realized that the flying artillery had restored the favorable
balance of offensive fire power. Marshal Hermann Goering's airmen in
Spain found that no defensive line, however well prepared with automatic
weapons, had much chance of withstanding a motorized assault after the
bombing planes had blasted a path with machine guns and fragmentation
bombs. The new artillery held a further advantage that Napoleon would
have envied, for it could also fly far back into the rear areas to destroy
supplies and cut off reinforcements.

While World War I standards still prevailed in the Spanish Civil War, aerial projectiles remained a minor factor. The German influence is shown by the statistics of 1938, when 9,000 tons of shells and 8,000 tons of bombs were used in Franco's autumn counteroffensive on the Ebro. The idea of the Stuka dive bomber had already been conceived, and Germany now went into mass production to prepare for the greater tests of geopolitics.

Tom Wintringham, who instructed republican volunteers in guerrilla tactics, tells in *The Story of Weapons and Tactics* how the blitzkrieg originated in Spain. Ludendorff had shown in 1918 that the defensive line, even the line of some depth, could be pierced by infiltration methods. He failed of a decision because the material means of his day were inadequate. Twenty years later his successors perceived that infiltration could be promoted from tactics to the sphere of strategy. Where Ludendorff had broken through corps fronts, the mechanized army of 1938 possessed the speed and firepower to penetrate the defensive line held by an entire nation.

Although few new weapons of importance had been invented since World War I, most of the old ones were multiplied in effectiveness. Planes developed to 300 miles an hour instead of 100, tanks 30 instead of 3. Artillery, mounted on rubber tires and sped forward by motor, showed an enormous gain in mobility over the iron-wheeled, horse-drawn guns of the recent past. The motor truck, then largely handmade and none too reliable, now flowed from the assembly line by the thousands to solve the transport and supply problems of a new mobile warfare.

With few exceptions, defensive weapons had not kept pace. The antiaircraft gun of 1938, equipped with range-finding instruments of uncanny precision, made its counterpart of the last war seem antiquated and feeble. Antitank guns showed a corresponding gain; but most armies kept the same model of rifle; and the machine gun had changed but little since 1918.

The defensive, in short, had lagged for twenty years while the potential speed of the offensive increased tenfold—from the three miles an hour of the marching army to the thirty miles of the mechanized host. The difference between these figures is largely the difference between the Western Front and the blitzkrieg.

After reaching these conclusions, the Germans in Spain experimented to determine the best procedure of piercing an opposing line for strategic purposes. They decided, according to Wintringham, that a breakthrough on a front only 1,000 yards wide offered all the possibilities of decision;

but to allow for the unexpected, 2,000 yards was adopted as the standard frontage of attack. In a great offensive two or three such assaults were to be launched about two miles apart, all efforts being co-ordinated with a view to penetrating as far as the enemy's supply and communication centres in the first rush. Although this conception violated age-old axioms warning against an attacker exposing his flanks, the Germans reckoned on the speed of their tanks as well as the fire power of accompanying dive-bombers to nullify the danger. They also foresaw that adversaries demoralized by a blitzkrieg surprise would probably be more concerned at the moment about their own flanks.

Of all Germany's future enemies only the Soviet Union appears to have learned valuable lessons from the Spanish Civil War. Despite the secrecy with which the Red Army guarded all plans, its generals evidently agreed with the Germans that the strongest fortified line could be broken by the mechanical assault. Only the defense in depth—a depth never dreamed of by World War I soldiers—could hope to slow down and entangle the steel-shod columns.

This precept was taught to recent civilians—Spanish peasants and workers who had the courage to turn ruined villages into improvised little fortresses after the mechanized forces swept past. Soon the attackers had to send back strong detachments to cope with the snipers preying upon their flanks and rear. One such strongpoint could be reduced without too much cost; but when every village became, in military jargon, an "island of resistance," the attack was bled of its impetus by the detachments needed to battle their way from house to house in bitter street fighting. Neither tanks nor armored cars were of much use in such operations, and the assailants usually suffered heavier losses than the defenders.

Many centuries ago the Iberian tribesmen of these tawny uplands flung themselves recklessly at the elephants brought by the Carthaginian invaders until they learned how to rout the huge beasts. The tanks of 1937 were no less terrifying to a novice, but man himself, indomitable as ever, remains the decisive factor of war. Thus for all the complex mechanical monsters of the day, no weapon is more worthy of respect than that human, derisive and withal effective tank destroyer, the "Molotov cocktail." Consisting simply of oil-soaked cotton waste taped to a wine bottle containing gasoline, it was ignited and thrown to shatter against the tank. The spreading blaze, feeding on the oil film covering the surface, often turned the machine into an oven which cre-

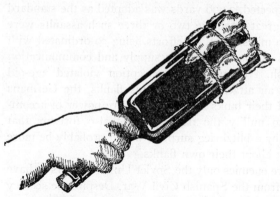

Molotov Cocktail

mated the crew within. Tanks were also crippled by *dynamiteros* who hurled sticks of fused explosives under the tracks; and even a fence post daringly thrust between the caterpillar and bogey wheels might put a landship out of action.

For it is a paradox that as war grows more mechanical, the value of a pair of human hands mounts ever higher in strategic calculations. China had already shown what guerrilla warfare could do to cancel the profits of mechanized invasion, and Spain added a second lesson.

THE NAZI MILITARY ORGANIZATION

In 1935, when Hitler repudiated the arms restrictions of the Versailles Treaty, each of the three branches of the German military service had its own general staff and commander-in-chief. All were subordinate to General Werner von Blomberg as minister of war and commander-in-chief of the Wehrmacht.

The Wehrmacht had been established to prevent the usual interservice bickerings by co-ordinating land, sea and air operations. Interservice planning was to be conducted by the Wehrmachtant, with General Wilhelm Keitel at the head.

By 1938, thanks to his bloodless victories, Hitler had enough personal power to sack Blomberg and abolish his posts. Thus the commanders of the three arms of the military service became Hitler's immediate subordinates. This result was brought about by a reorganization of the Ministry of War. Renamed the High Command of the Wehrmacht (*Oberkommando der Wehrmacht*, commonly known as the OKW), it was the instrument with which Hitler gradually gained complete control over German land operations.

Admiral Erich Raeder managed to retain some independence of action for the Navy, largely because Hitler was not interested in sea operations. The flamboyant Goering, as commander of the Luftwaffe, had so much personal influence over Hitler that he could bypass Keitel in decisions affecting air operations. With these exceptions, the power of Hitler to make strategic decisions soon became absolute.

"Keitel himself was completely subordinate to Hitler," comments Telford Taylor in *The March of Conquest*, a study of the Nazi military organization by the New York lawyer who served in 1946 as U.S. Army brigadier general and chief counsel for the prosecution in the Nuremberg war crimes trials. "His military talents were of a low order, and he had no prestige or influence among his fellow generals, who dubbed him 'Lakeitel,' a play on the German word *Lakai*, meaning 'lackey.' "

The German field army numbered 106 divisions in the summer of 1939. General Walther von Brauchitsch headed the High Command of the Army (*Oberkommando des Heeres*, or OKH) and General Franz Halder was chief of the Army General Staff. Field commanders were directly subordinate to OKH, which in turn came increasingly under the thumb of OKW as Hitler added to his personal power at the expense of German generals who were no match for him in beer-hall politics.

The field army of 1938 comprised nearly two million effectives. Their arms and equipment made the gear of 1914 seem as antiquated as the flintlock muskets of Napoleon's armies. At the outset of World War I only 2,700 machine guns, or a maximum of 50 to a division, were to be found in the whole German Army—less than half the number considered necessary for an armored division of 1939. In order to meet the German threat the reorganized United States Army set the following standards:

Triangular Infantry Division (16,024 officers and men)	*Armored Division* (12,700 officers and men)
7,327 .30-caliber rifles	2,017 .30-caliber rifles
61 60-mm. mortars	21 60-mm. mortars
179 .30-caliber machine guns	3,647 .30-caliber machine guns
179 machine and sub-machine guns, .45 and .50 caliber	2,670 machine and sub-machine guns, .45 and .50 caliber
18 81-mm. mortars	20 81-mm. mortars
8 75-mm. guns	8 75-mm. guns
36 105-mm. guns	36 105-mm. guns
12 155-mm. howitzers	411 37-mm. tank and antitank guns
60 37-mm. antitank guns	97 scout cars, 642 half-track trucks, 20 mortar carriers, 273 light
16 scout cars	tanks, 108 medium tanks, 78 maintenance trucks

These figures represented the ideal even if not always the real strength of infantry and armored divisions in western Europe on the eve of World War II.

The Germans of 1939 had broken abruptly with the past by equipping their infantry with motorized, rubber-tired artillery which could be rushed into action at speeds up to fifty miles an hour. Where other armies stressed specialization, they developed in their 105-mm. piece a combination gun and howitzer to meet infantry demands. Likewise, the "88" was used as a triple-purpose weapon in Spain, where it performed the functions of a field gun, antitank gun and antiaircraft gun.

The psychological influence of drill was not overlooked, and many of the old close-order German formations were dropped on the theory that they grounded the soldier unconsciously in line and defensive doctrines instead of offensive tactics. In their place the Germans introduced such training methods as advances against actual machine-gun bullets whipping the air a few inches overhead, or realistic simulated attacks on models of enemy fortifications.

Although the word "blitzkrieg" had already crept into the popular vocabulary, the full implications of the threat were not understood even by the British and French General Staffs, as events were soon to prove. Major F. O. Miksche, a Czechoslovak officer who served on the General Staff of the Spanish republican army, has given one of the best descriptions in his book *Attack*. For all preparations had been so well worked out by the Germans in Spain that veterans of the Civil War were not surprised by the results of 1939 and 1940.

The important thing to remember about the blitzkrieg is its combination of a lateral with a forward movement, giving the effect of a fast-moving machine which grinds while it slices. The direction of the three breakthrough attacks was not necessarily straight ahead—more often they slanted off on an angle which followed the path of least resistance. And as these spearheads made their rapid thrusts, other and lesser attacks were aimed at one side or another to widen the gap.

The name "lightning war," according to Miksche, was applied in description of the zigzag course as well as speed of assaults which are continually changing direction. Thus the pattern of the blitzkrieg through an expanse of enemy territory gave the impression of thunderbolts splitting the darkness. Surprise and deception were gained by this method, for the enemy could only be sure that the next thrust will be aimed at the point where his resistance appears to be weakest.

While the French still clung to the first World War theory of the fortified line, German military treatises spoke in terms of *Flächen und Lückentaktik*—"tactics of the space and gap." Hence the ten- or twelve-mile front of the blitzkrieg meant no more than the starting point for an explosion of local actions seeking to reduce an entire area in the shortest possible time.

As compared to the Wehrmacht, the French Army of 1940, though taking very seriously its reputation as the best in Europe, can only be regarded as an instrument of World War I. The well-worn tactical fabric of 1918 had been patched with more modern materials, but the nation economized on planes, armor and antiaircraft guns while spending 12½ billion francs on passive defense as represented by the Maginot Line.

Impression of the Blitzkrieg

Even before 1940 it might have occurred to civilians as well as soldiers that the great underground fortress could not stop bombing planes, and its epitaph has been suitably written by Major Miksche in *Attack*:

> The Maginot Line was a formidable barrier, not so much against the German Army as against French understanding of modern war.

As evidence Miksche points out that in a motorized age French soldiers were still thinking in terms of railway strategy. During the last conflict the munitions for every great offensive, sometimes amounting to half a million tons, were first unloaded at railheads located well behind the line. Horse-drawn vehicles and the comparatively few motor trucks of the day then brought the material forward to the base dumps. Another reloading became necessary before the supplies reached the attacking troops, so that the element of surprise was usually lost. Finally, the dumps could not be concentrated for fear of bombing or shelling, and their dispersal tended to widen the frontage of every offensive at the cost of decisive results.

Twenty years later the French still depended largely on steam transportation while their hereditary enemy had changed over to gasoline. Thus the Germans were able to concentrate both men and supplies as far as 150 miles behind the front, and by threatening many points simultaneously they multiplied the chances of surprise. When the time came to strike, they could move much more swiftly against opponents tied to railway lines which had been built to meet the military needs of the last century.

American Amphibious Tactics

The German General Staff made allowances, of course, for British intervention on the side of France. It was expected that at least six or eight divisions would be sent across the Channel shortly after hostilities began, and the British Navy has in every age merited respect. Britain's air power seemed so inferior, however, that Goering scarcely deemed it worthy of consideration. This estimate, as events were to prove, was an error that would cost the Luftwaffe dearly.

There could be little doubt in 1938 that the United States would aid Britain and France in every possible way, perhaps even to the extent of declaring war on Germany and Japan. But American pacifist sentiment was strong, and it also appeared that the United States would uphold its tradition of being militarily unprepared on the eve of war.

Certainly the OKW and OKH did not suspect that ever since 1933 the U.S. Navy and Marine Corps had been developing amphibious combat techniques that were destined to open up Europe, Africa and the Japanese-held islands of the Pacific to invasion without suffering a single major defeat. General J. F. C. Fuller has summed up these techniques in his history, *The Second World War*, as being "in all probability . . . the most far-reaching tactical innovation of the war."

The costly failure of the Gallipoli expedition in 1915 had been widely interpreted to mean that large-scale amphibious offensives were doomed to disaster by modern fire power. Among the dissenters was a brilliant young U.S. Marine Corps officer, Lieutenant Colonel Earl H. Ellis.

He predicted in 1921 that Japan would strike first and win the initial victories of a war with the United States which the island empire's ambitions made inevitable. Ellis maintained that a successful counter-offensive must be based on a sweep to Japan by means of amphibious assaults on Japanese-held islands of the Pacific.

He wrote a detailed plan contemplating an invasion route from Hawaii to the Marshalls, the eastern Carolines and the Palau group as the first stages of an advance to the Marianas, the Bonins and eventually Japan itself. This was essentially the route followed more than two decades later.

Some of Ellis' strategic ideas were adopted by the Joint Board of the Army and Navy (forerunner of the Joint Chiefs of Staff) for offensive operations in the Pacific. In 1922 the marine officer, who spoke Japanese fluently, took an indefinite leave of absence and used his own funds to tour the Japanese-mandated islands as a supposed commercial traveler. He died mysteriously the following spring in the Palaus, the cause being reported as "sudden illness" by the Japanese authorities.

Ellis left secretly classified writings which did much to keep alive the American interest in amphibious tactics. In 1927 the Joint Board of the Army and Navy committed itself by giving the Marine Corps the mission of "special preparation in the conduct of landing operations." All the resources of the small, peacetime Corps were devoted during the next six years to the occupation of Nicaragua and various Caribbean Islands. But modern amphibious warfare came into being on December 8, 1933, with the creation of a new organization to be known as the Fleet Marine Force. It was assigned the responsibility for the seizure, occupation and defense of naval objectives.

Obviously, the landing of troops on enemy-held beaches is an undertaking fraught with risks. As evidence of how little thought had been given to it by American military leaders up to this time, a Navy manual of 760 pages contained only five treating of amphibious landings. In the lack of a hornbook, the Marine Corps made it a first task to write one. All available officers of the base at Quantico, Virginia, were organized into committees for the creation of tactics and techniques where none had been before.

An amphibious assault landing is neither a land, sea nor air operation; it is a combination of all three. Aircraft, ships and ground forces must be closely co-ordinated, especially at the critical moment when the landing force makes the transition from one element to another. There were object lessons in profusion but few encouraging precepts to guide the marine committees at Quantico. Nevertheless, they finished the *Tentative*

Manual for Landing Operations in time for publication in 1934. It was adopted with revisions by the Navy; and parts of the Navy manual in turn were incorporated into the Army's first basic field manual for landing operations.

Marine landing exercises were held every year with the fleet, and new amphibious bases were set up for training purposes on both coasts. Simulated combat landings soon revealed that new tools as well as techniques were needed, and the Marine Corps encouraged inventors to submit models. Thus the LCVP (landing craft, vehicle, personnel) was developed by trial and error from a retractable boat of shallow draft and protected propeller which Andrew J. Higgins built originally for the use of fur trappers in the Louisiana marshes. With Marine Corps backing, he experimented until he designed a landing craft with a bow ramp for the quick discharge of troops, trucks and small tanks.

An amphibian vehicle invented by Donald Roebling for rescue work in the Everglades was the inspiration for the LVT (landing vehicle, tracked). Commonly known as the amtrac and equally at home on land or water, it had a capacity of 30 troops with combat gear.

Other strange craft went into mass production until the Navy and the Marine Corps had a fleet of vehicles and boats designed for amphibious assault operations. While these two branches of the service experimented with ship-to-shore landings, the U.S. Army worked out shore-to-shore landing techniques. The Army also contributed one of the most useful of the new vehicles in the DUKW (pronounced "duck" and probably derived from a code designation by its commercial manufacturer). A 2½-ton amphibian truck, it was designed for putting ashore artillery and ammunition.

With the development of the LST (landing ship, tanks), American amphibious planners had a craft large enough to take several thousand troops or to disgorge from its bow ramp an incredible number of tanks, trucks and troop-loaded LVTs. Nicknamed the Large Sitting Target because of its size and comparative slowness, the LST was to become the workhorse of the war in the Pacific.

New types of ammunition were developed by the Navy to increase the striking power of naval gunfire for amphibious operations. After the gunnery range of Culebra Island (off Puerto Rico) proved inadequate, the Navy purchased Bloodsworth Island in Chesapeake Bay. It became the first range to be used for amphibious gunfire training alone.

Air strikes, closely co-ordinated with naval gunfire, were to support the landing forces. Planes would also be employed for observation, spotting, reconnaissance and interdiction missions. Pilots were given intensive training in two-way radio communication and responding to such signals as ground panels of various colors.

It was not enough for the American planners to work out new tactics and techniques; they also found it necessary to train new specialists and even create new units. The critical moment of an amphibious operation, as they visioned it, would come when the assault waves approached the beaches, supported by air strikes and naval gunfire. In order to prevent utter chaos, trained men must be sent with the combat troops to maintain order. These specialists had such duties as marking the beaches, setting up communications centers, controlling traffic, directing labor parties, evacuating the wounded, and expediting the movement of troops, Once the beachhead had been won, the logistical phase of the operation would have top priority. For the drive inland must be nourished without delay with the vast quantities of ammunition, food, gasoline and water brought by the supply ships. Altogether, so many and diverse were the duties of the beach specialists that they were organized into a unit known as the shore party battalion, found only in a marine division.

More often than not, the new amphibious techniques derived from that uncommon quality called common sense. One of the Fleet Marine Force procedures was known as combat-loading—the loading of a transport with a unit's gear and supplies in the order they would be needed on the beach. Simple as this may seem, it had never been reduced to a science before; and it took a great deal of study before tables could be compiled to meet every foreseeable situation.

American preparations were obviously aimed at the Japanese Empire, which in the 1920's had fortified its mandated islands in the Pacific in spite of treaty regulations. In 1931 the Japanese took a long step further by seizing Manchuria. Placed under a puppet government and renamed Manchukuo, this large area of fertile land was capable of supplying many of the raw materials for a long war.

After digesting their acquisition, the Japanese forced a war on China in the summer of 1937. This time they met unexpected opposition which slowed the pace of aggression after preliminary victories. And though they overran whole provinces, the invaders had not yet conquered China when World War II broke out in Europe.

It might perhaps have been some comfort to the millions of anxious people in the democratic nations if they had realized that a potent new military system was being developed in the United States. But neither friend nor foe suspected any such thing at a time when Japan was building up a mighty empire in the Far East. As for Europe, the Nazi war machine appeared to be too powerful to allow much hope of a successful resistance.

GERMANY DIVIDES HER ENEMIES

So thoroughly had Nazi propaganda done its work, the radio listeners of the democratic nations would never have believed in their hour of humiliation that France and Czechoslovakia alone had the armed strength to stop Hitler. Colonel General Franz Halder, chief of the German General Staff from 1938 to 1942, confessed to his Allied captors in 1945 that Hitler had been bluffing. The blitzkrieg was a potentially effective tactical system. But at the time of the Munich Pact, the Third Reich had only 21 well-trained divisions, including two Panzer units, as compared to 45 trained Czech divisions well equipped with armor. Halder and his fellow generals believed that if it had come to war in 1938, their country's prospects would have been "nothing less than catastrophic."

Germany's army officers, with their aristocratic pretensions, were the victims during the late 1930's of a delusion that they could control the former corporal after he had served their purposes as rabble-rouser. France could have cooked his goose when he took the responsibility for occupying the Rhineland. But the bluff succeeded. And as success followed success, the officers of the General Staff found themselves under Hitler's thumb. They dared not overthrow a leader whose seeming ability to win bloodless victories by sheer intuition made him adored by the German people.

Perhaps the most costly error of the democratic nations lay in the assumption that war did not begin until the armies were set in motion. Hitler took full advantage of this blind spot by applying the tactics of infiltration in the economic and political spheres. Headed by the reliable Dr. Schacht, forces of financial storm troopers invaded the nations of eastern Europe for a threefold purpose—the storing up of German supplies for a new war, the creation of internal dissension which could later be exploited, and the detaching of these countries from their "Little Entente" alliance with France.

Much as the mechanized columns sought a weak spot in the opposing line, the economic warriors raised and lowered prices until discontented minorities accused their governments of favoritism or fraud. The countries themselves were set against one another in a sharp competition for the trade of Germans who profited from the rivalry while setting the stage for the political invasion soon to follow.

Hitler's Reich, buying when other nations were desperately eager to sell, importing labor when others had unemployment problems, seemed to have discovered some new secret of prosperity. The explanation, of course, could be found in the fact that Germany had gone on a war economy which must end only in collapse or conquest. But millions of Europeans were disturbed if not convinced; for the democratic nations, just emerging from a long period of business depression, made a sorry showing in contrast.

These preliminary moves were as much a part of the blitzkrieg as the final climactic dash of the tanks across the frontier. After the economic phase the Germans made their appeal to the prejudices which men esteem only second to their purses. With democracy weathering a crisis, every nation had its factions of malcontents who found relief from personal frustrations in such doctrines as Anglophobia, anti-Semitism and totalitarianism. By means of rewards and subsidies the invaders made allies out of the leaders—the Quislings, Henleins and De la Rocques who were to be used as local *Gauleiters*. Once the political breakthrough had been accomplished, Nazi propagandists attacked from the flanks and rear in an effort to create a minority large enough to call for "protection."

In 1936, when the bloodless war of infiltration began, the path of German conquest actually was blocked by potential military foes—the Soviet Union, Czechoslovakia, Poland and Yugoslavia in the east, Britain and France in the west. Three years later this combination had been so successfully undermined by economic and political attacks alone that on the eve of World War II Germany faced only Poland in the east, Britain and France in the west.

The Third Reich had meanwhile acquired two allies. When the League of Nations declared economic sanctions against Benito Mussolini in 1935 for his invasion of Abyssinia, he was thrown into the arms of Hitler. Both of them intervened in the Spanish Civil War a year later to test their new tanks and planes, and in November, 1936, they signed the Anti-Comintern (Anti-Soviet) Pact with Japan which established the Berlin-Rome-Tokyo Axis.

The *Anschluss* of Germany and Austria in 1938 was a shock to the democratic nations. But it could be pleaded that Hitler was merely uniting two nations with the same language and culture. Moreover, Dr.

Joseph Goebbels, the Nazi propaganda minister, painted a convincing picture of a willing Austria which did not lack elements of truth.

Two weeks later the spotlight was on Czechoslovakia. After setting up Konrad Henlein as the leader of a German minority in the Sudeten area, the Nazi dictator cynically upheld the principle of self-determination which had been the basis of the despised Versailles Treaty. Neville Chamberlain flew to Munich three times in the early autumn of 1938 and conferred with Hitler in the hope of averting war. In the end

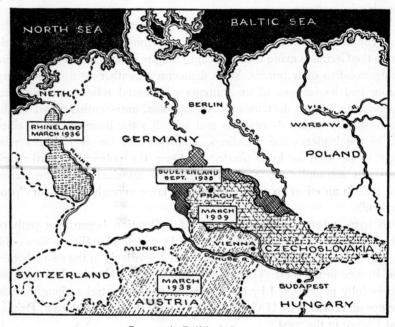

Germany's Political Conquests

the British prime minister and the French premier, Edouard Daladier, had to choose between a dishonorable peace and sacrificing Czechoslovakia. They betrayed a powerful ally and returned to be greeted by cheering crowds in London and Paris.

The leaders of the democratic nations, to be sure, did not have the advantage of hindsight, which constitutes the wisdom of historians. Nor did they appear to be any better endowed with foresight, judging by the lagging progress of British and French military preparations.

Daladier was only too well aware of the spirit of defeatism permeating the French Army from command to rank and file. Chamberlain, for his part, could not forget that England had only seven modern antiair-craft guns for the defense of London, and fewer than a hundred planes fit to cope with the aircraft of the Luftwaffe. Both leaders had good reason to believe that their peoples could not be led into war, so great was the dread of terror bombing.

Thus at Munich was lost the greatest opportunity of saving the world from the horrors of World War II. In a day of mass production, arms which had once taken years to manufacture could be turned out in months, as Britain herself was soon to demonstrate at Luftwaffe expense. The Munich Conference presented Adolf Hitler with an additional six months in which to build up his war machine. And in the spring of 1939, without bothering much about pretexts, he assumed absolute control over Czechoslovakia as his columns marched into Prague. This move gave him enormous supplies of first-class new arms—the tanks and artillery and automatic weapons of the Skoda munitions works—and placed him in a strategic position to envelop Poland from three sides. As the next victim, that nation was induced by a slice of territory to share in the guilt of the Nazi occupation of the whole of Czechoslovakia.

In less than three years, without firing a shot, Hitler had expanded the area of Germany from 181,500 square miles to 259,000, and increased the population from 60,000,000 to 80,000,000. Only one great hope, gilded by wishful thinking, remained to comfort the radio listeners of the democratic nations. They reassured themselves that the Third Reich and Soviet Russia must inevitably collide in the near future and fight it out to mutual destruction. This pleasing prospect was dashed on August 23, 1939, by the stunning announcement that Hitler and Stalin had signed a treaty of nonaggression! The shock would have been even more sickening had it been known that the two dictators also signed a secret protocol dividing Poland between them.

Only Britain, France and the United States, all three unprepared both morally and materially for such an ordeal, were left among the Great Powers to resist future Axis encroachments. But the Nazi propagandists had not been idle even in these last strongholds of parliamentary rule. Each had its surly little factions which took advantage of free speech to avow Fascist principles. Each had its larger groups of isolationists who could be taught to parrot such slogans as "England is ready to fight to the last Frenchman!" or "England expects that every American will do his duty!" Each had its still more numerous elements of the population which were honestly bewildered. For these puzzled and groping citizens, including thousands of youths who recalled only years of economic stress, the Nazis and Communists reserved a more subtle propaganda touch known as "polarization"—the inculcation of the idea that outworn democratic institutions no longer mattered in a world powerfully attracted to the opposite political poles of Fascism and Communism.

Looking back over the past two decades, it could be plainly seen that since 1919 Germany had been preparing for a conflict which was essentially a resumption of World War I. The nonaggression pact with Russia removed Hitler's worries about fighting a two-front war, and a week later his armoured columns rolled over the frontier of Poland without a declaration of hostilities. The date was September 1, 1939—the anniversary of the victorious double envelopment at Sedan in 1870 which had been for two generations of Germans a symbol of their warlike might.

PART EIGHT
WORLD WAR II

☆

PART EIGHT

WORLD WAR II

I

HITLER'S CONQUEST OF EUROPE

Yes, we are barbarians! We shall rejuvenate the world!
This world is nearing its end. It is our mission to cause
unrest. The important thing is the overwhelming shock
of the fear of death.

—HITLER

BRITAIN and France had defensive alliances with Poland, and it was a question whether they would leave this ally in the lurch as they had Czechoslovakia. On September 3 both nations delivered an ultimatum to the German Foreign Office, demanding a suspension of hostilities before midnight. When no answer was received, Britain and France declared war on Germany.

Never in modern history has the outbreak of war found the peoples of all participating nations so reluctant. This reaction was perhaps to be expected in London and Paris. But even in Berlin the streets were filled with people staring somberly at bulletins announcing the first Nazi successes in Poland. This time the Führer had not been able to win a victory by intuition alone.

Poland's unhappy situation is evident from a glance at the accompanying map, showing German and German-occupied territory as shaded areas. So well had Hitler's economic and political blitzkrieg been co-ordinated with the military that Poland was half beaten in Czechoslovakia. Without firing a shot Germany had placed the next victim within the jaws of the strategic vise formed by East Prussia and Slovakia. Most of the nation's industries were located in this region, which obviously must be evacuated. The only feasible line of defense, in fact, ran north and south behind the Narew, Vistula and San rivers.

These harsh realities were not overlooked by Polish strategists. But in the belief that they could fight delaying actions until Britain and France sent aid, they divided their army of about 800,000 into five main

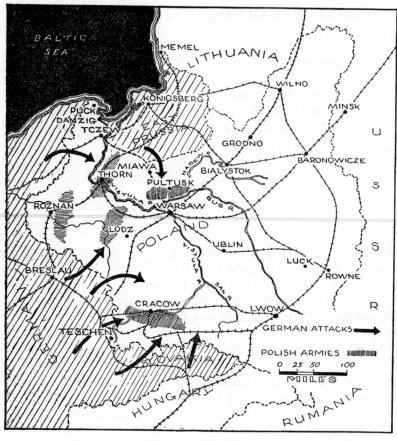

Blitzkrieg in Poland

groups, stationed near Pultusk, Cracow, Thorn, Lodz and Poznan. The first two were to defend the flanks as the others fell back toward the river lines, inflicting as many losses as possible before giving up the industrial cities.

Nothing could have suited the German generals better, for they aimed at the annihilation of armies rather than the occupation of territory. With full knowledge of the Polish dispositions, they planned two enormous double envelopments to be carried out by a total of 1,400,000 troops —the inner pincers to cut off the Thorn, Lodz and Poznan groups as the outer pincers closed in from Slovakia and East Prussia to complete the encirclement.

This is exactly what happened, for the German plans were translated into action with scarcely a slip. The difference in numbers cannot be estimated in terms of bayonets, since the invaders brought 10 tank divisions against an armored brigade, and 3,000 planes against 500. In the first two days their terrific bombing attacks destroyed most of the Polish aircraft on the ground while smashing railway junctions, landing fields and lines of communication. Meanwhile the swiftly moving mechanized units needed only hours to overcome defenses which the Poles had thought would hold for days. Within a week the Lodz, Thorn and Poznan groups had been cut to pieces, and the Cracow and Pultusk groups lasted only a few more days. By September 18 Poland was hopelessly crushed, with only the consolation that Warsaw had repulsed a German armored division in the suburbs. But even though the capital held out against bombs and artillery until the end of the month, its brave resistance had little effect on the final outcome.

The velocity of the Nazi conquest shattered any Polish hopes of military aid from France and England. To add to the prostrate nation's agony, the forces of Hitler's recent ally closed in from the rear to seize a large strip of eastern Poland. Few observers suspected at the time that the Third Reich and the Soviet Union were already preparing for their ultimate clash, and the new aggression added to the gloom in the democratic nations.

Hitler's columns gave such an impression of invincibility in Poland that Nazi weaknesses were not suspected. Not until after the war was it revealed that practically all of the German generals had been opposed to the Polish venture on the grounds that the aggressors were insufficiently prepared. Even the most skeptical of the doubters could not have feared that the Third Reich would be unable to beat Poland alone, despite the brief period of training given some of the recently conscripted troops. The question was whether Hitler could win his gamble in western Europe, where only nine active and ten reserve divisions of second-rate troops were left on guard against a French and British attack from the rear.

Once again Nazi propaganda won a moral victory, for the fortress-minded Allies had been led to believe that Germany's West Wall, or "Siegfried Line," was a barrier comparable to the Maginot Line, then considered impregnable. Actually it was an expendable zone, abounding in tank traps and designed to cushion rather than stop an enemy offensive. Whether it could have withstood an all-out French and British attack in 1939 is open to speculation. As it was, those nations watched the overwhelming of Poland without lifting a hand.

At least the British were warned by the ability of the Luftwaffe to plunge an entire nation into confusion, and preparations began immediately to build up the island's defenses against air attack. Otherwise, the Allies learned little from Poland's tragedy. While crediting the people with great courage, they assumed that lack of tanks and a poor strategic situation had been fatal in a plains region which invited mechanized attack. When their turn came, the Allies counted on larger, better equipped armies behind the Maginot Line and Belgian fortified belt to turn back the mechanized tide.

The Winter of the Phony War

During the first five months of World War II the British Army lost exactly six men killed in action. Bewildered spectators called this phase the "phony war" or "sitzkrieg" as ironical tales were circulated about secure soldiers knitting socks for bombed civilians. Yet even at this stage anyone who knew Germany's military history might have suspected that plans were afoot for further aggressions. It might also have been assumed that the enemy had not been idle during an interlude when France and Britain did so little to improve their prospects.

The fact is that Hitler had issued orders as early as October 9, 1939, in his *Directive No. 6 for the Conduct of the War,* for "an attacking operation on the northern wing of the western front, through the areas of Luxembourg, Belgium and Holland. This attack must be carried out with as much strength and at as early a date as possible."

Great Britain and France, of course, were to be the objectives. Hitler went to the unusual length of stating his reasons. Soviet Russia, he said, could not long be trusted as an ally, and the best safeguard was to give another and more impressive demonstration of Nazi armed might. This would also have the desirable effect of bringing Mussolini openly into the war. Germany's casualties in Poland had been only abut 10,000 killed and 30,0000 wounded, and the quick victory had restored morale in the homeland.

On this occasion the Führer met unwonted opposition from his generals. Rundstedt, Leeb, Reichenau, Halder and Brauchitsch all insisted that the Wehrmacht was far from ready for such a test. Hitler accused them of disloyalty in this "crisis of mutual confidence" but could not overcome their objections. As time went on, he named various potential dates in November, December and January for the opening of the great offensive, but a winter of unusual cold and fog seemed to confirm the generals' doubts. By February the Führer was apparently resigned to further postponements, though he never forgave several of his dissenting subordinates. It was like him, moreover, to take the credit for a winter of reorganization and training that added greatly to the striking power of the Wehrmacht.

The French and British soldiers along France's northern frontier found the interminable waiting more trying than combat. An atmosphere of complete boredom prevailed in the lines as patrols went out nightly on seemingly meaningless missions, seldom encountering an enemy in the emptiness of no man's land.

There was little air activity outside of a few British and German raids on opposing naval bases. During the entire winter the only breaks in the monotony occurred on the sea. The most memorable fight took place in South American waters between the German pocket battleship *Graf Spee* and the British cruisers *Exeter, Ajax* and *Achilles*. These outgunned ships survived a terrific pounding from the German 11-inch rifles, but their 6-inch fire damaged the *Spee* beyond hope of repair at sea. In the harbor of Montevideo Captain Hans Longsdorff found that his ship could not be made seaworthy within the 72 hours permitted by international law to a belligerent in a neutral port. While the British heavy cruiser *Cumberland* awaited his appearance at sea, he steamed out into the River Plate estuary, and great crowds of Sunday sightseers watched the scuttled *Spee* blow up and sink.

The British aircraft carrier *Courageous* was sent to the bottom by submarines before the war was a month old, and in October, 1939, the U-47 penetrated Scapa Flow to sink the British battleship *Royal Oak*. In retaliation, two of Admiral Raeder's destroyers were so badly damaged by the British submarine *Salmon* that they did not get back into action until the following year. And the worst blow of all came when a German bombing plane sank the German destroyers *Leberecht Mass* and *Max Schultz*. Although Raeder stormed at the lack of unified control, Goering refused to put any of his aircraft under naval supervision.

Total War in Poland

In Poland, as Telford Taylor has remarked in his *March of Conquest,* there was nothing phony about the total war waged by the conquerors. Before the last Polish soldier surrendered, Hitler, Heinrich Himmler and Reinhard Heydrich had agreed upon a sweeping program with a view to making the Poles a leaderless subject people. Jews were to be used for forced labor or herded into ghettos, since the first mass extermination camps were not ready until 1940.

In a country which has never had a large middle class, Himmler proposed to reduce the population to the level of peasants by destroying the clergy, nobility and intellectuals. Such a program could not be put into effect without the German Army's giving some measure of co-operation. No attempt was made, therefore, to conceal the mass executions and systematic looting. On the contrary, a deliberate effort was made to keep the officers informed. Hence it can be said authoritatively that from the beginning the German officers, with their supposedly rigid standards of honor, knew what was going on in Poland. They simply turned their backs.

Hitler himself gave them advance notice. At a meeting of Wehrmacht officers just before the invasion of Poland, he announced that policies "not to the taste of German generals" would be put into effect. They were not to interfere, he said, but must "restrict themselves to their military duties."

The Nazi dictator could always depend on his SS (*Schutzstaffel*) troops to carry out such policies without qualms. Only selected members of the Nazi party were enrolled in these units, which were considered the elite of the Wehrmacht—a political and military corps of fanatical fighters rewarded with special favors and privileges.

On the first day of the Polish invasion Hitler issued a secret order to his personal physician, Dr. Karl Brandt, directing him to organize a nation-wide program in Germany for the administering of a "mercy death" to thousands of incurables and other "useless eaters." The next step would come when selected German physicians, operating in the name of science, conducted experiments among subject peoples to determine how much cold, heat or pain the victims could stand before succumbing.

There is no doubt that some of the German generals were disgusted, but few had the moral courage to voice disapproval of the atrocities.

Among the few was General Georg von Kuechler, who tried unsuccessfully during the invasion of Poland to have SS troopers punished for a massacre of Jews. The following spring, newly promoted, he was back in Poland. Evidently he had seen the light meanwhile, for one of his first orders stressed "the necessity of ensuring that every soldier of the Army, particularly every officer, refrain from criticizing the ethnic struggle being carried out in the Government-General—for instance, the treatment of the Polish minorities, of the Jews, and of church matters. The final solution of the ethnic struggle . . . calls for unique harsh measures."

Poles who happened to be in the path of the Russian invasion found no escape from total war. Stalin's officers soon demonstrated that they could loot and organize mass executions as systematically as the Germans. They had had a great deal of practice in their homeland during the Red Army purges of 1937-1938.

The Russo-Finnish War

Soviet Russia contracted a war of its own on November 30, 1939. Stalin, straining every resource to prepare for war with Germany, feared for the security of Leningrad, which could be shelled by long-range guns from Finnish soil. Anticipating that Finland might be Germany's ally, the Russian dictator tried to negotiate for a more favorable strategic situation. He demanded that Finland lease or sell him five areas for their military value, and the valiant refusal of the small nation brought on war.

The outcome was never in doubt, but the Finns won the world's admiration with their intelligent as well as heroic resistance. Mechanized equipment met its first test under arctic conditions as the mercury dropped to 40° below zero (Fahrenheit) in one of northern Europe's coldest winters. And just as the mud of Spain had shown the limitations of tanks, so the snows of Finland taught lessons.

At the outset, unsuccessful naval attacks cost the Russians three destroyers, two submarines and auxiliary ships, sunk by Finnish coastal batteries which severely damaged a battleship. Russian penetrations by land fared no better at first. The invading columns were drawn deeper and deeper into the forest by white-clad Finnish groups which retired after burning and destroying everything the enemy could use. Ski patrols struck at field kitchens and supply trucks until the hardy Red Army troops were so starved and exhausted as to be no match for their outnumbered foes.

Ironically, the invaders were victims of the strategy their forefathers had used against Napoleon. When they advanced far enough into a frozen land of lakes and woods, the Finns cut them to pieces in detail. In the battle of Suomussalmi, one Russian division surrendered, another was annihilated, and a third was reduced to stragglers by Finnish forces they outnumbered three to one. Tanks were only an encumbrance in snowdrifts, and stragglers perished by the hundreds in the subzero cold. At a cost of 900 killed and 1,700 wounded, the Finns inflicted losses of

Blood on the Snow in Finland

27,500 killed, 1,500 prisoners and an unknown number of wounded on the invaders at Suomussalmi.

Finnish counterattacks on the northeastern shore of Lake Ladoga drove two Red infantry divisions and a tank brigade back to Pitkaranta, where they were surrounded. Airborne supplies proved insufficient and the survivors of an infantry division and the tank brigade surrendered. The remaining division was neutralized until the end of the war.

Two Russian armies were employed in the Karelian Isthmus to crush the Finns by sheer weight. Their attacks on the Mannerheim Line failed with terrible casualties among assault troops blocked by mine fields, tank traps and machine-gun emplacements hidden by a new snowfall. Early in January the battered Russians called a halt and devoted the rest of the month to reorganizing and preparing for a supreme effort in February, 1940.

Thirteen divisions were concentrated on the Karelian Isthmus to wear the Finns down by relentless pressure. Air strikes, artillery bombardments and infantry attacks went on constantly in daylight hours. The Russian tanks came on in masses, pushing rollers ahead of them to detonate mines and pulling sledges filled with infantrymen. In one four-day period the attackers claimed to have fired 300,000 artillery rounds into the works of sleepless, exhausted defenders.

The end was inevitable. A breakthrough on February 13 forced the Finns to make a fighting withdrawal and establish a line in the Viipuri area. Russian columns crossed the ice of the Gulf of Finland and outflanked the new positions. The Finns fought on a few more days against hopeless odds, but on March 13 hostilities ceased when Marshal Mannerheim accepted the harsh Russian terms.

Finland reported 60,000 casualties, including 18,000 killed. Russian losses were announced as 48,795 killed and 158,836 wounded, but neutral observers believed that the actual total exceeded a quarter of a million. Not only had the Red rank and file been expended callously in attacks, but most of the troops had no clothing fit for a northern winter.

The results of the Russo-Finnish War were to have an influence on the German invasion of Russia in the summer of 1941. The Red Army had been a mystery to the outside world, but its poor showing in Finland convinced German observers that it had been overrated.

THE INVASION OF DENMARK AND NORWAY

Only a few weeks after the end of hostilities in Finland, German land, sea and air forces overwhelmed Denmark and Norway. Needless to say, the plans for these operations had been laid long before. This was the only concept which did not originate with Hitler, who was gradually "sold" on its merits. As a further claim to distinction, it was the single campaign in which the German Navy took the leading part.

For once, Raeder and Goering agreed as both saw the advantages of seizing Scandinavian naval and air bases. The admiral took the lead in convincing Hitler that force must be used to ensure Germany's domination over a critical area on which the Reich depended for 11,000,000 of its annual 15,000,000 tons of iron ore. Most of it was shipped by rail via Kiruna from Swedish mines to Narvik and other Norwegian ports, and thence through Norwegian territorial waters to the Baltic. If Britain should first take these ports, warned Raeder, she could not only stop the vital flow of ore but also blockade the Baltic and the North Sea.

On October 10, when the proposal was broached to Hitler, he was occupied with plans for attacking France and Great Britain. As postponements became necessary, the Führer listened with increasing favor to Raeder's suggestions. The operation had an additional appeal to him because of the possibilities for putting into effect his racial theories.

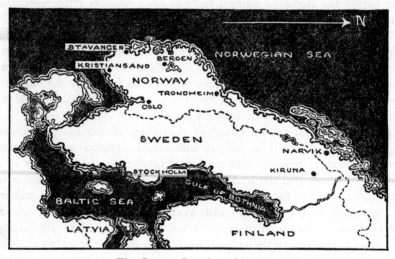

The German Invasion of Norway

German professors, who found vindications for Hitler's doctrines just as their forerunners had upheld Bismarck's, decided that among Europe's "inferior" peoples, the Scandinavians came nearest to equality with Germany's *Herrenvolk*. Hence the new aggressions were planned to some extent as cultural blitzkriegs. In contrast to the persecutions of Poles and Jews, the world would be shown how mildly the invaders could treat approved peoples. The advantages of seizing a merchant marine had a more practical appeal, as did the prospect of submarine bases nearer to British shipping lanes. From a military viewpoint, the blow of April 9, 1940, was also planned to unhinge the Allies both psychologically and strategically before Hitler struck to divide France and Britain.

Norway had a large merchant marine but no army, navy or air defenses fit to cope with a large-scale invasion. Denmark was even more vulnerable. Nazi plans called for an attack on the six chief Norwegian ports: Oslo, Kristiansand, Stavanger, Bergen, Trondheim, and Narvik. Air support, consisting of 1,000 planes, was to be the reliance of Nazi naval forces which included two pocket battleships, eight light cruisers and 20 destroyers. It was a small fleet for such a task, but Raeder counted on surprise to paralyze the defenders until Nazi land forces could gain a foothold.

He was not disappointed in this expectation. The shock of invasion proved so terrific that Denmark was mastered by surprise alone on the morning of April 9, 1940. In Norway air power came to the aid of treachery and deception as waves of transport planes at three-minute intervals landed 3,000 storm troopers in an hour at the Oslo airport. By afternoon the capital was in the hands of the Nazis as their band played for the stunned citizens.

Major Vidkun Quisling, former defense minister at the head of the Norwegian Fascist minority, made his name a universal epithet by ordering shore batteries at Bergen not to fire on invading warships and transports. A second army officer, Colonel Sundlo, welcomed the German merchant ships which had smuggled troops and artillery into Narvik. Other vital ports, airfields and railway junctions were taken with the aid of German guides who had been succored in Norway as undernourished children after World War I. Having thus learned the language and local conditions, they were able to betray their former foster parents with unique efficiency.

Newspaper accounts at the time made it appear that Norway had been delivered by spies and traitors rather than conquered. Despite a few instances of treachery, the result owed to a German land, sea and air campaign in which performance came up to plan. Within 24 hours the seaports representing the six main objectives were under Nazi control. Airborne troops took Oslo and Stavanger without a fight. These victories gave the Luftwaffe two airfields 600 miles north of its bases in western Germany.

The only failure may be traced to the Nazi assumption that the Norwegians would not resist. They were placated by eminently correct behavior on the part of invading troops commanded by General von Falkenhorst. They were offered the opportunity of continuing under their own monarch as wards rather than foes of the Third Reich. But they made it evident, after recovering from their first shock, that they intended to fight. King Haakon found a refuge in England, and the

Allied cause was aided by such ships of the Norwegian merchant marine as could escape.

The Allies were at a handicap against an enemy not bound by considerations of neutrality or international law. Had the British and French made a similarly ruthless use of superior naval forces to seize Narvik first, the Germans might have been hard put to recover the initiative at the risk of having their annual supply of iron ore seriously reduced. As it was, the Allies had to wait until after the Germans struck before sending troops to the aid of a sorely beset small nation. By that time— April 17 to 19—it was too late for the two British brigades and one French regiment to dislodge the Nazis in the Trondheim area. The Allies evacuated their force during the night of May 1-2, leaving south and central Norway in the hands of the enemy.

Operations at Narvik were more successful. Norwegian troops reinforced by British and French contingents, including French Foreign Legion units, made up a task force of about 25,000 which retook the seaport on May 28. The victory was short-lived, for reverses in France caused the Allies to be evacuated during the night of June 8-9 along with the Norwegian king and government officials. Norway's last organized troops laid down their arms, though guerrilla resistance went on in the mountains throughout the next four years.

In the naval warfare which accompanied land operations, the British took great risks and incurred heavy losses, largely from Nazi bombing planes. An aircraft carrier, two cruisers, nine destroyers and eight submarines were sunk in addition to six cruisers and eight destroyers damaged. It was a high price but the British could better afford it than could the Germans with losses of three cruisers, ten destroyers, twelve merchant ships and eight submarines, plus one pocket battleship and four cruisers severely damaged. The small German Navy was so hard hit that the few remaining ships had scarcely more than nuisance value.

The climax of the naval fighting took place on April 13 when the old British battleship *Warspite,* of Jutland fame, steamed majestically up narrow Narvik Fjord, followed by nine destroyers. They brought eight Nazi destroyers to bay and sank all at a cost of only three destroyers damaged.

HOLLAND AND BELGIUM OVERRUN

In the Norwegian campaign the reproach of "too little and too late" could be defended by the British and French on strategic grounds. The enemy had gained such a firm foothold in the first few days that it would have been a grave risk to send more than a token expeditionary force. The Germans were able to pour twice as many troops into Norway, and after a hopeless campaign the Allies withdrew with honor. In twenty-three days Hitler had subjected another country, and before his foes could recover their balance he threw the Nazi military machine into second gear by invading Belgium and the Netherlands without warning during the night of May 9-10, 1940.

Except for damaged prestige, the Allies had landed and evacuated their Norwegian force with few losses. Better yet, they had not committed themselves as deeply as the Germans might have expected. But in the next phase of Hitler's far-flung campaign France and England were compelled to take more serious risks. Moral considerations made it imperative that their armies hasten to the rescue, yet Belgium and the Netherlands had maintained such an anxious neutrality that no concerted plans had been discussed. Until recent months, indeed, Belgium had carried impartiality so far as to station troops along the French as well as the German frontier.

The fury of the opening assault left no doubt that the final bid for supremacy had come at last. The French General Staff, still guided by precepts of 1914, laid its defense plans accordingly. Then the Schlieffen Plan had nearly succeeded because the Allies were slow to foresee the menace of the wheeling German right wing, and in 1940 General Maurice Gamelin repaired the omission by advancing on the enemy's flank in Belgium.

The invasion began with a terrific dawn assault by the Luftwaffe on airports, supply depots and communication centres. For forty-eight hours the direction of the two main thrusts seemed to bear out the French idea of history repeating itself. Again, as in 1914, the enemy struck at the crossings of the Meuse and Albert Canal near Liége, and the blow at the Netherlands could be interpreted as an amendment to the Schlieffen Plan. Hence the Allies seemed strategically justified as they advanced in a left wheel of four main armies pivoting on the Maginot Line. One French army swept north of Brussels to the Dutch border as another, containing most of the armored and mechanized forces, drove toward Breda. The British force, under General Lord Gort, pushed northeast from the Meuse Valley to threaten the flank of any German spearhead entering France by the historic route of Liége and Namur. On the right the Second and Ninth French armies defended the approaches from Belgium and the Ardennes.

The movements of Plan D were carried out with a celerity which the Allies were soon to regret. Within a few hours it began to appear that the Netherlands could not hold out long enough to be reinforced. Even in areas where the sluices had been opened, the invaders came on in inflated rubber boats. Spies and traitors delivered some key points, as in Norway, but the German progress owed chiefly to rehearsed plans put into effect with supreme audacity. Parachute troops, officially accused of wearing Dutch uniforms, created tactical history by landing to seize Rotterdam's airport and strategically vital bridges. And while airborne troops failed to capture Queen Wilhelmina and her ministers at The Hague, the attempt showed how thoroughly a small, unprepared country could be demoralized.

The five days of Holland, from the Dutch viewpoint, were a nightmare of chaos filled with explosions, bomb flashes and sudden enemy appearances far behind a "front line" which existed only in the minds of generals fighting the last war over again. But the seeming chaos was controlled by the invaders with icy precision, and on the morning of May 14 the little nation had no choice but to capitulate. After the submission the victors issued a warning of terrorism to their remaining opponents by gutting the business district of Rotterdam with hundreds of 2,200-pound bombs. Eight hundred people were killed and 78,000 made homeless.

The Allies, repeating the errors of 1914, had expected the Liége fortifications to hold up the enemy for days at the crossings of the Meuse. Hence the fall within twenty-four hours of Eben-Emael, key fortress of the Liége system, gave rise to speculations as to the "secret weapon" used by the victors. Actually, the Germans had improved their time during the winter of "phony war" by rehearsing such attacks with models. Before dawn on May 10 German gliders landed troops directly on the superstructure. Trained specialists moved swiftly to blow up the cupolas, put the ammunition hoists out of commission and toss grenades into the muzzles of the guns. It was too late to save Eben-Emael by the time the sirens shrieked in the darkness, and Stuka dive bombers were already silencing the other forts. Soon the paratroops had been strengthened by ground forces which crossed the Meuse in rubber boats, and by noon of the 11th the entire Liége system had been forced to surrender.

This is merely one example of the planning and precision which went into hundreds of co-ordinated attacks delivered simultaneously the first morning. The Allies often suspected betrayal or novel weapons when they were beaten by a combination of skill and surprise which gave the invaders an overwhelming tactical superiority.

Plan D of the Allies called for a northward movement to a line north and east of Brussels, stretching from the Meuse to the Dutch frontier. The Maginot Line was Gamelin's reliance for defending his right flank. Since this barrier extended only as far west as Longwy, he de-

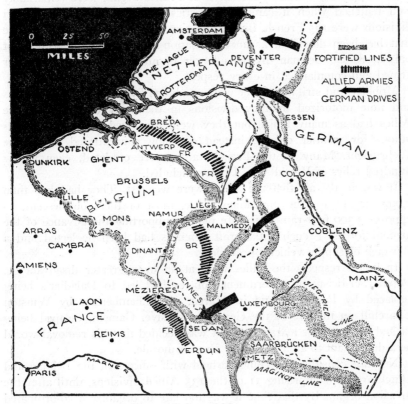

German Drives of May 10, 1940

pended on his Ninth and Second armies, behind the Ardennes and the Belgian fortifications, to hold up an enemy advance long enough for the Allied forces in Belgium to strike a decisive blow at the enemy's right flank.

Within 48 hours of the first German attacks, Gamelin had cause to suspect that Plan D would prove to be as futile as Plan XVII had been in 1914. For it grew increasingly apparent that the Nazi generals did not intend to expose their right flank while executing a wide right wheel in the Schlieffen manner. On the contrary, their armored columns were driving through the Ardennes toward the Meuse.

THE BATTLE OF FRANCE

The opposing forces, as the battle of France began, were remarkably well matched when it came to statistics. Opposed to the 136 Nazi divisions were 135 French, British, Belgian and Dutch divisions—a force that has been described as an aggregation rather than an army. Not only were the German divisions larger in numbers; they were better armed and commanded in every respect.

Mobility and striking power were combined by ten armored divisions and nine motorized infantry divisions in the army of invasion. The Allies had as many tanks, but they were employed in separated battalions for frontier defense instead of being concentrated, as in the Wehrmacht. Many of the French tanks were outdated, even a few hundred relics of World War I being included.

It was in the air that the Allies were weakest. They had less than 2,000 aircraft for the impending battle, most of them obsolescent, to oppose 3,500 first-rate Luftwaffe planes supporting the advance of the ground forces. French antiaircraft defenses had been neglected and a shortage of supply vehicles prevailed.

In moral respects the Allies were at an even greater disadvantage. Popular criticism of government policies had led to Daladier's being replaced by Paul Reynaud in March, and Chamberlain by Winston Churchill on the eve of the German offensive. Gamelin escaped being sacked by a narrow margin when it was decided that his removal would be a depressant to an already low French morale.

No staff consultations could be held with officers of the Belgian and Dutch armies, comprising 31 of the 135 Allied divisions, until after the invasion began. By that time it was too late to organize a co-ordinated defense.

The main feature of the Nazi plan, which had been amended many times, was the decision to aim the assault on France through the Ardennes with a view to opening up crossings of the Meuse south of Liége. When a wide enough breakthrough had been achieved, three Nazi columns of invasion would deliver the decisive attacks. The eastern column would swing left to move on the Maginot Line from the rear. The central column would drive south toward the Aisne. For the western column was reserved the death blow—a swing toward the Channel to strike the bulk of the Allied forces from the rear and smash them against the anvil of the German armies in northern Belgium and the Netherlands.

Plan GELB was, as Hitler boasted, a Schlieffen Plan in reverse; and the result could very well have been a battle of annihilation that would dwarf the symbolic German triumph of 1870. For it was a more grandiose Sedan the Germans planned in 1940, even to selecting that historic Meuse River town for their main breakthrough.

Charles de Gaulle, who commanded a French tank division with valor and distinction, had repeatedly warned his countrymen that the Ardennes were no barrier to armored units in spite of hills and narrow, winding roads. The Germans seemed to have thought this route too obvious, since they went to elaborate lengths for deception.

General von Kleist's group, with four of the ten armored divisions and the pick of the motorized infantry, was given the assignment of driving toward the Meuse. By the evening of May 10 his columns were well into Luxembourg. His order of the day read in part as follows:

> This side of the Meuse there can be no rest or halt for a man of this column. The organization must advance night and day without stopping, without looking right or left, and without yielding for a moment its calm control. . . . Our losses will be smaller if we do not allow the enemy time to get his bearings and make plans for the defense.

French cavalry were first to report that the German drive through the Ardennes was not a feint but the main effort. These troopers gave the Nazi armored columns their first opposition before retiring across the Meuse with heavy losses on the evening of May 12 and destroying the bridges. Up to this time the spotlight had been on the battle of Flanders, although it was already plain that Holland and Belgium could not hold out for long.

It cannot be charged that Gamelin failed to take immediate measures. Eleven divisions, including some armored forces, were ordered to the aid of General Corap's Ninth Army. According to past standards of railway warfare, these forces moved swiftly, since the first units were due to arrive on May 14 and the last before the 21st. The tragedy of France's unpreparedness was revealed when the motorized enemy reached the Meuse on the 13th to deliver the breakthrough attack at four o'clock that afternoon.

For the third time in as many generations, Sedan was the scene of decision in a war between France and Germany. It was not chosen for its historic interest, but because a northward bend in the river gave the invaders the opportunity for flanking artillery fire. The Nazi planners believed, moreover, that a breakthrough this far south would make the French anxious for the security of Paris.

At noon on the 13th General Heinz Guderian moved up three of the four armored divisions. The German 88's poured in a devastating fire as hundreds of dive bombers pounded the defenders for four hours. The French put up a brave fight but could repulse only one of the four crossings attempted by the Germans at four o'clock. The first ferry was in operation two hours later.

The tactics could have been no surprise to anyone who had read German treatises. The prescribed blitzkrieg assaults were launched on a 12-mile front by combat groups using tanks, Stuka dive bombers and motorized artillery. Before dark on May 13 the river had been crossed at three points, and like a flood enlarging a hole in a dam the mechanized torrent poured through the narrow gap. Within twenty-four hours the advance units covered nineteen miles as a second blitzkrieg attack broke through near Dinant, just over the Belgian frontier. By May 16 the Panzer divisions had reached Rethel, forty miles from Sedan, and another twenty miles on the 17th took them to the Oise.

This may be accepted as the actual date of France's downfall, for the invaders had now swung so far to the west that Gamelin's main armies were doomed to a fight for survival rather than victory.

PURSUIT AND ANNIHILATION

Up to May 15 the Allies in Belgium were still carrying out Plan D, and some of the French units had pushed far enough north to cross the Dutch border just before the collapse. On the morning of the 15th it was clear that the Allied rear was in danger, but the retirement southward began too late. By that time the French Ninth and Second armies were being cut to pieces, despite the effectiveness of armored counterattacks launched by De Gaulle's thinned tank division. The Germans had opened up a 40-mile hole in French defenses along the Meuse, and into France poured a column so long that the head was crossing the river before the tail had left Germany.

On May 18 the Kleist group drove across World War I battlefields from St.-Quentin to Péronne. Laon, Amiens and Doullens fell the next day. By the 21st the German armored columns had reached the Channel, cutting off the main Allied army in Belgium.

From May 17 to 25 anyone looking down from an airplane would have seen all Flanders and northwest France as a fiery caldron of bomb explosions and burning villages. The Allies, faithful to their strategic ideals, still hoped to form a defensive line somehow, somewhere. Radio announcers, trying to leaven the awful lump of dismay, hinted that once a stand had been made, mighty steel squadrons would meet in head-on shock. But such a prospect was not included in the invaders' plans. On the principle of using strength against weakness, they avoided tank battles and sent their armor against opposing infantry for purposes of infiltration. Far from seeking a collision, they made it their strategic object to rend the Allied forces into tactical morsels which could be masticated by their own infantry, following close behind the Stukas and Panzers.

When the Germans reached the Channel, nearly a million French, British and Belgian troops were surrounded on three sides by foes pressing in from Calais, Ostend, Ghent and Lille. In their own rear the invaders had already annihilated the French Ninth Army and most of the Second by forcing the surrender of the remnants which had not been previously cut to pieces. Other Nazi forces stood on the Somme and Aisne, poised for a drive on Paris, while still others had worked around to the rear of the Maginot Line.

Sick at heart, the peoples of the democratic nations could only await the final catastrophe after the surrender of King Leopold and his Army. The Belgian collapse exposed the entire left flank of Allied forces crowded into a narrow triangle with their backs to the sea. So dark was the hour that it seemed an authentic miracle when a concentration of British sea and air power brought off the evacuation of 338,223 men from Dunkirk, the sole remaining port. The survivors included all but about 30,000 of the original British expeditionary force as well as some French divisions. The whole of their arms and equipment had to be abandoned to pursuers who speedily "mopped up" Flanders, adding to a bag of prisoners which amounted to well over a million by June 1.

The Dunkirk evacuation, which will be given due attention in the following chapter, allowed a week's grace to General Maxime Weygand, greatest living exponent of the Foch school, who had replaced the hapless Gamelin. While the German armies regrouped for the pursuit and annihilation phases of Plan RED, the Allied peoples dared hope that a defensive line might still be established. The septuagenarian French general did everything possible to create defenses in depth, bristling with tank traps. But the invaders were so overwhelming that they swept to the Marne in simple frontal attacks. Italy's declaration of war and the fall of Paris followed in rapid succession, and on June 16 unhappy France asked for an armistice. Like lost and bewildered children, a people broken in spirit placed their last faith in the paternal leadership of Marshal Henri Pétain, and the eighty-four-year-old hero of Verdun had only the solution of despair.

Three generations of Frenchmen had trusted in vain to the military occultism of a General Staff which proved to be a sphinx without a secret. The failure of 1870 had been redeemed by the valor of armed citizens, while in 1914 enough allies had been at hand to turn defeat into victory. But there was no balm for the wounds of fallen France in 1940. Civilians could only share the blame with professional soldiers, for Weygand's operations had been handicapped by the greatest mass flight of modern history.

All the roads leading south were choked with pitiful hordes of refugees from northern France and Belgium. Peasants, shopkeepers, old men, women and children—they strained rearward, like so many lemmings, toward some unknown destination.

France might have taken warning from Poland, where every effort had been made to create panic among civilians. Yet eight months later it became evident that Paris had given little thought to the problem of citizen morale. While the refugees poured southward, scourged as if with bloody whips by Nazi bombs and machine-gun slugs, the French radio blared forth jazz music or cooking recipes. Soon the officials themselves were seized by the prevailing spirit of panic, and many of them joined the dismal migration. During the worst of the crisis the roads were choked with noncombatants, so that supplies and reinforcements could not reach the troops. This factor alone might have been enough to cause the final downfall, even if there had not been so many other elements of political and military weakness.

Up to this time the invaders had shown a cautious respect for world opinion as compared to their atrocities in Poland. But there was not the shadow of military excuse for the machine-gunning and dive-bombing of French civilian refugees by Luftwaffe aircraft. On the contrary, this slaughter resulted in needless road blocks as dead and wounded civilians slowed the German pursuit.

In retrospect, the "Maginot Line mentality" was blamed for France's catastrophe. It would be more just, however, to blame the failure to make a proper strategic use of that belt of steel and concrete. A shield is not much protection without a sword, and the Maginot Line was never intended to assume the entire burden of frontier defense. Its original purpose was to compensate for France's dwindling manpower by narrowing the front and channelizing the path of Germanic invasion. This would have made it possible to maintain a central mass of manoeuvre which could be rushed to any part of the front in hours. Unfortunately for France, Gamelin departed so far from this concept as to place his poorest troops opposite the Ardennes, while his reserves were so distributed that it took from three to ten days for them to reach the front by rail. Before the campaign was a week old, time had beaten France— the lost months before the war, the lost days of the early phase, and finally the lost hours against a foe who did not lose minutes.

Still, it would be unfair to heap too much blame on poor Gamelin's inept generalship. Joffre and Foch must also be held to stern account. For the class of 1914 had consisted of 750,000 Frenchmen, while in 1939 only 450,000 answered the call to arms. The gaps in the ranks of the nation's defenders represented the 300,000 unborn sons of the "human grapeshot" who had been sacrificed to the offensive doctrines of 1914 and 1915.

II

BRITAIN FIGHTS FOR SURVIVAL

*We shall draw from the heart of suffering itself the means
of inspiration and survival.*

—CHURCHILL

LATE in June, as Hitler visited the tomb of Napoleon in Paris, he could also claim to have mastered Europe. Like his predecessor, he had allied himself with Russia while reducing the western nations of the Continent to military subjection or a timid neutrality. Only the British Isles defied him, and Hitler had wings to cross the few miles of water which had balked Napoleon. Already the invaders of France were singing a ballad which proclaimed not only their ambition but also the envy behind a century's German hatred of British institutions:

> For we sail 'gainst England!
> Our flag, see it wave from the mast,
> Of Germany's strength it speaks;
> We want to halt at last
> The Englishman's sneering laugh.

Love of tradition is often held to be a symptom of national decline, and in 1940 England still paid a watchman five pounds a year to sound the alarm if Napoleon appeared off the Dover cliffs. This sentry must have witnessed an even more dramatic scene during the last days of May.

For tradition became the strength of a proud people who had not even forgotten the Spanish Armada. Pleasure boats, yachts, coal barges, fishing craft and warships made up a strange flotilla which crossed and recrossed the Channel to snatch broken battalions from the bombs of the Luftwaffe. Two days of fog, blanketing a sea as smooth as a mill-pond, aided in the rescue; and as the greatest boon of all, the Royal Air Force won a brief local supremacy.

British pilots were closer to their bases than Germans who had not yet found time to occupy captured airfields, while the marshy ground and canals near Dunkirk slowed up the mechanized forces. Thus the miracle of the evacuation is explained in practical terms—excepting only a factor which defies material analysis. For the British people, united by peril, had recaptured a national spirit which seemed dormant if not dead. No longer did they trust in the blockade, German oil shortages or any other comfortable road to victory. The long period of self-delusion ended abruptly when Winston Churchill, replacing Chamberlain as prime minister, addressed the House of Commons:

> If you ask what is our policy, it is to wage war by sea, land and air with all our might. I have nothing to offer but blood, toil, tears and sweat.

Despite the new British morale, the legend of the Dunkirk spirit being generated entirely by spontaneous combustion is dismissed as a myth by David Divine in *The Nine Days of Dunkirk*. "The 'Dunkirk spirit,' " he comments, "was not a vast incandescent flame of sacrifice and high endeavor that swept the country. Like the flow of little ships, it was something that awoke spontaneously but that had to be guided, encouraged, supported—like a small red heart of embers that must be blown upon. . . . Churchill blew upon them."

THE DUNKIRK EVACUATION

The British Admiralty put Operation DYNAMO into effect in the early evening of Sunday, May 26, 1940. It was expected, according to the order, that as many as 45,000 British soldiers might be taken away from Dunkirk in two days before enemy action put an end to the evacuation.

Four hours before receiving the directive, Admiral Sir Bertram Ramsay had already sent the first ships. In the tradition of Nelson placing the telescope to his blind eye, the forthright admiral took the responsibility at his Dover headquarters for a decision which resulted in the first

27,696 men being rescued. They were on their way home before midnight.

The operation went on full blast throughout the following week. Although Goering had promised to blight any such attempt, the Luftwaffe met its initial frustration. Night bombing was in its infancy, which gave Dunkirk a few hours of respite at that season of long days. There was also the factor that bombs exploding on the sandy beaches and in the shallow water were limited in destructiveness. But the chief reason for the Luftwaffe's failure was the temporary superiority of an out-

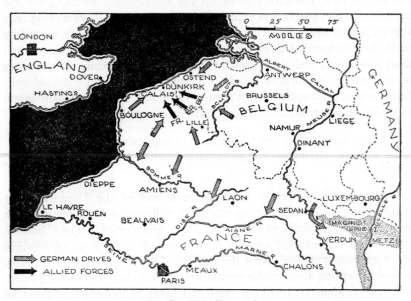

The Dunkirk Evacuation

numbered Royal Air Force. The new Spitfires proved more than a match for the Messerschmitts, and a second-rate British two-man fighter, the Boulton-Paul Defiant, had its fleeting hour of glory. Its inferiority to the faster German fighters had not yet become apparent, and the Defiant was deadly against Nazi bombers.

Among the many Dunkirk myths was the story that Hitler himself permitted the broken battalions to escape, hoping thus to woo Britain and promote a separate peace. The fact is that Field Marshal Gerd von Rundstedt had called a four-day halt, approved by Hitler, of his Army Group A. Fully half of his tanks and vehicles were destroyed or in need of repairs, following the drive across northern France. After the interlude, when the Germans did try to take Dunkirk from the land side, they ran into the last-ditch resistance of British and French troops fighting desperately behind canals and marshes. Lord Gort and his soldiers have seldom been given enough credit for their part in the "miracle of Dunkirk." Their perimeter kept shrinking as the result of enemy pressure, but it held long enough to allow the bulk of the threatened forces to escape, leaving their arms behind.

To Admiral Ramsay's strange fleet, however, belongs most of the glory. The 848 ships, many of them manned by civilian volunteers, comprised practically anything and everything that would stay afloat a few hours. No fewer than 226 of the 693 British ships were sunk, ranging from the destroyer *Basilisk* to the appropriately named 10-foot cockleshell *Dinky*. Losses among the 155 French, Belgian and Dutch ships were in the same proportion.

Here it may be wondered, in view of the havoc that submarines might have wrought, why the German Navy played such an impotent part at Dunkirk. The answer is that the German Navy had virtually ceased to exist for the time being, most of its units being under repair or at the bottom of the sea in Norwegian waters. The only operative ships were a heavy cruiser, two light cruisers, four destroyers and three submarines, though several major units were under construction.

June 1 was the peak of Operation DYNAMO, with the dramatic total of 64,429 men being rescued while the Royal Air Force fought the Luftwaffe to a standstill. One of the memorable spectacles of that June day was a British infantry company drawn up in a perfect column of fours in waist-deep water, coolly awaiting its turn for rescue. There were also instances of panic, but fewer than might be supposed, considering that men of four nations, speaking three languages, participated in the operation.

On the night of Monday, June 3, DYNAMO came to an end as the last 26,175 of the 338,226 rescued troops were lifted. Remaining in the area, according to German claims, were 40,000 men taken as prisoners.

HUMBLE PIE FOR NAZI GENERALS

Although the luster of the Nazi victory was somewhat dimmed by the escape of so many potential captives, plans were afoot in the Wehrmacht for a gigantic celebration. A parade through the streets of Paris was proposed, with Bastille Day on July 14 being named as the tentative date. But even Hitler was not so lacking in decency as to approve a jubilation on the national holiday of a brave fallen nation. Besides, he did not wish to take the risk of the parade being interrupted by British bombs.

Such an insult to France would have been contrary to the spirit of the comparatively moderate armistice terms—moderate, at least, from a German viewpoint. A large area of France was allowed to remain unoccupied; the French Navy was merely to be laid up and demobilized; and the Italian Fascists were sharply curbed in their demands for French territory.

From the French viewpoint, of course, the situation might have been summed up in the words of Francis I, "All is lost save honor." Much the same thing was said in 1940 by one of the French armistice delegates, General Charles Huntziger, when he learned that his country would be shorn of Alsace, Lorraine and other slices of territory. *"Les conditions sont dures,"* he commented, *"mais il n'y a rien contre l'honneur."*

Hitler's attitude toward conquered France was based on a constraint alien to his nature. He realized that too much harshness might result in making a French rallying point of North Africa, with its reservoir of hardy native troops. Thus it was that France, the archenemy, got off easier than Belgium and the Netherlands, which were occupied and exploited without a pretense of conciliation.

As for the victory parade in Paris, it came to nothing in consequence of the Führer's sudden return to his Black Forest retreat. He had already made up his mind as to the kind of celebration he would have, and the prospect was malicious enough to give him a good deal of anticipatory pleasure.

There was, to be sure, a parade conducted in Berlin on July 18 by a single infantry regiment. But neither Hitler nor his generals bothered to attend such an insignificant affair. The real Roman triumph was scheduled for the following evening in Berlin's Kroll Opera House.

All the officers of the German hierarchy were there in acceptance of an invitation which amounted to a command. As Hitler glanced at the rows of stiffly seated middle-aged men in dress uniforms, their chests blazing with decorations, he had no illusions about the opinion these military aristocrats had once held of the "Austrian guttersnipe." They had scarcely concealed their disdain for the World War I corporal when they thought they could use him as a rabble-rouser and cast him aside after he had served their purposes.

Even as late as the Polish triumph they had still retained enough authority to block his first plans for an attack on France and Britain. But now, less than a year later, it was another story. Hitler's cheaply bought victories in Norway and France had established him with Germany's industrial leaders and people beyond any prospect of the Wehrmacht officers daring to oppose him.

The Führer was never more gracious than when he rose to make his speech. As became the fountain of all honors, his own chest was bare of medals. He thanked the German officers for their loyal support; and as he continued, it grew more and more obvious that he was taking full credit for the plans and decisions of victory. The officers were merely being thanked as contributors whose suggestions had proved helpful.

When the Führer finished, he passed out decorations in token of his appreciation. Or perhaps "shoveled out" would be more appropriate, since it was insultingly plain that he meant to cheapen the medals by distributing them with such prodigality. Promotions were so many that new titles had to be applied, such as the one created for Goering, *Reichsmarschall des Grossdeutschen Reiches.* Thirteen marshals' batons were awarded. Seven men were advanced to the rank of full *General,* one to *Generaladmiral,* and nineteen to *General-oberst.*

Although Hitler had already acquired a retinue of sycophants, there were still Prussian officers of the old school who resented his debasing of military rank. They could do nothing but hide their feelings, for the servant of 1936 had become the master of 1940. The German officer corps had lost its honor in Poland, and it lost its pride on that July night in the Kroll Opera House.

The Failure of Operation Sea Lion

British morale rose to such heights after Dunkirk that Churchill felt it necessary to inject a warning note. "Wars," he said, "are not won by evacuations."

Britons realized that the country had never had such a dynamic war leader since the days of the elder Pitt. The comparison was inevitable, for Churchill with his eloquence and histrionic flair had many of the foibles as well as strong points of the Great Commoner. Both men believed fervently in the historic destiny of the English-speaking peoples, and since Pitt no Briton had ever appealed so forcefully to the New World as Churchill, whose mother had been born an American. Both men had risen to power in an hour of alarming national reverses, but

Churchill faced an even more formidable task as he labored to save the empire which Pitt had done so much to create. At least the homes and liberties of Englishmen were not directly imperiled in 1757, while in 1940 Churchill's words reveal the extent of the menace after Dunkirk:

> We shall defend our island whatever the cost may be. We shall fight on the beaches. We shall fight on the landing grounds. We shall fight in the fields and streets and in the hills. We shall never surrender and even if, which I do not for a moment believe, this island or even a part of it is subjugated and starving, then our empire across the seas will carry on the struggle until in God's good name the New World in all its strength and might sets forth to the rescue and liberation of the Old.

Months later, when the information could safely be made public, the prime minister disclosed that England was as unarmed at this time as a modern nation could be. Most of the armored and mechanized equipment had been abandoned in Flanders, and the loss of 1,000 guns left the island dangerously short of modern artillery. Even small arms and ammunition were lacking in a country which had never dreamed of such an emergency, so that Britons gratefully accepted an assortment of rifles, pistols and shotguns contributed by sympathizers in the United States.

This was the situation early in June, when London newspapers discussed the prospect of moving the seat of government to Canada. Britain could not dismiss as unfeasible the possibility of a German cross-Channel invasion, and all manner of preparations were being made with limited resources to defend the beaches and the roads leading inward.

Hitler seems to have given his first serious thought to the subject on July 2, 1940, after concluding that Britain would not make a separate peace. Ten days later, according to Ronald Wheatley's *Operation Sea Lion,* the views of OKH were expressed by Jodl and Keitel in a paper entitled "First Thoughts on a Landing in England." The naval supremacy of the island was conceded, as was the improbability of gaining a surprise.

"The landing," it was proposed, "must therefore take place in the form of a river crossing in force on a broad front. In this operation, the role of artillery must fall to the Luftwaffe; the first wave of landing troops must be very strong; and in place of bridging operations, a sea lane completely secure from naval attacks must be established in the Dover Straits."

It was suggested that troops of seven divisions (later increased to thirteen) should be landed between Dover and Bournemouth. Halder and Brauchitsch endorsed the proposal after discussing it with Raeder; and on July 16 Hitler approved it under the name of Operation SEA LION (*Seelöwe*). In his *Directive No. 16, Preparations for a Landing Operation Against England,* he stated his purpose in the first sentence: "As England, in spite of her hopeless military situation, still shows no sign of willingness to come to terms, I have decided to prepare, and if necessary to carry out, a landing operation against her."

Apparently the OKH planners had no doubts of success, so intoxicated were they on the heady wine of conquest. Elaborate schemes were advanced for the annihilation of British armies after gaining a foothold, but the inconvenient question of crossing the Channel was usually sidestepped or taken for granted. Although great mass-produced concrete troop-carrying tanks were proposed, capable of high speeds under water, these visionary monsters never reached the blueprint stage. When it came to landing craft actually available, the best that Raeder could offer were ancient flat-bottomed barges which would have to be towed.

American amphibious planners held that hours and even minutes counted in getting the assault force ashore to seize a beachhead. Hitler's land-minded generals allowed eleven days for the crossing of the first ten complete divisions.

The only glimmer of realism was the insistence of the OKH that German control of the air must be gained as a preliminary. Goering, as usual, promised results. And Operation SEA LION, a fantasy which never materialized, was sidetracked in August when the battle of Britain began.

THE MARNE OF WORLD WAR II

Although Hitler scoffed at Britons who hailed an evacuation as if it were a victory, Dunkirk had a tremendous influence on future strategy. There for the first time the Luftwaffe lost control of the air temporarily. And while the reverse could not be called serious, it disturbed aviators who had been shooting down the obsolescent and outnumbered planes of France with the ease of hunters bagging crippled ducks.

The Nazi air generals no longer despised the Royal Air Force after Dunkirk, but they did not realize that the British rate of aircraft production had passed that of Germany early in 1940. Even so, the total number of British planes was below the 4,000 of the Luftwaffe, which reached its peak during the battle of France. There were more than a million men in German air units, nearly half of them serving as anti-aircraft troops.

German land advances of recent campaigns had been made possible by precision bombings which knocked out opposing bases and communications at the outset. An amphibious operation depended to an even greater extent on "softening up" the enemy; and when the blow fell on August 8, Goering's airmen concentrated first on the island's ports and shipping. Thus for the first time in history a decisive battle was to be fought entirely in the new tactical element, as Tennyson had visioned so long ago in his poem "Prophecy":

> And there rained a ghastly dew
> From the nations' airy navies
> Grappling in the central blue.

The early phase lasted ten days, according to *The Battle of Britain,* a report published by the British Air Ministry. The Luftwaffe not only failed in its strategic object but suffered unexpected losses from RAF fighter opposition. As the next logical step the winged invaders struck with all their might at the airdromes which harbored the British planes, and the critical second period of great daylight assaults went on from August 24 to September 5. The Luftwaffe took an even more emphatic beating during these two weeks. On September 6, therefore, the precepts of Warsaw and Rotterdam were applied as the Germans launched a month's attack of frightfulness on the civilian population of London. This phase reached its peak on the 15th, when no less than 185 of Goering's planes were shot down, according to British reports. Such losses could not be long endured, and during the last three weeks of October the battle limped into its fourth period with the badly battered Luftwaffe confining its efforts chiefly to night raids on London and other cities. British morale soared higher in the consciousness of victory; for despite the heavy casualties and damage, a common peril united all classes when even the king and queen risked death in the bombing of Buckingham Palace.

These are the bare strategic outlines of the 84-day battle. They cannot give an impression of the huge air fleets which pounded incessantly at the island—great "sandwich formations" of German machines flying in six or eight "decks." At heights of 15,000 and 20,000 feet the outnumbered British fighters ripped into these aerial phalanxes to bring down an average of four planes for one. After such a defeat an amphibious operation would have been suicidal, so that Churchill was justified in his tribute to Britain's airmen, "Never in the field of human conflict was so much owed by so many to so few."

The Germans had spared no pains to make the Luftwaffe vastly superior to any possible combination of foes. When the nation went into full-scale mass production in 1938, Goering could be absolutely sure that Britain and France had nothing to match his Messerschmitt fighters or his Junkers, Heinkel and Dornier bombers. On the tactical principle that fighters should protect bombers in formation, the former were armed with two machine guns in each wing plus a 20-mm. cannon firing through the propeller hub. Hence it did not seem necessary to provide much armor.

As late as January, 1939, the British appeared to be the least formidable of Germany's foes in the air. Ironically, this very delay proved a blessing, according to Newman's *The Tools of War,* when the island began a belated production of machines which outclassed Goering's. For the Blenheims were more adequately armored than the German bombers, while the Hurricanes and Spitfires, with their four machine guns in each wing, had more fire power than the German fighters. Moreover, the Spitfire was faster than the Messerschmitt 109, and the Hurricane more manoeuvrable.

Dunkirk gave the Luftwaffe its first intimation that the enemy's planes were more modern. During the following ten weeks British craftsmen, toiling twelve hours a day, reduced the German margin of numerical superiority. The island also profited from the respite by perfecting a national system of air-raid defenses which played as vital a part in the battle of Britain as the valor of RAF pilots.

Poland's sad example first warned the British, who proceeded to divide the island into districts, each under a "controller" in charge of fighting planes, antiaircraft batteries, balloon barrages, detection devices and weather data. No general had more responsibility, for it was this officer, seated in his operations room, who took command of a three-dimensional battle in which seconds counted. At the first radar warning of raiders approaching three miles nearer every minute, he decided how many fighters, kept waiting at the "ready" or "stand-by," to put into the air above his district. Weather, mileage, gasoline and ammunition all entered into an equation that must be solved instantly. And once the machines were aloft, once the antiaircraft guns and balloon barrages were doing their part, the controller became chief-of-staff of a battle fought several miles overhead as he talked to the pilots by means of the two-way radio.

To add to the complexities, the efforts of the various districts had to be co-ordinated in minute detail. For it is understandable that if too many planes were sent up to meet a raid, the next enemy wave might find most of the fighters refueling on the ground, a helpless prey to bombers. The Luftwaffe varied its tactics from day to day in every conceivable manner without finding a key to the defense. The damage to London was considerable, especially in the dock area, but at no time were the city's vital services—gas, water, electricity, transportation— fatally impaired. This result owed to the heroic efforts of firemen who took all the risks of front-line troops in past wars.

German soldiers have been justly praised for their thoroughness. Yet in the battle of Britain—the Marne of the second World War—they were beaten by efficiency as well as highhearted courage. After having terrorized five nations, the Stukas proved too slow for Spitfires and Hurricanes, which reaped a deadly harvest. Nor did the Heinkels and Dorniers fare much better when the Germans tried tight formations protected by fighters at great altitudes. The British fighters literally cut some of the Messerschmitts in two with their eight machine guns before diving into the bombers.

Counting only enemy planes shot down in daylight, with full confirmation, the British Air Ministry reported the destruction of 2,375. All told, the defenders lost 600 fighters, from which 312 pilots parachuted to safety. The island's civilians paid a much heavier price—14,281 killed and 20,325 injured.

Poetic justice has seldom operated more dramatically, for the airmen who had bombed Warsaw and Rotterdam owed their defeat in large measure to a strategy of terrorism. On the moonlight night of November 14 the Germans dropped 400 tons of bombs on a small area in the heart of Coventry. A few weeks later, on December 29, they nearly succeeded in destroying London as thousands of incendiary bombs caused the worst conflagration the city had known since the great fire of 1666. Yet at Coventry the important manufacturing plants on the city's outskirts were left almost intact, and in London whole blocks of slum dwellings were leveled while warehouses and factories suffered only incidentally.

The Germans, in short, had learned little from their failure in the battle of Britain. And during the next four months, as the defense gained in skill and strength, even the casualties of demoralization raids showed a steady decline:

	Killed	Wounded
November, 1940	4,588	6,202
December, 1940	3,793	5,044
January, 1941	1,502	2,012
February, 1941	789	1,069

Before the battle of Britain ended, the Royal Air Force was striking back at German objectives. Industrial cities such as Essen, Cologne and Hamburg were the first targets. At this early date the British lacked the aircraft to deliver heavy blows, but at least their bombing raids gave the enemy a foretaste of the wrath to come.

As for Operation SEA LION, it died a quiet death in September, unmourned by German staff officers. There were wild tales that Hitler's legions actually had attempted a Channel crossing, only to perish wholesale as victims of various British secret weapons. But the fact is that the Führer lost interest in the late summer of 1940, when he first considered the prospect of launching an attack on Soviet Russia.

Britain's Naval Strength

In July Churchill made an audacious and farseeing move. With invasion expected daily, and with arms and trained men lacking, the prime minister sent his first contingents of troops to North Africa.

Britain's naval resources were stretched perilously thin at this time. The antisubmarine operations of the last war had made use of 527 destroyers, while only 178 were available for the greater tasks of 1939. In nearly every other classification the terms of the Washington Treaty for the limitation of naval armaments left the British fleet weaker than in 1918. It must also be remembered that the French and Italian fleets were allies at that date, while in 1940 the one was an enemy and the other an unfriendly "neutral."

The war's first surprise weapon had already appeared in the German magnetic bomb, sown by planes or submarines. Merely the approach of a steel ship closed an electric circuit, thus activating the machinery which caused the explosion. Within three weeks, however, British scientists found a simple yet effective antidote in the "degaussing girdle" —a coil of wire, charged with a faint current, which neutralized the mine by creating a magnetic field equal but opposite to that of the earth.

The submarine menace was not to be so easily scotched. During the last quarter of 1940 the sinkings mounted until they reached an average of 80,000 tons a week. This meant that the U-boats were destroying three ships for every one the British could build; and even the ten million tons acquired from Norway, Greece and the Netherlands could but postpone the day of reckoning.

At least Britain no longer stood alone in the crisis, for the United States had arrived at the stage of open and avowed aid. It is a moot question as to when the Republic actually entered the war, but President Roosevelt's broadcast of December 29, 1940, did not fall far short of declaring hostilities:

> There can be no reasoning with an incendiary bomb. We know now that a nation can have peace with the Nazis only at the price of total surrender. . . . Democracy's fight against world conquest is being greatly aided, and must be more greatly aided, by the re-armament of the United States and by sending every ounce and every ton of munitions and supplies that we can possibly spare to help the defenders who are in the front lines. . . . We must be the great arsenal of democracy. . . . There will be no "bottlenecks" in our determination to aid Great Britain. No dictator, no combination of dictators, will weaken that determination by threats of how they will construe that determination.

It would be fitting to describe 1940 as the year of appeasement. The word became a term of opprobrium when applied to the policies of another nation, yet all the Great Powers were tarred with the same brush. Britain, hoping to postpone a conflict in the Far East, placated Japan by closing the Burma Road during the rainy season, thus cutting off supplies to China. Japan in turn signed a nonaggression pact with Russia while secretly preparing for aggression in the Pacific. The United States, as the intended victim, provided Japan with scrap iron which intelligent observers knew would doubtless be made into bombs for use against Americans. The Soviet Union regarded such capitalistic evasions with scorn, but the Soviet Union sent trainloads of grain to Germany in order to gain time for the inevitable struggle between the two countries. And Germany, though dominating most of Europe, chose to turn the other cheek rather than provoke a war with a United States supplying arms to Britain.

President Roosevelt made capital of the Nazi reluctance by using Hitler's own tactics against him. For the American moves of 1940 and 1941 bear an amusing resemblance to Nazi prewar aggressions—a series of unfriendly acts, each too unimportant to cause a break, but contributing to a total effect which threatened the victim's national aims. Thus in rapid succession came such American measures as the transferring of fifty old destroyers to Britain in exchange for leased West Indies bases, the closing of Axis consulates, the "freezing" of Axis funds, the sequestration of Axis ships, and the training of British pilots in the United States. Most important of all was the Lend-Lease Bill, which amounted to the sharing of weapons and ships on equal terms with Britain.

As a "nonbelligerent," in fact, the United States could actually give more aid than if a state of war existed. Even during the battle of Britain as many as three hundred planes a month were sent across the Atlantic; and by 1941 American ships were delivering American tanks, planes and guns to the British forces in Egypt.

To add to the confusion of the international situation, two recent allies came to blows while antagonistic nations were appeasing one another. In July, 1940, British squadrons sank several warships in an attempt to bottle up the French fleet at Oran and Alexandria. This clash led to the breaking off of diplomatic relations between London and Vichy as the aged Pétain assumed dictatorial powers. Two months later General Charles de Gaulle, leader of the "Free French" forces aiding Britain, persuaded Churchill that Dakar could be occupied without a fight. Instead, the unexpected resistance of that strategic West African port precipitated a two-day gunnery duel, and in retaliation French planes bombed Gibraltar.

Hitler had allowed Mussolini only a few territorial crumbs from the spoliation of France; and with Britain weak in the Mediterranean area, the Fascist dictator invaded Egypt from his Libyan bases. Other forces, striking northward from Italian Somaliland, threatened Red Sea and Suez Canal communications, while the Italian fleet and air force tried to cut the Mediterranean supply line.

In the past, as Bismarck once remarked, Italy's appetite had been better than her teeth. But in 1940 it could not be denied that Mussolini had built up the most showy fleet, army and air force in the Mediterranean area. His people had supported him loyally in an Ethiopian campaign which overcame great geographical difficulties as well as the disapproval of the League of Nations; and the merit of his new armored forces could scarcely be discounted on the strength of reverses in the Spanish Civil War.

Never in history had the British Navy faced such tremendous responsibilities with such inadequate strength. In 1939, as in 1914, no admiral could pretend to know the potentialities of the new or improved sea weapons. Since World War I destroyers had quadrupled in power, so that they mounted 5-inch guns and cost from five to ten million dollars to build. Submarines, which were popularly supposed to be no more resistant than eggshells, could now survive an astonishing amount of punishment from depth charges.

The experience of Jutland had proved the battle cruiser to be too vulnerable, and such relics as Britain's gigantic *Hood* were regarded as doubtful assets. In general the world's navies had returned to the pre-

1914 concept of light and heavy cruisers, with the former mounting 6-inch guns and the latter 8-inch guns as primary armament. Both types showed a vast gain over their World War I predecessors in both protection and fire power.

Although the battleship had also been much improved between wars, her tactical enemies had multiplied at a disproportionate rate. Not only were the mine, the destroyer and the submarine more formidable than in 1914, but the motor torpedo boat must be reckoned an entirely new menace. These frail little wooden craft sacrificed both guns and armor to make room for powerful engines capable of doing fifty land miles per hour. Mounting only machine guns in addition to torpedo tubes, such giant killers depended on speed for defense as well as offense.

There was less need for conjecture about the aircraft carrier. Long before the Spanish Civil War added its lessons, tests had proved that the battleship could be sunk by the dive bomber or torpedo plane.

An island sea such as the Mediterranean favored the chances of the Italian fleet and air force, both of which were adapted to a hit-and-run strategy rather than slugging. The cruisers and battleships were faster than their British counterparts, and Italian admirals had led the world in the development of the motor torpedo boat. The nation's geographical position allowed it to depend on Mediterranean islands instead of carriers, so that land-based planes were in a position to dart out from the African and Asiatic as well as the European coast. The British had only their base at Malta to protect convoys running the length of a hostile sea.

But in a war full of surprises the predictions of the "experts" were often upset. Britain, which had most to dread from the bomber and torpedo plane, found salvation in those very weapons. It would appear that the island's poets have been air-minded in all ages; for the new naval strategy was foreseen in a strange prophecy written by Thomas Gray, author of "Elegy Written in a Country Churchyard," in the year 1737:

> The time will come, when thou shalt lift thine eyes
> To watch a long-drawn battle in the skies. . . .
> England, so long the mistress of the sea,
> Where winds and waves confess her sovereignty,
> Her ancient triumphs yet on high shall bear
> And reign, the sovereign of the conquered air.

The first proof came on the moonlight night of November 11. When the alarm sounded, the Italian fleet lay at anchor in the great double harbor of Taranto, secure from any naval attack. Yet within twenty minutes nearly half of the capital strength of Mussolini's navy was put out of action. Torpedo planes from the British carriers *Eagle* and *Illustrious* scored hits on three battleships, two cruisers, a destroyer and several cargo ships. And though most of these units were soon repaired, the numerical as well as moral superiority passed to Admiral Sir Andrew Cunningham's fleet.

From that moment he gave the enemy no rest. Only two weeks after the Taranto victory his carriers located the Italian remnants off the coast of Sardinia as they sought a new refuge. Again the torpedo planes struck by surprise, and British long-range gunnery played a part in damaging a battleship, two cruisers and two destroyers. On December 11 Cunningham's bombers relentlessly sought out the enemy in the harbor of Naples, where new hits were claimed on several cruisers and destroyers.

In these operations the all-seeing eye of radar played an important part on both sides. Called the "worst kept secret of the war," it had such a decisive effect on the battle of Britain that censorship could not prevent leaks.

Only a scholar could fully comprehend the basic principles. For the layman it is sufficient to know that a radio beam is projected to send back an echo, upon striking an object, which is at once transformed into a visual image on a screen. Thus the traditional "fog of war" is pierced by an eye which can detect a ship miles away at sea.

From the air it is possible for fliers to follow a coastline through the darkness, and to find their way to cities and harbors. It is likewise possible for the defenders to rely on warning, since the uses of radar are not limited to the offensive.

BRITISH VICTORIES IN AFRICA

The opposing forces in the North African desert were preparing for an offensive when the British struck first, at dawn on December 9, 1940. General Sir Archibald Wavell, the author of a delightful book on the attributes of generalship, gained such a crushing surprise at Sidi Barrani that 40,000 British troops destroyed double their numbers of men and tanks. Only one out of five Italian divisions escaped intact as a British armored column swung around to Marshal Graziani's rear. During the first week's fighting the Italians retreated 80 miles, and this triumph was but the prelude. Before March 1 Wavell had all but shattered the Italian empire in Africa. Sidi Barrani, Bardia, Tobruk, Derna and Bengasi fell to fast-moving forces which reached El Agheila to complete a sweep of more than 500 miles.

The Italian armies in East Africa were likewise reduced to a losing defensive on their own soil. These campaigns attracted less notice than the northern operations, yet one British motorized column of 20,000 men advanced 1,500 miles in 94 days against a much more numerous foe in mountain and desert country. Nearly 200,000 Italian troops, including native auxiliaries, were so divided and demoralized by the combined British forces that most of the remnants surrendered before the end of 1941. And on April 6, with the occupation of Addis Ababa, Lieutenant General Sir Alan Cunningham (brother of the commander of

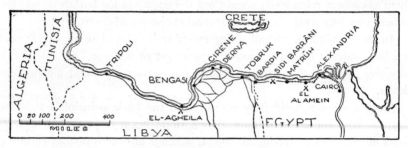

The African Desert Campaigns

the British Mediterranean Fleet) and his motley army of some 70,000 British, Free French, Belgians, Sikhs, Bengalis, Ethiopians and South Africans restored to Haile Selassie the kingdom that Mussolini had forcibly annexed in 1936.

In Libya the British air, naval and ground forces worked together in perfect unison. For the original surprise could hardly have succeeded without the preliminary attacks of RAF bombers which blinded Graziani's army by knocking out its aerial bases. The number of planes destroyed on the ground is convincing evidence—87 at Tobruk alone, and 75 at Bengasi. By Italian admission about half of the 171 planes lost in the annihilation of one entire air corps were wrecked before they could rise from the field.

Graziani lost so many trucks that he had little chance to recover his strategic balance after the rout at Sidi Barrani. The British command of the air contributed no more to the final result than a command of the sea which sometimes gave Wavell's advance the appearance of an amphibious operation. Convoys unloaded food, water and ammunition as the Army advanced along the desert littoral, while other British naval units cut off most of the Italian sea-borne supplies. Wavell's logistical advantage enabled him to turn the campaign into one prolonged pursuit. While his men stormed Derna, advance armored units had already isolated Tobruk, for such fortified bases proved to be traps for an Italian army systematically destroyed in detail.

Only three months were required to shatter the myth of a "new Rome" which Fascism had taken such pains in creating. From November 30 to February 11, according to an official London announcement, Wavell's army alone completed "the capture or destruction of the whole Italian army in East Libya, estimated to exceed 150,000 men." Among the 133,000 prisoners were an admiral and 19 generals, though the casualties of the victors amounted to only 438 killed, 87 missing and 1,249 wounded.

It is not taking credit from the great British victory to point out that Mussolini's conscripted peasants and factory workers did not show much enthusiasm for battle. They entered upon their captivity with few regrets, judging from the smiles flashed for press photographers. The "Sawdust Caesar," in short, had not won the loyalty of the men he harangued with bombastic oratory.

The Italian Navy, on the other hand, could claim suicidal feats of heroism which compare with any German exploits of the war. A deficiency of skill rather than zeal accounts for the Italian defeat in the one naval battle of the Mediterranean. On the morning of March 28 Admiral Cunningham learned that the enemy fleet had divided into two squadrons, to the north and southwest of Crete. The latter force, consisting of the new battleship *Vittorio Veneto* supported by cruisers and destroyers, was lured by the British destroyer screen toward Cunningham's three battleships. Just in time the Italians scented the trap, but while showing their heels to a slower enemy they could not escape the planes of the carrier *Formidable.* Three torpedoes hit the *Vittorio Veneto,* reducing her speed to eight knots. Hence the British warships were able to overtake their prey in the darkness, and at 4,000 yards their guns sank three 10,000-ton cruisers and three destroyers silhouetted in the glare of searchlights.

The battle of the Ionian Sea was gained without the loss of a single British ship or man. The presence of the aircraft carrier was the decisive factor, forcing a crippled squadron to accept action on the enemy's terms. This lesson had a second demonstration in May, when the British sank the newest and most formidable of Germany's few capital ships. Air reconnaissance warned that the *Bismarck* was about to put to sea from Bergen with the cruiser *Prinz Eugen*. Further reports from aviators brought the aged battle cruiser *Hood* to the aid of two British cruisers in the strait between Iceland and Greenland. The *Hood* offered battle, but a long-range shot found her magazine, and the world's largest warship blew up with nearly all her crew. More powerful British units were meanwhile hastening to the scene, guided by reconnaissance planes. Even so, the fleet German battleship eluded her pursuers for thirty hours and might have escaped if torpedo planes had not scored hits which diminished her speed and damaged her steering gear. Two British battleships and a cruiser closed in about 400 miles from Brest, and the *Bismarck* went down after a fearful pounding from torpedoes and armor-piercing shells. The *Prinz Eugen* reached Brest only to be crippled by bombing planes.

III

WAR IN THE BALKANS AND RUSSIA

Words have no relation to actions—otherwise what kind of diplomacy is it? . . . Good words are a mask for the concealment of bad deeds. Sincere diplomacy is no more possible than dry water or wooden iron.

—STALIN

AT THREE o'clock on the morning of October 28, 1940, the Italian minister in Athens delivered an ultimatum giving Greece three hours in which to open the country to Italian troops. Before the time limit expired, Mussolini's forces had already crossed the frontier.

To the surprise of the world in general and Italy in particular, the invaders met a fierce and effective resistance. Soon the glories of Marathon were being revived by modern Spartans and Athenians who probably would have carried the war to a victorious conclusion if Mussolini's ally had not intervened.

The fact that valor was supported by hardy and intelligent tactics added to the luster of the performance. The shades of Bourçet, Masséna and all departed mountain fighters must have rejoiced at the spectacle in the Albanian hills as the Greeks defeated tanks and dive bombers with mules and pack howitzers. For the principles of mountain warfare have varied but little down the ages, and Premier Metaxas of Greece applied them better than adversaries who trusted too much in a blitzkrieg formula.

Not only did the blitzkrieg have its limitations, but the Italians neglected several of the most important elements. Depending too much on superior numbers and equipment, they did not begin with the terrific aerial assaults which had accounted to a great extent for Nazi successes. Only a few ports and roads were bombed, so that the Greeks managed to concentrate without serious interference. Next, the invaders forgot that good mountain warfare had been based on infiltration and envelopment before anyone thought of the blitzkrieg. As a consequence, the cramped

War in the Balkans and Crete

Italian columns, pushing into the narrow valleys, were taken in flank by smaller but more mobile forces holding the commanding heights. In a country of few roads, the tanks bogged down in mud and snow, making slower progress than the mules on which the Greeks depended. Surprise envelopments cut off the spearheads of invasion, and by the end of the first month 10,000 prisoners were the only Italians left on Greek soil.

The initiative passed to troops who proved that even in an age of mechanized warfare the David and Goliath story is not dead. Greece could equip only twelve divisions even according to World War I standards, but ever since Mussolini's annexation of Albania in 1939 Metaxas had been planning this campaign. In Italian territory his forces changed from the defensive to the offensive without varying their tactics. Shunning frontal attacks while advancing over rude trails along the ridgelines, they kept the retreating enemy in constant peril of envelopment. Vione and other ports of entry had to be evacuated after being outflanked, for the Greeks had penetrated 40 miles into Albania before Christmas.

Britain could send few troops to her new ally, but new bases on Greek soil enabled the RAF to gain command of the air. Italian ports were pounded unmercifully, and Mussolini's convoys had to run the risk of both aerial and naval attacks. Meanwhile, an unusually severe winter aided the Greeks, whose women shoveled snow to make paths for the tireless infiltrations along the ridgelines.

The death of Greece's seventy-year-old premier from a throat operation in January, 1942, seemed only to incite his troops to further prodigies. Mussolini visited the Albanian front early in March to inspire his battered divisions. Reinforcements having been sent across the Adriatic at heavy cost, he ordered a renewal of the offensive to wipe out defeats which had already resulted in casualties estimated by the Greeks at 120,000 and probably numbering about half as many. His troops made their supreme effort on March 12, but by this time the Greeks were much better armed with weapons captured in Albania. They stopped the Italians in six days and Mussolini's scornful Teutonic allies came to his rescue both in the Balkans and in Africa.

The battle of Britain had cheated Hitler of an early and complete triumph. But the Germans still held the initiative, and as an improvement over World War I they were the blockaders instead of the blockaded. In April, 1941, their submarines sank 589,273 tons of Allied shipping, and 497,847 tons in May. This rate of destruction, if continued, must sooner or later starve Britain into submission. Nearly all of Europe's resources were meanwhile at the disposal of conquerors who looted occupied countries and bullied neutrals into compliance.

Hitler's forces never came nearer to their goal of Continental dominion than in 1940. Even the victims of war can forgive ruthlessness more readily than flabbiness, and thousands of Europeans wondered if Berlin's "New Order" did not, after all, offer new political truths for old governmental lies. Perhaps only a conqueror's sword, they reasoned, could have cut the knots of tradition which seemed to bind the democratic nations hand and foot.

Such half-formed ideas were confirmed by the conduct of the first German troops in occupied regions. Lean, hard young men, they exhibited a discipline which contrasted dramatically with the panics of the vanquished. At this moment Hitler had within his reach a moral as well as a material triumph. Then came a horde of Nazi military and political camp followers in the wake of the fighting men. Their portable printing presses turned out a special invasion currency which even the most ignorant shopkeeper could recognize as the means of systematically despoiling a nation. And with these notes stuffing their pockets, the representatives of the New Order soon proved to be more interested in champagne and silk stockings than ideas.

The invaders, in short, displayed the same qualities of greed, dishonesty and sensual self-indulgence that the conquered peoples had blamed for their own downfall. But if Hitler had failed politically, there could be no doubt in the spring of 1941 that he still held the military trumps. Even the British Empire seemed small as compared to a Nazi-dominated Europe in which a quarter of a billion people were toiling to supply Axis armies with weapons and supplies.

German Intervention in the Balkans

The question as to where the next German blow would fall was answered by Hitler's preliminary moves. Choosing to gain his ends by threats rather than force, he reduced Hungary, Rumania and Bulgaria in turn to the status of satellites. Yugoslavia and Greece were obviously next as the shadow of the swastika fell over the Balkans, and the former showed the familiar signs of acceptance. In the Balkans, however, popular emotion could still overthrow political reason, and the news of Yugoslavia's "diaper revolution" on March 27, 1941, upset the German plans. So called because it started among schoolboys, the uprising spread until the Army silenced the advocates of compromise in a bloodless coup which placed the seventeen-year-old King Peter on the throne.

Now followed ten days of tension as Hitler prepared to deal with this challenge. There could be no doubt as to the ultimate result, even though British reinforcements had landed in Greece.

At dawn on April 6 the Luftwaffe bombed Belgrade from rooftop height and 17,000 civilians died in the ruins. It took the German ground forces only ten days to demonstrate how a blitzkrieg should be conducted in mountain country. Using a small tank designed for such work, the armored divisions raced into the valleys as parachute units seized key points in advance, leaving the mopping up to specially trained mountain troops. The Yugoslav infantry, depending on oxen for transport, was soon split up into isolated groups fighting bravely but without much central direction. At Sarajevo, of World War I fame, the last Yugoslav army was encircled, and on April 18 the Germans announced that serious resistance had been overcome—a claim which guerrillas would dispute all the rest of the war.

The invasion of Greece ended in a German victory on April 30. So encouraging was the early resistance that the odds against the Greeks and British seemed to have been overcome by sheer valor. But only a token force could be spared from General Wavell's army, including a single armored brigade; and the RAF lacked both planes and landing fields to challenge the Nazi command of the air. Greece defied the new enemy with full knowledge that neither her armies nor her strategic position offered any reasonable prospect of a successful defense. From the beginning, therefore, the Allies could only hope to fight a delaying action, thus forcing the enemy to make a major effort out of a campaign which only a month before had promised to be a parade.

General Sir Henry Maitland Wilson's force consisted largely of Australians and New Zealanders. They fought the Nazi armored forces to a standstill for two days in the center, while the Greeks put up a struggle against the columns striking in the east toward the Aegean. But the Yugoslav front collapsed much sooner than had been expected; and the whole defensive position in Albania and northern Greece had to be abandoned, including the Metaxas Line.

April 12, 1941, dated the beginning of a stubborn retreat. Military stores had been removed in anticipation of Salonika's fall, but the Greek forces in the area were cut off and compelled to surrender. By this time the Luftwaffe had destroyed the last of the RAF landing fields, so that the Allies were left entirely without air support.

The British on the right and the Greeks on the left were still capable of an orderly withdrawal as they formed a new line stretching westward from Mount Olympus. This was the last effort of the Greeks, who were rapidly disintegrating from exhaustion. The Australians and New Zealanders fell back to historical Thermopylae, and on April 21 Athens advised General Wilson to withdraw entirely. By dint of rear-guard operations the evacuation was carried out from small ports and beaches in southern Greece as British warships took off 50,662 men out of an original 57,757.

In combination with the Balkan invasion the Germans compelled the British to stretch their thin resources to cope with diversions. An Axis-instigated revolt in Iraq was put down by inadequate British forces. As a more grave threat, the Mediterranean life line had been nearly severed after the Luftwaffe stationed squadrons of bombers in Sicily. Malta endured almost daily poundings which soon earned it a reputation as "the most bombed spot on earth." Stone caves sheltered the population and naval forces, but convoys in the Mediterranean took such ruinous losses that the British supplies for the African armies were routed chiefly around the Cape of Good Hope—the longest supply line ever maintained for such important operations.

As early as February, 1941, the Germans had landed troops in North Africa. These contingents were made up of picked men conditioned to desert hardships by artificial heat. By March an entire armored division and parts of two others had reached Libya, and on the 24th they struck at El Agheila to keep Wavell occupied during the Balkan invasion. The strain on his depleted resources was made evident by retreats which Cairo dispatches tried to disguise. But euphemisms could not hide the fact that Wavell was losing ground faster than he had gained it. From Bengasi the British fell back all the way to the Egyptian border; but despite the capture of several generals by German raiders, the losses in prisoners and matériel were not serious. Tobruk remained in British hands, and the enemy could only threaten a port well supplied from the sea. The presence of this stronghold in the Axis rear discouraged further advances, not to mention the air superiority which the RAF had wrested from the Luftwaffe.

The Aerial Conquest of Crete

The loss of territory meant little in mobile desert warfare, for Wavell had beaten the Italians by destroying armies rather than gaining ground. The German capture of Crete in May, 1941, struck a much heavier blow at British security.

Hitler's original intention had been to end his Balkan campaign with the surrender of Greece. But the desirability of setting up advanced air bases in Crete was so appealing that he authorized an airborne invasion.

As a prelude, German bombers worked over the British airfields at Maleme, Rethymnon and Herakleion for two weeks, flying as many as 300 sorties a day. Crete's defenders numbered 29,500 men, most of them

British and Greek soldiers evacuated from Greece with only their rifles. A few reinforcements had landed from Egypt, but heavy arms consisted only of eighteen antiaircraft guns, four 3.7-inch howitzers, six medium tanks and sixteen light tanks. Even shovels were so lacking that General Sir Bernard C. Freyberg's men had to use their helmets to dig foxholes in many instances.

The German plan was arithmetically simple. Three objectives were to be attacked, regardless of losses, until a foothold could be gained in one. Then the Luftwaffe would be able to pour in reinforcements faster than British forces could concentrate in an island 160 miles long from which all planes had been removed to save them from destruction.

This is exactly what happened. Even so, the first paratroops and glider-borne contingents endured such losses that the issue was in doubt for two days. In combination with the airborne landings, the Nazis launched their single amphibious operation of World War II. Two battalions of mountain troops and contingents of regular infantry were to be landed by two squadrons of coastal steamers and motor-driven fishing boats. Unfortunately for this effort, the Germans had overlooked the elementary principle that a successful amphibious assault depends on command of the sea as well as the air. The only protection was to be provided by aircraft, and it did not suffice as British destroyers tore into improvised landing craft crowded with German troops. So many were sunk that not a man reached the shores of Crete and only a handful of survivors found a refuge on Greek islands. It was from the outset an amateurish attempt doomed to costly failure.

The defenders of Crete put up a good fight, but once the airborne troops had captured the airfield at Maleme the end was in sight. New arrivals swelled the Nazi numbers to 35,000 picked troops, much better armed than the British.

British troop losses were some 13,000 killed, wounded and missing in addition to 2,000 naval casualties on the four cruisers and six destroyers sunk during the operation. About 16,500 men were evacuated to Egypt after a retreat over the mountains to the southern coast at Spakia.

The Germans made an obvious attempt to minimize troop losses which could hardly have been less than 10,000 in view of the complete failure of the amphibious operation. Of the 650 German transport planes employed, 151 were destroyed and 120 badly damaged.

"From now on," exulted Goering, "no island is safe!" This boast was premature, for Hitler was so alarmed by the heavy casualties, including the virtual destruction of his only airborne division, that he had no stomach for future operations of the sort. As a consequence, the British and American armed forces were allowed to take a commanding lead in the organization and training of airborne divisions.

Much more absorbing in the spring of 1941 was the question of Hitler's next move. With Greece and Crete as bases, plus the airfields in Syria made available by Vichy France, he was in a position to drive the British from the Mediterranean area. But the Nazi dictator had bigger fish to fry. On June 22, barely three weeks after his victory in Crete, he announced his decision after his troops had already shot down the frontier guards and surged into Russia. It was to be war on a scale never known before—geopolitical war for the conquest of the Heartland.

Russian Aggressions of 1939-1940

While Nazi Germany was gobbling up new territory in great gulps, the Soviet Union had been busily nibbling away in eastern Europe. There was little to choose between the two nations when it came to ethics. Russia, according to *U.S. Department of Defense Sheet 1-H*, violated her own treaty agreements 26 times during the 40 years from 1918 to 1958. Seven of the violations took place from September, 1939, to June, 1940. The agreements and violations of these ten months are as follows:

July 25, 1932—Russia signs nonaggression pact with Poland.

Sept. 17, 1939—Soviet troops invade Poland.

May 5, 1934—U.S.S.R.-Poland peace pact extended for ten years.

Sept. 29, 1939—U.S.S.R. signs agreement with Germany to partition Poland.

Jan. 21, 1932—U.S.S.R. and Finland sign nonaggression treaty.

Nov. 30, 1939—Russian troops invade Finland.

Sept. 28, 1926—Russia makes nonaggression pact with Lithuania.

June 15, 1940—Russia invades and annexes Lithuania.

Feb. 5, 1932—Soviet Union signs nonaggression treaty with Latvia.

June 16, 1940—Soviet forces invade Latvia, later annexed.

May 4, 1932—U.S.S.R. and Estonia sign a nonaggression treaty.

June 16, 1940—U.S.S.R. troops occupy Estonia as a prelude to annexation.

June 9, 1934—Russia guarantees sovereignty of Rumania.

June 27, 1940—Russia invades and occupies two Rumanian provinces.

"Signer, beware!" was the attitude of Soviet Russia toward treaties. There was no attempt to deny this policy except on occasions when a new pact was being negotiated. Lenin himself had said, "Promises are like piecrust, made to be broken."

From the Communist party viewpoint, Stalin was to be credited with superb statecraft in his aggressions of 1939-1940. As commander-in-chief of the Red Army and Navy, he was advised by the Stavka, or General Headquarters of the Armed Forces. This was Russia's nearest approach to a general staff, being composed of the chiefs of political bureaus as well as such major branches of the armed forces as infantry, artillery, aircraft and armor. Periodical meetings were held, but Stalin had the last word in decisions of importance.

His theories of war had been largely formed by a scholarly, sixty-year-old Russian soldier who lay near to death from a surgical operation in the autumn of 1941. Field Marshal Boris Shaposhnikov was little known outside the Soviet Union, having shown all his life a preference for remaining in the background. This quality of self-effacement had doubtless made possible the career of a former aristocrat and Czarist officer who became Stalin's military adviser.

In 1915 Grand Duke Nicholas recognized the ability of the studious young officer from the Urals by promoting him to a colonelcy on the General Staff. Shaposhnikov was not sympathetic to the causes of the Revolution, though he accepted its results by offering his services after the Bolsheviks came into power. Trotsky did not fall behind the grand duke in appreciation, and in 1928 Stalin chose Shaposhnikov as his chief-of-staff.

The development of the Red Army dates from that year. Shaposhnikov reorganized Russia's West Point, the Frunze Military Academy, until it ranked as a progressive institution. Crude young Revolutionary commanders who had risen from the ranks were compelled to pass courses which Timoshenko considered a worse ordeal than all his campaigns. Shaposhnikov lectured at many of these seminars, and his three-volume work of staff problems, *Brain of the Army,* was adopted as a standard text.

The Opposing Forces

Hitler had decided to attack the Soviet Union even before the battle of Britain ended. By an odd line of reasoning he concluded that a successful war with Russia would deprive Britain of her only potential ally on the

Continent, whereupon he would deal with the stubborn island later. Even the specter of a war on two fronts no longer haunted him, since he was confident that he could overwhelm the Soviet Union in a single summer. The project was uppermost in his thoughts during the last three months of 1940, and on December 18 he issued his top-secret *Directive No. 21* for Operation BARBAROSSA. The first two sentences announced his purpose:

> The German Armed Forces must be ready to crush Soviet Russia in a rapid campaign, even before the termination of the war with Britain. The Army will have to assign all available units to this task, with the reservation that the occupied countries must be protected against surprise attacks.

Hitler was so powerful by this time that officers differing with him did so at the risk of being sacked. As a consequence, he was more often the recipient of servile flattery than honest criticism. His low opinion of the Red Army was based largely on its poor showing in Finland, and he underestimated such war potentials of the Soviet Union as its population, difficult terrain, extremes of weather, natural resources and industrial plants, not to mention the fortitude of the Russian soldier as demonstrated in past wars.

Not much was known about the Red Army in 1941, and even after the war the information was limited to what Stalin wished the capitalistic world to know. The command and staff had not fully recovered from the purges of 1937-1938, when half the senior officers were liquidated—3 marshals, 13 army commanders, 57 corps commanders, 110 divisional and 220 brigade commanders. The Finnish debacle, however, had provided timely object lessons which were taken to heart.

The Russian infantry division of about 11,000 men consisted of three rifle regiments, two artillery regiments, and such lesser units as light tank, antitank, engineer, signal and medical. Cavalry divisions, numbering 7,000 men, were made up of four horse regiments, one mechanized cavalry regiment, and a mixed artillery regiment.

Artillery divisions comprised one antiaircraft, one light and two medium regiments equipped with 76-mm., 122-mm., and 152-mm. guns. This arm was the Red Army's strength, and as a lesson of the Finnish War, giant 280-mm., 305-mm. and 406-mm. howitzers were being manufactured in 1941 and would soon give the Army a terrific striking power.

The Soviet Union had some 8,000 aircraft. Most of them were obsolescent, however, their operations being limited to low-flying tactical support of the ground forces.

When it came to command and staff, there was of course no comparison between the Red Army and the German generals who had led the Wehrmacht to victory in three wars. Their Russian opposites had much to learn.

Turning to the Wehrmacht, it was essentially the same instrument that had won speedy and thrifty victories in Poland, Norway and France. More Panzer divisions had been created by reducing the number of tanks to 180, but Hitler had not increased an artillery strength that was light in proportion to his armor and aircraft.

Logistical problems were solved with the wonted German efficiency, and by May, 1941, an average of 300 trains a day moved ammunition and other supplies to the Eastern Front. Early in June the build-up for Operation BARBAROSSA was completed. According to *The History of World War II*, an excellent survey by historians of the United States Military Academy, the deployment of the German forces was as follows:

DIVISIONS

EASTERN FRONT

	Panzer	Motorized	Infantry	Total
OKH reserve (Brauchitsch)	2	1	6	9
Army Group North (Leeb)	3	2	23	28
Army Group Centre (Bock)	9	5	39	53
Army Group South (Rundstedt)	5	2	38	45
Total, Eastern Front	19	10	106	135

OTHER THEATERS

	Panzer	Motorized	Infantry	Total
Army Group Southeast (List)			7	7
Afrika Korps (Rommel)	1		1	2
Army Group West (Witzleben)	1		38	39
Denmark			1	1
Norway (Falkenhorst)			10	10
Total, other theaters	2		57	59
Total, German divisions	21	10	163	194

Included among the 163 infantry divisions were six mountain, one cavalry and nine security divisions.

The Luftwaffe contributed some 3,000 aircraft to Operation BARBA-ROSSA, including 400 dive bombers, 900 fighters, 1,000 long-range bombers and 700 patrol and reconnaissance planes. The pilots had more experience than those of the Red Army, and German aircraft were much superior.

Another factor to be considered is the moral momentum of German troops who believed themselves invincible. Up to this time Hitler could boast an unequaled record as a conqueror. The Nazi dictator had overwhelmed Poland in 27 days, Denmark and Norway in 23, Holland in 5, Belgium in 18, France in 39, Yugoslavia in 12, Greece in 21, and Crete in 11. This is in contrast to the hundred days it took Stalin to defeat Finland.

As Hitler entered upon his greatest military adventure, he was as much the ideologist as the strategist. One of his fanatical aims was the blowing up of the Kremlin, and he intended to raze Leningrad and Stalingrad—not because of their strategic importance but because he regarded them as shrines of Communism.

According to his ideological creed, the Slavs were an inferior race and the Russians the most inferior of the Slavs. It was foreordained, therefore, that civilians in the path of the German advance would receive no tender treatment.

A Front 2,000 Miles Long

Only two nations with military resources such as those of the U.S.S.R. and the Third Reich could have clashed on a front 2,000 miles long, stretching from the Arctic Ocean to the Black Sea. Plan BARBAROSSA assigned Leningrad, Moscow and the Ukraine as the objectives of Army Groups North (Leeb), Centre (Bock) and South (Rundstedt), respectively. German strategy emphasized infantry penetrations which could be exploited by the armored divisions with great double envelopments. The purpose was to cut off, surround and destroy the Russians in great masses rather than allowing them to retreat, thus luring the invaders into the interior as Napoleon's army had been.

Field Marshal Fedor von Bock, with the largest Panzer and motorized forces, was to make the main effort on the central front. During the first ten days his Panzer divisions advanced 200 miles while the Luftwaffe virtually drove Russian aircraft from the sky with losses estimated at 2,000 planes. Red Army ground force casualties were on a corresponding scale; and after mopping up the vast double envelopment of Russians in the Minsk-Bialystok area, the Germans reported the capture of 323,000 prisoners, 3,000 tanks and 1,800 guns.

So far, though the deadly array of weapons appalled civilians, the light casualty lists of World War II had been remarkable. The British had smashed Mussolini's African Empire at a price of fewer than a thousand slain, while the Germans conquered all France at a smaller cost than

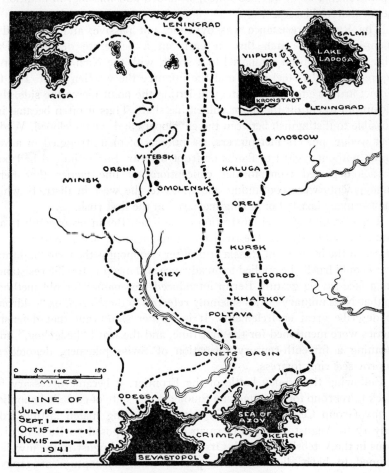

The First Six Months in Russia

their fathers paid for a few square miles at Verdun in 1916. Nevertheless, the battle of Smolensk was to prove that such thrifty successes were possible only when the offensive held the trumps. In Russia the Wehrmacht met for the first time a determined adversary superior in numbers and not fatally inferior in equipment. The resulting casualties were shocking as compared to previous operations of World War II. Early in August, 1941, a Moscow communiqué admitted the loss of 600,000 men, 4,000 planes and 5,000 tanks. The Germans estimated their total casualties up to August 26 at 441,000 killed, wounded and missing, in addition to heavy matériel losses.

The Russian resistance was dynamic, not passive, and the invaders themselves were often thrown back on a desperate defensive. Past blitzkriegs had been compared to a spear, with the Nazi armored forces representing the steel point and the infantry the wooden shaft. But the Soviet armies adopted a strategy of letting the point pierce the side, then closing in to cut off the more vulnerable shaft. Thus it often became impossible to distinguish between the envelopers and the enveloped. Wedge met wedge, pincers met pincers, as millions of men struggled in a vast arena without regard to flanks or front or rear. So far indeed had both armies departed from former conceptions of line tactics that fierce engagements were continuing 200 miles to the west in districts which the Germans boasted of having mastered in the first rush.

The first hint of Nazi frustration came when Berlin propagandists announced petulantly that the British had invented the word "blitzkrieg" to discredit the invaders of Russia! For after two months the term "lightning war" could hardly be applied to an advance still meeting terrific resistance. As a face-saving gesture Berlin introduced new names for old methods, so that Nazi military critics solemnly referred to the *Kessel,* or "caldron," to describe great encirclements. It is further significant that defensive tactics were mentioned for the first time, and the word "hedgehog," once meaning a fifteenth-century formation of Swiss pikemen, denoted an improvised ring fortress.

Following the 26-day battle of the Frontier, it became necessary for Bock to regroup for the attack on Smolensk. In spite of curtailed supplies, Army Group Centre engaged in another slugging match lasting from July 17 to August 16 as 60 German divisions opposed 70 Russian divisions in the Vitebsk-Smolensk-Orsha triangle. On August 10 the invaders claimed to have eliminated this pocket with the capture of 310,000 prisoners, 3,200 tanks and 3,200 guns. Although they had driven 400 miles into Russia, it was disturbing to find that they were behind Napoleon's timetable in 1812! On August 11, Chief-of-Staff Halder noted in his diary:

On the fronts not involved in the offensive movement reigns the quiet of exhaustion. What we are now doing is the last desperate

attempt to prevent our front line becoming frozen in position warfare. . . . The whole situation makes it increasingly plain that we
have underestimated the Russian Colossus. . . .

There was no direct co-operation between Bock and Rundstedt, whose
forces were separated by the Pripet Marshes, so that both were harassed
constantly by flank attacks. Army Group South had made slower progress
than the other two; and on August 21, after several conflicting orders,
Hitler announced a decision which may have cost him his expected capture of Moscow. The battle of Smolensk was still in progress when he
halted the drive on Moscow and transferred one of Bock's armored
groups to Rundstedt in the south and another to Leeb in the north.

"The most important aim to be achieved before the onset of winter,"
stated Hitler's *Directive 34,* "is not to capture Moscow but to seize the
Crimea and the industrial and coal region on the Donets and to cut off
the Russian supply from the Caucasus area; in the north the aim is to
cut off Leningrad and join with the Finns."

Army Group Centre was "to assign for this mission such forces as will
assure that the aim . . . will be accomplished; the Army Group must still
be able to repulse enemy attacks against the centre of the front from
positions which permit economy of forces."

Bock and Guderian urged a continuation of the offensive against
Moscow, which they felt confident of taking. But Hitler was obdurate,
and after being stripped of two armored groups Bock was reduced to a
passive defensive only 200 miles short of the Russian capital.

The Battle of Kiev

Although the drive in the south got off to a good start, it met stiff
resistance as it approached the Soviet industrial district in the Dnieper
bend. Kiev was reached by the middle of July, but the entire German plan
was upset when the resistance continued. Six weeks passed without
gains comparable to those made in the centre. This situation could not
be charged to Rundstedt's generalship; it was the result of fanatical
Russian opposition for the purpose of gaining time to remove industrial
plants and equipment whenever possible from the Donets Basin.

Kiev and Odessa were still holding out when Army Group South was
reinforced by Guderian's armor, transferred from Bock's army. German
affairs in the Ukraine prospered immediately. By the last week in
August bridgeheads had been established across the Dnieper. The battle
of Kiev reached a climax September 12 to 19 when Rundstedt completed

the most lucrative envelopment of the war. Five Soviet armies were virtually annihilated with losses of 665,000 prisoners, 3,718 guns and 886 tanks, according to German claims.

Before the liquidation of the Kiev pocket was finished, other German columns advanced into a strategic vacuum of abandoned Russian industrial cities laid waste in accordance with a ruthless scorched-earth policy. Even when the reinforcing units from Army Group Centre were withdrawn, Rundstedt's columns overran the devastated Donets Basin and drove on to capture Kharkov. Odessa was evacuated by Russian divisions which put up a futile defense of the isthmus leading to the Crimean Peninsula. There the Germans were stopped, more by their own exhaustion than by enemy resistance, just short of the historic fortress of Sevastopol. Their farthest penetration in the south had taken them to the suburbs of Rostov on the Don. By that time, early in November, autumnal rains had turned the roads into bogs; Rundstedt's troops had reached the limit of weariness, and his vehicles were in urgent need of repair or replacement.

Less spectacular gains were reported by Field Marshal Ritter von Leeb's Army Group North. Along the Baltic littoral the roads were bad, even by Russian standards, and marshes or lakes often canalized the routes of attack. Nevertheless, Leeb's armies forged ahead; and on September 8 they captured a fortress on Lake Ladoga, which cut the land approaches to Leningrad from the south and east. A breakthrough to the shore of the Gulf of Finland, southwest of Leningrad, tightened the German grip on the city and isolated the Russian Eighth Army on the peninsula southwest of the Kronstadt naval base.

During the next three days Leeb's all-out effort to storm Leningrad was blocked by the resistance not only of Red Army soldiers but also of civilians, regardless of age or sex. On the 12th an unseasonable snow came to the aid of the defense; and during the following week most of the German armor was removed from the Leningrad area, as if in admission that the attack had turned into a siege.

Hitler himself, in a memorandum of September 29, 1941, accepted a stalemate for the time being. He declared, however, that he had "decided to have Leningrad wiped from the face of the earth. . . . The intention is to close in on the city and blast it to the ground by bombardment of artillery of all calibers and continuous air attacks."

This ferocious sentence was never carried out, since the requisite Nazi guns and aircraft were always needed elsewhere. By December 1, 1941, only eight German divisions were left in the Leningrad and Kronstadt areas. Few of the aims of Army Group North had been accomplished. Contact had not been made with the Finns fighting Russia, nor had Leeb's forces been able to close entirely the ring around Leningrad. Connections with the rest of Russia were maintained across Lake Ladoga by ship during the summer and over the ice in winter. Thus the beleaguered city held out until January, 1944, when it was reoccupied by the Red Army.

The Battle of Moscow

Hitler's victories had not been bought cheaply, for at the end of September his casualties were officially listed as 116,900 killed, 409,600 wounded, and 24,500 missing—a total of 551,000, which exceeded the losses of all previous German operations combined. In thousands of instances the invaders had the Führer's racial theories to thank. A not-unusual fate for a captured Russian village was the execution of suspected guerrillas without a trial, the seizing of young women for soldiers' brothels, and the utilization of women and old men for forced labor. Civilian resistance was punished with the burning of villages and mass slaughter of the inhabitants.

It is understandable that great numbers of peasants and villagers should have been driven into the woods and swamps as partisans who preyed upon Nazi detachments and supply trains far back in the rear areas. The large proportion of missing in German casualty lists attests to invaders who simply vanished and whose bones are still moldering in some Ukrainian forest.

Stalin took the credit for this underground resistance as something organized by the Red Army before the war. This was true to a limited extent, since specially trained agents actually were parachuted by night into selected areas with a mission of organizing partisans and arranging for supply by air. For the most part, however, the resistance movement was a spontaneous uprising of desperate men and women who were the victims of Nazi brutality.

When given the opportunity, the Russians often welcomed the invaders. Secret opposition to Soviet policies was widespread, and there are good grounds for suspecting that the prisoners taken by the invaders included thousands of Red Army deserters. Hence it is a reasonable conjecture that if Hitler's armies had come as deliverers they might actually have overrun the U.S.S.R. to the Volga before winter. As it was, the Soviet dictator could have asked for no greater boon than this colossal political blunder resulting from Hitler's ethnic doctrines.

Budenny had been relieved by Timoshenko in the south and General Gregori Zhukov took command in the centre as the battle of Moscow opened during the first week of October, 1941. Fourteen Panzer and seven motorized divisions were included among the 69 Nazi divisions which Bock commanded. He estimated Zhukov's total at twelve armies composed of some 90 divisions, most of them understrength.

Hitler announced in an order of October 2 that "the preliminary conditions have been achieved to enable us to carry out the final powerful blow which is going to lead to the annihilation of the enemy before winter. . . . Today begins the last, the great battle of the year."

Throughout the next two weeks the opposing armies were locked in deadly combat. The capture of ground was secondary as compared to the destruction these mincing machines could inflict on each other. In this furious maelstrom, where the fighting sometimes reached a depth of 50 miles, the value of a human life was measured only by its ability to destroy another life. All the skill, imagination and technology of the twentieth century had at last been brought to a stark and dreadful contest in attrition.

The first phase ended in a great double envelopment which cut off 600,000 Russians in the Briansk-Vyazma pocket, according to Nazi estimates. But pressure was mounting on Bock's flanks, and partisan activity in his rear was cutting off badly needed supplies. Worse yet, from the German viewpoint, heavy autumnal rains in late October brought the advance almost to a standstill until the middle of November.

The final drive on Moscow, supported by 3,000 pieces of artillery and all available aircraft, opened on November 16. During the next two weeks every weapon and tactic developed so far in the war was used without regard to losses. Even the humble Molotov cocktail played a part in stopping Nazi armored columns. For the first time the Luftwaffe was challenged by the Red Air Force, and the new Yak fighter proved to be the equal of the Messerschmitt. Snow and subzero cold fought on the side of the Russians as ill-equipped Germans took terrific nightly artillery poundings.

The advance Nazi units came near enough to Moscow to see the nightly flashes of the city's antiaircraft guns. But it was apparent by the end of November that Bock's armies could not cover the last few miles. And on December 4 the invaders virtually admitted defeat by omitting any mention of the drive on Moscow in their daily communiqué.

THE RUSSIAN COUNTEROFFENSIVE

The Wehrmacht had met its first major reverse. Freezing temperatures had as much to do with the result as Russian arms, for Hitler had been too confident of a summer victory to prepare for a winter campaign. Joseph Goebbels, the propaganda minister, appealed to Germany for warm clothing; but the offerings reached the front too late to prevent widespread suffering. He estimated that German frost casualties alone during the winter of 1941-42 numbered 112,627, of which 14,357 required major amputations.

Damage to equipment was in proportion. German trucks and locomotives were immobilized for days by the extreme cold, which the Russians took into consideration in the manufacture and operation of their vehicles.

The strain of the battle of Moscow had been too much for the health of Bock and Field Marshal von Brauchitsch, nominal commander of the Wehrmacht, and both asked to be relieved. Hitler was now commander-in-chief in name as well as deed, and on December 19 he issued this order:

"Every man must fight where he stands. No falling back where there are no prepared positions in the rear."

Guderian and General Erich Hoeppner, commander of the Fourth Armored Group, were relieved by Hitler because they retreated without authority. The Führer also accepted the resignation of Rundstedt, who was refused permission to withdraw to a defensive position after his advance units were driven back from the outskirts of Rostov.

"Hitler, the visionary, saw that a retreat could only end as did that of Napoleon," comments General J. F. C. Fuller in his *Military History of the Western World.* "Although it was his obstinacy which had brought the campaign to the brink of disaster, it was his obstinacy which was to save it from plunging into the abyss. His refusal to draw out of Russia or to west of Smolensk undoubtedly saved his army from an even greater catastrophe than that of 1812."

The atmosphere of apprehension both in Berlin and at the front is indicated by the official Nazi suppression of Caulaincourt's *Memoirs,* containing a harrowing firsthand account of the destruction of Napoleon's *Grande Armée* in Russia. Adding to the gloom was the news of the United States' declaring war on the three Axis powers, for Hitler had made every effort to conciliate a nation whose potential at manufacturing arms and raising troops he respected.

Viewed as a whole, the advance of the Wehrmacht into Russia merits recognition as one of history's greatest military achievements. Even so, it was equaled by the defensive operations during the winter of 1941-42 which saved the Wehrmacht from destruction.

The German plan aimed at utilizing the main advance railway supply depots as "hedgehogs," each large enough for the sheltering of thousands of troops. No attempt was made to defend the space between entrenched camps bristling with artillery and armor around a 360° perimeter. The troops lived on the dumps, which were supplemented by airborne supplies as well as the trickle arriving by rail.

The front thus became a line of strategic islands in a wasteland of steppes, forests and charred villages. Late each morning a pale sun groped out of the mist and another gray day broke over the endless expanse of snow, only to be swallowed up at four o'clock by the blackness of another subzero night. Men went mad in this monotony of hardship, and the fortitude of German troops who survived the winter of 1941-42 deserved a better cause.

Planned withdrawals were completed in the centre, where General Gunther von Kluge had relieved Bock, just before Zhukov launched a counteroffensive late in December with fresh Siberian reinforcements. The Germans were hard hit and Kaluga fell with a large bag of prisoners to Russians who fought their way within 50 miles of Smolensk. In the south Field Marshal Walther von Reichenau, who had relieved Rundstedt, was staggered by Timoshenko's blows but managed to make a fighting retirement to hedgehogs strong enough to beat off attacks.

As the snow deepened, the Russians were limited to harassing operations conducted by Cossack divisions. Mounted troops, each drawing a sled on which an infantry soldier rode, were supported by sledge-drawn artillery. They captured several of the smaller hedgehogs but Kaluga was the only major strongpoint to be overwhelmed.

By February it was apparent that the Wehrmacht would pull through, but the winter was an ordeal that no participant would ever forget. German casualties from December 31 to February 20 were 175,636, according to Halder. This made a total of 1,005,336 since the opening day of the invasion, including 210,572 dead. There are no reliable figures as to Russian losses for this period, which probably were as high as 3,000,000 killed, wounded and missing. But the Soviet Union had already demonstrated its ability to put new divisions into the fight, and Lend-Lease arms from England and America would soon be compensating for Russian deficiencies in matériel.

There is little doubt that Moscow might have been taken if Hitler had not diverted most of the armor from Army Group Centre for six weeks. But it is equally probable that this result would not have won the war, even granting that Moscow was the hub of communications and the spiritual heart of Russia.

"Russia is so vast and the Russian government was so determined," wrote General Gunther Blumentritt, chief-of-staff of the German Fourth Army, "that the war would simply have gone on, taking new forms, in the huge spaces of that country. The best we could have expected was partisan warfare on an enormous scale in European Russia, quite apart from the great expanse of Asia which is also Russian territory."

IV

THE WAR IN THE PACIFIC

The only thing now to do is to lick hell out of them.

U.S. SENATOR BURTON K. WHEELER

ON THE Sunday morning of December 7, 1941, Japanese carrier-borne bombers attacked the American fleet at anchor in Pearl Harbor. Again, as at Port Arthur in 1904, Japan's armed forces struck while the nation's diplomats were masking the attempt by discussing peace. But in 1941 treachery paid richer rewards. Within a few minutes the dawn assault so altered the balance of sea power in the Pacific that the United States was beaten down to an anxious defensive.

In all modern history no nation had ever suffered such a naval catastrophe. For after that Sunday morning visitation no less than five twisted and burning battleships were disabled, and three others damaged. Altogether, 18 warships suffered hits in an assault which killed 2,403 men and wrecked 188 planes. The Pacific fleet and its great base had been all but knocked out in the first hour of undeclared war.

The extent of the disaster had of course to be concealed from the enemy, and first reports admitted only the loss of the obsolescent battleship *Arizona,* the capsizing of the *Oklahoma,* and the sinking of a target ship, mine layer and three destroyers. Not until April, 1944, did Admiral Ernest J. King, commander-in-chief of the United States fleet, deem it safe to tell the whole story. Long before that date the other twelve warships had been restored to active service.

Even at the time, while safeguarding their appalling secret, Navy officials reacted with courage and dignity. Without mincing words, Secretary Knox added to the first shock by announcing that "the United States forces were not on the alert against the surprise air attack."

Three days after Pearl Harbor the Japanese added to their naval superiority in the Pacific by sinking the *Repulse* and *Prince of Wales,* the only two British capital ships in the Far East.

These vessels had arrived at Singapore the week before. After learning that a weakly escorted Japanese convoy of troopships had been sighted on the way to Malaya, Admiral Philips decided to contest the invasion. His audacity bordered on recklessness in the lack of fighter coverage, and luck went against him when an enemy aerial scout reported the presence of the warships. Land-based Japanese dive bombers and torpedo planes flocked in for the kill, and within two hours the *Repulse* and *Prince of Wales* had been sent to the bottom—the first capital units of the war to be destroyed in full action by air power alone.

The Philippine Islands constituted a third barrier to Japanese ambitions—a potential American bastion on the flank of an enemy advance southward. But during the first devastating week it became obvious to trained observers that General Douglas MacArthur's small army could offer only delaying actions. Most of the American planes were destroyed on the ground in the first few days; and even if naval reinforcements had been available, they could not be maintained without aerial protection. This left only the prospect of retreat as Japanese amphibious forces were landed in Luzon after the destruction of the Cavite naval base by bombing attacks.

THE SAMURAI OF 1941

The first reaction of fury which the Pearl Harbor assault aroused in the United States was followed by incredulity. Such adjectives as "suicidal" and "megalomaniacal" were used by editorial writers when referring to a Japanese plan of conquest on a front from Shanghai to Honolulu. Among the other absurd notions cherished during the preceding twenty years, Americans had been solemnly assured in pseudoscientific articles that the slant-eyed Orientals could never qualify as pilots of fighter planes.

Illusions of this sort now began to crumble as rapidly as did the American, British and Dutch defenses in the Pacific. For the Japanese efforts in China had not prepared the democratic nations for the marvelously planned and executed amphibious assaults of December, 1941. Nor was it generally realized that fewer than 100,000 ill-equipped white soldiers, supported by several hundred modern planes and a scattered force of cruisers and destroyers, were doomed to be overwhelmed in detail by an "ocean blitzkrieg" bringing a crushing superiority to every point.

In 1938, while Hitler screamed about German might, Japanese propagandists were more subtle. With delicate strokes they painted a picture of a small, impoverished, flower-loving nation which had neither the desire nor the resources to menace Western countries. Japan was limned as a resolute little buffer state between democracy and Bolshevism, with the Manchukuo and China "incidents" being explained as efforts to check the spread of Communism.

With a population of 139,700,000, including Korea, Formosa and Manchukuo, the island empire had nearly double the human resources of the Third Reich. While using obsolescent planes against the Chinese, the nation's engineers were perfecting the Zero fighters and Nakajima torpedo bombers which would be withheld until the hour had struck. Japan's officers, who considered themselves the direct heirs of the Samurai tradition, were training troops for the jungle tactics which would later be used in Malaya and the Solomons. By the summer of 1940, eighteen months before Pearl Harbor, the process had gone so far that Japan's decentralized industries were placed on a full war basis by state decree.

The minds and bodies of the Japanese people had long been prepared for a conflict which might last ten years or more. An example of the hardening process applied to conscripts—perhaps the most rigorous training ever imposed in modern history—was reported five years before Pearl Harbor by an American officer, Captain Harold Doud, then serving on a language detail with the Japanese Army. In the *Infantry Journal* of January-February, 1937, he described the war games of peacetime regiments:

These exercises were remarkable chiefly for the long distance marches and the long periods without rest or sleep. One day we marched thirty-seven miles. Twice the troops went three days and two nights without sleep except what could be snatched during ten-minute halts and brief lulls in the situation. Sometimes the men slept while walking. . . . the last four-day period was the most strenuous. *We started out at five in the morning and marched almost continuously until ten the next morning. In that time we covered fifty-six miles.*

It is understandable that Captain Doud should have recalled the ordeal in italics. When he suggested that some of the soldiers might have slept at nightfall, the Japanese commander replied, "Oh no! That is not necessary. They already know how to sleep. They need training in how to stay awake."

This criticism might have been applied with more justice to the English-speaking peoples between 1919 and 1941. With a magnificent disdain for military values, President Wilson had allowed hundreds of mandated islands in the Pacific to be awarded to Japan after World War I. Mere dots on the map, these atolls provided naval bases in addition to a chain of "unsinkable aircraft carriers." Thus in 1941 a Japanese fighter plane equipped with spare gasoline tanks could proceed from island to island on its own power to strategic outposts extending in a vast semi-circle to the south and east.

Most of these secret preparations were made in defiance of regulations to which Japan had solemnly subscribed. Tokyo's contempt for such restrictions was shown even more flagrantly after the Washington Treaty of February, 1922, in which the major naval powers of the world agreed to limit armaments. Hailed in some quarters as a triumph of international good will, this contract rewarded Japanese duplicity while sorely handicapping Britain and the United States at the outbreak of World War II.

In 1937, when the terms of the Treaty of Washington expired, Congress refused to fortify Guam for fear of offending Japan—an attitude which undoubtedly had the support of constituents who showed any concern. Since 1935 General MacArthur had insisted that the Philippines could be held, yet not until 1941 were belated and insufficient efforts made to remedy defaults of the past.

At least the armed forces atoned for the nation's self-deception with their lives. Guam, isolated in the Japanese sphere, went down fighting after four days. Wake, defended by 378 marines with twelve planes and six 5-inch guns, created a new saga of American valor by repulsing all naval and aerial attacks for two weeks. Although the defenders had no shelter from enemy fire, they sank four enemy destroyers and damaged four before being overwhelmed on December 23. A week later Cavite and Manila were abandoned by MacArthur, who decided to retire before larger Japanese forces converging from beaches to the north and south.

Germany did not overlook an opportunity to isolate her new adversary, and the sinking of a tanker off Long Island began a submarine campaign which accounted for 327 ships, largely American, in the western Atlantic before the end of June, 1942. Added losses on the Murmansk route and in the northern Atlantic brought the Allied and neutral total for the war up to ten million tons by this date.

The Fall of Singapore

During the first days of 1942 the peoples of the United Nations could console themselves only with the news from Russia and Africa. The Red Army's winter counteroffensive had given proof of Russia's endurance. And in the African desert warfare another advance had been made by the British at the expense of Marshal Rommel.

General Sir Claude Auchinleck, who had replaced Wavell when that commander took charge in India, began an offensive late in November after receiving supplies and reinforcements. Tobruk was relieved after having been cut off for seven months, but Rommel evaded all attempts to encircle him. His German and Italian forces retired intact, after the loss of 14,000 prisoners and scores of tanks, as the victors raced on to Bengasi. During the mopping-up operations the British bagged an additional 13,500 captives by storming Bardia and Halfaya.

Neither in Russia nor in Africa, however, could the United Nations boast of decisive results. Soviet communiqués left no doubt that the chief object of Stalin's winter offensive was to establish stronger defensive positions for the expected renewal of Nazi attacks after the spring thaws. Nor had Auchinleck's triumph over Rommel been any more conclusive than the Nazi victories earlier in 1941. As yet Wavell had won the only real decision in Africa by destroying the Italian armies.

Certainly there was nothing illusory about Japanese progress in the Far East. Shanghai obviously could not be held, and Hong Kong surrendered after a defense of eleven days. The enemy's southward sweep now profited from the complaisance of Vichy France in allowing Indo-China to be occupied in July.

As a result the Japanese had established aerial and naval bases in Indo-China long before December 7, and the prompt capitulation of Thailand opened the way to Burma and Malaya. At this point the scope of the invaders' plans was revealed. While still fighting a large-scale guerilla war in China, they were prepared to launch co-ordinated attacks on Rangoon, Singapore, Bataan, Java and a vast group of South Pacific islands presenting a front of 3,000 miles from east to west.

So staggering was this concept that the peoples of the United Nations could fix their eyes on only one objective. Singapore became at once a symbol of Allied resistance, and few observers suspected that their hopes had been built upon the shifting sands of rhetoric. Familiar journalistic phrases such as "the mighty bastion of the Far East" had given the British and American public an optimism which seems to have been shared by a great many military men. Certain it is that the responsible officers believed the base to be safe from a land attack through the jungles—just as many American officers had believed that the Japanese would not dare to send their aircraft carriers against Pearl Harbor. Even when the invaders made their first landings on the coast some 275 miles north of Singapore, censors permitted the most confident predictions to be published.

Such psychological blind spots had of course been taken into military account by the Japanese. They realized that the jungle itself could be used as the shield of invasion, and it was an army of from 80,000 to 100,000 specialists which moved down the peninsula. Every man and weapon had been chosen for some particular task, as the defenders soon realized. The taunt of "monkeys," applied to the little Japanese warriors, proved only too apt as stealthy combat groups seemed to swing from tree to tree. Their faces painted green for camouflage in the jungle shadows, the agile and tireless invaders neglected no trick which might bewilder a more formal opponent. British officers were called out by name from their quarters, only to be shot down by a concealed marksman. Soldiers had to be constantly on the alert against confusing shouts in the English language which foemen had learned as part of their tactics.

The day's infiltration usually began about midnight and lasted until three in the afternoon for the main forces. Then the troops were well nourished and rested for nine hours as equally well-rested comrades kept the British awake with harassing tactics. To add to the effect on strained nerves, radio loud-speakers created false alarms with a din of machine-gun fire, mortar bursts and cries of distress, all of which had been recorded in Japan long before the war.

The marvel is only that defenders driven to the limits of exhaustion managed to keep their forces intact and retreat in some order from adversaries penetrating to their flanks and rear. Rivers aided the enemy's infiltration methods as the Japanese floated through on rafts at night, and larger contingents were sometimes landed on both coasts behind the British lines. When no other means of infiltration prevailed, the invaders did not hesitate to sacrifice troops in a frontal rush, so that the sound of enemy firing would guide their comrades.

It is to the credit of the British that they learned how to cope with most of these ruses. Even so, they remained at a disadvantage in weapons as well as tactics. The Japanese had developed sniping into a fine art, while their mortars and small tanks were created especially for jungle fighting. Hence the progress down the peninsula was a steady march, and on January 30 the last of the defenders were evacuated across the narrow Johore Strait, separating Singapore from the mainland.

All month the city and base had been well-nigh defenseless under terrific bombing attacks. Neither antiaircraft guns nor interceptor planes had been supplied in reasonable numbers, and Japanese confidence is indicated by the fact that certain buildings and installations were spared for future use. Meanwhile the silent 16-inch guns pointed seaward as a melancholy reminder that a fortress without adequate aerial forces is an anachronism.

Jazz syncopation from the loud-speakers throbbed in the shattered streets as a relief from the explosions. This was the dying city's requiem after the Japanese landed on the island itself in hundreds of steel barges. Artillery fire now supplemented bombs, so that recent British reinforcements and new planes proved to have arrived just in time to be sacrificed. By February 15 the last hope of resistance had faded, and the unconditional surrender of some 70,000 troops to General Yamashita became the greatest military disaster ever suffered up to that time by the British Empire.

THE END IN JAVA AND THE PHILIPPINES

The expert timing and co-ordination of the Japanese drives was never better exhibited than in Burma. Obviously the presence of British troops in Rangoon offered a serious threat to the flanks and rear of forces advancing in Malaya. Yet so accurately did the invaders judge the situation that they ignored the peril of a counterattack for a month while "softening up" Burma with bombing raids. When at last they struck on January 14, the fifth-column efforts of discontented natives helped to smooth the path of conquest. Again the Japanese superiority in jungle fighting was demonstrated, and on March 7 the outnumbered British were forced to begin the evacuation of Rangoon and all southern Burma.

Two days later the fall of Java was announced. This news came as an even more sickening blow, for the Dutch masters of the East Indies had proved from the beginning to be grim realists. Their lack of planes and guns cannot be charged to negligence, since four-fifths of the military supplies purchased from Britain and the United States could not be delivered by nations which were similarly handicapped.

Dutch submarines went into action after the news of Pearl Harbor, averaging a sinking a day for weeks. Dutch planes and destroyers were ready on January 10 when the invaders struck at Borneo and Celebes to gain control of the sea approaches to Java. Two Japanese warships and two transports were put out of action; and when the landings could not be prevented, the Dutch applied an inexorable scorched-earth policy.

After gaining a foothold in the centre of the island chain, the Japanese aimed their next blows at flanks as widely separated as New York and San Francisco. Amphibious forces occupied New Britain and New Ireland, while far to the west bombing raids destroyed Dutch airfields on Sumatra as a prelude to conquest. Then on January 23 the invaders suffered their first losses in Macassar Strait after renewing the attack on the centre. Dutch planes first sighted a large convey. They scored hits on eight warships and transports, and that night American destroyers raced through the convoy like wolves rending a flock of sheep. Allied sea and air attacks continued for four days and nights, so that thousands of troops could be estimated as casualties.

The Japanese, to balance the scale, boasted of having captured two hundred Allied cargo ships since the outbreak of war; and their enormous gains in matériel and territory justified daring risks. The surviving transports of the Macassar Strait fleet poured more troops into Borneo and Celebes, bringing Java within the range of the new airfields.

This success illustrates the pattern of amphibious infiltration which the invaders applied so ably in the East Indies. First, risks were taken in order to occupy a few key positions. Then aerial bases were established at top speed, so that the next objectives could be "prepared" more economically by attacks from land-based Mitsubishi bombers. The profits of this strategy were accumulative, since the risks diminished in proportion to the multiplication of new landing fields.

The Allies, lacking the planes, troops and warships to defend such an area, could do little to oppose landings in Bali, Timor and Sumatra. In preference to being weak everywhere the defenders chose to be as strong as possible in Java; and the decisive action occurred on the sea when the Japanese made their initial attempt at invasion. On February 27 their fleet of forty transports, escorted by nine cruisers and two destroyer flotillas, was encountered in the Java Sea. Karel Doorman, the Dutch admiral commanding a mixed Dutch, British, American and Australian force of five cruisers and sixteen destroyers, took the initiative in spite of his material inferiority. The outcome of the first clash rather favored the Allies, but the retiring Japanese squadron lured Doorman into a submarine ambush with fatal results. Two cruisers and a destroyer were lost, and during the pursuit of the next few days the Allied squadron was all but annihilated as a fighting force, with only four destroyers escaping undamaged.

This disaster sealed the doom of Java. The original three spearheads of invasion were soon reinforced; and despite the sacrificial efforts of outweighed Dutch land forces, a ten-day campaign ended all organized resistance.

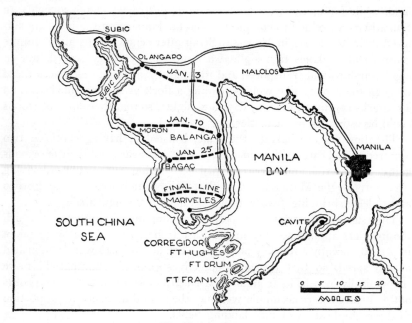

The End in Bataan

The conquest of the island barrier meant that the great land mass of Australia must now be held at any cost as the base for an Allied counteroffensive. Toward this end the continued resistance in the Philippines was of inestimable value in gaining military time, the commodity which Japan's foes needed most of all. Although Luzon had been the objective of the first large-scale drive of the Pacific war, the defenders of the hilly Bataan peninsula were still inflicting humiliating losses on Japanese prestige as well as personnel. Larger enemy forces were employed than in any other effort, yet after three months the little army of 40,000

American and Filipino troops showed no signs of yielding to superior numbers.

Much of the credit for these results should go to General Douglas Mac-Arthur. A divisional commander in World War I, he earned distinction afterwards as a peacetime soldier. Problems of Philippine defense had long been his major interest; and after assuming command of the islands in 1935, he retired from the Army two years later to organize a native constabulary. This well-trained force became the nucleus of belated defensive efforts in 1941 when MacArthur was recalled to command of the islands and provided with limited reinforcements and supplies from the United States.

By this time the improvement in the art of generalship since the preceding conflict had been made evident on all fronts. As a scholar of war, Wavell attacked in 1940 because he was too weak to risk a defensive, and his victories over the Italians mark him as one of the great soldiers of British history. Under him such field generals as Gott, Freyberg and Jock Campbell set a tradition of personal valor which made them heroes to their own rank and file. For the new tactics of mobility had nearly eliminated the sedentary officer of 1917, and morale gained as the ancient bond between the commander and his men was restored.

MacArthur's high qualities of leadership were shown in the Bataan retreat. Throughout January the incessant Japanese attacks were repulsed with heavy casualties as the Americans and Filipinos fell back to prepared positions. The infiltration methods which had succeeded in Malaya and Burma were broken up by the counterattacks of a dynamic defensive, and at the end of the month the invaders came to a halt of frustration.

The final American lines extended across the tip of the peninsula, opposite the island fortress of Corregidor. Yet General Homma's forces made no further progress in February, despite their superiority in all material respects. Neither bombings nor bombardments could shake the defense, and attempts at amphibious landings in MacArthur's rear were beaten off. Meanwhile, American submarines and patrol torpedo boats took a heavy toll of Japanese warships as well as cargo vessels, so that the Luzon invasion had already become the enemy's most costly effort.

Homma was succeeded on March 9 by Yamashita, the conqueror of Singapore. Japanese reinforcements added to the odds against Americans and Filipinos, who had been on short allowances of food since early in January. Only one supply ship in three now managed to run the blockade, and the defenders were without air support.

Japanese morale had long been upheld by legends of American softness and self-indulgence, yet the half-starved remnants on the tip of the peninsula held out a month against all of Yamashita's blows. Even after the lines were breached by attackers who disregarded losses, the epic of Bataan lasted another forty-eight hours before resistance ceased on April 9. In the end the little army had been beaten by hunger, malaria and exhaustion.

The troubles of the victors did not end here. Manila Bay could not be used until the guns of Corregidor were silenced, and not until May 6 was the overcrowded island bombed and starved into surrender. Lieutenant General Jonathan Wainwright might have been evacuated, but he elected to share the fate of his men.

America's Sinews of War

If the peoples of the United Nations had underrated Japan at first, they now reacted to the opposite extreme. For it could not be denied that within a few months the aggressors had laid violent claim to an area comprising more than three million square miles and a population of 403,560,000—one-fifth of all the people on earth! The resources of this empire in tin, oil and other raw materials were fabulous. And if the various Oriental peoples could be politically welded into Tokyo's Co-Prosperity Sphere—an obvious copy of Hitler's New Order—Japan might well emerge as the world's most formidable war power.

Naturally, the brunt of the defense fell upon the United States at this time. The Republic's errors and shortcomings had been glaringly revealed in recent months, but it was not so well understood that American military muscles were fast developing.

Ever since 1939 President Roosevelt had used his great political talents to take all possible defense measures in spite of the well organized opposition of isolationists. It was the nation's further good fortune in this emergency to have as its first soldier a man uniquely fitted for the responsibility, General George C. Marshall. Beginning in September, 1939, with a regular army of 200,000 men trained and equipped according to standards of 1919, Marshall bridged the tactical gap of two decades in the next two years. His increases in the numbers of troops were not as important as a multiplication of firepower which made the new armored and triangular infantry divisions the most potentially effective units of their kind in the world. Owing largely to his labors as organizer, the country had an army in the spring of 1942 which lacked little except battle experience.

But preparations for total war are not limited to the military. The products of the laboratory and factory are equally essential, and in 1940 the scientists of the United States were mobilized under the leadership of a board headed by Dr. Vannevar Bush, president of the Carnegie Institution. No fanfare of publicity announced this step, yet within a few months six thousand of the nation's most able young researchers went to work on war problems. A dramatic secrecy and anonymity shrouded their efforts, and no rewards beyond a normal peacetime salary awaited workers whose victories had a vital effect on strategy. Likewise, the industrialists of an industrial country changed abruptly from normal production to a complete war economy. So prodigious were their efforts that President Roosevelt's call for an output of 50,000 planes a year—a figure which seemed preposterous to both friend and foe in 1940—had been made to appear a moderate demand within thirty months.

Thus on March 16, 1942, when Washington announced that a substantial expeditionary force had already reached Australia, the achievement owed to scientists and manufacturers as well as generals.

The following day it became known that General MacArthur had been recalled from Bataan to take charge of the Allied forces based in Australia. The striking personality of this commander made him a popular choice; but anyone could deduce that the United States Navy would fight the first battles if the long and tenuous supply line were to be maintained. This branch of the service was better prepared for its tests than the shortcomings of a few officers at Pearl Harbor might have indicated. Sheer material inferiority reduced the Pacific fleet to an unwelcome defensive after that disaster, yet its first revenge came as early as February 1 when a task force raided the Marshall and Gilbert islands. A similar raid on Wake followed later in the month, and on March 4 American carrier-borne planes surprised Marcus Island, only 960 miles southeast of Tokyo.

These brisk actions were soon obscured by the daring of the blow struck on April 18, when Tokyo itself and three other Japanese cities were bombed in broad daylight. The attempt was of course intended for moral effect rather than material results, and as a master showman President Roosevelt made the most of the enemy's bewilderment. Not until a later date did Washington disclose that General James H. Doolittle and some eighty other aviators had created tactical history by taking off from a carrier with Mitchell two-motored bombers whose wing tips had only four feet clearance. Eighteen tons of bombs were dropped by fliers who skimmed over enemy housetops after covering 850 miles in a gale. Eighteen of the participants were captured or killed, the remainder being smuggled to safety after landing in China.

Although this stirring feat helped to wipe out bitter memories, wars are not won by moral effects alone. There remained the tremendous problem of holding Australia and its supply line, since enemy domination of the island continent would go far toward securing recent Japanese conquests. Already the invaders of New Britain had established a strong base at Rabaul, and the occupation of the northeast New Guinea coast in March brought Australia within the range of land-based bombers.

Now the strategists of both sides fixed their gaze on a point in the Coral Sea to the southeast of New Guinea where the American life line crossed the line of a Japanese advance southward from the Truk and Rabaul bases. Both sides hastened to seize islands suitable for land-based planes; and by April the Americans were building airfields in New Caledonia as the enemy landed in the Solomon and Louisiade groups.

The opening round of naval warfare in the Pacific took place off the Louisiade Archipelago on May 7, 1942, when opposing carrier striking forces met in the battle of the Coral Sea. Aircraft from the U.S. carrier *Lexington* damaged the light Japanese carrier *Shoho* so severely that she sank. A Japanese cruiser and a tanker were also sent to the bottom, and the carrier *Zuikaku* was set on fire. The Americans could claim only an inconclusive victory, however, for the carrier *Lexington* was hard hit and had to be destroyed. It was, as Admiral Ernest J. King pointed out, "the first major engagement in naval history in which surface ships did not exchange a shot."

THE BATTLE OF MIDWAY

In both tactical and strategic respects the Americans could claim an indecisive victory as the foe retreated northward. The next phase of the Japanese plan depended, of course, on future American moves. If, as the enemy anticipated, Admiral Chester W. Nimitz chose to keep his forces in the Coral Sea, they would be of no use to him when the Japanese aimed their main blows in the central Pacific. Then in the event of success the victors could return to dispose of Australia without interference from American forces reduced to the defense of their own mainland.

A more momentous decision never faced navy strategists, and all important units were recalled from the Coral Sea to Pearl Harbor about the middle of May. After being refueled and refitted at that great base, they steamed westward toward Midway.

Up to this point, despite their Coral Sea defeat, the Japanese had not made a serious error in strategy. For years the nation's naval writers had imagined a future sea battle in which the hated Yankees, like the Russians at Tsushima, would blunder into enemy waters with a huge fleet burdened by transports. Paradoxically, this was exactly the sort of force which the Japanese themselves now sent into enemy waters—the greatest armada so far of World War II, consisting of 7 battleships, 8 cruisers, 48 destroyers, 16 submarines and 12 transports loaded with 5,000 troops. The carrier force included the four largest and newest of the Japanese Navy, the *Akagi, Kaga, Hiryu* and *Soryu*. Altogether, counting tankers and oilers, a fleet of 100 vessels plowed the waves toward the central Pacific.

Two opposing theories of airplane construction and tactics were now to be put to the test. Japanese designers turned out lightly armored bombers which depended for protection on Zero fighters. The fighters in turn depended on speed, manoeuvrability and firepower, being provided with neither armor nor self-sealing gasoline tanks. Although these lacks have been charged to an Oriental disregard for human life, the real explanation is to be found in the strategic situation. The Japanese, being so well endowed with "island carriers," had sacrificed protection to gain mobility, believing that they could win a quick victory before their losses became serious. This policy seemed justified in their early clashes with Allied foemen flying slow and outdated machines.

The Americans had an entirely different strategic problem. Forced to cover great distances without benefit of island bases, they had little choice but to develop long-range, heavily armored bombers capable of holding their own without fighter protection. Thus was evolved the first dreadnought of the air in the Flying Fortress—a four-motored machine planned primarily for independent missions in the vast reaches of the Pacific. The same policy was applied to American fighters and medium bombers, all of which were more sturdy and self-sufficient than their corresponding Japanese numbers.

These contrasting theories of aerial warfare were to decide another naval battle in which the opposing warships never exchanged a salvo—a battle first waged on the drawing boards of Japanese and American aircraft plants. The invading fleet held a material superiority in every respect, including carriers, over an American force which did not include a single battleship. But the defenders had the advantage of the small Midway airfield with its Flying Fortresses, medium bombers, and fighters.

Postwar Japanese writings indicate that the successes of the past six months had resulted in a dangerous degree of overconfidence. Curiously enough, Japan's strategists had a more realistic outlook immediately after their one-sided victory at Pearl Harbor. The heroic fight put up a few days later by the U.S. Marines of Wake won the sober respect of Japanese who had previously deluded themselves that Americans were not capable of a battle to a finish.

Admiral Isoroku Yamamoto, commander-in-chief of the Japanese Navy, concluded in the spring of 1942 that the time was ripe for luring the main U.S. fleet to its destruction, whereupon Washington would be willing to accept a peace of compromise. His strategic plan envisioned a left-wing attack on Dutch Harbor, the U.S. naval base in the Aleutians, for the purpose of drawing American naval forces northward. Then, a day later, the main Japanese effort would take the form of a right-wing assault on Midway with a view to making that island a base for further offensive operations. A task force including two light carriers was to make the left-wing feint while the bulk of the fleet struck at Midway.

This plan was based on two assumptions which proved false. Yamamoto believed that some of the American naval forces in the South Pacific would not be able to reach Midway in time to participate. It was further assumed that the carrier *Yorktown* had been so badly damaged in the battle of the Coral Sea as to be inoperative.

The enemy did not know, of course, that Admiral Nimitz had learned of the Japanese plan on May 14 by means of deciphered code messages. He issued orders immediately for a concentration of U.S. naval forces at Pearl Harbor, and by a mighty effort the repairs of the *Yorktown* were completed in time for her participation.

Nimitz divided his fleet into two task forces: No. 16 commanded by Rear Admiral Raymond A. Spruance; and No. 17 under Rear Admiral Frank Fletcher. The total American strength, consisting of three carriers, eight cruisers, 14 destroyers and 19 submarines, was far below the enemy's in all respects save one. That was in numbers of aircraft, since the U.S. carriers could launch 225 to the Japanese 250, and Nimitz also had the advantage of the land-based American planes on Midway.

The Japanese carriers, after having been first sighted on June 3, were 240 miles west of Midway when they launched their first strike at dawn the following morning. The island was warned by radar and all planes took to the air. At 6:15 A.M. the 26 aircraft of the marine fighter squadron met the Japanese vanguard and shot down an unknown number of planes at a cost of 15 of their own. Midway was hard hit but the runways of the airfields were soon repaired.

The first American attack on Japanese carriers took place at 7:10 A. M., when seven land-based torpedo aircraft out of ten were destroyed without a hit to their credit. A few minutes later the enemy's excellent fighter defense repulsed a squadron of 30 marine dive bombers from Midway with losses of 11 planes. No better success attended a high-level attack by 16 Flying Fortresses.

These strikes by island-based planes convinced Admiral Chuichi Nagumo, commanding the Japanese carriers, that another attack must be made on Midway. In preparation, he ordered that 93 stand-by planes be sent below, so as to clear the flight decks for the recovery of aircraft from the second Midway strike.

This attempt never materialized, for the Japanese carriers now were subjected to a series of attacks from aircraft of the U.S. carriers. The battle had reached a critical stage, and it appeared for an hour that the American forces were about to take the decisive beating 'hat Admiral Yamamoto had envisioned.

It was midmorning when the *Hornet* and *Enterprise* launched their planes, just as the Japanese carriers made a sharp turn northward. This manoeuvre succeeded so well that the *Hornet's* leading 35 dive bombers never sighted the enemy at all. After a futile search, shortage of fuel made a Midway landing necessary for those which did not splash. The 15 TBDs (torpedo bombers)of the *Hornet,* having lost their fighter escort in a cloud layer, attacked without them. All were destroyed. Of their 30 pilots and crewmen, but one survived.

The *Enterprise* TBDs did not fare much better. A squadron of 14 also lost contact with its fighters and only four pilots returned from a futile attack. A like fate overtook a torpedo squadron from the *Yorktown* when ten of its twelve planes were shot down.

Altogether, only six out of 41 American torpedo bombers had survived. Not a single hit had been scored on the enemy. "Yet it was the stark courage and relentless drive of these young pilots of the obsolete torpedo planes that made possible the victory that followed," commented Samuel Eliot Morison in Vol. IV of his *History of U.S. Naval Operations in World War II.* "The radical manoeuvring that these imposed on the Japanese carriers prevented them from launching more planes. And the TBDs by acting as magnets for the enemy's combat air patrol and pulling Zekes [Japanese fighters] down to near water level, enabled the dive bombing squadrons that followed a few minutes later to attack virtually unopposed by fighter planes, and to drop bombs on full deck-loads in process of being refueled."

Only a few minutes after the last TBD attacks, 35 dive bombers from the *Enterprise* roared into action without fighter escort. One squadron closed in on the carrier *Akagi,* Admiral Nagumo's flagship, while 40 aircraft were refueling on the flight deck. Two direct hits made an inferno of these planes and those in the hangars below. It proved impossible to extinguish the flames and Nagumo transferred his flag to the cruiser *Nagara.* The carrier was abandoned and destroyed by a Japanese torpedo.

The *Enterprise*'s second squadron made short work of the *Kaga* just as her aircraft had finished refueling. Little resistance was met by the American planes, which left the ship in flames. She blew up and sank after being abandoned.

Dive bombers from the *Yorktown* landed three 1,000-pound bombs squarely on the deck of the *Soryu* in the midst of refueling planes. This carrier, too, had to be abandoned. After burning for five hours she went to the bottom.

Only the carrier *Hiryu* struck a blow for the Japanese. Upon sighting the *Yorktown,* she launched a strike of 18 dive bombers and six fighters, followed two hours later by ten torpedo aircraft and six fighters. Twelve of the dive bombers were shot down, but the *Yorktown* took three hits which left her unmanageable. The second Japanese attack scored with two torpedoes and the ship was abandoned. Even so, the *Yorktown* would have been saved if a Japanese submarine had not sunk her two days later.

The *Hiryu* survived her sister carriers by only a few hours. Late in the afternoon of June 4 the dive bombers of the *Enterprise* caught up with her, and four hits left the ship in flames. After the transfer of her crew, Japanese destroyers gave her the coup de grâce.

Seldom have the fortunes of battle taken a more drastic turn. The Japanese forces which apparently had victory within their grasp at 10 A.M. were decisively beaten by 5 P.M., with all four carriers and their 250 planes destroyed at a cost of 19 American dive bombers. Counting other American losses, the total for the battle of Midway was a carrier, a destroyer and some 150 aircraft.

At sunset on June 4 the Japanese began a full retirement. Only foul weather the following day saved them from further serious losses during the American pursuit. As it was, dive bombers from the carriers sank the cruiser *Mikuma* and made a wreck of the cruiser *Mogami,* so that she was out of action for months.

On June 7—precisely six months after "the day of infamy"—the pursuit ended and the fleet returned to Pearl Harbor. What was to prove the most decisive naval battle of the war in the Pacific had gone against the

Japanese, whose main hope lay in a quick victory before the American industrial potential could shift the balance of power in the Pacific.

Although the American TBDs were inferior, Nimitz had an advantage in radar and in that amazing machine, built by American cryptographers and code-named "Magic," which made Japanese messages an open book. In the long run, however, the invaders could blame faulty strategy for their defeat. By attacking Midway first, they left the American carriers free to launch decisive blows. If the carriers could have been knocked out first, Midway would have been a certain prey to be overwhelmed at leisure.

The Japanese left-wing diversion resulted in more or less of a fiasco for both sides. On June 3, when the two light carriers launched 56 fighters and medium bombers for an attack on Dutch Harbor, only 19 ever found the objective in bad weather. The phrase "fog of war" took on a literal meaning as Japanese carrier planes and U.S. land-based planes groped for one another. After two days of such efforts, with seven Japanese and eight American planes lost in action, the invading squadron turned homeward. The only lasting result was the landing of Japanese battalions on Kiska and Attu in the western Aleutian chain.

V

THE END OF THE BEGINNING

Machines do not fight; men do.

—MARSHALL ANDREWS

T HE global character of the conflict was strikingly revealed in the early summer of 1942. By June it became evident that Russia, northern Africa and the South Pacific would soon be areas of decision. Despite recent and limited successes won by the United Nations, the Axis forces still held the initiative in each of these vast theaters. That they would make full use of their material advantages could not be doubted, for time still fought against Allies who had only begun to recover from losses due to their initial unpreparedness.

It would not be too much to say that Western civilization stood on the defensive. Such expressions had been degraded by propagandists of World War I until they lost all integrity. Yet in the middle of the twentieth century, peoples conquered by the Axis Powers were actually being enslaved and massacred. Although the announcement was withheld until 1944, Washington learned that hundreds of the troops captured on Bataan had died from the effects of privation and brutal treatment. The Germans, as if keeping open a door of escape, were more cautious. While granting British and American prisoners most of their rights, they adopted a cold-blooded official policy of depopulating whole districts in Russia, Poland and the Balkans.

THE CRISIS OF AUGUST, 1942

The new conditions of global warfare had already weakened General Auchinleck's forces as Japanese successes caused 50,000 of his Australian veterans to be withdrawn for the defense of their homeland. Meanwhile, the Germans were winning the battle of supply in a warfare which has been described as a "quartermaster's nightmare." The Luftwaffe made the Mediterranean route so precarious for occasional convoys that all materials from England or America had to be sent around Capetown. This was the climax of Malta's ordeal, and even the enemy marveled at the tenacity of a defense which not only survived daily bombings but shot down as many as 63 raiders in a single day. British planes and submarines also sank dozens of Axis ships crossing from Sicily, though in the end Rommel profited from his shorter route.

The RAF continued to rule the air in the African desert warfare, and Brigadier Jock Campbell's tank columns stung the Axis flank and rear repeatedly. Forays of even greater audacity were made by small bands of picked men who had been trained in commando tactics—a phrase which sums up every art of hand-to-hand killing ever known to an Iroquois warrior or a Chicago gangster. The Germans standing guard over Europe had come to dread commando attacks ranging from Norway to France, and on the African front Marshal Rommel himself narrowly escaped capture in a raid on his headquarters.

The fifty-year-old organizer of the Afrika Korps was perhaps the foremost representative of the new type of German general. A captain in 1918, he hitched his wagon to Hitler's star during the violent postwar years and rose rapidly to the level of corps commander at the outbreak of World War II. Audacious and energetic, he proved after his Libyan defeat that he knew more about armored warfare than his opponents. Reorganizing his forces at El Agheila, he struck by surprise late in January to drive the enemy out of Bengasi, where valuable stores were left behind. Cairo tried to shrug off the reverse, and Rommel actually did take another beating in May when the British anticipated his flank attack south of Tobruk and drove him back with a concentration of superior forces. His position seemed shaky on the last day of the month as Auchinleck congratulated the victors, "Well done, Eighth Army! . . . Don't let him get away."

But Rommel had no intention of getting away. While his engineers made secret gaps in the opposing mine field, he brilliantly outmanoeuvred an overconfident foe with his "caldron" tactics of the next ten days. Then with appalling suddenness the British were lured into a tank ambush on "Black Saturday," June 13, 1942, and by Churchill's admission 230 out of 300 machines were destroyed by hidden 88-mm. guns.

The battle of Libya was lost in those few hours. Next day the British began a retreat which fell little short of a flight, leaving behind a force of 25,000 men at Tobruk. But the desert port was not destined to repeat its triumph of the previous winter. Before the garrison could organize its defense, Rommel crashed through the perimeter to compel the surrender of nearly two divisions and enormous supplies in a day.

Once again, as in 1940, the RAF saved the British cause. Every available plane, regardless of age or condition, was summoned from the entire Middle East. Red-eyed pilots, staggering with weariness, flew an incredible number of daily sorties, or individual missions, in heat and dust storms. With enemy bombs falling about them, ground crews toiled day and night, taking their sleep in snatches of a few minutes. And if the British had been beaten in tank and artillery tactics, they now taught the Luftwaffe a costly lesson in aerial warfare. Scores of German planes were destroyed on the ground, and the remainder so thoroughly outfought that Rommel was robbed of his ultimate triumph. An endless column of British trucks choked the road to Alexandria— "soft transport" which might have been the helpless prey of bombers— yet Auchinleck's remnants retired intact under their air umbrella.

The retreat ended at El Alamein, 70 miles from the great British naval base. There the pursuers were stopped as much by their own exhaustion and extended supply line as by the beaten army. Nevertheless, Rommel made it apparent that he was gathering his strength for a final effort. During these tense July and August days the Germans struck medals and printed occupation money to be used for the looting of Egypt. Mussolini arrived with bands and a white charger for the triumphal entry and Axis radio propagandists began to prepare the Egyptian people with promises of "liberation."

The German Spring Offensive in Russia

The news from Russia at this time was equally depressing. The Red Army, battling desperately all summer, had been unable to halt the enemy sweep across the eastern Ukraine. Thus in August the invaders reached the Volga near Stalingrad while penetrating deep into the Caucasus to threaten Soviet oil supplies.

Until late in the spring the Wehrmacht had been content to yield the initiative to Stalin in order to amass the supplies and reserves for this effort. The German winter defense line, planned to hold the railways west of Leningrad, Moscow and Kharkov, consisted of an integrated system of strongholds surrounded by fortified villages protruding like quills in every direction to expose assailants to crossfire and encirclement. The Soviet gains in territory were largely at the expense of an elastic defense between these "hedgehogs," few of which could be reduced. Hitler admitted that his unprepared armies had suffered cruel hardships, but the Russians paid a high price for their advances. This conclusion is based on Moscow's estimate of 4,500,000 Soviet casualties in the first year of the war, plus the loss of 9,000 planes and 15,000 tanks.

Here it may be noted that if the casualties of both armies reached unprecedented totals, so also did the numbers made whole by military surgery. In past conflicts the triumphs of war's healers had been judged from a humanitarian standpoint, but in 1942 the strategic aspects could not be overlooked. Neither the Wehrmacht nor the Red Army could have afforded such a fearful wastage if a high percentage of the wounded had not been restored to the ranks.

While sulfa and other new drugs of World War II have been more dramatically publicized, greater credit is deserved by blood plasma and aerial ambulances. Military surgeons of the first World War realized that additional thousands of men might have been saved by prompt transfusions, but the means were then lacking. Hence it would be hard to overrate the importance a generation later of the "blood banks," supplied by donations from civilian volunteers, which enabled plasma to be preserved until the moment of need. This victory over time is equaled only by the part played by aviation in cases where minutes mean the difference between life and death. Official United States figures, to cite one national example, reveal that 173,527 sick and wounded soldiers were evacuated to base hospitals by planes in 1943 alone, with only 11 deaths occurring in flight. More than 3,000 emergency cases were flown to the United States from such distant theaters as the South Pacific.

Owing to such methods, the German and Russian armies endured casualty lists which would have been fatal in the last war. Broken machines, like broken men, were restored to duty with highly organized efficiency. Mobile repair units, often working under fire, performed miracles of reclamation, while the great machine shops of the rear areas might be described as the base hospitals of matériel. Behind the battlefront, of course, the ceaseless warfare of production extended to the core of each warring nation, involving every man, woman and child in its operations. So vital was this phase that the probable outcome of the 1942 campaigns could have been predicted by anyone knowing the statistics. Before spring Germany had mobilized an industrial army of more than 2,500,000 foreign workers—not only satellite peoples such

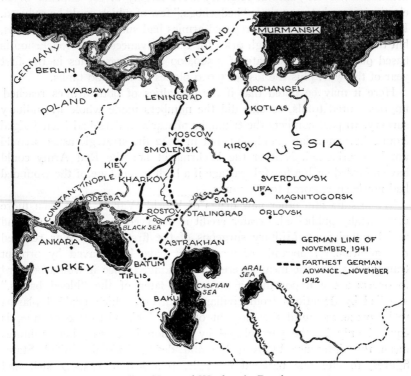

Two Years of Warfare in Russia

as Italians and Hungarians, but also Czechs, Danes, Poles and Frenchmen who had been coerced by the threat of starvation for their families. Add to this total at least an equal number of toiling war prisoners, and some idea may be gained of Germany's advantages over Russia, which had lost a third of its factories and population during the first four months of invasion. Only the strategic forethought of Soviet leaders in removing many war industries to distant Volga and Ural regions enabled the nation to survive.

Still, it could not be said that Russia stood alone. Britain and the United States took serious risks on their own fronts to send materials, even though government-controlled Moscow newspapers complained of late and inadequate deliveries from convoys which sometimes lost half their ships on the Murmansk route. This dissatisfaction is understandable, coming from a nation fighting for life, yet the amounts of 1942 were not to be despised. On May 10, 1944, Churchill announced that his country had sent 5,031 tanks and 6,778 planes to Russia since October, 1941. Between that date and March, 1944, American Lend-Lease aid amounted to nearly a billion delivered tons, including such items as 8,800 planes, 5,200 tanks and tank destroyers, 190,000 trucks and 7,000,000 pairs of boots.

In a global war the donors of course profited militarily. British industries, given a respite from raids, were able to multiply production. The increased output of giant Stirling and Lancaster bombers made possible an aerial offensive which far surpassed all German efforts. In four consecutive nights a total of 800 tons of explosives blasted the shipbuilding yards and aircraft plant in Rostock. The Skoda works at Pilsen had their turn, and on the night of May 30 the war's first raid by 1,000 planes was hailed as a tactical landmark. Whole districts of Cologne were leveled in an hour by incendiaries and two-ton "blockbusters," and enthusiasts declared that the war could be won by air power alone.

Russia in turn profited as enemy production was reduced and enemy fighter planes tied down to home defense. Even so, the odds against the invaded nation were heavy when the Germans adopted a new limited strategy. Instead of aiming at the destruction of Soviet armies, they now hoped to cripple the nation by capturing territory and cutting communications. For this purpose the Caucasus with its oil resources was deemed the area of least probable resistance. The Nazis, still coining new names for old tactics, employed a revised offensive formation known as the "mailed fist"—a shell of armor enclosing a core of infantry combat groups for the initial breakthrough. Actually the blitzkrieg methods of 1940 had merely been improved and applied on a larger scale. The armor created the gap, and the combat groups fanned out on either flank with all the weapons in the Nazi armory—dive bombers, flame throwers, paratroops and dual-purpose 105-mm. gun-howitzers.

At this date it remained the tactical mystery of World War II that no army had as yet made any extensive use of poison gas. Never in history has a proved weapon been discarded for ethical reasons, and it may be concluded that all armies dreaded a return to the immobility of 1917.

The hopes aroused by Stalin's winter offensive were quickly dimmed as the invaders seemed able to advance at will. Apparently the Russians had been deceived into expecting another great attack on Moscow, so that large forces under Marshal Zhukov were successfully neutralized in the centre while the enemy made steady progress in the south at Timoshenko's expense.

Again the Soviet forces resorted to a desperate strategy of turning their cities into islands of resistance. Sevastopol kept a large Nazi army occupied for 250 days before succumbing on July 1. More weeks of bloody street fighting slowed up the foe at Rostov, which did not fall until the end of the month after every house had been made into a little fortress.

In this emergency the Red Army produced one of the war's most effective new weapons in the Sturmovik—a ground-strafing plane designed to fly at heights of from 80 to 500 feet and knock out enemy tanks. Combining the functions of a fighter and a bomber, this machine depended on the rocket-firing principle. Attached to the underside of the wings, the projectile was released at the climax of the dive to strike a tank with a terrific force of penetration. Since the rocket principle eliminated all recoil, a heavier projectile could be used than any shell fired from an aerial cannon.

The most prodigious Soviet efforts and sacrifices could not check the advance, though the Nazis fell behind schedule after fighting their way across the Don opposite Stalingrad. Faster progress was shown in the Caucasus by armored forces meeting only infantry and cavalry. Cossack horsemen, armed with mortars and automatic weapons, made up the strength of an elastic defense which gave ground at the rate of 18 miles per day as the bulk of Timoshenko's forces stood in the great bend of the Don. Not until the middle of August, after severe losses, could the Germans claim to have secured their bridgeheads, and by this date the invaders of the Caucasus had neared the Grozny oil fields, almost within sight of the Caspian.

Never did Hitler's legions seem more invincible. In fourteen months they had advanced more than a thousand miles from their starting point. Viewed simply as a logistical feat, the maintaining of such a supply line has few parallels in history, not to mention the constant resistance which the Nazis overcame in the rear as well as the forward zone. Thus in August, 1942, their line extended 3,000 miles from north to south;

and United Nations observers were pessimistic as Marshal von Bock's forces swiftly concentrated against Stalingrad. It was scarcely to be expected that this unfortified industrial city could repulse the foe after the great fortress of Sevastopol had failed. Nazi control of the Volga seemed inevitable, and next the invaders would be in a position to attack Moscow from the rear after seizing the oil resources of the Caucasus.

U.S. Marine Landings on Guadalcanal

Naturally, these gigantic operations humbled the war in the South Pacific. Such was the impressiveness of mass in a Clausewitzian age that even the English-speaking peoples often underrated the importance of holding Australia. Yet if Britain and the United States owed much to Russia at this time, it is equally true that Russia was being defended by the Americans and Australians fighting against odds in the Pacific.

Likewise, the Western nations sometimes lost sight of the part played by the resistance of China since 1937 under the leadership of General and Madame Chiang Kai-shek. The numbers of foemen liquidated or at least neutralized in these guerrilla campaigns may never be known. Already the Japanese had paid their persistent adversaries the tribute of adopting many of the irregular tactics used by the Chinese.

Operations in the South Pacific became of primary importance in the summer of 1942 as the invaders renewed their attack on Australia and its life line. From the northeast coast of New Guinea a Japanese column toiled over 6,500-foot passes of the Owen Stanley range in an overland advance on Port Moresby, the Allied base. To complete the strategic pincers, other Japanese troops were now building a large airfield on the northern shore of Guadalcanal in the Solomon group. From this position land-based planes could support amphibious forces attacking New Caledonia as a first step toward the isolation of Australia.

American commanders had no wish to pit their carrier-borne aircraft against land-based planes, as would be the prospect if the enemy were allowed to finish the Guadalcanal airfield. On the other hand, the resources for an amphibious operation in the Solomons were simply not available at this time.

The Americans solved the strategic dilemma by attacking without the resources. And on August 7 the name of an obscure South Sea island first impinged upon the national consciousness as the marines landed on Guadalcanal by complete surprise.

The pitfalls which await a premature judgment of military operations were never better illustrated than at this time. Although the public could have no intimation, Britain and the United States were then at the height of their preparations for an invasion of northern Africa. During the Washington Conference of December, 1941, Churchill and Roosevelt had decided that the war in Europe must be given first consideration. Thus it is not surprising that August found the Allies accumulating men and supplies for the African expedition of November.

As a consequence, the Guadalcanal attack was an orphaned operation

The Fight for Guadalcanal

from the beginning. Sheer urgency had led to the decision, and assailants so lacking in men and materials could only hope that the enemy also would choose to fight a campaign of "limited liability." This hope seemed to be supported by the results of the first day. Without much trouble, marine landing parties exploited their surprise to seize the strip which the Americans renamed Henderson Field. It is an amusing footnote that navy strategists had waited until the enemy had done nine-tenths of the work, so that only a few more days of effort were needed before American bombers and fighters arrived from New Caledonia.

In combination with the Guadalcanal landings, other marine units seized Tulagi Harbor on Florida Island after putting down much stiffer opposition. As the first American amphibious operation of the war, Guadalcanal revealed that much remained to be learned if the new tactical system was to live up to its promise. Only the lack of effective resistance saved the attackers from heavy casualties as the punishment for lack of co-ordination between amphibious elements.

Americans often did not realize that their Marine Corps was a force without a counterpart in the world. European navies had marines for limited duties on shipboard or in naval bases, but neither the numbers nor the training were provided for large-scale offensive operations. In contrast, the U.S. Marines endeavored to live up to such slogans as "First to fight" and "America's force in readiness." Imposing a strict discipline, the "soldiers of the sea" were made up entirely of volunteers until the last months of the war. Six complete marine divisions with their own artillery and aircraft were then taking part in the Pacific.

So far the American successes on Guadalcanal had surpassed all expectations. But after recovering from the first shock, the Japanese made it plain that they intended to fight for the island. Dive bombers and torpedo planes, attacking the following day while the transports were unloading, damaged two ships. That evening the enemy's cruisers and destroyers were sighted, and in the middle of the night a surprise blow dealt the most crushing defeat that a United Nations naval force had known since the battle of Java. In this one-sided action off Tulagi, recorded by the Navy as the battle of Savo Island, one Australian and three American heavy cruisers were caught off guard and sunk by shells and torpedoes which damaged three other warships. Not a single Japanese unit was sunk.

At this moment American officers doubtless envied totalitarian leaders who do not have to account to their followers. The Allied peoples were in no mood for another Bataan or even another Dunkirk. Yet the possibility of either had to be faced, and navy censors did not announce the sinkings for two months. Not until his report of April, 1944, did Admiral King disclose the seriousness of the American situation after the Savo Island reverse:

> The loss of the four cruisers . . . and the subsequent loss of two aircraft carriers left us inferior in strength for several months. The Japanese did not take advantage of this opportunity to engage in a fleet battle with the balance of power on their side, probably because they did not know—and we did not let them know—how severe our losses were.

The enemy followed up the Savo Island victory by making it hot for American transports which had to be withdrawn before finishing their unloading. This meant that the outnumbered marines, hemmed in by foes on Lunga Plain, must look forward to subsisting on captured enemy food before the end of the month. Stores of aviation gasoline also were insufficient, and the defenders had to make use of captured enemy arms and ammunition to supplement their own.

BRITISH VICTORY IN THE DESERT

Only such a trite expression as "the dark before the dawn" could have described the outlook of the United Nations during September and most of October. China was isolated. The Americans appeared to have gone beyond their strategic depth in the Solomons. The British Eighth Army, fighting with its back to Alexandria, awaited the renewal of Rommel's offensive. At Stalingrad the hard-pressed Russians retreated from street to street as Berlin announced another triumph.

On October 15 no war leader of the world, least of all Adolf Hitler, could have supposed that from November 1 to 19 the Axis forces would go down to defeat in Russia, in Egypt and in the Solomons. During this same period the Anglo-American armies landed in Algeria and Morocco.

The various generals and their staffs, of course, did not view this climax as being either sudden or dramatic. They had found the road to victory a long uphill climb. Adversity taught the Eighth Army a new tactical maturity, and after a summer of reorganization a much more formidable force emerged. Refugee Greek, Polish and Free French soldiers were combined with Highlanders, Yorkshiremen, Cockneys, Australians, New Zealanders, South Africans, Sikhs and Gurkhas. In August General Sir Harold Alexander was appointed supreme commander in the Middle East, and General Sir Bernard Law Montgomery named to the command of the Eighth Army. This team worked miracles with the beaten troops in moral as well as material respects.

The war produced no more colorful figure than Montgomery—an Anglican bishop's son who combined a military career with a mystical Old Testament piety. Flamboyant and didactic, resented by his colleagues while being applauded by his men, he toured the Alamein front in a tank with the nickname "Monty" painted on the sides in flaring Gothic letters. But the ascetic, sharp-eyed little commander proved that he was more than a showman. Driving the army through a merciless course of training in desert summer heat, he hardened the green troops of Auchinleck's defeat. Meanwhile he insisted that the British be as well armed as the Afrika Korps, whose tanks and medium artillery had enjoyed a decisive advantage in firepower. The result was an increase in the numbers of 25-pounders and American-made "General Sherman" tanks mounting a 75-mm. gun.

The mine fields of the British front extended 40 miles from the seacoast to the Qattara depression, a wasteland which barred the way for tanks. Between these anchors the two armies fenced ceaselessly during the autumn weeks, each seeking its opening. Then as the United Nations anxiously awaited Rommel's blow, the British took the initiative at El Alamein in response to Montgomery's order of the day on October 23:

> When I assumed command of the Eighth Army I said that the mandate was to destroy Rommel and his army, and that it would be done as soon as we were ready. We are ready now. The battle which is now about to begin will be one of the decisive battles of history. It will be the turning point of the war.

Confident as this harangue may seem, the British general redeemed every word. At ten o'clock that night 800 guns flamed into action with a barrage reminiscent of 1915. The infantry and engineers plodded methodically into the enemy's lines as traffic police directed the movements. Behind the infantry the tanks were poised for a limited advance when lanes had been cleared in the mine field. Several menacing bulges were made in the Axis front during the next seventy-two hours by troops who advanced at night and dug in to defend their gains.

Rommel had taken an inopportune moment to confer in Berlin, and his subordinates allowed themselves to be bluffed by such an ancient ruse as a concentration of dummy vehicles. When he flew back on October 26 the battle was already half lost. During the next four days the Axis commander lashed out wildly with armored counterattacks, but Montgomery had the situation well in hand.

For a week the British general had been tapping here and there along the enemy front with the air of an artisan seeking the weak spot in a wall. Then on November 1 Rommel provided the opening by splitting his armor. British tanks roared into the gap at blitzkrieg speed and swung out laterally in the Axis rear. The Afrika Korps made its dying effort in the next day's tank battle, only to be soundly beaten. The breakthrough reached its climax on November 3 as the Axis remnants took to flight after jettisoning all impediments, human or inanimate. As an example of cordiality between Axis allies, the Germans seized the water of the Italian troops and left them behind to suffer from thirst until the British made them prisoners.

About 70,000 Axis soldiers, including a dozen generals, fell into the hands of victors who also took hundreds of tanks, planes, guns and trucks. The RAF and American fliers now pounded the routed enemy as Montgomery ordered a pursuit.

Amphibious Landings in Africa

England's church bells had hardly ceased ringing for El Alamein when the news came of another great victory in Africa—the successful landings of Allied troops from November 8 to 11 at Casablanca, Oran

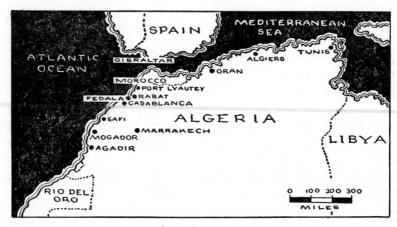

Operation TORCH

and Algiers. The British and Americans had kept their secret well, and only when it was too late did the Germans learn of the amphibious forces which gained control of a thousand miles of African coastline in a 76-hour series of attacks.

Operation TORCH was carried out by three task forces. The western group, Task Force 34, consisting of 102 ships and 35,000 troops under the command respectively of Rear Admiral Henry K. Hewett and Major General George S. Patton, Jr., was made up entirely of Americans. The components sailed on varying dates from a dozen ports along the U.S. Atlantic seaboard. Yet the rendezvous at sea was effected precisely on schedule some 450 miles SSE of Cape Race, Newfoundland.

The great majority of the crewmen, according to naval historian

Samuel Eliot Morison's *Operations in North African Waters*, "had been civilians in 1940, and thousands had never been to sea before. . . . An appreciable number of the blue-jackets on every ship were eighteen years old or younger. These boys were eager, competent and alert. They volunteered for work beyond their assigned duties; and three days' fighting was to prove, if it needed proof, that young Americans of this generation, brought up to hate war, are the best potential fighters in the world."

Task Force 34 was the nation's greatest war fleet up to this time. While it plowed its way across the Atlantic, the eastern and central task forces of the Mediterranean landings were assembling in United Kingdom ports under the command of Admiral Sir Andrew B. Cunningham. The ground force units for the attacks on Oran and Algiers consisted of 49,000 American and 23,000 British troops, and most of the ships were British. The two attacks were planned to go into effect regardless of what happened to the Atlantic coast operation.

The over-all plan contemplated a political as well as a military bid for victory. For the Allies hoped to gain the acquiescence of Admiral Darlan and other Vichy French leaders who were believed to be secretly in sympathy with Hitler's enemies.

As for tactics, each of the three task forces planned a double envelopment of the target area by means of landings on either side. Task Force 34 struck at Casablanca with simultaneous attacks on Safi, 140 miles to the south; at Fedala, 15 miles to the north; and at points still farther north for the capture of Port Lyautey with its airfield.

Although the Moroccan landings achieved a surprise, the local French commanders sternly refused to obey Admiral Darlan's order of November 8 to cease resistance—a directive issued on his own responsibility. Three days of hard fighting resulted for the American ground forces, and the warships had to slug it out with the French squadron and shore batteries. At a cost of five ships which suffered one hit each, the invaders disabled the battleship *Jean Bart* and three cruisers. The French also lost four destroyers and eight submarines, sunk or missing. Meanwhile, the U.S. ground forces secured all their main objectives in three days.

It can hardly be said that the French surrendered. After putting up a gallant defense until honor was satisfied, they simply went over to the side of the Allies, where most of them belonged in spirit. The guns had been silent only a few hours when American and French officers dined together in Casablanca, toasting one another in the name of a common cause against Axis domination.

French resistance was much lighter in the Mediterranean. Darlan's cease-fire order was generally obeyed at Algiers and had a deterring influence on the defenders of Oran. All objectives in both areas were taken in three days with comparatively moderate casualties.

Thus were Hitler and Mussolini introduced to the American amphibious tactics which would make it possible within two years for Allied armies to invade their homelands. It can hardly be said, however, that these tactics showed any such promise in November, 1942. Although three of the participating U.S. Army infantry divisions had been intensively trained for amphibious landings, inexperience resulted in a bedlam of confusion on the beaches. The LST and other amphibious workhorses had not yet made their appearance in the European theater, and the makeshift plyboard landing craft proved all too vulnerable to submerged rocks and enemy fire. Altogether, the North African landings were clumsy as compared to later amphibious operations; and the thrifty victories must be attributed in part to light resistance by Frenchmen whose hearts were not in the fight.

The repercussions of Operation TORCH were felt in France when Hitler ordered a German occupation of the Vichy government's territory and the French reacted with the scuttling of the fleet at Toulon. All eyes were now fixed on the map of North Africa. By ignoring the logistical problems which worry generals, a breakfast-table strategist could envision the invaders of Algeria pounding eastward into Tunisia and Tripoli. The prospect naturally occurred to Anglo-American commanders, but the Germans had an advantage in their Sicilian air bases. Troop-carrying planes needed only hours to land enough men to hold Tunis and Bizerte, though the Anglo-American forces lost the race by the narrowest of margins. Rommel had meanwhile succeeded in making good his escape, so that more fighting remained to be done in Africa.

Early in January Prime Minister Churchill and President Roosevelt met in the famous Casablanca Conference. Their decision to grant only terms of unconditional surrender was severely criticized by their own countrymen after the war on the grounds that it forced the enemy to a more desperate resistance by depriving him of all hope of compromise. Although the cogency of this argument can hardly be questioned, many of these same postwar critics were in favor of the Casablanca decision at the time. It is always difficult in later years to recall the emotional climate of total war, and peoples of the United Nations were little disposed in January, 1943, to grant concessions to enemies who had plunged the world into one of the most horrible wars of history.

AMERICAN VICTORY IN THE SOLOMONS

After three years of being starved for good news the United Nations were now feasting. For only a week after the African landings Pacific Fleet Headquarters announced a great naval victory in the battle of Guadalcanal.

This success, like the British triumph at El Alamein, came as the reward of long effort. All told, the contest in the Solomons consisted of six naval actions from August 8 to November 30 which were listed as battles. Viewed as a whole, the struggle emerges as an unceasing hundred-day battle fought on both land and sea for the control of Australia.

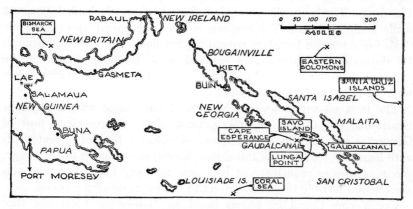

The Naval Warfare of the South Pacific

After scoring first in the Savo Island clash the Japanese met the American challenge with more than their usual energy. Two weeks later a second action, known as the battle of the Eastern Solomons, took place about 250 miles northeast of the island chain. An American two-carrier striking force located two enemy formations, including a battleship and three carriers, advancing on Guadalcanal. The nearest force sighted the Americans simultaneously, so that neither side had any advantage in reconnaissance. Land-based bombers from Henderson Field reinforced the naval planes, and a Japanese carrier, destroyer and transport were sunk before the enemy retreated with losses of 90 aircraft.

In August the Japanese began to land supplies and from 500 to 1,000 reinforcements nearly every night by means of the "Tokyo Express"—a force of light cruisers and destroyers which stole in under cover of darkness from anchorages in the Western Solomons. Meanwhile a swarm of submarines infested the waters south of the islands to cut off American supplies and reinforcements. During a comparative lull the carrier *Wasp* had to be abandoned and destroyed by her own crew after taking hits from three Japanese torpedoes.

The agony of Stalingrad loomed large in the headlines at the time, yet the Americans in the foxholes of Guadalcanal were also undergoing an ordeal. Infiltration raids made sleep a rare blessing for the invaders. The nightly Tokyo Express seldom failed to shell their positions, and Japanese planes dropped bombs at frequent intervals. Major General Alexander A. Vandegrift, the marine commander, drew up two regiments and their few pieces of artillery in a perimeter for the defense of Henderson Field. On the 20th of August 2,500 newly landed Japanese made a night assault. The marines stopped the enemy frontally while throwing a reserve battalion around his left flank to cut off withdrawal. By daybreak the encirclement resulted in a smashing defeat for the Japanese, who left 900 dead and 15 prisoners behind. The marine losses were 34 killed and 75 wounded.

The next all-out attack on the airfield took place on the night of September 12-13. The Japanese penetrated to the command post of General Vandegrift in a three-pronged advance but were beaten off with losses of 300 dead. In this action, known as the battle of the Ridge, the 2,000 enemy remnants lost half their numbers from starvation and disease in a terrible two-week retreat to the west end of the island.

Considering that U.S. planes based on Henderson Field had shot down 314 enemy aircraft by October 24, it is understandable that the Japanese should have launched a third assault that night. It succeeded no better than the first two attempts. And as American reinforcements and supplies began to arrive in larger increments, it grew increasingly plain that the enemy's only hope lay in a victory on the sea.

On the night of October 11 the American cruisers and destroyers had carried out a manoeuvre that was the talk of bright midshipmen before airplanes were invented. In the darkness they crossed the enemy's T diagonally as the white glare of their searchlights leaped across the water at a range of five miles. American gunners, firing with deadly accuracy, soon had their targets further illuminated by the glow of burning enemy ships. For it took only forty minutes in the battle of Cape Esperance to sink a cruiser and a destroyer and damage two other cruisers at a cost of one American destroyer sunk and a cruiser damaged.

Owing to the Navy's policy of withholding bad news, few people in the United States had any conception of the odds against their forces even after this timely little victory. The next day Japanese air raids on Guadalcanal reached a new peak of intensity as American infantry reinforcements landed. That night enemy battleships shelled the American positions for two hours with 14-inch guns. On October 14 the Japanese were able to put ashore an estimated 10,000 troops in daylight, though their boldness was punished by the loss of two transports.

Vice-Admiral William F. Halsey now took command of naval forces, and aerial reinforcements as well as patrol torpedo boats came to the rescue at Guadalcanal. On October 26 another Japanese striking force, including two large aircraft carriers and two battleships, was sighted about 300 miles northeast of the island by a two-carrier American force. In the ensuing action, known as the battle of the Santa Cruz Islands, both opposing carriers were damaged and more than a hundred planes shot down. Nevertheless, the engagement resulted in a defeat for American warships, which were pursued all night. The carrier *Hornet* received fatal hits from bombs and aerial torpedoes, and a destroyer was also lost. The carrier *Enterprise,* a battleship and a light cruiser were damaged.

At a later date it became known that the Americans had but a single undamaged carrier left in the Pacific after this unfortunate action. The enemy was in no better situation and the next two battles were fought by surface units.

The strain was lessened early in November when the marines were again reinforced by army units, but as usual the enemy added to his numbers. Both sides were now throwing all available land and sea forces into the struggle, and the inevitable fight to a finish began on the afternoon of November 12.

For a week it had been evident that the Japanese were massing warships, troops and planes for a full-scale invasion. The prelude took place when American fliers and antiaircraft guns repulsed an aerial torpedo attack on transports engaged in unloading. Only one enemy plane survived out of 31 bombers and fighters.

During the night of November 12-13 an American force of cruisers and destroyers escorted the empty transports out to sea, only to encounter three enemy columns, which included two battleships as well as cruisers and destroyers. Without hesitation Rear Admiral Daniel J. Callaghan, flying his flag on the heavy cruiser *San Francisco*, took his column between the two main enemy formations and opened the attack with the radio order, "We want the big ones."

The most furious surface fighting of the war occurred during the next twenty-four minutes. Four enemy ships burst into flames from the first salvos at a range of barely 3,000 yards. The surprised Japanese even fired at one another as their searchlights were shot out. After sinking an enemy cruiser, the *San Francisco* found herself trading salvos with a battleship at 2,500 yards. The American cruiser damaged her opponent heavily in this unequal contest, but Callaghan was killed and his crippled ship forced to limp back to the protection of shore batteries. Rear Admiral Norman Scott met his death on the bridge of the *Atlanta,* for during the first fifteen minutes only three American destroyers emerged undamaged from a force which included eight destroyers and four cruisers.

After planes from Henderson Field had finished the deadly work begun by the warships, a Japanese battleship, two cruisers and six destroyers had been sunk. Another battleship and six destroyers were damaged.

Air action played the chief part in the battle's second phase on November 14. Planes from the *Enterprise* and Henderson Field struck repeatedly at the enemy's main invasion force, destroying eight transports and four cargo ships.

The final act opened shortly after midnight when a Japanese force which included two battleships slipped into the channel between Florida and Savo islands. The enemy evidently hoped to surprise a weak cruiser and destroyer force, but the answering shots were fired by the guns of the *South Dakota* and *Washington* as well as smaller warships. Aircraft saw no action even as "spotters" in the old-fashioned gunnery duel that followed. Nor did the torpedo attack of the Japanese destroyers have much success. The American "battlewagons" put the enemy to flight, after a battleship and a destroyer were left sinking in flames. The recently repaired *South Dakota* took heavy damage but continued to fire as long as a target remained.

A few minor air actions ended the world's greatest surface sea battle since Jutland. In addition to the grand total of 16 Japanese ships sunk, the enemy's personnel losses were staggering as a consequence of transports sent to the bottom. Ship losses comprised two battleships, one cruiser, six destroyers and ten transports. Three cruisers, six destroyers and two transports were damaged. The cost to the Americans was two light cruisers and seven destroyers sunk and eight ships damaged, among them a light cruiser which later sank.

These comparative figures establish Guadalcanal as the battle that broke the back of the Japanese offensive in the South Pacific. Nevertheless, the enemy made a last major attempt to strengthen his land forces. On the night of November 30 two light cruisers were sighted off Guadalcanal with a column of destroyers and several transports and cargo ships. American cruisers, destroyers and patrol torpedo boats struck back savagely in another night gunnery duel fought without benefit of aircraft. The Japanese got the better of an inconclusive clash with losses of a destroyer while sinking one U.S. cruiser and damaging three others.

Even this postscript did not bring the Guadalcanal operations to an abrupt end. The Tokyo Express continued to make occasional runs during the next six weeks, though earnestly dodging battle with American naval forces. Such ventures grew increasingly risky in waters controlled by United States planes or patrol torpedo boats, so that the Japanese were soon reduced to dropping supplies by parachute.

Little fighting took place during the ensuing two months, for the enemy was able to land fewer than a thousand troops. American reinforcements poured into Guadalcanal until 58,000 soldiers and marines were combined in January, 1943, into the new XIV Corps, commanded by Army Major General Alexander M. Patch, who had relieved General Vandegrift in December.

Mopping-up operations continued until the first week of February, when the Tokyo Express made its final runs. This time the purpose was not to land reinforcements but to take off the 3,000 troops remaining from the 42,500 who had fought on Guadalcanal. Of the balance, 24,000 had been killed, 15,000 had died of disease, starvation or wounds, and 500 had been captured. Total American casualties included 1,743 killed and 4,953 wounded, of whom 1,242 killed and 2,655 wounded were marines.

A sizable squadron might have been formed of the ships lost by Japanese whose powers of replacement were limited as compared to those of the United States. Even more serious was the loss of hundreds of aircraft along with experienced pilots who were harder to replace than the planes. But perhaps the worst blow of all was in the moral sphere, for this was Japan's first large-scale reverse of the war on land. All ranks, including the modern Samurai in command, had believed implicitly in the superiority of the hardy little Japanese warrior over the "pampered" American soldier. This faith seemed to be upheld by the results of the war's first eight months, for even such a defeat as Midway could be charged to errors and the fortunes of war. But at Guadalcanal the losers could find no face-saving excuses. On land, on the sea, in the air—even in such a specialty as jungle combat—they were fought off their feet by Western foemen who had been outweighed during the early weeks.

Altogether, Guadalcanal merits a place as one of the decisive battles not only of World War II but of American history. There the Japanese southward drive was stopped and the enemy lost the strategic initiative.

The effects were felt in Papua. Just a week after the Guadalcanal landing, the Japanese drive over the Owen Stanley Mountains had begun, with Port Moresby on the southern coast as an objective. On September 14 the 11,000 attackers were stopped only 35 miles short of their goal by Australian infantry. General MacArthur rushed American troops from Australia to take part in a counteroffensive. The Allied crossing of the mountains was attended by severe hardships aggravated by supply shortages. Disease had caused more casualties than the Japanese when Lieutenant General Robert L. Eichelberger arrived on December 1 to take command of disease-ridden and dispirited U.S. troops reduced to one-sixth of a C ration per day. His reforms restored morale and on December 14 the Allies captured Buna, their first objective. Australian and American attacks continued until the Buna area was cleared of the enemy. This was the opening round in MacArthur's drive, which would not end until all the Japanese in New Guinea had been neutralized.

Not only did the Papua operation run parallel in chronology to the Guadalcanal campaign; it profited from the fact that two and a half divisions of Japan's best troops, originally intended for service in Papua, were sent to Guadalcanal instead.

RUSSIAN VICTORY AT STALINGRAD

Only one more assurance was needed to fill the cup of the United Nations to overflowing, and its inception may be dated just four days after the climax in the South Pacific. On November 18, with the effect of a tolling bell, the newspapers announced the eighty-seventh day of Stalingrad's defense. The following day the Soviet forces broke through on both enemy flanks to begin a double envelopment which ended with the annihilation of 312,650 Nazis.

As if by mutual consent, the struggle for Stalingrad had turned into the Verdun of World War II. Again, as in 1916, the German invaders fastened themselves like leeches on one strategic area for the purpose of bleeding a nation to death. That area was the Volga Valley, and the

Soviet Union accepted the challenge by proclaiming a defense to the last man.

Much larger forces had contended at both Smolensk and Moscow, for it does not appear that the total numbers of both sides at Stalingrad ever exceeded a million. On the Volga the Nazis were represented by the veteran Sixth Army, which had first distinguished itself in May, 1940, by leading the assault on Flanders. The Russians relied on their Sixty-second Army, made up largely of battle-hardened Siberian troops.

The rival commanders likewise personified the military trends of their respective countries. Fedor von Bock had been one of the monocled *Junker* officers who betrayed their caste and traditions when the Nazis came into power. His opponent, Gregori Zhukov, was one of Russia's new peasant generals who rose from a private's rank. Broad-faced and shaven of poll, he had saved the capital in 1941 by grimly keeping enough men and guns in reserve to exhaust the attackers.

Stalingrad had none of Moscow's advantages as a modern fortress. Two and a third miles wide at most, the open manufacturing city extended for fifteen miles along the river.

Inferiority in production, more than any other factor, accounted for the Russian retreat to the Volga. For the nation's output of war materials had been reduced by nearly half during the war's first few months, even though miracles were accomplished in removing machinery from industrial cities about to fall into the enemy's hands. The handicap was most severely felt in shortages of tanks and planes. While Russian newspapers angrily denied any grave weakness in these respects, the Luftwaffe's command of the air was apparent. So far the best Soviet aerial efforts had been defensive, and Moscow claimed a more effective system than the protective devices which won the battle of Britain. In the field, however, the enemy's dive bombers were usually able to blast the way for the "mailed fist" of armor enclosing motorized infantry. Thus the invaders finally stormed the great bend of the Don and covered the remaining 70 miles to the Volga.

The Russian situation did not improve, paradoxically, until it reached the desperate stage of fighting in the urban area of Stalingrad. Only picked German troops could cope with the tough Siberian infantry in street fighting. Hence the "siege" of Stalingrad was more accurately a battle waged from factory to factory and cellar to cellar. In such a struggle the Germans profited little from their advantages in armor and planes, while the Russian artillery superiority promised to be decisive.

Students of history had already suspected that the Nazi Napoleon fell considerably short of his French model. So overwhelming were the advantages conceded to Hitler by Allied unpreparedness that a veteran Russian soldier, General Rokossovsky, has been quoted as saying, "I fought the fathers and now I am fighting the sons. You will think I am being sentimental about the good old days, but I honestly think the fathers were better soldiers."

Certainly it would be hard to imagine Falkenhayn, Ludendorff or any other German general of World War I placing his armies in such a position as the Nazis occupied in October, 1942. Where the line of the previous autumn had been shortened until it took a fairly straight course from the Black Sea to the Baltic, the invaders were now much over-extended in the south. Not only was their 1942 line some 700 miles longer, but it protruded in a salient at Stalingrad which invited counter-attack on both flanks. Hitler's generals warned him repeatedly of the danger at the risk of dismissal, and Halder actually was dismissed after a stormy interview in which he urged the Führer to break off the Stalingrad offensive. Intuition now prevailed over strategic judgment in German operations, and in a Munich speech of November 8 Hitler spoke of Stalingrad as having already been captured:

> By taking it we cut off thirty million tons of Russian traffic, including nine million tons of oil. There flows the entire wheat crop gathered from the Ukraine and the Kabin, also manganese ore.

Even as he spoke these words Zhukov's forces were preparing a great counterstroke. German reinforcements had been drawn from the entire southern front at Hitler's urging to make possible the heavier battalions which slugged their way from street to street. The Russians were now fighting a holding battle in the ruined city while concentrating on both wings for the blow which fell on November 19. Five thousand massed guns created holes for the Soviet tanks and infantry which surrounded twenty-two divisions. Moscow's first reports were received with skepticism, since past claims of encirclement had so often been too optimistic. But this time the Russian attackers actually did have the enemy in a deadly grip. Within four days the Germans were completely enclosed and facing supply problems after their foes repulsed a relieving Panzer force.

The end was prolonged two months as the Führer exhorted his trapped soldiers to resist. This phase might better have been called the "siege" of Stalingrad, for the Nazis were scantily supplied by transport planes with food and ammunition. Soon the surrounded army had been cut in two, and the halves in turn chopped up into still smaller groups. Of the forces hemmed in on November 19, only a core remained on the last day of January when the Russians accepted the surrender of Marshal von Paulus and fifteen generals. During the entire operation, according to Russian figures, the German losses amounted to 175,000 dead and 137,650 prisoners in addition to 750 planes, 1,550 tanks, 6,700 guns, three armored trains and 1,125 railway cars.

These forces had paid the penalty of Hitler's insistence on seizing territory rather than destroying Russian armies. By overextending himself, he put his southern forces in a vulnerable position; and rather than pull them out while there was still time, he chose to sacrifice the Sixth Army to his own mad obstinacy.

THE RED ARMY ON THE OFFENSIVE

After long months of defeat, the results of the twenty days of November, 1942, were so encouraging that United Nations commentators sometimes tended to give them too much credit. Winston Churchill tried to suggest a more realistic evaluation when he warned that this phase was only "the end of the beginning."

For the Axis Powers had merely been checked rather than crushed at El Alamein, Guadalcanal and Stalingrad. Even after their reverses they retained a favorable balance in most strategic respects, although their margin of time narrowed as Allied production increased.

That the German military machine still had a formidable potential was demonstrated during the last stages of the battle of Stalingrad when the Nazis managed to extricate themselves from the Caucasus. It was a remarkable military feat in view of the perils and difficulties, but Hitler's forces were allowed no breathing spell. Winter was the Red Army's element, and without a pause the Russians launched an offensive on a 700-mile front from Orel to the Caucasus. During the first ten weeks they made gains of from 100 to 350 miles, often through deep snows. One by one, the Nazi "hedgehogs" fell to troops using skis and motorized sledges. Kursk, Kharkov and Rostov had been recaptured by the middle of February; and as a greater triumph, the Red Army lifted the 515-day siege of Leningrad.

Ever since August, 1941, when the Germans cut its last links with the rest of the Soviet Union, the beleaguered city had survived only by bringing supplies across frozen Lake Ladoga in the winter and running the blockade with swift boats in the summer. More than 1,750,000 deaths from epidemics were recorded among a war-swollen population deprived of regular gas, water and electricity. The relief of Leningrad thus seemed the crowning achievement of an offensive in which the Russians claimed to have slain 850,000 foes and captured 343,525 since November 19.

In view of such successes, the shock was the more disillusioning when the Germans suddenly struck back in March, 1943. Twelve fresh armored and infantry divisions strengthened the armies attacking in the south on a 200-mile front. Within two weeks Kharkov had been recovered by forces which advanced 80 miles before the spring rains put an end to further movement.

Once again, despite the winter's reverses, the Wehrmacht gave every appearance of might when it chose its own time. Stalingrad and subsequent defeats could be explained as the consequences of Hitler's meddling, while the German troops were obviously not as well equipped for winter operations as their foes. As yet the Red Army had not been able to stop a summer offensive, and United Nations observers could only look forward with apprehension to coming months.

Late in June the Nazis were massing troops on the 200-mile central Russian front from Orel to Belgorod. The invaders placed much dependence in their new 60-ton Mark VI tank, the famous "Tiger" model. As an added tactical surprise they introduced a 70-ton, caterpillar-tread, self-propelled gun carrier, the so-called "Ferdinand," with frontal armor 200 millimeters thick. Both of these monsters were designed to make way against Soviet guns and the rocket projectiles of Sturmovik planes.

The long-awaited German 1943 summer offensive in Russia began on July 5 as Hitler's legions surged forward. During the first week Berlin announced gains—some of them admitted by Moscow—which made it seem that the Nazi triumphs of the past two summers would be duplicated.

The Red Army, due to the secretive policy of Moscow, remained more or less of a mystery in United Nations circles. Allied correspondents were not allowed at the front, and Soviet communiqués proved no more trustworthy than those of Berlin. Not until after the war was it known that the Soviet armed forces at this time comprised 500 infantry divisions. And though most of them were understrength, they had outstanding artillery support.

The German offensive lasted just eight days. Then, on the night of July 13, hundreds of Soviet guns, brought up over muddy roads, split the darkness with one of the most tremendous bombardments of the war. At dawn, under a gray and drizzling sky, the Soviet infantry advanced on a 25-mile front north and east of Orel.

No greater test of Russian strength could have been chosen than this central bastion of the German front. A vast system of integrated strong points, pillboxes and heavily gunned concrete blockhouses, the Orel "hedgehog" had been created to hold up the largest army for weeks. Yet the Soviet attackers gained 25 miles in the first three days, advancing behind 42-ton tanks manufactured in the Urals, or Lend-Leased British and American armor. Neither the Tiger nor the Ferdinand could make way against the accurate Soviet artillery, and at the end of twelve days Orel had been half enveloped as new Russian attacks exploded up and down the entire front—south of Leningrad, against the Belgorod salient, and opposite Taganrog on the Sea of Azov.

The numbers involved were tremendous, even judged by previous standards set on this front. By the end of the month the Berlin radio, complaining of a numerical disadvantage, estimated that 600 divisions on both sides had been thrown into the fray.

So vast was the struggle that Orel seemed a minor prize when it finally fell on August 6. Kharkov, Briansk and Poltava had become the new objectives of the relentless Soviet sweep. The great battle for the liberation of Russia had begun, and the Wehrmacht was never again to regain the initiative except for desperate and short-lived counter-attacks.

Allied Gains in New Guinea

From Russia, where divisions were counted by the hundreds, it was a far cry to the small forces which fought for large objectives in the South Pacific. The Japanese conceded Papua to General MacArthur after their defeats in the Buna area, and a struggle for all New Guinea began as both sides rushed in reinforcements.

Allied control of the air gave MacArthur the advantage in this race. The airmen of Major General George C. Kenney's Fifth Air Force flew in whole units to a zone of operations which used up troops with tragic rapidity. One American reinforced battalion, for instance, went into the lines near Buna with 1,200 men and was relieved four weeks later with

165. As usual, jungle heat, humidity and disease had put far more soldiers out of action than enemy bullets.

Inferiority in the air compelled the Japanese to take the risk of water transportation when sending reinforcements and supplies to New Guinea. They paid a stiff penalty on March 1, 1943, when an American airman sighted 17 enemy ships in the Bismarck Sea. Bombing attacks had already made the route to New Guinea so hazardous that Japanese ships usually edged down the New Britain coast under cover of storms. This time a break in the clouds betrayed them, and soon the Liberators, Mitchells, Fortresses and Australian Beaufighters swooped down on their prey. The Allied fliers attacked mercilessly for three days until seven transports and four escorting destroyers were sunk. In this action, known as the battle of the Bismarck Sea, 61 enemy planes were shot down and an estimated 3,000 troops drowned at a cost to the Allies of four aircraft.

A similar proportion of Japanese to Allied air casualties occurred in most of the encounters of 1943. In a sky battle of June 16 over Guadalcanal a force of 120 Japanese bombers and fighters had 107 planes shot down by 100 American fighters at a cost of six planes. The explanation of such one-sided victories is to be found partly in the ability of American pilots, partly in the merits of American construction. While the airmen of 1942 often flew slow and unresponsive types as compared to the nimble Zero fighters, the second year of the Pacific war saw the United States far ahead in the battle of production. The principal factor in this victory was the adaptability made possible by American modification centres. Pilots in New Guinea and Tunisia had the opportunity to suggest improvements based on the shifting needs of actual combat in various theaters. Within a few days these changes were being put into effect at Cheyenne, Denver or Omaha, so that even a plane just off the assembly line might be condemned as obsolescent until it met the standards of pilots and gunners.

Barely a year after Pearl Harbor the United States had overcome most of Japan's material advantages. The handicaps of 1942 seemed remote when American amphibious forces invaded fogbound Attu the following May, yet the results of the 20-day campaign were not altogether heartening. The attackers gained their objectives, for the menace to Alaska was largely removed by isolating Japanese-held Kiska after annihilating the 2,500 enemy troops on Attu. But most Americans, soldiers as well as civilians, were revolted at the necessity for waging a strife of extermination. Exhibitions of the hara-kiri spirit struck them as being subhuman rather than superhuman, degrading twentieth-century warfare to the level of a rat hunt.

It was a war of extermination, nevertheless, that MacArthur's forces were waging in New Guinea. Allied control of the air and sea made it possible for the American general to sweep westward along the coast, bypassing enemy centers of resistance and leaving the troops behind to "wither on the vine"—in other words, to starve without striking a blow. It was an effective strategy which the Japanese had brought upon themselves by their insistence on suicidal fights to the last man after a situation had become militarily hopeless.

In order to protect his rear, MacArthur ordered Admiral Halsey, operating for the time being under his control, to seize islands with potential airfields in the Western Solomons. His object was to neutralize the great enemy base at Rabaul and force the Japanese to extend their supply lines.

U.S. Army troops and marines landed in New Georgia on June 30, 1943. It took a 37-day campaign to secure the island, even though American aircraft destroyed some 350 enemy planes at a cost of 93 of their own. American troop losses amounted to 1,136 killed and 4,140 wounded as the price of wiping out the 8,000 Japanese defenders of the island.

North Africa Lost to Axis

From the Allied viewpoint, the situation in North Africa was not encouraging during the early weeks of 1943. After conducting a brilliant retreat, Rommel had found a refuge in the strong Mareth Line which the French originally built as a bulwark against Mussolini's ambitions. Large forces of Germans and Italians had meanwhile been pouring into Tunisia from Sicily, giving the Axis Powers the means of delaying the Allies for months in a mountainous terrain well suited to defense.

Winston Churchill had taken the lead in initiating a policy of frankness as compared to World War I. Even so, deception is the soul of strategy, and few Britons and Americans had any idea of the risks taken during the November landings in Africa. Impressive as an amphibious force of 850 ships may seem, the strength employed was not sufficient to cope with a determined resistance along a thousand miles of coast line. Politics came to the aid of tactics as some much-criticized bargains were struck with Vichy officials, but the Allies could not prevent the enemy from building up a stronger army in Tunisia than Rommel had ever commanded in Libya. Only an hour's flying time was required for transport planes which landed an estimated 2,400 troops a day; and though 90 Axis ships were sunk during the winter, the Allies had the handicap of much longer sea routes. Thus, while the British and American peoples waited impatiently, their armies had been waging a four-month battle of supply. Not until February were they ready for action, and by that time Rommel held strongly fortified positions on interior lines.

During this seeming interlude the Anglo-American forces under General Dwight D. Eisenhower had gone far toward conquering the age-old problems of co-operation between allies. Churchill and Roosevelt took the first steps during their historic January conference in Casablanca. Next, the usual weak joints between armies of different nationalities were cemented to an extent seldom known before in military chronicles. British and American officers, serving together on the same staffs, learned that harmony could be achieved in spite of quips to the effect that a common language enabled its possessors the better to understand one another's insults.

It was perhaps inevitable that the untried American troops should be first to feel the sting as Rommel demonstrated his ability to make rapid lateral shifts along interior lines. Unlike their countrymen who had been plunged into a fight for survival in the Pacific, the forces in Tunisia were probably the best-equipped soldiers in the world. Their want of experience was painfully remedied in February, when veteran Panzer units lured the newcomers into a tank ambush. The charging American machines were knocked out wholesale by suddenly unmasked 88-mm. guns; then the Nazi armor took up a pursuit which lasted until the Americans retreated through Kasserine Pass, leaving behind much matériel.

Although weaknesses in command had been largely to blame, the Americans were rapidly developing generals as well as battle-hardened troops. The real leaders were not always the figures in the spotlight. Such a quiet, hard-working tactician as Lieutenant General Omar Bradley had to wait longer for public notice, but in both Africa and Sicily his ability found recognition. It is perhaps no coincidence that this officer was an infantryman, both by training and by inclination. While tank clashes still gripped the popular imagination, battles of 1943 were likely to be decided by the plodding foot soldier. The land mine, more than any other defensive weapon, had been responsible for the limitations of armor. Some of the deadly new German types were almost impossible to locate with the usual instruments. Antitank guns also had improved in effectiveness, and the American "bazooka," using the rocket-firing principle, could be brought into action by only two men.

The iron cavalry of 1943, in short, could no more make headway

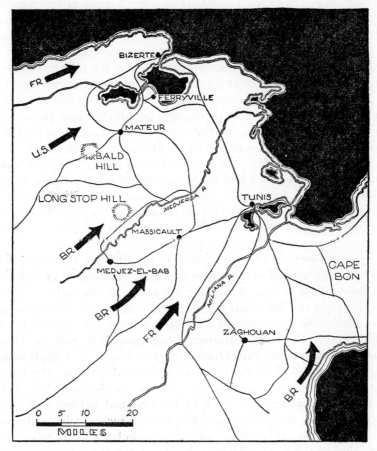

The Axis Loses Africa

against unbroken infantry—i.e., infantry supported by mine fields and antitank guns—than horsemen of the past could hope to ride down solid ranks of rifles and bayonets. In nearly every other respect the tank had inherited the ancient tactical functions of the mounted arm, so that armor came increasingly to be used for reconnaissance and pursuit.

General Montgomery's emphasis on infantry and artillery in combination with armor had much to do with his victory in the battle of El Alamein. And in March, 1943, the commander of the Eighth Army broke through the Mareth Line with similar tactics.

Again Montgomery took a week for his preliminaries, tapping here and there in search of weak spots. Then, after feinting at the Nazi left, he sent an armored flanking column in a wide sweep around the southern end to Rommel's right rear. This appeared to be the main blow, and the German shifted his armor to meet it. But Montgomery had not yet played his ace. After drawing off his adversary to the right, he suddenly launched the decisive blow at the Nazi left-centre—the very bulwark of the Mareth Line. To the accompaniment of a terrific barrage the British infantry smashed defenses in depth, and the armor raced through the gap in pursuit. Rommel had no choice but to withdraw to his final lines of defense, forming a semicircle around Bizerte and Tunis.

The struggle for Africa now entered its final phase. The Axis forces, though outnumbered, still had the advantages of position. Such heights as Bald Hill and Long Stop Hill, dominating wide areas, had been fortified with a view to delaying an advance for weeks. Throughout April the Allies took heavy losses in efforts to reduce these strong points. The Americans on the left, now fighting like veterans, waged a bitter 20-day battle over the hills and gullies of the El Guittar front. General Omar Bradley worked out a system of infantry infiltration in which his men followed the ridges, outflanking the enemy in the valleys. Late in April his right and left wings traded places—an unorthodox manoeuvre which resulted in the capture of Hill 609 and Bald Hill by fresh troops. Simultaneously the British stormed Long Stop Hill, and the climax approached as the Americans broke through to Mateur in a single bound.

Allied command of the air brought off the final decision. The British First Army, advancing on both sides of the Medjerda Valley, had a two-day aerial barrage laid down by bombers and fighters which flew 3,700 sorties, or individual missions. Four planes a minute dropped explosives on the Axis forces holding a critical area four miles wide which blocked the way to Massicault. On May 6 the infantry reported a very narrow breach, and General Alexander staked everything on a final spurt to the seacoast. His audacity was rewarded by perhaps the most perfect blitzkrieg of the war. The British spearhead drove through without regard to flanks, achieving such a surprise that motorized advance units captured German officers drinking in the sidewalk cafés of Tunis. The Americans reached Bizerte at almost the same moment, and on May 8 it remained only to gather in the prisoners.

Free French troops, who had taken a gallant part on both wings, had the satisfaction of seeing Nazi staff officers as demoralized as France's civilians had been in 1940. Rommel had left Tunisia because of illness, and his successor, General von Arnim, appeared to have reached the end of his resources. Obviously the beaten army might have waged a second Bataan in the rugged Cape Bon Peninsula, but veteran Panzer troops surrendered even to unarmed correspondents. About 200,000 captives were rounded up, two-thirds of them Germans, with most of their equipment intact.

The Allied term of self-reproach, "too little and too late," now might better have been applied to the Axis strategy in regard to Africa and Australia. At one time both of those great land masses could undoubtedly have been dominated by the aggressors at a smaller cost in men and materials than they eventually paid for losing them. The consequences to the United Nations would have been catastrophic, but it was the enemy who failed of perception.

VI

A SECOND FRONT IN EUROPE

This much is certain, he that commands the sea is at great liberty and may take as much or as little of the war as he will, whereas those that be strongest by land are many times nevertheless in great straits.

—SIR FRANCIS BACON

I N JULY, 1943, the world's attention was fixed on Sicily, where total forces amounting only to one-thirtieth of the numbers in Russia were contending for an island of limited strategic value. The significance of the operation lay in the fact that the Anglo-American allies had at last opened up a long-discussed second front in Europe. Stalin had been outspoken in his criticism of the delay, and his strictures were often echoed in Britain and the United States. Impatience was a natural reaction, but there is no evidence of tardiness on the part of the Western Allies. On the contrary, miracles of transport and supply had to be performed in order to launch a great amphibious assault barely two months after the victory in Tunisia.

The first blow was struck when Doolittle's bombers attacked the island of Pantelleria—the "Italian Gibraltar" whose 15-inch guns dominated the Sicilian straits. Flying fortresses and British warships joined in a concentrated pounding which lasted until the invasion troops prepared to storm the underground defenses. Before they landed, the Italian commander and 11,200 nerve-shattered survivors ran up the white flag on June 11, 1943. The next few days saw the surrender of the smaller Italian island strongholds of Lampedusa and Linosa.

The aerial assaults on Sicily and the Italian mainland continued with mounting fury, the chief targets being airfields and rail lines. On the night of July 9, the eve of D-day, the wind reached almost gale proportions as the great armada of warships and transports neared the objective. The storm subsided somewhat at dawn, but many of the troops were seasick as they stumbled out of the ramp-prowed invasion craft after thousands of paratroops had dropped out of the darkness. The unfavorable weather, however, proved to be the main factor in a surprise summed up by General Eisenhower's report of July 17:

> All the initial moves were carried out smoothly, and an astonishing lack of resistance was encountered on the shoreline. Captured Italian generals say we secured complete surprise. The airborne operations, which were executed about three hours ahead of the landing, were apparently the first real notice the defenders had of what was coming.

During the early hours confusion resulted in heavier losses than enemy action. Mistakes in planning, plus the havoc wrought by the storm, caused both ships and planes to be fired on by friendly guns which inflicted "serious" casualties. Nevertheless, 80,000 men, 7,000 vehicles, 300 tanks and mountains of supplies were landed from July 10 to 12, largely by 2½-ton American amphibian trucks.

The only threat to the invasion developed on the second day, when a heavy German armored counterattack was beaten off near Gela by American land and naval gunfire. Sicily had actually been won at a blow, for the invaders were able to occupy a fourth of the island during the first week. General Montgomery's British Eighth Army units pushed up the east coast past Syracuse, while the American forces drove westward toward Palermo, the key port, which fell on July 23. By the end of the month the enemy had been reduced to stubborn delaying actions in the mountains of the northeast corner.

Again, as in Africa, Lieutenant General George S. Patton, Jr., and the armored forces received the lion's share of the glory in American headlines. During the first few days the tanks made spectacular gains, but no less an authority than General Marshall reported that "in Sicily our armor raced around the island against feeble opposition and received few casualties." The real work of conquest was left to weary infantrymen using such weapons as mortars, carbines, automatic rifles, bazookas and grenades to evict a resourceful foe taking cover in rugged terrain.

Toward the end of the 39-day campaign the final victory was hastened by American amphibious landings in the rear of the foes retreating toward Messina, their last corridor of escape. On August 16 American

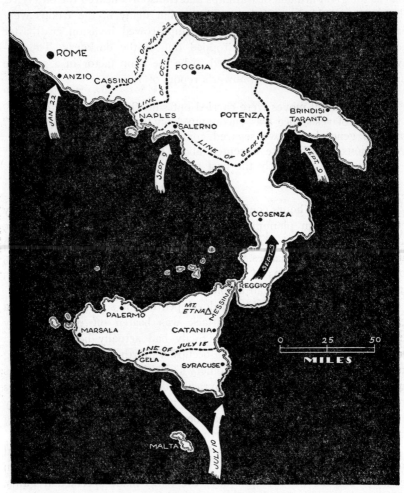

The Campaigns in Sicily and Italy

and British units met in this battered port, and organized resistance ended the following day. Thousands of Nazis were safely withdrawn to the mainland, despite the efforts of Allied planes. But the extent of the victory is expressed by the statistics—167,000 Axis casualties, including

37,000 Germans, inflicted at a cost of 16,769 Allied killed, wounded and missing.

The Germans had themselves to blame for the weak resistance put up by Italian troops who regarded the invaders as deliverers rather than enemies. Arrogant and overbearing as partners, Hitler's men had earned the hatred even of loyal Fascists. Throughout the entire war, in fact, the poor showing of Italian troops could be attributed less to unsoldierly qualities than to loathing of their Nazi overlords.

A climax was reached after the landings in Sicily, when King Victor Emmanuel proclaimed on July 25 that Mussolini had resigned. This news, soon followed by the report that Churchill and Roosevelt were conferring at Quebec, caused a stir of anticipation. Within a few more days came the announcement that units 'of the British Eighth Army had crossed the Strait of Messina under cover of heavy air and artillery bombardments, landing at the toe of the peninsula on September 3. Two beachheads were secured, and the invaders raced northward through Calabria.

After an uphill struggle of 27 months, ever since the British withdrawal from Greece in 1941, the Allies had at last won a foothold on the Continent. The success of the amphibious operations in Sicily made the threat of further Allied landings the more menacing. These victories had demonstrated at Axis expense how difficult it was to stop a surprise ship-to-shore assault conducted with American techniques and landing craft developed during the 1930's "from a concept and a prayer."

THE SURRENDER OF ITALY

Operations in the early summer of 1943 had made it plain that there was little co-operation between the allies of the Axis. Despite clever propaganda to the contrary, Germany and Japan were fighting separate wars. Italy had never relished the role of playing second fiddle to Germany, and Mussolini's resignation was followed by the announcement on September 8 of his country's unconditional surrender. On the following day Allied forces led by Lieutenant General Mark W. Clark landed at Salerno, just south of Naples, in an amphibious operation which threatened to cut off German defenders in the southern part of the peninsula.

Marshal Badoglio had begun secret negotiations with General Eisenhower early in August. At first the Italian offered only "complete neutralization," but as the collapse of his country became more apparent, the Allied terms found a grudging acceptance. The first units of the fleet

were surrendered on September 9, and savage Nazi reprisals led on
October 12 to an Italian declaration of war on Germany.

The high expectations aroused by these political triumphs were soon
dashed by military realities. Before the end of September it could be
deduced that the Allies had been taken as much by surprise as the
Germans. Neither the men nor the arms were available to reap the
full benefits of Italy's capitulation, and even the Salerno landings
narrowly escaped disaster. Far from being taken unawares, the Germans
had anticipated the time and place. The Panzers struck viciously and for
four days the amphibious troops were in a critical position. Only naval
gunfire and thousands of air sorties enabled them to hold the narrow
beachhead until airborne reinforcements secured the position.

A total of 189,000 troops and 108,000 tons of supplies were landed
within 16 days. During this period the patrols of the American Fifth
Army and British Eighth Army, both under the command of General
Sir Harold Alexander, met southeast of Salerno to form a ragged front
across the lower peninsula.

After the Nazi evacuation of Sardinia on September 20, the Allies
overran Corsica before October 4. Naples fell to them on October 1, and
that same day saw the occupation of the great system of Italian airfields
at Foggia.

Despite these gains, the Germans showed that they intended to fight
for every inch of Italian soil. Their able commander, Field Marshal
Albert Kesselring, had at his disposal enough veteran troops, plus
northern Italians enslaved as workers or auxiliary soldiers, to wage an
interminable series of delaying actions. The terrain was suited to this
strategy, since the mountains provided defensive positions while the sea
on either side limited Allied flanking operations.

Better Allied troops never fought on any front of the war. A cosmopolitan army, it included nearly every branch of the English-speaking
peoples—a unit of Hawaiian Japanese-Americans distinguished for valor,
Gurkhas, Sikhs, Free French divisions and Brazilians. The Volturno
was crossed on October 12, but the enemy had mined the roads, trails
and even stream beds which lay ahead. Wire entanglements, log-and-
earth strong points and mortar emplacements defended every approach,
slowing the advance to a crawl.

Of all the Nazi weapons, land mines probably did most to impede
the Allies. Some new types were fitted with nonmetallic cases to foil
electrical detectors, while others had mechanical delayed-action fuses to
explode them long after a road seemed safe. One of the most dreaded

antipersonnel mines was equipped with a spring which sent it five feet into the air to burst with maximum effect.

As an added handicap, the Anglo-American forces found that they had placed too much emphasis on armored warfare at the expense of infantry tactics. The penalties began to be exacted in November as Kesselring fell back to delaying positions 75 miles south of Rome. Dreary rains added to the Allies' difficulties, and before the end of the month the hopes inspired by Italy's surrender had proved illusory.

After the Volturno crossings, three months of costly mountain fighting brought the Fifth Army only about 30 miles nearer to Rome. General Eisenhower referred tartly to "armchair critics" in an interview, but it was apparent that the invasion had failed in many political as well as military respects. Far from tying down Nazi military strength in Italy, the invaders were themselves being tied down. Mussolini, rescued from captivity by German paratroops, was rallying Fascists to him behind the enemy lines, while the Allies had nothing positive to offer the southern Italians as a common cause.

On January 22, 1944, after 141 days of invasion, the strategic knot seemed to have been cut when British and U.S. amphibious troops landed on the beaches near Anzio. This surprise placed them only 25 miles south of Rome, well in the rear of the Nazis holding up the Allied advance.

The Anzio landings met little resistance during the first 48 hours. Then the enemy's swift and vigorous reaction made it evident that an amphibious attack does not carry with it a guarantee of victory. The Salerno landings had been so poorly planned that the Allies were hard pressed, and at Anzio the same mistake was made. Instead of driving inland immediately to seize favorable defensive terrain and hold it while reinforcements and supplies were being landed, the Allied soldiers again hugged the beachhead, where they made good targets. Nazi armor as well as infantry hemmed in the shallow perimeter, and deadly artillery fire from the near-by hills pounded both ships and troops. A month later the reinforced Allies, still no nearer to Rome, were fighting desperately to hold their own against Panzer counterattacks which reached a peak of fury on February 17, 1944.

The chief result of Anzio had been to create another small and precarious front, separated by miles of Nazi-held mountains from the Fifth and Eighth armies. These forces, too, had their troubles. An ancient hill town named Cassino became the new symbol of Allied frustration as the deadlock lasted into the spring months. Late in March, after days of futile house-to-house combat, 2,500 tons of bombs were dropped within a few hours, followed by 85,000 shells from guns as large as 240-mm. pieces. Yet even as radio announcers were exulting that Cassino had been "obliterated," Nazi combat groups appeared from deep cellars with their mortars and machine guns. For it has been the unvarying lesson of modern warfare that projectiles alone cannot wrest a position away from resolute infantry.

In April the fighting came to a standstill at Cassino, leaving the Allies only the comfort that their narrow Anzio foothold was firmly secured. Various explanations for these disappointing results were offered by strategists, but none is so convincing as the official comment of Henry L. Stimson, United States secretary of war.

"The simple fact is," he said, "that the Germans stopped us."

The Soviet Winter Offensive of 1943-44

In contrast to the deadlock on the Italian front, the Russians won one victory after another. Following the breakthrough at Orel in August, 1943, the Red Army kept the initiative in a succession of offensives up and down a 700-mile front. The recapture of Kharkov came on the 23rd. Briansk fell in the middle of September, and on the 25th the occupation of Smolensk marked a steady central advance of 250 miles since July 13.

Thousands of square miles in the Ukraine had been reclaimed before the retreating Nazis could harvest or burn the wheat. Early in October the Russians drove across the Dnieper; and on November 6 they won their greatest moral triumph since Stalingrad by storming into holy Kiev, the ancient capital.

Only a lull of a few weeks sufficed for the enormous task of reorganizing supply lines. Then in December the Red Army began its third winter offensive with attacks all the way from the Baltic to the Black Sea. The Crimea had already been isolated by advances in the south, leaving large Nazi forces cut off in the peninsula. Hitler's generals were being compelled to give up territory in order to save their hard-pressed armies; and on January 6, 1944, the Soviet columns crossed the border of prewar Poland, after winning back more than two-thirds of the half million square miles of Russian soil once held by the invaders.

In all modern history no other nation has ever recovered from such initial reverses as those suffered by the Soviet Union. It was as if most of the United States east of the Mississippi had been occupied during the first fifteen months of war, only to be redeemed during a like period following. The farthest Russian spearheads had now penetrated

800 miles west of Stalingrad—or, as the Moscow communiqués grimly put it, 500 miles east of Berlin.

The Russians, who themselves had gained a year's reprieve when Britain stood alone, were not silent about their sacrifices for the common cause. The Western Allies repaid the debt with interest in 1943 by maintaining two long and difficult supply lines which existed solely for the purpose of aiding the Soviet Union. In the icy waters of the north, British warships remained on constant duty to keep open the dangerous sea route to Murmansk. And in the mountains of Iran, the Americans of the Persian Gulf Command delivered to Russia's back door the Lend-Lease cargoes which had already come halfway around the earth in ocean freighters. New harbors, docks, warehouses, highways and rail lines had to be put into operation on this logistical front.

Not only were millions of tons of planes, tanks and trucks delivered to the Red Army; the Anglo-American Allies increased the military value of these weapons by strategic bombings which cut down the enemy's production. Moreover, it is a fair assumption that Russia's new tactical superiority in the air derived to no small extent from 1,550 British and U.S. planes added to the Soviet Air Force before May, 1944.

This fact is no reproach to a veteran army which made excellent use of all Lend-Lease materials. The Soviet artillery won the most praise from commentators, but the results of highly organized guerrilla warfare aided every advance. During a single month 33 enemy troop trains, two armored trains and a railway bridge were blown up in the Tarnopol region alone by bands operating behind the German lines. Some of the larger guerrilla forces fought with captured tanks and artillery, while maintaining their own supply lines with the help of materials dropped by Red Army planes.

The retreating Nazis hoped for a respite during the spring thaws, for mud usually ended all advances on the Eastern Front. But swamplike roads could not balk the hardy Soviet infantry, which had never lost the ability to march. New gains of 20 miles a day were sometimes made at the expense of Germans who had learned to depend too much on motor vehicles. Thus on April 2 one Russian army crossed the Rumanian border, while six days later another column reached the frontier of Czechoslovakia. Odessa fell on the 10th, having long been isolated, and on May 9 the Crimea was cleared of invaders by the capture of ruined Sevastopol.

JAPANESE DEFEATS IN THE PACIFIC

In the South Pacific the outer barrier of Japanese island defenses was breached during the winter of 1943-44 by a series of amphibious attacks. Following the successes of the early autumn, American soldiers and marines completed the conquest of the Solomons by landing on November 1 at Empress Augusta Bay in western Bougainville. A naval

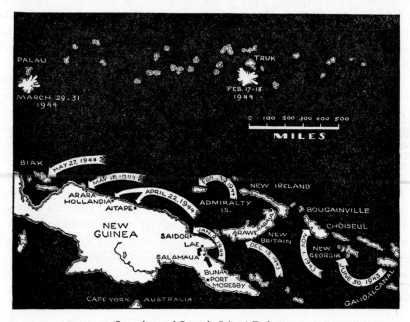

Invasions of Japan's Island Defenses

base and three new airfields placed the fighter planes of the invaders within 235 miles of Rabaul, the great Japanese base on New Britain.

While bloody jungle fighting went on at Bougainville—and it went on for many more weary months—New Britain itself was invaded on December 15 by U.S. Army troops who won a foothold at Arawe on the southwest coast. Nine days later new landings were made on the opposite side of the island, where American marines captured the enemy airdrome at Cape Gloucester. Rabaul now lay so exposed to air and naval attack that its usefulness as an advanced base came virtually to an end.

Up to this time all the important American amphibious operations in the Pacific had been conducted against large islands which offered the opportunity for feints and surprise landings. Amphibious techniques had improved with practice since the Guadalcanal operation, when the landing force was left without adequate arms and supplies because the transports had not been properly combat-loaded and protected. But other costly lessons remained to be learned the hard way, and errors in planning were punished by grievous casualties on the beaches of Tarawa.

This was the name applied to tiny Betio Island of Tarawa Atoll in the Gilberts group, more than a thousand miles northeast of Guadalcanal. For the preliminary bombardment Admiral Nimitz assembled the largest fleet ever to take part in an amphibious operation up to that time—seven battleships, seven heavy cruisers, thirty-four destroyers and eight escort carriers. By a coincidence, the three generals in charge of the troops were all named Smith. Major General Holland M. Smith USMC commanded the V Amphibious Force, divided into a Northern Landing Force under Major General Ralph C. Smith USA and a Southern Landing Force under Major General Julian C. Smith USMC.

About 5,500 of Japan's best soldiers held Makin and Tarawa atolls. Little effort was made to defend Makin, which was taken in the first assault without much trouble. It was on the square mile of Betio Island that the Japanese concentrated their forces after assisting nature with underwater concrete barriers so that an attack would be channelized into their fields of fire.

Although it hardly seemed possible that a single enemy soldier could have survived the bombardment of November 20, the Japanese found shelter in an elaborate system of deep underground blockhouses and caves. Veterans of well-executed Japanese amphibious attacks themselves, they were the better able to put up a stout defense when the American landing craft headed toward the beach on the following morning.

A hurricane of fire met the LCVPs and LVTs, some of which were blown up by mines and others wrecked by reefs or underwater obstacles. Hydrographical charts proved to have been inaccurate, and the marines were forced to wade in chest-deep water, where they made helpless targets for the deadly hail of Japanese machine-gun fire.

The survivors of three marine battalions landed on the narrow beach before dark. Unable to advance more than a few yards, they were pinned down behind a sea wall by Japanese fire while the surf washed in hundreds of American bodies. It was a terrible night for the men of the landing force, and all that saved them from annihilation was the Japanese

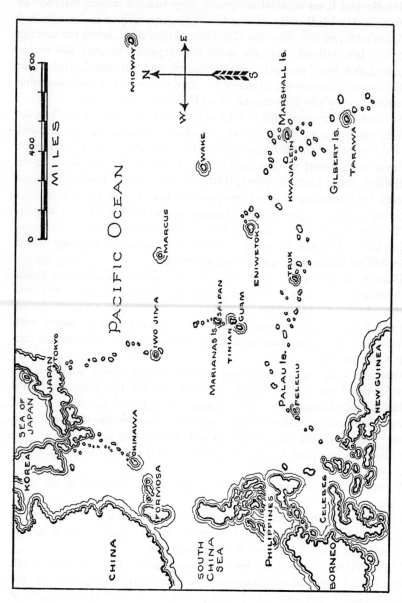

Steppingstones to Japan

failure to launch a counterattack while they had the advantage. But the Japanese had also taken severe punishment, and they remained in their caves, stunned by two days of U.S. naval bombardment.

Artillery, ammunition and a few tanks were landed that night, and the next morning saw the U.S. marine reserve battalions committed. They, too, suffered heavy casualties. Enough tanks and artillery were put ashore, however, to turn the tide of battle in favor of the attackers that afternoon. On the following morning, November 23, mopping-up operations began, and all organized resistance came to an end the next day. Of the 4,700 Japanese on Betio, 200 were taken prisoner and the rest fought until they were killed.

American losses of 985 killed and 2,193 wounded would have seemed low on the Russian front. They were disturbing to U.S. Navy and Marine Corps amphibious specialists, who made an exhaustive inquiry into the causes. They concluded that more accurate information about winds, tides, reefs and enemy installations must be a prerequisite in the future. They also agreed that the preliminary bombardment, terrific as it appeared, had failed to knock out a decisive proportion of enemy defenses.

The lessons learned in the Gilberts helped to reduce the price of invading the Marshall Islands on February 1, 1944. The preliminary bombardments were much more intense, with 15,000 tons of naval shells or bombs striking Kwajalein, Roi and Namur atolls. These blastings proved so effective that the troops swarmed ashore to gain their main objectives within a week, after killing twenty-eight Japanese for every American. On February 17, with the operation completed by the occupation of Eniwetok, the victors had gained a Pacific lagoon large enough to serve as an anchorage for a fleet. Better yet, they were in a position to send bombing planes against the Japanese naval base of Truk.

It has been suggested that a statue should be erected in honor of the caterpillar tractor as an instrument of conquest in the Pacific. Nothing could be more fitting, for every American success owed in some measure to the work of the Seabees—those naval construction battalions which built bases and airfields on captured islands. Composed of technicians representing 59 skills, they numbered 262,000 men early in 1944, or more than the whole Navy could muster before the war. These Jacks-of-all-trades followed closely behind the combat troops, slicing off hillsides and hacking out jungles with their bulldozers, so that planes could take off within a few days. The Japanese, though they toiled like ants, were at a disadvantage in this duel between hand labor and mechanical horsepower, which explains many of their failures.

American strategy was at its best in General MacArthur's westward sweep across the world's second largest island. After the capture of Finschhafen in September he occupied the Huon Peninsula before making a leap of 110 miles to land at Saidor on January 2, 1944. American regimental combat teams reduced the area so speedily that five days later an airstrip was in use.

Scarcely a year had passed since the fighting had ended on Guadalcanal, where the invaders had a material disadvantage at times in troops, planes and warships. At the crisis of that campaign only a single undamaged U.S. aircraft carrier remained in action, yet in the spring of 1944 the Navy announced the participation of fifty carriers against the Japanese. Numbers of warships and planes had multiplied in proportion, so that the foe faced the mightiest concentration of sea power ever directed against any nation in history.

This superiority helped MacArthur to bring off one of his most daring surprises. A date in April had been originally set for an invasion of the Admiralty Islands, important because of their harbors and airfields outflanking Rabaul. The American general was conducting a reconnaissance with elements of a single division on February 29 when he decided to risk a landing on Los Negros. The beachhead was held in spite of furious counterattacks, and the capture of Momote airdrome made it possible to conquer Los Negros, Manus and several adjoining islands.

The next combined land, air and water operation took the Americans 400 miles farther on April 22, leaving behind an estimated 50,000 Japanese troops to the eastward. Hollandia and Aitape, the new objectives, were seized with their airfields a week after the initial surprise. Humboldt Bay was transformed by the Seabees into an advanced naval base, and MacArthur moved his headquarters from Brisbane to Hollandia a few months later.

By this time the thrifty American pattern of conquest was familiar to the Japanese, who could only await the next move. Cut off from supplies, reinforcements or naval aid, they did not oppose new landings of May 17 at Arara and the Maffin Bay area.

Ten days later and 330 miles westward, another amphibious operation struck at Biak Island with its three airfields. Although the 8,000 defenders fought with customary Japanese tenacity, their defeat meant that MacArthur controlled the entire northern coast of New Guinea almost to the western tip.

From Biak to the Marshalls the new American positions formed an irregular crescent whose horns were separated by 3,000 miles. The Japanese system of outer island barriers had been smashed within a few months, proving that the "unsinkable aircraft carrier" was no match for mobile carriers which could strike with deception and surprise.

Never in modern chronicles had so large and strongly held an area been reduced with such economy. The full story is not told, moreover, until some account is made of the forces isolated behind the American strategic lines. These Japanese continued to resist whenever possible, but as a threat to Allied war aims they could be considered casualties. Of an original quarter of a million foemen in South Pacific regions, General MacArthur estimated that 142,000 had thus been neutralized— 60,000 on New Guinea, 50,000 on New Britain, 22,000 on Bougainville and 10,000 on New Ireland.

Nor were all the Japanese losses inflicted by amphibious operations. Early in 1944 came the first of those carrier strikes, supported by mighty task forces, which would soon blast the Japanese Empire from end to end. Rabaul had already been battered into helplessness by direct naval action, compelling enemy air and naval advance forces to withdraw to Truk. On February 17-18 that "impregnable" base was pounded for 48 hours by the shells, bombs and aerial torpedoes of a task force which included battleships.

The daring of this attack was exceeded during the last three days of March when a full-fledged battle fleet challenged the Japanese Navy by bombarding its Palau base, only 550 miles from the Philippines. So vast was the scope of the new Allied naval offensive that no enemy stronghold in the Pacific could count on immunity. Soon after an American squadron shelled Paramushiro, within flying distance of the northern Japanese mainland, a British and American task force launched a savage assault on Sebang Harbor in Sumatra, 6,000 miles to the southward.

Every Allied victory, naval as well as amphibious, owed to a consistent superiority in the air. United States naval statistics for 1943 listed a total of 2,212 Japanese and 351 American planes destroyed—a ratio of 6.3 to 1. The difference is partly explained by enemy deficiencies in both radar and radio. As an added factor, pilots were too hastily trained after the heavy losses of veteran airmen in 1942. But the chief reason is probably to be found in the vulnerability of lightly armored planes which lacked self-sealing fuel tanks. The Japanese Air Force was paying dearly for its policy of sacrificing protection to manoeuvrability.

Airborne Supply in Burma and China

At the Casablanca Conference it had been decided that more must be done to nourish operations on the two orphaned Allied fronts, Burma and China. The problems were dismaying. Japan's great initial sweep had cut the Burma Road, leaving General Chiang Kai-shek's armies isolated except for a trickle of airborne supplies over the "Hump" route of the Himalayas. China's situation grew desperate in her sixth year of war, and the Combined Chiefs of Staff agreed at the Casablanca Conference that an increased tonnage of supplies must be flown until a new all-weather road and oil pipe line could be built from India.

It could not be forgotten that during the first six months of 1942 Chinese guerrilla warfare had made it necessary for Japan to use more troops in that theater than in all the others combined. The Japanese occupation of Burma, however, shut off the supplies that had been coming over the Burma Road. As for the effectiveness of the Hump Route, it took three and a half tons of gasoline to fly in four.

A stalemate prevailed in China throughout 1943. The only offensive operations were conducted by the U.S. China Air Task Force, which shot down 351 enemy aircraft from February, 1942, to October, 1943, at a cost of 68. This organization, successor to the American Volunteer Group, became the Fourteenth Air Force under the command of Major General Claire L. Chennault.

At the Quebec Conference of August, 1943, the Southeast Asia Command was created, with Admiral Lord Mountbatten in command. General Joseph H. Stilwell, commanding the American China-Burma-India theater, was made his deputy and also chief-of-staff to Chiang Kai-shek, who retained control of operations in China. All air units in Burma, including the U.S. Tenth Air Force, were placed under the command of Major General George E. Stratemeyer and formed into the Eastern Air Command.

As a preliminary, formidable enemy forces had to be driven out of northern Burma, where they were well supplied by sea from Japan. The chief responsibility for this campaign fell upon the shoulders of Stilwell. A prewar authority on China, the American soldier spoke the language fluently. He had no illusions as to the difficulties ahead, having taken part in the dismal Allied retreat of 1942 from Burma—a rout which inspired his blunt comment, "I say we took a hell of a beating."

Stilwell began his campaign with only two Chinese divisions, which he trained in northeastern India. The climate and jungle terrain of Burma may be judged by the fact that some parts have an annual rainfall of 200 inches. No offensive could be attempted until after the monsoon ended and the floods receded. Meanwhile, the airborne cargo of the "oxygen route" over the Hump was doubled before winter, reaching a monthly average of 20,000 tons—more than the top capacity of the Burma Road. This meant that a few of the materials so direly needed by General Chiang Kai-shek were left over after the Fourteenth Air Force had been supplied.

With only a few hundred fighters and bombers at his disposal, Chennault made brilliant tactics take the place of numbers. Much larger

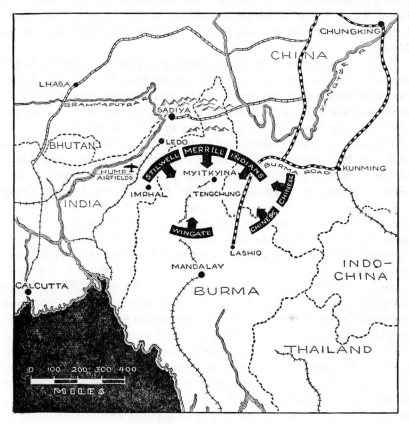

The Victory in Upper Burma

Japanese air forces, flying from bases in Formosa, Canton, Hangkow and Indo-China, were frequently caught at a local disadvantage by the veteran American airman. China's impoverished armies could scarcely have survived without this aid, for Chennault's bombs often had to substitute for artillery support.

The first moves toward recovering Upper Burma were made in the late autumn of 1943, when Stilwell's Chinese divisions advanced from Ledo into the Hukawng Valley. In February a second Allied column was composed of Brigadier General Frank D. Merrill's Marauders—specially trained American jungle fighters from veteran Pacific units who had responded to a call for volunteers. As these two forces fought their way southeast through spurs of the Himalayas, U.S. engineers followed within range of the guns, building a new macadam road from Ledo to connect with the old Burma Road at Tengchung by way of Myitkyina.

A third related operation placed Gurkhas and Indian guerrillas to the east of Merrill's combat team. Still farther east, two Chinese forces closed in on the opposite enemy flank. Five columns under Stilwell's direction were thus pushing southward in a great semicircle to envelop Myitkyina, the Japanese air base and key to northern Burma.

Materials for this campaign had to be landed in Calcutta, then transported to Ledo over a railway of two gauges. This meant that Allied armies eventually totaling 100,000 men were chiefly dependent on airborne supplies, free-drop or parachute, in the forward zone. Troop movements must also be made by plane at critical stages, so that the Tenth U.S. Air Force averaged nearly double the normal monthly flying time. "The re-entry into Burma," declared General Marshall, "was the most ambitious campaign yet waged at the end of an airborne supply line."

As Stilwell's five columns battled their way toward Myitkyina from the north, a sixth Allied force operated south of that objective. This was the famous band of Chindits—British and Indian jungle fighters trained by Major General Orde C. Wingate, the "Lawrence of Burma." Like the leader of the Arab revolt in World War I, the eccentric Englishman combined the qualities of scholar, mystic and adventurer. Unorthodox in his military theories, he conceived the plan of airborne landings far behind the enemy lines. The Chindits then hacked an airstrip out of the jungle, so that reinforcements as well as supplies could be flown in by U.S. airmen. And though Wingate died in a plane crash, his men cut the Japanese railway from Mandalay and prevented the foe from bringing up reinforcements.

The Marauders were meanwhile completing a 23-day march through mountains and jungles which remains one of the epics of the war. Emerging in three columns, Merrill's troops struck from the north, west and south to seize Myitkyina's main airfield in May, though it took 78 days of bloody fighting before the capture of the town could be announced on August 4. The victory left the Japanese remnants trapped between converging Allied forces, now being supplied and reinforced from the Myitkyina air base.

Another enemy column had launched a counterthrust by advancing into India to threaten the British base at Imphal and the vital railway to Ledo. This attempt was repulsed by British airborne troops, thus removing the peril to Stilwell's communications. His advance units then completed the campaign by making contact with the two Chinese forces pushing westward. The junction at Tengchung established a thin line across all Upper Burma, giving the Allies a hold which the Japanese were never able to shake.

THE SECOND FRONT IN THE SKY

During the first week of 1944 it was announced that General Eisenhower would have supreme command of the long-awaited Anglo-American invasion of western Europe. The only precedent for the attempt was disheartening. On August 19, 1942, a large-scale Canadian raid on Dieppe had proved a costly experiment. Led by tanks, highly trained Commandos penetrated the town, only to be trapped in a labyrinth of Nazi defenses and repulsed with casualties of 66 per cent.

Much more encouraging were the reports of the ceaseless offensive waged by British and American strategic bombers—"the second front in the sky," as it was termed by its enthusiasts. Any form of warfare which promises to shorten or soften a conflict is bound to have a wide popular appeal, and strategic bombing struck at the very roots of enemy production. A hundred tanks lost in battle could always be replaced; but if the munitions works that manufactured the tanks were knocked out in a single air raid, that result would mean more than a victory on the battlefield.

It was admitted that reverses took place in the air as well as on the ground. On the Sunday morning of August 1, 1943, for instance, a great daylight raid on the oil refineries of Ploesti, Rumania, was launched by Liberators of the U.S. Ninth Air Force, based at Bengasi, Libya, under the command of Major General Lewis Brereton. Surprise was lost by the 166 bombers which straggled in over the Rumanian plain at housetop level. By that time the air armada was in such disorder that the attacks were delivered piecemeal by pilots who became the targets for 558 antiaircraft guns and a swarm of German interceptor planes. Of the 166 aircraft 57 were lost. And while considerable damage was done,

Nazi slave laborers restored Ploesti to full production within a few weeks.

An American air raid of October, 1943, on German ball-bearing plants at Schweinfurt ended in losses of 30 per cent in pilots and planes. This object lesson led to the abandonment of bomber attacks without fighter escort.

Although the Allies had condemned the Germans for terror bombing of areas with few industrial targets, they did not hesitate to retaliate. At the Casablanca Conference of January, 1943, the Combined Chiefs of Staff issued a directive which defined the mission of strategic air power as "the progressive destruction of the German military, industrial and economic system, and the undermining of the morale of the German people to a point where their capacity for armed resistance is fatally weakened."

This directive named five main industrial targets in the following order of priority: (1) German submarine construction yards; (2) the German aircraft industry; (3) transportation; (4) the German oil industry; and (5) other targets of the enemy's war industry. Six months later so many Allied bombers were being shot down by enemy interceptors that the Combined Chiefs gave top priority to the destruction of German engine and component factories, repair and storage depots, and aircraft on the ground.

The Allied Bomber Command included the U.S. Eighth and Fifteenth Air Forces and the RAF Bomber Command. The British Lancasters being more lightly armored than American Flying Fortresses, the RAF was assigned the night shift for area bombing, which often meant the inflicting of heavy losses on civilians. For instance, over 70 per cent of Hamburg's heavily built-up area was destroyed in three raids by the Lancasters during July, 1943.

Daylight precision bombing was the province of the Americans, who had decided after the Schweinfurt debacle that bombers must have fighter escort all the way to the target. Allied attacks were to be co-ordinated, moreover, in an effort to reduce losses by deception and surprise.

The new theories had their test in November, 1943, after three weeks of intensive planning. In a preliminary daylight feint, Allied medium bombers attacked Nazi airfields in France. After enemy fighters had been drawn away from the Lowlands, 550 Liberators and Flying Fortresses took advantage of the opening to drop 1,200 tons of bombs on Wilhelmshaven. These heavy bombers were escorted by 450 U.S.

fighters—Thunderbolts and Lightnings equipped with belly tanks to make the long trip possible.

When the great armada returned to its English bases, the bombs of a third U.S. attack surprised Nazi fighters after they settled again on Lowlands fields. That night the RAF gave the foe no rest. First a few heavy bombers struck Cologne in a feint which accomplished its purpose of engaging enemy fighters from near-by fields. Then the main force found a comparatively clear way to Düsseldorf, where 2,000 tons of bombs were dropped in 27 minutes.

The total Allied losses of that day amounted to less than 3 per cent. This was the beginning of "round-the-clock" raiding, with U.S. bombers attacking by day and the British at night. Fighter escort and diversionary attacks became the rule as the air offensive approached a preinvasion tempo in the spring of 1944. Where air combat had once been avoided, Allied fighters challenged the Nazis to defend their shattered cities. Sometimes the Luftwaffe struck back with its old fury, but on one of many similar occasions 2,000 U.S. planes were allowed to bomb Brunswick without fighter resistance and to return without losing a single machine.

Altogether, 206,188 tons of bombs were dropped on Axis Europe during 1943, according to the *United States Strategic Bombing Survey*. Of this total, 131,688 tons were the ammunition of area raids.

Despite these impressive figures, it was revealed that German war production had actually risen in 1943, particularly during the second half of the year when bombing was heaviest! This postwar conclusion was seized upon by skeptics who contended that the claims of airmen as to enemy damage were much exaggerated. The explanation might have been found in such passages of the *Strategic Bombing Survey* as the following:

The Germans did not plan for a long war, nor were they prepared for it. Hitler's strategy contemplated a series of separate thrusts and quick victories over enemies that were even less prepared than Germany. . . . At the end of September [1941] Hitler, believing the war about won, ordered a large-scale reduction in armaments production.

British production of aircraft, trucks, tanks and other types of armament was larger than Germany's from 1940 to 1942. Not until the end of 1942 did Germany make a serious effort to increase war production. There was still no long-term planning or total mobilization such as prevailed in England and the United States. Albert Speer, with wide powers as German minister of armament production, increased the output of munitions in 1942, yet the manufacture of civilian goods was restricted only to a moderate extent.

The leaders of the Third Reich did not awaken to their danger until 1943. Then it was too late, despite the much-increased production of that year. Even during the first half of 1944 a gain could be shown in most types of armament; but Germany was now in the position of a reformed spendthrift living on his capital. By the second half of the year, aircraft plants were being too heavily bombed to meet Speer's quotas, which meant that not enough fighters were produced to defend the plants. Vicious circles of this sort were meanwhile strangling other forms of German war industry. A decline in the quality of pilots, for instance, might have been traced to a curtailment in training made necessary by a shortage of aviation gasoline as a consequence of strategic bombing.

Allied aircraft also deserved most of the credit for the check given German submarines. Since the first World War, when underwater raiders had nearly defeated the Allies, improvements had made the U-boats far more dangerous. The grand total of losses for Allies and neutrals throughout World War II added up to 4,770 ships of 21,140,000 gross tons—a figure equaling the tonnage of the British Empire's prewar merchant fleet, then the world's largest. The outlook was dark in the summer of 1942 when the Germans put into effect a system of resupply at sea by large cargo submarines.

"The losses by submarines off our Atlantic seaboard and in the Caribbean now threaten our entire war effort," wrote General Marshall to Admiral King in June, 1942. Fortunately for the Allies, a tactical antidote had recently been found in air patrols. United States Army and Navy planes watched over the coastal routes so effectively that no losses from U-boats were recorded in the Eastern, Gulf and Panama sea frontiers during the last quarter of 1942. RAF planes were meanwhile reducing sinkings in the waters around the British Isles.

By the spring of 1943 the Allies were protecting transatlantic convoys with small escort aircraft carriers and destroyers. Forming hunter-killer groups, the aircraft sought out the submarines and the destroyers pounded them relentlessly with depth charges. Thus the number of U-boat killings rose from 85 in 1942 to 237 the following year.

Germany had no merchant ships as prey for Allied underwater raiders, but British "midget" submarines slipped into Norway's Alten Fjord and disabled the 40,000-ton *Tirpitz* with torpedoes on September 22, 1943.

Germany's largest warship was further disabled by repeated aerial bombings, and on December 26 British naval guns sent the 26,000-ton *Scharnhorst* to the bottom. Not even nuisance value was left to Hitler's navy after these losses.

The Twenty Days of June, 1944

In February, 1944, the impending invasion of Europe was placed under the control of Supreme Headquarters, Allied Expeditionary Force, familiarly known as SHAEF. Duties in this command and staff organization were distributed as evenly as possible among American and British officers functioning together under General Eisenhower.

During the spring months the Allies used their control of the air to "soften up" the enemy for Operation OVERLORD, the code name for the invasion of Nazi-held Europe. By May the tactical air offensive grew to resemble a barrage blasting half a continent. German industries had become secondary objectives as Allied fliers concentrated on railways, airfields and coastal defenses in northern France.

Other indications made it clear to friend and foe alike that the day was near at hand. In an atmosphere of nightmarish speculation both sides lost no opportunity to wage a war of nerves. Nazi propagandists hinted darkly as to forthcoming secret weapons, while Allied broadcasters exhorted French "underground" forces already provided with small arms dropped from planes.

An ominous calm hung over the world's major fronts. The Red Army had been significantly quiet for two months, and events likewise seemed to be impending in the Pacific. The Allied forces in Italy made the first move, but even their long-delayed capture of Cassino on May 18 had the appearance of a mere local success. Not until the last days of the month did General Alexander find his opening, then the concerted offensive actually began with his advance on Rome.

In November, 1942, the war's first great turning point, the Allies had stopped the Axis drive toward world supremacy. And in June, 1944, they brought the struggle to a climax by launching an assault to break the inner defenses of Germany and Japan. Viewed separately, the blows fell in rapid succession over a period of twenty days:

June 4—Rome evacuated by the retreating Nazis.
June 6—Normandy invaded by the Anglo-American forces.
June 15—American landings in Saipan.
June 16—Beginning of strategic bombing in Japan.

June 18—Japanese defeat in a great naval battle.
June 23—Opening of the Soviet summer offensive.

Up to this time the Allied progress in Italy had averaged less than a mile a day. Little fault can be found with Alexander's generalship, but only costly slugging enabled his forces to link up the hitherto isolated Anzio and Cassino fronts. Even after this success it was obvious that Kesselring had evacuated Rome in order to fall back toward prepared positions.

For a few days the Allied advance resembled a pursuit, then the Nazi "rout" revealed itself more clearly as a series of delaying actions planned to exact a high price for every gain. Allied air superiority sometimes upset these calculations by strewing the roads with wrecked vehicles and hastening the retreat. Yet it could not be doubted that Rome's fall was only a beginning. More hard and bloody fighting lay ahead before Alexander could hope to reach the line of the Arno.

The magnitude of the Normandy invasion went far beyond any amphibious operation ever conceived before in history. Included in the Allied Expeditionary Force of 2,876,000 men were 39 divisions—24 infantry, 12 armored, and 3 airborne. Twenty were American, 14 British, 3 Canadian, 1 French and 1 Polish. There were also supporting units such as field artillery, engineers, signal and ordnance.

By May, 1944, the United Kingdom was, in General Eisenhower's words, "one gigantic air base, workshop, storage depot and mobilization camp." It would have been impossible to conceal preparations on such a scale, and the Allies made no attempt. On the contrary, they shouted the news from the housetops while waging a war of nerves on Germans who were kept guessing as to the time and place.

For more than a year Hitler had been building up his defenses along the French coast. He anticipated that the Allied invasion would be launched not later than the summer of 1944. On June 1 the Wehrmacht was deployed approximately as follows:

	Divisions	Aircraft
Russian front	140	1,040
France and Low Countries	58	1,100
Italy	23	260
Balkans	26	210
Denmark and Norway	5	50
Germany	13	1,440
	265	4,100

Hitler was already scraping the bottom of the manpower barrel. One of his divisions was composed entirely of men with stomach ailments, and other units consisted of non-German "volunteers" whose loyalty was open to doubt. By making use of such cannon fodder the Führer retained at this late date a strong reserve of young, dependable troops.

Field Marshal Gerd von Rundstedt shared the command in the West with Field Marshal Erwin Rommel during the spring of 1944. Curiously, it was Rommel, famed for his mobility, who advocated a static defense to stop an Allied invasion on the beaches. Rundstedt favored a strong reserve which could be shifted to any threatened point to destroy the Allied assault troops while they had one foot on land and the other in the sea.

Rommel enjoyed Hitler's confidence to a greater extent than did his colleague and his plan was adopted. Even the Panzer reserves were to be stationed just behind the beaches. "We must stop the assaulting forces in the water," he said, "[by] not only delaying but destroying all enemy equipment while still afloat."

Hitler and his two generals agreed that the main Allied landings would be made in the Pas de Calais area, which was precisely what Allied strategists were trying to make them believe. Dummy tent cities had been set up for that purpose in East Anglia and dummy landing craft appeared in the Thames.

At the eleventh hour Hitler guessed the right area but concluded that the Normandy landings would be secondary—a diversion to draw German troops away from the Pas de Calais beaches. He sent two more regiments to reinforce the units in Normandy but kept the bulk of his forces concentrated between the Seine and the Scheldt.

D-day of Operation OVERLORD had originally been set for June 5, but bad weather and high seas caused a 24-hour postponement. Shortly after midnight on the 6th the airborne troops took off in the darkness to make parachute or glider landings in enemy-held territory. Only the most breathless superlatives could have described the spectacle at dawn as 4,100 ships, not counting small craft, crossed from southern England to the Cotentin Peninsula. Overhead a total of 8,000 planes brought a 96-hour bombardment to a climax with an inferno of bomb explosions along the beaches. In the vanguard a fleet of six battleships, 22 cruisers and 93 destroyers provided naval gunfire. And in the rear of the beaches French underground forces were disrupting enemy wire communications and otherwise slowing up the movement of German reserves to the assault area.

The Fight for the Beaches

Four different H-hours were necessary for the four landing force teams—two British and two American—because of variations in tide and bottom. At sunrise, after a rough crossing, the assault troops poured ashore from the ramps of the landing craft. To their great surprise and relief, resistance was comparatively light at all points except OMAHA Beach in the American zone of operations.

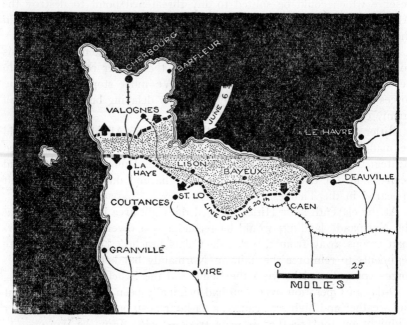

The First Two Weeks in Normandy

Enemy strength consisted of a Panzer and five infantry divisions deployed between Cherbourg and Caen. They gave the appearance of being stunned by the surprise and too confused for timely counterattacks.

As a consequence of scattered landings, the Allied airborne troops were not able to accomplish all their missions, and much of their equipment was lost. Nevertheless, their appearance was perhaps the main factor in disorganizing Germans who otherwise might have done more to prevent the Allied landings.

American casualties on UTAH Beach amounted to the astonishingly low figure of 137 killed and wounded. It was a different story on OMAHA

Beach, where the Germans had prepared their most formidable defenses. The landing forces were stopped at the water's edge by machine-gun and artillery fire from the high ground overlooking the beach. For two hours the Americans were pinned down behind the sea wall, but this landing was not to be another Anzio. Gradually the troops fought their way inland; and by noon, as reinforcements landed with tanks, the worst was over on OMAHA Beach.

The British and Canadian landings, to the left of the American zone, were all carried out successfully against the same incredibly light resistance as prevailed nearly everywhere on D-day. Once clear of the beaches, the invaders drove inland until they were stopped late that afternoon by a determined Nazi counterattack.

Five Allied divisions were ashore by nightfall. The next few days were devoted to landing more troops and tanks while closing the gap between the American and British beachheads. This aim was accomplished on June 12, in spite of stiffening resistance.

Again the Allies had reason to be grateful for Hitler's obstinacy, since he had clung to his conviction that the Normandy landings were secondary and the main attempt would be made in the Pas de Calais area. Thus the Allies were able to land 326,547 men in the first six days, in addition to 54,186 vehicles and 104,428 tons of stores. In the lack of a port, they were busily creating two artificial supply ports, each code-named MULBERRY, by towing concrete caissons across the Channel and sinking sixty old ships for breakwaters.

"From 9th June onwards," wrote General Hans Speidel, "the initiative lay with the Allies, who fought the battle entirely as it suited them." Both he and Rommel attributed the failure of German resistance to a paralysis resulting from the terrific Allied tactical bombing attacks.

But if the Allies had redeemed their invasion promises, the enemy soon showed that threats of a terrifying secret weapon had not been empty propaganda. During the night of June 13, strange missiles roared through the darkness over the London area, exploding with devastating effect. This was the world's introduction to the Nazi V-1 bomb, more often known as the robot bomb or buzz-bomb.

The first British reports were alarmingly soothing, but the robot's intended victims could have testified that it was one of the war's most dreadful weapons. Using the jet-propulsion principle, it had a maximum range of about 150 miles and a speed of some 300 miles per hour. A gyro device served to guide an ensemble consisting of a 16-foot wing-spread, a jet engine built above the tail, and an iron tube filled with explosives giving the effect of a one-ton bomb. And though the V-1 could not be aimed at specific targets, its accuracy was sufficient to cause destruction in crowded industrial districts.

Vigorous defense measures were adopted, most of them based on radar detection, but flak barrages and Spitfire patrols could provide only incomplete protection by exploding the missiles in air before they reached their destination. The fact had to be faced that the Nazi invention was capable of revolutionizing strategy. Jet propulsion had already passed the experimental stage in military aviation of all countries, so that speeds equaling the rate of sound were confidently predicted. Germany, applying the principle to long-range missiles, gave the world a dismaying glimpse into the possibilities of "push-button warfare" in the near future. Happily for the Allies, the V-1 came too late to affect the war's outcome.

As if in proof, the first robot explosions were followed next day by the announcement of the first raid by the mightiest bomber yet developed—the U.S. Superfortress. This plane was the answer to lessons taught by experience over enemy territory—a sky dreadnought large enough to carry enormous bomb loads over long distances at high altitudes, and self-sufficient enough to fend off interceptors with its heavy armor and fire power.

The secret of its design had been kept no better than that of radar, since it was not easy to hide a plane with a 141-foot wingspread, 16-foot propellers, four 2,200-hp. engines, and a fuselage length of 98 feet. On June 16 the monsters had their baptism of flak after flying 2,000 miles from Chinese bases to attack the Japanese steel city of Yawata. This meant that the island empire, with its huddled industries, could no longer escape the relentless attrition of strategic bombing by land-based planes.

Tokyo's fears were revealed by a new offensive in China. The loss of Upper Burma made it vital for the enemy to wipe out United States airfields before they could profit by increased supplies over the Hump route or the nearly finished Stilwell Road. Within a few weeks the Japanese drives gained enough momentum to occupy the rail junction of Hengyang, the most important Chinese city taken since the capture of Hangkow and Canton in 1938. Chennault's pilots flew double their normal sorties, but every day brought the foe nearer to Fourteenth Air Force bases.

The Battle of the Philippine Sea

This threat added to the significance of American landings in Saipan on June 15. For the key island of the Marianas, only 1,500 miles from

Tokyo, could be converted into a base for Superfortresses supplied by sea from the United States.

Japan's admirals reacted promptly by risking their first fleet action since Guadalcanal. The plan of attack probably derived from Midway, where Japanese invaders had been repulsed by a combination of land-based and carrier planes. In the new venture they hoped to reverse that defeat by striking from extreme range with carrier planes able to refuel at fields on Guam and Rota and strike again while returning to their ships. Thus the Japanese fleet would be kept out of reach of American aircraft, while surprising U.S. invaders assumed to be low on supplies and ammunition after the first critical days of Saipan.

This scheme, so plausible on the surface, took no account of the self-sufficiency of Vice-Admiral Marc A. Mitscher's Task Force 58, the most powerful unit of Admiral Spruance's Fifth Fleet. The Americans, having made themselves independent of fuel, ammunition and replacement problems, were able to turn the battle of the Philippine Sea into the third great Japanese naval disaster of the war.

On the morning of June 18 radar gave warning of approaching enemy aircraft then using the last of their gasoline. Spruance and Mitscher, divining the Japanese tactics, sent squadrons of bombers to smash air-fields on Guam and Rota, so that opposing planes would find it difficult to land. U.S. fighters swarmed out meanwhile from their carriers to bring down attackers by the score. Japanese machines which penetrated this screen had to deal with the Pacific war's heaviest anti-aircraft barrage.

By nightfall the attack had failed to the extent of a Japanese carrier sunk and 399 enemy aircraft destroyed. Two U.S. carriers and a battleship were slightly damaged and 27 planes lost.

The second phase of the battle took place the next evening, after Mitscher had steamed eastward all night and day under forced draft. At sunset he sent forth his carrier planes to "the point of no return" to bomb a retreating enemy fleet nearly stripped of defensive aircraft. A Japanese carrier and a tanker were sent to the bottom, and two carriers, three cruisers and three tankers took damaging hits. That night, in a hostile sea, the lights of Task Force 58 blazed defiantly to guide homing planes which had scarcely enough fuel for the long return trip. All but 49 pilots and crewmen were saved from 95 lost U.S. aircraft, most of them having been forced down with empty tanks.

The Japanese fared no better in the struggle for the 75 square miles of Saipan. After a 25-day campaign, with losses of 15,053 killed, wounded and missing, the invaders prevailed as Seabees toiled to create new airfields for Superfortresses which would soon be bombing Japan regularly. The defense of the island had cost the enemy 18,000 dead, 1,000 prisoners, 900 planes destroyed or damaged, and 58 ships and landing craft sunk.

Only one other announcement was needed to bring to a climax the twenty earth-shaking days of June. And on the 23rd came news of Stalin's long-expected offensive. Attacking on a 150-mile front in White Russia, where a huge Nazi salient represented most of the Soviet soil still held by the invaders, the Red Army struck with overwhelming power. Long-prepared German defenses crumbled under tremendous artillery bombardments, and at the end of twenty-four hours the guns of Moscow fired an unprecedented number of victory salutes.

Four days later, on June 27, the first stage of the Normandy campaign closed with the Nazi surrender of Cherbourg. The British and Canadian divisions of the left wing had taken Bayeux on the 11th and pushed toward Caen, where enemy resistance stiffened. The Americans were meanwhile driving westward across the peninsula, and on June 17 their advance units reached the opposite shore to seal off thousands of foemen. The German defenders of the wrecked seaport held out doggedly in underground positions, but a final four-day bombardment by 1,000 guns forced a capitulation. More than half a million Allied soldiers were now in the Cotentin Peninsula, and the invasion of Normandy had burgeoned into the battle for France.

VII

SURRENDER OF THE AXIS POWERS

The Hun is always either at your throat or at your feet.

—CHURCHILL

THE two MULBERRY ports have a good claim to being considered the war's greatest logistical triumph. After tugs had brought enormous steel and concrete caissons, seven miles of piering were towed from England as prefabricated units. Each artificial harbor weighed 750,000 tons and had about the capacity of the port of Dover.

Unfortunately for the Allies, a gale wiped out the American port on June 19 and damaged the other. Engineers made all possible repairs and soon had the British MULBERRY operative again. More dozens of ships were scuttled after the American occupation of Cherbourg to build a mole for the enlargement of port facilities. And by utilizing beaches the Allies were able to land nearly two million troops in three months along with 3,446,000 tons of ammunition and half a million vehicles.

At the end of the first ten days in Normandy, the American losses were 3,282 killed and 12,600 wounded. The explanation of this comparatively low casualty list may be found in the interdiction campaign waged by Allied airmen who sealed off the whole area from the Loire to the Meuse. Scarcely a bridge remained intact in all northern France, and bomb-pocked highways were choked with the wreckage of Nazi transport or armor.

So terrific was the air attack that one Panzer division took nineteen days to reach Normandy from central Galicia. More tragic, from the German viewpoint, was the failure of the Panzer Lehr Division, commanded by Lieutenant General Fritz Bayerlein and organized under Guderian's direction for the specific task of stopping the invasion. Possessing four times the striking power of an ordinary Panzer division, this unit of picked specialists took such punishment from the air that ten days were required to move from the Ghent area to Normandy. Nor did Bayerlein's troubles end upon arrival, for his division had been reduced to a mere fifteen tanks before the end of July.

There can be no question that an increased average of three tons of bombs a minute, night and day, did more than any other single factor to make the invasion a success. For the aerial encirclement of Germany was completed on June 2 when Allied fliers began shuttling between bases in England, Italy and Russia. Thus the enemy could be attacked in force from any direction, multiplying the defense problems of a fatally thinned Luftwaffe.

The amphibious victories of June seemed distant memories as the Allies inched their way forward through the hedgerows of Normandy in July. It was ideal defensive terrain and the Germans made the best of the sunken roads. Both Bradley and Montgomery paid dearly with casualties for every mile. Gains of less than five hundred yards in a day were reported by the Americans advancing toward St. Lô, and radio listeners in Allied nations recalled gloomily that a successful invasion had not led to a decision in Italy within a year.

Even on that front Florence was attacked in July by armies which had advanced as much as 15 miles a day since capturing Rome. In the Pacific the invasion of Guam was announced on the 21st, and in Poland the Red Army overran territory at the rate of 120 square miles every minute during the first thirty days of its offensive. Vilna, Brest-Litovsk and Bialystok were occupied in rapid succession by Russians who met almost no opposition. Before the end of the month Soviet guns had begun shelling Warsaw, and German-language primers were issued as General Chernyakhovsky's army neared the frontier of East Prussia.

Only in Normandy did Allied operations appear to have reached a standstill. The Germans, however, were not deceived. On July 6, as evidence of their gloom, Rundstedt was removed from supreme command in France, being replaced by Marshal von Kluge. Rommel, who also failed to justify the hopes placed in him, received a mortal wound when an American plane swooped down on his staff car, according to

Nazi reports. A few days later Berlin revealed that an attempt had been made to assassinate the Führer, and Churchill commented before the House of Commons:

> When I hear that after Hitler escaped his bomb he described his survival as providential, I think from a purely military point of view we can agree with him. Certainly it would be most unfortunate if the Allies were to be deprived in the closing phases of the struggle of that form of warlike genius by which Corporal Schickelgruber has so notably contributed to our victory.

Not until after the war was it learned that the attempt on Hitler's life had nearly succeeded. It was instigated by a group of officers who realized that the war was already lost for Germany and wished to spare their country the needless suffering of continued resistance. Hitler took a frightful vengeance by ordering the execution of every suspect. The story of Rommel's mortal wound in combat was a fabrication to cover up the fact that he committed suicide in October to save his family from persecution and disgrace. Kluge also took his own life, though neither he nor Rommel was directly implicated in the plot.

Rundstedt probably spoke for most of his colleagues in a telephone conversation of July 5. When OKW staff officers asked his opinion of the best strategy to pursue, the Third Reich's most able general growled, "End the war, you fools!" The next day he was removed from command.

THE ARGENTAN-FALAISE POCKET

While the battle of the hedgerows went on at a snail's pace, Bradley informed correspondents that he needed only three hours of perfect flying weather to break out of Normandy. The time came on the morning of July 25, when 3,000 U.S. planes dropped 3,390 tons of bombs on an area only five miles wide and two miles deep near St. Lô. The effects were afterwards described by General Bayerlein, commander of the shattered Panzer Lehr Division, to his American captors:

> My front lines looked like a landscape on the moon, and at least seventy per cent of my personnel were out of action—dead, wounded, crazed or numbed. All my frontline tanks were knocked out. Late in the afternoon the American ground troops began filtering in. I had organized my last reserves to meet them—not over fifteen tanks,

most of them from repair shops. The roads were practically impassable. Then next morning the bombing began all over again. We could do nothing but retreat.

American planes and guns took turns at bombarding, then hundreds of tanks led infantrymen pouring through the St. Lô funnel in trucks and half-tracks. After reaching open country Bradley's forces fanned out in three directions. So rapid was their advance that thousands of Nazis

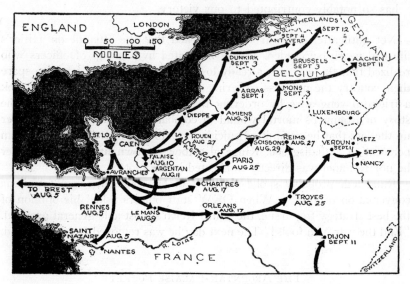

The Breakthrough at St. Lô

were cut off by the columns which raced through Coutances and Avranches into Brittany.

Montgomery's results were not so spectacular, though he contributed by fixing the Nazi strength south and west of Caen. From Avranches the U.S. forces cut straight across the base of the Brittany peninsula, driving a hundred miles in less than a week. When they reached the Bay of Biscay more thousands of foemen were sealed off, and such great harbors as Brest, Nantes and St.-Nazaire were isolated.

It would have been conservative strategy at this stage to consolidate gains by the capture of these much-needed supply ports. Instead, Eisenhower and SHAEF decided on bold new thrusts, while leaving behind a single corps to contain all the Germans in Brittany.

Bradley's command now comprised two armies—the First, led by Lieutenant General Courtney H. Hodges; and the newly created Third, under Lieutenant General Patton, which included most of the armor. The First was assigned the task of tying down the enemy, enabling the Third to dash eastward on the shortest route to Paris.

Marshal von Kluge, reluctantly carrying out Hitler's orders, launched a counterattack in an attempt to reach the sea at Avranches and split the American forces. Hodges' line was bent but not broken, and his stout resistance made it possible for Patton to push on through Rennes on August 3 and Le Mans six days later. From these points Third Army columns swung northward toward Argentan to threaten the rear of Kluge's whole army. Montgomery's Canadians were meanwhile driving southward from Caen toward Falaise to complete a great double envelopment which took the enemy by crushing surprise.

This was the famous "Argentan-Falaise pocket" in which 70,000 of Kluge's troops were killed or captured. In the lack of air cover, the Nazi counterstroke had been hopeless from the beginning. Fifteen divisions and parts of others were finally trapped in a shrinking pocket only 20 miles long and 10 wide. This area became a shambles as Allied bombers —so numerous that they had to take turns—struck at the crowded roads while Allied artillery poured in thousands of shells. Only about a third of the German Seventh Army escaped through a narrow corridor held open for eight hours.

Although it was a noble victory for the Allies, the fact that the pocket was not closed in time to trap the entire Seventh Army gave rise to a controversy which continued after the war. It has been the experience of history that adversity is a better cement for military alliances than success, and this occasion was no exception. Of Montgomery it had already been quipped, "In defense, indomitable; in attack, indefatigable; in victory, insufferable!" These words might with equal justice have been a toast to Patton, and it was in character when each intimated that the other had failed to close the Argentan-Falaise pocket.

War is a dull business on the whole and there is something to be said for the general who makes himself "colorful" by seeking personal publicity. Such commanders have a morale-building appeal to the public that more modest colleagues cannot claim; and Patton's ivory-handled pistols and shrill oaths were as famous as "Monty's" beret and ascetic tastes. Unfortunately, renown of this sort is likely to overshadow the accomplishments of equally talented but less vociferous generals. Hodges, the quiet, courteous U.S. First Army commander, was compared by his staff officers to Robert E. Lee in personality, yet he never received a tenth of Patton's headlines. Nor did Alexander ever gain the renown accorded to Montgomery.

THE LIBERATION OF FRANCE

While Bradley's First and Third armies pelted toward Paris on the heels of the foe, Montgomery's Second British and First Canadian armies struck northward along the coast toward Le Havre and Calais.

These pursuits had not been started when successful Mediterranean landings were made on August 15 by the U.S. Seventh Army of Lieutenant General Alexander M. Patch. Following a tremendous air offensive, the invasion fleet poured troops ashore southwest of Cannes in position for a drive up the Rhone Valley. This stroke imperiled the rear of all the German forces in France, so that the enemy could only hasten his escape at the cost of abandoning arms and equipment.

On August 25 the honor of occupying Paris was left to Free French forces commanded by General Le Clerc as Bradley's two armies passed the capital on the east and west. The part played by Allied tactical air power in the pursuit is beyond calculation. No better example could be found than the support given Patton's rapid advance. Little opposition barred the way, but on the right flank the menace of 30,000 fresh German troops across the Loire had to be taken into account. U.S. planes alone neutralized these foemen for three full weeks, hemming them in with bombs and machine-gun fire as surely as if they had been surrounded by tanks.

During the last days of August the sweep of the four Allied armies extended from the Channel to the Meuse. With few exceptions, only minor rear-guard actions were offered by Germans evacuating the most memorable battlefields of World War I—Verdun, St. Mihiel, Château-Thierry, Reims, Noyon and Amiens.

The pace of the advance is shown at its best by a single week's progress of Hodges' First Army. During these seven days his columns reversed nearly all the gains made by the Germans in four years of World War I. Field Marshal Walther Model had replaced Kluge when the Germans made a frantic effort to get across the Seine with their remaining forces. This was accomplished, according to a German account, "at the expense of losing the bulk of matériel, in an almost inextricable confusion of units, and with tremendous losses."

On August 26 and 27 Hodges regrouped his forces for the pursuit.

After crossing the Seine on the 27th and the Marne on the 28th, he drove through Soissons the following day. On September 1, the seventy-fourth anniversary of Sedan's surrender to Moltke, American shells were dropping into that historic town, and only twenty-four hours later Hodges had left the Belgian frontier behind. As a climax he brought off the most smashing victory of the Allied pursuit by cutting off five depleted Nazi divisions at Mons on September 3. In a few hours of furious battling, despite the weariness of his men, he drew a circle of armor and infantry which compelled the surrender of 22,000 enemy troops, while killing or wounding nearly as many more.

The task of reducing Brest was given on September 5 to the newly formed U.S. Ninth Army, commanded by Lieutenant General William H. Simpson and composed of troops operating in Brittany. It also had the mission of mopping up isolated pockets of resistance and protecting the flank of the Third Army along the Loire.

Patton was meanwhile pushing to the line of the Moselle near Metz, which he reached on the 7th. Supply proved more of a problem than enemy resistance, but American planes provided the solution by dropping gasoline. In that same area the most amazing dash of all ended on September 11 when patrols of Patch's Seventh Army made contact with the Third Army at Dijon. This junction completed a sprint of nearly 400 miles in the 27 days since the Mediterranean landings. Only light and scattered German counterattacks were met; and the Maquis, or French underground troops, led a popular uprising which soon resulted in the collapse of the Vichy government. Toulon, Marseille and Lyon fell in rapid succession, while on several occasions large Nazi detachments capitulated without striking a blow.

Montgomery's British and Canadians of the left wing kept pace with Hodges by driving from Normandy across Belgium in two weeks, entering the Netherlands on September 12. On the way Dieppe and Dunkirk were captured to pay off old scores, then the pursuers swept through Ostend, Brussels and Antwerp. These victories were celebrated by Englishmen who gained some measure of relief from V-1 bombs as their soldiers overran coastal launching bases. During the first eighty days 870,000 buildings had been razed or damaged, chiefly in the London area. An average of 100 robots a day were sent across the Channel, though alert defenses prevented nearly three-fourths of them from reaching their targets.

Nor were German reverses of these eventful days confined to western Europe. On the Italian front Pisa fell to Alexander on September 2, only two weeks after his occupation of Florence. The Russians had meanwhile opened up a new offensive in Rumania, capturing the Ploesti oil fields on August 30 and Bucharest the next day. An invasion of Bulgaria followed on September 8 as Soviet armies drove toward a junction with Marshal Tito's forces in Yugoslavia, where an effective guerrilla resistance had been maintained since 1941. At least 25 Nazi divisions in the Balkans were threatened, and the menace of a Russian advance up the Danube against Budapest had soon to be faced.

As the final moral blow, Germany itself was invaded on September 11 by Hodges' columns, barely two weeks after the crossing of the Marne. During their first forty-eight hours on enemy soil the Americans took Roetgen, in the outer defenses of the West Wall, and began the bombardment of Aachen.

The War Carried to Germany

At this date Germany stood revealed before the world as more hopelessly beaten than in the autumn of 1918. Losses in western Europe alone during the fifty days since St. Lô totaled half a million killed, wounded and prisoners, including the garrisons doomed to ultimate surrender. Casualties on the Eastern Front since June 23 were not far behind this figure. Despite such sacrifices, victorious Allied hosts battered at the gates of the Third Reich on five frontiers. New French armies, equipped with Lend-Lease weapons, had been organized under the leadership of General Charles de Gaulle; and other peoples of Nazi-occupied Europe would soon be liberated to add to the might of the victors.

Only in an age of total war could any government have been so mad as to continue a resistance promising only to defer the end a few months at the risk of the nation's future. Roosevelt and Churchill were of course blamed for insisting on an unconditional surrender. It is not likely, however, that the Nazi leaders would have accepted a compromise peace. Their hands were stained with the blood of several million prisoners who had been systematically "processed" through the gas chambers of concentration camps. There could have been no forgiveness even in their own country for such men when Germany recovered from her delirium. Hence they chose to drag the whole nation down with them to destruction in a gigantic Götterdämmerung.

German military fortunes, moreover, held forth a few prospects of mending. OKW strategists, knowing that Anglo-American armies must soon outrun their supply lines, had left garrisons in every large seaport with orders for a prolonged defense. Thus at the height of Allied victories Cherbourg remained the sole harbor, though the facilities of captured Dieppe and Le Havre were partially restored within a few weeks. Bordeaux, Nantes, Antwerp and St. Nazaire (or their estuaries) held out for weeks, while Calais, Brest and other ports were thoroughly wrecked before the garrisons surrendered.

The West Wall, which the Nazis themselves did not deem inpregnable, could at least be trusted to delay attackers and exact a heavy price in blood. These steel and concrete defenses, like those on the eastern German frontier, had the further merit of making it possible to use hastily trained boys and old men, thus saving first-line troops for counterattacks.

Finally, the Nazis were now ready to bombard England with another new secret weapon, the V-2 rocket. Neither London nor Berlin gave out any information until November, when 2,217 civilians were killed or injured; but the 558 casualties of the preceding month had already announced a new ordeal for a nation only recently rescued from large-scale robot bombardments.

The silent and eerie V-2, hurtling out of the stratosphere from launching bases in the Netherlands, had even more dreadful potentialities. A tapered and wingless projectile 45 feet long (minus the explosive head) and 6 to 7 feet in diameter, it attained a speed beyond the rate of sound, and a trajectory estimated as high as 60 miles above the earth. Neither planes nor antiaircraft guns were of any avail against the giant rocket, and victims heard no sound before it buried itself to explode with about the effect of a two-ton bomb.

With the new weapon added to Germany's assets, the necessity for Allied haste was increased. It had now become a question of whether the victors could maintain their momentum, and the Arnhem-Eindhoven aerial attack of September 17 must be reckoned one of history's most glorious failures.

On that Sunday morning the skies over Holland were suddenly filled with thousands of red, blue, white and yellow parachutes. More thousands of troops, as well as guns, jeeps and tanks, followed in a glider train 235 miles long to descend behind the German lines.

The effort aimed at no less a result than outflanking the northern limits of the West Wall and establishing bridgeheads on the Meuse, the Rhine and the Lower Rhine before the enemy recovered from his summer's disasters. Lieutenant General Sir Miles Dempsey's British Second Army had already extended a narrow salient nearly to the three river barriers. If the bridges could be seized in an audacious surprise, no fixed defenses as yet barred the way to the enemy capital 300 miles eastward.

More than 2,800 planes and 1,600 gliders were used by Lieutenant General Lewis H. Brereton's First Allied Airborne Army. Americans landing near Eindhoven quickly won the Rhine and Meuse bridges, made contact with Dempsey's forces and repulsed counterattacks. Ten miles farther north, 8,000 "Red Devils" of the British contingent failed through no fault of their own to solve a more difficult tactical problem. Denied the expected support from British ground troops, they were driven from the Lower Rhine bridge, surrounded by superior numbers, and subjected to a terrible nine-day ordeal from which only about 2,000 escaped death or capture.

Prompt counterattacks on Dempsey's thin corridor, cutting off reinforcements, had been the chief cause for the limited results. The consequences were soon felt in such slow and costly operations as the reduction of Aachen, which did not surrender until October 21. Nearly six weeks of bombardment and street fighting were necessary to take a city normally containing 165,000 people, though the defenders consisted largely of German second-line reserves led by storm troopers.

THE BATTLE FOR LEYTE GULF

In the Pacific theater the American conquest of Guam and Tinian in July, 1944, provided more bases in the Marianas for the strategic bombing of Japanese war industries by Superfortresses. General MacArthur had meanwhile extended his control of New Guinea to the western tip by a successful invasion of the Vogelkop Peninsula.

That the ultimate aim of American strategy was the Philippines could not be doubted on September 15 when the marines landed on Peleliu in the Palau Islands and soldiers swarmed ashore on Angaur and Morotai. All three objectives lay some 500 miles south of Mindanao, providing air bases for an invasion of the Philippines.

Peleliu proved to be an unexpectedly hard nut to crack. Only about six miles long and three wide, the coral rock was too small for manoeuvre and too large to be swallowed at a tactical gulp. One of the most repulsive pieces of real estate on earth, it abounded in Japanese caves large enough for a battalion of infantry supported by camouflaged artillery. A 27-day campaign of extermination, at a cost of 1,241 marine dead, was necessary before Peleliu could be officially declared "secured." Although

11,000 Japanese had been killed, mopping-up operations continued, as on Guam and Saipan, for weeks afterwards.

Whether Peleliu was worth the price in casualties was a question reserved for the long list of postwar controversies. Its airfield had not yet been secured when Admiral Mitscher's Task Force 58 "prepared" the enemy in the Philippines on October 11 by beginning a nine-day carrier attack on airfields of Formosa and Luzon. More than 900 planes were destroyed at a cost of only 45 U.S. aircraft.

On October 20, before the Japanese could recover, an armada of combat and transport vessels landed large forces on Leyte, the central bastion of the Philippines. Admiral Halsey's covering force included battleships, cruisers, destroyers and rocket ships, and 18 carriers gave air support.

During the first few days a drumfire bombardment of shells, bombs and rockets aided the troops in securing beachheads on the east coast. General MacArthur estimated that 14,405 casualties were inflicted on the defenders within a week at a cost of 2,160 American killed, wounded and missing.

But the decisive action was to be fought on the sea, where the Japanese were prepared to take supreme risks in defense of the Philippines. Elements of their main fleet were first sighted by U.S. submarines, which radioed warnings after sinking two cruisers. The remaining Japanese warships came on in a three-headed advance aiming to surprise the two American fleets during the confusion of landing supplies on the Leyte beaches. This attempt led to the fourth great naval action of the Pacific war: a running fight of three days, October 24 to 27, over a front of 700 miles.

The central enemy force, including five battleships, planned to penetrate the narrow San Bernardino Strait, between Samar and Luzon, in an effort to smash Admiral Thomas Kincaid's warships and soft-shelled transports off Leyte. As the other arm of a converging attack, the southern enemy force took the route of Surigao Strait, between Leyte and the small islands off Mindanao. Thus it was hoped that Kincaid could be caught between two fires at a disadvantage in both numbers and situation.

Japanese admirals had not overlooked Admiral Halsey's Third Fleet, including Mitscher's Task Force 58, in the Philippine Sea east of Luzon. Anticipating that he would send most of his carrier planes to the rescue of Kincaid, a northern enemy force rounded Luzon with four carriers protected by two battleships and five cruisers. When Halsey's flattops

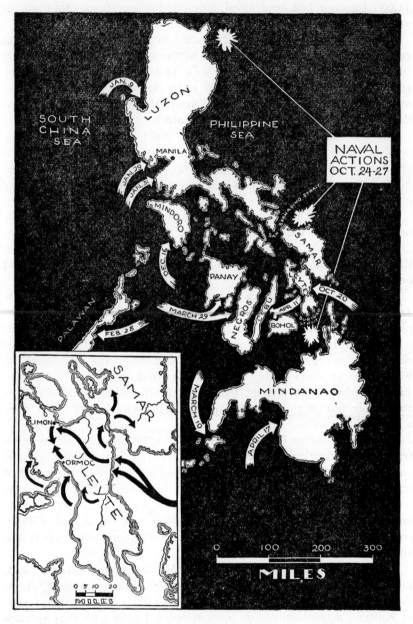

Return to the Philippines

were stripped of aircraft, these Japanese carriers planned to send their planes to the attack of the Third Fleet.

In all three co-ordinated attempts the enemy also counted on airfields in the Philippines. Not only were land-based planes available in large numbers to support the naval efforts, but carrier planes would be able to refuel on land.

American carrier planes struck the first blow by damaging units of the oncoming Japanese central and northern forces. Japanese carrier and land-based planes took severe punishment in this exchange, though the U.S. light carrier *Princeton* went down after repeated bomb hits.

The southern enemy force slipped through narrow Surigao Strait in the darkness, only to be ambushed by PT boats and destroyers. Five U.S. battleships, all of them repaired veterans of Pearl Harbor, then opened fire at a range of eight to ten miles. After losing two battleships, the Japanese took to flight as U.S. planes pounded the survivors mercilessly.

That same night Halsey and Mitscher steamed westward toward Luzon to meet the northern enemy force with most of the American carrier strength. The Japanese, who had expected to surprise unprotected flattops, were hoist by their own petard. Their decks were bare, with the planes refueling on Luzon, when Third Fleet bombers attacked to sink or damage all four carriers and score hits on both battleships at a cost of ten U.S. aircraft.

Kincaid's call for help came before this action ended. Halsey, who had taken long chances in leaving Leyte, immediately turned southward against the enemy's central force. The threat of his carriers sent the Japanese back through San Bernardino Strait after a battle in which Kincaid lost three destroyers and two escort carriers.

Japanese losses in the battle for Leyte Gulf were four carriers, three battleships, nine cruisers and eleven destroyers. One American light carrier, two escort carriers, two destroyers, and one destroyer escort were sunk.

Thus perished the remnants of the world's third largest fleet, the victims not only of American shells and bombs but also of Japanese failure to understand modern sea power. Niggardly strategists when they held the advantage, the heirs of Tsushima made poor use of the year's material advantage gained at Pearl Harbor. Overcautious when audacity might have paid, they frittered away their strength at Midway and Guadalcanal. Then, turning overbold in their weakness, they gambled frantically on the complex plans which led to disaster in the battles of the Philippine Sea and Leyte Gulf.

THE INVASION OF THE PHILIPPINES

The first week's land operations on Leyte seemed to promise a quick victory. Filipino guerrillas, who had been supplied for two years by U.S. submarines, proved effective allies. Thus at the outset the invaders overran half the island and gained control of the 5,040 square miles of near-by Samar.

Past amphibious operations had shown, however, that the Japanese were never vanquished painlessly. The defenders of Leyte decided to make a major stand after withdrawing to the jungle-clad mountains and rice paddies of the western side. General Yamashita, the conqueror of Singapore and Bataan, poured in some of the empire's most famous units as reinforcements. In spite of 35,000 casualties, plus frightful troop losses on transports sunk by U.S. planes, the Japanese were actually stronger at the end of the fourth week than on invasion day. Violent tropical downpours turned the terrain into ankle-deep mud, compelling the American forward troops to depend on native bearers for supply. Mechanized attacks were of course impossible under such conditions, and everything favored the defense in small war waged by large forces with such weapons as rifles, grenades, mortars and flame throwers.

The capture of Limon late in November, 1944, represented a hard-won step on the way to Ormoc, the enemy port of supply and reinforcement. An amphibious landing on the west coast finally led to the reduction of that objective on December 11, though three more weeks of bloody fighting ensued before the seven U.S. divisions closed out organized Japanese resistance.

During these cleanup operations, two American regiments invaded the island of Mindoro on December 16. Enemy opposition was comparatively light, and within a few days U.S. planes and PT boats had new advance bases.

This landing was obviously a prelude to a large-scale attempt on near-by Luzon, and on January 9, 1945, nearly 70,000 men of Lieutenant General Walter Krueger's U.S. Sixth Army won a foothold on Lingayen Gulf. Fifteen miles of beaches were secured the first day by attackers who lost no time in pushing into the central Luzon plain. Yamashita might perhaps have met the threat more effectively if new American landings had not compelled him to scatter his efforts. For on the 29th another amphibious force seized the tip of the Bataan Peninsula, where the outweighed Americans of 1942 had made their last stand. Only forty-eight hours later airborne troops descended southeast of Manila, hemming in the city from still another direction and ending its usefulness as an enemy port.

Supported by terrific aerial bombardments, the three American columns closed in from the north, northwest and south. On February 23, after days of house-to-house fighting, General MacArthur announced the liberation of the capital. Paratroops, who had meanwhile landed on Corregidor, reduced that island stronghold so speedily that Manila began functioning as an American port in March, 1945.

Fighting continued on Luzon, for Yamashita had retreated to the mountains with his remnants. But overwhelming American sea and air power made possible a rapid succession of landings on other key islands— Palawan in February, followed by Panay, Negros, Cebu and Mindanao in March. Japan had already lost the Philippines for all strategic purposes, though three months of difficult tactical operations remained for the Americans and their Filipino allies.

This was a timely gain, for the enemy's autumn and winter offensive in China gradually engulfed most of the Fourteenth Air Force bases. Before January the plight of Chiang Kai-shek's armies had become so grave that it appeared doubtful whether they could survive their eighth year of war. Two Japanese columns bored their way toward the heart of the ancient empire from the south and east, making it necessary for Chennault to abandon airfields. Internal strife was added to Chiang Kai-shek's other woes as the opposition of Chinese Communists reached a stage not far removed from civil war.

Only in Burma could the Anglo-American forces extend a helping hand. As the British Fourteenth Army drove southward from Myitkyina, other British units made amphibious landings at Akyab on January 5, threatening the Japanese hold on Mandalay and central Burma. There gains meant less to Chiang Kai-shek than the completion of the Stilwell Road. On January 28 the first convoy of trucks crossed the Burma-China frontier, and that same month Hump airborne cargo reached a total of 46,000 tons—three times the peak capacity of the old Burma Road.

Loss of Momentum in Europe

In the European theater the high hopes of September, 1944, were doomed to disappointment during the following three months as the Allies made slow and painful progress. The question as to the conduct of the final attack had already led to differences of opinion which dwarfed the Argentan-Falaise controversy. Again the British generals were ranged on one side and the Americans on the other. Montgomery held that "one powerful full-blooded thrust across the Rhine and into the heart of Germany, backed by the whole of the resources of the Allied armies, would be likely to achieve decisive results." He believed that the most feasible axis for such a drive lay in the British zone of operations, through Belgium to a crossing of the Rhine north of the Ruhr.

General Eisenhower maintained, on the contrary, that the Allied troops could best be employed on a broad front, where they would stretch the depleted German forces and create an opportunity for a breakthrough. He contended that Allied supplies were not sufficient for Montgomery's plan, even if all were alloted to his 21st Army Group, and that the capture of Antwerp, the foremost port of Europe, must be a prerequisite to any large-scale, sustained operation. As it was, the 7,000 trucks of the "Red Ball Express," moving some 8,000 tons of supplies a day, could not meet the ordinary demands of the combat forces.

SHAEF decided on a broad-front strategy, so that the possibilities of Montgomery's visionary thrust must remain forever in the realm of conjecture.

On September 15, 1944, the 48 Allied divisions on the Continent, all of which needed replacements, were divided among these nationalities— American, 25; British, 12; French, 7; Canadian, 3; Polish, 1. On the left, Montgomery's 21st Army Group, comprising 15 divisions, held a 150-mile zone. In the centre, Bradley had control of a 250-mile front with the 21 divisions of his 12th Army Group. And on the right, the 100-mile zone of U.S. Lieutenant General Jacob L. Devers' 6th Army Group was manned by six French and four American divisions.

German opposition stiffened immediately when Hitler's troops were fighting in defense of their own soil. An enemy who had seemed demoralized in the middle of September sold every inch of ground dearly in hard-fought delaying actions of the next three months. Marshal von Rundstedt, recently restored to command, accomplished these results while holding the bulk of his first-line troops in reserve. General Patton's armored divisions were kept occupied until late November at the task of reducing Metz and the Moselle defenses. Rundstedt managed even to deprive the Allies of an adequate supply port until November, though as early as September 21 General Eisenhower had reported to Washington:

Right now our prospects are tied up closely with our success in capturing the approaches to Antwerp. All along the line main-

tenance is in a bad state . . . but if we can get to using Antwerp it
will have the effect of a blood transfusion.

Weeks of bloody fighting were necessary before units of Lieutenant
General Henry D. Crerar's First Canadian Army could clear out the
defenders of Walcheren and other islands of the 50-mile estuary. British
warships and troops joined in amphibious attacks on forts resisting with

The Watch on the Rhine

suicidal fury. And when at last Antwerp began unloading cargo vessels,
the enemy rained both V-1 and V-2 bombs on the harbor area.

From late September to December 15, the U.S. First and Ninth armies
were able to advance only eight to twelve miles north of Aachen. The
initial objective was the little river Roer. As a preliminary, Allied aircraft were given the mission of knocking out the Roer dams, near the
town of Schmidt, which gave the enemy the means of flooding the
valley. The planes were unable to penetrate the antiaircraft defenses, and
Bradley's ground forces came up against fierce opposition.

Fourteen divisions, soon increased to 17, were employed in the zone of the First and Ninth armies. Ten fought in line on a 24-mile front at the height of the offensive. Beginning on November 16, more than 9,300 tons of bombs were dropped on German fortified positions by 1,204 U.S. and 1,188 British bombers. Large towns such as Jülich and Düren were obliterated, but every pile of rubble in this devastated area seemed to be converted into an organized strong point.

The gloomy Hürtgen Forest, covering roughly the Aachen-Düren-Monschau triangle, held up three American divisions for ten weeks and cost them a total of 13,067 casualties. On December 15, when Bradley's forces finally reached the Roer, operations of the last month alone had resulted in 21,650 casualties for the First Army and more than 10,000 for the Ninth.

During the first two weeks of December the Third Army established bridgeheads across the river Saar and drove within five miles of the western outskirt of Saarbrücken, the great industrial center. Patton was now up against some of the strongest fortifications of the West Wall, and attacks were postponed until more logistical support could be provided. The Third Army, which had taken 37,000 prisoners in the Metz and Saar campaigns, suffered 29,000 casualties.

On the right of the Allied line, General Devers' plan had called for the U.S. Seventh Army to advance on the Epinal-Saverne-Strasbourg Axis and the French First Army on the Belfort-Mulhouse Axis. The fighting continued in the Vosges with small Allied gains throughout October and the first two weeks of November. On the 13th the Seventh Army, which had been built up to eight divisions, launched its main attack in a snowstorm. The next day General de Tassigny's French troops broke through the enemy's defenses on a 20-mile front, taking both Belfort and Mulhouse and driving to the Rhine by the 22nd.

In the Seventh Army zone the Americans captured Saverne on the 22nd and swung eastward to occupy Strasbourg the next day, though the city's outer ring of forts did not fall until November 27. By the middle of December the 6th Army Group had crossed the German frontier on a 22-mile-front. All the other Allied forces were also in position to regroup and deal the final blows when Marshal von Rundstedt suddenly seized the initiative in the year's greatest surprise.

THE BATTLE OF THE BULGE

Only Pearl Harbor could compare with the shock at dawn on December 16, 1944, when a quarter of a million of the Third Reich's best troops struck in the Ardennes. Their objective was Antwerp by means of an expected Meuse breakthrough.

It was Hitler's last gamble. He had initiated planning in September, against Rundstedt's advice, for an offensive originally bearing the incredible code name of CHRISTROSE. So confident was the Führer of success that he was willing to stake the reserve of first-rate troops he had held to defend East Prussia and Berlin against a Russian attack.

Only six U.S. divisions—two of them consisting of green troops and two others of weary Hürtgen Forest remnants—were in line to oppose the onslaught of 20 Nazi divisions (soon increased to 24) of the Fifth and Sixth Panzer armies and the Seventh Army, largely infantry. Gasoline and ammunition had been hoarded by the Germans for weeks. Troop movements were conducted with the utmost secrecy, and Allied intelligence officers were as much surprised as the outweighed troops in the path of the huge King Tiger tanks when the Germans attacked on a 40-mile front between Monschau and Echternach.

The date had been set by OKW in the hope that bad weather would keep the Allied planes grounded. This gamble paid off richly with a week's snow, rain and fog during the short winter days. Terrain and weather made for confusion on both sides, so that the battle seemed to the participants to be waged by groping combat groups without much rear-area control.

Rundstedt, whose fate it was to put into action the plans he advised Hitler against, believed that his only chance for even a temporary victory lay in a dash which would carry him to Liége within the first few days. He was balked by the unexpected American opposition at the two chief communications centers, St. Vith and Bastogne. The first was like a peninsula forcing the flood of armored invasion to take another course; it was eventually overrun, but not until after it had diverted the direction of the attack to the south of Liége. As for Bastogne, it was the island of resistance which held out, depriving the Nazis of essential routes, until American reinforcements could arrive in decisive strength.

Some of the defending units were outnumbered as much as six to one at the outset. They were at a further disadvantage because of German weapon superiority in several important respects. This knowledge would have been disillusioning to American citizens, long led to believe that their soldiers faced no such handicaps. Every large unit of the war's most headline-conscious army had its public relations officers, and Office of War Information writers added to the barrage of words. American typewriters could be heard at moments above the guns, but too much of the output was intended to dazzle or obscure rather than enlighten. Newspaper correspondents, who might have been more candid critics, found themselves between the devil of army censorship and the deep blue sea of army public relations.

At least it was no secret to American soldiers in the Ardennes that their Sherman tanks were as vulnerable as cardboard against the enemy's 67-ton King Tigers with seven-inch steel hides. Only the speedy M-26

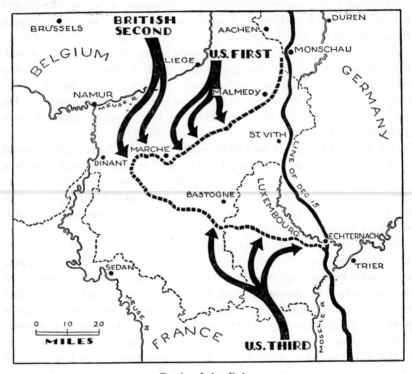

Battle of the Bulge

could cope with the monsters, and these U.S. tank destroyers were not yet available in sufficient numbers. The smokeless and flashless powder used in German ammunition gave the enemy another advantage, and the German machine pistol was the envy of American infantrymen. Much less excusable, from the viewpoint of ordnance research, was the superiority held throughout the war by the German 88-mm. gun, whose three functions had been revealed during the Spanish Civil War and lauded in American books published as early as 1942.

The American forces did have an ammunition advantage, however, in the new proximity, or VT (variable time), artillery fuse used for the first time in the battle of the Bulge. Consisting of a small, self-powered radio transmitter and receiver fitted into the nose of a shell, it enables the projectile to be exploded automatically upon arriving within effective distance of a target. The discharge of the gun sets the mechanism in operation. During the flight the transmitter broadcasts a continuous wave. The target itself sends back a reflection which operates on this wave to trip an electronic switch in the shell, thus shooting a current through the detonator to cause the explosion at ideal distance for effect.

Artillery alone held the enemy back at times in the critical St. Vith area as proximity shells destroyed German armor and transport on the narrow, winding roads. American troop reactions varied from sacrificial courage to panic, which is not surprising in view of the large proportion of men with too much or too little battle experience. There were enough stouthearted soldiers, at any rate, to stop the Germans at critical points in one of the greatest fights against material odds in American history.

Art frequently comes to the aid of fact in tales of military heroism. But the stark truth needs no adornment as a tribute to the men who held at Monschau, Echternach, St. Vith and Bastogne. Outnumbered and sometimes surrounded, these troops were never outfought. And it is due to their valor that Rundstedt failed in spite of driving more than 50 miles into the American lines.

The attempt to split the Allies politically failed when Montgomery was given command of Americans north of the salient. The geographical attempt failed because of Bradley's generalship in rushing reinforcements to imperiled areas, so that three new U.S. divisions were in the fight on the fourth day. General Patton's talents never shone more brightly than on December 20, when he withdrew units engaged on the Saar and speeded them to the Bastogne area. One company of Third Army tank destroyers that had been engaged east of the Saar in the morning of the 22nd opened fire on the enemy near Echternach that evening after completing a motor march of 69 miles.

A change in weather brought the turning point on the 23rd, when Allied tactical air power turned the crowded salient into a graveyard of German transport. U.S. guns were soon able to interdict supply roads, compelling the Germans to change their plans and make Dinant the first objective instead of Liége. Hitler insisted on continuing the operation, in spite of Rundstedt's warnings, though it was obvious on Christmas Day that he was beaten. At that time he was outnumbered by the one airborne, four armored, and nine infantry divisions in the U.S. First Army zone. The Führer would not admit defeat until January 16, 1945, when it took all of Rundstedt's skill to pull his shattered units out of the salient. His losses were 120,000 killed, wounded and prisoners. American casualties amounted to 77,000, many of them incapacitated by the bitter cold.

Allied generals admitted that the battle of the Bulge had set back their offensive eight weeks, but the cost to the enemy was heavier. Germany had been stripped of reserves in her hour of need, and the nation's morale was beaten down to a realization of imminent disaster. Germans kept on fighting only because of a submissiveness that has so often betrayed them into making sacrifices for an unworthy cause.

THE END IN GERMANY

During the first days of 1945 Germany faced the peril of invasion from south and east as well as west. Warsaw and Budapest were her bulwarks against Russian winter offensives which could be expected hourly. Large German forces had been resisting in the encircled Hungarian capital for weeks, and a counterthrust in January resulted in another battle of the Bulge at the expense of Soviet armies which gave ground but kept their hold on the city. Then on Friday, the 12th, the Eastern Front flamed into activity as Zhukov's armies advanced behind drumfire bombardments from the west bank of the Vistula.

Gains of forty miles were made in two days. Warsaw, Lodz and Cracow fell during the first week to columns pushing across the snow-covered plains of Poland, while in East Prussia both Tilsit and symbolic Tannenberg had to be evacuated.

On November 6 Stalin had been able to announce to his people the restoration of the entire Soviet frontier along its 1,800-mile length. January 20 became an equally important date in Russian chronicles as the first forces crossed the frontier of Germany proper. Six armies numbering more than three million men were now driving forward on an 800-mile front. Far in the north Finland had been invaded to the border of Norway; and in the south the reduction of Budapest on February 13, after a siege of fifty days, cost the enemy 159,000 killed and captured, according to Russian figures. But no other event could compare with the news that Soviet columns had reached the Oder on the twenty-third day of their offensive, about 33 miles east of Berlin.

That same Sunday morning, February 4, Churchill, Roosevelt and

Stalin began an eight-day conference at Yalta in the Crimea. At their Teheran meeting the three Allied leaders had decided on the strategy of a co-ordinated invasion of Germany. Now with that result accomplished and the end in sight, they "agreed on common policies and plans for

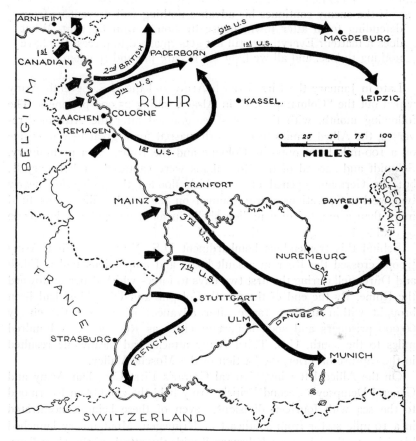

The Last Days of Germany

enforcing the unconditional surrender terms which we will impose upon Germany."

Only 300 miles separated the Russian and Anglo-American forces closing in on the Reich. This distance was annihilated by air power as British and U.S. planes dropped 17,000 tons of bombs on Nazi cities in a single February week. German radio exhortations made it evident that

Hitler had virtually been supplanted as dictator by Heinrich Himmler, who wielded the dreaded police power of the Gestapo. Goebbels, the propaganda minister, appealed to his countrymen for the "holy rage" of a scorched-earth resistance:

If the enemy continues his advance nothing will prevent us from defending town after town, house by house, ruin by ruin. What does it matter? Everything still left gets smashed to pieces. We have nothing to lose, and all we fight for is bare life and freedom.

Late in January the First French Army and the U.S. Seventh Army wiped out the "Colmar pocket" in Alsace, taking 25,000 prisoners. The following month, with their lines reorganized after the Ardennes reverses, the Allied armies to the north massed for a great new offensive on a 100-mile front opposite Cologne and the Ruhr. As a preliminary, Schmidt and several of the Roer dams were captured on February 8; but the Germans opened others which flooded the valley for nearly two weeks. Operations were resumed on the 22nd. Allied guns fired more than a quarter of a million shells in an hour, and nearly 10,000 tactical and strategic air sorties were flown before nightfall.

Behind this tremendous bombardment U.S. Ninth and First Army troops crossed the Roer in assault boats and amphibious tanks. Jülich and Düren fell during the first two days to forces which drove on toward the Rhine. By the end of the month Cologne and Düsseldorf had been brought within artillery range after advances which cost the enemy 66,000 prisoners and such important cities as Roermond. A hundred miles to the south, U.S. Third Army attacks had meanwhile resulted in the capture of Trier, the bastion of the Moselle Valley.

On the Allied left wing, General Crerar's First Canadian Army and General Dempsey's Second British Army held the zone from Roermond to the sea with fourteen divisions, seven of these being concentrated in a 10-mile sector from southeast of Nijmegen. Montgomery launched his drive to the Rhine on February 8 with the attack of the Canadians, who were gradually reinforced by fresh British divisions. Although they lost 1,100 prisoners the first day, the Germans fought back obstinately. They were aided by rains which turned the river valleys into bogs and compelled the Canadians and British to wade through knee-deep icy water. On February 13 a Canadian battalion reached the Rhine, but it took until the 28th before Montgomery had full control of the left bank in his zone.

By the end of the first week in March the Allies controlled most of the west bank from Holland to the Moselle. The ruins of Cologne were occupied on the 7th, and that same day brought one of those dramatic moments which too seldom enliven the chronicles of war. At 3:50 P.M. a platoon of an American armored division surprised Germans who planned at four o'clock to blow up the Ludendorff bridge at Remagen. Led by a lieutenant, the tankmen shot down a few guards, raced across the 1,200-foot structure, and cut the wires of demolition charges. Thus the span was captured only slightly damaged, so that Germany's historic water barrier proved less of a handicap than the Roer.

The enemy seemed too stunned for effective measures, and during the next 239 hours an endless column of American guns, tanks and troops poured across. On the tenth day the bridge collapsed from the effects of dive bombing, but the Allies were quick to take further advantage of their fabulous good fortune. South of Mainz, infantry of the U.S. Third Army made a daring crossing of the Rhine on March 22 which was soon enlarged into a bridgehead 15 miles wide. On the third day Patton's armor broke through to a depth of 27 miles after seizing an undamaged bridge over the Main, and the fall of Coblenz was announced on the 27th.

At the northern end of the line both the British Second Army and the U.S. Ninth Army established bridgeheads on March 24 with the aid of airborne assaults. Three days later the U.S. Seventh Army and the French First Army were over the river; and the Nazis could only withdraw all remaining units from the west bank as Rundstedt was replaced by Kesselring.

During the critical week of the Rhine crossings 21,430 bomber assaults and 29,981 fighter sorties were made by U.S. aircraft alone. By the last day of March eight Allied armies, comprising 1,250,000 men, faced 60 thinned enemy divisions on the east bank. The Germans, anticipating a major thrust in the Ruhr, massed most of their strength in the industrial area. This decision proved to be one of their most fatal errors of the war, for Eisenhower and Bradley outgeneraled them by sweeping to either side.

The Remagen bridgehead burgeoned into another St. Lô when U.S. First Army columns turned southeast instead of making the expected northward moves. Reaching the superhighway, Hodges' armored forces sped 40 miles a day as they swung in a circle to the north and west. On April 1, when they met U.S. Ninth Army units near Paderborn, the Germans in the Ruhr had been completely surprised and encircled.

More than 300,000 prisoners were bagged in this pocket during the next two weeks by victors who left behind containing troops and raced on into the heart of Germany.

The battle of the Ruhr put an end to effective enemy resistance. The First and Ninth armies pressed on toward Leipzig and Hanover at the rate of 20 to 30 miles a day. In the south the Third Army headed for the Danube Valley; the U.S. Seventh drove toward Munich and the British Second advanced on Bremen, while the Canadian First cleaned up the coastal areas on the left wing.

President Roosevelt died at the height of a pursuit limited chiefly by problems of transport and supply. Germany was being cut to pieces hourly by forces which met resolute opposition at only a few points. Vienna fell to the Russians on the 13th, and five days later the U.S. Third Army crossed the border of Czechoslovakia. An even greater climax came on the 25th as American and Soviet advance forces made contact at Torgau, where Frederick the Great won his last victory. That same afternoon Zhukov's columns completed their encirclement of Berlin, and desperate fighting began in the streets and subways.

The downfall of any powerful nation is a tragic spectacle, but few observers were moved to pity for Germany. Advancing armies had discovered concentration camps in which civilians were stripped naked, herded into execution chambers and cremated in specially built furnaces. The garments of these "processed" men, women and children were sorted in warehouses; their teeth were extracted for gold fillings, and their ashes went to fertilize German fields.

Such horrors had been deliberately planned to carry out a national policy aiming at the extermination of whole populations. At least ten million Europeans, on a basis of postwar estimates, are believed to have perished as the victims of torture, starvation or wholesale slaughter. German scientists and physicians were among the executioners, and neither statesmen nor army officers can be absolved from some degree of acquiescence.

The world's long nightmare ended first in Italy. The Allies crossed the Po to capture Genoa on April 27th, and both Venice and Milan fell two days later. In Milan the victors encountered the riddled corpse of Mussolini, who had been shot by Italian patriots. German resistance collapsed with startling suddenness at the end of the month, anticipating the official capitulation of May 2.

On that date the Russians announced the fall of Berlin. Goebbels, Himmler and Hitler were reported to have committed suicide; and the masses which had once deified the Führer were outspoken in reviling him—not because of his crimes against humanity, but because he lost the war.

No such chaos had been seen in Europe since the downfall of France. All the roads of the Reich were choked with homeless civilians, deserting soldiers and freed foreign slave laborers. Whole Nazi armies capitulated with their weapons intact during the first week of May, and on the 6th a national radio proclamation admonished any remaining forces to lay down their arms.

The final anticlimactic scene was enacted at 2:41 the next morning in a brick schoolhouse at Reims. General Gustav Jodl signed the articles of unconditional surrender for Germany, and peace came to Europe after five years, eight months and six days of the most destructive conflict in history.

The End in Japan

The rest of the world might pause to celebrate the boon, but the English-speaking peoples had another great war on their hands. American air forces began moving immediately from Europe to the Pacific, and Churchill promised the might of Britain.

Germany had been forced to depend largely on synthetics after conquering the productive capacity of a highly industrialized continent. Japan's problem was exactly the reverse. After conquering endless supplies of raw materials, Japan could depend only on the limited manufacturing potential of the home islands.

If the two Axis Powers had managed to pool such resources—if they had been true political and geographical instead of unilateral partners—the difficulties of their enemies might have been multiplied. But in the strategic sphere the Allies were able to wage a war on interior lines, with the bombing plane serving as the most effective weapon against Germany, and the submarine as well as the bombing plane against Japan.

After Guadalcanal, when the Anglo-American forces passed to the offensive, the strategy of conquering Japan resolved itself into four co-ordinated steps: (1) destroying enemy sea and air power; (2) cutting the home islands off from the raw materials of a conquered empire; (3) blasting the nation's manufacturing potential; (4) actual invasion as a last resort.

In order to accomplish the first two it was necessary to conquer the steppingstones as represented by Japanese-held islands. New Guinea on the left and the Gilberts and Marshalls on the right marked the two far-flung wings of the American advance.

The third stage began with the seizure of Saipan, Guam and Tinian, which provided air bases within practical bombing distance. During the autumn and winter months of 1944 the fleets of B-29 raiders covered the 1,500 miles to their targets with ever-increasing frequency and effectiveness. On November 24 Tokyo had its first attack by land-based planes, and after that date no industrial city in the island empire could hope for security.

By the early weeks of 1945 carrier strikes on the home islands were supplementing the efforts of the Superfortresses. Twice Admiral Mitscher's Task Force 58 steamed boldly to points within range of enemy fighters before sending out swarms of bombers to attack Japanese factories, railways and airfields.

There remained one persistent handicap to the raids of land-based bombers. The attackers need an air base on the route from the Marianas to Japan which could provide refueling facilities, fighter escort and photographic reconnaissance. The tiny Japanese island of Iwo Jima, preying on the Superfortresses with its interceptors, was just such a prize. Almost exactly midway between Saipan and Tokyo, it offered enough strategic advantages to be deemed worth a heavy tactical price.

From the middle of January onward, anyone could have deduced that this enemy possession had been marked for invasion. Day after day, at the sacrifice of surprise, carrier planes, warships or land-based bombers "softened up" an area measuring only 5 by 2¾ miles at its greatest extent. Then two divisions of U.S. Marines (soon increased to four) poured ashore on February 19 to begin one of the bloodiest struggles in their nation's history, comparing with Gettysburg in its casualties.

Naval gunfire and air support were all that could have been asked. But Iwo Jima's confines gave no scope for anything except frontal attacks against buried enemy blockhouses with concrete walls four feet thick. From a tactical point of view, the fight could have been likened to a death struggle between antagonists locked in a cloak closet. By the end of the first week 40,000 Americans and 20,000 Japanese were contending day and night in an area of less than 15 square miles, so that the explosions often shrouded the whole island in smoke, ashes and dust. The ordeal went on with scarcely a pause until March 16, when the last of the defenders were slain at a total cost of 4,189 American killed, 15,308 wounded and 441 missing.

The sacrifices made by the marines saved thousands of lives during the next six months. As a halfway base, Iwo Jima became a haven for crews of crippled B-29's unable to complete the flight to the Marianas. Fighter escort and photographic reconnaissance so added to the effects of strategic bombing that the war was undoubtedly shortened.

New carrier strikes pointed to the next bold step in strategy. On March 26 preliminary landings were made on the small Kerama Islands only a few miles from Okinawa, the largest of the Ryukyu chain trailing southward from Japan proper. And on April 1—the Easter Sunday morning of German encirclement in the Ruhr—the U.S. Tenth Army of Lieutenant General Simon Bolivar Buckner, Jr., landed on Okinawa itself, putting ashore 100,000 soldiers and marines from a fleet of 1,400 warships and transports.

This attempt was the most ambitious project in the Pacific since Luzon. Sixty miles long, and two to twenty miles in width, Okinawa lay only 370 miles from Kyushu, the southernmost Japanese main island, and about the same distance north of Formosa. Possession of such an advanced base would not only provide airfields within fighter range of Japan, but also a springboard for invasion.

The first stages were alarmingly easy. The Japanese put up little resistance for forty-eight hours. Okinawa was cut squarely in two before April 5 by forces which overran 80 square miles, or about one-fifth of the entire area. Then, as at Leyte, opposition stiffened abruptly. Never before in Pacific operations had the Americans been met with such masses of artillery. Well-hidden and -aimed enemy guns up to medium calibers supported infantry taking cover in caves and tombs, and by the second week the invaders were making slow progress.

A recent Allied invention had solved the most ancient of artillery problems, the disturbing force of recoil. By means of a compensating blast to the rear, a 57-mm. cannon formerly weighing 3,000 pounds could be carried and fired by two men. Even a "75" needed a tripod no heavier than a machine-gun mount for a range of four miles, though the rearward flash remained a drawback.

Another American innovation went back to Biblical times for its inspiration—steel catapults which hurled drums of fire into Japanese caves. New infantry flame throwers and flame-throwing tanks shot jets of such white-hot intensity that foemen were turned into ghastly living torches. White phosphorous artillery shells exploded to splash the enemy with living flame that could not readily be extinguished; and U.S. aircraft used new incendiary bombs containing a compound known as "napalm"—a powder mixed with gasoline to form a searing jelly. So intense were the flames that they snuffed out all oxygen in the immediate vicinity, and many of the casualties died of heat and suffocation rather than burns.

The VT, or proximity, artillery fuse saved thousands of American lives on Okinawa when the enemy expanded the *kamikaze* tactics first tried in the Philippines. Flying short-range planes with a ton of explosive in the warhead, Japanese pilots sacrificed their own lives to crash-dive into a target. United States naval releases tried to minimize the effects, but the invaders of Okinawa realized that the *kamikaze* threat held serious potentialities. Antiaircraft fire might bring down most of the attackers, but it needed only a single crash on the flight deck to turn a carrier into an inferno of exploding gasoline and bombs.

On April 7 Japan's largest battleship made what might be described as a suicide raid on U.S. warships off Okinawa. Accompanied by two light cruisers and nine destroyers, the 45,000-ton *Yamato* failed to surprise her intended victims, and carrier planes of Task Force 58 sent the flaming hull to the bottom. Both cruisers and three of the destroyers also were sunk.

Japanese *kamikaze* planes were more effective. During the Okinawa invasion alone the U.S. Navy suffered one-seventh of its personnel losses for the entire war—4,907 killed and missing, plus 4,824 wounded. In ship losses, with 30 sunk and 223 damaged, the campaign proved to be the most costly single effort of naval history up to this date.

The war ended in Europe, and still the Okinawa fighting dragged on week after week as the invaders drove the foe into the southern end of the island. American generalship was more sharply criticized here than in any other Pacific campaign, but the tactical difficulties were formidable. Strong enemy forces had imposed a warfare of extermination in an area too cramped for manoeuvre, and only steady slugging could prevail.

Not until June 21, after General Buckner met a soldier's death, could complete occupation be claimed. The enemy had lost 98,564 killed and 4,500 prisoners in the 82-day campaign. American casualties of 6,990 killed or missing and 29,598 wounded were less severe in proportion to total numbers than those suffered in the Saipan, Peleliu and Iwo Jima operations.

Only a few days later, on July 5, MacArthur announced that "the entire Philippine Islands are now liberated and the Philippine campaigns can be regarded as virtually closed." Reversing the usual ratio, only 17 U. S. divisions had all but annihilated 23 enemy divisions in mountain and jungle country favoring the defense. The able American general, whose statistics seldom erred on the side of understatement, estimated the total Japanese losses at 409,261 as compared to American casualties of 11,921 killed, 401 missing and 42,569 wounded.

Ancient China, after ninety-five months of invasion, turned on the foe in June with an offensive which regained much of the ground lost during the preceding year. Plodding forward inexorably, Chiang Kai-shek's soldiers recaptured Luchow to prove that many past defeats had been due to logistical poverty. Now with the Hump Route and the Stilwell Road providing almost adequate supplies, one army advanced into Indo-China on a 100-mile front as another pushed to within 150 miles of Shanghai. In spite of these gains, the specter of civil war between Chinese Nationalists and Communists grew ever nearer.

The Japanese had already lost nearly all Burma after the fall of Mandalay and the central region on March 20. British forces pressed on to occupy Rangoon on May 3 as the beaten army retreated for a last-ditch stand in Thailand and Malaysia. Australian troops were meanwhile invading Borneo to recapture oil fields which had been lost to the Allies since 1942.

Such outlying resources were of little further use to a foe now blockaded at home. After Okinawa the American sea and air force drew an ever-tightening noose around the Japanese main islands, gradually strangling an enemy who found it difficult to maintain communications even with Formosa and China. American submarines operated in the Sea of Japan and American carrier or land-based planes preyed on all manner of craft from freighters down to junks and fishing boats.

Strategic bombing mounted in fury. During July, at a cost of 11 planes, 40,000 tons of explosives or incendiaries were dropped on Tokyo, Kobe, Osaka, Nagoya and 35 other manufacturing cities. More than 150 square miles of Japan's war industries were destroyed as new low-level tactics cut losses to less than 1 per cent. Bomb loads had been increased to an average of 7.5 tons per plane, with as many as 500 Superfortresses taking part in a mission.

Postwar analysts agreed, however, that the submarine was the weapon that had done most to conquer Japan. Americans had become so accustomed to a defensive attitude that they scarcely realized how daring and effective their own underseas raiders were. "Dud" torpedoes had been a handicap during the early months of the war; but once the defects were remedied, the blows to Japanese transportation of raw materials reduced the island empire to sore straits by the early months of 1945.

Carrier strikes on Japanese cities had become an old story, so that the enemy's crippled warships were no longer safe in any port. Then on July 14 a once-formidable sea power knew the final humiliation when Admiral Halsey's big guns pounded a steel plant on Honshu, only 275 miles from Tokyo. Continuing down the east coast, where they were joined by British units, the battleships of the Third Fleet poured shells into coastal installations of Cape Nojima, at the very mouth of Tokyo Bay.

The lack of resistance made it plain that U.S. sea and air forces had accomplished all strategic aims except actual invasion. This last measure, too, had been planned in detail. Already MacArthur and Nimitz were beginning to mass troops, planes and warships in Okinawan and Philippine bases for a preliminary operation known as OLYMPIC—an invasion of Kyushu, the southernmost Japanese island, by the Sixth U.S. Army in the autumn of 1945. After that objective had been isolated, the final blow was to be struck in the spring of 1946 with Operation CORONET— an invasion of Honshu and envelopment of the Tokyo-Yokohama district by the Eighth and Tenth armies with the First in reserve.

There was no doubt of eventual success, but it could also be anticipated that casualties would be heavy. The losses inflicted by *kamikaze* tactics at Okinawa had been serious enough, and the enemy still held in reserve an estimated 8,000 planes and 2,000,000 first-line troops for a suicidal defense of the homeland. But even as American generals and admirals planned for invasion, the nation's secret army of scientific researchers made such a step unnecessary. In the early morning hours of July 16 an isolated area of the New Mexico desert suddenly became the most decisive front of the war. For a few seconds the lives of thousands hung in the balance; then a single explosion changed the course of tactical history, as was revealed three weeks later by President Truman's announcement of August 6:

> Sixteen hours ago an American airplane dropped one bomb on Hiroshima, an important Japanese army base. That bomb had more power than 20,000 tons of TNT. . . . It is an atomic bomb. It is a harnessing of the basic power of the universe. . . . What has been done is the greatest achievement of organized science in history.

So tremendous was the impact of this news that the war itself seemed minor in comparison. Atomic research for Allied military purposes began in 1941 when American, British and Canadian scientists pooled their knowledge at the request of Roosevelt and Churchill. Three small cities were built in the United States to furnish plants and laboratories, and $2 billion went into experiments conducted by 65,000 scientists and technicians. The best-kept secret of the war, its progress had gone far enough in the summer of 1945 to justify a test made by a group of researchers with a bomb mounted in a steel tower. This structure was completely vaporized by an explosion which sent a pillar of flame and cloud 40,000 feet into the night sky, lighting the desert with a blinding flash seen at Albuquerque, 120 miles away.

The effects of the first military use were so awesome that no American could exult. For hours on August 6 Hiroshima was hidden by a gigantic pall of smoke and dust which balked reconnaissance planes. Then aerial photographs revealed that an estimated 60 per cent of the built-up area had been destroyed, and Japanese reports placed the casualties at nearly a third of the city's 344,000 inhabitants.

At last the dream of the ages had come true—a secret weapon powerful enough to end a war at a stroke. Yet the realization was more like a nightmare, for after that fateful Monday everything seemed unreal. Even time lost its meaning as events rushed toward a climax with a velocity which left observers stunned. On Wednesday the Soviet Union declared war on Japan; on Thursday a second atomic bomb left a ghastly crater in the seaport city of Nagasaki; and on Friday, only ninety-two hours after the blast at Hiroshima, the Japanese Empire sued for peace.

Several tense days passed as radio messages were exchanged between Tokyo and Washington. Then on August 14—three years, eight months and one week after Pearl Harbor—the fighting ended in the Pacific.

This rapid sequence gave the impression that the atomic bomb alone had been the cause of Japanese capitulation. Actually, as postwar revelations proved, Emperor Hirohito and his more moderate advisers had admitted defeat in July. The new weapon merely hastened the submission of a nation beaten to its knees by strategic bombing, amphibious attacks, losses to submarines, and the destruction of sea and air power.

The final victory of the United Nations was confirmed on the deck of the U.S. battleship *Missouri* in Tokyo Bay. With General MacArthur presiding, the Japanese representatives signed the terms of unconditional surrender at nine o'clock on the morning of September 2, 1945. Radio reports of the brief ceremony were heard in the United States and Europe on September 1, the sixth anniversary of the invasion of Poland and the seventy-fifth anniversary of the surrender of Napoleon III at Sedan.

VIII

THE SEQUEL IN KOREA

Organizations created to fight the last war better are not going to win the next.

—LIEUTENANT GENERAL JAMES M. GAVIN

ONCE again the world faced the fact, which every war-weary generation must face anew, that peace is not a mantle which can shelter its wearers from strife. War is usually the symptom of man's failure to make the most of his opportunities in time of peace, and the basic causes are not always cured by a resort to arms. They are more often neglected during the emergency, only to reappear, complicated by new problems, during a convalescence known as the "period of postwar disillusionment."

The monetary cost of the Allied victory reached a figure beyond the comprehension of anyone except an international financier. Britain was reduced to a debtor nation, and four years of invasion had left France exhausted, with many of her cities and ports in ruins.

The United Nations, accustomed to vigorous leadership during the struggle, were again without inspiring guidance. Roosevelt had died, his great energies burned out by the effort to win the war. Churchill had been beaten at the polls by British voters who still adored him for his magnificent contributions during the crisis. Stalin had returned to power politics after the defeat of Germany, so that eastern Europe became the scene of one Soviet *fait accompli* after another.

The English-speaking peoples took no joy in finding themselves the most powerful military force on earth in the autumn of 1945. Comprising a small fraction of the globe's inhabitants, they had built up armies, navies and air fleets more mighty than all the others. Had they been obsessed with a lust for conquest it is a fair speculation that they possessed the means.

Far from having any such ambition, both Britain and the United States were uneasy under the new burden of responsibility. The awful secret of Hiroshima weighed heavily, for the public did not need to be reminded that today's military asset might become tomorrow's liability. Any citizen able to add two and two could perceive that the atomic bomb, plus jet and rocket propulsion, added up to future long-distance missiles which could conceivably conquer a strong nation in a few hours.

It would be necessary to go back to the year 1249 to find a comparable turning point in the history of war. But even the introduction of gunpowder does not offer a perfect analogy, since the first firearms were little more deadly than weapons dating back to Biblical times. Nor did gunpowder have a rapid evolution, considering that the TNT of a modern age is only about twice as powerful as the explosives of the Middle Ages.

Yet in a single August day the world of 1945 had to adjust itself to a new destructive force more than twelve thousand times as powerful as any improvement on TNT.

It is small wonder that the thought of ensuing months showed evidences of panic. Statesmen, educators, clergymen and soldiers of the English-speaking nations gave out gloomy statements; and the scientists who had created the new weapon seemed equally bewildered.

Among these apprehensive voices, no modern Richelieu was heard, no Wolsey, not even a Mazarin. For the political leadership of the new Atomic Age had not perceptibly advanced beyond the centuries when men depended solely on the horse for horsepower. That fact, more than any other, might have been interpreted as the real peril of the future— the slow progress made in humanitarian directions as compared to gains in mechanical and scientific respects.

Public expressions of anxiety in Britain and the United States were reminiscent of the wave of fear which followed the bombing of Barcelona in March, 1938. Then, too, intellectual leaders of both nations viewed the future with forebodings. Soldiers had little hope to offer. Psychologists predicted that whole populations would be driven mad. Clergymen, pacifists, bankers and educators agreed that "defenseless" flesh and blood could never endure new horrors without a precedent in past warfare.

After eight months of such misgivings, Chamberlain and Daladier went to Munich with an unmistakable mandate from the peoples of their nations. On their return to London and Paris the two statesmen were hailed as world benefactors, for the betrayal of Czechoslovakia seemed a cheap price to pay for deliverance.

Britons and Frenchmen were humiliated to learn after the war that Hitler's Third Reich was in more actual danger at the time of the Munich Pact than the nations he had hoodwinked. On a basis of comparative military strength, France and Czechoslovakia alone had the material means to overcome him if his bluff had been called.

Fear of strategic bombing, in short, drove the democratic nations to the point of allowing Germany enough time for an infinitely more terrible and costly war. When at last the ordeal had to be met, many of these alarms proved distorted. Cities were not "defenseless" with such aids as radar, interceptor planes and antiaircraft fire. During the crisis of 1940, moreover, Britons discovered the most unassailable defense ever known against any weapon—the stout hearts of a resolute and united nation.

No lesson of World War II had more to offer the Atomic Age than this sequence of related events. Finally, it could not be forgotten that the weapon so dreaded by the democratic nations in 1938 became the very sword of vengeance which did so much to defeat Germany and Japan in 1945.

SOVIET POSTWAR AGGRESSIONS

After the war the victors set the precedent of trying German and Japanese war leaders, both civilian and military, on charges of personal guilt. These proceedings were an abrupt departure from the past, and some doubt arose in the Allied nations as to their justification. It was argued that the accused were not properly represented in court, and that the accusers were actually punishing defeat. Nevertheless, executions of enemy war criminals took place, and men convicted of lesser crimes were sent to prison. The best-known figure of them all cheated the gallows, however, when Hermann Goering swallowed poison in his cell at Nuremberg.

Americans and Britons soon learned to their sorrow that they had exchanged one totalitarian enemy for another. Admittedly, they could not have defeated Germany without the aid of the Soviet Union, which had made greater sacrifices. Nor could the Communists have survived without the arms delivered to their back door by democratic allies. But a common cause did not, as it was hoped, make for friendly peacetime relations.

The cold ruthlessness of Soviet power politics was demonstrated before the war ended. After encouraging Warsaw underground forces to revolt in August, 1944, the Russians withheld promised aid while German occupation troops put down the uprising with a frightful slaughter. Red Army communiqués reported meanwhile that the Soviet advance had been halted by German defenders of the city. This was Stalin's way of ridding himself of Polish patriots who would doubtless have opposed his postwar plans for their country.

At the Yalta Conference (February, 1945) the last of the "Big Three" meetings attended by Roosevelt, the Soviet dictator put a price on Communist military aid in the Far East. The return of southern Sakhalin and a lease of the Port Arthur area were promised him to redress the "wrongs" of 1905. Stalin, for his part, consented to sign a treaty of friendship with Nationalist China which he had no intention of honoring.

Moscow waited six months to declare war on an already vanquished Japan. During the final six days of a conflict previously fought to a finish by the United States, the Red Army reaped a prodigious harvest of loot in Manchuria at a cost of negligible casualties.

Soviet armies accepted the surrender of 148 Japanese generals and nearly 600,000 troops. These unfortunates were sent to Siberia to endure as much as ten years of forced labor. Conversion to Communism was often made the price of release, so that the prisoners would return to form a troublesome political faction in their homeland.

Manchuria was stripped of a billion dollars' worth of heavy machinery, turbines and rolling stock. The value of Japanese forced labor during the next ten years was estimated at a like sum. Yet the Russians were not satisfied, and only General MacArthur's firmness kept them from sharing in the occupation of Japan.

Korea was divided into roughly equal halves, with the 38th parallel as a boundary line, for purposes of Russian and American occupation. Immediately the Russians in the northern zone began the organization of a Communist puppet nation armed and trained for aggression.

Four administrative zones, American, British, French and Russian, were set up in both Germany and Austria. Berlin was sliced into four sectors on a similar basis.

At the war's end the democratic nations had been confronted with a gigantic *fait accompli* when the Red Army remained in control of the area it had "liberated" during its westward drive. Eight nations—Albania, Bulgaria, Czechoslovakia, Finland, Hungary, Poland, Rumania, and Yugoslavia—were thus created into a cushion of Communist-dominated satellite and buffer states extending from the Arctic Ocean to the Adriatic and Black Seas. Less than a year after the defeat of Germany, Winston Churchill referred in an address of March 5, 1946, to the "Iron Curtain" which shut off the light from these nations in the shadow of the hammer and sickle.

A Declaration of Cold War

Americans of all political beliefs were aroused to a sense of danger. And on March 12, 1947, President Truman appeared before Congress with a declaration of cold war on totalitarian aggression in these words:

> One of the primary objects of the foreign policy of the United States is the creation of conditions in which we and other nations will be able to work out a way of life free from coercion. . . . We shall not realize our objectives, however, unless we are willing to help free peoples to maintain their free institutions and their national integrity against aggressive movements that seek to impose upon them totalitarian regimes. This is no more than a recognition that totalitarian regimes imposed upon free peoples, by direct or indirect aggression, undermine the foundations of international peace and hence the security of the United States.

The President asked Congress to appropriate $400,000,000 for economic and military aid to Greece and Turkey, both of them threatened with Communist infiltration. He pointedly reminded the legislators that this ounce of prevention, expensive as it might seem, was only "one-tenth of one per cent" of the $341 billion spent by the United States in World War II as a cure for totalitarianism.

Truman was criticized for bypassing the United Nations, the new world forum organized early in 1946 after adopting the name of the Axis opponents in World War II. Temporary quarters were found in New York, where a magnificent glass-brick building was being erected as a permanent home. The hopes placed in this "parliament of man" were dimmed by the abuse of the veto in the Security Council by Soviet representatives for the purpose of silencing discussion and obstructing procedures. Nevertheless, the United Nations was to recover from its growing pains and become an influence for peace.

Something more potent than discussion was needed in 1947, however, to help devastated Europe recover from the postwar economic ills which threatened to plunge France and Italy into Communism. The remedy was suggested by Secretary of State George C. Marshall, former

U.S. Army chief-of-staff, in an address of June 5, 1947, at Harvard University. He proposed that the war-blasted nations themselves agree on a program of self-help and mutual aid to be financed "so far as may be practicable" by the United States.

The Marshall Plan, as it soon came to be known, had its beginnings in invitations to 24 nations to attend a conference in Paris. As was expected, the eight Communist-dominated countries of eastern Europe declined with suspicious unanimity. Notes of acceptance were received from Austria, Belgium, Britain, Denmark, Eire, France, Greece, Iceland, Italy, Luxembourg, the Netherlands, Norway, Portugal, Sweden, Switzerland and Turkey.

Naturally, there was a good deal of opposition within the United States to this "share-the-American-wealth plan." It was argued that "Uncle Santa Claus" had already poured more than $12 billion into Europe since June, 1945, in the form of loans or grants. Despite these strictures, Congress took the calculated risk and passed a Marshall Plan appropriation of $6,098 million for grants of the first year.

The news of this fund could only have been galling to devastated nations under the Russian heel, for the Soviet Union had done little or nothing to aid their recovery. On June 24, 1948, Stalin retaliated by closing Berlin to non-Russian traffic. This meant that the forces of the three Western Powers must pull out unless they could find some means of supplying themselves and the German people in their sectors.

They could and did. Their transport planes put into effect the Berlin airlift, dubbed "Operation VITTLES." Garrison troops and 2,500,000 civilians were supplied with 2,343,310 tons of food and coal over an eighteen-month period by airmen who also organized a counterblockade of the Russian zone.

This tremendous achievement resulted in a great moral victory for the Western nations. Only a show of armed force could have impressed the Soviet Union, and they had given a convincing demonstration of air power.

American dollars, as the front-line troops of the cold war, had meanwhile won a noteworthy victory in Italy. Choosing between Communism and the benefits of the Marshall Plan, now known as the European Relief Program (ERP), the Italian people voted overwhelmingly against Communism. It was an unexpected setback for Moscow. And though American opponents of ERP referred to it as "Operation RAT-HOLE," it proved during its first three years to have restored an encouraging degree of economic health to western Europe.

Several of the recipient nations announced as early as 1950 that their industrial output exceeded that of 1938, the last year of peace prior to World War II. They were the exceptions, however, and in 1951 the Mutual Security Agency (MSA), under W. Averell Harriman, dispensed economic and military aid to the tune of $7,428 million.

THE NORTH ATLANTIC TREATY ALLIANCE

A new spirit of solidarity drew together the nations of western Europe. Perhaps the most impressive result was the fifty-year defensive pact signed at Brussels on March 17, 1949, by Britain, France, Belgium, the Netherlands and Luxembourg.

The following month, at American invitation, twelve nations met in Washington to sign the North Atlantic Treaty after a respectful bow to the United Nations. The United States, Canada, Britain, France, Italy, Belgium, the Netherlands, Luxembourg, Norway, Denmark, Iceland and Portugal agreed that an attack by an aggressor on one would be regarded as an attack on all. Action would be taken by the signatories, either individually or in concert, to the extent deemed necessary, including "armed force."

Americans of 1950 could look back with pride at the progress made by their country during the preceding five years at the unfamiliar and distasteful task of fighting a cold war. The revolution wrought in American foreign policy has been summed up by Thomas A. Bailey in his *Diplomatic History of the United States*:

> The United States had reversed its Monroe Doctrine in relation to Greece by accepting the Truman Doctrine. It had forsaken nonintervention by promoting the Marshall Plan. It had tossed overboard the no-alliance tradition by signing the Atlantic Pact. It had adopted peacetime conscription and a wartime military budget. It had embarked upon all such departures with extreme reluctance but basically in response to the instinct of self-preservation. The new American policies—all defensive in their outlook—were actually authored more by the men in the Kremlin than by the men in Washington. The American people had hoped for a peaceful world after World War II, but the aggressions of the Soviets simply would not permit them to drop their guard.

It had not been an easy road to travel for Americans paying the highest taxes in the nation's history. Many of them recalled bitterly, without taking account of extenuating circumstances, that they were again financing nations which had repudiated World War I debts. Recipients of American grants, far from showing appreciation, often grumbled because the amounts were not large enough. Every wall in Europe seemed to be scribbled with the familiar taunt, "Yankee, go home!" and not all the scribblers were Communists. In short, it may have been more blessed to give than receive during these years, but it took a great deal of Christian forbearance.

On the other hand, Americans could not forget that most of the recipient nations of western Europe had been ravaged not only by Nazi invasion but also by the bombings and artillery fire of Allied counteroffensives. When Congress voted billions to these nations, the legislators were acting in obedience to a mandate from a great majority of the American people.

Among the other American "firsts" of the cold war, the North Atlantic Treaty was the first military alliance ever concluded by the United States in time of peace. It had a salutary effect on the Soviet Union, which lifted the Berlin blockade on condition that the "Big Four" ministers meet at Paris. Nothing came of this conference (May 23 to June 20, 1949) except the yielding of the U.S.S.R. with respect to drafting a treaty of peace with Austria.

If Stalin had hoped by these concessions to block ratification of the North Atlantic Alliance, he was doomed to disappointment. Despite the opposition of an isolationist bloc, Congress approved the pact by large majorities. President Truman's request for $1.45 billion with which to arm the new allies met with more resistance, but after cuts and restorations both Houses passed the measure in September, 1949.

General Dwight D. Eisenhower was "drafted" from his duties as president of Columbia University in 1950 and made commander-in-chief of NATO (the North Atlantic Treaty Organization). As a concession to American isolationists, the sending of U.S. troops to Europe was limited to four divisions. Two more nations joined the following year when Greece and Turkey were admitted.

Infusions of American capital had had such a stimulating effect that several NATO nations announced that they needed no more economic aid. There was no relief for American taxpayers, however, since military appropriations swelled as rapidly as economic grants shrank.

By 1950 the Western nations under the leadership of the United States had a good claim to an incomplete victory in the first five years of the cold war. But it had not been gained without reverses on some fronts. The most costly setback took place in China, where the Communists finally prevailed over the Nationalists in spite of American aid. The struggle for mastery had been going on intermittently since the

1930's. In 1942, while fighting Japanese invaders, Chiang Kai-shek had said:

> You think it is important that I have kept the Japanese from expanding. . . . I tell you it is more important that I have kept the Communists from spreading. The Japanese are a disease of the skin; the Communists are a disease of the heart.

The Nationalist defeat was the more tragic because it was largely the consequence of inept leadership. Washington authorized credits to Nationalist China of $2 billion from 1945 to 1948, and vast stores of U.S. arms and equipment were turned over to Chiang Kai-shek's forces.

Too much of the money, unfortunately, was misspent or found its way into private pockets. Most of the arms eventually fell into the hands of Mao Tse-tung's Communists when entire divisions of their opponents surrendered in the final campaigns without firing a shot. A firsthand report was made on November 16, 1948, by Major General David G. Barr, senior officer of the United States Military Advisory Group in China:

> No battle has been lost since my arrival due to lack of ammunition and equipment. Their [the Chinese Nationalists'] military debacles in my opinion can all be attributed to the world's worst leadership and many other morale-destroying factors that lead to a complete loss of the will to fight.

If that doughty warrior Chiang Kai-shek had been a better strategist, the result might have been different. But the Nationalists fought an unimaginative war of position. They clung to cities for their political rather than military value, while Mao Tse-tung made the destruction of opposing armies the primary aim of his strategy. The morale of his adversaries sank so low after three years of reverses that Dean Acheson, U.S. secretary of state, could comment, "The Nationalist armies did not have to be defeated; they disintegrated."

By the autumn of 1949 the Chinese mainland was lost to Chiang Kai-shek, who found a refuge with his remaining forces on Formosa. Thus had another Communist nation come into being and its population of five hundred million topped even Soviet Russia's human resources.

A greater moral blow was dealt at this time to Americans who had supposed that their country was the sole possessor of atomic weapons. This consolation was snatched away on September 23, 1949, when

President Truman announced that Russia had recently exploded an atomic bomb. Although the Soviet Union had been given information by British and American scientists who betrayed their trust, Russian researchers would soon have succeeded on their own. In fact, it was an added blow when the Western nations were confronted with the evidence that Soviet scientists had been much underrated.

Some long chances had already been taken in the cold war, and now the NATO nations must assume the calculated risk of a twentieth-century Armageddon—a war in which the adversaries would hurl atomic thunderbolts across the seas at each other until their largest cities were reduced to tombs for millions of slain. And just at this stage the United States suddenly found itself involved in a hot war when a supposed "police action" in Korea turned into the fourth largest military effort of American history.

The Challenge in Korea

On June 25, 1950, without a declaration of war, the armies of the Soviet puppet state known as the North Korean People's Republic crossed the 38th parallel to attack the Republic of Korea. The United Nations now faced the same dilemma that had confronted the League of Nations in 1931, when Japan invaded Manchuria. By its failure to take action the League wrought its own ruin, since it never recovered its lost prestige.

If the Communists had counted on a weak-kneed reaction in 1950, they were speedily disillusioned. On the very day of the Korean outbreak, the Security Council of the UN (with the Russian delegate absent) unanimously charged the Korean Reds with an unprovoked aggression and called for a cease-fire.

The United States had a strategic as well as political stake in developments. Communist control of the entire Korean peninsula would pose a threat to Japan, the great American base in the Far East. Hence on June 27, two days after the invasion began, President Truman ordered the U.S. Seventh Fleet and the Far East Air Force to resist the aggression. He also directed the Navy to defend the Chinese Nationalists on Formosa from attacks launched by Mao-Tse-tung's Reds.

That same day the Security Council called upon UN members for military assistance. The U.S. set the example on July 2, 1950, when Truman directed General MacArthur to send American occupation troops from Japan to the aid of the routed Republic of Korea (ROK) forces.

On the 4th the U.S. contingent saw its first action, and three days later the Security Council called for a unified command in Korea. General MacArthur's appointment as UN commander-in-chief was followed by the naming of Lieutenant General Walton H. Walker to head the Eighth U.S. Army.

Up to this point the firmness of the United Nations and the courageous steps taken by President Truman had won the respect and admiration of the Western world. Approval soon gave way to bewilderment in the United States as a consequence of the poor showing made by the first American troops in action. The explanation could be traced back to the postwar scramble of citizen-soldiers clamoring in 1945 to be discharged. Irresistible pressure was put on congressmen until the stampede to civilian life made it necessary to recruit men for occupation duty in Japan and Germany. By 1950 it hardly seemed possible that, only five years before, the United States had been represented by the mightiest armed host of its history. All the ground forces remaining in the Far East were four infantry divisions averaging 70 per cent of full strength. Most of their heavy arms had been "mothballed" and the troops had received little combat training.

The Korean Red Army numbered about 100,000 men, trained and equipped by the Russians. They made short work of a ROK army that was hardly more than a lightly armed constabulary. Seoul fell on the third day to six invading divisions led by a hundred Soviet T-34 tanks, and at the end of the first week ROK organized resistance had ceased to exist.

The United States entered the war with a battalion-size task force, flown from Japan, which was routed in its initial action. No better fortune attended the efforts of the next several American contingents, fighting against crushing material odds. As occupation troops, they were physically soft and morally unprepared for the shock of combat. Yet they were less to blame than the military system which placed them in such a predicament. Their largest artillery pieces, the 105s, were outranged by the enemy's 155-mm. howitzers. Their M-24 tanks could not cope with the enemy's heavier Soviet T-34s; nor could the American 2.36″ rocket launchers penetrate the steel hides of the enemy tanks.

It seemed incredible that a great industrial nation such as the United States could have let its ground forces deteriorate to this extent in five years. The fault lay not so much in neglect of military preparations as in a one-weapon defense policy. Ever since the day of Hiroshima the American public had been warned of the horrors of a surprise atomic attack which might wipe out great cities in an hour. These alarms were sounded even at a time when it was believed that potential enemies did not possess the atomic formula for catastrophe. Scientists, educators, military analysts, statesmen—the nation's leaders apparently felt that the public must be aroused to a sense of danger. So thoroughly did these alarmists do their work that the United States placed all its strategic eggs in one basket—preparations for an atomic war to be decided in the air by intercontinental bombers and guided missiles.

It was an expensive program, considering that the cost of an all-jet B-52 was $8,000,000, as compared to $600,000 for a B-29 in 1945. Billions of dollars went ultimately into the setting up of bases outside the country where radar installations would warn of an enemy sneak attack and U.S. interceptor aircraft would be the first line of defense.

The American public backed this one-weapon national defense policy by accepting the heaviest tax burden in the country's history. Defeat and disaster were the price paid in Korea by troops who had never been trained for a limited war against Far Eastern adversaries.

The only American successes of the first few weeks were won by the Navy and the Air Force, which destroyed all opposition in the air and on the sea. In the land operations General MacArthur had no choice but to trade space for time. Two skeleton U.S. infantry regiments had been flown from Japan by the middle of July, but they were capable only of delaying actions. During the next two weeks they fell back to a line stretching like a bent bow from Masan on the southern coast by way of Taegu to Pohang on the Japan Sea. This was the Pusan Perimeter, named for the supply port, and the Eighth Army dared not give up another inch of ground.

The first sea-borne reinforcements, an army division and a marine brigade, landed at Pusan on August 1 and 2, 1950. Meanwhile, the shattered ROK forces were being reorganized by their resolute old president, Syngman Rhee, and attached to the Eighth Army. General Walker now had a mobile reserve, and two sustained UN counterattacks in August gave proof that American weapons deficiencies were no longer a problem.

When prospects were darkest, General MacArthur looked forward confidently to ending the war at a stroke. He envisoned a combined operation in which X Corps—a unit of marines and army troops created expressly for this mission—would make an amphibious landing in the enemy's rear at the west coast port of Inchon. While this force drove inland to Seoul, the Eighth Army would attack northward from the Pusan Perimeter, and the meeting of the two UN columns would cut off decisive numbers of Korean Red troops.

The Joint Chiefs of Staff did not share MacArthur's faith, and only after a third request was he granted an amphibiously trained marine division with its own aircraft wing. He was equally persistent on August

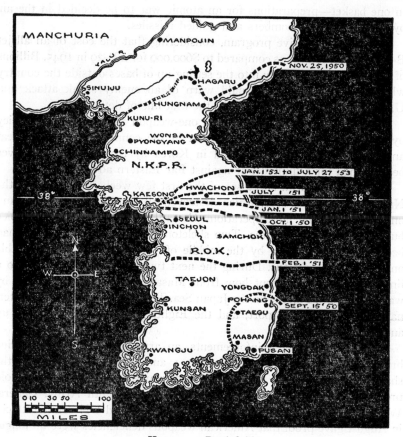

Korea as a Battlefield

23, 1950, at a briefing session in Tokyo's Dai Ichi building, when Navy and Marine Corps amphibious specialists warned him that an Inchon landing was fraught with perils. Mud shoals, winding channels and treacherous currents made navigation a hazard in the outer harbor. Wolmi-do, a fortified island, dominated the inner harbor, and its teeth must be extracted before attacking Inchon proper. Finally, scaling ladders would be needed for climbing the sea wall into the urban area, where two marine regiments had the task of fighting their way through the streets of an Asiatic seaport of 250,000 prewar population.

MacArthur listened courteously to the briefing officers but brushed all difficulties aside. "We shall land at Inchon," he said, "and I shall crush them!"

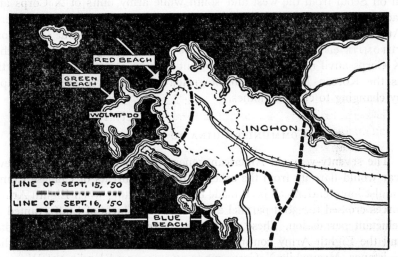

The Amphibious Landings at Inchon

His words were prophetic as well as dramatic. Navy and marine officers completed their planning in three weeks—the shortest planning period ever allotted to a major amphibious operation. Joint Task Force 7 made its way safely from Japan to Inchon's outer harbor after a narrow escape from a typhoon. While naval gunfire "softened up" the target area, the Navy and Marine Corps planes of Task Force 77 flew interdictory strikes.

A marine battalion hit GREEN Beach on the morning high tide of September 15, 1950, and took Wolmi-do with its shore batteries and causeway to the mainland. On the evening tide the two marine regiments of the landing force stormed ashore over the sea wall of RED Beach and the salt marshes of BLUE Beach. They gained control of the seaport before midnight, and meanwhile the dozers were unloading supplies from eight LSTs which had been grounded at dusk on the heels of the RED Beach landing force. It was the day's greatest calculated risk, for a single Korean Red mortar shell might have exploded among the drums of gasoline and created an inferno.

Inchon was fully secured the next day as the climax of a thrifty victory gained at an astonishingly low cost in casualties over opponents too stunned for effective resistance. Before the enemy could recover from his shock, the marines drove inland to seize Kimpo airfield, the largest in Korea. They crossed the broad Han in amphibian tractors and closed in on Seoul from the west and south while army units of X Corps attacked from the east. It took a week of hard fighting, with severe American losses, to overcome the reinforced defenders. But Operation CHROMITE ended successfully when the Eighth Army hammer met the X Corps anvil near Seoul. The ancient Korean capital fell on the 27th as the Korean Red Army disintegrated into fugitives seeking escape by changing to civilian clothes.

COMMUNIST CHINA TO THE RESCUE

The seventy-year-old American general had not foreseen that a new war would flare up from the ashes of the old. Threats of Chinese Communist intervention had been made by Mao Tse-tung when Eighth Army forces crossed the 38th parallel after the Joint Chiefs of Staff granted a reluctant permission. These mutterings were dismissed as propaganda, and the Eighth Army continued northward against weak and sporadic resistance. Meanwhile X Corps made an unopposed landing at Wonsan on the east coast after a sealift around the peninsula.

Even the first Chinese attacks were not interpreted as warnings. They took place on two occasions, in west and northeast Korea, and in each instance the attackers quickly withdrew. During the ensuing three November weeks, Mao Tse-tung's forces in Korea disappeared, as if swallowed up by the earth. As a feat in strategic legerdemain, it has few equals in history.

No sign of enemy movements alarmed the X Corps and Eighth Army columns advancing toward the river Yalu on both sides of the peninsula. Although intelligence reports estimated the CCF (Chinese Communist Forces) numbers as high as 150,000 along the northern frontier, it was believed that their mission was merely to guard the Yalu power plants. "Home by Christmas!" was the slogan on November 24, 1950, when General MacArthur launched the end-the-war offensive that he called a "massive compression envelopment."

This term seems optimistic in view of the fact that the two arms of the pincers, Eighth Army and X Corps, were separated by 80 miles of wildly mountainous terrain. On D-day, however, the UN columns advanced at will. Not until the night of November 25-26 was there any intimation of one of the greatest defeats ever suffered by American arms. Then the rout of a ROK corps on the right of the Eighth Army was the prelude to a CCF counteroffensive which sent the UN advance into reverse in both west and northeast Korea.

Chinese attacks nearly always took place at night and the tactics seldom varied. The weird notes of a shepherd's horn gave the signal, and gnomelike little men in padded cotton uniforms seemed to rise out of the very earth on an opponent's flanks. Although they had no supporting armor or aircraft and few artillery pieces, they made good use of such weapons as grenades, light mortars and submachine guns when combined with a surprise in the dark.

The uncanny ability of the Chinese at night infiltration was matched only by their fortitude and endurance. Although press releases mentioned "human sea" attacks, the invaders preferred to launch a series of company or even platoon efforts. Only when a gap had been opened did larger units pour through to exploit the advantage. On the defense the Chinese made the best of natural cover, and at "digging in" they had no equals.

The CCF strategic plan called for a major blow at the Eighth Army, which was in full retreat by November 27. Extensive withdrawals had been made necessary when the entire right flank was stripped by the disintegration of the ROK corps. Even so, the retirement proceeded in fairly good order until an error in judgment exposed major units of a U.S. Army division to a slaughter near Kunu-ri, a road junction some 40 miles north of Pyongyang.

The division staff and command had decided to take the risk of "bulling through" Kunu-ri Pass in an afternoon motor march rather than providing adequate flank protection. All went well until several thin-skinned vehicles were disabled by CCF fire from the high ground overlooking the narrow road winding through defiles. This brought the column to a jolting halt and presented "sitting duck" targets as more Chinese swarmed in for the kill. There were many instances of American heroism to atone for the command blunder, but the panic spread until it resulted in a dreadful tangle of immobilized tanks, trucks and jeeps. It was every man for himself as darkness put an end to the horror by enabling the survivors to escape.

So severely was the division punished that the remnants had to be pulled out of the line for a major reorganization. This disaster further weakened the Eighth Army's right flank, and large amounts of arms and vehicles were destroyed or abandoned as the retreat continued in subzero cold. Not until mid-December was a stand made along a defensive line a few miles south of the 38th parallel.

THE CHOSIN RESERVOIR BREAKOUT

In northeast Korea a secondary CCF offensive aimed at the envelopment and annihilation of a U.S. Marine division, four U.S. Army battalions, and a British commando unit "out on a limb" in the Chosin reservoir area, about 70 miles inland from Hungnam at the farthest point. The other major units of X Corps—two U.S. Army and two ROK divisions—were too dispersed to render timely aid.

Three CCF armies, comprising 11 infantry divisions of some 7,500 to 9,000 men each, had made their way into the area by secret night marches. They struck by surprise along the 35 miles of twisting mountain road from Yudam-ni to Chinhung-ni. The first CCF attacks occurred at Yudam-ni on the night of November 27-28, 1950. Within 24 hours the X Corps forces in the area had been sliced into six groups, each out of physical contact with the others.

From the 28th to the 30th, five of the threatened groups held their own in a desperate three-day defensive battle as temperatures sank to 26° below zero Fahrenheit. Successful resistance owed in nearly every instance to formation of a 360° perimeter and utilization of organic firepower along with artillery and air strikes. Only at Sinhung-ni, where three army battalions were overwhelmed by sheer numbers after a brave 48-hour stand, did the invaders achieve their purpose. About 700 survivors escaped over the Chosin Reservoir ice to Hagaru, and 380 wounded men were rescued by marines on jeep-drawn sleds.

The most critical battle took place at Hagaru, the marine forward base which must be held if the beleaguered forces were to fight their way out of the encirclement. On two nights the Chinese broke through the thinly manned perimeter, but gaps were restored by the counterattacks of marines reinforced with clerks, truck drivers and other service troops.

Major General Oliver P. Smith, the marine commander, directed the breakout from his forward command post at Hagaru. On December 1 the two marine infantry regiments and three artillery battalions at Yudam-ni seized the initiative and came out fighting. A quarter of a mile an hour was considered a good pace for a vehicle column that was in effect a walking 360° perimeter. Not until infantry flankers had cleared the enemy from front and sides did the march continue, with the artillery bringing up the rear. Marine and navy planes provided effective close

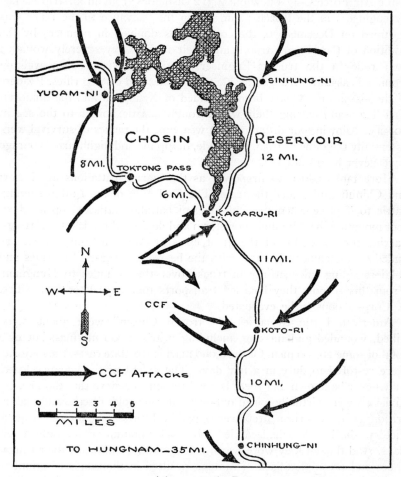

Advance to the Rear

air support throughout the daylight hours, and at night the column "buttoned up" in readiness to meet attacks from any direction.

It took three days to cover the 14 miles to Hagaru. On the way the stouthearted marine company at Toktong Pass was rescued after repulsing CCF onslaughts for five days and nights with the aid of unfailing artillery and air support. American casualties of 50 per cent had been suffered.

At Hagaru three more days were devoted to rest and regroupment while Air Force C-47's flew out 4,312 casualties from an airstrip hacked by engineers in the frozen plain. When the "advance to the rear" was resumed on December 6, the column was doubled in numbers by the addition of the Hagaru troops and their tanks. Only severely wounded men rode in the trucks. Engineers, artillerymen and even walking wounded casualties trudged beside the vehicles and carried rifles. Readers of the classics must have been reminded of Xenophon and the immortal Ten Thousand cutting their way through Asiatic hordes to the sea in 401 B.C. Allowing for differences in weapons, the tactics of survival were essentially the same in 1950. Fortitude, discipline and highhearted courage have never been outdated.

More tanks added to firepower as the marine battalions at Koto-ri and Chinhung-ni joined the train. The final fight of the 13-day running battle took place when the Chinhung-ni battalion attacked up a 3,600-foot mountain in a blinding snowstorm and destroyed the last CCF troops barring the way. One of the great epics of American military history ended on December 11, 1950, with the bearded, parka-clad marines and soldiers riding uneventfully in trucks over the 35 miles to Hungnam. From this seaport they boarded transports four days later as the first X Corps troops to be evacuated.

American battle casualties of "frozen Chosin" were about 5,500 killed, wounded and missing, including nearly 4,000 marines, out of a total of some 26,000 men. Of the 6,000 marine frostbite cases, the majority were restored to duty in a few days. The extent of the enemy's losses may never be known, but there is good reason to believe that the 11 CCF divisions were virtually wiped out—as much by cold, disease and malnutrition as by American firepower. Apparently in anticipation of a quick victory, the invaders had carried food and ammunition for only a few days. And though they wore warm cotton-padded uniforms, their canvas shoes and a complete lack of mittens resulted in thousands of crippling frostbite casualties.

It is significant that none of the 11 Chinese divisions was identified at the front again until the following March. As further evidence that the annihilators had been annihilated, no CCF opposition worthy of the name interfered with the great Hungnam redeployment of December 15 to 24, 1950.

The Eighth Army retreat having left X Corps isolated, General MacArthur ordered a complete withdrawal from northeast to south Korea. This sealift, aptly called "an amphibious operation in reverse," was the U.S. Navy's foremost achievement in the Korean War. Rear Admiral James H. Doyle, commanding Joint Task Force 90, did not intend to risk another Dunkirk, and the battleship *Missouri* headed the cruisers and destroyers pouring in preventive naval gunfire. The bombardment continued, along with naval and marine air strikes, in support of U.S. Army troops who held a shrinking perimeter until the last platoon embarked. Despite the vulnerability of such an operation, not a single American life was lost to enemy action. On Christmas Eve the evacuation ended with these impressive totals—105,000 UN troops, 91,000 Korean civilian refugees, 17,500 vehicles, and 350,000 measurement tons of gear, loaded out by 109 ships.

THE REGENERATION OF THE EIGHTH ARMY

Stunned incredulity was the reaction of the American public to the news from Korea. People who had been thinking in terms of atomic weapons and guided missiles found it incomprehensible that American troops could have been pushed around by an Asiatic peasant army lacking tanks and tactical aircraft. Seldom was it realized that the semi-guerrilla warfare of the CCF tactical system was at its best against a mechanized army in a mountainous terrain of few roads.

There were serious defects in the system, nevertheless, that the Chosin Reservoir campaign had revealed. The worst was a rigidity of approach which may be charged both to poor field communications and to a chain of command allowing few options below the division level. Once committed to an attack, the Chinese repeated the most costly tactical errors. At Hagaru, for instance, a CCF division forfeited a victory over a marine battalion by persistently attacking against strength in a thinly held perimeter where weak spots were apparent. For that matter, the over-all Chinese strategy was at fault; instead of striking at several groups simultaneously, the invaders might better have aimed a concentrated blow at Hagaru. The capture of that forward base, with its supply dumps and airstrip, would have deprived the marines of an essential rallying point and nourished Chinese efforts to isolate and destroy the other groups piecemeal.

Before these lessons could be evaluated, Mao Tse-tung's forces prepared to launch another great offensive while the Eighth Army was still

shaken by its reverses of December, 1950. American interdictory bombings, which had been so effective against mechanized forces in Europe
during World War II, could not prevent the enemy from bringing in
supplies by road and rail from Manchuria. Mountainous Korea, with its
main routes limited by terrain, should have been a happy hunting
ground for air interdiction; but damage to roads and bridges was repaired in an incredibly short time by coolie labor. Thus the enemy
contrived in three weeks of night movements to transport the tons of
matériel needed for a second major offensive.

Lieutenant General Matthew B. Ridgway completed a flight from
Washington to Korea on Christmas night and assumed the Eighth Army
command left vacant by the death of General Walker in a jeep accident.
"I must say in all frankness," he commented in his *Memoirs,* "that the
spirit of the Eighth Army as I found it on my arrival gave me deep
concern. There was a definite air of nervousness, of gloomy foreboding,
of uncertainty, a spirit of apprehension as to what the future held."

By this time the Korean conflict had become perhaps the most unpopular war of American history. It hardly seemed possible that only
six months before, Americans had almost unanimously approved President Truman's firm stand against Communist encroachments. Now the
intervention was known as "Truman's war" by his political opponents,
with the intimation that he had dragged an unwilling nation into a
futile military venture. The slanders of party politics had taken the place
of legitimate criticisms; and winning the next presidential election was
placed above winning the war against Communism in Korea.

The Administration's political foes were not isolationists; they simply
wanted a war of their own in another theater. On the grounds that the
Chinese Nationalist defeat had resulted from inadequate Administration
aid, they advocated an armed defense of Formosa that could only lead to
fighting on the Asian mainland. The charge of Administration neglect
had no support from American military observers in China during the
Civil War. Nor did the prospect of a major Formosa operation have
the endorsement of most of the nation's generals and admirals. Korea was
a thousand miles nearer to American bases in Japan; and as a peninsula
it offered more lucrative targets to American command of the air and
sea than did the Chinese mainland opposite Formosa.

This was not the first occasion in American military history when
operations in the field were adversely influenced by the feuds of party
politics on the home front. In fact, that recurring situation is perhaps
the chief inherent weakness of representative government in time of war.

There had been no flag waving or band music for troops sailing to Korea. They left behind them a nation doing business as usual, for only a comparatively few men and their families were making the sacrifices of war. Between battles in Korea, these troops read Stateside newspapers in which Mr. Truman's political opponents charged without evidence that Communists had infiltrated the State Department and the Department of Defense.

It is small wonder that many units in Korea were permeated with defeatism before General Ridgway arrived. The exceptions were units upheld by professional pride and tradition, such as the marines and veteran regular army regiments. Even some of the division commanders had cold feet at a time when Stateside editorial writers frankly discussed the prospect of withdrawing from Korea in admission of defeat by a Communist army fighting at a disadvantage in arms.

Ridgway saved the nation from this disgrace. He made daily tours of the Eighth Army front in an open jeep during subzero weather to warn officers and men that he would not put up with defeatism. On his fourth night in Korea, he sat down in his room and wrote his "declaration of faith," quoted here in part:

To me the issues are clear. It is not a question of this or that Korean town or village. Real estate is, here, incidental. . . .

The real issues are whether the power of Western civilization, as God has permitted it to flower in our own beloved lands, shall defy and defeat Communism; whether the rule of men who shoot their prisoners, enslave their citizens and deride the dignity of man, shall displace the rule of those to whom the individual and individual rights are sacred; whether we are to survive with God's hand to guide and lead us, or to perish in the dead existence of a Godless world.

If these be true, and to me they are, beyond any possibility of challenge, then this has long since ceased to be a fight for freedom of our Korean allies alone and for their national survival. It has become, and it continues to be, a fight for our own freedom, for our own survival, in an honorable, independent national existence.

On his daily rounds Ridgway "spoke the language" of the troops at the front. For it is not a coincidence that three of the foremost moral and intellectual leaders of the U.S. Army during the post-World War II decade were paratroop commanders who had jumped with their men in Normandy—Ridgway, James M. Gavin, and Maxwell D. Taylor. Sharing the perils and hardships of the troops gives a general an understanding of war that can never be gained otherwise, and the Eighth Army responded warmly to the energetic new chief who wore a live grenade for a boutonniere.

The CCF blow fell in the bitter cold of New Year's Eve. Although Ridgway had done wonders to restore morale during his first six days, the enemy drove through half-trained ROK units to a depth endangering the entire Eighth Army. The commanding general in his jeep took personal charge of setting up roadblocks to halt fleeing Korean allies. At his request, Syngman Rhee harangued the ROKs by radio and persuaded most of them to return to the firing line. It was too late, however, to stop the Chinese offensive. Both Inchon and Seoul were evacuated as the Eighth Army fell back to a new defensive line some 50 to 80 miles south of the 38th parallel.

"We came back fast," admitted Ridgway, "but as a fighting army, not as a running mob. We brought our dead and wounded with us, and our guns, and our will to fight."

The retreat had scarcely ended before he organized a reconnaissance in force by a regimental combat team. No enemy troops were encountered and it is not likely that Ridgway anticipated any such result. He was merely taking the first step toward giving the Eighth Army back its pride.

Next came a limited advance by a division. Then a forward movement on a corps front. And on February 23, 1951, the whole Eighth Army jumped off to the attack in Operation KILLER. A CCF counterattack on the central front caused only a brief setback, and Operation RIPPER was launched on March 7, 1951.

Ridgway insisted that acquiring real estate was secondary to the hurt the Eighth Army could do the Communists. Holding every inch of ground was not desired if more Communists could be put out of action by retiring to a stronger position. Without fear of undermining aggressive spirit, the commanding general ordered the establishment of phase lines in the rear for this purpose.

Even though gaining ground was incidental, the Eighth Army recovered Inchon and Seoul in an advance which took it past the 38th parallel. Captured CCF documents had revealed that the enemy was planning his Fifth Phase Offensive as an end-the-war drive in the spring of 1951. One of the objects of Ridgway's strategy, therefore, was to keep the Chinese off balance during their preparations.

On April 11 he was suddenly summoned to Tokyo to relieve General

Macarthur. The UN commander had been recalled by President Truman on charges that he ignored presidential directives to clear statements on national policy through the State Department.

Two Chinese Offensives Defeated

Lieutenant General James A. Van Fleet took command of the Eighth Army just a week before the opening round of the Chinese Fifth Phase Offensive on April 22, 1951. The enemy might have given the impression of victorious gains on D-day to anyone shifting colored pins on a map. Actually the UN troops were falling back to prepared phase lines on the east-central front, though in several instances the retreat was made urgently necessary by enemy pressure.

"Rolling with the punches" struck the troops as common-sense strategy in contrast to last-ditch stands, and the fighting spirit of the Eighth Army mounted. The enemy's strength consisted of expendable human tonnage, and he took frightful losses from opponents who traded battered real estate for Chinese lives.

The Eighth Army had earned the right to be known as one of the great armies of history. In this cosmopolitan array were combat and noncombat units of company to battalion size from Australia, Canada, Colombia, Ethiopia, France, Greece, India, the Netherlands, New Zealand, Norway, the Republic of Korea, Sweden, Thailand, Turkey, the Union of South Africa and the United Kingdom. The United States supplied the command and the bulk of the troops in a homogeneous organization.

Supporting the ground forces, the planes of the U.S. Fifth Air Force and 1st Marine Aircraft Wing—F-84 Thunderjets, F-51 Mustangs, F-80 Shooting Stars, F-86 Sabres, F9F Panthers and F4U Corsairs— flew 7,420 sorties during the eight days of the CCF offensive. By the end of April the Eighth Army had stopped the enemy cold in his drive on Seoul and established a strong, continuous defense line.

The Chinese tried again on May 16, this time on a 36-mile front in east Korea defended by one U.S. and two ROK divisions. The deep salient driven into the UN lines was so narrow as to be vulnerable to counterattack, and the enemy effort was brought to a standstill in four days.

Without pausing for a breathing spell, the Eighth Army launched a tremendous counterstroke during the last week in May. The Chinese, caught off balance after their two drives, were punished as never before.

Where it had been a rare event for a single CCF soldier to surrender voluntarily, more than 10,000 laid down their arms in one June week as remnants of riddled companies and even battalions. In some UN zones of operation the Chinese escaped only by dint of sacrificing their North Korean allies in hopeless rear-guard stands.

"In June, 1951, we had them whipped," commented General Van Fleet after the war. "They were definitely gone. They were in awful shape."

The Chinese wriggled out of this crisis by pretending a sudden interest in peace. Jacob Malik, the Soviet delegate to the United Nations, proposed truce talks and the Peiping radio hastily acquiesced. The United Nations could scarcely refuse to confer, and on July 10, 1951—a memorable date in the Korean conflict—UN and Communist delegates met at Kaesong. There the Chinese soon revealed that their purpose was to gain a respite which their thinned forces could use for digging defenses in depth and bringing up reinforcements and artillery.

After a two-month lull, some hard fighting took place in east-central Korea during September and October. On October 25 the course of the war was changed by the resumption of truce talks for the first time since the Communist delegates had walked out in anger, late in August. This time the hamlet of Panmunjom, near Kaesong, was chosen as the site of a "talkathon" which continued throughout the war.

The delegates agreed on November 23 to a so-called cease fire along a line of demarcation based on "points of repeated contacts." General Van Fleet instructed his corps commanders on November 27 that the demarcation line would be permanent a month later if no full armistice had been concluded. Thus by January 1, 1952, the war had become static. During the next 19 months Korea was scarred with opposing trans-peninsular systems of trenches and bunkers, and operations settled down into a petty warfare of raids and patrols reminiscent of the Western Front in 1915.

American artillery batteries saluted the new year by firing a "toast." "The thud of the snow-muffled howitzers," commented a U.S. Marine Corps historical survey, "was also a fitting farewell to the past year of a war that was not officially a war. Indications were that it would be concluded by a peace that was not a peace, judging from the attitude of the Communist delegates at Panmunjom. And meanwhile . . . Eighth Army troops would keep on fighting in accordance with the terms of a cease-fire that was not a cease-fire."

Tactical Innovations of the Korean War

Although this strange conflict now groped back to the warfare of a past generation, it anticipated the future with two of the foremost tactical innovations of the twentieth century—modern body armor and the combat helicopter.

Contrary to a popular impression, body armor has never entirely disappeared from history. During the early months of the American Civil War, thousands of Union troops bought riveted steel breastplates manufactured by Connecticut firms. Most of them were soon thrown away by the foot soldiers, however, as excess personal baggage.

Weight and rigidity also caused the rejection of 32 World War I prototypes submitted to the U.S. Army at General Pershing's request. Steel helmets were adopted by the armies of the Western Front, but body protection had to wait for the era of lightweight plastics.

American aviation bombing crews of World War II depended on flak suits and curtains. As for the infantry, an army-navy committee agreed in 1943 on the feasibility of two lightweight materials—12-ply basketweave nylon, and layers of glass cloth filaments laminated into ⅛-inch plates. The war ended before a U.S. infantry unit could begin combat tests on Okinawa, but in 1947 the Navy and Marine Corps set up a field laboratory for experiments at Camp Lejeune, North Carolina.

The outcome was the adoption of an eight-pound, zippered, sleeveless vest made of nylon with sheaths for curved plates of laminated glass cloth filaments, front and back. The need for such protection had been proved by World War II surgical statistics revealing the following incidence of wounds:

Nonfatal		*Fatal*	
Head	10%	Head	20%
Chest	10%	Chest	50%
Abdomen	10%	Abdomen	20%
Upper Extremity	30%	Upper Extremity	05%
Lower Extremity	40%	Lower Extremity	05%

Artillery, mortar and grenade fragments, along with submachine-gun slugs, figured in 60 per cent of the casualties, the remainder being caused by rifle or machine-gun bullets. Statistics from 57 infantry divisions in World War II indicated that the infantry, comprising 68.5 per cent of the total strength, suffered 94.5 per cent of the casualties.

Tests proved that the Marine Corps M-1951 vest, first to be worn in combat, was capable of "stopping a .45 caliber USA pistol or Thompson sub-machine gun bullet; all the fragments of the USA hand grenade at three feet; 75 per cent of the USA 8-mm mortar at 10 feet; the full thrust of the American bayonet." These figures are from the official description, which warned that the vest afforded no protection against rifle or machine-gun bullets.

Without armor protection, the skin of the abdomen can be pierced by a missile exerting a pressure of 250 pounds or more to the square inch. Body armor spreads the impact over a larger area, so that fatal wounds are reduced to serious, serious wounds to light, and light wounds to bad bruises.

Troop acceptance was enthusiastic. The U.S. Army soon produced a vest of its own, made entirely of nylon pads, and by the spring of 1952 nearly all American and Allied troops were protected in combat.

The most comprehensive statistics were compiled from February to August, 1953, by an army field research team on a basis of vests worn by 20,000 soldiers for a total of 400,000 hours. The 1,500 complete wound ballistics studies, most of them involving X-ray examination, and the hundreds of autopsies indicated that body armor had prevented from 60 to 70 per cent of chest and abdominal wounds. When penetrations did occur, they were much reduced in severity.

Seldom if ever has an important tactical innovation been produced at such a comparatively modest cost. The total research bill was only a few million dollars for a vest that could be manufactured commercially for $40. Although the general public praised it from a humanitarian viewpoint, military men foresaw tactical gains. For if the vest could prevent or reduce in severity 50 per cent of artillery, mortar and submachine-gun wounds, it meant in effect that half the enemy's most deadly antipersonal weapons had been silenced.

The lifesaving potentialities of body armor were multiplied by another tactical innovation, the combat helicopter. Surgeons had found that time was all-important in the treatment of men suffering from the shock of serious wounds. The chances of recovery were much increased if the patient could be rushed to the aid station, and the helicopter was obviously an improvement over stretcher and ambulance evacuation in mountain terrain. Where those means might take a day, helicopters could often fly a badly wounded man to a base hospital in an hour.

The development of rotary-wing aircraft had come too late for World War II, in which they played a very minor part toward the end. During the postwar years the U.S. Navy and Air Force organized squadrons for rescue and liaison work, but Lieutenant General Gavin's efforts on behalf of the Army were frustrated by Department of Defense rulings. The Marine Corps, last of all to fly a helicopter, sought a means of adapting its amphibious warfare studies to the Atomic Age.

Amphibious tactics which had taken ten years to evolve were rendered obsolescent in ten seconds by the bomb of Hiroshima. The tests of Operation CROSSROADS in July, 1946, left no doubt that the naval concentrations of Iwo Jima and Okinawa would be as ruinously blasted by a foe employing atomic weapons as were the 73 obsolete warships in Bikini Lagoon.

The marines saw the possibility of a tactical antidote in naval dispersion made possible by vertical troop landings from helicopters, which could fly in any one of 360 directions or hover motionless under flapping rotors. First to see combat duty were the three-place HO3S-1 Sikorsky aircraft combined with small fixed-wing planes in a marine observation squadron. In August, 1950, they proved their usefulness under fire on such diverse missions as casualty evacuation, liaison, command flights, wire laying, artillery spotting and rescue work. The general's steed of the past was replaced by the noisy "chopper," which could take him to any part of the front in a fraction of the time needed for jeep travel. During the attacks on Seoul after the Inchon landing, the marine commanding general was able to supervise closely the operations of a division fighting on both sides of an unbridged tidal river 1,200 feet wide.

Forebodings as to the helicopter's vulnerability proved to have erred on the gloomy side. Rotary-wing aircraft found their protection in flying at low altitudes, shielded by the terrain from enemy mortars and artillery. Enemy tactical aircraft were not a problem in Korea, and seldom did a smashup result from small-arms fire. Bullet holes were the rule rather than the exception on some types of missions, yet only two pilot fatalities occurred during the first six months of the HO3S-1 and the Bell HTL-2 in Korea.

Front-page headlines in American newspapers recorded one "first" after another to the credit of the marine helicopter transport squadron which reached Korea in the late summer of 1951. It consisted of fifteen HRS-1 Sikorsky aircraft, each with a payload of 1,420 pounds at sea level or a troop-lifting capacity of four to six combat-equipped troops in addition to the pilot.

Tactical history was made by the lift of a company of 224 marine infantrymen with their own gear and 17,772 pounds of supplies over a 15-mile route to the top of an 884-meter ridge. The operation was completed in 65 flights lasting four hours, though the march could not have been made on foot in a day.

Next, a week's supplies for a battalion were flown to the front over terrain so rough that hundreds of Korean porters had previously been employed. Then came Operation BUMBLEBEE—the 12-mile lift of an entire battalion of 958 men with full combat equipment. Twelve helicopters did the job in 156 flights requiring 5 hours and 50 minutes. The total weight transported was 229,920 pounds.

After this pioneer effort, it became routine to fly a battalion to the front and bring back the battalion relieved of duty. Former equations of tactical and logistical mobility were revised by the helicopter, which demonstrated that two front-line regiments could be entirely supplied from dumps eight miles in the rear. Drums of diesel fuel, barbed wire, rations, water, ammunition and mail made up the 1,612,306 pounds flown during a period of five days.

Other U.S. armed services were quick to adopt a work-horse of such proved ability. During the final months of the war, the Army led in numbers of helicopters, and both Navy and Air Force added to their quotas.

THE END IN KOREA

Except for such innovations as body armor and helicopters, the last nineteen months in Korea were uneventful. Not a single large-scale operation interrupted the routine clashes of small war while the delegates at Panmunjom contined their talks, unable to agree. CCF defenses in depth went back an average of 14 miles, so that the hills were honeycombed with tunnels, underground strong points and hidden gun emplacements. A UN breakthrough could have been achieved only at a prohibitive cost in casualties. And even if such an attempt had succeeded, not much would have been gained by advancing to the Yalu. As for invading Manchuria and China, there was the risk of alarming the Soviet Union and bringing on World War III.

It would be shortsighted, nevertheless, to conclude that nothing was accomplished in Korea. The United Nations had realized their main aim, which was to make a stand against the encroachments of the Communist world. If such a stand had been made against the Japanese, the Germans and the Italians during their encroachments of the 1930's,

World War II might have been prevented or at least fought to better advantage. For the experience of those years proved that there is no appeasing aggressors who respect only armed force.

Defeat at the hands of Asiatic peasant armies during the early months in Korea was a bitter pill, but it was perhaps the only medicine that could have shocked Americans out of a complacency stemming from a supposed advantage in atomic weapons. Stalin made a noteworthy contribution to American security by inciting the war in Korea. For it took the actuality of combat to arouse the nation to the urgent need of strengthening armed forces that had been allowed to decline since 1945.

A million Americans served in Korea; they and their allies of many nations found it a strange war in 1952 and 1953. Electric lights gleamed in prefabricated bunkers. Huge refrigeration plants made it possible to serve fresh meats and vegetables to troops who were rotated after a few months of combat duty. It was a "de luxe war," but it was also one of the deadliest wars of American history for citizen-soldiers. Action during the nineteen months of stalemate consisted chiefly of desperate encounters in the darkness of no man's land. Americans whose grandsires had fought Indians were up against the same tactics of concealment, stealth and lethal surprise.

Rotation meant that combat-experienced troops were soon replaced by novices. It is to the credit of the Americans, therefore, that they gave a good account of themselves. S. L. A. Marshall, the historian of the fighting man in Korea, interviewed hundreds of the U.S. Army survivors of the Pork Chop Hill action in the spring of 1953. "The infighting which took place in the entrenched works of the outposts," he wrote in *Pork Chop Hill,* "was as hardpressed and bloody as Cold Harbor, Attu or the Argonne. The Americans won, not simply by the superior weight of their artillery, but because the infantry, man for man in the hand-to-hand battle, outgamed the Red Chinese."

It came as an anticlimax when the cease fire of July 27, 1953, went into effect. On the surface, nothing was decided; not a square inch of ground changed hands, and no decision was reached as to the future of the antagonistic Koreans on opposite sides of the 38th parallel. Yet events of ensuing years were to indicate that the Communist world had been taught a new respect for nations believing in individual rights. There had been no Munich this time. There had been no collapse of the United Nations, and it may be that World War III was deferred or even averted on the battlefields of Korea.

Communist losses were estimated at more than a million killed and wounded in addition to a high death rate from disease. In the lack of accurate ROK statistics, there is no reliable total for UN losses. American casualties were 30,306 killed or died of wounds, and 103,284 wounded.

There were also hundreds of prisoners who died or suffered in health as a consequence of Communist mistreatment. The gaunt and debilitated survivors had been the victims of malnutrition, abuse and exposure to cold in efforts to make them confess to germ warfare and other "atrocities" which had no foundation in fact.

The only clear-cut decision of the Korean War was recorded when the Panmunjom delegates agreed to give prisoners of both sides the opportunity of deciding for themselves whether they were to be sent back to the country of their origin. The result was a humiliating defeat for the Communists, despite the propaganda campaign they waged in the prison camps. A UN total of 229, largely Koreans, had been converted to Communism, while some 22,000 Chinese Reds cast their lot with Nationalist China on Formosa. An equal number of Red Koreans voted to begin life anew in the Republic of Korea.

Two Scorpions in a Bottle

Throughout the first fifteen years of the Atomic Age, the peoples of the Western nations viewed war almost exclusively in terms of surprise airborne nuclear attacks capable of wiping out great cities or even nations in a few hours. Until 1949 the United States remained in exclusive possession of the awesome secret. The Soviet Union exploded its first bomb in the late summer of that year; and shortly after the United States developed the hydrogen bomb, the Russian scientists had one of their own.

For the first time in military history, two nations had the means of almost completely destroying each other—but only at the suicidal price of enduring a like devastation from retaliatory attacks. This situation has been compared by Dr. Robert Oppenheimer, the American physicist, to a duel between two scorpions in a bottle.

Nuclear physics is not the private property of any nation. It is a world science and events of the 1950's proved that Americans had underestimated the Soviet Union, just as a past generation had misjudged Japan. Thermonuclear weapons depend for their effect on the means of delivery, and Russian scientists took the lead in the development of ballistic missiles. By 1960 there were three recognized categories:

ICBM—intercontinental ballistic missile, range of 1,500 to 5,000 miles;

IRBM—intermediate-range ballistic missile, range of 550 to 1,500 miles;

MRBM—mid-range ballistic missile, range of 200 to 700 miles.

These missiles rendered obsolescent the intercontinental bombing planes which had been the dependence of the United States ever since the explosion at Hiroshima. The possibility of a weapon becoming outdated before it reached the stage of production was demonstrated on December 2, 1959, when American newspapers announced that the Pentagon had called a halt on the B-70. Although this intercontinental bomber would have had a speed of 2,000 miles per hour, it was too slow as compared to guided missiles. Its future usefulness, according to commentators, lay in the field of troop-carrying mobility.

It is beyond the scope of this survey of war to speculate on a future in which clashes between nations might conceivably be waged by opposing scientists, with old-fashioned strategists and tacticians being relegated to the background. Victory in these test-tube Armageddons would be decided in the laboratory on a basis of the deadliest germs, gases and ballistic missiles.

This is an exaggerated picture, of course, but the realities of the post-World War II era were a violent departure from the military past. For the first time in history, the United States was vulnerable to a direct and decisive attack from across the seas. There could be no doubt that American death casualties in a nuclear war might reach a total of fifty million or more. It is also true that germ warfare and new poison gases had horrible potentialities in missile attacks, but American leaders kept their eyes fixed on the dreadful specter of atomic destruction. Warnings appeared at frequent intervals in the form of books, public addresses and magazine articles which were calculated to frighten the public out of its wits. Seldom, however, did these despairing jeremiads suggest any practical means of building bomb shelters or evacuating cities.

American statesmen, after learning that the Soviet Union had atomic capabilities, fell back on a "one big war" strategy, based on the assumed possession of the largest atomic stockpile. The United States was probably never in more danger than when the principle of "massive retaliation" found high-placed advocates in Washington. This policy was summed up by Vice-President Richard M. Nixon, as quoted in the *New York Times* of March 14, 1954:

> Rather than let the Communists nibble us to death all over the world in little wars we would rely in the future primarily on our massive mobile retaliatory power which we could use in our discretion against the major source of aggression at times and places that we chose.

Secretary of Defense Charles E. Wilson, as quoted in James M. Gavin's *War and Peace in the Space Age,* put it bluntly: "We can't afford to fight limited wars. We can only afford to fight a big one, and if there is one that is the kind it will be."

General Gavin, whose brilliant army career ended in resignation because he could not reconcile his views with Department of Defense policies, disagreed with Mr. Wilson:

> If we cannot afford to fight limited wars then we cannot afford to survive, for that is the kind of a war we will be confronted with. That is the only kind we can afford to fight. Certainly we don't want another Korea, not if it means exposing our forces to tactical defeat because of our preoccupation with a one-weapon-system strategy, nor because of self-imposed artificial restrictions upon the research and development programs of forces other than those associated with that one-weapon system.

General Maxwell D. Taylor, chief-of-staff of the U.S. Army, stressed the necessity of preparations for limited wars in his introduction to a Department of the Army pamphlet, *Bibliography on Limited War,* in February, 1958:

> In these days of dramatic satellite launchings and missile flights, public attention is to a large degree focused on the dangers of a possible general thermonuclear war. This concern is understandable, but it may cause us to overlook the equally serious threat of limited wars initiated by an aggressor under the protective cover of mutual nuclear deterrence. Limited aggression, if not arrested, could lead to the possible loss of much of the Free World, and if not quickly suppressed might spread into the general conflagration, which we hope to avoid. I consider, therefore, that our readiness to fight and win promptly any local conflict is of the utmost importance, not

only to discourage potential enemies from limited military adventures, but as one of the major deterrents to general atomic war itself.

Taylor, like Gavin and Ridgway before him, went into early retirement as a protest against the policies of the President and Department of Defense.

From 1954 to 1958 the United States had a succession of alarms and excursions, any one of which might have burgeoned into a limited war. The summer after the Korean conflict ended, U.S. marines were alerted simultaneously for possible interventions in Guatemala, where a Communist-inspired uprising endangered American nationals, and in Indo-China. Sumatra was the scene of trouble early in 1957, and the U.S. carrier *Princeton* sailed to protect American interests with a task force composed of a marine infantry regiment and transport helicopter squadron. A political riot in Venezuela the following year made it expedient to send combat-ready marines in the cruiser *Des Moines,* which anchored off the coast until the atmosphere cleared.

In none of these instances was it necessary to put troops ashore. During the summer of 1958, however, both marines and soldiers landed in Lebanon after unrest in the Middle East threatened to break out into a war involving several nations. At the same time, on the other side of the world, U.S. naval and air forces found themselves in an equally tense situation when Communist Chinese bombardments of Quemoy and other Nationalist-held coastal islands appeared to foreshadow an invasion of Formosa. United States naval aviators took no active part but provided the Chinese Nationalist fliers with air-to-air missiles which helped to bring the bombardments to an end by shooting down enemy observation planes. In Lebanon the mere presence of some 14,000 U.S. troops supported by tanks and aircraft was enough to restore order, and after an occupation of two and a half months the Americans departed without having fired a shot.

The battlefield experience of other nations indicated that the helicopter was the only advance over the weapons and tactics of World War II. On October 26, 1956, the hostility between Jew and Mohammedan in the Near East exploded into the so-called "Hundred Hours' War." Never in modern times has a nation been as totally mobilized as Israel, with its population of only 1,700,000. Women as well as men were called to the colors, and a soldier inducted on the eve of his wedding found consolation in the thought that his bride, the rabbi and the guests also would be mobilized.

Striking first, General Moshe Dayan's columns crossed the border and cut four Egyptian divisions to pieces in the Sinai Peninsula. Surprise, audacity and motorized celerity were the best weapons of victors who met little resistance. At a cost of 180 men killed and four captured, Israel took 6,000 prisoners in four days and reported 1,000 enemy dead. The remnants of the 45,000 Egyptians made their way home in a wild flight after throwing away their weapons.

The one-sided war had scarcely ended when Britain and France carried out a sudden invasion of Egypt on November 6, 1956, to settle a dispute which began with the seizure of the Suez Canal in June by the Egyptian dictator, General Gamel Nasser. British troops completed the first vertical amphibious combat landing of history when helicopters flew landing forces from Cypress to Port Said. Paratroops and water-borne contingents also took part in an amphibious operation which secured the city after a day of street fighting. The occupation forces withdrew a few weeks later, when the issue was submitted to the United Nations.

It was the misfortune of France to pull out of Indo-China in 1954, after seven years of defeat, only to wage another costly colonial war in Algeria. In both instances the French regulars were up against guerrilla tactics, which have been effective under favorable conditions in all ages of war. Military strength can make little headway against the mobility of furtive groups which strike by stealth and melt away into jungle or mountain hiding places. Nor is it likely that atomic weapons will detract from the timeless efficacy of guerrilla warfare.

THE OUTLOOK FOR CO-SURVIVAL

There could be no doubt that by 1959 the United States and the Soviet Union had reached deterrent stature in the field of atomic weapons. Russia had gained the advantage, however, in preparations for limited wars. While keeping pace in thermonuclear developments, the Soviet Union had managed to maintain an army of 175 divisions—as compared to 14 for the United States—and build a larger fleet of submarines than any other nation could boast. Progress in improved types of armor, aircraft and artillery had not lagged.

There was no support in fact, moreover, for the prevailing belief in Western nations that the Red Army drew upon a bottomless reserve of manpower. In rebuttal, Fritz Sternberg has commented with italics in *The Military and Industrial Revolution of Our Time:*

The fact is that this Russian manpower superiority is a myth. . . . The population of Russia is about 202 millions. But the combined populations of the European NATO powers total 261 millions, and the four big European NATO powers have a total population about equal to that of the Soviet Union. But in addition there is the population of the United States, which is over 175 millions. In other words, *the combined populations of the NATO Powers, including the United States, is about twice as great as the population of the Soviet Union.*

The Russian advantage in numbers of troops simply derived from the fact that a larger proportion of men were trained, and a larger proportion of the national income budgeted for that purpose.

The Soviet Union stood ready to fight a big war, a small war, or any other kind of war. The sufferings of World War II had left scars on the Russian psychology; and the outlook for the future, as seen from the windows of the Kremlin, was not reassuring. To the west were the NATO nations, and small reliance could be placed in the loyalty of such Communist-dominated buffer states as Poland, Czechoslovakia and Hungary. To the east was Communist China, an undependable ally and potential enemy, which would have a population of a billion in the year 2000. To the north, south and west were the American-leased bases on foreign soil which had the capability of launching IRBM projectiles at Russian cities. Even the depths of the sea were suspect, for in 1960 American submarines could launch the POLARIS, an ICBM of marvelous accuracy, while remaining submerged.

The Russians, in short, had their problems, too.

War, as well as politics, makes for strange bedfellows. In 1945 nobody would have dreamed that five years later the United States would be on friendly terms with Japan and Western Germany. By the same token, it was not inconceivable in 1959 that the United States and the Soviet Union might agree upon a mutually acceptable plan of coexistence.

Pessimism, unfortunately, is likely to give the illusion of realism in any such consideration. But Christian Herter was a realistic optimist when he predicted a "competitive peace" with Russia in a New York address of November, 1959. The two nations, said the U.S. secretary of state, must find "common ground rules for co-survival." On the other hand, Soviet treaty violations and encroachments could not be forgotten, and it behooved Americans to keep their powder dry.

The nation's defense requirements at this time might have been condensed into three—nuclear deterrent capability, sea and air power supremacy, and capability for limited wars. The first two were within reach while the third still balked American planners.

Ironical as it may seem, their most formidable obstacle was the very effectiveness of thermonuclear missiles. Where soldiers had been striving through the ages for more powerful weapons, the problem now was to *weaken* an atomic warhead until it could be used on the battlefield. The HONEST JOHN of 1954 (pictured on the title page of this section) was proclaimed the first U.S. "tactical" nuclear weapon, yet it generated twice as much destructive force as the bomb that gutted Hiroshima. It took deliberate inefficiency of a high order to produce a low-yield missile for regimental use, but within five years the DAVY CROCKETT established the possibility of an atomic warhead suitable for battalion or even company actions.

The United States had produced by this time a large "family" of nuclear weapons for employment in three elements—ground to air, air to ground, air to air, sea to ground, and ground to ground. It was a bewildering arsenal, as contemplated by the layman who realized that the world of the twentieth century was in labor with the greatest industrial revolution of modern centuries. Such factors as speeded-up transportation, automation, overpopulation, the conquest of poverty, the control of disease, and the growth of nationalism in Asia and Africa were bound to have as much influence on future wars as innovations in weapons.

Only one factor remained constant, and that was man himself, indomitable as ever but prone to err. His place in the future of war has been summed up by Hanson W. Baldwin, military editor of the *New York Times:*

"Neither policies nor machines will determine the history of tomorrow. Man is the measure of all things. . . . This, then, is the ultimate battlefield: the hearts and minds of men."

CHRONOLOGICAL TABLE

490 B.C.	Battle of Marathon.
480	Salamis—the world's first decisive sea battle.
371	Epaminondas, the "father of tactics," wins the battle of Leuctra.
338	Chaeroneia and the downfall of Ancient Greece.
331	Battle of Arbela—the Persian Empire conquered by Alexander and the Macedonian phalanx.
321	The Roman legion evolves from the disaster of the Caudine Forks.
281	Heraclea, the original "Pyrrhic victory."
216	Battle of Cannae—Hannibal wins the classic annihilation victory of history.
202	Zama—Hannibal defeated by Scipio Africanus.
168	Pydna—the tactical duel between the legion and the phalanx.
52	Siege of Alesia.
49	Caesar's Ilerda campaign.
31	Battle of Actium, dating a new age of sea warfare.
70 A.D.	Siege of Jerusalem.
120	Pax Romana upheld by the cohorts.
297	Rome defended by barbarians.
378	Adrianople—the military ruin of Rome.
451	Attila repulsed at Chalons.
536	Africa and Italy reconquered by Belisarius.
627	Persia defeated by Byzantine arms at Nineveh.
638	Persia, Egypt and Syria overrun by Saracens.
673	Constantinople besieged by the Saracens.
717	Western civilization preserved by Byzantine victory over the Saracens in an eighty-three-year war.
774–799	Charlemagne's campaigns against the pagans.
886	Vikings repulsed from the walls of Paris.
941	Battle of Silistria—defeated Russians brought under Byzantine cultural influences.
1071	Byzantine military system perishes at battle of Manzikert.
1066	Battle of Hastings.
1187	Jerusalem lost to Christendom at the decisive battle of Tiberias.
1191	Saladin defeated by Richard at Arsuf.
1204	Sack of Constantinople by the Crusaders.
1220	Bokhara and Samarkand captured by Jenghiz Khan.
1241	Mongol invasion of Europe.
1249	Formula of gunpowder announced by Roger Bacon.

1302	French chivalry defeated by Flemish burghers in battle of Courtrai.
1314	Scotland's independence preserved at Bannockburn.
1346	Battle of Crécy—a thousand years of cavalry supremacy ended by English longbowmen.
1386	Battle of Sempach—Swiss confederacy saved by a revival of the phalanx.
1402	Battle of Angora—Ottoman Turks defeated by Tatar conquerors of Russia and India.
1421	Hussite victories of Ján Zižka, first soldier of the age of gunpowder to use infantry, cavalry and artillery in tactical combination.
1429	Siege of Orleans raised by Joan of Arc.
1450	Formigny, the decisive battle of the Hundred Years' War, won by the first standing army of modern history.
1453	Constantinople falls to the Turks.
1476	Battle of Nancy—Burgundy reduced to a province by defeat at the hands of the Swiss.
1515	Battle of Marignano—the legend of Swiss invincibility destroyed by French cannon.
1525	Battle of Pavia—a new tactical age of pike and arquebus founded by Emperor Charles V.
1529	Siege of Vienna by the Turks.
1571	Battle of Lepanto—Islam defeated by Christendom on the sea.
1588	Wreck of the Spanish Armada.
1589	Battle of Ivry—the decisive engagement of the Huguenot wars won by Henry of Navarre.
1590–1609	Campaigns of Maurice of Nassau.
1618–1648	The Thirty Years' War.
1631	Gustavus Adolphus, the "father of modern warfare," gains his greatest victory at Breitenfeld.
1643	Battle of Rocroi—a century of Spanish infantry supremacy ended by Condé's triumph.
1642–1651	The Great Rebellion in England.
1645	Battle of Kilsyth—the climax of Montrose's "year of miracles."
1651	Battle of Worcester—"crowning mercy" of Oliver Cromwell's cavalry tactics.
1657	Battle of the Dunes—Condé beaten by Turenne on the decisive field of France's civil war.
1667	New age of linear tactics, based on the flintlock and bayonet, founded by Louis XIV and his war minister Louvois.
1674	Battle of the Texel—English and French fleets defeated by Admiral De Ruyter's Dutch squadron.
1675	Battle of Turkheim—Turenne's greatest victory.
1689–1697	War of the Grand Alliance.
1690	Battle of the Boyne.
1692	Battle of La Hogue—decline of the French navy built up by Colbert.

1692	Siege of Namur—Vauban's masterpiece.
1693	Battle of Neerwinden—William of Orange defeated by Luxembourg.
1701–1714	War of the Spanish Succession and Great Northern War, fought simultaneously, rank as the first world war of modern history.
1704	Battle of Blenheim—Louis XIV's military supremacy successfully challenged by Marlborough.
1709	Battle of Poltava—Charles XII defeated by Peter the Great.
1709	Battle of Malplaquet—invaded France saved by Marshal Villars.
1740–1748	War of the Austrian Succession.
1741	Battle of Mollwitz, beginning the aggressions of Frederick the Great.
1745	Fontenoy, the classic of the age of linear tactics, won by Marshal Saxe.
1745	Louisburg captured by American colonists.
1756–1763	The Seven Years' War, involving four continents in its operations.
1756	Battle of Lake George—first pitched battle fought on American soil.
1757	Leuthen decided by Frederick's big guns.
1757	Clive's conquest of India.
1758	Battle of Ticonderoga—Montcalm's victory over the British and Americans.
1759	Kunersdorf—Frederick's greatest disaster.
1759	Wolfe and Montcalm at Quebec.
1760	Amherst's capture of Montreal.
1775–1783	The American Revolution.
1777	Battle of Saratoga—American independence maintained by rifle tactics.
1781	Yorktown—Cornwallis surrenders to Washington.
1792–1800	French Revolutionary Wars.
1792	Cannonade of Valmy—landmark of a new era, September 20.
1793	Nation-in-arms proclaimed, August 23, as France resorts to conscription.
1794	Battle of Fleurus, June 26—France's foes beaten by the "horde tactics" of Carnot.
1795	Revolutionary France on the offensive.
1796	Dego-Montenotte, April 12-20—General Bonaparte wins his first campaign.
1796	Bonaparte defeats the Austrians in the five days of Castiglione, August 1-5.
1797	Rivoli, the decisive battle of the Italian campaign, won by Bonaparte, January 14.
1797	Mantua surrendered to Bonaparte, February 2.
1798	Bonaparte sails for Egypt, May 19.
1798	Battle of the Nile—France's Mediterranean fleet destroyed by Nelson, August 1.

1799   Battle of Novi, August 13—the French routed by Suvárov.
1799   Bonaparte assumes dictatorial powers after the *coup d'état* of the *18 Brumaire*—November 9.
1800   Battle of Marengo, June 14—the victory which won Bonaparte an emperor's crown.
1800–1815 The Napoleonic Wars.
1805   Battle of Trafalgar, October 21—Nelson's greatest victory.
1805   Battle of Austerlitz, December 2—Napoleon at the zenith of his career.
1806   Battles of Jena-Auerstedt—Prussia crushed by a Napoleonic invasion, October 14.
1807   Battle of Friedland, June 14—new French artillery tactics compel Russia to accept a Napoleonic peace.
1808   Invasion of Spain—a French army surrendered in the field by General Dupont at Baylen, July 23.
1809   Aspern-Essling—Napoleon's first defeat, May 21-22, inflicted by the Archduke Charles.
1809   Battle of Wagram, July 5-6—Napoleon gains a dubious victory over the Austrians.
1809   Talavera—Wellington's first success, July 27, in the Peninsular War.
1810   Battle of Bussaco—Masséna beaten by Wellington, September 27.
1812   Battle of Borodino, September 7—Napoleon's invasion of Russia.
1812   Battle of Salamanca, November 11—Wellington wins the decisive battle in Spain.
1812   Retreat from Moscow—Napoleon leaves the wreck of the Grande Armée, December 8, to recruit a new army in France.
1813   Battle of Dresden, August 27—Napoleon's last great victory.
1813   Battle of Leipzig, October 16-18—Napoleon crushed by the forces of an aroused Europe.
1814   Napoleon abdicates, April 11, after the "barren masterpiece" of his campaign in France fails to prevent the invaders from entering Paris.
1815   The Hundred Days (March 1-June 18) from Napoleon's landing in France to the end at Waterloo.
1818   Battle of Maipu, April 5—San Martín gains the independence of Chile.
1824   Battle of Ayacucho, December 9—the last royalist army in South America defeated by Bolivar's lieutenant, General Sucre.
1832   Publication of Clausewitz's *On War*.
1836   Percussion-firing muskets adopted by the British army.
1847   Mexico City surrendered to General Winfield Scott, September 13.
1851   Rifles using the new Minié ball issued to the British army.
1855   Florence Nightingale establishes the right of Crimean War casualties to decent care.

1859   Battle of Solferino—the Austrians defeated by Napoleon III's
            rifled artillery, June 24.
1861–1865   The American Civil War.
1862   Fort Donelson surrendered to Grant, February 16.
1862   Battle of Shiloh, April 6-7—the Union wins the first great
            engagement of the war.
1862   Jackson's "Valley campaign," March 23-June 9.
1862   Seven Days' Battle, June 26-July 2—Richmond saved by Lee's
            victory over McClellan.
1862   Battle of Antietam, September 17—Lee's first invasion of the
            North.
1863   Battle of Chancellorsville, May 1-3—Lee's greatest victory.
1863   Battle of Gettysburg, July 1-3—Lee's second invasion of the
            North ends in the moral epic of the war.
1863   Vicksburg surrendered to Grant, July 4, cutting the Confederacy
            in two.
1864   Grant's drive on Richmond begins in the wilderness, May 4,
            and ends at Cold Harbor, June 3.
1864   Grant's crossing of the James, July 12-15.
1864   International Red Cross founded by Henri Dunant at Geneva,
            August 8.
1864   Atlanta surrendered to Sherman, September 2.
1864   Battle of Nashville, December 15-16—General Thomas wins the
            most crushing victory of the war.
1865   Appomattox, April 9—Lee's surrender to Grant.
1866   Battle of Sadowa, July 3—Austria defeated by the Prussian
            needle gun in the one great action of the Seven Weeks' War.
1870–1871   The Franco-German War.
1870   Battle of Spicheren, August 1—the beaten French introduce the
            first machine gun of European warfare.
1870   Battle of Gravelotte-Saint Privat, August 18—the defeat which
            led up to Marshal Bazaine's surrender at Metz.
1870   Sedan, September 1—the surrender of Marshal Macmahon's
            army dates a new German age of total war.
1870   Battle of Coulmiers—armed civilians of the *Défense Nationale*
            win France's only victory of the war, November 9.
1871   Siege of Paris ends in armistice, January 28.
1888   First modern submarine launched by France.
1890   Captain Mahan publishes *The Influence of Sea Power upon
            History*.
1898   Two Spanish squadrons annihilated in Spanish-American War.
1899–1902   South African War—smokeless powder, field telegraph and
            uniforms of protective coloring work drastic changes in tactics.
1903   Flight of the Wright brothers.
1904–1905   Russo-Japanese War.
1904   Russian fleet attacked at anchor as Japanese diplomats en-
            courage hopes of peace, February 8.

1904	Battle of the Yalu, April 30—an Oriental Valmy results when European troops are beaten for the first time by Asiatics using modern military methods.
1904	Battle of the Yellow Sea, August 10—Admiral Togo's victory aided by first use of wireless.
1905	Port Arthur surrendered, January 2, after a siege costing the attackers nearly 100,000 casualties.
1905	Battle of Mukden, February 21-March 6—the machine gun, the barbed-wire entanglement and the field telephone lead to tactics of attrition.
1905	Battle of Tsushima, May 27—Admiral Togo annihilates Russia's Baltic fleet in the first great naval engagement of the age of steam.
1912–1913	Balkan Wars—first aerial bombings on land and sea.
1914–1918	World War I.
1914	Battles of the Frontier, August 4-28—German invaders of Belgium and France carry out Count von Schlieffen's long-prepared plan.
1914	Battle of Tannenberg, August 26-30—Germans win a "second Cannae" at the expense of Russian invaders of East Prussia.
1914	Battle of Lemberg, August 27-31—Austrians defeated with heavy losses by main Russian forces of invasion.
1914	Battle of the Marne, September 6-9—aerial reconnaissance and motor transportation are factors in a decisive Allied victory.
1914	"Race to the Sea," September 28-November 22—a deadlock of trench warfare develops after the Germans fail to seize the Channel ports.
1914	English civilians experience first aerial bombing of the war, December 24.
1915	Champagne offensive, February 16-April 3—Joffre and Foch launch the first of the year's "nibbling" offensives based on long bombardments.
1915	Dardanelles campaign, March 18-December 18—Allied amphibious forces fail to break the deadlock by opening up a new strategic flank.
1915	Ypres, April 22—first poison gas attack.
1915	Conquest of Serbia, October 6-November 12—Central Powers are linked from the North Sea to Persian Gulf after overrunning the Balkans.
1916	Battle of Verdun, first phase, February 21-June 23—Germans attempt to "bleed France to death" in a struggle of attrition.
1916	Battle of Jutland, May 31—British gain a strategic victory in the war's one great sea engagement.
1916	"Brusilov offensive," June 4-September 28—Russia's dying effort on the Eastern Front.
1916	Battle of the Somme, July 1-November 13—new British national army advances seven miles at a cost of 450,000 casualties.

1916	First tank attack, September 15, proves to be premature.
1916	Battle of Verdun, final phase, October 24-December 15—new French tactics regain most of the ground lost earlier in the year.
1916	Conquest of Rumania completed by the Central Powers, December 6.
1917	New German submarine campaign results in losses of 3,855,000 tons from January 1 to June 30.
1917	Mutiny imperils French lines after failure of "Nivelle offensive," April 18-May 4.
1917	Battle of Passchendaele, July 31-November 4—Haig fails in Flanders at a cost of 300,000 casualties.
1917	Russia's military collapse admitted by Allies after failure of final offensive in August.
1917	Caporetto, October 24-November 9—Italians routed with losses of 600,000 by Austro-German offensive from the Julian Alps.
1917	Tank tactics, based on surprise, prove their merit at Cambrai, November 20.
1918	Ludendorff's four spring offensives, March 21-June 12, inflict a million casualties on the Allies and threaten Paris.
1918	Allies achieve unity of command, April 14, as Foch is named generalissimo.
1918	German *Friedensturm*, or peace offensive, repulsed with heavy losses in the Champagne and Marne areas, July 15-18.
1918	Second battle of the Marne, July 18-August 2—Foch launches a Franco-American counteroffensive, wiping out the Soissons-Reims salient.
1918	British counteroffensive in Picardy, August 8-27, reduces the Amiens salient.
1918	Pershing's American forces overrun the St. Mihiel salient, September 12-14.
1918	Allies attacking from Salonika force Bulgaria to her knees, September 15-29.
1918	Allenby's battle of annihilation in Palestine compels the capitulation of Turkey, September 19-30.
1918	New American offensive achieves a complete surprise on the Meuse-Argonne front, September 26.
1918	British break the Hindenburg Line on the St. Quentin-Cambrai front, September 27-October 5.
1918	Germany appeals for an armistice, October 3—military defeat admitted by Ludendorff and Hindenburg before morale collapses on home front.
1918	Italian advance from the Piave forces Austria to sue for an armistice, October 24-30.
1918	American troops reach Sedan in last drives of Meuse-Argonne offensive, November 1-10.
1918	Armistice of November 11 ends fighting on all fronts.
1919	Germany's new republican government recruits 400,000 *Freikorps* volunteers, January-June.

1919	Treaty of Versailles signed, June 28.
1919–1923	Ex-officers plot *Putsches* in Germany as campaigns of the "war in peace."
1922	Mussolini's "March on Rome."
1930	Unpaid state and private loans represent a huge German profit on reparations.
1931	The "Mukden Incident"—Japanese troops seize Manchuria, September 18.
1933	Adolph Hitler becomes chancellor in Germany.
1935	Mussolini invades Ethiopia, October 3.
1935	Germany restores military conscription in defiance of the Versailles terms.
1936	Hitler reoccupies the demilitarized zone of the Rhineland.
1936	Spanish Civil War begins, July 13.
1937	Italian mechanized forces defeated in battle of Guadalajara, March 8-14, as Italy, Germany and Russia send troops to Spain.
1937	German bombing of Guernica, April 26.
1937	"Marco Polo Bridge Incident," July 7, dates beginning of Sino-Japanese war.
1938	German occupation of Austria, March 12.
1938	German and Italian bombings of Barcelona, March 17-18.
1938	Munich Pact, September 30.
1939	Spanish Civil War ends with fall of Madrid, March 28.
1939	German occupation of Czechoslovakia, March 14.
1939	Mussolini invades Albania, April 7.
1939	German-Russian non-aggression pact, August 25.
1939	World War II begins with Nazi invasion of Poland, September 1.
1939	Blitzkrieg crushes last hope of effective Polish resistance, September 1-18.
1939	Russia invades Finland, November 30.
1939	Nazi "pocket battleship" *Graf Spee* scuttled after losing battle with British cruisers, December 18.
1940	Russian armored forces routed at Suomussalmi, January 8.
1940	Russians smash Mannerheim Line and force peace on Finland, February 1-March 13.
1940	German invasion of Norway and Denmark, April 9.
1940	Franco-British troops evacuate all Norway except Narvik region, May 2.
1940	German invasion of Holland and Belgium, May 10.
1940	Winston Churchill becomes prime minister in England, May 11.
1940	Main Nazi effort revealed as drive through the Ardennes into France, May 11.
1940	German break-through at Sedan, May 13.
1940	Holland capitulates, May 14.
1940	Allied forces cut in two by German drive toward the Channel, May 17.

1940   General Maxime Weygand replaces Gamelin as commander of Allied armies, May 19.

1940   German advance units reach the Channel, May 21.

1940   King Leopold orders capitulation of Belgian army, May 28.

1940   Dunkirk evacuation—335,000 British and French troops rescued by ships, May 30-June 3.

1940   Italy declares war on the Allies, June 10.

1940   Fall of Paris, June 14.

1940   Capitulation of France, June 17.

1940   French fleet at Oran seized or destroyed by British squadron, July 3.

1940   Battle of Britain, August 8-October 30—first decisive defeat for Germany as the Luftwaffe fails to break British aerial defenses.

1940   Mussolini invades Greece, October 28.

1940   Italian fleet bombed by British carrier-borne planes in Taranto Harbor, November 11.

1940   Battle of Sidi Barrani, December 9-16—Italian invaders of Egypt defeated by Wavell's British forces with heavy losses.

1940   Porta Edda falls, December 6, to Greek counteroffensive making steady gains in Albania.

1941   Bengasi captured by British forces, February 9—Italian army in Libya destroyed with losses exceeding 150,000.

1941   Italian Somaliland conquered by Allies, March 7.

1941   Greeks repulse Italian counteroffensive with losses of 50,000, March 15.

1941   Battle of the Ionian Sea (or Cape Matapan), March 28—Italians defeated by the British with heavy losses in greatest naval action of Mediterranean.

1941   German invasion of Greece and Jugoslavia, April 6.

1941   Last effective resistance in Jugoslavia overcome, April 16.

1941   Resistance ends in Greece, April 30, as survivors of British expeditionary force are evacuated.

1941   Germans capture Crete, May 20-29, in world's first aerial invasion.

1941   German battleship *Bismarck* sunk by British warships and planes, May 27.

1941   Nazis invade Russia, June 22.

1941   Battle of the Frontier, June 22-July 18—Soviet armies sacrifice territory in order to keep the bulk of their forces in reserve.

1941   Battle of Smolensk, July 21-September 27—Nazi invaders checked by the main forces of the Red army.

1941   Battle of Moscow, October 2-December 4—invaders of Russia fail to smash the Red army at Moscow, Leningrad and Rostov.

1941   First counterattacks of Russian winter offensive, December 6.

1941   American Pacific fleet attacked without warning at Pearl Harbor by Japanese carrier-borne planes, December 7.

1941 British warships *Repulse* and *Prince of Wales* sunk by Japanese torpedo planes, December 10.

1941 Luzon invaded by Japanese, December 22.

1941 American resistance ends on Wake, December 23.

1941 Hong Kong falls to Japanese, December 25.

1941 Bengasi recaptured by British, December 25.

1941 General MacArthur retreats to Bataan Peninsula, December 31, after evacuating Manila.

1941 Siege of Sevastopol lifted by Russian winter offensive, January 7.

1942 British abandon Malaya mainland, January 30, to Japanese jungle offensive.

1942 Surrender of Singapore, February 15.

1942 Battle of Java Sea, February 27-28—Allied squadron destroyed by Japanese.

1942 British evacuate Rangoon and southern Burma, March 7.

1942 Effective resistance ends on Java, March 10.

1942 Fall of Bataan, April 9.

1942 Tokyo bombed by American carrier-borne planes, April 18.

1942 Surrender of Corregidor, May 6.

1942 Battle of the Coral Sea, May 7-8—Americans win first round with Japanese naval forces.

1942 Nazi spring offensive begins in Russia, May 12.

1942 Battle of Midway, June 3-7—Japanese invasion fleet of eighty vessels repulsed with heavy losses by American carrier-borne and land-based planes.

1942 Simultaneous Japanese attack on Alaska, June 3, results in landings on Attu and Kiska.

1942 British armored forces defeated by Rommel, June 13, and pursued into Egypt.

1942 Tobruk falls to Rommel, June 21, with 25,000 prisoners.

1942 Sevastopol taken by Nazis, July 1.

1942 British make desperate stand at El Alamein, seventy miles from Alexandria, July 4.

1942 Americans land on Guadalcanal, August 7.

1942 Battle of Savo Island, August 8—first of the Solomons naval actions ends in a Japanese victory.

1942 Nazis cross the Don and penetrate to Grozny oil field in the Caucasus, August 15.

1942 Defense of Stalingrad begins, August 23.

1942 Japanese land attack on Guadalcanal repulsed by Americans, September 12-13.

1942 Axis forces hold the initiative on Stalingrad, Guadalcanal and El Alamein fronts, October 15.

1942 The twenty days of November—United Nations forces stop the Axis strategic offensive in the first great turning point of the global war, November 1-20.

1942 November 1-3—British Eighth Army wins complete victory over Rommel in the battle of El Alamein.

1942 November 8—Anglo-American forces land in Algeria and Morocco.

1942 November 13-15—Americans repulse Japanese invasion fleet with losses of twenty-eight ships in the decisive naval battle of Guadalcanal.

1942 November 19—Russian counteroffensive at Stalingrad encircles German Sixth Army.

1943 Buna occupied on January 3 by MacArthur's forces advancing from Port Moresby.

1943 Tripoli falls to British pursuing Rommel, January 22.

1943 Churchill and Roosevelt confer at Casablanca, January 27.

1943 Last Japanese troops on Guadalcanal evacuated, February 7.

1943 Kharkov recaptured after five hundred days of Nazi occupation, February 16.

1943 Japanese naval defeat in battle of the Bismarck Sea, March 1-3.

1943 British smash through Mareth Line, March 30, driving Rommel into Tunisia.

1943 Nazi defenders of Tunis and Bizerte annihilated by Anglo-American attack of May 6-8.

1943 Attu retaken by Americans, May 11-30.

1943 Italian island fortress of Pantelleria surrenders, June 11.

1943 The twenty days of July—second great turning point of the global war as United Nations forces seize the offensive, July 1-20.

1943 July 1-5—American landings in the central Solomons.

1943 July 10—Anglo-American forces invade Sicily with 2,000 warships and transports.

1943 July 13-20—Red army turns German summer offensive into a failure by wresting the initiative from the attackers.

1943 Palermo captured in Sicily, July 23.

1943 Munda occupied in New Georgia, August 5.

1943 Orel, great Nazi "hedgehog" of the centre, falls to Soviet advance, August 6.

1943 Americans land on Kiska, August 15, to find island evacuated by the Japanese.

1943 Organized resistance ends on Sicily after a thirty-nine-day campaign, August 17.

1943 Mussolini dictatorship collapses in Italy, August 25.

1943 First Allied foothold on European continent gained as British cross Straits of Messina, September 3.

1943 Italy surrenders unconditionally, September 8.

1943 Anglo-American forces seize beachheads on Salerno Bay, September 9.

1943 Lae captured by MacArthur in New Guinea, September 16.

1943 Sardinia occupied by Allies, September 20.

1943	Nazi battleship *Tirpitz* crippled by British "midget" submarines in Alten Fjord, September 22.
1943	Russian occupation of Smolensk, September 25, marks advance of 250 miles since middle of July.
1943	Naples and Foggia fall to Allies, October 1.
1943	Americans land on Bougainville, November 1.
1943	Kiev entered by Red army, November 6.
1943	Gilbert Islands invaded by Americans, November 21.
1943	Churchill, Roosevelt and Stalin confer at Teheran, November 28-December 1.
1943	Americans invade New Britain, December 15.
1943	British warships sink the Nazi battleship *Scharnhorst*, December 26.
1944	Red army crosses prewar border of Poland, January 6.
1944	Anglo-American landings at Anzio, January 22.
1944	Americans invade Marshall Islands, February 1.
1944	Americans invade Admiralty Islands, February 29.
1944	Red army crosses Rumanian border, April 2, and reaches frontier of Czechoslovakia, April 8.
1944	Odessa occupied by Soviet forces, April 10.
1944	MacArthur lands at Hollandia and Aitape, April 22.
1944	Sevastopol falls to Russian besiegers, May 9.
1944	Cassino evacuated by retreating Nazis, May 18.
1944	The twenty days of June—third great turning point of the global war as United Nations forces attack inner defenses of Germany and Japan, June 4-23.
1944	June 4—Rome falls to Anglo-American offensive.
1944	June 6—Normandy invaded by Anglo-American forces.
1944	June 15—American landings in Saipan.
1944	June 16—beginning of strategic bombing in Japan.
1944	June 18—Japanese defeat by Americans in naval battle of the Philippine Sea.
1944	June 23—opening of great Soviet summer offensive.
1944	Cherbourg captured by Americans, June 27.
1944	Caen falls to British, July 21.
1944	American attack breaks through at St. Lô, July 25.
1944	Americans take Rennes and overrun Brittany peninsula to the Loire, August 3-5.
1944	Fall of Myitkyina, after a seventy-eight-day fight, gives Allies a firm hold on Upper Burma, August 4.
1944	Allies trap 100,000 Germans in "Argantan-Falaise pocket," August 10-11, as enemy withdraws across Seine.
1944	Allies invade Mediterranean coast of France, August 15.
1944	Paris falls to great Allied advance, August 25.
1944	Bucharest occupied by Soviet forces, August 31.
1944	Americans cross frontier of Belgium, September 2.
1944	Pisa falls to Allied advance in Italy, September 2.

1944	Lyon occupied by Allies driving from Mediterranean, September 3.
1944	U. S. First Army crosses German frontier, September 11.
1944	British Second Army enters the Netherlands, September 12.
1944	Americans land on Morotai and two Palau islands, September 15.
1944	Allied aerial assault at Arnhem-Eindhoven, September 17.
1944	Red army crosses frontier of Hungary, October 6.
1944	Belgrade occupied by Soviet forces and Marshal Tito's Jugoslav guerrillas, October 14.
1944	Americans land on Leyte to begin MacArthur's invasion of the Philippines, October 20.
1944	Japanese fleet defeated in the second battle of the Philippine Sea, October 24-27.
1944	First Russian shells fall in Budapest, November 5.
1944	Stalin announces the restoration of the Soviet frontier along its entire 1,800-mile length, November 6.
1944	Allies begin offensive along the river Roer, November 16.
1944	Metz taken by U. S. Third Army, November 20.
1944	Strasbourg captured by French First Army, November 23.
1944	Tokyo bombed first time by land-based U. S. Superfortresses, November 24.
1944	Rundstedt opens great counterattack in the Ardennes, December 16, leading to the battle of the Bulge.
1944	Mindora invaded by the Americans, December 16.
1945	Luzon invaded by U. S. Sixth Army, January 9.
1945	Opening of great Soviet offensive in Poland, January 12.
1945	Warsaw falls to advancing Russians, January 17.
1945	Russians drive to the Oder, thirty-three miles east of Berlin, February 4.
1945	Roosevelt, Churchill and Stalin begin conference at Yalta, February 4.
1945	Budapest falls to Russians after a fifty-day siege, February 13.
1945	Iwo Jima invaded by U. S. marines, February 19.
1945	New Allied offensive opens in western Germany, February 22.
1945	Manila liberated by Americans, February 23.
1945	Cologne occupied by Americans, March 7.
1945	Americans seize bridge at Remagen, March 7, to win first crossing of the Rhine.
1945	Japanese resistance ends on Iwo Jima, March 16.
1945	Mandalay falls to British forces in Burma, March 20.
1945	Allies establish four new Rhine bridgeheads, March 22-27.
1945	Danzig falls to Soviet forces, March 30.
1945	U. S. First and Ninth armies meet near Paderborn, April 1, to encircle 300,000 Nazis in the battle of the Ruhr.
1945	Okinawa invaded by Americans, April 1.
1945	Japan's largest battleship, *Yamato*, sunk by Americans, April 7
1945	Hanover captured by Americans, April 10.

1945	Vienna falls to Soviet forces, April 13.
1945	U. S. forces enter Czechoslovakia, April 18.
1945	Bologna falls to U. S. Fifth Army, April 21.
1945	Berlin encircled by the Russians, April 25.
1945	American and Russian forces meet at Torgau, April 25.
1945	Bremen occupied by British, April 26.
1945	Mussolini executed by Italians, April 29.
1945	Fall of Venice and Milan, April 29.
1945	Munich occupied by U. S. Seventh Army, April 29.
1945	Berlin completely occupied by Russians, May 2.
1945	Nearly all Burma lost to Japanese as British capture Rangoon, May 3.
1945	Germany signs terms of unconditional surrender at Reims, May 7.
1945	Organized resistance ends on Okinawa after eighty-two-day campaign, July 21.
1945	MacArthur announces complete liberation of the Philippines, July 5.
1945	Halsey's Third Fleet bombards Japanese shores, July 14.
1945	Atomic bomb tested in New Mexico desert, July 16.
1945	First atomic bomb dropped on Hiroshima, August 6.
1945	Soviet Union declares war on Japan, August 8.
1945	Second atomic bomb dropped on Nagasaki, August 9.
1945	Japan sues for peace, August 10.
1945	Fighting ends in the Pacific, August 14.
1945	Japan signs terms of unconditional surrender on board U. S. battleship *Missouri* in Tokyo Bay, September 2.
1947	President Truman's declaration of cold war on the Soviet Union, March 12.
1947	Inception of the Marshall Plan, June 5.
1947	"Operation Vittles," the supply of Berlin by air, begins after Stalin closes the city to non-Russian traffic, June 24.
1949	Inception of North Atlantic Treaty Alliance, March 17.
1949	President Truman announces that Russia has exploded an atomic bomb, September 23.
1950	Invasion of the Republic of Korea by forces of the Soviet puppet state, North Korean People's Republic, June 25.
1950	President Truman orders U.S. air and naval forces in the Far East to resist the aggression. United Nations Security Council demands that Korean Reds withdraw, June 27.
1950	First U.S. ground forces land in Korea, July 4.
1950	Korean Reds defeated after successful U.S. amphibious combat landings at Inchon open the way to the recovery of Seoul, September 15-27.
1950	General of the Army Douglas MacArthur, supreme UN commander, launches "massive compression envelopment" with the object of advancing to the Yalu and ending the war, November 24.

1950	Chinese Communist surprise counteroffensive drives Eighth Army back in west Korea and compels retreat of UN forces in northeast Korea, November 26 to December 10.
1951	Second Chinese offensive makes necessary UN withdrawals to a line extending from 50 to 80 miles south of the 38th parallel, January 1 to 12.
1951	UN forces launch Operation KILLER, followed by Operation RIPPER, February 23 and March 4.
1951	Chinese Communist offensive fought to a standstill, April 22-29.
1951	Renewal of Chinese Communist offensive defeated in east Korea, May 16-21.
1951	UN counteroffensive gains ground and inflicts crippling losses on the enemy, May 25 to June 10.
1951	At request of hard-pressed Chinese, in desperate need of a breathing spell, truce talks at Kaesong lead to lull at the front, July 10 to August 27.
1951	Before front is "frozen" at request of truce-talk delegates meeting at Panmunjom, UN forces fight their way forward in a last offensive, September 1-24.
1952	Panmunjom delegates agree in November to permanent defensive lines, and static warfare begins, January 1.
1953	United States pledges atomic aid against aggressors at meeting of NATO in Paris, April 25.
1953	"Big Four" of NATO, the United States, Great Britain, France and West Germany, sign mutual defense treaty at Bonn, May 27.
1953	After a stalemate lasting since permanent lines were established, Korean War ends with a cease-fire agreement, July 27.
1953	Soviet Russia tests a hydrogen bomb, August 20.
1954	Armistice signed by France and Vietminh (Communist) ends seven-year guerrilla war in Indo-China, August 11.
1955	U.S. Secretary of State Dulles, in a New York address, announces the policy later known as "massive retaliation," January 12.
1955	U.S. Atomic submarine *Nautilus* makes first dive, January 20.
1956	The "hundred hour" Israeli-Egyptian war ends with rout of Egyptian forces in the Sinai peninsula, October 31 to November 4.
1956	British and French forces occupy Egypt for a month after successful airborne, water-borne and helicopter amphibious landings in Port Said on November 6.
1958	U.S. soldiers and marines occupy Lebanon, threatened with Communist infiltration, July 15 to September 29.
1959	Soviet Premier Nikita Khrushchev makes good-will tour of the United States, September 15-28.

ACKNOWLEDGMENTS AND SOURCES

One day in the fall of 1939, I mentioned to my publisher, the late Eugene F. Saxton, of Harper & Brothers, that I had accumulated nearly half a million words of indexed notes during the past six years while pursuing my hobby of reading military history. "That isn't a hobby," he said. "It's a book."

And so it was, thanks to the encouragement of a publisher who suggested the title and grubstaked the author with generous advances against royalties.

A good many other people have helped to make this book a reality. Second to none is my wife, Lois, who contributed the maps and illustrations under her professional name as an artist, L. K. Hartzell. She merits a halo, moreover, for sharing the home with the bulky notes, manuscript and correspondence of a thousand-page book. It was like bringing an infant up to massive maturity.

The first sources were books sent by insured mail to my New Hampshire country home on direct loan from the Harvard and Dartmouth college libraries. If I were to name all the other libraries deserving of thanks, my gratitude would be diluted by prolixity. The list would include not only the Library of Congress but also the many city and college libraries all over the country from which I received books through the Denver Bibliographical Center while living in that city. During the past ten years, as a historian of the United States Marine Corps in Washington, D.C., I have been the beneficiary of books on loan from the libraries of the Army, the Navy and the Marine Corps.

Perhaps an author should give thanks to his sources as well as to the libraries which made them available. Military scholarship, as we know it today, dates back only to the turn of the century. Oman in Britain, Dodge in America, Colin in France, Delbrück in Germany—they were the pioneers, and it is unfortunate that the last two have never been translated into English. During this same period, Mahan in America and Corbett in Britain were doing a like service for the annals of naval warfare.

Sometimes, as in the case of Oman's *Art of War in the Middle Ages,* a single work can illuminate an era. By the same token, if a reader were to be limited to a few volumes on warfare of the twentieth century, he could do no better than the operational histories of the First and Second World Wars, written by officers of the United States Military Academy and edited by Colonel T. Dodson Stamps and Colonel Vincent J. Esposito.

It would be ideal if these books could point the way to the official histories of the United States Army, Navy, Marine Corps and Air Force. More than a hundred volumes, written from original sources and distinguished for accuracy and objectivity, will eventually be published on the two World Wars and the Korean War. Similar works are being brought out by official historians of the United Kingdom, Australia, Canada, New Zealand and South Africa.

It is perhaps needless to mention that the present book is based almost entirely on published sources. Its purpose will have been fulfilled if it serves as an introduction to an ancient institution that has shaped so much of the history of the twentieth century. In such a general survey, aimed at the student rather than the scholar of war, it has seemed desirable to maintain a narrative flow, so that the book could be read without interruptions. This explains the lack of footnotes and accounts for the simplified operational maps. Reference has been made in the text to sources of unusual interest.

In the following pages will be found a list of sources arranged by parts. Asterisks refer to those whose publishers have kindly given permission to use quotations.

PART ONE: THE CLASSICAL AGE

Aristophanes. *The Eleven Comedies* (translator anonymous). New York: Liveright, 1927.*

Arrian. *Anabasis of Alexander* (Rooke, trans.). London, 1813.

Caesar, Gaius Julius. *Commentaries* (J. Rice Holmes, trans.). London, 1909.

Delbrück, Hans. *Geschichte der Kriegkunst im Rahmen der politischen Geschichte.* Vol. I, *Das Altertum,* and Vol. II, *Römer und Germanen.* Berlin: G. Stilke, 4 Vols., 1900-1920.

Dodge, Theodore Ayrault. *Alexander.* Boston: Houghton Mifflin, 1890.

———. *Hannibal.* Boston: Houghton Mifflin, 1891.*

———. *Caesar.* Boston: Houghton Mifflin, 1893.*

Fuller, Major General J. F. C. *Wars of the Diadochi.* Encyclopaedia Britannica, 14th Edition, Vol. IX, 1929.

Grote, George. *History of Greece.* London, 10 Vols., 1888.

Herodotus. *History of the Persian Wars* (W. P. Dickson, trans.). London, 1862.

Homer. *Iliad* (Alexander Pope, trans.). New York, 1880.

Jal, Auguste. *Archiologie Navale.* Paris, 1840.

Josephus, Flavius. *The Jewish War* (W. Whiston, trans.). New York, 1824.

Lewis, Charles Lee. *Famous Old World Sea Fighters.* Boston: Lothrop, Lee & Shepard, 1929.

Liddell Hart, Captain B. H. *A Greater than Napoleon: Scipio Africanus.* Edinburgh: Blackwood, 1926.

Livy (Titus Livius). *History of Rome* (George Baker, trans.). New York, 1836.

Mommsen, Theodor. *History of Rome* (W. P. Dickson, trans.). London, 4 Vols., 1887.

Napoleon III. *Histoire de Jules César.* Paris, 2 Vols., 1865.

Plutarch. *Complete Works.* New York, 1909.

Polybius. *General History* (Hampton, trans.). London, 1823.

Serre, Paul. *Études sur l'Histoire Militaire et Maritime des Grecs et des Romains.* Paris, 1888.

Tacitus. *Historical Works* (Arthur Murphy, trans.). New York: Dutton, 1932.

Thucydides. *History of the Peloponnesian War* (B. Jowett, trans.). London, 1883.

Torr, Cecil. *Ancient Ships.* Cambridge, 1895.

Vaudencourt, F. G. de. *Histoire des Campagnes d'Annibal en Italie.* Milan, 3 Vols., 1812.

Vegetius. *De Re Militari* (Jean Priorat, trans.). Paris, 1897.
Xenophon. *Anabasis, Cyropaedia* and *Hellenica* (H. G. Dakyns, trans.). London, 1890-1904.

PART TWO: THE CAVALRY CYCLE

Bury, John Bagnell. *History of the Later Roman Empire.* London, 2 Vols., 1889.
Carpini, Joannes de Plano. *Histoire des Mongols.* Paris, 1867.
Delbrück, Hans. *Geschichte der Kriegkunst im Rahmen der Politischen Geschichte.* Vol. III, *Das Mittelalter.* Berlin: G. Stilke, 1900-1920.
Denis, Ernest. *Huss et la Guerre des Hussites.* Paris: Leroux, 1930.
Gibbon, Edward. *The Decline and Fall of the Roman Empire.* New York, 6 Vols., 1872.
Hallam, Henry. *History of Europe during the Middle Ages.* New York, 2 Vols., 1900.
Hime, H. W. L. *Gunpowder and Ammunition, their Origin and Progress.* London, 1904.
Hodgkin, Thomas. *Italy and her Invaders.* Oxford, 3 Vols., 1890.
Howorth, Sir Henry. *History of the Mongols.* London, 5 Vols., 1876-1880.
Lane-Poole, Stanley. *Mohammedan Dynasties.* London, 1884.
Lenfant, Jacques. *Histoire de la Guerre des Hussites.* Amsterdam, 2 Vols., 1731.
Liddell Hart, Captain B. H. *Mongol Campaigns.* Encyclopaedia Britannica, Vol. XV, 14th Edition, 1929.
Lutzow, Count. *Bohemia, an Historical Sketch.* New York, 1909.
Michaud, Joseph Francois. *Histoire des Croisades.* Paris, 6 Vols., 1840.
Muyden, B. van. *Histoire de la Nation Suisse.* Lausanne, 3 Vols., 1896-1899.
Oman, Sir Charles W. C. *History of the Art of War in the Middle Ages.* London: Methuen, 2 Vols., 1924.*
Procopius of Caesarea. *History of the Wars* (H. B. Dewing, trans.). London: Heinemann, 6 Vols., 1914.*
Sykes, Brigadier General P. M. *A History of Persia.* London, 2 Vols., 1915.
Thompson, James Westfall. *An Economic and Social History of the Middle Ages.* New York: Century, 1928.*
Villehardouin, Geoffroy de. *Conquête de Constantinople* (E. Bouchet, trans.). Paris, 2 Vols., 1891.

PART THREE: THE MILITARY RENAISSANCE

Brantôme, Pierre de Bourdeille. *Memoirs.* Paris, 12 Vols., 1864-1896.
Buchan, John. *Oliver Cromwell.* Boston: Houghton Mifflin, 1934.*
————. *Montrose.* Boston: Houghton Mifflin, 1928.
Corbett, Sir Julian S. *Drake and the Tudor Navy.* London, 1888.
Creasy, Sir Edward Shephard. *History of the Ottoman Turks.* London, 2 Vols., 1878.
Dodge, Theodore Ayrault. *Gustavus Adolphus.* Boston: Houghton Mifflin, 1895.
Firth, C. H. *Cromwell's Army.* London, 1902.

Fletcher, C. R. L. *Gustavus Adolphus*. London, 1892.
Froissart, Jean. *Chronycles* (Sir John Bourchier, trans.). Oxford, 7 Vols., 1927-1928.
Gardiner, Samuel R. *History of the Great Civil War*. London, 4 Vols., 1893.
Gibbons, Herbert Adams. *The Foundation of the Ottoman Empire*. Oxford, 1916.
Hurtel, Georges. *Turenne: Les Institutions Militaires de son Temps*. Paris, 1884.
La Noue, Francois de. *Discours Politiques et Militaires*. Paris, 1854.
Motley, John Lothrop. *The Rise of the Dutch Republic*. Philadelphia, 3 Vols., 1898.
Oman, Sir Charles W. C. *History of the Art of War in the Sixteenth Century*. New York: Dutton, 1937.
Robertson, William. *History of the Reign of the Emperor Charles the Fifth*. London, 3 Vols., 1769.
Schiller, Johann Christoph von. *Wallenstein* (Alexander F. Murison, trans.). New York: Longmans, Green, 1931.*
Wedgwood, C. V. *The Thirty Years' War*. New Haven: Yale University Press, 1939.
Weygand, General Maxime. *Turenne*. Paris: Flammarion, 1929.

PART FOUR: ARMED DIPLOMACY

Bain, R. N. *Charles XII and the Collapse of the Swedish Empire*. London, 1895.
Brun, V. *Guerres Maritimes de la France*. Paris, 1861.
Carlyle, Thomas. *History of Frederick the Great*. New York, 6 Vols., 1871.
Churchill, Winston S. *Marlborough, his Life and Times*. New York: Charles Scribner's Sons, 6 Vols., 1932.*
Colin, Colonel Jean. *Les Campagnes du Maréchal de Saxe*. Paris, 3 Vols., 1900-1906.
Corbett, Sir Julian S. *England in the Seven Years' War*. London, 1907.
Custance, Sir Reginald. *The Ship of the Line in Battle*. London, 1912.
Forester, C. S. *Louis XIV, King of France and Navarre*. New York: Dodd Mead, 1928.
Fortescue, Sir John W. *Marlborough*. New York: Appleton, 1932.
Frederick II, King of Prussia. *Oeuvres de Frédéric le Grand*. Berlin, 30 Vols., 1846-1857.
Halévy, Daniel. *La Jeunesse du Maréchal de Luxembourg*. Paris, 1904.
Lloyd, General Henry. *Histoire de la Guerre d'Allemagne*. Paris, 1803.
Mahan, Captain Alfred T. *The Influence of Sea Power upon History, 1660-1783*. Boston: Little, Brown, 1890.*
Maude, Colonel F. N. *Seven Years' War*. Encyclopaedia Britannica, Vol. XX, 14th Edition, 1929.
Parkman, Francis. *A Half Century of Conflict*. Boston, 2 Vols., 1902.
———. *Montcalm and Wolfe*. Boston, 2 Vols., 1901.
Saxe, Marshal Count Maurice. *Mes Rêveries sur l'Art de Guerre*. Paris, 1756.
Schuyler, E. *Life of Peter the Great*. London, 1884.

Ségur, Pierre de. *La Jeunesse du Maréchal de Luxembourg.* Paris, 1904.
Thompson, James Westfall. *The Wars of Religion in France.* Chicago, 1909.
Vauban, Sébastien le Prestre de. *Oeuvres.* Amsterdam, 2 Vols., 1771.
Voltaire, Francois Marie Arouet de. *Précis du Siècle de Louis XIV.* Paris, 1826.

PART FIVE: THE REVOLUTION IN TACTICS

Adams, Henry. *The War of 1812.* (Excerpt from the nine-volume *History of the United States.*) (Major H. A. DeWeerd, ed.) Washington: Infantry Journal Press, 1944.
Alden, John Richard. *The American Revolution, 1775-1783.* New York: Harper, 1954.
Atkinson, Major C. F. *French Revolutionary Wars.* Encyclopaedia Britannica, 14th Edition, Vol. IX, 1929.*
Bonnal, M. *Carnot, d'apres les Archives Nationales.* Paris, 1888.
Colin, Colonel Jean. *La Tactique et la Discipline dans les Armées de la Révolution.* Paris, 1902.
———. *Études sur la Campagne de 1796-1797 en Italie.* Paris, 1898.
———. *L'Éducation Militaire de Napoléon.* Paris, 1901.
Caulaincourt, General de, Duke of Vicenza. *With Napoleon in Russia.* New York: Morrow, 1935.
——— *No Peace with Napoleon!* New York: Morrow, 1936.
Commager, Henry Steele, and Richard B. Morris. *The Spirit of '76: The Story of the American Revolution as Told by Participants.* 2 Vols. Indianapolis: Bobbs-Merrill, 1958.
Dodge, Theodore Ayrault. *Napoleon.* 4 Vols. Boston: Houghton Mifflin, 1904.
Fisher, George Sydney. *The Struggle for American Independence.* Philadelphia: Lippincott, 2 Vols., 1908.*
Fortescue, Sir John W. *Wellington.* New York: Dodd, Mead, 1925.
Freeman, Douglas Southall. *George Washington.* 6 Vols. New York: Scribner's, 1948-1955.
Fuller, Major General J. F. C. *British Light Infantry in the Eighteenth Century.* London: Hutchinson, 1925.
Graham, James. *General Daniel Morgan of the Virginia Line.* New York, 1856.
Greene, Francis Vinton. *General Greene.* New York, 1893.
Grouard, A. M. *Les Batailles de Napoléon.* Paris, 1900.
Guibert, Jacques. *Essai Général de Tactique.* Liége, 2 Vols., 1775.
Macdonell, A. G. *Napoleon and his Marshals.* 2 Vols. New York: Macmillan, 1934.
Mahan, Captain Alfred Thayer. *Major Operations of the Navies in the War of American Independence.* Boston: Little, Brown, 1913.
———. *The Influence of Sea Power upon the French Revolution and Empire, 1793-1812.* Boston: Little, Brown, 1892.
———. *The Life of Nelson.* Boston: Little, Brown, 1897.
Maude, Colonel F. N. *Napoleonic Campaigns.* Encyclopaedia Britannica, 14th Edition, Vol. XVI, 1929.*

Moore, Sir John. *Diary* (General Sir J. F. Maurice, ed.). London, 2 Vols., 1904.
Napoleon I. *Correspondence.* Paris, 28 Vols., 1857-1859.
Napoleon I. *Oeuvres de Napoléon à Saint Hélène.* Paris, 4 Vols., 1870.
Nickerson, Hoffman. *The Turning Point of the Revolution.* Boston: Houghton Mifflin, 1928.
Oman, Sir Charles W. C. *History of the Peninsular War, 1807-1813.* London, 6 Vols., 1902-1920.
Peckham, Howard H. *The War for Independence.* Chicago: University of Chicago Press, 1958.
Petre, F. Lorraine. *Napoleon and the Archduke Charles.* London, 1909.
Pratt, Fletcher. *Road to Empire: the Life and Times of Bonaparte the General.* New York: Doubleday, Doran, 1939.
Trevelyan, Sir George O. *The American Revolution.* New York, 4 Vols., 1899.
Tucker, Glenn. *Poltroons and Patriots: A Popular Account of the War of 1812.* 2 Vols. Indianapolis: Bobbs-Merrill, 1954.
Ward, Christopher. (John Richard Alden, ed.) *The War of the Revolution.* 2 Vols. New York: Macmillan, 1952.
Yorck von Wartenburg, Count Hans. *Napoleon as a General.* London, 2 Vols., 1902.

PART SIX: WAR'S MACHINE AGE

Alexander, General E. P. *Military Memoirs of a Confederate.* New York, 1908.
Atkinson, Major C. F. *Franco-German War.* Encyclopaedia Britannica, 14th Edition, Vol. IX, 1929.
Badeau, Adam. *Military History of U. S. Grant.* New York, 4 vols., 1881.
Ballard, Colin R. *The Military Genius of Abraham Lincoln.* Cleveland: World, 1954.
Bernardi, General Friedrich von. *Germany and the Next War.* London, 1914.
Bonnal, General Henri. *Sadowa.* Paris, 1901.
Brodie, Bernard. *Sea Power in the Machine Age.* Princeton: Princeton University Press, 1942.
Buguslawski, Captain A. von. *Tactical Deductions from the War of 1870-71* (Colonel J. J. Graham, trans.). London, 1872.
Chambers, Lenoir. *Stonewall Jackson: The Legend and the Man.* 2 Vols. New York: Morrow, 1959.
Clausewitz, General Karl von. *On War* (Colonel J. J. Graham, trans.). London, 2 Vols., 1873.
Elliott, Charles Winslow. *Winfield Scott: the Soldier and the Man.* New York: Macmillan, 1937.
Falk, Edwin A. *Togo and the Rise of Japanese Sea Power.* New York: Longmans, Green, 1936.
Freeman, Douglas Southall. *R. E. Lee.* 4 Vols. New York: Scribner's, 1934-1935.

Fuller, Major General J. F. C. *The Generalship of Ulysses S. Grant.* New York: Dodd, Mead, 1929.
Goltz, General Colmar von der. *The Nation in Arms* (Philip A. Ashworth, trans.). London, 1914.
————. *The Conduct of War* (Major G. F. Leverson, trans.). London, 1917.
Gorlitz, Walter. *The German General Staff, Its History and Structure, 1675-1945.* Brian Battershaw, trans. London: Hollis and Carter, 1953.
Grant, Ulysses S. *Personal Memoirs.* Cleveland: World, 1956.
Henderson, Colonel G. F. R. *Stonewall Jackson and the American Civil War.* London, 2 Vols., 1900.
Huddleston, F. J., and E. W. Sheppard. *Crimean War.* Encyclopaedia Britannica, 14th Edition, Vol. VI, 1929.*
Jomini, Baron Antoine. *Summary of the Art of War* (Major O. F. Winship, trans.). New York, 1854.
————. *Treatise on Grand Military Operations* (Colonel S. B. Holabird, trans.). New York, 1865.
Latour, Major A. Carriere. *Historical Memoir of the War in West Florida and Louisiana.* Philadelphia, 1816.
Lea, Homer. *The Valor of Ignorance.* New York, 1909.
Lewis, Lloyd. *Sherman: Fighting Prophet.* New York: Harcourt, Brace, 1932.
Livermore, Thomas. *Numbers and Losses in the Civil War in America.* New York, 1901.
McCormick, R. R. *Ulysses S. Grant, the Great Soldier of America.* New York: Appleton, 1934.
Mitre, General Don Bartolomé. *The Emancipation of South America.* London, 1893.
Moltke, Field Marshal Count Helmuth von. *The Franco-German War of 1870-71.* London, 2 Vols., 1891.
Moses, Bernard. *The Intellectual Background of the Revolution in South America.* New York, 1926.
Muzzey, David Saville. *The American Adventure: a History of the United States.* 2 Vols. New York: Harper, 1927.*
Picq, Colonel Ardant du. *Battle Studies* (Colonel John N. Greely and Major Robert G. Cotton, trans.). New York: Macmillan, 1921.*
Puleston, Captain William D. *Mahan.* New Haven: Yale University Press, 1939.
Robertson, William Spence. *History of the Latin American Nations.* New York: Appleton, 1932.
Rourke, Thomas. *Man of Glory: Simon Bolivar.* New York: Morrow, 1939.
Sherman, General W. T. *Memoirs.* New York, 1881.
Smith, J. H. *The War with Mexico.* New York: Macmillan, 1920.
Williams, Kenneth P. *Lincoln Finds a General.* 5 Vols. New York: Macmillan, 1953-1958.

PART SEVEN: WORLD WAR I

Borsky, G. *The Greatest Swindle in History: Story of the Reparations.* London: Müller, 1942.*

Brusilov, General A. A. *A Soldier's Notebook, 1914-1918.* London: Macmillan, 1930.

Buchan, John. *A History of the Great War.* 4 Vols. Boston: Houghton Mifflin, 1922.

Cameron, James. *1914.* New York: Rinehart & Co., 1959.

Churchill, Winston S. *The World Crisis.* 5 Vols., New York: Scribner's, 1923-1929.

Corbett, Sir Julian S. *History of the Great War, Based on Official Documents, Naval Operations.* London: Longmans, Green, 1920.

Cruttwell, C. R. M. F. *A History of the Great War, 1914-1918.* Oxford: Clarendon Press, 1934.*

Falkenhayn, General E. von. *General Headquarters, 1914-1916, and Its Critical Decisions.* New York: Dodd, Mead, 1919.

Falls, Cyril. *The Great War.* New York: Putnam's, 1959.

Foch, Marshal Ferdinand. *The Memoirs of Marshal Foch.* New York: Doubleday, Doran, 1920.

French, Field-Marshal Viscount. *1914.* Boston: Houghton Mifflin, 1919.

Fuller, Major General J. F. C. *Tanks in the Great War.* London: J. Murray, 1920.*

Gaulle, General Charles de. *The Army of the Future.* Philadelphia: Lippincott, 1941.*

Harbord, James G. *The American Army in France.* Boston: Little, Brown, 1936.

Hindenburg, Marshal von. *Out of My Life.* New York: Harper, 1921.

Hoffman, General Max. *The War of Lost Opportunities.* London: Paul, French, Trubner, 1924.

Joffre, Field Marshal. *The Personal Memoirs of Joffre.* New York: Harper, 1932.

Kluck, Alexander von. *The March on Paris and the Battle of the Marne.* New York: Longmans, Green, 1920.

Knox, Major General Sir Alfred W. *With the Russian Army, 1914-1917.* New York: Dutton, 1921.

Liddell Hart, Captain B. H. *The Real War, 1914-1918.* Boston: Little, Brown, 1930.*

———. *The Defence of Britain.* New York: Random, 1939.*

Ludendorff, General Erich. *Ludendorff's Own Story.* 2 Vols. New York: Harper, 1920.

March, General Peyton C. *The Nation at War.* New York: Doubleday, Doran, 1932.

Millis, Walter. *Road to War: America, 1914-1917.* Boston: Houghton Mifflin, 1935.

Mitchell, General William. *Our Air Force.* New York: Dutton, 1921.

Mowrer, Lillian T. *Rip Tide of Aggression.* New York: Morrow, 1942.*

Owen, Frank. *Tempestuous Journey: Lloyd George and His Times.* New York: McGraw-Hill, 1955.

Palat, General B. E. *La Grande Guerre sur le Front Occidental.* 12 Vols. Paris: Chapelot, 1917-1924.

Pershing, General John J. *Final Report of General John J. Pershing.* Washington: Government Printing Office, 1920.

——. *My Experiences in the World War.* New York: Stokes, 1931.

Pétain, General Henri Philippe. *Verdun.* New York: Dial Press, 1930.

Scheer, Admiral von. *The German High Seas Fleet in the World War.* London: Cassell, 1920.

Sims, Vice-Admiral W. S. *The Victory at Sea.* New York: Doubleday, Page, 1920.

Soward, F. H. *Twenty-five Troubled Years, 1918-1943.* New York: Oxford University Press, 1943.

Stamps, Colonel T. Dodson, and Colonel Vincent J. Esposito, eds. *A Short Military History of World War I.* With atlas. West Point: United States Military Academy, 1950.

Townshend, Major General Sir Charles. *My Campaign in Mesopotamia.* London: Thornton-Butterworth, 1920.

United States Army in the World War. A series of 17 volumes, edited by official historians, consisting of reprints, in whole or in part, of significant official documents which describe the organization of the American Expeditionary Forces, its policies, training, combat operations, and the postwar period, including the final reports of the AEF staff. Following are the volumes, all of which contain maps, photographs and tables to support the text:

1. *Organization of the American Expeditionary Forces.*
2. *Policy-Forming Documents: American Expeditionary Forces.*
3. *Training and Use of American Units with British and French.*

MILITARY OPERATIONS OF THE AMERICAN EXPEDITIONARY FORCES.

4. *Cambrai, Somme Defensive, Lys, Aisne Defensive, Cantigny, Château-Thierry, Montdidier Noyon.*
5. *Champagne-Marne. Aisne-Marne.*
6. *Oise-Aisne, Ypres-Lys, Vittorio-Veneto.*
7. *Somme.*
8. *St.-Mihiel.*
9. *Meuse-Argonne.*
10. *The Armistice Agreement and Related Documents.*
11. *American Occupation of Germany.*

REPORTS OF COMMANDER-IN-CHIEF, AEF, STAFF SECTIONS AND SERVICES.

12. *G-1.*
13. *G-2.*
14. *G-3, G-4, G-5, and Schools.*
15. *Staff Sections and Services.*
16. General Orders, GHQ, AEF.
17. Bulletins, GHQ, AEF.

Villari, Luigi. *The War on the Italian Front*. London: Cobden-Sanderson, 1932.
Wavell, General Sir Archibald. *Allenby*. New York: Oxford, 1941.

PART EIGHT: WORLD WAR II

Alexander, Field Marshal. *Report to the Combined Chiefs of Staff on the Italian Campaign, 1944-1945*. London: H. M. Stationery Office, 1951.
Arnold, Lieutenant General H. H., and Brigadier General Ira C. Eaker. *Winged Warfare*. New York: Harper, 1941.
Auphan, Rear Admiral Paul, and Mordal, Jacques. *The French Navy in World War II*. Annapolis: U.S. Naval Institute, 1959.
Bradley, General Omar N. *A Soldier's Story*. New York: Holt, 1951.
Bragadin, Commodore Marc'Antonio. *The Italian Navy in World War II*. Annapolis: U.S. Naval Institute, 1957.
Brereton, Lieutenant General Lewis H. *Brereton Diaries*. New York: Morrow, 1946.
British Air Ministry. *The Battle of Britain*. New York: Garden City Publishing Co., 1941.
British War Office. *The Campaigns in Greece and Crete*. London: H. M. Stationery Office, 1942.
Bullock, Alan. *Hitler*. New York: Harper, 1952.
Burr, John G. *The Framework of Battle*. Philadelphia: Lippincott, 1943.
Caldwell, Cy. *Air Power and Total War*. New York: Coward-McCann, 1943.
Ciano, Galeazzo. *Ciano's Diplomatic Papers* (Malcolm Muggeridge, ed.). London: Odhams, 1948.
Clifford, Alexander G. *The Conquest of North Africa, 1940-1943*. Boston: Little, Brown, 1943.
Churchill, Winston. *The Second World War*. 5 Vols. Boston: Houghton Mifflin, 1948-1951.
Dejong, Louis. *The German Fifth Column in World War II*. Chicago: University of Chicago Press, 1956.
Divine, David. *The Nine Days of Dunkirk*. New York: Norton, 1959.*
Doud, Captain Harold. "Sixth Months with the Japanese Infantry." *Infantry Journal*, January-February, 1937.*
Douhet, Giulio. *The Command of the Air* (Dino Ferrari, trans.). New York: Coward-McCann, 1942.*
Doorman, P. L. G. *Military Operations in the Netherlands*. London: Allen and Unwin, 1944.
Eichelberger, Robert L. *Our Jungle Road to Tokyo*. New York: Viking, 1950.
Eisenhower, Dwight D. *Crusade in Europe*. New York: Doubleday, 1948.
Fried, Hans. *The Guilt of the German Army*. New York: Macmillan, 1942.*
Fuller, Major General J. F. C. *The Second World War*. London: Eyre and Spottiswoode, 1948.*
Gaulle, General Charles de. *The Call to Honour*. New York: Viking, 1955.
Gavin, Major General James M. *Airborne Warfare*. Washington: Infantry Journal Press, 1947.*

Greenfield, Kent Roberts, ed. *Command Decisions*. World War II operations analyzed by sixteen historians of the Office of the Chief of Military History, Department of the Army. New York: Harcourt, Brace, 1959.

Guderian, General Heinz. *Panzer Leader*. New York: Dutton, 1952.

Haines, Charles Grove. *The Origins and Background of the Second World War*. New York: Oxford, 1943.

Halder, Franz. *Hitler as War Lord*. New York: Putnam's, 1950.

Halsey, Fleet Admiral William F. *Admiral Halsey's Story*. New York: Whittlesey, 1947.

Harvey, Ray Forrest. *The Politics of the War*. New York: Harper, 1943.

Hetherington, John. *Airborne Invasion*. New York: Duell, Sloan and Pearce, 1943.

Hinsley, F. H. *Hitler's Strategy*. Cambridge: Cambridge University Press, 1951.

Holles, Everett. *Unconditional Surrender*. New York: Howell, Soskin, 1945.

Hough, Frank O. *The Island War*. Philadelphia: Lippincott, 1947.*

Hungerford, Ernest. *Transport for War*. New York: Dutton, 1943.

Isely, Jeter, and Philip A. Crowl. *The U.S. Marines and Amphibious War*. Princeton: Princeton University Press, 1952.*

Inoguchi, Captain Rikihei, and Commander Tadashi Nakajima. *The Divine Wind: Japan's Kamikaze Force in World War II*. Annapolis: U.S. Naval Institute, 1958.

Kennedy, Major General Sir John. *The Business of War*. New York: Morrow, 1958.

Kerr, Walter. *The Russian Army*. New York: Knopf, 1944.

King, Admiral Ernest J. *Our Navy at War: Official Report Covering Combat Operations up to March 1, 1944*. Washington: United States News, 1944.

Leahy, Fleet Admiral William D. *I Was There*. New York: Whittlesey, 1950.

Lederrey, Colonel. *La Défaite Allemande à l'Est*. Paris: Kavauzelle, 1951.

Lee, Asher. *The German Air Force*. London: Duckworth, 1946.

Leeb, Field Marshal Ritter von. *Defense* (Stefan T. Possony and Daniel Vilfroy, trans.). Harrisburg, Pa.: Military Service Publishing Co., 1943.

Levine, Isaac Don. *Mitchell, Pioneer of Air Power*. New York: Duell, Sloan and Pearce, 1943.*

Liddell Hart, Captain B. H. *The Defence of Britain*. New York: Random, 1939.*

Lory, Hillis. *Japan's Military Masters*. New York: Viking, 1943.

Ludendorff, General Erich. *The Nation at War* (A. S. Rappaport, trans.). London: Hutchinson, 1936.*

Marshall, General George C. *The Winning of the War in Europe and the Pacific: Biennial Report of the Chief of Staff of the U.S. Army*. New York: Simon and Schuster, 1945.

Marshall, S. L. A. *Bastogne*. Washington: Infantry Journal Press, 1947.

Mellenthin, Major General F. W. von. *Panzer Battles*. Norman: University of Oklahoma Press, 1956.

Miksche, Major F. O. *Attack: A Study of Blitzkrieg Tactics*. New York: Random, 1942.*

Montgomery, Field Marshal the Viscount. *Normandy to the Baltic.* Boston: Houghton Mifflin, 1948.

Moorehead, Alan. *The End in Africa.* New York: Harper, 1943.*

Morison, Samuel Eliot. *History of U.S. Naval Operations in World War II.* Of the 14 volumes planned for this comprehensive work, all but one had been completed by 1959. Boston: Little, Brown, 1947-1959 ff.*

Mountbatten, Vice-Admiral, Earl of Burma. *Report to the Combined Chiefs of Staff by the Supreme Allied Commander, Southeast Asia, 1943-1945.* London: H. M. Stationery Office, 1951.

Nelson, Donald M. *Arsenal of Democracy.* New York: Harcourt, Brace, 1946.

Patton, General George S., Jr. *War as I Knew It.* Boston: Houghton Mifflin, 1947.

Rommel, Field Marshal Erwin. *The Rommel Papers* (B. H. Liddell Hart, ed.). New York: Harcourt, Brace, 1953.

Roscoe, Theodore. *United States Destroyer Operations in World War II.* Annapolis: U.S. Naval Institute, 1957.

———. *United States Submarine Operations in World War II.* Annapolis: U.S. Naval Institute, 1949.

Ruge, Vice-Admiral Friedrich. *Der Seekrieg: The German Navy's Story.* Annapolis: U.S. Naval Institute, 1957.

Ryan, Cornelius. *The Longest Day: June 6, 1944.* New York: Simon and Schuster, 1959.

Sayre, Joel. *Persian Gulf Command.* New York: Random, 1945.

Seversky, Major Alexander P. de. *Victory Through Air Power.* New York: Simon and Schuster, 1942.

Sherrod, Robert. *History of Marine Corps Aviation in World War II.* Washington: Combat Forces Press, 1952.

Snow, Edgar. *The Pattern of Soviet Power.* New York: Random, 1945.

Speidel, Hans. *Invasion: 1944.* Chicago: Regnery, 1950.

Stamps, Colonel T. Dodson, and Colonel Vincent J. Esposito, eds. *A Military History of World War II.* 2 Vols., with atlas. West Point: U.S. Military Academy, 1953.

Stettinius, Edward P. *Lend-Lease: Weapon for Victory.* New York: Macmillan, 1944.

Stilwell, General Joseph W. *The Stilwell Papers.* New York: Sloane, 1948.

Stimson, Henry L. *Prelude to Invasion.* Excerpts from official reports of U.S. Secretary of War. Washington: Public Affairs Press, 1944.

Strausz-Hupe, Robert. *Geopolitics: the Struggle for Space and Power.* New York: Putnam's, 1942.

Taylor, Lieutenant Samuel W. "As a German General [Bayerlein] Saw It." *Saturday Evening Post,* Oct. 20, 1945.*

Taylor, Telford. *The March of Conquest.* New York: Simon and Schuster, 1958.*

United States Air Force. *The Army Air Forces in World War II: Plans and Early Operations* (Wesley Frank Craven and James Lee Cate, eds.). 4 Vols.; others to follow. Chicago: University of Chicago Press, 1948-1951 ff.

United States Army, Department of, Office of the Chief of Military History.

The United States Army in World War II. A series planned to comprise 80 or more volumes when completed. (Kent Roberts Greenfield and Stetson Conn, eds.) Washington: Government Printing Office, 1940-1959 ff.

United States Marine Corps, Historical Branch. *History of the U.S. Marine Corps in World War II.* Vol. I, *Pearl Harbor to Guadalcanal,* by Lieutenant Colonel Frank O. Hough, Major Verle E. Ludwig, and Henry I. Shaw, Jr. Other volumes in preparation. Washington: Government Printing Office, 1958.

United States Navy, Office of the Chief of Naval Operations, Naval History Division. *Naval Chronology, World War II.* (John B. Heffernan, Rear Admiral USN [Ret.], ed.) (See also Samuel Eliot Morison and U.S. Naval Institute publications for books about the U.S. Navy in World War II.) Washington: Government Printing Office, 1955.

United States Strategic Bombing Survey. *The Effects of Strategic Bombing on the German War Economy.* Washington: Government Printing Office, 1945.

Wavell, General Sir Archibald. *Dispatch on the Operations in the Southwest Pacific from 15 January to 25 February 1942.* London: H. M. Stationery Office, 1943.

Werner, Max. *The Great Offensive.* New York: Viking, 1942.*

Wilmot, Chester. *The Struggle for Europe.* New York: Harper, 1952.

Wilson, General Sir H. Maitland. *Report by the Supreme Allied Commander, Mediterranean, to the Combined Chiefs of Staff on the Italian Campaign, 8 January to 10 May 1944.* Washington: Government Printing Office, 1946.

Wintringham, Tom. *New Ways of War.* New York: Penguin, 1940.

Wolff, Leon. *Low Level Mission: The Story of the Ploesti Raids.* New York: Doubleday, 1947.

Wynne, Captain G. C. *If Germany Attacks.* London: Faber, 1940.

THE SEQUEL IN KOREA

Blumenson, Martin. "MacArthur's Divided Command." *Army,* November, 1956.

Cagle, Commander Malcolm W., USN, and Commander Frank A. Manson, USN. *The Sea War in Korea.* Annapolis: U.S. Naval Institute, 1957.*

Geer, Andrew. *The New Breed* (U.S. Marine operations in Korea). New York: Harper, 1952 *

Gugeler, Captain Russell A., USA, ed. *Combat Actions in Korea.* Washington: Combat Forces Press, 1954.*

Karig, Captain Walter, USNR, Commander Malcolm W. Cagle, USN, and Lieutenant Commander Frank A. Manson, USN. *The War in Korea* (Naval Actions). Vol. VII, Battle Report Series. New York: Rinehart, 1952.*

MacArthur, General of the Army Douglas, USA. "MacArthur Makes His Reply." *Life,* Feb. 13, 1956.

Mao Tse-tung. "Strategic Problems of the Chinese Revolutionary War." Mimeographed pamphlet edited by Lieutenant Colonel F. B. Nihart, USMC. Quantico: Marine Corps Schools, 1951.*

Marshall, S. L. A. *The River and the Gauntlet.* New York: Morrow, 1952.
——. *Pork Chop Hill.* New York: Morrow, 1956.*
Miller, John Jr., Major Owen J. Carroll, and Margaret E. Tackley. *Korea, 1951-1953.* Washington: Government Printing Office, 1956.*
Montross, Lynn. *Cavalry in the Sky: The Story of U.S. Marine Combat Helicopters.* New York: Harper, 1954.
——. "Fleet Marine Force Korea." *U.S. Naval Institute Proceedings,* August and September, 1954.
Rigg, Lieutenant Colonel Robert, USA. *Red China's Fighting Hordes.* Harrisburg: Military Service, 1951.
Truman, Harry S. *Memoirs.* 2 Vols. New York: Doubleday, 1955-1956.
United States Army, Department of, Office of the Chief of Military History. *From the Naktong to the Yalu.* By Lieutenant Colonel Roy E. Appleman, USA.* Tentative title of manuscript at OCMS, 1959. Other volumes on Korean War in preparation by OCMS historians.
——. *The Korean Conflict: Policy, Planning, Direction.* By Lieutenant Colonel James F. Schnabel, USA.* Tentative title of manuscript at OCMS, 1959.
United States Marine Corps, Historical Branch. *U.S. Marine Operations in Korea.* Vols. I, II and III, by Lynn Montross and Captain Nicholas A. Canzona, USMC, 1954-1957. Two more volumes in preparation, 1959.
Walker, Richard L. *China Under Communism: The First Five Years.* New Haven: Yale University Press, 1955.
Westover, Captain John G., USA, ed. *Combat Support in Korea.* Washington: Combat Forces Press, 1955.
Whitney, Major General Courtney, USA (Ret.). *MacArthur: His Rendezvous with History.* New York: Knopf, 1956.

BIRTH OF THE ATOMIC AGE, 1946-1960

Andrews, Marshall. *Disaster Through Air Power.* New York: Rinehart, 1954.
Dinerstein, Herbert S. *War and the Soviet Union.* New York: Praeger, 1959.
Eliot, George Fielding. *Victory Without War, 1958-1961.* Annapolis: U.S. Naval Institute, 1958.
Garthoff, Raymond L. *Soviet Strategy in the Nuclear Age.* New York: Praeger, 1958.
Gavin, General James M. *War and Peace in the Space Age.* New York: Harper, 1958.
Henriques, Robert. *A Hundred Hours to Suez.* (The Israeli-Egyptian War.) New York: Viking, 1957.
Holcombe, Arthur N., chairman. "Organizing Peace in the Nuclear Age," by the Commission to Study the Organization of Peace. New York: New York University Press, 1959.
King-Hall, Stephen. *Defense in the Nuclear Age.* New York: Fellowship Publications, 1959.
Knorr Klaus, ed. *NATO and American Security.* Princeton: Princeton University Press, 1959.

Marshall, S. L. A. *Sinai Victory.* (The Israeli-Egyptian War.) New York: Morrow, 1958.

Millis, Walter, with Harvey C. Mansfield and Harold Stein. *Arms and the State: Civil-Military Elements in National Policy.* New York: The Twentieth Century Fund, 1958.

Morganstern, Oskar. *The Question of National Defense.* New York: Random, 1959.

Ridgway, General Matthew B. *Soldier: The Memoirs of Matthew B. Ridgway.* New York: Harper, 1956.

Sternberg, Fritz. *The Military and Industrial Revolution of Our Time.* New York: Praeger, 1959.

Taylor, General Maxwell D. *The Uncertain Trumpet.* New York: Harper, 1960.

United States Army, Department of. *Missiles, Rockets and Satellites.* 5 pamphlets. Washington, 1958.

GENERAL SOURCES

Aumale, Henri d'Orleans, Duc d'. *Les Institutions Militaires de la France.* Paris, 1867.

Bailey, Thomas A. *A Diplomatic History of the American People.* Sixth Edition. New York: Appleton-Century-Crofts, 1958.*

Brodie, Bernard. *A Layman's Guide to Naval Strategy.* Princeton: Princeton University Press, 1942.

Campana, J. *Les Progrès de l'Artillerie.* Paris: Lavauzelle, 1923.

Canonge, J. F. *Histoire et Art Militaire.* Brussels, 1904.

Colin, Colonel Jean. *Les Transformations de la Guerre.* Paris, 1902.

Corbett, Sir Julian S. *Some Principles of Maritime Strategy.* New York: Longmans, Green, 1911.*

Craig, Gordon A. *The Politics of the Prussian Army, 1640-1945.* Oxford: Clarendon Press, 1955.

Daugherty, William E., and Morris Janowitz, eds. *A Psychological Warfare Case Book.* Baltimore: Operations Research Office, Johns Hopkins Press, 1958.

Denison, Colonel G. T. *History of Cavalry.* London, 1907.

Dupuy, Colonel R. Ernest. *The Compact History of the U.S. Army.* New York: Hawthorne, 1956.

Earle, Edward Mead, ed. with Gordon A. Craig and Felix Gilbert. *Makers of Modern Strategy: Military Thought from Machiavelli to Hitler.* Princeton: Princeton University Press, 1944.

Ellis, Havelock. *My Confessional.* New York: Houghton Mifflin, 1934.*

Fiske, Rear Admiral Bradley A. *The Art of Fighting.* New York: Century, 1920.

Foch, Marshal Ferdinand. *De la Conduite de la Guerre.* Paris, 1915.

———. *The Principles of War* (Hilaire Belloc, trans.). London, 1918.

Fortescue, Sir John W. *A History of the British Army.* 14 Vols. London and New York: Macmillan, 1899-1930.*

Fuller, Major General J. F. C. *The Reformation of War*. London: Hutchinson, 1923.*
———. *The Dragon's Teeth*. London: Constable, 1932.*
———. *War and Western Civilization*. London: Duckworth, 1932.
———. *Generalship: Its Diseases and Their Cure*. Harrisburg: Military Service Publishing Co., 1936.
———. *Decisive Battles of the U.S.A.* New York: Beechhurst, 1953.
———. *A Military History of the Western World*. 3 Vols. New York: Funk and Wagnalls, 1955.*
Ganoe, William Addleman. *The History of the United States Army*. New York: Appleton, 1924.*
Gilbert, Major Gerald. *The Evolution of Tactics*. London, 1907.
Hamley, General Sir Edward B. *The Operations of War*. Edinburgh: Blackwood, 1922.
Henderson, G. F. R. *The Science of War*. New York, 1905.
Hicks, Major James E. *Our Arms and Weapons*. New York: Norton, 1941.
Hime, H. W. L. *The Origin of Artillery*. London, 1915.
James, William, *Memories and Studies*. New York: Longmans, Green, 1924.*
Kelly, Colonel E. H. *Fortification and Siegecraft*. Encyclopaedia Britannica, 14th Edition, Vol. IX, 1929.*
Lecomte, C. *Les Ingénieurs Militaires de France*. Paris, 1904.
Lewal, J. L. *Stratégie de Combat*. Paris, 1895.
Liddell Hart, Captain B. H. *The Decisive Wars of History*. Boston: Little, Brown, 1924.
———. *The Ghost of Napoleon*. New Haven: Yale University Press, 1934.*
Lloyd, Colonel E. M. *A Review of the History of Infantry*. London, 1908.
Maillard, L. *Eléments de la Guerre*. Paris, 1912.
Maude, Colonel F. N. *Cavalry: Its Past and Future*. London, 1903.
Michelet, Jules. *Histoire de France*. Paris, 17 Vols., 1893-1899.
Napoleon III and J. Fave. *Études sur le Passe et l'Avenir de l'Artillerie*. Paris, 6 Vols., 1846-1871.
Newman, James R. *The Tools of War*. New York: Doubleday, Doran, 1942.
Nickerson, Hoffman. *The Armed Horde, 1793-1939: a Study of the Rise, Survival and Decline of the Mass Army*. New York: Putnam's, 1940.
Phillips, Major Thomas R., ed. *Roots of Strategy* (selected writings of Sun Tzu, Vegetius, Saxe, Frederick, Napoleon). Harrisburg: Military Service Publishing Co., 1940.*
Potter, Commander E. B., USNR, ed. *The United States and World Sea Power*. Englewood Cliffs, N. J.: Prentice-Hall, 1955.
Stevens, William Oliver, and Allan Westcott. *A History of Sea Power*. New York: Doran, 1920.
Susane, General Louis. *Historie de l'Infanterie Francaise*. Paris, 5 Vols., 1876.
Upton, Emory. *The Military Policy of the United States*. Washington, 1917.
Vagt, Alfred. *A History of Militarism, Civilian and Military*. New York: Meridian, 1959.
Wintringham, Tom. *The Story of Weapons and Tactics*. Boston: Houghton Mifflin, 1943.

INDEX